P9-CRL-265

Second Edition

Economics In Our Times

Second Edition

Roger A. Arnold
California State University San Marcos

National Textbook Company
a division of NTC/Contemporary Publishing Group
Lincolnwood, Illinois USA

Cover Photos: *Clockwise from Top:* Stock Exchange/© CORBIS; Times Square/© CORBIS; Capital Building/© CORBIS; Alan Greenspan/© CORBIS; Money/© CORBIS; Globe/© PhotoDisc; Ken Griffey, Jr./© CORBIS; Computer/© CORBIS

Intext photo credits following index.

ISBN 0-538-69055-0

Published by National Textbook Company, a division of NTC/Contemporary Publishing Group, Inc.
4255 West Touhy Avenue, Lincolnwood (Chicago), Illinois 60646-1975 U.S.A.

©2001 NTC/Contemporary Publishing Group, Inc.
All rights reserved. No part of this book may be reproduced, stored in a retrieval system, or transmitted in any form or by any means, electronic, mechanical, photocopying, recording, or otherwise, without prior permission of the publisher.
Manufactured in the United States of America.

00 01 02 03 04 05 06 07 08 09 QB 0 9 8 7 6 5 4 3 2 1

About the Author

Professor Roger Arnold is first and foremost an economics educator, having taught a variety of economics courses at several major universities. He has also served for many years as Director for a Center for Economic Education. He currently teaches at California State University in San Marcos, California.

Professor Arnold received his Bachelor of Social Science degree from the University of Birmingham, England, and his Master's and Doctorate degrees from Virginia Polytechnic Institute and State University. He completed his Ph.D. dissertation under Nobel Laureate James M. Buchanan.

Professor Arnold is an experienced teacher, researcher, and writer. He has written numerous successful textbooks, as well as articles and columns for *The Wall Street Journal* and other respected publications.

Dedication

To my mother, B.J., who taught me the value of learning

Editorial Review Board

Professor Robert M. Herman
Moorpark College
Moorpark, California

Professor Dennis D. Muraoka
California State University
Long Beach, CA

Professor John M. Hail
Southwest Missouri State University
Springfield, MO

Patricia Dobbs
Crockett High School
Austin, TX

Kyleen Dobbs
Pflugerville High School
Pflugerville, TX

Sandi Haltom
R.L. Turner High School
Carrollton, TX

Second Edition Editorial Reviewers

Kimberly Allen
Northside High School
Warner Robins, GA

Sharon Amundson
Duncanville High School
Duncanville, TX

James Blomdahl
Mora High School
Mora, MN

H. Ray Buchanan
Greenhill School
Dallas, TX

Jim Chambers
Dubuque, IA

Robert Chambliss
Leon High School
Tallahassee, FL

Helen Chouinard
Lanier High School
San Antonio, TX

Gail Colbert
Economic Education Consultant
Woodbury, MN

Stacey Daniell
Western Hills High School
Fort Worth, TX

Art Equihua
Crown Point High School
Crown Point, PA

Kay Frazier
Eastern Hills High School
El Paso, TX

Irene Grant
North Salem High School
Salem, OR

Richard Ross Grubbs
O.D. Wyatt High School
Fort Worth, TX

Richard Gutierrez
Montwood High School
El Paso, TX

Gary Hammac
East Central High School
San Antonio, TX

William Heitsman
Hartsville High School
Hartsville, SC

Todd Hornaday
Bettendorf High School
Bettendorf, IA

David N. Jones
Beaver River Central High School
Beaver Falls, NY

Lynn Kaneps
Parker, TX

Jim Lachappelle
Liberty High School
Clarksburg, WV

Mike Mass
Peoria High School
Peoria, IL

Kevin Magavern
The Woodlands High School
The Woodlands, TX

Bill McCormick
Richland NE High School
Columbia, SC

David N. Moerbe
Boswell High School
Fort Worth, TX

Susan Morris
Frenship High School
Wolfforth, TX

Joseph A. Naumann
McCluer North High School
Florissant, MO

Matthew Pearce
Kickapoo High School
Springfield, MO

Michael Perrin
Odessa High School
Odessa, TX

Joaquin Ramos
Coronado High School
El Paso, TX

Steven Reff
University High School
Tucson, AZ

Suzanna Roberts
Galt High School
Galt, CA

Carl Schmidt
Monta Vista High School
Cupertino, CA

Ann Semler
North Shore Senior High School
Houston, TX

Claudia Shanaman
Columbia High School
Columbia, PA

Don Smith
Mountain View High School
Mesa, AZ

Edward Stacey
Oswego High School
Oswego, NY

Bruce Steger
Palm Bay High School
Melbourne, FL

Gail Stevens
Milby High School
Houston, TX

Ruth Strunc
Ennis High School
Ennis, TX

Janet Swartzbaugh
Philipsburg, OH

Ann Tepovich
Redwood High School
Larkspur, CA

Margaret Thompson
Northside High School
Fort Smith, AR

Mike Tilford
Mahomet Seymour High School
Mahomet, IL

Tim Wanamaker
Bay High School
Panama City, FL

Kayla Watkins
Abilene High School
Abilene, TX

Bob Wright
Vanguard High School
Ocala, FL

Previous Edition Reviewers

Nancy Corridon
Hendersonville High School,
Hendersonville, TN

Jamie Daily
Holmes High School,
San Antonio, TX

James W. Davis
Jasper High School,
Jasper, TX

Charles F. Depro
Sikeston Sr. High School,
Sikeston, MO

Patricia Dobbs
Crockett High School,
Austin, TX

Kyleen Dobbs
Pflugerville High School,
Pflugerville, TX

Sharon Ehrhorn
Kalaheo High School,
Kailua, HI

Rebecca Ennis
Sharpstown High School,
Houston, TX

Dr. Charles Fox
McLane High School,
Fresno, CA

Patricia Geyer
Johnson High School,
Sacramento, CA

Judy Haley
Pinetree High School,
Longview, TX

Sandi Haltom
R.L. Turner High School,
Carrollton, TX

Paul G. Haynes
Burlington High School,
Burlington, WI

Lynn Huselton
Plano East Senior High School,
Plano, TX

Colette Kolstad
Preble High School,
Green Bay, WI

Jim Lively
John Jay High School,
San Antonio, TX

Sharon Lynn
Marietta, GA

Alice Morgan
Solon High School,
Solon, OH

John O'Brien
Centennial High School,
Circle Pines, MN

Dennis Pate
Brentwood High School,
Brentwood, TN

Sarah Pepper
Washington High School,
San Mateo, CA

David Plyler
San Antonio, TX

Carl Rossi
Geibel High School,
Uniontown, PA

Dr. Deborah Savage
Austin High School,
Houston, TX

Richard Streit
Wahlert High School,
Dubuque, IA

James Tally
Judson High School,
Converse, TX

Steve Vanderbol
Joplin High School,
Joplin, MO

Laura Wagner
Bryan High School,
Bryan, TX

Vernon Wilder
Pleasant Grove High School,
Texarkana, AR

Contents in Brief

Contents

The Basics of Economics

Contents

Contents

Contents

UNIT 4

Contents

UNIT 5 Everyday Economics

Features

Technology & Innovation

Economics and History

Economics Around the World

Features

Features

Exhibits

Exhibits

Exhibits

Introduction

Economics can be either boring or exciting, depending on *how* it is presented. Increasingly, I have come to believe that the right way to present economics is to *surprise* students and readers.

Perhaps you come to the study of economics with low expectations; perhaps you think that economics will be a dull and dry subject. If so, you will be surprised when you see that:

- Economics often occurs in the unlikeliest places.
- Economic events, far removed from you, are linked to you.
- Economics can answer many of your questions.

Economics Occurs in the Unlikeliest Places

Most people think that economics occurs only on Wall Street, in Washington, D.C., on the factory floor, in a bank, or in a conference room at a major corporation. Economics is in all these places, but it is in so many more places, too.

In this book, I have tried to show you that economics often "pops up" at times and places that may surprise you. Economics pops up on a day at Disneyland, on Thanksgiving day, in the California gold rush, in Hollywood, in a rock 'n' roll band, on a television show, on a freeway, and even during sleep. Economics isn't only about unemployment, inflation, interest rates, stock prices, and taxes. It is about life. Once you learn this, you may find yourself getting excited about economics. You will probably want to learn more.

Economic Events, Far Removed from Us, Are Linked to Us

Throw a pebble across the surface of a lake, and you will see ripples. An economic action is like the pebble: it creates ripples that extend far beyond its point of origin. Sometimes, an economic event that has its point of origin in, say, Japan, India, or Mexico can affect you, living here in the United States.

In this book I have tried to show you how your life is affected by economic events that you may have thought could not affect you. In this book you will see how a change in the value of the Mexican peso, Japanese yen, Thai baht, and Turkish lira can influence how much you buy of various goods and services. You will see how a meeting in Vienna can change the price you pay for gasoline. You will see how an economic crisis in a country half way around the world can affect your chances of getting a weekend job. As you work your way through the text, you will learn that your world is really much bigger than you might have ever imagined. You always knew that what happened down the street, across town, or in your state's capital could affect your life. I want to show you that what happens in Tokyo, London, Mexico City, and Moscow can, and does, have a major impact on your life, too.

Economics Can Answer Many of Our Questions

You walk into a store and pay $14 for a CD. Would you like to know why you didn't pay a lower price, say, $4 for the CD? Economics has the answer.

You read that a movie star earns $20 million per film and that a secretary at a real estate firm earns $20,000 a year. Do you want to know why the movie star earns so much more than the secretary? Economics has the answer.

You are looking for a used car to buy. One used car you are considering costs $8,000, another costs $12,000. Do you want to know why one car is priced higher than the other? Economics has the answer.

You are thinking of taking out a loan to finance the purchase of your used car. Before you obtain the loan, the interest rate for the loan rises from 6 percent to 7 percent. Do you want to know why? Economics has the answer.

House prices are higher in San Francisco, California, than in Des Moines, Iowa. Do you want to know why? Economics has the answer.

Even though wages are lower in Mexico than in the United States, thousands of U.S. firms choose to stay in the U.S. and hire American workers. Wonder why? Can you guess where you might find the answer?

There are literally hundreds of such questions that you may not have answers to. It is a sure bet that many of those questions will be answered after you have studied economics.

Paul Samuelson (b. 1915) was the first American economist to win the Nobel Prize in Economics. He once said that setting out to explore the exciting world of economics for the first time is a unique thrill. You are about to set out to explore the world of economics for the first time. You may not know what awaits you, but those of us who have passed this way before know. We know that you are in for a very special time. You are going to be surprised at how much you will learn about your world in a matter of just a few months. And you know something else? You're going to be pleasantly surprised at how much fun you have along the way.

—Roger A. Arnold

Economics In Our Times

Second Edition

UNIT 1

The Basics of Economics

Chapter 1
What Economics Is About

Chapter 2
Our Free-Enterprise System: Markets, Ethics, and Entrepreneurs

Chapter 3
Demand

Chapter 4
Supply

Chapter 5
Markets: Supply and Demand Together

ANDRE
AGASSI

CHAPTER 1

What Economics Is About

What This Chapter Is About

This chapter introduces you to a few of the basic and most important concepts that form the foundation upon which much of the subject of economics is built. This chapter also discusses the *economic way of thinking,* which refers to the distinctive way economists view, interpret, and analyze the world.

Why This Chapter Is Important

Simple arithmetic functions are both useful and powerful. They are useful because almost every day you have some reason to add, subtract, multiply, or divide. Just think about how much harder your life would be if you did not know simple math.

These functions are powerful because they are the springboard to higher mathematics and to deeper understanding. You could not learn algebra, calculus, or geometry without knowing how to add, subtract, multiply, and divide. Without algebra, calculus, and geometry, safe bridges could not be built and satellites could not be put into space.

The economic concepts discussed in this chapter—scarcity, choice, and opportunity cost—perform functions similar to the roles of addition, subtraction, multiplication, and division. First, once learned, these concepts are continually used to interpret much of life. In fact, they are used so often that you will begin to wonder how you ever understood anything without them. Second, these concepts form the base upon which the economics you will learn in later chapters is built.

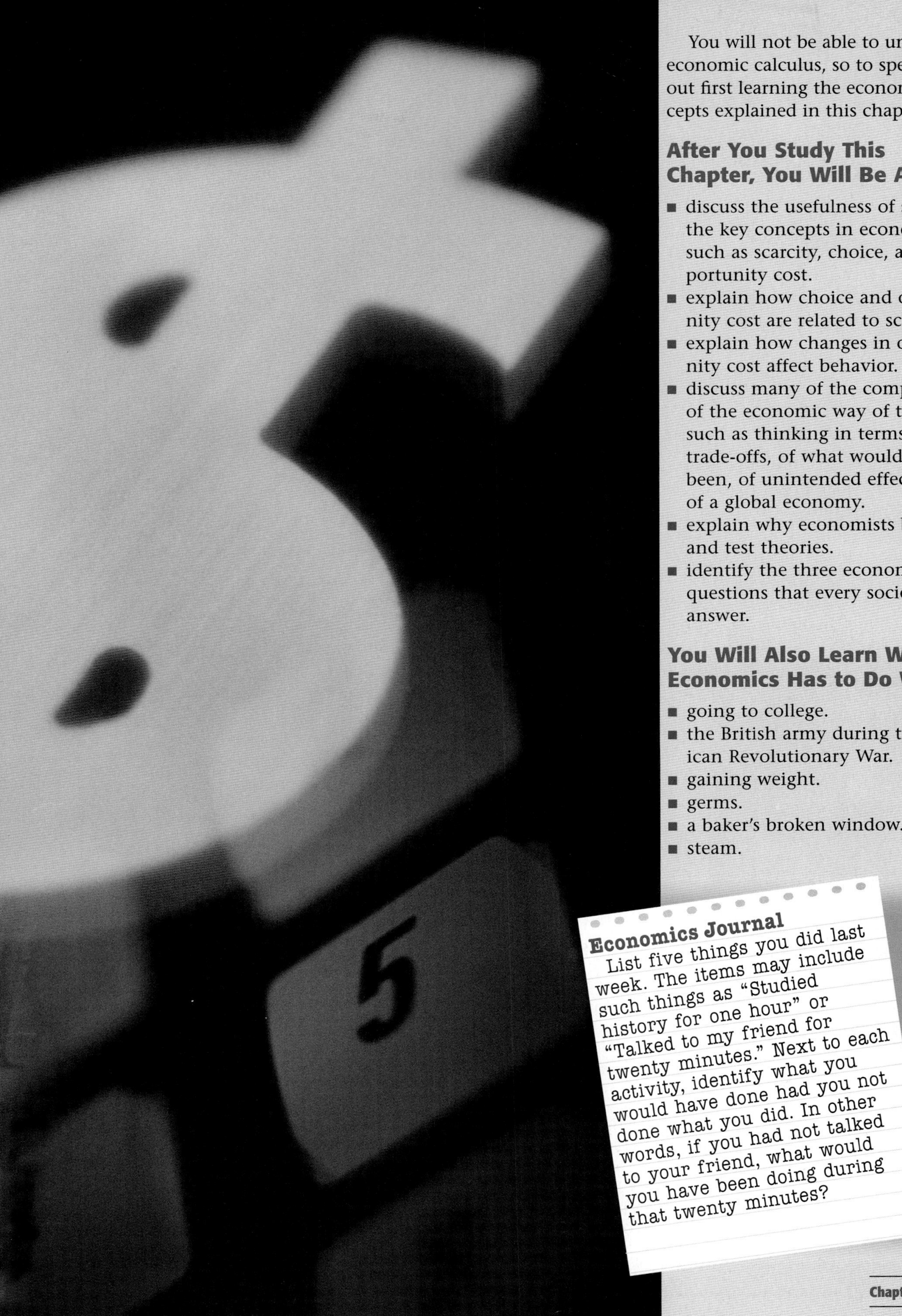

You will not be able to understand economic calculus, so to speak, without first learning the economic concepts explained in this chapter.

After You Study This Chapter, You Will Be Able To

- discuss the usefulness of some of the key concepts in economics, such as scarcity, choice, and opportunity cost.
- explain how choice and opportunity cost are related to scarcity.
- explain how changes in opportunity cost affect behavior.
- discuss many of the components of the economic way of thinking, such as thinking in terms of trade-offs, of what would have been, of unintended effects, and of a global economy.
- explain why economists build and test theories.
- identify the three economic questions that every society must answer.

You Will Also Learn What Economics Has to Do With

- going to college.
- the British army during the American Revolutionary War.
- gaining weight.
- germs.
- a baker's broken window.
- steam.

Economics Journal

List five things you did last week. The items may include such things as "Studied history for one hour" or "Talked to my friend for twenty minutes." Next to each activity, identify what you would have done had you not done what you did. In other words, if you had not talked to your friend, what would you have been doing during that twenty minutes?

SECTION 1

Scarcity, Choice, and Opportunity Cost

Three important concepts in economics are scarcity, choice, and opportunity cost. As you read this section, keep these key questions in mind:

- What is scarcity?
- How is choice related to scarcity?
- How is opportunity cost related to choice?
- Is there a difference between zero price and zero cost?

What Is Scarcity?

Key Terms

want
tangible
intangible
resource
scarcity
opportunity cost
rationing device
economics

People have **wants**—things they desire to have. They do not want just anything, however. They want things that they think will make them happy or satisfied. For example, people may want cars, houses, clothes, food, money to give to their favorite charities, more friends, better health, and countless other things.

You will notice that some things people want are **tangible** and some are **intangible.** Something is tangible if it can be felt or touched. A computer is tangible; you can touch it. Something is intangible if it cannot be felt by touch, such as a deep friendship. (See Exhibit 1-1 for more examples.)

A horse is tangible (it can be touched). What it may provide to its owner–friendship or companionship–is intangible.

Wants cannot be satisfied by wishing to have something. **Resources** are needed to produce goods or services. Nanette may want a computer, but she is not going to get one by simply wishing. It takes resources to produce a computer, and it takes money to buy one.

Like Nanette, we all have a problem in life, an economic problem: our wants are unlimited, while the resources available to satisfy these wants are limited. Stated differently, people's wants are greater than the resources available to satisfy their wants—a condition called **scarcity.** Scarcity is an economic fact of life, much as the law of gravity is a fact of life.

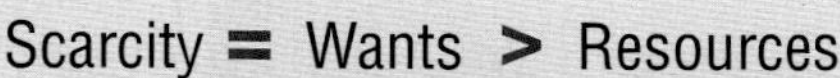

You may be wondering if people really do have unlimited wants. Perhaps you know someone you think has only a few wants (some food, a place to sleep, a few clothes, and that's all). You may think that people want only tangible goods (such as cars and houses), and once such needs have been met, they have no other wants. But people want other things,

want
A thing that we desire to have.

tangible
Able to be felt by touch. For example, a book is tangible: you can touch and feel it.

intangible
Not able to be felt by touch. For example, an economics lecture is intangible.

Exhibit 1-1

Tangible and Intangible Goods

Look at the two lists in this chart. Can you explain the difference between tangible and intangible goods in your own words?

Tangible goods	Intangible goods
• Car	• Friendship
• Home	• Health
• Computer	• Love
• Rollerblades	• Success
• Clothes	• Freedom
• CD player	• Respect

too, such as love, friendship, peace in the world, a cleaner environment, and more leisure time. Also, most people aren't completely satisfied even after getting what they want—they then want a *newer* car, a *bigger* house, *more* CDs. Frequently one want leads to another. If we take into account all the things that people may want—all the things from which people can possibly derive usefulness or satisfaction—it is likely that their wants will be unlimited. There is a stark contrast between unlimited wants and limited resources.

resource
Anything that is used to produce goods or services. For example, a person's labor may be used to produce computers, TV sets, and much more, and therefore a person's labor is a resource. There are four categories of resources: land, labor, capital, and entrepreneurship.

scarcity
The condition in which our wants are greater than the resources available to satisfy those wants.

Because of Scarcity, Choices Have to Be Made

Wants are unlimited, and resources are limited. Scarcity therefore exists, and choices have to be made. After all, if there are not enough resources to satisfy all our wants (yours, mine, and everybody else's), we have to choose which wants (of the unlimited number we have) we will satisfy. On an individual basis, it is similar to having a limited income. Maria earns $1,000 a month. She wants a new outfit, ten new books, a trip to Hawaii, a new car, and many other things. The problem is that she can't have everything she wants, given her income. She has to choose between the new outfit or the ten new books.

In a world of scarcity, choices have to be made. A person may have to choose between a new car and a trip, for example.

Consider the choices a society has to make because scarcity exists. Some groups of people want more health care for the poor, some want more police protection, some want more schools, and some a cleaner environment. As we know, wants are not realized simply by the asking. It takes resources to bring these things about. The problem, though, is that even if we could satisfy all the wants listed here, there would be more later. Even if we were to provide more health care to the poor, hire more police officers, build more schools, and clean up the environment, there would still be other things to do. There will always be more wants, and there will never be enough resources to satisfy our unlimited wants. We must choose how we are going to use our limited resources by choosing which wants we will try to satisfy and which wants will be left unsatisfied.

Scarcity ➡ Choices

opportunity cost
The most highly valued opportunity or alternative forfeited when a choice is made.

From Choices to Opportunity Costs

Every time you make a choice, such as choosing to buy a sweater instead of two compact discs, you incur an **opportunity cost.** The most valued opportunity or alternative you give up (or forfeit) to do something is that something's opportunity cost. Thus, the opportunity cost of your choosing to buy a sweater is two compact discs. (See Exhibit 1-2 for more examples.)

Choice ➡ Opportunity cost

Consider another example. Suppose Lionel spends $3,000 to buy a computer. What is the opportunity cost of the computer? Lionel must ask himself what he would have done with the $3,000 if he had not purchased the computer. If he would have spent the $3,000 on a big-screen television set, then he has given up the television to get the computer. The big-screen television set is the opportunity cost of the computer.

Exhibit 1-2

Opportunity Cost

The most valued opportunity or alternative you give up to do something is that something's opportunity cost.

What you do	What you would have done	Opportunity cost
Watch television	Read a book	The opportunity cost of watching televsion is reading a book.
Buy a computer	Take a vacation in France	The opportunity cost of buying a computer is taking a vacation in France.
Go to sleep at 9:00 p.m. instead of 11:00 p.m.	Watch a two-hour video	The opportunity cost of sleeping from 9:00 to 11:00 p.m. is watching a two-hour video.

Why Did the British Troops Wear Bright Red Uniforms in the American Revolutionary War?

When George Washington and the colonists fought the British, the colonists were dressed in rags, while the British troops were clad in fine, bright red uniforms. Commenting on this, people often say, "The British were foolish to have worn bright red uniforms. You could see them coming for miles."

Economists would not be so quick to label the British as foolish. Instead they would ask if there was some reason why the British troops wore bright red. For instance, David Friedman, an economist, thinks it is odd that the British, who at the time were the greatest fighting force in the world, would make such a seemingly obvious mistake. He has an alternative explanation, an economic explanation that gives us insight into the way economists think about things. Friedman's explanation is based on opportunity cost.

Friedman reasons that the British generals did not want their men to break ranks and desert, because winning the war would be hard, if not impossible, if a lot of men deserted. Thus, the generals had to think up a way to make the opportunity cost of desertion high for their soldiers. The generals reasoned that the higher the cost of desertion, the fewer deserters there would be.

How do you make the cost of desertion high? One thing you do is make the penalty for desertion severe, such as a stiff jail sentence or death. The British generals effectively told their soldiers that if they deserted, they would have to forfeit their freedom or their lives.

Of course, there is a problem here. A stiff penalty is not effective if deserters cannot be found. Therefore, the generals had to make it easy to find deserters, which they did by dressing them in bright red uniforms. In those days there were no electronic tracking devices or helicopters that could look for people from the air. About the only thing that a British general could do to increase the likelihood that a deserter would be found was to make him easy to see.

Certainly it was possible for a deserter to throw off his uniform and walk through the countryside in his underwear alone, but in the harsh winters of New England, doing so would guarantee death. He had almost no choice but to wear the bright red uniform. Maybe those bright red uniforms weren't that foolish an idea after all. Perhaps they were a way to raise the cost of desertion to potential deserters.

QUESTION TO ANSWER In battle, the British soldiers marched toward their enemy in neat rows. Was this foolish, or was there perhaps a sound economic reason for this formation?

Question: *Suppose Natasha spends $10,000 on a new car. If she had not spent the money on a new car, she could have*

1. *purchased $10,000 worth of clothes,*
2. *spent $10,000 traveling,*
3. *given $10,000 to charity, or*
4. *made a $10,000 down payment on a house.*

Because she could have done any of these things, aren't all of them the opportunity cost of buying the car?

Answer: *No. It is necessary to differentiate between what Natasha could have done and what she would have done.* Opportunity cost *refers to what Natasha would do if she did not buy the car. If she would spend the $10,000 traveling around the world, then traveling—and only traveling—is what she actually gives up by buying the new car.*

The Link between Scarcity, Choice, and Opportunity Cost

Let's summarize what we have said about scarcity, choices, and opportunity cost up to this point.

We first stated that because scarcity exists, choices have to be made. In other words, because our wants are greater than the resources available to satisfy our wants, we will have to choose which of our wants will be satisfied and which will remain unsatisfied.

Next, we stated that when we make a choice, we incur an opportunity cost. For example, when we choose to eat a slice of pizza instead of a hamburger, the cost of eating the pizza is not eating the hamburger.

The three concepts—scarcity, choice, and opportunity cost—are linked together. Scarcity implies choice, and choice implies opportunity cost. Logically, then, we conclude that there would be no opportunity costs for people to incur if there were no scarcity. In other words, it is because we live in a world characterized by scarcity that we incur costs. (See the photo at the left for a visual diagram of this concept.)

Question: *Suppose Roberto buys a ticket to an upcoming concert and, at the last minute, decides not to go. He gives the ticket to Brad, asking for nothing in return. If Brad goes to the concert, could we say that his going to the concert comes with zero opportunity cost? After all, he has not had to give up any money to go to the concert.*

Answer: *No. Brad gives up something, if not money, to attend the concert. He gives up the time he could be using in other ways. He gets into his car, drives 10 miles, stands in line, watches the concert for 90 minutes, walks back to his car, and drives home. He could be doing something else in the time it takes him to do all this. There is a difference between zero price (Brad paid nothing for the ticket; it was given to him) and zero opportunity cost.*

Make a Prediction

Suppose the U.S. Congress makes it illegal to use money (price) as a rationing device. Would some other rationing device arise to take its place? Explain your answer.

Another Consequence of Scarcity: The Need for a Rationing Device

rationing device
A means for deciding who gets what portion of the available resources and goods.

Individuals have wants; resources are necessary to satisfy wants. Since wants are greater than the resources available—that is, since scarcity exists—there needs to be some **rationing device,** some means for deciding who gets what portion of the available resources and goods. Price is a rationing device. If you are willing and able to pay the price for the resources (and goods and services that the resources go to produce), they are yours. If you are either unwilling or unable to pay the price, they are not yours. They are rationed out to those who are willing and able to pay.

Scarcity ➡ Rationing device

If scarcity did not exist, there would be no need for a rationing device, and people would not pay the dollar prices for resources and goods. In every transaction—buying pizza, buying groceries, or buying an airline ticket—scarcity is present.

Still Another Consequence of Scarcity: Competition

Today's world has much competition. People compete for jobs, states compete for businesses, and students compete for grades. The economist wants to know why this competition exists and what form it takes. First, the economist concludes, competition exists because of scarcity. If there were enough resources to satisfy all of our seemingly unlimited wants, people would not have to compete for the available but limited resources.

Second, the economist sees that competition takes the form of people trying to get more of the rationing device. If price is the rationing device, people will compete to earn dollars. People compete to earn dollars every day. Say three people are up for the same promotion at their business firm. Why do they want the promotion? Certainly added prestige and responsibility may be part of the answer, but still people are more likely to take promotions that come with more money.

What rationing device is used to decide who gets to eat pizza?

Suppose something other than price were used as the rationing device—muscular strength, for example. People with more muscular strength (measured by lifting weights) would receive more resources and goods than people with less muscular strength. In this situation, an

Would People Go to College If Scarcity Did Not Exist?

Evidence shows that as one's educational level rises, income rises, too. For example, in 1998, the average annual income for a person with only a high school diploma was $22,895, while the average annual income for a person with a bachelor's degree from college was $40,478. In other words, in 1998, college graduates earned an average of $17,583 more than high school graduates. Over time, this dollar difference tends to get larger, because average income increases at a faster rate for college graduates than for high school graduates.

What do these facts have to do with scarcity? Scarcity is the condition in which people's wants are greater than the resources available to satisfy those wants. Therefore, some rationing device must exist to decide who gets what quantity of the available resources. In the United States today that rationing device is U.S. dollars. The more dollars you have—in other words, the more of the rationing device you have—the more resources you can acquire, and the more of your wants you will be able to satisfy.

It follows that people will compete for dollars; that is, they will compete to get possession of the rationing device. One way people compete is by choosing to go to college. They know that by going to college they are likely to increase their annual and lifetime earnings, which, in simple language, means they will have more money. More money means more resources with which to satisfy their wants.

Of course, people also go to college for other reasons than to earn a higher income. They attend to obtain many nonmonetary benefits—to make friends, to develop a greater understanding about themselves and others, and to learn about subjects that they have always found interesting. Still, increasing annual and lifetime earnings is an important reason for going to college. To understand just how important, ask yourself whether as many people would go to college if there were no difference between the earnings of the average high school graduate and the average earnings of a college graduate. With no difference, the motivation for going to college would probably not be as strong for most people.

Also ask yourself if as many people would go to college if scarcity did not exist. In such a world, there would be no need for a rationing device and no need to compete for it. Stated differently, part of the reason people choose to attend college is because scarcity exists.

QUESTION TO ANSWER In recent years, the dollar difference between the average earnings of high school and college graduates has increased. Based on this information, would an economist predict that a smaller or a larger percentage of people would choose to attend college?

economics The science that studies the choices of people trying to satisfy their wants in a world of scarcity.

economist would predict that people would compete for muscular strength and would lift weights each day. The lesson is simple: Whatever the rationing device, people will compete for it.

A Definition of Economics

So far, you have learned about three important economic concepts—scarcity, choice, and opportunity cost—and you know something of the economic way of thinking. Now that you have started to think about economics, it's time for a formal definition of the term. **Economics** is the science that studies the choices of people trying to satisfy their wants in a world of scarcity.

Back to Opportunity Cost

You have learned that scarcity makes choice necessary, and that every time a choice is made, an opportunity cost is incurred. Economists add that a change in opportunity cost can, and often does, change a person's behavior. To illustrate, suppose Sunil has a part-time job at a local grocery store. Each day he goes to work at 2 P.M. and leaves at 6 P.M. Does he incur any opportunity costs when he chooses to work each day between 2 and 6 P.M.? He certainly does; whatever he would be doing if he weren't working is the opportunity cost of his working.

Naomi has an appointment to meet a friend at 12 noon, and she has a job interview at 2 P.M. For which appointment is she less likely to be late? Explain your answer.

Now let's increase the opportunity cost of Sunil's going to work. Suppose one day Sunil is on his way to work when someone stops him and offers to pay him $300 if he doesn't go to work that day. What will Sunil do? Will he continue on his way to work or take the $300 and not go to work? An economist would predict that as the opportunity cost of working at his part-time job increases relative to the benefits of working, Sunil is less likely to go to work. According to how economists think about behavior, whether Sunil's or your own, the higher the cost of doing something, the less likely it will be done.

Increase the opportunity cost of doing something ➡ Do less of it
Decrease the opportunity cost of doing something ➡ Do more of it

Section 1 Review

Defining Terms

1. Define
   a. scarcity
   b. opportunity cost
   c. economics
   d. want
   e. resource
   f. rationing device
2. Explain the difference between tangible and intangible goods.

Reviewing Facts and Concepts

3. Because scarcity exists, people must make choices. Explain why.
4. Give an example to illustrate the fact that a person may incur an opportunity cost without paying anyone any money.
5. Is the opportunity cost of attending high school the same for all high school students? Explain why or why not.

Critical Thinking

6. If price were not used as a rationing device, would something else have to be used? If so, what might it be?

Applying Economic Concepts

7. Gallagher is planning on going to college in a few months. The tuition is $2,000 a year. Assuming that Gallagher goes to college for four years, is the opportunity cost of his attending college $8,000? Why or why not?

SECTION 2

The Economic Way

You may think that your economics education will involve your learning specific definitions (What is opportunity cost?), theories (What causes unemployment or economic growth?), or facts (The national debt of the United States is so many billions of dollars). Certainly definitions, theories, and facts are all in this book and are part of your economics education. But the definitions, theories, and facts are not the most important part of your economics education. That role is played by the *economic way of thinking*. In other words, there is a certain way that economists think about, analyze, and view the world, and this economic way of thinking is the most important thing for you to learn in your economics course.

As you read this section, keep these key questions in mind:

- What does the economic way of thinking consist of?
- What is the difference between *microeconomics* and *macroeconomics*?

What costs do these girls incur by choosing to play basketball? What might some of the benefits be?

Key Terms

trade-off
global economy
microeconomics
macroeconomics

Thinking in Terms of Costs and Benefits

According to an economist, there are costs and benefits to almost everything we do. There are costs and benefits to learning economics, eating a hamburger, driving a car, asking a person out on a date, sleeping an extra hour, taking a vacation, or talking on the telephone.

According to the economist, a person will want to do whatever is under consideration only if the benefits are greater than the costs. For example, a person will buy a computer only if the benefits of buying the computer are expected to be greater than the costs of buying it. If the costs are perceived to be greater than the benefits, then the person will not purchase the computer.

A student graduates from high school and decides to go on to college. At college, she decides to major in psychology. What do we know about her choice of a major? According to the economist, we know that when she made the decision to major in psychology, she thought that the benefits of doing so would be greater than the costs.

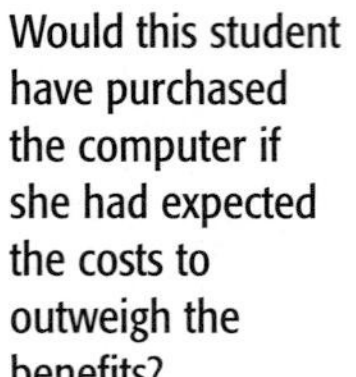

Would this student have purchased the computer if she had expected the costs to outweigh the benefits?

Thinking in Terms of Trade-Offs

Certain activities cause pollution. When we drive our cars, we pollute the air. One way to reduce the amount of pollution from cars is to develop more and better pollution-reducing technology. We have developed some already, but it has not eliminated pollution altogether. For example, although our cars today are equipped with pollution-reducing equipment, driving a car still produces some pollution. Given today's technology, then, the only way to get rid of absolutely all car pollution is to stop driving cars. Is it worth it?

If your answer is no, you already have a basic understanding of how an economist thinks. An economist believes that we can't have everything we want in the quantities we want. More of one thing often means less of something else. A situation in which more of one thing *necessarily* means less of something else is a **trade-off.** Economists identify many trade-offs in life. For example, more pollution-free air means less driving, and more driving means less pollution-free air. Taking more time to study for a test means having less time available to talk on the telephone with friends, and talking for a long time on the telephone means less time to study for the test.

If a country spends heavily on national defense, it will have less money to spend on other areas, such as health care and education. How are these trade-offs decided in the United States?

trade-off
A situation in which more of one thing necessarily means less of something else.

Think of a trade-off on a larger scale. A country wants to put more money into education. This strategy may be good, but putting more money into education means having less money available for medical research or national defense.

Thinking in Terms of What Would Have Been

Most people have the ability to think in terms of what *was* (the past), what *is* (the present), and what *will be* (the future). Economists think in these terms, too; then, they add at least one more category—thinking in terms of *what would have been.*

Suppose the federal government sets aside funds for a new interstate highway system. Thousands of people are hired to work on the project. Local newspapers in the towns along the highway write lots of stories on all the increased job activity. As a result, it looks as if more people are working on road construction, but no fewer people are working at anything else. It also appears that there are more highways, but no fewer cameras, computers, cars, and so on. Someone might think that we have gained the benefits of more jobs and highways without paying an opportunity cost.

We need to remind ourselves, however, that someone—namely, the taxpayers—had to pay for the new interstate highway system. What did the taxpayers give up by paying the taxes used to fund the new highway? They gave up the opportunity to buy more clothes, computers, books, and so on. We now begin to think in terms of all the products that would have been produced and consumed had the highway not

ECONOMICS *and the* INTERNET

Economists think in terms of both benefits and costs. For example, attending college has both benefits and costs. Usually, the benefits far exceed the costs. To learn more about colleges, go to the following Web site:
http://www.allaboutcollege.com

Once at the site, in the left margin you will see a list of various countries. Click on "United States." The next screen you see will list the fifty states and Washington, D.C. Click on the state in which you think you may want to attend college. From there, click on the names of a few colleges, and read about them. After spending some time looking at different colleges, identify what you think are the benefits and costs of attending college. Finally, do you think the benefits are greater than, less than, or equal to the costs?

When the federal government uses resources to build a new highway system, it follows that there are fewer resources available to do other things. This prompts the economist to ask, "What would have existed had the highway system not been built?"

been built. If, say, more clothes would have been produced instead of highways, it follows that more people would have worked in the clothing industry and fewer would have worked in highway construction. In short, we think in terms of *what would have been.* It is important to be able to think in terms of what would have been, because only then do we know the opportunity costs for what is.

Question: *Because the interstate highway system was built, people had to give up the opportunity to buy as many clothes, computers, books, and so on. The costs of the interstate highway system seem high. Does it follow that it would have been better if the federal government hadn't built the new interstate highway system?*

Answer: *Not necessarily. Remember, an economist thinks in terms of costs and benefits—not costs only. The things that "would have been" (had the interstate highway system not been built) relate to the costs of the highway system. It is still possible for the benefits of building the new interstate highway system to be greater than the costs. It does not necessarily follow that things would have been better if the federal government hadn't built the interstate system.*

Thinking in Terms of Unintended Effects

Has anything ever turned out differently from what you intended? No doubt you can provide numerous examples of these "unintended effects," as economists would call them. Suppose, for example, that on an average day a shoe store sells 100 pairs of shoes at an average price of $40 a pair, thereby earning $4,000. One day the store owner decides to raise the price of shoes from an average of $40 to $50. What does he intend or expect the effect of this action to be? He probably expects to increase his earnings from $4,000 a day to some greater amount, perhaps to $5,000 (100 pairs of shoes × $50 = $5,000). The store owner might be surprised by the results. At a higher price, it is very likely that he will sell fewer pairs of shoes. Suppose that at a price of $50 a pair, the owner sells an average of 70 pairs of shoes a day. What are his average daily earnings now? ($3,500, since 70 pairs of shoes × $50 = $3,500.) The owner did not intend for things to turn out this way; he intended to increase his earnings by raising the price of shoes. The decrease in his earnings is an unintended effect of his actions.

Consider another example of two nations, the United States and Japan, to illustrate the idea of unintended effects. Suppose that United States citizens are buying some Japanese goods (such as Japanese cars), and that Japanese citizens are buying some goods produced in the United States (such as U.S. computers). Then things change: the Japanese government decides to place a $200 tax (or tariff) on every U.S. computer sold in Japan. (A tax on foreign goods imported into a nation is called a *tariff*.) People in Japan who buy U.S. computers will have to pay $200 more than they would have paid without the tariff. Why might the Japanese government do this? It may want Japanese computers to outsell U.S. computers; it may want to generate higher profits and greater employment in the Japanese computer industry. To accomplish these goals, the government deliberately makes U.S. computers more expensive than Japanese computers by placing the tariff on U.S. computers. This action ends up hurting U.S. computer companies, because they sell fewer computers.

By raising the price of a pair of shoes, a storeowner may decrease, instead of increase, her earnings. Why?

The United States could decide to retaliate by placing a tariff on Japanese cars sold in the United States. Japanese cars will be more expensive, and fewer will be sold. This action will hurt Japanese car companies.

In summary, Japan initially takes an action—placing a tariff on U.S. computers sold in Japan—hoping that the Japanese people will buy more Japanese computers and fewer U.S. computers (the intended effect of the action). Let's say that the intended effect is realized: the Japanese people actually do buy more Japanese computers and fewer U.S. computers. But there is an unintended effect, too: the United States places a tariff on Japanese cars, which ends up hurting Japanese car companies. When the Japanese placed a tariff on U.S. computers, they did not intend for the United States to retaliate and place a tariff on Japanese cars.

If Japan places a tariff on U.S. computers imported into Japan, who is hurt? Who is helped?

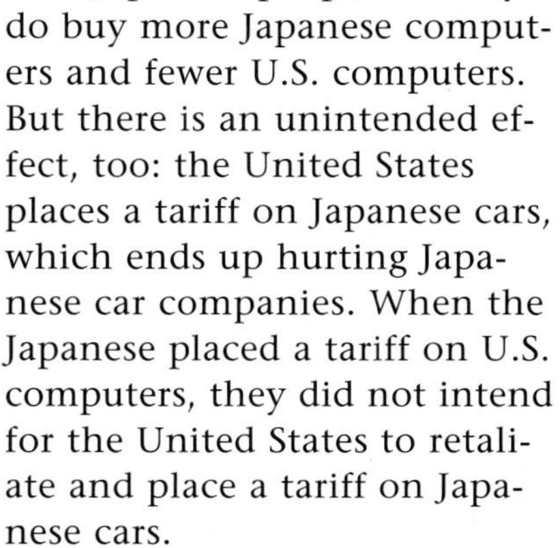

Do unintended effects matter? The answer is yes, they matter a great deal because they are part of the whole picture.

Economics Around the World

Why Is the Extended Family Common in India and Not in the United States?

People in different countries have different customs and traditions. For example, in India living in an extended family is customary. When a man and woman marry, they move in with one or the other's parents, and later if they have children, they continue to live with the parents. In contrast, the extended family is not customary in the United States today.

©1985 Da ecks. All rights reserved

Why is the extended family customary in India and not in the United States? Some people say it is because Indians are more family oriented than Americans, or because Indians have a longer tradition of the extended family than Americans do. These answers are not particularly informative. Saying that Indians are more family oriented than Americans is simply a way of describing, not explaining, the fact that the extended family is customary in India and not in the United States. Saying that Indians have a longer extended-family tradition than Americans does not explain *why* they have a longer tradition.

Let's look at the issue from an economic perspective. The economist might say that different generations are more likely to live together if it is more costly for the average member of the family to be independent. Stated differently, the more costly it is to "go it alone," the less likely one will live alone and the more likely one will live with family members.

The poorer a person is, the less likely he or she can make it alone. In short, it is harder for the average newlywed couple in India to rent their first apartment or buy their first home than it is for the average newlywed couple in the United States. In fact, it has been estimated that nearly 40 percent of the Indian population is too poor to afford even an adequate diet. Given the poverty in India, the extended family may simply be a means to survive.

Also, India has no well-developed social security system, and company retirement benefits are much less common than in the United States. Adults in their forties and fifties are more likely to have their aged parents live with them when the parents cannot survive on their own.

In fact, the extended family in India may simply be the Indian form of social security. The U.S. Social Security system is a pay-as-you-go system. Today's working population pays for today's retired population in return for the upcoming working population paying for them when they become the retired population. In India, adult children take care of their aged parents in return for having their children take care of them when they become old.

People often talk about customs and traditions as if they cannot be explained: They are what they are, and who knows why? To an economist, however, customs and traditions often have economic explanations.

QUESTION TO ANSWER In some countries, a siesta (a nap, usually taken at noon) is customary. In other countries, it is not. Do you think there is an economic explanation for the difference? If so, what is it?

That is why, for any action, economists think in terms of both intended and unintended effects.

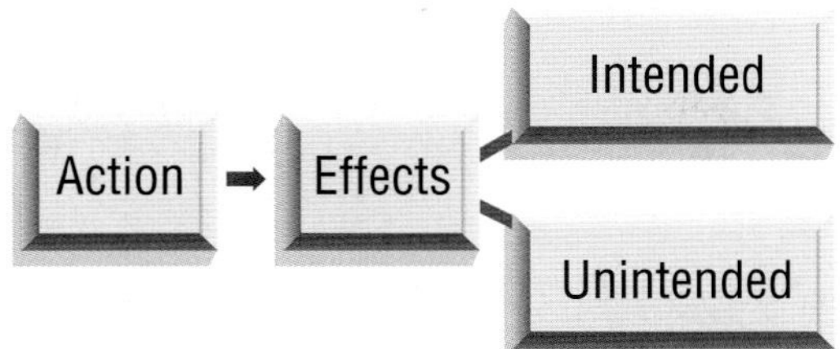

global economy An economy in which economic actions taken anywhere in the world may affect an individual's standard of living.

microeconomics The branch of economics that deals with human behavior and choices as they relate to relatively small units—an individual, a business firm, or a single market.

macroeconomics The branch of economics that deals with human behavior and choices as they relate to the entire economy.

Thinking in Terms of a Global Economy

Many economists think in terms of a **global economy,** an economy in which economic actions taken anywhere in the world may affect an individual's standard of living. To illustrate, economists often talk loosely about an economy's being "healthy" or "sick." When an economy is healthy, people are buying and selling goods, factories are being built, most people who want to work are working, and so on. When an economy is sick, people are not buying or selling goods as much, factories are not being built, and some people who want to work are unemployed.

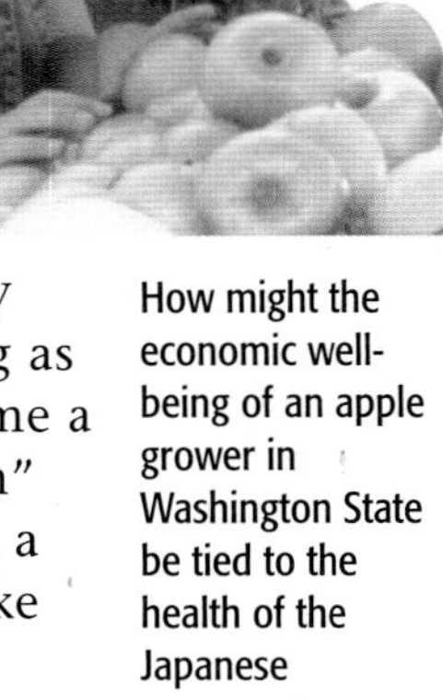

How might the economic well-being of an apple grower in Washington State be tied to the health of the Japanese economy?

Suppose that the Japanese, German, Mexican, and Canadian economies are sick. The people in these nations are not buying as much as they would buy if their economies were healthy. Some of the things they are no longer buying are things produced in other countries, such as the United States. Because people in the United States are not selling as many products in Japan, Germany, Mexico, and Canada, they do not earn as much income. Some U.S. workers may even lose their jobs because the businesses they work for are not selling as much to people in other nations. In turn, the U.S. economy may become a little sick. Obviously, people in the United States do not want to "catch" the economic illness of other nations, just as you do not want to catch a cold from the person sitting next to you in class. Unfortunately, just like real colds, economic "colds" are often contagious.

The good news is that economic health can be contagious, too. If the Japanese, German, Mexican, and Canadian economies get well and the people in these nations buy more goods, they may buy more U.S. goods, which will help U.S. businesses and workers.

Thinking in Terms of the Small and the Big

Economics is divided into two branches, **microeconomics** and **macroeconomics.** In microeconomics, economists look at the small picture. They study the behavior and choices of relatively small economic units, such as an individual or a single business firm. Economists who deal with macroeconomics look at the big picture, studying behavior and

Exhibit 1-3
Two Major Branches of Economics

Economists divide economics into two major branches: microeconomics and macroeconomics. Without reading about these two branches, guess which one looks at *small* economic units.

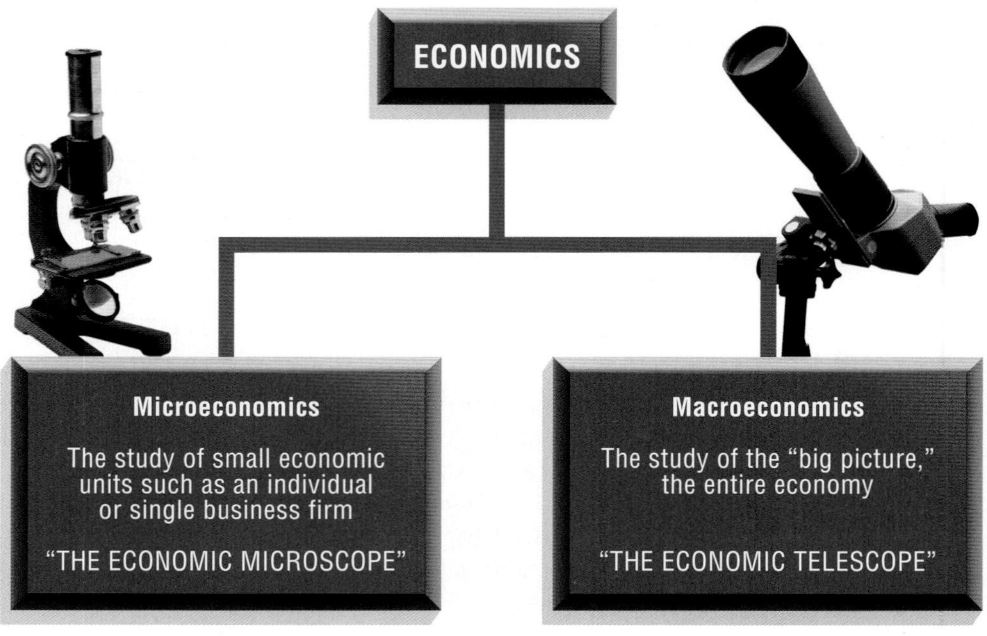

choices as they relate to the entire economy. (See Exhibit 1-3). For example, in microeconomics, an economist would study and discuss the unemployment that exists in a particular industry, such as the car industry; in macroeconomics, an economist would investigate the unemployment that exists in the nation. In microeconomics, an economist would look at the buying behavior of consumers in regard to a single product, such as computers; an economist dealing in macroeconomics would study the buying behavior of consumers in regard to all goods. We might say that the tools of macroeconomics are telescopes, while the tools of microeconomics are microscopes. Macroeconomics stands back from the trees to see the forest. Microeconomics gets up close and examines the tree itself, including its bark, its branches, and the soil in which it grows.

Section 2 Review

Defining Terms

1. Define
- **a.** trade-off
- **b.** global economy
- **c.** microeconomics
- **d.** macroeconomics

2. Use the word *trade-off* correctly in a sentence.

Reviewing Facts and Concepts

3. According to economists, there are costs and benefits to almost everything we do. Identify the costs and benefits of each of the following: going to the dentist for a checkup, doing your homework, and getting an extra hour of sleep.

4. Give an example of an unintended effect.

5. What is the difference between microeconomics and macroeconomics?

Critical Thinking

6. If there were zero opportunity cost to everything you did, would you ever face a trade-off? Explain your answer.

Applying Economic Concepts

7. How could you go about proving that you live in a global economy?

SECTION 3

Building and Testing Theories

Economists often build theories. This section explains why they build theories, how they build them, and what purpose the theories serve.

As you read this section, keep these key questions in mind:

- Why do economists build theories?
- What is a theory?
- How should we judge theories?

Key Term

theory

Some Questions Do Not Have Obvious Answers

Some questions have obvious answers, and others do not. To illustrate, if you hold a ball in your right hand and ask someone what will happen if you let go of it, the person will likely say that the ball will drop to the ground. Right answer. If the classroom clock reads 10:12 and you ask someone in the class what time it is, that person will say 10:12. Again, right answer.

Now suppose you ask someone any of the following questions:

- Why is the crime rate higher in the United States than in England?
- What causes the stock market to rise or fall?
- What causes some nations to be rich and others to be poor?

There are no obvious (or easy) answers to these questions.

Because some economic questions do not have obvious answers, economists build theories. Think of a theory as a mechanism that an economist uses to answer a question for which there is no obvious (or easy) answer. Here are only five of hundreds of questions for which economists have built theories:

1. What causes inflation?
2. What causes the unemployment rate to rise or fall?
3. How do business firms operate?
4. What causes the prices of goods and services to rise, fall, or remain stable?
5. Why do countries experience good economic times in some years and bad economic times in other years?

Gas prices will often rise and fall. An economist will build an economic theory to explain why gas prices fluctuate.

But What Is a Theory?

A couple of stories will help you understand the formal definition of *theory.*

Do you think that an understanding of the calorie theory can help this woman maintain her desired weight? Explain your answer.

Gaining Weight Suppose you are living in the days before anyone has heard the word *calorie.* Over a period of three years, you notice that your weight changes. At one time you weigh 140 pounds, then 145 pounds, then 155 pounds. You wonder why you are gaining weight.

Along comes a person who gives you a simplified explanation of what is happening. She says that there are things called "calories," and that we can measure food in terms of how many calories it has. Some foods have more calories than others. She then says that every day you use up, or expend, calories when you walk, run, clean the house, and so on. Finally, she says that your weight depends on how many calories you take in compared to how many you burn. If you consume more calories than you expend, you will gain weight.

This calorie theory is used to explain one's weight. You will notice that in this theory there is an explanation of how things work (how your body takes in and uses up calories) in order to answer a question. All theories have this structure. A theory always has some explanation of how things work in order to answer a question that does not have an obvious answer.

theory
An explanation of how something works, designed to answer a question for which there is no obvious answer.

The Definition of a Theory A **theory** is an explanation of how something works, designed to answer a question for which there is no obvious answer.

How Do We Judge Theories?

We should judge theories by how well they predict, not by how they sound to us. At one time, the round-earth theory sounded ridiculous to people, but it has been proved correct.

Many people evaluate a theory based on whether or not it seems reasonable. However, many theories that at first seemed very unreasonable to people turned out to be correct. Think about how it might have sounded to you if you had lived before microscopes were invented and someone told you that people were getting sick because of tiny "things" (which today we call *germs*) that no one could see. You might have thought that sounded ridiculous. Or suppose you had lived during the days of Christopher Columbus and someone proposed the round-earth theory to answer a question. You might have said, "There is no such thing as a round earth!"

Sometimes things that sound ridiculous and wrong to us turn out to be right. Germs that we cannot see can and sometimes do cause human sickness. The earth is indeed round (spherical).

Scientists believe that we should evaluate theories based not on how they sound to us, or whether they seem right, but on how well they *predict*. If they predict well, then we should accept them; if they predict poorly, then we should not.

What are the predictions of the calorie theory we discussed earlier? The theory predicts that the more high-calorie goods you eat and the less activity you have in your daily life, the more weight you will gain. And this is exactly what we do see. The calorie theory's predictions are supported by real-world evidence.

Summary on Theory

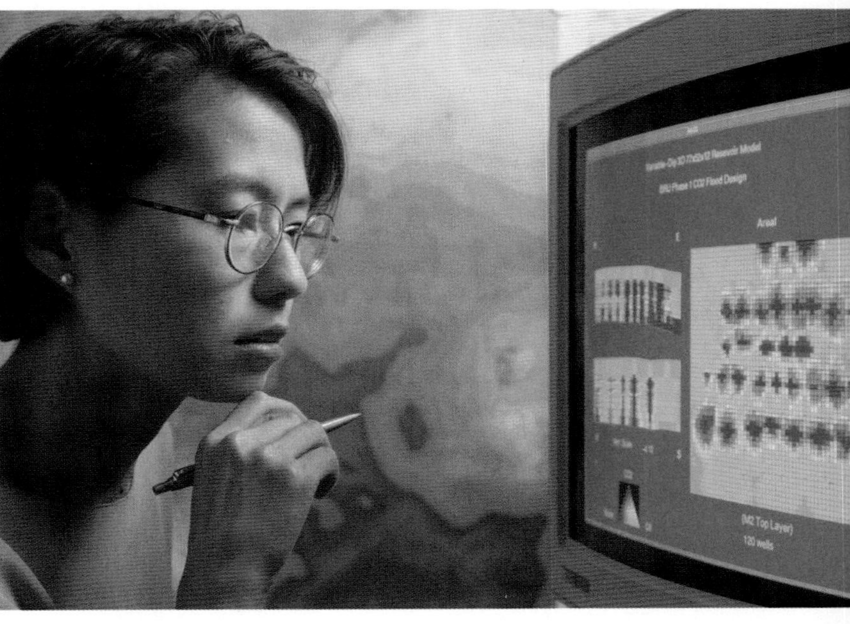

Some theories predict more accurately today, thanks to the advanced technology of computers.

Economists build theories to answer economic questions for which there are no obvious answers. All theories are explanations of how the theorist believes something works. For example, a theory about the economy will explain how the economy works; a theory about the human body will explain how the human body works. Theories are better judged by how well they predict than by how they seem or sound to us, because what sounds right may be wrong, and what sounds wrong may be right. No doubt, as you read this text, you will come across an economic theory here or there that you think sounds wrong. You are urged to adopt the scientific attitude and hold off judging any economic theory until you learn how well it predicts.

Finally, all theories leave certain factors out in explaining how something works. What is left out is what the theorist believes is unimportant and unnecessary.

Section 3 Review

Defining Terms

1. Define *theory.*

Reviewing Facts and Concepts

2. Why don't economists build theories to answer *all* questions? Why build theories for only those questions that have no obvious answer?

3. Smith proposes a certain theory to explain economic growth. Jones criticizes Smith's theory because, as she says, "it leaves too many factors out of the analysis." Comment on Jones's criticism of Smith's theory.

Critical Thinking

4. Suppose a biologist's theory on swans predicts that all swans are white. The biologist then tests the theory by searching for swans and noting their color. So far, all swans identified have been white. Does it follow that the theory is necessarily correct and that all swans are white? Explain your answer.

Applying Economic Concepts

5. Chia-Yu and Rachel are in the same geometry class. Until today, their teacher always came to class well groomed and well dressed. Today, she came to class with uncombed hair and a careless appearance. Chia-Yu and Rachel each came up with a theory to explain this change in appearance. Chia-Yu says that the teacher got up late, had less time to get ready for school than usual, and therefore did not have time to tend to her appearance. Rachel says that the teacher has made a conscious decision to change her looks. Instead of taking as much time with her appearance, she has decided to be a little more carefree and just go as she is. How might we test each of the two theories to see which comes closer to the truth?

SECTION 4

Four Types of Resources and Three Economic Questions

This section discusses four types of resources. It also lists and explains the three economic questions that every society has to answer. As you read this section, keep these key questions in mind:

- What are the four types of resources or factors of production?
- What is land, labor, capital, and entrepreneurship?
- What are the monetary payments to each of the four types of resources?
- What are the three economic questions that every society must answer?
- What is an economic system?
- What are the major differences between free enterprise and socialism?
- What is a mixed economy?

Land is one of the four factors of production. It includes all the natural resources found in nature, including animals and diamonds.

Four Resources

Key Terms

land
labor
capital
entrepreneurship
rent
wages
interest
profit
economic system
free enterprise
socialism
economic plan
income distribution
mixed economy

Scarcity is the condition in which our wants are greater than the resources available to satisfy those wants. In economics, a synonym for *resources* is *factors of production.* Resources, or factors of production, are what people use to produce goods. For example, wood and a machine are resources that may be used to produce a desk. Economists place resources in four broad categories: land, labor, capital, and entrepreneurship.

Land When the word **land** is mentioned, you may picture an acre of woods or a plowed field in your mind's eye. The resource *land* is more, however. It includes all the natural resources found in nature—such as water, minerals, undeveloped land (including the thousands of miles of desert in Nevada and California), animals, and forests.

Labor **Labor** refers to the physical and mental talents that people contribute to the production of goods and services. For example, a person working in a factory is considered to be the resource labor. A TV weatherperson telling you what the weather will be like tomorrow is considered to be the resource labor.

A construction worker is considered to be the resource labor.

land
All the natural resources found in nature. An acre of land, mineral deposits, and water in a stream are all considered land.

labor
The physical and mental talents that people contribute to the production of goods and services.

capital
Produced goods that can be used as resources for further production. Such things as factories, machines, and farm tractors are capital.

entrepreneurship
The special talent that some people have for searching out and taking advantage of new business opportunities and for developing new products and new ways of doing things.

Capital In economics, **capital** refers to produced goods that can be used as resources for further production. Such things as machinery, tools, computers, trucks, buildings, and factories are all considered to be capital. Each is used to produce some other good.

Entrepreneurship If someone asked you to point to the resource land, you might point to a forest. For the resource labor, you might point to yourself as an example. To show capital, you might point to a computer. But what would you point to if someone asked you to give an example of **entrepreneurship**? This resource is not so easy to identify.

The trucking business plays a major role in U.S. industry. Why are trucks considered the resource capital?

Entrepreneurship refers to the special talent that some people have for searching out and taking advantage of new business opportunities, as well as for developing new products and new ways of doing things. For example, Steven Jobs, one of the developers of the first personal computer, exhibited entrepreneurship. He saw a use for the personal computer and developed it, and hundreds of thousands of customers then purchased his product—the Apple computer.

Question: *Because only people can exhibit entrepreneurship, why isn't entrepreneurship considered a type of labor? In short, why aren't there only three resources—land, labor, and capital—instead of four?*

Answer: *Economists consider entrepreneurship sufficiently different from the ordinary talents of people to deserve its own category. Consider this explanation. Both an apple and celery are nonmeats, but we don't put them into the same category. An apple is a fruit, and celery is a vegetable. They are different enough to be placed in different categories. So it is with labor and entrepreneurship. The* ordinary *mental and physical talents of people are considered labor. The* special *talents that are directed toward searching out and taking advantage of new business opportunities, products, and methods are considered entrepreneurship.*

The Monetary Payments to Resources

When someone wants to use resources to produce a good—such as a house or car—that person has to pay for the resources. This fact implies that we can link monetary, or money, payments to the resources that are

Steven Jobs helped develop the first Apple computer. Why would an economist classify his accomplishment an example of entrepreneurship and not of labor?

Technology & Innovation

What Does a Steam Engine Have to Do With Where a Factory Locates?

Entrepreneurship refers to the special talent that some people have for searching out and taking advantage of new business opportunities, as well as for developing new products and new ways of doing things. In short, entrepreneurs are innovators and developers of new technology. Often, as a result of the innovations of entrepreneurs, the economy changes in fundamental ways, and as a result of fundamental changes in the economy, life changes.

Consider life in England before the introduction of the steam engine. Before steam power, work could be performed only by humans, animals, wind, or moving water. To use wind or moving water, people had to go where these resources could be found. Thus, the early factories in England had to be located in the countryside, where wind and water (streams) were most likely to be found. The goods produced in the factories were then carried over the open crude roads by horse and oxen, a time-consuming and expensive means of transportation. It was so expensive, in fact, that by the time the goods were produced and transported to the cities, the price of the goods was so high that only the richest could afford to buy them.

Thomas Newcomen developed the first practical steam engine in 1712. His invention meant that much less labor was needed to do manual work, so the cost of the resource labor was lowered.

In 1769, James Watt came up with a technological innovation that increased the efficiency of the steam engine that made it possible to locate a steam engine anywhere, not only near a source of fuel. Therefore, a factory could be located anywhere. Factories could be built near consumers to cut down on transportation costs. Lower labor and transportation costs meant prices were lower and more people could buy the goods that were produced in the factories.

The steam engine not only economized on human labor, influenced the location of factories, and brought many more goods within the reach of ordinary people, it also changed the political environment in England. Before the steam engine, political power was largely held by the landowning aristocracy. As a result of the steam engine, a prosperous industrial class began to emerge, and the monopolistic political power of the landed aristocracy was soon a thing of the past.

QUESTION TO ANSWER Economists think in terms of benefits and costs. What do you see as the benefits of the steam engine? The costs?

used to produce goods. Payment to a land resource is called **rent;** payment to labor is called **wages;** payment to capital is called **interest;** and payment to entrepreneurship is called **profits.** Stated differently, land earns rent, labor earns wages, capital earns interest, and entrepreneurship earns profits.

Suppose you want to build a house. You hire some workers (labor), you buy some tools (capital), and you buy a lot (land). You have to make monetary payments for each of the resources you buy. Let's say you pay $24,000 in total for the workers you hire (this figure includes what you pay yourself as a worker, too). You pay $10,000 for tools and $25,000 for the wooded lot in the city's newest development. These dollar figures represent the earnings from the resources of labor, capital, and land. Adding these figures yields a total of $59,000. Now suppose you sell the house to someone for $70,000. The difference between the cost of the house and the sales price of the house is $11,000, which is profit. Profit is the payment to the resource entrepreneurship.

Notice that we can take the sales price of the house ($70,000) and break it up into the payments to different resources: $24,000 to labor, $10,000 to capital, $25,000 to land, and $11,000 to entrepreneurship. Looking at things this way, we notice that the price a consumer pays for a good purchased is more than simply the money that the seller receives. Included in it are the monetary payments to different resources, or factors of production.

rent
The payment to the resource land.

wages
The payment to the resource labor.

interest
The payment to the resource capital.

profit
The payment to the resource entrepreneurship.

Three Economic Questions Every Society Must Answer

All nations in the world have something fundamental in common: all must decide how to answer three economic questions about the production and distribution of goods.

The first economic question every society has to answer is, *What goods will be produced?* Because of scarcity, no country can produce every

A farmer uses a tractor to plow the fields. To which of the three economic questions is this action relevant?

Jeff Bezos, Founder and CEO of Amazon.com Books

You can buy a popular book in two principal ways. You can get into your car, drive to a bookstore, search the shelves, buy the book, and return home; or you can purchase the book online.

Perhaps the best-known online bookstore is Amazon.com Books. Jeff Bezos, its founder and chief executive officer (CEO), graduated from Princeton University in 1986 with a degree in electrical engineering and computer science. In the spring of 1994, Bezos came across some information that changed his life: World Wide Web usage was growing at 2,300 percent a year. Bezos decided to start a company that would make use of the Web. He drew up a list of twenty-five products that he thought could easily be sold over the Web. At the top of the list were books.

Bezos headquartered Amazon.com in Seattle, Washington, to take advantage of its proximity to major book warehouses and the technical people needed to run an online bookstore. He named his bookstore "Amazon" and called it the "Earth's Largest Bookstore" because the Amazon River is the world's largest river in terms of the volume of its discharge basin. Big river, big bookstore.

QUESTION TO ANSWER How has Bezos affected the opportunity cost of buying books? If you are not familiar with Amazon.com, you may want to visit the Web site before you answer the question. The site address is: http://www.amazon.com

Web Designer

Hundreds of Web sites are added to the World Wide Web every day. A Web designer, sometimes called a Webmaster, is a person who develops and maintains a site on the World Wide Web. Web designers often work with graphic designers and writers who develop the content–art and text–for the site. Sometimes, however, Web designers themselves devise the art and write the text for a client. Then they code or program the site and maintain its links and content.

Jobs for Web designers are everywhere these days. Almost everyone wants to be on the Web–businesses, schools and universities, charitable organizations, special-interest groups, libraries, and so on. The academic background of Web designers is varied. Most are college graduates with majors such as computer science, journalism, and graphic design. Almost all know HyperText Markup Language (HTML), the language used to create World Wide Web pages, and JAVA, a cross-platform programming language that can be used to create animation and interactive features on Web pages. To learn more about work as a Web designer or Webmaster, you may want to go to the following site: http://www.websitebuilder.com

QUESTION TO ANSWER A few years ago, if you had told people you were a Webmaster, they would not have known what you were talking about. What does this tell you about the relationship between changes in technology and the types of jobs available?

good it wants in the quantity it would like. More of one good (say, television sets) leaves fewer resources to produce other goods (such as cars). No matter what nation we are talking about—the United States, China, or Brazil—each one has to decide what goods will be produced.

The next question every society has to answer is, *How will the goods be produced?* Will farmers using modern tractors produce food, or will farmers using primitive tools produce it? Will the food be produced on private farms, where production decisions are made by individual farmers, or will it be produced on collective farms, where production decisions are made by people in the government?

The third question is, *For whom will the goods be produced?* Will anyone who is able and willing to pay the prices for the goods be able to obtain them, or will government decide who will have the goods?

How a society answers these three economic questions defines its **economic system.** Stated differently, it is the function of an economic system to answer these three economic questions. There are two major economic systems: **free enterprise** and **socialism.** Free enterprise is an economic system in which individuals own most, if not all, the resources and control their use. In socialism, government controls and may own many of the resources. Sometimes free enterprise is called *capitalism* or a *market economy.* This book will mainly use the term *free enterprise,* but occasionally it will speak of a capitalist economic system or a market economy. Socialism is sometimes loosely referred to as a *command economy.* To be more accurate, a command economy is a particular type of socialist economic system, which will be discussed in some detail in a later chapter. This chapter discusses the broad outlines of free enterprise and socialism.

economic system
The way in which a society decides what goods to produce, how to produce them, and for whom goods will be produced.

free enterprise
An economic system in which individuals (not government) own most, if not all, the resources and control their use. Government plays a very small role in the economy.

socialism
An economic system in which government controls and may own many of the resources. Government plays a major role in the economy.

economic plan
A government program specifying economic activities, such as what goods are to be produced and what prices will be charged.

income distribution
The way all the income earned in a country is divided among different groups of income earners.

Major Differences between Free Enterprise and Socialism

Let's look at the major differences between free enterprise and socialism in a few areas.

Resources Resources are used to produce goods and services. In a free-enterprise economic system, these resources are owned and controlled by private individuals. In a socialist economic system, the government controls and may own many of the resources.

Government's Role in the Economy In a free-enterprise economic system, government has a small role to play in the economy. It does not make decisions on things like what goods and services will be produced or how they will be produced. Under socialism, government may make those decisions.

Economic Plans Under socialism, government decision makers may write an **economic plan,** a plan that specifies the direction economic activities are to take. For example, a plan may state that over the next five years, the nation's economy will produce more manufactured goods (such as cars and trucks) and fewer agricultural goods (such as wheat and corn). A free-enterprise economic system would have no such plan.

Income Distribution **Income distribution** refers to how all the income earned in a country is divided among different groups of income earners. In a free-enterprise economic system less attention is paid to the income distribution than in a socialist economic system. Government decision makers under socialism are more likely to use government's powers to redistribute income, usually directing it away from society's high earners. In the United States, although the income distribution is unequal, there is income mobility. For example, a University of Michigan study reported that of the people who were in the lowest fifth of the income distribution in 1975, only 5.1 percent were still there in 1991—and 29 percent were in the highest fifth.

THINKING Like an Economist

Some people look at countries and see differences. People speak French in France and English in the United States, for example. The crime rate is higher in the United States than in Belgium. The economist looks at countries and sees similarities. For example, the United States has to decide what goods will be produced, how the goods will be produced, and for whom the goods will be produced, and so do China, Russia, Mexico, Egypt, and every other country in the world.

Controlling Prices In a free-enterprise economic system, prices are allowed to fluctuate—that is, to go up and down. Government does not attempt to control prices. In a socialist economic system, government decision makers do control prices, although not all socialist systems control prices to the same extent. For example, government decision makers may think that the price of bread is too high at $2 a loaf and thus order that no one be allowed to buy or sell bread for more than $1.50 a

In China, the government intervenes to redistribute income. How might this practice affect a Chinese entepreneur who wants to design and manufacture a new and better product (for example, a new and better bicycle)?

loaf. Or they may feel that wage rates for unskilled labor are too low at $4 an hour and thus order that no one be allowed to "buy" or "sell" unskilled labor for less than $6 an hour. We will discuss arguments that have arisen about these and other matters in later chapters.

Economic Systems and Reality

In reality, a nation's economic system may contain some ingredients of free enterprise and some ingredients of socialism. For example, the United States is considered to have a free-enterprise economic system. After all, most of the resources are owned by private individuals, and there are no economic plans to speak of. But the U.S. government plays a larger role in the economy than it would play in a pure free-enterprise system, and some prices are controlled. Thus, while the United States is considered a free-enterprise nation, it has a few features of socialism. (See Exhibit 1-4.)

A similar point can be made for other nations. For example, China is considered to be a socialist economic nation. Many resources are owned by government, economic plans are customary, and some prices are controlled. But in some areas, China has been experimenting with free-enterprise practices, so to say that China is 100 percent socialist would be incorrect.

Sometimes, economies that have features of both free enterprise and socialism are called **mixed economies.** If we were to adopt this terminology, we would have to say that both the U.S. and Chinese economies are mixed economies. However, to call them both mixed economies is misleading. It makes them sound alike when they are not. The United States

mixed economy
An economy that has features of both free enterprise and socialism.

Exhibit 1-4

Differences between Free Enterprise and Socialism

The chart will help you summarize some of the major differences between free enterprise and socialism.

	Free Enterprise	Socialism
Resources	Owned by private individuals	Owned by government
Government's role in the economy	Small role	Major role
Economic plans	None	Written by government decision makers
Income distribution	Government pays little attention to equality or inequality of income distribution	Government pays much greater attention; may redistribute income
Controlling prices	May fluctuate—government doesn't control	Government controls prices to varying degrees

Exhibit 1-5

A Spectrum of Economic Systems

There are two major and radically different economic systems: free enterprise and socialism. Here, these two economic systems lie at opposite ends of a spectrum. Most nations' economies fall somewhere between socialism and free enterprise on this spectrum, although an economy is usually closer to one end than the other. For example, Nation D's economy is more nearly a free-enterprise system and less a socialist system than Nation B's economy.

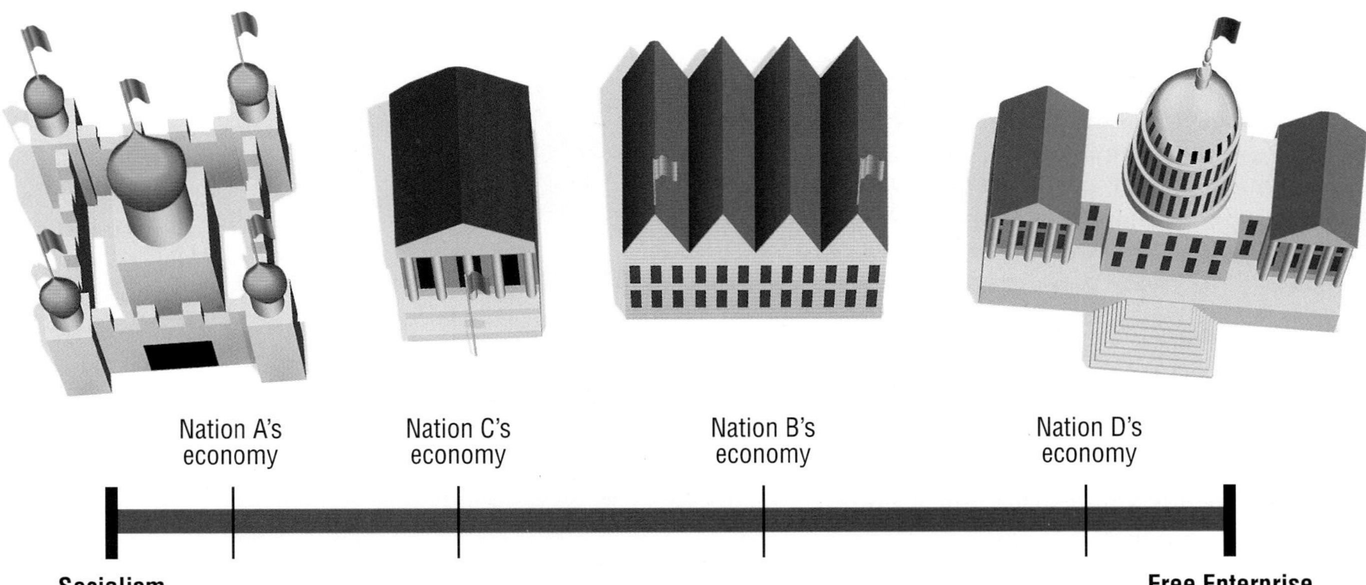

has much more free enterprise than China, and China has much more socialism than the United States; the economies of these two nations are quite different. It is clearer to refer to the United States as a free-enterprise nation and to China as principally a socialist nation, while noting that there are some socialist practices in the United States and some free-enterprise practices in China.

Very few countries operate as a pure free-enterprise or pure socialist system. Instead, they draw from both systems and become known as mixed economies. How much or how little they implement from each economy will dictate whether or not they are viewed by others as a free-enterprise or socialist nation. Exhibit 1-5 illustrates this.

Section 4 Review

Defining Terms

1. Define
- **a.** entrepreneurship
- **b.** interest
- **c.** profits
- **d.** economic system
- **e.** rent
- **f.** wages
- **g.** economic plan
- **h.** income distribution

2. If an economy has elements of more than one economic system, it is a ______.

Reviewing Facts and Concepts

3. Identify the following resources. Write "Ld" for land, "Lb" for labor, "C" for capital, and "E" for entrepreneurship.
- **a.** Francis's work as a secretary
- **b.** iron ore
- **c.** a farm tractor
- **d.** a computer used to write a book
- **e.** a comedian telling jokes on a television show
- **f.** a singer singing at an outdoor concert
- **g.** your teacher teaching you economics
- **h.** someone inventing a new product
- **i.** crude oil
- **j.** oil-drilling equipment

4. What are the three economic questions that every society must answer?

5. What is the difference between free enterprise and socialism when it comes to the ownership of most resources?

Critical Thinking

6. If most economies of the world are mixed economies, does it follow that most economies are the same? Explain your answer.

Applying Economic Concepts

7. What are some of the questions you would need answers to before you could accurately label an economy *free enterprise* or *socialist?*

Developing Economic

Skills

Illustrating Ideas with Graphs

A picture is worth a thousand words. It is with this familiar saying in mind that economists construct their graphs. With a few lines and some curves, much can be said. In this section, we examine a few of the graphs commonly used in economics.

Pie Charts (or Pie Graphs)

A pie chart is a convenient way to represent the parts of something that, added together, equal the whole. Suppose we consider a typical 24-hour weekday for Danny Chen. On a typical weekday, Danny spends 8 hours sleeping, 6 hours in school, 2 hours at football practice, 2 hours doing homework, 1 hour watching television, and 5 hours doing nothing (hanging out). It is easy to represent the breakdown of a typical weekday for Danny in pie chart form, as in Exhibit 1-6.

Exhibit 1-6

A Pie Chart

Homework
Football practice
Watching TV
Hanging out
School
Sleeping

As you will notice, pie charts give you a quick visual message that shows rough percentage breakdowns and relative relationships. For example, in Exhibit 1-6, it is easy to see that Danny spends much of his time sleeping (the "sleeping" slice of the pie is the largest slice). He spends the same amount of time at football practice as doing his homework and twice as much time doing his homework as watching television.

Exhibit 1-7

A Bar Graph

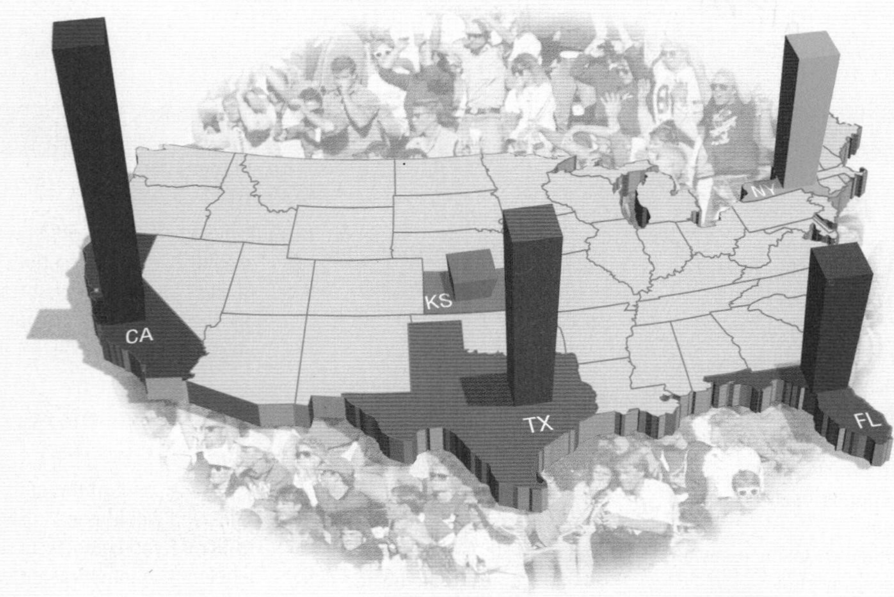

Bar Graphs

The bar graph is another visual aid that economists use to convey relationships. Suppose we want to represent the projected population of various states at the beginning of the year 2005, as in Exhibit 1-7. Among the many relationships shown, we can see that Texas is projected to have a slightly greater population than New York, and California is expected to have more people than either of those two states.

Line Graphs

Sometimes information is best and most easily displayed in a line graph. Line graphs are particularly useful to illustrate changes in a factor over some time period. Suppose we want to illustrate the variations in average points per game for a high school basketball team in recent years. As you can see from Part (a) of Exhibit 1-8, the basketball team was on a roller coaster during the years 1987 to 2000. The team's performance was not consistent from one year to the next.

Part (b) takes the data presented in Part (a) of Exhibit 1-8 and shows it in another way. This graph uses a different measurement scale on the vertical axis. With this scale, the distance between 20 and 40 points, the distance between 40 and 60 points, and so on are less than the distances in Part (a). Now the line that connects the average points per game in the different years is much more nearly straight, so the basketball team appears much less inconsistent than in Part (a). In fact, we could choose a scale that would allow us to end up with something close to a straight line. The point is this: Data shown in line graph form may convey different messages depending on the measurement scale used.

QUESTIONS TO ANSWER

1. Explain how pie charts give information illustrating relative relationships.
2. When would you most likely use a pie chart to illustrate something?
3. When are line graphs most useful?

Exhibit 1-8

Two Line Graphs Plot the Same Data

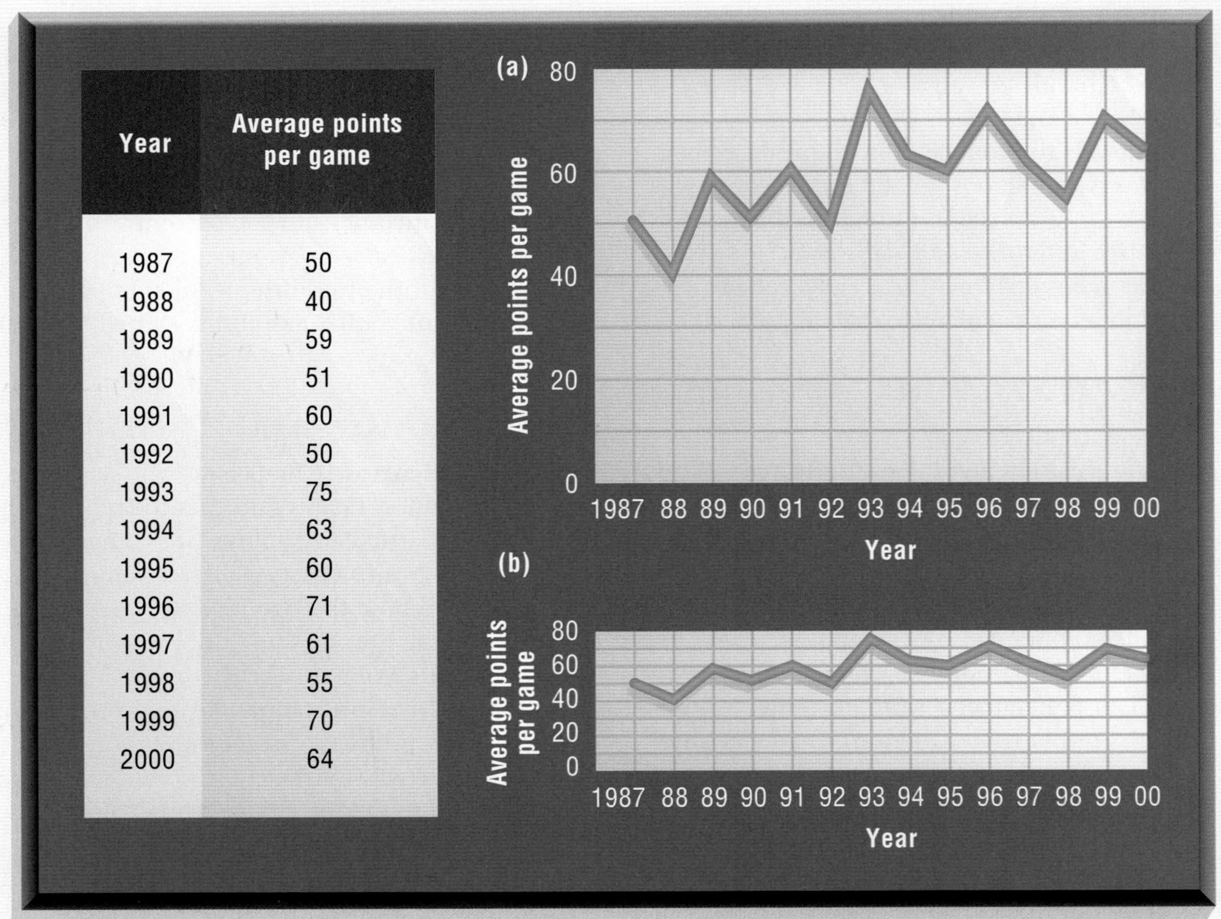

Year	Average points per game
1987	50
1988	40
1989	59
1990	51
1991	60
1992	50
1993	75
1994	63
1995	60
1996	71
1997	61
1998	55
1999	70
2000	64

CHAPTER 1 Review

Economics Vocabulary

Fill in the following blanks with the appropriate word or phrase.

1. The condition where wants are greater than the resources available to satisfy those wants is called _____.
2. Things that we desire to have are called _____.
3. _____ is the most highly valued opportunity or alternative forfeited when a choice is made.
4. _____ is the science that studies the choices of people trying to satisfy their wants in a world of scarcity.
5. The branch of economics that deals with human behavior and choices as they relate to relatively small units is called _____.
6. A(n) _____ is an explanation of how something works, designed to answer a question for which there is no obvious answer.
7. An _____ is the way in which a society decides what goods to produce, how to produce them, and for whom goods will be produced.
8. A(n) _____ is an economy that has features of both free enterprise and socialism.
9. The monetary payment to land is called _____.
10. The monetary payment to capital is called _____.

Review Questions

1. What is scarcity?
2. Explain this statement: Because scarcity exists, choices must be made.
3. Explain the link between scarcity and competition.
4. If you attend a public high school, there is no admission fee or tuition. Does it follow, then, that there is no opportunity cost to your attending school? Explain your answer.
5. Why is it preferable to think in terms of costs and benefits rather than in terms of benefits only?
6. Suppose there is a high cost to building more schools in your city or town. Does it necessarily follow that the schools should not be built? Explain your answer.
7. Suppose apples are currently selling for 50 cents each. Someone says that apple sellers can't make a decent living if they sell their apples so cheaply. He says there should be a law stating that no one can sell an apple, and no one can buy an apple, for less than 75 cents. He intends for the law to raise the income of apple sellers. What might be an unintended effect of this law? Explain your answer.
8. Why is it better to judge theories by how well they predict than by whether or not they sound right or reasonable to us?
9. How is a theory like a road map?
10. How does entrepreneurship differ from labor?
11. What is an economic system? What are the two major economic systems in the world today?
12. List three ways in which free enterprise and socialism are different.

Calculations

1. Bill decided to buy six books on history instead of four books on politics. It follows, then, that the opportunity cost of each history book was _____ books on politics.
2. The chapter mentioned that the price of a good can be viewed as the sum of the monetary payments to the various resources that produced the good. Using this background information, if wages are \$40, rent is \$20, interest is \$10, and there is a \$10 loss incurred on the sale of the good, then what is the price of the good?
3. The top fifth of income earners earn 45 percent of total income, and the bottom fifth of income earners earn 5 percent of total income. If the earnings of the top fifth are \$600 billion a year, what absolute dollar amount is earned by the bottom fifth?

Economics and Thinking Skills

1. **Application.** The person who developed Music Television (MTV) said that today's younger generation particularly enjoys two things: (1) television and (2) music, especially rock music. His idea was to combine the two, and MTV was born. Would you say that he was exhibiting entrepreneurship? Explain your answer.
2. **Application.** Think like an entrepreneur. Identify a new product or service that you believe many people will want to buy. Outline the details of the new product or service, and explain why you think people will want to buy it.
3. **Analysis.** Explain how scarcity is related to each of the following: (1) choice, (2) opportunity cost,

(3) a rationing device, and (4) competition.

4. **Cause and Effect.** "Because we have to make choices, there is scarcity." What is wrong with this statement?

Writing Skills

Write a one-page paper explaining how the world would be different if scarcity did not exist.

Economics in the Media

Find an example in your local newspaper of one effect of scarcity. Your example may come from an article, editorial, or advertisement.

Where's the Economics?

What does this classroom of college students have to do with scarcity?

Analyzing Primary Sources

Henry Hazlitt, economist and journalist, wrote a book called *Economics in One Lesson*, first published in 1946. It became famous for outlining some of the basic principles of economics. Hazlitt, in a simple story from the book, shows us that economists often think in terms of what would have been:

A young hoodlum, say, heaves a brick through the window of a baker's shop. The shopkeeper runs out furious, but the boy is gone. A crowd gathers, and begins to stare with quiet satisfaction at the gaping hole in the window and the shattered glass over the bread and pies. After awhile the crowd feels the need for philosophic reflection. And several of its members are almost certain to remind each other or the baker that, after all, the misfortune has its bright side. It will make business for some glazier [glass setter]. *As they begin to think of this they elaborate upon it. How much does a new plate glass window cost? Two hundred and fifty dollars? That will be quite a sum. After all, if windows were never broken, what would happen to the glass business? Then, of course, the thing is endless. The glazier will have $250 more to spend with other merchants, and these in turn will have $250 more to spend with still other merchants and so on ad infinitum. The smashed window will go on providing money and employment in ever widening circles. The logical conclusion from all this would be, if the crowd drew it, that the little hoodlum who threw the brick, far from being a public menace, was a public benefactor.*

Now let us take another look. The crowd is at least right in its first conclusion. This little act of vandalism will in the first instance mean more business for the glazier. The glazier will be no more unhappy to learn of the incident than an undertaker to learn of death. But the shopkeeper will be out of $250 that he was planning to spend for a new suit. Because he has to replace a window, he will have to go without the suit (or some equivalent need or luxury). Instead of having a window and $250, he now has merely a window. Or, as he was planning to buy the suit that very afternoon, instead of having both a window and a suit he must be content with the window and no suit. If we think of him as a part of the community, the community has lost a new suit that might otherwise have come into being, and is just that much poorer.

The glazier's gain of business, in short, is merely the tailor's loss of business. No new "employment" has been added. The people in the crowd were thinking only of two parties to the transaction, the baker and the glazier. They had forgotten the potential third party involved, the tailor. They forgot him precisely because he will not now enter the scene. They will see the new window in the next day or two. They will never see the extra suit, precisely because it will never be made. They see only what is immediately visible to the eye.[1]

1. The chapter explained that economists think in terms of what would have been. Identify this kind of thinking in the Hazlitt story.
2. What is the lesson to be learned from Hazlitt's story?
3. Why is it easier for people to see what is than what would have been?

---

1. *Henry Hazlitt,* Economics in One Lesson *(Arlington House Publishers, New Rochelle, New York, 1979), pp. 23–24.*

CHAPTER 2

Our Free-Enterprise System: Markets, Ethics, and Entrepreneurs

What This Chapter Is About

Today, many of us take life's conveniences for granted—washing machines to clean our clothes, radios to provide music in our cars, television sets to inform and entertain us, or computers to work on at school and on the job. These things and others that make our lives more pleasant and easier were developed mainly in free-enterprise economies. This chapter considers what the free-enterprise system is, how it operates, its ethical basis, and the roles government and entrepreneurs play in it.

Why This Chapter Is Important

Free enterprise can be examined in two ways. One way looks at it much the way Winston Churchill, a former prime minister of Great Britain, looked at democracy. To paraphrase Churchill, it's not that democracy is so good but that the other political systems are so bad. In other words, democracy is the best system we have. Some people feel the same way about free enterprise: it's not that free enterprise is so good but that it's merely the best system we have.

Others take a decidedly different view. To them, free enterprise is not only the best of a bad lot; it is good in an absolute sense. Free enterprise is not only an economic system that puts the "bacon on the table" but also a system that does so in an ethically desirable way.

No matter what you think of free enterprise, it is an economic system to reckon with. In the late 1980s and early 1990s, countries that had not

yet adopted free-enterprise ways began to do so. As an economic system, free enterprise has always played a major role in the development of economic wealth in the world, and it promises to play an even bigger role in the twenty-first century.

After You Study This Chapter, You Will Be Able To

- discuss how the free-enterprise economic system answers three key economic questions.
- list and discuss the five major features of free enterprise.
- identify the role that profit and loss play in a free-enterprise economy.
- discuss the relationship of free enterprise to the Bill of Rights, the Declaration of Independence, and the U.S. Constitution.
- identify the role of government in a free-enterprise economy.
- identify important economic relationships by using a circular flow diagram.

You Will Also Learn What Economics Has to Do With

- Thanksgiving and the Pilgrims.
- exercise equipment in the year 2025.
- hash browns and super-sized sodas.

Economics Journal

Average consumers have more goods and services available in countries that practice free enterprise than in countries that practice socialism. Think about the goods you consume on a monthly basis. Identify three of these goods that consumers in socialist countries (such as Cuba or North Korea) do not consume as regularly or at all.

SECTION 1

Free Enterprise

Chapter 1 stated that the way in which a society answers the three economic questions—What goods will be produced? How will the goods be produced? For whom will the goods be produced?—defines its economic system. This section discusses how the free-enterprise system answers these questions.

As you read this section, keep these key questions in mind:

- What goods will be produced in a free-enterprise economy?
- Who decides how goods will be produced in a free-enterprise economy?
- For whom will goods be produced in a free-enterprise economy?
- What are five major features of free enterprise?

Key Terms

private property
public property
incentive

Free Enterprise and the Three Key Economic Questions

The three key economic questions are answered in a free-enterprise economy as follows.

A recording company decides to put out a CD of a live performance. With this decision, which economic question is the company answering?

What Goods Will Be Produced? In a free-enterprise economy, business firms are free to choose which goods they will produce. They exercise their freedom of choice by producing those goods or products they predict consumers will be willing and able to buy at a price and quantity that will earn profits for the company. For example, suppose consumers are willing and able to buy goods A, B, and C at a price and quantity that will earn profits for business firms, but they are either unwilling or unable to buy goods D, E, and F at a price and quantity that will result in profits. Business firms will produce goods A, B, and C, and they will not produce D, E, or F.

How Will These Goods Be Produced? The individuals who own and manage the business firms decide how goods will be produced. For example, if the owners and managers of an automobile company want to use robots to produce cars, then they will purchase the robots and produce cars with them. If a company prefers that its secretaries use typewriters instead of personal computers, then typewriters will be used at this company.

For Whom Will the Goods Be Produced? In a free-enterprise economy, goods are produced for those people who are willing and able to buy them. Notice that it takes both willingness and ability to make

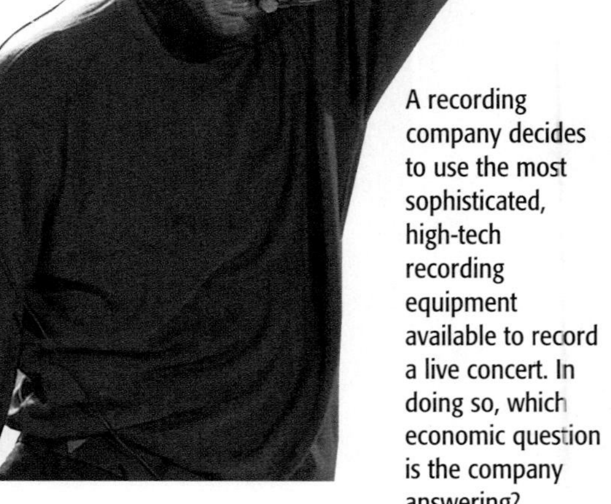

A recording company decides to use the most sophisticated, high-tech recording equipment available to record a live concert. In doing so, which economic question is the company answering?

a purchase. A person has the ability to buy a $20,000 car if that person has $20,000 to spend, but if the same person is unwilling to spend $20,000 for the car, he or she will not purchase the car. Also no purchase will occur if a person has the willingness to buy something but is unable to do so. For example, Shelly may be willing to spend $2,000 to buy a computer but may currently be unable to do so because she does not have the money.

A recording company launches an ad campaign to sell a new music CD to teens. Which economic question does this answer?

Five Features of Free Enterprise

Five major features or characteristics define free enterprise: private property, choice, voluntary exchange, competition, and economic incentives. (See Exhibit 2-1.)

MINI GLOSSARY

private property Any good that is owned by an individual or a business.

public property Any good that is owned by the government.

Private Property Any good—such as a car, house, factory, or piece of machinery—that is owned by an individual or a business is referred to as **private property.** Any good that is owned by the government—such as the Statue of Liberty—is referred to as **public property.** Under free enterprise, individuals and businesses have the right to own property. Furthermore, they may own as much property as they are willing and able to purchase, and they may sell whatever property they own.

Choice (or Freedom to Choose) Choice is a key element of free enterprise. Workers have the right to choose what work they will do and for whom they will work. Businesses have the right to choose the products they will produce and offer for sale. Buyers have the right to choose the products they will buy.

Exhibit 2-1
Characteristics of Free Enterprise

Economic systems are often defined by their characteristics. The five characteristics that define free enterprise are private property, choice (or freedom to choose), voluntary exchange, competition, and economic incentives.

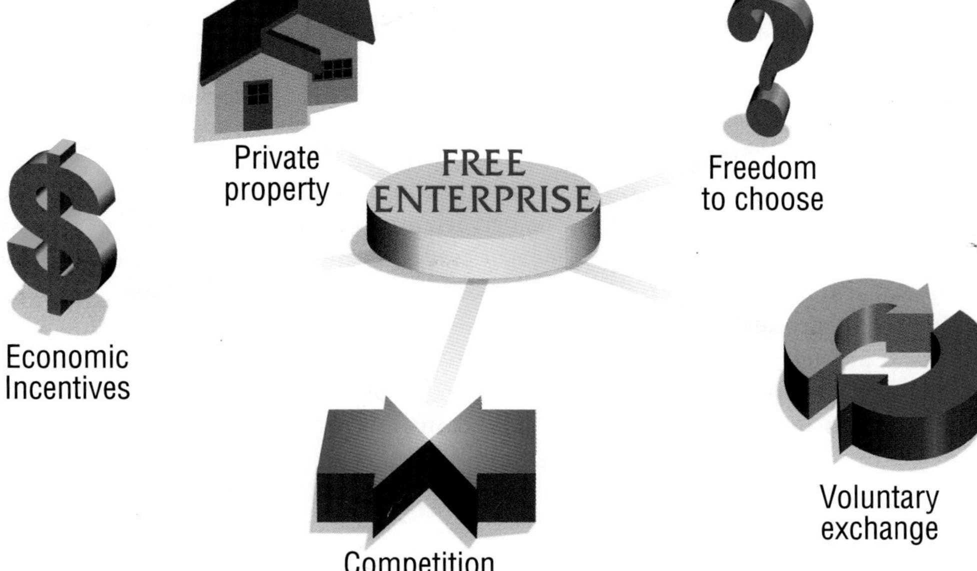

Pilgrims, Property, and Thanksgiving

Private property is one of the features of free enterprise. Many of the advocates of free enterprise argue that without private property, free enterprise could not produce as much wealth as it does.

Private property is not without its critics, though. Some people argue that private property breeds greed and selfishness. Common property—property held in common by the community— motivates people to be more civic minded, peaceful, and caring, they say. The advocates of private property retort that this notion of common property is idealistic and wrong. The truth is, they say, that common property often leads to poverty and unhappiness.

With this background, consider the Pilgrims in the early 1600s. When the Pilgrims left the "Old World" they formed a partnership in a joint-stock company with some London merchants. When the Pilgrims landed off the coast of Massachusetts in 1620, they followed the advice of the company and declared that all pastures and produce would be common property. The result was chaos and starvation; after the first winter, half the colonists were dead.

Bad weather is often blamed for what happened to the pilgrims, but the governor of the Plymouth colony, William Bradford, believed otherwise. He thought it had a lot to do with the fact that the pilgrims held *common property* instead of *private property.* Bradford, therefore, assigned every family in the colony a private parcel of land, on which the family could produce food that it sold for profit. In his diary, Bradford wrote that privatizing the land "had very good success for it made all the hands very industrious, as much more corn was planted than otherwise would have been." He also remarked on how unsuccessful the common property scheme had turned out to be when he said, somewhat philosophically, that it had proved the "vanity of that conceit of Plato's . . . that the taking away of [private] property and bringing community into a commonwealth [of common property] would make them happy and flourishing." It seemed that common property, far from making people happy and flourishing, had instead made them poor and hungry.

Some historians now say that it was probably Bradford's decision to turn common property into private property, more than a change in the weather, that produced the first plentiful harvest in the Plymouth colony—a plentiful harvest that was subsequently celebrated as Thanksgiving.

QUESTION TO ANSWER To get an idea of how private property affects incentives, consider two settings. In the first setting, you and five of your friends share the ownership of a car. In the second setting, you are the only owner of the car. In which setting are you more likely to take care of the car (for example, to make sure it is clean and in good running order)? Explain your answer.

Voluntary Exchange In free enterprise, individuals have the right to make exchanges or trades they believe will make them better off. For example, suppose Mei has $10, Michael has a book, and they trade. We conclude that Mei believes she is better off having the book than the $10, and Michael believes he is better off having the $10 than the book. Individuals make themselves better off by entering into exchanges—by trading what they value less for what they value more.

How an economist views self-interest and how the general public views it are often different. Much of the general public believes that nothing good can come from self-interest. For example, a self-interested seller might try to cheat or lie to a customer. Self-interested sellers try to make themselves better off at their customers' expense.

To the economist, it is often because sellers are self-interested that they will not cheat or lie to a customer. After all, such unethical behavior reduces the likelihood that the seller will stay in business, because he or she won't get return business. Also, sellers know that if they do cheat and lie to their customers, their competition–other sellers–will be more than happy to tell potential customers about it. It is in the self-interest of sellers to monitor each other.

Competition Under free enterprise, individuals are free to compete with others. Suppose you live in a town with five bakeries. You think you would like to open your own bakery and compete for customers with the other five bakeries. In a free-enterprise system, there is no person or law to stop you.

As a consumer living in a free-enterprise system, you are likely to benefit from competition between sellers. You will probably have a bigger selection of products from which to choose, and sellers will compete with each other for your dollars by increasing the quality of the goods they sell, offering lower prices, providing better service, and so on. Although consumers in a free-enterprise system may still have justified consumer complaints, the system usually provides major advantages. It may also have some disadvantages, which may or may not be present in other economic systems. We will examine consumer economic issues in a later chapter.

As a worker in a free-enterprise economy, you may benefit from competition in another way. The competition between employers for your labor services will often result in your earning a higher wage or income than if there were no competition. For example, suppose you are an accountant working for one of the five accountancy firms in town. A person opens up another accountancy firm and wants you to come to work for her. How might she get you to quit your present job and come to her firm? She may offer you a higher income than you are currently earning.

Competition in a free-enterprise economy may benefit you as a worker. The competition among employers for your labor services may push your wages up.

Adam Smith, Father of Modern Economics

Many economists consider Adam Smith to be the father of modern economics. Smith was born in Kircaldy, Scotland, on June 5, 1723, and he died on July 17, 1790. Smith studied at both Glasgow University in Scotland and Oxford University in England.

In 1776, the year the Declaration of Independence was signed, Smith published his famous *Inquiry into the Nature and Causes of the Wealth of Nations.* This book successfully answered the question, Why are some nations rich and others poor? Smith's short answer is that wealth occurs where free enterprise thrives and government plays a limited role.

QUESTION TO ANSWER Smith stated that "people of the same trade seldom meet together, even for merriment and diversion, but the conversation ends in a conspiracy against the public, or in some contrivance to raise prices." Based on this quote, do you think Smith was pro-business or pro-competition?

Economic Incentives An **incentive** is something that encourages or motivates a person toward action. Under free enterprise, money acts as an incentive to produce. If you produce goods and services that people are willing and able to buy, you receive money in return. Adam Smith, often considered the father of modern economics, understood the usefulness of economic (or monetary) incentives in a free-enterprise economy: "It is not from the benevolence of the butcher, the brewer, or the baker, that we expect our dinner, but from their regard to their own interest." In other words, business owners are interested in making themselves better off. Their desire to earn an income that they can use to purchase what they want strongly motivates them to produce for others.

The desire of business owners to make themselves better off also has positive effects for others, because to obtain an income, they must provide something of worth to others. In short, the essence of a free-enterprise economic system is that someone (the butcher, the brewer, or the baker) can get what he or she wants (more income) by offering to sell something that others want to buy.

incentive Something that encourages or motivates a person toward an action.

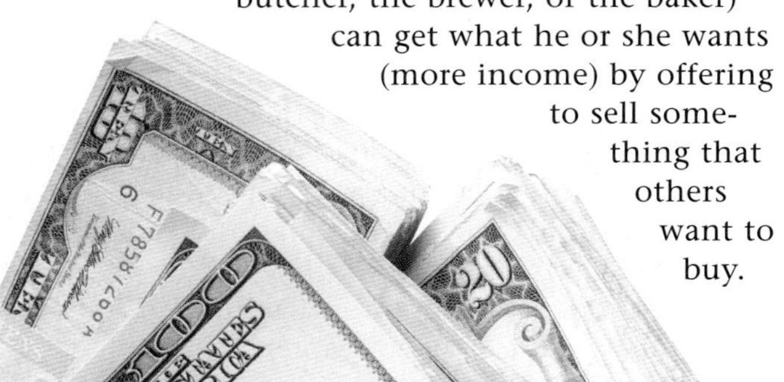

Money often acts as an incentive to motivate people toward an action. Can you think of any other incentives?

Section 1 Review

Defining Terms

1. Define
   a. private property
   b. public property
2. Use the word *incentive* correctly in a sentence.

Reviewing Facts and Concepts

3. In a free-enterprise economy, how would you answer the question, For whom are goods produced?
4. Under free enterprise, everyone has the right to own property. Does it follow that everyone will own property? Why or why not?
5. How does voluntary exchange benefit a person?
6. What advantages do consumers get from the competition between sellers?

Critical Thinking

7. Would Adam Smith agree that the benefits of free enterprise are a consequence of the human desire to make life better for others? Explain.

Applying Economic Concepts

8. Teachers want students to do their homework completely, carefully, and punctually. Identify an incentive that you think would promote student effort toward reaching these objectives.

SECTION 2 Free Enterprise: Emphasis on Profit and Loss

The previous section discussed how a free-enterprise system answers the three key economic questions and briefly described the five major features of free enterprise. This section turns to the role of profits and losses in a free-enterprise economy.

As you read, keep these key questions in mind:

- What roles do profits and losses play in a free-enterprise economy?
- What do profits, losses, and resources have to do with one another?

MINI GLOSSARY

profit
The amount of money left over after all the costs of production have been paid. Profit exists whenever total revenue is greater than total cost.

total revenue
The price of a good times the number of units of the good sold. Total revenue = price × number of units sold.

total cost
The average cost (or expense) of a good times the number of units of the good sold. Total cost = average cost × number of units sold.

average cost
Total cost divided by quantity. For example, if the total cost is $100 and the quantity is 10, then the average cost is $10. Average cost is often called *per-unit cost.*

loss
The amount of money by which total cost exceeds total revenue.

Key Terms

profit
total revenue
total cost
average cost
loss

Profits in a Free-Enterprise Economy

Suppose a computer company spends $2,000 to produce a computer and sells it for $3,500. The company earns $1,500 in profit. **Profit** is the amount of money left over after all the costs of production have been paid.

Profit can also be described in terms of total revenue and total cost. **Total revenue** is the price of a good times the number of units of the good sold:

Total revenue = Price of a good × Number of units sold

For example, suppose you sell radios at a price of $50 apiece. On Monday you sell five radios, so the total revenue for Monday is $250.

Total cost is the **average cost** of a good times the number of units of the good sold:

Total cost = Average cost of a good × Number of units sold

Suppose the average cost of the five radios you sell is $30 per radio. The total cost is $150. For the five radios, the difference between total revenue ($250) and total cost ($150) is $100. This $100 is profit. Notice that there is profit any time total revenue is greater than total cost. When the reverse holds—when total cost is greater than total revenue—there is a **loss,** stated in terms of the amount of money by which total cost exceeds total revenue. For example, suppose that in a given year, a clothing store has a total revenue of $150,000 and total costs of $200,000. If we subtract the store's costs from its revenues, we get −$50,000, a loss for the year.

Profit = Total Revenue > Total cost
Loss = Total cost > Total revenue

THINKING Like an Economist

Some people believe that if you favor a free-enterprise economy, you must be in favor of everything that businesspersons do. The economist thinks differently. She knows that businesspersons may want to hamper the free-enterprise economy. For example, suppose a U.S. car company wants the government to restrict the number of new foreign cars that can be imported into the country to be sold. In so doing, the U.S. car company hopes to lessen the competition it faces from foreign car companies. This act is not consistent with free enterprise, which promotes competition. In other words, being pro–free enterprise and being pro-business are not necessarily the same thing. Being pro–free enterprise is usually more nearly consistent with being pro-consumer and pro-competition.

At any time in a free-enterprise economy, some business firms are earning profits, and some are taking losses. Profits and losses are (1) signals to the firms actually earning the profits or taking the losses and (2) signals to firms standing on the sidelines.

Suppose the NBC television network airs a comedy show on Thursday night that earns high ratings. Because companies will pay more to advertise on high-rated shows, the comedy show creates high profits for NBC. The CBS network airs a crime show on Thursday night that receives low ratings and losses. What are NBC and CBS likely to do now?

NBC will probably do nothing but stand firm. The comedy show is earning high ratings, and the network is earning high profits. CBS, in contrast, will probably cancel its crime show, because the public does not like it. CBS might replace the crime show with a comedy, because NBC has already shown that a comedy does better than a crime show.

So far the third major network, ABC, has been on the sidelines watching what has been happening to NBC and CBS on Thursday night. ABC is thinking about developing a new program. Will what has happened to NBC and CBS influence ABC's decision as to what type of program it will develop? Yes, ABC will be more likely to develop a comedy than a crime show.

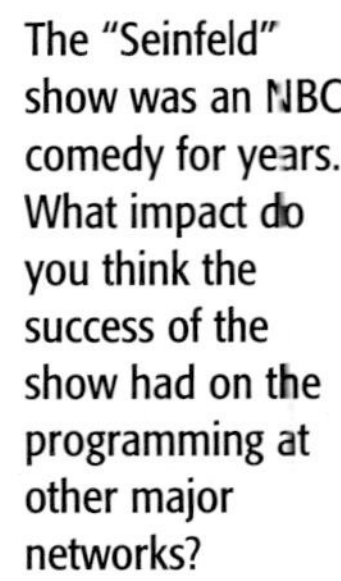

The "Seinfeld" show was an NBC comedy for years. What impact do you think the success of the show had on the programming at other major networks?

Let's summarize what has happened:

- First, the people at home decide what they want to watch on television.
- Second, many more people watch the NBC comedy show (giving it high ratings) than the CBS crime show (which gets low ratings).
- Third, companies pay more to advertise on high-rated shows than low-rated shows, so NBC earns profits on its Thursday show and CBS takes losses.
- Fourth, NBC realizes it has a winning show, so it keeps the comedy show on the air. CBS realizes it has a losing show, so it takes the crime show off the air.
- Fifth, ABC, on the sidelines, decides to copy NBC instead of CBS.

You recall that resources consist of land, labor, capital, and entrepreneurship. When CBS decides to take its crime show off the air and replace

Exhibit 2-2
The Flow of Resources

In a free-enterprise economy, resources are pulled toward profitable enterprises. Resources tend to be pushed away from businesses incurring losses.

it with a comedy show, what is happening to the resources that were previously used to produce the crime show? An economist would say the resources are being reallocated—moved from one place to another or used differently. The resources used to produce the crime show—the people who worked on the show, the cameras used to film the show, the accountants who kept the books—will probably be used to work on a comedy show instead of a crime show. Simply put, *resources flow toward profit; resources flow away from losses.* Profit is like a big magnet: it pulls resources toward it. Loss is like a big wind: it pushes resources away. (See Exhibit 2-2.)

Profit Is Never Guaranteed in a Free-Enterprise System

Suppose both CBS and ABC copy NBC and air comedy shows Thursday night. Are they guaranteed to earn profits on their comedy shows, just as NBC does? There is no guarantee that their shows will be popular and that they will earn profits.

However, let's suppose the shows are popular. The popularity of the CBS and ABC shows may then begin to take away some of NBC's audience, reducing the ratings of the NBC show and, in turn, its profits. NBC may no longer reap profits. Just because it earned profits in the past does not necessarily mean that it will earn profits in the future.

Section 2 Review

Defining Terms

1. Define
   a. total revenue
   b. total cost
   c. profit
   d. average cost
   e. loss

Reviewing Facts and Concepts

2. Explain how profits and losses affect where resources will be used.
3. If a business is currently earning high profits producing lamps, what are other firms that observe this fact likely to do? Explain your answer.
4. If price is $40, number of units sold is 450, and average cost is $33, what is the profit?

Critical Thinking

5. Many people think that profit benefits only the person who earns it—in other words, there is no social function to profit. Do you agree or disagree? Explain your answer.

SECTION 3

The Ethics of the Free-Enterprise System

Free enterprise gives us the ability to produce goods and services in vast quantities. In the words of Adam Smith, it can create "the wealth of nations." This ability is considered one of the major benefits of free enterprise. But is free enterprise an ethical economic system? This section considers the **ethics** of free enterprise—the principles of conduct, such as right and wrong, morality and immorality, good and bad.

As you read this section, keep these key questions in mind:

- What are some of the qualities or characteristics of an ethical economic system?
- What are some of the freedoms in free enterprise?

Ethics and Free Enterprise

Key Term

ethics

We often evaluate a person as being ethical or not. Can we do the same thing for an economic system? For example, can we determine whether the free-enterprise system is an ethical economic system? Another way of approaching this question is to ask, What characteristics or qualities would the free-enterprise system need to have to be an ethical system? What goals would it need to meet? (See Exhibit 2-3.)

First, the supporters of free enterprise state that an ethical economic system allows individuals to choose their own occupations or professions. An ethical system, they say, does not force people to do jobs or tasks that they would rather not do. On this count, the supporters of free enterprise argue that it is an ethical system, because no one is forced to work at a job he or she does not want. People are free to choose what to do. Although all workers may at times grumble about their jobs, this is not evidence that they would choose to do something else or that they are being forced to do their jobs. The ethical consideration is whether a person is being forced by someone to do the job.

Exhibit 2-3

An Ethical Economic System

1. Allows individuals to choose their own occupations or professions.
2. Produces goods/services preferred by both the majority and the minority.
3. Rewards or punishes producers based on how well or poorly they respond to the buying public.
4. Supports the right of the individual to be free.
5. Provides an opportunity for individuals to strengthen and develop their abilities.

Second, an ethical economic system produces the goods and services preferred by both the majority and the minority. The supporters of free enterprise argue that under that economic system, if the majority of the people want to buy cars that are light colored and medium sized, with CD players, then manufacturers will produce that kind of car. (After all, they do not want to produce goods that consumers are not willing

Hundreds of thousands of American restaurants serve hamburgers. The free-enterprise system will reward the restaurants that do the best job of satisfying their customers; the others will eventually go out of business.

to buy.) If a minority of people want big cars instead of medium-sized cars, then it is likely that some big cars will be produced, too. And if a different minority of people want small cars, some small cars will probably be produced.

Think of free enterprise at work in the restaurant business. In most U.S. cities of moderate size, there are many different types of restaurants—those that serve home cooking, fast food, ethnic foods, health food, and so on.

Under free enterprise, a wide variety of goods and services are available because free enterprise has responded both to the majority and to minorities.

Third, an ethical economic system rewards (or punishes) producers according to how well (or poorly) they respond to the preferences of the buying public. Free enterprise certainly does conform. Sellers that continue to give consumers what they want to buy in terms of type of good, quality of good, and price of good will likely earn profits and stay in business. Those that do not respond to public preferences end up taking losses and going out of business.

Fourth, the proponents of free enterprise argue that no economic system can be ethical if it limits people's freedom. In free enterprise, they say, people have numerous freedoms: the freedom to work where they want to work, the freedom to start their own businesses if they want, the freedom to acquire property, the freedom to buy and sell the goods they want to buy and sell, and even the freedom to fail.

ethics
The principles of conduct, such as right and wrong, morality and immorality, good and bad.

The free-enterprise system satisfies the preferences of the majority and the minority. Even though only a minority of Americans may prefer health food restaurants to mainstream restaurants, health food restaurants exist.

Suppose Harris Jackson takes his entire savings and opens a shoe store.

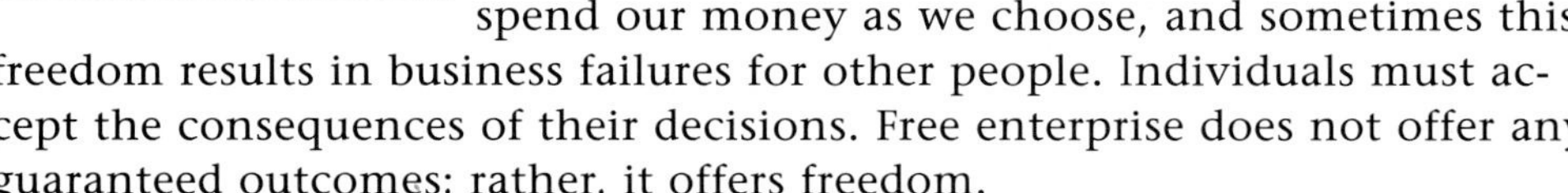

Six months later, Harris shuts down his business and declares bankruptcy. His problem was that very few people wanted to buy shoes from him. This happens in the U.S. free-enterprise system every day. Implicit in free enterprise is the freedom to spend our money as we choose, and sometimes this freedom results in business failures for other people. Individuals must accept the consequences of their decisions. Free enterprise does not offer any guaranteed outcomes; rather, it offers freedom.

Question: *There is a difference between having the freedom to do something and having the ability to do it. What use is the freedom to start your own business in a free-enterprise economy if you do not have the money to start the business? Without the ability, the freedom seems useless.*

Answer: *One response to this comment is that neither of the two major economic systems—free enterprise or socialism—can provide people with the ability to do anything, such as write a great novel, run the four-minute mile, or be a successful entrepreneur. However, economic systems may or may not give individuals the opportunity to realize their potential.*

The supporters of free enterprise argue that free enterprise does provide people with the opportunity, or freedom, to start a business. They also argue that free enterprise gives individuals the opportunity to strengthen and develop their abilities. Suppose a person does not currently have the money or the knowledge to open up her own business, and she is currently working at a low-wage job. Is she destined never to start her own business? Not necessarily.

She can begin today doing those things that are necessary to start her own business in the future. These steps may include working hard in her current job, saving some money, attending school to learn about the business she wants to start, and obtaining a business loan. The economic history of the United States, under free enterprise, is full of stories of people who were poor and uneducated (and, in many cases, did not know the English language), yet went on to start their own businesses and become economically successful.

Economic Principles in the Bill of Rights, the Declaration of Independence, and the Constitution

The Constitution, the Bill of Rights, and the Declaration of Independence hold a special place in the hearts and minds of most Americans. It can also be argued that these three documents have a special significance to free enterprise: each document has free-enterprise economic principles contained within it.

Remember that private property, choice, and competition are important features of free enterprise and that the essence of free enterprise is freedom. It is not difficult to find evidence that the Constitution, the Bill of Rights, and the Declaration of Independence are also about private property, choice, competition, and freedom, among other things.

The Bill of Rights, for example, notes that "private property [shall not] be taken for public use, without just compensation." In other words, if the government wants some land you own in order to put in a road, it cannot simply take that land from you. It must justly compensate, or pay, you for that land. This fact shows the high regard for private property in the Bill of Rights.

The signers of the Declaration of Independence listed many complaints against the king of Great Britain, George III. One complaint was that the king had prevented the thirteen colonies from "trad[ing] with all parts of the world." Surely the signers of the Declaration of Independence were angry at King George III for not allowing them to practice free trade—an essential ingredient of free enterprise—with the rest of the world.

Article 1, Section 8, of the U.S. Constitution says that "no tax or duty shall be laid on articles exported from any State." The Constitution favors preserving competition; if states had been allowed the right to impose a tax on each other's goods, competition within each state would have been

Those who framed the Constitution, the Declaration of Independence, and the Bill of Rights took great care to protect and preserve the freedoms that are a key part of a free-enterprise economy.

lessened. For example, suppose that people in both North Carolina and Virginia produce shoes. The North Carolina government imposes a tax on all shoes imported into North Carolina from Virginia. This makes the shoes produced in Virginia more expensive in North Carolina and thus less competitive there than the shoes produced in North Carolina. To preserve competition—an important feature of free enterprise—it was important to deny states the right to tax each other's goods.

Economic Rights and Responsibilities in a Free-Enterprise Economy

People have certain rights in a free-enterprise economy, but rights rarely come without responsibilities. What are the responsibilities of persons in a free-enterprise economy?

This young woman has earned the right to drive a car. What are the responsibilities that accompany that right?

Many people argue that the right to voluntary exchange comes with the responsibility of giving the other person accurate information about what is being exchanged. Suppose Steve wants to exchange (sell) his twelve-year-old house for the $170,000 that Roberto is willing and able to pay for it. In a free-enterprise economic system, Steve and Roberto have the economic right to complete this exchange, but Steve also has the responsibility to tell Roberto the particulars about the house. For example, if the house has termites or faulty plumbing, Steve should tell Roberto this fact. In other words, Steve has the responsibility of truthfully relating to Roberto the facts about the product he is considering buying. This disclosure is a matter of simple fairness or justice.

Consider another economic right in a free-enterprise economy: the right to private property. The responsibility associated with this right is the responsibility of using one's property only for legal purposes; it is a responsibility to respect and abide by the law. Suppose Isabella owns a car. She certainly has the right to use that car to drive to and from work, go on vacations, pick up friends at school, and so on, but she also has the responsibility of obeying the speed limit and driving carefully.

Finally, consider the economic right to compete in a free-enterprise system. The responsibility attached to this right is to compete in a truthful, legitimate manner. If both Tushar and Yolanda own pizzerias in town and are thus in competition with each other, both have the responsibility to be truthful about the other's business. Tushar should not lie to his customers that Yolanda's pizzeria was cited by the government health examiner for having insects in the kitchen. Yolanda must not lie and say that Tushar uses less cheese in his pizzas than he actually does.

Section 3 Review

Defining Terms

1. Define *ethics.*

Reviewing Facts and Concepts

2. "Under free enterprise, only the majority of people can buy the goods they prefer; the minority always end up buying those goods they would prefer not to buy." Do you agree or disagree with this statement? Explain your answer.
3. "Free enterprise guarantees economic success." Do you agree or disagree with this statement? Explain your answer.
4. Explain what responsibility goes with each of the following rights:
   a. the right to voluntary exchange
   b. the right to private property
   c. the right to compete

Critical Thinking

5. "In a free-enterprise system, it is possible that more trashy novels will be published and sold than serious, soul-inspiring works of literature. Any system that produces this outcome can't be ethical." Do you agree or disagree with this statement? Explain your answer.

SECTION 4

Entrepreneurs

Chapter 1 discussed entrepreneurship as one of the four broad categories of resources for an economy. An **entrepreneur** is a person who has a special talent for searching out and taking advantage of new business opportunities, as well as for developing new products and new ways of doing things. This section examines the role of the entrepreneur in a free-enterprise economy.

As you read this section, keep these key questions in mind:

- What is an entrepreneur?
- How does an entrepreneur help you?

It Is Not Easy to Be an Entrepreneur

Key Term

entrepreneur

To get some idea of what being an entrepreneur is like, try to imagine you are one. Our definition says an entrepreneur does any or all of three things: (1) searches out and takes advantage of new business opportunities, (2) develops new products, and/or (3) develops new ways of doing things.

How would you search out new business opportunities? No book in the library can give you a personalized answer. Even if such a book existed, by the time it was published and found its way into the library, the business opportunities listed in it would no longer be new. Most people, when confronted with the task of finding a new business opportunity, end up scratching their heads. Most people are not entrepreneurs; entrepreneurs are a tiny minority of the population.

entrepreneur
A person who has a special talent for searching out and taking advantage of new business opportunities, as well as for developing new products and new ways of doing things.

Think about the second task of an entrepreneur: developing new products. What new product can you think of developing? Most of us are accustomed to thinking in terms of products that already exist, such as televisions, computers, or cars. Thinking of a new product is not easy, especially one with a high potential for sales.

As for the third task of an entrepreneur, developing new ways of doing things, ask yourself what things people would want to do differently. Then ask, *How* could people do these things differently? You'll probably find that these questions are difficult to answer. Indeed, entrepreneurs have to overcome obstacles, solve problems, and answer challenging questions.

If an entrepreneur succeeds in coming up with an idea for a new product, develops and produces it, and then offers it for sale, how are we made better off? Think of entrepreneurs whose new products have helped you. For example, think about Steven Jobs, one of the developers of the personal computer. Was your life affected positively or negatively as a result of his entrepreneurship? Most would say we benefited from the introduction of the personal computer, along with the invention of the compact disc, the felt-tip pen, and the quartz digital watch.

The production of everything from penicillin to paper clips was made possible in some way by an entrepreneur. In what ways have entrepreneurs made your life easier and more satisfying?

What Will Life Be Like in the Year 2025?

Entrepreneurs are necessarily forward looking. Instead of concentrating on the past, or the present, they try to figure out what the future will look like. They then produce the new products that they think people in the future will be willing and able to buy.

Is there any way for us to know what the future really will hold? In some ways there is. Let's start with a fact. In the year 2000, 13.1 percent of the population was between the ages of fourteen and seventeen years old, and 6.6 percent of the population was between sixty-five and seventy-four. In the year 2025, people fourteen to seventeen years old are predicted to make up 12.1 percent of the population, and people sixty-five to seventy-four are predicted to make up 10.6 percent of the population. In other words, the future will be composed of relatively more older people and relatively fewer younger people than the present.

We can expect entrepreneurs to respond to this upcoming change in the age distribution of the U.S. population. Entrepreneurs, as discussed earlier in this chapter, are people who have a special talent for searching out and taking advantage of a new business opportunity. Certainly the "aging of the population" is a new business opportunity, and we can expect entrepreneurs in a free-enterprise economy to respond to it.

Relatively more entrepreneurial energy will probably be directed toward finding medicines that make people live longer and feel better. More exercise equipment that meets the needs of the elderly will probably be developed and produced. (Most exercise equipment developed and advertised today is geared toward younger people.) More books of interest to an elderly population may be published. Perhaps more radio talk shows geared toward an aging population will appear.

With the aging of the U.S. population, politics may change, too, due to the political entrepreneurs on the scene. No doubt issues such as Social Security, retirement benefits, and federal monies directed toward cancer research will be a bigger part of the political agenda.

QUESTION TO ANSWER In 2000, people thirty-five to forty-four years old accounted for 16.3 percent of the population. In 2025, you will be a member of this age group, but it will then account for only 12.7 percent of the population. Speculate on how life for this age group may be different when it makes up 12.7 percent of the population as opposed to today, when it makes up 16.3 percent of the population.

Entrepreneurs on the Freeway of Life

Almost half the population of the United States lives in thirty-nine metropolitan areas. Most of the people who live in those metropolitan areas have fairly long commutes to work. While 13 percent of all commuters spend forty-five minutes or more in their cars each day, it is not uncommon for many commuters in major metropolitan areas to spend one and a half to three hours in their cars each day commuting to and from work.

Think of people driving to work and spending forty-five minutes or more each day in their cars as a business opportunity. How could an entrepreneur—a person who has that special talent for searching out and taking advantage of new business opportunities—respond to these commuters?

Some entrepreneurs realized that people who spend at least forty-five minutes each day in a car have plenty of time to listen to a book being read to them, so they started producing books on tape. Listening to a book on tape has become an important part of the way many commuters pass their time.

McDonald's, the fast-food franchise, has responded to long commutes by making sure that its food can be eaten in a car. For example, McDonald's places its hash browns in a half-sized paper bag with the top sticking out so that drivers can eat with one hand and drive with the other. McDonald's also offers super-sized sodas with containers that fit easily into traditional car cup holders. Other fast-food franchises have started offering sandwiches in bread pockets or tightly wrapped paper so that drivers can easily and comfortably eat and drive without any mess.

The rush to produce a cellular telephone (introduced in 1983) may have been motivated partly by the desire of entrepreneurs to come up with a product that people with long commutes were likely to buy. Other entrepreneurs have been coming up with new uses for the cellular telephone. For example, the largest discount stock brokerage firm, Charles Schwab and Company, is trying to develop services that clients can access in their cars. One recently introduced service is a voice recognition system that provides stock quotations. Commuters in their cars can pick up their cellular telephones, punch in some numbers, and listen to a few stock quotations.

What's next? Microsoft, the giant software company, wants to put a computer in cars so that drivers can check their E-mail and listen to information from the Internet while they are driving.

QUESTION TO ANSWER As wages and salaries rise in real terms, the value of time rises, too. A person who earns $100 an hour finds that his or her time is more valuable than a person who earns $30 an hour. Entrepreneurs realize that when the value of time rises people want to economize on time. Microwave ovens, computers, and cellular telephones are all products that help people reduce the time it takes to complete a given task. Can you think of other relatively new products that help people economize on time?

Entrepreneurs, it would seem, play an important role in society by taking risks to develop new products or new ways of doing things that benefit the public. From a consumer's point of view, having more risk-taking entrepreneurs in a society likely means having more choices of goods and services in that society.

Finally, entrepreneurs have an ethical responsibility to put forth a product or service that consumers can benefit from and that will not harm them in any way. Also, entrepreneurs have the responsibility to deal honestly with people. For example, it is unethical to falsely advertise a new product, to claim that it can do certain things that it cannot really do.

Entrepreneurs, Profit, and Risk

"You can't get something for nothing." This saying is certainly true for entrepreneurship. We can't get people to risk their own time and money, to try to develop new products, and to innovate unless there is a chance that they can earn profit. With this in mind, how would you respond to someone who says, "Look at that entrepreneur. He's a billionaire; he's earned high profits for years. We ought to pass a law that people can earn no more than 5 percent profit on anything they produce and sell"?

You may be inclined to agree, thinking that with a law that limited profits, you would be able to buy goods and services at lower prices. Less profit for the billionaire entrepreneur, in other words, would simply mean more money in your own pocket.

Things don't always work this way, however. If potential entrepreneurs knew that they could earn only a 5 percent profit at best, they might not be willing to take the risks necessary to become actual entrepreneurs. With fewer entrepreneurs, there would be fewer new goods and services and fewer innovations for your benefit. Not all entrepreneurs are successful, of course. In fact, many entrepreneurs risk their time and money and end up with nothing. A few do end up with millions or even billions of dollars. It is the prospect of millions or billions of dollars that motivates entrepreneurs to assume the risks that are inherent in entrepreneurship.

Entrepreneur

In college you will find classes such as Economics 101, Sociology 101, English 101, and Accounting 101. What you won't find is Entrepreneurship 101; there is no such course. Many entrepreneurs believe that entrepreneurship cannot be taught the way biology, mathematics, or French literature are taught. Of course, entrepreneurs do need an education.

Becoming an entrepreneur entails both benefits and costs. The benefits are that you might be able to work for yourself, work when you want to, and work where you want to. You also could earn a lot of money. But these benefits don't come without high costs. Being an entrepreneur is extremely risky. You could take all your savings to start a new business or develop a new product, only to fall on your face. For almost every successful entrepreneur that you hear about, many do not make it.

QUESTION TO ANSWER Identify two present-day successful entrepreneurs whom you respect. Look into their backgrounds, and write a short paper describing what characteristics you think they have that led to their success.

Section 4 Review

Reviewing Facts and Concepts

1. What does an entrepreneur do?
2. How might an entrepreneur's risk-taking activities benefit society?

Critical Thinking

3. Economists speak of four categories of resources: land, labor, capital, and entrepreneurship. Suppose that in country A there is much more land, labor, and capital than in country B, but there are no entrepreneurs. In country B, however, there are many entrepreneurs. In which country would you prefer to live, and why?

SECTION 5 The Role of Government in a Free-Enterprise Economy

Advocates of free enterprise usually say that government should play a limited role in the economy. According to them, government should be limited to (1) enforcing contracts and (2) providing nonexcludable public goods. This section discusses both roles.

As you read this section, keep these key questions in mind:

- What would happen if government did not enforce contracts?
- What is a public good?
- In a free-enterprise economy, why won't individuals produce nonexcludable public goods for sale?

Key Terms

contract
private good
public good
excludable public good
nonexcludable public good
free rider

Government as Enforcer of Contracts

Think of what life would be like in a nation without government—no city government, no state government, no federal government. Suppose you own a construction company and regularly purchase supplies from people. On Tuesday, you enter into a **contract** with a person (an agreement between the two of you to do something). You agree to pay her $1,000 today if she delivers a shipment of wood to you on Friday. Friday comes, and there is no wood. Saturday, no wood. Sunday, no wood. On Monday you call the person to ask what has happened. She says that she has no intention of delivering the wood to you. "But you took my $1,000. That is theft!" you say. She just laughs at you and hangs up the telephone.

Some lawyers specialize in contract law. They know the "ins" and "outs" of various types of contracts.

What do you do now? You can't turn to the police, because police services are part of government, and there is no government. You can't take the person to court, because the court system also is a part of government.

You can see the need for some institution to enforce contracts. In our society today, government stands ready to punish persons who break their contracts.

Who is better off and who is worse off with government standing ready to enforce contracts? Just about everybody is better off. Only the contract breakers are worse off, because they can no longer break their contracts without at least the threat of punishment.

Could the free-enterprise system function without a government to enforce contracts? Most economists believe that it could function, but not nearly as well as it does now. Instead, it would be severely crippled. Without government to enforce contracts, economists argue, the risk of going into business would be too great for many people. (Would you go into business if you knew people could break their contracts with you and

MINI GLOSSARY

contract An agreement between two or more people to do something.

private good A good of which one person's consumption takes away from another person's consumption. A car is a private good.

public good A good of which one person's consumption does not take away from another person's consumption. National defense is a public good.

excludable public good A public good that individuals can be excluded (physically prohibited) from consuming.

nonexcludable public good A public good that individuals cannot be excluded (physically prohibited) from consuming.

not be punished?) Only a few people would assume the high risks of producing such items as television sets, houses, cars, and computers. The economy would be much smaller. Some economists believe that a free-enterprise system will be a large, thriving economy when government acts to enforce contracts and a small, sluggish economy when it does not.

A country decides to change its economic system from socialism to free enterprise. There is one problem, though: the country has a very poor institutional mechanism for enforcing contracts. Will free enterprise flourish in the country? Why or why not?

Government as Provider of Nonexcludable Public Goods

Goods are categorized as two major types—private goods and public goods. A **private good** is a good in which one person's consumption takes away from another person's consumption. For example, an apple and a computer are both private goods. If Micala takes a bite of an apple, there is that much less of the apple that someone else can consume. If Bill is working on the computer, then Janey cannot also be on the computer; in other words, Bill's use of the computer takes away from Janey's use of the computer.

In contrast, a **public good** is a good in which one person's consumption *does not* take away from another person's consumption. A movie in a movie theater and a lecture in college are public goods. If the movie is showing in a theater, then the fact that Vernon is watching the movie does not detract from Xavier's watching the movie. Both men can view the same movie to the same degree. If a teacher in college is lecturing on biology to thirty students, one student's consumption of the lecture does not take away anything from any other student's consumption.

Not all public goods are alike, however. There are **excludable public goods** and **nonexcludable public goods.** A public good is excludable if individuals can be excluded (physically prohibited) from consuming it. A public good is nonexcludable if individuals cannot be excluded from consuming it.

A computer is an example of a private good. While a business executive is using a company computer, her colleagues cannot use it.

Again, consider the movie in the theater. It is an excludable public good, because movie theater owners can (and do) prevent people from watching the movie. If you go to the movie theater and choose not to pay the ticket price, then the theater owner will not permit you to enter the theater. She will exclude you from viewing the movie.

A movie in a theater is an excludable public good. You can be excluded from viewing it if you do not pay the ticket price of admission.

What about a lecture in a college classroom? It is also an excludable public good. If you do not get admitted to the college or do not pay your tuition, the college can see to it that you do not sit in the college classroom and listen to the lecture.

The classic example of a nonexcludable public good is national defense, which consists of missiles, soldiers, tanks, and so on. Suppose that the U.S. government has produced a certain amount of national defense.

National defense is definitely a public good, because one person's consumption of it does not detract from another person's consumption. In this way, national defense is like a movie or a lecture.

In another way, however, national defense is not like a movie or a lecture. While the seller of a movie and the seller of a lecture can each exclude people from consuming what they have to sell, the producer of national defense cannot exclude people from consuming the good it produces. The U.S. government cannot exclude anyone in the United States from consuming its national defense because it is physically impossible, or prohibitively costly, to do so.

To illustrate, suppose an enemy's missiles are headed for the United States. The U.S. government decides to take action and fire on the incoming missiles. When it fires and destroys the incoming missiles, it protects Yang, who lives in a rather large city in an unnamed state, and it is also (automatically) protects many other people. It cannot be any other way.

To make the matter even more stark, suppose that one of the spies of the country that has launched the attack against the United States lives in the same city as Yang. The U.S. government may not want to protect this spy from the incoming missile attack, but it is physically impossible to protect some people and not others.

The United States cannot physically exclude people from being protected by its national defense system. The U.S. national defense system is a nonexcludable public good.

free rider
A person who receives the benefits of a good without paying for it.

Economists contend that in a free-enterprise economy, people will be willing to produce private goods and excludable public goods, but no one will want to produce nonexcludable public goods. Why not? Because once a nonexcludable public good is produced, no one will pay for it. People will not pay for something they cannot be excluded from consuming.

To illustrate, suppose a company builds a dam to stop the flooding on people's lands. After the dam is built, representatives of the company go to the people and ask them if they want to buy the dam's services (flood prevention). Each person says, "The dam is already in place, I am benefiting from it, and there is no physical way you can exclude me from benefiting from it. So why should I pay?" Economists call persons who receive the benefits of a good without paying for it **free riders.**

Would a private corporation have decided to build the Hoover Dam? Why or why not?

People know that they usually cannot get others to voluntarily pay for a nonexcludable public good, so they decide not to produce it. (Looking back, we can now see that the company that produced the dam in our example would probably never have produced the dam in real life.) In contrast, though, people in a free-enterprise economy will be quite willing to produce and offer to sell private goods and excludable public goods. First, all private goods are excludable. If you do not pay for an apple, computer, car, or book, then you do not get the good; you are excluded from it. If you do not pay for a movie or lecture, you do not get to consume these excludable public goods. In short, people in a free-enterprise

U.S. citizens help to decide which nonexcludable goods government will produce when they cast their votes for politicians who share their views.

economy will produce those things that they can withhold from buyers if they do not get paid for producing them.

In conclusion, a free-enterprise economy will produce private goods and excludable public goods, but it will not produce nonexcludable public goods. But suppose that people still want nonexcludable public goods, such as national defense or flood protection. If the free-enterprise economy will not produce these goods, who will? The government will provide nonexcludable public goods and pay for them with taxes. In fact, many economists argue that the government should provide nonexcludable public goods, because no one else will. The framers of the U.S. Constitution recognized the legitimate role of government in providing nonexcludable public goods, such as national defense. Here is the Preamble to the Constitution:

> *We, the People of the United States, in Order to form a more perfect Union, establish Justice, insure domestic Tranquility,* provide for the common defence, *promote the general Welfare, and secure the Blessings of Liberty to ourselves and our Posterity, do ordain and establish this Constitution for the United States of America.* (Emphasis added)

You might wonder how people communicate to their government what nonexcludable public goods, and how much of these goods, it should provide. In the U.S. system of government, one way people communicate what nonexcludable public goods, and how much of these goods, they want is through the political process. U.S. citizens have the right to vote, and they can influence what government does through the ballot box. For example, suppose the majority of the people want the U.S. government to provide less instead of more national defense. They will likely vote for politicians who voice this same preference and vote against politicians who do not share their preference. U.S. citizens also have the right to lobby their elected representatives directly, by writing letters or talking to the representatives in person.

Section 5 Review

Defining Terms

1. Define
   - **a.** free rider
   - **b.** contract
   - **c.** private good
   - **d.** public good
   - **e.** excludable public good
   - **f.** nonexcludable public good

Reviewing Facts and Concepts

2. Identify each of the following as a public or a private good: (a) a pair of shoes, (b) sunshine, (c) a pen, (d) a pizza, and (e) national defense.
3. Why won't a private business firm produce a nonexcludable public good?
4. How are nonexcludable public goods paid for?

Applying Economic Concepts

5. Give an example of a setting in which a free rider is present.

SECTION 6

The Circular Flow of Economic Activity: A Picture Is Worth a Thousand Words

We have examined the free-enterprise system in some detail in this chapter. We end with a picture of this system that shows the routes of economic activity in the economy. The picture represents the circular flow of economic activity.

As you read this section, keep these key question in mind:

- In an economy, what are the economic relationships between businesses and households?
- What are the economic relationships between government and households?
- What are the economic relationships between government and businesses?

Within the circular flow of economic activity, households buy goods from businesses and sell resources to businesses. Here we see some of the goods that households buy from businesses.

The Circular Flow

Key Terms

circular flow of economic activity
household

Look at Exhibit 2-4 which illustrates the **circular flow of economic activity** in the U.S. economy, or the economic relationships between different economic groups. At first sight, it simply looks like a picture with lines going every which way, but those lines tell a story:

1. It is customary to think of the U.S. economy as composed of businesses, government, and **households** (economic units of one person or more that sell resources and buy goods and services). In the exhibit, businesses, government, and households are visually represented in the center of the diagram.
2. There is an economic relationship between businesses and households. Businesses sell goods and services to households (purple arrow), for which households make monetary payments (blue arrow). For example, a consumer buys a sofa from a furniture company.
3. Businesses and households have another economic relationship: individuals in households sell resources (such as their labor services) to business firms (red arrow), and in return, businesses pay individuals for these re-

circular flow of economic activity
The economic relationships that exist between different economic groups in an economy.

household
An economic unit of one person or more that sells resources and buys goods and services.

Exhibit 2-4

The Circular Flow of Economic Activity in the U.S. Economy

The circular flow of economic activity shows the relationship between different economic groups. For example, in this circular flow diagram we see that households buy goods from businesses and sell resources to businesses. We see that both businesses and households pay taxes to government and receive benefits from government.

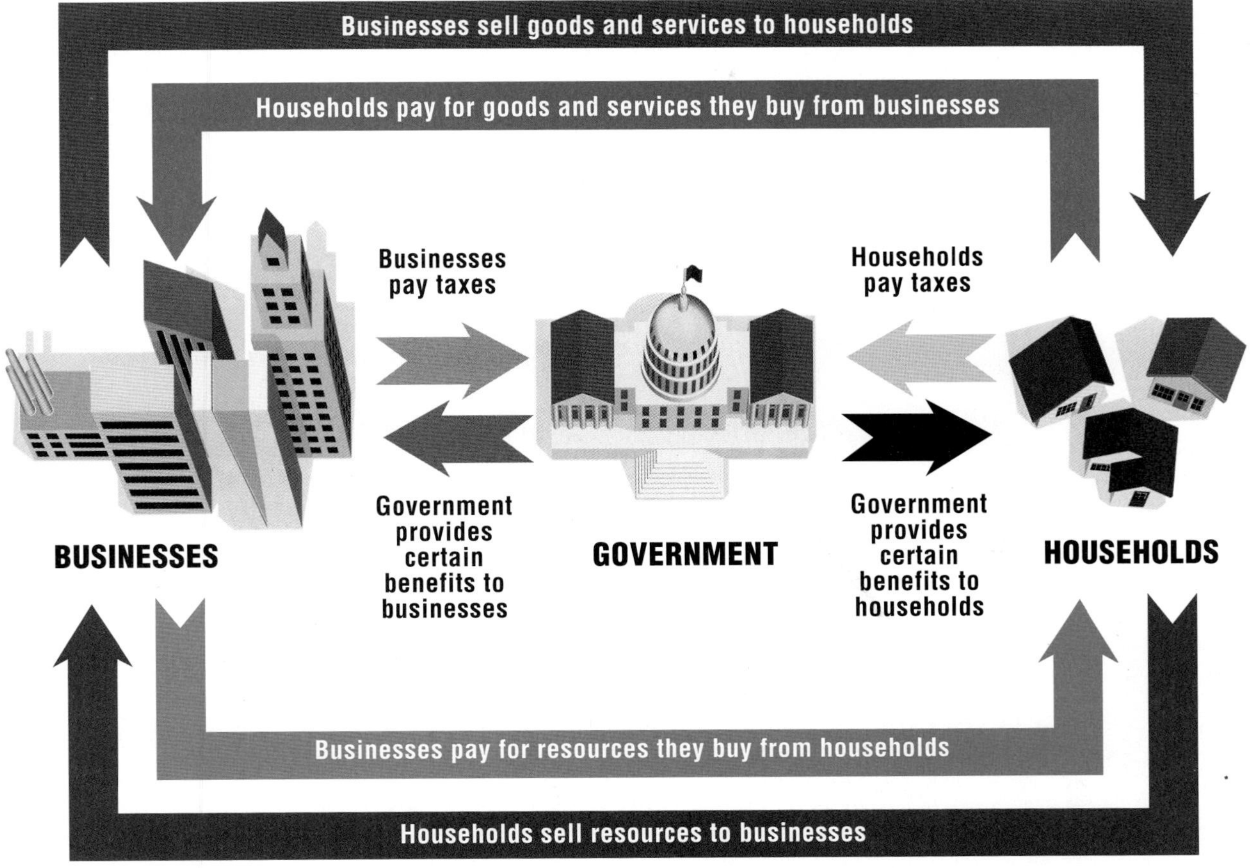

sources (green arrow). For example, a business pays a worker a day's wage.

4. Both businesses and households have a certain economic relationship with the government. Households pay taxes to the government (yellow arrow) and in return receive certain goods and services (black arrow). For example, the government provides individuals with roads, schools, and national defense. The same kind of relationship holds between businesses and the government: businesses pay taxes to the government (orange arrow), and the government provides certain goods and services to businesses (brown arrow).

If we look at Exhibit 2-4 as a whole rather than focusing on any of its parts, we see a representation of the economic activity that goes on in the U.S. economy. Notice in particular the relationships between different economic agents:

- *Businesses and households.* Households sell resources to businesses, and businesses pay for those resources. Also, businesses sell goods and services to households, and households pay for those goods and services.

- *Government and households.* Households pay taxes to the government, and the government provides goods and services to households.
- *Government and businesses.* Businesses pay taxes to the government, and the government provides goods and services to businesses.

Why Is the Circular-Flow Diagram Useful?

Suppose you are watching the news one night on television. An economist who works for the president of the United States is stating that the president is seriously considering raising people's taxes. Look at Exhibit 2-4 and ask yourself which arrow is going to be affected by this action. It is the yellow arrow labeled "Households pay taxes," which goes from households to the government. If all other things remain the same, this arrow is going to grow larger, because there will be more tax dollars flowing through it.

When people buy items in a store, they usually pay a sales tax. Which arrow in Exhibit 2-4 relates to people paying taxes?

Next, ask yourself this question: If there are more tax dollars flowing through the yellow arrow from households to government, are any fewer dollars going to be flowing through some other arrow? The answer is yes—through the blue arrow that moves from households to businesses. In other words, because households pay more of their income in taxes, they will have less of their income to buy things such as television sets, cars, and computers. (In turn, the government will have more money to spend on benefits such as nonexcludable public goods.)

In conclusion, the circular-flow diagram allows us to see how a change in one thing in the economy (such as taxes) will lead to a change somewhere else in the economy (such as in the amount households spend on goods and services produced by businesses).

Section 6 Review

Defining Terms

1. Define
   a. circular flow of economic activity
   b. household

Reviewing Facts and Concepts

2. According to the circular flow of economic activity, in what economic activities is the government engaged? (Look at Exhibit 2-4 to help you answer the question.)
3. According to the circular flow of economic activity, in what economic activities are households engaged?
4. According to the circular flow of economic activity, in what economic activities are businesses engaged?
5. Businesses both buy and sell goods or products. For example, a car company might buy tires, carpet, and radios to install in the cars that it sells. Pick a company, and identify two goods that it buys and one good that it sells. (Warning: Be sure that you identify a good that a company buys, not a resource. For example, the car company in our example might buy the labor of thousands of workers, but labor is not a good but a resource.)

Developing Economic **Skills**

Thinking Straight

To be a good economist, it is important to be a clear thinker. This feature identifies a few of the many "thinking pitfalls" we can fall into if we are not careful.

Unrepresentative Sample

Statistics deals with populations and samples. To illustrate, suppose the president gives a televised speech on Tuesday night. What do people think of it? All the people who heard the speech would be considered the *population*; for example, 70 million people. Pollsters are not likely to ask all 70 million people what they thought of the speech. Instead, they usually ask a relatively small number of people, called a *sample*.

Suppose that the vast majority of the people sampled (say, 700 out of 1,000) state they liked what the president had to say. Pollsters may conclude that if 70 percent of the sample liked the president's speech, it follows that 70 percent of the 70 million who heard the speech liked it.

Whether or not this conclusion is accurate depends on how closely the sample matches the characteristics of the population. For example, suppose the population consists of 70 percent urban dwellers and 30 percent rural dwellers; 60 percent college-educated persons and 40 percent high-school educated persons; 40 percent with an income over $50,000 a year and 60 percent with an income under $50,000, and so on. If the sample has the same characteristics, it is representative of the population; in that case there would be good reason to believe that if 70 percent of the sample liked the president's speech, 70 percent of the population liked it, too. But if the sample has very different characteristics from the population and it is unrepresentative of the population, it is not likely that the sample results hold for the population.

False Cause-and-Effect Relationships

Imagine hearing the following in a speech: "The budget deficit started to rise a few months ago, and now we see that interest rates are beginning to go up. It is clear to all of us that if we want to get interest rates down, we have to reduce the size of the deficit." The speaker implies that rising deficits *cause* rising interest rates.

People often make the error of thinking that what comes first necessarily causes those things that come later. The speaker here mistakenly believes that because budget deficits started to rise before interest rates started to rise, higher budget deficits must be the cause of higher interest rates. In reality, higher budget deficits may or may not cause higher interest rates. It is not necessarily the case that what comes first is the cause of what comes next. Say a person washes her car at 10:00 A.M., and at 1:00 P.M. that day it starts to rain. Did the person washing her car cause the rain? Obviously, it takes more than a particular time sequence to establish cause and effect.

Wrong Directions

Sometimes we mistake cause for effect. For example, suppose someone says, "The recent rise in the stock market has been good for the economy," inferring that a rising stock market is the cause of the economy's getting stronger. The truth may be just the opposite. It is easy to slip into the error of thinking that cause is effect and effect is cause.

QUESTIONS TO ANSWER

1. What is an unrepresentative sample?
2. Give an example that illustrates why things that come first do not necessarily cause things that come later.

CHAPTER 2

Review

Economics Vocabulary

Fill in the following blanks with the appropriate word or phrase.

1. The price of a good times the number of units of the good sold equals ____.
2. An ____ is something that encourages or motivates a person toward an action.
3. ____ relates to principles of right and wrong, morality and immorality, good and bad.
4. Any good that is owned by the government is considered ____.
5. An ____ is a person who has that special talent for searching out and taking advantage of new business opportunities, as well as for developing new products and new ways of doing things.
6. If a product's total cost is greater than total revenue, the firm has incurred a(n) ____.
7. One reason a private business firm will not supply a nonexcludable public good is because it cannot collect payment from ____.
8. A(n) ____ is an agreement between two or more people to do something.
9. A good of which one person's consumption does not take away from another person's consumption is called a(n) ____.
10. A computer is an example of a(n) ____ good.

Review Questions

1. How is the question, "How will goods be produced?" answered in a free-enterprise economy?
2. Explain how voluntary exchange can make individuals better off.
3. What are the five major features of a free-enterprise economy?
4. Calculate the profit or loss in each of the following situations (TR stands for total revenue, and TC stands for total cost). Be sure to put a minus (−) in front of a loss figure.
   a. TR = $400; TC = $322
   b. TR = $4,323; TC = $4,555
   c. TR = $576; TC = $890
   d. TR = $899,765; TC = $456,897
5. Company Z produces men's clothes. For the last 18 months, the company has been taking a loss. What is the loss "saying" to company Z? Stated differently, what message should be coming through loud and clear to company Z?
6. An economist would say that profit attracts resources. What does this mean? You may want to give an example to illustrate your point.
7. What do entrepreneurs do?
8. According to supporters of free enterprise, what should government do? Why should it do these things?
9. Is education a private or a public good? Explain your answer.
10. What does the circular-flow diagram illustrated in Exhibit 2-4 show, and how is it useful?

Calculations

1. For each letter (A through H) in Exhibit 2-5, provide the correct number or dollar amount.

Exhibit 2-5

Price	Quantity produced and sold	Average cost	Total cost	Profit
$10	100	$4	A	B
$15	C	$7	$700	$800
$12	10	$10	$100	D
E	F	$50	$1,000	$2,000
$ 4	G	$3	H	$100

2. A business firm earns $5,000 profit on 1,000 units of a good that it sells for $6.99 each. What is the average cost of the good?

Graphs

1. Look back at the circular-flow diagram in Exhibit 2-4 on page 59, and answer the following questions.
   a. Where do households get the funds to pay for the goods and services they buy from businesses?
   b. Where do businesses get the funds to pay for the resources they purchase from households?
   c. Where does the government get the funds to provide benefits to businesses and households?
2. Look at the circular-flow diagram in Exhibit 2-4. Suppose you are a member of the household sector, so you have to pay taxes to the government. Your total tax bill is $100. Now suppose you sign your

name on a $100 bill and give it to the government. Looking at Exhibit 2-4, can you determine any way that the same $100 bill could ever be back in your hands again? Explain your answer.

Economics and Thinking Skills

1. **Comprehension.** "There has to be some mechanism for deciding where resources will be used in an economy. Free enterprise is such a mechanism." Explain.
2. **Analysis.** There are five features of free enterprise that we discussed in this chapter. If you had to pick the most important two, which two would you pick? Explain your answer.
3. **Cause and Effect.** Adam Smith said, "It is not from the benevolence of the butcher, the brewer, or the baker, that we expect our dinner, but from their regard to their own interest." What is the cause of our getting our dinner?

Writing Skills

Carefully read the following debate between Turner and Suarez. Write an essay supporting the person you think makes the stronger points. It is important for you to address why you think one person's points are stronger than the other's.

Turner: Taxation is theft. The government should not be involved in taxing people.
Suarez: The government has to tax people in order to raise the funds to pay for nonexcludable public goods.
Turner: If people wanted these goods, they would gladly pay for them. The fact that people have to be forced, through the tax system, to pay for nonexcludable goods must mean that they do not want them.
Suarez: There is a problem here: people may want the nonexcludable public goods but not be willing to pay for them on a voluntary basis.
Turner: Who are you to decide what people do and do not want? Why not simply make these judgments based on people's behavior? If they really want something, they will purchase it. If they don't really want something, they won't purchase it. Let people's behavior be your guide to what it is the people want.
Suarez: Again, it is not that easy. People may want national defense, for example, but not be willing to pay for it because it is a nonexcludable public good. The government already provides national defense, and its benefits cannot be denied to anyone.
Turner: So what? Air cannot be denied to anyone, but we don't tax people to breathe it, do we?
Suarez: No, we don't, but air is provided free by nature. National defense is not provided free. We must pay for it if we want it.
Turner: You just said, "We must pay for it if we want it." The key word there was *if.* The fact that we are forced to pay for national defense, through the tax system, leads me to believe that we don't want it. I never have to be forced to do something I want to do. I am only forced to do things I don't want to do.
Suarez: I still say that taxation is necessary, because without it, we wouldn't have certain nonexcludable public goods.
Turner: And I still say that if we really wanted these goods, we would be willing to pay for them on a voluntary basis. We don't need taxes to get us what we don't want.

Economics in the Media

1. In recent years, a number of formerly socialist countries have been experimenting with free enterprise. A few examples are Russia, China, and many of the Eastern European countries. Find a recent newspaper article that addresses events in a country that is experimenting with free enterprise. Then identify any actions or events described in the article that either promote or retard free enterprise. (For example, suppose you read that Russian legislators have passed a law with the effect of turning some public property into private property. This action promotes free enterprise.)

Where's the Economics?

What does free enterprise have to do with this photograph?

CHAPTER 3

Demand

What This Chapter Is About

This chapter introduces and discusses one of the most important concepts in economics: demand. Demand is about *buying* goods and services.

When scientists want to study something closely, they put it under a microscope, and what was once invisible becomes visible. We will do much the same with the concept of demand as we put it under an economic microscope and report on what we see.

Why This Chapter Is Important

Certain people and institutions play important roles in your life. For example, your parents, teachers, and friends are important. Government also plays an important part in your life. It determines such things as when you can get a driver's license, the amount of taxes you must pay, and when you will be able to vote.

Markets also play an important role in your life. They determine what prices you pay for computers, cars, television sets, books, and clothes. Markets also determine what people earn as teachers, accountants, television and movie stars, baseball players, and software developers.

If you are interested in the prices you pay for the goods and services you buy or in why some people earn higher salaries than others, then you will be interested in learning how markets work. The first step is to learn about demand, the subject of this chapter.

After You Study This Chapter, You Will Be Able To

- state the law of demand.
- explain what it means when demand rises or falls.
- explain why, as the price of a good rises, people buy less of it.
- draw a demand curve.
- list and discuss the factors that can change demand.
- discuss the concept of elasticity of demand.
- explain the difference between elastic, inelastic, and unit-elastic demand.
- explain why a price rise sometimes results in an increase in total revenue and sometimes results in a decrease in total revenue.

You Will Also Learn What Economics Has to Do With

- Disneyland and Disney World.
- how a computer keyboard is arranged.
- rock stars.

Economics Journal

Make a list of five items that you buy each month. Next to each item, put its price and the quantity of the item you purchase. An example is "CDs, $15, 1 per month." Which items would you buy more of if their prices were lower? Which items would you buy less of if their prices were higher?

SECTION 1 Demand

Economists study **markets,** places where people come together to buy and sell goods or services. A **good** is a tangible item that gives a person utility or satisfaction. For example, cars, houses, clothes, and computers are goods for most people. A **service** is an intangible item that gives a person utility or satisfaction; history lectures and baseball games are services for most people.

Before a market exists, there must be at least one buyer and one seller. Stated differently, each market has a buying side and a selling side. The buying side is relevant to what is called *demand,* and the selling side is relevant to what is called *supply.* Our discussion of demand begins in this section, and the next chapter introduces supply.

As you read this section, keep these key questions in mind:

- What is demand?
- What is the difference between demand and quantity demanded?
- Why do price and quantity demanded move in opposite directions?
- What is the difference between a demand schedule and a demand curve?

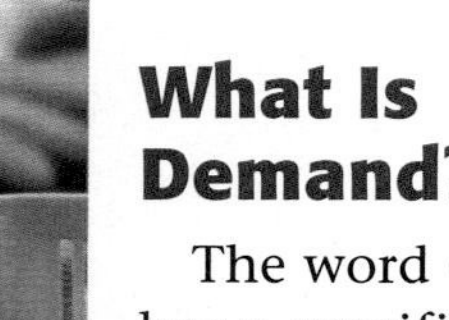

This woman is buying fruit at the market. In doing so she is expressing her demand for fruit—that is, her willingness and ability to buy.

What Is Demand?

Key Terms
market
good
service
demand
law of demand
quantity demanded
law of diminishing marginal utility
inverse relationship
demand schedule
demand curve

The word **demand** has a specific meaning in economics. It refers to the willingness and ability of buyers to purchase a good or service. *Willingness to purchase* a good refers to a person's want or desire for the good; having the *ability to purchase* a good means having the money to pay for the good. Both willingness and ability to purchase must be present for demand to exist. For example, Cruz may be willing to buy a car but be unable to pay the price, so there is no demand. Tanya may be unwilling to buy a car but be able to pay the price, in which case there still is no demand.

> Demand = Willingness and ability to purchase

GLOSSARY

market
Any place where people come together to buy and sell goods or services.

good
A tangible item that gives a person utility or satisfaction. Sometimes a good is referred to as a *product.*

service
An intangible item that gives a person utility or satisfaction.

demand
The willingness and ability of buyers to purchase a good or service.

law of demand
A law stating that as the price of a good increases, the quantity demanded of the good decreases, and that as the price of a good decreases, the quantity demanded of the good increases.

quantity demanded
The number of units of a good purchased at a specific price.

law of diminishing marginal utility
A law stating that as a person consumes additional units of a good, eventually the utility gained from each additional unit of the good decreases.

The Law of Demand

Suppose the average price of a compact disc rises from $10 to $15. Will individuals want to buy more or fewer compact discs at the higher price? Most people would say that individuals would buy fewer. Now suppose the average price of a compact disc falls from $10 to $5. Will individuals want to buy more or fewer compact discs at the lower price? Most people would say more. If you answered the questions the way most people would, you instinctively understand the **law of demand**, which says that as the price of a good increases, the quantity demanded of the good decreases, and as the price of a good decreases, the quantity demanded of the good increases. This relationship can be shown in symbols:

Law of Demand

(where P = price, and Qd = quantity demanded)

If P ↑ then Q_d ↓

If P ↓ then Q_d ↑

Question: *Is there a difference between demand and quantity demanded? These terms sound similar.*

Answer: *Yes. To an economist, the term* demand *means something different from the term* quantity demanded. *Demand refers to the willingness and ability of buyers to purchase a good or service. For example, an economist would say that Karen has a demand for popcorn, which means that Karen has both willingness and ability to purchase popcorn.* **Quantity demanded** *refers to the number of units of a good purchased at a specific price. For example, suppose the price of popcorn is $1 a bag, and Karen buys two bags. It follows, then, that two bags of popcorn is the quantity demanded of popcorn at $1 a bag. An easy way to remember the difference between demand and quantity demanded is that quantity demanded is always a number. In the example, it was the number 2 (two bags of popcorn).*

THINKING Like an Economist

Meng says, "The more money a person has, the more expensive the car the person will buy." He implicitly assumes that the ability to buy something means that the person has the willingness to buy it, too. This is not the way an economist thinks. The economist knows that one can have the ability to buy something but not the willingness. For example, Bill Gates has the ability to buy many things, but he doesn't buy everything he has the ability to buy.

Why Do Price and Quantity Demanded Move in Opposite Directions?

The law of demand says that as price rises, quantity demanded falls, and that as price falls, quantity demanded rises. Why is this the case? According to economists, it is because of the **law of diminishing marginal utility**, which states that as a person consumes additional units of a good, eventually the utility or satisfaction gained from each additional unit of the good decreases. For example, you may receive more utility (satisfaction) from eating your first hamburger at lunch than your second and, if you continue, more utility from your second hamburger than your third.

A Day at Disneyland or Disney World

The Walt Disney Company operates two major theme parks in the United States, Disneyland in California and Disney World in Florida. Each year millions of people visit each site.

The ticket prices to visit Disneyland and Disney World differ, depending on how many days you want to go. For example, Disneyland's Web site at http://www.disney.com/plan/passports lists the prices of a one-, two-, or three-day passport (ticket) to Disneyland. On one day checked, the price of a one-day passport was $41; the price of a two-day passport, $76; and the price of a three-day passport, $99.

Notice that the price of a one-day passport ($41), when doubled, would be $82. But Disneyland does not charge visitors double its one-day passport price for visiting two days; it charges $76. Similarly, triple the price of a one-day passport would be $123, but Disneyland charges $99 for a three-day passport. Why does Disneyland charge reduced rates for two- and three-day passports?

Disneyland is effectively telling visitors that if they want to visit the theme park for one day, they have to pay $41, but a second day will cost only $35 more, not $41 more. And if visitors want to visit the theme park for three days, the third day will cost $23 more, not $41 more. In short, for a three-day passport, Disneyland charges $41 for the first day, $35 for the second day, and $23 for the third day, for a grand total of $99.

The real question is, Why does Disneyland charge less for the second day than the first day, and why does it charge less for the third day than the second day? It's because of the law of diminishing marginal utility, which states that as a person consumes additional units of a good, eventually the utility from each additional unit of the good decreases. If the law of diminishing marginal utility holds for Disneyland, it means that individuals get more utility from the first day at Disneyland than the second day, and they get more utility from the second day than the third day. The less utility or satisfaction people get from something, the lower the dollar amount they are willing to pay for it. Thus, people would not be willing to pay as much for the second day at Disneyland as the first, and they would not be willing to pay as much for the third day as the second. Disneyland knows this and therefore prices its one-, two-, and three-day passports accordingly.

QUESTION TO ANSWER Can you think of a good or service that is priced the way visits to Disneyland are priced (that is, for two units of the good or service, you pay less than double what you pay for one unit)?

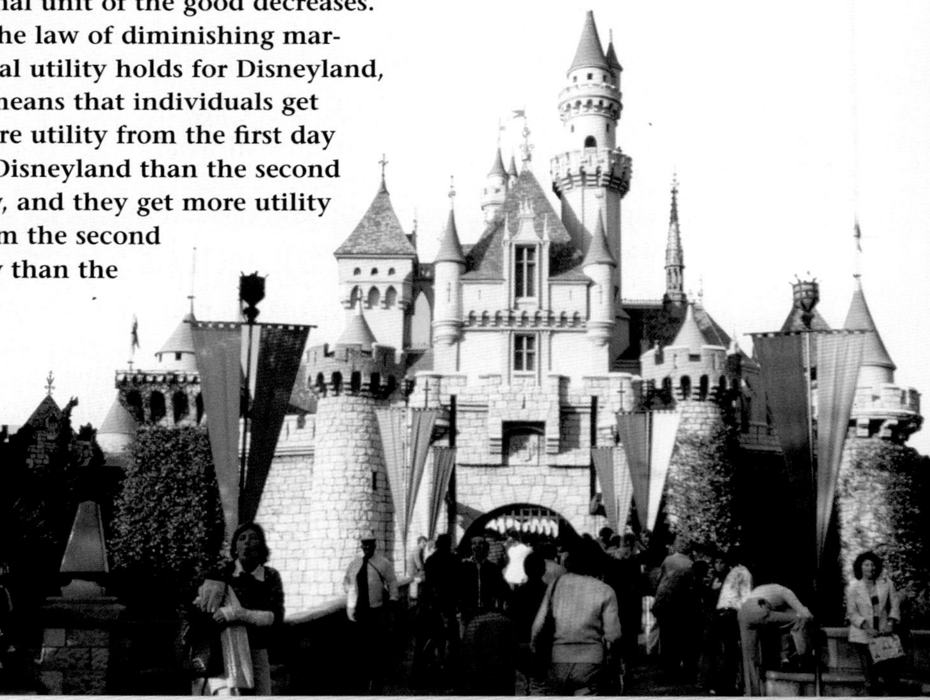

WELCOME TO THE
MARGINAL UTILITY CAFE

TODAY'S SPECIAL:
25¢ HAMBURGERS

GLASBERGEN

"LET'S SEE . . . THAT MAKES SEVEN BURGERS TOTAL SO FAR. WOULD YOU LIKE A FEW MORE? THEY ARE ONLY 25 CENTS EACH NOW."

Cartoon by Randy Glasbergen, © 2000.

What does this have to do with the law of demand? Economists state that the more utility you receive from a unit of a good, the higher price you are willing to pay for it; and the less utility you receive from a unit of a good, the lower price you are willing to pay for it. According to the law of diminishing marginal utility, individuals eventually obtain less utility from additional units of a good (such as hamburgers), so it follows that they will buy larger quantities of a good only at lower prices. And this is the law of demand.

A Demand Schedule: The Law of Demand by the Numbers

How would you represent the law of demand in numbers? First, recall what the law of demand says: as price goes up, quantity demanded goes down; and as price goes down, quantity demanded goes up. This up-down relationship is called an **inverse relationship.** Exhibit 3-1a shows a two-column chart that numerically represents an inverse relationship between price and quantity demanded. Looking at Exhibit 3-1a, we see that as we move down the "Price" column, the price falls (from \$4 to \$3 to \$2 to \$1). As this happens, quantity demanded rises (from 1 to 2 to 3 to 4). A numerical chart, such as this one, that illustrates the law of demand is called a **demand schedule.**

MINI GLOSSARY

inverse relationship
A relationship whereby two variables move in opposite directions. When one variable rises, the other falls.

demand schedule
The numerical representation of the law of demand.

When price falls, quantity demanded rises. This can be seen here as these young Frenchmen fill their carts with goods that have gone on sale.

Exhibit 3-1

Demand Schedule and Demand Curve

(a) A demand schedule for a good. Notice that as price decreases, quantity demanded increases.
(b) Plotting the four combinations of price and quantity demanded from Part a and connecting the points gives us a demand curve. Price, on the vertical axis, represents price per unit of a good. Quantity demanded, on the horizontal axis, always applies to a specific time period (a week, a month, a year, and so on).

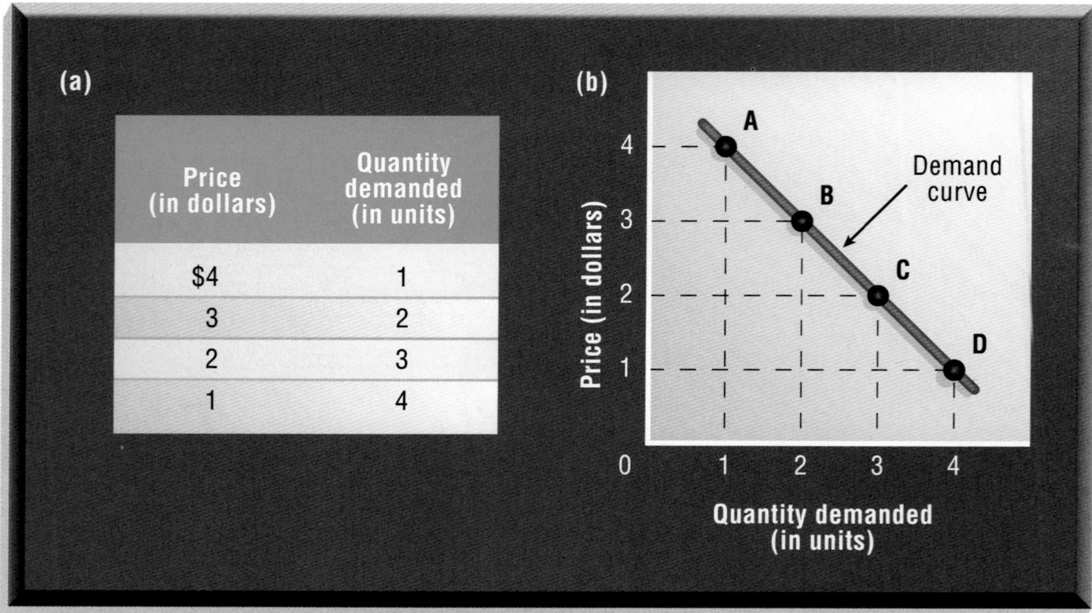

(a)

Price (in dollars)	Quantity demanded (in units)
$4	1
3	2
2	3
1	4

A Demand Curve: A Picture of the Law of Demand

demand curve The graphical representation of the law of demand.

How would you illustrate the law of demand in picture form? The simple way is to plot the data in a demand schedule. Exhibit 3-1b shows how the price-quantity combinations in Exhibit 3-1a are plotted. The first price-quantity combination, consisting of a price of $4 and a quantity demanded of 1, is labeled as point A in Part b of Exhibit 3-1. The second price-quantity combination, a price of $3 and a quantity demanded of 2, is labeled as point B. The same process continues for points C and D. If we connect all four points, from A to D, we have a line that slopes downward from left to right. This line, called a **demand curve,** is the graphic representation of the law of demand.[1]

1. Although points A through D lie along a straight *line,* many economists loosely refer to it as a demand *curve.* Don't let this confuse you. The standard practice in economics is to call the graphic representation of the relationship between price and quantity demanded a *demand curve,* whether it is a curve or a straight line.

Section 1 Review

Defining Terms

1. Define:
   - a. demand
   - b. quantity demanded
   - c. law of diminishing marginal utility
   - d. service
   - e. market
   - f. inverse relationship
   - g. demand schedule
   - h. demand curve
   - i. law of demand
   - j. good
2. Use the word *demand* correctly in a sentence. Use the term *quantity demanded* correctly in a sentence.

Reviewing Facts and Concepts

3. List three services and three goods.
4. Give an example of a demand schedule.

Critical Thinking

5. Why are demand curves downward sloping?
6. Yesterday the price of a good was $10, and the quantity demanded was 100 units. Today the price of the good is $12, and the quantity demanded is 87 units. Did quantity demanded fall because the price increased, or did the price rise because quantity demanded decreased?

Applying Economic Concepts

7. Tatiana says, "If society were to enact harsher penalties for criminal activity, there would be fewer crimes committed." Does she believe the law of demand holds for criminal activity? Explain your answer.

SECTION 2

Factors That Can Cause the Demand Curve to Shift

This section examines factors that can shift a demand curve to the left or right. These factors include income, preferences, and prices of related goods. The section begins by explaining what it means when a demand curve shifts to the left or right.

As you read this section, keep these key questions in mind:

- What does it mean when a demand curve shifts to the right?
- What does it mean when a demand curve shifts to the left?
- What is a normal good? An inferior good? A neutral good?
- What are substitutes? Complements?

What Does It Mean When the Demand Curve Shifts?

Look at the original demand curve, D_1, in Exhibit 3-2. Suppose this demand curve represents the current demand for orange juice. A week passes, and the demand curve for orange juice shifts to the right, to D_2. To understand what it means for the demand curve to shift, first look at point A on D_1, the original demand curve. This point represents 400 quarts of orange juice purchased at $1 per quart. Now look at point B on D_2, the new demand curve. Point B represents the same price as before, $1 per quart, but a greater quantity demanded, 600 quarts. What does a rightward shift in a demand curve, such as the shift from D_1 to D_2, mean? It means that buyers are willing and able to purchase more of a good at the original price and at all other prices. Demand has increased.

Key Terms

normal good
inferior good
neutral good
substitute
complement

Exhibit 3-2
Shifts in a Demand Curve

Moving from D_1 (original demand curve) to D_2 represents a rightward shift in the demand curve. Demand has increased. Moving from D_1 to D_3 represents a leftward shift in the demand curve. Demand has decreased.

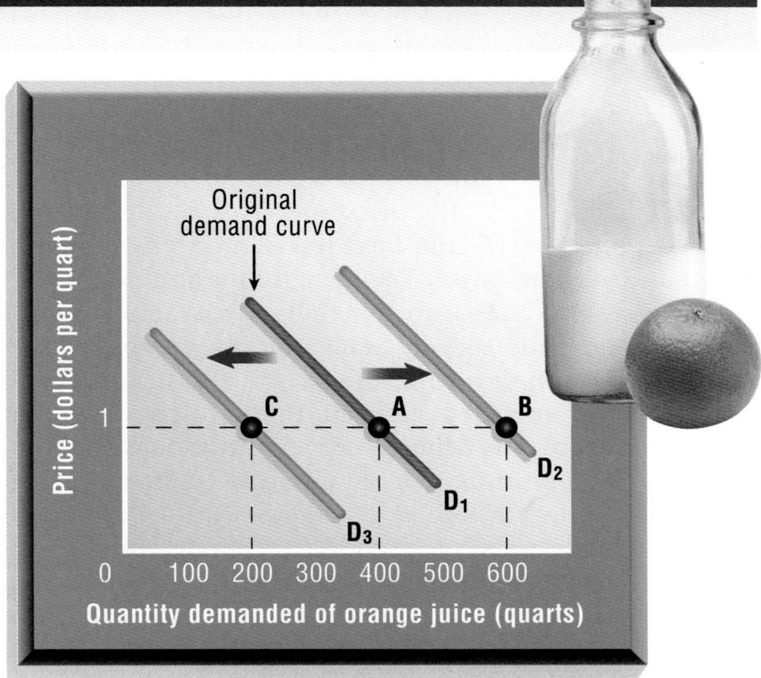

To identify what a shift to the left in a demand curve means, focus on points A and C in Exhibit 3-2. Again, looking at point A on D_1, we see that at a price of $1 per quart, 400 quarts of orange juice are purchased. Now look at point C on D_3, the demand curve after it has shifted to the left. At $1 per quart, buyers are now willing and able to purchase only 200 quarts. A leftward shift in a demand curve means that buyers are willing and able to purchase less of a good at the original price and at all other prices. Demand has decreased.

To summarize, when the demand for a good increases, the demand curve for that good shifts rightward. When the demand for a good decreases, the demand curve for that good shifts leftward.

Demand increases ➡ Demand curve shifts rightward
Demand decreases ➡ Demand curve shifts leftward

What Factors Cause Demand Curves to Shift?

Demand curves do not shift to the right or left without cause. They shift because of changes in income, preferences, prices of related goods, and number of buyers.

An economist thinks that for every effect there is a cause. For example, if the demand for a good rises, there has to be some cause. What is the cause? It could be a rise in income (if the good in question is a normal good), a change in peoples' preferences toward the good, a rise in the price of a substitute, or a fall in the price of a complement. Economists are constantly trying to identify the causes of the effects they observe.

Income As their income rises, people can buy more of any particular good. But remember that having the *ability* to buy more of a good does not necessarily mean having the *willingness* to buy more. For example, Andrew may receive an increase in his income and thus have a greater ability to buy jeans, but he may not be willing to buy more jeans.

If a person receives an increase in income and, as a result, buys more of a certain good, that good is called a **normal good.** The demand for a normal good rises as income rises and falls as income falls. For example, suppose Shawana currently earns $1,000 a month and buys three CDs a month at a price of $12 each. If her income rises to $1,200 a month and she buys four CDs a month at a price of $12 each, then CDs are a normal good for Shawana. Her demand curve for CDs shifts to the right.

If a person receives an increase in income and, as a result, buys less of a certain good, that good is called an **inferior good.** The demand for an inferior good falls as income rises and rises as income falls. For example, suppose Richard is currently earning $800 a month and buys five hot dogs a month at $1 each. If his income rises to $900 a month and he buys four hot dogs a month at $1 each, then hot dogs are an inferior good for Richard. His demand curve for hot dogs shifts to the left.

Finally, if a person receives an increase in income and buys neither more nor less of a good, that good is called a **neutral good.** The demand for a neutral good remains unchanged as income rises or falls. For example, if Cynthia receives a pay raise and buys neither more nor less toothpaste as a result, toothpaste is a neutral good for her. Her demand curve for toothpaste does not shift.

If your income rises, and you buy fewer hot dogs, then what kind of good would hot dogs be for you?

normal good
A good the demand for which rises as income rises and falls as income falls.

inferior good
A good the demand for which falls as income rises and rises as income falls.

neutral good
A good the demand for which remains unchanged as income rises or falls.

substitute
A similar good. With substitutes, the price of one and the demand for the other move in the same direction.

complement
A good that is consumed jointly with another good. With complements, the price of one and the demand for the other move in opposite directions.

Preferences People's preferences affect how much of a good they buy. A change in preferences in favor of a good shifts the demand curve to the right. A change in preferences away from a good shifts the demand curve to the left. For example, if people begin to favor spy novels and buy more of them than they did before, the demand curve for spy novels shifts to the right.

Prices of Related Goods The demand for a good is affected by the prices of related goods. There are two types of related goods, substitutes and complements. When two goods are **substitutes,** the demand for one good moves in the same direction as the price of the other good. For example, for many people, coffee is a substitute for tea. Thus, if the price of coffee increases, the demand for tea also increases as people substitute tea for the higher-priced coffee. Tea's demand curve shifts to the right, as shown in Exhibit 3-3b. Other examples of substitutes include corn chips and potato chips, Chrysler cars and Toyota cars, and two brands of margarine.

Two goods are **complements** if they are consumed together. For example, tennis rackets and tennis balls are used together to play tennis. With complementary goods, the demand for one moves in the opposite direction as the price of the other. As the price of tennis rackets rises, for example, the demand for tennis balls falls. Other examples of complements (or complementary goods) include cars and tires, lightbulbs and lamps, and golf clubs and golf balls.

Exhibit 3-3

Increased Demand for Tea after a Rise in the Price of Coffee

The price of coffee per cup increases from $1.50 to $2.00 in Part a. This price increase causes the demand for tea to shift to the right, as shown in Part b. Because the price of coffee and the demand for tea move in the same direction (both increase), coffee and tea are substitutes.

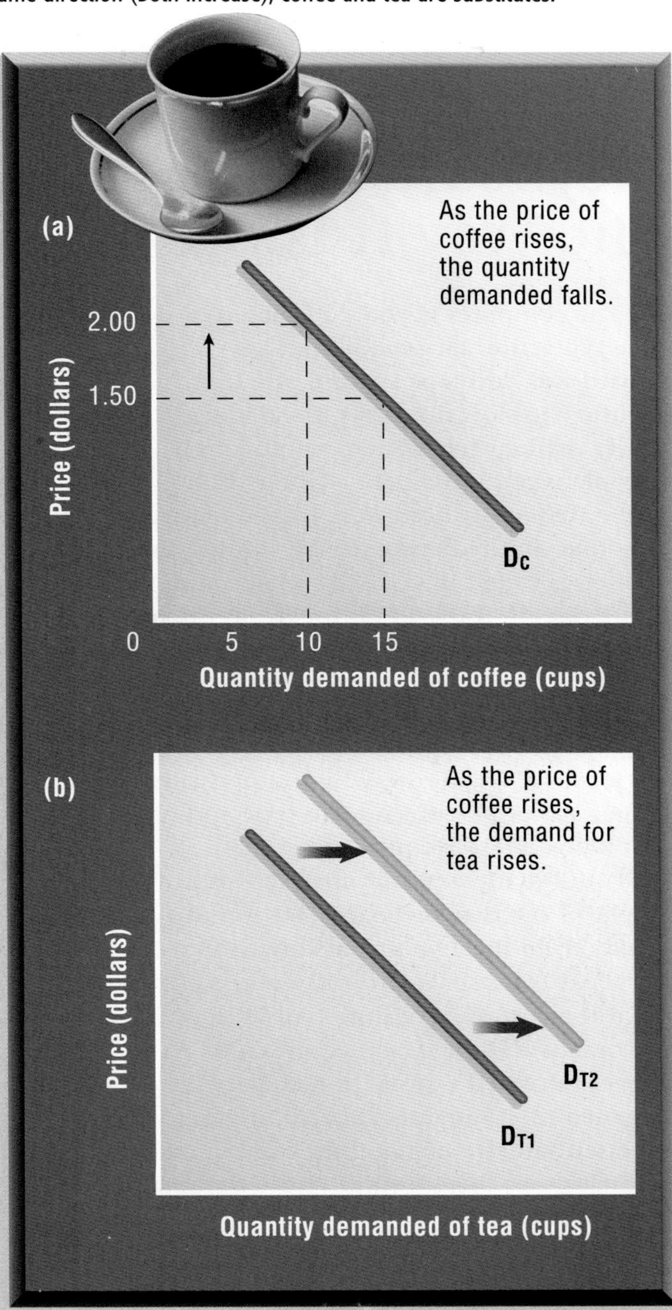

Number of Buyers The demand for a good in a particular market area is related to the number of buyers in the area. The more buyers, the higher the demand; the fewer buyers, the lower the demand. The number of buyers may increase because of a higher birthrate, increased immigration, or the migration of people from one region of the country to another.

Technology & Innovation

Why Is the Computer Keyboard Arranged the Way It Is?

The computer keyboard is based on the typewriter keyboard. That keyboard was developed in the nineteenth century to slow down typists, because the early manual typewriters would jam if people typed too quickly. Letters that were frequently used were placed far apart from one another on the keyboard. We still use this keyboard, which is called the QWERTY keyboard, after the first six letters in the second row (from the top) of the keyboard.

The alternative to the QWERTY keyboard is a keyboard developed by August Dvorak in the 1930s. The Dvorak keyboard placed the most frequently used letters in a single row, which supposedly made it much easier to learn how to type and made almost everyone a faster typist.

Paul David, an economist, researched the development of the two keyboards. He found a U.S. Navy study from the 1940s that showed that the Dvorak keyboard was so superior to the QWERTY keyboard that the cost of retraining typists from QWERTY to Dvorak would be recouped in ten days. But the Navy never retrained typists. In fact, very few people have learned the Dvorak keyboard. In other words, there is essentially no demand for the Dvorak keyboard, which raises the question, If the Dvorak keyboard offers a technology superior to the QWERTY keyboard, why isn't there a demand for it? Does the buying public sometimes turn its back on superior technology? Is that how things sometimes work?

Some economists think so. They argue that the first technology to take hold—even it if is not as good as a later technology—often has an advantage over others that follow. The QWERTY typewriter keyboard had a head-start advantage over the Dvorak typewriter keyboard because QWERTY was first, everyone was using it, and no one wanted to be the first to change to something else. The lesson is that the first technology adopted influences future buying decisions. In terms of the language of this chapter, demand (for various goods) is shaped by history.

Other economists disagree with this line of thinking. They argue that the buying public does not turn its back on superior technology. The fact that QWERTY was not replaced by Dvorak, say these economists, is evidence that Dvorak is not superior to QWERTY, despite what the U.S. Navy said in a 1940s report. If it were superior, people would have changed from QWERTY to Dvorak. As one economist said, "Really large mistakes offer profit opportunities. If there is a really crummy technology out there that we have locked into, then it will be worth it for someone to pay the cost" to get people to switch.

QUESTION TO ANSWER Do you think that the first technology, even though it may not be the best technology, has a clear advantage in the minds of the buying public over technologies that follow? Give examples to support your view.

Factors such as a higher death rate or the migration of people from one region to another can also cause the number of buyers to decrease.

Consider a bookstore at a mall and an online bookstore. If the online bookstore begins to sell its books for less than the mall bookstore, what will happen to the demand for books purchased at the mall bookstore? Explain your answer.

Question: *Suppose the price of pasta rises, and Sarah buys less pasta and more steak. Therefore, according to the text, pasta and steak are substitutes. The problem is that pasta and steak don't seem like substitutes. Hamburger and steak may be substitutes, but not pasta and steak. I'm confused. Can you help me understand this?*

Answer: *Substitutes are not decided before we have data on prices and purchases. Just because two goods (such as hamburger and steak) may seem similar, it doesn't mean they are substitutes. And just because two goods (such as pasta and steak) seem different, it doesn't necessarily follow that they are not substitutes. What matters is how the demand for one good changes as the price of the other good changes. If the price of one and the demand for the other move in the same direction, then the two goods are substitutes, according to the definition of the term.*

A Change in Demand versus a Change in Quantity Demanded

A *change (increase or decrease) in demand* refers to a *shift* in the demand curve, as illustrated in Exhibit 3-4a.

Change of demand = Shift in demand curve

For example, saying that the demand for apples has increased is the same as saying that the demand curve for apples has shifted rightward. The factors that can change demand (shift the demand curve) include income,

Exhibit 3-4

A Change in Demand versus a Change in Quantity Demanded

(a) A change in demand refers to a shift in the demand curve. A change in demand can be brought about by a number of factors (income, preferences, prices of related goods, and number of buyers). (b) A change in quantity demanded refers to a movement along a given demand curve, which is brought about only by a change in (a good's) own price.

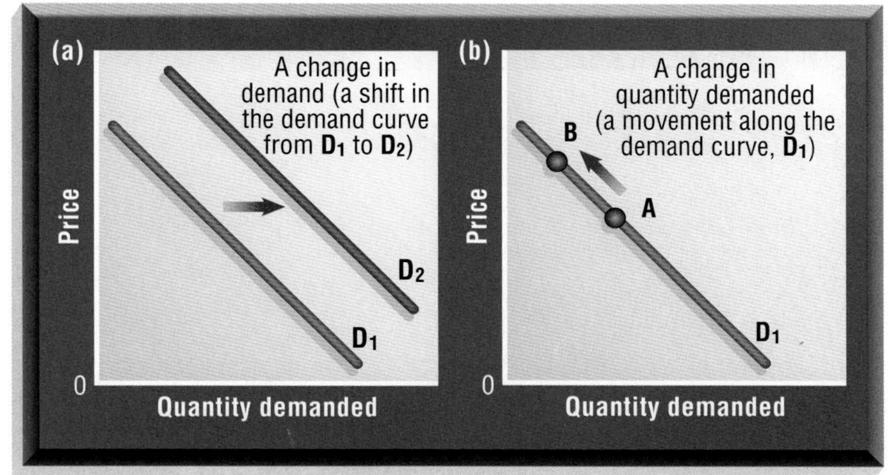

preferences, the prices of related goods (the prices of substitutes and complements), and the number of buyers.

A *change in quantity demanded* refers to a *movement* along a demand curve, as shown in Exhibit 3-4b.

Change in quantity demanded = A movement from one point to another point on the same demand curve

The Bureau of Labor Statistics (BLS) is an agency within the U.S. Department of Labor. The agency collects data on prices in the economy. To see if consumer prices are rising, falling, or remaining constant, go to the BLS Web site at http://stats.bls.gov/. Once there, click on "Economy at a Glance." Next, scroll down the page until you see "Consumer Price Index (CPI)." The CPI is a measure of the prices of the goods and services purchased by consumers. Have prices risen, fallen, or remained constant in the last month reported? If prices have risen or fallen, by what percentage have they risen or fallen?

The only factor that can directly cause a change in the quantity demanded of a good is a change in the price of the good—its own price. For example, a change in the price of computers brings about a change in the quantity demanded of computers, and a change in the price of lamps changes the quantity demanded of lamps.

The Responsibilities of Buyers

This chapter so far has discussed the economic activities of buyers. Buyers also have certain responsibilities they should meet. For example, a buyer who is thinking about buying a used car from someone has the responsibility to become informed about the car (ask questions) and to make sure the car is in working order. The buyer should not simply accept what the seller of the car says without question or evidence. Once she has agreed to purchase the car, she has the ethical responsibility to pay the seller the agreed-upon price. If the buyer of the car pays by check, she has the ethical responsibility to make sure the funds to pay for the car are in her checking account. It is both unethical and illegal to write a check without sufficient funds to cover it.

Section 2 Review

Defining Terms

1. Define:
   a. normal good
   b. inferior good
   c. substitute
   d. neutral good
   e. complement

Reviewing Facts and Concepts

2. Explain what it means if demand rises.
3. Jerry, a comedian, started out doing stand-up comedy and went on to perform on a very popular hit television series. As he went from stand-up comedian to TV star, his income increased substantially. During this time, he bought increasingly more cars (specifically, Porsches) to add to his collection. For Jerry, what kind of good are Porsches?

Critical Thinking

4. Identify a good that is a substitute for one good and a complement for another. (Hint: A Coca-Cola may be a substitute for a Pepsi and a complement for a hamburger.)

Applying Economic Concepts

5. In recent years the price of a computer has fallen. What effect is this likely to have on the demand for software? Explain your answer.

Graphing Economics

6. Graph the following:
   a. an increase in demand
   b. a decrease in demand

SECTION 3

Elasticity of Demand

This section discusses one of the most important concepts in economics: elasticity of demand. As you read this section, keep these key questions in mind:

- What is elasticity of demand?
- How do we compute elasticity of demand?
- What does it mean to say that the demand for a good is elastic? Inelastic? Unit elastic?
- What factors can change the elasticity of demand?
- Does a rise in price for a good necessarily bring about a higher total revenue?

What Is Elasticity of Demand?

Key Terms

elasticity of demand
elastic demand
inelastic demand
unit-elastic demand

The law of demand states that price and quantity demanded move in opposite directions. If price goes up, quantity demanded goes down; and if price goes down, quantity demanded goes up.

Now suppose price goes up from $1 to $1.10, a 10 percent rise in price. We know that quantity demanded will go down, but we don't know by how much. Quantity demanded could go down by 10 percent, by less than 10 percent, or by more than 10 percent.

The relationship between the percentage change in quantity demanded and the percentage change in price is **elasticity of demand.** We can look at it as a ratio:

$$\text{Elasticity of demand} = \frac{\text{Percentage change in quantity demanded}}{\text{Percentage change in price}}$$

In the equation, the numerator is percentage change in quantity demanded, and the denominator is percentage change in price. **Elastic demand** exists when the quantity demanded (the numerator) changes by a greater percentage than price (the denominator). For example, suppose the quantity demanded of lightbulbs falls by 15 percent as the price of lightbulbs is increased by 10 percent. An economist would say that because the numerator (15 percent) is greater than the denominator (10 percent), the demand for lightbulbs is *elastic*. Alternatively, an economist could say that elasticity of demand is greater than 1, because if you divide 15 percent by 10 percent, you get 1.5, which is greater than 1.

Inelastic demand exists when the quantity demanded changes by a smaller percentage than price—that is, when the numerator changes by less than the denominator. Suppose the quantity demanded of salt falls by 5 percent as the price of salt rises by 10 percent. The numerator (5 percent) is less than the denominator (10 percent), so the demand for salt is inelastic. An economist could say that elasticity of demand is less than 1 (if you divide 5 percent by 10 percent you get 0.5, which is less than 1).

elasticity of demand
The relationship between the percentage change in quantity demanded and the percentage change in price.

elastic demand
The type of demand that exists when the percentage change in quantity demanded is greater than the percentage change in price.

inelastic demand
The type of demand that exists when the percentage change in quantity demanded is less than the percentage change in price.

Exhibit 3-5

Elasticity of Demand

ELASTICITY OF DEMAND

IF DEMAND IS	THAT MEANS
Elastic	Quantity demanded changes by a larger percentage than price. For example, if price rises by 10 percent, quantity demanded falls by, say, 15 percent.
Inelastic	Quantity demanded changes by a smaller percentage than price. For example, if price rises by 10 percent, quantity demanded falls by, say, 5 percent.
Unit elastic	Quantity demanded changes by the same percentage as price. For example, if price rises by 10 percent, quantity demanded falls by 10 percent.

MINI GLOSSARY

unit-elastic demand
The type of demand that exists when the percentage change in quantity demanded is the same as the percentage change in price.

Finally, **unit-elastic demand** exists when the quantity demanded changes by the same percentage as price—that is, when the numerator changes by the same percentage as the denominator. For example, suppose the quantity demanded of picture frames decreases by 10 percent as the price of picture frames rises by 10 percent. The numerator (10 percent) is equal to the denominator (10 percent), so the demand for picture frames is unit elastic. According to an economist, elasticity of demand would be equal to 1 (10 percent divided by 10 percent equals 1). Exhibit 3-5 reviews the descriptions of elastic, inelastic, and unit-elastic demand.

Determinants of Elasticity of Demand

Why is the demand for some goods inelastic, while the demand for other goods is elastic? This section examines four factors that affect the elasticity of demand: the number of substitutes available, luxuries versus necessities, the percentage of income spent on the good, and time.

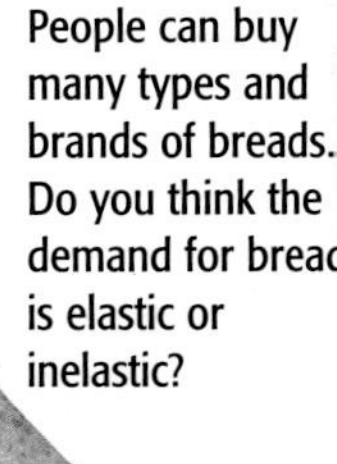

People can buy many types and brands of breads. Do you think the demand for bread is elastic or inelastic?

Number of Substitutes The demand for goods with many substitutes is likely to be elastic; the demand for goods with very few or no substitutes is likely to be inelastic. Consider two goods, heart medicine and bread. Heart medicine has relatively few substitutes; many people must have it to stay well. Even if the price of heart medicine went up by 50, 100, or 150 percent, quantity demanded probably would not fall by much.

In contrast, a particular brand of bread has many substitutes. If the price of brand X rises, a person can turn to brand Y, brand Z, or some other brand. We would expect that if the price of any one brand rises, the quantity demanded for that brand will fall off greatly, because people have other brands to turn to.

An expensive car is considered a luxury. Heart medicine is a necessity if one has a heart condition. The demand for which of the two goods, the expensive car or the heart medicine, is more likely to be elastic?

Luxuries versus Necessities Luxury goods (luxuries) are goods that people feel they do not need to survive. For example, a $50,000 car would be a luxury good for most people. Necessary goods (necessities), in contrast, are goods that people feel they need to survive. Heart medicine may be a necessity for some people. Food is a necessity for everyone. Generally speaking, if the price of a necessity, such as food, increases, people cannot cut back very much on the quantity demanded. (They need a certain amount of food to live.) However, if the price of a luxury good increases, people are more able to cut back on the quantity demanded. Between the two types of goods, luxuries and necessities, the demand for necessities is more likely to be inelastic.

Percentage of Income Spent on the Good Claire Rossi has a monthly income of $2,000. Of this amount, she spends $20 on soda and $400 on dinners at restaurants. In percentage terms, she spends 1 percent of her monthly income on soda and 20 percent of her monthly income on dinners at restaurants. Suppose the price of soda and the price of dinners at restaurants both double. What will Claire be more likely to change, the quantity demanded of soda or the quantity demanded of dinners at restaurants? She will probably change the quantity demanded of dinners at restaurants; she will feel this price change more strongly, because it affects a larger percentage of her income. Claire may shrug off a doubling in the price of soda, on which she spends only 1 percent of her income, but she is less likely to shrug off a doubling in the price of dinners at restaurants, on which she spends 20 percent.

If you spend a larger percentage of your income on eating out at restaurants than on soda, the demand for which good is more likely to be elastic?

In short, buyers are more responsive to price changes in goods on which they spend a larger percentage of their income. Thus the demand for goods on which consumers spend a small percentage of their income (soda, for Claire) is more likely to be inelastic than the demand for goods on which consumers spend a large percentage of their income (dinners at restaurants, for Claire).

Time As time passes, buyers have greater opportunities to change quantity demanded in response to a price change. If the price of electricity went up today and you knew about it, you probably would not change your consumption of electricity much today. By three months from today, though, you would probably have changed it more. As time passes, you have more chances to change your consumption by finding substitutes (natural gas), changing your lifestyle (buying more blankets and turning

Bill Gates

William H. Gates III is co-founder and chairman of Microsoft Corporation, the world's leading provider of software for personal computers. Bill Gates was born on October 28, 1955. He attended public elementary school and a private school in Seattle, Washington. He started programming computers when he was thirteen years old. In 1973, Gates entered Harvard University. He dropped out of Harvard when he was a junior and devoted his full time to Microsoft, a company he co-founded in 1975 with a boyhood friend, Paul Allen. In the spring of 2000, Gates was worth $77 billion, a dollar figure that changes as the value of Microsoft stock changes. Gates enjoys reading and playing golf and bridge.

QUESTION TO ANSWER Bill Gates's major business is selling software (although Microsoft does not sell only software). Computers and software are complementary goods. In recent years, the price of personal computers has been declining rapidly. Explain how this price decline will affect the demand for software (in general) and how it may affect Gates's income.

down the thermostat at night), and similar actions. The less time you have to respond to a price change in a good, the more likely it is that your demand for that good is going to be inelastic.

If the demand for basketballs is elastic, what will happen to total revenue as basketball prices rise?

The Relationship between Elasticity and Total Revenue

What does it matter if the demand for a particular good is elastic, inelastic, or unit elastic? Elasticity of demand matters, especially to business firms and other sellers, because it relates to total revenue. Remember that total revenue is the amount of money that a seller receives for selling a good. Specifically, it is the price of a good times the quantity sold. For example, if Javier sells 100 basketballs at $20 each, his total revenue is $2,000.

To illustrate how elasticity of demand relates to total revenue, we will consider four cases in detail. Case 1 will illustrate what happens when demand is elastic and a seller raises his price. Case 2 will illustrate what happens when demand is elastic and a seller lowers his price. Case 3 will illustrate what happens when demand is inelastic and a seller raises his price. Case 4 will illustrate what happens when demand is inelastic and a seller lowers his price.

Case 1: Elastic Demand and Price Rise Javier currently sells 100 basketballs a week at a price of $20 each. His total revenue (per week) is $2,000. Suppose Javier raises the price of his basketballs to $22 each, a 10 percent increase in price. The law of demand states that quantity demanded will fall. If the demand for the basketballs is elastic, the percentage change in quantity demanded must fall by more than the percentage rise in price—specifically, by more than 10 percent. Suppose the quantity demanded falls from 100 to 75, which is a 25 percent reduction.

"A seller is always better off selling his goods at higher prices than lower prices," someone says. An economist questions the word *always*. The economist knows that sometimes sellers are better off selling their goods at higher prices, and sometimes they are not. For example, if demand is inelastic and price increases, then total revenue increases, too. But if demand is elastic and price increases, then total revenue decreases.

What is Javier's total revenue at the new price and quantity demanded? It is $1,650, the new price ($22) multiplied by the number of basketballs sold (75). Notice that if demand is elastic, a price rise will lead to a decline in total revenue. Javier's total revenue went from $2,000 to $1,650 when he increased the price of basketballs from $20 to $22. An important lesson here is that a rise in price does not always bring about a rise in total revenue.

Elastic demand + Price rise = Total revenue decrease

Case 2: Elastic Demand and Price Decline In case 2, as in case 1, demand is elastic. This time, however, Javier lowers the price of his basketballs from $20 to $18, a 10 percent reduction in price. We know that if price falls, quantity demanded will rise. Also, if demand is elastic, the percentage change in quantity demanded is greater than the percentage change in price. Suppose quantity demanded rises from 100 to 130, a 30 percent increase. Total revenue at the new, lower price ($18) and higher quantity demanded (130) is $2,340. Thus, if demand is elastic and price is decreased, total revenue will increase.

Elastic demand + Price decline = Total revenue increase

Case 3: Inelastic Demand and Price Rise
Beginning with case 3, the demand for basketballs is inelastic. Now suppose Javier raises the price of his basketballs to $22 each, a 10 percent increase in price. If price rises, quantity demanded will fall. Furthermore, if demand is inelastic, the percentage change in quantity demanded must fall by less than the percentage rise in price. Suppose the quantity demanded falls from 100 to 95, a 5 percent reduction.

Javier's total revenue at the new price and quantity demanded is $2,090, which is the new price ($22) multiplied by the number of basketballs sold (95). Notice that if demand is inelastic, a price rise will lead to an increase in total revenue. Javier's total revenue went from $2,000 to $2,090 when he increased the price of basketballs from $20 to $22.

Inelastic demand + Price rise = Total revenue increase

Architect

Architects design buildings and other structures. Designing a building means more than simply drawing a picture of it on paper. It means specifying all elements of a building, such as its air conditioning, heating, plumbing, landscaping, and interior. These specifications often require architects to meet certain building codes and zoning laws.

To become an architect, you must first earn a degree in architecture. Upon graduation, you will probably be an intern architect with an architecture firm for three to seven years. Afterward, you will most likely take a twelve-hour, multipart, nationwide architecture examination to become a registered architect. About one-third of all architects work for an architecture firm or are self-employed. Others work for builders, developers, etc. In recent years, architects have not found much work designing single-family houses, because residential design is now handled primarily by large home builders who use standard architectural models.

QUESTION TO ANSWER In 1990, the U.S. Congress passed the Americans with Disabilities Act (ADA), which requires that architects design buildings and structures with everybody, at any stage of life, in mind. A building must be designed to accommodate everyone. As a result of the ADA, architects today are more involved than ever before with building codes, ordinances, and government.

Just as there is a demand for cars and computers, so is there a demand for architects. Similarly, so can certain factors change the demand for architects. Do you think the ADA increased, decreased, or left unchanged the demand for architects? Explain your answer.

Do Rock Stars Need to Know about Elasticity of Demand?

Rock stars need to know a lot of things. They need to know how to play musical instruments, sing, and perform on stage. But they also need to know about elasticity of demand. In fact, a large part of their earnings will depend on whether or not they know about elasticity of demand.

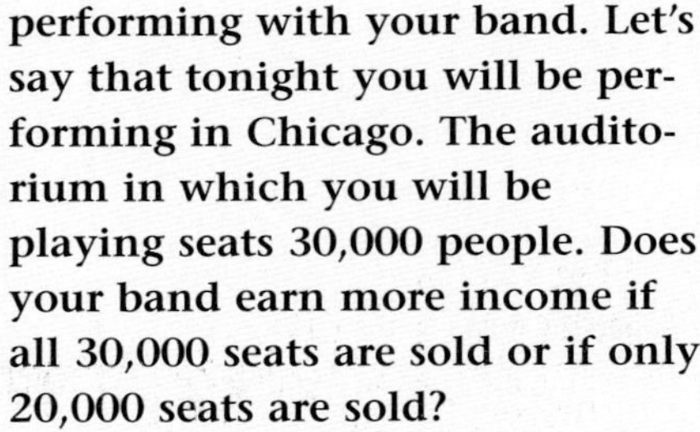

To illustrate, suppose you are a member of a famous musical group. You write songs, record them, and spend 200 days each year on the road performing with your band. Let's say that tonight you will be performing in Chicago. The auditorium in which you will be playing seats 30,000 people. Does your band earn more income if all 30,000 seats are sold or if only 20,000 seats are sold?

This seems like a silly question. It seems obvious that the band would be better off if it sold more tickets than fewer tickets. Certainly 30,000 would be better than 20,000, wouldn't it?

The obvious answer here is not necessarily correct. The answer really depends on an understanding of elasticity of demand. To illustrate, suppose that to sell all 30,000 seats, the price per ticket has to be $30. At this ticket price, total revenue, which is the number of tickets sold times the price per ticket, is $900,000.

If the demand for your Chicago performance is *inelastic*, a higher ticket price will actually raise total revenue. (Remember: Inelastic demand + Price rise = Increase in total revenue.) Suppose you raise the ticket price to $50. At this higher price you will not sell as many tickets as you sold when the price was $30 per ticket. Let's say you sell only 20,000 tickets. You have not "sold out" the auditorium, but it doesn't matter. At a price of $50 per ticket and 20,000 seats sold, total revenue is $1 million—or $100,000 more than it was when you sold out the auditorium.

Is a sold-out auditorium, then, better than an auditorium that is not sold out? Usually you would think so, but an understanding of elasticity of demand informs us that it may be better to sell fewer tickets at a higher price than to sell more tickets at a lower price. Who would have thought it? [a]

QUESTION TO ANSWER Suppose the demand for the Chicago performance had been elastic. If, at a price of $30 per ticket, all 30,000 seats were sold, would total revenue be higher or lower at $25 per ticket?

---

a. This analysis implicitly assumes that only one ticket price, $30 or $50, can be charged. If more than one ticket price can be charged, then some seats may be sold for $30, some for $40, some for $50, and so on.

Why is it important for store managers to know if demand for their products is elastic or inelastic before they raise or lower prices?

Case 4: Inelastic Demand and Price Decline Demand is again inelastic, but Javier now lowers the price of his basketballs from $20 to $18, a 10 percent reduction in price. We know that if price declines, quantity demanded will rise. We also know that if demand is inelastic, the percentage change in quantity demanded is less than the percentage change in price. Suppose quantity demanded rises from 100 to 105, a 5 percent increase. Total revenue at the new, lower price ($18) and higher quantity demanded (105) is $1,890. Thus, if demand is inelastic and price declines, total revenue will decrease.

Inelastic demand + Price decline = Total revenue decrease

The Case of Unit-Elastic Demand Sometimes demand is neither elastic nor inelastic; sometimes it is unit elastic. What is the relationship between unit-elastic demand and total revenue?

The answer to this question involves both the definition of *unit elastic* and the law of demand. If demand is unit elastic, by definition the percentage change in quantity demanded is equal to the percentage change in price. For example, if price changes by 10 percent, then quantity demanded changes by 10 percent. The law of demand states that as price rises, quantity demanded falls, and as price falls, quantity demanded rises.

If we take the definition of *unit elastic* and combine it with the law of demand, we must conclude that any change in price will be *equal to,* but move in the *opposite direction of,* the change in quantity demanded. In other words, if price goes up by 10 percent, quantity demanded will go down by 10 percent. If price goes down by 5 percent, quantity demanded will go up by 5 percent.

Exhibit 3-6

Relationship of Elasticity of Demand to Total Revenue.

If demand is elastic, price and total revenue move in opposite directions: as price goes up, total revenue goes down, and as price goes down, total revenue goes up. If demand is inelastic, price and total revenue move in the same direction: as price goes up, total revenue goes up, and as price goes down, total revenue goes down. If demand is unit elastic, as price changes (rises or falls), total revenue remains constant.

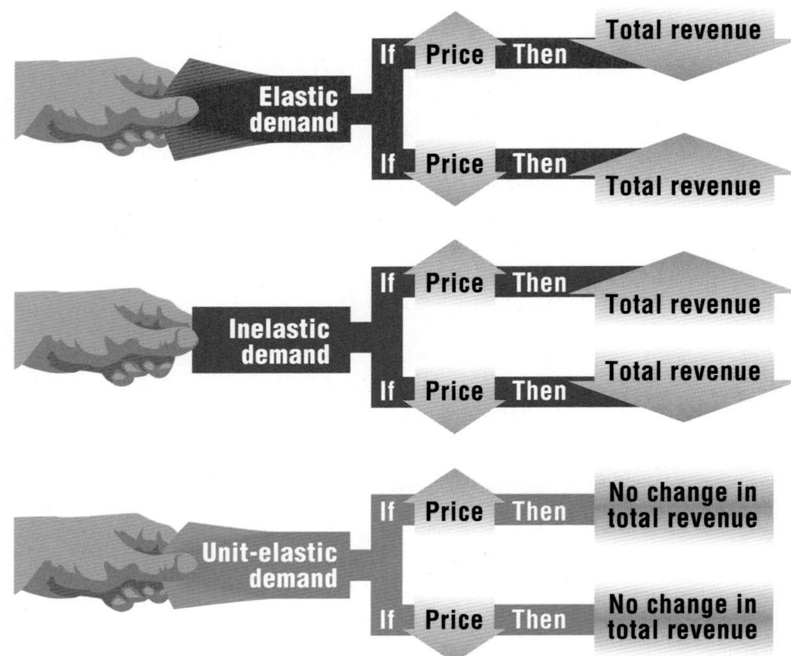

What, then, will be the effect on total revenue if demand is unit elastic and price either rises or falls? There will be no change in total revenue. The price change perfectly offsets total revenue by the change in quantity demanded. It would be similar to having one factor cause the temperature outside to rise by 6 degrees while at the same time another factor causes the temperature outside to fall by 6 degrees. Obviously, with *equal* forces moving in *opposite* directions, there would be no change in the temperature outside. Similarly, when demand is unit elastic, neither a price rise nor a price fall will lead to a change in total revenue. Exhibit 3-6 summarizes much of the material discussed in this section.

Section 3 Review

Defining Terms

1. Define:
   - a. elasticity of demand
   - b. unit-elastic demand
   - c. inelastic demand
   - d. elastic demand

Reviewing Facts and Concepts

2. Does a rise in price necessarily bring about a higher total revenue?
3. The price of a good rises from $4 to $4.50, and as a result, total revenue falls from $400 to $350. Is the demand for the good elastic, inelastic, or unit elastic?
4. Good A has ten substitutes, and good B has twenty substitutes. The demand for which good is more likely to be elastic? Explain your answer.

Critical Thinking

5. How is the law of demand (a) similar to and (b) different from elasticity of demand?

Applying Economic Concepts

6. A hotel chain advertises its hotels as "The Best Hotels You Can Find Anywhere." Does this ad have anything to do with elasticity of demand? If so, what?

Developing Economic

Skills

Thinking the *Ceteris Paribus* Way; or, It's Never Too Late to Learn Some Latin

To illustrate the law of demand, we might say, "As the price of coffee falls, people will buy more coffee." Now suppose Fernandez says, "I'm not sure that people will buy more coffee if the price of coffee falls. Suppose that at the same time the price of coffee falls, people learn that coffee causes cancer. People aren't going to buy more coffee just because its price has fallen if they now think that coffee can give them cancer."

Who is right? Is the law of demand right that people will buy more coffee if the price of coffee falls? Or is Fernandez right that even if the price of coffee falls, people won't buy more of it if they learn that it causes cancer?

You might be inclined to say that Fernandez is right. It seems only reasonable to believe that people won't run out and buy more of a cancer-causing agent just because it is cheaper than it used to be.

Even though Fernandez may be right, however, the law of demand is not wrong. The law of demand—which specifies that price and quantity demanded move in opposite directions—implicitly assumes that when price changes, *nothing else changes.* In Latin, the term used to denote that nothing else changes is *ceteris paribus* (pronounced "set eris pair abis"). In other words, when the law of demand states that as the price of coffee falls, people buy more coffee, it is implicitly assuming that nothing else in the world changes. It assumes that there is no more or less health information about coffee, there are no more coffee drinkers in the world (in fact, there are no more people in the world), the climate of the world is not changing, people don't earn a higher or lower income than they did previously, and so on. In other words, the only factor that changes is the price of coffee: it falls. And if the price of coffee falls and nothing else changes, then people will buy more coffee.

You might be wondering why economists would want to assume that when the price of coffee falls, nothing else changes. After all, other things change in the real world, so why should we assume things that we know are not true? The answer is that economists do not specify *ceteris paribus* because they want to say something false about the world; they specify it because they want to specify what they believe is the real-world relationship between two variables. Look at it this way: If you drop a ball off the roof of a house, it will fall to the ground—*unless someone catches it.* This statement is true, and probably everyone would willingly accept it as true. The following statement has an identical meaning: If you drop a ball off the roof of a house, it will fall to the ground, *ceteris paribus* (that is, if nothing else changes). The phrase "unless someone catches it" in the first sentence means the same as *"ceteris paribus"* in the second sentence. If one statement is acceptable to us, the other should be, too.

QUESTION TO ANSWER A person has been eating one bowl of regular ice cream every day for twenty days. After the twentieth day, the person realizes she has put on two pounds. In her attempt to lose weight, she switches to low-fat ice cream. After twenty more days, she has gained two more pounds. Does it follow that low-fat ice cream adds as much weight as regular ice cream? Explain your answer, based on your knowledge of how the *ceteris paribus* assumption is used in economics.

CHAPTER

3 Review

Economics Vocabulary

Fill in the following blanks with the appropriate word or phrase.

1. A(n) _____ is any place where people come together to buy and sell goods or services.
2. Something that is intangible and gives a person utility or satisfaction is called a(n) _____.
3. According to the law of demand, as the price of a good rises, the _____ of the good falls.
4. According to the _____, price and quantity demanded are inversely related.
5. According to the _____, as a person consumes additional units of a good, eventually the utility gained from each additional unit of the good decreases.
6. Demand is _____ if the percentage change in quantity demanded is less than the percentage change in price.
7. A downward-sloping demand curve is the graphic representation of the _____.
8. A(n) _____ good is a good the demand for which rises as income rises and falls as income falls.
9. If, as the price of good X rises, the demand for Y rises, then X and Y are _____.
10. When demand is _____, the percentage change in quantity demanded is the same as the percentage change in price.

Review Questions

1. Express the law of demand in (a) words, (b) symbols, and (c) graphic forms.
2. "The law of diminishing marginal utility holds that a person receives greater utility from consuming the first two units of a good than from consuming the first unit only." Is this statement true or false?
3. Write out a demand schedule for four different combinations of price and quantity demanded.
4. Margarine and butter are substitutes. What happens to the demand for margarine as the price of butter rises?
5. Explain what happens to the demand curve for apples as a consequence of each of the following.
   a. More people begin to prefer apples to oranges.
   b. The price of peaches rises (peaches are a substitute for apples).
   c. People's income rises (apples are a normal good).
6. "Sellers always prefer higher to lower prices." Do you agree or disagree? Explain your answer.
7. What is the difference between inelastic demand and elastic demand?
8. Explain how the law of diminishing marginal utility is related to the law of demand.
9. What is the difference between a demand schedule and a demand curve?
10. What does it mean when a demand curve shifts to the right? To the left?
11. In each of the following cases, identify whether the demand for the good is elastic, inelastic, or unit elastic.
    a. The price of apples rises 10 percent as the quantity demanded of apples falls 20 percent.
    b. The price of cars falls 5 percent as the quantity demanded of cars rises 10 percent.
    c. The price of computers falls 10 percent as the quantity demanded of computers rises 10 percent.
12. State whether total revenue rises or falls in each of the following situations.
    a. Demand is elastic and price increases.
    b. Demand is inelastic and price decreases.
    c. Demand is elastic and price decreases.
    d. Demand is inelastic and price increases.

Calculations

1. If the percentage change in price is 12 percent and the percentage change in quantity demanded is 7 percent, what is the elasticity of demand equal to?
2. The price falls from $10 to $9.50, and the quantity demanded rises from 100 units to 110 units. What does total revenue equal at the lower price?
3. What is the percentage rise in total revenue as a result of the price falling from $10 to $9.50 in the previous question?

Graphs

Use Exhibit 3-7 to answer Questions 1 through 3. In the exhibit, P = Price, and Q_d = Quantity demanded.

1. What does Exhibit 3-7a represent?
2. What does Exhibit 3-7b represent?
3. What does Exhibit 3-7c represent?

Exhibit 3-7

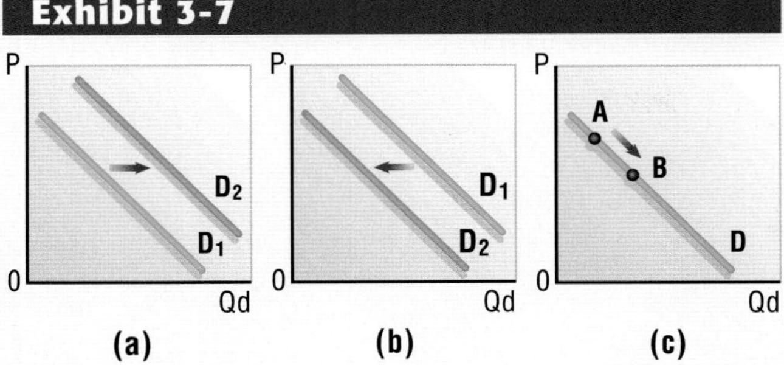

4. In Exhibit 3-8, a downward-pointing arrow (↓) means there is a decrease, an upward-sloping arrow (↑) means there is an increase, and a bar (—) over a variable means the variable remains constant (unchanged). Fill in the blanks for Parts a through c.

Exhibit 3-8

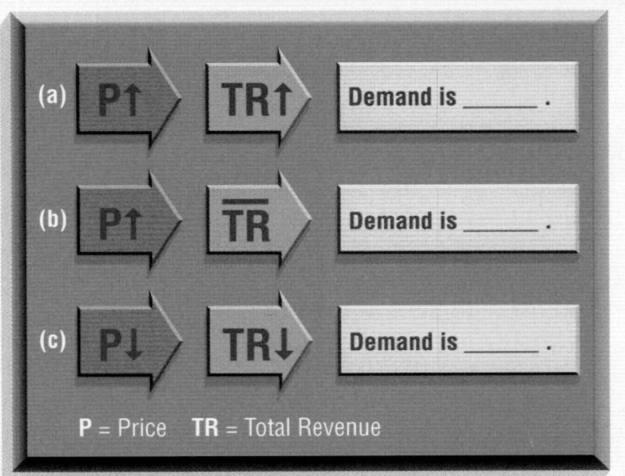

Economics and Thinking Skills

1. **Application.** Income in the economy is expected to grow over the next few years. You are thinking about buying stock in a company. Is it better to buy stock in a company that produces a normal, inferior, or neutral good? Explain your answer.
2. **Analysis.** What kind of relationship exists between price and total revenue if demand is elastic?
3. **Cause and Effect.** Look back at Exhibit 3-1b on page 70. Which factor (on which axis) is cause, and which factor is effect?

Writing Skills

Do you think most of the goods and services you buy during a year are normal goods, inferior goods, or neutral goods? Write a one-page paper that answers the question. Your paper should, among other things, define *normal, inferior,* and *neutral goods* and give evidence to support your answer.

Economics in the Media

1. Find an example of the law of demand, the law of diminishing marginal utility, or elasticity of demand in a newspaper or magazine. Your example may come from an article, editorial, or advertisement.
2. Find an example of the law of demand, the law of diminishing marginal utility, or elasticity of demand on television, in the movies, or on the radio.

Where's the Economics?

How will a decline in the price of one soft drink affect the demand for other soft drinks?

Analyzing Primary Sources

Alfred Marshall (1842–1924) was a British economist. His major work, *The Principles of Economics,* is considered one of the most important books in economics.[1] The excerpt from Marshall's book quoted here is from Book 3, Chapter 1, titled "Gradation on Consumers' Demand." Read the excerpt carefully, and then answer the questions that follow.

To obtain complete knowledge of demand for anything, we should have to ascertain how much of it he would be willing to purchase at each of the prices at which it is likely to be offered; and the circumstance of his demand for, say, tea can be best expressed by a list of the prices which he is willing to pay; that is by his several demand prices for different amounts of it.

1. Is Marshall speaking about (a) a demand schedule, (b) elasticity of demand, or (c) total revenue?
2. Give a numerical example to illustrate what Marshall means here.

1. Marshall, Alfred, *The Principles of Economics* (Amherst, NY: Prometheus Books, 1997).

CHAPTER 4

Supply

What This Chapter Is About

Just as a coin has two sides, so does a market. A coin has heads and tails, a market has a buying side and a selling side. The previous chapter discussed demand, which is the buying side of the market. This chapter discusses supply, the selling side.

Why This Chapter Is Important

Suppose you want to purchase a car. You go to the car dealership and look at the different cars. The car you would like to purchase has a price tag of $20,000. How did the dealership decide on this price? Why not $25,000 instead, or $15,000? What is so special about the $20,000 price tag?

Suppose you graduate from high school, go to college, and then get a job in your chosen field. Your first full-time job after college pays $45,000 a year. Why did your employer come up with $45,000 rather than $50,000 or $30,000? Consider that Michael Jordan, in his last year of playing professional basketball, earned approximately $30 million from his employer, the Chicago Bulls. How did the Bulls organization come up with $30 million?

If you want to understand how these dollar amounts are decided, you need to understand the material in this chapter, which has to do with *supply.* Think of supply as a crucial piece in the very important puzzle of why prices are what they are.

After You Study This Chapter, You Will Be Able To

- state the law of supply.
- draw a supply curve.
- explain what it means when supply increases or decreases.
- list and discuss the factors that can change supply.
- discuss the concept of elasticity of supply.
- explain the difference between elastic, inelastic, and unit-elastic supply.

You Will Also Learn What Economics Has to Do With

- who you will be nice to.
- living to be one hundred years old.
- the Beatles and the Rolling Stones.

Economics Journal

Make a list of three work tasks that you have been paid to complete. For example, if you have had a part-time job, list the job. If you have been paid to wash the family car, mow the lawn, or clean the house, list any of these activities. Beside each task, identify the dollar amount you were paid (on an hourly basis). Next, identify how long it took to complete the particular task. Here is an example: "Clean the house, $15, 3 hours." Next, would you have completed each task if you had been paid 25 percent less? Would you have worked as hard at completing the task if you had been paid 25 percent less?

SECTION 1 Supply

This section defines *supply,* states the law of supply, and derives both a supply schedule and a supply curve. As you read this section, keep these key questions in mind:

- What is supply?
- Are all supply curves upward sloping?
- What is the difference between a supply schedule and a supply curve?

These young workers develop software for personal computers, such as the laptops they are holding. The company they work for, Microsoft, *supplies* software since it is both willing and able to produce and sell software.

What Is Supply?

Like the word *demand,* the word **supply** has a specific meaning in economics. It refers to the willingness and ability of sellers to produce and offer to sell a good or service. It is important to keep in mind that there can be no supply of a good or service, and a person cannot be a seller, unless there is both willingness and ability to produce and sell. When we speak of *willingness* to produce and sell, we mean that the person wants or desires to produce and sell the good. When we speak of *ability* to produce and sell, we mean that the person is capable of producing and selling the good. For example, if Jackie is willing to produce and offer to sell a chair but is unable to do so, there is no supply. If Masako is able to produce and offer to sell a chair but is unwilling to do so, there is still no supply.

Key Terms

supply
law of supply
direct relationship
quantity supplied
supply schedule
supply curve

Supply = Willingness and ability to produce and sell

The Law of Supply

Suppose you are a supplier, or producer, of TV sets, and the price of a set rises from $300 to $400. Would you want to supply more or fewer TV sets at the higher price? Most people would say more. If you did, you in

supply
The willingness and ability of sellers to produce and offer to sell a good or service.

law of supply
A law stating that as the price of a good increases, the quantity supplied of the good increases, and as the price of a good decreases, the quantity supplied of the good decreases.

direct relationship
A relationship between two factors in which the factors move in the same direction. For example, as one factor rises, the other rises, too.

quantity supplied
The number of units of a good produced and offered for sale at a specific price.

supply schedule
A numerical chart that illustrates the law of supply.

stinctively understand the **law of supply,** which holds that as the price of a good increases, the quantity supplied of the good increases, and as the price of a good decreases, the quantity supplied of the good decreases. In other words, price and quantity supplied move in the same direction; that is, they are factors that have a **direct relationship.** We can write the law of supply in symbols:

If P ⬆ then Q_s ⬆
If P ⬇ then Q_s ⬇
where P = price and Q_s = quantity supplied

Consider two settings. In the first setting, high school students are not paid to get A's. In the second, they are paid $50 for each A. In which setting will there be more A's? How does your answer relate to the law of supply?

The Difference between *Supply* and *Quantity Supplied*

When economists use the word *supply,* they mean something different from what they mean when they use the words *quantity supplied.* Again, supply refers to the willingness and ability of sellers to produce and offer to sell a good or service. For example, a supply of new houses in the housing market means that currently there are firms that are willing and able to produce and offer to sell new houses.

Quantity supplied refers to the number of units of a good produced and offered for sale at a specific price. Let's say that a seller will produce and offer to sell five hamburgers when the price is $2 each. Five is the quantity supplied at this price. If the seller will produce and offer to sell six hamburgers when the price is $2.50 each, then six is the quantity supplied at this price.

If an economist uses the word "supply" in referring to cars or hamburgers, how is this different from talking about the same products and using the term "quantity supplied"?

A Supply Schedule

We can represent the law of supply in numbers, just as we did with the law of demand. The law of supply states that as price rises, quantity supplied rises. Exhibit 4-1a on page 93 shows such a relationship. As the price goes up from $1 to $2 to $3 to $4, the quantity supplied goes up from 10 to 20 to 30 to 40. A numerical chart like this one that illustrates the law of supply is called a **supply schedule.**

Everyday Economics

Are You Nicer to Nice People?

Business firms supply cars, clothes, food, computers, and much more. The quantity of each good or service they supply depends on price. According to the law of supply, the higher the price, the greater the quantity supplied.

What about everyday people going to high school or college, or working at a job? Can those people supply anything? They can supply many things, one of which is niceness. Moreover, they can supply different amounts of niceness. Consider yourself: you can be very nice to a person, moderately nice, a little nice, or not nice at all. What determines how much niceness you supply to people? (In other words, why are you nicer to some people than to others?)

One factor that may determine how nice you are to someone is how much someone "pays" you to be nice. It may be a stretch, but think of yourself as selling niceness, in much the same way you might think of yourself selling shoes, T-shirts, corn, or computers. The quantity of each item you supply depends on how much the buyer pays you.

If people want to buy niceness from you, what kind of payment will they offer? A person could come up to you and say, "I will pay you $100 if you will be nice to me," but usually things don't work that way. People buy, and therefore pay for, niceness not with the currency of dollars and cents but with the currency of niceness. In other words, the nicer they are to you, the more they are paying you to be nice to them.

Suppose a person can pay three prices of niceness: the very-nice price (high price), the moderately nice price, and the little-nice price (low price). [a] Now consider two persons, Caprioli and Turen. Caprioli pays you the very-nice price, and Turen pays you the little-nice price. Will you be nicer to Caprioli, who pays you the higher price, or to Turen, who pays you the lower price?

If you answer that you will be nicer to Caprioli, you are admitting that you will supply a greater quantity of niceness to the person who pays you more to be nice. You have found the law of supply in your behavior. Again, you are nicer to those persons who pay you more (in the currency of niceness) to be nice.

a. If it makes it easier, think of the very-nice price as $100 worth of niceness, the moderately nice price as $50 worth of niceness, and the little-nice price as $10 worth of niceness.

QUESTION TO ANSWER Do you think that when it comes to the quantity supplied of niceness, most people behave in a manner consistent with the law of supply?

supply curve
A graph that shows the amount of a good sellers are willing and able to sell at various prices. Only the upward-sloping supply curve is a graphic representation of the law of supply.

A Supply Curve

We can also illustrate the law of supply in graphic form by plotting the data in the supply schedule, as in Exhibit 4-1b. Point A is the first price-quantity combination from the supply schedule, consisting of a price of $1 and a quantity supplied of 10. Point B represents a price of $2 and a quantity supplied of 20; Point C, a price of $3 and a quantity supplied of 30; and Point D, a price of $4 and a quantity supplied of 40. Connecting points A through D creates a **supply curve,** a line that slopes upward from left to right and shows the amount of a good sellers are willing and able to sell at various prices. The upward-sloping supply curve in Exhibit 4-1b is the graphic representation of the law of supply.

Question: *It appears that there are three ways to represent the law of supply. It can be represented in symbol form ($P\uparrow\ Q_s\uparrow$ and $P\downarrow\ Q_s\downarrow$), in terms of a supply schedule, and in terms of a supply curve. Is this correct?*

Answer: *Yes, that is correct.*

A Vertical Supply Curve

The law of supply, which holds that as price rises, quantity supplied rises, does not hold for all goods and over all time periods. First, it does not hold for goods that cannot be produced any longer, such as Stradivarius violins. These violins were made by Antonio Stradivari more than two hundred years

Exhibit 4-1
Supply Schedule and Supply Curve

(a) A supply schedule for a good. Notice that as price increases, quantity supplied increases. (b) Plotting the four combinations of price and quantity supplied from Part a and connecting the points yields a supply curve.

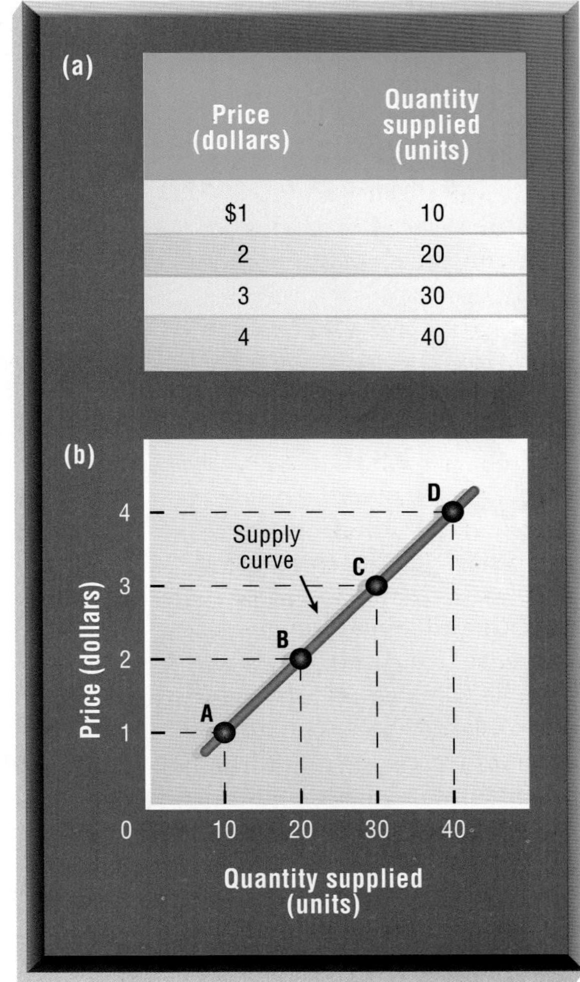

(a)

Price (dollars)	Quantity supplied (units)
$1	10
2	20
3	30
4	40

DRABBLE

DRABBLE reprinted by permission of United Feature Syndicate, Inc.

Exhibit 4-2

Supply Curves When No More Can Be Produced and When There is No Time to Produce More

As you can see, the supply curve is not upward sloping when additional units cannot be produced or when there is no time to produce additional units. In these cases, the supply curve is vertical. In Part a, the letter *X* at the base of the supply curve represents the quantity of Stradivarius violins that currently exist in the world.

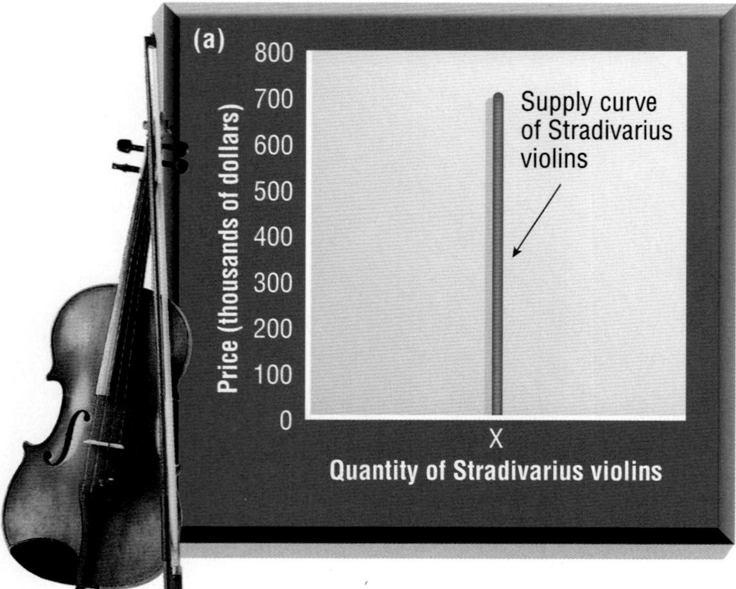

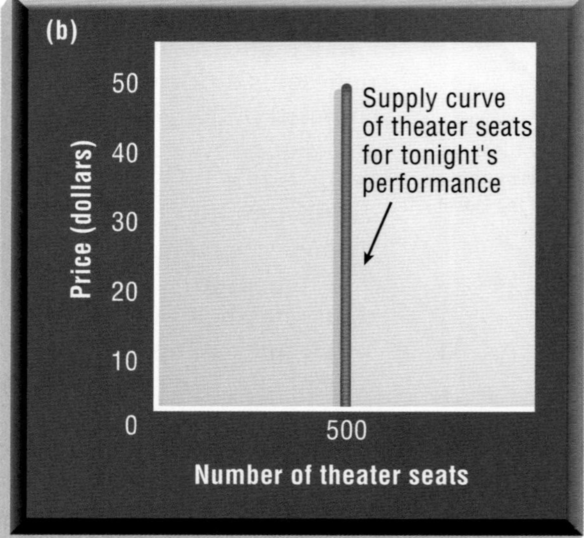

ago. It is impossible for an additional Stradivarius violin to be produced today, because Stradivari has been dead since 1737. No matter how high the price goes, the quantity supplied cannot increase to more than the total number of Stradivarius violins that currently exist. Thus, the supply curve of Stradivarius violins is not upward sloping but vertical, as shown in Exhibit 4-2a.

Second, the law of supply does not hold when there is no time to produce more units of a good. For example, a theater in St. Louis is sold out for tonight's play. Even if ticket prices were to increase from $30 to $40, there would be no additional seats tonight; there is no time to enlarge the theater and add more seats. For tonight's performance, the supply curve of theater seats is vertical, as illustrated in Exhibit 4-2b.

Section 1 Review

Defining Terms

1. Define
   - **a.** supply
   - **b.** quantity supplied
   - **c.** supply curve
   - **d.** supply schedule
2. Use the term *quantity supplied* correctly in a sentence. Use the word *supply* correctly in a sentence.

Reviewing Facts and Concepts

3. **a.** State the law of supply.
   b. Explain the direct relationship between the price of a good and the quantity supplied.
4. Do all supply curves graphically represent the law of supply? Explain your answer.
5. Identify a good for which there is an upward-sloping supply curve. Identify a good for which there is a vertical supply curve.

Critical Thinking

6. Three months ago the price of a good was $4, and the quantity supplied was 200 units. Today the price is $6, and the quantity supplied is 400 units. Did the quantity supplied rise because the price increased, or did the price rise because the quantity supplied increased?

Applying Economic Concepts

7. Suppose there are three McDonald's restaurants in your town, and each pays its employees $6 per hour. If McDonald's were to start paying $9 per hour to its employees, would more, fewer, or the same number of people want to work for McDonald's, according to the law of supply?

SECTION 2

Factors That Can Cause the Supply Curve to Shift

A supply curve can shift to the left or right. This section explains what the shift in the supply curve means and then discusses some of the factors that cause the shift, including resource prices, technology, taxes, and quotas.

As you read this section, keep these key questions in mind:

- What does it mean when a supply curve shifts to the right?
- What does it mean when a supply curve shifts to the left?
- What factors cause sellers to supply more or less of a good?

What Does It Mean When the Supply Curve Shifts?

Look at the original supply curve, S_1, in Exhibit 4-3. We'll say that this supply curve represents the current supply of personal computers. Three months pass, and the supply curve shifts to the right, to S_2. What does this mean?

Look first at point A on S_1, the original supply curve. This point represents 4,000 computers supplied at $1,000 per computer. Now look at point B on S_2, the new supply curve. Point B represents the same price as before, $1,000 per computer, but now the quantity supplied of computers is 6,000. The

Key Terms

technology
advancement in technology
per-unit cost
subsidy
quota
elasticity of supply
elastic supply
inelastic supply
unit-elastic supply

Exhibit 4-3

Shifts in a Supply Curve

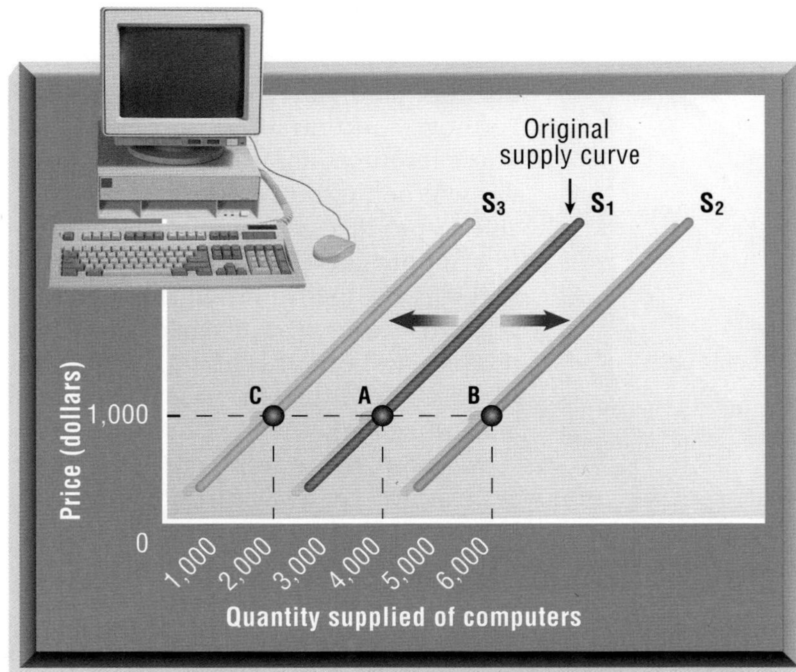

Moving from S_1 (the original supply curve) to S_2 represents a rightward shift in the supply curve. Supply has increased. Moving from S_1 to S_3 represents a leftward shift in the supply curve. Supply has decreased.

In 1921, a seller sold something to a buyer for $100. In 1998, a seller sold something to a buyer for $100. Were the two sales, in 1921 and 1998, equivalent? Not at all, because a dollar was worth more in 1921 than in 1998. In fact, a $100 purchase in 1921 was the equivalent of a $913 purchase in 1998. In other words, buying something for $100 in 1921 was the same as buying something for $913 in 1998. To find out what any dollar purchase in the past is equivalent to today, go to the Web site of The Dismal Scientist: http://www/dismal.com/toolbox/cpi_index.stm

What is a $100 purchase in 1945 equivalent to in the last year identified at the site?

rightward shift in the supply curve, from S_1 to S_2, means that sellers are willing and able to produce and offer to sell more of a good (computers) at the original price and at all other prices. Supply has increased.

What about a shift to the left in a supply curve? Start again at point A on S_1, where 4,000 computers are supplied at a price of $1,000 per computer. Now suppose the supply curve shifts leftward, to S_3. At $1,000 per computer, sellers are now willing to supply only 2,000 computers. The leftward shift in the supply curve means that sellers are willing and able to produce and offer to sell less of a good (fewer computers) at the original price and at all other prices. Supply has decreased.

Supply increases ➡ Supply curve shifts rightward
Supply decreases ➡ Supply curve shifts leftward

What Factors Cause Supply Curves to Shift?

Supply curves do not shift to the right or left without cause, any more than demand curves do. Something must change to cause a shift. Changes in resource prices, technology, taxes, subsidies, quotas, number of sellers, or weather can cause supply curves to shift. (See Exhibit 4-4.)

Exhibit 4-4
Shift Factors

Factors That Can Cause the Supply Curve to Shift

- Resource prices
- Technology
- Taxes
- Subsidies
- Quotas
- Number of sellers
- Weather (in some cases)

Resource Prices

Chapter 1 identified four resources, or factors of production: land, labor, capital, and entrepreneurship. For now, concentrate on land, labor, and capital. These resources are used to produce goods and services. When resource prices fall, sellers are willing and able to produce and offer to sell more of the good (the supply curve shifts to the right). The reason is that it is cheaper to produce the good. When resource prices rise, in contrast, sellers are willing and able to produce and offer to sell less of the good (the supply curve shifts to the left); it is more expensive to produce the good.

Suppose, for example, that the wage rate (labor cost) rises for employees working for a car manufacturer, while everything else remains the same. As a result, the car manufacturer will produce and offer to sell fewer cars; the supply curve shifts leftward.

Technology **Technology** is the body of skills and knowledge relevant to the use of resources in production. For example, the technology of farming

technology
The body of skills and knowledge concerning the use of resources in production.

advancement in technology
The ability to produce more output with a fixed amount of resources.

per-unit cost
The average cost of a good. For example, if $400,000 is spent to produce 100 cars, the average, or per-unit, cost is $4,000.

subsidy
A financial payment made by government for certain actions.

quota
A legal limit on the number of units of a foreign-produced good (import) that can enter a country.

today is much different from two hundred years ago. Today, unlike two hundred years ago, tractors, pesticides, and special fertilizers are used in farming.

An **advancement in technology** is the ability to produce more output with a fixed amount of resources. Again, consider farming. With the use of fertilizers and pesticides, farmers today can produce much more output on an acre of land than they could many years ago. This advancement in technology, in turn, lowers the **per-unit cost,** or average cost, of production for farmers. Farmers respond to lower per-unit costs by being willing and able to produce and offer to sell more output. In other words, the supply curve shifts to the right.

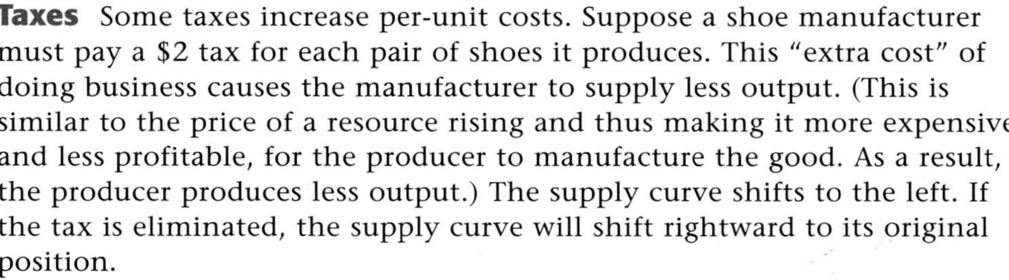

Modern farmers use pesticides and fertilizers. Are pesticides and fertilizers an advancement in the technology of farming? What effect will this have on farm output?

Taxes Some taxes increase per-unit costs. Suppose a shoe manufacturer must pay a $2 tax for each pair of shoes it produces. This "extra cost" of doing business causes the manufacturer to supply less output. (This is similar to the price of a resource rising and thus making it more expensive, and less profitable, for the producer to manufacture the good. As a result, the producer produces less output.) The supply curve shifts to the left. If the tax is eliminated, the supply curve will shift rightward to its original position.

Subsidies **Subsidies** have the opposite effect of taxes. A subsidy is a financial payment made by government for certain actions. Suppose the government subsidizes the production of corn by paying corn farmers $2 for every bushel of corn they produce. Because of the subsidy, the quantity supplied of corn is greater at each price, and the supply curve of corn shifts to the right. Removal of the subsidy shifts the supply curve of corn to the left.

Quotas **Quotas** are restrictions on the number of units of a foreign-produced good (import) that can enter a country. For example, suppose Japanese producers are currently sending, and want to continue to send, 100,000 cars to the United States each year. Now suppose the U.S. government imposes a quota on Japanese cars, say, at 80,000 a year. This quota means that no more than 80,000 Japanese cars can be imported into the United States. A quota decreases supply, so the supply curve shifts to the left. The elimination of a quota causes the supply curve to shift rightward to its original position.

Economists think in terms of incentives. More important, they believe that individuals respond to changes in incentives in predictable ways. Recall the discussion of taxes and subsidies with respect to supply. A tax on the production of a good is a "disincentive" to produce that good. Consequently, economists believe that fewer units of that good will be produced. In contrast, a subsidy on the production of a good is an "incentive" to produce that good. Consequently, economists believe that more units of that good will be produced as a result.

Technology & Innovation

What Happens If People Live to Be 100?

An advancement in technology is one factor that increases supply. Usually, when we talk about supply, we mean the supply of goods and services. But can an advancement in technology increase the supply of people? One way to increase the supply of people in the world is to increase the length of life. For example, if people start living an average of 100 years instead of 70 years, there are going to be more people in the world.

This takes us to Michael Rose, an evolutionary biologist at the University of California at Irvine who studies the aging process. Rose has found a way to increase the average life span of a fruit fly. The average fruit fly lives for about 70 days, but Rose's fruit flies live for 140 days.

If Rose and other like-minded scientists can do for human beings what they have done for fruit flies, then people in the future may live longer lives. According to some scientists working in the area of aging, ages of 100 or 150 years are not unreasonable.

Now suppose that scientists did figure out how to slow the aging process in humans, and people began to live longer. Furthermore, suppose that as a result of slowing the aging process, an average 80-year-old in the future felt the same way an average 50-year-old feels today. What economic effects would this have?

First, longer-living people would probably work for more years than we do today. People today often start full-time work when they are 22 years old and retire at around 65, a work life of 43 years. In the future, they may start work at 22 and retire at 85, a work life of 63 years.

People are resources, and resources go to produce goods and services. If there were more people working, there would be more goods and services. In other words, the current research on aging, if successful, would lead to a greater supply of goods and services in the world.

Does this mean that the average person living in the future will have more goods and services than the average person living today? It all depends on how fast the population grows relative to how fast the supply of goods and services grows. In a world of twenty people and twenty goods and services, the average person has one good or service. If the number of people grows faster than the supply of goods and services, the average number of goods per person will decline. In other words, the average person will be poorer in terms of goods and services. But if the supply of goods grows faster than the number of people, then the average number of goods per person will rise. The average person will be richer in terms of goods and services. Finally, if the supply of goods grows as fast as the number of people, the average number of goods per person will remain the same. People, on average, will become no richer and no poorer.

Thus, if current research on aging actually ends up slowing the aging process and lengthening life, there will be an increase in the supply of goods and services in the world. Whether this will make the average person richer, poorer, or neither still remains to be seen.

QUESTION TO ANSWER Do you think that slowing the aging process will result in increasing, decreasing, or leaving unchanged the average person's material standard of living?

Number of Sellers If more sellers begin producing a particular good, perhaps because of high profits, supply increases and the supply curve shifts to the right. If some sellers stop producing a particular good, perhaps because of losses, the supply curve shifts to the left.

Weather (In Some Cases) Weather can affect the supply of a good. Bad weather reduces the supply of many agricultural goods, such as corn, wheat, and barley. Unusually good weather can increase the supply.

An unusually long and severe dry spell can affect farm output. Will it also affect the supply of food at the grocery store?

A Change in Supply versus a Change in Quantity Supplied

A change in supply, which we just discussed, is not the same as a change in quantity supplied. A change (increase or decrease) in supply refers to a shift in the supply curve, as illustrated in Exhibit 4-5a.

Change in supply = Shift in supply curve

Saying that the supply of apples has increased is the same as saying that the supply curve for apples has shifted to the right. As you know, the factors that can change supply (shift the supply curve) include the prices of relevant resources, technology, a tax on the production of a good, subsidies, quotas, the number of sellers, and weather (in some cases).

Exhibit 4-5

A Change in Supply versus a Change in Quantity Supplied

(a) A change in supply refers to a shift in the supply curve. A change in supply can be brought about by a number of factors. (b) A change in quantity supplied refers to a movement along a given supply curve. A change in quantity supplied is brought about only by a change in (a good's) own price.

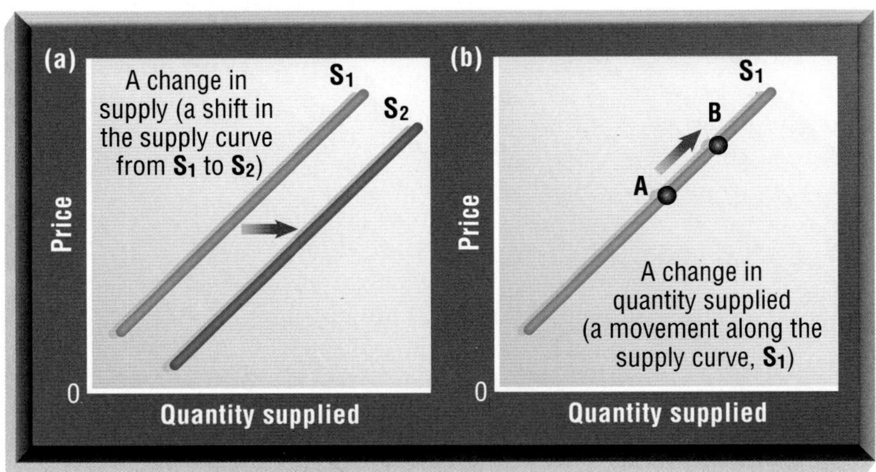

The Beatles

On February 9, 1964, Ed Sullivan, the host of the *The Ed Sullivan Show,* stepped onto the stage of the CBS Studios in New York City and announced, "Ladies and gentlemen—The Beatles." That Sunday night would net the highest ratings in U.S. television history (up to that point) for a single show: 73 million viewers. It would also begin what has become known as the "British invasion"—the "invasion" of the United States by British rock groups and popular culture.

Before we continue the story of the British invasion, let's go back to supply. One of the factors that increases the supply of a good or service is the number of sellers. The more sellers of a good or service, the greater the supply of that good or service. One key thing that can increase the number of sellers of a particular good or service is success. Success is copied. In economic terminology, success equals profit. Where there is profit, new sellers will emerge to try to capture some of that profit. (Sellers turn away from losses and gravitate toward profit.)

The Beatles, a British rock group, became a huge success in the United States. Their early musical releases, such as "I Want to Hold Your Hand," "She Loves You," and "Can't Buy Me Love," were immensely popular and profitable.

Soon the supply of British groups in the United States would rise. (The supply curve of British groups in the United States would shift to the right.) The Beatles had shown that a distinctly British group could conquer the United States and earn millions. Some of the British groups and singers that were part of the invasion were the Rolling Stones, the Dave Clark Five, The Who, the Yardbirds, Herman's Hermits, The Hollies, the Kinks, Procol Harum, Cream, Spencer Davis Group, the Animals, and Donovan. In fact, the Beatles had so thoroughly shown the popularity of British style that many U.S. groups went so far as to copy the look and, to a degree, the style of the British (for example, the Byrds and the Turtles). Other groups made sure they had British members; examples are Fleetwood Mac; Crosby, Stills & Nash; and the Monkees.

While many millions of teenagers danced to the songs played by the British groups, some parents were dismayed. The British groups had not only changed the sound of music in the United States but also had influenced the look, dress, and attitudes of many people.

Many young males began to wear their hair long (in imitation of groups like the Beatles and the Rolling Stones). One parent wrote to the Rolling Stones, "You should be given a good bath and then all that hair should be cut off. . . . Your filthy appearance is liable to corrupt teenagers all over the country."

QUESTION TO ANSWER The feature said that "success is copied." Can you think of other successful products in the past that have been copied?

Taxes, Tariffs, and America's Great Depression

The text discussion of the factors that affect supply included both taxes and subsidies. There is an old economic saying that "you get less of that which you tax and more of that which you subsidize." For example, if we tax work, people will work less than if we don't tax work. If we subsidize museums, we will get more museums than if we don't subsidize museums.

With this in mind, think of a tariff, which is a tax on imported goods. Governments can and do impose tariffs on foreign-produced (imported) goods. For example, the United States can impose or raise tariffs on Japanese-produced cars imported into the country.

We now go back in history, to around the time of the Great Depression. In January 1929, many members of Congress had become disturbed over the increase in imports into the United States. Willis Hawley, the chairman of the House Ways and Means Committee in the House of Representatives, introduced a bill in Congress to deal with this apparent problem. It came to be known as the Smoot-Hawley Tariff Act, which proposed substantially higher tariffs on many imported goods. It was thought that with higher tariffs on imported goods, Americans would buy fewer imports and more goods produced in the United States. This outcome, some thought, would be good for the country.

Although the Smoot-Hawley Tariff Act was not signed into law until June 17, 1930, its passage was likely, and many people in the country suspected it would become law long before it did. Some people thought it would be bad for business in the United States. They thought that other countries would retaliate with their own high tariffs (which they did), and that global trade would diminish, thus hurting the U.S. economy. (If other countries imposed high tariffs on U.S. goods, then Americans would not be able to sell as much abroad.)

Some economists blame the sharp decline in the stock market in 1929 —which some say dates the beginning of the greatest economic decline in the nation's history, the Great Depression—on the foregone conclusion that Congress would pass, and the president would sign, the Smoot-Hawley Tariff Act. Certainly, the stock market did plummet after the act was signed into law. Furthermore, many economists today believe that the act not only served as one of the catalysts of the Great Depression but also made the Great Depression last longer than it would have otherwise.

QUESTION TO ANSWER Economists say that we get less of that which we tax. If a tariff is a tax on imports, then what does a tariff, especially one that is retaliated against by other countries, give us less of?

A change in quantity supplied refers to a movement along a supply curve, as shown in Exhibit 4-5b on page 99.

The only factor that can directly cause a change in quantity supplied of a good is a change in the price of the good—its own price. For example, a change in the price of computers brings about a change in the quantity supplied of computers. A change in the price of books brings about a change in the quantity supplied of books.

MINI GLOSSARY

elasticity of supply The relationship between the percentage change in quantity supplied and the percentage change in price.

elastic supply The kind of supply that exists when the percentage change in quantity supplied is greater than the percentage change in price.

inelastic supply The kind of supply that exists when the percentage change in quantity supplied is less than the percentage change in price.

unit-elastic supply The kind of supply that exists when the percentage change in quantity supplied is the same as the percentage change in price.

Elasticity of Supply

Chapter 3 discussed elasticity of demand. There is **elasticity of supply,** too. Elasticity of supply is the relationship between the percentage change in quantity supplied and the percentage change in price. We can look at it as a ratio:

$$\text{Elasticity of supply} = \frac{\text{Percentage change in quantity supplied}}{\text{Percentage change in price}}$$

Notice that the equation has a numerator (percentage change in quantity supplied) and a denominator (percentage change in price). **Elastic supply** exists when the quantity supplied changes by a greater percentage than price—that is, when the numerator changes by more than the denominator. For example, suppose the price of lightbulbs increases by 10 percent, and the quantity supplied of lightbulbs increases by 20 percent. The numerator (20 percent) changes by more than the denominator (10 percent), so the supply of lightbulbs is elastic.

Inelastic supply exists when the quantity supplied changes by a smaller percentage than price—that is, when the numerator changes by less than the denominator. Finally, **unit-elastic supply** exists when the quantity supplied changes by the same percentage as price—that is, when the numerator changes by the same percentage as the denominator. Exhibit 4-6 on page 103 reviews the definitions of elastic, inelastic, and unit-elastic supply.

THINKING Like an Economist

There are two major types of changes that economists speak about: directional changes and magnitudinal (or quantitative) changes. A directional change relates to the direction one variable changes in response to a change in the direction of another variable. For example, the law of supply speaks to directional changes. It states that quantity supplied rises as price rises. A magnitudinal change relates to *how much* one variable changes in response to a given magnitudinal change in another variable. For example, elasticity of supply speaks to magnitudinal changes, because it deals with *how much* quantity supplied changes for a given (magnitudinal) change in price.

Question: *With respect to elasticity of supply, is it a change in the price of the good that causes a change in the quantity supplied, or is it a change in the quantity supplied that causes a change in price?*

Answer: *The change in price is the cause of the change in quantity supplied. In other words, the change in price comes first, and the quantity supplied responds to it. Change in price = cause; change in quantity supplied = effect.*

The Responsibilities of Sellers

Chapter 3 discussed the responsibilities of buyers. Sellers have responsibilities, too. Sellers have the responsibility to inform buyers about the

Exhibit 4-6

Elasticity of Supply

ELASTICITY OF SUPPLY

IF SUPPLY IS.	. . . . . .THAT MEANS
Elastic	Quantity supplied changes by a larger percentage than price. For example, if price rises by 10 percent, quantity supplied rises by, say, 15 percent.
Inelastic	Quantity supplied changes by a smaller percentage than price. For example, if price rises by 10 percent, quantity supplied rises by, say, 5 percent.
Unit elastic	Quantity supplied changes by the same percentage as price. For example, if price rises by 10 percent, quantity supplied rises by 10 percent.

goods they are thinking about purchasing. A used-car seller, for example, should inform a car buyer about the condition of the car. If a car begins to shake when it is going 50 miles an hour, the seller has the responsibility to tell this to the buyer. A seller also has the responsibility of selling the buyer a safe product. For example, if a used-car seller knows the tires on a car are worn and ready to burst, the seller has the responsibility of replacing the tires before selling the car.

Section 2 Review

Defining Terms

1. Define

a. elastic supply
b. inelastic supply
c. unit-elastic supply
d. per-unit cost
e. subsidy
f. quota
g. technology

Reviewing Facts and Concepts

2. Identify what happens to a given supply curve as a result of each of the following.
   a. resource prices fall
   b. technology advances
   c. a quota is repealed
   d. a tax on the production of a good is repealed
3. If supply increases, does the supply curve shift to the right or to the left?
4. Identify whether a given supply curve will shift to the right or to the left as a result of each of the following.
   a. resource prices rise
   b. a quota is placed on a good.
5. Give a numerical example that illustrates elastic supply.

Critical Thinking

6. The previous section explained how a supply curve can be vertical. If a supply curve is vertical, does it follow that supply is (a) elastic, (b) inelastic, (c) unit elastic, or (d) none of the above? Explain your answer.

Graphing Economics

7. Graph the following:
   a. an increase in supply
   b. a decrease in supply
   c. an increase in the supply of good X that is greater than the increase in the supply of good Y

Developing Economic Skills

Working with Supply and Demand Curves

Chapter 3 introduced the demand curve, and this chapter discussed the supply curve. Chapter 5 will put supply and demand together in one diagram and talk about a market. Before that step, however, it is important to make sure you have a good understanding of the details of demand and supply curves. Here are a few points to keep in mind.

A demand curve tells us the relationship between what is on the vertical axis (price) and what is on the horizontal axis (quantity demanded).

Think of a demand curve as saying something to you. If you look at Exhibit 4-7a, you can almost hear what the demand curve has to say. Notice that there are two axes: a vertical axis, "Price," and a horizontal axis, "Quantity demanded." The demand curve has something to "say" about these two factors: as price decreases, (from $10 to $5 in the exhibit), quantity demanded increases (from 100 units to 200 units). And when price increases, quantity demanded decreases. In other words, the demand curve tells us the relationship between price and quantity demanded: when one increases, the other decreases.

When a demand curve shifts, it tells us something new about quantity demanded.

Suppose a demand curve shifts to the right, from D_1 to D_2 in Exhibit 4-7b. What do demand curves "tell" us when this happens? They tell us something new about quantity demanded. The exhibit tells us that at the price of $10, buyers (demanders) now are willing and able to buy 150 units (of the good or service) instead of 100 units. In other words, when a demand curve shifts to the right, it says that buyers want to buy more at each and every price. Ask yourself what a demand curve says if it shifts to the left. Although this scenario is not drawn here, the demand curve says that buyers want to buy less than before at each and every price. A shift in a demand curve can be caused by changes in income, preferences, the prices of related goods, and the number of buyers.

There is a difference between a shift in a demand curve and a movement along a demand curve.

A movement along a demand curve is altogether different from a shift in a demand curve. Exhibit 4-7c illustrates a movement along a demand curve by the arrow between points A and B. What we see is a movement from one point (A) on the demand curve to another point (B) on the demand curve. Only a change in price can cause this movement. Notice in the exhibit that when the price is $10, the quantity demanded is 100 units (point A). When the price changes to $5, the quantity demanded increases to 200 units (point B). Remember that a move-

Exhibit 4-7

All About Demand Curves

(a) A demand curve; (b) A shift in a demand curve; (c) A movement along a demand curve.

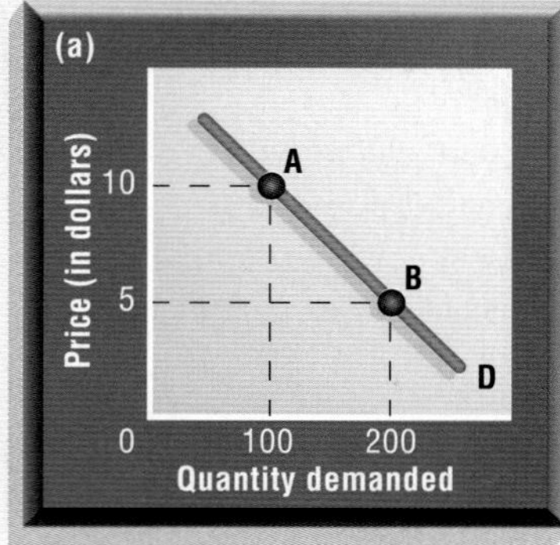

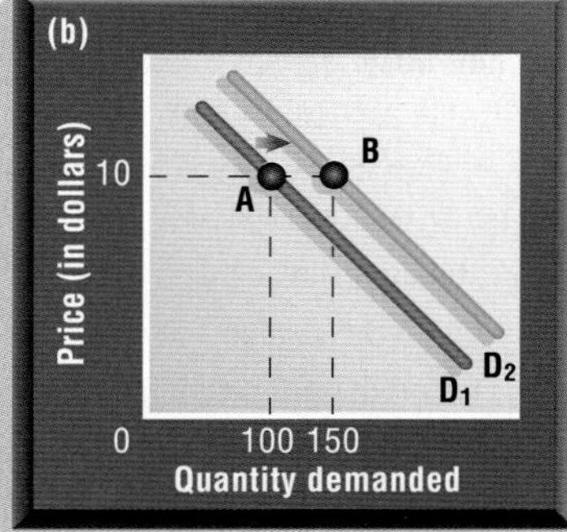

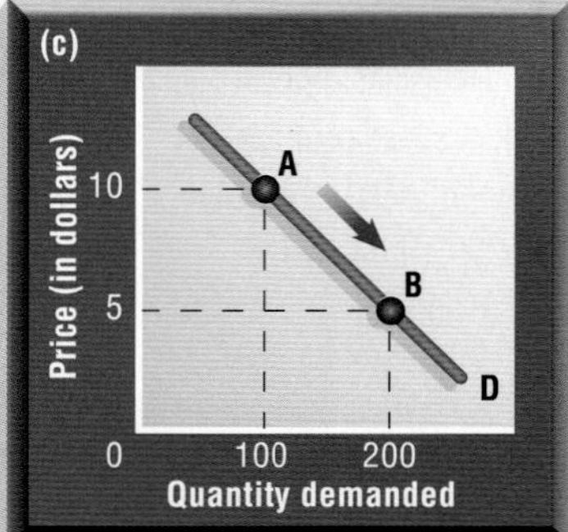

Exhibit 4-8

All About Supply Curves

(a) A supply curve; (b) A shift in a supply curve; (c) A movement along a supply curve.

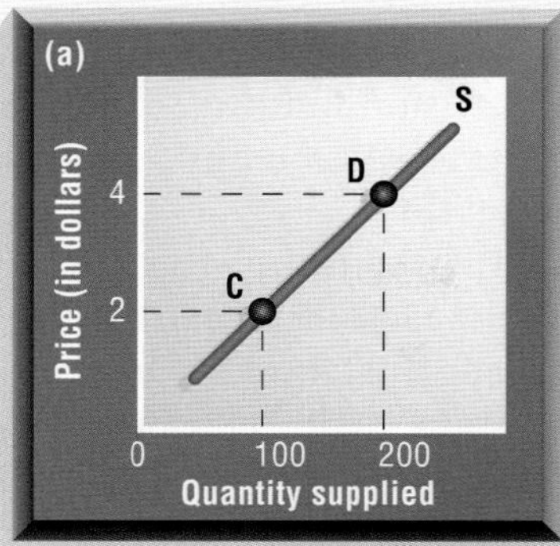

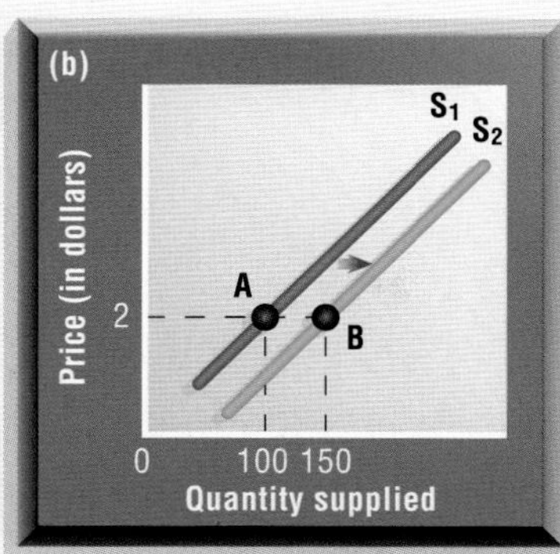

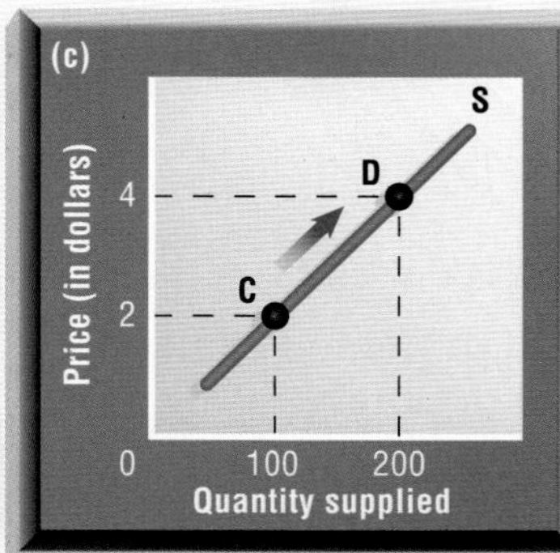

ment along a demand curve is caused only by a change in price—the price of that good.

A supply curve tells us the relationship between what is on the vertical axis (price) and what is on the horizontal axis (quantity supplied).

The supply curve also has something to say. Look at Exhibit 4-8a. Again, notice that there are two axes: a vertical axis, "Price," and a horizontal axis, "Quantity supplied." The supply curve says that as price increases (from $2 to $4 in the exhibit), quantity supplied increases (from 100 units to 200 units). In other words, the supply curve tells us the relationship between price and quantity supplied: when one increases, the other also increases.

When a supply curve shifts, it tells us something new about quantity supplied.

Suppose a supply curve shifts to the right—for example, from S_1 to the new curve S_2, in Exhibit 4-8b. When supply curves do this, they tell us something new about quantity supplied. The exhibit tells us that at a price of $2, sellers (suppliers) are willing and able to produce and offer to sell 150 units (of the good or service) instead of 100 units. In other words, when a supply curve shifts to the right, it says that sellers want to produce and sell more at each and every price. When a supply curve shifts to the left, it says that sellers want to produce and sell less at each price. A shift in a supply curve can be caused by factors such as changes in resource prices, technology, taxes, subsidies, quotas, number of sellers, and weather (in some cases).

There is a difference between a shift in a supply curve and a movement along a supply curve.

A movement along a supply curve is altogether different from a shift in a supply curve. Exhibit 4-8c shows a movement along a supply curve by the arrow between points C and D, indicating a movement from one point to another point on the supply curve. This movement is caused by a change in price. Notice in the exhibit that when the price is $2, the quantity supplied is 100 units (point C). When the price changes to $4, the quantity supplied increases to 200 units (point D). Remember, a movement along a supply curve is caused only by a change in price.

1. In Exhibit 4-7, which part (a, b, or c) shows a shift in a demand curve?
2. In Exhibit 4-8, which part (a, b, or c) shows a shift in a supply curve?
3. In Exhibit 4-8, which part (a, b, or c) shows a movement along a supply curve?
4. What does a shift in a demand curve tell us?
5. What does a shift in a supply curve tell us?
6. What does a demand curve tell us?
7. What does a supply curve tell us?
8. What can cause a movement along a supply curve? Can the same thing cause a shift in a supply curve? Explain your answer.
9. What can cause a movement along a demand curve? Can the same thing cause a shift in a demand curve? Explain your answer.

CHAPTER 4

Review

Economics Vocabulary

Fill in the following blanks with the appropriate word or phrase.

1. A(n) ____ is the numerical representation of the law of supply.
2. A(n) ____ is the graphic representation of the law of supply.
3. According to the law of supply, as price rises, ____ rises.
4. Supply is ____ if the percentage change in quantity supplied is greater than the percentage change in price.
5. Supply is ____ if the percentage change in quantity supplied is equal to the percentage change in price.
6. ____ refers to the number of units of a good produced and offered for sale at a specific price.

Review Questions

1. Explain the term *supply* as it applies to economics. What is the difference between supply and quantity supplied?
2. Express the law of supply in (a) words, (b) symbols, and (c) graphic form.
3. Luisa is willing but not able to produce and offer to sell plastic cups. Is Luisa a supplier of plastic cups? Explain your answer.
4. Are all supply curves upward sloping? Why or why not?
5. Write out a supply schedule for four different combinations of price and quantity supplied.
6. Identify whether the supply curve for each of the following would be vertical or upward sloping.
   a. desks in your classroom at this moment
   b. seats at a football stadium at this moment
   c. television sets over time
   d. Compaq computers over time
   e. Picasso paintings (*Hint:* Picasso is dead.)
7. What does it mean when a supply curve shifts to the right? To the left?
8. Between the price of $10 and $14, supply is inelastic. What does this mean?
9. Explain what happens to the supply curve of television sets as a consequence of each of the following.
   a. Resource prices fall.
   b. There is a technological advancement in the television industry.
   c. A tax is placed on the production of television sets.
10. Identify the factors that can change supply. Identify the factor that can change quantity supplied.
11. Explain the terms *incentive* and *disincentive*. Identify and describe an example of each. In addition, explain how the disincentive might affect the supply of a particular good.
12. In each of the following cases, identify whether the supply of the good is elastic, inelastic, or unit elastic.
    a. The price of books rises 10 percent, and the quantity supplied of books rises 14 percent.
    b. The price of bread rises 2 percent, and the quantity supplied of bread rises 2 percent.
    c. The price of telephones falls 6 percent, and the quantity supplied of telephones falls 8 percent.
13. There is a direct relationship between price and quantity supplied. Identify two other factors for which there is a direct relationship.
14. What factor causes movement along a demand curve?

Calculations

1. A house-building company spends $40 million to produce 400 houses. What is the average cost, or per-unit cost, of a house?
2. A $150 purchase in 1925 was the equivalent of a $1,425 purchase in 1999. How much would an item purchased in 1925 for $375 have cost in 1999?
3. Firm A sold 400 stereos for a total of $200,000, and Firm B sold 550 stereos for a total of $275,000. Which firm is charging more per unit? Graph the supply curve.
4. If the percentage change in price is 5 percent and the percentage change in quantity supplied is 10 percent, what is elasticity of supply equal to?
5. Currently the price of a good is $10, and the quantity supplied is 300 units. For every $1 increase in price, quantity supplied rises by 5 units. What is the quantity supplied at a price of $22?

Graphs

Use Exhibit 4-9 to answer the following questions. P = price, and Q_s = quantity supplied.

1. What does Exhibit 4-9a represent?
2. Which part of Exhibit 4-9 (Part a, b, or c) represents a change in supply due to an advancement in technology?

Exhibit 4-9

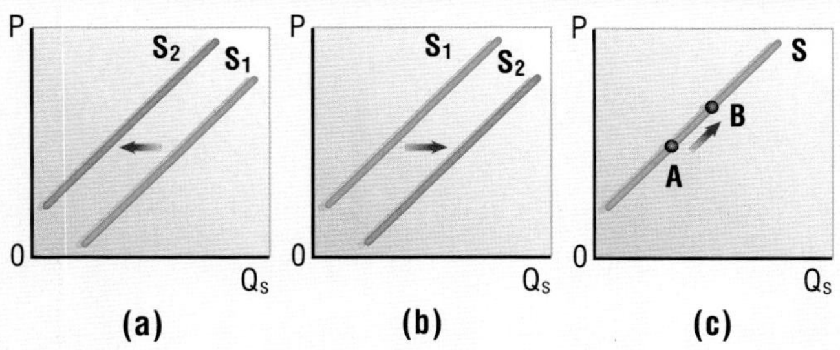

3. What does Exhibit 4-9c represent?
4. Which part of Exhibit 4-9 (Part a, b, or c) represents a change in supply due to a increase in resource prices?

Economics and Thinking Skills

1. **Application.** The law of supply pertains to many goods. For example, if the price of shoes rises, in time the quantity supplied of shoes will rise, too. Devise an experiment to test whether studying for an economics test is subject to the law of supply.
2. **Analysis.** How is elasticity of demand (discussed in Chapter 3) similar to, and different from, elasticity of supply (discussed in this chapter)?
3. **Cause and Effect.** Explain the process by which a tax, applied to the production of a good, changes the supply of the good.

Writing Skills

In the "Thinking Like an Economist" feature on page 97, it was stated that economists believe that people respond to changes in incentives. What is your view on the subject? Do you believe that people respond to changes in incentives? What evidence (scientific or anecdotal) is there to support your position? Write a one-page paper that answers these questions.

Economics in the Media

1. Find an example in a newspaper or magazine of something that has a vertical supply curve associated with it. For example, you may read about a concert that was recently performed at an auditorium in town. The supply curve for seats in the auditorium is vertical: that is, there is a fixed number of seats, and the number of seats does not change as ticket prices rise and fall.
2. Find an example in a newspaper or magazine that relates to a change in supply. For example, you may read that government plans to impose a quota on a particular good. As you learned in this chapter, quotas reduce the supply of goods.
3. The law of supply states that as the price of a good rises, the quantity supplied rises. Obviously, there is a direct relationship between price and quantity supplied. Find an example of a direct relationship on television or in the movies. For example, in the movie *Stealing Home,* with Mark Harmon and Jodie Foster, Harmon's character gets happier the more baseball he plays. Thus, there is a direct relationship between the amount of baseball the character plays and the amount of happiness he feels (more baseball, more happiness).

Where's the Economics?

How will the cold freeze affect the supply of oranges in the orange market?

Analyzing Primary Sources

Adam Smith (1723–1790), who was introduced in Chapter 2 of this text, is a leading figure in the history of economics. In his major work, *An Inquiry into the Nature and Causes of the Wealth of Nations,* he talks about many things, including supply, the major topic of this chapter. Read the following excerpt from Book 1, Chapter 7, and then explain what Smith is saying.

The quantity of every commodity brought to market naturally suits itself to the effectual demand. It is in the interest of all those who employ their land, labour, or stock, in bringing any commodity to market, that the quantity never should exceed the effectual demand; and it is the interest of all other people that it never should fall short of that demand.

CHAPTER 5

Markets: Supply and Demand Together

What This Chapter Is About

Every market has two sides: a demand side, which you learned about in Chapter 3, and a supply side, which you learned about in Chapter 4. This chapter puts demand and supply together and discusses a market. The discussion focuses on how markets function and on how they determine the prices you pay for everything from milk to cars.

Why This Chapter Is Important

Markets are a little like the air you breathe—they are everywhere. Any time you buy or sell anything, a market exists. When you buy a loaf of bread at the local grocery store or you buy a car, you are involved in a market transaction. If you have ever had a part-time job, you sold your labor services and were involved in a market transaction. There is no getting away from markets. They are everywhere, and you will deal with them for the rest of your life.

After You Study This Chapter, You Will Be Able To

- explain how supply and demand work together to determine price.
- explain what happens to price when there is a surplus.
- explain what happens to price when there is a shortage.
- explain what happens if price is not at its equilibrium level.
- use supply and demand to explain everyday events.

You Will Also Learn What Economics Has to Do With

- Elvis Presley's Cadillac.
- the California gold rush.
- a meeting in Vienna.
- congested freeways.
- trying out for a high school sports team.
- grade point averages (GPAs) and Scholastic Assessment Test (SAT) scores.

Economics Journal

List five goods that you purchased in the last year that were "on sale." Why do you think the retailers put these goods on sale?

SECTION 1

The Market: Supply and Demand Together

Supply and demand work together to determine price. The British economist Alfred Marshall (1842–1924) compared supply and demand to the two blades of a pair of scissors. Just as it is impossible to say which blade does the actual cutting, it is impossible to say whether demand or supply is responsible for the market price we observe. The fact is, price is determined by both sides of the market.

As you read this section, keep these key questions in mind:

- How do supply and demand together determine price?
- What happens to price if there is a surplus in the market?
- What happens to price if there is a shortage in the market?

SUPPLY DEMAND

An Auction: Supply and Demand at Work

Key Terms

surplus
shortage
equilibrium
equilibrium quantity
equilibrium price
inventory

To understand exactly how supply and demand work together to determine price, think of yourself at an auction where bushels of corn are bought and sold. This auction may be different from the auctions you have heard about or seen before. At this auction, price will be allowed to go up and down in response to supply and demand.

Suppose for now that the supply curve for corn is vertical, as in Exhibit 5-1. It cuts the horizontal axis at 40,000 bushels of corn, so no more and no fewer than 40,000 bushels of corn will be auctioned off. The demand curve for corn is downward sloping. Furthermore, suppose that in our auction, each potential buyer of corn is sitting in front of a computer that registers the number of bushels he or she wants to buy. For example, if Nancy Berkeley wants to buy 5,000 bushels of corn, she simply keys the number 5,000 into her computer.

Supply and demand are at work in auctions that take place on the Internet. http://www.ebay.com is the address of a popular Internet auction site. When you go to this site, the left side of your monitor shows a list of the various categories of goods that are being auctioned. List five of the categories. Next, click on one of the categories, and see what specific items are being auctioned. Be sure to notice the highest bid for each item, when the auction started, and when it ends.

The auction begins. (Follow along in Exhibit 5-1 as you read about what is happening at the auction.) The auctioneer calls out the price, $6.

- At $6 a bushel, the potential buyers think for a second, and then each registers the number of bushels he or she wants to buy at that price. The total is 20,000, which is the quantity demanded of corn at $6 per bushel. The quantity supplied, though, is 40,000. In economics, when quantity supplied is greater than quantity demanded, a **surplus** exists. At a price of $6 per bushel, the surplus equals 20,000 bushels (the difference between the quantity supplied and the quantity demanded). The auctioneer, realizing that 20,000 bushels of corn will go unsold at this price, decides to lower the price per bushel to $5.

surplus The condition in which the quantity supplied of a good is greater than the quantity demanded. Surpluses occur only at prices above equilibrium price.

shortage The condition in which the quantity demanded of a good is greater than the quantity supplied. Shortages occur only at prices below equilibrium price.

Exhibit 5-1

Supply and Demand at Work at an Auction

The auctioneer calls out different prices, and buyers record how much they are willing and able to buy. At prices $6 and $5, quantity supplied is greater than quantity demanded—there is a surplus. At prices $2 and $3, quantity demanded is greater than quantity supplied—there is a shortage. Only at a price of $4 is the quantity demanded equal to the quantity supplied—there is neither a surplus nor a shortage. (The supply curve is vertical at 40,000 bushels of corn because we have assumed that no more and no fewer than 40,000 bushels of corn will be auctioned off.)

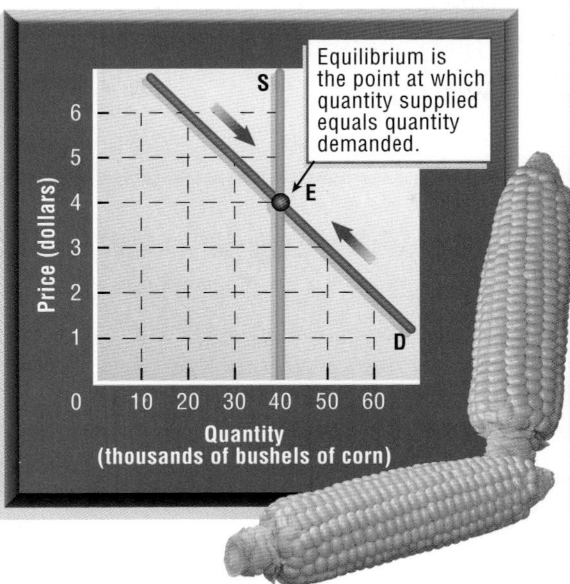

equilibrium The condition of being at rest or balanced. Equilibrium in a market exists when the quantity of a good that buyers are willing and able to buy is equal to the quantity of the good that sellers are willing and able to produce and offer for sale (that is, quantity demanded equals quantity supplied). Graphically, equilibrium in a market is shown as the intersection point of the supply and demand curves.

equilibrium quantity The quantity of a good that is bought and sold in a market that is in equilibrium.

equilibrium price The price at which a good is bought and sold in a market that is in equilibrium.

- At $5 a bushel, the quantity demanded increases to 30,000 bushels, but the quantity supplied of corn at this price still is greater than the quantity demanded. There is still a surplus of corn—specifically, 10,000 bushels. The auctioneer lowers the price again, this time to $2.
- At $2 a bushel, the quantity demanded jumps to 60,000 bushels and is greater than the quantity supplied. When quantity demanded is greater than quantity supplied, a **shortage** is said to exist. The auctioneer, realizing that he can't sell 60,000 bushels of corn because that quantity does not exist, decides to raise the price to $3.
- At $3 a bushel, quantity demanded falls to 50,000 bushels but is still greater than quantity supplied. A shortage still exists, although it is smaller than the shortage that existed at $2 per bushel. The auctioneer raises the price to $4.
- At $4 a bushel, the quantity demanded is 40,000, and the quantity supplied is 40,000. The auction stops. The 40,000 bushels of corn are bought and sold at $4 a bushel. The corn market is said to be in **equilibrium.** A market is in equilibrium when the quantity demanded of a good equals the quantity supplied. In this example, the quantity 40,000 bushels of corn is referred to as the **equilibrium quantity** (the quantity of a good bought and sold in a market that is in equilibrium), and $4 is referred to as the **equilibrium price** (the price at which a good is bought and sold in a market that is in equilibrium).

Alfred Marshall, Economist

Perhaps no other economist introduced the economics profession to as many widely used microeconomic tools as Alfred Marshall (1842–1924). As a child, his father overworked him at his studies and made him promise never to play chess (because he saw chess as a waste of time). He also tried to prevent him from studying mathematics because it was unnecessary for the ministry, which is the career he had chosen for his son. Alfred Marshall rejected his father's choice of a career. He went to Cambridge University and studied mathematics, physics, and economics.

Marshall popularized the diagrammatic approach in economics, which is used many times in this chapter.

Marshall is also known for many microeconomic tools, but two of the most important are supply and demand. Some economists before him thought that only the cost of production (reflected in supply) determined price; others thought that only demand determined price. Marshall, however, said that both supply and demand determine price. It is widely acknowledged today that Marshall had it right.

QUESTION TO ANSWER Suppose your job is to explain to someone how prices are determined. Will it be easier to do this with words only, or with words and a picture (of supply and demand curves)? What does your answer tell you about the contribution Marshall made to understanding economics through popularizing the diagrammatic approach?

Relationship of quantity supplied (Q_s) to quantity demanded (Q_d)	Market condition
$Q_s > Q_d$	Surplus
$Q_d > Q_s$	Shortage
$Q_d = Q_s$	Equilibrium

If there is a plentiful harvest of fruit, how will the supply of fruit in the grocery store be affected?

Moving to Equilibrium: What Happens to Price When There Is a Surplus or Shortage?

When the price was $6 a bushel and there was a surplus of corn, the auctioneer lowered the price. When the price was $2 and there was a shortage, he raised the price. The behavior of the auctioneer can be summarized this way: *If a surplus exists, lower the price; if a shortage exists, raise the price.* In so doing, the auctioneer moved the corn market into equilibrium.

Not all markets have auctioneers. (When was the last time you saw one in the grocery store?) But many markets act as if an auctioneer is calling out higher and lower prices until equilibrium price is reached. In many real-world markets, prices fall when there is a surplus and rise when there is a shortage. Why?

Why Does Price Fall When There Is a Surplus? With a surplus, suppliers will not be able to sell all they had hoped to sell, so their **inventories** (stock of goods on hand) grow beyond the normal level. Storing extra goods can be costly and inefficient; thus sellers want to reduce their inventories. Some will lower prices to do so; some will cut back on producing output; others will do a little of both. As shown in Exhibit 5-2, price and output tend to fall until equilibrium is achieved.

Why Does Price Rise When There Is a Shortage?

With a shortage, buyers will not be able to buy all they had hoped to buy. Some buyers will offer to pay a higher price to get sellers to sell to them instead of to other buyers. The higher prices will motivate suppliers to start producing more output. Thus, in a shortage, there is a tendency for price and output to rise until equilibrium is achieved (see Exhibit 5-2).

inventory
The stock of goods that a business or store has on hand.

THINKING Like an Economist

Economists think of *equilibrium* the way many people think of a magnet. A magnet draws things to it. Markets are drawn toward equilibrium. If there is a shortage in a competitive market, it won't last long. The shortage will turn into equilibrium. Similarly, a surplus in a competitive market won't last long, because the surplus will turn into equilibrium.

Exhibit 5-2

Moving to Equilibrium

If there is a surplus—as there is at a price of $15—price and quantity of output fall. If there is a shortage—as there is at a price of $5—price and quantity of output rise. At $10, there is neither a surplus nor a shortage, so there is no change in price or quantity of output.

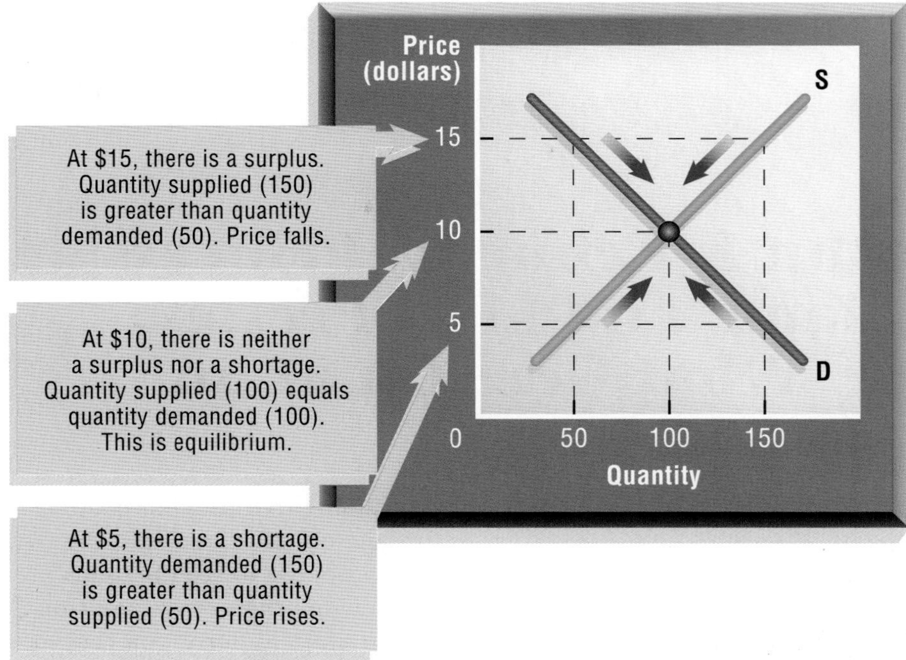

Review: Reading Graphs

To make sure you know how to determine quantity demanded and quantity supplied on a graph, start at a price of $15 in Exhibit 5-2. To find the quantity demanded, follow the dotted horizontal line over to the demand curve (D). Then follow the dotted vertical line downward to the horizontal (or quantity) axis (50). Thus, the quantity demanded is 50 at $15.

To find the quantity supplied at $15, again start at the price of $15 on the vertical axis, and follow the dotted horizontal line over to the supply curve (S). Then follow the dotted vertical line downward to the horizontal axis. The number here is 150, so the quantity supplied is 150 at $15.

Is there a surplus or a shortage at $15? Because the quantity supplied (150) is greater than the quantity demanded (50), there is a surplus. What happens to price if a surplus exists? Price falls.

Suppose a company's stock sells for $110 a share. The company produces a product that it sells in many countries. One day the company receives some bad economic news: Congress has passed legislation prohibiting it from selling its product in five countries to which it currently sells. Predict what will happen to the share price of this company's stock. Give an explanation for your prediction.

Changes in Equilibrium Price

So far, we have established that equilibrium price is determined by both supply and demand. In Exhibit 5-2, the equilibrium price is $10. For the equilibrium price to change, either supply or demand would have to change.

Demand Changes and Equilibrium Price Changes

Exhibit 5-3a on page 115 shows the demand for and supply of television sets. The original demand curve is D_1, the supply curve is S_1, equilibrium is at point 1, and the equilibrium price is $300. Now suppose the

John F. Kennedy, Princess Diana, and Elvis Presley; or, What Goes On at an Auction House?

Rare and unusual products are often bought and sold at auctions. A few of the goods sold at auctions have been dresses owned and worn by Princess Diana, a desk owned by President John F. Kennedy, and a Cadillac owned by Elvis Presley.

You may not have attended an auction at a major auction house such as Sotheby's or Christie's, but, for all practical purposes, this chapter has described what goes on there. Supply and demand are at work at the auction houses to determine the prices of the objects for sale, as well as who will and will not end up with the objects.

As a buyer at a major auction house, you will probably first leaf through the catalog to find what is up for auction, and then visit the auction house to see the items.

There are three ways you can bid on an item. First, you can go to the auction in person. You will need to register, at which time you will be asked to supply a bank reference and identification. You then will receive a paddle with your bidder number on it. The number on the paddle identifies who you are.

A second way to bid on items is by written bid. You decide on the maximum dollar amount you will pay for an item and give the written bid to the auction house, which then bids for you.

A third way to bid on items is by telephone. A person at the auction house will take your bids as the auction is in progress. This person may say to you, "The highest bid so far is $5,500. Do you want to bid higher?" Bidding usually starts at half the estimated price of the item published in the catalog. Bids usually follow a certain dollar increment, depending on the expected price range of the good being auctioned.

Think of an auction in terms of supply and demand. Generally, there is only one of whatever is being auctioned—one painting, one car, one estate, or one particular item of a famous person. Thus quantity supplied is usually one. There are usually many people who want to buy the one item. In other words, quantity demanded is greater than quantity supplied. What the auctioneer effectively does is to raise the price until there is only one person willing to buy the one item. At the end of the auction, quantity supplied equals quantity demanded, and both are one.

You may want to check out the Web page for one of the more famous auction houses, Christie's, at http://www.christies.com and see what is up for auction.

QUESTIONS TO ANSWER

1. The paddle at an auction has two purposes, only one of which we explicitly mentioned. What do you think the other purpose is?
2. Why do you think the auction house does not permit bids in $1 increments?

demand for television sets increases. (Recall from Chapter 3 the factors that can shift the demand curve for a good: income, preferences, prices of related goods, and number of buyers.) The demand curve shifts to the right, from D_1 to D_2. D_2 is now the relevant demand curve. At $300 per television, the quantity demanded (using the new demand curve, D_2) is 300,000, and the quantity supplied (using the one and only supply curve, S_1) is 200,000.

Because the quantity demanded is greater than quantity supplied, a shortage exists in the television market. Price then begins to rise. As it does, the television market moves to point 2, where it is in equilibrium again. The new equilibrium price is $400. We conclude that an increase in the demand for a good will increase price, all other things remaining the same.

Now suppose the demand for television sets decreases (see Exhibit 5-3b). The demand curve shifts to the left, from D_1 to D_2. At $300, the quantity demanded (using the new demand curve, D_2) is 100,000, and the quantity supplied (again using S_1) is 200,000. Because quantity supplied is greater than quantity demanded, a surplus exists. Price begins to fall. As it does, the television market moves to point 2, where it is in equilibrium again.

Exhibit 5-3

Changes in the Equilibrium Price of Television Sets

A change in equilibrium price can be brought about by (a) an increase in demand, (b) a decrease in demand, (c) an increase in supply, or (d) a decrease in supply.

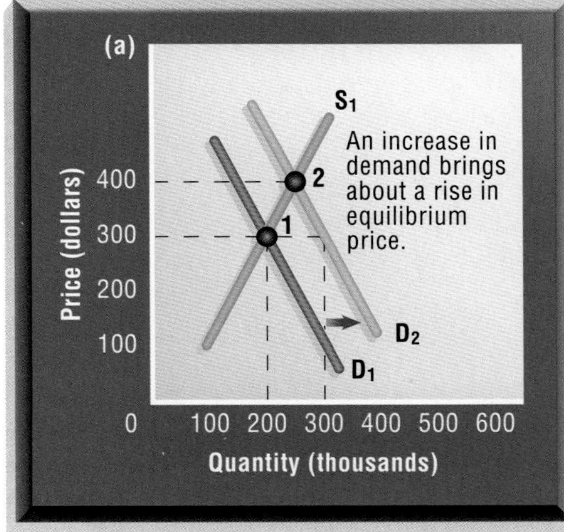

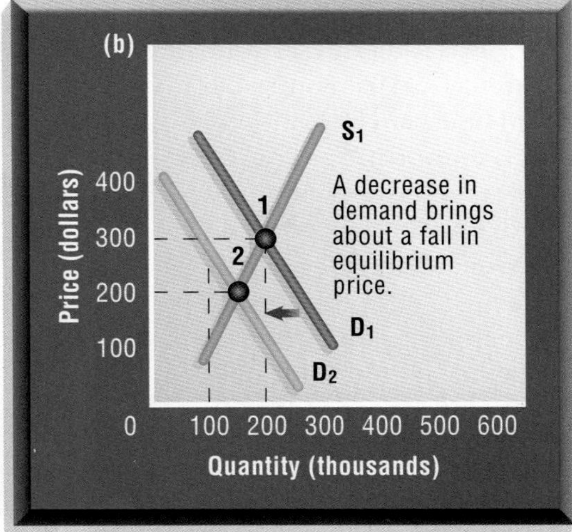

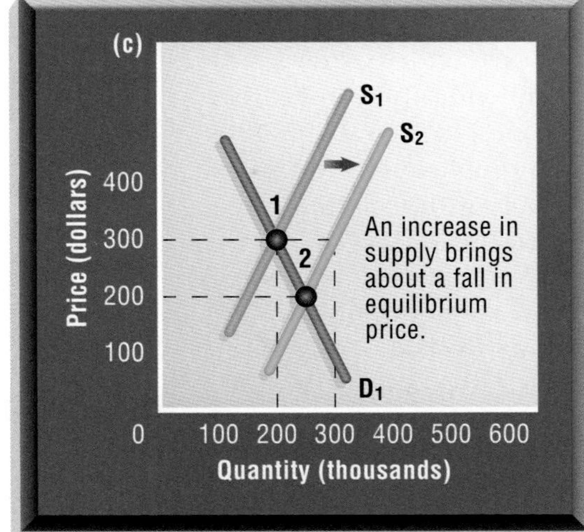

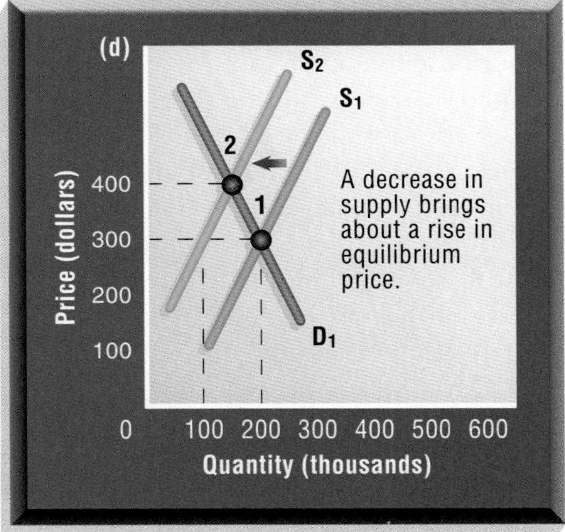

How to Reduce Air Pollution and Get Rid of a Car That Won't Sell

Suppose Ali wants to sell his seven-year-old car for $10,000, so he puts an ad in the newspaper. A few people take a look at the car, but no one buys it. One day Ali mentions this fact to his friend, Larry. Larry looks at the car and tells Ali that he would have an easier time selling the car if he put four new tires on it and painted it. Larry's solution to Ali's problem is a common one: if something doesn't sell at a given price, try to make it better so that it does.

There is no doubt that Larry has a point, but his solution to the problem isn't the only one possible. An economist who thinks in terms of price knows that there is another way to solve Ali's problem. It involves only lowering the price of the car.

Suppose five large factories are located near one another. Each day thousands of units of various goods are produced in these factories and shipped around the world. In the process of producing the goods, some smoke is emitted into the air. The residents who live downwind of the factories complain of air pollution.

What's the solution? Most people would say that environmental standards need to be set, regulations put into place. Perhaps the government needs to tell the factory owners to cut their smoke emissions by 25 percent during the next year.

An economist, however, thinks in terms of price and therefore knows that an environmental standard or regulation is not the only way to solve the problem. A change in price can work, too. Currently, the factory owners pay zero price to emit pollution into the air. Suppose the government started charging each factory $100 for each unit of pollution it emitted into the air. At $100 per pollution unit, would the factory owners emit less pollution into the air than they would if they paid nothing? Of course they would.

Both the car example and the factory pollution example deal with problems. Wherever there is a problem, someone will offer a solution. Often solutions have nothing to do with adjusting price.

This is where economists have something to offer. Economists think in terms of how price affects behavior. They know that if you change price, you change behavior, too. Lower the price of the car, and people who didn't want to buy the car at the higher price may want to buy it at the lower price. Raise the price of emitting pollution, and factories that once emitted a lot of pollution will emit less. In short, four new tires and a paint job can often solve the problem of a car that isn't selling, but a lower price can, too. Environmental standards and regulations can often solve the problem of too much pollution, but so can charging for that pollution.

QUESTION TO ANSWER Ali will be able to sell his car if he lowers the price to $9,000. Alternatively, he will be able to sell the car for $10,000 if he puts on four new tires and paints the car. Under what condition is Ali better off simply choosing to lower the price?

The new equilibrium price is \$200. A decrease in the demand for a good will decrease price, all other things remaining the same.

Supply Changes and Equilibrium Price Changes Now suppose the supply of television sets increases. (Recall Chapter 4's discussion of the factors that can shift the supply curve for a good, including resource prices, technology, taxes, and quotas.) The supply curve shifts to the right, from S_1 to S_2. At \$300, the quantity supplied (using the new supply curve, S_2) is 300,000, and the quantity demanded (using D_1) is 200,000. Quantity supplied is greater than quantity demanded, so a surplus exists in the television market. Price begins to fall, and the television market moves to point 2, where it is in equilibrium again. The new equilibrium price is \$200. Thus, an increase in the supply of a good will decrease the price, all other things remaining the same.

Now suppose the supply of television sets decreases, as in Exhibit 5-3d. The supply curve shifts leftward, from S_1 to S_2. At \$300, the quantity supplied (using S_2) is 100,000, and the quantity demanded (using D_1) is 200,000. Because quantity demanded is greater than quantity supplied, a shortage exists in the television market. Price begins to rise, and the television market moves to point 2, where it is again in equilibrium at the new equilibrium price of \$400. We conclude that a decrease in the supply of a good will increase the price, all other things remaining the same.

Changes in Supply and in Demand at the Same Time

The analysis just completed either (1) changed demand and left supply constant or (2) changed supply and left demand constant. In the real world, of course, both demand and supply can change at the same time. Let's look at a few cases and see how equilibrium price changes as a result.

Demand Increases and Supply Increases Look at Exhibit 5-4a on page 118. Suppose that D_1 and S_1 are initially operational, and the equilibrium price is \$300. Then both demand and supply increase. Demand increases from D_1 to D_2, and supply increases from S_1 to S_2. Notice that the increase in demand has been drawn as being greater than the increase in supply. In other words, the demand curve shifts further right (from D_1 to D_2) than the supply curve shifts right (from S_1 to S_2).

As we can see in the exhibit, equilibrium price rises from \$300 to \$400. In conclusion, if (1) both demand and supply increase and (2) demand increases more than supply increases, then equilibrium price increases.

Sellers often discount prices on certain items, including meat. Is a sale more likely to take place when there is a surplus or a shortage of a particular good?

Suppose again that we increase demand and supply, but this time supply increases by more than demand (see Exhibit 5-4b). Equilibrium price decreases from \$300 to \$200. In summary, if (1) both demand and supply increase and (2) supply increases more than demand increases, then equilibrium price decreases.

Now let's again increase both demand and supply,

Exhibit 5-4

Changes in Both Supply and Demand

Sometimes supply and demand change at the same time. In (a), both demand and supply increase, but demand increases more than supply. As a result, equilibrium price increases. In (b), both demand and supply increase, but this time supply increases more than demand. As a result, equilibrium price decreases. In (c), both demand and supply increase by the same amount, and equilibrium price remains constant. In (d), both demand and supply decrease, but demand decreases more than supply. As a result, equilibrium price decreases. In (e), both demand and supply decrease, but supply decreases more than demand. As a result, equilibrium price increases. In (f), both demand and supply decrease by the same amount, and equilibrium price remains constant.

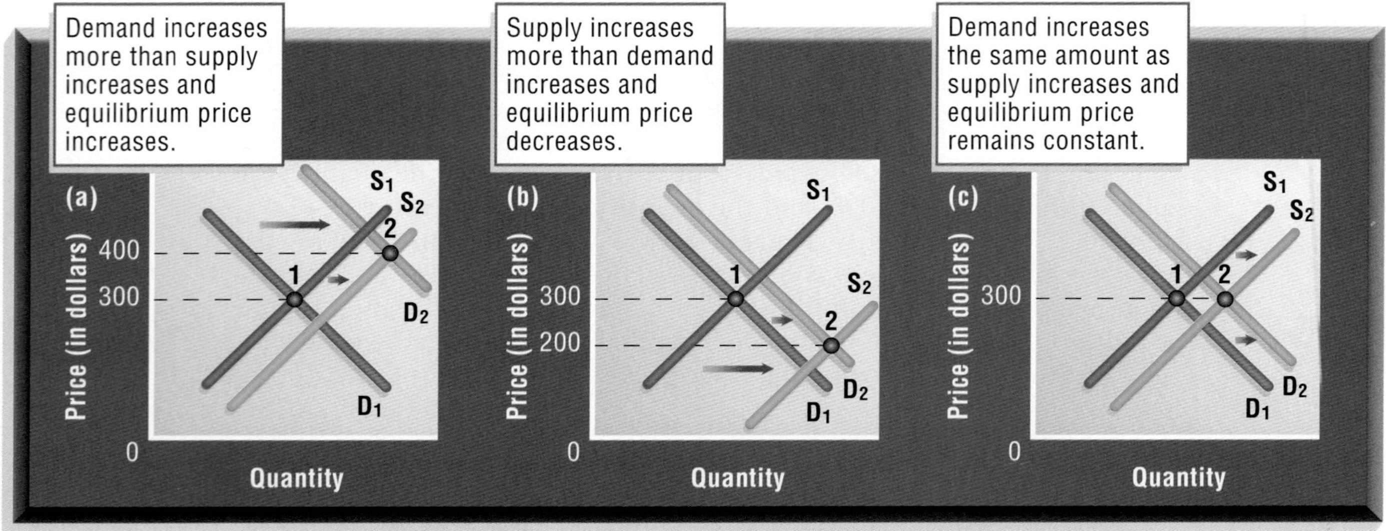

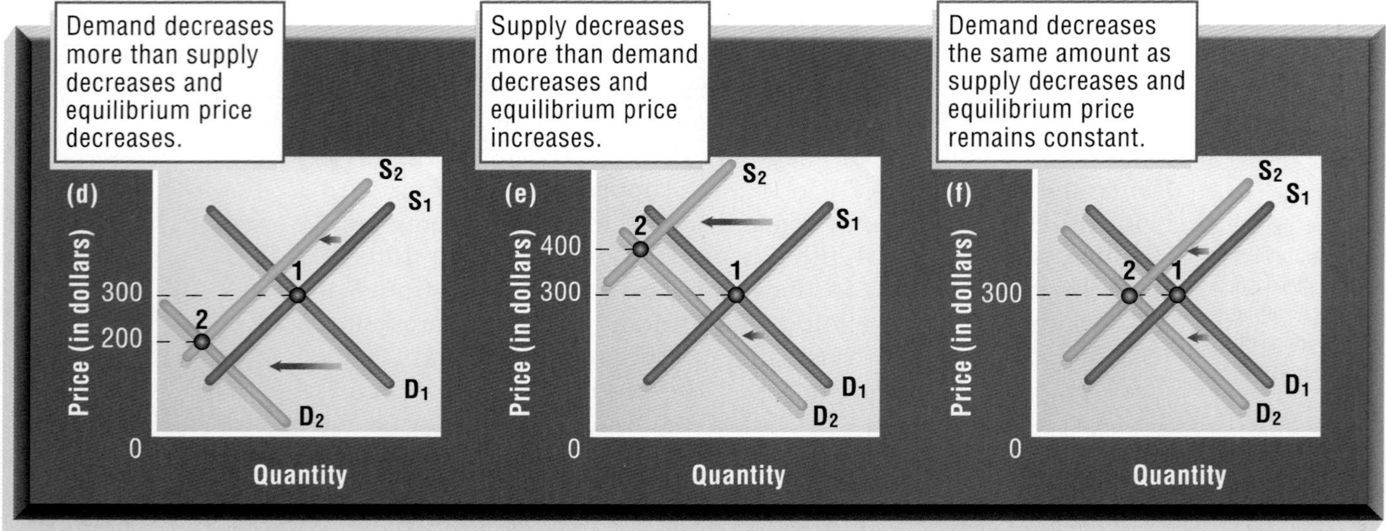

but this time by the same amount (see Exhibit 5-4c). Now equilibrium price remains constant at $300. Thus, if (1) both demand and supply increase and (2) demand increases the same amount as supply increases, then equilibrium price remains constant.

Demand Decreases and Supply Decreases Just as both demand and supply can increase at the same time, they can decrease at the same time, too, as shown in Exhibit 5-4 (parts d through f). In Exhibit 5-4d, demand decreases more than supply decreases, so equilibrium price decreases. In Exhibit 5-4e, supply decreases more than demand decreases, so equilibrium price increases. Finally, in Exhibit 5-4f, demand decreases the same amount as supply decreases, so equilibrium price remains constant.

Does It Matter If Price Is at Its Equilibrium Level or Not?

Think of two different worlds. In world 1 there are ten markets, each of which is in equilibrium. If all markets are in equilibrium, there are no shortages or surpluses of any good or service. In this world, there are no complaints from buyers or sellers. No buyer is complaining that because of the shortage, she can't buy something that she is willing and able to buy. No seller is complaining that because of the surplus, he can't sell something that he is willing and able to sell. Buyers are buying the quantities of the goods they want to buy, and sellers are selling the quantities of the goods they want to sell.

World 2 also has ten markets, but in five of the ten markets price is below equilibrium price, and in five of the ten markets price is above equilibrium price. In other words, half the markets are in surplus, and half are in shortage. In this world, both buyers and sellers are complaining. Buyers are complaining that because of the shortages, they can't buy some goods they are willing and able to buy. Sellers are complaining that because of the surpluses, they can't sell some goods they are willing and able to sell.

Things are dramatically different in world 1 and world 2. There are no shortages or surpluses in world 1, and there is nothing but shortage and surplus in world 2. Why is the first world so different from the second? In world 1 equilibrium price exists in every market, and in world 2 it does not exist in any market. To the economist, the level of price is important, because it determines whether or not people live in a world of shortages and surpluses.

Economists know that competitive markets, if left unhampered, eventually reach equilibrium. They also know that not all competitive markets reach equilibrium at the same speed. For example, the stock market may go from shortage to equilibrium in a matter of seconds or minutes, whereas the housing market may take months to make a similar move.

Section 1 Review

Defining Terms

1. Define
   a. shortage
   b. surplus
   c. equilibrium (in a market)
   d. equilibrium quantity
   e. equilibrium price
   f. inventory

Reviewing Facts and Concepts

2. If demand increases and supply is constant, what happens to equilibrium price?
3. If supply decreases and demand is constant, what happens to equilibrium price?
4. If supply increases and demand is constant, what happens to equilibrium price?
5. If the shortage is 40 units and the quantity supplied is 533 units, then what does quantity demanded equal?
6. If supply decreases by more than demand decreases, what happens to equilibrium price?

Critical Thinking

7. A producer makes 100 units of good X at $40 each. Under no circumstances will he sell the good for less than $40. Do you agree or disagree? Explain your answer.

Graphing Economics

8. Graph the following:
   a. demand increases in a market
   b. supply decreases in a market
   c. demand decreases in a market
   d. demand increases by more than supply increases in a market

SECTION 2

Where Supply and Demand Show Up

Supply and demand is not simply an abstract theory that appears only in economics textbooks like this one. Supply and demand are real-world forces that appear in numerous places every day. This section identifies some of those places.

As you read this section, keep these key questions in mind:

- Why do people wait in long lines to buy tickets for some rock concerts?
- Why does a house cost more in San Francisco than in Louisville, but a candy bar costs the same in both cities?
- Why does it cost more to go to the movies on Friday night than on Tuesday morning?
- What does traffic congestion have to do with supply and demand?
- What does trying out for a high school sport have to do with supply and demand?
- What is the necessary condition to earn a high income?

Why Some Rock Concerts Have Long Lines

Suppose tickets for a rock concert go on sale at 8 A.M. on Saturday. A long line of people forms even before the ticket booth opens. The average person has to wait an hour to buy a ticket. Some people don't get to buy tickets at all, because the concert sells out before they get to the ticket booth.

People frequently wait in long lines to buy tickets to rock concerts or to movies. Does a long line indicate equilibrium price or a price below equilibrium price?

Why is there a long line of people waiting to buy tickets to the rock concert, but there is not a long line of people waiting to buy food at the grocery store or TVs at the electronics store? Also, why are some of the people waiting to buy tickets to the rock concert turned away, but no one who wants to buy bread is turned away at the grocery store, and no one who wants to buy a TV set is turned away at the electronics store? The market for the rock concert tickets (at least in this instance) must differ somehow, but how?

In the long line of people waiting to buy concert tickets, some people were turned away. Translate this observation into economics. In economic terms, when some people go away without being able to buy what they came to buy, it means that quantity demanded exceeds quantity supplied; there is a shortage in the market.

You learned earlier that if there is a shortage in a market, price will rise. Eventually, it will

How a Meeting in Vienna Can Change the Price You Pay for a Gallon of Gasoline

Nobody wants to see $10 oil again.
—Qatari Oil Minister Abdullah al-Attiyah

Saudi Oil Minister Ali al-Naimi said the new restrictions were aimed at lifting oil prices back to $18 a barrel.
—Wire service report

At the end of 1998 and the early part of 1999, the price of oil fell to around $13 a barrel. Many of the members of the Organization of Petroleum Exporting Countries (OPEC) and non-OPEC oil-producing countries were saddened by this fact. OPEC consists of eleven countries (Algeria, Indonesia, Iran, Iraq, Kuwait, Libya, Nigeria, Qatar, Saudi Arabia, the United Arab Emirates, and Venezuela). Some of the major non-OPEC oil-producing countries include Russia, Mexico, and Oman.

In March 1999, the oil ministers of the OPEC countries got together in Vienna, Austria, to talk about the low price of oil and what they could do to get the price up to about $18 a barrel. They concluded that each of their countries could cut back on the supply of oil. A few of the non-OPEC oil-producing countries decided to do the same. (If demand is constant and supply falls, price rises.) The OPEC countries, along with a few non-OPEC countries, agreed to cut back their production of oil for about a year. Their objective was to reduce oil production by about 16 percent over the year.

Soon the oil cutbacks came, and as the laws of supply and demand predict, the price of a barrel of oil began to rise. In a matter of days the price of oil was in the range of $15 to $17. Soon after, U.S. motorists noticed a rise in the price of gasoline at the pump, from around $1.05 a gallon to about $1.30 a gallon.

It should be noted that OPEC has both successfully and unsuccessfully tried to raise the price of oil before. Whether or not it is successful depends on whether all countries live up to their cutback agreements or not. For example, if eleven countries agree to cut back the supply of oil, and then each begins to cheat on the agreement, the supply of oil is not likely to fall very much, if at all. If they can all hold to their agreement, however, the oil supply will fall, and prices will rise.

QUESTION TO ANSWER Graphically represent the effects of the OPEC agreement to cut production.

Exhibit 5-5
Rock Concert Ticket Price

The seller of rock concert tickets sells 10,000 tickets at a price of $40 each. At this price, there is a shortage; the seller has charged too low a price. A price of $60 per ticket would have achieved equilibrium in the market. The supply curve is vertical at 10,000 seats in this graph because this is the total number of seats in the auditorium. Even if a higher price is offered per ticket, no additional seats will be forthcoming.

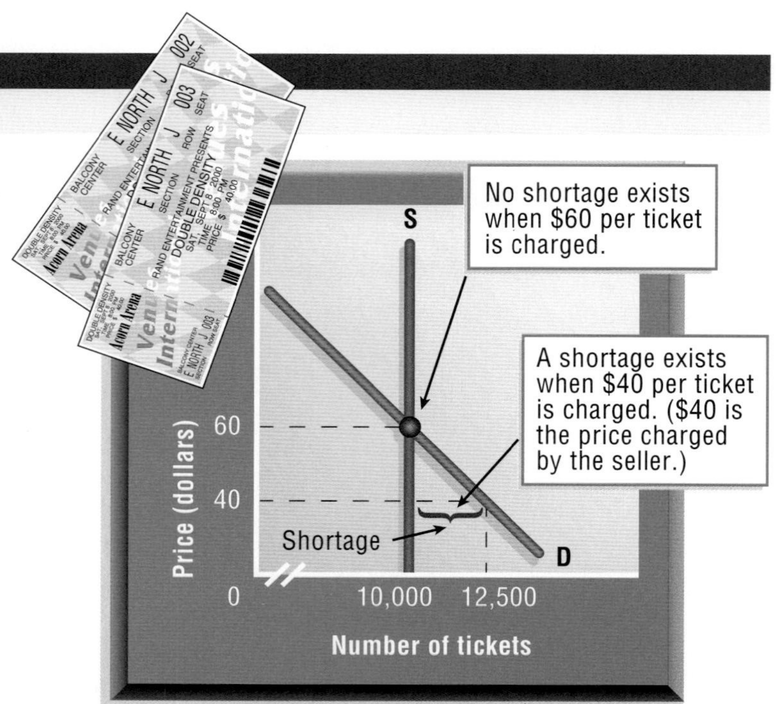

rise to its equilibrium level. The problem in the rock concert example, though, is that the tickets were bought and sold before the seller realized there was a shortage of tickets. In hindsight, the seller knows that the price charged for the tickets was too low, and this pricing caused a shortage. If the seller had charged the equilibrium price, there would have been no shortage, no long lines, and no one turned away without a ticket. As shown in Exhibit 5-5, the seller charged $40 a ticket. At this price, quantity demanded (12,500) was greater than quantity supplied (10,000). If the price had been $60 a ticket, quantity supplied (10,000) would have equaled quantity demanded (10,000), and there would have been no shortage.

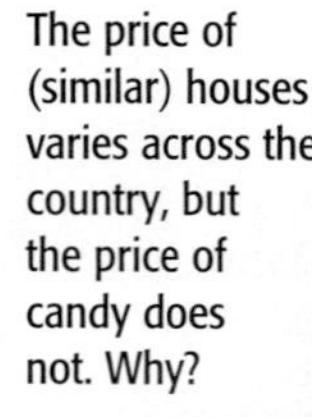

The price of (similar) houses varies across the country, but the price of candy does not. Why?

Why didn't the seller charge the higher equilibrium price, instead of a price that was too low? The seller might have charged the equilibrium price had he or she known it. Think back to the auctioneer example. Note that the auctioneer did not call out the equilibrium price at the start of the auction. He called out $6, which was too high a price. There was a surplus at that price. Later, he called out $2, which was too low a price, causing a shortage. It was only through trial and error that the auctioneer finally hit upon the equilibrium price. The seller of the rock concert tickets may not have had the luxury of trial and error.

Candy Bars, Bread, and Real Estate Prices

In general, no matter where you go in the United States, the price of a candy bar (pick your favorite brand) is the same. A candy bar in Toledo, Ohio, is the same price as a candy bar in Miami, Florida. The same holds, to a large degree, for a loaf of bread.

The California Gold Rush: or, An Egg for $36, a Glass of Water for $1,800

James Marshall, a carpenter, was building a sawmill for John Sutter, a Swiss immigrant who arrived in California in 1839. On a chilly morning on January 24, 1848, Marshall was busy at work when something glistening caught his eye. He reached down and picked up the object. Marshall said to the workers he had hired, "Boys, by God I believe I have found a gold mine." Marshall later wrote, "I reached my hand down and picked it up; it made my heart thump, for I was certain it was gold. The piece was about half the size and shape of a pea. Then I saw another." In time, Marshall and his workers came across more gold, and before long people from all across the United States and many other countries headed to California to try it themselves. In short, there was a rush for gold in California.

The story of the California gold rush can be told from various perspectives, one of which is supply and demand. It is interesting to investigate the gold rush days in terms of how the demand or supply for certain goods and services changed and how, as a result, prices changed, too. Before the discovery of gold at Sutter's mill, a metal pan sold for 20 cents, which is the equivalent of $3.60 today. After the news that gold had been discovered, the demand for metal pans (which were used to "pan" for the gold) increased sharply. The price followed—rising to $15, which is equivalent to $270 today.

Land prices rose dramatically in San Francisco at the time. Before gold was discovered, San Francisco was a small hamlet with only a few hundred people. The gold rush brought great population growth to the area—so great that real estate that cost $16 (the equivalent of $288 today) before gold was discovered jumped to $45,000 (the equivalent of $810,000 today) just eighteen months after the discovery of gold.

Near the gold mines, the prices of food and clothing also sharply increased. For example, a loaf of bread in New York sold for 4 cents at the time (equivalent to 72 cents today), whereas the price was 75 cents (the equivalent of $13.50 today) near the mines. Eggs sold for about $2 each (the equivalent of $36 today) and boots for $100 a pair (the equivalent of $1,800 today).

Many people who came to California to discover gold came along the Oregon-California Trail. The trip was extremely long and hard, and water was in extremely short supply. For long stretches of the trip there was no water at all. It was not uncommon for people trekking westward to pay $1 for a glass of water (the equivalent of $18 today). In some cases, the price of a glass of water rose to a whopping $100 (the equivalent of $1,800 today).

QUESTION TO ANSWER Price can rise if (1) demand rises, (2) supply falls, or (3) demand rises and supply falls. What explains the rise in the price of each of the following (mentioned in the feature)?

a. water
b. metal pans
c. land

Now consider real estate prices—in particular, the price of a house in San Francisco, California, and the price of a similar house in a similar neighborhood in Louisville, Kentucky. The house in San Francisco will sell for approximately two to three times the price of the house in Louisville. Why, when it comes to candy bars and bread, does a good sell for approximately the same price no matter where it is purchased in the United States, whereas a house purchased in San Francisco is so much more expensive than a similar house in Louisville?

What are some of the factors that this shop owner will consider as he decides the price to charge for his candy?

Supply and demand give us the answer. Consider the case of the candy bar. There is both a demand for and a supply of candy bars in both Toledo and Miami. Let's say the price of a candy bar is higher in Toledo because the demand for candy bars is higher in Toledo.

Suppose that the price of a candy bar is $2 in Toledo and $1 in Miami. Given the price difference, the suppliers of candy bars will prefer to sell more of their product in Toledo than in Miami, so the supply of candy bars will increase in Toledo and decrease in Miami. Because the supply of candy bars will have increased in Toledo, the price of a candy bar will decrease (say, from $2 to $1.50); and because the supply of candy bars will have decreased in Miami, the price of a candy bar will increase (say, from $1 to $1.50). Only when the prices of candy bars are the same in Toledo and Miami will suppliers no longer have an incentive to rearrange the supply of candy bars in the two cities. The same analysis holds for the price of bread in two cities. When suppliers can shift supply from one location to another, price will tend to be uniform for products.[1]

Foreign currency exchange booths can be found in airports around the world. What do supply and demand have to do with the value of a dollar, peso, or yen?

Now consider houses in different cities. Housing prices are much higher in San Francisco than in Louisville because in San Francisco the demand for houses is higher, relative to the supply of houses, than it is in Louisville. If houses were candy bars or bread, suppliers would shift their supply from Louisville to San Francisco. However, houses are built on land, and the price of the land is part of the price of a house. Naturally, suppliers cannot pick up an acre of land in Louisville and move it to San Francisco.

Thus, where the supply of a good cannot be moved in response to a difference in price between cities, prices for this good are likely to remain different in these cities.

Yen, Rubles, and Pesos

There are many different currencies in the world: Mexican pesos, French francs, Russian rubles, British pounds, Japanese yen, and so on. If you want foreign currency, you have to buy it much the same way you have to buy a computer if you want one. For example, you might have to pay $1.70 to buy a British pound, 60 cents to buy a German mark, 18 cents to buy a

1. For simplicity, our analysis does not take into account transportation costs. In reality, however, prices of candy bars and bread are still the same everywhere, having adjusted for transportation costs.

French franc, and seven-tenths of a penny to buy a Japanese yen. There is a dollar price for each foreign currency.

The price of foreign currency is not always the same. Sometimes a British pound or a German mark is more expensive than at other times. For example, you might have to pay $1.70 for a British pound one week, $1.85 the next week, and $1.45 in a month. What causes the price of a British pound, or any other currency, to change? The answer is supply and demand. Whenever the demand for or the supply of a currency changes, its price changes, too. For example, if the demand for Japanese yen increased because more people wanted to buy Japanese goods, then the price of a yen (in terms of a dollar) would rise. Instead of paying seven-tenths of a penny for a yen, you might have to pay eight-tenths of a penny.

Supply and Demand at the Movies

Seeing a movie at the movie theater does not always cost the same. If you want to see a movie on Friday night, you may have to pay $7, but for the same movie at 11 o'clock Tuesday morning you may have to pay only $3.50. The difference has to do with supply and demand. Certainly the supply of seats in the theater is the same Friday night as Tuesday morning. The demand, however, is different. The demand to see a movie on Friday night is higher than on Tuesday morning, and the higher demand makes for a higher price.

Why is it cheaper to go to the movies at 11 A.M. on Tuesday than at 7 P.M. Friday night?

Supply and Demand on a Freeway

Supply and demand are easy to see at a rock concert, a movie theater, or the grocery store. But supply and demand also appear in places we wouldn't initially think to look, such as on a freeway. To illustrate, suppose there is a certain supply of freeway space—150 miles. There is also a demand for freeway space; people have a demand to drive on freeways.

Suppose every freeway or highway in your state is turned into a toll road. Furthermore, suppose the toll is mistakenly set at $2 above equilibrium. What do you predict will happen as a result?

The demand to drive on a freeway is not always the same, of course. It is higher at 8 A.M. on Monday, when people are driving to work, than at 11 that night. Exhibit 5-6a on page 126 shows one supply curve and two demand curves. The supply curve, S_1, represents the supply of freeway space (say, 150 miles). The demand curve D(11 P.M.) represents the demand for freeway space at 11 P.M. Monday, and the demand curve D(8 A.M.) represents the demand for freeway space at 8 A.M. Monday. You will notice that the demand at 8 A.M. is greater than the demand at 11 P.M. [D(8 A.M.) > D(11 P.M.)].

What do most people have to pay to drive on the freeway? For most freeways across the country, the price is zero; most freeways do not have

Exhibit 5-6

Supply and Demand on a Freeway

(a) The demand for freeway space differs at two times, 8 A.M. and 11 P.M. Monday. If zero price is charged to drive on the freeway, there is a shortage of freeway space at 8 A.M. (freeway congestion), but not at 11 P.M. A toll of $1.50 eliminates freeway congestion at 8 A.M. (b) The supply of freeway space is increasing, which eliminates freeway congestion at 8 A.M. (c) There is a lower demand for freeway space with carpooling than without. Sufficient carpooling eliminates freeway congestion at 8 A.M.

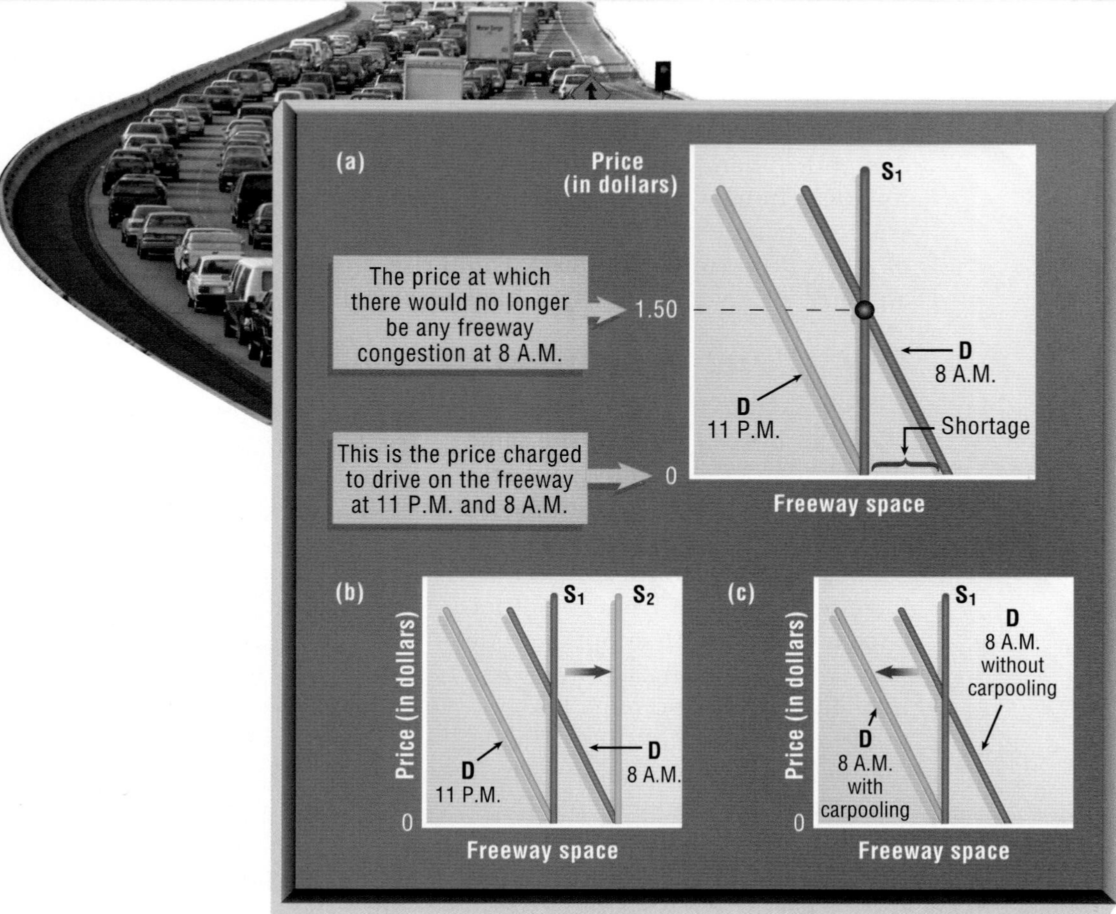

tolls.[2] In Exhibit 5-6a, you will notice that zero price is the equilibrium price if it is 11 P.M. on a Monday. The demand curve for freeway space and the supply curve of freeway space intersect at zero price at 11 P.M. on Monday. In other words, at this time there is neither a shortage nor a surplus of freeway space.

Now look at the situation at 8 A.M. At zero price—no toll—the quantity demanded of freeway space is greater than the quantity supplied. At zero price, there is a shortage of freeway space. In everyday language, the freeway is congested. A congested freeway is simply the physical manifestation of a shortage of freeway space.

What is the solution to freeway congestion? Two common solutions are building more freeways and having people carpool. One speaks to the supply side of the freeway market and the other, to the demand side. When people say that we ought to build more freeways, they want to push the supply curve (of freeway space) to the right (see Exhibit 5-6b). If the supply of freeway space shifts from S_1 to S_2, there is no longer a shortage of freeway space at zero price at 8 A.M. The problem of freeway congestion is solved.

If more people carpool, then for all practical purposes the demand for freeway space falls (see Exhibit 5-6c). In other words, if people carpool to such an extent that the demand for driving on the freeway drops by as

2. People do pay taxes to build freeways, but this fact is not relevant here. People are not paying a price to drive on freeways, at least nontoll freeways.

How Might Highway Tolls Change Everyday Life?

On page 126, the text discussed various methods of eliminating freeway congestion. One way was to add to the supply of freeways by building more. A second way was to try to decrease the demand for freeway travel (especially at peak times) by getting people to carpool. A third way was to charge tolls on freeways. The tolls would be set at equilibrium levels so that driving on the freeway on Monday at 8 A.M. would cost more than driving on the freeway on Monday at 11 P.M.

A few states are beginning to experiment with tolls on freeways. For example, Southern California has one freeway on which tolls are charged. This freeway has much less traffic than most other (non-toll) freeways, and drivers never complain of congestion or traffic jams.

Ten years from today, the U.S. population will be larger, and more drivers will be competing for the available freeway space. If nothing is done, freeway congestion will worsen. Government may try to get people to carpool more, although carpooling has not been very successful in the past and may not be in the future. A continued failure would leave only building more freeways and charging tolls.

The critics of freeway tolls argue that charging tolls won't really solve the freeway congestion problem, because most of that congestion comes on weekday mornings between 7 and 9 and on weekday evenings between 4 and 7. These are the hours that people travel to and from work. In other words, as long as the typical workday is from 8 A.M. to 5 P.M. Monday through Friday, there will be freeway congestion no matter whether there are tolls or not.

However, with a system of tolls in place, the workday might change. If there were tolls, and those tolls were higher at 8 A.M. and 5 P.M. than at 9 A.M. and 6 P.M., some businesses would no doubt change their work schedules. They might allow their employees to work from 9 to 6 instead of 8 to 5. We might even see work schedules such as 6 to 3 or 10 to 7. In a tight labor market, when companies have a hard time finding good employees, they are usually willing to compete for employees in many different dimensions. It isn't difficult to believe that they might adjust work hours, too.

Tolls might affect not only our work schedules but also when we go shopping, when we drive to see a friend, or when we go to a baseball game. For example, many major league baseball teams are located in large metropolitan areas with heavy traffic at certain times of the day. These teams often play games on Friday around 7 P.M. Thus, most people have to start on their way to the stadium around 5 or 6 P.M., when there is a lot of traffic congestion because people are still heading home from work. If there were a system of tolls, and tolls were set at their equilibrium levels, the tolls to drive on the freeway at, say, 7 P.M. would likely be lower than at 5 or 6 P.M. Would the owners of major league baseball teams reschedule their games to, say, 8 P.M. on Fridays? They might very well do this, because after all, they are interested in selling tickets.

QUESTION TO ANSWER The critics of tolls say that tolls discriminate against the poor. What do you think?

much as is shown in the exhibit, then there is no longer a shortage of freeway space at zero price at 8 A.M. The problem of freeway space again is solved.

Of course, as is probably evident now, there is a third way to get rid of freeway congestion. It has nothing to do with building more freeways or carpooling. Freeway congestion can be eliminated by charging equilibrium tolls. In other words, as shown in Exhibit 5-6a, a toll of $1.50 would eliminate freeway congestion at 8 A.M.

Trying Out for a High School Sport

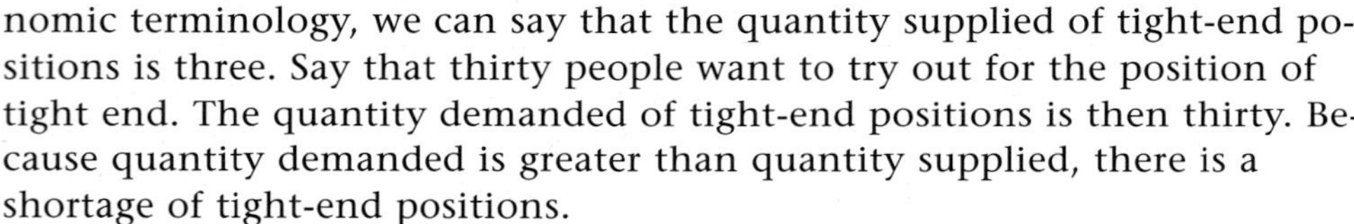

Do supply and demand have anything to do with making the school volleyball team?

Suppose you want to try out for a high school sport, such as football, volleyball, or golf. How competitive do you have to be to get on the team? It depends on how many open positions there are on the team you want to try out for, as well as how many people are going to try out for the available positions. In short, how competitive you must be is a matter of the supply of positions and the demand for positions.

Suppose you want to try out to be on the high school football team, specifically the position of tight end. The team's coach says he wants three people who can play tight end. In economic terminology, we can say that the quantity supplied of tight-end positions is three. Say that thirty people want to try out for the position of tight end. The quantity demanded of tight-end positions is then thirty. Because quantity demanded is greater than quantity supplied, there is a shortage of tight-end positions.

When there is a shortage of anything in a competitive market, the price of that thing rises. The team's coach, of course, is not going to accept money from the students who want to try out for the team. What he will do is raise the nonmoney price of being a tight end in a different way. People will have to "pay" to be a tight end with hard work and skill. Stated differently, they will have to pay in terms of their expected performance; they will have to be very good to get on the team.

Would they have had to be as good to get on the team if there had been only five people who wanted to be a tight end? Not at all. In that case, the shortage of tight-end positions would have been smaller (if quantity demanded = 5 and quantity supplied = 3, then the shortage is 2), and the nonmoney price of being a tight end would not have risen as much to bring supply and demand into equilibrium. Thus, the greater demand (for positions on a sports team) relative to the supply (of positions), the higher the nonmoney price of getting on the team (the better a person has to be to get on the team). The performance you need in order to get on a team where thirty people are trying out for three spots is greater than what you need in order to get on a team where five people are trying out for three spots.

If what we are saying is true, would you expect that big high schools (large student bodies) or small high schools (small student bodies) would be more likely to have more competitive teams, all other things being equal? The answer is big high schools. Look at it this way: Each high school has only one football team. In other words, the supply of positions on each team at each school is the same. But demand is not the same at each school. The demand to be on the team at a school with a large student body will be greater than the demand to be on the team at a school with a small student body. (More people will try out for each position at a big school than a small school.) The nonmoney price a person has to pay to be on the team at a big school will be higher than at a small school.[3]

GPA, SAT Scores, and College

You do not need the same grade point average (GPA) or Scholastic Assessment Test (SAT) score to get into all colleges. One college may require a GPA of 2.5 and an SAT score of 950, while another requires a GPA of 3.5 and an SAT score of 1200. Why the difference? Again, the answer is supply and demand. The higher the demand to get into a particular college, the higher its entrance requirements.

To illustrate, take two colleges, college A and college B. Each college will admit 2,000 students to its entering freshman class next year. Each college charges $4,000 a semester in tuition. Thus, the quantity supplied of open spots and the tuition are the same at each college. But suppose the demand to go to college A is three times the demand to go to college B. There are 4,000 applicants for 2,000 spots at college B, but there are 12,000 applicants for 2,000 spots at college A.

If the demand to get into college A is greater than the demand to get into college B, and everything else between the two colleges is the same, will this student need a higher SAT score to get into college A or B?

The shortage at college A is greater than the shortage at college B, so the nonmoney price to get into college A will rise by more than it will rise at college B. The nonmoney price of getting into college is usually measured in terms of high school academic performance (in other words, GPA and SAT scores). The greater the demand to get into a college relative to supply, the higher the GPA and SAT scores required to get into that college, or the higher the "price" a student must pay in terms of grades.

Radio Host

There are different kinds of radio hosts. Some specialize in talk—perhaps about politics, human relationships, religion, or sports. Some radio hosts mainly play music. The salary range for radio hosts is wide. Disc jockeys in small radio markets may earn very little, while radio hosts in large markets or who are syndicated may earn millions of dollars.

There are many more people who want to work in radio than there are positions available. One way to increase your chances of getting a job in radio is by gaining experience. Assistants or interns starting at small stations gain experience of all kinds: learning about electronic equipment, reading the news, writing scripts, and so on. Many radio stations like to hire college graduates who have majored in speech, communications, journalism, business, or public relations. Others hire graduates of broadcasting schools. A successful radio host needs a good, clear, likable voice; creativity; and the ability to ad-lib on the air.

QUESTION TO ANSWER If the number of radio stations increases in the next ten years, how will this affect the demand for radio hosts?

3. It does not necessarily follow that football teams from big schools usually defeat football teams from small schools. Winning a football game depends on more than just the quality of the players; it also depends on the quality of the coaches. A small school may have a better coach than a large school and because of this factor will win more games. We are not considering this factor in our analysis.

WALNUT COVE

Reprinted with special permission of King Features Syndicate.

Necessary Conditions for a High Income: High Demand, Low Supply

As consumers, we are used to paying prices. We pay a price to buy a computer, some soda, or a shirt. We sometimes receive prices, too. As a seller of a good, you receive the price that the buyer pays.

Many people do not sell goods; instead, they sell their labor services. The person who works at a fast-food restaurant after school or an attorney at a law firm is selling labor services. The "price" employees receive for what they sell is usually called a *wage*. A wage, over time, can be referred to as a *salary* or *income*. A person who earns a wage of $10 an hour receives a monthly income of $1,600 if he or she works 160 hours a month.

A wage is determined by supply and demand, just as the price of oranges, apples, or TV sets is. It follows, then, that for someone to receive a high wage, demand must be high and supply low. The higher the demand relative to supply, the higher the wage will be.

To earn a high wage, then, is to perform a job in great demand that not many other people can do. If few know how to do it, supply will be low. Low supply combined with high demand means you will receive a (relatively) high wage.

Consider the wage of a restaurant server versus a computer scientist. There is a large demand for both servers and computer scientists. However, there is a large supply of servers and a not-so-large supply of computer scientists, so computer scientists earn more than servers.

Section 2 Review

Reviewing Facts and Concepts

1. On a freeway there is sometimes traffic congestion (bumper-to-bumper traffic) and sometimes very little traffic. Explain why.

2. Housing prices are higher in city X than in city Y. Using the concepts of supply and demand, explain why.

3. Identify whether a shortage, a surplus, or equilibrium exists in the following settings:

a. There are fewer applicants for the first-year class at college X than spaces available.

b. People who wanted to attend a baseball game were told that tickets had sold out the day before.

c. Houses for sale used to stay on the market for two months before they were sold. Now they are staying on the market for up to six months, and they still aren't selling.

Critical Thinking

4. Carmelo says, "A movie theater charges the same price for a very popular movie as it does for a very unpopular movie. Obviously, the movie theater doesn't charge more when demand for the movie is higher than when it is lower." Shelby counters by saying, "Movie theaters often call the more popular movies *special engagements* and do not accept any discount tickets for them." If Shelby is correct, does her point negate Carmelo's? Explain your answer.

Applying Economic Concepts

5. This section stated that people will earn high incomes if they can supply labor services that not many other people can supply, and for which there is a large demand. If you choose to go to college, how will this affect your supply position?

Developing Economic Skills

Understanding the Two Jobs That Price Performs

We know that prices in many markets are determined by supply and demand. But once price is determined—for example, once price is at its equilibrium level of, say, $10—does it do anything? The answer is yes; price rations goods, and it conveys information.

Price Acts as a Rationing Device

Saturday Price 25¢ each

Following Saturday Price 40¢ each

Wants are unlimited, but resources are limited. In short, scarcity exists. Furthermore, because resources are limited and the production of goods requires resources, goods are also limited. Consequently, a rationing device is needed to determine who gets what part of the available limited resources and goods. As a rationing device, price rations scarce resources to those persons who pay the price for the resources.

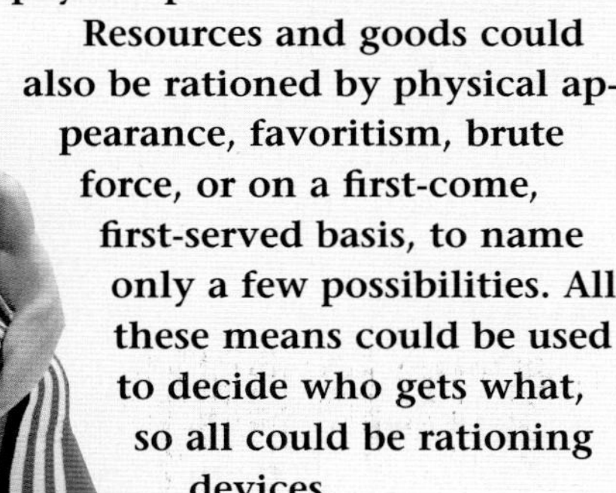

Resources and goods could also be rationed by physical appearance, favoritism, brute force, or on a first-come, first-served basis, to name only a few possibilities. All these means could be used to decide who gets what, so all could be rationing devices.

Some people wonder why *need* isn't used as a rationing device. Such a world would have a few problems. First, who would determine need? Second, what is it that people really need? Third, if need were the rationing device, would people have any incentive to work and produce? With price as the rationing device, people have to produce goods and services to earn the income necessary to buy goods.

Price Acts as a Transmitter of Information and Therefore Affects Behavior

Think of what you do when you get new information. Suppose that just before you leave your house to go to school or shopping, you hear a weather report: beginning in an hour, rain all day. With this new information, you decide to wear a jacket and take an umbrella.

Just as a weathercaster on television can convey certain information to you, so can price. And just as you may change your behavior based on what the weathercaster says, you may change your behavior based on what price "says."

Imagine that on Saturday, Noelle walks into a local grocery store and purchases 20 oranges at 25 cents each. On Sunday, unknown to her, a cold spell hits Florida and wipes out one-quarter of the orange crop. The cold spell shifts the supply curve of oranges to the left and leads to a rise in the price of oranges. Next Saturday, Noelle returns to the grocery store and notices that the price of oranges has risen to 40 cents each. Because of the higher price, she decides to buy only 12 oranges instead of 20. (Her demand curve for oranges is downward sloping; she buys fewer oranges at higher prices than at lower prices.)

It is clear that a change in price has affected Noelle's buying behavior, but what information has price transmitted in the process of affecting behavior? By moving up and down, price transmits information on the relative scarcity of a good.

When a good becomes relatively more scarce, Noelle acts the same way she would act if she had heard what the higher price had to say: she buys less.

1. The supply of a good increases; consequently, the price of the good decreases. What information is price transmitting about the relative scarcity of the good?
2. The demand for a good rises; consequently, the price of the good rises. What information is price transmitting about the relative scarcity of the good?

CHAPTER

5 Review

Economics Vocabulary

Fill in the following blanks with the appropriate word or phrase.

1. A(n) _____ exists when quantity supplied is greater than quantity demanded.
2. A(n) _____ exists when quantity demanded is greater than quantity supplied.
3. A market is in _____ when quantity demanded equals quantity supplied.
4. The price that exists in a market when quantity demanded equals quantity supplied is called the _____.
5. The quantity that exists in a market when quantity demanded equals quantity supplied is called the _____.
6. In a market, if quantity supplied is currently greater than quantity demanded, a firm's _____ are above normal levels.

Review Questions

1. Explain why price falls if there is a surplus.
2. Look at the prices listed in Exhibit 5-1 on page 111. At what prices is there a surplus? What is the equilibrium price and the equilibrium quantity?
3. "All markets are necessarily in equilibrium at all points in time." Do you agree or disagree? Explain your answer.
4. What might we see when a market is experiencing a shortage? (*Comment:* It is not enough to say that quantity demanded is greater than quantity supplied, because this is simply a definition of *shortage.* You must identify a tangible event of a shortage.)
5. Pens sell for about the same price in every city in the country, but houses do not. Why?
6. Alfred Marshall compared supply and demand to the two blades of a pair of scissors. What point was he trying to make?
7. Identify what will happen to equilibrium price and equilibrium quantity in each of the following cases:
   - **a.** demand rises and supply is constant
   - **b.** demand falls by more than supply rises
   - **c.** supply rises by more than demand rises
   - **d.** supply falls and demand is constant
8. Suppose you are a manager of a grocery store. How would you know which goods were in shortage? In surplus?
9. Both the demand for and the supply of a good rise. Under what condition will the price of the good remain constant?
10. Suppose gold is selling at $300 an ounce in London and at $296 an ounce in New York. How will the supplies of gold in the two cities be reallocated? What effect will this reallocation have on the price of gold in each city? Explain your answer.
11. You wake up one morning to learn that the value of the dollar is lower than it was yesterday. Yesterday a dollar would buy 118 yen, and today a dollar will buy only 110 yen. Is it possible that the demand for dollars increased (all other things remaining the same) and that this explains why the dollar has lost some value?
12. Some National Basketball Association (NBA) players receive annual incomes of several million dollars. Explain their high salaries in terms of supply and demand.

Calculations

1. Price is $10, quantity demanded is 100 units, and quantity supplied is 130 units. For each dollar decline in price, quantity demanded rises by 5 units, and quantity supplied falls by 5 units. What is the equilibrium price?

Graphs

1. Identify the exhibit in the chapter that illustrates the following.
   - **a.** a decrease in supply that is less than a decrease in demand
   - **b.** an increase in supply that is greater than an increase in demand
   - **c.** an increase in demand, supply constant
   - **d.** a decrease in supply, demand constant
2. Graphically represent the following.
   - **a.** a decrease in demand, supply constant
   - **b.** an increase in supply, demand constant
   - **c.** a decrease in demand equal to a decrease in supply
3. Explain what is happening in the following parts of Exhibit 5-7.

a. Part a
b. Part b
c. Part c
d. Part d

Exhibit 5-7

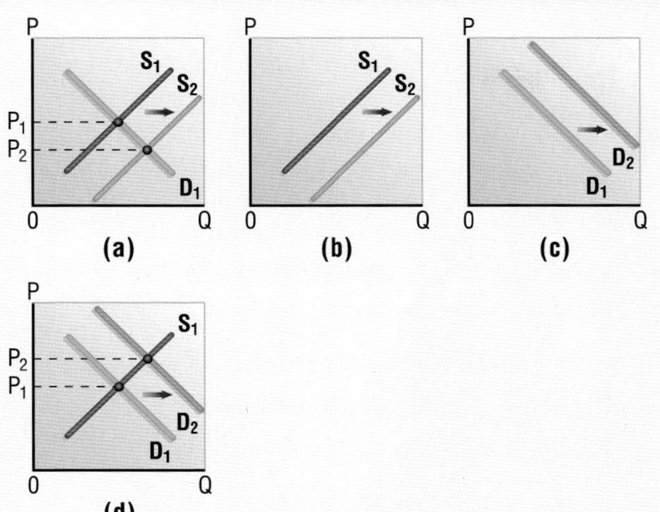

Economics and Thinking Skills

1. **Analysis.** Suppose that in 1998 the average price of a meal at a restaurant was \$15, and 50,000 restaurant meals were bought and sold. In 1999 the average price of a meal at a restaurant was \$16, and 60,000 restaurant meals were bought and sold. Which of the three following events can explain a higher price and more meals purchased and sold? Explain your answer.
   a. The supply of restaurant meals increased.
   b. The demand for restaurant meals decreased.
   c. The demand for restaurant meals increased.
2. **Cause and Effect.** Suppose the equilibrium price of bread is \$2 a loaf. The federal government mandates that no loaf of bread can be purchased or sold for more than \$1 a loaf. As a result of the mandate, how will the market for bread be different than when bread could be purchased and sold for \$2? Explain your answer.

Writing Skills

Section 2 of the chapter and many of the boxed features presented applications of supply and demand. Supply and demand is all around: at the movies, on the freeway, and at a rock concert. To fully understand supply and demand, it is important to work with it. Identify some event in your life that can be explained or analyzed in terms of supply and demand. Write a two-page paper (with diagrams) discussing this event.

Economics in the Media

Find an example in your local newspaper of a market in which demand or supply changes (and therefore price changes). Your example may come from an article, editorial, or advertisement.

Where's the Economics?

How does an unusually bountiful corn harvest affect the price of an ear of corn?

Analyzing Primary Sources

Earlier this chapter mentioned Alfred Marshall, the British economist who compared supply and demand to the two blades of a pair of scissors. In the following excerpt from *The Principles of Economics,* Marshall's most famous and influential book, he states the three faculties that a good economist needs:

The economist needs the three great intellectual faculties—perception, imagination and reason: and most of all he needs imagination, to put him on the track of those causes of visible events which are remote or lie below the surface, and of those effects of visible causes which are remote or lie below the surface.

1. According to Marshall, what are the three intellectual faculties that an economist needs?
2. According to Marshall, what function does imagination serve?

UNIT 1

Debate the Issues

Working After School: What Are the Trade-offs?

Through our study of economics, we learn that there are trade-offs in life. More of one thing often means less of something else. Spending more money on clothes means less money for entertainment. More time spent studying means less time to hang out with your friends.

One of the major trade-offs high school students face is whether or not to work after school. Some people argue that high school students should work after school; others argue against it, saying their time is better spent studying. Let's hear what five people have to say.

Rebecca Clark, a junior in high school: I work after school and on the weekends at a fast-food restaurant here in town. It may be hard to believe, but I actually like the work. I meet a lot of nice people, I earn some money, and I am developing a good work ethic. When I first went to work, I thought it was going to be easier than it turned out to be. I thought I was just going to have some fun and make some money. But I've learned that to do a job well you have to be conscientious, follow orders closely, and focus on what you are doing. These are qualities that I think will benefit me throughout my life. I think I am a better person because I work. My parents are concerned about how work takes time away from my studies, but I never was much of a student. If I weren't working, I might be just wasting my time. I might even get into some trouble.

Tommy Sanchez, a senior in high school: I know I could work after school, but I choose not to. Working after school would come at too high a price for me. If I worked after school, I wouldn't have as much time to study. I want to get into a really good college and to do that I need to have high grades. If I worked, I probably couldn't get the A's that I am currently getting in my courses. The way I look at it, I will have 40 or 50 years to work. I am young now and I like learning, and the more I learn, the brighter my future will be. I think I would be sacrificing my future if I worked after school now.

My older brother didn't work at a job when he was in high school. He spent most of his time studying. As a result, he got high grades and a good score on the SAT. What is even more important is that he got into Yale. He received a top-quality education at Yale and made many good future business contacts. In fact, he now works in a company owned by the father of one of his best friends at Yale.

Some of my friends talk about the money they make in their after-school jobs. They can buy a lot of things that I can't. They buy better clothes, and some of them have even bought a car. I'd like to have a car, too, but I don't want to take away from my studies right now to get a job just so I can buy a car.

EXAM TUESDAY 4 PM!

Bob Neidelman, parent: I think it is important for teens to develop a sense of responsibility and that's why I have urged my daughter to get a job after school and on the weekends. I worked when I was her age, and I learned a lot from what I did. Mainly, I learned the value of a dollar. I know that people say teens should not work, that they should devote more time to their education, but the truth of the matter is there are different types of education. There is the book-learning type of education, where a person learns geometry, calculus, English literature, and history. And then there is the education that you receive from getting out in life and working. When you work, you learn how to get along with people. You learn to persevere in order to get a job done. These are important things to learn. In the long run they'll be more important to her than learning how to solve calculus problems.

Nancy Drummon, guidance counselor: I think working after school is good for some students and not for others. It really depends on the trade-offs the particular student faces. For instance, I often get students in my office who work but who are doing poorly in their courses. I tell them they would be better off if they didn't work, but instead spent their time after school studying and trying to get their grades up.

But I've got other students who are doing well in their courses and feel they can continue to do well even though they get jobs. I see working as a good idea. Not only will they learn some things in their work that they might not otherwise learn, but they will have a little extra spending money, too. There are things they want to do and buy, and working gives them the opportunity to do those things.

In short, I think that whether or not a student should work depends on the individual student. Not all students face the same trade-offs. What is right for one student may not be right for another.

Amy Yoshii, college student: I worked all through high school, and I really regret it now. I worked for all the wrong reasons. I worked simply to get the money to buy the same things my friends were buying. My friends were spending a lot of money on clothes, so I thought I had to, too. I thought that if I didn't, my friends would look down on me, and might even stop being my friends. I worked to get a down payment for a car. Once I bought the car, I had to continue to work so I could make the payments and keep it running. There were many weekends when I was dead tired from working. I'd come home Sunday night, after working all day Saturday and all day Sunday, and have to study for a biology or calculus test. I can't tell you how many times I just went to bed, telling myself I would get up early and study. The alarm clock would ring, and I'd shut it off. I paid the price in lower grades. I could have gotten A's if I had had more time to study, but instead I got B's and a few C's.

I got into college, and I am doing better now, but college hasn't been easy for me. I think if I had worked less in high school, and studied more, college would have been more enjoyable, and easier.

I've learned that it is extremely important to prioritize—a person just can't do too many things and do them well. The world we live in values education a lot. You can't cut corners when it comes to your education. Working just gets in the way. My advice to any high school student is if you don't *have* to work, *don't.* Don't work just to get some extra money so you can buy a few extra things. Study more, work less. You'll be glad you did in the long run.

What Do You Think?

1. Who do you most nearly agree with? Why?
2. Do you think there is a trade-off between education and work? Why or why not?

UNIT 2

Microeconomics: Business, Markets, and Economic Decisions

CHAPTER 6

Business Decisions: Costs, Revenues, and Profits

What This Chapter Is About

This chapter discusses business firms. It explains why business firms exist and describes the different types of business firms. It also discusses how business firms decide the number of units of a good to produce and the number of employees to hire.

Why This Chapter Is Important

To understand the life you are living, it is important to understand the institutions that play a big role in our society. One of those institutions is *business.* Almost every day of your life you come into contact with some kind of business—for example, when you buy food at a restaurant or you buy a pencil, pen, CD, or computer at a store. If you have a part-time job, it is probably with some kind of business. This chapter begins to examine this institution with which we all have so many dealings.

After You Study This Chapter, You Will Be Able To

- explain why firms exist.
- describe the three major forms of business organization: the sole proprietorship, the partnership, and the corporation.
- describe the structure of a corporation.
- explain the difference between bonds and stocks.
- explain the difference between variable costs and fixed costs.
- compute total cost, average total cost, marginal cost, and marginal revenue.
- explain how firms decide what quantity of output they will produce.
- explain how firms decide how many workers to hire.

You Will Also Learn What Economics Has to Do With

- determining the right amount of time to study for a test.
- the five richest Americans in history.
- hamburgers and fries in the 1940s.

Economics Journal

Make a list of the businesses you deal with most often as a consumer and (if relevant) as an employee. Next to each business, identify the good(s) or service(s) it produces and sells. Finally, identify the business on your list that you think is the most consumer oriented. What makes it more consumer oriented than the others?

SECTION 1

About Business Firms

Why do business firms exist? Are there different types of business firms? This section answers these two questions.

As you read this section, keep these key questions in mind:

- Why do business firms exist?
- What is a sole proprietorship?
- What is a partnership?
- What is a corporation?

Key Terms

business firm
shirking
monitor
residual claimant
sole proprietorship
personal income tax
corporate income tax
unlimited liability
partnership
general partner
limited partner
corporation
stockholder
stock
asset
limited liability
dividend
board of directors
bylaws
bond
face value
par value
coupon rate
cooperative
franchise
franchiser
franchisee

Why Do Business Firms Exist?[1]

Business firms exist whenever people working together can produce more than the sum of what individuals working alone can produce. Suppose there are ten individuals, each of whom fishes for a living. Each day each person catches 100 fish. The daily sum of fish caught by these ten individuals is therefore 1,000 fish. One day one of the ten individuals says to the others, "Instead of fishing alone, why don't we form a team and fish together? We can specialize in doing different things. One person will make the nets, another person will navigate the boat, some people will cast the nets, and so on. I think that if we work together—if we form a team, so to speak—we will be able to catch 2,000 fish a day."

Let's suppose this person is correct; ten people working together can catch more fish (2,000) than the sum of these ten people working alone (1,000 fish). The doubling of the fish catch is reason enough for the people to work together as a team. Another name for this team is

Fishing alone, these two men would probably not be able to catch this many fish. What do we call an enterprise in which people pool their efforts to increase their productivity?

1. The theory of the firm we discuss was advanced by economists Armen Alchian and Harold Demsetz in "Production, Information Costs, and Economic Organization," *American Economic Review* 62 (December 1972) 777–795.

business firm An organization that uses resources to produce goods and services, which are sold to consumers, other firms, or the government.

shirking The behavior of a worker who is putting forth less than the agreed-to effort.

monitor The person in a business who coordinates team production and reduces shirking.

a business firm. A business firm of people working together can be more effective than a group of people all working individually.

> People working together can produce more than the sum of what people working alone can produce ➡ ➡ Reason to form a firm
>
> ---
>
> People working together cannot produce more than the sum of what people working alone can produce ➡ ➡ No reason to form a firm

The Structure of Firms

Let's suppose that the ten fishers agree to form a firm and fish together each day. They also agree to split their catch evenly among the ten of them. If they catch 2,000 fish a day, for example, each person will get 200 fish to sell. Each fish sells for $1, so each person's income will be $200 a day.

Things go smoothly for a while. Each day the ten fishers work together catching fish, and each day they catch 2,000 fish. Then one day one of the ten individuals, Jake, feels lazy. He comes to work late, takes long breaks, and generally doesn't work as hard as he should. We say he is **shirking**, or putting forth less than the agreed-to effort. Because of Jake's shirking, the fish catch falls to 1,800. Divided ten ways, each person receives 180 fish, or an income of $180, that day.

Notice that one person, Jake, shirked, but all ten people had to pay for his shirking. Everyone's income fell by $20 because Jake shirked. When he shirked, Jake received the full benefits of shirking, but he paid only one-tenth of the costs of shirking. Nine-tenths of the shirking costs were paid by the remaining nine persons in the fishing firm.

There are two car dealerships, A and B. In A, the members of the sales staff are paid a fixed monthly amount of $2,000 plus a $200 bonus for each car they sell. In B, the salespersons are paid a fixed monthly amount of $2,500, but they do not receive a bonus for each car they sell. In which setting will a member of the sales staff be more likely to shirk?

When a person receives the full benefits of his shirking but pays only a fraction of the costs, there is likely to be a lot of shirking. No doubt there will be more people shirking than only Jake, and this shirking will further reduce the fish catch. In other words, instead of 1,800 fish a day, the catch will fall to 1,600 as more people shirk, then to 1,400 as even more people shirk, and so on. The increased fish catch (2,000 instead of 1,000), however, was the reason the ten individuals came together to form a team in the first place. If there are no added fish, there is no reason for the firm to exist.

How can the ten members stop the shirking and continue to reap the added fish catch? One way is to choose one among them to be the **monitor**—the person in the firm who coordinates team production and seeks to reduce shirking (the boss, in other words). To be effective, this boss must have the ability to fire and hire people. If Jake is shirking, the boss must be able to fire him and replace him with someone who will not shirk. The threat of dismissal is what reduces shirking in a firm.

Much like the captain of a ship, the monitor coordinates the team's production.

How can the monitor, or boss, be kept from shirking? One possibility is to give the monitor an incentive not to shirk by making him or her a **residual claimant** of the firm. A residual claimant receives the excess of revenues over costs (profits) as income. If the monitor shirks, then profits are likely to be lower (or even negative); therefore, the monitor will receive less income.

In summary, firms come into existence when individuals working together can produce more than the sum of what individuals can produce alone. Once a firm is formed, people in the firm will shirk. The increased shirking reduces the added output of the firm. To deal with this problem, a monitor who has the ability to hire and fire employees is chosen. To make sure the monitor doesn't shirk, he or she is made the residual claimant.

Many sole proprietorships are smaller firms, like restaurants or farms, where a single owner works and has few employees. Can you think of any sole proprietorships located near you?

Types of Firms

Business firms commonly fall into one of three legal categories: sole proprietorships, partnerships, and corporations. Each is discussed in turn.

Sole Proprietorships

A **sole proprietorship** is a business that is (1) owned by one individual, (2) who makes all the business decisions, (3) receives all the profits or takes all the losses of the firm, and (4) is legally responsible for the debts of the firm. Many family farms are sole proprietorships, as are many other businesses such as barbershops, restaurants, and carpet-cleaning services. Sole proprietorships in the United States outnumber partnerships and corporations combined. In the late 1990s, nearly three out of every four firms were sole proprietorships. In contrast, sole proprietorships account for a relatively small percentage of total business revenues—approximately 6.1 percent. Corporations account for the largest percentage of total business revenues—approximately 89 percent.

Advantages of Sole Proprietorships

There are certain advantages to organizing a business as a sole proprietorship.

1. *Sole proprietorships are easy to form and to dissolve.* To start a sole proprietorship, you need only meet certain broadly defined governmental regulations. Some firms must meet health and zoning regulations; for example, if you are starting a restaurant, you must be sure that the restaurant is clean (a health regulation) and that it is located in an area where restaurants are permitted (a zoning regulation). Also, you need to register the name of the business with local governmental officials. To dissolve a sole proprietorship, you need only to stop doing business.
2. *All decision-making power resides with the sole proprietor.* If you are the owner

residual claimant
A person who shares in the profits of a business firm.

sole proprietorship
A business that is owned by one individual, who makes all business decisions, receives all the profits or incurs all the losses of the firm, and is legally responsible for the debts of the firm.

personal income tax
A tax paid on a person's income.

corporate income tax
A tax paid on a corporation's profits.

unlimited liability
The legal responsibility of a sole proprietor of a business or of partners in a business to pay any money owed by the business. The proprietor's or partner's personal assets may be used to pay these debts.

partnership
A business that is owned by two or more co-owners, called partners, who share any profits the business earns and are legally responsible for any debts incurred by the firm.

of a sole proprietorship, you alone can make all the business decisions. There are no stockholders or partners to consult when you are deciding whether to expand your business, buy more supplies, advertise on the radio, and so on. Decisions can be made quickly and easily, since only one person counts—the sole proprietor.

3. *The profit of the firm is taxed only once.* Among the different types of taxes in the United States are sales taxes, property taxes, corporate income taxes, and personal income taxes. If you are the owner of a sole proprietorship, the profit you earn is counted as your income, and only **personal income taxes** (taxes paid on your income) apply to it. Proprietorships do not pay **corporate income taxes** (taxes paid on a corporation's profits). As you will see, neither do partnerships. Only corporations pay corporate income taxes.

Disadvantages of Sole Proprietorships Sole proprietorships have disadvantages, too:

Often sole proprietorships have a limited life. Do you know why?

1. *The sole proprietor faces unlimited liability. Liability* is a legal term that has to do with the responsibility to pay debts. Saying that sole proprietors have **unlimited liability** means that their personal assets may be used to pay off the debts of the firm. For example, suppose Arzlani opens her own cookie shop in the shopping mall. A year passes, and she is taking a loss on the business. She is also in debt to her suppliers—the person from whom she buys flour, the person from whom she rents the shop, and so on. Because Arzlani has unlimited liability, her personal assets—such as her car and her house—may have to be sold to pay off her business debts.

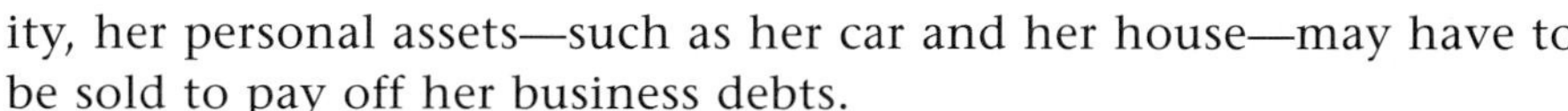

2. *Sole proprietors have limited ability to raise funds for business expansion.* Sole proprietors do not find borrowing funds easy, because lenders are not eager to lend funds to business firms whose success depends on one person. The sole proprietor's sources of money are often limited to personal funds and the funds of close friends and family members.
3. *Sole proprietorships usually end with the retirement or death of the proprietor; they have a limited life.* When the owner of a sole proprietorship dies, the business "dies" as well. From the point of view of the business community and the firm's employees, this is a disadvantage. Employees usually like to work for firms that offer some permanency and the possibility of moving upward.

Partnerships A **partnership** is a business that is (1) owned by two or more co-owners called *partners,* (2) who share any profits the business earns and (3) who are legally responsible for any debts incurred by the firm. Simply put, you may think of a partnership as a proprietorship with more than one owner. Partnerships include such businesses as some medical offices, law offices, and advertising agencies.

Advantages of Partnerships The advantages of partnerships include the following:

1. *In a partnership, the benefits of specialization can be realized.* If, for example, one partner in an advertising agency is better at public relations and another is better at artwork, each can work at the tasks for which he or she is best suited. The ad agency then has a better chance of succeeding than if only one person ran it.
2. *The profit of the partnership is the income of the partners, and only personal income taxes apply to it.* The owners of a partnership, like the owner of a sole proprietorship, pay only personal income taxes. Corporate income taxes do not apply to them.

Partnerships allow each partner to do what she does best.

Disadvantages of Partnerships Partnerships also have some disadvantages, which include the following:

1. *The general partners' liability is unlimited.* There are two types of partners, **general partners** and **limited partners.** General partners are partners who are responsible for the management of the firm. They face unlimited liability, just as sole proprietors do. But in a way, unlimited liability is even more of a disadvantage in a partnership than it is in a sole proprietorship. In a sole proprietorship, the proprietor incurs his or her own debts and is solely responsible for them. In a partnership, one general partner might incur the debts, but all general partners are responsible for them. For example, if partner Matson incurs a debt by buying an expensive piece of medical equipment without the permission of partners Bradbury and Chan, that is too bad for partners Bradbury and Chan. They are still legally responsible for the debts incurred by Matson, their partner.

   While a general partner has unlimited liability, a limited partner does not. A limited partner's liability is restricted to the amount he or she has invested in the firm. Limited partners usually do not participate in the management of the firm or enter into contracts on behalf of the firm.
2. *Decision making in a partnership can be complicated and frustrating.* Suppose that Smithies, a partner in a law firm, wants to move the partnership in one direction, to specialize in corporate law. Yankelovich wants to move it in another direction, to specialize in family law. Who makes the decision in this tug-of-war? Possibly no one will make the decision, and things will stay as they are, which may not be a good thing for the growth of the partnership.

Some partners never seem to agree. Have you ever disagreed with a teammate or partner?

general partner
A partner who is responsible for the management of the firm and who has unlimited liability.

limited partner
A partner who cannot participate in the management of the firm and who has limited liability.

Corporations A **corporation** is (1) a legal entity that can

Jerry Yang is a stockholder in Yahoo! Are stockholders the owners of the firm?

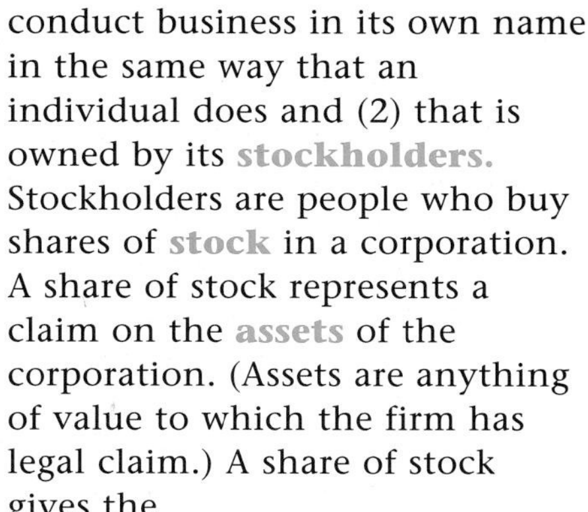
conduct business in its own name in the same way that an individual does and (2) that is owned by its **stockholders.** Stockholders are people who buy shares of **stock** in a corporation. A share of stock represents a claim on the **assets** of the corporation. (Assets are anything of value to which the firm has legal claim.) A share of stock gives the purchaser a share of the ownership of the corporation.

What does it mean when we say that a corporation is a legal entity that can conduct business in its own name? For purposes of the law, a corporation is a living, breathing entity (like an individual), even though in reality a corporation is not a living thing. Let's say that a thousand people want to form a corporation and call it XYZ Corporation. The law treats XYZ Corporation as if it were a person. What this means in practice can be seen through an example. Suppose XYZ Corporation has a debt of $3 million and it has only $1 million with which to pay the debt. Legally, the remainder of the debt ($2 million) cannot be obtained from the owners (stockholders) of the corporation. It is the corporation that owes the money, not the owners of the corporation. The owners of the corporation have limited liability.

Each year *Fortune* magazine ranks the top 500 corporations in the United States according to revenue. In recent years, the largest revenue-earning corporation in the United States has been General Motors. If you want to find the most recent list of the Fortune 500, go to the Fortune 500 Web site at http://www.fortune.com/fortune/. Once there, click on "Fortune 500." List the top 10 U.S. corporations according to revenues.

corporation
A legal entity that can conduct business in its own name in the same way that an individual does. Ownership of the corporation resides with the stockholders.

stockholder
A person who owns shares of stock in a corporation. The stockholders of a corporation are the owners of the corporation.

stock
A claim on the assets of a corporation that gives the purchaser a share of the ownership of the corporation.

asset
Anything of value to which the firm has a legal claim.

No business is protected from declining sales—not a sole proprietorship, partnership, or corporation.

Question: *How many corporations, partnerships, and sole proprietorships are there in the United States?*

Answer: *There are about 4.6 million corporations, 1.7 million partnerships, and 17 million sole proprietorships. As an aside, you may be interested in knowing that in 1999, the largest 500 corporations in the United States earned $6.3 trillion in revenues, $410 billion in profits, and employed over 10 percent of the U.S. workforce.*

limited liability
A condition in which an owner of a business firm can lose only the amount he or she has invested (in the firm). Stockholders of a corporation have limited liability.

dividend
A share of the profits of a corporation distributed to stockholders.

Advantages of Corporations The advantages of corporations include the following:

1. *The owners of the corporation (the stockholders) are not personally liable for the debts of the corporation; they have limited liability.* To say that the stockholders have **limited liability** means that they cannot be sued for the corporation's failure to pay its debts. They are not personally responsible for these debts. For example, if Turner is a stockholder in corporation X, and corporation X cannot pay off its creditors, Turner does not have to sell her personal assets (her house, car, and so on) to pay the debts of the corporation. She can lose only her investment and nothing more. For example, if she bought fifty shares of stock in the corporation at a price of $10 each, her investment is $500. She may never see this $500 again, but she will lose no more.
2. *Corporations continue to exist even if one or more owners sell their shares or die.* The corporation itself is a legal entity. Its existence does not depend on the existence of its owners.
3. *Corporations are usually able to raise large sums of money by selling stock.* Because of limited liability, people are more willing to invest in a corporation than in other business forms. The price of a share of stock may be small, so many more people can afford an investment. Furthermore, they can invest as much or as little as they want; for example, a person may buy either 10 or 1,000 shares of stock in a corporation. In addition, because corporations can sell bonds and issue stock, they have ways of raising money that do not exist for proprietorships or partnerships. (We look at bonds and stocks in more detail later in the chapter.)

Anyone can buy stock in a corporation and check its progress on the Internet.

Disadvantages of Corporations The disadvantages of corporations include the following:

1. *Corporations are subject to double taxation.* Suppose XYZ Corporation earns $3 million profit this year. This profit is subject to the corporate income tax. If the corporate income tax rate is 25 percent, then $750,000 is paid in taxes, and $2.25 million remains for **dividends** and other uses. Dividends are shares of the corporation's profits distributed to stockholders.

   Suppose that half of the $2.25 million profit after taxes is distributed to stockholders as dividends. This distribution is considered income for the stockholders and is taxed at personal income tax rates.

Economics and History

The Five Richest Americans in History

Many individuals throughout history have reaped riches by starting a business. In *The Wealthy 100: From Benjamin Franklin to Bill Gates*, Michael Klepper and Robert Gunther ranked the one hundred wealthiest Americans in history. To determine how wealthy a person was or is, the authors looked at the person's wealth as a percentage of the entire economy. Here are the top five (in order):

History records Bill Gates and Andrew Carnegie as two of the five richest Americans.

1. *John D. Rockefeller.* In 1913, Rockefeller had a total wealth of $900 million, which was 1/65th of the entire economy. In today's terms, this sum would be equivalent to having $189.6 billion. Rockefeller sensed an impending boom in oil and built his first oil refinery in Cleveland in 1863. Soon he had built the largest oil refinery business in the country.
2. *Andrew Carnegie.* In 1901, Carnegie had a total wealth of $250 million. In today's terms, it would be equivalent to having $100.5 billion. In 1848, Carnegie came to the United States from Scotland and worked for the Pennsylvania Railroad as a telegrapher. Carnegie built a steel-producing company that, by the early 1890s, produced more steel than all of Great Britain.
3. *Cornelius Vanderbilt.* In the mid-1800s, Vanderbilt had a total wealth of $105 million ($95.9 billion in today's terms). In 1929 he started a steamship line, which he sold in the 1860s, when he got into the business of railroads. He controlled the Hudson River Railroad, the New York Central, and the Lake Shore & Michigan Southern.
4. *John Jacob Astor.* In the early 1800s, Astor had a total wealth of $20 million ($78 billion today). Astor started his own fur-trading business. When that business started to decline, he turned his business eye to real estate. He was hoping that the growing New York City would soon expand outward to where he owned property. His hope was realized, and his property was worth millions.
5. *William (Bill) H. Gates.* In the spring of 2000, Gates was worth $77 billion, a figure that changes depending on the value of the Microsoft stock he owns. When he was nineteen years old, Gates dropped out of Harvard University and cofounded Microsoft with his high school friend Paul Allen. In 1980, IBM asked Gates to design an operating system for its computers. Microsoft has produced some of the most popular software programs in the world.

QUESTION TO ANSWER Andrew Carnegie, the second richest American in history, wrote down his rules for succeeding in life. Here is some of what he said: "First, never enter a bar-room [a bar]. Do not drink liquor as a beverage. . . . Fourth, do not think a man has done his full duty when he has performed the work assigned him. A man will never rise if he does only this. Promotion comes from exceptional work. . . . Fifth, whatever your wages, save a little. Live within your means." What is your opinion of Carnegie's rules?

In short, the $3 million profit was subject to both the corporate income tax and the personal income tax—two taxes, or double taxation. Contrast this situation with the profit earned by a proprietorship, which is subject to only one tax, the personal income tax.

2. *Corporations are complicated to set up.* Corporations are more difficult to organize than sole proprietorships and partnerships, as we discuss next.

board of directors
An important decision-making body in a corporation. It decides corporate policies and goals, among other things.

bylaws
Internal rules of a corporation.

Exhibit 6-1 summarizes the advantages and disadvantages of corporations and compares them with the advantages and disadvantages of proprietorships and partnerships.

How to Form a Corporation Forming a corporation is a fairly complicated procedure. Here are a few key points related to the formation of a corporation:

1. *Promoters and the prospectus.* Promoters are those persons who take the first steps to form the corporation. One of their tasks is to issue a *prospectus,* a document that contains information and facts about the new corporation, especially as related to its financial operations. Promoters often give the prospectus to persons they believe would be interested in purchasing stock in the corporation.

Exhibit 6-1

Advantages and Disadvantages of Different Types of Business Firms

Type of business firm	Examples	Advantages	Disadvantages
Sole Proprietorship	• Local barbershop • Many restaurants • Family farm • Carpet-cleaning service	• Easy to form and to dissolve. • All decision-making power resides with the sole proprietor. • Profit is taxed only once.	• Proprietor faces unlimited liability. • Limited ability to raise funds for business expansion. • Usually ends with retirement or death of proprietor.
Partnership	• Some medical offices • Some law offices • Some advertising agencies	• Benefits of specialization can be realized. • Profit is taxed only once.	• Partners face unlimited liability (one partner can incur a debt and all partners are legally responsible for payment of the debt). • Decision-making can be complex and frustrating.
Corporation	• IBM • AT&T • General Motors	• Owners (stockholders) have limited liability. • Corporation continues if owners sell their shares of stock or die. • Usually able to raise large sums of money.	• Double taxation. • Corporations are complicated to set up.

The board of directors will often meet to discuss corporate strategy.

2. *Articles of incorporation.* A document called the *articles of incorporation* gives basic information about the future corporation, such as its name and the purpose for which it is being organized. This document must be filled out and submitted to the appropriate state officials in the state in which the corporation will be registered. A filing fee must also be paid. The persons who complete these tasks are called *incorporators.*
3. *Corporate charter.* If the articles of incorporation are approved by state officials, the state grants the new corporation a corporate charter. This charter entitles the corporation to conduct business.
4. *Organizational meeting.* Once the corporate charter has been obtained, the first organizational meeting of the corporation takes place. At this meeting, the **board of directors** of the corporation is chosen. This decision-making body decides corporate policies and goals, among other things. At the organizational meeting corporate **bylaws** (internal rules of the corporation) are also passed.

The Corporate Structure As a group, the stockholders are the most important persons in a corporation. They are its owners, and they elect the members of the board of directors. Voting for the board of directors is usually an annual event, with each stockholder having the right to cast as many votes as he or she has shares of stock. For example, a person with one share of stock has one vote, whereas a person with 10,000 shares of stock has 10,000 votes.

Presidents of corporations are often chosen by the board of directors.

The board of directors, as we have said, is an important decision-making body in a corporation that determines corporate policies and goals. It decides what products the corporation will produce and sell, what percentage of the profits of the firm will go to stockholders (as stock dividends), and what percentage will go for modernization and expansion. Also, the

Economics & People

William Randoph Hearst, Founder, the Hearst Corporation

William Randolph Hearst is given credit today for almost single-handedly creating U.S. journalism and thus changing the mass media in the United States. He was born on April 29, 1863, to George Hearst, a self-made multimillionaire with mining and ranching interests, and Phoebe Apperson Hearst, a Missouri schoolteacher. In 1880, his father accepted a small daily newspaper, the *San Francisco Examiner,* as payment for a gambling debt. In the mid-1880s, William wrote his father from Harvard University, where he was attending college, asking him if he could take over control of the *Examiner.*

Hearst, a creative and imaginative newspaperman, wanted to produce newspapers that people would buy and told his editors and reporters, "Readers don't like to be forced to read sentences or paragraphs two or three times to understand what the writing is trying to say. Nor are they likely to be impressed if you write meandering and oblique sentences full of words they don't understand. . . . If a story doesn't make sense to your customers, it's pretty safe to say they'll ignore it." Today, the Hearst Corporation owns many newspapers and magazines.

QUESTION TO ANSWER Do you think Hearst's perception of the newspaper-reading public was accurate for his time? Do you think it is accurate today?

Exhibit 6-2
Structure of a Typical Corporation

Stockholders occupy the top position in a corporation. They elect the board of directors, which in turn chooses the corporation's top officers (the president and others). Vice presidents answer to the president, department heads answer to vice presidents, and all other employees either directly or indirectly answer to department heads.

Stockholders
Board of directors
Secretary | President | Treasurer
Vice president | Vice president | Vice president
Dept. head | Dept. head | Dept. head | Dept. head | Dept. head | Dept. head | Dept. head
All other employees

board of directors chooses the corporation's top officers, including the president, one or more vice presidents, the secretary, and the treasurer. These officers carry out the day-to-day operations of the corporation. To do so, they often appoint other vice presidents, as well as department heads, who supervise all other employees in their departments. Exhibit 6-2 shows this structure.

Financing Corporate Activity All firms, whether proprietorships, partnerships, or corporations, can raise money by borrowing from banks and other lending institutions. Only corporations, however, have two other avenues. They can sell bonds (sometimes referred to as *issuing debt*), and they can issue (or sell) additional shares of stock.

Think of a **bond** as a statement of debt issued by a corporation—an IOU, or piece of paper on which is written a promise to pay. For example, when AT&T issues a bond, it is promising to pay a certain amount of money at a certain time. Here is the process at work:

1. Quentin buys a bond issued by AT&T in the year 2000 for $10,000. The $10,000 is now in the possession of AT&T (the corporation might use the money to help buy new equipment), and the bond (a piece of paper) is in the possession of Quentin.
2. The bond that Quentin has in his hands has a few things written on it. For one thing, it has a dollar figure written on it, called the **face value** (or **par value**) of the bond. We'll say it is $10,000. There is also a percentage written on the bond, called the **coupon rate** of the

bond
A statement of debt issued by a corporation. The corporation promises to pay a certain sum of money at maturity and also to pay periodic fixed sums until that date.

face value (par value)
The dollar amount specified on a bond.

coupon rate
A percentage of the face value of a bond that is paid out regularly (usually quarterly or annually) to the holder of the bond.

cooperative
A business that provides services to its members and is not run for profit. Usually, a cooperative is formed when a group of persons (the members) want to pool their resources to gain some benefit that they, as individuals, could not otherwise obtain.

bond. The coupon rate is the percentage of the face value of a bond that is paid out regularly to the bondholders. For Quentin's bond, we'll say the coupon rate is 10 percent. Finally, there is a maturity date written on the bond—the date the bond matures, or is paid off by AT&T. We'll say this date is 2005.

3. The bond is a legal promise that AT&T has made to Quentin. The promise has two parts. First, AT&T has promised to pay the face value of the bond at the maturity date. Second, it has promised to pay the coupon rate, times the face value of the bond, each year until the maturity date. The coupon rate is 10 percent, and the face value of the bond is $10,000; 10 percent of $10,000 is $1,000, so Quentin receives $1,000 in the year 2000 and in each year through 2005. (This $1,000 is called the *annual coupon payment.*) In 2005, Quentin receives not only $1,000 but also the face value of the bond, $10,000, because 2005 is the maturity date of the bond.

What is the difference between stocks and bonds?

Instead of selling bonds, AT&T could have issued stock to raise money. Remember that a share of stock is a claim on the assets of the corporation that gives the purchaser a share of the ownership of the corporation. Whereas the buyer of a corporate bond is *lending* funds to the corporation, the buyer of a share of stock is acquiring an *ownership right* in the corporation. Simply put, if you buy a bond from a corporation, you are a lender, not an owner. If you buy shares of stock in a corporation, you are an owner, not a lender.

There is one key difference between bondholders and stockholders: the corporation is under no legal obligation to pay stockholders. Bond purchasers have lent money to the corporation, so the corporation must repay these loans, along with extra payments (such as the $1,000 Quentin received each year), to the bond purchasers for the use of their money. But stockholders have not lent funds to the corporation; instead, they have bought a part of it. If the corporation does well, the value of their stock will rise, and they will be able to sell it at a price higher than the price they paid for it. However, if the corporation does not do well, the value of their stock will fall, and they will most likely have to sell it for less than the purchase price.

Other Business Organizations: Cooperatives and Franchises

Sole proprietorships, partnerships, and corporations are not the only types of business organization; they are simply the most common. Two other types of business organization are the cooperative and the franchise.

Cooperatives A **cooperative,** or co-op, is a business that provides services to its members and is not run for profit. Usually, a cooperative is formed when a group of persons (the members) want to pool their resources to gain some benefit that they, as individuals, could not otherwise obtain. For example, sellers often offer reduced prices to buyers who purchase in bulk. Individual consumers can take advantage of these reduced prices by forming a consumer cooperative, which can buy large quantities of consumer items (food, home appliances, and so on) at reduced prices and then pass the savings on to its members through lower prices.

Franchises The franchise is a form of business organization that has become more common in the last twenty-five years. A **franchise** is a contract by which a firm (usually a corporation) lets a person or group use its name and sell its goods or services. In return, the person or group must make certain payments and meet certain requirements. For example, McDonald's Corporation offers franchises. Individuals can buy the right to use McDonald's name and to sell its products, as long as they meet certain requirements. The corporation, or parent company, is called the **franchiser;** it is the entity that offers the franchise. The person or group that buys the franchise is called the **franchisee.** A few well-known franchises are McDonald's, Burger King, Wendy's, Pizza Hut, Domino's Pizza, and Taco Bell.

It might surprise you to learn that the franchise type of business organization is relatively new. Why did franchises become such a popular business form in the late twentieth century?

The franchise agreement works this way: (1) The franchisee pays an initial fee. (In the late 1990s, the initial fee for a McDonald's franchise was $45,000.) (2) The franchisee often pays a royalty, or percentage of the profits, to the franchiser for a number of years. (3) The franchisee usually agrees to meet certain quality standards decided on by the franchiser. (For example, all McDonald's franchises cook Big Macs for the same length of time.) In return, the franchisee receives from the franchiser the right to use the parent company name, the right to sell a certain product, financial assistance, assistance in training employees and personnel, and national advertising.

Franchises offer several advantages to franchisees. For many franchisees, national advertising is especially important. Consider how many hours of national TV advertising McDonald's annually buys. This advertising benefits its franchisees from Maine to California. Furthermore, with a well-established company such as McDonald's or Burger King, the franchisee buys a business that has been proved successful. Consider the risk of starting your own restaurant compared with the risk of opening a McDonald's or a Burger King. The U.S. Department of Commerce reports that the failure rate is about twelve times higher for independently owned businesses than for franchises.

Of course, franchise business arrangements are not always smooth sailing. Sometimes the franchiser fails to provide the financial and training support the franchisee expects, and occasionally the franchisee does not provide the quality of service and product that the franchiser expects. Are franchises the wave of the future? We don't know for sure. What we do know is that, in the last twenty-five years, franchises have proved to be a very successful form of business organization.

MINI GLOSSARY

franchise
A contract by which a firm (usually a corporation) lets a person or group use its name and sell its goods in exchange for certain payments being made and certain requirements being met.

franchiser
The entity that offers a franchise.

franchisee
The person or group that buys a franchise.

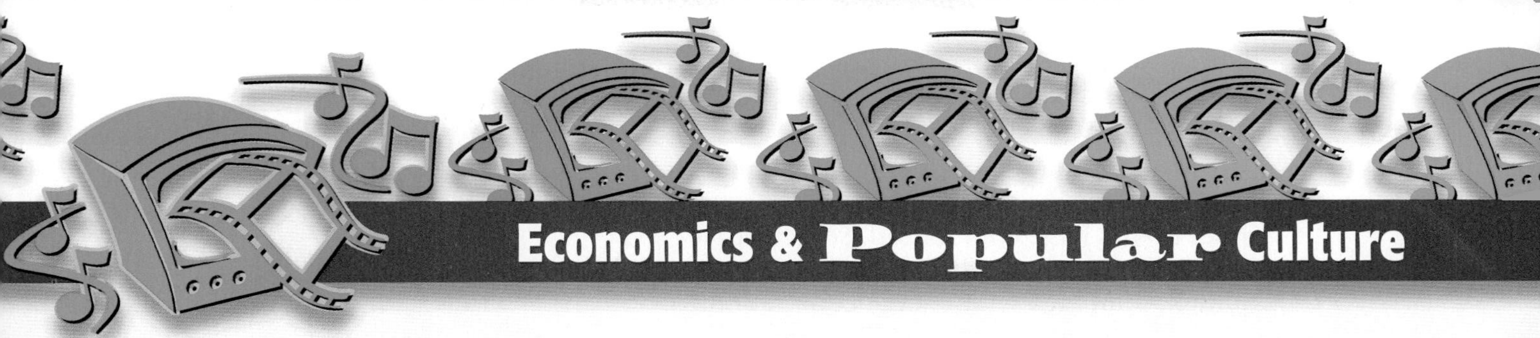

Hamburgers and Fries in the 1940s

Brothers Dick and Mac McDonald owned a drive-in restaurant in San Bernardino, California, in the late 1940s. It was a good business, earning annual revenues of $200,000, but they wanted the business to grow. So they replaced carhops (people who come out to cars to take orders) with self-service at a counter. They also reduced their menu from twenty-five to eleven items: hamburgers, cheeseburgers, three soft-drink flavors, milk, coffee, potato chips, pies, french fries, and milk shakes. The revamped restaurant was a big hit and annual revenues quickly grew to $350,000.

Ray Kroc, a milk shake mixer salesman, heard of the McDonald brothers' success. He decided to pay them a visit, hoping to sell them some milk shake mixer machines. After all, he had heard that the McDonald brothers were selling 20,000 milk shakes a month. When Kroc arrived at the restaurant, he saw throngs of customers. He knew that what he saw before him was a gold mine. Kroc told the McDonald brothers that they should open up several more restaurants. They were interested in the idea of more restaurants, but not in opening the restaurants themselves. Kroc volunteered.

Kroc formed a franchising company on May 2, 1955. The first franchised McDonald's opened on April 15, 1955, in Des Plaines, Illinois. The license fee for McDonald's in those days was $950 per restaurant; the royalty (or service) fee was 1.9 percent of restaurant sales. Of the 1.9 percent, 0.5 percent went to the McDonald brothers. In the late 1950s, Kroc bought out the McDonald brothers and was in complete control of McDonald's.

The growth in McDonald's over the years has been phenomenal. Today, McDonald's serves 43 million people each day (over 20 million of whom are in the United States), has about 26,000 restaurants in 119 countries (over 13,000 in the United States), and opens up a restaurant somewhere in the world every five hours of every day. Also, McDonald's hires hundreds of thousands teenagers each year.

QUESTION TO ANSWER The current McDonald's franchise application asks this question: "Will you devote your full time to this business?" Why do you think McDonald's wants to know an applicant's answer to this question?

The Small Business Administration

A small business firm usually has a much smaller operation (fewer employees, less revenue) than a large corporation. Some people think that the small business firm is at a disadvantage compared with a large corporation. For example, the small firm might not have the money or the management expertise that a large corporation has, which could put the small firm at a competitive disadvantage.

Congress set out to protect small businesses in 1953 by passing the Small Business Act. This act set up the Small Business Administration (SBA), whose job is to assist small businesses. The SBA, for example, often directly lends money to people who want to start a new small business or expand an old one. It also guarantees loans that a small business might obtain from a bank. (When the SBA guarantees a loan, it makes it easier for the owner of a small business to obtain a loan from a bank.) The SBA also provides loans to small businesses that have been damaged by natural disasters, such as hurricanes or earthquakes. Furthermore, the SBA has set up programs to promote economic opportunities for minority groups; for example, it makes special loans to individuals with disabilities, and makes sure that women have equal access to all its services.

The SBA often helps small businesses affected by natural disasters.

If you are thinking of starting your own small business, it would be in your best interest to contact the SBA and find out what assistance—financial and otherwise—is available to you. You will usually find the SBA listed in the telephone book under "United States Government." You can also visit the SBA's Web site: **http://www.sbaonline.sba.gov/**.

What Is the Ethical and Social Responsibility of Business?

Do businesses have an ethical and social responsibility, and if so, what is it? Some people think that businesses have an ethical responsibility to use their profits to meet socially worthwhile objectives. Milton Friedman, the winner of the 1976 Nobel Prize in economics, views the ethical and social responsibility of businesses differently: "There is one and only one social responsibility of business—to use its resources and engage in activities designed to increase its profits so long as it stays within the rules of the game, which is to say, engages in open and free competition, without deception or fraud." Friedman implicitly speaks to the ethical responsibility of businesses and explicitly to their social responsibility. As Friedman sees it, the ethical responsibility of business is to play by the rules of the game: to (1) engage in open and free competition and (2) not deceive or commit fraud upon the buying public. According to Friedman, then, if a company tried to use government to stifle its competition, that company would not be engaging in open and free competition and therefore would be acting unethically. If a company lied to the buying public about its product, saying the product could provide certain benefits that it actually could not provide, it would be acting unethically. In short, according to Friedman, a business is acting ethically if it engages in open and free competition, does not try to prevent its competitors from doing the same, and does not lie or misrepresent its product to the buying public.

After a business has met these ethical standards, says Friedman, its job is simple: it should earn as much profit as possible by selling the public something it wants to buy. A business should forget about giving money to the Red Cross, the homeless, or the children's wing of a hospital. All this is outside its social responsibility. Instead, a business should earn profit, turn the profit over to its stockholders (in the form of dividends), and then let these stockholders decide what they want to do with their money. If they want to give it to the homeless or needy children, that is up to them to decide. The following is what Friedman has to say on the subject:

Few trends could so thoroughly undermine the very foundations of our free society as the acceptance by corporate officials of a social responsibility other than to make as much money for their stockholders as possible. This is a fundamentally subversive doctrine. If businessmen do have a social responsibility other than making maximum profits for stockholders, how are they to know what it is? . . . One topic in the area of social responsibility that I feel duty bound to touch on, because it affects my own personal interests, has been the claim that business should contribute to the support of charitable activities and especially to universities. Such giving by corporations is an inappropriate use of corporate funds in a free-enterprise society. The corporation is an instrument of the stockholders who own it. If the corporation makes a contribution, it prevents the individual stockholder from himself deciding how he should dispose of his funds.

Businesspeople have an ethical responsibility to play by the rules.

Section 1 Review

Defining Terms

1. Define
- **a.** unlimited liability
- **b.** stock
- **c.** asset
- **d.** corporation
- **e.** partnership
- **f.** bylaws
- **g.** dividend
- **h.** bond

Reviewing Facts and Concepts

2. Under what condition will individuals form a firm?

3. Which type of business organization is the most numerous in the United States?

4. Which type of business organization accounts for the largest share of total business revenue?

5. What does it mean to say that corporations face double taxation?

6. Explain the difference between a limited partner and a general partner.

7. Why would a company make a boss (monitor) a residual claimant of the firm?

Critical Thinking

8. Do you think the initial fee for all franchises (McDonald's, Wendy's, Burger King, and so on) is the same? Why or why not?

9. Do you agree or disagree with Milton Friedman's position on the ethical and social responsibility of business? Explain your answer.

Applying Economic Concepts

10. If the face value of a bond is \$10,000 and the coupon rate is 5 percent, what is the annual payment to the bondholder?

SECTION 2 Costs

Suppose you are in the business of producing cars. Do you know offhand how many cars you would produce? Would it be 1,000, 2,000, or 100,000? How would you go about determining the "right" quantity to produce? You may have a feeling that you should not produce too few or too many, but how would you know what too few and too many were? To begin to answer these questions, we need to look more closely at costs and revenues. We begin with costs.

As you read this section, keep these key questions in mind:

- What are fixed costs? Variable costs?
- What do total costs equal?
- How do we compute fixed cost, variable cost, average total cost, and marginal cost?

Fixed and Variable Costs

Key Terms

fixed cost
variable cost
total cost
average total cost
marginal cost

All businesses have costs, but not all costs are the same. For example, suppose Maria Torres owns a business that produces a certain kind of toy. In her business, Torres needs a plant, or factory, in which the toy can be produced. She also needs insurance, employees, machines, certain materials for producing the toy (such as plastic and rubber), paper, pens, computers, electricity, and much more.

Consider one of the many things Torres needs—a plant. Currently, she rents a plant from Terry Adams. The rental contract specifies that Torres agrees to pay Adams $2,000 rent each month for twelve months.

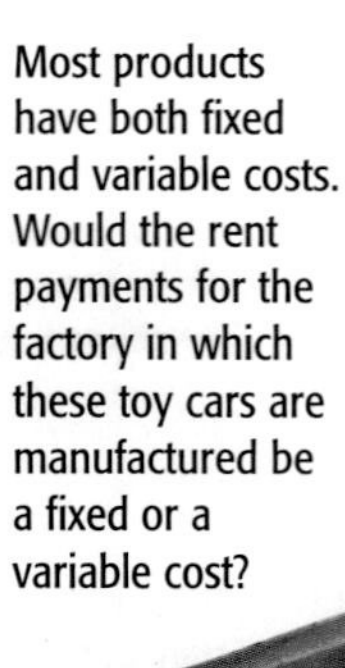

Most products have both fixed and variable costs. Would the rent payments for the factory in which these toy cars are manufactured be a fixed or a variable cost?

ONE BIG HAPPY

Reprinted by permission of Rick Detorie and Creators Syndicate, Inc.

fixed cost A cost, or expense, that is the same no matter how many units of a good are produced.

variable cost A cost, or expense, that changes with the number of units of a good produced.

total cost The sum of fixed costs plus variable costs.

average total cost (per-unit cost) The total cost divided by the quantity of output

What if Torres does not want to rent the plant after she has paid only three months' rent? Must she pay rent for the remaining nine months? Given the contract that Torres and Adams have entered into, the answer is yes. In other words, no matter whether Torres produces 1 toy, 1,000 toys, 10,000 toys, or even zero toys in the plant each month, she still has the legal obligation to pay rent of $2,000 a month for twelve months.

Costs, or expenses, that are the same no matter how many units of a good are produced are called **fixed costs.** The $2,000 rent is a fixed cost for Torres for a period of twelve months.

Now suppose Torres employs ten workers and pays each $50 a day. Her labor cost per day is $500. One day, she gets a special order for many hundreds of toys. To meet the order, she hires five additional workers at $50 per day. As a result, her labor cost rises by $250, to a total of $750. Notice that the increase in labor cost goes along with an increase in the number of toys being produced. Costs, or expenses, that vary, or change, with the number of units of a good produced are called **variable costs.**

If we add fixed costs to variable costs, we have **total costs:**

$$\text{Total costs} = \text{Fixed costs} + \text{Variable costs}$$

Suppose we want to compute total costs for a month. If fixed costs are $2,000 for the month and variable costs are $750, then total costs are $2,750 for the month.

Average Total Cost

Suppose a teacher gives a test to five students. The grades are as follows: 80, 90, 100, 60, and 75. The total number of points—the sum of the individual grades—is 405. To find the average grade, we divide the total, 405, by the number of students, 5. The average grade on the test is 81.

Similarly, to compute the **average total cost** (ATC), or per-unit cost, simply divide total cost (TC) by the quantity of output (Q):

$$\text{Average total cost (ATC)} = \frac{TC}{Q}$$

For example, if total cost is $6,000 and 1,000 units of a good are produced, then average total cost is $6 ($6,000 ÷ 1,000 = $6).

Marginal Cost: A Very Important Cost Concept

Every company must compute the marginal cost for its products. Why is this important?

Suppose Torres currently produces 1,000 units of a toy, and total cost is $6,000. She then decides to produce an additional unit of the toy; in other words, she produces one more toy. As a result, total cost rises from $6,000 to $6,008. What is the change in total cost that results from this change in output? It is $8; that is, total cost went from $6,000 to $6,008 when output went from 1,000 units to 1,001 units. The change in total cost that results from producing an additional unit of output is called **marginal cost.** In other words, *marginal cost is the additional cost of producing an additional unit of a good.* In our example, the marginal cost is $8. When you think about marginal cost, focus on the word *change.* Marginal cost describes a change in one thing (total cost) caused by a change in something else (quantity of output).

In economics, the triangle symbol (Δ) means "change in."

Thus, when we write

$$\text{Marginal cost (MC)} = \frac{\Delta TC}{\Delta Q}$$

we mean "marginal cost equals the change in total cost divided by the change in quantity of output." We can place the numbers from our example in this equation. ΔTC, the change in total cost, is $8 ($6,008 − $6,000 = $8). ΔQ, the change in quantity produced, is 1 (1,001 − 1,000 = 1):

Marginal cost (MC) = $8 ÷ 1 = $8

The marginal cost is $8. Exhibit 6-3 reviews the five cost concepts discussed in this section.

marginal cost
The additional cost of producing an additional unit of a good; the change in total cost that results from producing an additional unit of output.

Exhibit 6-3

Five Cost Concepts

Type of cost	Description	Example
Fixed Cost (FC)	Cost, or expense, that does not change as output changes	A firm's monthly rent is a fixed cost.
Variable Cost (VC)	Cost, or expense, that changes as output changes	The amount a firm spends on employees' wages is usually a variable cost.
Total Cost (TC)	Fixed costs plus variable costs (FC + VC)	If fixed costs equal $2,000, and variable costs equal $4,000, then total cost equals $6,000.
Average Total Cost (ATC)	Total cost divided by quantity of output $\left(\frac{TC}{Q}\right)$	If total cost equals $6,000, and quantity equals 1,000 units, then average total cost equals $6.
Marginal Cost (MC)	Change in total cost divided by change in quantity of output $\left(\frac{\Delta TC}{\Delta Q}\right)$	If total cost equals $6,000, when quantity equals 1,000 units, and total cost equals $6,008, when quantity equals 1,001 units, then marginal cost equals $8.

Section 2 Review

Defining Terms

1. Define

a. fixed costs

b. variable costs

c. marginal cost

Reviewing Facts and Concepts

2. Give an example of a fixed cost and a variable cost.

3. A firm produces 125 units of a good. Its variable costs are $400, and its total costs are $700. Answer the following questions:

a. What do the firm's fixed costs equal?

b. What is the average total cost equal to?

c. If variable costs were $385 when 124 units were produced, then what was the total cost equal to at 124 units?

Critical Thinking

4. This section discussed both average total cost and marginal cost. What is the key difference between the two cost concepts?

Applying Economic Concepts

5. An airline has 100 seats to sell on a plane traveling from New York to Los Angeles. It sells its tickets for $450 each. At this price, 97 tickets are sold. Just as the plane is about to take off, a person without a ticket says he is willing to pay $150, but not one penny more, to buy a ticket on the plane. The additional cost of the additional passenger (to the airline)—that is, the marginal cost to the airline—is $100. Is it in the best interest of the airline to sell the person a ticket for $150? Explain your answer.

SECTION 3

Revenue and Its Applications

Now that we have examined costs, we turn to a discussion of revenues. Then we look at costs and revenues together to determine how much of a good a firm will produce.

As you read this section, keep these key questions in mind:

- What is total revenue?
- What is marginal revenue?
- Why does a business firm compare marginal revenue with marginal cost when deciding how many units of a good to produce?

Total Revenue and Marginal Revenue

Key Terms

marginal revenue
law of diminishing marginal returns

In Chapter 2, *total revenue* was defined as the price of a good times the quantity sold. For example, if the price of a book is $5 and 100 are sold, then total revenue is $500. Consider the following: (1) Harris sells toys for a price of $10 each. (2) Harris currently sells 1,000 toys. (3) This means that Harris's total revenue is $10,000. If Harris sells one more toy for $10, what is the change in total revenue that results from the change in output sold?

Companies need to know the total revenue for their operation.

To answer this question, we first calculate what the total revenue is when Harris sells 1,001 instead of 1,000 toys; it is $10,010. We conclude that the total revenue changes from $10,000 to $10,010 when an additional toy is sold. In other words, there is a change in total revenue of $10.

The change in total revenue (TR) that results from selling an additional unit of output is **marginal revenue** (MR). In other words, marginal revenue is the additional revenue from selling an additional unit of a good. In the example, $10 is the marginal revenue. We can write it this way:

$$\text{Marginal revenue (MR)} = \frac{\Delta TR}{\Delta Q}$$

Marginal revenue equals the change in total revenue divided by the change in the quantity of output sold.

MINI GLOSSARY

marginal revenue
The additional revenue from selling an additional unit of a good; the change in total revenue that results from selling an additional unit of output.

Deciding How Much to Produce: Comparing MC with MR

Unit 1

Unit 2

Unit 3

Unit 4

How does a car company decide whether or not to produce another car?

Firms must answer many questions. One important question is how much of a good or service to produce. For example, does a car company produce 100, 1,000, or 10,000 cars? Should a computer company produce 10,000, 100,000, or 200,000 computers?

Firms compare marginal revenue with marginal cost when deciding how much output to produce and sell. The process amounts to common sense: as long as marginal revenue is greater than or equal to marginal cost, the firm wants to produce an additional unit of output. The firm does not want to produce an additional unit of output when marginal cost is greater than marginal revenue.

To illustrate, consider Exhibit 6-4. Row 1 tells us which unit of the good we are discussing. Row 2 tells us the marginal revenue for that unit. Row 3 tells us the marginal cost for that unit. Row 4 notes whether the firm would produce the unit of the good under consideration.

For the first unit of the good, marginal revenue is $5, and marginal cost is $2. In other words, the added revenue from selling the first unit of the good is greater than the added cost of producing the first unit of the good. Obviously, under these circumstances, the firm would want to produce and sell the first unit of the good. The firm also wants to produce and sell the second and third units, because again, the added revenue from producing and selling these units of the good is greater than the added cost of producing them. For the fourth unit, marginal revenue equals marginal cost, so the firm is impartial between producing and selling the good and not producing and selling it. Customarily, economists assume that a firm produces the unit of the good for which marginal revenue equals marginal cost. Finally, for the fifth unit

Exhibit 6-4

What Quantity of Output Does the Firm Produce?

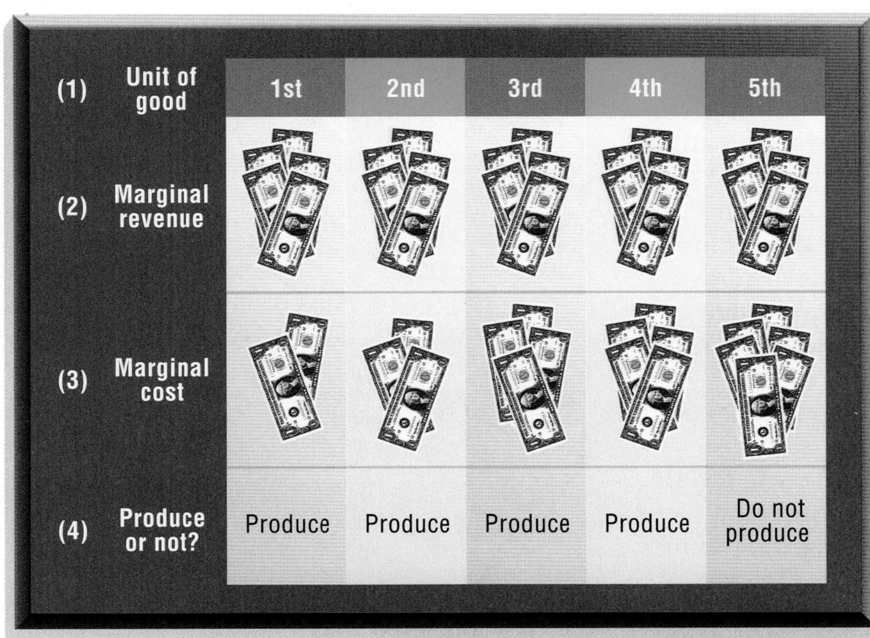

The firm continues to produce output as long as marginal revenue is greater than or equal to marginal cost. It does not produce those units of the good for which marginal cost is greater than marginal revenue. In the exhibit, the firm produces the first through the fourth units of the good, but not the fifth unit.

What Is the Right Amount of Time to Study for a Test?

A business firm can produce anywhere from 1 to 100,000 units of a good. What is the right amount? As the chapter explains, it is the amount of the good at which marginal revenue equals marginal cost.

To determine the right amount of something, an economist would say we need to consider marginal costs and marginal benefits. There are costs and benefits to studying, sleeping, eating, working, vacationing, and so on. How much of any activity is too little, how much is too much, and how much is the right amount? That's simple, says the economist: the right amount of anything is the amount at which the marginal benefits equal the marginal costs.

Suppose the marginal (additional) benefits of studying start out high and decrease with time. Exhibit 6-5 illustrates this with a downward-sloping marginal benefit curve (for studying). This curve says that you benefit more from the first minute of studying than the second minute, more from the second minute than the third, and so on.

Assume that the marginal costs of studying are constant over time. In other words, you are giving up as much by studying the first minute as the second minute, and so on. In the exhibit, the marginal cost curve (of studying) is horizontal to illustrate this point.

A quick look at Exhibit 6-5 says that the right amount of time to study is two hours. If you study less than two hours (say, one hour), you will forfeit all the net benefits (marginal benefits greater than marginal costs) you could have reaped by studying an additional hour. If you study more than two hours, you are entering into the region where marginal costs (of studying) are greater than marginal benefits. This means that the right amount of time studying is two hours. The rule is this: Do something as long as marginal benefits are greater than marginal costs, and stop when they are equal.

QUESTION TO ANSWER Suppose Exhibit 6-5 represents your marginal benefits and marginal costs of studying. In other words, the right amount of time for you to study is two hours. Then one day, your economics teacher talks about the benefits of learning economics. Afterward, you realize that there are more benefits to learning economics than you had thought. Will this change the amount of time you study economics? Explain your answer in terms of Exhibit 6-5.

Exhibit 6-5

The Marginal Benefits and Marginal Costs of Studying

What is the right amount of time to study? Study as long as the marginal benefits of studying are greater than the marginal costs, and quit when the marginal benefits equal the marginal costs In the diagram, this time comes at two hours of studying.

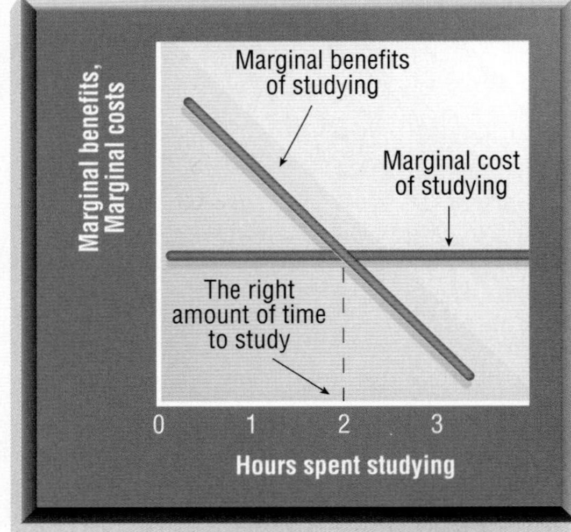

of the good, marginal cost is greater than marginal revenue, so the firm does not want to produce and sell this unit. We conclude that the firm will produce 4 units of the good. This is the quantity at which marginal revenue equals marginal cost.

You may be wondering why it isn't better for a firm simply to produce and sell whatever quantity of goods customers would buy. For example, if a firm could sell 13,000 cars but no more, then why wouldn't it simply produce and sell 13,000 cars? In other words, why wouldn't firms produce and sell every car that someone is willing to buy? A firm does not follow this strategy because sometimes the costs of producing a particular unit of a good are greater than what the firm hopes to earn by selling the good. Suppose that the firm could sell the 13,000th car for no more than $11,000, but it would cost the firm $14,000 to produce the car. Should it produce and sell the car? Definitely not. Remember, a firm concerns itself not only with how many dollars come into the firm but also with how many dollars go out.

MR > MC ➡ Produce
MC > MR ➡ Do not produce

Profit, Marginal Revenue, and Marginal Cost

A firm will produce and sell an additional unit of a good if marginal revenue is greater than or equal to marginal cost, but it will not produce and sell an additional unit of a good if marginal cost is greater than marginal revenue. After all, the objective of business firms is to maximize profit. Remember from Chapter 2 that profit exists when total revenue is greater than total cost. For example, if total revenue is $400,000 and total cost is $320,000, then profit is $80,000. The firm wants profit to be as large as possible, and one way to maximize profit is to make sure it produces and sells an additional unit of a good as long as doing so adds more to total revenue than to total cost. Again suppose that a business firm's total revenue is $400,000, total cost is $320,000, and profit is $80,000. Now suppose it produces and sells an additional unit of a good. The additional revenue from selling this unit of the good (the marginal revenue) is $40, and the additional cost of producing this unit of the good (the marginal cost) is $10. Total revenue will rise to $400,040 ($400,000 + $40 = $400,040), and total cost will rise to $320,010 ($320,000 + $10 = $320,010). What will happen to profit? It will increase to $80,030 ($400,040 − $320,010 = $80,030). Thus, whenever the firm produces and sells an additional unit of a good and marginal revenue is greater than marginal cost, it is adding more to its total revenue than to its total cost, and therefore it is maximizing profit.

Two owners of a business talk over whether or not to produce more units of a good. Are marginal revenue and marginal cost relevant to their discussion? Explain.

THINKING Like an Economist

The comparison of marginal revenue (MR) with marginal cost (MC) to determine how many units of a good to produce is typical of the type of thinking used in economics. It is thinking in terms of benefits and costs.

Marginal revenue can be seen as the additional benefits of selling another unit of a good, and marginal costs as the additional costs of producing another unit of a good. The firm simply compares these (additional) benefits and costs and decides what to do. If additional benefits are greater than additional costs, the firm produces an additional unit of the good. If additional costs are greater than additional benefits, it does not produce an additional unit.

Human Resources Specialist

Businesses want to hire qualified employees who are well suited for the jobs at hand. They hire human resources specialists who recruit and interview employees and advise on hiring decisions. Human resources specialists also provide training and deal with compensation, benefits, and so on.

In the late 1990s, human resources specialists held about 544,000 jobs and were employed in every industry in the United States. For jobs in human resources, employers usually look for college graduates who have majored in business administration, communication, and public administration, among other fields. Many colleges have programs that lead to a degree in personnel, human resources, or labor relations.

QUESTION TO ANSWER Top management may be involved only with the final interview of key employees. Background work is done by human resources specialists. How do you think top managers monitor human resources specialists to make sure they do not shirk their responsibilities?

How to Compute Profit and Loss

When a firm computes its profit or loss, it determines total cost and total revenue and then finds the difference:

1. To compute total cost (TC), add fixed cost (FC) to variable cost (VC): TC = FC + VC.
2. To compute total revenue (TR), multiply the price of the good (P) times the quantity of units (Q) of the good sold: P × Q = TR.
3. To compute profit (or loss), subtract total cost (TC) from total revenue (TR): profit (or loss) = TR − TC.

To illustrate, suppose variable cost is $100 and fixed cost is $400. It follows that total cost is $500. Now suppose that 100 units of a good are sold at $7 each; total revenue is then $700. If we subtract total cost ($500) from total revenue ($700), we are left with a profit of $200.

MINI GLOSSARY

law of diminishing marginal returns A law that states that if additional units of a resource (such as labor) are added to another resource (such as capital) that is fixed in supply, eventually the additional output produced (as a result of hiring an additional worker) will decrease.

Hiring Additional Workers and the Law of Diminishing Marginal Returns

Among the decisions a business firm has to make is whether or not it should hire an additional worker. For example, suppose it currently has ten workers. Should it hire one more? If so, and the number of workers increases to eleven, should it hire still one more worker?

According to economists, this decision involves the **law of diminishing marginal returns.** This law states that if we add additional units of a resource (such as labor) to another resource (such as capital) that is in fixed supply, eventually the additional output produced (as a result of hiring an additional worker) will decrease. Look at Exhibit 6-6. Reading across the first row, we see that when there are zero workers, there is no output. When one worker is added, the quantity of output (shown in the second column) is 5 units. The third column shows the additional output produced as a result of hiring an additional worker. Since output is zero with no workers and 5 units with one worker, we conclude that hiring an additional (the first) worker increased output by 5 units.

When a second worker is added, the quantity of output (shown in column 2) increases to 11 units. How much did output increase as a result of an additional (the second) worker? The answer is 6 units, as shown in column 3. If a third worker is added, output rises to 18 units, and the additional output produced as a result of the hiring of an additional (the third) worker is 7 units, as shown in column 3.

Before we go on, notice what has been happening in column 3: the numbers have been increasing, from 0 to 5, then 6, then 7. But notice that when a fourth worker is added, output increases to 23 units, but the additional output produced is 5 units—less than the additional output pro-

Sometimes hiring additional workers is worth the additional cost.

Exhibit 6-6

The Law of Diminishing Marginal Returns

As more workers are added (column 1), the quantity of output produced each day rises (column 2). At first, the additional output produced as a result of hiring an additional worker rises (see the first four entries in column 3), but it turns down with the addition of the fourth worker. It is with the fourth worker that diminishing marginal returns are said to set in.

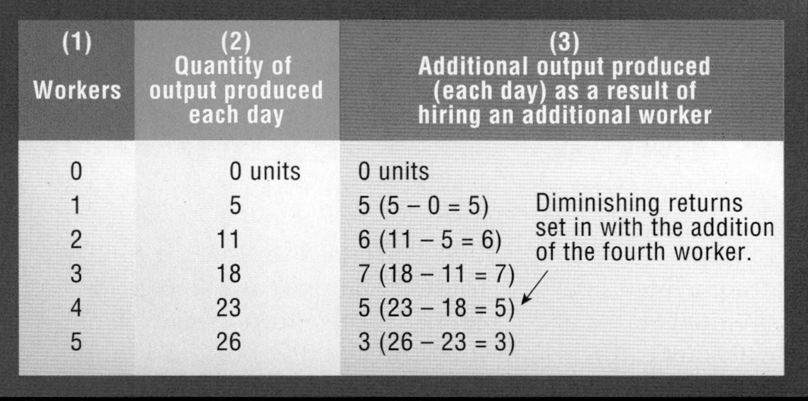

(1) Workers	(2) Quantity of output produced each day	(3) Additional output produced (each day) as a result of hiring an additional worker
0	0 units	0 units
1	5	5 (5 – 0 = 5)
2	11	6 (11 – 5 = 6)
3	18	7 (18 – 11 = 7)
4	23	5 (23 – 18 = 5)
5	26	3 (26 – 23 = 3)

Diminishing returns set in with the addition of the fourth worker.

duced (7 units) as a result of adding the next-to-last (the third) worker. What we are observing here is the law of diminishing marginal returns, which states that eventually the additional output produced (as a result of hiring an additional worker) will decrease. We added another worker (the fourth worker) here, and the additional output (shown in column 3) decreased from 7 to 5 units. In short, diminishing marginal returns set in with the addition of the fourth worker.

Do you think the firm should have hired a fourth worker? It depends on the cost and benefit of hiring the fourth worker. The benefit is that output rises by 5 units. Suppose the firm can sell these 5 units for $30 each, for a total of $150. Now the firm has to compare this $150 with the cost of hiring a fourth worker. Suppose the firm has to pay this fourth worker $70; it would seem that it is worth hiring a fourth worker. In other words, because of the fourth worker, 5 additional units of output are produced, which can be sold for $150, but the firm has to pay the worker only $70. By hiring the fourth worker, the firm is better off by $80.

Section 3 Review

Defining Terms

1. Define

a. marginal revenue

b. law of diminishing marginal returns

Reviewing Facts and Concepts

2. The additional output obtained by adding an additional worker is 50 units. Each unit can be sold for $2. Is it worth hiring the additional worker if she has to be paid $150 a day? Explain your answer.

3. Price is $20 per unit no matter how many units a firm sells. What is the marginal revenue for the 50th unit? Explain your answer.

Critical Thinking

4. This section explained how a firm computes profit. Specifically, it computes total cost and total revenue and then finds the difference. Suppose a firm wants to compute its profit *per unit.* In other words, instead of computing how much profit it earns in total, it wants to know how much profit it earns per unit. How could the firm go about computing profit per unit? (*Hint:* The answer has something to do with average total cost.)

Graphing Economics

5. Suppose the marginal benefits of playing tennis are constant for each minute of the first twenty minutes and then steadily decline for each additional minute. The marginal costs of playing tennis are constant. Furthermore, marginal costs are equal to marginal benefits at the forty-fifth minute. Diagrammatically represent the marginal benefits and marginal costs of playing tennis.

Why U.S. Firms Do Not Always Locate in Mexico

When discussing trade between countries, someone might say, "We, in the United States, can't do away with tariffs (taxes on imports), or quotas (quantitative restrictions on imports), because if we do, U.S. firms will leave the country and set up shop in foreign countries where labor is cheaper. After all, if a U.S. firm can go to, say, Mexico, hire labor at half the cost of hiring U.S. labor, produce a good, and then send it back into the country tariff free, it will do so. Without tariffs or quotas, every firm in the United States would head for foreign shores."

Is this true? Suppose the United States imposed no tariffs or quotas on any goods brought into the country for sale. Would U.S. firms head for foreign countries? Certainly many foreign countries have lower wages than the United States, but this is only one benefit to U.S. firms of going to a foreign country and hiring foreign labor. There are costs, too. U.S. firms would compare benefits and costs and then decide what to do.

Suppose that if a U.S. firm stays in the United States and hires U.S. workers, it will have to pay $10 an hour. If it goes to Mexico and hires Mexican labor, it will have to pay $5 an hour. Wages are two times higher in the United States than in Mexico, so why wouldn't the U.S. firm head for Mexico? The answer is that labor productivity may not be as high in Mexico as in the United States. In the United States, the average worker, working with various capital equipment, can produce 30 units of good X every hour. In Mexico, the average worker can produce 10 units of good X every hour. Now is it really worth it for the U.S. firm to go to Mexico?

The firm needs to compute its output per dollar of labor cost, which it does by dividing labor productivity by the hourly wage:

$$\text{Output per dollar of labor cost} = \frac{\text{Number of units labor produces per hour}}{\text{Wage rate}}$$

In the United States, the company pays a worker $10 an hour and receives 30 units of good X in return. In other words, it produces 3 units per $1 of labor cost. In Mexico, the firm pays a worker $5 an hour and receives 10 units of good X in return, so it produces 2 units per $1 of labor cost. Knowing this, the firm obviously will locate in the United States, because it is cheaper. The firm produces more output per dollar in the United States than in Mexico.

QUESTION TO ANSWER In this feature, a firm compares labor productivity with wage rates to determine where it will locate. How is this comparison similar to a firm comparing marginal revenue with marginal cost to determine how much of a good it will produce?

Developing Economic

Skills

Calculating Costs and the Average-Marginal Rule

You need to know how total, average, and marginal costs are computed, and then to understand the relationship between any average and marginal magnitude. This relationship between average and marginal is summed up in what economists call the *average-marginal rule.*

Total Cost

Computing total cost is easy—we simply add. For example, suppose variable costs are $400 and fixed costs are $300 and we want to compute total cost. We simply sum the two cost figures and get $700.

Average Total Cost

Computing average cost is easy—we simply divide. For example, to compute average total cost, we divide total cost by output. If total cost is $700 and output is 25 units of some good, then average total cost is $28.

Marginal Cost

Computing marginal cost is easy—we find the change in any total magnitude and the change in output and simply divide. For example, suppose total cost is $700 at an output of 25 units and $740 at 26 units. What is the marginal cost of the additional (twenty-sixth) unit? The change in total cost is $40 and the change in the number of units is 1, so marginal cost is $40.

The Average-Marginal Rule

What happens to average total cost if marginal cost is above it? below it? The answer is given by the average-marginal rule, which states: If the marginal is below the average, the average declines; if the marginal is above the average, the average rises.

To illustrate the average-marginal rule, let's first consider a noncost setting. Consider test grades in a school course. Suppose on your first test you earn 90 points. It follows that with only one test, your average grade (in the course) is 90. On your second test you receive 100 points. The 100 represents your marginal grade: it is the grade you earn on the additional (the next) test. Now compute your new average grade, which is 95 (190/2). Why did your average rise from 90 to 95? It is because your marginal grade (100) was above your average grade (90).

Suppose now that you receive 82 points on your third test. The 82 represents your marginal grade. Now compute your average, which is 90.7. Why did your average fall from 95 to 90.7? It is because your marginal grade (82) was below your average grade (95).

The changes in your average grade from 90 to 95 to 90.7 are consistent with the average-marginal rule. When the marginal grade was above the average grade, the average grade increased and when the marginal grade was below the average grade, the average grade decreased.

The average-marginal rule holds not only for grades but for costs, too. If marginal cost is below average total cost, average total cost declines; if marginal cost is above average total cost, average total cost rises.

1. The average income in city X is $50,000 a year. Jess moves into the city, and his annual income is $60,000 a year. Will the new average in city X (with Jess included) be higher or lower than the old average income (without Jess)? Explain your answer.
2. Suppose the marginal cost of producing good X is less than the average total cost of producing good X. What will happen to the average total cost of producing good X? Explain your answer.

CHAPTER 6

Review

Economics Vocabulary

Fill in the following blanks with the appropriate word or phrase.

1. In a sole proprietorship and partnership, owners have _____ liability, whereas in a corporation, owners have _____ liability.
2. The stockholders of the firm choose the _____.
3. Total cost equals _____ plus variable cost.
4. The additional cost of producing an additional unit of a good is called _____.
5. The _____ states that if additional units of a resource are added to a resource that is fixed in supply, eventually the additional output produced will decrease.
6. Another term for *average total cost* is _____.
7. The entity that offers a franchise is called the _____.
8. Ten percent of the face value of a bond is paid out regularly, so 10 percent is the _____ of the bond.
9. A(n) _____ for a firm is anything to which the firm has a legal claim.
10. The tax that a person pays on his or her income is called the _____ tax.

Review Questions

1. List and explain two major differences between a corporation and a partnership.
2. What does it mean when people say that corporations are taxed twice? (To what taxes are we referring?)
3. Suppose a bond has a $10,000 face value and a coupon rate of 8 percent. What is the dollar amount of each annual coupon payment?
4. Specify the condition under which a firm will be formed.
5. In setting 1, Mayang works for herself. She gets to keep or sell everything she produces. In setting 2, Mayang works with five individuals. Here, she gets to keep one-fifth of everything she produces and of everything that everyone else produces. In which setting is Mayang more likely to shirk? Explain your answer.
6. What is the relationship between a bondholder and the firm that issued the bond? What is the relationship between a stockholder and the firm that issued the stock?
7. How does a cooperative differ from a corporation?
8. In general, what is the difference between fixed and variable costs?
9. Explain why a firm continues to produce those units of a good for which marginal revenue is greater than marginal cost.
10. A firm will produce and sell units of a good if marginal revenue is greater than marginal cost. Does this strategy have anything to do with the firm's objective to maximize profit? Explain your answer.
11. How does a firm compute its profit or loss?

Calculations

1. Calculate the marginal cost for the additional unit in each of the following cases. (TC = total cost, and Q = quantity of output.)
   a. Q = 100, TC = $4,322; Q = 101, TC = $4,376
   b. Q = 210, TC = $5,687; Q = 211, TC = $5,699
   c. Q = 547, TC = $10,009; Q = 548, TC = $10,123
2. Calculate the average total cost in each of the following cases. (TC = total cost, and Q = quantity of output.)
   a. Q = 120, TC = $3,400
   b. Q = 200, TC = $4,560
   c. Q = 150, TC = $1,500
3. The marginal benefit of playing chess (in money terms) is $10 for the first game of chess, $8 for the second, $6 for the third, $4 for the fourth, $2 for the fifth, and $0 for the sixth. The marginal cost of playing chess (in money terms) is always $5. What is the right number of games of chess to play? Explain your answer.
4. Look at Exhibit 6-6 on page 165. Suppose it costs a firm $45 a day to hire the fifth worker. What does the price of the good (the firm produces) have to be before it is worth hiring the fifth worker?

Graphs

In Exhibit 6-7, Q = quantity of the good, MC = marginal cost, and MR = marginal revenue. Which part or parts (a–c) in Exhibit 6-7 illustrate the following?

1. Jim pays more to produce the second unit of the good than the first, more for the third than the second, and so on.

2. The additional "benefits" of producing the fourth unit of the good are the same as the additional benefits of producing the fifth unit of the good.
3. Marginal revenue is constant over quantity of the good produced.
4. Marginal revenue declines as the firm sells additional units of the good.

Exhibit 6-7

$ MR MC 0 1 2 3 4 5 6 Q (a)

$ MR MC 0 1 2 3 4 5 6 Q (b)

$ MR MC 0 1 2 3 4 5 6 Q (c)

Economics and Thinking Skills

1. **Application.** When Dairy Queen first entered into franchise agreements, it did not require franchisees to handle all the Dairy Queen products (some carried hamburgers and some did not). In contrast, McDonald's franchise agreements do require its franchisees to handle all the McDonald's products. If you were a franchiser, what kind of franchise agreement would you want, and why?
2. **Analysis.** What does profit depend upon?
3. **Cause and Effect.** How is marginal cost related to average total cost? (*Hint:* To help you answer the question, do the following. First, construct a numerical example that shows how average total cost changes if marginal cost is above it versus below it. Then step back from your numerical example and notice the relationship between marginal cost and average total cost.)

Writing Skills

Research the life of one of the five persons mentioned in the feature "Economics in History: The Five Richest Americans in History." Write a two-page paper on the person, in which you discuss how the person's business activities (in the past) may affect you today.

Economics in the Media

Find the portrayal of a top business executive on a television show or in a movie. Describe the role of the executive in the show or movie. What does he or she do? How does he or she act? How accurate do you think the portrayal is of real life? Explain your answer.

Where's the Economics?

What kind of costs do employees represent for the firm?

Analyzing Primary Sources

This chapter discussed shirking, monitors, residual claimaints, and profit. All four of these concepts are discussed in a short passage by economist Thomas Sowell in his famous work *Knowledge and Decisions:*[2]

Viewed in retrospect, residual claims are not very significant as a percentage of national income (about 10 percent) or as a return on investment (about 10 percent per annum). As a percentage of the selling price of goods, residual claims can be quite trivial. Supermarkets average about a penny profit on a dollar's worth of groceries, and only the huge volume of business they do every day brings this up to a profitable operation. It is not as a retrospective sum that residual claims have a major impact on the economy. It is as a prospective incentive that it profoundly affects behavior and the efficiency of production. If residual claimants were guaranteed in advance the very same sums which they end up earning, the whole economic system would function differently. With everyone in the economic system essentially on guaranteed salaries, the monitoring problems would be massive.

1. Sowell uses a synonym for *profits* in the passage. What is it?
2. What does Sowell mean when he says, "With everyone in the economic system essentially on guaranteed salaries, the monitoring problems would be massive"?

2. Thomas Sowell, *Knowledge and Decisions* (New York, Basic Books, 1996), p. 66.

CHAPTER 7

Competition and Markets

What This Chapter Is About

The topic of discussion in the last chapter was the firm. Firms operate within a certain type of setting—specifically, a market setting, which economists call a **market structure.** A market structure is defined by its characteristics, such as the number of sellers in the market (many versus few), the product that sellers produce and sell (Do all sellers sell the same product or slightly differentiated products?), how easy or difficult it is for new firms to enter the market, and so on.

According to economists, there are four market structures: perfect competition, monopoly, monopolistic competition, and oligopoly. A firm may find itself producing and selling goods in any one of the four market structures. The major purpose of this chapter is to describe each of the four market structures.

Why This Chapter Is Important

There are two prices: the price the seller asks for and the price the buyer pays. In some markets, these two prices are not the same. For example, a car buyer sees the $30,000 sticker price of a car he is interested in. This is the price the seller is asking. The buyer says he will pay only $27,000. The seller counters with $29,000, and then the buyer counters with $28,000. The seller accepts. The price the buyer pays ($28,000) is less than the price the seller was initially asking ($30,000).

In the clothing market, things are different. When you go into a store to

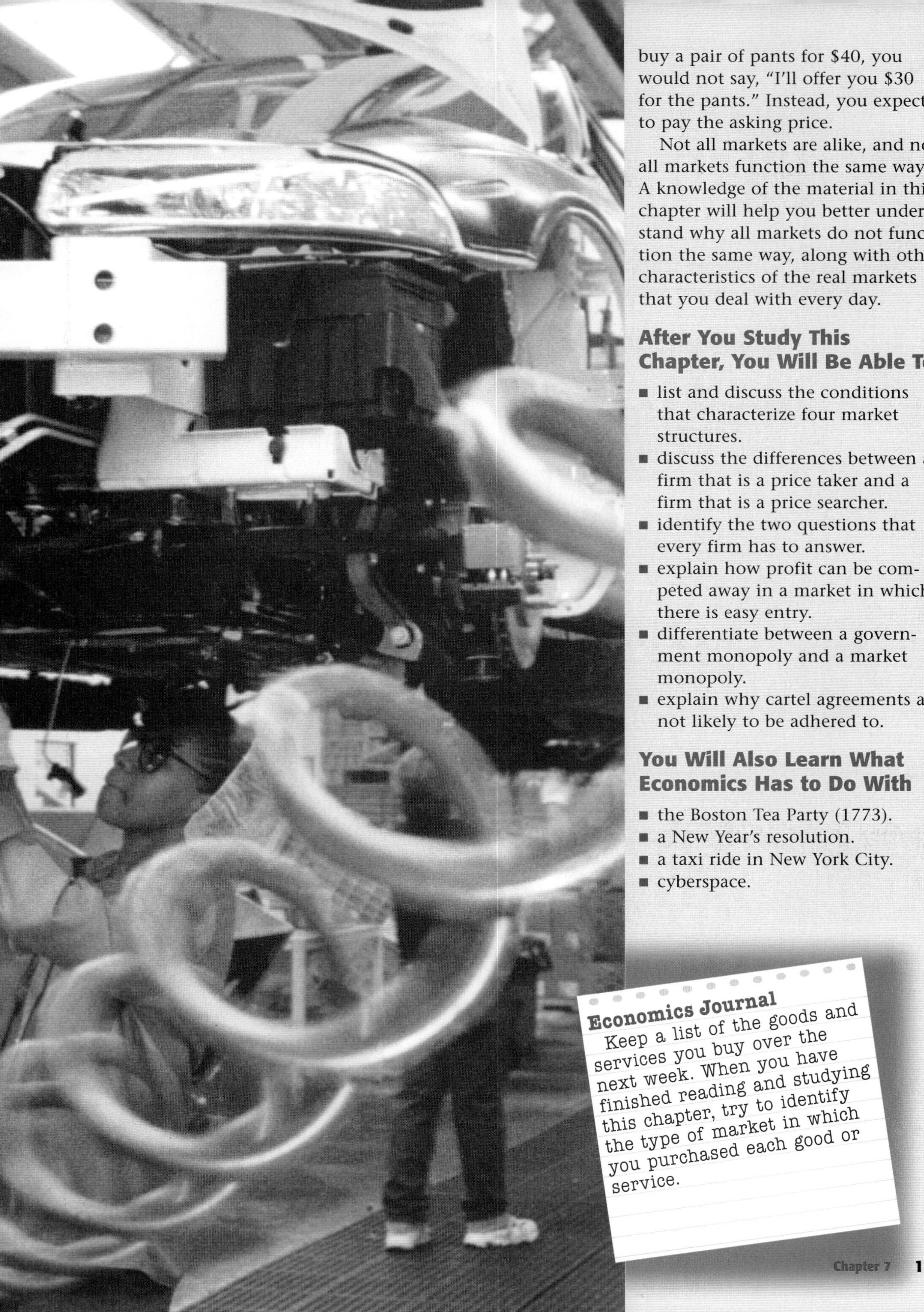

buy a pair of pants for $40, you would not say, "I'll offer you $30 for the pants." Instead, you expect to pay the asking price.

Not all markets are alike, and not all markets function the same way. A knowledge of the material in this chapter will help you better understand why all markets do not function the same way, along with other characteristics of the real markets that you deal with every day.

After You Study This Chapter, You Will Be Able To

- list and discuss the conditions that characterize four market structures.
- discuss the differences between a firm that is a price taker and a firm that is a price searcher.
- identify the two questions that every firm has to answer.
- explain how profit can be competed away in a market in which there is easy entry.
- differentiate between a government monopoly and a market monopoly.
- explain why cartel agreements are not likely to be adhered to.

You Will Also Learn What Economics Has to Do With

- the Boston Tea Party (1773).
- a New Year's resolution.
- a taxi ride in New York City.
- cyberspace.

Economics Journal

Keep a list of the goods and services you buy over the next week. When you have finished reading and studying this chapter, try to identify the type of market in which you purchased each good or service.

SECTION 1 Perfect Competition

As has been said, firms can find themselves in one of four market structures. The first market structure we discuss is perfect competition.

As you read this section, keep these key questions in mind:

- What are the characteristics of perfect competition?
- What are some examples of perfectly competitive markets?
- What does it mean to say that a firm has no control over price?

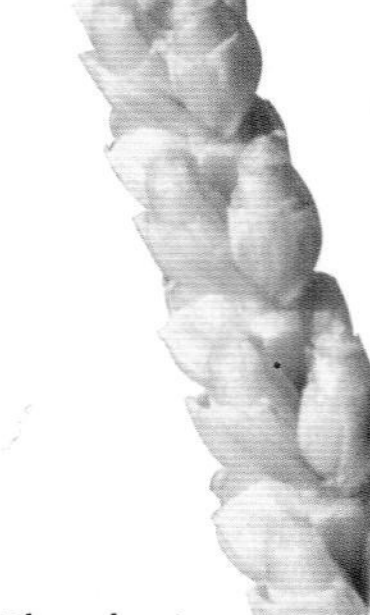

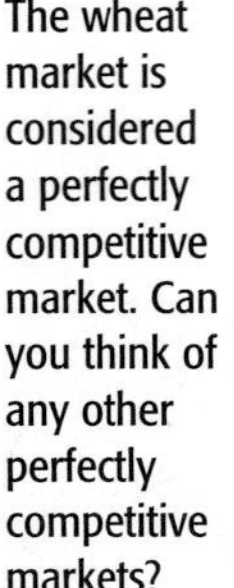

The wheat market is considered a perfectly competitive market. Can you think of any other perfectly competitive markets?

The Characteristics of Perfect Competition

Key Terms
market structure
perfect competition
price taker

Market structures are defined by certain conditions or characteristics. Four conditions characterize **perfect competition.**

1. *There are many buyers and many sellers.* In a perfectly competitive market, there are many buyers and many sellers for the good under consideration. For example, in the wheat market, many people buy wheat, and many people (wheat farmers) sell wheat.
2. *All firms sell identical goods.* There is no difference (as far as the buyer is concerned) between the goods one firm sells and those other firms sell. For example, a buyer may look upon Farmer Jones's wheat as identical to Farmer Smith's wheat.
3. *Buyers and sellers have all relevant information about prices, product quality, sources of supply, and so on.* All buyers and sellers in a perfectly competitive market know everything that is relevant to them about buying and selling. For example, Farmer Jones knows who else is selling wheat, the price at which the wheat is being sold, the quality of the wheat, and so on.
4. *There is easy entry into the market and easy exit out of the market.* Any seller who wants to enter a perfectly competitive market can do so; no government regulations or laws prohibit entry. Also, any time sellers want to leave the market, they can do so.

MINI GLOSSARY

market structure The setting in which a seller finds itself. Market structures are defined by their characteristics, such as the number of sellers in the market, the product that sellers produce and sell, and how easy or difficult it is for new firms to enter the market.

Farmers operate in perfectly competitive markets. Is there easy entry into and exit out of perfectly competitive markets?

What Do We Conclude from the Four Conditions?

Given the four characteristics of a perfectly competitive market, we conclude that the sellers in a perfectly competitive market are **price takers.** Price takers are sellers who can sell all their output at the equilibrium price but can sell none of their output at any other price. To illustrate, suppose Farmer Smith, a wheat farmer, has produced 1 million bushels of wheat, and the equilib-

perfect competition
A market structure in which (1) there are many buyers and many sellers, (2) all firms sell identical goods, (3) buyers and sellers have all relevant information about buying and selling activities, and (4) there is easy entry into the market and easy exit out of the market.

price taker
A seller that can sell all its output at the equilibrium price but can sell none of its output at any other price.

rium price of wheat is $4 per bushel. If Smith is a price taker, he can sell all 1 million bushels of his wheat at $4 per bushel, but he can't sell even 1 bushel at $4.01 a bushel.

Why can't Smith sell even 1 bushel of wheat at a price above the equilibrium price? The answer lies in the first three conditions of perfect competition identified earlier. First, buyers will know if Smith tries to sell his wheat for more than the equilibrium price, because according to condition 3, buyers have all the information relevant to buying. Second, buyers will turn down the price of $4.01 and simply buy from the other sellers who are selling wheat at $4. After all, according to condition 1, there are many sellers to choose from. Why should buyers buy from Smith at $4.01 a bushel when they could buy from other sellers at $4 a bushel? Third, buyers don't mind buying from other sellers, because other sellers, according to condition 2, are selling the identical product that Smith is selling. Wheat is wheat.

If it sounds odd that Smith can sell all his wheat at the equilibrium price but none at 1 penny more, consider another setting where this situation exists—the stock market. Suppose Kolpolovic, who owns 1,000 shares of Disney stock, decides one day to sell the stock. The current equilibrium price of the stock is $30. Kolpolovic can sell all her stock at $30, but she won't be able to sell even 1 share of stock for $31. If she tries to sell her stock for $31 per share, no one will want to buy it. After all, what buyer would buy from Kolpolovic for $31 a share when she could buy from someone else for $30 a share? Kolpolovic, as a seller of stock, is a price taker.

Can Price Takers Sell for Less Than the Equilibrium Price?

We know that price takers can sell their entire product at the equilibrium price but not even 1 unit of their product at 1 penny more than the equilibrium price. But can price takers sell any of their product at less than the equilibrium price? For example, if the equilibrium price of wheat is $4 a bushel, can Farmer Smith sell any of his wheat at, say, $3.99? Yes, he *can* sell his wheat at $3.99, but he *won't,* because it would not benefit him. After all, if he can sell all his wheat at $4 a bushel, why lower the price? There is no monetary incentive for Smith to offer his wheat for sale at less than the equilibrium price. He does better by selling at, instead of at less than, the equilibrium price.

We conclude that price takers will sell their product at only one price, the equilibrium price. They *can't* sell any of their product for more than the equilibrium price, and they *won't* sell any of their product for less than the equilibrium price.

This farmer covers his wheat crop, preparing to deliver it to market. Explain why he *can't* sell his wheat for more than the equilibrium price, and *won't* sell it for less.

Must a Perfectly Competitive Market Meet All Four Conditions?

Many agricultural markets (for example, wheat and corn markets) and the stock market are perfectly competitive markets. It just so happens that these markets also meet the four conditions of perfect competition. Consider the stock market. In the stock market there are many buyers and sellers, so condition 1 is satisfied. All sellers sell the identical product, shares of a particular stock, so condition 2 is satisfied. Buyers and sellers of stock have access to a wealth of information via newspapers, stockbrokerage firms, investment research firms, and the like, so condition 3 is satisfied. Anyone who wants to get into or out of the stock market can do so easily, so condition 4 is satisfied.

Many agricultural markets are perfectly competitive markets. Why is the corn market perfectly competitive?

If would seem, by our description of the stock market, that a market is perfectly competitive *only if* it meets all four conditions of perfect competition, but that is not so. A market may not satisfy one or more of the four conditions and still be perfectly competitive. What determines whether a market is perfectly competitive or not is whether firms (sellers) in the market are price takers or not. If they are price takers, then the market is perfectly competitive; if they are not price takers, then the market is not perfectly competitive.

To illustrate, consider the fictional widget market. First, in this market there are many buyers and only a few sellers. Second, each seller sells a good that is very similar (but not identical) to what is sold by the other sellers. Third, buyers and sellers have a lot of information that is relevant to the market, but they certainly do not have *all* information. Fourth, entry into and exit from the market is relatively easy. Fifth, firms that produce and sell widgets are price takers.

Is the stock market a perfectly competitive market? Are sellers of stock *price takers*?

Is the widget market a perfectly competitive market? On the one hand, we notice that the widget market does not meet all four conditions of perfect competition. For example, there are only a few sellers in the widget market, not many sellers. On the other hand, firms (sellers) in the widget market are price takers. Is it more important to meet all four conditions or to be a price taker? According to an economist, it is more important to be a price taker. As long as firms in a market are price takers, then the market need not meet all four conditions of perfect competition to be considered perfectly competitive.

The reason the conditions of perfect competition are identified in the first place is that when these conditions are met by a market, sellers in that market are often price takers. In other words, usually but not always, the four conditions and price taking go together.

What Does a Perfectly Competitive Firm Do?

Every firm has two major questions to answer:

1. How much of our product do we produce?
2. What price do we charge for our product?

How does a perfectly competitive firm answer these questions? Chapter 6 explained how any firm answers the first question: it produces the quantity of output at which marginal revenue equals marginal cost.

How does the perfectly competitive firm answer the second question? It has no choice on what price to charge for its product. It has to sell its product at the equilibrium price, because it is a price taker. If the equilibrium price is $10, then that is the price it charges, not $10.01 or $9.99. In summary, perfectly competitive firms produce the quantity of output at which marginal revenue equals marginal cost, and they charge the equilibrium price (determined in the market by supply and demand) for that product.

Every firm has to answer two questions: (1) How much of our product do we produce? and (2) What price do we charge?

Profit in a Perfectly Competitive Market

Suppose there are 200 firms (sellers) in market X, a perfectly competitive market. Each of the firms is producing good X and selling it for its current equilibrium price, $10. Furthermore, all 200 firms are earning profits. Will things stay as they are currently? Not likely.

According to condition 4, there is easy entry into a perfectly competitive market. Firms that are not currently in market X will notice that firms in market X are earning profits. The firms not in market X will want to earn profits, too. There is nothing stopping them from earning the profits: all they have to do is enter market X. After all, it is easy to enter market X, a perfectly competitive market.

As new firms enter market X, the number of firms in the market rises, say from 200 to 250. With more firms, the supply of good X increases. And when the supply of a good rises, equilibrium price falls. Furthermore, as price falls, so does profit. Profit, remember, is total revenue (price times number of units sold) minus total cost. In this case, as price falls, so do total revenue and profit.

Firms will enter market X until there is no longer a reason to do so—when there is no more profit. When profit has fallen to zero and total revenue is exactly equal to total cost, firms will no longer have a monetary incentive to enter into market X.

In a perfectly competitive market, then, profit acts as a signal to firms not in the market. It says, "Come over here and get me." As new firms gravitate toward the

If there is easy entry into the microchip market, and new firms enter that market, what will happen to the supply of microchips?

You read in the newspaper that high profits are being earned by many of the firms in the computer market. Assuming that there is easy entry into the computer market, what do you predict will happen to profits in the future? Explain your answer.

profit, they increase the supply of the good that is earning profit and thus lower its price. As they lower its price, the profit dissipates. The process ends when there is no longer an incentive for firms to enter the market to obtain profit:

Profit exists ➡ New firms enter the market ➡ Supply rises ➡ Price falls ➡ Price falls until there is no longer an incentive for firms to enter the market

Profits May Be Taxed Away

Suppose we go back to the point in time when the 200 firms in market X were all earning profits. Now suppose a member of Congress says, "The firms in market X are earning huge profits. They do not deserve them; they just happened to be in the right place at the right time. The demand for the product they produced increased, and price followed. Soon after price went up, the companies started earning high profits. We ought to tax these profits, and I propose a special tax on these profits of 100 percent."

If Congress begins to tax profits at a higher rate, how might this affect you as a consumer?

Congress goes along with this member, enacts a special tax on the profits of the firms in market X, and taxes away these profits. With the profits taxed away, there is no reason for firms not currently in market X to enter it. But if no new firms enter market X, the supply of good X will not rise, and the price of good X will not then fall. This leaves consumers paying a higher price than they would have had to pay if the profits of the 200 firms had not been taxed away.

The tax had an intended and unintended effect. Its intended effect was to tax away the profits of the 200 firms. The unintended effect was that consumers ended up paying a higher price for good X than they would have paid without the tax.

Section 1 Review

Defining Terms

1. Define
   a. price taker
   b. market structure

Reviewing Facts and Concepts

2. What does it mean to say that there is easy entry into a market and easy exit out of the market?
3. What quantity of output does a perfectly competitive firm produce? What price does it charge for its product?

Critical Thinking

4. Some of the 200 firms in market X, a perfectly competitive market, are incurring losses. How will these losses influence (a) exit out of the market, (b) the supply of the good produced in the market, and (c) the price of the good? Explain your answers.

Applying Economic Concepts

5. How can a seller determine whether it is a price taker or not?

SECTION 2

Monopoly

Monopoly, this section's topic, is the opposite of perfect competition. As you read this section, keep these key questions in mind:

- What are the characteristics of a monopoly?
- What are examples of barriers to entry?
- Do monopolists ever face competition?

The Characteristics of Monopoly

Here are the three conditions that characterize a **monopoly:**

1. *There is one seller.* Contrast this with perfect competition, where there are many sellers.
2. *The single seller sells a product for which there are no close substitutes.* Because there are no close substitutes for its product, the single seller— the monopolist—faces little, if any, competition.
3. *There are extremely high barriers to entry, which means that entry into the market is extremely difficult.* In a perfectly competitive market, it is easy for a firm to enter the market. Entering a monopoly market is very hard, if not impossible. There are extremely high **barriers to entry,** things that keep new firms out of the market. The nature of these barriers is discussed shortly.

There is a vast desert and only one place to buy water. Is the owner of the water a monopolist?

How Monopolists Differ from Perfect Competitors

Suppose firm Z is a monopoly firm that produces and sells good Z. Currently, it charges $10 per unit and sells 10,000 units a month. If firm Z raises the price of its product to $12, will it still be able to sell some of its product? The answer is yes. After all, there are no close substitutes (condition 2) for good Z and no other seller that sells good Z (condition 1). However, firm Z won't be able to sell as many units of good Z at the higher price ($12) as at the lower price ($10). For example, it may sell 9,000 units if it charges $12 a unit, whereas it sold 10,000 units when it charged $10 a unit.

Firm Z, the monopoly firm, is a **price searcher.** In contrast with a price taker, a price searcher can sell some of its product at various prices (for example, at $12, $11, $10, $9, and so on). Whereas a price taker has to "take" one price—the equilibrium price—and sell its product at that price, the price searcher has a list of prices from which to choose.

Key Terms

monopoly
barrier to entry
price searcher
public franchise
natural monopoly

MINI GLOSSARY

monopoly A market structure in which (1) there is a single seller, (2) the seller sells a product for which there are no close substitutes, and (3) there are extremely high barriers to entry.

barrier to entry Anything that prohibits a firm from entering a market.

price searcher A seller that can sell some of its output at various prices.

Which of the many possible prices is the best price? To answer this question, back up and consider the two questions that the monopoly firm, like any firm, has to answer: (1) How much do we produce? (2) How much do we charge? The monopoly firm, like any firm, will produce that quantity of output at which marginal revenue equals marginal cost. Suppose that for a particular monopoly firm this quantity turns out to be 20,000 units. What is the best price to charge for each unit? The best price turns out to be the highest price at which all 20,000 units can be sold. If at $14, only 15,000 units of the 20,000 units are sold, then $14 is not the best price. But if at $13, all 20,000 units can be sold, then $13 is the best price. Again, the monopoly firm seeks to charge the best price possible, which is the highest price at which it can sell its entire output.

The monopoly firm, however, faces a problem: it does not know what its best price is. It has to search for it through a process of trial and error. It may charge one price this week, only to change it next week. Over time, a monopoly firm finds the highest price at which it can sell its entire output.

How Selling Corn or Stock Differs from Selling Cable Television Service

Perhaps nothing brings home the difference between a perfectly competitive seller (a price taker) and a monopoly seller (a price searcher) than placing yourself in the role of each. First, suppose you are a corn farmer in Iowa. You have just harvested 100,000 bushels of corn, and you want to sell them as quickly as possible. It's easy to determine at what price you sell your corn: you just check the newspaper or listen to the crop report on the radio or TV news to see what price corn is selling at. That's the price you take for your corn.

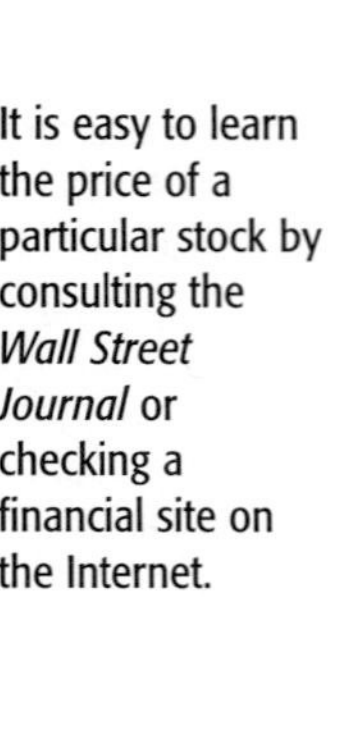

It is easy to learn the price of a particular stock by consulting the *Wall Street Journal* or checking a financial site on the Internet.

Now, suppose you own 100 shares of stock that you want to sell. How do you decide at what price to sell your stock? Again, it's easy: you just check the price of your stock by looking in the newspaper, accessing the Internet, or calling up a stockbroker. Whatever price is quoted is the price at which you sell your stock.

Now say you own a cable television company. In many towns only one cable company is allowed to serve a certain geographic area; therefore, you are a monopolist. The cable wire has been laid across town, and you are ready for business. What do you charge for your cable service? The answer is not so easy this time. There is no "cable television report," the way there is a crop report. No newspapers list cable television prices the way they list stock prices. Thus, while it is rather easy for firms to determine their selling prices in perfectly competitive markets, price determination is not so easy in monopolistic markets.

The Boston Tea Party

The original meaning of *monopoly* was an exclusive right to sell something. For example, a king might grant someone in his favor a monopoly, which entitled the person to be the sole producer and seller of a good. The king could fine or imprison anyone who dared to compete. It would be similar today to granting a particular company the right to be the only producer and seller of computers, cars, or houses.

The issue of monopoly is important in the early history of the United States. In 1767 the British Parliament passed the Townshend Acts, which imposed taxes (duties) on various products that were imported into the American colonies. These taxes were so hated in the colonies that they prompted protest and noncompliance. They were repealed in 1770, except for one: the British Parliament left the tax on tea to show the colonists that it had the right to raise tax revenue without seeking colonial approval. To get around the tax, the colonists started to buy tea from Dutch traders.

Then, in 1773, the British East India Company was in financial trouble. The company sought a special privilege—a monopoly—from the British Parliament. Parliament complied and passed the Tea Act, which granted the British East India Company the sole right (the monopoly right) on all tea exported to the colonies. The act declared that the only tea that colonists could legally buy was tea that was carried on East India Company ships and sold through its agents.

The combination of the tax on tea and the grant of monopoly to the East India Company greatly angered many of the colonists. On a cold December 16 night in 1773, sixty colonists dressed up as Mohawks and boarded three ships in Boston Harbor. On board the ships were 342 chests of tea owned by the East India Company. The colonists opened the chests and threw the tea into Boston Harbor.

This act so infuriated King George III and the British Parliament that they decided to retaliate against the colonists. In 1774, Parliament passed the Coercive Acts, which hurt the colonists in many ways. The acts threatened the economic life of the colonists by stipulating that the Boston port would be closed and enforced by a blockade until the taxes and damages were paid on the tea. The acts also allowed the king to appoint government officials in the colonies who until then had been elected by the colonists. Local authorities were given the right to find suitable quarters (in colonists' houses) for British troops. The Coercive Acts made the colonists angrier than before. Two years later, the colonists declared their independence from England, and the American Revolutionary War began.

QUESTION TO ANSWER How does the definition of *monopoly* in this feature differ from the definition stated earlier in this chapter?

Is the Sky the Limit for the Monopolist?

Suppose a pharmaceutical company has recently invented a new medicine that cures arthritis. With respect to this medicine, the pharmaceutical company is a monopolist; it is the only seller of a medicine for which there are no close substitutes. Can the pharmaceutical company charge any price it wants for the medicine? For example, can it charge $5,000 for one bottle (24 pills) of medicine? If your answer is yes, ask yourself if the company can charge $10,000 for one bottle. If your answer is still yes, ask yourself if the company can charge $20,000 for one bottle.

The purpose of these questions is to get you to realize that there is a limit to how high a price a monopolist can charge. The sky is not the limit. At some high prices in our example, no one is willing to buy the medicine.

Exhibit 7-1

Is the Sky the Limit for the Monopolist?

Once a monopoly firm has decided on its quantity of output, it is limited to the highest price it can charge (per unit) for the product. Specifically, it is limited by the height of the demand curve. In this case the monopoly firm has decided to produce 500,000 bottles of medicine. The highest price it can charge (per unit) and sell this output is $100 per bottle.

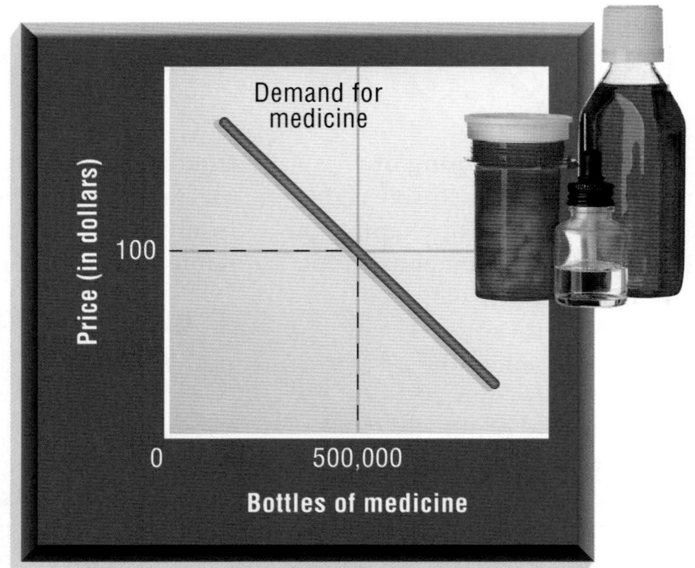

The monopolist is limited by the height of the demand curve it faces. Suppose the demand curve in Exhibit 7-1 is the demand curve for the medicine that cures arthritis and that the pharmaceutical company has decided to produce 500,000 bottles of medicine. As you can see, the highest price (per bottle) that can be charged for each bottle of 500,000 bottles is determined by the height of the demand curve, $100 per bottle. The sky is not the limit; the height of the demand curve (at the quantity of output the firm wants to sell) is the limit.

A Monopoly Seller Is Not Guaranteed Profits

Most people think that if a firm is a monopoly seller, it has to earn profits. This is not true, however; no monopoly seller is guaranteed profits. A firm earns profits only if the price it sells its good for is above its average total cost.[1] For example, if a firm sells its good for $10 and average total cost (per-unit cost) is $6, then it earns $4 profit per unit. If it sells 1,000 units, its profit is $4,000.

The monopolist sells its product for the highest price possible, but there is no guarantee that this price is greater than the monopoly seller's average total cost. If it is not, the monopoly seller does not earn any profits. If average total cost for the monopoly seller is actually higher than the highest possible price for which it sells its product, the monopoly seller earns a loss (not a profit). If this situation continues, the monopoly seller will go out of business.

1. If it makes things easier, think of price as "per-unit price" and average total cost as "per-unit cost."

Technology & Innovation

Is the Internet the Enemy of Monopolists?

Many college campuses have only one bookstore. Professors tell the campus bookstore manager the books they want their students to buy, and the bookstore orders the books. During the first weeks of classes, students usually go to the bookstore and buy the books they need. They often complain about the high price of textbooks; it is not uncommon for textbooks to sell for between $80 and $100.

Many college students have felt that to a large degree, the campus bookstore acts as a monopolist. It is a single seller of a good (required textbooks) for which there are no substitutes (the student has to buy the book the professor is using in class, not a book that is similar), and usually the university administration will not allow more than one bookstore on campus (so barriers to entry are high). In a way, we might consider the campus bookstore a geographic monopoly: it is the single seller of a good with no good substitutes and high barriers to entry in a certain location—the university campus.

Enter the Internet, which has, to a large degree, destroyed many geographic monopolies. College students no longer have to buy their textbooks from their campus bookstore; they can buy them from an online bookstore like Amazon.com, which promises a discount on books it sells. In other words, the Internet has essentially eliminated the barrier to entering any campus's textbook market.

Similarly, some people think that the Internet has eliminated geographic monopolies in cars, although the case is less strong here. Suppose you live in a town where there is only one Ford dealership. It is true that the dealership may be the sole seller of Fords within a certain area (say, a radius of 40 miles), but there is a substitute for a Ford (for example, a Honda). Nevertheless, it is possible for a single Ford dealership to have a certain degree of monopoly power. If you want a Ford, you are inclined to go to that Ford dealership.

Again, the Internet has changed that situation. First, there are online sites where you can obtain the invoice price of any car you are thinking about buying. Second, you can contact Ford dealers in nearby areas via the Internet and ask them if they are willing to sell you a Ford for, say, $1,500 over invoice price. Now, instead of negotiating with the only Ford dealership in town, you can negotiate with several dealerships over the Internet.

QUESTION TO ANSWER The Internet is used to weaken geographic monopolies in textbooks and cars. Can you identify any other kinds of geographic monopolies threatened by the Internet?

Barriers to Entry

Suppose firm X is a monopolist. It is currently charging a relatively high price for its product and earning large profits. Why don't other businesses enter the market and produce the same product as firm X? As noted, there are high barriers to entry into a monopoly market. They include legal barriers, a monopolist's extremely low average total costs, and a monopolist's exclusive ownership of a scarce resource.

MINI GLOSSARY

public franchise A right granted to a firm by government that permits the firm to provide a particular good or service and excludes all others from doing so.

Legal Barriers Legal barriers to entry in a monopoly market include public franchises, patents, and copyrights. A **public franchise** is a right granted to a firm by government that permits the firm to provide a particular good or service and excludes all others from doing so. Potential competition is thus eliminated by law. For example, as stated earlier, in many towns only one cable company is allowed to service a particular geographic area (for example, the west side of town). This company has been given the exclusive right to produce and sell cable television. If an organization other than the designated company were to start producing and selling cable television, it would be breaking the law.

In the United States, a patent is granted to the inventor of a product or process for twenty years. For example, a pharmaceutical company may have a patent on a medicine. During this time, the patent holder is shielded from competitors; no one else can legally produce and sell the patented product or process. Some people argue that patents are necessary to encourage innovation, because few people would waste their time and money trying to invent a new product if their competitors could immediately copy the product and sell it.

Copyrights give authors or originators of literary or artistic productions the right to publish, print, or sell their intellectual productions for a period of time. With books, either the author or the company that published the book holds the copyright. For example, the publishing company holds the copyright to this textbook—it owns the right to reproduce and sell copies of this book. Anyone else who copies the book or large sections of it to sell or simply to avoid buying a copy is breaking the law.

Copyright laws and patents are designed to protect the original work of authors, musicians, inventors, and others. Why are these laws important?

Extremely Low Average Total Costs (Low Per-Unit Costs)

Chapter 6 described average total cost as total cost divided by quantity of output, also called *per-unit cost.* For example, if total cost is $1,000 and quantity of output is 1,000 units, then average total cost is $1 per unit.

In some industries, firms have an average total cost that is extremely low—so low that no other firm can compete with this firm. To see why, let's consider the relationship of average total cost and price. A business will earn a per-unit profit when it sells its product for a price that is higher than its average total cost.

Some companies may have such a low average total cost that they are able to lower their prices to a very low level and still earn profits.

A Taxi Ride in New York City

It is easy for new firms to enter some markets and difficult for them to enter others. Difficulty in entering a market is usually caused by the existence of some barrier to entry. Of course, not all barriers to entry are the same. One kind is created through legal means. For example, when the government specifies that no firm can compete with the U.S. Postal Service in the delivery of first-class mail, it has effectively created a legal barrier to entering the business of delivering first-class mail.

With this as background, suppose you go to New York City. You visit Rockefeller Center and Madison Square Garden; you take a tour of the Empire State Building and the Statue of Liberty; you go to a Broadway play at night. In your travels around New York City, you notice taxicabs picking up and delivering people. You wonder what you or anyone else would need to do to enter the taxicab market in New York City.

Let's list the things that sound reasonable. You would need a car and a driver's license. Perhaps the city of New York would want to make sure that you did not have a criminal record, so you might need to pass a personnel check.

In reality, the Taxi and Limousine Commission in New York City requires that you also have a taxi license, called a *taxi medallion.* It is sort of like a business license: you need it to lawfully operate a taxicab business in New York City. In 1999 the price of a taxi medallion was $215,000.[a]

The high price of a taxi medallion acts as a barrier to entering the taxicab market in New York City. Who gains and who loses as a result of this barrier to entry? The beneficiaries are clearly the current owners of taxicab businesses. Because of such a high barrier to entering the taxicab business, the supply of taxis on the streets of New York City is less than it otherwise would be. If supply is lower than it would be, then prices are higher. In other words, the price of a taxi ride in New York City is likely to be less if a taxi medallion cost, say, $300 than if it cost $225,000. At the latter price, fewer people will be entering the taxicab business and expanding the supply of taxis for hire. The losers are (1) people who would like to enter the taxicab business but cannot and (2) the taxi riders who pay higher prices because of the somewhat restricted entry into the taxicab business.

a. The price of a taxi medallion changes over time. For example, in 1976 it was about $45,000; in 1988 it was about $125,000; and in 1999 it was $215,000. The number of medallions issued is fixed by state legislation at around 12,000, a number that has remained constant for about fifty years. To obtain information about current medallion prices, you may visit the Taxi and Limousine Commission Web site at http://www.ci.nyc.ny.us./html.tlc/

QUESTION TO ANSWER As a result of the high price of a taxi medallion, taxi fares are higher than they would be if taxi medallion prices were lower. Do you agree or disagree?

Consequently, competitors may be forced out of business. Suppose seventeen companies are currently competing to sell a good. One of the companies, however, has a much lower average total cost than the others. Say company A's average total cost is $5, whereas the other companies' average total cost is $8. Company A can sell its good for $6, earn a $1 profit on each unit sold. Other companies cannot compete with it. In the end, company A, because of its low average total cost, is the only seller of the good; such a firm is called a **natural monopoly.**

What might explain why some companies have lower average total costs than other companies that produce the same good?

MINI GLOSSARY

natural monopoly A firm with such a low average total cost (per-unit cost) that only it can survive in the market.

Exclusive Ownership of a Scarce Resource It takes oranges to produce orange juice. Suppose one firm owned all the oranges; it would be considered a monopoly firm. The classic example of a monopolist that controls a resource is the Aluminum Company of America (Alcoa). For a long time, this company controlled almost all sources of bauxite (the main source of aluminum) in the United States, making Alcoa the sole producer of aluminum in the country from the late nineteenth century until the 1940s.

Government Monopoly and Market Monopoly

As we have seen, sometimes high barriers to entry exist because competition is legally prohibited, and sometimes they exist for other reasons. Where high barriers take the form of public franchises, patents, or copyrights, competition is legally prohibited. In contrast, where high barriers take the form of one firm's low average total cost or exclusive ownership of a resource, competition is not legally prohibited. In these cases, there is no law to keep rival firms from entering the market and competing, even though they may choose not to do so.

Some economists use the term *government monopoly* to refer to monopolies that are legally protected from competition. They use the term *market monopoly* to refer to monopolies that are not legally protected from competition.

Section 2 Review

Defining Terms

1. Define

- **a.** barrier to entry
- **b.** natural monopoly
- **c.** price searcher

Reviewing Facts and Concepts

2. When it comes to determining the quantity of goods to produce, a monopolist is like a perfect competitor. How so?

3. A monopolist is a price searcher. For what price is the monopolist searching?

Critical Thinking

4. Firm A is a perfectly competitive firm, and firm B is a monopoly firm. Both firms are currently earning profits. Which firm is less likely to be earning profits in the future? Explain your answer.

Applying Economic Concepts

5. The demand for the good that firm A sells does not rise or fall during the month, yet firm A raises its price at the beginning of the month and lowers its price at the end of the month. What might explain firm A's pricing behavior?

SECTION 3

Monopolistic Competition

Between perfect competition at one extreme and monopoly at the other, there are two types of markets: monopolistic competition and oligopoly.

As you read this section, which discusses monopolistic competition, keep these key questions in mind:

- What are the characteristics of monopolistic competition?
- What are some examples of monopolistic competition?
- Are monopolistic competitors price takers or price searchers?

monopolistic competition
A market structure in which (1) there are many buyers and many sellers, (2) sellers produce and sell slightly differentiated products, and (3) there is easy entry into and easy exit from the market.

Key Term
monopolistic competition

The Characteristics of Monopolistic Competition

Three conditions characterize **monopolistic competition**:

1. *There are many buyers and many sellers.* A monopolistic competitive market has many buyers and many sellers, as does a perfectly competitive market.
2. *Firms produce and sell slightly differentiated products.* In a perfectly competitive market, all firms produce and sell identical products. In a monopoly there is only one firm, and it produces a unique product—one for which there are no close substitutes. A monopolistic competitive market has many firms, each producing a product that is slightly different from other firms' products. For example, McDonald's hamburgers and Burger King's hamburgers are slightly differentiated products.
3. *There is easy entry into and exit from the market.* Monopolistic competition resembles perfect competition in having no barriers, legal or otherwise, to entry or exit.

McDonald's and Burger King sell hamburgers, but McDonald's hamburgers are slightly differentiated from Burger King's hamburgers. Are McDonald's and Burger King monopolistic competitors?

Monopolistic Competitive Firms Are Price Searchers

Monopolistic competitive markets thus have some things in common with perfectly competitive markets: both markets have many buyers and many sellers as well as easy entry and exit. Because of these commonalities, it would be easy to conclude that just as a seller in a perfectly competitive market is a price taker, so must a seller in a monopolistic competitive market be a price taker. That, however, is the wrong conclusion. Monopolistic competitive sellers are price searchers, largely because they sell a slightly differentiated product (condition 2). Suppose firm A is a

monopolistic competitive firm or seller. It is currently producing and selling good A at $40 per unit. At this price, it sells 1,000 units a week. If it raises its price to $45, it is likely to still sell some of its product (say, 700 units), because what it sells is not identical to any other product in the market. In other words, consumers will not be able to shift wholly from buying good A to buying an identical good; good A is slightly different from all other goods.

In summary, because monopolistic competitive firms produce and sell slightly different products, they are price searchers. They can sell some of their product at various prices.

There are many coffee shops. Is a coffee shop a monopolistic competitive firm?

What Do Monopolistic Competitive Firms Do?

Like perfectly competitive firms and monopoly firms, monopolistic competitive firms have to answer two questions: (1) How much do we produce? and (2) What price do we charge? They answer the first question the same way every firm answers it: they produce the quantity of output at which marginal revenue equals marginal cost. They answer the second question the same way monopoly sellers answer it: by searching for the highest price per unit at which they can sell their entire output. If they have produced 10,000 units of their good, they search for the highest per-unit price at which they can sell all 10,000 units.

How Are Monopolistic Competitors' Products Different?

When we say that one product is slightly different from another product, to what are we referring? When we say that McDonald's hamburgers are slightly different from Burger King's hamburgers, for example, the word *different* refers to taste and appearance. McDonald's hamburgers look and taste slightly different (to most people) from Burger King's hamburers. Products can differ in other ways, too.

This late 1990s gas station has chosen a rather unique and creative way to differentiate its product. Why do you think this strategy might be effective, or not effective?

For example, consider a particular brand of gasoline sold at a gas station at Third Avenue and Main Street and at a gas station at Ninth Avenue and Main Street. Is the gasoline at the two stations identical? Certainly the physical properties are the same, but the gasoline is sold at different locations, and the locational differences may affect the choices of the buyers of the gasoline. For example, suppose the gas station at Third and Main is in a dangerous neighborhood, and the gas station at Ninth and Main is in a safe neighborhood. Consumers may perceive gas sold in a safe neighborhood as slightly different from gas sold in a dangerous neighborhood. In other words, the location at which a product is sold may be enough to differentiate one physically identical product from another.

The location of a seller may matter to buyers. Do you prefer to buy gas at some locations instead of other locations?

Monopolistic competitors' products, then, can be different in any way that is perceived as different by consumers. If location makes a difference to consumers, then two physically identical products sold at different locations are slightly different products. If different credit terms, sales service, or delivery options make two physically identical products different in the minds of consumers, then they are slightly different products. In short, when it comes to buying products, the physical properties of a product may not be all that matters to consumers. How the product is packaged, where it is purchased, from whom it is purchased, and whether or not it is delivered may all matter (make a difference) to consumers.

Many Monopolistic Competitors Would Rather Be Monopolists

Suppose you own a business that is considered a monopolistic competitive firm. Your business is one of many sellers, you sell a product slightly differentiated from the products of your competitors, and there is easy entry into and exit from the industry. Would you rather your business were a monopolist firm instead? Wouldn't it be better for you to be the only seller of a product than to be one of many sellers?

Most business owners would say it is indeed better to be a monopolist firm than a monopolistic competitive firm, because they believe that as a monopolist they would face less competition. How do monopolistic competitors go about trying to become monopolists?

Some monopolistic competitors use advertising. If a monopolistic competitor can, through advertising, persuade the buying public that its product is more than slightly differentiated from those of its competitors, it stands a better chance of becoming a monopolist. For example, many firms produce men's and women's jeans, and many people think the jeans produced by these firms look very much alike. How, then, does any one of

the firms differentiate its product from the pack? Some companies add designer labels to their jeans to suggest that they are uniquely desirable—that one would want to wear only Levi's jeans, or only Guess jeans. Or through advertising, a firm could try to persuade the buying public that its jeans are worn by the most famous, best-looking people living and vacationing in the most exciting places in the world. Whether or not the advertising is successful in meeting its objective is not the issue here. The point is that through advertising, firms sometimes try to differentiate their products from their competitors' products.

Firms will sometimes try to differentiate their products (from their competitors' products) by adding a designer label. Do designer labels influence your buying decisions?

What Matters Is How Much Competition a Seller Faces

One of the major differences between sellers in different market structures is how much competition a seller in each market faces. How much competition a seller faces—much, some, very little, none—principally depends on two factors: how close to unique a seller's product is, and how easy it is for new sellers to enter the market.

How much competition a seller faces depends on two factors: (1) how unique a seller's product is and (2) how easy it is to enter the market. Do you think the makers of aspirin face much competition?

Consider a seller in each of the three market structures with respect to these two factors. In perfect competition, a seller does not produce and sell a unique product at all: it produces and sells a product identical to that of other sellers. The seller is in a very competitive position, because if it raises the price of its product by only 1 penny over equilibrium price, consumers can turn to other sellers to purchase the identical product. A seller in a perfectly competitive market faces stiff competition from other sellers currently in the market, as well as potentially stiff competition from new sellers who may join the market. After all, in perfect competition, there is easy entry into the market. In short, a seller in a perfectly competitive market faces stiff competition from both current sellers and potential sellers.

THE BORN LOSER ® by Art and Chip Sansom

THE BORN LOSER reprinted by permission of Newspaper Enterprise Association, Inc.

Things are somewhat different for the monopolistic competitive seller. This seller does not face as much competition from current sellers, because it produces and sells a product that is slightly different from that of other sellers. A rise in the price of its good will not cause all its customers to leave it and head for its competitors, because it sells a product that is slightly different from that of its competitors. Still, the monopolistic competitor has the same problem as the perfect competitor when it comes to potential competitors: there is easy entry into a monopolistic competitive market, just as in a perfectly competitive market. New sellers can be just around the corner waiting to take away some of a current monopolistic competitor's business.

How much competition does a monopoly seller face? It faces less competition than either a perfect competitor or a monopolistic competitor. It sells a product for which there are no close substitutes. Consumers buying from monopoly sellers have fewer options available to them than they do when they buy from perfect competitors or monopolistic competitors. For example, if a monopolistic competitor raises price too high, provides poor service, or lowers quality, many consumers will choose to walk away and buy from the seller's competition. But it's not that easy to walk away from a monopoly seller, because no sellers sell a close substitute for the monopoly seller's products. In short, the monopoly seller does not have to be afraid of competition, because there really is not much. Furthermore, competition is not likely to increase, because there are barriers to entering the monopoly market.

Section 3 Review

Reviewing Facts and Concepts

1. What are the three conditions that characterize monopolistic competition?
2. How might monopolistic competitors' products be slightly different?
3. Monopolistic competition shares some things with perfect competition and some things with monopoly. Explain.

Critical Thinking

4. In what way or ways are a monopoly, a monopolistic competitor, and a perfect competitor alike?

Applying Economic Concepts

5. Identify an action of a real-world monopolistic competitor that is trying to turn itself into a monopolist.

SECTION 4

Oligopoly

The fourth market structure is oligopoly. As you read about it in this section, keep these key questions in mind:

- What are the characteristics of oligopoly?
- What are some examples of oligopoly?
- Are oligopolists price takers or price searchers?
- What are cartel agreements?

Steel is a homogeneous product produced in an oligopolistic market.

The Characteristics of Oligopoly

Key Terms

oligopoly
cartel agreement

The following three conditions characterize **oligopoly:**

1. *There are few sellers.* An oligopolistic market has only a few sellers. Each seller is aware that its actions affect the other sellers and that the actions of the other sellers affect it. For example, General Motors and Ford Motor Company are considered oligopolists. Economists assume that General Motors and Ford know that what each does influences what the other does. General Motors knows, for example, that if it comes out with a new, sporty car and lowers prices on its existing cars, Ford may follow suit.
2. *Firms produce and sell either identical or slightly differentiated products.* Steel is a homogeneous or identical product produced in an oligopolistic market; in other words, every firm's steel is the same as every other firm's steel. Cars are a slightly differentiated product produced in an oligopolistic market. Ford's cars are slightly different from cars of General Motors.
3. *There are significant barriers to entry, which means that entry into the market is difficult.* Often, firms in the market have such low average total costs that new firms are afraid to enter the market and compete. Patents and exclusive control over an essential resource also act as barriers to entry. Exhibit 7-2 lists the conditions that characterize each of the four market structures discussed in this chapter.

oligopoly
A market structure in which (1) there are few sellers, (2) sellers produce and sell either identical or slightly differentiated products, and (3) there are significant barriers to entry.

Exhibit 7-2

Conditions that Characterize Various Market Structures

Market structure	Number of sellers	Type of product	Barriers to entry	Control over price	Examples of products and services sold in this type of market
Perfect competition	Many	Identical	No barriers	No control	Wheat, corn, stocks
Monopoly	One	Unique	Extremely high barriers	Considerable amount of control	Water, electricity, delivery of first-class mail
Monopolistic competition	Many	Slightly differentiated	No barriers	Yes, but not as much as in monopoly	Clothing, meals at restaurants
Oligopoly	Few	Identical or slightly differentiated	Significantly high barriers	Yes, but not as much as in monopoly	Cars, cereal

Oligopoly Firms Are Price Searchers

Like monopoly and monopolistic competitive firms, oligopoly firms are price searchers, for several reasons. First, oligopolists may produce slightly differentiated products (condition 2). Second, it is difficult for new firms to enter the market (condition 3). And third, oligopolists have some measure of control over price. In short, oligopolists can sell some of their output at various prices.

U.S. automobile manufacturers face stiff competition from German, Japanese, and other foreign car manufacturers.

How Much Competition Do Oligopolists Face?

The last section developed a way to think about sellers in various markets. We think about, or categorize, sellers according to how much competition they face. In turn, how much competition a seller faces depends on how close to unique a seller's product is and how easy it is for new sellers to enter the market and compete with it. With this as background, let's discuss oligopoly.

How close to unique is an oligopolist's product? According to the conditions that characterize oligopoly, an oligopolist's product is not unique. Some oligopolists produce an identical good (steel), and others produce a slightly differentiated product (cars). We would expect, then, that an oligopolistic seller faces fairly intense competition from current sellers. For example, Ford Motor Company faces stiff competition from General Motors and Chrysler, two U.S. companies. In the world market for cars, Ford faces extremely stiff competition from Japanese car companies such as Toyota, Nissan, Honda, and Mitsubishi.

Where the oligopolistic seller does not face too much competition is from potential sellers. It is difficult to enter an oligopolistic market, so current oligopolistic sellers are shielded from new sellers to some degree.

Identifying Oligopolistic Industries

Economists determine whether a market is oligopolistic by looking at the percentage of sales accounted for by the top four firms in the industry. If only a few firms account for a large percentage of sales, then the market is considered oligopolistic. For example, suppose there are ten firms in an industry, and the total revenue of the industry is $100 million. The four firms with the highest sales generate $80 million in revenue. In other words, the top four firms account for 80 percent of total revenues in the industry (because $80 million is 80 percent of $100 million), and the industry is dominated by the top four firms. It is an example of an oligopolistic market.

Now consider a real-world example. The U.S. automobile industry is largely made up of General Motors, Ford Motor Company, and Chrysler Corporation. Together, these three firms account for about 90 percent of American-made cars sold in the United States. Other examples of oligopolistic markets include industries that produce cigarettes, tires and inner tubes, cereal breakfast foods, farm machinery, and soap and detergents.

The car market and the breakfast cereal market are both considered oligopolistic markets.

Oligopoly and Interdependence: Looking over Your Shoulder

Oligopoly differs from other market structures in terms of the number of sellers. There are many sellers in both perfect competition and monopolistic competition, and only one seller in monopoly. Only in oligopoly are there only a few sellers.

Will a seller act differently if it is one of only a few sellers than if it is one of many? There is some evidence that when a seller is one of only a few sellers, it is more likely to base its behavior on what other sellers do than if it is one of many sellers. Consider the airline market, which is con-

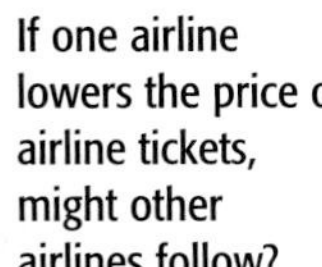

If one airline lowers the price of airline tickets, might other airlines follow?

cartel agreement An agreement that specifies that the firms that entered into the agreement will act in a coordinated way to reduce the competition among them.

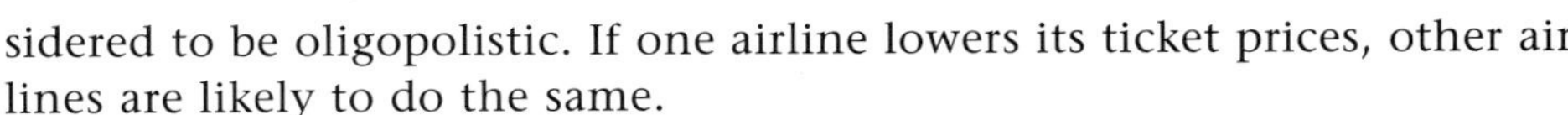

sidered to be oligopolistic. If one airline lowers its ticket prices, other airlines are likely to do the same.

Cartels

It is easier for the few sellers in an oligopolistic market to get together and discuss common issues than for the many sellers in either a perfectly competitive or a monopolistic competitive market to do the same. Why would sellers that compete with each other want to get together in the first place? One of the various reasons may be that they want to get together to try to eliminate or reduce the competition they present to one another.

If the CEOs of companies enter into a cartel agreement, they are breaking the law. Are cartel agreements anticompetive agreements? Do you think they hurt the consumer?

To illustrate, suppose there are three major car companies. Each year they compete with one another on such things as price, quality, style, and service. Over the years they realize that the competition between them actually helps the car consumer and hurts them. In the boardroom of one of the car companies, the chief executive officer (CEO) says, "Every time our competitors lower prices, we have to do the same thing; every time they come up with a new sport-utility vehicle or a better or safer sedan, we have to do the same thing. All this competition is great for the consumer, but it's not so good for our profits."

Suppose the CEO calls a meeting with the CEOs at the other two major car companies. They get together for a nice lunch somewhere and talk over their problems. At the end of the lunch they all agree that the competition among them is helpful to consumers but not so helpful to them, so they should try to reduce some of this competition. Specifically, they decide to keep prices where they currently are (no more discounts) and to stop coming up with new car models for the next two years.

The three CEOs have entered into a **cartel agreement,** an agreement that

Suppose automobile companies entered into a cartel agreement. How might car production be affected?

specifies that they will act in a coordinated way to reduce the competition among them and (they hope) raise their profits. In the United States, cartel agreements are illegal. But suppose that they were not illegal, so nothing prevented the CEOs from making the cartel agreement. What then? Many people would say that the CEOs would be successful at reducing their competition and increasing their profits. In other words, the cartel agreement would harm consumers and help the three car companies.

This answer assumes that the three car companies would actually hold to the cartel agreement. However, firms that enter into cartel agreements often break them. To see why, put yourself in the place of one of the three automobile company CEOs. You have just gotten back to your office after lunch with the other CEOs. You start to think about the cartel agreement you have just entered into and say to yourself, "I know I promised not to lower prices and not to develop any new model cars, but suppose I forget what I promised. Suppose I develop new car models and release them to the market next year. If my competitors hold to the cartel agreement, they will not release new models next year, and I will be the only car company with new models. My company should be able to take business away from our competitors. Instead of not competing with my competitors, why don't I just try to run them out of business?"

There is a strong monetary incentive, on the part of each of the CEOs, to break the promise made with the other CEOs. Each is likely to break the agreement in the hope of getting rid of his or her competition, once and for all. If all three break the agreement out of self-interest, there is no agreement. The three car companies are back where they started, competing with each other.

Even if cartel agreements were not illegal, therefore, they probably would not be much of a problem for consumers. Certainly sellers in the same market might try to make cartel agreements and would want them to hold, but it is not likely that they would hold. After all, once the agreement had been made, each seller that entered into it would have a sharp monetary incentive to break it and make itself much better off at the expense of its competitors. It's nearly impossible for companies to turn their backs on the chance to get rid of their competition.

The Organization of Petroleum Exporting Countries (OPEC) is one of the most successful cartels in history. Still, at times, members have cheated on the cartel. Visit the OPEC Web site http://www.opec.org and click on "About OPEC."

QUESTIONS TO ANSWER
1. To what is OPEC dedicated?
2. What countries make up OPEC?
3. What percentage of the world's oil is supplied by OPEC members?

Firms in the same industry must compete for customers. This puts firms in the same industry at odds with each other. Does NBC News wish CNN had never been created?

Is It Buyers against Sellers or Sellers against Sellers?

The noneconomist may think that the best interests of consumers or buyers are pitted against the best interests of producers or sellers. They may believe that buyers want to buy high-quality products at low prices. Sellers want to produce cheap products and sell them for high prices. Whatever is good for buyers is bad for sellers, and whatever is good for sellers is bad for buyers. In short, buyers and sellers are on different sides of the fence; it's sellers against buyers.

Putting things this way makes it sound as if buyers and sellers are natural enemies and that there is a war between them. However, this view does not accurately represent the forces at work. The real war may not be between buyers and sellers but among sellers. Sellers may indeed be on one side of the fence and buyers on the other side, but not all the sellers on the same side of the fence are happy with one another. Some want to get rid of other sellers so that there will be fewer sellers on the selling side of the fence. General Motors wants to get rid of Toyota so there will be fewer car companies. Dell, Inc., wants to get rid of Compaq so there will be fewer computer manufacturers. NBC wants to get rid of CBS, and NBC, CBS, and ABC wish that cable television had never come to exist.

Sellers may (initially) have interests opposed to those of consumers, but that does not mean sellers will get what they want at the expense of consumers. Often, what keeps sellers in line is other sellers—either other sellers currently in the market or sellers who may one day enter the market. In other words, it is the threat of actual or potential competition from other sellers that ends up aligning the interests of sellers with buyers.

Section 4 Review

Defining Terms

1. Define
   a. oligopoly
   b. cartel agreement

Reviewing Facts and Concepts

2. Why might a firm that voluntarily entered into a cartel agreement decide to cheat on (or breach) the agreement?
3. Why are oligopolistic firms price searchers?

Critical Thinking

4. If perfectly competitive firms are price takers and monopoly, monopolistic competitive, and oligopolistic firms are price searchers, then it follows that there are three times as many firms in the real world that are price searchers as are price takers. Do you agree or disagree? Explain your answer.

Applying Economic Concepts

5. Someone tells you that the firms in a particular industry are all selling their products for the same prices. Does it follow that the firms have entered into a cartel agreement?

Developing Economic

Skills

The Economics Paper: Finding a Topic

Suppose your economics teacher gives you the assignment of writing an essay on a topic of your choice. What topic would you choose? How would you go about researching it? How would you write it? These are some of the important questions we will answer as we discuss how to write a research paper, beginning in this chapter and continuing through Chapter 9. This chapter discusses how to find an economics topic to research and write about. Chapter 8 explains how to research the topic. Chapter 9 discusses how to write and rewrite the paper.

Before you start to look for a topic, take a moment to think about the purpose of the essay and your intended audience. Is your assignment to report the factual information that you have learned about your topic or to express an opinion and develop an argument that will support your case? Who is going to read your essay? Your choice of topic might be very different if you were writing for a school newspaper than if you were writing for your teacher. A few minutes spent thinking about your purpose and intended audience will help as you set about looking for a topic.

There are a number of ways to find a topic. You might make a list, as you read, of questions that you would like answered. For example, you have been reading about a number of topics in this book, such as supply and demand, opportunity costs, the free-enterprise system, prices, scarcity, business firms, and profit. Go back to a topic that you found interesting, and as you reread the pages, write down a question after every two or three paragraphs. For example, here are some of the questions that might come to mind as you read about business firms:

1. Why do some business firms earn higher profits than others do?
2. What determines where business firms will locate?
3. Do U.S. business firms face much competition from foreign business firms?
4. Do business firms do things differently today than, say, twenty years ago?

It is important to find questions that you find interesting. After all, you're the one who will be spending the time to research and write the essay. Besides, if you aren't interested in the topic of your essay, do you really think someone reading it will find it interesting?

At this stage, you should not be concerned with whether your questions make sense. You should simply write down the questions that come to mind. Free yourself to ask anything you want. Then, once you have written down a few questions, go back to see if any of the contains a topic to write about. For example, look at Question 3. This question contains a topic: "U.S. businesses and foreign competition." This phrase, then, could be the title of your economics paper.

When looking for a topic, do not limit your reading to economics textbooks. Economics topics can be found in news and business magazines (such as *Time, Newsweek, Forbes,* and *Fortune*), newspapers, encyclopedias, and elsewhere.

Perhaps you have trouble coming up with questions as you read. If so, think about the fact that newspaper reporters often think in terms of the following questions: Who? What? Where? When? How? and Why? For example, a news reporter who was assigned a story about a fire might begin by trying to get answers to those questions. She might ask, Who reported the fire? What damage has been done? Where did the fire start? When was the fire reported? How did the fire get so large? Why did the firefighters have trouble getting the blaze under control?

This method of asking questions about who, what, where, when, how, and why is effective in economics, too. It reminds us to ask questions that we might not ordinarily ask. Returning to the topic of business firms, for example, you might ask, What is the world's largest business firm? What does it produce? Where is it located? How did it become so large? It is unlikely that all six questions will be reasonable ones to ask about all economics topics, but many of these questions will serve as useful prompts to start you on your way to finding a good essay topic.

A common mistake of many students is to choose a topic that is too broad. For example, after reading this chapter, a student might consider writing about the topic "competition." That is an enormous topic about which many people have written entire books. You couldn't begin to address that topic within the scope of a brief paper, and any attempt would be very frustrating. In choosing an appropriate topic for your paper, try to narrow the question down to one that you can realistically expect to answer by the time you have finished and that you can answer in time to meet your assignment deadline.

Remember that selecting a topic is one of the most important aspects of writing an essay. Make sure you take the time to think about your audience, the purpose of the essay, and what is expected. Write down a lot of questions about an area that interests you, and one of these questions probably will contain a topic about which you will want to write. Taking the time to select an appropriate topic will pay off.

QUESTIONS TO ANSWER

1. Go back through this chapter and, for each numbered section, write three or four questions that you would like to have answered. Remember, free up your mind to ask any question that is interesting to you.
2. From the questions you generated in Question 1, choose one question from each section to rewrite in the form of a title for an economics paper. Follow the example developed in this feature.

CHAPTER 7

Review

Economics Vocabulary

Fill in the following blanks with the appropriate word or phrase.

1. The conditions that characterize _____ include the following: many sellers and many buyers; all firms sell an identical product; there is easy entry into the market and easy exit out of the market; and buyers and sellers have all relevant information about prices, product quality, sources of supply, and so on.
2. A(n) _____ is a seller that can sell all its output at the equilibrium price but none at 1 penny higher.
3. The conditions that characterize _____ include one seller, no close substitutes for the good the seller sells, and high barriers to entry.
4. A(n) _____ can sell some of its output at various prices, although it sells less output at higher prices.
5. A(n) _____ is a right granted to a firm by the government that permits the firm to provide a particular good or service and excludes all others from doing so.
6. A(n) _____ is a monopoly that is legally protected from competition.
7. A company that ends up being the only seller of a good because of its low average total cost is called a(n) _____.
8. The conditions that characterize _____ include many buyers and many sellers, firms that produce and sell slightly differentiated products, and easy entry into and exit from the market.
9. The conditions that characterize _____ include few sellers, firms that produce and sell either identical or slightly differentiated products, and significant barriers to entry.
10. An agreement among firms that specifies that they will act in a coordinated way to reduce the competition between them is called a(n) _____ agreement.

Review Questions

1. In perfect competition, buyers and sellers have all relevant information about prices, product quality, sources of supply, and so on. Give an example to illustrate what this means.
2. Firm A is a perfectly competitive firm. Why can't it sell its product for 1 penny higher than the equilibrium price?
3. Why don't perfectly competitive firms ever sell for less than the equilibrium price?
4. Explain how profits are competed away in a perfectly competitive market.
5. What are the two questions that every firm has to answer?
6. Why is a monopoly seller a price searcher?
7. In at least one sense, a perfectly competitive firm is like a monopoly firm. Each firm sells its product for the highest price possible. Do you agree or disagree? Explain your answer.
8. How can low average total costs (per-unit costs) act as a barrier to entry?
9. To become an attorney, a person must graduate from law school and pass a bar examination in one of the fifty states. Is the bar examination a barrier to entering the law market? Why or why not?
10. What keeps any profits the monopoly seller is earning from being competed away?
11. Do perfectly competitive firms decide how much to produce in a different way than monopoly firms do? Explain your answer.
12. Firms in a monopolistic competitive market produce slightly different products. In what ways might these products be slightly different?
13. What are the two principal determinants of how much competition a seller in a market faces?
14. Why might a cartel agreement be more likely in an oligopolistic market than in a monopolistic competitive market?
15. Explain why a firm that entered into a cartel agreement would cheat on or break that agreement.

Calculations

1. The average total cost for a firm is $4, price is $8, and quantity of output sold is 100 units. Compute the firm's profit.
2. A monopoly seller produces and sells 1,000 units of a good at a price of $49.99 per unit. Its total cost is $30,000. How much profit does it earn?
3. Consumers are willing to pay a maximum per-unit price of $10 if 1,000 units of a good are offered for

sale, and a maximum per-unit price of $8 if 1,500 units of the good are offered for sale. A monopoly seller offers 1,500 units for sale, and its per-unit cost is $9 per unit. Assuming the monopoly seller sells its output at the highest per-unit price possible, does it earn profit? If so, how much?

4. A firm can sell 1 unit of good X at $40, and it can sell one additional unit for every $1 reduction in price. Its marginal cost is constant at $34. How many units of the good should the firm produce?

Graphs

1. If you were to graph marginal revenue in Question 4 (in "Calculations") would you get a downward-sloping or upward-sloping curve? Explain your answer.
2. Exhibit 7-3a has partly described what happens in a competitive market when firms earn high profits. Fill in the missing boxes A through C.
3. Exhibit 7-3b has partly described what happens in a competitive market when firms in a market earn losses. The chapter did not explicitly describe this process, but it did describe what happens when firms earn high profits. Based on your knowledge of what happens when firms earn high profits, fill in the missing boxes D and E.

Exhibit 7-3

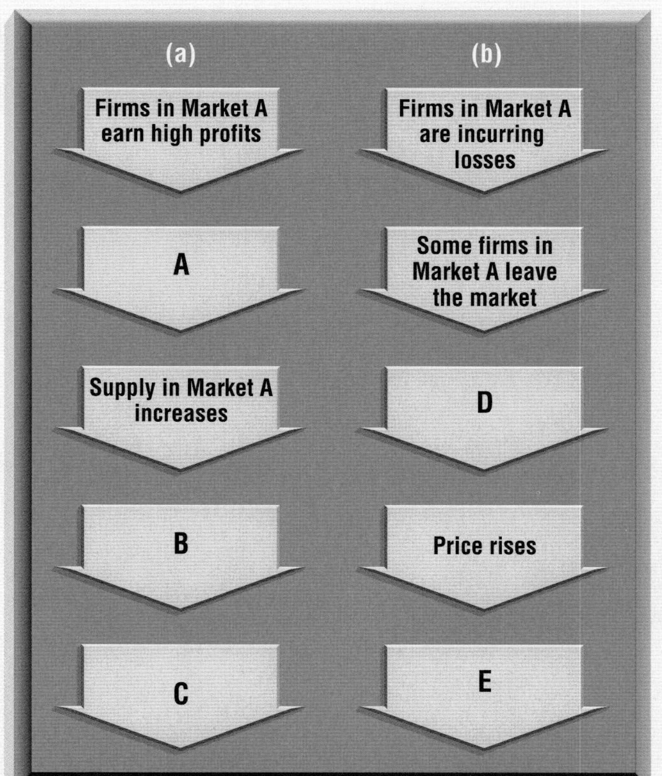

Economics and Thinking Skills

1. **Application.** Lam goes to a car dealership to look at cars. The salesperson shows him the cars he wants to see and drive. The salesperson asks Lam what he does for a living. Is there an economic reason for asking this question? If so, what is it?
2. **Analysis.** Firm A has been producing and selling good A in market A for ten years. Recently, other firms have moved into market A and started to produce good A. Firm A has asked the government to restrict the number of firms that can enter the market. Why would firm A want to restrict entry into the market?
3. **Comprehension.** State, in your own words, why cartel agreements do not usually hold up.

Writing Skills

Write a one-page paper in which you outline and discuss similarities and differences between a perfectly competitive firm and a monopoly firm.

Economics in the Media

1. Find an example of either an oligopoly or a monopoly in your local newspaper.
2. In today's newspaper, find yesterday's equilibrium price of a share of any stock listed on the New York Stock Exchange. If you had owned the particular stock and had wanted to sell it, could you have sold it for a higher price than the equilibrium price? Explain your answer.
3. Find an example of a legal barrier to entry, a cartel agreement, a monopoly, a perfectly competitive seller, or an oligopolist on television or in a movie.

Where's the Economics?

What market structure is relevant to the photo? Explain your answer.

CHAPTER 8

Employment and Wages

What This Chapter Is About

There are many markets in the economy: the car market, computer market, corn market, stock market, labor market, and education market, to name only a few. This chapter discusses the labor market, the market in which wages are determined. It discusses the demand for and supply of labor, and how wages are determined. It also discusses the history of the labor union movement in the United States.

Why This Chapter Is Important

Millions of people go to work every day. They work as cab drivers, computer programmers, attorneys, salespersons, construction workers, and accountants, among other things. These persons are part of the civilian labor force. The *civilian labor force* consists of men and women sixteen years old or older who are either working at jobs or actively searching for jobs. One day soon you will be part of the civilian labor force, if you are not already. When that day arrives, you will probably think a lot about what you are paid in the labor market. This chapter will help you understand the labor market and why people get paid what they do.

After You Study This Chapter, You Will Be Able To

- explain why some persons earn higher wages than others.
- describe the employment effects of the minimum wage law in the labor market.
- describe how labor unions try to affect the demand for and supply of their labor.
- explain how labor unions affect union and nonunion wages.
- explain the difference between the employment rate and the unemployment rate.

You Will Also Learn What Economics Has to Do With

- sleep.
- major league baseball pitchers.
- TV and movie stars.

Economics Journal

Each day for a week, identify one job you think you might like to have when you are twenty-nine years old. After each job, write why you would like that job. Next, identify what you think a person in that job earns today. For example, if you say that you would like to be a computer software engineer for a big company when you are twenty-nine, enter what you think a person with that job today earns on an annual basis.

SECTION 1 What Determines Wages?

Why do some people earn higher wages or incomes than others? A baseball player may earn a million dollars a year, whereas a secretary earns much less, as do computer programmers, truck drivers, and almost everyone else. Who or what determines the amount people earn as workers in the labor force? In a competitive labor market, the answer is simple: supply and demand.

As you read this section, keep these key questions in mind:

- What does the demand curve for labor look like?
- What does the supply curve for labor look like?
- Why do wage rates differ?

Many people complain that professional athletes such as Ken Griffey Jr. earn too much money. How do you think an economist would respond to this complaint?

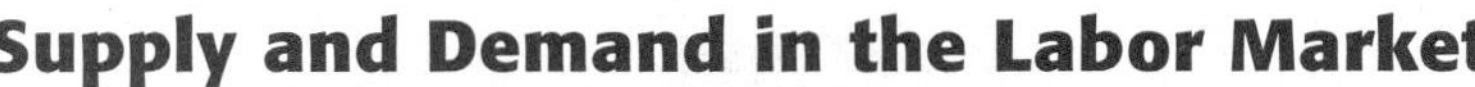

Supply and Demand in the Labor Market

Key Terms

wage rate
derived demand
minimum wage law

Chapter 3 discussed demand, and Chapter 4 introduced supply. They discussed these concepts as related to the determination of prices for goods or products—such things as apples, cars, and houses. Labor is not a product; it is a resource, or factor of production. However, supply and demand can also be used to analyze how the price of a resource, or factor of production, is determined.

There are people who *demand* labor (usually referred to as *employers*) and people who *supply* labor (usually referred to as *employees*). It follows, then, that labor has a demand curve and a supply curve. The price of labor is called the **wage rate.**

wage rate
The price of labor.

The demand curve for labor is downward sloping, as shown in Exhibit 8-1. A downward-sloping demand curve implies that employers will be willing and able to hire more people at lower wage rates than at higher wage rates. For example, employers are willing and able to hire more workers if the wage rate is $7 per hour than if the wage rate is $10 per hour.

Exhibit 8-1

The Demand for Labor

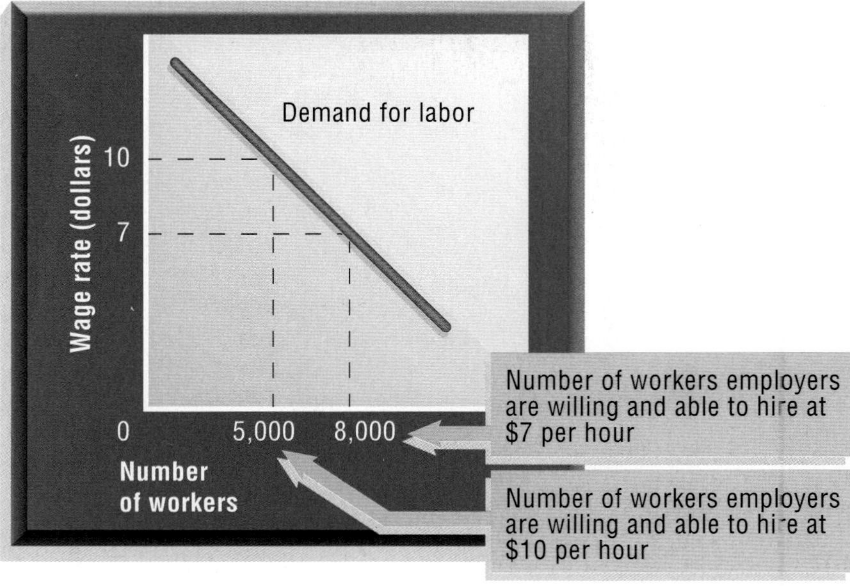

Exhibit 8-2
The Supply of Labor

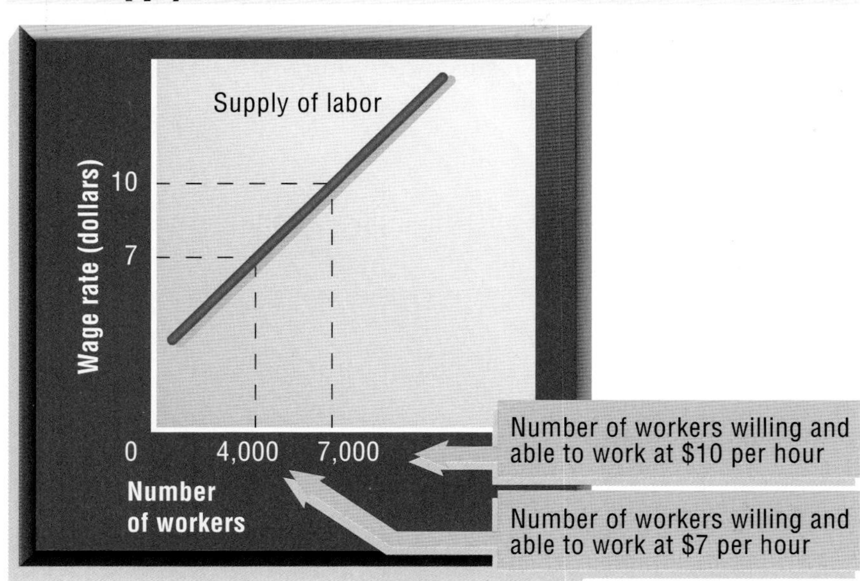

The supply curve for labor, in contrast, is upward sloping, as shown in Exhibit 8-2. More people will be willing and able to work at higher wage rates than at lower wage rates. In the exhibit, more people are willing and able to work if the wage rate is $10 per hour than if the wage rate is $7 an hour.

How the Equilibrium Wage Rate Is Established

Recall from Chapter 5 that the equilibrium price is the price at which the quantity demanded of a good equals the quantity supplied. Suppose $14 is the equilibrium price of compact discs; at this price, the number of compact discs that sellers are willing and able to sell equals the number of compact discs that buyers are willing and able to buy.

Similarly, in the labor market, the equilibrium wage rate is the wage at which the quantity demanded of labor equals the quantity supplied of labor. Stated differently, it is the wage rate at which the number of people employers are willing and able to hire is the same as the number of people who are willing and able to be hired. In Exhibit 8-3a, when the wage rate

Exhibit 8-3
Finding the Equilibrium Wage Rate

(a) At $9 per hour, the number of people willing and able to work (7,000) is greater than the number employers are willing and able to hire (3,000). We conclude that $9 is not the equilibrium wage rate. (b) At $7 per hour, the number of people employers are willing and able to hire (6,000) is greater than the number willing and able to work (4,000). We conclude that $7 is not the equilibrium wage rate. (c) At $7.75 per hour, the number of people willing and able to work (5,000) is the same as the number employers are willing and able to hire (5,000). We conclude that $7.75 is the equilibrium wage rate.

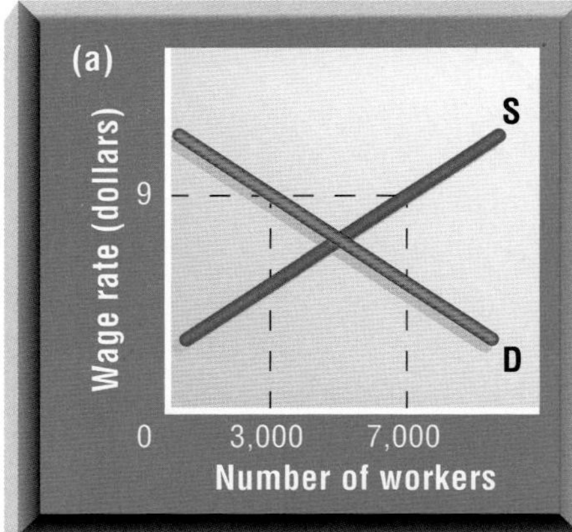

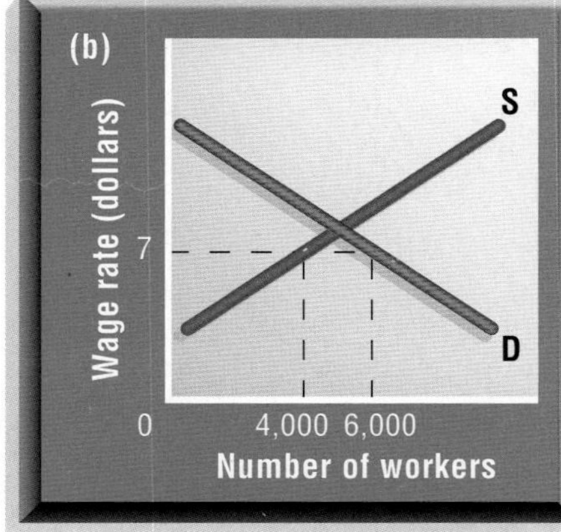

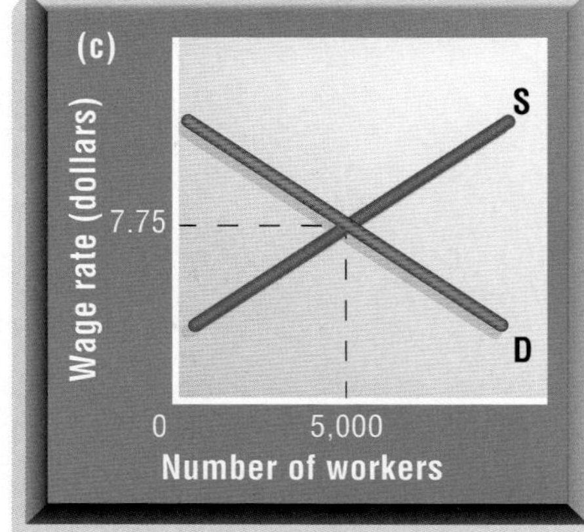

is $9, the number of people who are willing and able to work (quantity supplied equals 7,000) is greater than the number of people employers are willing and able to hire (quantity demanded equals 3,000). It follows that $9 is not the equilibrium wage rate; at $9, there is a surplus of labor.

In Chapter 5, you learned that when there is a surplus of a good, its price falls. Things are similar in a competitive labor market. When there is a surplus of labor, the wage rate falls:

Quantity supplied of labor > Quantity demanded of labor = Surplus of labor
Surplus of labor ➡ Wage rate falls

Now consider Exhibit 8-3b. The wage rate is $7, and the number of people employers are willing and able to hire (6,000) is greater than the number of people who are willing and able to work (4,000). Thus, $7 is not the equilibrium wage rate. At $7, there is a shortage of labor, so the wage rate rises:

If some people earn higher wages than others, then either the demand for their labor services is higher or the supply of their labor services is lower.

Quantity demanded of labor > Quantity supplied of labor = Shortage of labor
Shortage of labor ➡ Wage rate rises

In Exhibit 8-3c, the wage rate is $7.75, and the number of people employers are willing and able to hire (5,000) equals the number of people who are willing and able to work (5,000). We conclude that $7.75 is the equilibrium wage rate. At this wage rate there is no tendency for the wage rate to rise or fall, because there is no shortage or surplus of labor.

Why Wage Rates Differ

Supply and demand help us to understand why some people earn higher wages than others. First, suppose that the demand for every type of labor is the same—the demand for accountants is the same as the demand for construction workers, and so on. Now suppose we learn that the equilibrium wage rate for accountants is higher than that for construction workers. If demand for the two types of labor is the same, how can we explain the difference in wage rates? Obviously, the supply of accountants and the supply of construction workers must not be the same. If accountants earn more than construction workers, it must be because the supply of accountants is less than the supply of construction workers. We conclude that *wage rates can differ because the supply of different types of labor is not the same.*

Suppose instead that the supply of different types of labor is the same—for example, the supply of bank tellers is the same as the supply of car mechanics. If car mechanics earn more than bank tellers, what would explain the difference? Obviously, the demand for bank tellers and car mechanics must not be the same. We conclude that *wage rates can differ because the demand for different types of labor is not the same.*

We can combine these two conclusions and state that in general, *wage rates may differ because the demand for different types of labor is not the same or because the supply of different types of labor is not the same.*

Will Increased Immigration Lead to Higher or Lower Wages?

Millions of immigrants come to the United States each year. Those who are admitted by the U.S. government are usually referred to as *documented immigrants.* In 1997, for example, 800,000 documented immigrants were admitted to the United States. Immigrants who are not admitted legally by the U.S. government are usually referred to as *undocumented immigrants.* Approximately 5 million undocumented immigrants came to the United States in 1997.

In the near future, documented immigrants admitted to the country each year will probably number between 500,000 and 1 million. Demographers expect undocumented immigration to rise, so the total number of immigrants will probably rise in the years to come. Some people argue that increased immigration will increase the supply of labor in the country and thus lead to lower wages.

There is no doubt that increased immigration will affect the supply of labor, but it must be remembered that it will affect the demand for labor, too. The demand for labor is derived from the demand for the product that labor produces. With increased immigration, the larger population will translate into a higher demand for food, housing, clothes, entertainment, education, and other services. A higher demand for these goods and services will then translate into a higher demand for the workers who produce these goods.

In summary, increased immigration will affect both the supply of and the demand for labor. What will be the effect on wages? The outcome will depend on whether the increase in demand is greater than, less than, or equal to the increase in supply. If the demand for labor increases by more than the supply of labor increases, increased immigration will lead to higher wages. If demand increases by less than supply increases, increased immigration will lead to lower wages. And if demand increases by the same amount as supply increases, increased immigration will not change wages.

QUESTION TO ANSWER Under what condition will increased immigration leave wages unchanged?

Money Benefits versus Nonmoney Benefits

Suppose Smith is offered two jobs, A and B. In job A, he will earn an annual income of $100,000 and in job B, $40,000. Which job will he choose? Most people would say that he will choose job A because it pays a higher income. Smith won't necessarily choose job A, however, because a higher income (more money per year) is not the only thing that matters to people. Also important are what people are doing in their jobs, who their co-workers are, where they have to work, how many hours a week they have to work, how much vacation time they receive, and more. In short, if everything between the two jobs, A and B, is the same except that job A pays $100,000 and job B pays $40,000, then certainly Smith will choose job A over job B. However, usually not everything is the same between two jobs.

Jobs come with both money and nonmoney benefits. Might a person choose a lower-paying job if it gave him or her more vacation time than a higher-paying job?

Let's suppose that Smith chooses job B (the lower-paying job) over job A. He tells us that he chose the lower-paying job because he likes the job so much more. In job B he is doing something that he has always wanted to do, he works with nice people, he gets one month of vacation each year, and he is enormously stimulated by what he does. In contrast, in job A he would have been doing something both boring and tedious to him, he would have worked with people he did not really like (especially his boss), and he would have had only two weeks of vacation each year. On top of all this, he would have had to work ten hours more each week in job A than he has to work in job B, and he would have had much less job security. Thus, job A pays more than job B, but job A does not have the nonmoney benefits that job B has.

In short, all jobs come with both money benefits and nonmoney benefits. Look at it this way:

Benefits in a job = Money benefits (income) + Nonmoney benefits

Certainly job A comes with higher money benefits (higher income) than job B, but (as far as Smith is concerned) it also comes with lower nonmoney benefits than job B. Because Smith chose job B (the $40,000 job) over job A (the $100,000 job), the nonmoney benefits in job B must have been higher than the nonmoney benefits in job A.

How much higher must they have been, in a dollar amount? The answer is at least $60,000 higher. To understand why, consider what Smith has "paid" by choosing job B over job A. He has paid $60,000 a year, because he has given up the opportunity to earn $60,000 more a year in job A. Therefore, the nonmoney benefits of job B must have been worth at least $60,000 to Smith.

Suppose that the nonmoney benefits in job A equal $0, and the nonmoney benefits in job B equal $1 more than $60,000, or $60,001. This means the benefits of job A equal $100,000 ($100,000 in money benefits or income plus $0 in nonmoney benefits), but the benefits of job B equal $100,001 ($40,000 in money benefits plus $60,001 in nonmoney benefits).

Once nonmoney benefits are taken into account, job B is the job with the greater benefits. We can say that it "pays" more, as long as we understand that a person in a job is paid in terms of both money and nonmoney benefits.

The Demand for a Good and Wage Rates

Eva lives in Detroit and works in a factory helping to produce cars. Suppose the demand for cars decreases (see Exhibit 8-4a). What do you think will happen? If the demand for cars decreases, car companies do not need to hire as many people to produce cars, so the demand for workers decreases (see Exhibit 8-4b). As the demand for workers decreases and the supply stays constant, the wage rate decreases. As the demand for workers increases and the supply stays constant, the wage rate increases.

Exhibit 8-4

The Demand for Cars, the Demand for the Workers Who Produce the Cars, and Their Wage Rates

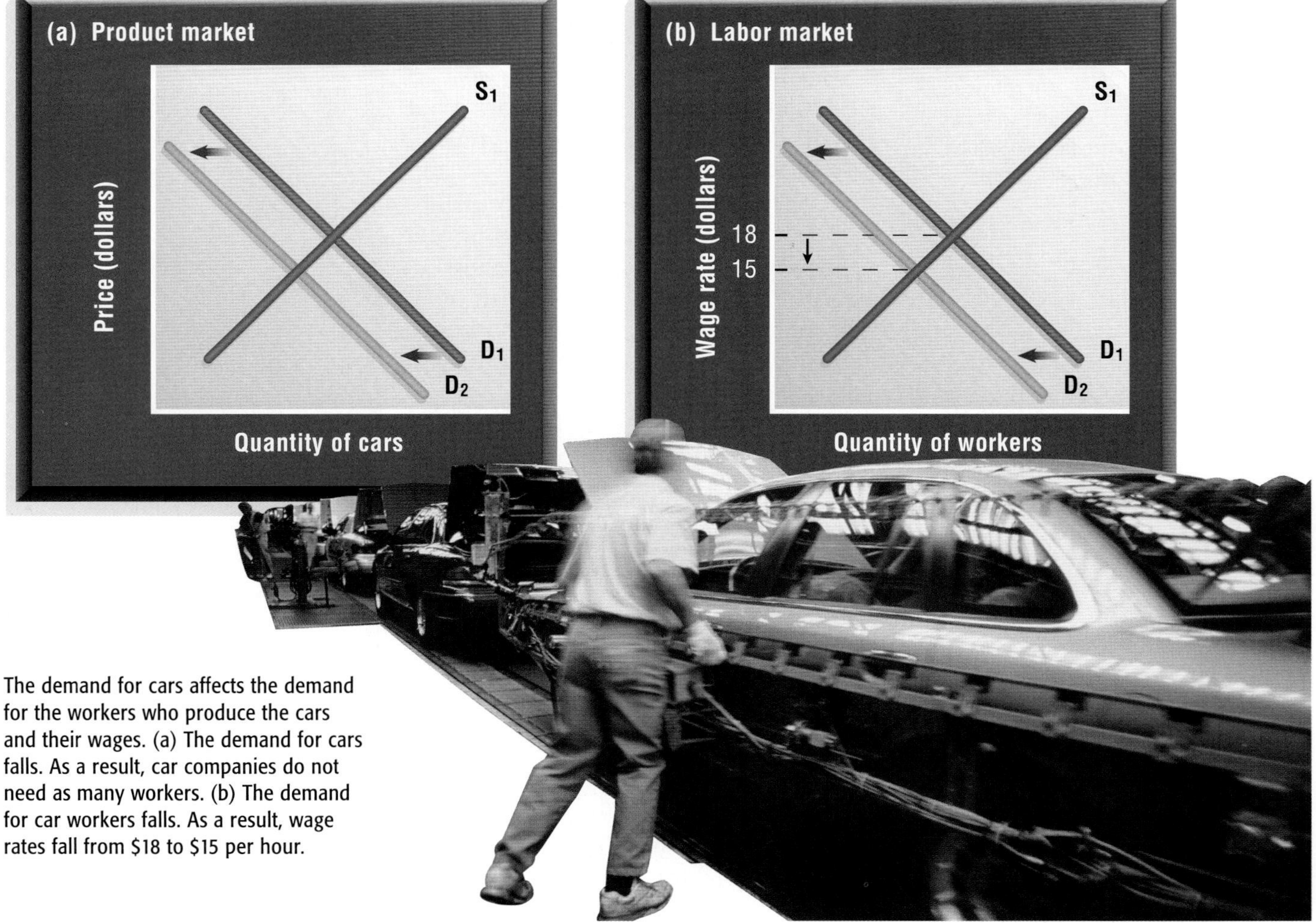

The demand for cars affects the demand for the workers who produce the cars and their wages. (a) The demand for cars falls. As a result, car companies do not need as many workers. (b) The demand for car workers falls. As a result, wage rates fall from $18 to $15 per hour.

Demand for the good (that labor produces) falls	➡	Demand for labor falls	➡	Wage rates fall
Demand for the good (that labor produces) rises	➡	Demand for labor rises	➡	Wage rates rise

Jim is offered two jobs, A and B. Job A pays $50,000 a year, and job B pays $60,000 a year. The nonmoney benefits in the two jobs are the same. Cindra is offered two jobs, C and D. Job C pays $50,000 a year, and job D pays $60,000 a year, but the nonmoney benefits in the two jobs are not the same. Is it as easy to predict which job Cindra will choose as it is to predict which job Jim will choose? Why or why not?

Because the demand for labor is dependent upon the demand for the good or service labor produces, the demand for labor is often referred to as a **derived demand.** A derived demand is a demand that is the result of some other demand.

derived demand
A demand that is the result of some other demand.

Factors That Determine Wage Rate

If you are reading this book as part of a high school course, you are somewhere between the ages of fourteen and eighteen. Let's jump ahead fifteen years, when you will be between twenty-nine and thirty-three years old. At that time, you will be working at some job and earning some wage rate or salary. You could be earning anywhere between, say, $20,000 and $500,000 a year. What will determine the amount you will earn?

Your wage rate (and salary) will depend on a number of things, one of which is the demand for your labor services. The demand for you may be high, low, or medium. The higher the demand for you, the higher your wage rate will be. Obviously, you want the demand for you to be as high as possible.

Two factors will make the demand for your labor services high: (1) the demand for the good you produce and (2) your productivity. The greater the demand for the product you produce, the greater the demand for your labor services. If you produce accounting services and accounting services are in high demand, then you are in high demand, too. If you play professional basketball and professional basketball is in high demand, then you are in high demand, too. If you produce telephones and telephones are in low demand, then you will be in low demand, too.

The second factor that relates to the demand for you as an employee is your productivity. The more productive you are at what you do, the greater the demand. Suppose that two people can produce accounting services. One, however, can produce twice as many accounting services per hour as the other. It follows, then, that the faster accountant will be in greater demand by accounting firms.

Professional basketball players such as Shaquille O'Neal earn relatively high salaries. Do you know why?

How Much Sleep You Get May Depend on How Much You Earn

As educational achievement rises, so does one's income. For example, in the late 1990s, the average annual income of a person with only a high school diploma was $21,431, whereas the average annual income of a person with a bachelor's degree from college was $36,980. The average income of a person with a master's degree was higher, at $47,609, and even higher for a person with a doctorate, at $64,550. Assuming that a person works forty hours a week, fifty weeks a year, the person with a high school diploma earns $10.71 an hour, the person with the bachelor's degree earns $18.49 a hour, the person with the master's degree earns $23.80 an hour, and the person with the doctorate receives $32.27 an hour.

Chapter 1 described the opportunity cost of something as the most valued opportunity or alternative you have to give up (or forfeit) to do something. For example, if you were not reading this chapter right now, you would be talking to a friend on the telephone; thus, "talking to a friend on the telephone" is the opportunity cost to you of reading this chapter.

Now let's see if we can tie together opportunity cost, educational achievement, and wage rates with the number of hours a person sleeps. We know that as educational achievement rises, a person's wage rate rises. It is possible to view a person's wage rate as the opportunity cost of not working. In other words, a person who earns $20 an hour when she is working is forfeiting this amount when she chooses not to work. It follows, then, that people who earn relatively high wages have higher opportunity costs of not working than do people who earn relatively low wages. For example, the person with the doctorate (who earns $32.27 an hour) forfeits more than the person with only the high school diploma (who earns $10.71 an hour) when he does not work.

One of the things we do when we do not work is sleep. It follows that the opportunity cost of sleeping is higher for the person with more education and higher wages than for the person with less education and lower wages. An economist would predict that the higher the opportunity cost of sleeping, the less one will sleep. If the economist is correct, we should see that individuals who are more educated and earn higher incomes will sleep less than those who are less educated and earn lower incomes.

> More education ➡ Higher wages ➡
> Higher opportunity cost of not working ➡
> Higher opportunity cost of sleeping ➡ Sleep less

Two economists, J. Biddle and D. Hammermesh, did present evidence that on average, sleep is related to education and wage rates. They found that more-educated people earn more and sleep less than less-educated people who earn less. They sleep fourteen minutes less for each year of additional schooling. In short, more education may be good for your wallet, but it's not so good for your sleep.

QUESTION TO ANSWER Blackwell has a high school diploma, earns $10 an hour, and sleeps eight hours a night. Nitobe has a doctorate, earns $50 an hour, and sleeps eight hours and thirty minutes a night. Both Blackwell and Nitobe are the same age. If our evidence is correct, does it mean that the Biddle and Hammermesh evidence must be incorrect?

THE BORN LOSER ® by Art and Chip Sansom

The BORN LOSER reprinted by permission of Newspaper Enterprise Association, Inc.

A number of factors can influence your productivity. One factor is your innate ability; you may simply have been born with a great ability to organize people, play baseball, sing a song, or write a story. A second factor is how much effort you put into developing your skills. You may have worked hard developing and perfecting your ability to produce a service, whether it is attorney services, teaching services, or medical services. Third, your productivity is affected by the quality and length of your education. The higher the quality of your education and the more education you have, the more productive you will be (all other things being equal). In fact, statistics show that as one's educational level rises, so does one's income. In summary, the demand for you (as an employee) will rise with the demand for the product or service you produce and your productivity.

Concert pianists often earn high salaries. What do their high salaries have to do with the number of people who can play the piano with great skill?

Of course, your wage (or salary) in the future depends not only upon how high or low the demand for you is in the future but also upon the number of people who can do what you do. In short, it also depends on supply. For example, the demand for you may be very high, but if the supply is very high, too, you are not likely to earn a high wage. High wages are the result of high demand combined with low supply.

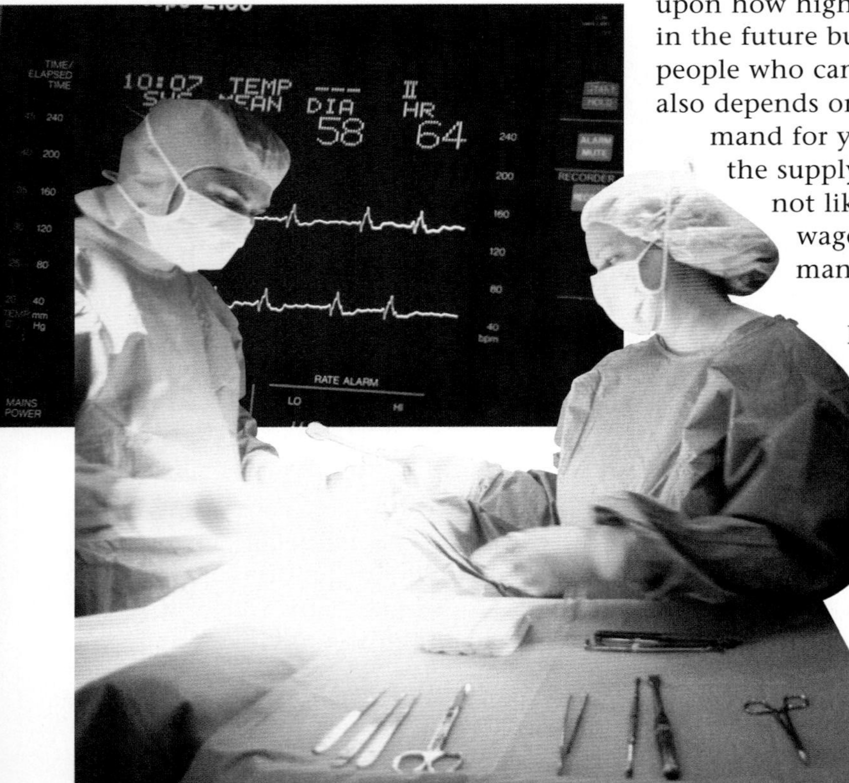

Surgeons usually earn high salaries because the demand is high for what they do and not many people can do what surgeons do.

Why is supply high in some labor markets and low in others? The supply of labor offered in a particular labor market is a function of a number of factors, one of which is the ability to perform a particular service. For example, more people can work as restaurant servers than as brain surgeons. Similarly, more people can drive trucks than can argue and win difficult law cases before the United States

Are TV, Movie, and Sports Stars Worth the Many Millions They Earn?

A television news anchor announces a particular sports star's new salary: $10 million a year. The anchor goes on to say that a particular TV star will now earn $1 million an episode, and a movie star will get $20 million for his next movie.

These are very large salaries, and it is natural to ask whether the people who receive them are worth the money they are paid. Is anyone worth $1 million an episode or $10 million to play one season of baseball?

Would an economist say these high salaries are justified? Let's explore the question by laying out a possible set of facts. Suppose you are the president of NBC, and a star of one of your hit shows is asking for $1 million an episode. Whether or not you pay it depends on whether or not the star is worth $1 million an episode. But how do you determine if she is or is not?

First, you ask yourself what would happen to the ratings of the show if the star were no longer on it. Suppose you think the ratings would drop. If they dropped, you could not charge as much for a 30-second commercial. Currently, a 30-second spot on a top-rated television show sells for about $350,000. If there are ten 30-second commercials, revenue is $3.5 million.

Suppose that without the star on the television show you think that ratings would drop so that you could charge only $200,000 for a 30-second commercial. With ten commercials, this price would reduce revenue to $2 million. In short, with the star the network earns revenue of $3.5 million an episode, and without the star it would earn revenue of $2 million per episode, a difference of $1.5 million. If the star left, revenue would drop by $1.5 million.

Is it worth paying $1 million to the star to prevent losing $1.5 million in revenue? Stated differently, is it better to pay $1 million or to lose $1.5 million? Obviously, it is better to pay $1 million than to lose $1.5 million. Thus, in this case the star is worth $1 million an episode. As long as the additional revenue that the star generates (in this case, an additional $1.5 million) is greater than the star's salary (in this case, $1 million), then the star is worth what she is paid.

QUESTION TO ANSWER There is sometimes a large difference between what a star earns and what others who work with the star earn. For example, in 1998, Michael Jordan, the star player for the Chicago Bulls basketball team, earned more than 100 times the salary of the lowest-paid player on the team. Why do you think there is such a large difference between what a star earns and what those who work with the star earn?

Supreme Court. These statements do not put a value judgment on work as a restaurant server or truck driver. They simply report the fact that some tasks can be completed by more people than others. All other things being equal, the fewer people who can do what you do, the higher your wage (or salary) will be.

> Your wages will be higher than others' wages when
> - the demand for the good you produce is higher than the demand for other goods
> - your productivity is higher than others' productivity
> - few people can do what you do

A major league baseball pitcher, for example, often earns many millions of dollars each year in income because he possesses the three factors necessary to generate a high income. First, he is part of a team that produces baseball, a product that is in high demand. Each year many millions of people express their demand for baseball by attending baseball games and watching them on television. Second, major league baseball pitchers are productive; they can (usually) produce strikes and pitches that batters find difficult to hit. In so doing, they make the game of baseball more exciting. Third, not many people can do what they do (supply is low). In short, as was stated earlier, when there is a combination of (1) high demand for the good or service produced, (2) high productivity, and (3) the situation where not many people can do what one does, the result is a high salary.

If relatively few people are either able or willing to work on skyscrapers (too dangerous), how will this fact affect the wages of those who are able and willing?

Government and Wages

The **minimum wage law** sets a wage floor—that is, a level below which hourly wages rates are not allowed to fall. The law, passed during the Great Depression of the 1930s, initially established a minimum wage of 25 cents an hour. In 2000, the minimum wage was $5.15 an hour. Some states, such as California, Washington, and Massachusetts, have set their minimum wage rate higher than the federal rate.

minimum wage law A federal law that specifies the lowest hourly wage rate that can be paid to workers.

The U.S. Congress determines the minimum wage. Earlier, however, you read that supply and demand determine wage rates. What is going on? The fact is that supply and demand are not always *allowed* to determine wages. To illustrate, suppose that in a particular labor market the equilibrium wage rate is $3.10 an hour. In other words, the demand curve and the supply curve of labor intersect at a wage rate of $3.10. Congress then argues that a wage rate of $3.10 an hour is too low, and it orders employers to pay employees at least $5.15 an hour. This rate is now the minimum wage. It becomes unlawful to pay an employee less than this hourly wage.

Many people would agree with Congress that a wage of $3.10 an hour is simply too low. Economists, however, are not so interested in whether Congress is justified or not in setting a minimum wage as they are in knowing the effects of government's setting the minimum wage rate above the equilibrium wage rate. For example, will employers hire as many workers at the minimum wage rate of $5.15 as they would at the equilibrium wage rate of $3.10? Remember, the demand curve for labor is downward sloping. As the wage rate falls, employers will hire more workers; and as the wage rate rises, they will hire fewer workers. Thus, a minimum wage rate set by Congress above the equilibrium wage rate will result in employers being willing and able to hire fewer workers.

Minimum Wages and Gangs

Why do some high schoolers get into gang activity, especially selling illegal drugs? Someone might reply, "There's a good reason why some kids get into gang activity and selling drugs—economics. Take a fifteen-year-old with very few job skills. His options are flipping hamburgers at a fast-food restaurant for the minimum wage or earning a lot of money selling drugs. Some kids are going to see the large difference in income and choose to sell drugs for the gang."

That answer is riddled with errors, though. One misconception is about the amount of money earned by the foot soldiers in gangs who actually sell drugs on the streets. Most people think that the foot soldiers earn a lot of money—certainly many times more than what they could earn flipping hamburgers. The truth is that they do not.

Two researchers, Steven Levitt, an economist at the University of Chicago, and Sudhir Venkatesh, a sociologist at Harvard University, studied gang activity in a midwestern city.[1] The researchers obtained access to a drug gang's books, which listed such things as how much crack cocaine the gang had sold, how much members had spent on weapons, and how much they had paid to street pushers.

1. "An Economic Analysis of a Drug-Selling Gang's Finances," by Steven D. Levitt and Sudhir Alladi Venkatesh, NBER Working Paper Series, No. 6592, National Bureau of Economic Research, Cambridge, Massachusetts, 1998.

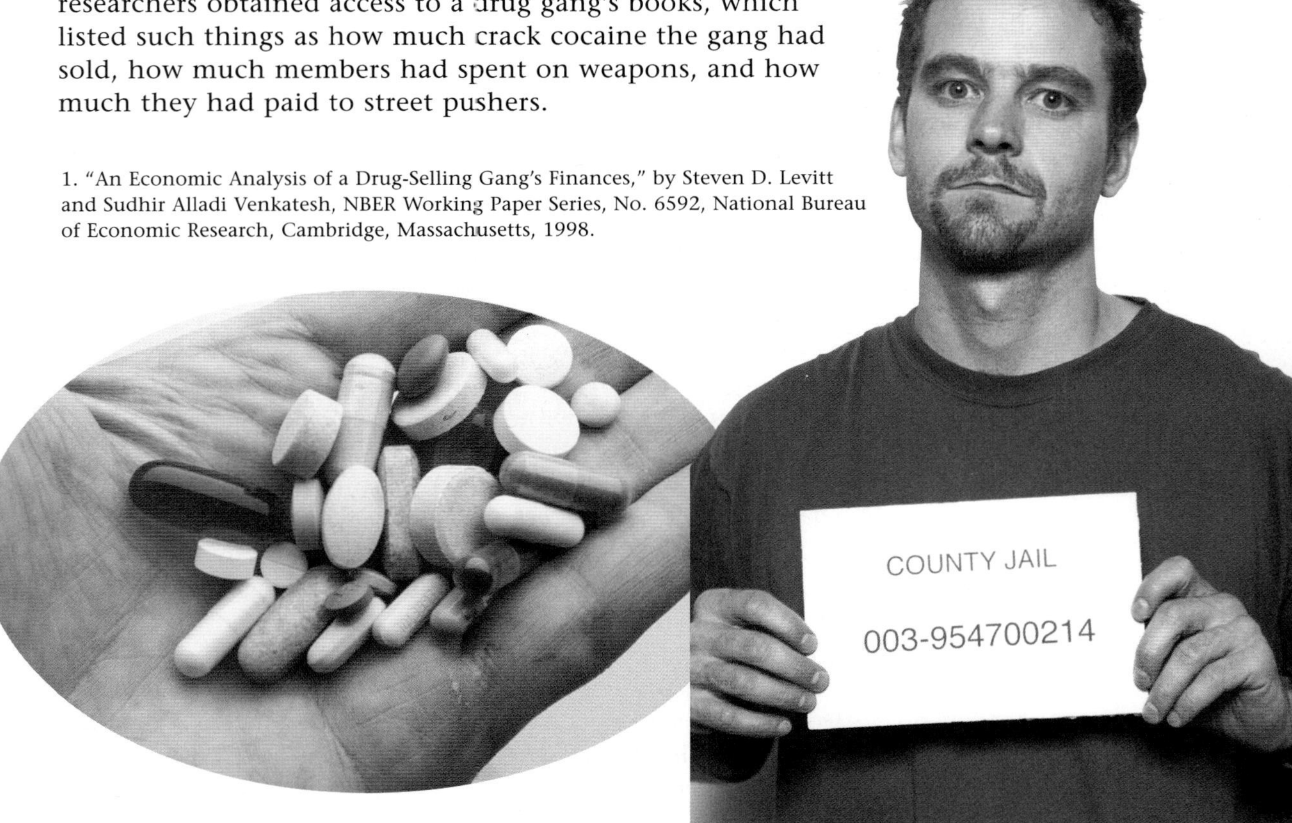

Contrary to popular belief, the foot soldiers in gangs who sell or deliver illegal drugs do not earn much money. Many earn less than the minimum wage—and end up in prison, too.

THINKING Like an Economist

Many people think that economists see things only in terms of dollars and cents, and all that matters to them is money. In reality, economists think in terms of utility or satisfaction, and they know that money is not the only thing that gives people utility or satisfaction. For example, the money benefits of a job are not the only thing people consider when deciding to accept a job or not. The nonmoney benefits of the job matter, too. In short, economists think in terms of benefits, not just money benefits.

The researchers learned that the average street pusher earned $6 an hour at the beginning of their study and about $11 an hour at the end. But remember, this is the *average wage* for a street pusher. Some earned less than the average. Levitt and Venkatesh say, "For much of the period examined, the actual wage earned by low-level street-corner sellers (as opposed to the average wage over all levels of the gang), is less than the minimum wage." Why are they paid so little? The researchers write, "While these wages are almost too low to be believable, there are both theoretical arguments and corroborating empirical evidence in support of these numbers. From a theoretical perspective, it is hardly surprising that foot-soldier wages would be low given the minimal skill requirements for the job and the presence of a 'reserve army' of potential replacements among the rank and file." In other words, the supply of this type of labor is so large relative to the demand that the job pays very little.

This young woman is smiling because her boss just increased her money income. Is it guaranteed that her real income has risen, too?

Money Wages versus Real Wages

Suppose Patel earns $9 an hour in 1999 and $12 an hour in 2000. In terms of the goods and services she can buy, is she better off in 1999 or in 2000? The obvious answer is that she is better off in 2000, when she earns the higher wage rate. This answer, however, assumes that the prices of the goods she buys in 1999 and 2000 are the same, but they may not be. Prices may be higher in 2000 than 1999. Whether she is better off in 2000 than 1999 depends on how much her wages have risen relative to how much prices have risen.

Suppose the only good that Patel buys is chocolate bars. In 1999, chocolate bars sell for $1 a bar. With a wage rate of $9 an hour, Patel can buy 9 chocolate bars an hour. In 2000, chocolate bars are $2 a bar; with $12 an hour, Patel can buy 6 chocolate bars an hour. The point is that we can measure a person's wage rate in terms of money (for example, $9 or $11) or in terms of what it buys. Measuring a person's wage rate in terms of money gives us the person's *money wage*. Measuring a person's wage rate in terms of what it buys gives us the person's *real wage*.

Can a person's money wage rise while the person's real wage falls? This is exactly what happened to Patel when she went from earning $9 to $12 an hour, but her real wage fell from 9 chocolate bars an hour to 6 chocolate bars an hour. Everyone talks in terms of money wages ("I earn $10 an hour"), but our real wage is far more important because it measures what we can do with the money wage we receive.

We are paid in money wages, so how do we compute our real wages so that we can see how much better off or worse off we are in terms of buying power from one period to the next? We computed Patel's real wage in 1999 versus 2000 by simply dividing the money wage in each year by the price of a chocolate bar in each year. In the real world, of course, people do not simply buy chocolate bars; they buy a variety of goods. The government measures the "average price" of these goods, usually called a *price index*. One particularly well-known price index is the Consumer Price Index, or CPI. Perhaps you have heard a television newscaster say, "The government reported today that the CPI rose by 4 percent over the year." In other words, prices, on average, are 4 percent higher this year than last year.

The government computes the CPI on an annual basis. Therefore, we can compute our real wage by simply dividing our money wage in a given year by the CPI in the same year:

$$\text{Real wage} = \frac{\text{Money wage}}{\text{CPI}}$$

For example, suppose in 1996 a person earned a wage rate of $20 an hour, and the CPI was 146.2. The person's real wage was 0.137. In percentage terms, it is 13.7 percent—but 13.7 percent of what? In the chocolate bar example, it would be 13.7 percent of one chocolate bar. But we aren't talking about chocolate bars here; we are talking about many goods. Think of the 0.137, then, as 13.7 percent of one unit of a composite good. This composite good is a little food, a little housing, and a little entertainment all rolled up into one.[2] With $20 an hour, then, a person can purchase 13.7 percent of one unit of the composite good.

Now suppose the person's wage rate rises to $30 in 2002. Furthermore, let's suppose that the CPI in 2002 turns out to be 170.4. What, then, is the person's real wage? If we divide $30 by 170.4, we get 0.176, or 17.6 percent of one unit of a composite good.

Is the person's real wage higher in 1996 or in 2002? The answer is 2002. In 1996, his real wage rate is 13.7 percent of one unit of a composite good, and in 2002 it is 17.6 percent of one unit of a composite good.

The prices of goods and services are rising, but money wages do not seem to be rising at the same pace. What will happen to real wages in the near future?

2. Because we are speaking about "average prices," we must talk about "average goods." A composite good is simply another name for an average good.

Section 1 Review

Defining Terms

1. Define

a. wage rate

b. derived demand

c. minimum wage law

2. Give an example of a money wage and a real wage.

Reviewing Facts and Concepts

3. In a competitive labor market, suppose the quantity demanded of labor is greater than the quantity supplied. What will happen to the wage rate? Explain.

4. John is paid $7 an hour, and Kimsan is paid $23 an hour. In general, why does Kimsan earn more than John?

5. Mauricio accepts a job that pays $35,000 a year instead of a job that pays $80,000 a year. What do the nonmoney benefits in the $35,000 job equal (at minimum)? Explain your answer.

Critical Thinking

6. If major league baseball becomes less popular, what will happen to the salaries of major league baseball players? Explain your answer.

Applying Economic Concepts

7. Over the last three years, Rachel's money wage increased by 10 percent, and prices increased by 13 percent. Has Rachel's real wage increased, decreased, or remained stable? Explain your answer.

SECTION 2

Labor Unions and the Labor Market

A **labor union** is an organization that seeks to increase the wages and improve the working conditions of its members. In 1998, 13.9 percent of all workers were members of a labor union. This figure was down a little from 1997, when 14.1 percent of all workers were in a labor union. Today, approximately 16 million workers are members of unions. This section discusses the practices and effects of labor unions.

As you read this section, keep these key questions in mind:

- How might labor unions affect the demand for and supply of union labor?
- What is a union shop?
- What is the purpose of a strike?

Key Terms

labor union
closed shop
Taft-Hartley Act
union shop
strike
right-to-work law

Some Practices of Labor Unions

One objective of a labor union may be to obtain higher pay for its members. The union then must direct its activities to increasing the demand for its labor, decreasing the supply of its labor, or both.

The Demand for Union Labor As stated earlier, if the demand for a good decreases, then the demand for the labor that produces the good decreases, too. For example, if the demand for cars decreases, then the demand decreases for the workers who produce cars. If the demand for cars increases, of course, the demand increases for the workers who produce cars.

With that in mind, suppose you are a union worker in the U.S. automobile industry, centered in Detroit, Michigan. Would you want the demand for American-made cars to increase, stay constant, or decrease? Obviously, you would want the demand for American-made cars to increase, because you know that if it increases, the demand for your labor increases, too. And as the demand for your labor increases, your wage rate increases, all other things remaining the same.

Your labor union thus might try to increase the demand for the product it produces. It might launch an advertising campaign urging people to purchase only union-produced goods. For example, television commercials have urged people to "look for the union label"—in other words, buy union-made goods.

Labor unions sometimes call strikes. Is this an attempt to affect the demand for, or supply of, labor?

A labor union's motto is "Buy goods made in te U.S.A." Is the motto relevant to the demand for, or supply of, labor?

MINI GLOSSARY

labor union An organization that seeks to increase the wages and improve the working conditions of its members.

What Do Employees around the World Earn?

There is a difference between hourly wages (hourly earnings) and hourly compensation costs. For example, a person may earn a wage rate of $13 an hour but also receive year-end bonuses, health insurance paid for by the employer, paid vacations, and so on. The sum of all the dollar benefits that an employer provides its employees is the hourly compensation cost, which is always higher than the hourly wage. Exhibit 8–5 shows the hourly compensation costs in U.S. dollars for production workers in manufacturing in selected countries.

QUESTION TO ANSWER How can hourly compensation costs rise if wages are constant?

Exhibit 8-5

Hourly Compensation Costs, Selected Countries

Source: U.S. Bureau of Labor Statistics.

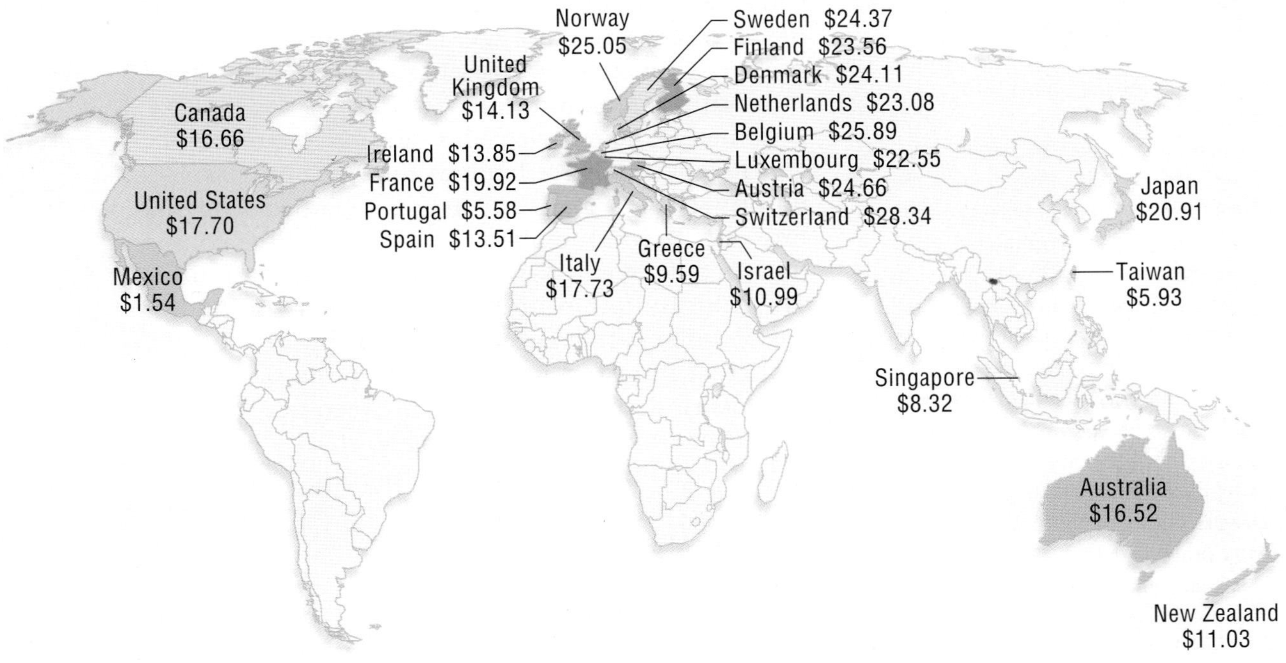

Economics & People

César Chávez, U.S. Migrant Farm Worker, Labor Leader

César Estrada Chávez (1927–1993) was born into a California family that was part of the migrant community, traveling from farm to farm to pick fruits and vegetables during harvest. Once Chávez completed the eighth grade, he quit school and worked full-time in the fields. Chávez protested the low pay and poor working conditions of the migrant workers. He formed a labor organization, the National Farm Workers Association (NFWA), which later became the United Farm Workers (UFW).

In 1965, Chávez and the NFWA led a strike of California grape pickers to demand higher wages. During the strike, Chávez encouraged all Americans to boycott table grapes as a show of support. In 1968, Chávez began a fast to call attention to the cause of the migrant worker. In 1970, with 17 million people supporting the grape boycott, the growers signed an agreement with Chávez's union; the strike had lasted five years. Today Chávez is given credit for bringing to the attention of the U.S. public the poor working conditions of migrant workers and for initiating the process that led to improved working conditions.

QUESTION TO ANSWER Often, boycotts are not successful. Can you think of the reason why?

Also, when U.S. union workers are in competition with workers in other countries (as, for example, U.S. car workers are in competition with Japanese car workers), an advertising campaign might urge people to buy goods "made in the U.S.A."—another union slogan in the recent past.

Unions also know that if they can increase the productivity of their membership, employers will have a greater demand for their workers. Productivity relates to how much output labor can produce. For example, if Yuan can produce more radios per hour than Smith, we would say that Yuan is more productive than Smith. Firms have a higher demand for more productive workers. Because of this, some unions provide new entrants with training programs meant to increase their productivity.

This young woman is a member of a union shop. Did she have to join the union before she was hired?

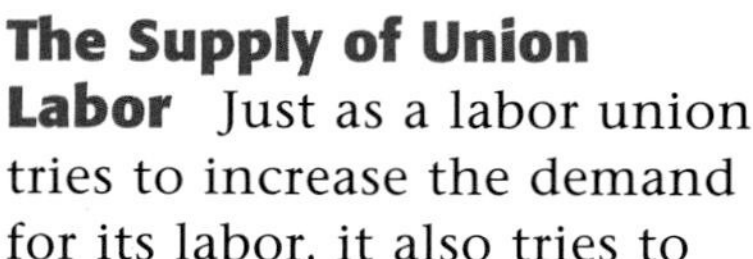

The Supply of Union Labor Just as a labor union tries to increase the demand for its labor, it also tries to decrease labor supply. Suppose you work as a truck driver. Would you prefer to be one of a thousand truck drivers in the United States or one of ten thousand truck drivers? Your answer probably is one of a thousand, because you know that the lower the supply of truck drivers, the higher your wage rate, all other things remaining the same.

Some people criticize labor unions for trying to control the supply of labor at times. In the past, some unions supported **closed shops,** organizations that hire only union members. To work for these companies, people would first have to join the labor union. The labor union, in turn, might hold down the number of workers that could join (and thus work in the particular industry) in order to keep the supply of workers in that industry low and keep wage rates high. The union could perhaps do this by limiting membership or requiring long training periods. Today, the closed shop is illegal. It was prohibited by the **Taft-Hartley Act,** passed by the U.S. Congress in 1947.

The **union shop,** however, is legal in many states. A union shop does not require individuals to be union members in order to be hired, but it does require employees to join the union within a certain period of time after being hired. Labor unions favor union shops, because if everyone working in a particular trade or industry has to become a member of the union within a certain period of time, the labor

MINI GLOSSARY

closed shop An organization that hires only union members.

Taft-Hartley Act An act, passed in 1947 by the U.S. Congress, which made the closed shop illegal and gave states the right to pass right-to-work laws. These right-to-work laws prohibit employers from establishing union membership as a condition of employment.

union shop
An organization that requires employees to join the union within a certain period after being hired.

strike
A work stoppage called by members of a union to place pressure on an employer.

right-to-work law
A state law that prohibits the practice of requiring employees to join a union in order to work.

union gains greater control over the supply of labor. For example, consider the **strike,** a work stoppage called by union members to put pressure on an employer. It is easier for the union to call a strike if everyone in a particular trade or industry is a member of the union.

Today, twenty-one states have passed **right-to-work laws,** which make it illegal to require union membership for purposes of employment. In short, in states with right-to-work laws, the union shop is illegal. Exhibit 8-6 lists the states that have passed right-to-work laws.

Question: *Are union workers a bigger percentage of workers in countries other than the United States?*

Answer: *Generally speaking, the United States is a country of low union density (union membership as a percentage of employment) compared with Canada, Australia, Japan, and most of Western Europe. According to the U.S. Bureau of Labor Statistics, France and the United States have the lowest unionization rates, while Sweden and Denmark have the highest levels of union membership (around 75 to 80 percent for each country).*

Unions' Effects on Union and Nonunion Wages

On average, do union workers receive higher pay than comparable nonunion workers? (By saying *comparable* nonunion workers, we are comparing union and nonunion workers who do essentially the same work.) One important economics study concluded that over the period from 1920 to 1979, the average wage of union members was 10 to 15 percent higher than that of comparable nonunion labor. That is, for every $100 earned by nonunion labor, comparable union labor earned between $110 and $115. In 2000, the U.S. Bureau of Labor Statistics reported that mean weekly earnings for union workers were one-third higher than for nonunion workers.

There is an economic reason for believing these results. A simple example is illustrated in Exhibit 8-7. Suppose there are 100 persons in the labor force. Currently, 25 of these persons are members of a union, and 75 are not. We assume that each of the 100 persons can work in either the union

Exhibit 8-6
States That Have Right-to-Work Laws

In the twenty-one states that have right-to-work laws, the union shop is illegal.

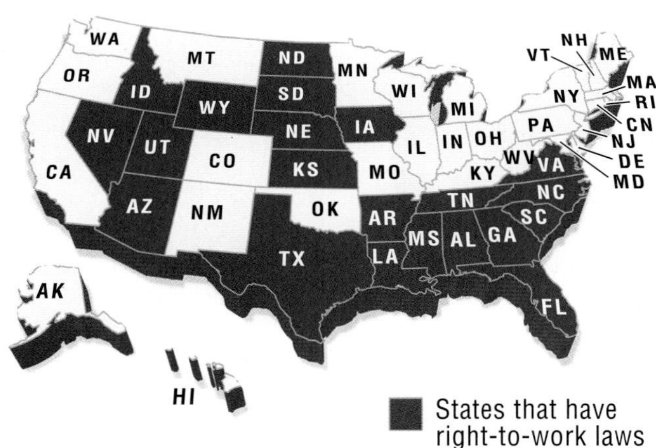

Exhibit 8-7

Unions' Effects on Union and Nonunion Wages

Given:
1. 25 workers in union sector
2. 75 workers in nonunion sector
3. Wage rate of $8 in both sectors

↓

Labor union calls a strike. Result is higher union wage rate of $9.

↓

As a result of the higher union wage rate, firms in the union sector of the economy fire five union workers.

↓

These five fired union workers seek work in the nonunion sector.

↓

Supply of labor in the nonunion sector rises and, as a result, the nonunion wage rate falls.

↓

Conclusion:
Unions cause wage rates to rise for union workers and to fall for comparable nonunion workers.

How might a successful strike by a union affect *union* wages? How might a successful strike by a union affect *nonunion* wages?

or the nonunion part of the economy. Furthermore, we assume that each of the 100 persons currently earns a wage rate of $8.

Suppose now that the labor union (of which 25 persons are members) calls a strike and ends up bargaining its way to a wage rate of $9. At $9 per hour, the businesses that currently employ union labor workers do not wish to employ as many persons as they wished to employ at a wage rate of $8, so a few of the union workers get fired. Let's say that 5 workers get fired.

The 5 union workers who have been fired seek jobs in the nonunion part of the economy. As a result, the supply of persons in the nonunion part rises (from 75 to 80). An increase in the supply of labor puts downward pressure on wage rates in the nonunion part of the economy. The wage rate moves down from $8 to $7.50.

Most studies support the conclusion that union labor earns more than comparable nonunion labor. For example, throughout most of the 1980s and

In the late 1990s, miners who were members of a labor union earned $60 more a week than miners who were not members of a labor union.

1990s, weekly earnings were higher for union labor than for comparable nonunion labor in the mining, construction, manufacturing, retail, and services parts of the economy. The dollar differences varied, though. In 1998, for example, there was a difference of $60 in mining, whereas there was a difference of approximately $300 in construction.

Two Views of Labor Unions

Some people see labor unions as an obstacle to establishing reasonable work standards. Other people see labor unions as a valuable collective voice for their members.

There are two major views of labor unions' effects on production and efficiency. The traditional view holds that labor unions are an obstacle to establishing reasonable work standards and thus make companies that employ union labor less competitive. For example, suppose some members of a plumbers' union work for a manufacturing company. The union may insist that only a plumber in this company (and no one else) can change the washer on a leaky faucet. Union critics argue that such rigid staffing requirements are unreasonable and that they make these companies less competitive in a world economy. When a company loses its competitive edge, it may go out of business.

A newer view says that the labor union is a valuable collective voice for its members. There is evidence that in some industries, union firms have a higher rate of productivity than nonunion firms. Economists explain this by saying that the labor union plays a role as a collective-voice mechanism for its members. Without a labor union, some argue, workers who were disgruntled with their jobs, who felt taken advantage of by their employers, or who felt unsafe in their work would leave their jobs and seek work elsewhere. This "job exiting" comes at a cost. It raises training costs for the firm and results in lengthy job searches during which those searching for jobs are not producing goods. Such costs can be reduced, it is argued, when a labor union acts as a collective voice for its members. Instead of individual employees' having to discuss ticklish employment matters with their employers, the labor union does it for them. Overall, the labor union makes the employees feel more confident, less intimidated, and more secure in their work. Such positive feelings usually mean happier, more productive employees.

A Brief History of the Labor Movement

National unionism began to emerge in the United States after the Civil War. Since labor unions greatly impact the U.S. economy, you should be aware of some of the key events in the development of these unions.

The Knights of Labor In 1869, a union called the Knights of Labor was organized. Seventeen years later, in 1886, its membership totaled approximately 800,000. The Knights of Labor welcomed anyone who worked for a living—farmers, skilled workers, and unskilled workers—with a few exceptions, such as liquor dealers. The group called for higher wages and an eight-hour working day.

On May 4, 1886, approximately 100,000 members of the Knights of Labor demonstrated in front of the McCormick Harvester Works in Haymarket Square in Chicago. Someone tossed a bomb into the crowd, causing a riot in which several people were killed. Public sentiment soon turned against the Knights of Labor, although no wrongdoing on its part was proved. The union began to lose membership, and in 1917 it collapsed.

On May 4, 1886, at Haymarket Square in Chicago, labor demonstrations to protest the killing of a union worker turned into a bloody riot. The riot had a negative impact on the membership and on the power of the Knights of Labor.

The American Federation of Labor The American Federation of Labor (AFL) was formed in 1886 under the leadership of Samuel Gompers, who ran the organization until his death in 1924. Gompers believed that the AFL should consist mainly of skilled workers. Membership was approximately 2 million in 1904, rising to 5 million in 1920 and then falling to 3 million in 1930. Its activities were almost solely directed to lobbying for better pay and improved working conditions for its members.

Early Court Decisions In the early days of the labor union movement, the courts had treated unions as illegal conspiracies. Union leaders were regularly prosecuted and sued for damages. For example, in an important case decided by the Supreme Court of Massachusetts in 1842, the court ruled that unions were not illegal, but that certain union practices were. Later, the Sherman Antitrust Act, which was passed by Congress in 1890, began to be applied to labor unions, although many persons said that Congress had only intended it to be applied to businesses. The Sherman Act declared that "every person who shall . . . combine or conspire with any other person or persons, to monopolize any part of the trade or commerce . . . shall be guilty of a misdemeanor."

Samuel Gompers, shown here (standing) with the executive council of the American Federation of Labor, believed that the AFL should include mainly skilled workers.

During the early 1900s, injunctions were used against labor unions to prevent strikes and some other activities. (Injunctions are court orders that were originally designed to prevent damage to property when it was thought that other court processes would be too slow.) Because of the use of injunctions by employers during this period, labor unions found it very difficult to strike.

The Norris-LaGuardia and Wagner Acts The legal climate in which labor unions operated changed dramatically in 1932 with the passage of the Norris-LaGuardia Act by the U.S. Congress. The main thrust of the act was to restrain the use of injunctions. It declared that workers should be "free from the interference, restraint, or coercion of employers" in choosing their union representatives.

Senator Robert F. Wagner sponsored the Wagner Act. The Wagner Act has been called the single most important piece of labor legislation enacted in the United States in the twentieth century.

In 1935 Congress passed the Wagner Act, which required employers to bargain in good faith with workers; the act also made it illegal for employers to interfere with their employees' rights to organize or join a union. In addition, the act set up the National Labor Relations Board (NLRB) to investigate unfair labor practices.

Union membership grew by leaps and bounds as a result of the Norris-LaGuardia and the Wagner Acts.

The Congress of Industrial Organizations Because of the better legal climate for labor unions after passage of the Norris-LaGuardia and Wagner Acts, a push was made to unionize major industries such as steel and automobiles. This trend caused some discontent within the AFL. The union was largely made up of craft unions—unions of individuals who practice the same craft or trade (for example, everyone within a particular craft union may be a plumber, an electrician, or the like). Some people within the AFL wanted to unionize people only into craft unions. Others wanted industrial unions—unions that include everyone in a particular industry, whether or not they all practice the same craft. For example, people doing many different jobs in the automobile industry would belong to the same union. In 1938, John L. Lewis of the United Mine Workers broke with the AFL and formed the Congress of Industrial Organizations (CIO). The CIO successfully unionized the steel, rubber, textile, meat-packing, and automobile industries along industrial union lines.

John L. Lewis formed the Congress of Industrial Organizations (CIO). What difference of opinion led Lewis and others to split with the AFL and form the CIO?

For a time, both the AFL and the CIO increased their memberships. After World War II, however, membership in the CIO began to decline. Some thought that the bickering between the two unions was the cause. In 1955, the AFL, a craft union, and the CIO, an industrial union, merged under the leadership of George Meany into the AFL-CIO.

The Taft-Hartley Act The congressional sentiment that made the Wagner Act possible in 1935 began to shift after World War II. A few particularly damaging strikes in 1946 set the stage for the Taft-Hartley Act in 1947. This act gave states the right to pass right-to-work laws, which prohibit unions from requiring employers to make union membership a condition of employment.

In the 1960s and 1970s public employee union membership increased. Should public employees, such as firefighters, have the right to strike?

The Landrum-Griffin Act Congress passed the Landrum-Griffin Act in 1959 with the intent of policing the internal affairs of labor unions. The act calls for regular union elections and secret ballots, and it requires union leaders to report on their unions' finances. It also prohibits former convicts and communists from holding union office. The Landrum-Griffin Act was passed because during the late 1950s, the U.S. public became concerned over reports that some labor union leaders had misappropriated funds and were involved in corruption.

The Growth in Public Employee Unions A public employee union is a union whose members work for the local, state, or federal government. By far the most important development in the labor movement in the 1960s and 1970s was the sharp growth in public employee union membership. The main issue raised by public employee unions is the right to strike. These unions feel they should be able to exercise this right, but their opponents argue that public sector strikes—by police officers or firefighters, for example—could have a crippling effect on society.

Section 2 Review

Defining Terms

1. Define
   a. Taft-Hartley Act
   b. strike
   c. right-to-work law
   d. union shop
2. What is the purpose of a labor union?
3. What is the difference between a union shop and a closed shop?

Reviewing Facts and Concepts

4. Labor union A wants to increase the demand for its member workers. Identify two things the union can do to try to achieve this outcome.
5. Is the union shop illegal in right-to-work states?
6. What did the Norris-LaGuardia Act accomplish?

Critical Thinking

7. Do you think it was right for the courts, in the early days of labor unions, to issue injunctions that prevented strikes and other union activities? Why or why not?

Applying Economic Concepts

8. The members of labor union X produce cars in the United States for sale in the United States only. The U.S. Congress is contemplating imposing a quota (a quantitative restriction) on the number of foreign-produced cars that can be sold in the country. Are the members of labor union X likely to support or not support this action? Explain your answer.

SECTION 3

Measuring Unemployment

The chapter so far has been discussing people who work at jobs in the labor force. Not everyone who wants to work is working, however. Some people are unemployed. The discussion now turns to the facts and figures of unemployment.

As you read this section, keep these key questions in mind:

- What two major categories make up the noninstitutional adult civilian population?
- What two categories make up the civilian labor force?
- How do we calculate the unemployment rate?
- How is the employment rate calculated?

Who Are the Unemployed?

Key Terms

unemployment rate
employment rate

Exhibit 8-8 discusses employment status in the United States. Start with the total population of the United States. Next, divide the population into two broad groups. One group consists of persons who are under sixteen years of age, in the armed forces, or in a mental or correctional facility. The other group, which consists of all others in the total population, is called the *noninstitutional adult civilian population.*

Now take the noninstitutional adult civilian population and divide it into two groups: persons *not in the labor force* and persons in the *civilian labor force.*

Exhibit 8-8

Breakdown of the Total U.S. Population by Employment Status

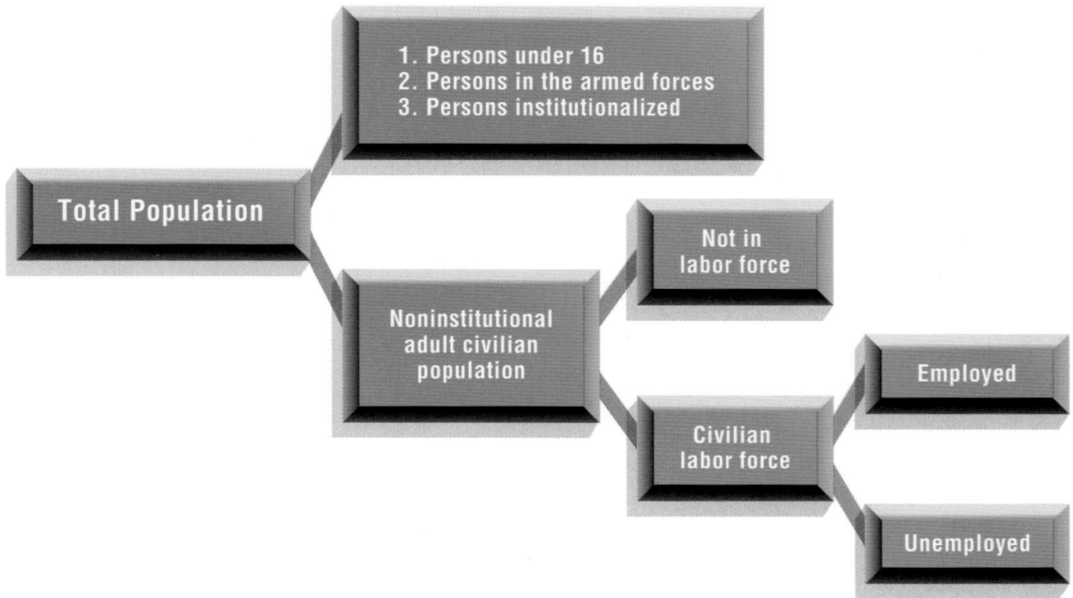

The persons not in the labor force are those who are neither working nor looking for work. Retired persons fall into this category, as do those engaged in homemaking in their own homes and persons who choose not to work.

Persons in the civilian labor force can be categorized as being either *employed* or *unemployed.*

Civilian labor force = Unemployed persons + Employed persons

How Do You Know If You're Employed or Unemployed?

How do you know if you're employed or unemployed? On the surface, this question is silly. You might say that you know if you're employed or unemployed by simply knowing whether you have a job. If you do, you are employed. If you do not, you are unemployed.

Unfortunately, things are not this simple. Suppose Frank, age twenty, worked twelve hours last week as an "unpaid" worker on his father's farm. Furthermore, Frank is not looking for work. Would you consider him to be employed or unemployed? Some people would say Frank is unemployed, because he is not earning a wage; others would say he is employed, because he is working at a job.

Persons who are retired, engaged in homemaking in their homes, or who choose not to work (for whatever reason) are not in the civilian labor force.

To clarify the situation, let's turn to the official government definitions of *unemployed* and *employed persons.* A person is employed if he or she did any of the following:

1. Worked at least one hour as a paid employee during the past week.
2. Worked in his or her own business or profession.
3. Worked at least fifteen hours per week as an "unpaid" worker on a family-owned farm or business.
4. Was temporarily absent from work for reasons of illness, vacation, bad weather, child-care problems, maternity or paternity leave, a labor-management dispute, job training, or family or personal reasons.

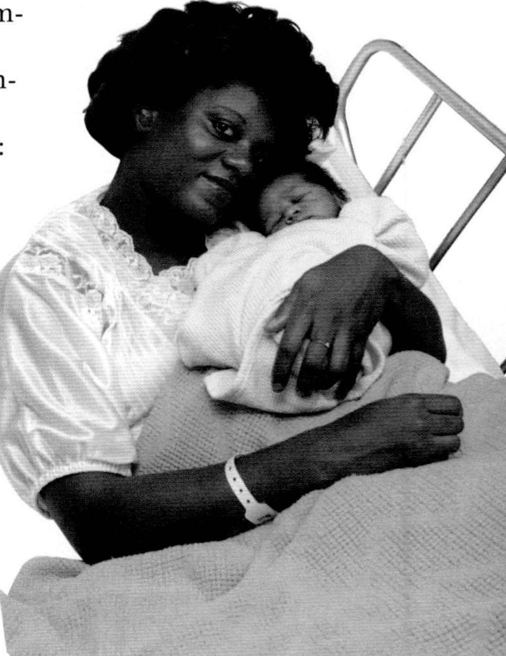

A mother on maternity leave from work is considered employed.

A person is unemployed if any of the following is true:

1. He or she did not work during the past week, actively looked for work within the past four weeks, and is currently available for work.
2. He or she is waiting to be called back to a job after having been laid off.
3. He or she is waiting to report to a job within thirty days.

MINI GLOSSARY

unemployment rate The percentage of the civilian labor force that is unemployed. Unemployment rate = unemployed persons ÷ civilian labor force.

employment rate The percentage of the noninstitutional adult civilian population that is employed. Employment rate = employed persons ÷ noninstitutional adult civilian population.

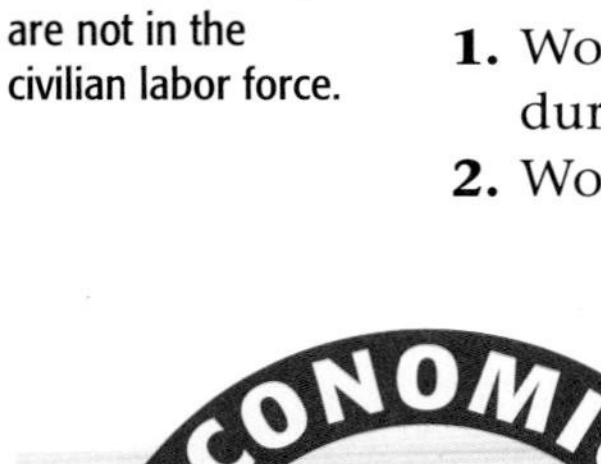

ECONOMICS and the INTERNET

Go to the Economics Statistics Briefing Room at
http://www.whitehouse.gov/fsbr/employment.html
and report the current numerical data for the following:

1. the civilian labor force
2. the number of unemployed persons
3. the unemployment rate
4. average weekly hours
5. average hourly earnings

A person who works at least fifteen hours per week as an unpaid worker on a family-owned farm is considered employed.

Let's return to Frank, who worked twelve hours as an unpaid worker on his father's farm. Is Frank employed? According to our definition of an employed person, Frank would have had to work at least fifteen hours as an unpaid worker on his father's farm to be considered employed. Because he worked only twelve hours, he cannot be considered employed. Does this mean, then, that Frank is unemployed? The answer is no, because he does not meet any of the three criteria just given for an unemployed person.

If Frank is neither employed nor unemployed, what is he? A glance at Exhibit 8-8 shows that Frank is *not in the labor force*. First, Frank is not employed, nor is he unemployed. According to the exhibit, Frank then cannot be part of the civilian labor force. If he is not part of the civilian labor force but is still a part of the noninstitutional adult civilian population (which he is, because he is not under sixteen, in the armed forces, or institutionalized), then he must fall into the "not in the labor force" category.

Unemployment and Employment Rates

The **unemployment rate** is the percentage of the civilian labor force that is unemployed. It is equal to the number of unemployed persons divided by the civilian labor force.

$$\text{Unemployment rate} = \frac{\text{Unemployed persons}}{\text{Civilian labor force}}$$

For example, if the number of persons unemployed is 1 million and the labor force is 10 million, then the unemployment rate is 10 percent.

The **employment rate** is the percentage of the noninstitutional adult civilian population that is employed. It is equal to the number of persons employed divided by the number of persons in the noninstitutional adult civilian population:

$$\text{Employment rate} = \frac{\text{Employed persons}}{\text{Noninstitutional adult civilian population}}$$

Physical Therapist

Accident victims and individuals with disabling conditions such as low back pain, arthritis, and fractures often go to physical therapists. These health care professionals provide services that help restore function, improve mobility, relieve pain, and prevent or limit permanent physical disabilities. They often consult and practice with physicians, dentists, nurses, speech-language pathologists, and others. Some specialize in certain areas, such as pediatrics, geriatrics, or sports medicine. In the late 1990s there were approximately 120,000 physical therapists in the United States, and one out of four worked part-time. About two-thirds were employed in either hospitals or offices.

All states require physical therapists to pass a licensure examination after graduating from an accredited educational program. According to the American Physical Therapy Association, there are about 170 accredited physical therapy programs across the country. The U.S. Bureau of Labor Statistics predicts that physical therapists will be among the fastest-growing occupations through the year 2006.

QUESTION TO ANSWER The elderly population of the United States is growing as a percentage of the entire population. How will this affect the demand for physical therapists?

Tomorrow's Jobs

The U.S. Bureau of Labor Statistics often makes projections about jobs in the future. Here are some projections for the period from 1996 to 2006.[3]

- The labor force will grow 11 percent between 1996 and 2006, which is half the rate that it grew during the period from 1976 to 1986.
- The labor force will continue to grow faster than the population.
- The labor force growth for Hispanics, Asians, and other races will be faster than for blacks, whites, and non-Hispanics.
- Between 1996 and 2006, women's share of the labor force is projected to slowly increase, from 46 to 47 percent.
- Workers over age forty-five will account for a larger share of the labor force as the baby boom generation ages.
- Business, health, and education services will account for 70 percent of the growth within the service industry.
- Health care services will account for 3.1 million new jobs between 1996 and 2006, the largest numerical increase of any industry.
- Computer and data processing services will add more than 1.3 million jobs from 1996 to 2006.
- Of the twenty-five occupations with the largest and fastest employment growth, high pay, and low unemployment, eighteen require at least a bachelor's degree.
- The three fastest-growing occupations are in computer-related fields.
- Occupations that require a bachelor's degree are projected to grow the fastest—nearly twice as fast as the average for all occupations.

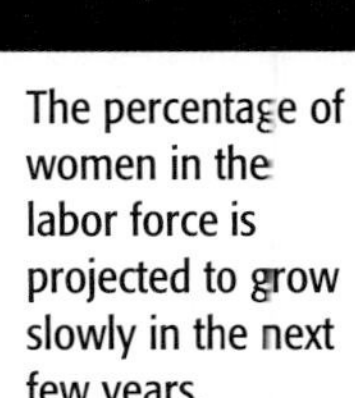

The percentage of women in the labor force is projected to grow slowly in the next few years.

Tomorrow's jobs will increasingly require a college degree.

3. The information here is taken from "Tomorrow's Job," a report published by the U.S. Bureau of Labor Statistics (Web site address where this report was found: http://stats.bls.gov/oco/oco2003.htm).

Section 3 Review

Defining Terms

1. Define
   a. unemployment rate
   b. employment rate

Reviewing Facts and Concepts

2. The noninstitutional adult civilian population is 100 million, the civilian labor force is 66 million, and the number of unemployed is 4 million. How many persons are not in the labor force?
3. Jason worked on his family's farm last week for about six hours. He did not receive any pay. Is Jason part of the civilian labor force? Explain your answer.
4. The noninstitutional adult civilian population is 120 million, the number of unemployed persons is 5 million, and the number of employed persons is 60 million. What is the unemployment rate?

Critical Thinking

5. Clark got fired from his job on January 5. He looked for another job from January 6 through April 20. He could not find anyone who wanted to hire him. It is now June 5, and Clark neither has a job nor is actively searching for a job. Is Clark unemployed? Explain your answer.

Applying Economic Concepts

6. If the unemployment rate is 10 percent, does it follow that the employment rate is 90 percent? Explain your answer.

Developing Economic Skills

The Economics Paper: Doing the Research

The previous chapter discussed how to find a topic for an economics paper. We chose "U.S. businesses and foreign competition" as our topic. The next step is the research. A researcher is also an investigator.

Where do you begin as a researcher? First, you must define your goal. You probably have a number of questions about the chosen topic. You need answers to your questions. Your goal, then, is to learn enough about the topic that you have selected to answer many, if not all, of your questions.

The place to begin your research is the library, and a key person to speak with there is the librarian. You might tell the librarian, "I want to write a paper on U.S. businesses and foreign competition. Here are a few of the questions I would like to answer in my paper. Where would you suggest I begin my research?" Librarians are experts at finding information; they are some of the best investigators around.

To research your topic, search the computerized library catalog using the *subject index*. To do this you need to identify a couple of key words that pertain to the topic—perhaps *foreign competition, U.S. businesses,* and *foreign firms in the U.S.* The librarian might be able to suggest other key words for your search.

Locate the books, and examine them to see if they have information relevant to your topic by checking the index at the back of the book. Look for the same key words you used to search the subject index of the card catalog.

You can also search for information in newspapers and magazines using a database, information in electronic form that can be accessed through a computer. If your library subscribes to a database service on newspapers, you can type in key words pertaining to your topic. The computer screen will then display a list of articles that contain information on your chosen subject from the newspapers in the database.

Other excellent sources of information are encyclopedias and dictionaries of economics, such as the *International Encyclopedia of the Social Sciences* and the *Fortune Encyclopedia of Economics,* edited by David R. Henderson.

As you conduct your research, it is important that you take clear and detailed notes. Each time you find some information that pertains to the topic, write down a summary of what you have found. Also note where you found your information. Keep detailed bibliographic references, including the name of the source, the author, the publisher, the city of publication, the date of publication, and the page where you found the information. This information will help you when it comes time to write the paper. If you copy passages from any source, be sure to note that they are quotations so that you can give proper credit in your paper. If you use someone else's words or ideas, you must let your reader know that you are doing so.

Finally, keep in mind that research often requires a lot of tedious work. Often you will spend hours looking for a book that ends up being of little use to you when writing your paper. Research is not about finding the book or coming across the person who can give you all the answers. It is about making the best use of all the resources available to you.

1. Choose an economics topic to research. (You may consider one of the topics you chose when working on the "Developing Economics Skills" feature in Chapter 7.) Next, visit your school library, city library, or both, and write a list of five sources that seem relevant to your topic. If any of your sources are books, identify the pages you think will be most useful. (Check the index.)
2. Learn how to locate information by subject using your school library's computerized catalog. Write an explanation of this process.

CHAPTER

8 Review

Economics Vocabulary

Fill in the following blanks with the appropriate word or phrase.

1. The _____ sets a level below which wage rates are not allowed to fall.
2. A(n) _____ is an organization that hires only union members.
3. The _____ is the percentage of the civilian labor force that is unemployed.
4. The _____ is the percentage of the noninstitutional adult civilian population that is employed.
5. A(n) _____ is an organization that requires employees to join the union within a certain period of time after being hired.
6. The _____, which was passed in 1947, gave the states the right to pass right-to-work laws.

Review Questions

1. In a competitive labor market, what happens to the wage rate when there is a surplus of labor? A shortage of labor?
2. John earns a higher wage rate than Wilson. It necessarily follows that the demand for John's labor services is greater than the demand for Wilson's labor services. Do you agree or disagree? Explain your answer.
3. If the minimum wage rate is higher than the equilibrium wage rate, fewer people will be hired because the cost of labor is too high. Do you agree or disagree? Explain your answer.
4. What are unions' effects on union wages? On nonunion wages? Explain your answers.
5. Identify two factors that can change the demand for labor.
6. If an individual is offered two jobs, one of which pays more than the other, the individual will always choose the higher-paying job. Do you agree or disagree? Explain your answer.
7. How is a person's quality and level of education related to his or her wages?
8. If the average major league baseball player earns less than the average professional basketball player, is this situation necessarily because the demand for baseball players is lower than the demand for basketball players? Explain your answer.
9. Can a person's money wage decrease at the same time his or her real wage increases? Explain.
10. Outline the traditional and the new view of labor unions.
11. What were the demands of the Knights of Labor?
12. Outline the details of the Wagner Act.
13. What is a public employee union?
14. Are persons "not in the labor force" considered to be in the civilian labor force?
15. Explain how a person can be working but not be employed.
16. What is the unemployment rate?
17. Is it possible for the unemployment rate to rise as the number of unemployed persons falls? Explain your answer.
18. If the demand for labor increases by the same amount as the supply of labor increases, will wages rise, fall, or remain the same?
19. If the demand for labor increases by less than the supply of labor increases, will wages rise, fall, or remain the same?

Calculations

1. Alicia turned down a job that pays $60,000 a year for a job that pays $32,000 a year. The nonmoney benefits in the lower-paying job equal at least what dollar amount?
2. In year 1, Bob earns $1,000 a month when the CPI is 130. In year 2, Bob earns $1,500 a month when the CPI is 135. In which year is Bob's real income higher? What percentage higher?
3. Total population = 145 million; noninstitutional adult civilian population = 135 million; persons not in the labor force = 10 million; unemployed persons = 7 million. Using these data, compute the following.
   a. the unemployment rate
   b. the employment rate
   c. the civilian labor force
   d. the total number of persons who are under the age of sixteen, in the armed services, or in an institution

Graphs

Graphically represent the following.

1. The equilibrium wage rate is currently $10 an hour. The demand for labor increases by more than the

supply of labor increases. The new equilibrium wage rate is $12. Be sure to label your axes.

2. The demand for labor falls by more than the supply of labor rises.
3. The demand for labor rises by the same amount as the supply of labor rises.
4. In Exhibit 8-9, the original demand and supply curves are labeled D_1 and S_1, and the new demand and supply curves are labeled D_2 and S_2. In Parts a through d, identify what will happen to the equilibrium wage as a result of the change in demand, supply, or both.

Exhibit 8-9

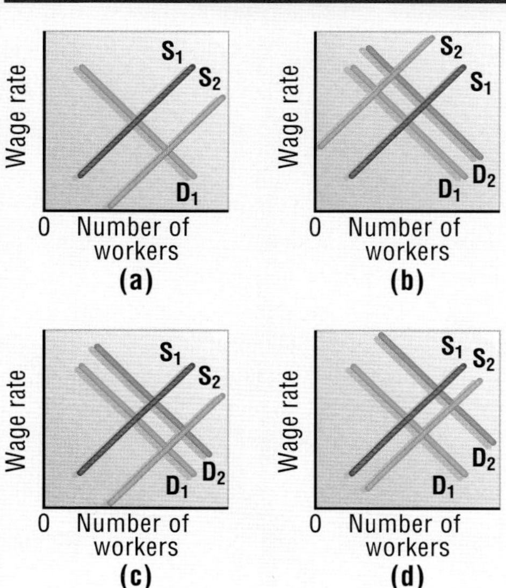

Economics and Thinking Skills

1. **Application.** Suppose you are an economist hired by a labor union that is currently negotiating wages with management. Current union members are paid $18 an hour. The objective of the labor union executives is to make sure that over the next year, their members' wages do not fall in real terms. The CPI in the current year is 179, and the expected CPI next year is 190. What (money) wage would maintain the real wage of the union members?
2. **Analysis.** Three jobs, A, B, and C, all pay the same salary, $70,000 a year. What additional information do you need to decide which of the three jobs is the best job for you?
3. **Cause and Effect.** Is higher labor productivity an effect of higher wages or a cause of higher wages? Explain your answer.

Writing Skills

The early history of the labor union movement is full of interesting stories. Go to the Internet and read *The Battle of Matewan* at http://www.matewan.com/battle.htm. After you have studied the story, write a two-page paper outlining the details.

Economics in the Media

Pick a television or movie star who is currently earning a relatively high salary. Explain what the star does. Next, explain why the person earns such a large salary.

Where's the Economics?

How would increased public demand for basketball games affect the average salary paid in baseball?

Analyzing Primary Sources

Samuel Gompers, the president of the American Federation of Labor between 1886 and 1924, was a leading spokesman for the labor union movement. He advocated shorter working hours, higher wages, safe and sanitary working conditions, and workplace democracy. Before he died, Gompers wrote a farewell message to be read after his death. The following is part of the message:

"Say to them that as I kept the faith I expect they will keep the faith. . . . Say to them that a union man carrying a card is not a good citizen unless he upholds the institutions of our great country, and a poor citizen . . . if he upholds the institutions of our country and forgets the obligations of his trade association. "

- Do you agree or disagree with Gompers's statement? Explain your answer.

CHAPTER 9

Government and Business

What This Chapter Is About

Every day you deal with two major institutions, government and business, in many ways. This chapter discusses some of the ways that government and business deal with each other in the United States—specifically, the many governmental policies designed to influence behavior. Both antitrust and regulatory policies are described in this discussion of the role of government in the U.S. free-enterprise system.

Why This Chapter Is Important

The eighteenth-century economist Adam Smith was a major advocate of the free-enterprise system. Still, he believed that businesspersons rarely get together without talking about how they can make themselves better off at their customers' expense. He said, "People of the same trade seldom meet together, even for merriment and diversion, but the conversation ends in a conspiracy against the public, or in some contrivance to raise prices."

There are indeed cases in which business firms conspire against the public and contrive to raise prices. Most economists agree that government has a role to play in trying to prevent this kind of action and, if it has already occurred, in punishing the persons responsible. We have to be careful, however, not to slip into the error of thinking that every time business and government are involved in some matter, it is business that is wrong and government that is right. Also, we should remember that sometimes government and business do things together that end up hurting the public.

This chapter considers the many ways in which government and business interact. Because government and business are important parts of your life, an enhanced understanding of each will increase your understanding of the world in which you live.

After You Study This Chapter, You Will Be Able To

- describe the Sherman Antitrust Act, Clayton Act, Federal Trade Commission Act, Robinson-Patman Act, and Wheeler-Lea Act.
- explain the types of natural monopoly regulation.
- explain how an economist thinks about regulation.
- explain how government deals with negative externalities.

You Will Also Learn What Economics Has to Do With

- Hollywood.
- eviction notices.
- bogus marriages.
- being late to class.

Economics Journal

Read through a newspaper each day for a week. Make a list of the stories you find that have to do with both government and business. Write down the title of each story or article. Next to the title, explain what the story is about.

SECTION 1

Antitrust Law

One of the stated objectives of government is to encourage competition so that monopolists do not have substantial control over the prices they charge. The government tries to meet this objective through its **antitrust laws,** laws meant to control monopoly power and to preserve and promote competition. This section examines five of the major antitrust laws.

As you read this section, keep these key questions in mind:

- What do the antitrust acts deem illegal?
- What are the criticisms of the antitrust acts?

Key Terms

antitrust law
merger
trust
price discrimination

The Sherman Antitrust Act

The Sherman Antitrust Act (or, simply, the Sherman Act) was passed in 1890, a time when there were numerous mergers between companies. A **merger** occurs when one company buys more than half the stock in another company, putting two companies under one top management. At the time of the Sherman Act, the organization that two companies formed by combining to act as a monopolist was called a **trust,** which in turn gave us the word *antitrust.*

The Sherman Act contains two major provisions:

1. "Every contract, combination in the form of trust or otherwise, or conspiracy, in restraint of trade or commerce . . . is hereby declared to be illegal."
2. "Every person who shall monopolize, or attempt to monopolize, or combine or conspire with any other person or persons to monopolize any part of the trade or commerce . . . shall be deemed guilty of a misdemeanor."

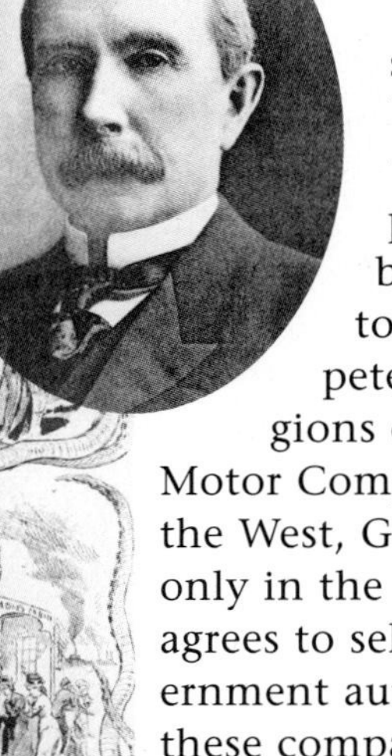

One of the most famous trusts in U.S. history was the Standard Oil Trust, controlled by John D. Rockefeller.

Together, these two provisions state that either attempting to become a monopolist or trying to restrain trade is illegal. Suppose three companies that sell basically the same product get together and promise not to compete with one another in certain regions of the country. Perhaps Ford Motor Company agrees to sell cars only in the West, General Motors agrees to sell cars only in the South and East, and Chrysler agrees to sell cars only in the North. Government authorities would likely rule that these companies were conspiring to eliminate competition and that such actions were illegal under the Sherman Act. The

antitrust law Legislation passed for the stated purpose of controlling monopoly power and preserving and promoting competition.

merger A joining of two companies that occurs when one company buys more than half the stock in the other company. As a result, the companies come to act as one.

trust A combination of firms that come together to act as a monopolist.

price discrimination What occurs when a seller charges different buyers different prices for the same product when the price differences are not related to cost differences.

word *likely* was used in the last sentence because the Sherman Act is somewhat vague. For example, the act never explains which specific acts constitute "restraint of trade," although it declares such acts illegal.

The Clayton Act

The Clayton Act of 1914 made certain business practices illegal when their effects "may be to substantially lessen competition or tend to create a monopoly." The following practices were prohibited by the act:

1. *Price discrimination.* **Price discrimination** occurs when a seller charges different buyers different prices for the same product and when the price differences are not related to cost differences. For example, if a company charges you $10 for a product and charges your friend $6 for the same product, and there is no cost difference for the company in providing the two of you with this product, then the company is practicing price discrimination.

   You might argue that this goes on every day, sometimes very innocently. For example, suppose ten-year-old Jonathan has a lemonade stand in front of his house. He advertises that he will sell a glass of lemonade for 50 cents. George, a neighbor, comes along and buys a glass for 50 cents. Then Karen, a girl Jonathan likes, comes along, and Jonathan sells her a glass of lemonade for only 5 cents. Is Jonathan price discriminating? Probably. Does the Clayton Act apply to him? Probably not. Remember, the act says that price discrimination is illegal only when it has the effect of substantially lessening competition. It is doubtful that Jonathan's pricing policy in his neighborhood is substantially lessening competition in the lemonade industry.

Suppose these young girls charge one customer a higher price for lemonade than another customer. Does the Clayton Act apply to their act of price discrimination?

2. *Tying contracts.* A tying contract is an arrangement whereby the sale of one product depends on the purchase of some other product or products. For example, suppose the owner of a company that sells personal computers and computer supplies agrees to sell computers to a store only if the store owner agrees to buy paper, desk furniture, and some other products, too. This agreement is a tying contract, and it is illegal under the Clayton Act.
3. *The acquisition of competing companies' stock if the acquisition reduces competition.* If Ford Motor Company acquired stock in General Motors, its competitor, the government might rule this acquisition illegal. Again, it is important to note that an acquisition must substantially lessen competition before the Clayton Act applies. If Ford owned one share of General Motors, it would hardly substantially lessen competition.

4. *Interlocking directorates.* An interlocking directorate is an arrangement whereby the directors of one company sit on the board of directors of another company in the same industry. For example, such an arrangement would exist if Jones, Brown, and Smith were on the board of directors of Chrysler and were also on the board of directors of Ford.

The Federal Trade Commission Act

What does the Clayton Act say about the directors of one company sitting on the board (of directors) of another company?

The Federal Trade Commission Act, passed in 1914, declared that "unfair methods of competition in commerce" were illegal. In particular, the act was designed to prohibit aggressive price-cutting acts, sometimes referred to as *cutthroat pricing.* For example, suppose you own a business that produces and sells tires. A competitor begins to drastically lower the prices of the tires it sells. From your viewpoint, your competitor may be engaged in cutthroat pricing. From the viewpoint of the consumer, your competitor is simply offering a good deal. The officials who are supposed to enforce the Federal Trade Commission Act will have to decide. If they believe your competitor is cutting its prices so low that you will have to go out of business and that it intends to raise its prices later, when you're gone, they may decide that your competitor is violating the act.

Some economists have noted that the Federal Trade Commission Act, like other antitrust acts, contains vague terms. For instance, the act does not precisely define what "unfair methods of competition" consist of. Suppose a hotel chain puts up a big, beautiful hotel across the street from an old, tiny, run-down motel, and the old motel ends up going out of business. Was the hotel chain employing "unfair methods of competition" or not?

One tire manufacturer drastically lowers the prices of the tires it sells to its customers. Is it involved in cutthroat pricing? The officials who enforce the Federal Trade Commission Act will have to decide.

The Robinson-Patman Act

The Robinson-Patman Act was passed in 1936 in an attempt to decrease the failure rate of small businesses by protecting them from the competition of large and growing chain stores. At that time in our economic history, large chain stores had just arrived on the scene. They were buying goods in large amounts and were sometimes being offered price discounts from their suppliers. The chain stores began to pass on the price discounts to their customers. The small businesses were not being offered the price discounts and thus found it increasingly difficult to compete with the chain stores. The Robinson-Patman Act prohibited suppliers from offering special discounts to large chains unless they also offered the discounts to everyone else.

Many economists believe that rather than preserving and strengthening competition, the Robinson-Patman Act limited it. The act, they say, seemed more concerned about a particular group of competitors (small businesses) than about the process of competition.

The Robinson-Patman Act, passed in 1936, is sometimes called the Anti-Chain-Store Act. Part of the act was designed to protect the small independent retailer from large chain-store competition, which was causing small business failures, and therefore, putting many people out of work.

Exhibit 9-1

Major Antitrust Acts

Major antitrust acts in U.S. history include the Sherman Act, the Clayton Act, the Federal Trade Commission Act, the Robinson-Patman Act, and the Wheeler-Lea Act.

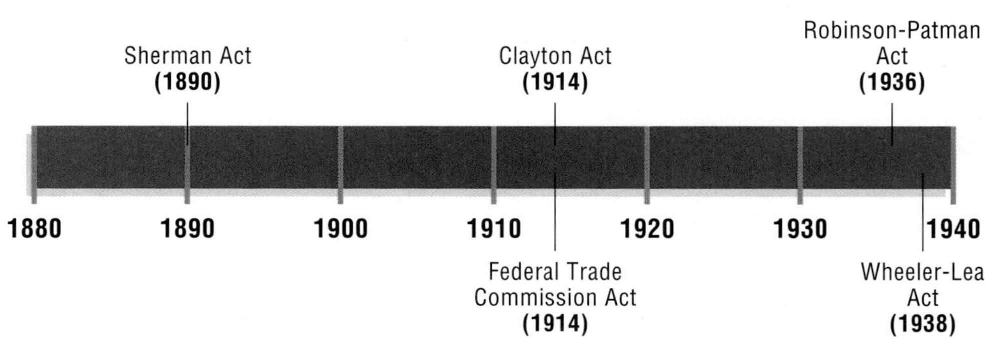

ECONOMICS and the INTERNET

The Antitrust Division of the U.S. Department of Justice enforces many of the antitrust laws. Go to its Web site at http://www.usdoj/atr and discover who the current assistant attorney general of the Antitrust Division is. Then click on "Antitrust Case Filings" at the bottom of the page. You will be taken to a page that lists many of the cases that the Antitrust Division has recently filed against companies. Choose any one of the many cases. Read through it, and write a one-page paper outlining the specific charge against the company that is being made by the Antitrust Division.

The Wheeler-Lea Act

The Wheeler-Lea Act, passed in 1938, empowered the Federal Trade Commission (FTC), a government agency, to deal with false and deceptive acts or practices by businesses. Major actions by the FTC in this area have involved advertising that the agency has deemed false and deceptive.

One Major Unanswered Question in Antitrust Policy

It is not always clear where lines should be drawn in implementing antitrust policy. Which firms should be allowed to enter into a merger, and which firms should be prohibited? What constitutes restraint of trade? Which firms should be called monopolists and broken into smaller firms, and which firms should be left alone?

As we might guess, not everyone answers these questions the same way. In short, some points of antitrust policy are still unsettled. One controversy deals with how broadly or narrowly a market is defined. For example, suppose company X manufactures and sells cereal. Is company X in the cereal market, or is it in the breakfast foods market? The cereal market is, of course, a smaller market than the breakfast foods market, because breakfast foods are not only cereal but also everything else people eat for breakfast (eggs, bacon, biscuits, pastries, fruit, and so forth).

How broadly or narrowly a market is defined can have a lot to do with whether a firm is considered a monopoly or not. For example, in an important antitrust suit in 1945, a court ruled that Alcoa (Aluminum Company of America) was a monopoly because it had 90 percent of the virgin aluminum ingot market. If the market Alcoa operated in had been broadened to include stainless steel, copper, tin, nickel, and zinc (some of the goods aluminum had to compete with), it is unlikely that Alcoa would have been ruled a monopoly.

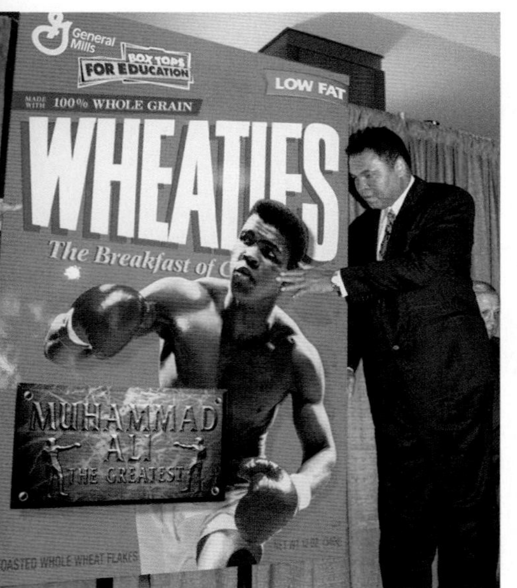

Is a particular cereal manufacturer part of the cereal market or the breakfast foods market? The answer is relevant to issues of antitrust.

In a more recent case, in 1997, two office superstores, Staples, Inc., and Office Depot, sought to enter into a merger. The FTC challenged the merger, stating that it would lead to less competition and higher prices for consumers. The FTC based its argument on what it considered to be the relevant market—namely, the office superstore market. Staples and Office Depot said that the FTC was defining the market much too narrowly. They argued that the relevant market was any business that sold office products, which would include superstores, discount stores, drugstores, and wholesale clubs. While Staples and Office Depot together made up a rather large percentage of the office superstore market, they composed only 6 percent of the much broader market they said was relevant to their merger. In the end, the argument of Staples and Office Depot was not accepted, and they gave up their attempt to merge.

Technology & Innovation

Why Is Hollywood the Film Capital of the World?

Thomas Alva Edison was born in 1847 and died in 1931. The world Edison was born into was very different from the world he died in, and to a large degree the difference was due to Edison himself. In his 84 years, he was granted 1,093 patents—among them 389 for electric light and power, 195 for the phonograph, 150 for the telegraph, 141 for storage batteries, and 34 for the telephone.

Edison also played a major role in the development of the movie industry. Along with an employee, William Dickson, Edison invented the kinetophonograph, which was capable of showing a moving picture that was synchronized with a phonograph record. The kinetoscope, also an Edison invention, was a device in which users put a coin and then watched a short motion picture through a hole.

Edison built the first building that was used solely to make movies. A hole in the ceiling allowed the sun to shine through and illuminate the stage. The entire building was on a set of tracks so it could be moved around to follow the sun. The first film Edison produced was a fifteen-minute movie called *The Great Train Robbery*. Over the years he produced over two thousand short films.

There is evidence that Edison and some others tried to gain complete control over the movie industry in its early days. The Motion Pictures Company, sometimes called the Movie Trust or the Edison Trust, was a group of ten film producers and distributors. The company possessed most of the available motion picture patents for camera and projection equipment. The Movie Trust entered into a contract with Eastman Kodak Company, which manufactured film, to sell film only to members of the Movie Trust. It is reported that the Movie Trust refused to lease or sell equipment to certain independent filmmakers and theater owners. It also forbade the identification of actors in their movies; the Movie Trust thought that if the actors were known, they would demand higher salaries.

An agreement between Thomas Edison (right) and George Eastman (left) was one of several factors causing independent filmmakers to relocate to Southern California, ultimately making Hollywood the movie capital of the world.

One of the independent movie producers the Movie Trust tried to put out of business was Carl Laemmle. Laemmle, along with other independent producers, decided to leave the East Coast, where the Movie Trust had the greatest control, and go to southern California—specifically, Hollywood. In 1917, the Movie Trust was dissolved by court order, but by then the movie industry had a new home. Laemmle, for example, had founded Universal Studios in Hollywood in 1912.

What if the Movie Trust had *not* engaged in anticompetitive tactics? Would Hollywood be the capital of the film world today? It is doubtful. Had it not been for those tactics, the film capital would probably be on the East Coast, around New York City.

QUESTIONS TO ANSWER One of the first films Thomas Edison made was of a research laboratory employee, Fred Ott, sneezing. The short film can be seen at the Web site http://memory.loc.gov/ammem/mi-edisonquery.html. Search for the Edison sneeze.

1. On what day was the sneeze recorded?
2. Identify the name of Edison's movie studio.

Are Antitrust Laws Always Applied Properly?

People are inclined, perhaps, to believe that when the government enforces the antitrust laws, it does so properly. Government may be seen as riding into the market on a white horse, preventing monopolies from running roughshod over consumers. In reality, the record of government in this area is mixed. Sometimes government, through its enforcement of the antitrust laws, promotes and protects competition, and sometimes it does not.

Consider the case of Utah Pie. In 1967, the Salt Lake City–based Utah Pie Company charged that three of its competitors in Los Angeles were practicing price discrimination, which is deemed illegal by the Clayton Act. Specifically, the three competitors were charged with selling pies in Salt Lake City for lower prices than they were selling them near their plants of operation. The Supreme Court ruled in favor of Utah Pie.

What were the facts? Were the three competitors from Los Angeles running Utah Pie out of business? Were they hurting consumers by charging low prices? Some economists have noted that Utah Pie actually charged lower prices for its pies than did its competitors and that it continued to increase its sales volume and earn a profit during the time its competitors were supposedly exhibiting anticompetitive behavior. These economists suggest that Utah Pie was simply trying to use the antitrust laws to hinder its competition.

Was Harvard University conspiring with some other select universities to fix prices? The U.S. Department of Justice thought so.

Now consider a case in which most economists believe that the antitrust laws were applied properly. For many years, the upper-level administrators of some of the top universities—Brown, Columbia, Cornell, Dartmouth, Harvard, MIT, Princeton, University of Pennsylvania, and Yale—met to discuss such things as tuition, faculty salaries, and financial aid. There seemed to be evidence that these meetings occurred because the universities were trying to align tuition, faculty raises, and financial need. For example, one of the universities wanted to raise faculty salaries by more than the others but was persuaded not to do so. Also at these meetings, the administrators would compare lists of applicants to find the names of students who had applied to more than one of their schools (for example, someone might have applied to Harvard, Yale, and MIT). The administrators would then adjust their financial aid packages for that student so that no university was offering more than another.

The U.S. Justice Department charged the universities with a conspiracy to fix prices. Eight of the universities settled the case by agreeing to cease colluding (making secret agreements that effectively reduce competition)

Economics & People

John Sherman, U.S. Senator and chief sponsor of the Sherman Antitrust Act

John Sherman was born on May 10, 1823, in Lancaster, Ohio. He was a younger brother of General William Tecumseh Sherman, who played a major role in the Civil War. John Sherman practiced law in Ohio before entering politics. He served in the U.S. House of Representatives (1855–61) and in the U.S. Senate (1861–77, 1881–97) and was secretary of the Treasury under President Rutherford B. Hayes (1877–81).

John Sherman was considered a fiscal expert, and he often favored conservative, middle-of-the-road financial policies over others. He was the chief sponsor of the Sherman Antitrust Act of 1890. He said trusts and monopolies amounted to "a kingly prerogative, inconsistent with our form of government . . . if we will not endure a king as a political power, we should not endure a king over production, transportation, and sale of any of the necessaries of life."

QUESTION TO ANSWER Do you think that your life today is better or worse because of the Sherman Antitrust Act? Explain your answer.

on tuition, salaries, and financial aid. MIT pursued the case to the U.S. Supreme Court. In 1992, the Supreme Court ruled against MIT, saying that it had violated antitrust laws.

The United States versus Microsoft

On May 15, 1998, the U.S. Department of Justice issued a complaint against the software company Microsoft, Inc. The Justice Department charged that Microsoft was a monopolist in the personal computer operating systems (OS) market. The operating system that Microsoft manufactures and sells is Windows, which, according to the Justice Department, is used on over 80 percent of all Intel-based personal computers in the world.

Bill Gates, co-founder of Microsoft, defends the actions of Microsoft against charges by the U.S. Department of Justice.

The Justice Department claimed that Microsoft was using its dominance in the operating systems market to maintain its monopoly position (inferring that Microsoft was doing something to eliminate its competition from actual and potential operating systems) and to establish a monopoly position in the Internet browser market. How was it doing this? The Justice Department claimed that Microsoft, which packages its Internet browser (Internet Explorer) with Windows, required computer manufacturers to agree—as a condition for receiving licenses to install Windows on their products—not to remove Microsoft's browser and not to allow a more prominent display of a rival browser (such as Netscape Navigator). In other words, unless a computer manufacturer agreed to Microsoft's terms, Microsoft would not license Windows to the manufacturer. Manufacturers were put in a stranglehold position, the Justice Department argued, because a computer without Windows wasn't worth much.

The Justice Department also claimed that Microsoft refused to display the icons of any Internet service providers (such as AOL) on the main Windows screen unless the Internet service provider would first agree to withhold information about non-Microsoft browsers from its customers.

In the antitrust case, Microsoft argued that it was not a monopolist in the operating systems market, or if it was, it certainly didn't act like one. A monopolist sits back and rests on its laurels, knowing that no one can challenge it. Microsoft said that it was a part of a cutthroat software industry where today's industry leaders could go out of business tomorrow if they didn't stay competitive and innovative. It argued that none of its business practices hurt any consumers (after all, it was giving away its Internet browser for free with Windows) and that all were necessary to its survival.

Furthermore, Microsoft argued that packaging its browser with Windows was not an attempt to monopolize any market; instead it was an attempt to provide the buying public with a better, more complete product.

On Friday, November 5, 1999, Judge Thomas Penfield Jackson, the judge who heard the case against Microsoft, issued his findings of fact. Findings of fact simply present the facts of the case as the judge sees them; it does not constitute a ruling in the case. In his findings of fact, Judge Jackson essentially agreed with the case the Justice Department made against Microsoft. Judge Jackson said that Microsoft is not only a monopolist in

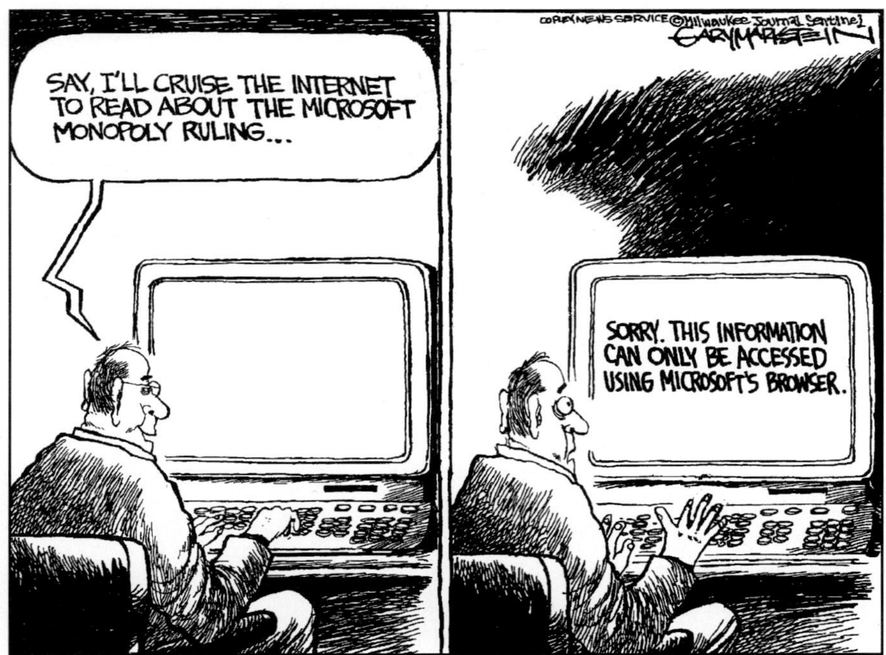

Reprinted by permission of Copley News Service. © 2000 Milwaukee Journal Sentinel. All rights reserved.

the operating-systems (OS) market, but that it used its monopoly power to thwart competition. Specifically, it tied its operating system (Windows) together with its browser (Internet Explorer), not for purposes of efficiency, nor to satisfy consumers, but in order to establish a monopoly position in the browser market and to preserve its monopoly position in the operating-systems market.

Soon after Judge Jackson issued his findings of fact, he asked Judge Richard Posner, chief judge of the U.S. Court of Appeals in Chicago, to attempt to mediate a settlement between Microsoft and the Department of Justice. If a settlement was reached, then there would be no need for the judge to issue a ruling in the case. Settlement talks broke down after four months. On Monday, April 3, 2000, Judge Jackson issued his ruling: Microsoft had violated the Sherman Antitrust Act. The judge wrote: "Microsoft placed an oppressive thumb on the scale of competitive fortune, thereby effectively guaranteeing its dominance" and that Microsoft was guilty of "unlawfully tying its Web browser" to Windows. On June 7, 2000 the judge ordered that Microsoft be split into two firms, one for the Windows operating system and the other for applications software. Microsoft vowed to appeal the judge's order.

Section 1 Review

Defining Terms

1. Define
   a. antitrust law
   b. merger
   c. price discrimination
   d. trust

Reviewing Facts and Concepts

2. A company advertises its product in a deceptive manner. Which act would apply to this action?
3. Which act declares illegal "unfair methods of competition" in commerce?
4. How broadly or narrowly a market is defined can have a lot to do with whether a firm is considered a monopoly or not. Do you agree or disagree? Explain your answer.

Critical Thinking

5. A firm sells its product at a lower price in city A than in city B. Is the firm necessarily a price discriminator?

Applying Economic Concepts

6. A car wash advertises "Every Tuesday Is Ladies' Day," where women can have their cars washed for $3 less than men can have their cars washed. Is this an example of price discrimination? Explain your answer.

SECTION 2

Regulation

Business firms in the U.S. free-enterprise system must abide by rules, or regulations, set up by government. In the 1990s, nearly 60,000 persons were employed in 27 regulatory agencies of the U.S. government. Many others were employed in smaller regulatory agencies in the federal government, and tens of thousands were employed by state and local regulatory agencies. One area in which government regulation is prominent is natural monopoly, discussed in this section.

As you read this section, keep these key questions in mind:

- What are the two principal ways of regulating a natural monopoly?
- How does the public choice theory of regulation differ from the capture theory of regulation?

Key Term

public utility commissions

Natural Monopoly Regulation

Chapter 7 defined a *natural monopoly* as a firm that has such low average total costs that it can outcompete all other firms in the industry and thus become the sole survivor. Examples of natural monopolies include local gas, water, and electricity firms. In many U.S. cities, the local government grants the right to a natural monopoly firm to supply natural gas, electricity, or the like. Government does so on the stated grounds that permitting, say, a number of gas firms to compete in an area would result in many of the firms going out of business. In the process, scarce resources would have been wasted. Many local government officials argue that it is better to permit only one company to provide a particular good or service and then to regulate that one firm. There are two principal ways in which government can and does regulate natural monopolies: price regulation and profit regulation.

Local gas, water, and electricity firms (utilities) are often considered natural monopolies.

MINI GLOSSARY

public utility commission A government group that regulates public utility companies (such as electric, water, and gas companies).

Price Regulation Instead of allowing the regulated natural monopoly to charge any price it wants, **public utility commissions** (government groups that regulate public utility companies) or other government groups can set the price the monopoly can charge. These commissions need to be careful, because if they set a price that is below costs, the natural monopoly will go out of business. Critics point out, though, that if the price is set above costs, the monopolist will have no incentive to hold costs down. For example, suppose a government commission rules that a regulated monopolist can charge $1 over costs for every unit sold. In this case, would the regulated monopolist be concerned if its costs increased? Probably not. According to the government commission's rule, it can charge a higher price if its costs increase.

Public Relations Specialist

Public relations specialists serve as advocates for businesses, governments, universities, hospitals, and other organizations. Their objective is to present the organization they work for in the most positive light possible. Some public relations specialists work as lobbyists; that is, they put forth their organization's best interests before elected officials and try to shape government policy in the process. Generally, though, public relations specialists handle such functions as media, community, consumer, and governmental relations; political campaigns; and interest group representation.

Most public relations specialists are college graduates who studied communications, journalism, law, public relations, advertising, or some related field. Many gained their first experience in the field by working as interns. Experience–the more, the better–is necessary in this field.

QUESTION TO ANSWER How might a company that has an antitrust suit brought against it by the U.S. Justice Department employ a public relations specialist?

Profit Regulation Another way in which government can regulate a natural monopoly is by specifying that it can earn only a certain rate of profit. Again, though, the monopolist may have little incentive to watch its costs. If it knows a certain profit rate is guaranteed no matter what, it may not care whether costs go up or not.

Theories of Regulation

Suppose a natural monopoly firm is outcompeting all firms in the area. Once all the other firms have gone out of business, the natural monopoly raises its prices. Its attitude is, "We're the only guy in town. You have to buy from us and pay our prices."

Government then steps in to protect the consumer and decides to regulate the natural monopoly firm. Instead of letting the natural monopoly firm charge whatever it wishes to charge, the public utility commission sets reasonable prices. The natural monopoly firm ends up earning a reasonable profit, and consumers end up with lower prices.

In this scenario, government is the knight on the horse who rides into town and takes care of the problems for the little guy (the consumer). Economists often refer to this as the *public interest theory* of regulation. According to this theory, the regulators not only want to, but do, act in the best interests of the public.

But is this the way things work out in the real world? Some economists think not. There are two principal theories that explain why regulators might not act in the best interests of the consumer: the capture theory of regulation and the public choice theory of regulation.

Capture Theory of Regulation Economists who support the capture theory of regulation say that eventually the regulated firm will capture and control

Exhibit 9-2
Types of Natural Monopoly Regulation

There are essentially two types of natural monopoly regulation: price regulation and profit regulation.

Types of Natural Monopoly Regulation

- **Price Regulation**: Regulators set the price the natural monopoly can charge.
- **Profit Regulation**: Regulators set the rate of profit the natural monopoly can earn.

the regulatory body. For example, the public utility companies that are regulated by the public utility commission will end up controlling the public utility commission. In other words, the public utility commission will end up doing what the firms it is regulating want it to do. The following points have been put forth to support this theory:

Government regulatory activities deal with issues of price, safety, and pollution, among others.

1. In many cases, persons who have been in an industry are asked to regulate that industry, because they know the most about it. Such regulators are likely to feel a bond with people in the industry, see their side of the story more often than not, and thus be inclined to cater to them.
2. At regulatory hearings, members of the industry attend in greater force than do taxpayers or consumers. The industry turns out in force because the regulatory hearing can affect it substantially and directly; in contrast, the effect on individual taxpayers and consumers is usually small and indirect. Thus, regulators are much more likely to hear and respond to the industry's side of the story.
3. Members of the regulated industry make a point of getting to know the members of the regulatory agency. They may talk frequently about business matters and perhaps socialize. The bond between the two groups grows stronger over time, which may have an impact on regulatory measures.
4. After they retire or quit their jobs, regulators often go to work for the industries they once regulated.

Public Choice Theory of Regulation The other theory about whether regulators really do what is best for consumers is the public choice theory of regulation. Economists who uphold this theory suggest that to understand the decisions of regulatory bodies, we must first understand how decisions affect the regulators themselves. For example, a regulation that increased the power of the regulators and the size and budget of the regulatory agency would not be viewed the same way as a regulation that decreased the agency's power and size. The public choice theory of regulation predicts that the outcomes of the regulatory process will tend to favor the regulators instead of either business interests or the public.

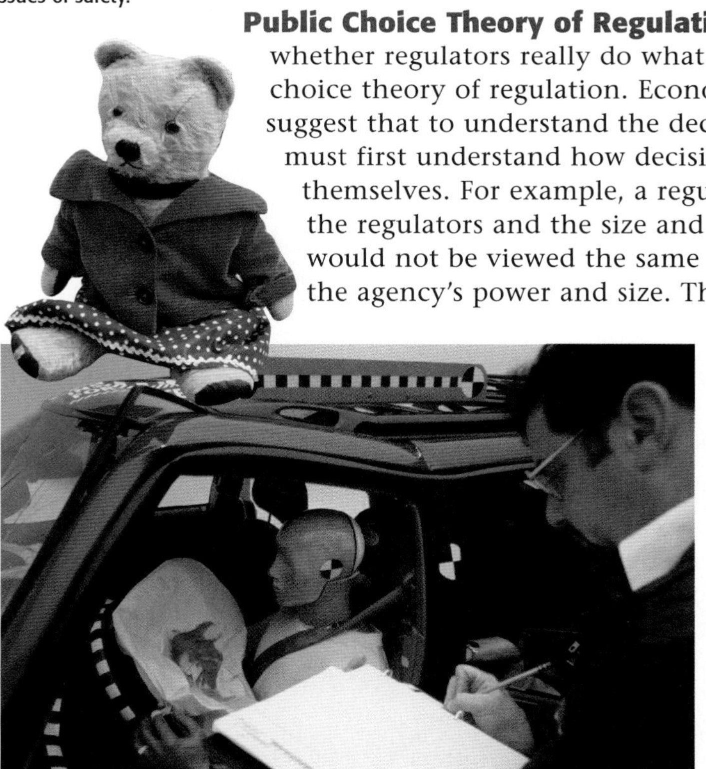

Government is involved in social regulation, which often deals with issues of safety.

Social Regulation

When the word *regulation* is used, different people often think of different things. Some people may think of the price and profit regulation that is part of regulating a natural monopoly, which we just discussed. Others may think of what has been referred to as *social regulation*. Social regulation is regulation that is concerned with the conditions under which goods and services are produced and the safety of these items for the consumer. For example, the Occupational Safety and Health Administration (OSHA) is a regulatory government agency that is concerned with protecting workers against occupational injuries and illnesses. The Consumer Product Safety Commission (CPSC) specifies minimum standards for potentially unsafe products. For example, a business firm cannot simply make any type of toy to sell, but only toys that are not likely to harm the children who use them. The Environmental Protection Agency (EPA) regulates the amount of pollution business firms can emit into the air or rivers.

The government requires manufacturers to seal many dangerous substances with child-proof lids. What might be the benefits of safety caps to this child? The costs?

As with almost any type of government regulation, not everyone agrees on the worth of social regulation. Some people argue that the bulk of social regulation is too costly to taxpayers and only indicates an intrusive, meddlesome government. The proponents of social regulation believe that while the costs are high, the benefits are even higher. They say, for example, that highway fatalities would be 40 percent higher in the absence of automobile safety features mandated through regulation, that mandated child-proof lids have resulted in 90 percent fewer child deaths caused by accidental swallowing of poisonous substances, and that government regulations on the use of asbestos save between 630 and 2,553 persons from dying of cancer each year.

The proponents of social regulation also argue that government regulation and monitoring of business is important because atrocious things can happen without it. For example, they cite the case of Beech-Nut Nutrition Corporation, a baby food manufacturer that in 1987 pleaded guilty to 215 felony counts. (A felony is a major crime.) The company had sold millions of containers of sugar water and flavoring that it had labeled "100 percent apple juice." The case of Cordis Corporation is also often cited. Cordis Corporation produced and sold thousands of pacemakers that it knew were defective.[1] Many of the pacemakers failed, and the company ended up pleading guilty to twenty-five criminal violations.

Government regulation, whether it has to do with prices and profits, consumer information, working standards, or anything else, continues to be a major topic of debate. The next section explains why.

The Costs and Benefits of Government Regulation

Suppose a business firm is polluting the air with smoke from its factories. The government passes an environmental regulation requiring that this business firm purchase antipollution devices that cut down on the smoke emitted into the air. What are the benefits of this kind of regulation? First, there is cleaner air. Cleaner air may lead to fewer medical problems in the future. For example, in some U.S. cities, the pollution from

1. A pacemaker is an electronic device implanted in the body and connected to the wall of the heart. It is designed to provide a regular, mild, electric shock that stimulates contraction of the heart muscle and restores a normal heartbeat.

Exhibit 9-3

How an Economist Sees Regulation

An economist realizes that there are both benefits and costs to regulation.

cars and factories causes people to cough, feel tired, and experience eye discomfort. Some of these people have continuing medical problems from constantly breathing dirty air. Government regulation that ends up reducing the amount of pollution in the air surely helps these people.

Regulation may also benefit the environment and thus the people who enjoy a clean environment. For example, some air pollution can harm birds and destroy certain types of plants and trees. With cleaner air, there may be more birds singing and prettier trees to view.

Regulation, however, does not come with benefits only. It comes with costs, too. For example, a business firm that has to incur the cost of anti-pollution devices has a rise in its overall costs of production. Simply put, it is costlier for this business firm to produce its product than before the regulation was imposed. The business firm may produce fewer units of its product, which raises its product price and results in some workers losing their jobs.

Regulations come with benefits and costs. For example, a regulation may give us a cleaner environment at the cost of some workers losing their jobs.

If you are a worker who loses your job, you may view the government's insistence that business install pollution devices differently than if you are a person suffering from weak lungs. If you have weak lungs, less pollution may be the difference between your feeling well or sick. If you are a worker for the business firm, less pollution may end up costing you your job. Ideally, you may prefer to have a little less pollution in your neighborhood, but not at the cost of losing your job.

Where do economists stand on these issues? Are they for or against government regulation of the type described? They are neither for nor against such regulation; the job of the economist is continually to make the point that there are both benefits and costs to regulation. To the person who sees only the costs, the economist asks, But what about the benefits? And to the person who sees only the benefits, the economist asks, But what about the costs? The economist then goes on to outline the benefits and costs as accurately as possible.

Landlords, Renters, and Eviction Notices

Economists know that one change often brings another. Suppose that apartment landlords must give their renters one month's notice before evicting them, but a state senator thinks renters should get four months' notice. So the senator drafts legislation making it illegal to evict a tenant without four months' notice. Landlords lobby against the proposed legislation, while most renters and members of the general public lobby in its favor.

Noneconomists might think this way: Renters will be better off with the four months' notice than with only one month's notice. They will have more security. Landlords, of course, will be worse off.

Noneconomists make the mistake of thinking that the *only thing* that would change as a result of the legislation is that renters would simply get three extra months of notice. Economists know that this is unlikely, because they know a change in one factor often causes a change in another. Consider what a change in rental regulations would do to the supply of and demand for apartments. As a result of forcing landlords to give four months' notice rather than one, the law would increase the likelihood of economic losses for landlords. As a result, some landlords would decide to get out of the apartment rental business. As a consequence, the supply of apartments would decrease.

On the demand side of the market, though, the demand for apartments would rise. Chapter 3 discussed various factors that affect the demand for a good or service. One of the factors was people's preferences. As preferences become more favorable toward a good or service, the demand for it rises; and as preferences become less favorable toward a good or service, the demand for it falls. Giving renters four months' notice instead of one would positively affect people's preferences for apartment living. The demand for apartments would rise.

In summary, the change in rental regulations would lower the supply of apartments and raise the demand for apartments. A fall in supply combined with a rise in demand would lead to higher equilibrium rent. For example, apartment rent might rise from $600 to $700 a month because of the change in regulations.

In short, a change in how much notice landlords must give renters would not leave everything else in the world unchanged. It would lead to a change in the rental price of apartments. We would move from a world in which apartments were $600 a month and landlords had to give one month's notice to tenants to a world in which the rent was higher (say, $700) and landlords had to give four months' notice to tenants.

What is the lesson to be learned? First, rental regulations, which on the surface appear to be pro-renter, may end up hurting renters more than they help them. Second, in an economic sense, a change that appears at first glance to affect only one thing may affect other things, too.

QUESTIONS TO ANSWER

1. Suppose that only 5 percent of all renters fail to pay their rent and are therefore likely to be evicted. Does the change in the rental regulation from one month's notice to four months' notice help or hurt the remaining 95 percent of all renters? Explain your answer.
2. Would you be in favor of allowing landlords to offer various apartment contracts to renters, specifying less notice for eviction in return for lower rent? Explain your answer.

Unintended Effects of Regulation

In addition to outlining the benefits and costs of regulation, the economist tries to point out the sometimes unintended consequences of regulation. To illustrate, the government often regulates the manufacturers of automobiles by imposing fuel economy standards on cars. For example, the government may state that new cars must get an average of 40 miles per gallon instead of, say, 30 miles per gallon. Many people say that this regulation is good. They reason that if car companies were made to produce cars that got better mileage, people would not need to buy and burn as much gasoline. With less gasoline burned, less pollution would be produced.

It is not guaranteed to work out this way, though. If car companies produced cars that were more fuel efficient, people would have to buy less gasoline to take them from one place to another. The cost per mile of traveling would fall, so people might begin to travel more. Leisure driving on Saturday and Sunday might become more common, people might begin to drive farther on vacations, and so on. If people began to travel more, the gasoline saving that resulted from the higher fuel economy standards might be offset or even outweighed. More gasoline consumption due to more travel would mean more gas burned and more pollutants ending up in the air. In other words, a regulation requiring car companies to produce cars that get better fuel mileage might have an unintended effect.

Exhibit 9-4

Effects of Regulation

When a government regulation is issued, the people who specified and passed the regulation often were aware of only the intended effects of the regulation. According to economists, this is only half the picture. There are often unintended effects, too. Sometimes the unintended effects are undesirable.

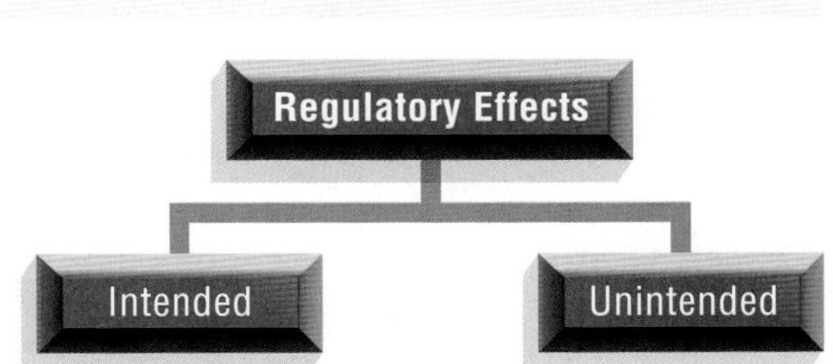

Section 2 Review

Defining Terms

1. Define
   a. natural monopoly
   b. public utility commission

Reviewing Facts and Concepts

2. A public utility commission states that a natural monopoly firm in the area can charge $2 above its per-unit costs for every unit of the service it provides to the public. In other words, if per-unit costs are $4, the natural monopoly firm can charge $6 per unit. What is an unintended effect of this policy?
3. What is social regulation?
4. How does the economist view government regulation?

Critical Thinking

5. "If the government imposes higher fuel economy standards, the amount of pollution produced by automobiles will undoubtedly become less." Do you agree or disagree? Explain your answer.

Applying Economic Concepts

6. Suppose you live in a country where medicine containers do not come with safety caps. Instead, they have easy twist-off caps. To protect children from getting into their parents' medicine, a government regulation is passed requiring the manufacturers of medicine containers to place safety caps on all their containers, making it impossible for little children to take off the caps. In addition, many adults find the safety caps very difficult to remove. Can you identify an unintended effect of the government's regulation specifying that all medicine containers must have a hard-to-remove safety cap? Explain your answer.

SECTION 3

Externalities

A person's or a group's actions can produce side effects that are felt by others. In general, side effects that affect the well-being of third parties are called **externalities,** because the costs or benefits are external to whoever caused them. Externalities may be negative or positive. This section considers both types.

As you read this section, keep these key questions in mind:

- What is a negative externality?
- What is a positive externality?
- What can be done about negative externality problems?

MINI GLOSSARY

externality A side effect of an action that affects the well-being of third parties.

negative externality An adverse side effect of an action that is felt by others.

Key Terms

externality
negative externality
positive externality

Negative Externalities

Suppose it is 3 A.M., and you are fast asleep. Suddenly, you awaken to the sounds of a radio blasting away. You get up, open the window of your bedroom, and realize that the loud music is coming from your neighbor's house. Your neighbor is taking an action—playing the radio loudly—that has an adverse side effect on you. Economists call this adverse side effect a **negative externality,** or a negative third-party effect.

A person is sleeping and next door the radio is being played loudly. Is this a negative or a positive externality?

Consider another example of a negative externality. The owners of a house rarely mow their lawn or cut their shrubbery. The people who live in the houses nearby complain that not only is this property not kept up and therefore unpleasant to look at, but the property also lowers the value of their own houses. One neighbor, who lives across the street, says, "I need to sell my house, but I'm going to have a hard time doing it because the people across the street don't keep up their property. No one wants to live across from an eyesore. I will probably have to lower the price of my house before anyone will even start to think about buying it." Undoubtedly, the owners of the property that is not kept up are acting in a way that adversely affects their neighbors. The adverse side effect is a negative externality.

Bees can make an orchard more productive. Is this a negative or a positive externality?

Erica Richards is a beekeeper who lives near an apple orchard. Erica's bees occasionally fly over to the orchard

Cigarettes, Taxes, and Gangs

There is hardly a person in the United States who does not know that cigarette smoking is bad for one's health. In time, smoking can kill you. Programs have been initiated at both the federal and state levels to combat cigarette smoking. Government-sponsored ads on television urge people not to smoke, and people at both the state and federal government levels have called for higher taxes on cigarettes and other tobacco products.

Some economists also argue for higher taxes on cigarettes, based on the theory of externalities. To illustrate, consider Bambrick, who smokes a pack of cigarettes a day. He smokes in his home, and his children are adversely affected by the secondhand smoke; they get smoke in their lungs and cough a lot. Bambrick is imposing a negative externality on his children.

As you will learn in this chapter, one way to deal with a negative externality is to tax the activity that generates it. If a tax is imposed on packs of cigarettes, cigarette smoking will be more expensive, and Bambrick will smoke less. (We assume he has a downward-sloping demand curve for cigarettes: the higher the price of cigarettes, the lower the quantity demanded of cigarettes.) When Bambrick smokes less, he will impose fewer negative externalities on his children.

Returning now to the issue of taxes, suppose that in the future, states do raise taxes on cigarettes and other tobacco products. Furthermore, suppose that some states raise the taxes on cigarettes much more than other states. For example, California imposes a $3 tax on cigarettes, but nearby Arizona imposes a 50-cent tax. It follows that a pack of cigarettes will be more expensive in California than in Arizona.

What will happen as a result? Consider what happened in the 1960s when some of the northeastern states raised taxes on cigarettes. The price differential among cigarettes in different states prompted wholesale smuggling. People bought cigarettes in states such as North Carolina, where taxes were low, packed them into trucks, and drove them to states such as New York, where taxes were relatively high. In short, the tax differences gave way to price differences that stimulated illegal cigarette smuggling.

Europe has been faced with similar problems. For example, it has been reported that Germany's high cigarette tax has led to smuggling; 50,000 cartons of cigarettes can net a smuggler $550,000 in profits. There have even been reports of turf battles between different gangs for control of the street sale of smuggled cigarettes. Would the United States face the same consequences if states imposed widely different taxes on cigarettes?

QUESTION TO ANSWER Would there be less cigarette smuggling if all states imposed the same amount of taxes on cigarettes than if they did not? Explain your answer.

Exhibit 9-5
Externalities

There are two types of externalities: negative and positive.

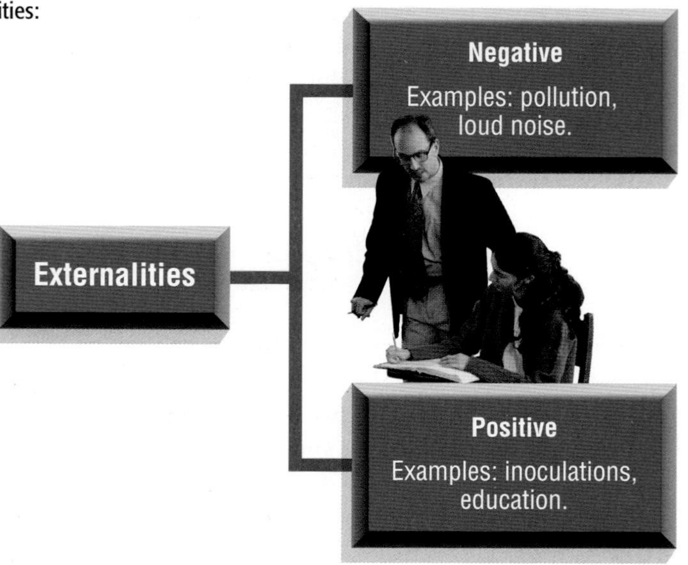

and pollinate the blossoms, in the process making the orchard more productive. Thus, Erica takes an action—keeping bees—and a benefit external to the action is felt by some other person. Because Erica's beekeeping activity results in an externality that benefits someone else, it is referred to as a **positive externality,** or a positive third-party effect.

Another example of a positive externality occurs when Yolanda visits a physician and is inoculated against polio. Now she can be sure that she will not become sick with polio. But Yolanda's actions also benefit other people: people who come into contact with Yolanda are protected from getting polio from her. As far as the community as a whole is concerned, Yolanda's inoculation against polio is a positive externality.

positive externality A beneficial side effect of an action that is felt by others.

Government and Positive Externalities

Some people argue that education generates positive externalities. They say that when you attend school, you not only learn things that will directly help you in life and in the workplace but you also become a better citizen and a more informed voter. Becoming a better citizen and a more informed voter ends up benefiting more people than just yourself.

Let's analyze your own case. You are in high school taking this economics course. Because of the course, it is hoped, you will become more knowledgeable about economics issues than you would have been otherwise. One day, you are listening to two politicians running for the U.S. Senate from your state; they are debating some economics issues on television. One politician makes inaccurate statements on almost all the issues, while the other accurately portrays the economics issues. You decide to vote for the politician who is accurate on the issues, because you feel she will

Some people believe that one person's education benefits more than the person being educated. Is there a positive externality here?

more likely end up promoting economic policies that are good for the United States.

Your informed vote increases (by a tiny percentage) the probability that the politician who understands economics will get elected. If she is elected, whom have you helped? You have helped yourself, no doubt, but you have also helped all the other people who will now benefit by having a person knowledgeable about economics shape government policy instead of an uninformed person. In short, your education has helped not only you but others, too. In economics terminology, your education has produced a *positive externality*.

Suppose population density in the United States increases in the next two decades. Do you predict more or fewer negative externalities as a result? Explain your answer.

At this point, some people argue that because your education can help other people, these other people ought to pay something for the benefits they derive from your education. One solution might be to have the members of society pay taxes to support the schools you attend. In other words, as this argument goes, because the public benefits from your education and the education of other persons like you, it should pay toward that education. The public-school system is a result of this thinking.

Persons who attend public schools do not directly pay for the education they receive (although they indirectly pay if their parents pay property taxes, which are largely used to fund public education). Instead, their education is paid for with taxpayer money. That is, the education of public-school students is subsidized. Some people argue that government should subsidize those activities—like education—that generate positive externalities for society at large.

Government and Negative Externalities

If you are on the receiving end of a negative externality—if you are awakened at 3:00 A.M. by loud music, or the smoke a factory is emitting is getting into your lungs—you will probably feel that negative externalities are bad. But what can be done? Some people argue that it is government's duty to minimize the "bad" in society—in other words, to reduce the incidence of negative externalities. Government can do so in three principal ways: through the court system, regulation, and taxation.

The Court System It is a fall day. Frank lives in a house with many trees in the yard. The leaves have fallen, and Frank rakes them up into a pile. Instead of tossing them into a trash can, he decides to burn them. The smoke from the burning leaves drifts over to Ruben's house. Ruben, it so happens, is allergic to smoke. He walks over to Frank's house and asks Frank to stop burning the leaves, because he is allergic to smoke. Frank says that he has a right to burn his leaves on his property. Ruben says that he has a right to a smoke-free neighborhood. Frank repeats that he has the right to burn his leaves on his property, even if the smoke adversely affects someone else.

Ruben decides to take Frank to court, where the lawyers for the two parties argue the case. In the end, the court has the duty to decide (1) whether the smoke is a negative externality (in fact, it was at the time) and (2) who has the right to do what. Specifically, even if the smoke is a negative externality, does Frank have the right to burn the leaves on his property? Or does Ruben have the right to a smoke-free environment in his neighborhood?

One person burns leaves in her yard and the smoke from the burning leaves adversely affects nearby neighbors. What's the best way to deal with this negative externality?

Regulation Pollution—specifically, the pollution emitted from both cars and factory smokestacks—is considered a negative externality. In many cases, government regulates the amount of pollution that can be emitted into the air. For example, most states require car owners to meet pollution standards, and government often limits the amount of pollution that factories can emit into the air. Government may also deem it illegal to dump chemicals into rivers and lakes.

Taxation You may recall from Chapter 4 that some taxes raise the per-unit costs of production and cause a leftward shift in the supply curve. Stated differently, some taxes reduce output and raise prices. (Whenever the supply curve shifts left and demand is constant, price increases and the quantity of output decreases.) All this is simple supply-and-demand economics, but what does it have to do with negative externalities?

Pollutants may be emitted into the air as a result of a firm producing steel. What is the best way to deal with this negative externality?

Suppose a business firm is producing steel. As a by-product, pollutants are discharged into the air through a smokestack. Instead of imposing an environmental regulation on the steel-producing firm to clean up the air, government decides to impose a tax. For every ton of steel produced, the firm has to pay $100 in taxes.

As a result of the tax, the business firm will find it costlier to produce steel. The firm is likely to end up producing less steel, which means fewer pollutants discharged into the air. In other words, the tax on steel has indirectly reduced the amount of negative externality (pollutants in the air) by making the production of steel more costly.

What Is the Cost of Arriving Late to Class? or, the Economics of Tardiness

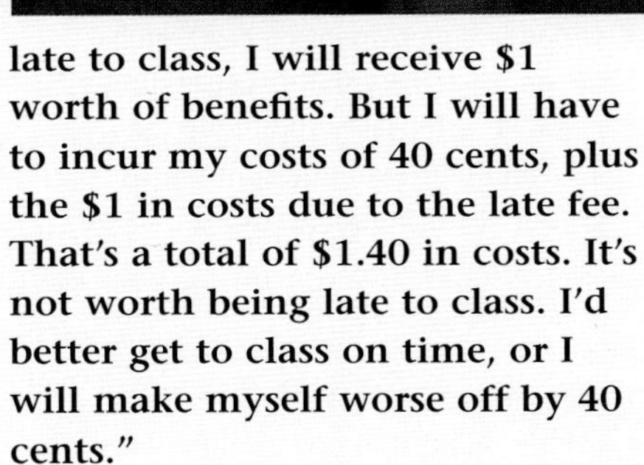

Class started five minutes ago. You are sitting at your desk, listening to the teacher, and taking notes. The teacher is discussing an unusually challenging topic today, and you are listening attentively. Then the classroom door opens. You turn at the sound and see Warren, one of your classmates, arriving late to class. For a few seconds, your attention is diverted from the lecture. When you refocus your attention on the teacher, you realize that you have missed an essential point of the lecture. You are a little irritated by this.

The scenario described is a *negative externality.* Warren undertook an action—he arrived late to class—and you were adversely affected. Most likely he considered only his private benefits and costs of arriving to class late, not that you might be affected adversely or that his action might impose a cost on you.

Most people, at this point, would say that Warren probably couldn't help but arrive at class late. Perhaps he inadvertently got delayed somewhere or was called to the office.

Certainly those things could have happened to Warren, but tardiness is also sometimes the result of a conscious decision. To illustrate, suppose Warren is finishing up lunch when the school bell rings. He knows he has five minutes to get to his class. He makes the conscious decision to keep talking to a friend, knowing that he will be a few minutes late to class. Because he chose to be late to class, he must perceive the benefits of his lateness as being greater than the costs he will have to pay. To put dollar amounts on costs and benefits, let's say it is worth $1 in benefits for him to be late and worth only 40 cents in costs. Because benefits are greater than costs, he chooses to be late.

When Warren arrives late to class, however, you are adversely affected; you incur some cost (say, $1). What can the teacher do to get Warren to consider the fact that his tardiness adversely affects others? Suppose it were permissible to charge students a "late fee" if they arrived late to class. The teacher could say to Warren, "When you are late, you adversely affect others. How much do you adversely affect others? One dollar's worth. So here is what I plan to do: when you arrive late to class, you must pay me $1."

If this system were implemented, when the bell rang Warren would be thinking, "If I am late to class, I will receive $1 worth of benefits. But I will have to incur my costs of 40 cents, plus the $1 in costs due to the late fee. That's a total of $1.40 in costs. It's not worth being late to class. I'd better get to class on time, or I will make myself worse off by 40 cents."

The teacher in the example acts much the way government does when it imposes a tax on an activity that generates a negative externality. The tax makes the activity more costly for the actors, so they undertake the activity less often.

QUESTION TO ANSWER When a teacher says she will penalize students who disrupt class (for example, by taking off points on the next test), might this be an attempt to get the disruptive students to "pay" for the costs their behavior imposes on others? Explain your answer.

THINKING Like an Economist

The discussion of externalities reminds us that some activities produce negative side effects for others. For example, a factory that emits smoke into the air adversely affects the health of those who live nearby. For these people, the smoke is a negative externality.

Many people argue that the market system is incapable of doing anything about the problem of negative externalities. They say that the market fails whenever it does not take into account and adjust for externalities—negative or positive. There is, simply put, *market failure.*

When markets fail to address the externality issue, government may have a role to play. The economist warns that, just as markets may fail, so might government. For example, suppose government places a high tax on an activity that is generating a negative externality (polluting the air), and consequently some firms go out of business and thousands of jobs are lost.

Once again, the economist thinks here in terms of costs and benefits. When there is market failure, there is little doubt that potential benefits might be realized through government action. However, will government take the actions that will turn the potential benefits into actual ones, and will the costs of these actions be less than the benefits?

We have to be careful in our analysis, though. Taxation, like regulation, sometimes comes with unintended consequences. An illustration will analyze automobile production instead of steel production. Say that in year 1, there are no taxes on the automobile industry. In year 2, government places a tax of $500 per car on the auto industry. In other words, for every new car a firm produces, it must pay the government $500 in taxes. Do you think the auto industry will produce more cars in year 1 or year 2? The correct answer is year 1, all other things remaining the same. Taxes of the sort described here raise the cost of producing and selling cars, and car firms react by producing fewer cars.

A tax on new car production may have an unintended effect: a higher percentage of old, higher-polluting cars on the roads. Explain.

At this point, you might point out that because there are fewer cars, there will be less pollution. This statement overlooks something important, though. Although fewer new cars are produced and purchased, people may simply drive their old cars longer, and old cars emit more pollution than new cars. Thus, the tax on the production of new cars will reduce the number of new cars on the road relative to the number of old cars, and if miles driven do not change, we can expect more, not less, pollution from cars. Taxation, like regulation, does not always have its intended effect.

Section 3 Review

Defining Terms

1. Define
- **a.** externality
- **b.** negative externality
- **c.** positive externality

Reviewing Facts and Concepts

2. Give an example of a negative externality and a positive externality.

3. Explain how the court system can be used to deal with negative externalities.

4. Explain how taxes can be used to deal with negative externalities.

Critical Thinking

5. Burning gasoline causes carbon monoxide (pollution), so the less gasoline that is burned, the less pollution there will be. With this in mind, suppose the government raises the fuel-efficiency standards on new cars. Instead of cars getting an average of 27 miles per gallon, suppose new cars get an average of 40 miles per gallon. Will the new, higher fuel-efficiency standard necessarily reduce car pollution? Explain your answer.

Applying Economic Concepts

6. Your neighbor plays his CD player too loudly at night and, as far as you are concerned, imposes a negative externality on you. How would you deal with this negative externality problem?

Developing Economic

Skills

The Economics Paper: Writing and Rewriting It

Chapter 7 explained how to find an economics topic on which to write, and Chapter 8 discussed how to research the topic. This chapter discusses how to write and then rewrite the paper.

Writing the Paper

Before you begin writing, you should prewrite, a process of generating and organizing ideas. One way to prewrite is to brainstorm, writing down everything that comes to mind about the topic. Once you have written down as many statements or ideas as you can, look at them to see if there is any theme that links them all.

Once you have identified that theme, it is now time to structure your paper. Structuring your paper involves figuring out the best way to tell your story. One useful way to organize your thoughts is to use index cards. Follow this procedure:

Step 1. Write down each of the main points you want to make in your paper on a separate index card.
Step 2. Organize the cards in the order in which you want to discuss each point.
Step 3. Using your index cards, pretend you are giving an oral report. You may either say the words out loud or silently to yourself. The important point is to "hear" yourself "write" the paper.
Step 4. Consider reordering your main points so your paper is better organized. This is where the use of index cards makes things easy. Now repeat Step 3. Continue reordering your main points and orally presenting your paper until you have found the best way to present the information.
Step 5. Using your sequenced index cards as your guide, write the paper. And remember, *writing* requires *thinking* and *preparation*—the free, unconstrained thinking used in prewriting and the focused thinking used in structuring.

Rewriting the Paper

If you remember only one thing about writing, let it be this: good writing is the result of rewriting. The process of rewriting begins with reading your paper sentence by sentence. After reading each sentence, ask yourself whether you have clearly communicated what you intended.

After reading each paragraph, try to identify its main message. Then ask yourself if you have communicated that message clearly.

Now go back and rewrite the sentences and paragraphs that need to be rewritten. Try to use as few words as possible to communicate your message. Much of rewriting is getting rid of unnecessary words. Next, go through the paper again, sentence by sentence, correcting any grammatical and spelling errors.

Finally, read the paper from beginning to end without stopping. Then ask yourself whether a person picked at random would find it clear, organized, and interesting. If it fails this test, ask yourself why.

Someone reading the previous paragraph might say, "I'm not sure how to fix my writing. Can you give me some rules to follow?" There are many rules to writing clear and grammatically correct prose, but perhaps the most important is to make your writing clear, simple, and direct. To achieve that goal, avoid the excessive use of adverbs and adjectives. Eliminate long, complex sentences that confuse the point you are trying to make. State things clearly, so no one will mistake your meaning. Use simple words that do not get in the way of your message.

QUESTIONS TO ANSWER

1. What is a person trying to accomplish by prewriting?
2. What is a person trying to accomplish through structure?

CHAPTER

9 Review

Economics Vocabulary

Fill in the following blanks with the appropriate word or phrase.

1. The objective of the ____ is to control monopoly power and preserve and protect competition.
2. A(n) ____ is a combination of firms that come together to act as a monopolist.
3. ____ occurs when a seller charges different buyers different prices for the same good or service even though there are no cost differences between the buyers.
4. A(n) ____ is an arrangement whereby the sale of one product depends on the purchase of some other product or products.
5. Economists consider both the ____ and ____ of regulation.
6. A(n) ____ is a side effect of an action that affects the well-being of others.
7. A(n) ____ is a firm that has such low average total costs that it can outcompete all other firms in the industry and thus remain as the sole survivor.
8. Another term for a negative third-party effect is a(n) ____.
9. A(n) ____ is the joining of two companies into one; it occurs when one company buys more than half the stock in the other company.
10. A government group that regulates public utility companies is called a(n) ____.
11. A(n) ____ is a beneficial side effect of an action that is felt by others.

Review Questions

1. What is one major criticism of the Sherman Antitrust Act?
2. Which antitrust act states that "every contract, combination in the form of trust or otherwise, or conspiracy, in restraint of trade or commerce . . . is hereby declared to be illegal"?
3. Explain how an interlocking directorate worked. Which antitrust act outlawed interlocking directorates? Explain the reasons why such directorates were prohibited.
4. False or deceptive advertising violates which antitrust act?
5. "Economists are against regulation." Do you agree or disagree? Explain your answer.
6. Explain the reasoning of the Federal Trade Commission when it challenged, and then prohibited, the merger of Staples and Office Depot. Explain the reasoning given by the two stores in support of their planned merger.
7. Explain how taxation may be used to eliminate a negative externality problem.
8. What were the details of the Utah Pie case? How did the Supreme Court decide the case?
9. Suppose company Z has been charged with being a monopoly. The company asks you to defend it in court. How would you define the market in which company Z operates? Explain your answer.
10. Explain the term collusion, and cite a particular instance of collusion.
11. What is the difference between the capture theory of regulation and the public choice theory of regulation?
12. Justify the public-school system on positive externality grounds.
13. What is a tying contract, and which antitrust act deems it illegal?
14. Sudhir studies for his biology test late into the night and oversleeps the next morning, thus missing the test. Is there a negative externality here? Explain your answer.

Calculations

1. A natural monopoly produces 100,000 units of a good and has total costs equal to $5 million. A public utility commission decides to set a price for the natural monopoly. What is the lowest price it can set for the natural monopoly and not have the monopolist go out of business? Explain your answer.
2. Suppose the following holds: A gallon of gasoline is $1.20; the average driver drives 50 miles a week; the average car gets 25 miles per gallon; and for each gallon of gas purchased and used, 1 unit of pollution is emitted. It follows that the cost per mile to drive is 4.8 cents. Now suppose that technology changes so that the average car gets 50 miles per gallon. If gasoline prices do not change, the cost per mile to drive drops to 2.4 cents. How many more miles a week would the average driver

have to drive so that the level of pollution remained constant? Explain your answer.

Economics and Thinking Skills

1. **Application.** Suppose you work in the Antitrust Division of the U.S. Department of Justice, and the following case is brought to your attention. Company X claims that a major competitor, company Y, has lowered its prices and is trying to drive company X out of business. What is difficult about knowing whether or not the Federal Trade Commission Act applies to this case?
2. **Analysis.** Company X is regulated by a public utility commission. The commission can impose five possible regulations, A through E, on company X. The company wants regulation E, and it does not want A through D. The commission ends up imposing regulation E on the company. Does it follow that the capture theory of regulation is correct? Explain your answer.
3. **Cause and Effect.** Give an example of a regulation that causes an unintended effect.

Writing Skills

Write a one-page paper identifying two negative externalities that have adversely affected your life.

Economics in the Media

1. Find an example in your local newspaper of one of the following: a negative externality, positive externality, or recent antitrust decision or case. Your example may come from an article, editorial, or advertisement.
2. Watch a news program, and find an example of price discrimination, a negative externality, social regulation, or an unintended effect of regulation.

Where's the Economics?

What economics issue does the photo below illustrate?

UNIT 2

Debate the Issues

Should There Be a Minimum Wage?

Like many high school students, you may have a job and work after school. If so, there is a good chance that you earn the minimum wage, which is set by the U.S. Congress. It is against the law for employers to pay workers less than the minimum wage. If the minimum wage is $6.15 an hour, then it is unlawful for an employer to pay an employee $5.00, $5.50, or $6.00 an hour.[1]

Do you think that a minimum wage is good for workers and good for the economy, too? Some people argue in favor of it; other people argue against it. Some people argue that the minimum wage should be raised; other people argue that it should not be. Let's listen in on a conversation between Mike and Mrs. Peters. Mrs. Peters owns a small bakery in town. Mike, seventeen years old, works at the hardware store three doors down from the bakery. Mike currently earns the minimum wage.

Mrs. Peters: How are you doing today, Mike? What can I get for you?

Mike: I'll have a chocolate éclair and a milk. And, by the way, I'm doing pretty well today. On my way to work I heard that Congress is thinking of raising the minimum wage. That will mean more money for me.

Mrs. Peters: I think the minimum wage is one of the things that sound better than it is.

Mike: What do you mean? What could possibly be wrong with the minimum wage?

1. There are some exemptions for the minimum wage. For example, there is a subminimum wage that holds for certain employees over certain periods of employment (such as those persons who earn tips in their jobs).

Mrs. Peters: Well, for one thing, it goes against the whole idea of free enterprise. Under free enterprise, employers and employees should be able to make their own deals. They shouldn't have government telling them how much to pay.

Mike: But if there weren't a minimum wage, employers would pay their employees next to nothing. Perhaps instead of my earning $6 an hour, I'd earn $2 an hour.

Mrs. Peters: Okay, let's say that you are earning $6 an hour. Along comes the government and tells your employer that he has to pay you $7.50 an hour. Jim may decide to fire you. It may be worth it for Jim to pay you $6 an hour, but not $7.50 an hour. Has the minimum wage helped you? I don't think so. I think it has priced you out of a job.

Mike: But it's possible that I'll keep my job as the wage goes from $6 to $7.50. Fact is, I may be worth $7.50 an hour, but Jim is paying me only $6 an hour so he can earn higher profits. What the minimum wage does is simply force Jim to pay me what I'm worth.

Mrs. Peters: If you were really worth $7.50 an hour, you would be earning $7.50 an hour right now. The boss who thinks you are worth $7.50 an hour would simply offer you that amount to come work for him instead of working for Jim.

That's how he would compete you away from Jim.

But let's go with what you say. Let's suppose that Congress tells your employer he has to pay you $7.50 an hour. And let's suppose you keep your job. That doesn't mean some people won't lose their jobs. Everyone knows that employers hire more people at lower wages than at higher wages. As wages go up, they are going to hire fewer people. In other words, some of the people working at the lower wages will be fired.

Mike: I don't think anyone has to lose his job as the wage goes up. Employers will simply end up with lower profits.

Mrs. Peters: That might work if you're talking about Microsoft or General Motors, but what about Joe's Pizza or the corner deli? Some companies are just squeaking by, so that any mandated cost increase will hurt them. They will try to cut their costs by firing some people.

The other thing is that not all businesses are faced with the same set of circumstances. Circumstances may differ from one region of the country to another. The economy may be booming in the Southwest and businesses can easily pay higher wages. But the economy may be sluggish in the Midwest and businesses can't pay higher wages. A set minimum wage, that every business has to pay, no matter what its circumstances, doesn't take this into account.

Mike: I don't know, I hear what you are saying, but I still think that without the minimum wage, too many employers would squeeze their employees.

Mrs. Peters: Mike, there are whole industries in this country where the minimum wage is not relevant. No one is paid the minimum wage that works for an accounting firm, no one is paid the minimum wage that works as a computer scientist, no one is paid the minimum wage that works as an attorney. All these people earn much more than the minimum wage. Do they earn more than the minimum wage because government has ordered the companies to pay them more than the minimum wage? Not at all. The government hasn't said a thing. The companies simply pay them more because they can't hire these people without paying more. It is a matter of supply and demand, Mike. Companies have to pay the wages that are determined in the market by the forces of supply and demand.

Mike: Oh, come on. You know there is a big difference between what an attorney earns and what I earn. The minimum wage law isn't there to protect attorneys, accountants, and computer scientists. It is there to protect the little guy. The guy without much skill or experience.

Mrs. Peters: But, that's just the point. The minimum wage doesn't protect this person. It often just prices him out of a job. You can't make employers pay more for a person than that person is worth to them. If a person is worth only $5 an hour to an employer, and the government says you have to pay this person $7 an hour, you know what is going to happen? That person is going to go without a job.

What Do You Think?

1. Who do you think makes the stronger argument, Mike or Mrs. Peters? Defend your answer.
2. What are Mike's strong points? weak points? What are Mrs. Peters's strong and weak points?
3. Go to http://www.dol.gov/dol/esa/public/minwage/chart.htm to learn what the current minimum wage is. Do you think the minimum wage should be raised? Why or why not?

UNIT 3 Macroeconomics: The Economy

CHAPTER 10

Money

What This Chapter Is About

When someone mentions the word *money,* you might think of a $20 bill. Money is cold, hard cash to most of us, but there is more to money than that. At one time in the world's history, for example, there was no money anywhere. How did money come into existence? And what does money do? You might say that we use it to buy the things we want. But does it do anything else? Can money be used to pay off a debt? Can it be saved? If it is saved, what is it saved for?

How is the world different with money than it would be without it? Suppose that tomorrow morning you woke up, and there was no money in the world. It had disappeared. How would the world be different? Would it be a better or a worse place to live? Would people be less greedy, more greedy, or about the same as they were before? Would there be as much production? Would there be as many people working?

As you can see, many questions lie below the surface of a discussion of money. Money is that $20 bill, no doubt, but it is also much more. In this chapter, you'll begin to find out just how much more there is to the story of money.

Why This Chapter Is Important

Money influences our lives in more ways than most of us think. It influences the degree of economic activity in the economy, the level of interest rates, prices, exchange rates, and so

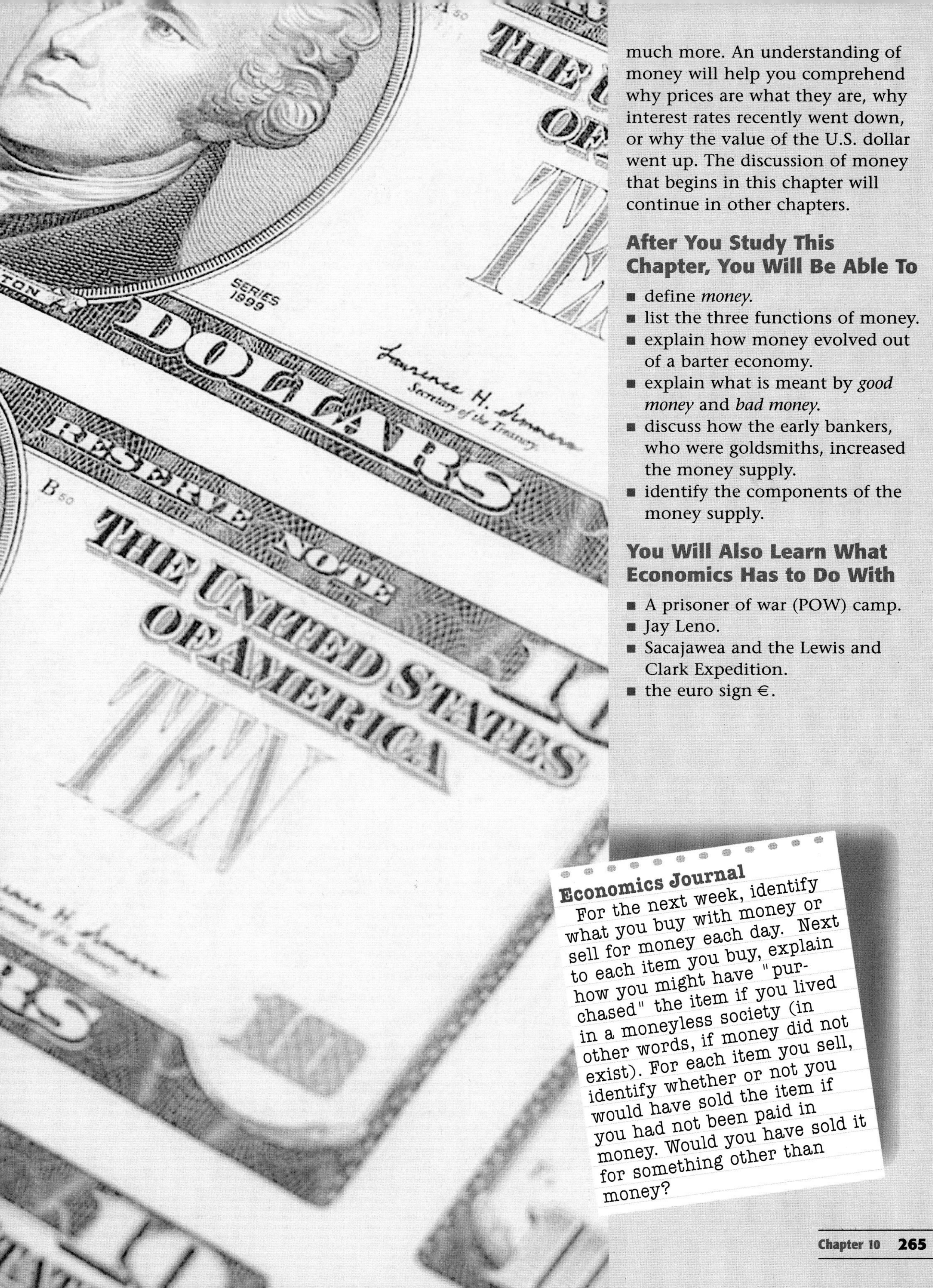

much more. An understanding of money will help you comprehend why prices are what they are, why interest rates recently went down, or why the value of the U.S. dollar went up. The discussion of money that begins in this chapter will continue in other chapters.

After You Study This Chapter, You Will Be Able To

- define *money.*
- list the three functions of money.
- explain how money evolved out of a barter economy.
- explain what is meant by *good money* and *bad money.*
- discuss how the early bankers, who were goldsmiths, increased the money supply.
- identify the components of the money supply.

You Will Also Learn What Economics Has to Do With

- A prisoner of war (POW) camp.
- Jay Leno.
- Sacajawea and the Lewis and Clark Expedition.
- the euro sign €.

Economics Journal

For the next week, identify what you buy with money or sell for money each day. Next to each item you buy, explain how you might have "purchased" the item if you lived in a moneyless society (in other words, if money did not exist). For each item you sell, identify whether or not you would have sold the item if you had not been paid in money. Would you have sold it for something other than money?

SECTION 1

The Origins Of Money

You were born into a world where people use money to make everyday transactions—to buy a loaf of bread, a book, or a pair of socks. Your parents, grandparents, and great-grandparents were born into the same kind of world. But some of your relatives (in the distant past) lived at a time when there was no money. They made transactions by trading one good or service for some other good or service, such as bread in exchange for meat or help at building a hut in exchange for cloth. This system of trading goods and services for other goods and services is called a **barter economy.** This section discusses the problems in a barter economy and then explains how money evolved out of such an economy.

As you read this section, keep these key questions in mind:

- What is a barter economy?
- How did money emerge out of a barter economy?
- What is money?
- What gives money its value?
- What are the functions of money?

As you know from studying American history, Native Americans frequently traded with the European explorers, settlers, and pioneers. What goods and services exchanged hands in this barter economy?

Key Terms

barter economy
double coincidence of wants
transaction costs
money
face value
Gresham's law
medium of exchange
unit of account
store of value
fractional reserve banking

A Barter Economy

Living in a barter economy is not easy. To understand what makes barter difficult, pretend you are living long ago. There is no money, and the only way you can get what you want is to trade something you have for it. Suppose you produce utensils such as forks, spoons, and knives. No one can live on utensils alone, so you set out to trade your utensils for bread, meat, and other necessities. You come across a person who bakes bread and ask if he is willing to trade some bread for some utensils. He says, "Thank you very much, but no. I have all the utensils I need." You ask him what he would like instead of utensils. He says he would like to have some fruit, and that if you had fruit he would be happy to trade bread for fruit.

You go on your way and find another person with bread. You ask her if she wants to trade bread for utensils. Like the first person, she says no, but she would be happy to trade bread for meat if you had any. You do not, so you move on to find another person who, you hope, will be willing to trade bread for utensils.

barter economy
An economy in which trades are made in goods and services instead of in money.

double coincidence of wants
The situation in which each of two parties to an exchange has what the other wants. In a barter economy, it is a requirement that must be met before a trade can be made.

transaction costs
The costs associated with the time and effort needed to search out, negotiate, and consummate an exchange.

The problem here is that you and the people you are coming across do not have a **double coincidence of wants**—the situation in an exchange where each of the two parties has what the other wants. You would have a double coincidence of wants if you found a person who had bread (what you want) and wanted what you had (utensils).

Double coincidence of wants	=	You have what Jane wants, and Jane has what you want

In short, the necessary condition for exchange or trade to take place is that people have a double coincidence of wants. What makes living in a barter economy so hard is that many of the people you want to trade with don't want to trade with you. In other words, people with whom you do not have a double coincidence of wants often confront you.

Trade, then, is very time consuming. It could take all day, if not longer, to find a person who wants to trade bread for utensils. Economists state the problem this way: the **transaction costs** of making exchanges are high in a barter economy. For our purposes here, think of the transaction costs as the time and effort you have to spend before you can make an exchange. If the transactions costs could somehow be made lower, trading would be easier.

The Emergence of Money: Lowering Transaction Costs of Exchanges

How can an individual living in a barter economy reduce the transaction costs of making exchanges? Consider the following scenario. In a barter economy with, say, 100 goods, some goods are more readily accepted in exchange than others. For example, good A might be accepted (on average) every tenth time it is offered in exchange, while good B might be accepted every seventh time. If you want to reduce the transaction costs of making exchanges, you offer good B for trade. But to offer good B in exchange, you have to have it in your possession. Now someone offers to trade good B for your utensils. You don't really want to consume good B (in the same way that you want to consume bread), but you realize that good B will be useful in making exchanges. It will reduce the transaction costs of making exchanges, so you accept it. Perhaps tomorrow you will use good B to lower the transaction costs of getting what you want.

Once some people accept a good because it reduces the transaction costs of exchange, others will follow. Think of why this is true. After you accept good B, it has greater acceptability than it used to have. This greater acceptability makes good B more useful to, say, Pheng than it was previously. Specifically, it is more useful because it now reduces the transaction costs of making barter exchanges by even more than it previously did.

Through the course of history, people have used many different materials—gold, silver, copper, beads, and even rocks—as money.

If Pheng now accepts good B, it simply makes it more likely that someone else will now accept good B, and so on. Eventually, everyone will accept good B in exchange. When this time arrives—when good B is widely accepted in exchange—good B is called **money.** Money is any good that is widely accepted in exchange and in the repayment of debts. Historically, goods that have evolved into money include gold, silver, copper, rocks, cattle, and shells, to name only a few.

MINI GLOSSARY

money
A good that is widely accepted for purposes of exchange and in the repayment of debt.

Self-Interest and Money

The story of the emergence of money from a barter economy is a story in which individual self-interest plays a big role. People in a barter economy simply wanted to make their everyday trading easier; they wanted to reduce the transaction costs of bartering. Thus they saw that it was in their best interest to begin to accept one prticular good among all goods that was most widely accepted in exchange. As a result of all individuals pursuing their self-interest, the barter economy disappeared and the money economy appeared.

Question: *Kings and queens of long ago had their likenesses stamped on gold coins. Is this evidence that the kings and queens actually created money?*

Answer: *No. Kings and queens might have stamped their likenesses on money, but neither kings nor queens, nor any government, invented money. Money predates formal government. It simply emerged out of the self-interested actions of people, each of whom was trying to make his or her own life easier.*

The text's account of how money evolved out of a barter economy emphasizes the spontaneous and unplanned nature of the process. No one came up with the idea for money and then put the idea into action. Instead, people living in a barter economy were simply trying to reduce the time and effort it took them to make their everyday exchanges, and as a result, money evolved. Money was an unintended consequence of people's actions.

Economists believe that there are many unintended consequences of people's actions. Like money, some of these consequences are beneficial. For example, consider the chemist who wants to become rich. He spends long hours working to develop a medicine that will reduce the pain arthritis sufferers feel. He sets one thing as his objective (becoming rich) and ends up doing something else besides (relieving people's pain).

What Gives Money Value?

Is a $10 bill considered to be money? To answer the question, you simply need to ask yourself whether or not the $10 bill is widely accepted for purposes of exchange. If it is, then it is money; if it is not, then it is not money. The $10 bill is widely accepted for purposes of exchange, of course, and therefore it is money.

What is it that gives money (say, the $10 bill) value? Like the bread or cloth in a barter economy, our money has value because of its general acceptability. Money has value to you because you know that you can use it to get what you want. You can use it to get what you want, however, only because other people will accept it in exchange for what they have.

To illustrate, suppose that tomorrow morning you wake up and begin to walk to school. On the way, you stop by the convenience store to buy a doughnut and milk. You try to pay for the food with two $1 bills. The owner of the store says that he no longer accepts dollar bills in exchange for what he has to sell. This story repeats itself all day with different store owners; no one is willing to accept dollar bills for what he or she has to sell. Suddenly, dollar bills have less value to you. If you cannot use them to get what you want, they are simply paper and ink, with little value at all.

Money in a Prisoner of War Camp

During World War II, an American, R. A. Radford, was captured and imprisoned in a prisoner of war (POW) camp. During his stay he noted that the Red Cross would periodically distribute to the prisoners packages that contained goods such as cigarettes, toiletries, chocolate, cheese, margarine, and tinned beef. Not all the prisoners had the same preferences: some liked chocolate but did not like cigarettes, whereas others liked cigarettes but did not like cheese. Soon, the prisoners began to barter-trade with each other. One prisoner, who had cigarettes and wanted more chocolate, would try to find another prisoner who wanted less chocolate and more cigarettes.

As this chapter explained, barter is a more time-consuming and difficult way to trade than trading with money. Soon the prisoners no longer bartered goods; they used money instead. The money was not U.S. dollars, French francs, German marks, or British pounds. In fact, it was not any national money at all; cigarettes emerged as the money in the POW camp. They were widely accepted for purposes of exchange. Soon chocolate bars, cheese, and other goods were quoted in "cigarette prices": 10 cigarettes for a chocolate bar, 20 cigarettes for cheese, and so on.

QUESTIONS TO ANSWER

1. How is a cigarette in a POW camp like a dollar bill?
2. Why did the cigarette rather than the chocolate or cheese, become money?

A historical example can further illustrate the point. Between 1861 and 1865 in the South, Confederate notes (Confederate money) had value, because Confederate money was accepted by people in the South for purposes of exchange. Today in the South, Confederate money has little value (except for historical collections), because it is not widely accepted for purposes of exchange. You cannot pay for your gasoline at a service station in Alabama with Confederate notes.

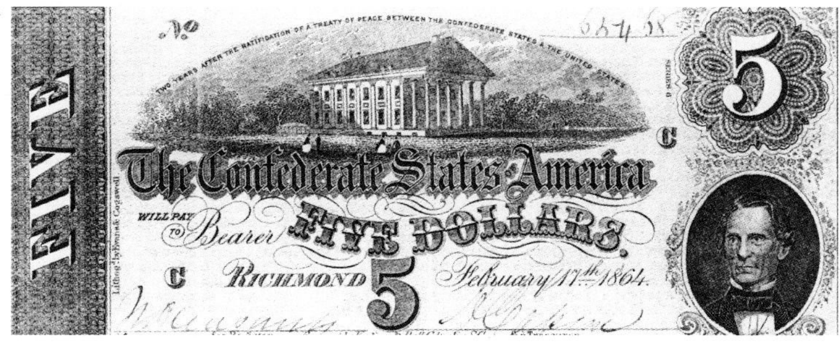

If you knew someone who was willing to accept a Confederate note in exchange for a good or service, would that mean that Confederate dollars could be considered money? Explain.

Prices double in an economy. Is there any reason to believe that money will either no longer be used as a medium of exchange or as a unit of account? Explain your answer.

What Are the Benefits of Using Money?

The transaction costs of exchange are lower in a money economy than in a barter economy. In a barter economy, not everyone you want to trade with wants to trade with you; you don't have a double coincidence of wants with everyone. In a money economy, in contrast, everyone you want to buy something from wants what you have—money. Everyone is willing to trade what they have for money. Because you have a double coincidence of wants with everyone in a money economy, but not with everyone in a barter economy, the transaction costs of making exchanges are lower in a money economy than in a barter economy.

Money lowers the transaction costs of making exchanges. A person can pay for a cart full of goods in a matter of a few minutes. Imagine how long it would take this woman to acquire all of these groceries in a barter economy.

More Goods, Services, and Leisure Lower transaction costs translate into less time needed for you to make a given level of exchange in a money economy than in a barter economy. For example, if it would take you four hours to obtain milk, bread, and fruits in a barter economy, it would take much less time (a few minutes) to obtain the same goods in a money economy. Using money, then, would free up some time for you. With that extra time, you could produce more of whatever it is you produce (accounting services, furniture, computers, or novels), consume more leisure, or both. In a money economy, then, people produce more goods and services and consume more leisure than they would in a barter economy. The residents of money economies are richer in goods, services, and leisure than the residents of barter economies.

Specialization The residents of money economies are more specialized, too. If you lived in a barter economy, it would be difficult and time consuming to make everyday transactions. You probably would produce many things yourself rather than deal with the hardship of producing only one good and then trying to exchange it for so many other goods. In other words, the higher the transaction costs of trading, the less likely you would want to trade, and the more likely you would produce the goods that you would otherwise have to trade for.

In a money economy, however, it is neither difficult nor time consuming to make everyday transactions. The transaction costs of exchange are low relative to what they are in a barter economy. You have the luxury of specializing in the production of one thing (writing poetry, writing computer programs, delivering economics lectures), selling that one thing for money, and then using the money to buy whatever good or service you want to buy. If you produce only economics lectures, you do not have to worry that the person you want to buy a car from won't sell you a car because he doesn't want your economics lectures. You won't be trading your economics lectures for a car; you will be trading money for a car, and you can be sure the car salesman wants money.

Think about the necessities of life: food, drink, shelter. Do you think that the producers of these necessities would have been interested in trading their goods for plays, even those written by Shakespeare, in a barter economy? What impact would this have on specialization?

Would William Shakespeare have written plays if he had lived in a barter economy? He may have, but the probability is lower in a barter economy than in a money economy. How do you have time to write plays when you have to dedicate so much of your time to trying to find someone with whom you have a double coincidence of wants? Shakespeare might have had to bake his own bread, sew his own clothes, and build his own house had he lived in a barter economy, which would not have left much time for writing plays.

What holds for Shakespeare holds for other people, too. Would cars, computers, telephones, and airplanes exist if we still lived in a barter economy? It is doubtful. Many of the products and great works of art that we take for granted required people to spend long periods of time producing them. People had to specialize in the production of that one product, that one great work of art, or that one invention. In a barter economy, they would have probably chosen not to specialize. They would have had to produce many of the goods they wanted to consume, because specializing in the production of one good and then trying to trade that one good for hundreds of other goods would have been just too difficult.

Gresham's Law: Good Money, Bad Money

face value
The stated denomination on paper money or coins. For example, the face value of a nickel is 5 cents, and the words *five cents* actually appear on a nickel.

Did you know that money can be either good or bad? The following story illustrates how. Silver coins were used as money in the days of King Henry VIII of England. One day, King Henry issued an order to reduce the silver content of coins. Coins that before 1543 had been 92.5 percent pure silver were reduced to 33.3 percent pure silver by 1545, but their **face value** (stated denomination) was not reduced. In other words, a 1543 coin had more silver in it than a 1545 coin, but the two coins had the same money denomination. (The same thing happened in the United States in the 1960s. A dime minted before 1965 has a higher silver content than a dime minted in 1965 or after, although both pre-1965 dimes and post-1964 dimes represent 10 cents.)

Would Jay Leno Be Funny in a Barter Economy?

Suppose Jay Leno lived in a barter economy. Would he be funny?

Before we answer that question, let's look at what Leno does on an average day, living in a money economy. He wakes up in the morning, eats breakfast, and then drives to the NBC studios in Burbank, California. Once there, he gets ready for his late-night television show, which he will tape at 5:30 P.M. Pacific time. On his show he will tell jokes, make funny comments, and generally try to keep people laughing.

Would Leno try to keep people laughing if he lived in a barter economy? On a hypothetical typical day in a barter economy, he wakes up, eats breakfast, and then tries to see if he can trade a few jokes for some food. He meets a man who bakes bread. He asks the man if the man will trade some of his bread for a few laughs. The man tells Leno he is not interested in making this trade. In economic terms, Leno and the man do not have a double coincidence of wants. Leno spends the rest of the day looking for people who have food and are willing to trade it for a few laughs. At the end of the day he finally finds such a person.

After a few days, Leno realizes that having only one thing to trade in a barter economy—jokes—is problematic. He decides to produce some of his own food so he will not have to trade for so many things. In economic terms, if trading is difficult, people reduce the number of trades they have to make by producing much of what they want to consume.

After deciding to produce some of his own food, Leno's average day changes. He spends most of his day planting seed to grow corn and apples, baking bread, and raising cows. He has little time to think up jokes or to hone his comedic routine.

Why is Leno's life so different in a money economy from what it would be like in a barter economy? In a money economy he specializes in producing only one thing—jokes. In a barter economy, he would produce many things—corn, apples, meat and milk from cows, and a few jokes. Thus, in a money economy Leno specializes, and in a barter economy he would not.

In fact, few people would specialize in a barter economy to the degree they do in a money economy. They would not specialize for the same reason that Leno would not specialize: it's too risky. When you produce only one thing, it is extremely unlikely that you are going to obtain your preferred bundle of goods through barter trade. After all, what is the probability that everyone whose goods you want will want the one thing that you produce?

In a money economy, in contrast, everyone is willing to trade what they have for money. There is no issue of double coincidence of wants, so people can specialize in one good or service. There is not as much risk to specializing as there would be in a barter economy, so people produce one thing (jokes, attorney services, corn, and so on), sell it for money, and then use the money to make their preferred purchases.

QUESTION TO ANSWER What do you see as the benefits and the costs of specialization?

Gresham's law
An economic law stating that bad money drives good money out of circulation. (Bad money has the same face value as good money, but a lower precious metal content.)

medium of exchange
Anything that is generally acceptable in exchange for goods and services.

unit of account
A common measurement in which values are expressed.

store of value
Something with the ability to hold value over time.

After King Henry's change in the coins, people began to circulate only the newer, lighter coins and to hoard the older, heavier coins. After all, silver is valuable, and silver coins can be melted down and the silver sold. If two coins have the same face value but one has more silver than the other, it is better to spend the coin with the lower silver content and keep the coin with the higher silver content.

When King Henry VIII's daughter, Elizabeth, became queen, she wondered why the people in her kingdom were spending one type of silver coin and not the other. A financial adviser to Queen Elizabeth I, Sir Thomas Gresham (1519–1579), gave her an explanation similar to the one you have just read. Gresham's explanation is captured in the statement, "Bad money drives good money out of circulation." Today, this statement is known as **Gresham's law.**

The Functions of Money

Money has three major functions. It functions as a medium of exchange, a unit of account, and a store of value.

Money as a Medium of Exchange A **medium of exchange** is anything that is generally acceptable in exchange for goods and services. As we have seen, then, the most basic function of money is as a medium of exchange. Money is present in almost every exchange made.

Money as a Unit of Account A **unit of account** is a common measurement in which values are expressed. Money functions as a unit of account, which means that all goods can be expressed in terms of money. For example, we express the value of a house in terms of dollars (say, $180,000), the value of a car in terms of dollars (say, $20,000), and the value of a computer in terms of dollars (say, $3,000).

Money as a Store of Value A good is a **store of value** if it maintains its value over time. Money serves as a store of value. For example, you can sell your labor services today, collect money in payment, and wait for a future date to spend the money on goods and services. You do not have to rush to buy goods and services with the money today; it will store value to be used at a future date.

To say that money is a store of value does not mean that it is necessarily a constant store of value. To illustrate, let's say there is only one good in the world, apples, and the price of an apple is $1. Julio earns $100 on January 1, 2000. If he spends the $100 on January 1, 2000, he can buy 100 apples. But suppose instead that he holds the money for one year, until January 1, 2001. Furthermore, suppose the price of apples has doubled, to $2. Thus, on January 1, 2001, Julio can buy only 50 apples. The money has lost some of its value between 2000 and 2001. If prices rise, the value of money declines. Therefore, although money acts as a store of value, it is not a constant store of value.

When economists say that money serves as a store of value, they do not mean to imply that money is a constant store of value or that it always serves as a store of value equally well. Money is better at storing value at some times than at other times. (Money is "bad" at storing value when prices are rapidly rising.)

Exhibit 10-1
The Major Functions of Money

Function	Definition	Example
Medium of exchange	Anything that is generally acceptable in exchange for goods and services.	John uses money to buy haircuts, books, food, CDs, and computers. Money is the medium of exchange.
Unit of account	Common measurement in which values are expressed.	The price of a candy bar is $1, and the price of a book is $14. The exchange value of both goods is measured by dollars (unit of account). Notice that exchange values can be compared easily when money is used. In this example, the book has 14 times the exchange value of the candy bar.
Store of value	An item that maintains value over time.	Phil has a job and gets paid $100. He could use $100 to buy a ski jacket that he wants, but he decides not to. Instead, he saves the $100 and buys the ski jacket six months later. For Phil, money has acted as a store of value over the six-month period.

For a summarized comparison of the three major functions of money, see Exhibit 10-1 above.

Goldsmiths were often the early bankers because they had safe storage facilities.

The Early Bankers

Our money today is easy to carry and transport, but it was not always that way. For example, when money was principally gold coins, carrying it was neither easy nor safe. Gold is heavy, and transporting thousands of gold coins is an activity that could easily draw the attention of thieves. Thus, individuals wanted to store their gold in a safe place. The person most individuals turned to was the goldsmith, someone already equipped with safe storage facilities. Goldsmiths were the first bankers. They took in other people's gold and stored it for them. To acknowledge that they held deposited gold, goldsmiths issued receipts called *warehouse receipts* to their customers. For example, Adams might have had a receipt from the goldsmith Turner stating that he had deposited 400 gold pieces with Turner. (Similarly, today your bank gives you a receipt when you deposit money.)

Before long, people began to circulate the warehouse receipts in place of the

Is it Money or a Boggs' Bill?

J.S.G. Boggs is an artist. He is not an artist who draws bowls of fruit, landscapes, or houses in the countryside. He is an artist who draws money. He calls his art "Boggs' bills." At first glance, a Boggs' bill looks much like a dollar bill. It has some important differences, however. For example, on the back of a dollar bill are the words "The United States of America." On a Boggs' bill it might be "The United States of Florida." On the back of a dollar bill, across the number 1, the word "One" is printed. On a Boggs' bill the word "Fun" might appear instead.

J.S.G. Boggs has said that he is not a counterfeiter, but an artist. He makes no attempt at trying to deceive people. When he hands a merchant a Boggs' bill, he tells the merchant that he is not handing him currency, but a piece of art that may look somewhat like currency. He often asks if the merchant is willing to sell him what he wants for a Boggs' bill. Some merchants do, most do not.

The Secret Service, whose job is not only to protect the president of the United States, but also to "arrest any person committing any offense against the laws of the United States relating to coins and currency," believes that Boggs is in violation of Title 18 of the Federal Criminal Code and Rules. This federal law prohibits the production of any likeness to money, with the exception of reproductions in black and white or those that are less than 75% or more than 150% the size of real money. Boggs argues that his art is not a likeness of money because often one side of a Boggs' bill is blank.

There are two issues in question with respect to Boggs' bills. The first is whether or not he is in violation of Title 18. The courts must decide. The second is whether or not what he produces is money. This matter is for economists to decide. According to economists, *money is any good that is widely accepted for purposes of exchange and in the repayment of debt.* Are Boggs' bills widely accepted for purposes of exchange? The answer is a most definite no. Most sellers do not trade their goods for Boggs' bills. There is no doubt about it, then: Boggs' bills are not money.

QUESTIONS TO ANSWER

1. If you want to see a Boggs' bill, you can go to http://www.jsgboggs.com/. Some people say that Boggs draws money because of the notoriety he receives from doing it. What do you think?
2. If Boggs' bills are not money, can Boggs be a counterfeiter?

gold itself (gold was not only inconvenient for customers to carry, but also inconvenient for merchants to accept). For instance, if Adams wanted to buy something for 400 gold pieces, he might give a warehouse receipt to the seller instead of going to the goldsmith, obtaining the gold, and then delivering it to the seller. Using the receipts was easier than dealing with the gold itself for both parties. In short, the warehouse receipts circulated as money—that is, they became widely acceptable for purposes of exchange.

Goldsmiths began to notice that on an average day, few people came to redeem their receipts for gold. Most individuals were simply trading the receipts for goods. At this stage, warehouse receipts were *fully backed* by gold. The receipts simply represented, or stood in place of, the actual gold in storage.

Some goldsmiths, however, began to think, "Suppose I lend out some of the gold that people have deposited with me. If I lend it to others, I can charge interest for the loan. And since receipts are circulating in place of the gold, I will probably never be faced with redeeming everyone's receipts for gold at once." Some goldsmiths did lend out some of the gold that had been deposited with them and collected the interest on the loans. The consequence of this lending activity was an increase in the supply of money, measured in terms of gold and paper receipts. Remember, both gold and paper warehouse receipts were widely accepted for purposes of exchange.

A numerical example can illustrate how the goldsmiths' activities increased the supply of money. Suppose there are only 100 gold coins in the world; the money supply is represented by 100 gold coins. Now suppose the owners of the gold deposit their coins with the goldsmith. To keep things simple, suppose the goldsmith gives out 1 paper receipt for each coin deposited. In other words, if Flores deposits 3 coins with a goldsmith, she receives 3 warehouse receipts, each representing a coin.

What do bankers do with much of the money that people deposit with them?

The warehouse receipts begin to circulate instead of the gold itself, so the money supply consists of 100 paper receipts, whereas before it consisted of 100 gold coins. But still the number is 100.

Now the goldsmith decides to lend out some of the gold and earn interest on the loans. Suppose Roberts wants to take out a loan for 15 gold coins. The goldsmith grants the loan. Instead of handing over 15 gold coins, though, the goldsmith gives Roberts 15 paper receipts.

What has happened to the money supply? Before the goldsmith went into the lending business, the money supply consisted of 100 paper receipts. Now, though, the money supply has increased to 115 paper receipts. The increase in the money supply (as measured by the number of paper receipts) is a result of the lending activity of the goldsmith.

The process described here was the beginning of **fractional reserve banking.** Under a fractional reserve banking system, such as the one that currently operates in the United States, banks (like the goldsmiths of years past) create money by holding on reserve only a fraction of the money deposited with them and lending the remainder.

fractional reserve banking A banking arrangement in which banks hold only a fraction of their deposits and lend out the remainder.

Section 1 Review

Defining Terms

1. Define
   a. barter economy
   b. double coincidence of wants
   c. transaction costs
   d. money
   e. face value
   f. Gresham's law
   g. medium of exchange
   h. unit of account
   i. store of value
   j. fractional reserve banking

Reviewing Facts and Concepts

2. Give an example in which two individuals have a double coincidence of wants.
3. What gives money its value?
4. Money serves as a *unit of account.* Give an example to illustrate what this means.
5. What does it mean to say that the United States has a fractional reserve banking system?

Critical Thinking

6. What role does self-interest play in the emergence of money from a barter economy?

Applying Economic Concepts

7. There are two dimes, A and B, that have the same face value (10 cents). Dime A has a greater silver content than dime B. According to Gresham's law, dime B will be used for everyday transactions, and dime A will be hoarded. Why do people hoard high-silver-content dimes? When they are hoarded, they can't be used to buy things. What good is a dime if it can't be used to buy something?

SECTION 2

The Money Supply

In the previous discussion of early banking, both gold and warehouse receipts were part of the money supply. Both were widely accepted for purposes of exchange. In today's world, people do not circulate warehouse receipts or gold. What does the money supply consist of today? This section answers that question.

As you read this section, keep these key questions in mind:

- What does the money supply consist of?
- What is a Federal Reserve note?

Key Terms

money supply
currency
Federal Reserve note
demand deposit
savings account
near-money
debit card

Components of the Money Supply

The **money supply** in the United States, or the total supply of money in circulation, is composed of (1) currency, (2) checking accounts, and (3) traveler's checks.[1]

Money supply =
Currency + Checking accounts + Traveler's checks

1. *Currency.* **Currency** includes both coins (such as quarters and dimes) minted by the U.S. Treasury and paper money. The paper money in circulation consists of **Federal Reserve notes.** If you look at a dollar bill, you will see at the top the words "Federal Reserve Note." The Federal Reserve System, which is the central bank of the United States (discussed in the next chapter), issues Federal Reserve notes.
2. *Checking accounts.* Checking accounts are accounts in which funds are deposited and can be withdrawn simply by writing a check. Sometimes check-

MINI GLOSSARY

money supply The total supply of money in circulation, composed of currency, checking accounts, and traveler's checks.

currency Coins issued by the U.S. Treasury and paper money (called Federal Reserve notes) issued by the Federal Reserve System.

Federal Reserve note Paper money issued by the Federal Reserve System.

Do you think the employee at this clothing store will accept the customer's check for the amount of her purchase as payment? Is a check money?

1. Actually, this list is referred to as the M1 ("M-one") money supply. There are other, broader measures of the money supply (such as the M2 money supply) which include all the M1 supply as well as other monies, such as small savings accounts. We do not discuss them in this text.

You can find money supply figures at many sites on the Internet. One is a site for the Board of Governors of the Federal Reserve System. **http://www.federalreserve.gov/releases/H6/hist/** Go there, and you will see the heading "Money Stock and Debt Issues Measures." In the list of tables below this heading, click on Table 1. There you will see figures for various money supply measures. The money supply measure discussed in this chapter is officially referred to as the "M1 money supply." Find the most recent dollar figure for the M1 money supply. Next, look at Table 2. Identify the growth rate in the M1 money supply for the last twelve months.

ing accounts are referred to as **demand deposits,** because the funds can be converted to currency on demand and given to the person to whom the check is made payable. For example, suppose Malcolm has a checking account at a local bank with a balance of $400. He can withdraw up to $400 currency from his account, or he can transfer any dollar amount up to $400 to someone else by simply writing a check to that person.

3. *Traveler's checks.* A traveler's check is a check issued by a bank in any of several denominations ($10, $20, $50, and so on) and sold to a traveler (or to anyone who wishes to buy it), who signs it at the time it is issued by the bank and then again in the presence of the person cashing it.

Of the three major components of the U.S. money supply, the checking account component is the largest. For example, in March 2000, there were $585 billion in checking accounts, $516 billion in currency, and $8 billion in traveler's checks. The money supply was $1,109 billion (see Exhibit 10-2).

Exhibit 10-2

Components of the Money Supply

The money supply consists of currency, checking account (balances), and traveler's checks. The amounts shown represent the money supply in March, 2000.

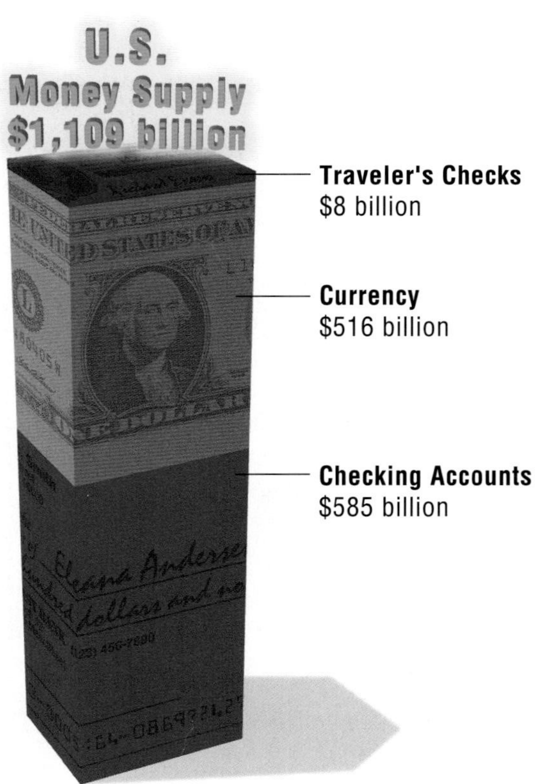

demand deposit A deposit that can be withdrawn in currency or transferred by a check to a third party on the initiative of the owner.

savings account An interest-earning account.

near-money Assets, such as nonchecking savings accounts, that can be easily and quickly turned into money.

Turning some near-monies (such as a nonchecking savings account) into money is not difficult.

Is a Savings Account Money?

A **savings account** is an interest-earning account. For example, if you have $400 in your savings account and the annual interest rate you are paid is 6 percent, in a year your savings account will increase to $424. There are some savings accounts on which you can write checks and some on which you cannot. Savings accounts on which you can write checks fall into the category of checking accounts, which were discussed earlier. A passbook savings account is an example of a nonchecking savings account. When you deposit your money into a passbook savings account, you are given a small booklet in which deposits, withdrawals, and interest are recorded.

A nonchecking savings account is not considered money because it is not widely accepted for purposes of exchange. You cannot go into a store, show the salesperson the balance in your passbook savings account, and buy a $40 sweater. However, nonchecking savings accounts are considered **near-money.** Near-money is anything that can be relatively easily and quickly turned into money. You cannot buy a sweater by telling the salesperson that you have so much money in your passbook savings account (near-money), but you can go to the bank and request that your nonchecking savings be given to you in currency.

THE BORN LOSER ® by Art and Chip Sansom

THE BORN LOSER reprinted by permission of Newspaper Enterprise Association, Inc.

Will the Euro Sign (€) Become As Well Known As the Dollar Sign ($)?

There are many different monies in the world: dollars, pesos, yen, rubles, and so on. On July 1, 2002, there will be fewer monies; on that day many of the countries of Europe will no longer use their national currencies but will instead use the euro.

The euro was officially adopted as the money of the European Union on January 1, 1999. The European Union consists of fifteen member countries, but only eleven of those countries (Austria, Belgium, France, and Germany, to name a few) joined the euro zone on that day, irrevocably fixing their national currencies to the euro. For example, the French franc was set at 6.55 francs to 1 euro. No euro notes or coins were issued that day, but noncurrency transactions (such as stock market transactions) could be made in euros.

Euro notes and coins will begin to be issued on January 1, 2001, at the latest and will be used alongside national currencies until June 30, 2002. Beginning on July 1, 2002, only euros will be used as money in the countries in the euro zone.

One major reason the euro was adopted was to reduce the costs of Europeans doing business with each other. For example, consider that before the introduction of the euro, if a German firm wanted to trade with a French firm, it would have to convert its currency (marks) into French currency (francs). With one currency, the euro, there is no need for this; both the German and French firms use the same money.

Think of what it might be like in the United States if each of the fifty states had its own money. Would trade between states be easier or harder than it is today? Most people think it would be much harder. It is the same for Europe, people say. Many European countries principally trade with each other, and having multiple monies makes this trade more difficult than having just one money.

As an aside, the symbol for the euro, €, looks like an *E* with two horizontal, parallel lines across it. It was inspired by the Greek letter *epsilon,* in reference to the cradle of European civilization, and to the first letter of the word *Europe.* The parallel lines represent the stability of the euro. The official abbreviation for the euro is EUR.

QUESTION TO ANSWER Currency exchange rates are published each day in the newspaper. Check today's paper, and see what a euro trades for in terms of U.S. dollars.

Credit cards are not money because they are not used to repay debt. What is the actual relationship between credit cards and debt?

Are Credit Cards Money?

At first sight, a credit card appears to be money. After all, it is often referred to as "plastic money," and most retailers accept credit cards as payment for purchases. But on closer examination, we can see that a credit card is not money.

Consider Tina Quentin, who decides to buy a pair of shoes. She hands the shoe clerk her Visa card and signs for the purchase. Essentially, what the Visa card allows Tina to do is take out a loan from the bank that issued the card. The shoe clerk knows that this bank has, in effect, promised to pay the store for the shoes. At a later date, the bank will send Tina a credit card bill. At that time, Tina will be required to reimburse the bank for the shoe charges, plus interest (if her payment is made after a certain date). Tina is required to discharge her debt to the bank with money, such as currency or a check written on her checking account.

In conclusion, then, a credit card is not money. Money has to be both widely used for exchange and be used in the repayment of debt. A credit card is not used to repay debt but rather to incur it. It is an instrument that makes it easier for the holder to obtain a loan. The use of a credit card places a person in debt, which he or she then has to pay off with money.

Sacajawea

The new dollar coin, first introduced into circulation in 2000, has the image of Sacajawea on its obverse (front) side. Sacajawea was a Native American woman who, at the age of eleven, was captured by a Hidatsa raiding party and taken from her fellow Shoshones. Later, she was either bought or won in a bet by a French-Canadian trader, Toussaint Charbonneau, who made Sacajawea his wife. When she was fifteen years old, explorers Meriwether Lewis and William Clark hired Charbonneau, not so much for his exploratory skills as for those of his wife. Because she knew several Indian languages she was able to help Lewis and Clark acquire the horses they needed. She also knew the rugged country and its vegetation and taught them how to find edible roots. Once, she single-handedly rescued Clark's journals from the Missouri River when their boat capsized. Without the journals, much of the record of that first year of the expedition would have been lost to history.

Sacajawea died at the age of twenty-five. Clark, who was always deeply indebted to Sacajawea, took responsibility for educating her son and daughter.

QUESTION TO ANSWER This chapter discussed the term *transaction costs* in its exploration of money. In what way did Sacajawea lower the transaction costs of exploring for Lewis and Clark?

Debit Cards

The **debit card** is becoming increasingly popular with people purchasing goods. A debit card allows funds to be withdrawn from automated teller machines, as well as funds to be transferred from one person's checking account to another's. Debit cards are used at many grocery stores and gas stations. For example, grocery store customers at the checkout stand can run their debit cards through a desktop device much like the devices stores currently use to verify credit card purchases. The clerk at the store enters the amount of the food purchase. The customer then enters a secret personal identification number (PIN), permitting access to his or her checking account. The customer then commands a transfer of funds (equal to the food purchase) from the checking account to the store's account, probably at another bank. As soon as the store has verified that the funds transfer has been completed, the customer leaves with the merchandise. The operation takes a matter of seconds.

Debit cards are becoming increasingly popular because of their many uses.

MINI GLOSSARY

debit card A card that can be used to withdraw funds at automated teller machines and to pay for purchases by electronically transferring funds from one account to another (where the seller has the appropriate equipment). Debit cards look like credit cards.

Section 2 Review

Defining Terms

1. Define
   - a. money supply
   - b. currency
   - c. Federal Reserve note
   - d. demand deposit
   - e. savings account
   - f. near-money
   - g. debit card

Reviewing Facts and Concepts

2. What is the largest component of the money supply?
3. What is the difference between near-money and money?

Critical Thinking

4. Credit cards are widely accepted for purposes of exchange, yet they are not money. Why not?

Applying Economic Concepts

5. Take a look at a Federal Reserve note. On it, you will read the following words: "This note is legal tender for all debts, public and private." What part of the definition of *money* does this message pertain to?

Developing Economic Skills

Calculating Relative Prices

In a barter economy there is no money, so the value of all goods must be expressed in terms of all other goods. Let's say there are three goods in a barter economy: apples, paper, and pencils. If we wanted to know the "price" of apples, it would be quoted in terms of both paper and pencils. For example, a person might say that 1 apple has a price of either 10 sheets of paper or 2 pencils. This means that if you have either 10 sheets of paper or 2 pencils, you can "buy" 1 apple.

When you are finding the price of one good (say, an apple) in terms of another good (say, pencils), you are said to be finding the relative price of a good. In our example, the relative price of 1 apple was 2 pencils. Even though you live in a money economy and not in a barter economy, it is still important to know how to compute relative prices. In fact, you do not know the cost of anything until you can compute relative prices.

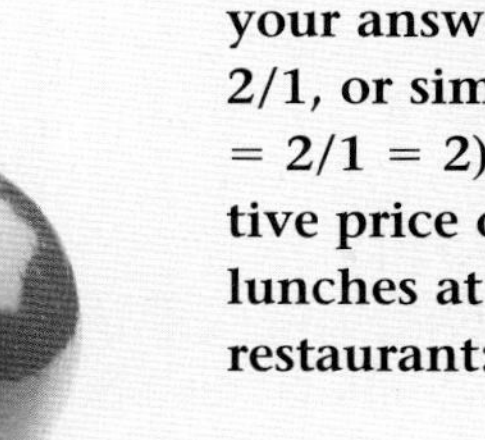

To illustrate, suppose one day you buy a book for \$15. Later that day, someone asks you the cost of the book. You say \$15, but that is not a complete answer to the question. Remember, according to an economist, the cost of something is what you forfeit, or give up, in order to obtain that something. The opportunity cost of the book is what you would have purchased if you had not purchased the book. Suppose you would have used the money to eat lunch at your favorite restaurant, where you pay an average of \$7.50 for lunch. Now what is the opportunity cost of the book? This question is no different from the question, What is the relative price of the book?

Computing relative price in a money economy is simple.

1. *In a money economy, think of the good for which you want to find the relative price as the numerator in a ratio, and any other good as the denominator in a ratio.* We want to know the price of the book, so we put "book" in the numerator and "lunch" in the denominator:

   Book/Lunch

2. *Place the dollar amount of each good alongside the good:*

   \$15 book/\$7.50 lunch

3. *Find the ratio.* This ratio is your answer. The ratio is 2/1, or simply 2 (\$15/\$7.50 = 2/1 = 2). Thus, the relative price of the book is 2 lunches at your favorite restaurant:

   1 book = 2 lunches

   Two lunches, then, is the opportunity cost of the book.

1. One apple trades for 5 marbles. What is the relative price of 1 marble? (In other words, what do you have to pay in terms of apples to buy 1 marble?)
2. One egg trades for 1 orange. What is the relative price of 1 orange?
3. Ten hats trade for 20 shirts. What is the relative price of 1 shirt?
4. Fifty pencils trade for 25 erasers. What is the relative price of 1 pencil?
5. Five paintings by Khan trade for 20 paintings by McDonald. What is the relative price of 1 painting by McDonald?
6. The price of a lamp is \$40; the price of a picture frame is \$15. What is the relative price of the picture frame?
7. The price of a table is \$123; the price of a computer stand is \$78. What is the relative price of the table?
8. If the price of apples rises and the price of oranges remains the same, what happens to the relative price of apples? Explain your answer with numbers.

CHAPTER 10

Review

Economics Vocabulary

Fill in the following blanks with the appropriate word or phrase.

1. A(n) _____ is an economy in which trades are made in terms of goods and services instead of money.
2. The costs associated with the time and effort needed to search out, negotiate, and consummate an exchange are called _____.
3. Jack has apples and wants oranges. Karen has oranges and wants apples. Jack and Karen have a _____.
4. The _____ of a dime is 10 cents.
5. _____ states that bad money drives good money out of circulation.
6. Coin and paper money are _____.
7. Anything that is generally accepted in exchange for goods and services is a _____.
8. A common measurement in which values are expressed is a(n) _____.
9. A(n) _____ is paper money issued by the Federal Reserve System.
10. A banking arrangement in which banks hold only a fraction of their deposits and lend out the remainder is referred to as _____.
11. The _____ is composed of currency, checking accounts, and traveler's checks.
12. A(n) _____ is withdrawable on demand (in the form of currency) and transferable by means of a check.
13. A(n) _____ is an interest-earning account.
14. An asset that can easily and quickly be turned into money is called _____.
15. A(n) _____ is a card that can be used to withdraw funds at automated teller machines and to pay for purchases by electronically transferring funds from one account to another.
16. _____ is the characteristic of something that holds value over time.

Review Questions

1. Is a double coincidence of wants more likely or less likely to occur in a barter economy than a money economy? Explain your answer.
2. A person goes into a store and buys a pair of shoes with money. Is money here principally functioning as a medium of exchange, a store of value, or a unit of account?
3. Jim puts $100 cash in a box in his office and keeps it there for one year. Is this money principally functioning as a medium of exchange, a store of value, or a unit of account?
4. Explain how money emerged out of a barter economy.
5. "Money has value if it is backed by gold. If money is not backed by gold, then it has no value." Do you agree or disagree? Explain your answer.
6. Explain how goldsmiths increased the money supply. (*Note:* The money supply consists of gold and warehouse receipts for purposes of this question.)
7. Why is a checking account sometimes called a *demand deposit?*
8. What is currency?
9. Why is there greater specialization in a money economy than in a barter economy?

Calculations

1. Suppose there are two kinds of dimes: pre-1965 dimes and post-1965 dimes. Each dime has a face value of 10 cents. The pre-1965 dimes have a silver content of 0.01 ounce, and post-1965 dimes have no silver content. Gresham's law predicts that bad money will drive good money out of circulation: post-1965 dimes will drive pre-1965 dimes out of circulation. What is the lowest ounce-price of silver that must exist before it makes more sense to melt the pre-1965 dimes for their silver content than to use them in exchange? Explain your answer.
2. In a tiny economy, there are 25 dimes, 10 nickels, 100 one-dollar bills, 200 five-dollar bills, and 40 twenty-dollar bills in circulation. In addition, traveler's checks equal $500, balances in checking accounts equal $1,900, and balances in savings accounts equal $2,200. What is the money supply? Explain your answer.

Economics and Thinking Skills

1. **Application.** Gresham's law is usually applied to money, stating that bad money drives good money out of circulation. Some people believe Gresham's

law also applies to things other than money. Give an example of something you think Gresham's law might apply to other than money.

2. **Cause and Effect.** Did the emergence of money (out of a barter economy) cause people to become self-interested, or did self-interest cause the emergence of money?

Writing Skills

The chapter discussed the fact that if it were not for money, people would not specialize as much as they do today, and if they did not specialize as much, we would not have many of the goods and services we currently enjoy. Would William Shakespeare or Ludwig van Beethoven have produced their great works in a barter economy? Write a one-page paper identifying something you enjoy today that you think would not exist if you currently lived in a barter economy. Explain why you think this item would not exist in a barter economy.

Economics in the Media

In the business section of many newspapers (one of which is the *Wall Street Journal*), you will find the most recent money supply figures. Find the most recent money supply figure in a newspaper or business publication. If possible, identify the dollar amount of the three major components of the money supply: currency, checking accounts, and traveler's checks.

Where's the Economics?

Which of the three functions of money is most strongly represented in the photo?

Analyzing Primary Sources

Milton Friedman won the Nobel Prize in economics in 1976. Friedman was an expert in many economics subjects, but one of his main areas of expertise was money. In 1992, he published a book entitled *Money Mischief*. Here is a short excerpt from that book:

One reason why money is a mystery to so many is the role of myth or fiction or convention. I started this book with the chapter on stone money precisely in order to illustrate that point. To make the same point in a way that is perhaps more relevant to the everyday experience of most of us, consider two rectangles of paper of about the same size. One rectangle is mostly green on the backside and has a picture of Abraham Lincoln on the front side, which has the number 5 in each corner and contains some printing. One can exchange pieces of this paper for a certain quantity of food, clothing, or other goods. People will willingly make such trades. The second piece of paper, perhaps cut from a glossy magazine, may also have a picture, some numbers, and a bit of printing on its face. It may also be colored green on the back. Yet it is fit only for lighting the fire.

Whence the difference? The printing on the five-dollar bill gives us no answer. It simply says, "Federal Reserve Note/The United States of America/Five Dollars" and, in smaller print, "This note is legal tender for all debts, public and private . . . "

The short answer—and the right answer—is that private persons accept these pieces of paper because they are confident that others will. The pieces of green paper have value because everybody thinks they have value. Everybody thinks they have value because in everybody's experience they have had value. . . . The United States could barely operate without a common and widely accepted medium of exchange (or at most a small number of such media); yet the existence of a common and widely accepted medium of exchange rests on a convention: our whole monetary system owes its existence to the mutual acceptance of what, from one point of view, is no more than a fiction.[2]

1. According to Friedman, what gives money value?
2. Friedman says at the end of the passage, "Our whole monetary system owes its existence to the mutual acceptance of what, from one point of view, is no more than a fiction." What does he mean? To what is he referring?

2. Milton Friedman, *Money Mischief* (New York: Harcourt Brace Jovanovich, 1992), pp. 9–10.

CHAPTER 11

Banking and the Federal Reserve System

What This Chapter Is About

This chapter discusses banking and the Federal Reserve System. It explains how banks and the Federal Reserve together can and do change the money supply. Later chapters will explain how changes in the money supply affect you in your many roles in life, including buyer, seller, borrower, lender, and employee.

Why This Chapter Is Important

You know that the Supreme Court is an important institution and that the decisions the members of the Court make affect our daily lives. You also know that Congress is another important institution that makes decisions affecting our daily lives. But have you heard of the Federal Reserve System, popularly referred to as *the Fed?* It, too, is an important institution, and the decisions the members of the Fed's Board of Governors make also affect our daily lives—at times, more than the decisions of the Supreme Court or Congress. The Fed conducts U.S. monetary policy. It can increase or decrease the money supply with a few simple tools. As you read this chapter and chapters to come, you will realize just how important and far reaching the effects of changes in the money supply can be.

After You Study This Chapter, You Will Be Able To

- explain the structure of the Federal Reserve System.
- discuss how banks create demand deposits (money).
- identify and explain the ways in which the Fed can change the money supply.

You Will Also Learn What Economics Has to Do With

- airplanes full of money.
- the yellow brick road in *The Wizard of Oz*.
- banking on the Internet.

Economics Journal

Over the next two weeks, note in detail your dealings with a bank. For example, if you go to a bank to make a deposit, explain how you made the deposit. Did you go inside the bank and make the deposit, or did you make it by using an automatic teller machine (ATM)? Also, if you made a withdrawal from a bank, explain how you made it. Did you use the bank's ATM, or did you go into the bank and make the withdrawal?

SECTION 1 The Federal Reserve System

The **Federal Reserve System**—popularly called **the Fed**—is the central bank of the United States. Other national central banks include the Bank of Sweden, the Bank of England, the European Central Bank, and the Bank of Japan. This section outlines the structure of the Federal Reserve System and discusses some of its major responsibilities.

As you read this section, keep these key questions in mind:

- How many persons sit on the Board of Governors of the Federal Reserve System?
- What is the Federal Reserve System (the Fed)?
- How does the check-clearing process work?

Dr. Alan Greenspan, who became chairman of the Federal Reserve Board in 1987, began his fourth four-year term as chairman in June, 2000. Many economists and government leaders believe that Dr. Greenspan's leadership helped fuel the U.S. economy's record growth during his tenure.

The Structure of the Federal Reserve System

Key Terms

Federal Reserve System (the Fed)
Board of Governors of the Federal Reserve System
Federal Open Market Committee (FOMC)
reserve account

In 1913, the Federal Reserve Act was passed in Congress. This act set up the Federal Reserve System, which began operation in 1914. Today, the principal components of the Federal Reserve System are (1) the Board of Governors, and (2) the twelve Federal Reserve district banks.

Board of Governors The **Board of Governors of the Federal Reserve System** controls and coordinates the Fed's activities. The board is made up of seven members, each appointed to a fourteen-year term by the president of the United States with Senate approval. The president also designates one member as chairman of the board for a four-year term. The Board of Governors is located in Washington, D.C.

Federal Reserve System (The Fed) The central bank of the United States.

Board of Governors of the Federal Reserve System The governing body of the Federal Reserve System.

Federal Open Market Committee (FOMC) The 12-member policy-making group within the Fed. This committee has the authority to conduct open market operations.

The Twelve Federal Reserve District Banks The United States is broken up into twelve Federal Reserve districts. Exhibit 11-1 shows the boundaries of these districts. Each district has a Federal Reserve district bank. (Think of the Federal Reserve district banks as "branch offices" of the Federal Reserve System.) Each of the twelve Federal Reserve district banks has a president.

An Important Committee: The FOMC The major policy-making group within the Fed is the **Federal Open Market Committee (FOMC).** A later part of this chapter will consider what the FOMC does, but for now you need only note that the FOMC is made up of twelve members. Seven of the twelve members are the members of the

Exhibit 11-1

Federal Reserve Districts and Federal Reserve Bank Locations

The boundaries of the Federal Reserve Districts, the cities in which a Federal Reserve bank is located, and the location of the Board of Governors (Washington, D.C.) are all noted on the map.

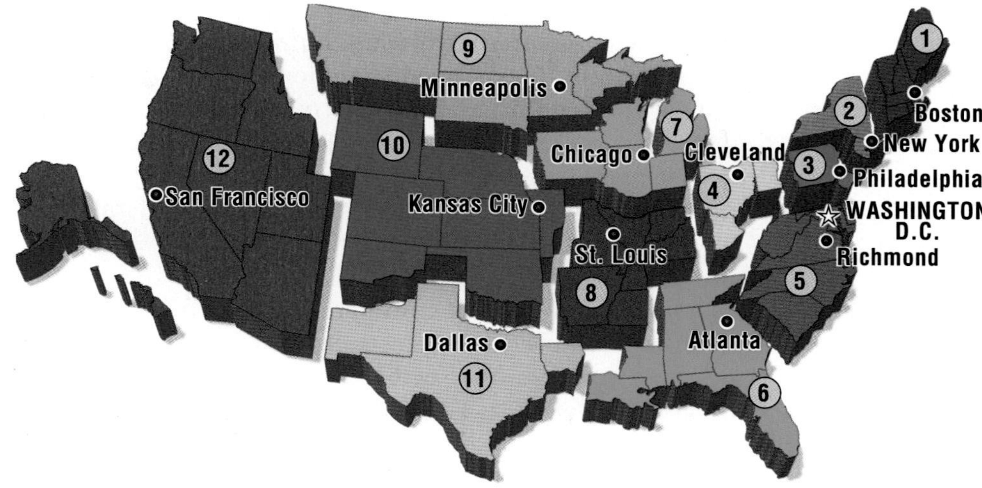

Board of Governors. The remaining five members come from the ranks of the presidents of the Federal Reserve district banks.

Functions of the Federal Reserve System

The following is a brief description of six major responsibilities of the Fed.

1. *Control the money supply.* A full explanation of how the Fed controls the money supply comes later in the chapter.
2. *Supply the economy with paper money (Federal Reserve notes).* As stated in Chapter 10, the pieces of paper money we use are *Federal Reserve notes.* Federal Reserve notes are printed at the Bureau of Engraving and Printing in Washington, D.C. The notes are issued to the twelve

The Federal Reserve Board makes decisions that affect the U.S. economy's money supply, but the Fed does not print Federal Reserve notes. What government agency is responsible for actually printing our paper money?

reserve account A bank's checking account with its Federal Reserve district bank.

Federal Reserve district banks, which keep the money on hand to meet the demands of the banks and the public. For example, suppose it is the holiday season, and people are going to their banks and withdrawing greater-than-usual numbers of $1, $5, and $20 notes. Banks need to replenish their supplies of these notes, and they turn to their Federal Reserve district banks to do so. The Federal Reserve district banks meet this cash need by supplying more paper money. (Remember, the twelve Federal Reserve district banks do not print the paper money; they only supply it.)

3. *Hold bank reserves.* Each commercial bank that is a member of the Federal Reserve System is required to keep a **reserve account** (think of it as a checking account) with its Federal Reserve district bank. For example, a bank located in Los Angeles would be located in the twelfth Federal Reserve district, which means it deals with the Federal Reserve Bank of San Francisco. The local bank in Los Angeles must have a reserve account, or checking account, with this reserve bank. Soon we will see what role a bank's reserve account with the Fed plays in increasing and decreasing the money supply.
4. *Provide check-clearing services.* When someone in San Diego writes a check to a person in Los Angeles, what happens to the check? The process by which funds change hands when checks are written is called the *check-clearing process.* The Fed plays a major role in this process. Here is how it works (see Exhibit 11-2 on page 292):
   - **a.** Suppose Harry Saito writes a $1,000 check on his San Diego bank and sends it by mail it to Ursula Pevins in Los Angeles. To record this transaction, Harry reduces the balance in his checking account by $1,000. In other words, if his balance was $2,500 before he wrote the check, it is $1,500 after he wrote the check.
   - **b.** Ursula receives the check in the mail. She takes the check to her local bank, endorses it (signs it on the back), and deposits it into her checking account. The balance in her account rises by $1,000.
   - **c.** Ursula's Los Angeles bank

This person is writing a check to a friend. Explain how his check clears the bank.

Carter Glass, U.S. Senator and "Father of the Federal Reserve System"

The Federal Reserve System was born out of the Federal Reserve Act of 1913, which was largely framed and sponsored by Carter Glass (1858–1946), who is often referred to as the "father of the Federal Reserve System."

Glass followed his father's path to become owner-operator of the *Lynchburg Daily News* and the *Daily Advance,* among other newspapers, before being elected to the U.S. House of Representatives in 1902. He was appointed to the U.S. Senate in 1920, succeeding Thomas Martin from Virginia, who died in late 1919. Glass was a U.S. senator from Virginia until his death.

Glass was the chairman of the Banking and Currency Committee when his friend Woodrow Wilson became president. Soon after Wilson was in office, the Federal Reserve Act was passed.

Glass was the principal author of the Glass-Stegall Act of 1933. This act established the Federal Deposit Insurance Corporation (FDIC), which guarantees individuals' deposits in banks up to a certain dollar amount.

QUESTION TO ANSWER Read a brief biography of Carter Glass at the Federal Reserve Bank of Minneapolis Web site **http://www.mpls.frb.org/pubs/region/97-12/glass-bio.html**. Then answer this question: Besides being a member of the House of Representatives and a U.S. senator, what other high government office did Glass hold?

Flying in with the Money

A banker at a commercial bank located about 200 miles from the Federal Reserve Bank of Minneapolis was frantic. There was a large crowd outside his bank, and the people wanted their money, now. The banker got on the phone and called the Federal Reserve Bank in Minneapolis. He told the people at the Minneapolis Fed that there was a "mad run" on his bank. If the Fed did not come to his rescue soon, he would be out of currency and unable to give the customers of his bank their money.

Where was their money? Why didn't he have it to give to them? As this chapter explains, banks have to have on hand only a fraction of their customers' deposits, according to the reserve requirement.

The Federal Reserve System responded to the call for currency. The Federal Reserve Bank of Minneapolis chartered a small plane, and two Fed officials took it, along with a half-million dollars in small-denomination bills, to the nearby town.

Upon approaching the town, the pilot flew the plane over Main Street to dramatize its arrival in the town: the Federal Reserve was flying in to the rescue. The plane landed at a nearby field. From the field, the Fed officials were escorted into town by the police, and the money was stacked in the bank's windows. The sight of all the money calmed the bank's customers, who were now assured they could get their money if they wanted. A banking panic was averted in a very dramatic way.

QUESTION TO ANSWER How would you define a *banking panic*?

SOURCE: This feature is based on "Born of a Panic: Forming the Federal Reserve System," *The Region,* August 1998. (*The Region* is a publication of the Federal Reserve Bank of Minneapolis.)

sends the check to its Federal Reserve district bank, which is located in San Francisco. The Federal Reserve Bank of San Francisco *increases* the reserve account of the Los Angeles bank (Ursula's bank) by $1,000 and *decreases* the reserve account of the San Diego bank (Harry's bank) by $1,000.

d. The Federal Reserve Bank of San Francisco sends the check to Harry's bank in San Diego, which then reduces the balance in Harry's checking account by $1,000. Harry's bank in San Diego either keeps the check on record or sends it along to Harry with his monthly bank statement.

5. *Supervise member banks.* Without warning, the Fed can examine the books of member commercial banks to see what kind of loans they have made, whether they have followed bank regulations, how

Exhibit 11-2

The Check-Clearing Process

1. Harry and Ursula
Harry Saito writes a $1,000 check on his San Diego bank and sends it to Ursula Pevins in Los Angeles.

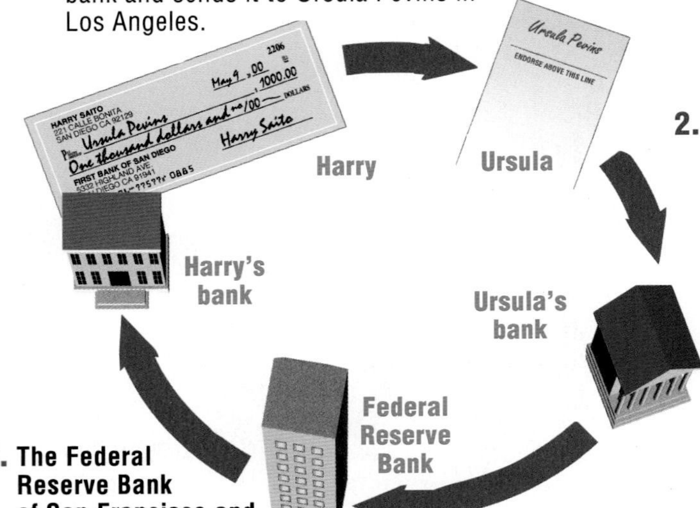

2. Ursula and her Los Angeles bank
Ursula endorses the check and deposits it in her local (Los Angeles) bank. The balance in her checking account rises by $1,000.

Ursula's bank

Federal Reserve Bank

3. The Los Angeles bank and the Federal Reserve Bank of San Francisco
Ursula's local (Los Angeles) bank sends the check to the Federal Reserve Bank of San Francisco, which increases the reserve account of the Los Angeles bank by $1,000 and decreases the reserve account of the San Diego bank by $1,000.

4. The Federal Reserve Bank of San Francisco and the San Diego bank
The Federal Reserve Bank of San Francisco sends the check to Harry's bank in San Diego, which then reduces the balance in Harry's account by $1,000.

accurate their records are, and so on. If the Fed finds that a bank has not been following established banking standards, it can pressure the bank to do so.

6. *Serve as the lender of last resort.* A traditional function of a central bank is to serve as the "lender of last resort" for banks suffering cash management problems. For example, let's say that bank A has lost millions of dollars and finds it very difficult to borrow from other banks. At this point, the Fed may step in and act as lender of last resort to bank A. In other words, the Fed may lend bank A the funds it wants to borrow when no one else will.

Section 1 Review

Defining Terms

1. Define
   a. Federal Open Market Committee (FOMC)
   b. Federal Reserve System (the FED)
   c. Board of Governors of the Federal Reserve System
   d. reserve account

Review Facts and Concepts

2. In what year did the Fed begin operating?
3. Explain how a check is cleared.
4. What does it mean when we say the Fed is the lender of last resort?

Critical Thinking

5. Economists speak about printing, issuing, and supplying paper money. Are these different functions? Where is each function performed?

Applying Economic Concepts

6. Do you think banks need the Fed to act as "lender of last resort" more often during good economic times or bad economic times? Explain your answer.

SECTION 2 The Money Creation Process

Chapter 10 explained that the early bankers were goldsmiths, who could increase the money supply (made up of gold and warehouse receipts) by extending loans to people. Instead of long-ago goldsmiths, this section considers modern-day bankers working at desks with computers. You will see, though, that the goldsmiths of yesterday and the bankers of today are not much different from each other in their ability to change the money supply.

As you read this section, keep these key questions in mind:

- What do total reserves equal?
- What are required reserves? Excess reserves?
- What do banks do with excess reserves?

A Few Preliminary Facts

Key Terms
total reserves
required reserves
reserve requirement
excess reserves

The following points and definitions are crucial to an understanding of the mechanics of how banks create money.

1. The previous section mentioned that each member bank has a *reserve account,* a checking account that a commercial bank has with its Federal Reserve district bank. If we take the dollar amount of a bank's reserve account and add it to the cash the bank has in its vaults (called, simply enough, *vault cash*), we have the bank's **total reserves.**

MINI GLOSSARY

total reserves The sum of a bank's deposits in its reserve account at the Fed and its vault cash.

required reserves The minimum amount of reserves a bank must hold against its deposits as mandated by the Fed.

reserve requirement A regulation that requires a bank to keep a certain percentage of each dollar deposited in the bank in its reserve account with the Fed or in its vault (as vault cash).

Total reserves	=	Deposits in the reserve account at the Fed	+	Vault cash

For example, if bank A has \$15 million in its reserve account with the Fed and \$4 million in its vault, then its total reserves equal \$19 million.

2. Total reserves can be divided up into required reserves and excess reserves. **Required reserves** are the amount of reserves a bank must hold against its checking account deposits, as mandated by the Fed. For example, suppose bank A holds checking account deposits (checkbook money) for its customers totaling \$100 million. The Fed requires, through its **reserve requirement,** that bank A hold a percentage of this total amount in the form of reserves—that is, either as deposits in its reserve account at the Fed or as vault cash (because both of these are reserves). Suppose this percentage is 10 percent. This means that bank A is required to hold 10 percent of

The money this bank keeps in its vault is called *vault cash.* To determine the bank's total reserves, you would need to add the amount of its vault cash to what other amount?

$100 million, or $10 million, in the form of reserves. This $10 million is called *required reserves.*

Required reserves = Reserve requirement × Checking account deposits

excess reserves Any reserves held beyond the required amount; the difference between total reserves and required reserves.

3. **Excess reserves** are the difference between total reserves and required reserves.

   Excess reserves = Total reserves − Required reserves

   For example, if total reserves equal $19 million and required reserves equal $10 million, then excess reserves equal $9 million. See Exhibit 11-3 for a review of these points.
4. Banks can make loans with their excess reserves. For example, if bank A has excess reserves of $9 million, it can make loans of $9 million.

How Banks Create Checking Account Deposits (Demand Deposits) to Increase the Money Supply

Chapter 10 said that the money supply is the sum of currency (coins and paper money), checking account deposits, and traveler's checks. For example, if there is $300 billion in currency, $500 billion in checking account deposits, and $10 billion in traveler's checks, the money supply is $810 billion.

You will recall that checking account deposits are sometimes referred to as *demand deposits,* because a checking account contains funds that can be withdrawn not only by a check but also on demand.

Exhibit 11-3

Reserves—Total, Required, and Excess

Kind of reserves	What it equals	Numerical example
Total reserves	Total reserves = Deposits in the reserve account at the Fed + Vault cash	Deposits in the reserve account = $15 million Vault cash = $4 million **Total reserves = $19 million**
Required reserves	Required reserves = Reserve requirement × Checking account deposits	Reserve requirement = 10 percent Checking account deposits = $100 million **Required reserves = $10 million**
Excess reserves	Excess reserves = Total reserves − Required reserves	Total reserves = $19 million Required reserves = $10 million **Excess reserves = $ 9 million**

Economics on the Yellow Brick Road

At different times in U.S. history, the money supply was backed by gold. Under a pure gold standard, before paper money can be issued there has to be gold to back it up. This means that the country's gold supply would limit the amount of paper money that could be issued.

In 1893, the United States fell into an economic depression: the stock market crashed, banks failed, workers were laid off, and many farmers lost their farms. Some people blamed the depression on the gold standard. They said that it was too confining and that it prevented the issuing of the amount of money needed to get people out of the depression. They argued for a gold and silver standard instead. If the money supply were based on the amount of both gold and silver instead of only on the amount of gold, the money supply could be larger.

One of the champions of this silver movement, as it was referred to, was William Jennings Bryan, the Democratic candidate for the U.S. presidency in 1896. Bryan had established himself as a friend to the many Americans who had been hurt by the depression, especially industrial workers and farmers. Bryan's views on having the money supply backed by both gold and silver, instead of gold alone, were shared by L. Frank Baum, a writer. Baum blamed the gold standard for the hardships faced by farmers and workers and wrote a book in which he expressed his views. That book was *The Wonderful Wizard of Oz,* the basis for the 1939 movie *The Wizard of Oz.*

In both the book and the movie, Dorothy is said to represent Bryan. As Dorothy begins her travels to the Emerald City, which represents Washington, D.C., she travels down a yellow brick road, which symbolizes the gold standard. On the way to the Emerald City she meets a scarecrow (the farmers), a tin man (industrial workers), and a cowardly lion (the Populist Party of the time). Dorothy's dog, Toto, who travels with her to the Emerald City, is supposed to represent the Democratic Party (as we said, Bryan was a Democrat).

In the book and the movie, Dorothy battles with the Wicked Witch of the West, who wears a golden cap (again, symbolizing the gold standard). The witch wants Dorothy's silver shoes because of their magical quality, just as silver was supposed to magically get the country out of the depression. (The silver shoes were changed to "ruby slippers" in the movie.) Dorothy ends up killing the witch, thus ending the gold standard. She clicks her silver shoes together and returns home to Kansas, where all is right with the world.

QUESTIONS TO ANSWER

1. What point was Baum trying to make about the gold standard in his book?
2. Some people believe that a gold standard is useful and beneficial because it limits the government's power to issue paper money. What do you think?

THINKING Like an Economist

The noneconomist often mistakenly thinks that money is simply currency (coins and paper money). To the economist, money is a generally accepted medium of exchange. This chapter and the previous one explained that currency, checking account deposits, and traveler's checks are all money. You will notice that all three are widely accepted for purposes of exchange.

Banks (such as your local bank down the street) are prohibited from printing currency. Your bank cannot legally print a $10 bill. However, banks can create checking account deposits (checkbook money), and if they do, it increases the money supply.

For example, suppose the money supply is $810 billion, composed of $300 billion in currency, $500 billion in checking account deposits (demand deposits), and $10 billion in traveler's checks. Now suppose banks create an additional $20 billion in checking account deposits, raising checking account deposits from $500 billion to $520 billion. As a result, the money supply increases from $810 billion to $830 billion.

This section will show you how banks can create checking account deposits and thus increase the money supply.

We start with a fictional character, Fred. (His name rhymes with *Fed* for a reason you will learn later.) Fred has the magical ability of snapping his fingers and creating, out of thin air, a $1,000 bill. (You will also learn later why this ability is not really as magical as it seems.)

On Monday morning at 9 o'clock, outside bank A, Fred snaps his fingers and creates a $1,000 bill. He immediately walks into the bank, opens up a checking account, and tells the banker that he wants the $1,000 deposited into his checking account. The banker gladly complies. Entry a in Exhibit 11-4 shows this deposit.

What does the bank physically do with the $1,000 bill? It places it into its vault, which means the money has found its way into vault cash. Vault cash, remember, is part of total reserves. (Total reserves = Deposits in the reserve account at the Fed + Vault cash.) Thus, if vault cash goes up by $1,000, total reserves rise by the same amount.

To keep things simple, let's assume that bank A had no checking account deposits before Fred walked into the bank. Now it has $1,000. Also, let's say that the Fed has set the reserve requirement at 10 percent. What are bank A's required reserves? Required reserves equal the reserve requirement multiplied by checking account deposits. Since 10 percent × $1,000 = $100, bank A has to keep $100 of its checking account deposits in reserve form—either in its reserve account at the Fed or as vault cash. (See Entry b in Exhibit 11-4.)

Your local bank cannot print bundles of paper money such as you see here. Your bank can, however, increase the money supply by increasing checking account deposits.

Exhibit 11-4
The Banking System Creates Demand Deposits (Money)

In this exhibit, the reserve requirement is 10 percent. We start with Fred, who has the ability to create money out of thin air. He snaps his fingers and creates $1,000 in currency and then deposits it in Bank A. The $1,000 is new reserves for Bank A and is also a new checking account deposit. Required reserves equal $100, and excess reserves equal $900. Excess reserves can be used by the bank to create new loans or demand deposits (new money). The process continues for Banks B, C, D, E, and so on. In the end, we see that the banking system creates $9,000 in new checking account deposits (new money) based on Fred's initial deposit of $1,000 of new money.

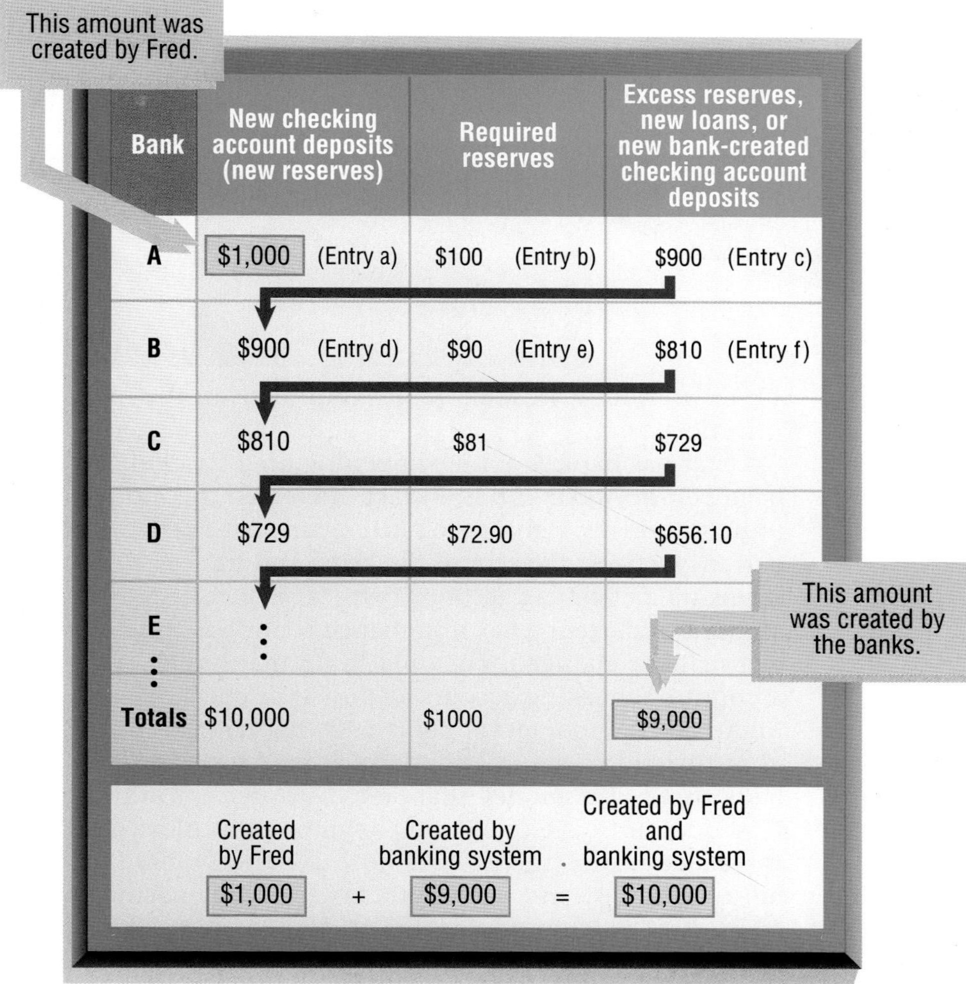

Bank	New checking account deposits (new reserves)	Required reserves	Excess reserves, new loans, or new bank-created checking account deposits
A	$1,000 (Entry a)	$100 (Entry b)	$900 (Entry c)
B	$900 (Entry d)	$90 (Entry e)	$810 (Entry f)
C	$810	$81	$729
D	$729	$72.90	$656.10
E ⋮	⋮		
Totals	$10,000	$1000	$9,000

Currently, however, bank A has more than $100 in its vault; it has the $1,000 that Fred handed over to it. What, then, do its excess reserves equal? Because excess reserves equal total reserves minus required reserves, it follows that the bank's excess reserves equal $900, the difference between $1,000 (total reserves) and $100 (required reserves). (See Entry c in Exhibit 11-4.)

What Does the Bank Do with Excess Reserves?

What does bank A do with its $900 in excess reserves? It creates new loans with the money. For example, suppose Alexi walks into bank A and asks for a $900 loan. The loan officer at the bank asks Alexi what she wants the money for. She tells the loan officer she wants a loan to buy a television set, and the loan officer grants her the loan.

Some people may think that at this point the loan officer of the bank simply walks over to the bank's vault, takes out $900 in currency, and hands it to Alexi. This usually does not happen, however. Instead, the loan officer opens up a checking account for Alexi at bank A and informs her that the balance in the account is $900. (Again, see Entry c in Exhibit

You might borrow money from your local bank to buy a new television set. How would your loan affect the money supply?

11-4.) In other words, banks give out loans in the form of checking account deposits.

What has bank A done by opening up a checking account (with a $900 balance) for Alexi? It has, in fact, increased the money supply by $900. To understand this, remind yourself again that the money supply consists of currency, checking account deposits, and traveler's checks. When bank A opens up a checking account (with a balance of $900) for Alexi, the dollar amount of currency has not changed, nor has the dollar amount of traveler's checks changed. The only thing that has changed is the dollar amount of checking account deposits, or checkbook money. It is $900 higher, so the money supply is $900 higher, too.

At this point you might ask, "But isn't the $900 Alexi receives from the bank part of the money that Fred deposited into the bank? In other words, Fred does not have the $1,000 anymore, but Alexi has $900 of it." This is not exactly correct. Fred does not have the $1,000 in currency anymore, but he certainly still has $1,000. After all, the balance in his checking account is $1,000. On top of this, Alexi now has $900 in her checking account. That's an additional $900 created by the bank that did not exist before.

Question: *Does a bank have to create a loan with its excess reserves?*

Answer: *No, it does not have to create a loan, but it probably will. Extending loans is how banks earn interest income. In other words, it is in a bank's monetary interest to use excess reserves to extend loans.*

The Story Continues

So far, Alexi has been granted a loan in the form of a $900 balance in a new checking account. She now goes to a retail store and buys a $900 television set. She pays for the set by writing out a check for $900 drawn on bank A. She hands the check to the owner of the store, Roberto.

At the end of the business day, Roberto takes the check to bank B. For simplicity's sake, we assume that checking account deposits in bank B equal zero. Roberto, however, changes this situation by depositing the $900 into his checking account. (See Entry d in Exhibit 11-4.)

At this point, the check-clearing process (described earlier) kicks in. Bank B sends the check to its Federal Reserve bank, which increases the balance in bank B's reserve account by $900. At the same time, the Federal

Technology & Innovation

Banking on the Internet

When your parents first started banking, and certainly when your grandparents first started banking, the procedure was different from banking procedures today. Customers would always go to a teller at a bank to withdraw funds from their checking and savings accounts and to deposit funds into these accounts.

Banking began to change in the 1980s with the heavy use of automatic teller machines (ATMs). No longer did a bank's customers have to walk into the bank to conduct business; they could deposit and withdraw funds via an ATM.

Banking changed even more in the 1990s, when the Internet made it possible for banks to go online. Today there are numerous banks online, and because of changes in economic legislation, these banks can provide their customers many more services than they did in the past. For example, besides providing standard banking services to their customers, banks now can provide insurance and stock quotations, help with purchases of stocks and bonds, help with paying bills, and much more.

To see how online banking works, begin at one of the more popular search engines. Type in "online banking." The names of numerous online banks will appear on the screen. Click on one, and read what the bank has to offer. You will see that users will be able to check their checking and savings accounts online, fill out a credit application, apply for a credit card, buy stocks and bonds, and pay many of their bills (such as utility bills). The technology that has given us the Internet has made all this possible.

QUESTION TO ANSWER What do you perceive as being some of the costs and benefits of online banking?

Reserve bank decreases the funds in bank A's reserve account by $900. Once the Federal Reserve bank has increased the balance in bank B's reserve account, total reserves for bank B rise by $900. (Total reserves = Deposits in the reserve account at the Fed + Vault cash.) (Again, see Entry d in Exhibit 11-4.)

What happens to the checking account deposits at bank B? They rise to $900, too. Bank B is required to keep a percentage of the checking deposits in reserve form. If the reserve requirement is 10 percent, then $90 has to be maintained as required reserves. (See Entry e in Exhibit 11-4.) The remainder, or excess reserves ($810), can be used by bank B to extend new loans or create new checking account deposits (which are money). (See Entry f in Exhibit 11-4.) The story continues in the same way with other banks (banks C, D, E, and so on).

How Much Money Was Created, and Who Created What?

So far, bank A has created $900 in new loans or checking account deposits, and bank B has created $810 in new loans or checking account deposits. If we continue by bringing in banks C, D, E, and so on, we will find that all banks together—that is, the entire banking system—create $9,000 in new loans or checking account deposits (money) as a result of Fred's deposit. This dollar amount is boxed in Exhibit 11-4. This is $9,000 of new money—money that did not exist before Fred snapped his fingers, created $1,000 out of thin air, and then deposited it into a checking account in bank A.

The facts can be summarized as follows:

1. Fred created $1,000 in new paper currency (money) out of thin air.
2. After Fred deposited the $1,000 in bank A, the banking system as a whole created $9,000 in additional checking account deposits (money).

Thus, Fred and the banking system together created $10,000 in new money. Fred created $1,000 in currency, and the banking system created $9,000 in checking account deposits. Together, they increased the money supply by $10,000.

If you know that this bag of money contains 1,000 one-dollar bills, you would probably say the contents of the bag is worth $1,000. What value might a banker put on the bag if you deposited its contents in his bank?

A Simple Formula

You can use the following simple formula to find the (maximum) change in the money supply ($10,000) brought about in the example:

$$\text{Change in money supply} = \frac{1}{\text{Reserve requirement}} \times \text{Change in reserves of first bank}$$

In the example, the reserve requirement was set at 10 percent (0.10). The reserves of bank A, the first bank to receive the injection of funds, changed by $1,000. Put the data into the formula:
Change in the money supply = 1/0.10 × $1,000 = $10,000

Section 2 Review

Defining Terms

1. Define
   a. total reserves
   b. required reserves
   c. reserve requirement
   d. excess reserves

Reviewing Facts and Concepts

2. Fred creates $2,000 in currency with the snap of his fingers and deposits it in bank A. The reserve requirement is 10 percent. By how much does the money supply increase?
3. Bank A has checking account deposits of $20 million, the reserve requirement is 10 percent, vault cash equals $2 million, and deposits in the reserve account at the Fed equal $1 million. What do required reserves equal? What do excess reserves equal?

Critical Thinking

4. The numerical examples in this section always had banks creating loans (new checking account deposits) equal to the amount of excess reserves they held. For example, if bank A had $900 in excess reserves, it would create new loans equal to $900, not something less. In reality, banks may not lend out every dollar of their excess reserves, but they do come very close. Why would a bank want to lend out nearly all (if not all) of its excess reserves?

Applying Economic Concepts

5. Is a $100 check money? Explain.

SECTION 3

Fed Tools for Changing The Money Supply

When the Fed changes the money supply, it is said to be implementing **monetary policy.** The Fed can change the money supply in three ways: (1) by changing the reserve requirement, (2) by conducting open market operations, and (3) by changing the discount rate. This section considers these three ways of changing the money supply.

As you read this section, keep these key questions in mind:

- How does a change in the reserve requirement change the money supply?
- How does an open market operation change the money supply?
- How does a change in the discount rate change the money supply?

MINI GLOSSARY

monetary policy The deliberate control of the money supply by the Fed.

Key Terms

monetary policy
open market operations
federal funds rate
discount rate

Changing the Reserve Requirement

Look again at the formula to find a change in the money supply:

$$\text{Change in money supply} = \frac{1}{\text{Reserve requirement}} \times \text{Change in reserves of first bank}$$

Now consider the following three cases. In each case, the money supply is initially zero, and \$1,000 is created out of thin air. The difference in the three cases is the reserve requirement, which is 5 percent in the first case, 10 percent in the second, and 20 percent in the third. Let's calculate the change in the money supply in each of the three cases.

Case 1. (Reserve requirement = 5 percent); Change in money supply = 1/0.05 × \$1,000 = \$20,000.

Case 2. (Reserve requirement = 10 percent); Change in money supply = 1/0.10 × \$1,000 = \$10,000.

Case 3. (Reserve requirement = 20 percent); Change in money supply = 1/0.20 × \$1,000 = \$5,000.

Note that the money supply is the largest (\$20,000) when the reserve requirement is 5 percent. The money supply is the smallest (\$5,000) when the reserve requirement is 20 percent.

What happens if the Fed changes the reserve requirement? Again, using the numbers in the three cases, we can see that if the Fed increases the reserve requirement from 5 percent to 10 percent, the money supply decreases from $20,000 to $10,000. If the Fed decreases the reserve requirement from 20 percent to 10 percent, the money supply increases from $5,000 to $10,000.

Thus, the Fed can increase or decrease the money supply by changing the reserve requirement. If it increases the reserve requirement, the money supply decreases; if it decreases the reserve requirement, the money supply increases.

Lower reserve requirement ➡ Money supply rises
Raise reserve requirement ➡ Money supply falls

Open Market Operations

This chapter has mentioned an important committee in the Federal Reserve System, the Federal Open Market Committee, or FOMC. This committee of twelve members conducts **open market operations** (the buying and selling of government securities by the Fed). Before we can discuss these operations in detail, however, some background information that relates to government securities and the U.S. Treasury is necessary.

MINI GLOSSARY

open market operations Buying and selling of government securities by the Fed.

A major job of the U.S. Treasury is to collect the vast sums of money that the federal government needs to do its work. By observing this Treasury worker, can you guess what the Treasury Department's major source of revenue is?

The U.S. Treasury is an agency of the U.S. government. The Treasury's job is to collect the taxes and borrow the money needed to run the government. Suppose the U.S. Congress decides to spend $1.2 trillion on various federal government programs. The U.S. Treasury has to pay the bills. It notices that it has collected $1.1 trillion in taxes, which is $100 billion less than Congress wants to spend. It is the Treasury's job to borrow the $100 billion from the public. To borrow this money, the Treasury issues or sells government (or Treasury) securities. A government security is no more than a piece of paper promising to pay a certain dollar amount of money in the future; think of it as an IOU statement.

These government securities are bought by members of the public. For example, Lynn buys a government security for $9,000 that promises to pay $10,000 in a year. In buying the security, Lynn is, in fact, lending $9,000 to the Treasury, which it promises to pay back the next year with interest.

The Fed (which is different from the Treasury) may buy government securities from any member of the public or sell them. When the Fed buys a government security, it is said to be conducting an *open market purchase*. When it sells a government security, it is said to be conducting an *open market sale*. These operations affect the money supply.

The Fed conducts an open market purchase of a government security. Predict what will happen to the money supply.

Open Market Purchases Let's say that you currently own a government security, which the Fed offers to purchase from you for $10,000. You agree to sell your security to the Fed. You hand it over, and in return you receive a check made out to you for $10,000.

It is important to realize where the Fed gets this $10,000. It gets the money "out of thin air." Recall Fred, who had the ability to snap his fingers and create a $1,000 bill out of thin air. Obviously, no such person has this power. The Fed, however, does have this power—it can create money out of thin air.

How does the Fed create money out of thin air? Think about the answer in this rough form: You have a checking account, and the Fed has a checking account. There is a balance in each account. The Fed can take a pencil and increase the balance in its account at will—legally. However, if you decide to pencil in a new balance and then write a check for an amount you don't have in your checking account, your check bounces. Fed checks do not bounce.

Let's return to the example of an open market purchase. Once you have the $10,000 check from the Fed, you take it to your local bank and deposit it in your checking account. The total dollar amount of checking account deposits in the economy is now more than before the Fed purchased your government security. Furthermore, no other component of the money supply (not currency or traveler's checks) is less. Thus, the overall money supply has increased. In conclusion, when the Fed conducts an open market purchase, the money supply increases.

Open market purchase ➡ Money supply rises

Open Market Sales Suppose the Fed has a government security that it offers to sell you for $10,000. You agree to buy the security. You write out a check to the Fed for $10,000 and give it to the Fed. The Fed, in return, turns the government security over to you. Next, the check is cleared, and a sum of $10,000 is removed from your account in your bank and transferred to the Fed. Once this sum is in the Fed's possession, it is removed from the economy altogether. It is as if it disappears from the face of the earth.

The total dollar amount of checking account deposits is less than before the Fed sold you a government security. An open market sale reduces the money supply.

The Fed conducts an open market sale. Predict what will happen to the dollar amount of reserves in the banking system. Explain your answer.

Open market sale ➡ Money supply falls

Banks, like individuals, take out loans. The interest rate a bank pays for its loan depends on where it gets the loan. Explain.

federal funds rate
The interest rate one bank charges another bank for a loan.

discount rate
The interest rate the Fed charges a bank for a loan.

Changing the Discount Rate

Suppose bank A wants to borrow $1 million. It could borrow this dollar amount from another bank (say, bank B), or it could borrow the money from the Fed. If bank A borrows the money from bank B, bank B will charge an interest rate for the $1 million loan. The interest rate charged by bank B is called the **federal funds rate.** If bank A borrows the $1 million from the Fed, the Fed will charge an interest rate, called the **discount rate.**

Whether bank A borrows from bank B or from the Fed depends on the relationship between the federal funds rate and the discount rate. If the federal funds rate is lower than the discount rate, bank A will borrow from bank B instead of from the Fed. (Why pay a higher interest rate if you don't have to?) If, however, the discount rate is lower than the federal funds rate, bank A will probably borrow from the Fed.

Whether bank A borrows from bank B or from the Fed has important consequences. If bank A borrows from bank B, no new money enters the economy. Bank B simply has $1 million less, and bank A has $1 million more. But if bank A borrows from the Fed, the Fed creates new money in the process of granting the loan. Here is how it works: The bank asks for a loan, and the Fed grants it by depositing the funds (created out of thin air) into the reserve account of the bank. For example, suppose the bank has $4 million in its reserve account when it asks the Fed for a $1 million loan. The Fed simply changes the reserve account balance to $5 million; that's all there is to it. As a result, the bank has more reserves.

Thus, if the Fed lowers its discount rate relative to the federal funds rate, and if banks then borrow from the Fed, the money supply will increase.

Lower the discount rate ➡ Money supply rises

Go to the Web site of the Board of Governors of the Federal Reserve System (http://www/bog.frb.fed.us/). Once there, click on "Research and Data," and then click on "Statistics: Releases and Historical Data." Under "Daily Releases" you will see "Selected Interest Rates–Daily Update." Click on this item. What is the most current federal funds rate? What is the most current discount rate? (The discount rate is noted under "discount window borrowing.")

Are All Central Banks Alike?

The money supply is an important factor in the economy. For example, a change in the money supply can change the total amount of spending in the economy. In general, a larger money supply leads to more spending, and a smaller money supply leads to less spending. In turn, changes in the amount of spending affect economic activity and prices.

If the money supply is an important factor in the economy, then it follows that the institution that largely controls the money supply is important. In the United States, that institution is the Federal Reserve System. In other countries, it is the central bank.

Not all central banks are alike. One way they differ is in the degree of independence they possess. For example, in the past many economists have argued that the central bank in Germany, the Bundesbank, is more independent of the German government than the Bank of England is from its government.

Does it matter what degree of independence a central bank has? Some economists have found that, in general, the more independent a central bank (the more independent of politics, in particular), the lower the country's average annual rate of inflation. This finding is shown in Exhibit 11-5. Notice that on the horizontal axis, independence is measured from left to right. The further right on the axis, the more independent the central bank is from the country's political process. The vertical axis measures the average annual inflation rate from 1955 to 1988 for several countries. Notice that countries such as Switzerland, Germany, and the United States have relatively independent central banks, and that the average annual inflation rates in these countries are lower than those of New Zealand, Spain, and Italy, which have relatively less independent central banks. In other words, as far as inflation goes, it appears that the more independent the central bank is of politics, the lower the country's average annual inflation rate.

Exhibit 11-5

Central Bank Independence and Average Annual Inflation Rates

Generally, the more independent a country's central bank, the lower the country's average annual inflation rate. The average annual inflation rate shown is for the period 1955–1988.

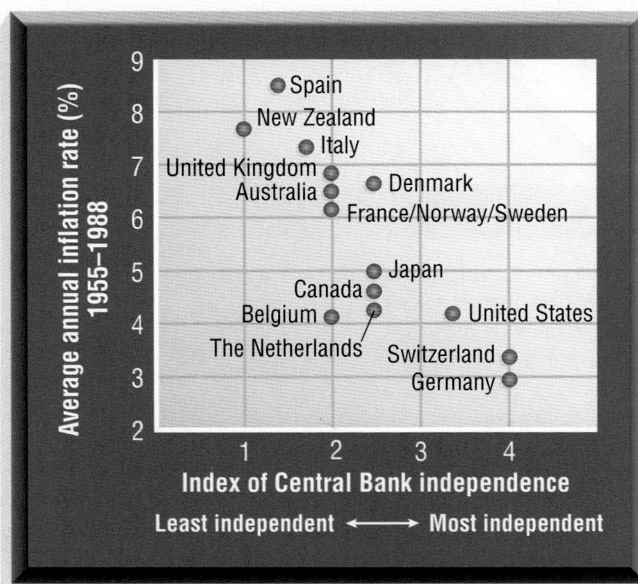

QUESTION TO ANSWER Does the general inverse relationship identified between central bank independence and the average annual inflation rate hold when we compare Belgium and the United States? Explain your answer.

If the Fed raises its discount rate so that it is higher than the federal funds rate, banks will begin to borrow from each other rather than from the Fed. There will come a day, though, when the banks will have to repay the funds they borrowed from the Fed in the past (say, funds they borrowed many months ago), when the discount rate was lower. When the banks repay these loans, money is removed from the economy, and the money supply drops. We conclude that if the Fed raises its discount rate relative to the federal funds rate, the money supply will eventually fall. See Exhibit 11-6 for a review of the ways in which the Fed can change the money supply.

Raise the discount rate ➡ Money supply falls

Question: *The Fed has three tools at its disposal to change the money supply. Does it use one of the three tools more than the others?*

Answer: *Yes. The tool the Fed uses most often to change the money supply is open market operations.*

Exhibit 11-6
Fed Monetary Tools and Their Effects on the Money Supply

The following Fed actions increase the money supply: purchasing government securities in the open market, lowering the reserve requirement, and lowering the discount rate relative to the federal funds rate. The following Fed actions decrease the money supply: selling government securities in the open market, raising the reserve requirement, and raising the discount rate relative to the federal funds rate.

Fed monetary tool	Money supply
Open market operation	
Buys government securities	Increases
Sells government securities	Decreases
Reserve requirement	
Raises reserve requirement	Decreases
Lowers reserve requirement	Increases
Discount rate	
Raises discount rate (relative to the federal funds rate)	Decreases
Lowers discount rate (relative to the federal funds rate)	Increases

Section 3 Review

Defining Terms

1. Define

a. discount rate

b. federal funds rate

c. open market operation

d. monetary policy

Reviewing Facts and Concepts

2. The Fed wants to increase the money supply. (a) What can it do to the reserve requirement? (b) What type of open market operation can it conduct? (c) What can it do to the discount rate?

3. The Fed conducts an open market sale. Does the money for which it sells the government securities stay in the economy? Explain your answer.

Critical Thinking

4. When the Fed conducts an open market purchase, it buys government securities. As a result, the money supply rises. Could the Fed raise the money supply by buying something other than government securities? For example, suppose the Fed were to buy apples instead of government securities. Would apple purchases (by the Fed) raise the money supply? Explain your answer.

Applying Economic Concepts

5. If the Fed wants the money supply to rise by a ridiculously high percentage—say, 1 million percent—could it accomplish this objective? Explain your answer.

Developing Economic

Skills

Identifying Economic Trends

A *trend* is a general tendency or inclination in a particular direction. To illustrate, suppose Robert is currently graduating from high school. During his four years in high school, his grade point average, or GPA, looked like this:

Freshman year GPA = 2.45
Sophomore year GPA = 3.33
Junior year GPA = 3.45
Senior year GPA = 3.89

Robert's GPA has been rising during his time in high school. Here, then, is a trend—an upward trend in Robert's academic performance.

Consider another example. Suppose that this year, in a city in the Midwest, 2 feet of snow fell in the winter. Last year 3 feet of snow fell. Three years ago 4 feet of snow fell, and four years ago 5 feet of snow fell. There is a trend toward less snow.

It is important to know the difference between a trend and a one-time change in the direction of some variable. For example, suppose the average daytime temperature in San Diego in January is 63 degrees. One day in January in San Diego, the average temperature happens to be 45 degrees. Is this a trend toward cooler temperatures in San Diego? Not at all. It is simply one day when the temperature fell below average.

Economists often try to identify trends in economic data. Four of the many variables for which they try to identify trends are (1) the money supply, (2) the average annual growth in the economy, (3) the unemployment rate, and (4) the inflation rate. For example, the average annual growth rate in the money supply in the 1960s was 3.86 percent. It was higher in the 1970s, at 6.51 percent, and even higher in the 1980s, at 7.66 percent. Was there a trend in the average annual growth rate in the money supply? Yes, and the trend was upward.

Now consider the average annual growth rate in the economy for the various decades. Sometimes the economy gets bigger at a faster rate than at other times. For example, in the 1960s, the average annual growth rate of the economy was 4.40 percent. In the 1970s, the economy grew an average of 3.20 percent each year. In the 1980s, the average annual growth rate was slightly lower than in the 1970s (2.77 percent). Was there a trend to the average annual growth rate in the economy? There certainly was, and it was downward.

When an economist identifies a trend in economic data that is going in the "wrong" direction, one of his or her jobs is to try to figure out how to reverse the trend. If a trend in a variable is going in the "right" direction, an economist will try to figure out what has changed to make the trend change. For example, the average annual inflation rate was relatively high in the 1970s, lower in the 1980s, and still lower in the 1990s. An economist is interested in knowing what happened to bring this desirable trend about.

QUESTIONS TO ANSWER

1. Global warming is defined as "an increase in the earth's average atmospheric temperature that causes corresponding changes in climate and that may result from the greenhouse effect." Is there anything in the definition of *global warming* that indicates a trend? If so, what?
2. Harry has promised himself that he will exercise three to four times each week. Today was his first day of exercising. Is this a trend? Explain your answer.

CHAPTER

11 Review

Economics Vocabulary

Fill in the following blanks with the appropriate word or phrase.

1. When the Fed buys or sells government securities, it is conducting a(n) _____.
2. The major policy-making group within the Fed is the _____.
3. The governing body of the Federal Reserve System is the _____.
4. Total reserves minus required reserves equals _____.
5. _____ are the minimum amount of reserves a bank must hold against its checking account deposits, as mandated by the Fed.
6. If excess reserves are $50 million and required reserves are $10 million, then _____ must equal $60 million.
7. The required reserves a bank must hold can be kept as vault cash or as deposits in its _____ with the Fed.
8. _____ refers to the deliberate control of the money supply by the Fed.
9. The interest rate that one bank charges another bank for a loan is called the _____.
10. The interest rate that the Fed charges a bank for a loan is called the _____.
11. The _____ is the central bank of the United States.
12. The regulation the Fed sets specifying the percentage of each deposited dollar a bank must keep in its reserve account with the Fed or in its vault (as vault cash) is called the _____.

Review Questions

1. Explain how a check clears. Illustrate this process using two banks in the Federal Reserve district in which you live.
2. List the locations of the twelve Federal Reserve district banks.
3. State what each of the following equals:
   a. total reserves
   b. required reserves
   c. excess reserves
4. The chapter noted that when banks create new checking account deposits (by extending new loans to borrowers), they are in effect *creating money.* What is the reason for equating a checking account deposit with money?
5. Determine which of the following Fed actions will increase the money supply: (a) lowering the reserve requirement, (b) raising the reserve requirement, (c) conducting an open market purchase, (d) conducting an open market sale, (e) lowering the discount rate relative to the federal funds rate, (f) raising the discount rate relative to the federal funds rate.
6. Banks cannot print money, but they can create money. Explain.
7. What do we mean when we say that the Fed can create money out of thin air?
8. Explain how an open market purchase increases the money supply.
9. What is the relationship between changes in the reserve requirement and changes in the money supply?
10. According to Exhibit 11-1, in which Federal Reserve district do you live?
11. Suppose the Fed sets the discount rate much higher than the existing federal funds rate. With this action, what signal is the Fed sending banks?
12. Identify the functions of the Fed.

Calculations

1. A bank has $600 million in checking account deposits, and the reserve requirement is 12.5 percent. What do required reserves equal?
2. A bank has $100 million in its reserve account at the Fed and $10 million in vault cash. The required reserve requirement is 10 percent. What do total reserves equal?
3. The Fed conducts an open market purchase and increases the reserves of bank A by $2 million. The reserve requirement is 20 percent. By how much does the money supply increase?
4. The Fed conducts an open market purchase and increases the reserves of bank A by $10 million. The reserve requirement is 10 percent. By how much does the money supply increase?

Graphs

1. Look at the map of the United States in Exhibit 11-7. There are twelve circles, and in each circle there is a letter. Supply the number of the Federal Reserve district that corresponds to each letter. For

example, does *A* represent the first Federal Reserve district, the second, the third, or which one?

Exhibit 11-7

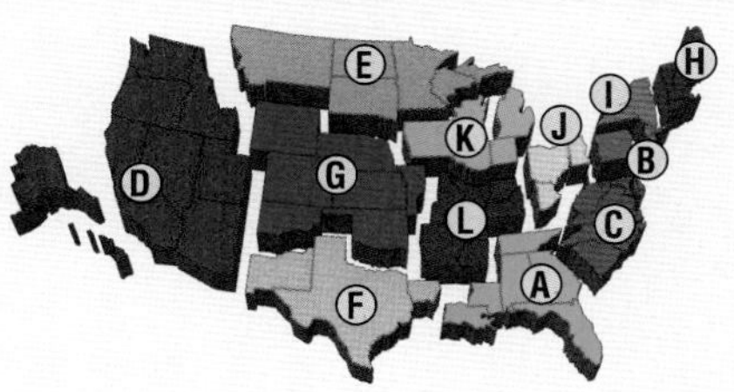

2. In Exhibit 11-8, fill in the blanks (a, b, and c).

Exhibit 11-8

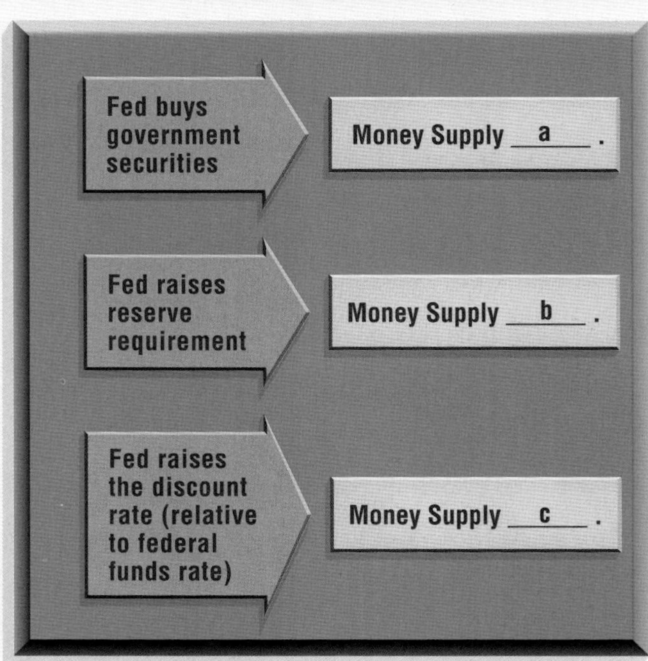

Economics and Thinking Skills

1. **Application.** Bank A has lent out all its excess reserves, and a borrower walks into the bank. The borrower asks for a $400,000 loan. Assuming the bank manager wants to lend $400,000 to this person, can she do this?
2. **Analysis.** Look at a $1 bill (Federal Reserve note). On the left-hand side of the front, there is an emblem. The name of the Federal Reserve district bank that issued the note is written in small letters on the emblem. Federal Reserve district banks issue notes to the banks in their districts. With this in mind, consider the following: There are two towns in two different Federal Reserve districts. One is a tourist town, and the other is not. In which of the two towns would you expect to find more Federal Reserve notes *not* issued by the Federal Reserve district bank in the district in which the town is located? Explain your answer.
3. **Cause and Effect.** In year 1, reserves (in the banking system) equal $100 billion, and the money supply equals $1,000 billion. In year 2, reserves equal $120 billion, and the money supply equals $1,200 billion. Did the greater money supply in year 2 cause the higher dollar amount of reserves, or did the higher dollar amount of reserves cause the greater money supply? Explain your answer.

Writing Skills

Check in your school library to see if you can find information on any of the following topics: (1) the origin of the Federal Reserve System, (2) how the Bureau of Engraving and Printing prints paper money, or (3) the economic views of the current chair of the Board of Governors of the Federal Reserve System. (You will need to check encyclopedias, magazines, and books.) Next, write a two- to three-page paper on one of the topics.

Economics in the Media

1. Find an article about the Fed in any current newspaper. Write two paragraphs explaining the article.
2. Find mention of the Federal Open Market Committee (FOMC), the current chair of the Board of Governors of the Federal Reserve System, the lender of last resort responsibility of the Fed, monetary policy, the discount rate, or the federal funds rate on any television news show. Identify the context of the story.

Where's the Economics?

How can a bank increase the money supply if it cannot print money?

CHAPTER 12

Measuring Economic Performance

What This Chapter Is About

Economics can be divided into two branches: microeconomics and macroeconomics. Microeconomics deals with human behavior and choices as they relate to relatively small units—the individual, the firm, or a single market. Units 1 and 2 of this book discussed microeconomics. Macroeconomics deals with human behavior and choices as they relate to the entire economy. It is the focus of Unit 3.

This chapter begins the study of macroeconomics, with an emphasis on the "big picture." Instead of the output of a single firm, we examine the output of the entire economy. Rather than the price of a single good (say, apples), we consider the prices of all goods. Instead of analyzing how taxes affect one firm or one industry, we see how taxes affect the economy. It is macroeconomic news that you usually read about in the newspaper and hear about on the radio. This chapter begins with two of the basics: the economy's output and overall prices in the economy.

Why This Chapter Is Important

Gene Epstein writes a column entitled "Economic Beat" for one of the most influential business and economic magazines in the world, *Barron's*. On May 10, 1999, he wrote: "As recently as April 30, investors found good evidence that the Commerce Department's GDP report can move the market. On that Friday morning, it was announced that gross

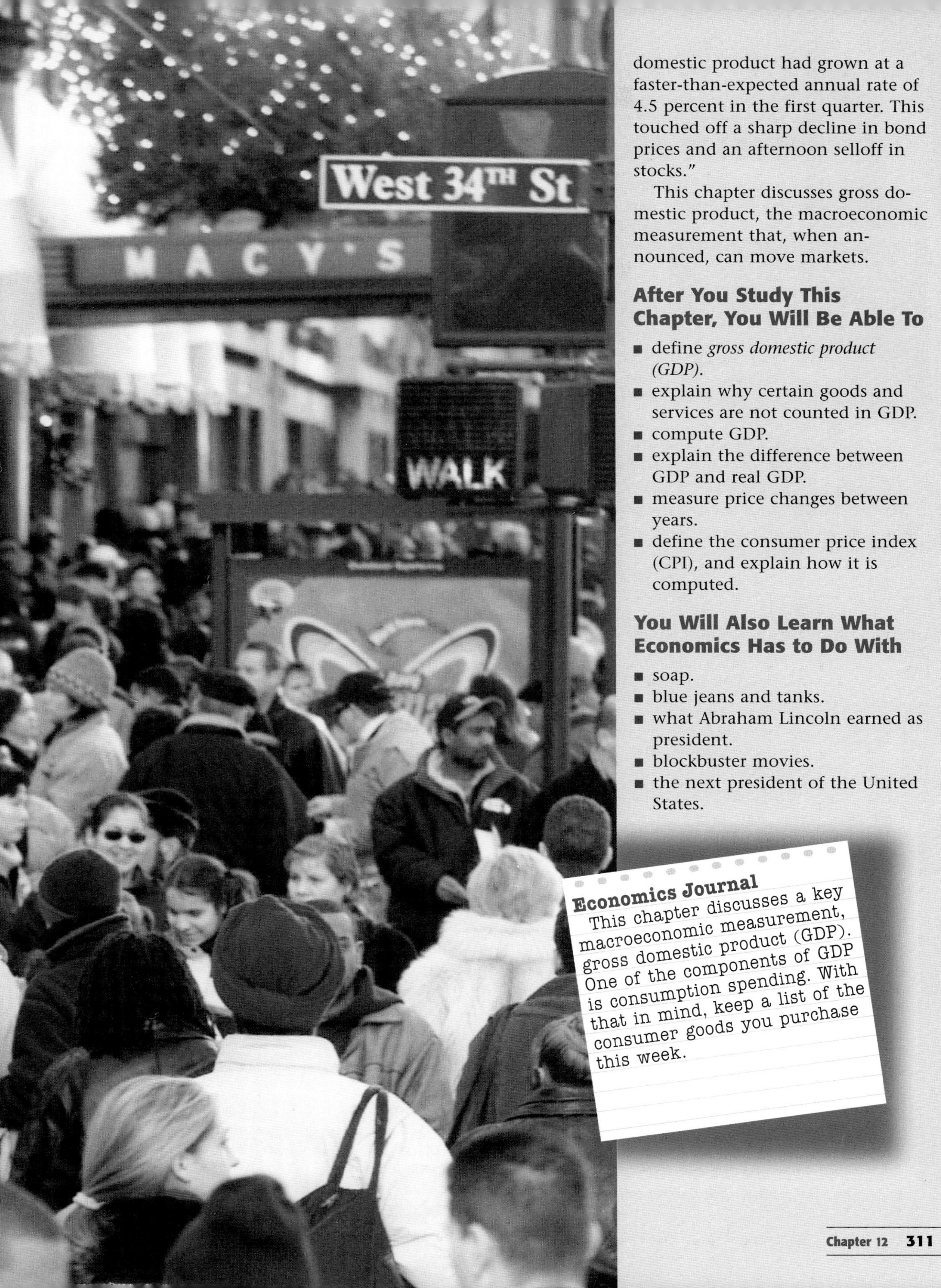

domestic product had grown at a faster-than-expected annual rate of 4.5 percent in the first quarter. This touched off a sharp decline in bond prices and an afternoon selloff in stocks."

This chapter discusses gross domestic product, the macroeconomic measurement that, when announced, can move markets.

After You Study This Chapter, You Will Be Able To

- define *gross domestic product (GDP)*.
- explain why certain goods and services are not counted in GDP.
- compute GDP.
- explain the difference between GDP and real GDP.
- measure price changes between years.
- define the consumer price index (CPI), and explain how it is computed.

You Will Also Learn What Economics Has to Do With

- soap.
- blue jeans and tanks.
- what Abraham Lincoln earned as president.
- blockbuster movies.
- the next president of the United States.

Economics Journal

This chapter discusses a key macroeconomic measurement, gross domestic product (GDP). One of the components of GDP is consumption spending. With that in mind, keep a list of the consumer goods you purchase this week.

SECTION 1 National Income Accounting

You are listening to the car radio. The newscaster says that according to a newly released government report, the economy has been growing, and prices are rising only slightly. What exactly does it mean when someone says that the economy has been growing? And when someone says that prices are rising only slightly, what does that mean? Does it mean that all prices are rising slightly, or just some prices? And what is meant by *slightly*?

This section begins our examination of economic measurements. Regarding these measurements, it is perhaps easiest to think of the economy as you would your own body. If you go to the doctor and tell her that you are sick, she will take some measurements—she will take your temperature, run some blood tests, take your blood pressure, and so on. She will try to assign numbers to things. "You are running a fever," she may say, "because your temperature is 101.8 degrees."

Economists try to measure things, too, for the same reason doctors measure things—to learn how the patient (or the economy) is doing. Economists usually measure gross domestic product (GDP) and prices. This section explains what gross domestic product is and how it is measured. The chapter later considers prices.

As you read this section, keep these key questions in mind:

- What is GDP?
- Why are only final goods and services computed in GDP?
- What is omitted from GDP?

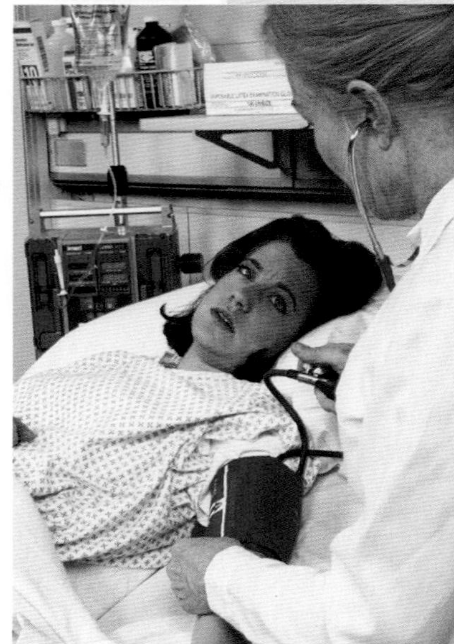

Taking her patient's blood pressure is one of several measurements this doctor can use to determine the patient's health. Economists also use measurements, such as the GDP, to determine the health of the economy.

Gross Domestic Product

Key Terms

gross domestic product (GDP)
double-counting

Gross domestic product (GDP) is the total market value of all final goods and services produced annually in an economy. For example, suppose there is a tiny economy in which only three goods are produced, in these quantities: ten computers, ten cars, and ten watches. Furthermore, suppose the price of a computer is \$2,000, the price of a car is \$20,000, and the price of a watch is \$100. If we wanted to find the GDP of this small economy—that is, if we wanted to find the total market value of the goods produced during the year—we would multiply the price of each good times the quantity of the good produced and then sum the dollar amounts. (See Exhibit 12-1 on page 313.)

1. *Find the market value for each good produced.* That is, multiply the price of each good times the quantity of the good produced. For example, if ten computers are produced and the price of each is \$2,000, then the market value of computers is \$20,000.
2. *Sum the market values.*

Exhibit 12-1
Gross Domestic Product (GDP)

In our very tiny example economy, the only goods produced are computers, cars, and watches. To calculate the GDP, we would multiply the quantity of each good by its price, then sum the dollar amounts.

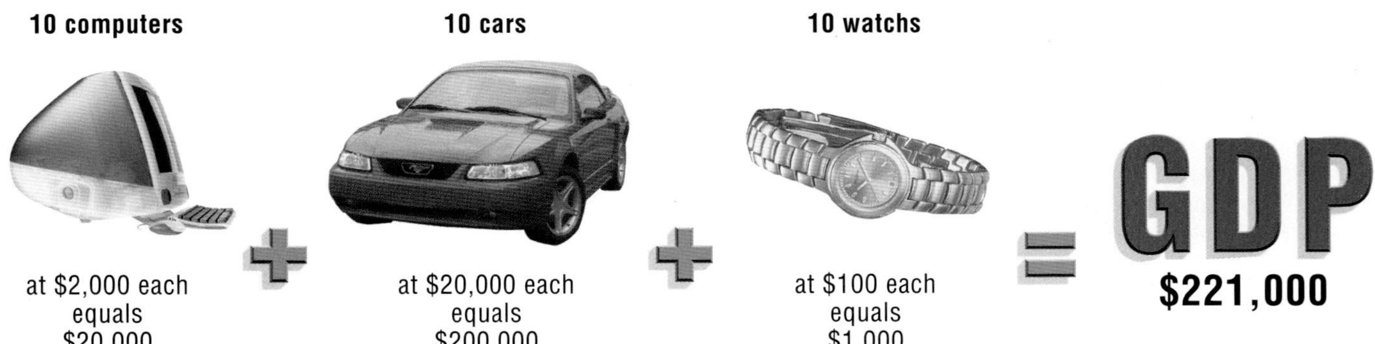

Here are the calculations:
Market value of computers = $2,000 × 10 computers = $20,000
Market value of cars= $20,000 × 10 cars = $200,000
Market value of watches = $100 × 10 watches = $1,000

Gross domestic product = $20,000 + $200,000 + $1,000 = $221,000

This total, $221,000, is the gross domestic product, or GDP, of the tiny economy.

Why Final Goods?

The definition of GDP specifies "final goods and services"; GDP is the total market value of all final goods and services produced annually in an economy. Economists often distinguish between a *final good* and an *intermediate good.*

A final good is a good sold to its final user. When you buy a hamburger at a fast-food restaurant, for example, the hamburger is a final good. You are the final user; no one uses (eats) the hamburger besides you. An intermediate good, in contrast, has not reached its final user. For example, consider the bun that the restaurant buys and on which the hamburger is placed. The bun is an intermediate good at this stage, because it is not yet in the hands of the final user (the person who buys the hamburger). It is in the hands of the people who run the restaurant, who use the bun, along with other goods (lettuce, mustard, hamburger meat, and so on), to produce a hamburger for sale.

What *final goods* can you identify in this photo? What intermediate goods did the restaurant need to buy to create these final goods?

When computing GDP, economists count only final goods and services. If they counted both final and intermediate goods and services, they would be **double-counting,** or counting a good more than once.

Suppose that a book is a final good and that paper and ink are intermediate goods used to produce the book. In a way, we can say that the book is paper and ink (book = paper + ink). If we were to calculate the GDP by adding together the value of the book, the paper, and the ink (book +

gross domestic product (GDP) The total market value of all final goods and services produced annually in an economy.

double-counting Counting a good more than once in computing GDP.

Copy Editor

Copy editors review, rewrite, and edit the work of writers. Anywhere you find professional writing, you will find copy editors—at book publishing firms, magazines, TV stations, radio stations, newspapers, and many other organizations. Copy editors can also work on a freelance basis for many different clients.

Copyediting requires a college degree, usually in communications, journalism, English, or some other liberal arts specialty. It requires an exceptionally good working knowledge of grammar, punctuation, spelling, and sentence style. Some copy editors work in highly specialized fields—such as engineering, medicine, linguistics, or chemistry—and therefore also need a working knowledge of the field. Copy editors must be able to express ideas clearly and logically and have a strong desire to write. Creativity, curiosity, attention to detail, a broad range of knowledge, self-motivation, and perseverance are valuable traits for a copy editor to have.

QUESTION TO ANSWER Suppose an author copyedits her own work instead of hiring a copy editor. Will GDP be higher or lower as a result?

paper + ink), we would, in effect, be counting the paper and ink twice. Because the book is paper and ink, once we count the book, we have automatically counted the paper and the ink. There is no need to count them again.

What GDP Omits

Some exchanges that take place in an economy are omitted from the GDP measurement. We discuss them next.

Illegal Goods and Services In order for something to count as part of GDP, that something has to be capable of being counted. Illegal trades are not capable of being counted, for obvious reasons. For example, when someone makes an illegal purchase, there is no record of the transaction.

If this gardener gets paid in cash to plant some flowers and shrubs, does this payment become part of the GDP? Does it matter whether or not there is a sales receipt? Explain.

Transactions of Legal Goods and Services for Which There Is No Record Suppose a gardener goes to someone's house and offers to mow the lawn and prune the shrubbery for $25 a week. The person agrees. The gardener then asks that he be paid in cash instead of by check and that no written record of the transaction be made. In other words, there will be no sales receipt. Again the person agrees. The payment for these gardening services does not find its way into GDP. With cash payment and no sales receipt, there is no evidence that a transaction was ever made.

Some Nonmarket Goods and Services Some goods and services are traded, but not in an official market setting. Let's say that Eileen Montoya cooks, cleans, and takes care of all financial matters in the Montoya household. She is not paid for doing all this; she does not receive a weekly salary from the family. Because she is not paid, the value of the work she performs is not counted in GDP.

Why do you think the sale of used cars is *not* included in the GDP?

Sales of Used Goods Suppose you buy a used car tomorrow. Will this purchase be recorded in this year's GDP statistics? No, a used car does not enter into the current year's statistics, because the car was counted when it was originally produced.

Stock Transactions and Other Financial Transactions Suppose Elizabeth Sullivan buys 500 shares of stock from Keesha Wilson for a price of $100 a share. The total price is $50,000. The transaction is not included in GDP, because GDP is a record of goods and services produced annually in an economy. A person who buys stock is not buying a product but rather an ownership right in the firm that originally issued the stock. For example, when a person buys Coca-Cola stock, he is becoming an owner of the Coca-Cola Corporation.

Does the Social Security check that this mail carrier is about to deliver contribute to the GDP? Why or why not?

Government Transfer Payments In everyday life, one person makes a payment to another usually in exchange for a good or service. For example, Enrique may pay Harriet $75 to buy her old CD player. When the government makes a payment to someone, it often does not get a good or service in exchange, and the payment is then said to be a *government transfer payment.* For example, the Social Security check that 67-year-old Frank Simmons receives is a government transfer payment. Simmons, who is retired, is not currently supplying a good or service to the government in exchange for the Social Security check. Because GDP accounts for only current goods and services produced, and a transfer payment has nothing to do with current goods and services produced, transfer payments are properly omitted from GDP statistics. See Exhibit 12-2 for a review of items omitted from GDP.

Exhibit 12-2
What the GDP Omits

Item	Example
Illegal goods and services	A person buys an illegal substance.
Legal goods and services for which there is no record of the transaction	A gardener works for cash, and no sales receipt exists.
Some nonmarket goods and services	A family member cooks, cleans, and mows the lawn.
Sales of used goods	You buy a used car.
Stock transactions and other financial transactions	You buy 100 shares of stock in a company.
Government transfer payments	Frank Umchuck receives a Social Security check.

Exhibit 12-3

Gross National Product Does Not Equal Gross Domestic Product

The citizenship of the producer is relevant to computing GNP. The residency of the producer is relevant to computing GDP.

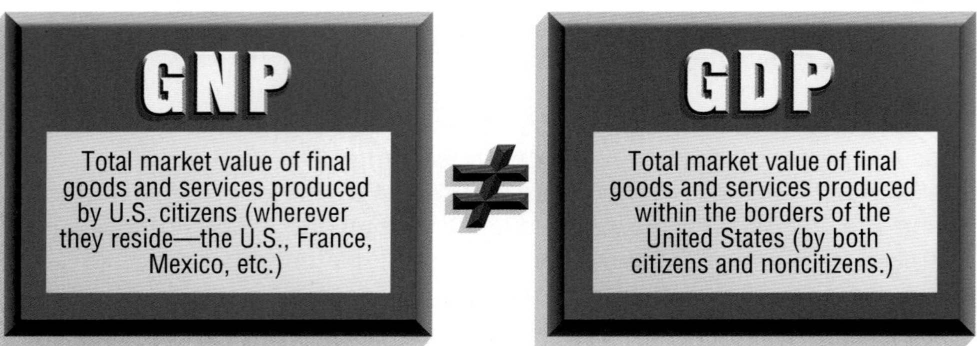

The Difference Between GDP and GNP

Economists, government officials, and members of the public talk about GDP when they want to discuss the overall performance of the economy. They might say, "GDP has been on the rise" or "GDP has been declining a bit." It was not always GDP that these individuals talked about, though. Until about a decade ago, it was GNP—*gross national product.*

What is the difference between GDP and GNP? GNP measures the total market value of final goods and services produced by U.S. citizens, no matter where in the world they reside. GDP, in contrast, is the total market value of final goods and services produced within the borders of the United States, no matter who produces them.

Suppose a U.S. citizen owns a business in Japan. The value of the output she is producing in Japan is counted in GNP because she is a U.S. citizen, but it is not counted in GDP because it was not produced within the borders of the United States. Now suppose a Canadian citizen is producing goods in the United States. The value of his output is not counted in GNP because he is not a U.S. citizen, but it is counted in GDP because it was produced within the borders of the United States. (See Exhibit 12-3 above.)

Section 1 Review

Defining Terms

1. Define

a. gross domestic product (GDP)

b. double-counting

Reviewing Facts and Concepts

2. In a simple economy, three goods are produced during the year, in these quantities: ten pens, twenty shirts, and thirty radios. The price of pens is $4 each, the price of shirts is $30 each, and the price of radios is $35 each. What is GDP for the economy?

3. Why are only final goods and services computed in GDP?

4. Which of the following are included in the calculation of this year's GDP?

a. Twelve-year-old Bobby mowing his family's lawn

b. Terry Yanemoto buying a used car

c. Barbara Wilson buying 100 shares of Chrysler Corporation stock

d. Stephen Sidwhali's receipt of a Social Security check

e. An illegal sale at the corner of Elm and Jefferson

Critical Thinking

5. What is the difference (for purposes of measuring GDP) between buying a new computer and buying 100 shares of stock?

Applying Economic Concepts

6. The government does not now include the housework that a person does for his or her family as part of GDP. Suppose the government were to include housework. How might it go about placing a dollar value on housework?

SECTION 2

Measuring GDP

We know what GDP is and how to measure it in a small economy, such as one with only three or four goods. But how is GDP of the giant U.S. economy measured? This section explains how. As you read this section, keep these key questions in mind:

- What are the four sectors of the economy?
- What are consumption, investment, government purchases, export spending, and import spending?
- How is GDP measured?
- What is per-capita GDP?

MINI GLOSSARY

consumption Expenditures made by the household sector.

investment Expenditures made by the business sector.

government purchases Expenditures made by the government sector. Government purchases do not include government transfer payments.

export spending The amount spent by the residents of other countries for goods produced in the United States.

Key Terms

consumption
investment
government purchases
export spending
import spending

How Is GDP Measured?

Economists break the economy into four sectors: the household sector, the business sector, the government sector, and the foreign sector. Next, they state a simple fact: the people in each of these sectors buy goods and services—that is, they make expenditures.

Economists give names to the expenditures made by each of the four sectors. The expenditures made by the household sector (or by consumers) are called **consumption.** The expenditures made by the business sector are called **investment,** and expenditures made by the government sector are called **government purchases.** (Government purchases include purchases made by all three levels of government—local, state, and federal.) Finally, the expenditures made by the residents of other countries on goods produced in the United States are called **export spending.** Exhibit 12-4 gives examples of goods purchased by households, businesses, government, and foreigners.

Consider all the goods and services produced in the U.S. economy in a year: houses, tractors, watches, restaurant meals, cars, computers, radios, compact discs, and much, much more. Suppose someone from the household sector buys a compact disc. This purchase falls into the category of *consumption.* When someone from the business sector buys a large machine to install in a factory, the purchase is considered an *investment.* If the U.S. government purchases a tank from a company that produces tanks, the purchase is considered a *government purchase.* And if a person living in Sweden buys a U.S.–produced sweater, this purchase is considered spending on U.S. exports and therefore is registered as *export spending.*

If these jeans were made in the U.S. and sold to Asian and European wholesalers, the jeans would represent what type of expenditure?

As these commuters buy train tickets, they are making what type of expenditure?

Exhibit 12-4

The Expenditures Made by the Four Sectors of the Economy

Sector of the economy	Name of expenditures	Definition	Examples
Household	Consumption	Expenditures made by the household sector on goods for personal use	TV sets, telephones, clothes, lamps, cars
Business	Investment	Expenditures made by the business sector on goods used in producing other goods; also includes business inventories	Tools, machines, factories
Government	Government purchases	Expenditures made by federal, state, and local governments	Paper, pens, tanks, planes
Foreign	Exports	Expenditures made by foreigners for American-made goods	Cars, wheat, computers
	Imports	Expenditures made by Americans for foreign-made goods	Cars, radios, computers

It stands to reason that all goods produced in the economy must be bought by someone in one of the four sectors of the economy. It follows that if economists simply sum the expenditures made by each sector—that is, if they sum consumption, investment, government purchases, and export spending—they will be close to computing the GDP.

They are only close, however; they still need to adjust for U.S. purchases of foreign-produced goods. For example, if Cynthia in Detroit purchases a Japanese-made television set for $500, this $500 TV purchase would not be included in GDP because GDP is a measure of goods and services produced annually in an economy. Specifically, the U.S. GDP is a measure of goods and services produced annually in the territorial area we know as the United States. Cynthia's TV was not produced in the United States, so it is not part of U.S. GDP. Spending by Americans for foreign-produced goods is called **import spending.**

import spending
The amount spent by Americans for foreign-produced goods.

To compute U.S. GDP, then, we need to sum consumption (C), investment (I), government purchases (G), and export spending (EX) and then subtract import spending (IM). We can now write GDP in symbol form:

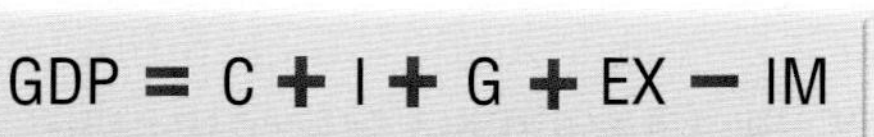

$$GDP = C + I + G + EX - IM$$

For example, in the first quarter of 2000, consumption in the United States was $6,602 billion, investment was $1,719 billion, government purchases were $1,707 billion, export spending was $1,059 billion, and import spending was $1,390 billion. Thus we can calculate GDP to be $9,697 billion (see Exhibit 12-5).

Exhibit 12-5
Computing GDP (First Quarter, 2000, in billions of dollars)

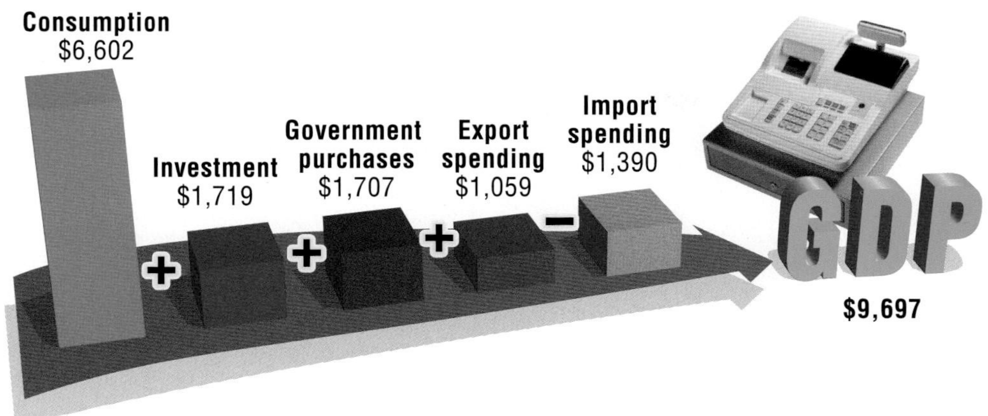

Question: *Is there a difference between an* export *and* export spending *and between an* import *and* import spending*?*

Answer: *Yes. Usually when people use the word* export *they are talking about a good. For example, because the U.S. produces and sells cars to people in the rest of the world, a car is an export for the United States. The dollar amount that residents of other countries pay for the U.S. goods they purchase (in other words, for U.S. exports) is called* export spending.

Similarly, an import *is usually considered to be a good. For example, coffee is an import for the United States. The dollar amount that Americans pay for the foreign-produced goods that they buy is called* import spending.

To recap: an export is a good and export spending is a certain dollar amount; an import is a good and import spending is a certain dollar amount.

Keep in mind that when we use the words export spending *and* import spending, *we are using these words to refer to the United States. For example, when we say that export spending was $1,059 billion in 2000, we mean that residents of foreign countries bought $1,059 billion worth of goods from the United States. When we say that import spending was $1,390 billion in 2000, we mean that Americans bought $1,390 billion worth of goods from other countries.*

This coffee is being shipped to the U.S. In computing the U.S. GDP, should you add or subtract the market value of the coffee?

Suppose that this merchant is able to sell only 90 of the 100 sombreros that are priced at $10 each. Would economists add $900 or $1,000 to the GDP?

You hear on the news that import spending has increased sharply in recent months. What do you predict this increase will do to GDP? Explain your answer.

Is Every Good That Is Produced Also Sold?

Our definition of GDP is the total market value of all final goods and services *produced* annually in an economy. However, we measured the GDP by finding out how much the four sectors of the economy *spend* on goods and services. Suppose something is produced but not purchased. Is it included in GDP or not? For example, a car company produces 10,000 new cars this year, but the household sector chooses to buy only 8,900 of the 10,000 cars. That means that some cars (1,100) were produced but not sold. Do these cars get counted in GDP?

The answer is yes, because the government statisticians who measure GDP assume that everything that is produced is purchased by someone. For purposes of calculating GDP, the government statisticians assume that the car company "purchased" the 1,100 cars that the car company did not sell.

GDP versus Quality of Life

In 1998, the U.S. GDP was more than six times larger than the GDP of France (see Exhibit 12-6). Does it follow that because Americans live in a country with a higher GDP than the French, Americans are better off than the French? If your answer is yes, then you have made the mistake of equating a higher GDP with being better off or having greater well-being. Greater production of goods and services is only one of the many factors that contribute to being better off or possessing greater well-being.

Look at the issue on an individual basis. Franklin has $1 million in the bank, owns a large home, drives a luxury car, and works seventy hours per week. He has little time to enjoy nature or his family. In contrast, Harris has $100 in the bank, owns a small home, drives an old car, and works thirty hours a week. He has much time to enjoy life. Who is better off—

Exhibit 12-6
GDP of Selected Nations (1998)

Source: U.S. Bureau of the Census. Figures are based on purchasing power parity exchange rates.

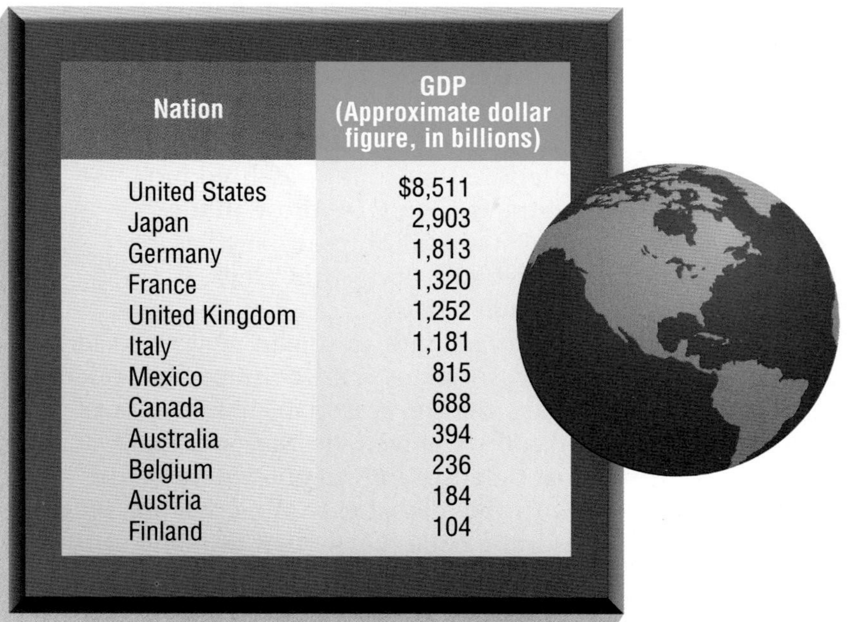

Nation	GDP (Approximate dollar figure, in billions)
United States	$8,511
Japan	2,903
Germany	1,813
France	1,320
United Kingdom	1,252
Italy	1,181
Mexico	815
Canada	688
Australia	394
Belgium	236
Austria	184
Finland	104

This French vendor does not seem too concerned that France's GDP falls far short of the U.S. GDP. What possible reasons can you give for his positive attitude about his business and the French economy in comparison to the U.S. economy?

Franklin or Harris? In terms of expensive goods, there is no doubt that Franklin has more than Harris; in this one respect, Franklin benefits more than Harris. In terms of leisure time, though, Harris is better off than Franklin. In overall terms—taking everything into account—we cannot say who is better off. We just do not know.

Similarly, we simply cannot say whether Americans are better off than the French on the basis of their GDPs. All we can say for sure is that Americans live in a country in which greater production exists. Being better off takes into account much more than simply how much output is produced.

In assessing a country's GDP, its population also must be considered. Country X may have double the GDP of Country Y, but if its population is three times as large, then on a per-person basis each person has fewer goods and services (on average) in country X than in country Y. In short, bigger GDP does not necessarily mean bigger per-capita GDP.

$$\text{Per-capita GDP} = \frac{\text{GDP}}{\text{Population}}$$

In recent years some economists have tried to devise an economic measurement that comes closer than GDP to measuring such intangibles as happiness or well-being. For example, economists William Nordhaus and James Tobin have developed what they call MEW (measures of economic welfare). MEW adds to GDP many of those things that are presently excluded but nonetheless increase our overall standard of living—for example, the value of leisure time and household production. MEW also subtracts from GDP those things that decrease our overall standard of living, such as pollution costs and "regrettable necessities" such as police protection and national defense.

THINKING Like an Economist

Economists understand that life is full of trade-offs. More of one thing may mean less of something else. For example, a higher GDP may come at the expense of less leisure.

The MEW measurement assumes a utopian view of society and is controversial. For one thing, Nordhaus and Tobin exclude defense expenditures. Their assumption is that no reasonable country buys national defense for its own sake; if there were no war or risk of war, there would be no need for national defense, and no one would be the worse off. Other economists disagree with the idea of excluding defense expenditures, arguing that the same reasoning could be applied to many of the other components of GDP. For example, it could be said that no one wants a hospital for its own sake. If there were no accidents or illnesses, there would be no hospitals, and no one would be the worse off. But of course, we need hospitals. In summary, the construction of MEW is an attempt to measure economic welfare more closely. Whether MEW does a better job at this than GDP is debatable; nevertheless, the search continues for more finely tuned economic measurements.

Trying to better measure overall economic welfare, some economists subtract from the GDP the cost of police protection, such as the protection provided by these English bobbies. Do you think this is a good idea?

Section 2 Review

Defining Terms

1. Define
   a. consumption
   b. investment
   c. government purchases
   d. export spending
   e. import spending

Reviewing Facts and Concepts

2. Why is import spending subtracted from the sum of consumption, investment, government purchases, and export spending in computing GDP?
3. Suppose consumption is \$2,000 billion, investment is \$700 billion, government purchases are \$1,200 billion, export spending is \$100 billion, and import spending is \$150 billion. What does GDP equal?
4. A computer company produces 25,000 computers this year and sells 22,000 to its customers. According to government statisticians, however, all 25,000 computers have been purchased. How do the statisticians reach this conclusion?

Critical Thinking

5. Suppose country X has a GDP that is three times larger than that of country Y. Are the people in country X better off than the people in country Y? Explain your answer.

Applying Economic Concepts

6. A family has six people, five of whom produce goods and services that are sold directly to consumers. One person in the family is too young to work. How would you go about measuring the family's "GDP"?

SECTION 3

Real GDP

In a simple economy with only one good, we compute GDP by multiplying the price of the good times the quantity of the good sold. For example, suppose the good is watches, and the price is $100. If the quantity of watches produced is fifty in a given year, then GDP is $5,000.

Suppose that the next year the quantity of watches stays steady at fifty, but the price rises to $200. GDP is now $10,000—double what it was last year. Notice that although GDP is higher in the second year than in the first year, the quantity of watches produced in both years is the same, fifty. Only the price of watches is different. Thus, it is possible for GDP to rise from one year to another even if there is no increase in the quantity of goods produced.

If the number of watches produced stays the same, but the price goes up, will the GDP change? Will the *real* GDP change?

Because of this fact, economists often adjust GDP for price changes so that they can separate price changes from output changes. In other words, they calculate the real GDP.

As you read this section, keep these key questions in mind:

- If GDP is higher in one year than another, do we automatically know why it is higher?
- What is real GDP?

The Two Variables of GDP: P and Q

Key Terms

base year
real GDP

When we computed GDP in a simple, one-good economy, we multiplied two variables to find GDP: price (P) and quantity (Q). If either of the two variables rises and the other remains constant, GDP will rise.

To illustrate, look at the following chart:

Price	Quantity	GDP
$10	2	$20
$15	2	$30
$10	3	$30

With a price of $10 and a quantity of 2, GDP is $20. When the price rises to $15 but the quantity is held constant at 2, GDP rises to $30. Finally, if the price is constant at $10 and the quantity increases to 3, GDP again is $30. Clearly, an increase in either price or quantity will raise GDP.

Cotton, Soap, Infections, and Real GDP

One way to produce more goods and services, and therefore have a higher real GDP, is to have more people working. Obviously, it takes labor (people) to produce goods and services. The more people who are working, all other things being equal, the more real GDP there will be.

It is also an obvious fact that people cannot work if they are dead. In the past, many people died early in life, often of things that are readily and easily cured today, such as bacterial infections.

To take a short detour, take the case of Nathan Rothschild, who in 1836 was said to be the richest man in the world. Rothschild had left London for Frankfurt, Germany, to attend the wedding of his son. At the time, he was suffering from an inflammation on his lower back, which a German physician had diagnosed as a boil. Rothschild got steadily worse, and his physician in London was summoned to Frankfurt. When his doctor could not cure the problem, a German surgeon was brought in to see what he could do. He opened and cleaned the wound, but it was too late. The "boil" was an abscess, and the poison from it had gotten into Rothschild's body. On July 28, 1836, the richest man in the world died of an infection that today is routinely cured by antibiotics.

Rothschild's fate was not uncommon in the early 1800s. People also commonly died of gastrointestinal infections, which were often transmitted from human waste to hands to food to digestive tracts. The main reasons for this transmission were woolen underwear (which caused people to itch) and a lack of mass-produced soap.

This situation changed with the Industrial Revolution. Two of the chief products of the Industrial Revolution were cheap, washable cotton (which does not scratch) and mass-produced soap made from vegetable oils. Together, these two products dramatically reduced the transmission rates of gastrointestinal infections. Consequently, people ended up living and working longer. Working longer meant that more goods and services would be produced.

SOURCE: Based on David S. Landes, introduction to *The Wealth and Poverty of Nations* (New York: W. W. Norton, 1998).

QUESTION TO ANSWER Can you identify any health developments in the past decade that may result in people working longer?

Suppose someone then told you that GDP was $20 one year and $30 the next year. You would have no way of knowing whether GDP increased because price increased, because quantity of output increased, or because both price and quantity increased. But suppose there was a way to hold price constant. If price was held constant and GDP increased, would you know what caused the rise in GDP? If price is held constant, then any rise in GDP must be due to a rise in quantity, of course.

How can we keep price constant? Economists do it by computing GDP for each year—1998, 1999, 2000, and so on—using the prices that existed in one particular year in the past chosen as a point of reference for comparison, called the **base year.** Economists who compute GDP this way are said to be computing **real GDP** (GDP measured in base-year, or constant, prices).

GDP is equal to price in the current year times quantity in the current year. But real GDP is equal to price in the base year times quantity in the current year:

$$\text{GDP} = P_{\text{Current year}} \times Q_{\text{Current year}}$$
$$\text{Real GDP} = P_{\text{Base year}} \times Q_{\text{Current year}}$$

To illustrate, let's again assume that we have a simple, one-good economy that produces only watches. Look at Exhibit 12-7 (on the next page). Column 1 of the exhibit lists several years, column 2 gives the price of watches in these years, and column 3 gives the quantity of watches produced in these years. Column 4 shows GDP for each year. (GDP equals the current-year price times the current-year quantity of watches.)

Real GDP is shown in column 5. To calculate it, we multiply the price of watches in the base year of 1987 by the current-year quantity. For example, to get real GDP in 1999, we take the quantity of watches produced in 1999 and multiply it by the price of watches in 1987.

A quick look at real GDP figures tells us that because real GDP in 1999 ($160,000) is higher than that in 1998 ($152,000), the quantity of watches produced in 1999 must have been greater than the quantity of watches produced in 1998. A look at the quantities in column 3 confirms this assumption. Also, because the real GDP figure for 2000 ($148,400) is lower than that for 1999 ($160,000), the quantity of watches produced in 2000 must have been lower than the quantity of watches produced in 1999. Again, column 3 confirms this.

base year
In general, a benchmark year—a year chosen as a point of reference for comparison. When real GDP is computed, the outputs of different years are priced at base-year levels.

real GDP
Gross domestic product (GDP) that has been adjusted for price changes; GDP measured in base-year, or constant, prices.

Joseph Alois Schumpeter, Economist

In one of his most famous works, *Capitalism, Socialism, and Democracy,* the economist Joseph Schumpeter (1883–1950) asks whether or not capitalism can survive. His answer is no. Schumpeter was a strong believer in capitalism and thought that it would die because of its successes, not its failures. Over time capitalism would produce more and more real GDP, and people living under capitalism would become so wealthy that a large intellectual class would arise that would make its living attacking capitalism. In other words, the intellectual class would attack the very system that gave it the freedom to attack it.

Schumpeter also predicted that in a capitalist society, new innovations would cause old technologies, skills, and equipment to become obsolete. He called this process "creative destruction." In the end, though, this "creative destruction" was good for the people who lived under capitalism, because it provided them with a continually rising standard of living.

QUESTION TO ANSWER Do you see any evidence of "creative destruction" in today's world? Explain your answer.

Exhibit 12-7

Computing GDP and Real GDP in a Simple, One-Good Economy

Column 4 computes the GDP for a simple, one-good economy. The price in the current year is multiplied by the quantity produced in the current year. Column 5 computes real GDP by multiplying the price in 1987 (the base year for purposes here) by the quantity produced in the current year. Economists prefer working with real GDP to working with GDP because they know that if real GDP in one year is higher than real GDP in another year, output is greater in the year with the higher real GDP.

(1) Year	(2) Price of watches	(3) Quantity of watches produced	(4) GDP	(5) Real GDP
1987	$80	—	Price in current year × Quantity in current year	Price in 1987 × Quantity in current year
1998	$120	1,900	$120 × 1,900 = $228,000	$80 × 1,900 = $152,000
1999	$150	2,000	$150 × 2,000 = $300,000	$80 × 2,000 = $160,000
2000	$190	1,855	$190 × 1,855 = $352,450	$80 × 1,855 = $148,400

The Base Year

In computing real GDP for 1998, 1999, and 2000, we multiplied the quantity of watches produced in each year times the price of watches in 1987, the base year. Thus, another way to define *real GDP* is *GDP in base-year prices* or, if 1987 is the base year, for example, *GDP in 1987 prices*.

Section 3 Review

Defining Terms

1. Define
   a. base year
   b. real GDP

Reviewing Facts and Concepts

2. Gross domestic product is $6,000 billion in one year and $6,500 billion the next year. Is output necessarily higher in the second year than in the first? Explain your answer.
3. Why do economists compute real GDP?
4. When real GDP increases, which variable, P or Q, is increasing?

Critical Thinking

5. Can GDP go up at the same time that real GDP goes down? Explain your answer.

Applying Economic Concepts

6. An economist wants to know if the "average person" in country X has more goods and services to consume than the "average person" in country Y. Do you recommend that the economist look at per-capita GDP or per-capita real GDP? Explain your answer.

SECTION 4

Measuring Price Changes

We have seen that economists measure changes in output from one year to the next by comparing real GDP for these years. If real GDP for 1998 is $6,000 billion and real GDP for 1999 is $6,500 billion, for example, economists know that in 1999 the economy produced $500 billion worth of goods and services over and above what it produced in 1998.

Changes in output are not the only thing in which economists are interested. They are also interested in changes in prices. We discuss here how economists calculate changes in prices.

As you read this section, keep these key questions in mind:

- What is the consumer price index?
- How is the consumer price index calculated?

Honda's president has just announced a price increase for Honda's automobiles. Because prices for most goods and services frequently change, economists use various methods to compute changes and analyze their effects on the economy.

Key Terms

price index
consumer price index (CPI)
aggregate demand curve
aggregate supply curve

Calculating the Change in a Single Price

Suppose that in 1999 a Honda Accord was priced at $20,000, and in 2000 a Honda Accord was $21,500. By what percentage did the price of a Honda Accord increase? Here is the formula we use to determine the percentage change in price:

$$\text{Percentage change in price} = \frac{\text{Price in later year} - \text{Price in earlier year}}{\text{Price in earlier year}} \times 100$$

If we fill in the numbers, we get the following:

$$\text{Percentage change in price} = \frac{\$21{,}500 - \$20{,}000}{\$20{,}000} \times 100 = \frac{\$1{,}500}{\$20{,}000} \times 100 = 7.5\%$$

In this example, we found the percentage increase in a single price from one year to the next. Economists are much more interested, though, in what has happened to prices in general than in what has happened to a single price. Before they can calculate the change in prices from one year to the next, they need to compute a **price index,** the average price level. The most widely cited price index is the **consumer price index (CPI).** You might have heard a newscaster say, "Today it was reported in Washington that the consumer price index has risen 3.2 percent on an annual basis." We now consider how the CPI is computed and what it means.

MINI GLOSSARY

price index
A measure of the price level, or the average level of prices.

consumer price index (CPI)
The most widely cited price index.

The Consumer Price Index

The CPI is calculated by the U.S. Bureau of Labor Statistics. The bureau uses a sampling of thousands of households and determines what these consumers have paid for a representative group of goods called the *market basket.* This amount is compared with what a typical "consumer unit" paid for the same market basket in 1982–1984. (A consumer unit is a household of related or unrelated individuals who pool their money. In the last survey, the average consumer unit was made up of 2.6 people.)

Calculating the CPI involves this process:

1. Calculate the total dollar expenditure on the market basket in the *base year* and the total dollar expenditure on the market basket in the *current year.*
2. Divide the total current-year expenditure by the total base-year expenditure, and multiply by 100.

You can locate economic data at many sites on the Internet. One good Web site is maintained by the Bureau of Labor Statistics, or BLS, http://stats.bls.gov/top20.html. To get some of the most popular data at the BLS, go there, and click on "Overall BLS Most Requested Series." Next, find the following:

a. The CPI for all urban consumers (called CPI-U); base year 1982–1984.
b. The CPI-U/less food and energy.

Exhibit 12-8 illustrates an example. To simplify things, we'll say that the market basket is made up of only two goods instead of the hundreds of items that it actually contains. Our market basket will contain ten CDs and five T-shirts.

The total dollar expenditure on the market basket in the *base year* is found by multiplying the quantities of goods in the market basket (column 1) times the prices of the goods in the base year (column 2). A look at column 3 shows us that $130 was spent on CDs and $20 was spent on T-shirts, for a total dollar expenditure of $150.

Exhibit 12-8
Calculating the Consumer Price Index

Step 1:
Calculate the total dollar expenditure on the market basket in the base year and the current year. These amounts are calculated in column 3 ($150) and column 5 ($180), respectively.

(1) Goods in the market basket	(2) Price in base year	(3) Base-year expenditure (1) × (2)	(4) Price in current year	(5) Current-year expenditure (1) × (4)
10 CDs	$13	10 × $13 = $130	$15	10 × $15 = $150
5 T-shirts	$4	5 × $4 = $20	$6	5 × $6 = $30
		$150		$180
		Total dollar expenditure on the market basket in the base year		Total dollar expenditure on the market basket in the current year

Step 2:
Divide the total dollar expenditure on the market basket in the current year by the total dollar expenditure on the market basket in the base year, and then multiply by 100.

$$CPI_{\text{current year}} = \frac{\text{Total dollar expenditure on the market basket in current year}}{\text{Total dollar expenditure on the market basket in base year}} \times 100$$

$$= \frac{\$180}{\$150} \times 100$$

$$= 120$$

Next, the total dollar expenditure on the market basket in the *current year* is found by multiplying the quantities of goods in the market basket (column 1) times the prices of the goods in the current year (column 4). A look at column 5 shows us that \$150 was spent on CDs and \$30 was spent on T-shirts, for a total dollar expenditure of \$180.

Now, we divide the total current-year expenditure, \$180, by the total base-year expenditure, \$150, and then multiply by 100:

$$\frac{\$180}{\$150} \times 100 = 120$$

The CPI for the current year is 120.

Notice that the CPI is just a number. What does this number tell us? By itself, the CPI number tells us very little. It is only when we compare one CPI number with another that we learn something. (See Exhibit 12-9.) For example, in the United States in 1996, the CPI was 156.9. One year later, in 1997, the CPI was 160.5. The two CPI numbers can be used to figure out the percentage by which prices increased between 1996 and 1997 in the same way we determined the percentage increase for a single price:

$$\text{Percentage change in CPI} = \frac{\text{CPI in later year} - \text{CPI in earlier year}}{\text{CPI in earlier year}} \times 100$$

If we fill in the numbers, we get the following:

$$\text{Percentage change in CPI} = \frac{160.5 - 156.9}{156.9} \times 100 = \frac{3.6}{156.9} \times 100 = 2.29\%$$

Exhibit 12-9

CPI, 1990-99

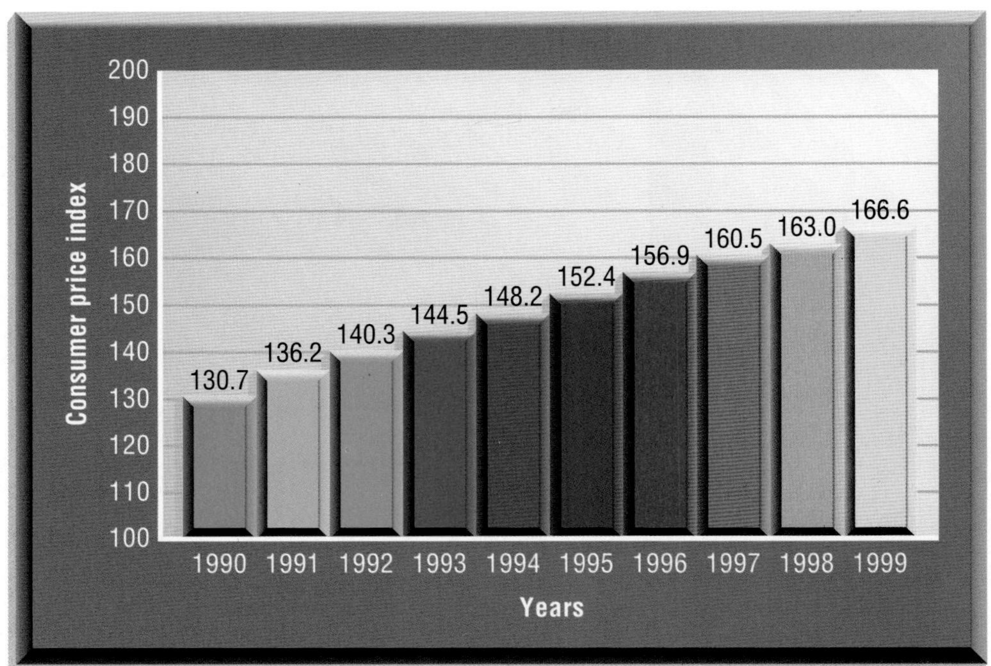

What Did Abraham Lincoln Earn as President?

In 2000, when Bill Clinton was president, he earned $200,000. In 1863, when Abraham Lincoln was president, he earned $25,000. Does it follow that President Clinton was paid eight times more than President Lincoln?

At first glance, it may seem that Clinton was paid more than Lincoln, but we need to keep in mind that when Lincoln was president the prices of goods and services were much lower than when Clinton was president. In other words, $25,000 in 1863 would buy much more than $25,000 in 2000.

To get some idea of what a $25,000 salary in 1863 would equal in today's dollars, economists use the following formula:

$$\text{Salary in today's dollars} = \text{Salary in earlier year} \times \frac{\text{CPI}_{\text{Today}}}{\text{CPI}_{\text{Earlier year}}}$$

Suppose that by "today" we mean 2000. We want to find out what Lincoln's 1863 salary is equal to in 2000. The CPI in 2000 was 171.2, and the CPI in 1863 was about 9. Filling in the formula, we see that Lincoln's salary in 1863 was equivalent to earning $475,555 in 2000.

$$\text{Salary in today's dollars} = \$25{,}000 \times \frac{171.2}{9} = \$475{,}555$$

In other words, President Lincoln, in 1863, earned more than twice as much as President Clinton earned in 2000.

QUESTION TO ANSWER A house cost $18,000 in 1960, and the CPI in 1960 was 29.6. What is the price of the house in 2000 dollars (CPI in 2000 = 171.2)?

Exhibit 12-10

$$\text{Salary in today's dollars} = \$25{,}000 \times \frac{171.2}{9} = \$475{,}555$$

aggregate demand curve A curve that shows the quantity of goods and services that buyers are willing and able to buy at different price levels.

Determining the Quantity of Goods and Services and the Price Level

Chapter 3 explained that there are two sides to every market—a demand side and a supply side. We represent the demand in a market with a downward-sloping demand curve and the supply in a market with an upward-sloping supply curve. As you may recall, equilibrium price and quantity in a market are determined by the forces of supply and demand. What holds for a market holds for an economy, too; any economy has a demand side and a supply side, as illustrated in Exhibit 12-11 below. The demand side is represented by the **aggregate demand curve,** which shows the quantity of goods and services that buyers are willing and able to buy at different price levels.

Exhibit 12-11
Aggregate Demand and Aggregate Supply

Equilibrium in an economy comes about through the economic forces of aggregate demand (AD) and aggregate supply (AS). The economy is in equilibrium at Point A in the exhibit.

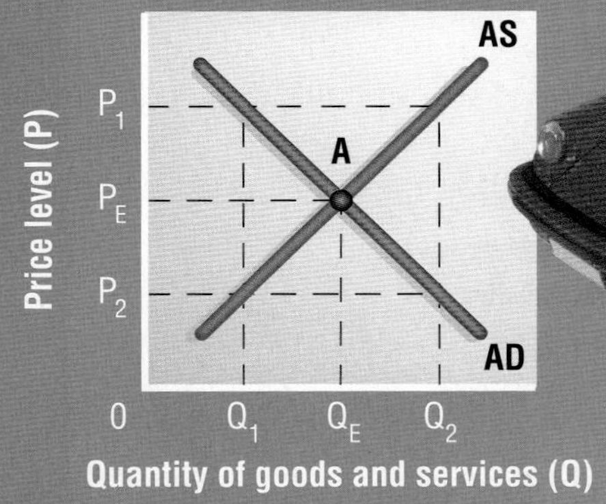

Price level (P)

P_1 P_E P_2

AS A AD

0 Q_1 Q_E Q_2

Quantity of goods and services (Q)

	When price level is	Buyers are willing and able to buy	Sellers are willing and able to sell	Remarks
Look at AD only	P_1	Q_1	—	Buyers are willing and able to buy more at lower price levels than at higher price levels.
	P_2	Q_2	—	
Look at AS only	P_1	—	Q_2	Sellers are willing and able to produce and sell more at higher price levels than at lower price levels.
	P_2	—	Q_1	
Look at AD and AS	P_1	Q_1	Q_2	Buyers are willing and able to buy less than sellers are willing and able to produce and sell.
	P_2	Q_2	Q_1	Buyers are willing and able to buy more than sellers are willing and able to produce and sell.
	P_E	Q_E	Q_E	At equilibrium, buyers are willing and able to buy the same amount as sellers are willing and able to produce and sell.

The Biggest Box Office Attraction of All Time—It's Probably Not What You Think

A list of the top fifty movies of all time puts movies such as *Titanic, Stars Wars, Independence Day, E.T., Jurassic Park,* and *Home Alone* at the top of the list. For example, *Titanic* had total gross earnings of $601 million, and *E.T.* earned $400 million. In comparison, *Indiana Jones and the Temple of Doom* earned $180 million, and *The Sound of Music* earned $163 million.

There is a problem with comparing the gross receipts of movies, though. The gross receipts for a particular movie are calculated by adding up the cost of all the tickets sold for that movie. But the "top 50" movies were released in different years, which means the ticket prices varied. For example, in 1940 the average price of a movie ticket was 24 cents; in 1960, it was 69 cents; and in 1980, it was $2.69. This helps us see that $1 of gross for *Titanic*, released in 1997, is not equal to $1 of gross for *Sound of Music*, released in 1965.

To truly compare the success of these movies, we would have to convert each movie's gross receipts into today's dollars. If we say that "today" is 2000, we have to convert dollars in the past into 2000 dollars. When we do this, the top movie of all time turns out to be none other than *Gone with the Wind*, released in 1939. In 2000 dollars, its gross receipts were $2.46 billion, in comparison with *Titanic*'s gross receipts of $640.6 million (in 2000 dollars). Second place goes to a 1937 release, *Snow White and the Seven Dwarfs*, with gross receipts in 2000 dollars of $2.25 billion.

QUESTION TO ANSWER The list of the top fifty movies of all time is released periodically, but there is no attempt to convert the gross receipts of each movie into today's dollars. Why do you suppose this is?

And the Next President of the United States Is . . .

Every four years in the United States, a presidential election is held. There are usually two major presidential candidates (one from the Democratic Party and one from the Republican Party) and a number of third-party candidates, but the press coverage focuses on the two major candidates. In the months before a presidential election, journalists follow the two major candidates across the country and record not only what they say about the issues but also every misstep, scandal, and piece of gossip. Then, on election day, the voters go to the polls and elect or reelect a president.

Why do the voters vote the way they do for president? The numerous possible answers range from the style of the candidate ("He is at ease with himself and others") to his foreign policy proposals ("He will keep us out of war"). But do people really vote for a president based on these factors, or do they only say (or believe) they vote based on these things? Perhaps people simply vote based on the state of the economy in the months preceding the election. If the economy is good, they vote for the incumbent or his party's candidate. If the economy is bad, they vote for the challenger.

A number of economists have built economic models suggesting that they can predict presidential elections based primarily on two variables: per-capita real GDP (which is real GDP divided by population) and the inflation rate (as perhaps measured by changes in the consumer price index). If the per-capita real GDP is growing in the three quarters (nine months) preceding the election and inflation is low in the three years preceding the election, people will vote for the incumbent or the person who represents the incumbent's party. Otherwise, they will vote for the challenger.

Do models like this predict results well? One model, the Fair Model, was developed by Ray Fair, an economist at Yale University. His model has three key economic variables, two of which we have already mentioned. His model has a high success rate, although it has not predicted every recent presidential election accurately. Still, the model has predicted well enough for many economists, as well as some political pundits, to admit that the state of the economy is a major determinant of who is elected president of the United States.

QUESTION TO ANSWER Why do you think the state of the economy preceding the presidential election might largely determine the outcome of the election? In other words, why might the state of the economy determine the candidate for whom people vote?

Berry's World

"Isn't this great about the drop in consumer prices? If we had jobs, we could take advantage of it."

BERRY'S WORLD reprinted by permission of Newspaper Enterprise Association, Inc.

(Sometimes the quantity of goods and services is simply referred to as *output*.) The supply side is represented by the **aggregate supply curve,** which shows the quantity of goods and services, or output, that producers are willing and able to supply at different price levels. The equilibrium price level and equilibrium quantity of goods and services are determined by the forces of aggregate demand and aggregate supply.

MINI GLOSSARY

aggregate supply curve
A curve that shows the quantity of goods and services that producers are willing and able to supply at different price levels.

The forces of aggregate demand and supply determine the equilibrium price level and equilibrium quantity of goods and services (equilibrium output) in an economy. The equilibrium price level (P_E in Exhibit 12-11 on page 331) and the equilibrium quantity of goods and services, or output (Q_E in Exhibit 12-11), come to exist over time. For example, at P_1 the quantity demanded of goods and services (Q_1) is less than the quantity supplied of goods and services (Q_2), and there is a surplus of goods and services. As a result, the price level drops. As a result of a lower price level, people buy more goods and services, and producers produce less. The surplus begins to disappear because of these actions on the part of buyers and sellers. (Buyers are helping to eliminate the surplus by buying more, and sellers are helping to eliminate the surplus by producing less.)

At P_2, the quantity demanded of goods and services (Q_2) is greater than the quantity supplied (Q_1), so there is a shortage of goods and services. Thus, the price level rises, people buy fewer goods and services, and producers produce more. The shortage begins to disappear because of the actions of buyers and sellers. (Buyers are helping to eliminate the shortage by buying less, and sellers are helping to eliminate the shortage by producing more.) Only at P_E is the quantity of goods and services supplied equal to the quantity of goods and services demanded; both are Q_E.

Section 4 Review

Defining Terms

1. Define
  a. price index
  b. consumer price index (CPI)
  c. aggregate demand curve
  d. aggregate supply curve

Reviewing Facts and Concepts

2. The market basket is composed of six books, five shirts, four blouses, and two pairs of shoes. The price of books is $10 each, the price of shirts is $20 each, the price of blouses is $23 each, and the price of shoes is $40 per pair. What is the total dollar expenditure on the market basket?

3. The CPI is 103 in year 1 and 177 in year 2. By what percentage have prices increased between the two years?

4. Suppose the CPI was 143 in year 1 and 132 in year 2. Did prices rise or fall between year 1 and year 2?

Critical Thinking

5. What can cause the equilibrium price level to rise? What can cause the equilibrium quantity of goods and services (in the economy) to fall? (*Hint:* Look at Exhibit 12-11.)

Applying Economic Concepts

6. Smith earned $40,000 in 1996 and $50,000 in 1997. The CPI was 156.9 in 1996 and 160.5 in 1997. Using the data presented, how can Smith figure out if his earnings went up by more than, less than, or equal to the change in prices? (If you have trouble answering this question, you may want to first read the feature "Developing Economics Skills: Using Percentages to Make Comparisons.")

Developing Economic **Skills**

Using Percentages to Make Comparisons

During the period 1987 to 1997, medical care prices rose by 80 percent, while food prices increased by 39 percent. Comparing the price change in one thing with the price change in another in this way can be useful. To illustrate, suppose you are a farmer. As a farmer, you produce certain food goods to sell. You also buy certain goods and services in your role as consumer. What might be of interest to you is the percentage change in the price of what you sell (food products) compared with the percentage change in the price of what you buy (all kinds of consumer goods and services).

To compute the change in the prices of what the farmer buys, we can look at the consumer price index (CPI) in different years. For example, in 1997 the CPI was 160.5, and in 1998 it had risen to 163.0. We use the formula that follows (the same one given earlier in the chapter) to compute the percentage change in prices:

$$\text{Percentage change in CPI} = \frac{\text{CPI in later year} - \text{CPI in earlier year}}{\text{CPI in earlier year}} \times 100$$

$$= \frac{163.0 - 160.5}{160.5} \times 100$$

$$= \frac{2.5}{160.5} \times 100$$

$$= 1.56\%$$

In 1997 the price index for food goods that farmers sell was 107, and in 1998 it had fallen to 101. We use the formula that follows to compute the percentage change in prices:

$$\text{Percentage change in prices of food goods that farmers sell} = \frac{\text{Price index in later year} - \text{Price index in earlier year}}{\text{Price index in earlier year}} \times 100$$

$$= \frac{101 - 107}{107} \times 100$$

$$= \frac{-6}{107} \times 100$$

$$= -5.61\%$$

Having made our computations, we see that the prices of the goods farmers buy increased (1.56 percent) and the prices of the goods farmers sell fell (−5.61 percent) during 1997–1998.

1. Valerie's objective is to cut back on buying clothes and entertainment in order to save money. Last month, she spent $136 on clothes and $98 on entertainment. This month, she has spent $129 on clothes and $79 on entertainment. Compute the percentage change in spending for each good, and then compare the changes. Is Valerie cutting back more in spending on clothes or entertainment?
2. Suppose the price index for the goods Juan sells is 132 in year 1 and 145 in year 2. The price index for the goods he buys is 124 in the first year and 135 in the second year. How much have prices increased between the two years for the goods he sells? For the goods he buys?

CHAPTER 12

Review

Economics Vocabulary

Fill in the following blanks with the appropriate word or phrase.

1. The total market value of all final goods and services produced annually in an economy is called _____.
2. The total market value of all final goods and services produced annually by the citizens of a country, no matter where in the world they reside, is called _____.
3. Counting a good more than once in computing GDP is called _____.
4. The household sector makes expenditures called _____.
5. The business sector makes expenditures called _____.
6. Real GDP is measured in _____ prices.
7. The _____ shows the quantity of goods and services that buyers are willing and able to buy at different price levels.
8. _____ and _____ go together to determine the equilibrium price level and the equilibrium quantity of goods and services in an economy.
9. _____ is GDP that has been adjusted for price changes.
10. _____ refers to expenditures made by the household sector.
11. Expenditures made by the business sector are called _____.

Review Questions

1. Define and give examples of the following:
   a. consumption
   b. investment
   c. government purchases
2. Why does the GDP omit government transfer payments?
3. What is the difference between GDP and GNP?
4. Why does GDP omit illegal transactions?
5. Why does GDP omit stock transactions?
6. What is the difference between an intermediate good and a final good?
7. Why does an economist prefer to work with real GDP figures over GDP figures?
8. What is a consumer unit?
9. Which spending component of GDP is the largest?
10. What happens to GDP if import spending rises and no other spending component of GDP changes?

Calculations

1. Using the following data, compute the GDP: consumption = $3,212 billion; government purchases = $800 billion; export spending = $230 billion; import spending = $127 billion; and investment = $654 billion.
2. A tiny economy produces 10 units of good X and 15 units of good Y. Base-year prices for these goods are $1 and $2, respectively. Current-year prices for these goods are $2 and $3. What is the CPI?
3. Using the data in Question 2, what does real GDP equal?
4. In Exhibit 12-8 on page 328, change the prices in column 2 to $14 for CDs and $6 for T-shirts. Change the prices in column 4 to $17 for CDs and $8 for T-shirts. Now calculate the CPI.
5. The CPI is 143 in year 1 and 132 in year 2. By what percentage have prices fallen?

Graphs

Look at Exhibit 12-12. For each letter (A, B, C, etc.), provide the correct dollar amount.

Exhibit 12-12

Goods in market basket	Price in base year	Base-year expenditure	Price in current year	Current-year expenditure
10 x	$4	B	C	$50
12 y	A	$120	$12	D

Total dollar expenditure on market basket in current year = E

Total dollar expenditure on market basket in base year = F

Economics and Thinking Skills

1. **Application.** The market basket the government uses to compute the CPI may have different goods in it than your own market basket. How would you go about computing the CPI for your market basket? Explain your answer.
2. **Cause and Effect.** Does a higher GDP cause higher prices, or do higher prices cause a higher GDP? Explain your answer.

Writing Skills

Find a recent copy of the *Economic Report of the President* in your library or on the Internet
http://www.gpo.ucop.edu/catalog/erp00.html
(Note that you should put the last two digits of the current year in the spot where *00* now appears in the address.) The report contains chapters on different economic topics. Choose one of the chapters to read; then write a two-page paper that briefly explains the content of the chapter.

Economics in the Media

1. Find a story or article in your local newspaper that addresses one of the following: GDP, real GDP, CPI, consumption spending, investment spending, or government spending. Explain what was said in the story or article.

Where's the Economics?

This woman is trimming the hedges in her yard. If she paid a gardener to trim them, would GDP rise? Explain your answer.

Analyzing Primary Sources

The Bureau of Labor Statistics publishes the consumer price index. In one of its online publications
http://stats.bls.gov/cpifaq.htm
it answered some commonly asked questions about the CPI. Here is an excerpt:

1. *What is the CPI?*
   The Consumer Price Index (CPI) is a measure of the average change over time in the prices paid by urban consumers for a fixed market basket of consumer goods and services from A to Z. The CPI provides a way for consumers to compare what the market basket of goods and services costs this month with what the same market basket cost a month or a year ago.
2. *Is the CPI a cost-of-living index?*
   No, although it frequently and mistakenly is called a cost-of-living index. The CPI is an index of price change only. It does not reflect the changes in buying or consumption patterns that consumers probably would make to adjust to relative price changes.
3. *What goods and services does the CPI cover?*
   The CPI represents all goods and services purchased for consumption by urban households. We have classified all expenditure items into over 200 categories, arranged into 8 major groups. In addition, the CPI includes various user fees such as water and sewerage charges, auto registration fees, vehicle tolls, and so forth. Taxes that are directly associated with the prices of specific goods and services (such as sales and excise taxes) are also included. But, the CPI excludes taxes not directly associated with the purchase of consumer goods and services (such as income and Social Security taxes).

   The CPI does not include investment items (such as stocks, bonds, real estate, and life insurance). These items relate to savings and not day-to-day living expenses.

   For each of the over 200 item categories, the Bureau has chosen samples of several hundred specific items within selected business establishments, using scientific statistical procedures, to represent the thousands of varieties available in the marketplace. For example, in a given supermarket, the Bureau may choose a plastic bag of golden delicious apples, U.S. extra fancy grade, weighing 4.4 pounds to represent the "Apples" category.
4. *How are CPI prices collected and reviewed?*
   Each month, Bureau of Labor Statistics (BLS) field representatives visit or call thousands of retail stores, service establishments, rental units, and doctors' offices, all over the United States to obtain price information on thousands of items in the CPI market basket.

Questions to Answer

1. Are sales and excise taxes included in computing the CPI?
2. Why doesn't the CPI include spending on stocks, bonds, real estate, and life insurance?
3. How many times a year does the Bureau of Labor Statistics collect price information necessary to compute the CPI?

CHAPTER 13

Inflation, Deflation, and Unemployment

What This Chapter Is About

The United States has experienced inflation, deflation, low unemployment, high unemployment, and moderate unemployment. This chapter will identify some of the causes and effects of inflation, deflation, and unemployment.

Why This Chapter Is Important

Economists say that an understanding of economics will not keep you out of the unemployment line, but if you're there, at least you'll know why. The same is true for inflation and deflation. An understanding of economics will not help you avoid rising or falling prices, but at least you will know why they are rising or falling. Sometimes understanding the *why* of things can be very satisfying.

After You Study This Chapter, You Will Be Able To

- explain what inflation is.
- measure the inflation rate.
- discuss a few specific causes of demand-side and supply-side inflation.
- identify the general conditions necessary for inflation to occur.
- explain what deflation is.
- explain the differences between frictional, structural, natural, and cyclical unemployment.
- explain why full employment does not correspond to zero unemployment.
- identify the relationship between a fall in aggregate demand and the unemployment rate.

You Will Also Learn What Economics Has to Do With

- prices in Germany that rose by 41% a day in 1923.
- grade inflation.
- standing in line in Cuba.

Economics Journal

Identify ten goods that you have purchased over the last year. Next, identify which goods you think have gone up, down, or remained unchanged in price over the past few months. Have more goods gone up in price than have gone down or stayed constant?

SECTION 1

Inflation

This section defines inflation, shows how it is measured, and discusses its causes and effects. As you read this section, keep these key questions in mind:

- What is inflation?
- How is inflation measured?
- What causes inflation?
- What are the effects of inflation?

You might more easily remember that *inflation* means the average price level is increasing if you think of what happens to hot air balloons when you *inflate* them (they go up).

Key Terms

inflation
demand-side inflation
supply-side inflation
velocity
simple quantity theory of money
hedge

What Is Inflation?

Because there are many goods in an economy, there are many prices in an economy (the price of apples, of cars, of pencils, of computers, and so on). An average of all these prices is called the *price level*. When someone says that the price level has increased, it means that the prices of goods produced and sold in the economy are higher, on average. It does not necessarily mean that every single price is higher—only that on average, prices are higher.

Inflation is defined as an increase in the price level. Stated a little differently, inflation is an increase in the average level of prices.

How Do We Measure Inflation?

How is it determined whether the economy has experienced inflation? If the price level has increased, then there has been inflation; if it has not increased, there has not been inflation.

Chapter 12 explained that the consumer price index (CPI) is used to measure the price level. Suppose the CPI last year was 110, and the CPI this year is also 110. Has there been inflation between the two years? The answer is no, because the price level (as measured by the CPI) has not increased.

Suppose, though, that the CPI was 110 last year and is 121 this year. There now has been inflation between the two years, because the CPI has risen.

We can find the inflation rate between two years by using the same formula we used in Chapter 12 to find the percentage change in the CPI:

$$\text{Inflation rate} = \frac{\text{CPI in later year} - \text{CPI in earlier year}}{\text{CPI in earlier year}} \times 100$$

MINI GLOSSARY

inflation
An increase in the price level, or average level of prices.

Filling in the numbers, we get the following:

$$\text{Inflation rate} = \frac{121 - 110}{110} \times 100 = 10\%$$

Because there is a positive change (rise) in the CPI, there is inflation; the inflation rate is 10 percent.

Demand-Side Versus Supply-Side Inflation

Chapters 3 and 4 discussed supply and demand in a market setting. When the demand for a good increases and supply remains the same, price increases; and when the supply of a good decreases and demand remains the same, price increases. Chapter 12 introduced the concept of supply and demand in an economy. The demand side of the economy was represented by aggregate demand, and the supply side of the economy was represented by aggregate supply.

Inflation, which is an increase in the price level, can originate on either the demand side or the supply side of the economy. Consider Exhibit 13-1a, which depicts an aggregate demand curve (AD_1) and an aggregate supply curve (AS_1). The equilibrium price level is P_1. Suppose aggregate demand increases; the aggregate demand curve shifts rightward, from AD_1 to AD_2. Consequently, the price level increases, from P_1 to P_2. Because the price level has increased, there is inflation. We conclude that if aggregate demand increases and aggregate supply stays the same, inflation will occur. When an increase in the price level originates on the demand side of the economy, economists call it **demand-side inflation.**

demand-side inflation
An increase in the price level that originates on the demand side of the economy.

Exhibit 13-1
Inflation

Inflation is an increase in the price level. An increase in the price level can be caused by an increase in aggregate demand, or AD (shown in Part a), or by a decrease in aggregate supply, or AS (shown in Part b). When an increase in the price level originates on the demand side of the economy, it is called *demand-side inflation;* when it originates on the supply side of the economy, it is called *supply-side inflation.*

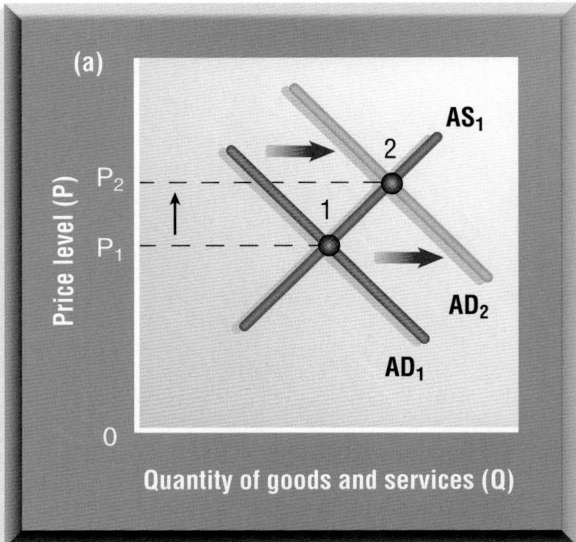

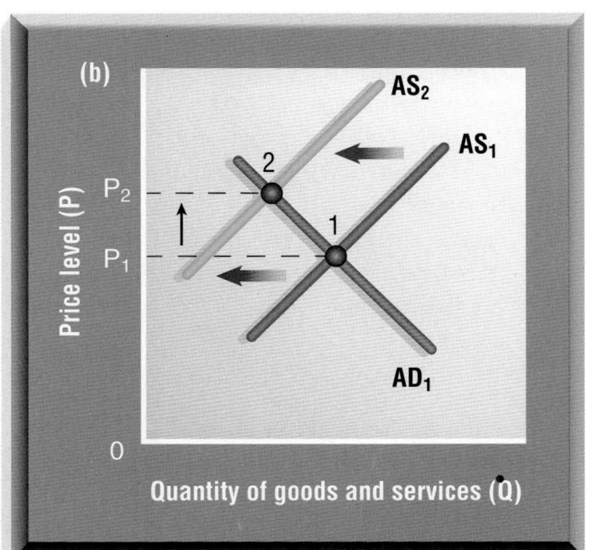

One of the things that can cause demand-side inflation is an increase in the money supply. For example, suppose the Fed increases the money supply. The result is more money in the economy, and demand in the economy rises. As a consequence of the increased demand, the price level increases.

Exhibit 13-1b shows a decrease in aggregate supply, from AS_1 to AS_2. As a result of this decrease, the price level increases, from P_1 to P_2. Again, because the price level has increased, there is inflation. Thus, if aggregate supply decreases and aggregate demand stays the same, inflation will occur. An increase in the price level that originates on the supply side of the economy is called **supply-side inflation.** One of the things that can cause supply-side inflation is a major drought that lowers the output of agricultural goods. As a result the supply of goods in the economy is smaller, and the price level increases.

supply-side inflation
An increase in the price level that originates on the supply side of the economy.

How might dry, parched soil be related to the amount of money this man has to pay for certain goods?

Question: *Can there still be inflation if both aggregate demand and aggregate supply increase?*

Answer: *Yes, if aggregate demand increases by more than aggregate supply increases. For example, look at Exhibit 13-2. Initially, the economy is at point 1, and the price level is P_1. Then both the increasing aggregate demand curve and the increasing aggregate supply curve shift rightward, to AD_2 and AS_2, respectively. Notice, though, that aggregate demand increases more; its curve shifts rightward by more than the aggregate supply curve shifts rightward. In this case the price level increases from P_1 to P_2, and there is inflation.*

Exhibit 13-2
Aggregate Demand Increases by More Than Aggregate Supply

When aggregate demand AD increases by more than aggregate supply (AS), the price level (P) increases; we have inflation.

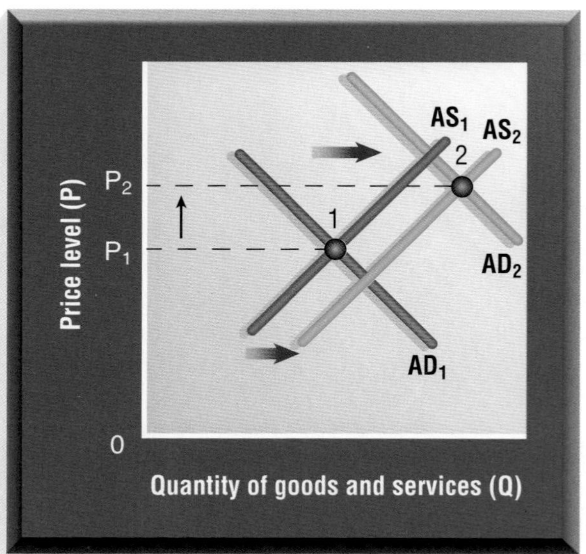

Grade Inflation: When Is a B+ No Better Than a C?

Inflation can sometimes be deceptive. To illustrate, suppose that Lavotka produces and sells motorcycles. The average price for one of his motorcycles is $10,000. Unknown to Lavotka, the Fed increases the money supply. Months pass, and then one day Lavotka notices that the demand for his motorcycles has increased. He raises the price of his motorcycles and earns a higher dollar income.

Lavotka is excited about earning more income, but he soon realizes that the prices of many of the things he buys have increased, too. Food, clothing, and housing prices have all gone up. Lavotka is earning a higher dollar income, but he is also paying higher prices. In relative terms, his financial position may be the same as it was before he increased the price of his motorcycles; for example, if his income went up by 10 percent, and prices also increased by 10 percent, he would be no better off.

Grade inflation also exists. Suppose that instead of teachers giving out the full range of grades, A through F, they start to give out only grades A through C. As a result, the average grade given out rises, and there is grade inflation. (Just as price inflation is a higher average price, grade inflation is a higher average grade.)

Grade inflation can be just as deceiving as price inflation. To illustrate, suppose you get higher grades without studying more. Your average grade goes from a C to a B+. Your relative standing in school has not gone up, however, unless only your grades, and no one else's grades, have risen (or your grades have risen by more than other persons' grades). Because everyone is getting higher grades, you may just be maintaining your relative position. In other words, if you are now earning a B+ instead of a C, other people may be earning an A instead of a B+. In a class of thirty students, with the teacher giving out the full range of grades (A through F), you might have been ranked tenth in the class. Now, in the same class of students, with the teacher giving only grades A through C, you might be earning higher grades but still be ranked 10th in the class.

QUESTION TO ANSWER What do you think might be the cause of grade inflation?

The Simple Quantity Theory of Money

The simple quantity theory of money presents a clear picture of what causes inflation. Before examining this theory, though, we must know something about velocity and the exchange equation.

MINI GLOSSARY

velocity
The average number of times a dollar is spent to buy final goods and services in a year.

simple quantity theory of money
A theory that predicts that changes in the price level will be strictly proportional to changes in the money supply.

Velocity The average number of times a dollar is spent to buy final goods and services is called **velocity.** To illustrate the concept of velocity, consider a tiny economy with only five \$1 bills. In January, the first of the \$1 bills moves from Maria's hands to Nancy's hands to buy a newspaper. Then, in June, it goes from Nancy's hands to Bob's hands to buy a bagel. And in December, it goes from Bob's hands to Tu's hands to buy a used paperback book. Over the course of the year, this \$1 bill has changed hands three times. The other \$1 bills also change hands during the year. The second bill changes hands five times; the third, six times; the fourth, three times; and the fifth, three times. Given this information, we can calculate the number of times the average dollar changes hands in purchases. We do so by finding the sum of the times each dollar changed hands ($3 + 5 + 6 + 3 + 3 = 20$ times) and then dividing by the number of dollars (5). The answer is 4, which is the velocity in this example.

The Exchange Equation This is the exchange equation:

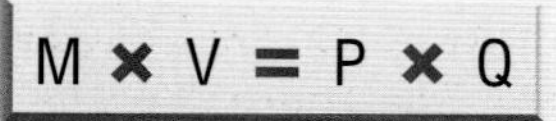

M stands for the money supply, P stands for the price level or average price, Q stands for the quantity of output (quantity of goods and services), and V stands for velocity. M times V must equal P times Q. To see why, think of the equation on a personal basis. Suppose you have \$40; this is your money supply (M). You spend the \$40 one time, so velocity (V) is 1. You spend the \$40 on 5 books, so 5 is the quantity of goods and services you purchase—it is your Q in the exchange equation. Now ask yourself what P must equal, given that M is \$40, V is 1, and Q is 5. If you spend \$40 on 5 books, the average price per book must be \$8. P must be \$8, because \$8 times 5 books equals \$40. Here is the exchange equation using the numbers in this example:

$$M(\$40) \times V(1) = P(\$8) \times Q(5 \text{ books})$$

$$\$40 = \$40$$

THINKING Like an Economist

Economists use a three-step approach. First, they find something they want to explain. Second, they construct a theory to try to explain it. Third, they seek out real-world evidence that will tell them whether the theory is correct.

Look at this three-step approach in light of our discussion of inflation. First, economists wanted to discover what causes inflation. Second, they constructed the simple quantity theory of money to explain inflation. (The theory held that inflation is caused by increases in the money supply.) Third, they gathered evidence that would either support the theory or disprove it. This approach—find something to explain, construct a theory to explain it, and then gather evidence to see whether the theory is correct—is used by economists in many situations.

The Simple Quantity Theory of Money The **simple quantity theory of money** is used to explain inflation. It predicts that changes in the price level will be strictly proportional to changes in the money supply. The theory begins by making two assumptions: that velocity (V) is constant and that the quantity of output or goods and services (Q) is constant. Let's set V at 2 and Q at 100 units.

These numbers will remain constant throughout our discussion.

Suppose the money supply (M) equals \$500. If V is 2 and Q is 100 units, then the price level must equal \$10:

$$M(\$500) \times V(2) = P(\$10) \times Q(100 \text{ units})$$
$$\$1{,}000 = \$1{,}000$$

Now suppose the money supply increases from \$500 to \$1,000, a doubling of the money supply. As stated earlier, velocity and output are constant. Velocity (V) is still 2, and output (Q) is still 100 units. The price level (P), however, increases to \$20:

$$M(\$1{,}000) \times V(2) = P(\$20) \times Q(100 \text{ units})$$
$$\$2{,}000 = \$2{,}000$$

In other words, if the money supply doubles (from \$500 to \$1,000), the price level doubles (from \$10 to \$20; see Exhibit 13-4 on the next page). This result is what the simple quantity theory of money predicts: changes in the money supply will bring about strictly proportional changes in the price level. For example, if the money supply increases by 100 percent, the price level will increase by 100 percent; and if the money supply increases by 20 percent, the price level will increase by 20 percent. Early economic writers used the simple quantity theory of money to explain inflation. The theory states that inflation (an increase in the price level) is caused by an increase in the money supply.

Predict what will happen to the price level as a result of each of the following.

a. The money supply decreases.
b. Velocity increases.
c. The quantity of goods and services decreases.

Exhibit 13-3
Money and Prices

According to the simple quantity theory of money, if velocity and the quantity of output are constant, more money leads to higher prices.

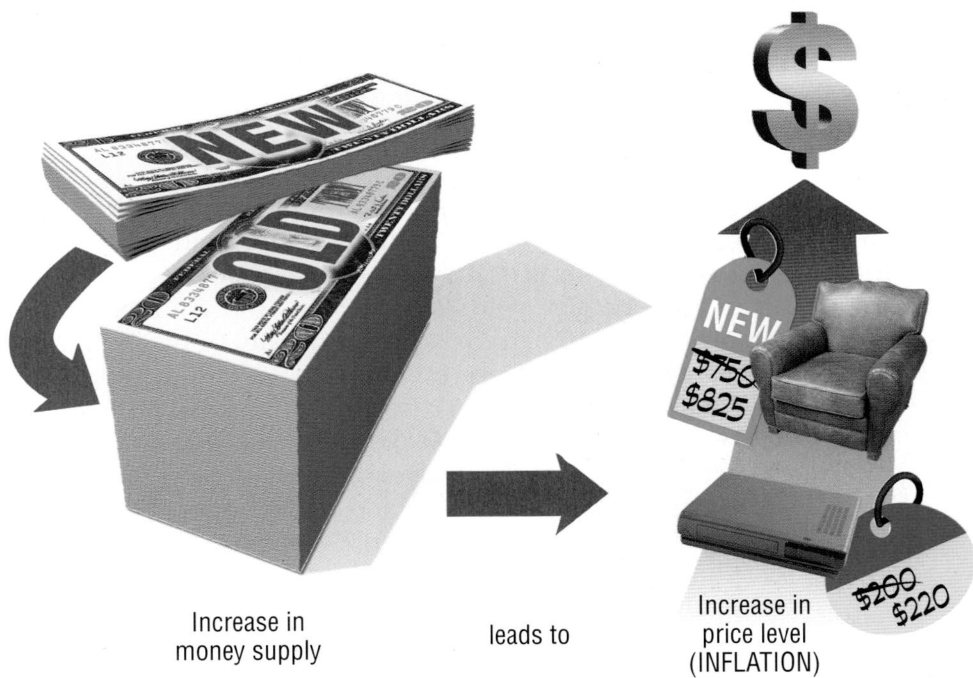

Exhibit 13-4
The Simple Quantity Theory of Money

This exhibit outlines the basics of the simple quantity theory of money. Start with $M \times V = P \times Q$. Then, if V and Q are held constant, it follows that a change in the money supply (M) will lead to a proportional change in the price level (P). The numbers used in the exhibit support this conclusion.

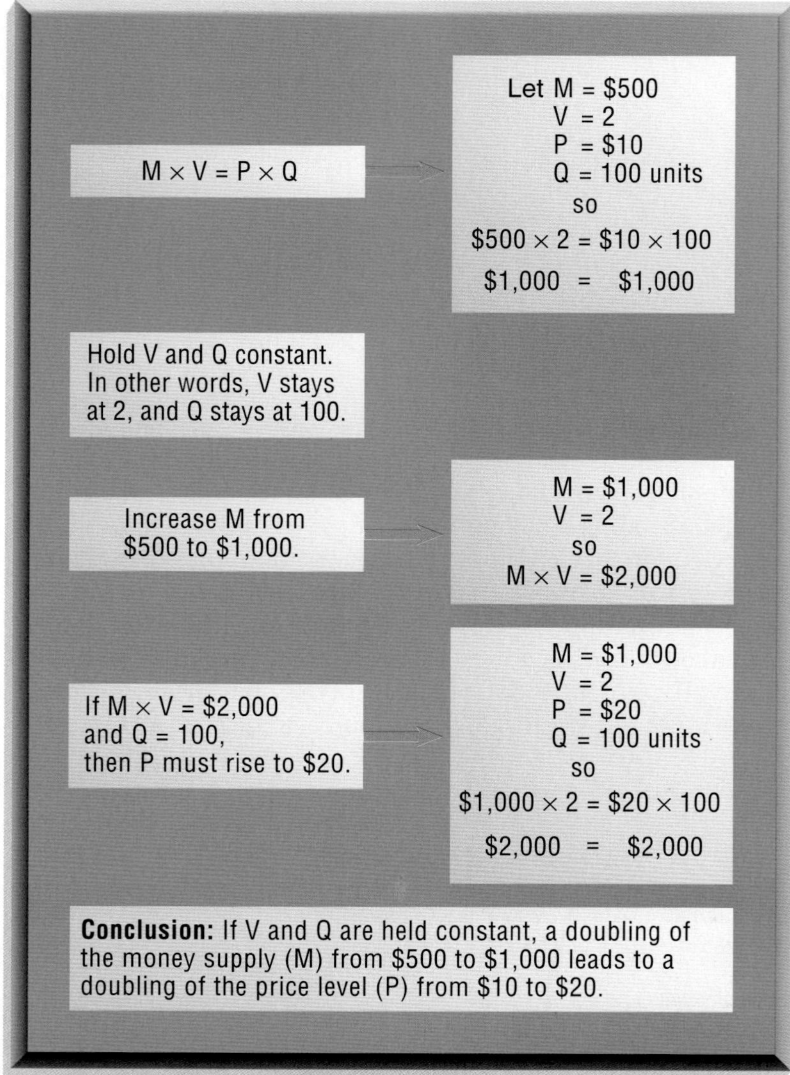

Real-World Applications The simple quantity theory of money predicts that changes in the money supply will bring about *strictly proportional* changes in the price level. In the real world, however, this strict proportionality does not usually hold. An increase in the money supply of, say, 10 percent does not usually bring about a 10 percent increase in the price level.

Usually, *the greater the increase in the money supply, the greater the increase in the price level.* For example, a nation that increased its money supply by 30 percent would usually have a greater increase in its price level (its inflation rate) than a nation that increased its money supply by 20 percent. This finding is consistent with the "spirit" of the simple quantity theory of money. After all, the theory says that changes in the money supply bring about strictly proportional changes in the price level, so it follows that larger changes in the money supply should bring about larger changes in the price level.

A Tripling of Prices Each Day

Suppose you woke in the morning and decided to buy an apple. You paid 25 cents for the apple. Later that day the price for an apple was 50 cents. Still later in the day, the price was 75 cents. A world in which prices rise dramatically during a day sounds unbelievable, but some people have lived in such conditions.

When the price level rises sharply and quickly, economists say that there is *hyperinflation* (very high inflation). Generally, economists reserve the word *hyperinflation* to describe episodes where the monthly inflation rate is greater than 50 percent. At this rate, what cost \$1 would cost \$130 a year later.

To a large extent, hyperinflation first started appearing only in the twentieth century. For example, in 1923 prices in Germany were rising by 41 percent a day. In 1946 in Hungary, prices were tripling each day.

Hyperinflation is caused by an extremely large and rapid growth in the supply of money. Think of things in terms of the simple quantity theory of money. In the short run, velocity and the quantity of goods and services are nearly constant, so changes in the price level are strictly proportional to changes in the money supply. If the money supply rises by, say, 1,000 percent, there is likely to be a change in the price level of around 1,000 percent.

During the German hyperinflation, the supply of money increased by a factor of 7.32×10^9. During the Hungarian hyperinflation, the supply of money increased by a factor of 1.19×10^{25}. In the past, a government might increase the supply of money by such a large percentage to pay for government expenditures.

One effect of hyperinflation is that employees would rather be paid in goods than in money. Would you want to be paid in money if the prices of the goods you wanted were rising very fast? During the hyperinflation in Germany, employees were paid twice a day, and they would shop in the middle of the workday, before the money they were paid with would lose any more value.

Another effect of hyperinflation is that it destroys the wealth of many people. People can hold their wealth in money or in goods. People who hold a lot of their wealth in the form of money lose much of that wealth through hyperinflation. To illustrate, suppose you have \$100,000 in a savings account. A hyperinflation rate of 50 percent a month lowers the value of that \$100,000 by 50 percent each month.

Costantino Bresciani-Turroni, an Italian economist, has argued that the German hyperinflation destroyed much of the wealth of the middle classes in Germany and so made it easier for the Nazis to gain power. If Bresciani-Turroni is correct, it follows that rapid increases in the money supply are more destructive than anyone could imagine.

QUESTION TO ANSWER Money functions as a store of value, a medium of exchange, and a unit of account. Which function is most likely to diminish or be eliminated by hyperinflation?

Many senior citizens have a fixed income. Why is this a problem during periods of inflation?

The Effects of Inflation

We tend to think that inflation affects only the buyer of goods, as when a person pays $60 instead of $50 a week for groceries. In truth, however, people are affected by inflation in many other ways as well.

Inflation and Individuals on Fixed Incomes Denise has lived on a fixed income for the last ten years; that is, every year for the past ten years, her income has been the same. However, each year for the past ten years, the price level has increased; there has been inflation. Thus inflation has lowered the purchasing power of Denise's money. She can buy fewer units of goods with a given amount of money than she could previously buy, and her material standard of living is reduced.

Inflation and Savers On January 1, Lorenzo puts $2,000 into a savings account that pays 6 percent interest. On December 31, he removes $2,120 from the account ($2,000, which is the original amount, and $120 in interest). Suppose that during the year prices have not increased at all (the inflation rate is 0 percent). Saving has made Lorenzo better off, because at the end of the year he can purchase $120 more of goods and services than he could at the beginning of the year.

Now suppose instead that during the year, prices increased by 10 percent (the inflation rate was 10 percent). How much money would Lorenzo need at the end of the year to buy exactly what $2,000 could buy at the beginning of the year? If prices had increased by 10 percent, he would need 10 percent more money, or a total of $2,200. But instead of having $2,200, Lorenzo has only $2,120 from his savings account; he must settle for purchasing $80 less of goods and services than he could at the beginning of the year. Because the inflation rate (10 percent) was greater than the interest rate (6 percent) that Lorenzo earned on his savings, he ended up worse off. It is clear that inflation hurts savers.

If inflation persists, however, it is customary for financial institutions to compete for customers by offering an interest rate that has been adjusted upward by the inflation rate. Suppose financial institutions would offer a 4 percent interest rate next year if prices were going to stay the same as this year (that is, if there were no inflation). However, they anticipate a 5 percent inflation rate during the year. Many institutions will begin to compete for customers by offering a 9 percent interest rate, the sum of the interest rate they would offer if prices did not change and the anticipated inflation rate (4% + 5% = 9%).

Suppose someone tells you that she paid $30,000 for a house in 1960. That sounds like very little to pay for a house, but 1960 was a long time ago, when prices were not as high as they are today.

To figure out what you would have to pay today to buy the same house that was bought in 1960 for $30,000, go to http://woodrow.mpls.frb.fed.us/economy/calc/cpihome.html on the World Wide Web.

There you will find the "Consumer Price Index Inflation Calculator." Click on it, and fill in the relevant data. Then answer this question: What would you have to pay in the most recent year identified to buy the same house that was bought for $30,000 in 1960?

Standing in Line in Cuba

Consider a mythical land where all prices are set by government officials. A haircut is $5, a quart of milk is $1, and a watch is $40. Now suppose that in this mythical land the monetary authority sharply increases the money supply. According to the simple quantity theory of money, we would expect the prices of goods and services to rise soon. For example, a haircut might rise to $10, a quart of milk to $2.50, and so on.

Remember, though, that in this mythical land government officials set all prices. If they do not want the price of a haircut to rise, they will not raise it. No matter how much money the monetary authority puts into circulation, the price of a haircut stays at $5.

In this mythical land, there is no inflation, because prices are not permitted to rise. No matter how much the money supply grows, prices remain constant.

This mythical land is not really so mythical. Any country in the world where prices and wages are set by government edict—in other words, any country with widespread price controls—is this mythical land.

One such place is Cuba. Most prices and wages there are set by government officials. Markets do not determine prices through the forces of supply and demand; government officials do. They decide what milk will cost, what bread will cost, and so on.

In recent years the government of Cuba has claimed that the Cuban economy has experienced no inflation. Of course, there is no way it could have inflation, given that prices are not permitted to rise. It would be like having a fever and a broken thermometer. No matter how high your fever, your temperature always registers 98.6 on the thermometer. Does it follow that because your fever is not registering on the thermometer, you do not really have a fever? Not at all.

In countries where prices are set and cannot legally rise, inflation takes a particular form. Instead of prices rising, there are longer lines of people waiting to buy goods. Instead of prices rationing goods, the first-come-first-served (FCFS) rule rations goods. In a world where FCFS is used as a rationing device, long lines of people appear.

In some countries inflation is measured by the percentage increase in the price level. In Cuba, however, inflation has to be measured by the length of the line of people demanding to buy goods. The longer the line, the higher the "inflation rate."

QUESTION TO ANSWER Would you rather have inflation register as higher prices or longer lines? Explain your answer.

Some people try to offset the effects of inflation by buying goods such as gold and fine art.

Inflation and Past Decisions

Inflation often turns past decisions into mistakes. Consider the building contractor who last year signed a contract to build a shopping mall for $30 million. He agreed to this dollar figure based on his estimates of what it would cost to buy the materials and hire the labor to build the mall. He estimated $28 million in costs. All of a sudden, inflation hits. Prices of labor, concrete, nails, tile, and roofing rise. Now the contractor realizes it will cost him $31 million to build the mall. He looks back on his decision to build the mall for only $30 million as a mistake—a costly mistake for him.

MINI GLOSSARY

hedge
To try to avoid or lessen a loss by taking some counterbalancing action.

Inflation and Hedging against Inflation What do individuals in an inflation-prone economy do that individuals in a stable-price economy do not do? They try to **hedge** against inflation. In hedging, people try to avoid or lessen a loss by taking some counterbalancing action. They try to figure out what investments offer the best protection against inflation. Would gold, real estate, or fine art be the best hedge? People travel to distant cities to hear "experts" talk on inflation. They subscribe to numerous newsletters that claim to predict future inflation rates accurately. All this action obviously requires an expenditure of resources. Resources, we remind ourselves, that are expended in the effort to protect against inflation can no longer be used to build factories or produce houses, shoes, or cars. Thus, one effect of inflation is that it causes individuals to try to hedge against it, thereby diverting resources away from being used to produce goods.

Section 1 Review

Defining Terms

1. Define
   a. inflation
   b. demand-side inflation
   c. supply-side inflation
   d. velocity
   e. simple quantity theory of money
   f. hedge

Reviewing Facts and Concepts

2. The CPI is 167 in year 1 and 189 in year 2. What is the inflation rate between the two years?
3. "An increase in the money supply is more likely to cause supply-side inflation than demand-side inflation." Do you agree or disagree? Explain your answer.
4. If financial institutions do not compensate savers for inflation, what effect does inflation have on savers?

Critical Thinking

5. A theory that predicts that changes in the money supply bring about strictly proportional changes in the price level also predicts that larger changes in the money supply should bring about larger changes in the price level. Do you agree or disagree? Explain your answer.

Applying Economic Concepts

6. The simple quantity theory of money assumes that velocity and the quantity of goods and services are constant. Suppose we drop the latter assumption, and something happens so that the quantity of goods and services in the economy falls. What will happen to the price level?

SECTION 2

Deflation

This section discusses deflation. As you read this section, keep these key questions in mind:

- What is deflation?
- What causes deflation?

Deflating a hot air balloon has the same effect on a balloon that *deflation* has on prices (they go down).

What Is Deflation?

Key Term
deflation

Deflation is the opposite of inflation. **Deflation** is defined as a decrease in the price level, or the average level of prices. We measure deflation the same way we measured inflation, by finding the percentage change in prices or the CPI between years. For example, suppose the CPI in year 1 is 150, and it is 145 in year 2. What is the change in the CPI? Here is the formula again:

deflation
A decrease in the price level, or average level of prices.

$$\text{Deflation rate} = \frac{\text{CPI in later year} - \text{CPI in earlier year}}{\text{CPI in earlier year}} \times 100$$

Filling in the numbers yields the following:

$$\text{Deflation rate} = \frac{145 - 150}{150} \times 100 = -3.3\%$$

Because there is a negative change in the CPI (downward), there is deflation. The deflation rate is 3.3 percent.

AD/AS and Deflation

Just like inflation, deflation can originate on either the demand side or the supply side of the economy. Consider Exhibit 13-5a on the next page, which shows an aggregate demand curve (AD_1), and an aggregate supply curve (AS_1). The equilibrium price level is P_1. Suppose the aggregate demand curve decreases and shifts from AD_1 to AD_2. Consequently, the price level decreases from P_1 to P_2. Because the price level has decreased, we have deflation. We conclude that if aggregate demand decreases and aggregate supply stays the same, deflation will occur. One of the things that can

Exhibit 13-5
Deflation

Deflation can be caused by a decrease in aggregate demand (shown in Part a), or by an increase in aggregate supply (shown in Part b).

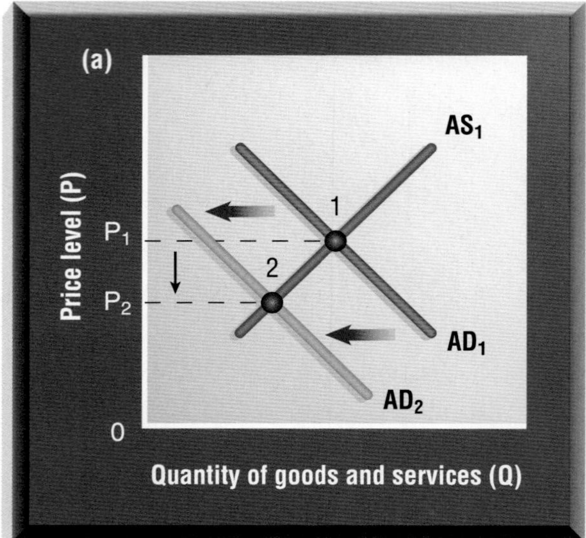

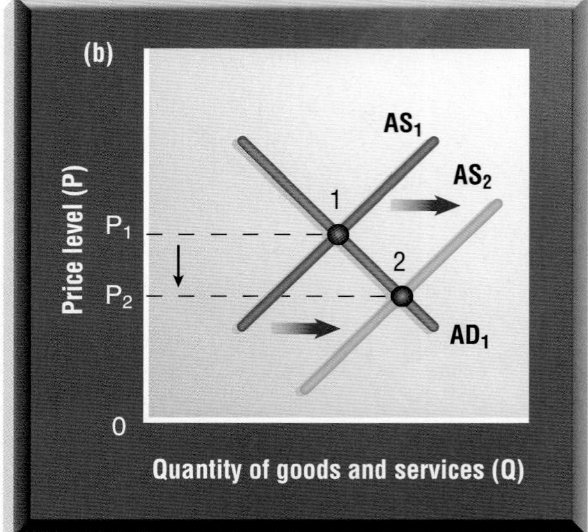

cause aggregate demand to fall is a decrease in the money supply, so a decrease in the money supply can cause deflation.

Next, consider an increase in aggregate supply, from AS_1 to AS_2 in Exhibit 13-5b. As a result, the price level drops from P_1 to P_2. Again, because the price level has decreased, we have deflation. If aggregate supply increases and aggregate demand stays the same, deflation will occur. One of the things that can cause deflation (from the supply side) is an increase in technology that makes it possible to produce more goods and services with the same level of resources.

Simple Quantity Theory of Money and Deflation

Just as the simple quantity theory of money can be used to explain inflation, it can be used to explain deflation, too. Suppose the money supply (M) equals \$500, velocity (V) equals 2, and quantity of goods and services (Q) is 100 units. We know that M × V must equal P × Q, so the price level (P) must equal \$10.

$$M(\$500) \times V(2) = P(\$10) \times Q(100 \text{ units})$$
$$\$1{,}000 = \$1{,}000$$

Suppose the money supply drops to \$250, all other things remaining the same. What happens to the price level? It must drop to \$5:

$$M(\$250) \times V(2) = P(\$5) \times Q(100 \text{ units})$$

In other words, a fall in the money supply will bring about deflation (assuming that velocity and the quantity of goods and services do not change).

A Major Effect of Deflation

When prices fall, they do not all fall at the same time. This situation often presents a problem. For example, suppose Latoya produces wooden

If the price of wooden tables falls, but the price of glue and wood remain the same, these workers may lose their jobs. Explain.

tables. To produce wooden tables, she needs wood, glue, and laborers. In short, in her business Latoya is interested in four prices: the prices of wooden tables, wood, glue, and laborers. She is interested in the price of wooden tables because this relates to her total revenue. For example, if the price of wooden tables is $100 and she sells 50, her total revenue is $5,000. But if the price of wooden tables is lower, at $40, her total revenue is $4,000.

Latoya is interested in the price of wood, glue, and laborers because these prices relate to her total cost. The higher these prices, the higher her overall costs.

Suppose that the money supply in the economy drops, and deflation occurs. Furthermore, not all prices fall at the same time. The price of wooden tables falls first, and the prices of wood, glue, and laborers fall many months later.

What happens to Latoya as a result of the price of wooden tables falling but the prices of wood, glue, and laborers staying constant (for a few months)? Her total revenue falls, but her total costs stay the same. As a result, her profits fall—so much that Latoya ends up getting out of the business of producing wooden tables. She closes up shop, lays off the workers she currently employs, and looks for different work.

In short, when prices do not fall at the same time, deflation can lead to firms going out of business and workers being laid off. Because it is unusual for all prices to fall at the same time, these results are common in deflation.

Section 2 Review

Defining Terms

1. Define *deflation.*

Reviewing Facts and Concepts

2. Are inflation and deflation measured the same way? Explain your answer.
3. Explain how a change in aggregate demand and aggregate supply can cause deflation.

Critical Thinking

4. Suppose there are ten goods in an economy, and the prices of four goods go down while the prices of six goods go up. From the information given, is it possible to determine whether inflation or deflation has occurred? Explain your answer.

Applying Economic Concepts

5. What does deflation do to the value of money? Illustrate your answer with an example.

SECTION 3

Unemployment

Many people seem to think that unemployment is avoidable. If we could only implement the "correct" economic policies, some people argue, the unemployment rate (as it is now measured) would drop to 0 percent. That thought is pure fantasy, as this section explains. The text also discusses four categories of unemployment: frictional, structural, natural, and cyclical.

As you read this section, keep these key questions in mind:

- What is frictional unemployment?
- What is structural unemployment?
- What is natural unemployment?
- What is cyclical unemployment?
- How is aggregate demand related to the unemployment rate?

Key Terms

frictional unemployment
structural unemployment
natural unemployment
full employment
cyclical unemployment

The Unemployment Rate

Suppose the unemployment rate is 6%. If there are 140 million persons in the civilian labor force, how many are unemployed?

Chapter 8 showed how the government calculates the unemployment rate:

$$\text{Unemployment rate} = \frac{\text{Unemployed persons}}{\text{Civilian labor force}}$$

For example, if the number of persons unemployed is 5 million and the labor force is 100 million, then the unemployment rate is 5 percent. It is this unemployment rate that you will read about in a newspaper or hear mentioned on a news show. Sometimes it is referred to as the *official unemployment rate.*

Look again at the numerator of the unemployment rate, "unemployed persons." Suppose this number is 5 million. Not every one of the 5 million unemployed persons is unemployed for the same reason. In economics, there are three different categories of unemployed persons. Persons are said to be frictionally unemployed, structurally unemployed, or cyclically unemployed.

Frictional Unemployment

Every day in the United States, people make millions of buying decisions. Consequently, the demand for some goods is rising, and the demand for other goods is falling.

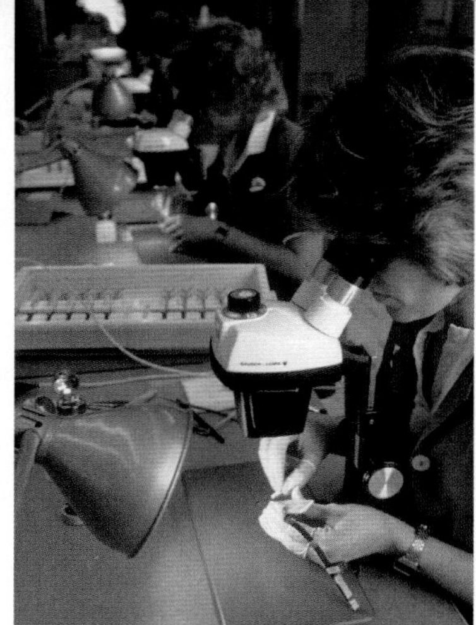

A frictionally unemployed worker has skills that will transfer, for example, from one electronics company to another.

This shifting affects the number of people producing different goods. To illustrate, suppose there are two goods: Dell computers and Compaq computers. During April, the demand for Compaq computers rises, and the demand for Dell computers falls. As a result, Dell decides to fire some workers, and Compaq decides to hire some additional workers.

Suppose you are a worker fired from Dell. In time, you may find work at Compaq (doing what you did at Dell), but in the meantime you are said to be *frictionally unemployed.* **Frictional unemployment** occurs when a person is unemployed as a result of changing market (demand) conditions and has transferable skills.

Frictional unemployment will always exist, because there will always be changing market conditions; the demand for some goods will increase as the demand for other goods decreases. Frictional unemployment is simply the result of buyers expressing their freedom to buy what they want when they want it. As long as buyers have freedom, some people will be unemployed.

frictional unemployment The condition of workers who have lost their jobs because of changing market (demand) conditions and who have transferable skills.

Structural Unemployment

Now consider an example with Compaq, which produces computers, and Ford Motor Company, which produces cars. In April, the demand for Compaq computers rises, and the demand for Ford cars falls. Compaq begins to hire additional workers, and Ford fires some workers. A worker fired by Ford may in time find work at Compaq (doing something different from what he did at Ford), but in the

Attorney

Attorneys, or lawyers, act as both advocates and advisers. As an advocate, an attorney represents a client in a civil or criminal trial. As an adviser, an attorney counsels his or her clients as to their obligations, rights, and particular courses of action in business and legal matters. All attorneys must interpret the law, whether they are advising or advocating.

To become a practicing attorney you must obtain a college degree and graduate from a law school accredited by the American Bar Association or the proper state authorities. After graduation, you must pass a written bar exam administered by the state in which you plan to practice law. To enter law school you must first take the Law School Admission Test (LSAT), which is similar to the Scholastic Assessment Test (SAT) that students usually take before attending college.

Why might a structurally unemployed worker, who goes from a car company to a computer company, be out of work longer than a frictionally unemployed worker who goes from a computer company to another computer company?

meantime he is structurally unemployed. **Structural unemployment** is a worker's condition if he or she is unemployed as a result of changing market (demand) conditions and he or she does not currently have the skills necessary to work for a company that is hiring workers. The worker may have to retrain to get a new job.

Like frictional unemployment, structural unemployment will always exist. After all, there will always be changing market conditions, as well as people fired who do not currently possess the skills necessary to obtain the available jobs.

Natural Unemployment

Natural unemployment is the sum of frictional and structural unemployment. For example, if 3 million persons were frictionally unemployed and 2 million persons were structurally unemployed, 5 million persons would be naturally unemployed.

$$\text{Natural unemployment} = \text{Frictional unemployment} + \text{Structural unemployment}$$

How would we calculate the percentage of the civilian labor force that is naturally unemployed? We would simply take the number of persons naturally unemployed (5 million) and divide it by the number of persons in the civilian labor force. Suppose the labor force consists of 100 million persons. The natural unemployment rate is then 5 percent.

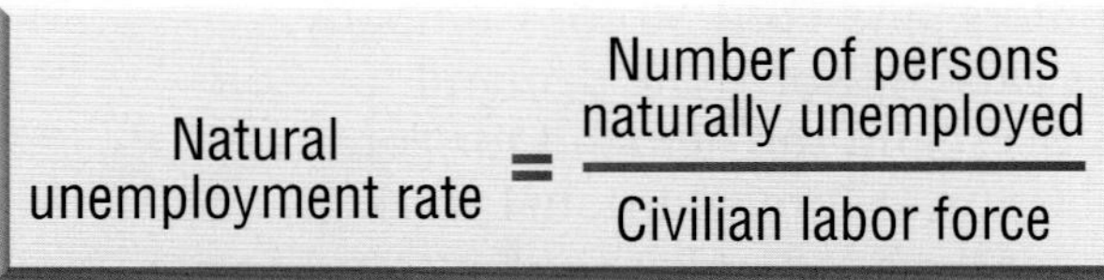

This construction worker is employed today, but may be unemployed next month. Whether he is frictionally or structurally unemployed, he will be counted in the official unemployment rate.

Economists have estimated the natural unemployment rate for the United States to be between 4.0 and 6.5 percent. They go on to say that when the nation's unemployment rate (that is, the official unemployment rate that is computed by the federal government) is equal to the natural unemployment rate, **full employment** exists in the economy. For example, if the natural unemployment rate is 5 percent and the unemployment rate is 5 percent, the economy is operating at full employment.

You may think it is odd that economists claim the economy is operating at full employment when

MINI GLOSSARY

structural unemployment The condition of workers who have lost their jobs because of changing market (demand) conditions and whose skills do not match the requirements of available jobs.

natural unemployment Unemployment that is caused by frictional and structural factors in the economy.

full employment The situation that exists when the official unemployment rate equals the natural unemployment rate.

cyclical unemployment The difference between actual or official unemployment and natural unemployment.

a 5 percent unemployment rate exists. You may have thought that full employment means that the unemployment rate is 0 percent: there are no unemployed persons. According to economists, however, there will always be some people unemployed due to frictional and structural reasons. There will always be people changing jobs, because the demand for goods and services is increasing in one place and decreasing in another. To economists, a zero unemployment rate is unrealistic.

Question: *What is* natural *about natural unemployment?*

Answer: *Recall that natural unemployment is the sum of frictional and structural unemployment. Changing market conditions cause frictional and structural unemployment, which means that the demand for some goods is increasing while the demand for other goods is decreasing. In short, natural unemployment is due to people deciding to buy more of some goods and less of other goods. Economists think this tendency is very natural and will go on forever.*

Cyclical Unemployment

Suppose there are 10 million persons unemployed in the United States and that 1 million of them are frictionally unemployed and 2 million are structurally unemployed. It follows that, out of the 10 million unemployed persons, 3 million are naturally unemployed. But what about the remaining 7 million? According to economists, these 7 million persons are *cyclically unemployed.* Stated differently, **cyclical unemployment** is the difference between official unemployment and natural unemployment. If we want to talk in terms of unemployment *rates,* then the cyclical unemployment rate is the difference between the official unemployment rate

Exhibit 13-6

Types of Unemployment

Here we identify the different types of unemployment.

Types of Unemployment	Description
Frictional unemployment	Workers have lost their jobs because of changing market (demand) conditions and have transferable skills.
Structural unemployment	Workers have lost their jobs because of changing market (demand) conditions, and their skills do not match the requirements of available jobs.
Natural unemployment	Unemployment that is caused by frictional and structural factors in the economy. Natural unemployment is the sum of frictional and structural unemployment.
Cyclical unemployment	The difference between official unemployment and natural unemployment.

and the natural unemployment rate. For example, if the unemployment rate in the United States is 8 percent and the natural unemployment rate is 5 percent, then the cyclical unemployment rate is 3 percent. (Exhibit 13-6 on the previous page summarizes the types of unemployment.)

Why would a person be cyclically unemployed? Obviously, it cannot involve demand simultaneously increasing for some goods and decreasing for other goods. If such were the case, these persons would be either frictionally or structurally unemployed. Cyclical unemployment must be caused by something else.

Most economists think that an increase in the number of persons who are cyclically unemployed is due to a decrease in aggregate demand—in other words, a decrease in the *total* demand for goods and services. The next section discusses that theory.

The Unemployment Rate and Aggregate Demand

Most economists believe that the unemployment rate will increase if aggregate demand decreases. To understand why, start with an economy operating at full employment. Suppose that the Fed reduces the money supply, which in turn leads to a reduction in aggregate demand in the economy. In other words, the Fed's action has reduced the overall amount of spending.

As overall spending drops, some firms begin to sell less, and so they cut back on their production. Consequently, they fire some workers. As workers get fired, the unemployment rate rises. Thus, a decrease in aggregate demand has resulted in an increase in the unemployment rate.

Instead of Firing Workers, Can't Wages Be Lowered?

Suppose a company has 1,000 workers and pays each one $15 an hour. Then, because of a drop in spending in the economy, the company sells fewer goods. In reaction, it cuts back on production. At this point, fewer workers will be needed, so some are usually fired.

Aggregate demand is high when people spend money. If aggregate demand decreases, unemployment may increase.

You may be wondering why can't all workers keep their jobs and agree to accept lower wages. Instead of paying 1,000 workers $15 an hour, the company could pay 1,000 workers $11 an hour. That way, none would have to lose their jobs; all would simply work for lower wages. But things don't always work this way, for several reasons.

When demand decreases, managers are often faced with some difficult choices. Explain.

First, not all workers will agree to lower wages. Jim, for example, has been with the company for twenty-five years and has seniority. He knows that if there are cutbacks or firings, he will be one of the last persons to go. Will he accept lower wages so that some others won't get fired, or will he want to keep his higher wages even if it means that some will be fired? Because Jim isn't going to be one of the persons fired, he may prefer to keep his old, higher wages.

Second, managers may also resist lower wages. Production is down, and it is the manager's job to either fire some workers or reduce the wages of the entire workforce. She may believe that if she lowers everyone's wages, worker morale will drop, and everyone will dislike her. If she fires some workers and maintains the wages of the remaining workers, only the fired workers will be unhappy. But the fired workers won't be around—they'll be somewhere else looking for a job. Simply put, managers may prefer to fire some workers and keep wages up than to pay all workers a lower wage.

Section 3 Review

Defining Terms

1. Define
   a. frictional unemployment
   b. structural unemployment
   c. natural unemployment
   d. full employment
   e. cyclical unemployment

Reviewing Facts and Concepts

2. "The economy has not achieved full employment until the unemployment rate is 0 percent." True or false? Explain your answer.

3. Explain why some business firms may prefer to fire some workers rather than lower the wages of all employees.

Critical Thinking

4. "Natural unemployment is the result of changes in people's preferences for various goods and services." Do you agree or disagree? Explain your answer.

Applying Economic Concepts

5. During your lifetime you may become unemployed at some point; however, you would prefer to be frictionally unemployed rather than structurally unemployed. How might you reduce your chances of becoming structurally unemployed?

Developing Economic

Skills

Interpreting Economics Cartoons

"A picture is worth a thousand words." This often-repeated saying aptly states the goal of editorial cartoonists. Using the cartoon, a unique medium, cartoonists entertain us and shape our opinions just as others use print, music, or the electronic media. Often, an editorial cartoon consists of a funny picture, but it involves much more than superficial humor; it allows the cartoonist to communicate a message in a direct and powerful manner.

Have you ever looked at an editorial cartoon and not understood what it was the cartoonist was trying to express? If you answered yes, welcome to the club! Some cartoons do not make a point as well as others. Or perhaps you do not have the proper background to understand fully what the cartoonist is trying to communicate. Most of the time, though, we do get the point, and whether we agree or disagree with the cartoonist, we are generally better informed for having seen the cartoon.

Confused Economists

An old joke among economists goes something like this: If you placed all the economists in the world end to end, they would never reach a conclusion. Keep this joke in mind as you examine the cartoon on this page. Do you notice confusion, disagreement, and chaos? The birds in the tree certainly do. This cartoon effectively communicates the notion, held by many people, that economists cannot agree on anything. In reality, however, economists agree on many things.

Economists often classify issues as either positive or normative. Positive economic issues can be proved true or false, and economists generally agree on these issues. For example, saying the rate of inflation is 3.2 percent can readily be proved by examining statistics, so this is a positive economic statement. Normative economic statements are opinions that cannot be proved true or false. Saying the inflation rate *should* be 2.5 percent is an opinion; therefore, it is an example of a normative statement. Just as friends may have differences of opinion, so do economists. Remember, their disagreements typically deal with normative issues, not positive ones.

Reprinted by permission of the Kansas City Star. © 2000

"What makes you think these guys are economists?"

Doughnut Shop

Some cartoons are not intended to editorialize, but they still use economic principles to make a point and have some fun. Inspect *The Far Side* cartoon, and try to identify the economic concepts it illustrates. Probably the first thing that comes to mind is profit. The shop owner is puzzled because his revenues are not high even though he is

"Well, shoot. I just can't figure it out. I'm movin' over 500 doughnuts a day, but I'm still just barely squeakin' by."

"movin' over 500 doughnuts a day." When he states he is "barely 'squeakin' by," he is referring to the low profit he is making. To determine profit, we subtract total costs from total revenue. Clearly, if his total revenue were higher, he would be making more profit. Another less-obvious concept is that of ethics. An ethical employee would not steal from the company, but it is implied in the picture that the helper has yet to meet a doughnut he did not like.

Economics Lecture

The *Frank and Ernest* cartoon, another example of a cartoon making fun of economics, introduces the concept of velocity. Velocity refers to the average number of times a dollar is spent to buy final goods and services during a year. Frank and Ernest are attending a lecture on the topic of velocity. However, the comic strip characters act as if learning this economic concept is no big deal. After all, one spends his paycheck two or three times over before he is even paid. (He must have very good credit.)

QUESTIONS TO ANSWER

1. Explain how editorial cartoons differ from other methods of expression.
2. Describe the difference between positive and normative economic statements. Give an example of each.
3. Create your own editorial cartoon using one of the themes addressed in this feature or one of your own themes.
4. Find an example of an editorial cartoon in a recent paper. Examine it carefully, and then write a brief report explaining what the cartoonist is trying to say.
5. In the comic strip section of the newspaper, find cartoons that deal with economic themes such as scarcity, opportunity cost, demand, supply, or money. Bring them to class and explain the economic concepts and how the cartoons illustrate the concepts.

FRANK AND EARNEST reprinted by permission of Newspaper Enterprise Association, Inc.

CHAPTER 13

Review

Economics Vocabulary

Fill in the following blanks with the appropriate word or phrase.

1. Aggregate demand rises, and the price level rises. This scenario is an example of ____.
2. Aggregate supply falls, and the price level rises. This is an example of ____.
3. The average number of times a dollar is spent to buy final goods and services in a year is called ____.
4. The ____ predicts that changes in the price level will be strictly proportional to changes in the money supply.
5. When people ____ against inflation, they are trying to avoid or lessen a risk by taking some counterbalancing action.
6. ____ is the sum of frictional and structural unemployment.
7. When the official unemployment rate equals the natural unemployment rate, ____ exists.
8. ____ is a decrease in the price level or average level of prices.
9. ____ refers to the condition of workers who have lost their jobs because of changing market (demand) conditions and who have transferable skills.
10. ____ refers to the condition of workers who have lost their jobs because of changing market (demand) conditions and whose skills do not match the requirements of available jobs.

Review Questions

1. What is the difference between inflation and deflation?
2. Can both inflation and deflation be caused by changes in aggregate demand? Explain your answer.
3. Give an example of a person who is frictionally unemployed.
4. Inflation reduces the value or purchasing power of money. What does this mean?
5. Explain how deflation can lead to an increase in unemployment.
6. What might happen on the demand side of the economy to cause inflation?
7. What are the assumptions of the simple quantity theory of money? What is its prediction?
8. In year 1 the Fed increases the money supply 10 percent, and in year 4 it increases the money supply 20 percent. Following which year is the inflation rate likely to be higher if the simple quantity theory of money predicts well? Explain your answer.
9. Can both inflation and deflation be caused by changes in aggregate supply? Explain your answer.
10. Explain why the unemployment rate might rise if aggregate demand falls.
11. Explain how inflation affects both individuals on fixed incomes and savers.
12. A war breaks out in a country, and factories are destroyed. Is this situation more likely to cause demand-side or supply-side inflation? Explain your answer.

Calculations

1. The CPI is 145 in year 1 and 154 in year 2. What is the inflation rate between the two years?
2. The CPI is 155 in year 1 and 123 in year 2. What is the deflation rate between the two years?
3. The money supply is $2,000, velocity is 2, and the quantity of goods and services is 500 units. According to the exchange equation, what is the average price of a good?
4. The natural unemployment rate is 5 percent, the structural unemployment rate is 2 percent, and the official unemployment rate is 9 percent. What is the frictional unemployment rate? The cyclical unemployment rate?

Graphs

1. Illustrate the following:
   a. demand-side inflation
   b. supply-side inflation
2. Which panel(s) in Exhibit 13-7 illustrate(s) each of the following?
   a. a change in the economy resulting in a higher price level and a lower quantity of goods and services

b. a change in the economy resulting in a lower price level and a lower quantity of goods and services

c. a change in the economy resulting in a higher price level and a greater quantity of goods and services

Exhibit 13-7

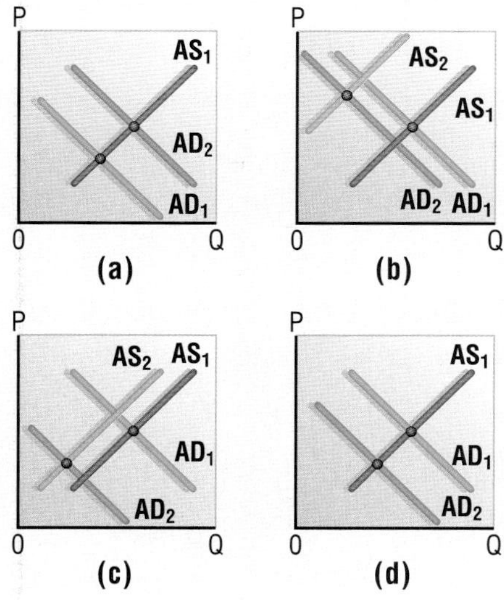

Economics and Thinking Skills

1. **Application.** Explain how knowledge of the exchange equation can be used to explain both inflation and deflation.
2. **Analysis.** Can there be inflation in the face of an increase in the quantity of goods and services? Explain your answer.
3. **Cause and Effect.** Do higher interest rates cause higher inflation, or does higher inflation cause higher interest rates? Explain your answer.

Writing Skills

Suppose you are working at job A when you become unemployed. Unfortunately, you do not possess the skills to transfer into an industry that is currently hiring people. In other words, you are structurally unemployed. In a one-page paper, explain what you would do to become employed again.

Economics in the Media

1. Find a newspaper article that discusses inflation, deflation, or the unemployment rate. Identify and discuss the details of the article.
2. Find a story on a television news show that either mentions or discusses the CPI or the unemployment rate. Explain the context in which the mention or discussion takes place.

Where's the Economics?

In deflation, what happens to the value of goods (such as houses) relative to the value of money?

CHAPTER 14

Business Cycles and Economic Growth

What This Chapter Is About

This chapter discusses two of the most important topics in economics: business cycles and economic growth. Business cycles deal with the ups and downs in the economy. Economic growth concerns increases in real GDP and rising standards of living.

Why This Chapter Is Important

During the course of your life you can be sure you will experience two things as a member of the economy. First, you will experience business cycles. Economic activity will be going along fine; then it will decline, bottom out, and pick up again. In other words, you will experience the ups and downs of the economy.

Second, you will experience economic growth, which will probably occur slowly and over time. But it will make a huge difference to the life you live. When you learn about business cycles and economic growth, you learn about the environment in which you will spend much of your life.

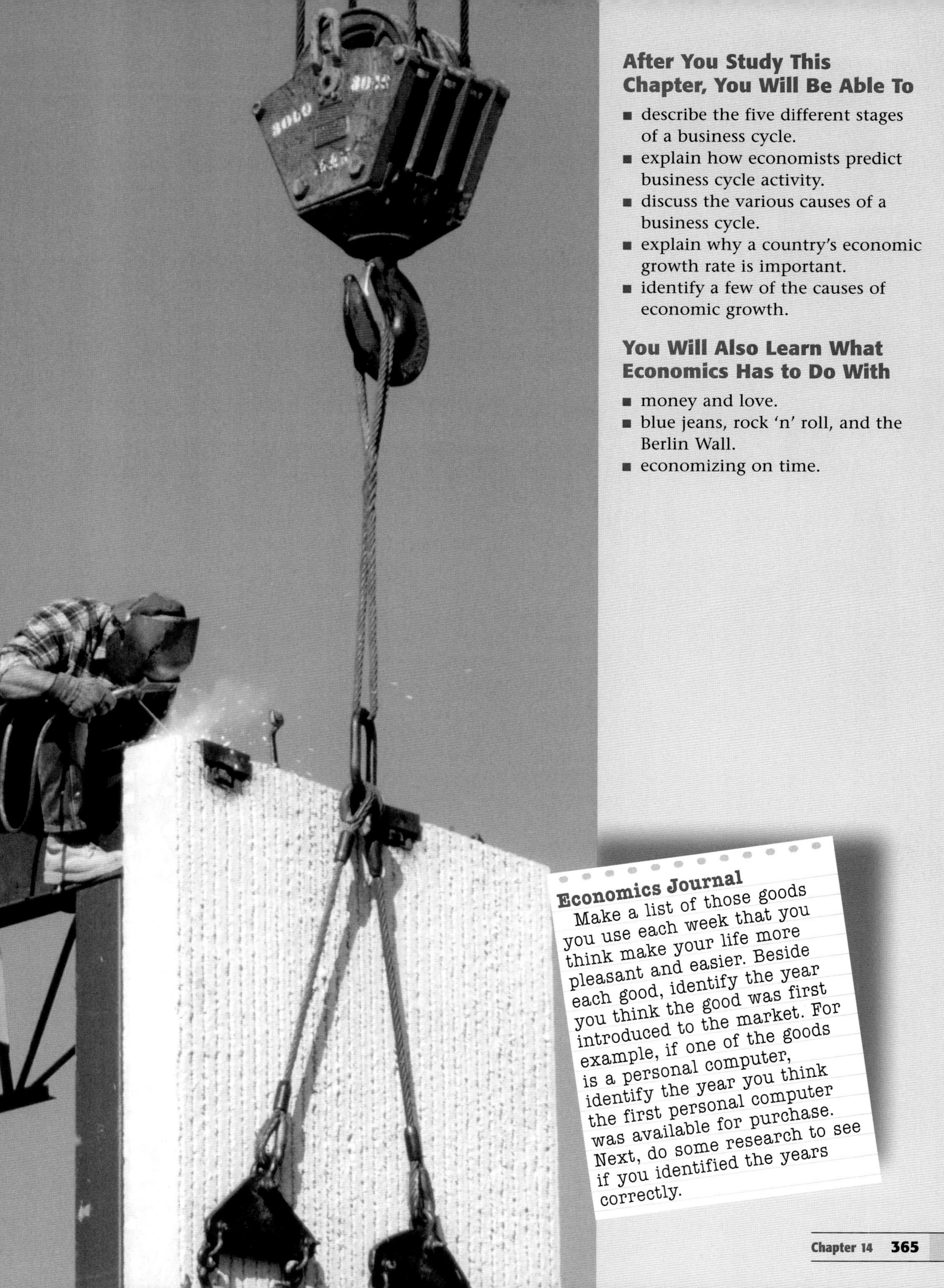

After You Study This Chapter, You Will Be Able To

- describe the five different stages of a business cycle.
- explain how economists predict business cycle activity.
- discuss the various causes of a business cycle.
- explain why a country's economic growth rate is important.
- identify a few of the causes of economic growth.

You Will Also Learn What Economics Has to Do With

- money and love.
- blue jeans, rock 'n' roll, and the Berlin Wall.
- economizing on time.

Economics Journal

Make a list of those goods you use each week that you think make your life more pleasant and easier. Beside each good, identify the year you think the good was first introduced to the market. For example, if one of the goods is a personal computer, identify the year you think the first personal computer was available for purchase. Next, do some research to see if you identified the years correctly.

SECTION 1 Business Cycles

A business cycle relates to the ups and downs in economic activity, as measured by changes in real GDP. As you read this section, keep these key questions in mind:

- What is a business cycle?
- How do economists forecast business cycles?
- What causes business cycles?

A business cycle can be likened to a roller coaster. Can you explain the comparison?

What Is a Business Cycle?

Key Terms
business cycle
recession

Chapter 12 discussed both GDP and real GDP. As you recall, GDP is the total market value of all final goods and services produced annually in an economy. Real GDP is simply GDP adjusted for price changes. To calculate real GDP, we take the quantity of goods and services produced in an economy in a current year and multiply by the prices that existed in a base year:

$$\text{Real GDP} = P_{\text{Base year}} \times Q_{\text{Current year}}$$

If real GDP is on a roller-coaster—rising and falling and rising and falling—the economy is said to be incurring a **business cycle.** Economists usually talk about four or five phases of the business cycle. Five phases are identified here and in Exhibit 14-1 on page 367:

1. *Peak.* At the *peak* of a business cycle, real GDP is at a temporary high (Q_1 in Exhibit 14-1).
2. *Contraction.* If real GDP decreases, the economy is said to be in a *contraction.* If real GDP declines for two consecutive quarters (there are four quarters in a year), the economy is said to be in a **recession.**
3. *Trough.* The low point in real GDP, just before it begins to turn up, is called the *trough* of the business cycle.
4. *Recovery.* The *recovery* is the period when real GDP is rising; it begins at the trough and ends at the initial peak. For example, the recovery in Exhibit 14-1 extends from the trough to where real GDP is again at Q_1.
5. *Expansion.* The *expansion* refers to increases in real GDP beyond the recovery. In Exhibit 14-1, it refers to increases in real GDP above Q_1.

business cycle
Recurrent swings (up and down) in real GDP.

recession
A slowdown in the economy marked by real GDP falling for two consecutive quarters.

Exhibit 14-1
The Phases of the Business Cycle

The phases of a business cycle include the peak, contraction, trough, recovery, and expansion. A business cycle is measured from peak to peak.

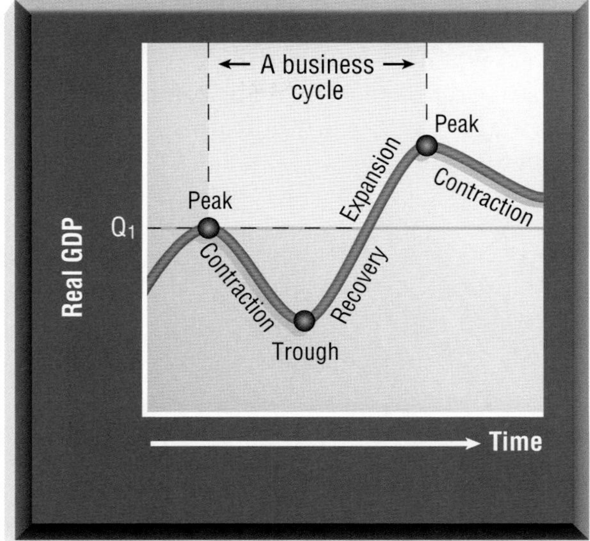

An entire business cycle is measured from peak to peak. The typical business cycle is four to five years, although a few have been shorter and some have been longer.

Question: *Has the United States experienced many business cycles?* If so, how long is the average business cycle?

Answer: *Between 1854 and 1991, the United States went through thirty-one entire business cycles. The average business cycle during this time was fifty-three months. The average time from the first peak to the trough—that is, the average time of the contraction—was eighteen months. The average time from the trough to the next peak—that is, the average time of the recovery plus the expansion—was thirty-five months. As an aside, one of the longest contractions in U.S. history was from August 1929 to March 1933, the years of the Great Depression.*

The carefree flappers reflect the state of the economy in 1926, before the Great Depression. During the Depression, veterans helped distribute food to those in need.

Follow-up Question: *What is the difference between a* recession *and a* depression*?*

Answer: *A depression is a recession that is major in* both *scale* and *duration. In short, a depression is a* deep *and* long *recession.*

Forecasting Business Cycles

Think of yourself when you have the flu. Your illness usually has three stages: (1) when you are coming down with the flu, (2) when you have the flu, and (3) when you are getting over the flu but still do not feel like your old self. In each stage, there is an indicator of what is happening.

In the first stage, when you are coming down with the flu, you feel a little sluggish and tired. We might call this condition a *leading indicator* of the flu, in that it precedes the flu; it lets you know what is coming.

In the stage when you have the flu, you feel achy, and you might have a fever. We could call this condition a *coincident indicator* of the flu, in that it coincides with having the flu.

Finally, during the period when you are getting over the flu, your temperature returns to normal. You are slightly more alert, but you do not have all your energy back. We could call this condition a *lagging indicator* of the flu. Thus, we have established a few indicators of your health and sickness.

Similarly, economists have devised a few indicators of the health and sickness of the economy—*leading, coincident,* and *lagging indicators*—that are said to do what their names suggest: *lead* economic upturns or downturns (in real GDP), *coincide* with economic upturns or downturns, and *lag* behind economic upturns and downturns.

A fever can be called a coincident indicator of the flu; it coincides with the upturns and downturns of the illness. Similarly, in the economy, coincident indicators coincide with economic upturns and downturns.

Irving Fisher, Economist

How hard is it to predict downturns in the economy? For Irving Fisher (1867–1947) it was rather hard, which says a lot about how hard it is for others.

Fisher, who taught at Yale University, was one of the most respected economists of his day. But even he did not predict the Great Depression. Just two days before the major stock market crash, the "first shot" of the Great Depression, Fisher said that the stock market would continue to rise and that no problems lay ahead for the economy. Taking his own advice, Fisher lost a lot of money in the stock market.

Was Fisher a bad economist? Not at all; in fact, he is regarded as one of the best economists who has ever lived. The problem lies with the difficulty of making consistently accurate economic predictions, even for the best economist.

You probably have been acquainted with some of Fisher's work without even knowing it. Fisher was also an inventor. One of his creations was the "visible card index," the early model of the Rolodex.

QUESTION TO ANSWER If all economists could make consistently accurate predictions about the stock market, what would you expect to see in the world?

Even though this young lady is recovering from her illness, she probably still has a few symptoms. What might be a "lagging indicator" of her illness?

NON SEQUITUR by WILEY

Reprinted with permission of Universal Press Syndicate. All rights reserved.

We would expect a leading indicator to rise before an upturn in real GDP and to fall before a downturn in real GDP. A coincident indicator should reach its high point coincidentally with a peak of a business cycle and reach its low point with the trough of a business cycle. Finally, we would expect a lagging indicator to reach its high sometime after the peak of a business cycle and to reach its low sometime after the trough of a business cycle.

Leading economic indicators tend to be more often cited in the news than either coincident or lagging indicators, perhaps because people seem particularly interested in predicting or forecasting the future. They want to know what lies ahead—contraction or expansion? What will the economic future hold?

Are stock prices a leading, coincident, or lagging indicator?

Dow's milestones

Time it took for the industrial average to go from:

1,000 to 2,000 — 5,168 days

9,000 to 10,000 — 357 days

The National Bureau of Economic Research (NBER) is a private, nonprofit, nonpartisan research organization dedicated to promoting a greater understanding of how the economy works. The main office of the NBER is in Cambridge, Massachusetts. One of the many things that the NBER does is determine the dates of the different phases of the business cycle. For example, it might determine that the peak of a given business cycle was in a certain month and year. Go to the NBER Web site http://www.nber.org. Click on "Business Cycles Dates." There you will find the troughs and peaks for past business cycles. Consider now the years of the Great Depression in the United States, 1929 to 1933. According to the NBER, how many months was the Great Depression, from peak to trough?

A few of the leading indicators include stock prices, the money supply (in inflation-adjusted dollars), consumer expectations, and average weekly hours worked in manufacturing. For example, a stock market that is up generally reflects good economic times ahead, and a stock market that is down generally reflects bad economic conditions to come. An increase in average weekly hours worked reflects good times ahead. The reasoning is that when good things are happening in the economy—when sales and profits are expected to rise—companies will adjust upward the number of hours their employees work before hiring more people. Similarly, a decline in average weekly hours worked reflects bad times ahead. When this indicator goes down, it usually means that sales and profits are expected to fall, and companies are cutting back on the number of hours their employees work. Exhibit 14-2 identifies the ten leading economic indicators.

The chair of the Board of Governors of the Federal Reserve System goes before Congress and says that the Fed is likely to sharply cut back the growth rate of the money supply in the next few months. What do you predict for the future course of real GDP? The unemployment rate?

What Causes the Business Cycle?

Since the end of World War II, the United States has gone through nine business cycles.[1] What causes a business cycle? As you might expect, different economists identify different causes of the business cycle. We discuss a few theories here.

Money Supply Some economists believe that changes in the money supply cause economic contractions and expansions. For example, when either the absolute money supply drops or the growth rate in the money supply declines, people end up buying fewer goods and services, and the economy falls into a contraction. In contrast, when

1. National Bureau of Economic Research, Cambridge, Massachusetts.

Exhibit 14-2
The Ten Leading Economic Indicators

1. Average weekly hours, manufacturing.
2. Average weekly initial claims for unemployment insurance.
3. Manufacturers' new orders, consumer goods and materials.
4. Vendor performance, slower deliveries, diffusion index.
5. Manufacturers' new orders, nondefense capital goods.
6. Building permits, new private housing units.
7. Stock prices, 500 common stocks.
8. Money supply, M2.
9. Interest rate spread, 10-year Treasury bonds, less federal funds.
10. Index of consumer expectations.

the money supply rises there is more buying, and an economic expansion commences.

These economists say the ups and downs of the business cycle are caused by the erratic behavior of the monetary authorities or the Fed. Sometimes the Fed puts the monetary accelerator to the floor, dramatically increasing the money supply and causing expansion. At other times it slams on the monetary brakes, causing the money supply to drop and the economy to dive into a contraction.

A slowdown in residential construction can cause a business cycle. Explain how this could happen.

Business Investment, Residential Construction, and Government Spending

Some economists point to changes in business investment, residential construction, or government spending as the cause of a business cycle. For example, a contraction might result from a cutback in business investment or government spending that lowers aggregate demand in the economy. With lower aggregate demand, firms do not sell as many goods and services, so they end up firing workers. Fired workers do not have the income they once had, so overall income in the economy falls. And with a lower income, people do not buy as many goods. Thus the initial cut in spending stimulates even further declines in spending, and the economy falls deeper into recession. Things are reversed when either the business sector or government starts to spend more.

Can a good economy help get a politician reelected? Explain your answer.

Politics Some economists believe that at least some business cycles have been caused by politicians trying to get reelected to office. Suppose it is a year or so before the members of Congress will be running for reelection. They know that their chances of reelection are greater if the economy is in good shape on election day. To this end, they pass more spending bills in Congress, hoping to

The Great Depression and the Way People View the Economy

The most severe contraction that the U.S. economy has endured began in 1929 and ended in 1933 (the worst years of the Great Depression). In fact, that contraction was so deep and long that many people believe it changed the way people viewed a free-enterprise economy.

Before the Great Depression, politicians, economists, and members of the general public believed the economy was self-correcting or self-regulating. The economy could "heal itself" if it got "sick." Just like the human body can cure itself of certain ailments (such as a cold or the flu), so could the economy cure itself if it found itself in a contraction or a business slump. For example, in a business slump, wages and interest rates fall, and firms start hiring more workers and start investing more. In time, a bad situation turns into a good one. Obviously, if the economy is self-correcting, there is little, if any, role for government to play. There is no need for government to intervene and try to fix the economy, because the economy will soon fix itself.

The Great Depression changed this view of the economy. For many people, it was proof that a free-enterprise economy was not only unstable but also unable to heal itself. Government intervention in the economy came to be viewed as necessary to prevent it from collapsing.

Some economists have argued against this view. Milton Friedman, for example, argued that the Great Depression was not so much the fault of a free-enterprise economy as it was the fault of the Federal Reserve System. He argued that it was the Fed's cutting back the money supply by about one-third during the years of the Great Depression, and not the free-market economy, that made the contraction so severe.

Friedman's view is accepted by many economists today, but it was not widely understood in the 1930s through the 1960s by economists, politicians, or members of the public. People in those decades saw the Great Depression as proof of the instability and waste that could arise in a free-enterprise economy. This change from viewing the economy as self-regulating to seeing it as unstable and wasteful opened the door to the government's playing an interventionist and management role in the economy. Many government programs ("New Deal" programs) that began during the administration of President Franklin Delano Roosevelt probably would not have had wide public support before the Great Depression. Coming when they did, however, Roosevelt's government programs were seen by many as ultimately saving people from the ravages of a free-enterprise economy run amok.

QUESTION TO ANSWER Anton says that people change their view of how the world works only after experiencing a crisis that their view cannot explain. Frances says that people change their view of how the world works only through education. Which person are you more likely to agree with, and why?

During the Gulf War many Kuwaiti oil wells were set on fire to destroy the oil. How did this affect the U.S. economy?

increase aggregate demand in the economy. With greater aggregate demand, they reason, firms will sell more goods and services and hire more workers. People will have jobs and income. And when times are good, voters are likely to reward the people in office who (they believe) made this possible.

Of course, things may get out of hand after the election. The greater aggregate demand can cause inflation (as we saw in Chapter 13). Congress may then reverse its strategy by trying to cut spending to lower aggregate demand and cool off the economy. If Congress cuts spending too much, though, the economy could slide into a contraction.

Innovation Some economists believe that major innovations are the seeds of business cycles. For example, a company develops a major new technology or product, and its sales skyrocket. To stay competitive, other companies must try to copy what the innovator has done or come up with a better innovation themselves. For a time, these copycat firms invest heavily to maintain their market positions relative to the innovator. In time, though, investment spending tends to slow, and the economy turns down.

Supply Shocks Some economists argue that the contraction phase of the business cycle is brought about by major supply-side changes in the economy that reduce the capacity of the economy to produce. For example, a war can destroy factories and people and lower the productive capacity of an economy. Or consider a major cutback in oil production brought on by conflict in the Middle East. With less oil, which is an important resource in the production process, the productive capability of the economy declines. Firms end up producing less, so they fire some of their workers. Real GDP goes down, and the unemployment rate goes up.

Section 1 Review

Defining Terms

1. Define
   a. business cycle
   b. recession

Reviewing Facts and Concepts

2. What are the five phases of a business cycle?
3. If the initial peak of a business cycle was January 1, year 1, the trough was July 1, year 2, and the final peak was July 1, year 4, how long was the contraction (in months)?
4. What is a coincident indicator?

Critical Thinking

5. One leading indicator is average weekly hours worked. If this indicator rises, what does it indicate about the future performance of the economy? Explain your answer.

Applying Economic Concepts

6. One explanation of the business cycle is that changes in business investment, residential construction, or government spending cause the business cycle. If this explanation is correct, how could you use this information to determine whether it is a good time or bad time to buy stocks in the stock market?

SECTION 2

Economic Growth

This section is about economic growth. As you read this section, keep these key questions in mind:

- What is the difference between absolute real economic growth and per-capita real economic growth?
- Do small differences in economic growth rates matter?
- What causes economic growth?

What Is Economic Growth?

Key Terms

absolute real economic growth
per-capita real economic growth
production possibilities frontier (PPF)

The term *economic growth* refers to either absolute real economic growth or to per-capita real economic growth. **Absolute real economic growth** is an increase in real GDP from one period to the next. For example, if real GDP was $6,000 billion in year 1 and $6,500 billion in year 2, the economy has witnessed absolute real economic growth. **Per-capita real economic growth** is an increase from one period to the next in per-capita real GDP, which is real GDP divided by population:

An increase in the quantity of goods produced (TVs, computers, cars, etc.), with no change in population, leads to an increase in per-capita real GDP.

$$\text{Per-capita real GDP} = \frac{\text{Real GDP}}{\text{Population}}$$

Do Economic Growth Rates Matter?

Suppose that the absolute real economic growth rate is 4 percent in one country and 3 percent in another country. The difference in these growth rates may not seem very significant, but if these growth rates are sustained over a long period, the people who live in each country will see a real difference in their standard of living. For example, if a country's economic growth rate is 4 percent each year, real GDP will take eighteen years to double. But if a country has a 3 percent annual growth rate, real GDP will take twenty-four years to double. In other words, a country with a 4 percent growth rate can double its real GDP in six fewer years than a country with a 3 percent growth rate.

absolute real economic growth
An increase in real GDP from one period to the next.

per-capita real economic growth
An increase from one period to the next in per-capita real GDP, which is real GDP divided by population.

production possibilities frontier (PPF) All possible combinations of two goods that an economy can produce in a certain period of time, under the conditions of a given state of technology, no unemployed resources, and efficient production.

The Rule of 72

How did we figure out that a country with a 3 percent growth rate will double its size in twenty-four years but that a country with a 4 percent growth rate will double its size in eighteen years? We used the Rule of 72, which says that the way to find out the time required for any variable to double is simply to divide its percentage growth rate (expressed as a whole number, not as a decimal) into 72:

$$\text{Rule of 72} = \frac{72}{\text{Growth rate}} = \text{Number of years for a variable to double}$$

Growth and a Production Possibilities Frontier

One of the key concepts in economics is the **production possibilities frontier (PPF).** Let's assume that there are only two goods in the world, guns and butter. If all the resources of the economy are used to produce guns, 80 guns can be produced in a year. If all the resources of the economy are used to produce butter, 130 units of butter can be produced.

Besides these two maximum amounts of guns and butter, the following combinations of the two goods can be produced in a year: 72 units of butter and 60 guns; 104 units of butter and 40 guns, and 120 units of butter and 20 guns. If we plot the different combinations of the two goods the economy can produce when it uses all its resources, we obtain the production possibilities frontier in Exhibit 14-3. A society can produce any combination of goods on or below its PPF. Anything beyond the frontier, though, is currently beyond the society's reach. In other words, the PPF is all possible combinations of two goods that an economy can produce in a certain period of time, under the conditions of a given state of technology, no unused resources, and efficient production.

Traditionally in economics, the term *guns* is used to represent military goods, such as tanks and bombs, and the term *butter* is used to represent civilian goods, such as TV sets, cars, and computers.

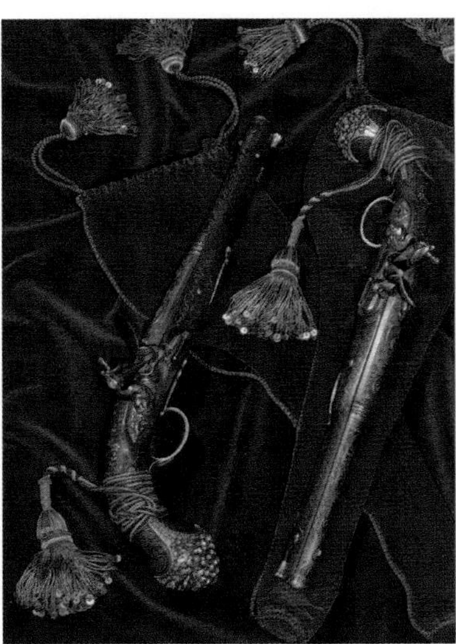

Exhibit 14-3

Deriving a Production Possibilities Frontier

The economy can produce any of the five combinations, labeled A–E, of the two goods. These combinations are plotted, and the curve that connects points A–E is called the production possibilities frontier (PPF).

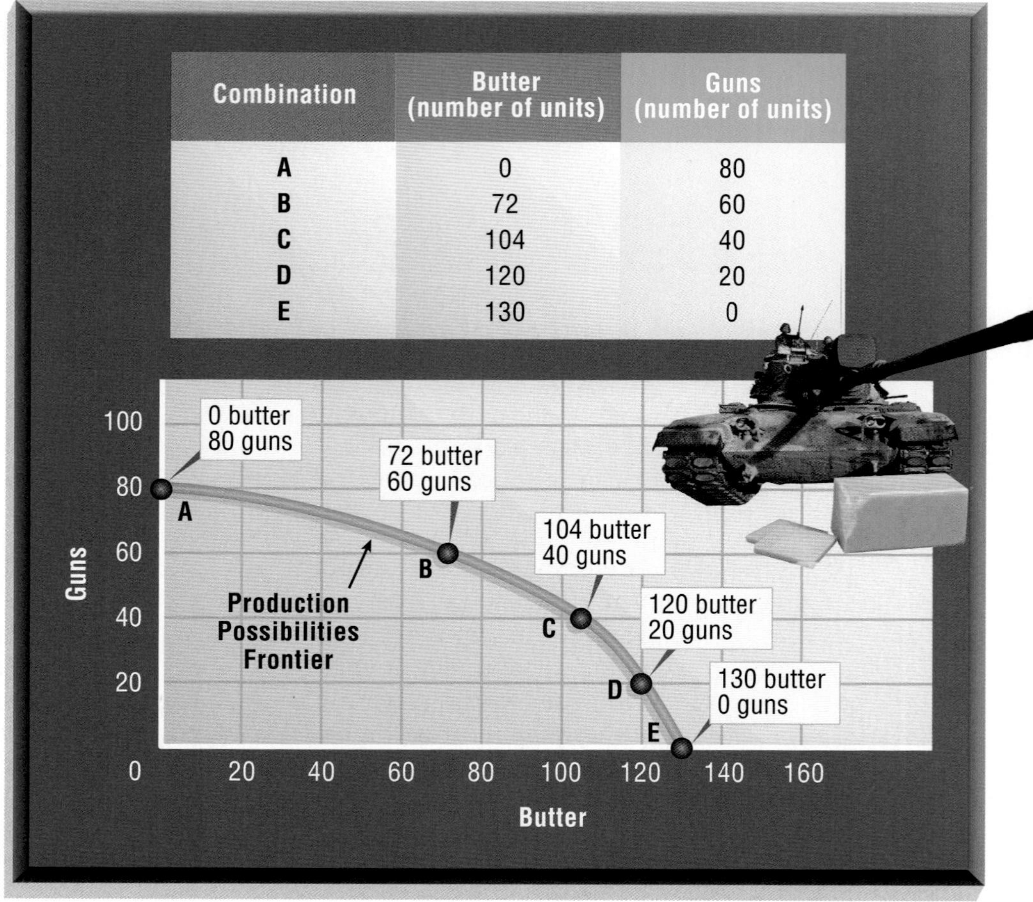

Combination	Butter (number of units)	Guns (number of units)
A	0	80
B	72	60
C	104	40
D	120	20
E	130	0

Two Kinds of Economic Growth

Economic growth can occur from a position either below or on the PPF.

Economic Growth from a Position below the PPF An economy can be located on or below its PPF. For example, an economy could be located at either point A or point B in Exhibit 14-4a on page 377. Suppose an economy is located at point A, a point below the PPF. Obviously at this point there are some unused resources in the economy, because only when the economy is on the PPF are all resources fully used. At point A the economy is producing 100 units of butter and 100 guns, but it can produce more with the resources it has; it can produce 150 units of butter and 200 guns by using all its resources and producing at point B.

A movement from point A to point B is evidence of economic growth. More of both goods are produced at point B than at point A. Real GDP is higher at point B than point A.

Before we continue to discuss economic growth, let's compare the unemployment rate at point B with the unemployment rate at point A. Obviously, the unemployment rate at point B is the natural unemployment rate; the economy is at full employment at point B. We know this because point B is on the PPF, which means all resources are fully employed.

Exhibit 14-4

Economic Growth from a Position Below and On a PPF

Economic growth can occur from a position below the PPF (Part a) or from a position on the PPF (Part b).

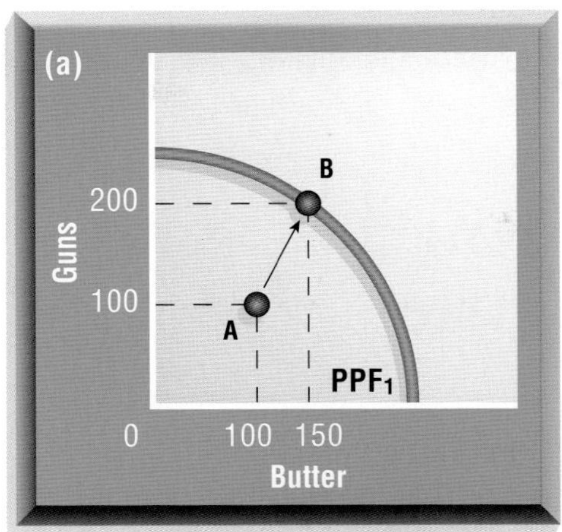

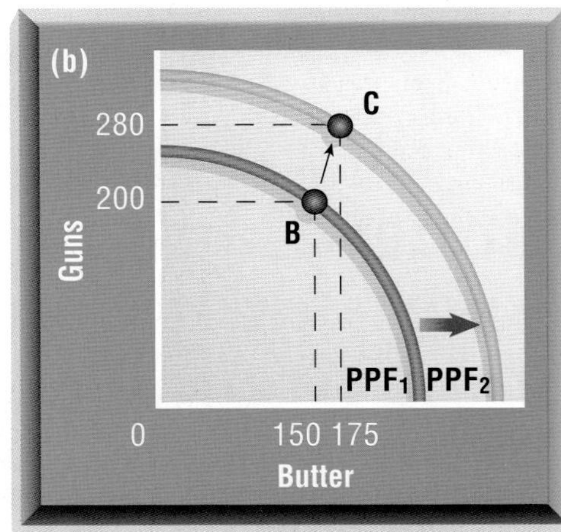

By comparison, then, the unemployment rate at point A has to be higher than the unemployment rate at point B. If the unemployment rate is 5 percent at point B, it may be 7 percent at point A.

Thus, to achieve economic growth, the economy must move from point A to point B. Obviously, the unemployment rate that exists at point A must be lowered. In other words, lowering the unemployment rate and moving toward full employment will move the economy away from point A and toward point B. On the road from A to B, economic growth is occurring.

Many policies can be implemented to reduce the unemployment rate. One policy that was discussed in Chapter 13 was increasing aggregate demand; increases in aggregate demand can increase the real GDP and lower the unemployment rate (at least in the short run).

Economic Growth from a Position on the PPF Now suppose the economy is located at point B in Exhibit 14-4b, on PPF_1, producing 150 units of butter and 200 guns. How does an economy that is currently on its production possibilities frontier experience economic growth? Obviously, the only way is to shift its PPF to the right, say, from PPF_1 to PPF_2. In other words, if an economy is already on its PPF, the only way it can experience economic growth is if its PPF shifts rightward. Then, as we see in Exhibit 14-4b, the economy can move from point B to point C (where more goods are produced and the real GDP is higher).

What Causes Economic Growth?

What factors cause economic growth of the type shown in Exhibit 14-4b, that is, economic growth brought on by a rightward shift in the PPF? A few factors that can affect growth are natural resources, labor, capital, technological advances, and incentives.

Natural Resources With more natural resources, a country can produce more goods and services. For this reason, people often think that countries with a plentiful supply of natural resources experience economic growth, whereas countries that are short of natural resources do not. In reality,

Money Can't Buy You Love, But It Can Settle Some Arguments

The idea behind a production possibilities frontier (PPF) is simple: with a limited number of resources, an economy can produce only so many goods and services. Similarly, with a limited income, individuals can buy only so many goods and services. To illustrate, suppose that Juanita and Bill have a combined income of $800 a week. Let's say that they can spend their income on only two goods, clothes and entertainment. Furthermore, suppose the average price of a unit of clothing and a unit of entertainment is $40.

If all $800 is spent on clothes, or all $800 is spent on entertainment, 20 units can be purchased. Exhibit 14-5 shows these two end-points. The line that runs between these two points is called the *budget constraint.*

Now suppose that Bill wants to be at point A (15 units of entertainment and 5 units of clothes), and Juanita wants to be at point B (15 units of clothes and 5 units of entertainment).

They argue for days. Bill says they should be at point A, and Juanita says point B. They decide to compromise at point C, purchasing 10 units of clothes and 10 units of entertainment.

A greater income will allow both Bill and Juanita to get exactly what they want. For example, if their combined income rises from $800 to $1,200 a week, they can move from point C to point D. At point D, Bill is consuming his ideal amount of entertainment (15 units), and Juanita is consuming her ideal amount of clothes (15 units).

More money income (assuming that prices are constant) is to a family what economic growth is to a society. It can make everyone better off and no one worse off.

QUESTION TO ANSWER Initially, a movement from point C to point D will make both Bill and Juanita better off. Might Bill and Juanita in time start to argue over where they should locate on the $1,200-a-week budget constraint? Explain your answer.

Exhibit 14-5
Juanita and Bill, Entertainment and Clothes

If Juanita and Bill are earning $800 a week, Bill wants to be at point A, and Juanita wants to be at point B. However, each person compromises, and they locate at point C. More money income makes it possible for both to get what they would get at their preferred points. Here, additional income moves them from the $800-a-week budget constraint to the $1,200-a-week budget constraint. Bill can now get what he wanted at point A (15 units of entertainment), and Juanita can get what she wanted at point B (15 units of clothes).

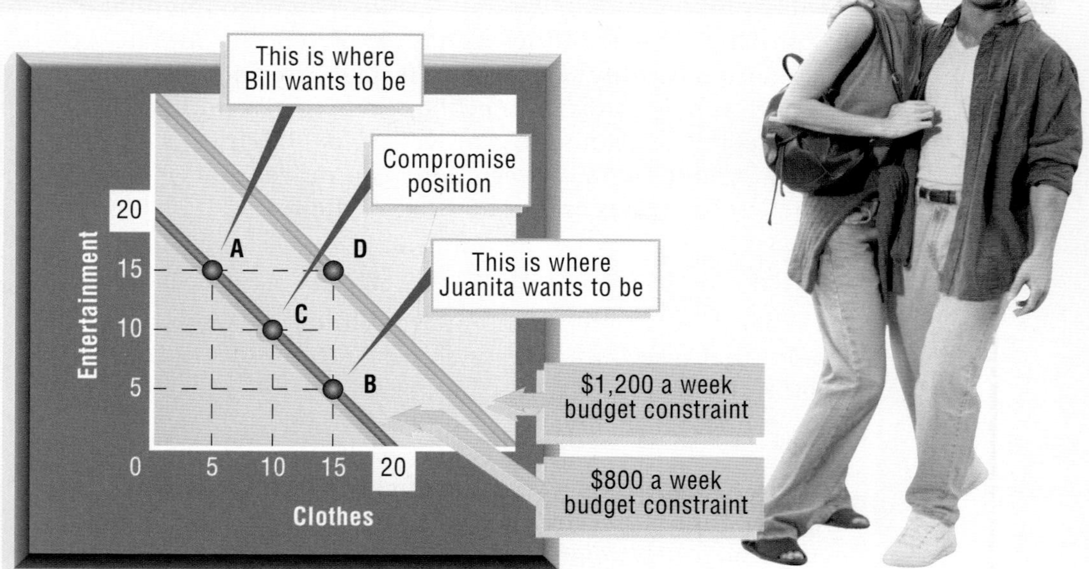

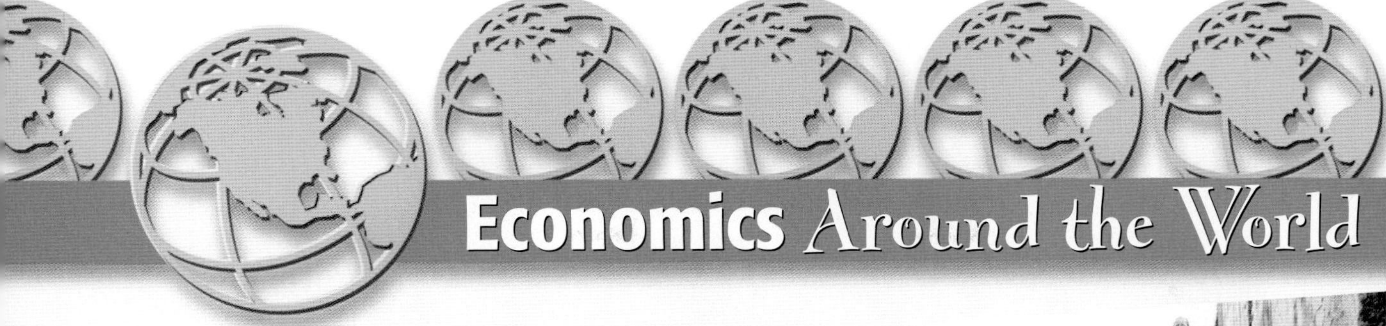

Blue Jeans, Rock 'n' Roll, and the Berlin Wall

The Berlin Wall once stood as the symbol of communism and of the Cold War. Today the Berlin Wall is gone, and the Cold War is over. What happened? Some people say that the former Soviet Union recognized that it could never compete with the U.S. military, and decided to stop investing so much in the military arms race.

Not everyone agrees with this theory, however. Some say that rock music and blue jeans had more to do with the decline of the Soviet Union than did military might. Exhibit 14-6 illustrates this idea. The production possibilities frontier (PPF) in the exhibit has blue jeans, rock music, and other consumer goods on the vertical axis and military goods on the horizontal axis. Suppose that Soviet consumers want to be at point A, with 100 units of military goods and 600 units of consumer goods. However, the Soviet leadership wants to be at point B, with 400 units of military goods and 180 units of consumer goods.

If the Soviet leadership decided to be at point B, consumers would be disgruntled. Through economic growth, however, the Soviet leadership could reduce the level of discontent. To see how, look at point C, where there are more blue jeans and rock music (400 units) than at point B, and more military goods, too. Consumers still would not be where they wanted to be, but they would be closer at point C than at point B.

The problem was that the Soviet Union was not growing very much in the 1970s and 1980s, so point C was not available as a possible move. Thus, the tension between the Soviet leadership and consumers was deepening. Finally, a revolt against communism took place—and things began to change. What lesson can be learned, in terms of the PPF? A country that locates itself at a point on the PPF where the majority of people do not want to be is likely to experience greater political instability than a country that locates at a point where the majority of people do want to be.

Exhibit 14-6

The PPF and the Collapse of the Former Soviet Union

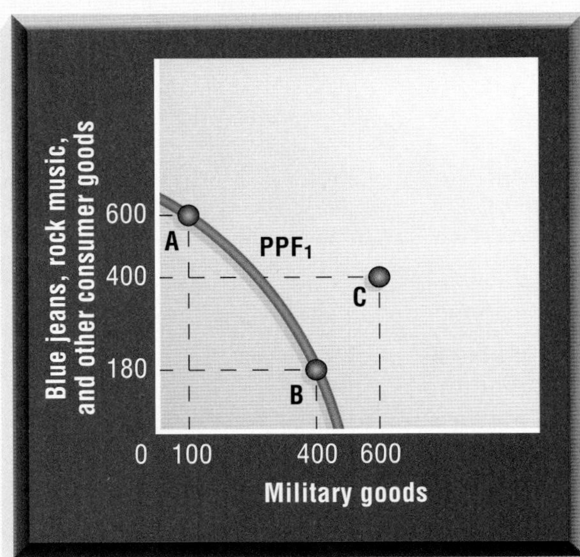

QUESTION TO ANSWER Suppose the U.S. government took over the role of telling firms what to produce, how many units to produce, and so on. Would U.S. consumers be angry? If so, how would they show their anger?

Singapore has experienced economic growth despite being short of natural resources.

however, some countries with an abundant supply of natural resources have experienced rapid economic growth in the past (such as the United States), and some have experienced no growth or only slow growth. Also, some countries that are short of natural resources, such as Singapore, have grown very fast. Natural resources are neither sufficient nor necessary for economic growth. However, it is still more likely for a country rich in natural resources to experience growth, all other things being equal. In other words, if there are two countries, A and B, and everything is the same between the two countries except that A has more natural resources than B, then A is likely to grow more than B.

Labor With more labor, it is possible to produce more output. More labor by itself, however, is not what matters most to the economic growth. More important is the productivity of the labor. Government statisticians measure labor productivity by dividing the total output produced by the number of hours it takes to produce the output:

Using a machine (capital good) increases the productivity of this worker.

$$\text{Labor productivity} = \frac{\text{Total output produced}}{\text{Total hours it takes to produce total output}}$$

For example, if \$6 trillion of output is produced in 200 billion labor hours, then labor productivity is \$30 per hour.

An increase in labor productivity causes economic growth. The real question, then, is how an economy can achieve an increase in labor pro-

Exhibit 14-7
Cause and Effect

The direct relationship of labor productivity and economic growth can be seen in this cause and effect illustration.

ductivity. One way is through increased education and training. Another way is through capital investment. Combining workers with more capital goods tends to increase the labor productivity of the workers. For example, a farmer with a tractor is more productive than a farmer without one, and an accountant with a computer is more productive than an accountant without one.

Capital As just mentioned, capital investment can lead to increases in labor productivity and therefore to increases in output or real GDP. But more capital goods do not fall from the sky. Recall from an earlier chapter that getting more of one thing often means forfeiting something else. To produce more capital goods, which are not directly consumable, present consumption must be sacrificed. Consider Robinson Crusoe, alone on an island and fishing with a spear. He must give up some of his present fish to take out the time to weave a net (a capital good) with which he hopes to catch more fish.

Exhibit 14-8 shows that for the period 1970 to 1990, those countries with higher investment rates largely tended to have higher per-capita real GDP growth rates. For example, investment was a higher percentage of GDP in Austria, Norway, and Japan than it was in the United States, and those countries experienced a higher per-capita real GDP growth rate than the United States did.

Exhibit 14-8
Investment and Per-Capita Real GDP Growth for Selected Countries, 1970–1990

Generally, those countries with higher investment rates tend to have higher per-capita real GDP growth rates.

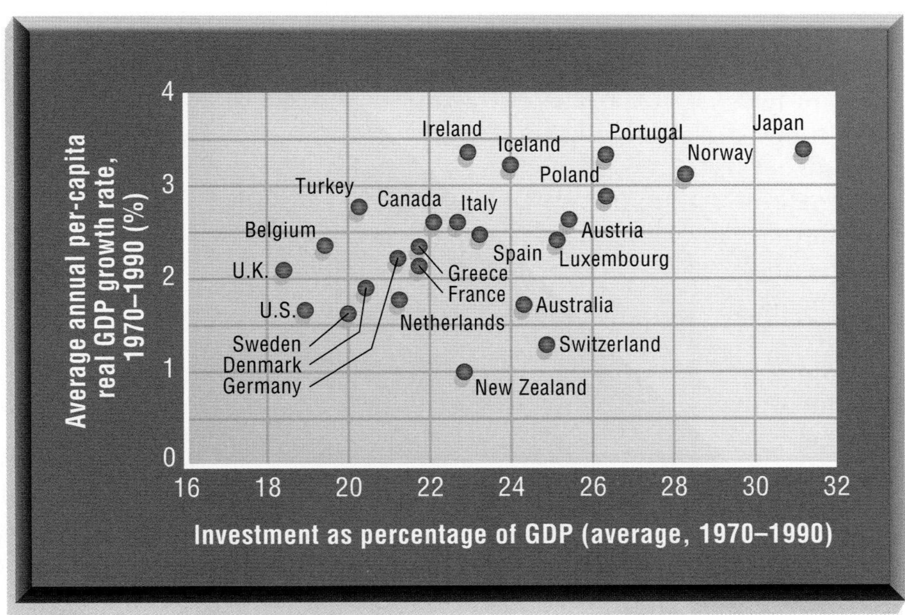

Technology & Innovation

How Economizing on Time Can Promote Economic Growth

Every time someone introduced an innovation, he did two things. By increasing his own productivity, he generated a surplus for society as well as for himself: he used fewer of society's scarce resources for the same result or produced more without increasing the amount of scarce resources he consumed.

Henri Lepage, *Tomorrow Capitalism*[a]

It is possible for society to shift the production possibilities frontier (PPF) to the right, and create economic growth. One way society can do so is through a technological change or innovation that makes it possible to use fewer resources to produce a particular good. To illustrate, suppose there are 100 units of a given resource. Currently it takes 10 units of the resource to produce 20 units of good X, and 90 units of the resource go to produce 900 units of other goods.

Now suppose there is a technological change or innovation that makes it possible to produce 20 units of good X with only 5 units (instead of 10 units) of the resource. Now 95 units (instead of 90 units) of the resource can go to produce other goods. With more resources going to produce other goods, more other goods can be produced. For example, perhaps now with 95 units of the resource going to produce other goods, 950 units of other goods can be produced. In short, a technological advance or innovation that saves resources in the production of one good makes growth possible.

Now consider the resource of *time*. Time, like labor and capital, is a natural resource; it takes time (in much the same way it takes labor or capital) to produce goods. Thus, any technological advance that economizes on time frees up some time to be used to produce other goods. Consider a simple, everyday example. With today's computers, people can do things like make calculations, write books, type reports, and design buildings in much less time than in the past, which frees up the time to do other things. Having more time to produce other things promotes economic growth.

a. Lepage, Henri, *Tomorrow Capitalism* (LaSalle, Illinois: Open Court Publishing Co., 1982).

QUESTION TO ANSWER How does the Internet promote economic growth?

Technological Advances Technological advances make it possible to obtain more output from the same amount of resources. Compare the amount of work that can be done by a business that uses computers with the amount accomplished by a business that does not.

Technological advances may be the result of new capital goods or of new ways of producing goods. The use of computers is an example of a technological advance that is the result of a new capital good. New and improved management techniques are an example of a new way of producing goods.

Technological advances usually result from companies and countries investing in research and development (R&D). R&D is a general term that encompasses such things as scientists working in a lab to develop a new product and managers figuring out, through experience, how to motivate employees to work to their potential.

Incentives Some economists have argued that per-capita real economic growth first appeared in areas that directed people to effective economic projects. In other words, economic growth developed where people were given the incentive to produce and innovate.

Consider two incentive structures: in one, people are allowed to keep the full monetary rewards of their labor, and in the other, people are allowed to keep only half. Many economists would predict that the first incentive structure would stimulate more economic activity than the second, all other things being the same. Individuals invest more, take more risks, and work harder when the incentive structure allows them to keep more of the monetary rewards of their investment, risk taking, and labor.

The Kirov Works in St. Petersburg once produced military equipment. Now it produces farm machinery. How might this change affect economic growth in Russia?

Two Worries about Future Economic Growth

Two worries commonly crop up in discussions of economic growth. One concerns the costs of growth. Some individuals argue that more economic growth means more pollution, more factories, more crowded cities, more emphasis on material goods and getting ahead, more rushing around, more psychological problems, more people using drugs, more suicides, and so on. They argue for less growth instead of more.

Others maintain there is no evidence that economic growth (or faster, as opposed to slower, economic growth) causes any or all of these problems. They argue that growth brings many positive things: more wealth, less poverty, a society that is better able to support art projects and museums, and so forth.

The debate between those who favor more growth and those who favor less is complex. Economists have joined in, as have psychologists, biologists, sociologists, and many others. The debate promises to continue for a long time.

Newspaper Reporter

Newspaper reporters gather information and write stories about local, state, national, and international events and present points of view on various current issues. Reporters often have a hectic work life. They have to research stories quickly, meet numerous deadlines, and go places they would rather not go. Their working hours may differ from day to day, and they may work long hours into the night.

The benefits of the job include excitement, feeling as if you make a difference, and meeting interesting people. Reporters often see themselves as current-day historians.

Many reporters major in journalism, English, history, economics, or political science in college. Besides a college degree, reporters need to have good writing and listening skills. Experience is important, so interested students might work for their high school or college newspaper.

QUESTION TO ANSWER Some jobs are more closely linked to the ups and downs of a business cycle than others. For example, when the economy is down, many unskilled jobs seem to disappear. Do you think that when the economy is contracting, many reporters lose their jobs? Explain your answer.

Strip mines, such as this one in the heart of the Amazon forest, have always been criticized by environmentalists. They argue that strip mining destroys natural resources and habitats and scars the landscape for decades. Are we in danger of running out of natural resources?

The second worry concerns the relationship between economic growth and the future availability of resources. Some people believe that continued economic and population growth will hasten the time when there will be no more natural resources, clean air, or pure water, and no more land for people to live on comfortably. These people urge social policies that will slow growth and preserve what we have.

Critics of this position often charge that such "doomsday forecasts," as they have come to be called, are based on unrealistic assumptions, oversights, and flimsy evidence. For example, economist Julian Simon has pointed out that contrary to popular opinion, population growth does not hinder economic growth, nor does it increase the incidence of famine. Furthermore, he points out that natural resources are not becoming increasingly more scarce. In fact, Simon had a wager with Paul Ehrlich, author and professor of population studies and biological sciences, about the relative price of natural resources in the period 1980–1990. Ehrlich said that natural resources were becoming increasingly more scarce and therefore would rise in price during this period. Simon, to the contrary, said that natural resources were becoming more plentiful and would actually fall in price. Simon won the bet easily.

Section 2 Review

Defining Terms

1. Define
   - **a.** absolute real economic growth
   - **b.** per-capita real economic growth
   - **c.** production possibilities frontier (PPF)

Reviewing Facts and Concepts

2. Can real GDP rise as per-capita real GDP falls? Explain your answer.
3. You put $1,000 into a savings account that pays an interest rate of 6 percent annually. How many years before your savings has doubled?

Critical Thinking

4. Natural resources are neither necessary nor sufficient for economic growth. Explain.
5. Can labor productivity decline as total output is rising? Explain your answer.

Applying Economic Concepts

6. How can a PPF be used to show the different choices a society has?
7. What do you see as the costs of economic growth? The benefits?

Developing Economic Skills

Applying the Production Possibilities Frontier

Exhibit 14-9 represents a production possibilities frontier (PPF) for two kinds of goods, military goods and consumer goods. Suppose that this PPF holds for the United States, and that currently the United States is operating at point C. At point C, it is producing a certain amount of military goods and a certain amount of consumer goods.

Some U.S. citizens propose that the United States should produce more military goods and fewer consumer goods. They argue that we live in a dangerous world and that we have to protect ourselves. They argue that the United States should shift from point C in Exhibit 14-9 to, say, point B, where there are more military goods. The PPF makes clear, though, that at point B there are fewer consumer goods.

Now consider some other U.S. citizens who argue that the United States should produce more consumer goods and fewer military goods. They propose that the United States move from point C to, say, point D. At point D, there are more consumer goods but, of course, fewer military goods.

Common sense tells us that in an economy that operates on its PPF, more of one good means less of some other good. For example, suppose the president of the United States proposes that the health care system be restructured. He says that millions of persons do not have health insurance, and some are not receiving medical attention. In the president's proposed health plan, these persons would receive health insurance and medical attention.

The United States has the resources to provide every person in the country with needed medical attention. However, if the United States is operating on its PPF and if the quality of medical attention is not to be lowered, it is impossible to provide more people with health insurance and medical attention without sacrificing some other goods and services.

Does the recognition of this fact dampen our optimism about providing medical care to those who need it? Perhaps for some people it does. We would like to think that we can accomplish one goal without reducing our ability to accomplish any other goal, but the world does not always work this way. An understanding of what is possible—and what is not—often comes to us through the PPF. It may not always be pleasant, but thinking in terms of the PPF does keep us grounded in reality, which is no small accomplishment.

Exhibit 14-9

Choices and the Production Possibilities Frontier

We assume this production possibilities frontier holds for the United States. The nation has to operate at some point on the PPF; it cannot operate at more than one point at a time.

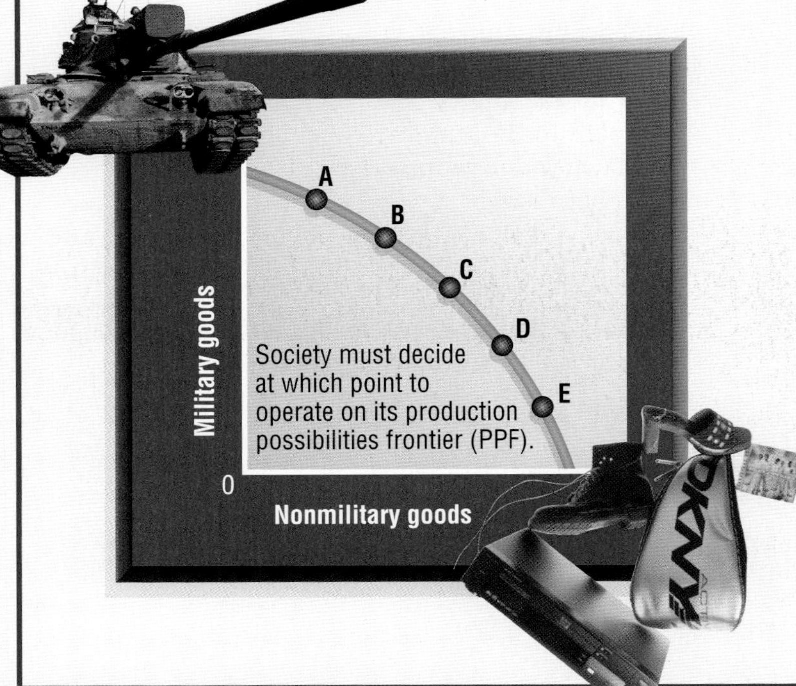

QUESTIONS TO ANSWER

1. You can do many things in a day: work, go to school, watch TV, and so on. How is this like an economy that can produce many different goods in a year?
2. There is a saying in economics: "There is no such thing as a free lunch." We might change it to say, "There is no such thing as free medical care for everyone." Would these statements be made by a person who thinks in terms of a PPF or a person who does not? Explain.

CHAPTER 14

Review

Economics Vocabulary

Fill in the following blanks with the appropriate word or phrase.

1. Real GDP is at a temporary high if it is at the _____ of a business cycle.
2. The _____ of a business cycle refers to increases in real GDP beyond the recovery.
3. If real GDP is at the low point of the business cycle, it is in the _____.
4. A(n) _____ indicator can be used to predict or forecast business cycles.
5. An increase in real GDP from one period to the next is referred to as _____ growth.
6. Real GDP divided by population is called _____.
7. A(n) _____ refers to recurrent swings in real GDP.
8. A(n) _____ consists of all possible combinations of two goods that an economy can produce in a certain period of time, under the conditions of a given state of technology, no unemployed resources, and efficient production.
9. If real GDP has fallen in two consecutive quarters, the economy is said to be in a(n) _____.

Review Questions

1. How can politics cause the business cycle?
2. Why are leading economic indicators more often cited in the news than coincident or lagging indicators?
3. How is economic growth related to labor productivity?
4. Diagrammatically represent the peak, trough, contraction, expansion, and recovery of a business cycle.
5. Explain how a change in the supply side of the economy can cause the contraction phase of a business cycle.
6. How do incentives affect economic growth?
7. Explain how the Fed can cause a business cycle.
8. Identify two ways of increasing labor productivity.
9. Can an economy witness both positive absolute real economic growth and negative per-capita real economic growth at the same time? Explain your answer.

Calculations

1. Real GDP in year 1 is $4,233 billion, and in year 2 it is $4,456 billion. The population is 178 million in year 1 and 182 billion in year 2. What is the per-capita real GDP in each year? Has there been per-capita real economic growth?
2. You place $5,000 in a savings account that pays an annual interest rate of 5 percent. How many years will it be before you have doubled your initial deposit?
3. Brown's annual income, which is $50,000, is growing at the rate of 10 percent a year. How many years will it be before her income has doubled?
4. If there is positive absolute real economic growth and negative per-capita real economic growth, what is the relationship between the change in real GDP and the change in population?

Graphs

1. In Exhibit 14-10 identify each of the following:
   a. point A
   b. point B
   c. point C to D
   d. point A to D
   e. point B to C

Exhibit 14-10

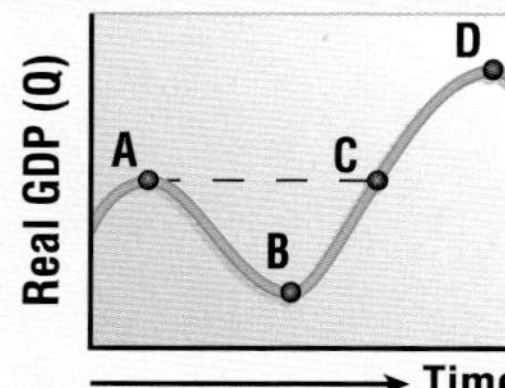

2. Look at Exhibit 14-11. Is the unemployment rate higher at point A or point B? Explain your answer.

Exhibit 14-11

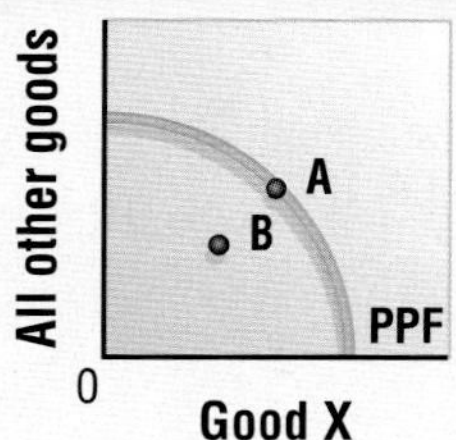

Economics and Thinking Skills

1. **Application.** What might be a leading indicator of your achieving a high grade on your next economics test?
2. **Analysis.** Suppose government spending remains constant over ten years. Is this fact evidence in support of or contrary to the theory that says politics can cause business cycles? Explain your answer.
3. **Cause and Effect.** Illustrate how an increase in population can cause both absolute real economic growth and per-capita real economic growth.

Writing Skills

If you were born in the early to mid-1980s, you have experienced a 3 percent annual absolute real economic growth rate over your lifetime. Write a one-page paper identifying how you think your life would be different today if there had been no growth during your lifetime.

Economics in the Media

1. Find an article in the newspaper that discusses the business cycle, any phase of the business cycle, any of the causes of the business cycle, or economic growth. Discuss the details of the article.
2. Find mention on a television news show of something you think will promote economic growth. For example, perhaps there is a short feature on tax incentives, new capital goods, or new management techniques. Explain how you think economic growth will be promoted by what you have identified.

Where's the Economics?

What is the relationship between the increased use of capital goods (such as robotics) and economic growth?

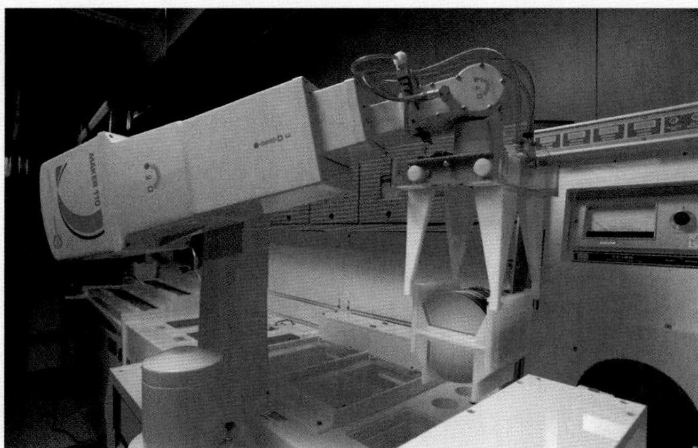

Analyzing Primary Sources

Paul Romer, a professor of economics at Stanford University, is well known for his innovative work in growth theory. In recent years, Romer has provided economists with a new way to look upon economic growth. Here is a short excerpt from a commencement address he delivered in 1996:[a]

Change and growth are linked together in the same way that risk and return are linked in the stock market. It is not possible to create more economic value merely by doing more and more of the same old things we have done in the past. In this century, we would not have been able to improve standards of living much if we had simply tried to make extra copies of the farms and factories that we had when the century began. . . .

Growth in the value of the economic output can be achieved only by finding different, more valuable ways to make use of the fixed resources given to us here on earth. Once, the only use we could find for iron oxide, ordinary rust, was as a pigment in cave paintings. Later, the only use for silicon was in glass. Now we use iron oxide to store data on computer disks and use silicon to make computer chips. A careful look around at the technological opportunities we face suggests that there are vastly many—almost incomprehensibly many—discoveries like these that remain for us to exploit. Because of these discoveries we will never face limits to growth. But we will be able to take full advantage of these discoveries and exploit these new uses for old materials only if we change the way we organize our lives and our work. And these changes can be disruptive. Some workers will find that their skills are not as valuable as they once were. Some will have to change jobs as firms shrink or fail. Some may have to change careers. There is little demand for cave painters or glass blowers these days, but there is a demand for computer literate graphic artists and for semiconductor fabrication technicians.

1. According to Romer, how does growth occur?
2. According to Romer, how do we create "more economic value"?

a. Paul Romer, "Risk and Return," commencement address delivered at Albertson College, June 1, 1996.

CHAPTER 15

Government and the Economy: Fiscal and Monetary Policy

What This Chapter Is About

Government can intervene in the economy in numerous ways. Two principal means are through fiscal policy and monetary policy. Fiscal policy deals with changes in taxes and government spending, whereas monetary policy deals with changes in the money supply. These two types of policies are discussed in this chapter.

Why This Chapter Is Important

In the past, people in the United States thought that government had no right to try to manage the economy. Government was simply there to provide goods (such as national defense) that the economy could not produce itself. Today, many people believe that if there is something wrong with the economy, the government should get to work on it. Government should manage the economy. Specifically, if there is inflation, government should get rid of it; if the level of unemployment is too high, government should lower it; if economic growth is weak, government should give the economy a boost; and so on.

Do monetary and fiscal policy always work as hoped? Not always. This chapter helps you understand the technical details and effects of monetary and fiscal policy.

After You Study This Chapter, You Will Be Able To

- explain what fiscal policy is.
- explain how fiscal policy may be used to reduce unemployment and inflation.
- discuss crowding out and explain how it bears on the effectiveness of fiscal policy.
- explain how monetary policy may be used to reduce unemployment and inflation.
- discuss the relationship between erratic monetary policy and stagflation.

You Will Also Learn What Economics Has to Do With

- *Star Wars.*
- 1964.
- the quality of your life.
- psychiatrists in Japan.

Economics Journal

The Federal Reserve System implements monetary policy in the United States. Watch the nightly news for a week. Write down each time you hear either the Fed or monetary policy mentioned. Beside each entry, describe the details of the report or story.

SECTION 1

Fiscal Policy

Fiscal policy refers to changes government makes in spending or taxation (or both) to achieve particular economic goals. Some economists believe that fiscal policy can be used by government to solve the twin problems of inflation and unemployment. We will examine their theories here, as well as what the critics say.

As you read this section, keep these key questions in mind:

- What is fiscal policy?
- What type of fiscal policy does government use to try to reduce unemployment?
- What type of fiscal policy does government use to try to reduce inflation?
- What are crowding out and crowding in?
- How can taxes affect the supply side of the economy?

Types of Fiscal Policy

Key Terms

fiscal policy
expansionary fiscal policy
contractionary fiscal policy
crowding out
crowding in
after-tax income
Laffer curve

Fiscal policy deals with government spending and taxes. If government spending is increased, taxes are reduced, or both, government is said to be implementing **expansionary fiscal policy.** The objective of this type of policy is to increase total spending in the economy in order to reduce the unemployment rate.

If government spending is decreased, taxes are raised, or both, government is said to be implementing **contractionary fiscal policy.** The objective is to reduce total spending in the economy in order to reduce inflation. (The two types of fiscal policy discussed here are summarized in Exhibit 15-1 on page 391.)

What type of fiscal policy would be implemented to reduce unemployment? To reduce inflation?

fiscal policy Changes government makes in spending or taxation to achieve particular economic goals.

expansionary fiscal policy An increase in government spending or a reduction in taxes.

contractionary fiscal policy A decrease in government spending or an increase in taxes.

Exhibit 15-1
Two Types of Fiscal Policy

If government increases its spending, decreases taxes, or both, it is implementing expansionary fiscal policy. If government decreases its spending, raises taxes, or both, it is implementing contractionary fiscal policy.

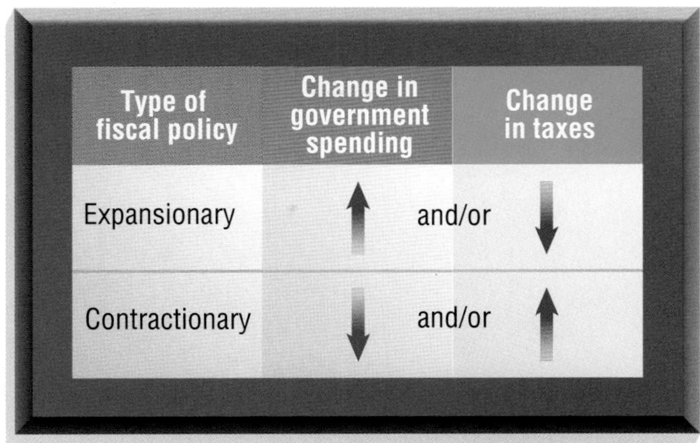

Type of fiscal policy	Change in government spending		Change in taxes
Expansionary	↑	and/or	↓
Contractionary	↓	and/or	↑

Expansionary Fiscal Policy and Unemployment

Suppose the official unemployment rate is 8 percent and the natural unemployment rate is 5 percent. Government sets a goal of reducing the unemployment rate, hoping to reduce it to 5 percent and thus achieve full employment. How might the use of fiscal policy help government meet this goal? Here is how some economists say it works:

- A high unemployment rate is the result of people not spending enough money in the economy. In other words, if people spend more money, firms sell more goods, and they have to hire more people to produce the goods.
- To reduce the unemployment rate, Congress should implement expansionary fiscal policy—that is, it should increase government spending, lower taxes, or both. If it chooses to increase government spending instead of lowering taxes, government can choose to spend more on health care, education, national defense, and many other needed programs.
- As a result of government's increasing its spending, there will be more spending in the economy. To illustrate, suppose that at current prices the government is spending $1,200 billion, business is spending $800 billion (buying factories, machines, and materials), and consumers are spending $4,000 billion (buying television sets, clothes, computers, and other goods). Total spending at current prices is $6,000 billion. Government decides to increase its spending by $200 billion, to $1,400 billion. Now total spending increases to $6,200 billion.
- As a result of the increase in total spending, firms sell more goods.
- When firms start to sell more goods, they have to hire more workers to produce the additional goods. The unemployment rate goes down as a result of more people working.

According to some economists, when government increases its spending and no sector of the economy lowers its spending, the unemployment rate falls. Explain how this happens.

The Issue of Crowding Out

crowding out The situation in which increases in government spending lead to reductions in private spending.

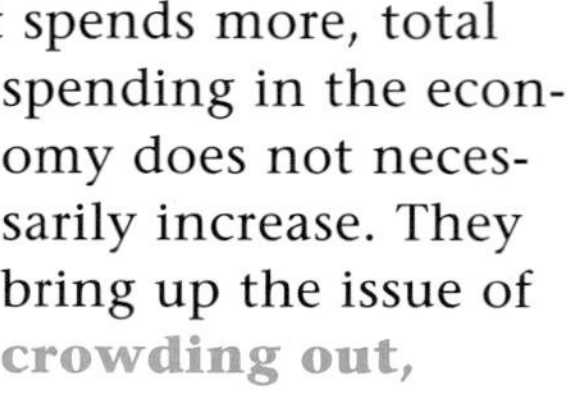

Some economists do not agree that things will turn out the way they were just presented. They say that when government spends more, total spending in the economy does not necessarily increase. They bring up the issue of **crowding out,** which occurs when increases in government spending lead to reductions in private spending (spending made in the private sector by consumers and businesses).

If the government increases spending on public education, some private schools might close their doors. Why?

For example, suppose that currently in the economy, $60 million is spent on an average day. We'll say that $45 million is spent by the private sector (households and businesses buying such things as television sets, houses, and factories), and $15 million is spent by government (buying such things as defense and education). Suppose now that government decides to increase its spending on education, thus raising its average daily spending to $17 million. What is the consequence? Does total spending rise to $62 million ($17 million in public spending plus $45 million in private spending)? Not necessarily, say some economists. Because government spends more on education, people may decide to spend less on education. Specifically, because government spends more on public schools and public-school teachers, people may decide there is less need for them to spend as much on private schools and private-school teachers. As a result, private spending will drop from $45 million to $43 million. Total spending therefore will remain at $60 million ($17 million in government spending plus $43 million in private spending).

In this example, where an increase of $2 million in government spending causes a $2 million decline in private spending, we have *complete crowding out;* each dollar increase in government expenditures is matched by a dollar decrease in private spending. With complete crowding out, an increase in government expenditures does not lead to an increase in total spending in the economy. Thus, it does not affect unemployment.

Consider another example. Suppose that government spends an extra $2 million, and consumers and businesses spend less—but not $2 million less. This situation is an example of *incomplete crowding out,* which occurs when a decrease in private spending only partially offsets an increase in govern-

Star Wars

The economy is made up of four sectors: household, business, government, and foreign. Suppose the total spending of these four sectors is $6,000 billion. Now suppose that government wants to increase the total spending in the economy. To this end, it raises its spending from $700 billion to $900 billion. Does it follow that total spending rises by the $200 billion increase in government spending? Not necessarily; if there is crowding out, the government's spending more may simply cause households to spend less so that total spending stays constant.

With this as background, consider a blockbuster movie like the *Star Wars* movie, *Episode I: The Phantom Menace.* This movie was released on Wednesday, May 19, 1999. On that day it earned $28.5 million. On its first weekend, it earned $64.8 million. In its first five days, it earned $105 million.

Looking at these dollar amounts, some people would say that the blockbuster *Star Wars: Episode I* would increase spending on movies. However, an increase is not inevitable after a blockbuster release. There may be some crowding out in movies, which may work in one of two ways.

To illustrate the first way, suppose the movie-going public spends $70 million each weekend on ten movies. This dollar amount is evenly distributed across all ten movies, so each movie earns $7 million. A blockbuster, however, increases its share of the $70 million. It earns $20 million and the nine remaining movies evenly divide up the remaining $50 million. In other words, spending on the blockbuster comes at the expense of other movies. Blockbuster spending crowds out nonblockbuster spending, in much the same way that government spending can crowd out household spending.

Of course, things don't have to work this way. Because of the blockbuster, total spending on movies on the blockbuster weekend may rise. In other words, the movie-going public may increase the amount it spends on movies in the first few weekends after a blockbuster is released. Spending may rise to, say, $90 million each weekend for three consecutive weekends. Once the "blockbuster effect" has worn off, however, spending falls below the usual $70 million per weekend—say, to $50 million per weekend for a few weekends. The blockbuster spending has still crowded out nonblockbuster spending, although not as quickly. This crowding out occurs over a six-week period instead of during a given week.

Alternatively, a blockbuster may not crowd out nonblockbuster movie spending but may crowd out nonmovie spending. To illustrate, suppose that because of a blockbuster, spending on movies actually does rise over a year. The new weekend average goes from $70 million to $80 million. But because people are spending more on movies, they spend less on other things. In other words, movie spending crowds out nonmovie spending. One sector in the economy (the movie sector) expands as another sector contracts.

QUESTION TO ANSWER A blockbuster movie is released on a given weekend, and the owner of the coffee shop next door to the theater says, "We're going to get a lot of business this weekend; in fact, I think this new blockbuster will increase our annual revenues." Is the coffee shop owner correct about the blockbuster increasing *annual revenues?*

THINKING Like an Economist

Ask an economist a question, and you are likely to get a *conditional answer.* For example, suppose you ask an economist if expansionary fiscal policy will bring about more spending in the economy. He might say that it will, *given the condition that complete crowding out does not occur.* In other words, if complete crowding out occurs, then expansionary fiscal policy will not increase spending in the economy; but if complete crowding out does not occur, then expansionary fiscal policy will increase spending in the economy. Some people, hearing this conditional answer, may think the economist simply cannot give a direct answer, but this is not the case at all. The economist is simply specifying the conditions under which expansionary fiscal policy works and the conditions under which it does not work.

Consider a similar situation: We might ask a physician if the medicine she is prescribing for us will make us feel better. She might say that if we are not allergic to the medicine and if we take it in the prescribed dosage, it will make us feel better. But if we are allergic to the medicine or if we do not take it as prescribed, it will not make us feel better. The physician is specifying the conditions under which the medicine will work. The answers to economic questions are similarly conditional.

ment spending. If this situation occurs, an increase in government spending does raise the total spending in the economy.

For example, again suppose that current spending in the economy is $60 million a day—$45 million in private spending and $15 million in government spending. Government spending increases to $17 million, and as a result private spending falls, but by $1 million rather than $2 million. Now private spending is $44 million, government spending is $17 million, and total spending is $61 million; total spending has increased.

Keynes on the Economy

John Maynard Keynes (1883–1946), who is considered one of the greatest economists of all times, was educated in England at Cambridge University, where he received a degree in mathematics in 1905. His major work in economics, *The General Theory of Employment, Interest and Money,* was published in 1936. This book changed the way many economists thought about the economy. In the book, Keynes argued that too little spending in the economy was the cause of high unemployment. Before Keynes, most economists thought it was impossible for insufficient (too little) spending within an economy to cause a high level of unemployment. They said that if people were initially spending too little, firms would simply lower prices, people would see the lower prices, and they would start buying more goods. For example, if car manufacturers were selling too few cars, they would lower the price of cars, and people would then buy more cars.

John Maynard Keynes argued that too little spending in the economy was the cause of high unemployment. Would Keynes be in favor of expansionary fiscal policy at such times? Explain your answer.

Keynes said that things might not always work this way. Specifically, he argued that even if people were not spending much money, firms might not lower prices. In other words, the car manufacturer that is not selling many cars may not lower the price of cars so that it can sell more.

But why wouldn't the car manufacturer lower car prices? Keynes hints that the answer involves the wages the car manufacturer pays to its workers. If workers would take a cut in wages, then the car manufacturer would see its costs go down, and it would lower car prices. But if wages do not go down, the car manufacturer might not lower prices. In other words, the

Employees are sometimes affected when companies cut costs. Explain why.

car manufacturer is waiting for a decrease in the wage rates it has to pay its workers before it will lower prices.

Why aren't wage rates decreasing? You would think that a representative of the car manufacturer could go to the workers and say, "I am not selling many cars, but there is a way to sell more cars: I can lower prices. But before I can lower prices, I need to lower my costs. Paying your wages is a large part of my costs. If you would accept lower wages, I could lower car prices, and people would buy more cars. If not, I might have to lay off some workers. What do you say?"

Keynes said that the workers would initially say no and would resist wage cuts. They might think that the car manufacturer was simply trying to pay them less because it wanted to earn higher profits, that business was not really that bad, and that the manufacturer had no intentions of lowering car prices very much. In other words, the workers might think the story was simply a ploy to lower wages.

In an effort to cut costs, GM laid off workers and closed this plant in Flint, Michigan, in 1980.

What's left to do then? If wages are not coming down quickly and sellers are not reducing prices, people may actually be laid off from their jobs because consumers are not spending enough for full employment to exist. Keynes argued that at this point, what had to be done was to raise total spending in the economy. Recall our earlier discussion of expansionary fiscal policy. Simply put, it was up to government to either increase its spending or lower taxes so that total spending in the economy would increase.

Critics argue that Keynes's proposal to enact expansionary fiscal policy did not take into account crowding out: if government spends more, consumers and businesses will spend less, and therefore there will be little, if any, change in total spending in the economy. Also, say the critics, Keynes opened the door to government involvement in the economy. They argue that once government was given the responsibility of using expansionary fiscal policy to reduce unemployment, it would abuse its newfound power. Instead of only increasing government spending to reduce unemployment, government would also want to increase government spending to "buy" votes at election time—whether or not there was an unemployment problem.

Contractionary Fiscal Policy and Inflation

Chapter 13 stated that inflation (increases in the price level) can occur when the aggregate demand in the economy grows faster than the aggregate supply in the economy. Stated differently, inflation is the result of too much spending in the economy relative to the quantity of goods and services available for purchase. Some economists have characterized inflation as "too much money chasing too few goods." Many of these economists argue that the way to get prices down in the economy is to reduce spending, which they say can be done through *contractionary fiscal policy.* Here are the points they make:

Cartoon by Randy Glasbergen, © 2000.

- Inflation is the result of too much spending in the economy. In other words, if people spent less money, firms would initially sell fewer goods. The firms would end up with a surplus of goods in their warehouses. To get rid of their goods, they would have to lower prices.

When government cuts its spending, it often gives rise to protests by the people affected. Here students at Louisiana State University protest government spending cuts.

- To get prices down, Congress should implement contractionary fiscal policy by decreasing government spending, raising taxes, or both. Let's suppose that government cuts its spending.
- As a result of the fall in government spending, there will be less spending in the economy. To illustrate, suppose that at current prices the government is spending $1,200 billion, business is spending $800 billion, and consumers are spending $4,000 billion. Total spending at current prices is $6,000 billion. Government decides to cut its spending to $200 billion. Now total spending decreases to $5,000 billion.
- As a result of the decrease in total spending, firms initially sell fewer goods.
- As a result of selling fewer goods, firms have surplus goods on hand. The inventories in their warehouses and factories are rising above a desired level, so to get rid of the unwanted inventory (the surplus goods), firms lower prices.

The Issue of Crowding In

As with expansionary fiscal policies, some economists do not agree that things will turn out the way they are supposed to with contractionary fiscal policies. They say that if government reduces its spending, total spending in the economy will not necessarily decline. They point out that **crowding in** occurs when decreases in government spending lead to increases in private spending. To illustrate, suppose government decreases its spending on public education by $2 million. As a result, people turn to private education, increasing their purchases of it by $2 million. This dollar-for-dollar trade-off is referred to as *complete crowding in;* for every dollar decrease in government spending on education, there is a dollar increase in private spending on education. Because of complete crowding in, there is no change in total spending in the economy. Thus, if complete crowding in occurs, a decrease in government spending will not lead to a decrease in total spending in the economy, so it will not bring prices down.

crowding in The situation in which decreases in government spending lead to increases in private spending.

It is possible that *crowding in* is not complete. In other words, it is possible to have *incomplete crowding in* or *zero crowding in.* If there is zero crowding in, for every $1 cut in government spending, private spending remains constant. With incomplete crowding in, for every $1 cut in government spending, private spending rises by less than $1. For example, for every $1 decrease in government spending on education, private spending on education may rise by, say, 60 cents. With either zero or incomplete crowding in, a decrease in government spending will lead to a decrease in total spending in the economy, so it will bring prices down.

Flight Attendant

Major airlines are required by law to have flight attendants on every flight for safety reasons. The primary job of the flight attendant is to see that safety regulations are adhered to, and they also try to make passengers as comfortable as possible.

Usually one hour before departure, flight attendants are briefed by the pilot in command on such things as emergency evacuation procedures, expected weather conditions, crew coordination, and length of flight. They then check first-aid kits, emergency equipment, and the entire cabin to make sure everything is in order. The lead flight attendant, usually called a *purser,* oversees the other flight attendants while performing many of the same duties.

Flight attendants must have a high school diploma, although airlines generally prefer those who have attended college. In addition, to be a flight attendant a person must be poised, tactful, and resourceful; be in excellent health; be able to speak well; and meet a certain height requirement. Most airlines require new flight attendants to complete four to six weeks of intensive training. New attendants are usually put on reserve status until they have been working for a period of time. They fill in for flight attendants who are ill or work on flights that have been added due to increased business.

QUESTION TO ANSWER How might a decrease in total spending in the economy affect the job security of flight attendants?

Government can choose to change taxes, which can affect both the spending and producing sides of the economy.

(Exhibit 15-2 below summarizes the effectiveness of fiscal policy under various conditions.)

Fiscal Policy and Taxes

The discussion up to this point has concerned either an increase or a decrease in government spending. Assuming there is no crowding out or crowding in, changes in government spending affect the spending (demand) side of the economy. For example, if there is no crowding out, an increase in government spending increases total spending in the economy. If there is no crowding in, a decrease in government spending lowers total spending in the economy.

Exhibit 15-2
The Effectiveness of Fiscal Policy

Part a: If crowding out is complete, expansionary fiscal policy is not effective at reducing unemployment. If crowding out doesn't occur or is incomplete, expansionary fiscal policy is effective at reducing unemployment. Part b: If crowding in is complete, contractionary fiscal policy is not effective at reducing inflation. If crowding in doesn't occur or is incomplete, contractionary fiscal policy is effective at reducing inflation. The conclusion: Fiscal policy does not work under all conditions; it works only under some.

	Objective	Policy	Condition existing	Does the policy affect total spending in the economy?	Does the policy meet the objective (as stated in the first column)?
(a)	**Reduce unemployment**	Expansionary fiscal policy (as measured by an increase in government spending)	No crowding out	Yes	Yes
	Reduce unemployment	Same as above	Complete crowding out	No	No
	Reduce unemployment	Same as above	Incomplete crowding out	Yes	Yes
(b)	**Reduce inflation**	Contractionary fiscal policy (as measured by a decrease in government spending)	No crowding in	Yes	Yes
	Reduce inflation	Same as above	Complete crowding in	No	No
	Reduce inflation	Same as above	Incomplete crowding in	Yes	Yes

Besides changing its spending, government can also change taxes. Changes in taxes, though, can affect two sides of the economy rather than just one. Changes in taxes can affect the spending (demand) side of the economy and the producing (supply) side of the economy.

How Taxes Can Affect the Spending (Demand) Side of the Economy

As discussed in an earlier chapter, economists designate four sectors in the economy: the household sector, the business sector, the government sector, and the foreign sector. For this discussion, we consider only the household sector and also assume that there is no crowding out or crowding in.

The spending of the household sector is called *consumption.* For example, if consumption expenditures in the economy last year amounted to $4,000 billion, it means the household sector spent $4,000 billion on various goods and services.

Lower taxes can lead to increased spending for a family such as this one. Explain how increased spending can result in lower unemployment.

Members of the household sector get most of the money they spend on goods and services from their income. However, people do not get to spend all the income they earn; part of it goes to pay taxes. The part left over is called **after-tax income.**

after-tax income The part of income that's left over after taxes are paid.

Let's say that the average household spends 90 percent of its after-tax income and saves the rest. Now suppose the average household earns $60,000 a year and pays $15,000 in taxes. The household has an after-tax income of $45,000. If the household spends 90 percent of its after-tax income, then $40,500 ($\$45{,}000 \times 0.90 = \$40{,}500$) is spent on goods and services. If there are, say, 50 million households, the entire household sector spends the following on consumption: 50 million $\times$ $40,500, or $2,025 billion.

What happens if government lowers taxes? For example, suppose it lowers taxes such that the average household no longer pays $15,000 in taxes but rather pays $10,000 in taxes. After-tax income now rises from $45,000 to $50,000. If the average household continues to spend 90 percent of its income, it now spends $45,000 ($\$50{,}000 \times 0.90 = \$45{,}000$) on goods and services. If we multiply this times 50 million households, we get $2,250 billion. In other words, as a result of a decrease in taxes, consumption spending has risen from $2,025 billion to $2,250 billion. If no other sector's spending in the economy falls, then total spending in the economy rises as a result of a tax cut.

As a result of the increase in total spending, firms sell more goods. And when firms start to sell more goods, they hire more workers to produce the additional goods. The unemployment rate goes down as a result of more people working.

Would things work in the opposite direction if taxes were raised? Most economists think so. A rise in taxes would lower after-tax income, thus lowering consumption spending. A reduction in consumption spending, in turn, would lower total spending in the economy.

Technology & Innovation

How the Internet Lowers Taxes

In 1999 an estimated 87 million people in North America and 150 million people worldwide had Internet access. Many millions of these people were buying online. For example, during the 1998 holiday season, an estimated 43 percent of all Internet users purchased something online, whether a book, a clothing item, a CD, flowers, and so on. Many more millions of people are expected to shop over the Internet in the future. If this happens, people who might have paid taxes on their purchases may end up not paying taxes.

Under the Constitution of the United States, states are prohibited from taxing interstate commerce. They can only tax the selling activities of companies that have a presence in the same state as the consumer. For example, if a customer in California buys a good sold by a firm located in California, this transaction is subject to California sales tax. Both the consumer and the firm reside in California, so the state of California can tax the transaction. In contrast, if a consumer lives in North Dakota and buys something from a firm in California, the transaction is not subject to California sales taxes, because the transaction occurs *between* states (the buyer is in one state and the seller in another).

In the past, businesses tried to locate near their customers to cut down on travel and communication costs. After all, if you want to buy clothes, books, or a computer, you might choose a store near you. Because of the Internet, however, a business no longer has to locate in your neighborhood to be near you; it can effectively locate on the Internet. Now stores are as close to you as your home computer. In short, the technology of the Internet has made it possible for a business to physically locate anywhere in the world it wants to and have "branches" everywhere there is a computer and a connection to the Internet.

To see how this affects the taxes you pay, consider a company like Amazon.com, which sells books online. If there were no Internet, Amazon would likely have to open up bookstores all over the country. Every time customers went into one of those bookstores and bought books, they would have to pay sales tax. In reality, when you buy a book online from Amazon (unless you live in a state where Amazon has a book warehouse), you do not pay any sales tax. (Of course, you have to pay shipping and handling charges instead.)

The governors of many states have argued that the Internet is hurting their sales tax revenues, and they have asked that they be able to tax Internet transactions. So far, such taxation has not been allowed. We will wait to see what happens in the future.

QUESTION TO ANSWER A company is physically located in Texas and sells clothes over the Internet. A person in Tennessee orders clothes from the Texas clothier and does not pay any sales tax on the purchase. Do you think the person in Tennessee should pay a sales tax to Tennessee, to Texas, or to neither state? Explain your answer.

How Taxes Can Affect the Producing (Supply) Side of the Economy

How much would anyone work if income taxes were 100 percent? In other words, if out of every dollar a person earned, he or she had to pay the full dollar in taxes, how many hours a week would the person work? Of course, no one would work if he or she had to pay 100 percent of earnings in taxes. It stands to reason, then, that people would work more as the income tax rate came down from 100 percent. For example, people might work more at a 90 percent tax rate than at a 100 percent tax rate, more at an 80 percent tax rate than at a 90 percent tax rate, and so on.

We can also look at this concept in terms of after-tax income. The higher your after-tax income, the more you are willing to work; the lower your after-tax income, the less you are willing to work. In other words, we would expect a much more industrious, hard-working, long-working labor force when the average income tax rate is, say, 20 percent than when it is 70 percent. It follows, then, that there will be a greater supply of goods and services in the economy (the aggregate supply curve shifts right) when taxes are lower than when they are higher.

Would this worker be more willing to work if the income tax rate was 75% or 30%? Explain your answer.

Tax Rates and Tax Revenues

Many people think that a tax cut results in lower tax revenues for the government, but this is not necessarily the case. Tax cuts can lead to lower or to higher tax revenues.

To illustrate, suppose Smith is a representative taxpayer who earns $2,000 each month. On his monthly income, he pays an average tax rate of 40 percent, which means he pays $800 in taxes and is left with an after-tax income of $1,200.

$$\text{Taxes paid} = \text{Average tax rate} \times \text{Income}$$

Now suppose the average tax rate is cut to 35 percent. Does it follow that tax revenues will decline? They only necessarily decline if income stays constant (35 percent of $2,000 is less than 40 percent of $2,000). As was stated earlier, tax cuts often stimulate more work, and more work leads to more income. Suppose, as a result of the tax cut, Smith works more and earns $2,500 a month.[1] Now he pays 35 percent of $2,500 in taxes, or $875, and he is left with an after-tax income of $1,625.

Thus, at a tax rate of 40 percent Smith paid $800 in taxes, but at a tax rate of 35 percent he paid $875 in taxes. Again, if Smith is the representative taxpayer, a tax rate cut will actually increase tax revenues. The government will take in more tax money with a tax cut, not less money, because the rise in income was greater than the tax cut. Income rose from $2,000 to $2,500 a month, which is a 25 percent increase. The tax rate cut was from 40 to 35 percent, which is a 12.5 percent cut. In other words, as long as income rises by more than the taxes are cut, tax revenues will rise.

1. Not everyone works more after a tax cut, but as long as some people do, the results hold.

The 1964 Tax Cut

It was 1962, and John F. Kennedy was president of the United States. Walter Heller, one of Kennedy's economic advisers, started telling the president that the economy needed a tax cut (a form of expansionary fiscal policy) to keep it from sputtering. In December, in a speech before the Economic Club of New York, President Kennedy said, "An economy hampered by restrictive tax rates will never produce enough revenue to balance our budget just as it will never produce enough jobs or enough profits."

In January 1963 he said, "It has become increasingly clear that the largest single barrier to full employment . . . and to a higher rate of economic growth is the unrealistically heavy drag of federal income taxes on private purchasing power, initiative and incentive."

Kennedy proposed expansionary fiscal policy—in the form of a tax cut—to get economic growth up and the unemployment rate down. He proposed lowering the top personal income tax rate, the bottom personal income tax rate, the corporate income tax, and the capital gains tax. He was assassinated in Dallas before Congress passed his tax program, but Congress did pass it.

In 1964, when the tax bill passed, the unemployment rate was 5.2 percent; in 1965, it was down to 4.5 percent; in 1966, it was down further, to 3.8 percent. The tax cut is widely credited with bringing the unemployment rate down.

As for economic growth, in 1964, when the tax cut was passed, it was 5.8 percent; one year later, in 1965, the growth rate was up to 6.4 percent; and in 1966, the growth rate was even higher, at 6.5 percent. Again, the tax cut received much of the credit for stimulating economic growth.

QUESTION TO ANSWER Does a tax cut affect the demand side of the economy, the supply side, or both? Explain your answer.

Congress will soon implement a 10 percent cut in income taxes. Based on available evidence, it looks like a change in after-tax income will only slightly increase the amount of labor that people will supply in the economy. What do you predict will happen to tax revenues? Explain your answer.

Consider what could have happened, though. Suppose Smith's income had risen from $2,000 to $2,100 (a 5 percent rise in income) instead of to $2,500. At a tax rate of 35 percent and an income of $2,100, Smith pays $735 in taxes. In other words, he pays lower taxes at a lower tax rate. If he is the representative taxpayer, it follows that lower tax rates generate lower tax revenues, because the rise in income (5 percent) is less than the tax rate cut (12.5 percent).

A group of economists, called *supply-side economists,* believe that cuts in high tax rates can generate higher tax revenues, whereas cuts in low tax rates generate lower tax revenues. To illustrate, Exhibit 15-3a starts at a relatively high tax rate of 90 percent. A tax rate cut to 80 percent raises tax revenue from $700 billion to $1,000 billion. Lower tax rates go together with higher tax revenues.

Exhibit 15-3
A Hypothetical Laffer Curve

The Laffer curve represents the relationship between tax rates and tax revenues that some economists believe exists. Starting at relatively high tax rates, a *tax rate cut* will generate *higher tax revenues.* For example, this is shown in (a): the tax rate is cut from 90 percent to 80 percent and tax revenues rise. Starting at relatively low tax rates, a *tax rate cut* will generate *lower tax revenues.* For example, this is shown in (b): the tax rate is cut from 20 percent to 10 percent and tax revenues fall. The Laffer curve is named after economist Arthur Laffer.

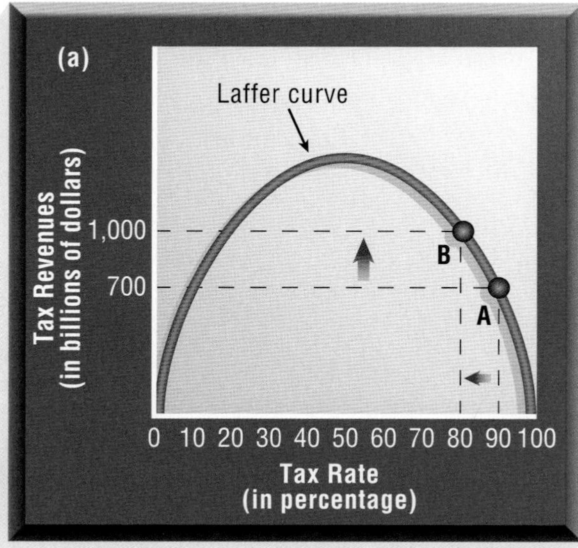

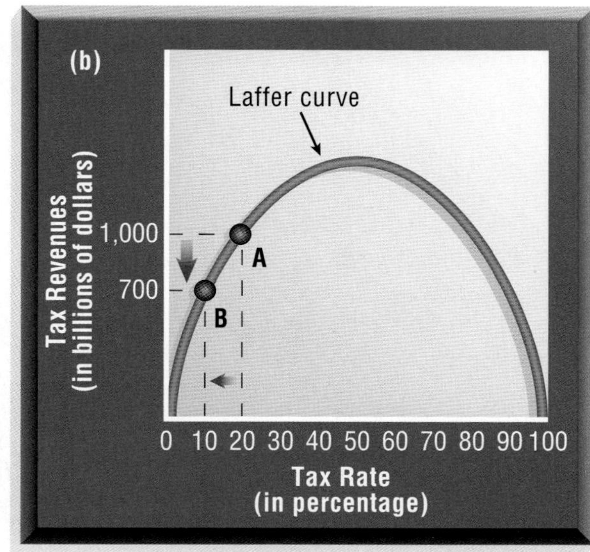

MINI GLOSSARY

Laffer curve The curve, named after economist Arthur Laffer, that shows the relationship between tax rates and tax revenues. According to the Laffer curve, as tax rates rise from zero, tax revenues rise, reach a maximum at some point, and then fall with further increases in tax rates.

Alternatively, Exhibit 15-3b starts at a relatively low tax rate of 20 percent. A tax rate cut to 10 percent lowers tax revenue from $1,000 billion to $700 billion. This time, lower tax rates are accompanied by lower tax revenues.

The curve in Exhibit 15-3 is called the **Laffer curve,** after economist Arthur Laffer. The Laffer curve simply illustrates the relationship that some economists believe exists between tax rates and tax revenues.

In Exhibit 15-3, you will notice that tax revenue is maximized at a tax rate of 50 percent. No one knows if this is true or not; specific tax rates were added to the Laffer curve drawn here merely for explanatory purposes. As far as anyone knows, tax revenue may be maximized at some tax rate higher or lower than 50 percent.

Section 1 Review

Defining Terms

1. Define
   a. fiscal policy
   b. expansionary fiscal policy
   c. contractionary fiscal policy
   d. crowding out
   e. crowding in
   f. after-tax income
   g. Laffer curve

Reviewing Facts and Concepts

2. What is contractionary fiscal policy, and for what purpose is it likely to be implemented?
3. Give a numerical example of complete crowding out.
4. While changes in government spending principally affect the demand side of the economy, a change in taxes can affect both the demand side and the supply side of the economy. Do you agree or disagree? Explain your answer.

Critical Thinking

5. Is expansionary fiscal policy always effective at increasing total spending in the economy and decreasing unemployment? Explain your answer.

Applying Economic Concepts

6. Someone says, "If the federal government cuts income tax rates, tax revenues will rise." Might this person be wrong? Explain your answer.

SECTION 2

Monetary Policy

The preceding section described how government uses fiscal policy to try to reduce unemployment and inflation. This section discusses monetary policy.

As you read this section, keep these key questions in mind:

- What type of monetary policy is used to reduce unemployment?
- What type of monetary policy is used to reduce inflation?
- How does monetary policy reduce unemployment and inflation?

Types of Monetary Policy

Key Terms

expansionary monetary policy
contractionary monetary policy

If the Fed increases the money supply, it is implementing **expansionary monetary policy.** Its objective is to increase total spending in the economy in order to reduce the unemployment rate. If the Fed decreases the money supply in order to reduce total spending in the economy and reduce the growth rate in the price level (reduce inflation), it is implementing **contractionary monetary policy.**

MINI GLOSSARY

expansionary monetary policy An increase in the money supply.

contractionary monetary policy A decrease in the money supply.

Expansionary Monetary Policy and Unemployment

Many economists believe expansionary monetary policy works to lower the unemployment rate in the following manner:

- The Fed increases the money supply.
- A greater money supply is usually associated with greater total spending in the economy. (There is more money to spend.)
- As a result of increased spending in the economy, firms begin to sell more products.
- As firms sell more products, they hire more workers, thus lowering the unemployment rate.

If this man is unemployed because of too little spending in the economy, can the Fed affect his chances of finding a job? Explain your answer.

The issue of crowding out does not arise in monetary policy. When the federal government (acting through the U.S. Congress) spends more (an expansionary fiscal policy), some other sector of the economy may well spend less. With monetary policy, this situation need not exist. If the Fed increases the money supply, no one need spend less; there is simply more money to spend.

Because crowding out is not an issue with expansionary monetary policy, many economists argue that an increase in the money supply will increase total spending in the economy and therefore indirectly lower the unemployment rate.

Contractionary Monetary Policy and Inflation

Many economists believe contractionary monetary policy works to reduce inflation in the following manner:

- The Fed decreases the money supply, perhaps by conducting an open-market sale. (Open-market sales are discussed in Chapter 11.)
- A smaller money supply is usually associated with lower total spending in the economy. (There is less money to spend.)
- As a result of the decrease in spending in the economy, firms begin to sell less.
- As firms sell fewer products, their inventories in the warehouses rise. To get rid of surplus goods, firms reduce prices. (Or, at minimum, they stop raising prices.)

Exhibit 15-4 below summarizes expansionary and contractionary monetary policies.

Would these shoppers spend more under expansionary monetary policy or contractionary monetary policy? Explain.

Monetary Policy and the Exchange Equation

The exchange equation, introduced in Chapter 13, states that the money supply (M) times velocity (V) is equal to the price level (P) times the quantity of goods and services produced (Q):

$$M \times V = P \times Q$$

Some economists say that the objective of monetary policy, pure and simple, is to maintain a stable price level—in other words, keep P constant in the exchange equation. If this objective is met, there is neither inflation (P rising) nor deflation (P falling).

Suppose maintaining a stable price level is the objective. How should the Fed go about meeting it? To answer this question, we must realize that if $M \times V = P \times Q$, then

$$\%\Delta M + \%\Delta V = \%\Delta P + \%\Delta Q$$

where Δ stands for "change in." In other words, the percentage change in the money supply plus the percentage change in velocity equals the percentage change in the price level plus the percentage change in the quantity of goods and services.

Exhibit 15-4
The Effectiveness of Monetary Policy

Expansionary monetary policy is used to reduce unemployment; contractionary monetary policy is used to reduce inflation.

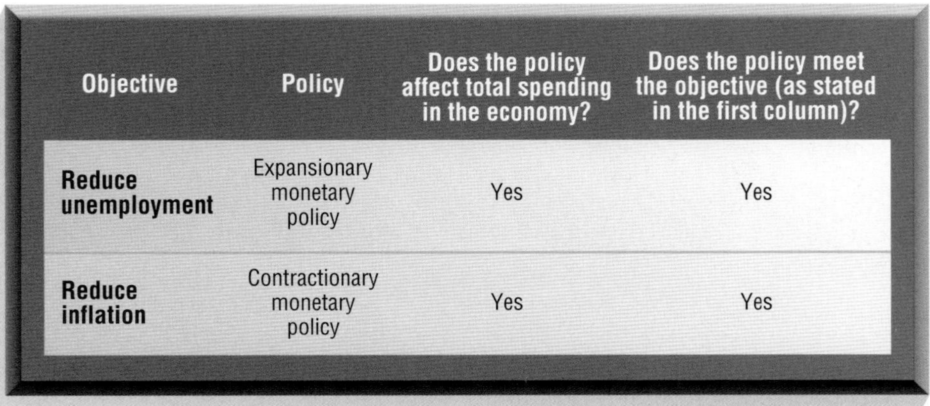

Objective	Policy	Does the policy affect total spending in the economy?	Does the policy meet the objective (as stated in the first column)?
Reduce unemployment	Expansionary monetary policy	Yes	Yes
Reduce inflation	Contractionary monetary policy	Yes	Yes

The Federal Open Market Committee (FOMC) largely determines monetary policy in the United States. Visit the Web site for the FOMC http://www.bog.fed.us/fomc/ Who are the current members of the FOMC?

The equation can be rearranged in a way that shows what the percentage change in the money supply equals. Subtracting $\%\Delta V$ from both sides yields:

$$\%\Delta M = \%\Delta P + \%\Delta Q - \%\Delta V$$

With this equation in mind, suppose that the *average* annual changes in velocity and quantity of goods and services are as follows:

1. $\%\Delta V = 1$ percent
2. $\%\Delta Q = 3$ percent

Furthermore, assume that the objective is to hold the price level stable:

3. Objective: $\%\Delta P = 0$ percent

Now, given 1 through 3, how much should the Fed increase the money supply so that the price level does not change? The answer is 2 percent:

$$\begin{array}{ccccccc} \%\Delta M & = & \%\Delta P & + & \%\Delta Q & - & \%\Delta V \\ \downarrow & & \downarrow & & \downarrow & & \downarrow \\ 2\% & = & 0\% & + & 3\% & - & 1\% \end{array}$$

Some economists propose that monetary policy should be implemented this way, that is, put on automatic pilot. The Fed should simply compute the average annual change in velocity and in the quantity of goods and services, set the percentage change in prices equal to 0 percent, and calculate the money supply change accordingly. The Fed should not fiddle with the money supply from month to month or year to year. It should not increase it sometimes and decrease it other times.

Will such a policy always yield stable prices? Probably not, because some years V and Q will change by more or less than the average annual rate. For example, if the average annual change in velocity is 1 percent, some years it might change by, say, 2 percent or 0.5 percent. Economists who support this type of monetary policy, however, say that the changes in V and Q will be close enough to their average annual changes that we will come close to keeping prices stable if we simply put money supply changes (monetary policy) on automatic pilot.

Section 2 Review

Defining Terms

1. Define

- **a.** expansionary monetary policy
- **b.** contractionary monetary policy

Reviewing Facts and Concepts

2. Explain how expansionary monetary policy can lower the unemployment rate.

3. The objective is to keep prices stable. Suppose the average annual change in velocity is 1 percent, and the average annual change in the quantity of goods and services is 4 percent. By what percentage should the Fed increase the money supply?

Critical Thinking

4. What evidence would be inconsistent with the theory that predicts lower inflation through contractionary monetary policy?

Applying Economic Concepts

5. Suppose the Fed sets as its single objective the stabilization of the price level. To this end, it decides to automatically increase the money supply by 2 percent each year based on an average annual change in velocity of 1 percent and an average annual change in the quantity of goods and services of 3 percent. If current-year velocity is above its average annual rate, what will happen?

SECTION 3

Stagflation: The Twin Maladies Appear Together

So far in the discussion of inflation and unemployment, it was assumed that the economy experienced either inflation or high unemployment, but never both at the same time. Real-world economies, however, sometimes do experience inflation and high unemployment at the same time, which is known as **stagflation.** In the late 1970s and early 1980s, stagflation was a major economic problem in the United States.

As you read this section, keep these key questions in mind:

- When the money supply rises, why does the output of goods and services rise before prices?
- When the money supply falls, why does the output of goods and services fall before prices?
- What causes stagflation?

MINI GLOSSARY

stagflation
The occurrence of inflation and high unemployment at the same time.

Rising Unemployment and Inflation

Key Terms

stagflation
stop-and-go, on-and-off monetary policy

For many years, economists believed that the economy would experience either high inflation or high unemployment, but not both at the same time. Moreover, they believed that inflation and unemployment moved in opposite directions. As the inflation rate increased, the unemployment rate decreased; and as the inflation rate decreased, the unemployment rate increased. They thought that inflation and unemployment were on opposite ends of a seesaw.

Real-world data appeared to support this view. For example, during most of the 1960s, inflation and unemployment moved in opposite directions. But in the 1970s, the inflation-unemployment trade-off disappeared for a few years. Instead of moving in opposite directions, inflation and unemployment began to move in the same direction—specifically, they both began to increase. The economy began to experience high inflation and high unemployment, or stagflation.

During Jimmy Carter's term as president, inflation and unemployment were both on the rise.

Exhibit 15-5

Evidence of Stagflation

The nations listed in the exhibit experienced stagflation—as evidenced by both higher inflation rates and higher unemployment rates—in the 1970s. Notice that the inflation rate and the unemployment rate are higher in the later period (1974–1979) than in the earlier period (1963–1973), which is stagflation at work.

Nation	Years	Average annual inflation rate (%)	Average annual unemployment rate (%)
Canada	1963–1973	4.6	4.8
	1974–1979	9.2	7.2
France	1963–1973	4.7	2.0
	1974–1979	10.7	4.5
Italy	1963–1973	4.0	5.2
	1974–1979	16.1	6.6
Japan	1963–1973	6.2	1.2
	1974–1979	10.2	1.9
United Kingdom	1963–1973	5.3	3.0
	1974–1979	15.7	5.3
United States	1963–1973	3.6	0.8
	1974–1979	4.7	3.2

Stagflation has occurred in other nations, as shown in Exhibit 15-5. For example, in Canada from 1963 to 1973, the average annual inflation rate was 4.6 percent, and the average annual unemployment rate was 4.8 percent. Then, during the 1974–1979 period, both inflation and unemployment increased. The average annual inflation rate rose to 9.2 percent, and the average annual unemployment rate rose to 7.2 percent. The same thing was also happening in France, Italy, Japan, and the United Kingdom.

An increase in the money supply can affect the output of goods. Explain how this happens.

How Money Changes Affect the Economy: Output First, Prices Second

Some economists believe that stagflation is the result of a stop-and-go, on-and-off monetary policy. Before we examine their position, though, it is important that we look at the sequence of effects that monetary policy has on the economy.

Most economists agree that changes in the money supply affect both prices and the output of goods and services, but that output is affected before

Economic Woes, Ethnic Violence, and Psychiatrists

The most serious risk is that deep recession could lead to widespread ethnic violence and a breakdown of social and political order.

—*The Economist*, March 7, 1998

In the late 1990s, many East Asian countries were having severe economic problems. For example, Indonesia had high unemployment and even higher inflation (stagflation). Many people did not know the cause of their economic woes; they did not know who or what to blame. In their search for culprits, they began to attack the ethnic Chinese in the country, who make up only 3 percent of the country but control about 70 percent of the country's wealth.[a] The situation got so bad in Indonesia that at one point 89 million people in the country could afford only one meal a day. Many of the hungry people took to the streets and started looting the shops and warehouses owned by the ethnic Chinese.

In Japan, bad economic times had different consequences. One result was that more Japanese people began to see psychiatrists. Bad economic times meant more business for Japan's psychiatrists. One psychiatrist, Takashi Sumioka, began to specialize in treating people with "restructuring syndrome"[b]—people who complain of tiredness, insomnia, and depression caused by finding themselves jobless in an economy that no longer seems to need their skills.

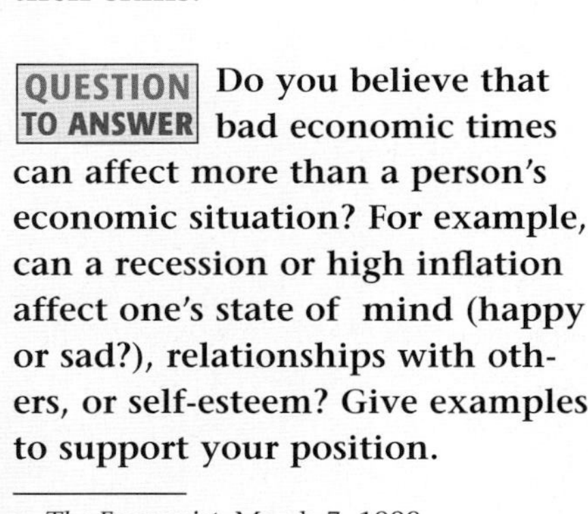

QUESTION TO ANSWER Do you believe that bad economic times can affect more than a person's economic situation? For example, can a recession or high inflation affect one's state of mind (happy or sad?), relationships with others, or self-esteem? Give examples to support your position.

a. *The Economist,* March 7, 1998.
b. "Japan's Worry about Work," *The Economist,* January 23, 1999.

Why might there be a lag between an increase in the money supply and an increase in prices?

prices. For example, when the Fed increases the money supply, total spending in the economy increases. As a result, firms sell more goods. Consequently, they begin to hire more laborers and produce more output. It is only later that prices rise.

Why does output rise before prices? Because when firms begin to sell more, they do not know at first whether this increase is temporary or permanent. Thinking it may be temporary ("It was a good sales week, but next week may not be so good"), firms do not yet want to change prices. If they raise prices and later learn that the higher sales were only a quirk, they may become less competitive.

Consider Yoko, who owns a pizza restaurant. In an average week, she sells 400 pizzas at an average price of $6. This week, she sells 550 pizzas. Yoko does not know why she did so well this week. People may be getting tired of hamburgers, or people may be getting tired of eating at home, or the Fed may have raised the money supply and increased total spending.

Yoko could immediately raise the price of her pizzas from $6 to $8, but suppose her higher-than-average sales do not last. If this week's higher sales are only temporary and she raises her price to $8 (while her competitors keep their prices the same), Yoko may hurt her business. She is therefore likely to be cautious and wait and see what happens. If sales continue at 550 a week, maybe after a few weeks she will raise her price. But if sales drop back to 400 a week, she will keep the price as it is. We can conclude that given an increase in the money supply, output is likely to go up before prices do.

An increase in hiring and output may follow an increase in the money supply. At what point do prices increase?

Similarly, when there is a decrease in the money supply, output is affected before price. To illustrate, suppose that instead of selling her average of 400 pizzas this week, Yoko sells only 250 pizzas. She does not know why sales are lower than average; she just knows they are. She reduces her output of pizzas and perhaps cuts back on overtime for her employees. She does not immediately reduce the price, though, because she cannot be sure if the lower-than-average sales will continue. She does not want to lower the price until she is sure that the demand for her good has fallen. We conclude

"All I Want Is Good Monetary Policy"

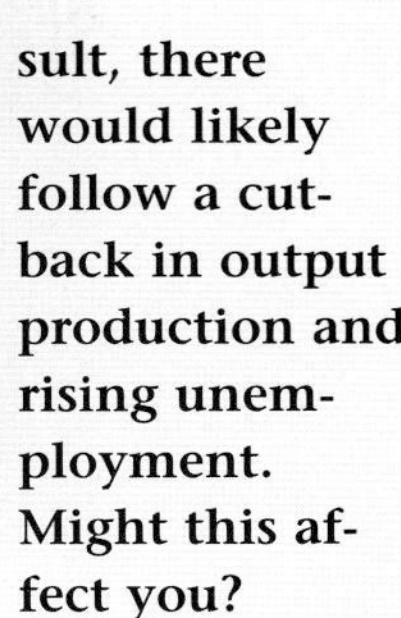

Does monetary policy affect the quality of your life? Most people do not think of monetary policy as affecting their lives much. They feel their lives are affected by how many friends they have, what they are studying in school, where they work, how busy they are, how happy they are, and so on. If you asked people what would make their lives better, rarely, if ever, would they reply, "My life would be better with better monetary policy."

The truth, however, is that the quality of life people enjoy is not unrelated to the quality of the monetary policy implemented in the country in which they live. Those who live in a country that practices bad monetary policy have lives much different from the lives of those living where good monetary policy is the rule.

For example, suppose you lived in a country with stop-and-go, on-and-off monetary policy—a world where there is stagflation. Would the high inflation and high unemployment in such a place affect you? It would indeed affect what you would pay for the goods you wanted to buy, if you would even be able to afford some of the goods; it would also affect whether you had an after-school job, along with the job security of your parents, uncles, aunts, sisters, and brothers.

Suppose you lived in a country where the monetary authorities continually increased the rate of growth of the money supply. In this country where the inflation rate was extremely high, would your life be affected?

Suppose you lived in a country where the monetary authorities made mistakes and periodically cut the money supply sharply. As a result, there would likely follow a cutback in output production and rising unemployment. Might this affect you?

The point is simple: Most of us do not think about the quality of the monetary policy in the country in which we live. We think about those things that are close to us and that we see each day, such as school, work, friends, family, and so on. These things do affect our lives, but monetary policy does, too. The quality of the monetary policy implemented in the country in which we live can determine the quality of our lives. Bad monetary policy can lead to hyperinflation, recessions, economic depressions, and high unemployment. These economic states, in turn, often cause people to feel anxiety, uncertainty, or depression. Thus, the quality of the monetary policy strongly affects the lives we live.

QUESTION TO ANSWER How would the life of a sixteen-year-old high school student be different in country A, where the monetary authorities successfully stabilized the price level with monetary policy, than in country B, where the monetary authorities practiced stop-and-go, on-and-off monetary policy?

Some economists believe that a fall in the market supply of oil can cause stagflation.

that given a decrease in the money supply, output is likely to go down before prices do.

What Causes Stagflation?

As was said earlier, some economists believe stagflation is caused by a **stop-and-go, on-and-off monetary policy** (an erratic monetary policy). They describe what happens as follows:

- The Fed increases the money supply. It pushes the monetary accelerator to the floor, which first raises output and then raises prices.
- Time passes. The increased money supply has raised the price level—that is, it has caused inflation.
- At the same time people are dealing with the high inflation, the Fed reduces the money supply. It presses on the monetary brakes. As a result, output is affected first, and it falls. Because there is less output, fewer people are required to work in the factories. Unemployment rises.

Notice that in the economy, inflation is coupled with a cutback in output and an increase in unemployment. The previous monetary policy (money supply up) caused the high inflation, and the current monetary policy (money supply down) caused the high unemployment. The economy is experiencing the effects of both monetary policies, or stagflation.

Not all economists agree with this description of the cause of stagflation or believe it is the only cause. Some economists maintain that a marked decrease in aggregate supply (perhaps due to a fall in the market supply of a major resource, such as oil) can also cause stagflation.

stop-and-go, on-and-off monetary policy An erratic monetary policy. The money supply is increased, then decreased, then increased, and so on. It is similar to driving a car by putting the accelerator to the floor, then slamming on the brakes, then putting the accelerator to the floor, then slamming on the brakes again, and so on.

Section 3 Review

Defining Terms

1. Define
   - **a.** stagflation
   - **b.** stop-and-go, on-and-off monetary policy

Reviewing Facts and Concepts

2. When the money supply increases, output rises before prices. Why?
3. Explain in detail what causes stagflation.

Critical Thinking

4. Because firms adjust output before prices, what information do they lack?

Applying Economic Concepts

5. What effect, if any, do you think stagflation plays in the reelection prospects of the president of the United States?

Developing Economic

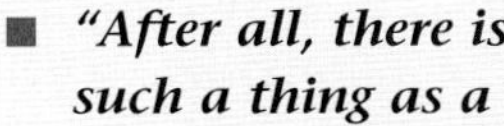

Skills

Understanding Economists in the News

Economists are sometimes interviewed on television news shows. For example, an economist might be asked on a nightly news show whether she thinks the inflation rate will rise, or whether unemployment will go down. Upon completion of this course, you should have a good idea of what economists are talking about when they answer such questions. However, sometimes economists use key phrases that may be difficult to understand without an explanation. The following are a few of these phrases, along with their explanations:

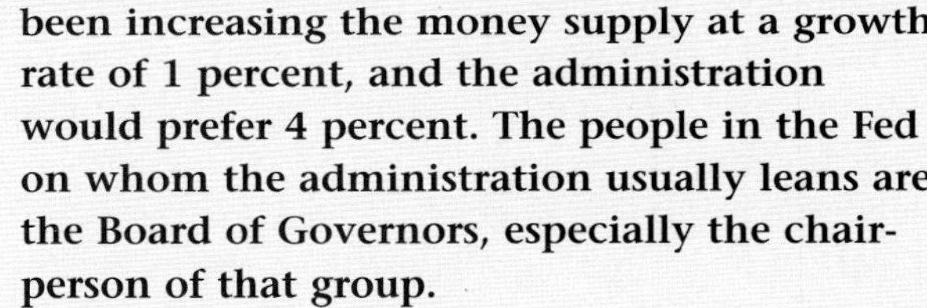

- *"After all, there is such a thing as a boom-and-bust cycle."* An economist who makes this statement is referring to the business cycle, discussed in Chapter 14. As you may remember, the business cycle relates to swings (up and down) in real GDP. The "boom" in the economist's statement refers to an upswing in real GDP (real GDP is increasing). The "bust" refers to a downswing in real GDP (real GDP is decreasing).
- *"The money stock increased by 11 percent last year." Money stock* is simply a synonym for *money supply.*
- *"The bond market likes what is going on in Washington." Washington* usually refers to the president of the United States, Congress, and the Fed. The phrase "what is going on" refers to what is being done in the area of economic policy. The president and Congress decide fiscal policy; the Fed decides monetary policy. When the bond market "likes" monetary and fiscal policy, there are usually a lot of people buying bonds, so the price of bonds is rising.
- *"The stock market likes what is going on in Washington."* The explanation here is the same as that of the previous statement concerning bond markets, except it refers to the stock market instead of the bond market.
- *"Fiscal policy is tight."* This statement refers to contractionary fiscal policy.
- *"Fiscal policy is loose."* This statement refers to expansionary fiscal policy.
- *"Monetary policy is tight."* This statement refers to contractionary monetary policy.
- *"Monetary policy is loose."* This statement refers to expansionary monetary policy.
- *"The administration is leaning on the Fed." The administration* refers to the president's administration. It usually consists of the president, his economic advisers, and the secretary of the Treasury. When the administration is leaning on the Fed, it is usually trying to get the Fed to increase the money supply growth rate. For example, the Fed may have been increasing the money supply at a growth rate of 1 percent, and the administration would prefer 4 percent. The people in the Fed on whom the administration usually leans are the Board of Governors, especially the chairperson of that group.
- *"The Fed is pumping up the money supply."* This statement means the Fed is increasing the money supply at a relatively high rate.
- *"The economy is in the upward-sloping portion of the Laffer curve."* Look back at Exhibit 15-3, Parts a and b, on page 403. In Part a, points A and B are on the downward-sloping portion of the Laffer curve. In Part b, points A and B are on the upward-sloping portion of the curve. If the economy is in the upward-sloping portion, decreases in tax rates will lower tax revenues, and increases in tax rates will raise tax revenues.

QUESTIONS TO ANSWER

1. What does it mean if monetary policy is loose?
2. To what does "boom and bust" refer?
3. What is another term for the *money supply?*

CHAPTER

15 Review

Economics Vocabulary

Fill in the following blanks with the appropriate word or phrase.

1. The scenario in which government spending increases by $1 and, as a result, private spending decreases by $1 is called _____.
2. If the Fed decreases the money supply, it is implementing _____ policy.
3. If the Fed increases the money supply, it is implementing _____ policy.
4. The scenario in which government spending decreases by $1 and, as a result, private spending increases by $1 is called _____.
5. _____ is the simultaneous occurrence of inflation and high unemployment.
6. _____ refers to changes government makes in spending, taxation, or both to achieve particular macroeconomic goals.
7. The _____ expresses the relationship that some economists believe holds between tax rates and tax revenues.
8. Income minus taxes is _____.
9. If the government increases its spending or lowers taxes, it is implementing _____ policy.
10. If the government decreases its spending or raises taxes, it is implementing _____ policy.
11. Erratic monetary policy is sometimes called _____.

Review Questions

1. Explain how complete crowding in affects contractionary fiscal policy.
2. In general, what is the cause of stagflation? Specifically, what causes the inflation part of stagflation? What causes the unemployment part of stagflation?
3. If the official unemployment rate is above the natural unemployment rate, expansionary fiscal policy will always reduce it. Do you agree or disagree? Explain your answer.
4. Explain the process by which expansionary monetary policy reduces the unemployment rate.
5. Explain the process by which contractionary monetary policy reduces inflation.
6. How can changes in income tax rates affect both the supply side and the demand side of the economy?
7. Rosa Jenkins, who owns a hotel, has rented out a higher-than-average number of rooms this week. Why is she likely to wait awhile before she raises the room rent?
8. Describe the process by which expansionary fiscal policy reduces unemployment (assuming there is no crowding out or incomplete crowding out).
9. Explain why expansionary monetary policy is probably not a solution to stagflation.
10. Do lower tax rates mean lower tax revenues? Explain your answer.

Calculations

1. Suppose the average tax rate is 20 percent, and tax revenues are $800 billion. What does (taxable) income equal?
2. Suppose government would need to raise total spending in the economy by $100 billion to substantially lower the unemployment rate. Furthermore, suppose there is incomplete crowding out; specifically, for every $1 the government spends, private spending falls by 80 cents. By how much would government have to increase its spending in order to raise total spending in the economy by $100 billion?
3. Suppose the average tax rate is 25 percent, and tax revenues equal $600 billion. If the average tax rate falls to 20 percent, how much will (taxable) income have to *increase* in order to keep tax revenues unchanged?
4. According to the Laffer curve, what two tax rates will generate zero tax revenues?

Graphs

1. If the objective is to maintain price stability, by what percentage should the money supply change in cases A through D in Exhibit 15-6?

Exhibit 15-6

	A	B	C	D
$\%\Delta V$	0	-1	+2	-2
$\%\Delta Q$	+2	+2	+3	+3

2. Using Exhibit 15-7, answer the following questions.
   a. What happens to tax revenues as the tax rate is lowered from E to D?
   b. What happens to tax revenues as the tax rate is increased from A to B?
   c. What is the tax rate at which tax revenues are maximized?
   d. What happens to tax revenues as the tax rate is increased from D to E?

Exhibit 15-7

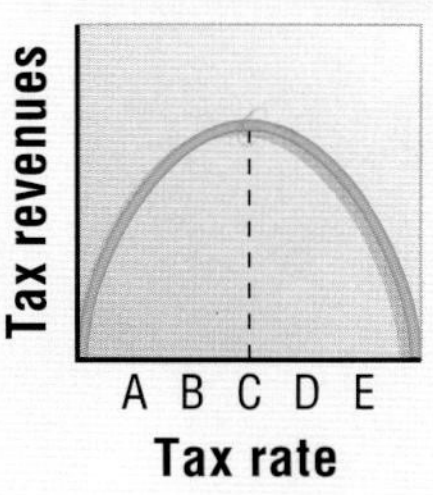

Economics and Thinking Skills

1. **Application.** It is sometimes said that making consistently accurate predictions in economics is difficult. Based on your reading of this chapter, give an example that illustrates this point.
2. **Analysis.** If expansionary fiscal policy is ineffective at raising total spending in the economy and lowering the unemployment rate, what condition must hold? Explain your answer.
3. **Cause and Effect.** Suppose that over a period of five years, velocity, the money supply, the quantity of goods and services, and the price level all rise. What caused the price level to rise? Explain your answer.

Writing Skills

Based on your reading of the chapter, write a one-page paper that addresses this question: Why do economists differ in their views on the effects of fiscal policy actions?

Economics in the Media

1. Find an article in the local newspaper that addresses fiscal policy, monetary policy, tax revenues, or tax rate cuts. Identify the major ideas of the article.
2. Find a story on a television news show that addresses tax rates, tax revenues, or monetary policy. Identify the major ideas of the story.

Where's the Economics?

Suppose Congress decides to spend more on various government programs in order to lower the unemployment rate. Under what condition will it fail to meet its objective?

Analyzing Primary Sources

John Maynard Keynes is said to have revolutionized economics with his book *The General Theory of Employment, Interest and Money,* published in 1936. Here is a short excerpt from the book:

> *In particular, it is an outstanding characteristic of the economic system in which we live that, whilst it is subject to severe fluctuations in respect of output and employment, it is not violently unstable. Indeed it seems capable of remaining in a chronic condition of sub-normal activity for a considerable period without any marked tendency either towards recovery or towards complete collapse. Moreover, the evidence indicates that full, or even approximately full, employment is of rare and short-lived occurrence. Fluctuations may start briskly but seem to wear themselves out before they have proceeded to great extremes, and an intermediate situation which is neither desperate nor satisfactory is our normal lot. It is upon the fact that fluctuations tend to wear themselves out before proceeding to extremes and eventually to reverse themselves, that the theory of business* cycles *having a regular phase has been founded.*

1. According to this statement, does Keynes believe that an economy can fall into a very severe recession or even an economic depression? Explain your answer.
2. According to Keynes, is the economy usually at full employment? Explain your answer.

CHAPTER 16

The Government Budget: Spending and Taxing

What This Chapter Is About

This chapter takes a close look at the federal government's taxing and spending activities. It describes what taxes the federal government applies, how the government spends tax revenues, the effects of both a budget surplus and a budget deficit, and the national debt.

Why This Chapter Is Important

The federal government affects your life in many different ways, two of which are its taxing and spending decisions. What kinds of taxes the government imposes and the sizes of those taxes affect important parts of your life, such as what you buy and how much you work. How the government spends the tax revenues affects you, too. For example, how much it spends on education directly affects you now and in the future.

After You Study This Chapter, You Will Be Able To

- explain the difference between the benefits-received principle and the ability-to-pay principle.
- discuss how proportional, progressive, and regressive income taxation differ.
- explain the budget process.
- explain the relationship between budget deficits and the national debt.
- explain how the national debt relates to future generations.

You Will Also Learn What Economics Has to Do With

- the first Social Security beneficiary.
- showing off.
- the Rolling Stones.

Economics Journal

Keep a list of the goods and services that you purchase for one week. Next to each good or service, write the dollar amount of the sales tax you pay. For example, on a $10 book you might pay a sales tax of 50 cents; on a $40 item of clothing, you might pay a sales tax of $2.

SECTION 1

Taxes

This section discusses taxes in general and the federal income tax in particular. It also discusses two principles of taxation, the benefits-received principle and the ability-to-pay principle.

As you read this section, keep these key questions in mind:

- What types of taxes exist?
- How do proportional, progressive, and regressive income taxation differ?
- How does the federal government spend its tax revenues?
- What is a fair tax?

Key Terms

national debt
proportional income tax
progressive income tax
regressive income tax

Major Federal Taxes

The government has three levels: federal, state, and local. At the federal level, there are three major taxes: the personal income tax, the corporate income tax, and the Social Security tax. In 2000, the federal government took in tax revenues of $1,883 billion.[1] Of this total, about 91 percent was from personal income, corporate income, and Social Security taxes. Exhibit 16-1 on page 419 shows the estimates of the Congressional Budget Office (CBO, which will be discussed later) for the tax revenue that each of the three taxes will raise from 2001 to 2006.

These people are filling out the forms for filing their personal income taxes. If you have a job, have you paid income taxes?

Personal Income Tax The personal income tax is the tax a person pays on his or her income. There is a federal personal income tax, applied by the federal government, and many (but not all) states have a personal income tax. At the federal government level, the personal income tax raised $899 billion in 2000, which accounted for approximately 47 percent of total federal tax revenue that year. In other words, for every 1 dollar the federal government received in taxes in 2000, 47 cents of that dollar came from the personal income tax.

Corporate Income Tax The tax corporations pay on their profits is the corporate income tax. The federal government applies a corporate income

1. The data for 2000 (found throughout the chapter) are estimates. The federal government regularly revises its estimates and, as time passes, estimates are replaced by actual numbers.

Exhibit 16-1
Federal Tax Projections, 2001–2006 ($ billions)

Here are the federal tax projections made by the Congressional Budget Office for the years 2001–2006.

Taxes	2001	2002	2003	2004	2005	2006
Personal income	$ 986	$1,026	$1,068	$1,112	$1,162	$1,217
Corporate Income	189	187	190	194	200	208
Social Security	684	714	742	770	808	842
Other	157	169	177	187	191	198
Total	**2,016**	**2,096**	**2,177**	**2,263**	**2,361**	**2,465**

tax, as do many states. At the federal government level, the corporate income tax raised $189 billion in 2000. This amount was about 10 percent of the total federal tax revenue in 2000.

Social Security Tax The Social Security tax is a federal government tax placed on income generated from employment. Half of the tax is placed on the employer, and half is placed on the employee. In 2000, at the federal government level, the Social Security tax raised approximately $636 billion, or about 34 percent of the total federal tax revenue. (See Exhibit 16-2 below.)

Three Other Major Taxes

Federal income taxes are not the only taxes people pay. Three other major taxes are excise taxes, sales taxes, and property taxes.

Excise Tax Excise taxes are taxes placed on the purchase of certain goods. For example, there are excise taxes on tobacco products and gasoline. Every time people buy gasoline at a gas station, they pay an

Exhibit 16-2
Where the Money Comes From

For each dollar the federal government raises from taxes, 47 percent comes from the personal income tax, 10 percent comes from the corporate income tax, 34 percent comes from the Social Security tax, and 9 percent comes from other federal taxes. (These percentages are for 2000.)
Source: U.S. Bureau of the Census.

Is Showing Off Too Costly?

Thorstein Veblen (1857–1929), an economist, believed that people sometimes buy goods for the wrong reasons. He coined the term *conspicuous consumption*—that is, purchasing designed to show off or to display one's status.

Consider the fact that today you can buy several different makes of watches, two of which are a Timex and a Rolex. A Timex costs under $100, and a Rolex costs many thousands of dollars. Both brands of watches keep good time, but the Rolex does something else: it "says" that you have the money to buy something very expensive. In other words, a Rolex is a status symbol.

Does our culture today promote status? Some economists believe that it does. The race for status, these economists contend, is a relative race and is wasteful.

Some economists argue that the race for status comes with certain opportunity costs, one of which is lost leisure. If we try to leapfrog each other, we work harder and longer to achieve a status position we could all achieve at lower cost.

Another opportunity cost of the race for status may be that society has to do without certain goods that it wants. For example, suppose society wants the government to spend more money on medical research, education, and infrastructure. Currently, three individuals—A, B, and C—are locked into a race for status with the other two. Since A is richer than B, and B is richer than C, A can buy more status goods (big houses, fancy cars, etc.) than B, who can buy more status goods than C.

Suppose the government proposes that it increase taxes on each of the individuals by 10 percent. A, B, and C argue against the higher tax rate because this will reduce their ability to buy status goods. They fail to realize, however, that while higher tax rates may make it less likely that each individual can buy as many status goods, their relative positions in the race for status will not change. After the higher taxes are paid, A will still have a higher after-tax income than B, who will have a higher after-tax income than C. Higher taxes will not stop the race for status, nor will higher taxes prevent anyone from showing off. The higher taxes will simply reduce the amount of money that the individuals can spend in their race to show off.

Are any benefits derived from the higher taxes? According to some economists, the additional tax revenue can finance more medical research, education, and infrastructure. In other words, there may be some benefits from using higher taxes to slow down the race for status.

One criticism of this reasoning is that the additional tax funds may not be used in the way people want them to be used. The funds may go for "public conspicuous consumption," such as expensive federal buildings, and other similar things. The critics also point out that higher taxes dampen people's incentives to produce, which may lead to less economic growth and wealth in the future. Finally, the critics point out that if the race for status is hobbled by higher taxes, the race will not slow down; it will simply take a different form. Instead of competing for status in terms of goods, people will compete for status in terms of power over others. In the end, the critics argue, it may be better to have people compete for status by buying goods than by trying to control others.

QUESTION TO ANSWER Do people in your high school try to achieve status by purchasing certain goods? If so, what goods?

excise tax. The federal government applies excise taxes, as do many states.

Sales Tax Whereas excise taxes are applied to the purchase of a few goods, sales taxes are applied to the purchase of a broad range of goods—cars, computers, clothes, books, and so on—when they are purchased. State governments typically raise tax revenue through sales taxes. There is no federal (national) sales tax.

Property Tax Property tax is a tax on the value of property (such as a home). It is a major revenue raiser for state and local governments.

Taxes and Workdays

Individuals, then, pay an assortment of taxes, including personal income taxes and Social Security taxes to the federal government, sales taxes to the state, and property taxes to the local government. How many days each year does the average person have to work to pay all his or her taxes? It was calculated that if a person began work on January 1, 2000, he or she would have to work until May 3, 2000, before earning enough to pay all taxes owed. Exhibit 16-3 shows how long the average taxpayer had to work to pay taxes in selected years.

Where Does the Money Go?

In 2000, the federal government spent approximately $1,765 billion. How was this money spent? The federal government breaks down its spending according to categories, a few of which are briefly discussed here.

The Internal Revenue Service provides a set of tax tables at its Web site http://www.irs.ustreas.gov/prod/ind_info/tax_tables/index.html Go to the site, and find out how much a single person who has a taxable income of $75,000 pays in income taxes.

You will notice in Exhibit 16-3 that the number of days spent working to pay taxes increased over time. Do you think it will continue its upward trend? Explain your answer.

Exhibit 16-3

How Many Days Do You Have to Work to Pay Your Taxes?

This exhibit shows the number of days the representative taxpayer has to work to pay his or her taxes in selected years. In 1950, it was 90 days. In 2000, it was 124 days.

Year	Number of days spent working to pay all federal, state, and local taxes	Time period
1950	90	January 1–March 31
1960	101	January 1–April 11
1970	109	January 1–April 19
1980	111	January 1–April 21
1990	112	January 1–April 22
2000	124	January 1–May 3

Who Pays the Tax?

Since the inception of Social Security, the Social Security tax has been split between the employer and the employee. For example, in 1999, the Social Security tax rate was 12.4 percent. Half of this tax, or 6.2 percent, was placed on the employer, and the other half was placed on the employee. In other words, the employee was expected to pay $6.20 per $100 of gross earnings (up to a limit), as was the employer.[a]

It is commonly believed that if a tax is placed on someone, then that someone actually pays the tax. There is a difference, however, between the placement of a tax and the payment of a tax. Just because the government places a tax on Smith, it does not necessarily follow that Smith pays the tax. The same is true for the Social Security tax: just because the government places half the tax on the employer does not necessarily mean that the employer pays the tax.

To illustrate, suppose the Social Security tax is $2 a day and that it is fully placed (100 percent) on the employer. In other words, the government effectively says to the employer, "For every employee you hire, you must pay a tax of $2 a day."

An earlier chapter explained that wage rates are determined by supply and demand. For example, the demand for labor and the supply of labor go together to determine the wage rate. Suppose that the equilibrium wage rate before the tax is placed on the employer is $10 an hour. What will the tax that is placed on the employer do to the employer's demand for labor? A tax will lower the employer's demand for labor. Employers will not want to hire as many employees if they have to pay a $2 tax per employee per day as they will want to hire if they do not have to pay the tax.

In other words, as a result of the Social Security tax being fully placed on the employer, the demand for labor falls. Consequently, the wage rate also falls, say, from $10 an hour to $9 an hour.

So, in our example, have employees paid for any of the Social Security tax? Yes, they have paid in terms of lower wages. In other words, without the tax, employees' wages would be higher ($10 an hour) than they are with the tax ($9 an hour). Some of the Social Security tax is paid for by the employees in the form of lower wages, even though all the tax was placed on the employer.

QUESTION TO ANSWER There are two sides to a market, a demand side (buying side) and a supply side (selling side). If a tax is placed on one side of the market, it can affect the other side. Do you agree or disagree? Explain your answer.

Tax is placed fully on employer ➡ Employer's demand for labor falls ➡ Wage rate falls ➡ Conclusion: Some of the tax is paid for by the employee in terms of lower wages.

a. The 12.4 percent tax rate does not include Medicare; if we add Medicare, the tax rate rises to 15.3 percent.

National defense accounts for 15.5 percent of federal government spending. Should the government spend more or less on defense? Explain.

National Defense In 2000, the federal government spent $274 billion on national defense. This amount was 15.5 percent of total federal government spending in that year. In other words, out of every dollar the federal government spent in 2000, 15.5 cents went to national defense. This money largely goes to pay the men and women in the armed services and to buy and maintain military weapons.

Income Security *Income security* refers to government programs such as housing assistance, food and nutrition assistance for the poor, unemployment compensation (for those persons who have lost their jobs), and federal employee retirement and disability payments. The federal government spent $258 billion on income security in 2000, or about 14.6 percent of total federal government spending.

Health The federal government spent $152 billion on health care, exclusive of Medicare (discussed next) and hospital and medical care for veterans, in 2000. This sum was 8.6 percent of total federal government spending. Some of this money went for health care research, but the bulk of it went for health care services.

Medicare and Social Security payments account for over a third (35.3%) of all government spending.

Medicare In 2000, the federal government spent $216 billion on Medicare, which is hospital and medical insurance for Social Security beneficiaries aged sixty-five and over. This amount was 12.2 percent of total federal government spending.

Social Security The federal government in 2000 spent $408 billion on Social Security payments, which largely go to retired persons. These payments were 23.1 percent of total federal government spending.

Education, Training, Employment, and Social Services In 2000, the federal government spent $63 billion in the category of education, training, employment, and social services (about 3.6 percent of total federal government spending). Most of this money went for elementary, secondary, and higher (college and university) education.

Ida May Fuller, First Beneficiary of Monthly Social Security Benefits

The legislation that gave birth to Social Security, the Social Security Act of 1935, was signed into law on August 14, 1935. Soon after the law took effect, some beneficiaries received one-time payments. For example, some people retired within days of the law going into effect and thus received only a few pennies in benefits. (Social Security benefits are determined by how long a person has paid Social Security taxes.)

However, the first person to receive a monthly Social Security check was Ida May Fuller. Born on September 6, 1874, on a farm outside Ludlow, Vermont, Fuller attended school in Rutland, Vermont, where one of her classmates was Calvin Coolidge, the thirtieth president of the United States. Fuller worked both as a schoolteacher and a legal secretary. She contributed a total of $24.75 in taxes into the Social Security system over three years. Fuller retired when she was sixty-five years old and began collecting monthly benefits in January 1940 with an initial check for $22.54. She lived to be 100 years old and collected a total of $22,888.92 in Social Security benefits.

QUESTION TO ANSWER What was Ida May Fuller's percentage return on her Social Security taxes?

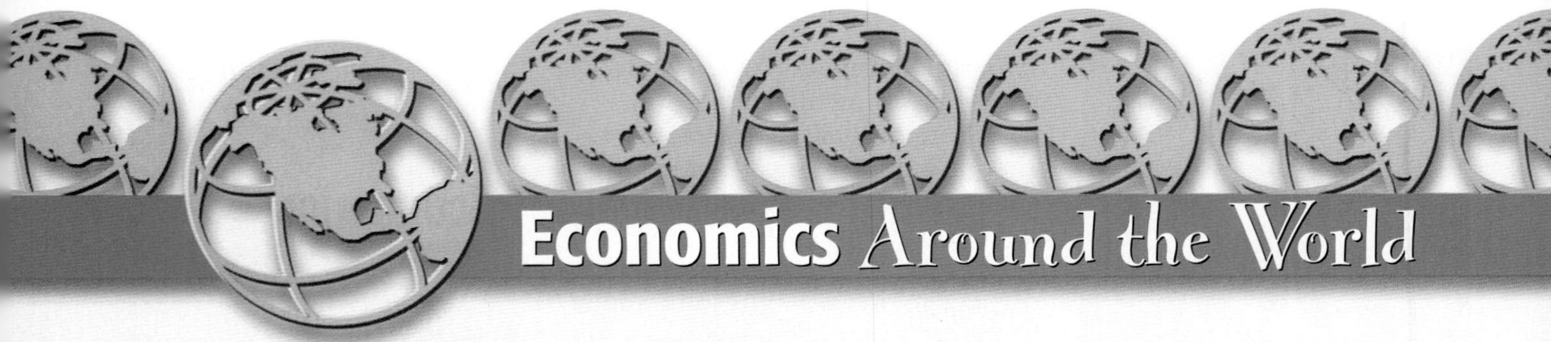

The United Kingdom, Taxes, and the Rolling Stones

In 1977, the government of the United Kingdom passed into law the Foreign Earnings Deduction. As a result, British citizens living and working in foreign countries did not have to pay British income taxes as long as they did not spend more than sixty-two days in the United Kingdom.

Now fast-forward to 1998. The Rolling Stones, one of the most famous rock bands in history, were on a world tour. They were scheduled to play four dates in the United Kingdom. Ordinarily they would not have had to pay British taxes on their world tour earnings because of the Foreign Earnings Deduction. However, that deduction had been repealed in 1998 because it was seen as a giveaway to the rich. As a result of the repeal, the Rolling Stones would have had to pay $20 million in British taxes if they had played the four U.K. dates. If they were forced to pay these taxes, the entire tour would have taken a loss.

Mick Jagger said that the Stones would play the four U.K. dates for charity if they could have the tax deduction. His request for the tax deduction was denied, so the four British tour dates were canceled.

Do taxes affect behavior? They certainly affected the behavior of the Rolling Stones.

QUESTION TO ANSWER Caroline earned $500,000 last year, half in country X, where she resides, and half in country Y. Do you think Caroline should pay income taxes in country X on all her income or only on the $250,000 she earned in country X? Explain your position.

SOURCE: Adapted from editorial, "The Jagger Curve," *Wall Street Journal,* June 9, 1998.

Net Interest on the National Debt When the government spends more money than it receives in tax revenues, it is said to run a budget deficit. For example, if the government spends $1,200 billion and its tax revenues are $1,000 billion, the budget deficit is $200 billion. The government has to borrow the $200 billion, in much the same way that people have to borrow money if their expenditures are greater than their income. The federal government has borrowed much money over the years; in 2000, its total debt—referred to as the **national debt**—was $5.7 trillion. The federal government has to pay interest on this debt, in much the same way that people have to make interest payments on their general credit card bills (such as Visa or MasterCard). In 2000, the interest payment the government had to make on the national debt was approximately $215 billion, or 12.1 percent of total federal government spending (see Exhibit 16-4 on page 425). To see projected government spending for the years 2001 through 2006, see Exhibit 16-5 on page 426.

An interest payment of $215 billion is extraordinary. We can get some idea of its size by comparing the interest payments on the national debt to

national debt
The sum total of what the federal government owes its creditors.

Exhibit 16-4
Where the Money Goes

For each dollar the federal government spends, 15.5 percent goes for national defense; 14.6 percent for income security; 8.6 percent for health; 12.2 percent for Medicare; 23.1 percent for Social Security benefits; 3.6 percent for education, training, employment, and social services; 12.1 percent for net interest; and 10.3 percent for other things, such as the court system, agricultural programs, transportation, and veterans' benefits. Data are for 2000.
Source: U.S. Bureau of the Census.

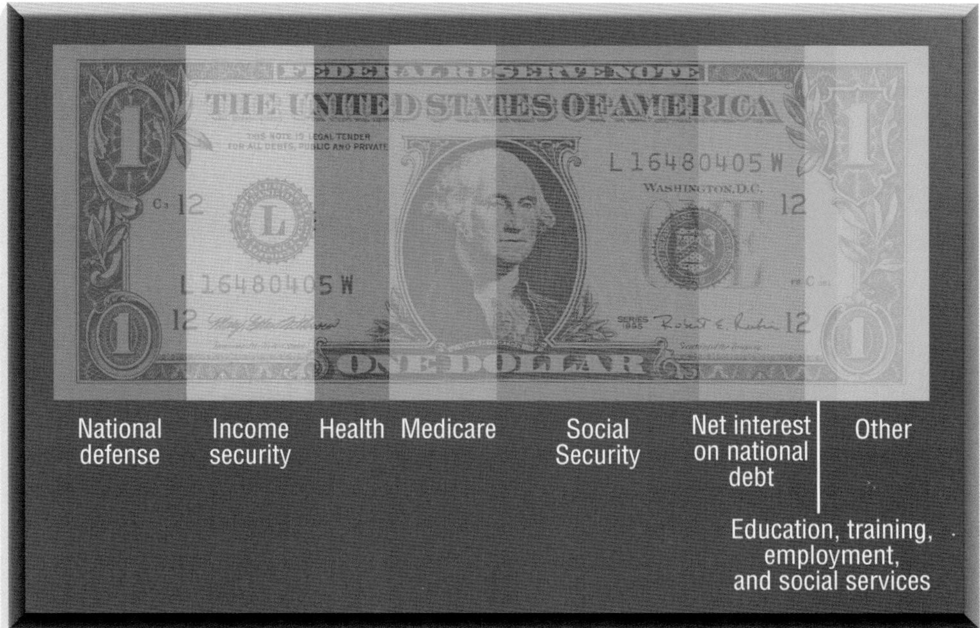

the amount of money spent on other things. For example, while in 2000 the federal government spent $215 billion in interest payments on the debt, it spent less than this total amount on education, housing assistance for the poor, nutrition assistance for the poor, health care services (unrelated to Medicare), and the administration of justice (such as courts) combined.

Economists look at things in terms of opportunity cost. They ask, "What is the opportunity cost of the $215 billion in interest payments paid on the national debt?" In other words, if there were no national debt, and thus interest payments did not have to be made, how might things be different? The federal government could have used the $215 billion to help the poor or build more schools. Or if the government chose not to spend this $215 billion, then taxes could have been lower by $215 billion. If taxes had been lower, people would have had more money to spend the way they saw fit (on houses, cars, computers, clothes, and so on), thereby generating more employment in certain industries.

No one knows for sure exactly how things would have been different had the $215 billion not been spent on interest payments. But, then, that is not the point. The point here is that certain alternatives are necessarily forfeited because of the large national debt.

The Budget Process

Just as individuals may have budgets in which they specify how they will spend their incomes—such as $300 a month for food and $100 a month for clothes—the federal government has a budget, too. In the federal budget, the federal government specifies how it will spend the money it has. It may decide to spend $250 billion on national defense, $100 billion on health care, and so on.

Exhibit 16-5

Government Spending Projections, 2001–2006 ($ billions)

Here are the federal government spending projections made by the Congressional Budget Office for the years 2001–2006.

	2001	2002	2003	2004	2005	2006
Government spending	$1,839	$1,888	$1,950	$2,017	$2,093	$2,140

Preparing a budget and passing it into law is a long process. It begins with the president of the United States, who, with others in the executive branch of government, has the job of preparing the budget. The president's budget, as the federal budget is initially called at this stage, recommends to Congress how much should be spent for such things as national defense, income security programs, education, and agricultural programs. The president must submit the budget to Congress on or before the first Monday in February of each year.

The budget for fiscal year 2001, which the president transmitted to Congress on February 7, 2000, covers the fiscal year beginning October 1, 2000. You can learn more about budgets for various fiscal years and the budget process in general at the Web site w3.access.gpo.gov/usbudget/.

After the president sends his proposed budget to Congress, members of Congress (such as Dick Armey, shown here at the podium) voice their opinions, and the opinions of their constituents, on the budget. Why do you think the president and Congress often disagree on budget issues?

Once the president's budget is in the hands of Congress, it is scrutinized by the members of the many congressional committees and subcommittees. Within Congress, the Congressional Budget Office advises the members of the committees and subcommittees on technical details of the president's budget. At this time, there may be disagreements between the president and members of Congress relating to how money should be spent; for example, the president may want to spend more money for health care than many members of Congress think should be spent. Disagreements may also arise over how much tax revenue is likely to be raised over the next few months. Perhaps the president and his staff may have estimated that the federal government will have $1,700 billion in tax revenues to spend, but Congress has estimated tax revenues to be $1,600 billion. The president and Congress try to resolve their differences. (Both the executive and legislative branches of government must estimate tax revenues, because they do not know for certain what economic conditions will be like, and tax revenues depend on the state of the economy. For example, if the economy is sluggish and many millions of people are out of work, there will be less income earned, and thus income taxes will be down.) Between the time when the president first submits his budget to Congress and when Congress actu-

HAGAR THE HORRIBLE

Reprinted with special permission of King Features Syndicate.

ally votes on the budget, many details of the president's budget may be changed to reflect compromises between the president and Congress.

Where are the American people in the budget process? Do they have a role to play? Some political pundits have pointed out that once the president submits his budget to Congress, the people get a chance to hear about it. There are usually numerous newspaper stories and newscasts about the president's proposals. The American people have a chance to write or call their congresspersons and express their preferences on the president's budget. Also during this time, special-interest groups may lobby members of Congress and express their preferences on the president's budget.

Congress has the obligation of passing a budget by the beginning of the fiscal, not the calendar, year. (A calendar year begins on January 1 and runs through December 31; a fiscal year can begin on the first day of another month and run for the next twelve months. The fiscal year under which the federal government operates begins on October 1 and runs through September 30.) Once Congress passes the budget, the details of spending outlined in the budget become law for that fiscal year. And the whole process begins again in only a few months.

The president and Congress do *not* establish the budget in isolation. The American people respond to national news stories about the budget in a variety of ways, including, in some cases, public demonstrations.

What Is a Fair Share?

Most people say that it is only right for everyone to pay his or her fair share of taxes. The problem is, How do we decide what a fair share is? And who is to decide? Historically, two principles of taxation touch on this issue: the benefits-received principle and the ability-to-pay principle.

Benefits-Received Principle The benefits-received principle holds that a person should pay in taxes an amount equal to the benefits he or she receives from government expenditures. For example, if you drive often on

Tax Cuts and the Rich

People are interested not only in the amount of taxes they pay but also in who pays what percentage of taxes. For example, it is interesting to learn that the top 1 percent of income earners in 1997 paid 33.2 percent of all federal income taxes. The top 5 percent of income earners that year paid 51.9 percent of all federal income taxes. Exhibit 16-6 shows what percentage other groups paid.

Now suppose that Congress passes a tax cut. How would you expect a tax cut to affect a particular group of earners? For example, after a tax cut do you think the rich would pay a share of the federal income taxes that is larger, smaller, or about the same as before the tax cut? For an answer, let's look at two major tax cuts in U.S. history. The first occurred during the 1920s. At that time, anyone earning $50,000 or more was considered rich. As a result of the tax cuts, the share of total income taxes for this group went from 44.2 percent in 1921 to 78.4 percent in 1928.

Again, in the early 1980s, Congress passed a major cut in federal income taxes. Before this tax cut, the top 10 percent of income earners paid 48 percent of all federal income taxes. Several years after the tax cut, they paid 57.2 percent. As for the top 1 percent of income earners, before the tax cut they paid 17.6 percent of all federal income taxes. Several years later they paid 27.5 percent. So you can see that a tax cut can have a very different effect from what you might expect on the percentage of tax paid by a particular group of earners.

You might wonder, if a group of earners pays a certain percentage of the taxes, do they receive an equal amount of the total income? For example, we learned that in 1997 the top 1 percent of income earners paid 33.2 percent of all federal income taxes. Does this mean that this group also earned 33.2 percent of total income? The answer is no. In 1997, the top 1 percent of income earners earned 17.4 percent of total income and paid 33.2 percent of all federal income taxes.

Exhibit 16-6

Which Groups Pay the Most Taxes?

Income group—percentage of income earners by amount earned	Group's share of federal income taxes
Top 1%	33.2%
Top 5%	51.9%
Top 10%	63.2%
Top 25%	81.7%
Top 50%	95.7%
Bottom 50%	4.3%

QUESTION TO ANSWER Did the top 1 percent of income earners pay a larger or smaller percentage of federal income taxes in 1997 as compared with the 1980s?

Among other things, our taxes pay for national defense and for building and maintaining roads and highways. Why might different taxing methods be used to pay for these goods and services?

government-provided roads and highways, you ought to pay for the upkeep of the roads. (This goal is usually met through the excise tax on gasoline. People who drive a lot buy a lot of gas, so they pay more in gas taxes than people who drive very little. Because gas tax revenues are used for the upkeep of the roads, the major users of the roads end up paying the bulk of road upkeep costs.)

Ability-to-Pay Principle With some government-provided goods, it i easy to figure out roughly how much someone benefits. For instance, ir the roads-and-highways example, we can assume that the more a person drives on the road or highway, the more benefit he or she obtains from it. With other government-provided goods, however, it is not as easy to relate benefits received to taxes paid. For example, consider national defense. We could say that almost all Americans benefit from national defense, but we would have a hard time figuring out how much one person benefits relative to another person. Does Jackson, down the street, benefit more than, less than, or the same as Stein, who lives up the street? The benefits-received principle is hard to implement in such cases.

Often, the ability-to-pay principle is used instead. This principle says that people should pay taxes according to their abilities to pay. Because a rich person is more able to pay taxes than a poor person, a rich person should pay more taxes than a poor person. For example, a millionaire might pay $330,000 a year in income taxes, whereas a person who earns $30,000 a year might pay $8,000.

Proportional, Progressive, and Regressive Income Taxes

Income taxes can be proportional, progressive, or regressive.

Proportional Income Taxation With a **proportional income tax,** everyone pays taxes at the same rate, whatever the income level. For example, if Kuan's taxable income is $100,000, she will pay taxes at the same rate as Arehart, who has a taxable income of $10,000. Suppose this rate is 10 percent. Kuan then pays $10,000 in income taxes, and Arehart

proportional income tax
An income tax that everyone pays at the same rate, whatever the income level.

Exhibit 16-7
Three Income Tax Structures

Proportional	Progressive	Regressive
Same tax rate for every taxpayer and tax rate remains constant as taxable income rises.	Tax rate rises as taxable income rises.	Tax rate falls as taxable income rises.

pays $1,000. Notice that Kuan, who earns ten times as much as Arehart, pays ten times as much in taxes ($10,000 as opposed to $1,000). However, Kuan pays at exactly the same rate—10 percent—as Arehart. Sometimes a proportional income tax is called a *flat tax,* because everyone pays the same flat tax rate.

Progressive Income Taxation A **progressive income tax** is a tax that people pay at a higher rate as their income levels rise. To illustrate, suppose Davidson pays taxes at the rate of 10 percent on a taxable income of $10,000. When his income doubles to $20,000, he pays at a rate of 12 percent. A progressive income tax is usually capped at some tax rate; it rises to some rate and then stops. For instance, perhaps no one will pay at a rate higher than 39.6 percent, no matter how high the income.

progressive income tax
An income tax whose rate increases as income level rises. Progressive income tax structures are usually capped at some rate.

regressive income tax
An income tax whose rate decreases as income level rises.

Regressive Income Taxation With a **regressive income tax,** people pay taxes at a lower rate as their income levels rise. For example, Lowenstein's tax rate is 10 percent when her income is $10,000 and 8 percent when her income rises to $20,000.

Question: *Does the United States today have a progressive, regressive, or proportional federal income tax?*

Answer: *The U.S. federal income tax is progressive.*

Section 1 Review

Defining Terms

1. Define
   a. proportional income tax
   b. progressive income tax
   c. regressive income tax
   d. national debt

Reviewing Facts and Concepts

2. What three federal taxes together account for approximately 91 percent of federal government tax revenues?
3. Which federal tax raises the greatest tax revenue?
4. What percentage of the year did the average taxpayer have to work in 2000 to pay all his or her taxes?

Critical Thinking

5. "It is possible for a high-income earner to pay more in taxes than a low-income earner under a regressive income tax." Do you agree or disagree? Explain your answer.

Applying Economic Concepts

6. Is a sales tax regressive, proportional, or progressive? Explain your answer.

SECTION 2

The Budget: Deficits and Surpluses

The federal budget can be in one of three states: balanced, in deficit, or in surplus. This section discusses the meaning and effects of each.

As you read this section, keep these key questions in mind:

- What is a balanced budget? a budget deficit? a budget surplus?
- What is the relationship between deficits and the national debt?
- What are some issues connected with budget surpluses?

Budgets: Balanced and in Deficit

Key Terms
budget deficit
budget surplus

Adam Smith, the eighteenth-century economist, said, "What is prudence in the conduct of every private family, can scarce be folly in that of a great kingdom." In other words, if it is right and reasonable for a family to do something, it is probably also right and reasonable for a great nation to do the same thing. For example, if it is right for a family to save and to make sure it does not stay in debt, then it is right for a nation to do the same. For many years this notion, which originated with Adam Smith, carried over to the discussions of U.S. federal budget policy. Most people believed that the federal budget should be balanced—that is, government expenditures should be equal to tax revenues. **Budget deficits,** which occur when government expenditures exceed tax revenues, were acceptable, but only during wartime.

budget deficit The situation in which federal government expenditures are greater than federal government tax revenues.

Conditions began to change around the time of the Great Depression (1929–1933), a period of great economic distress in this country. During

During the early years of our country, budget deficits were considered acceptable only during wartime. Is this still true today?

The Great Depression changed the way people thought about the U.S. budget. Explain.

this time, unemployment skyrocketed, the production of goods and services plummeted, prices fell, banks closed, and companies went bankrupt. Until this time, many people in the United States had thought that the free-enterprise economy was a stable, smooth mechanism and that it was not subject to violent and abrupt downturns. The economic downturn of the Great Depression gave these people cause for doubt and upset their cherished notions of how an economy worked. Slowly, many previously accepted ideas of budget policy began to be discarded. One notion in particular that fell by the wayside was the idea that the federal budget should be balanced. Slowly, people began to accept budget deficits as a way of reducing unemployment.

What do budget deficits have to do with reducing unemployment? Suppose the federal budget is balanced. Government spending is $1,200 billion, and tax revenues are $1,200 billion. However, unemployment is high, say, around 10 percent. The president, along with Congress, wants to reduce the unemployment rate by implementing expansionary fiscal policy (increase government spending or decrease taxes). Together, they decide to increase government spending to $1,250 billion. Tax revenues, we'll assume, remain constant at $1,200 billion. In this instance, expansionary fiscal policy has led to a budget deficit; government spending ($1,250 billion) is greater than tax revenues ($1,200 billion). The federal budget deficit is $50 billion.

Many people came to see budget deficits as necessary, given the high unemployment that plagued the economy. According to them, the choice was simple:

THINKING Like an Economist

Suppose the economy is faced with high inflation. Political leaders turn to economists and ask them what should be done. The economists say that contractionary fiscal policy should be put into effect. Specifically, government spending should be cut or taxes raised. The economists say this strategy will reduce inflation. The government officials swallow hard, because they know that while this may be good economic advice, it is bad political advice. Few politicians win elections by proposing to cut people's benefits or raise their taxes.

An economist is aware that what may be the "best medicine" for the economy may turn out to be so bitter tasting that politicians will not want to prescribe it to the electorate. There is sometimes a tension between economics and politics, and politics is often a stronger force than economics.

Exhibit 16-8

Federal Budget Deficits, 1988–1997

The United States experienced a federal budget deficit every year from 1970 through 1997. In this exhibit we show the budget deficits for 1988–97.
Source: Economic Report of the President, 1999.

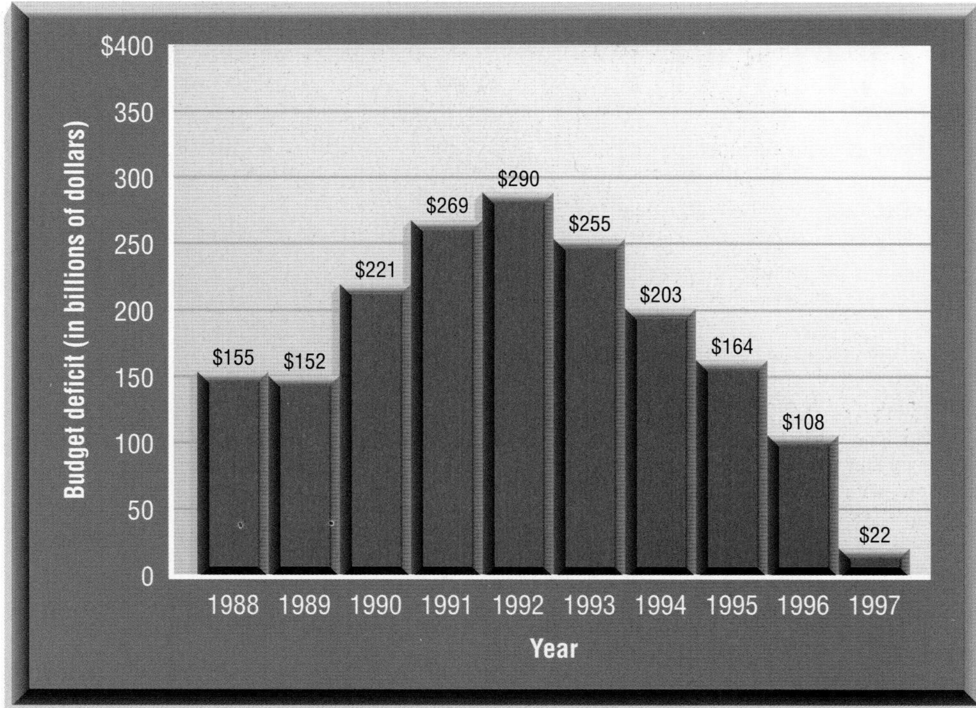

(1) either keep the federal budget balanced and suffer high unemployment (and the reduced output of goods and services that is a consequence of it) or (2) accept the budget deficit and reduce the unemployment rate. For many people, it was "better to balance the economy than to balance the budget." Exhibit 16-8 shows budget deficits from 1988 through 1997.

Question: *Do all economists agree that it is better to have a budget deficit and reduce unemployment than to maintain a balanced budget?*

Answer: *No. One reason is that not all economists believe that expansionary fiscal policy, which can sometimes create a budget deficit, is effective at reducing unemployment. Chapter 15 discussed this issue in relation to the topic of crowding out. Some economists believe that complete crowding out will prevent expansionary fiscal policy from being effective at reducing the unemployment rate.*

In June of 2000, this graduate's share of the national debt was $20,578. Explain what the national debt is.

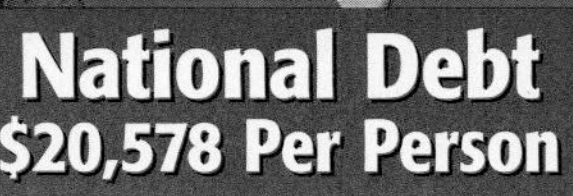

Budget Deficits Lead to National Debt

The only way an individual can spend more than he or she earns is to borrow the difference and incur a debt. (We are ruling out monetary gifts to this person.) For example, if Harry earns $30,000 a year and spends $32,000, he would have had to borrow $2,000. This $2,000 is Harry's debt.

What is true for Harry is true for the federal government. If it spends more than it receives in tax revenues, it has to borrow the difference and incur a debt. Of course, another way to say this is that every time the federal government runs a deficit, it has to borrow money and incur a debt. In

Records of the national (public) debt can be found at the Web site of the Department of the Public Debt http://www.publicdebt.treas.gov/ What was the national debt on the day you checked?

short, deficits lead to debt. The debt of the federal government is called the *national debt.*

The federal government had a budget deficit each year for almost three decades, from 1970 to 1997. In June, 2000, the national debt was approximately $5.64 trillion. If we divide the national debt by the U.S. population, we get *per-capita national debt,* which is $20,578. The per-capita national debt is sometimes referred to as each citizen's share of the national debt.

Budget Deficits, National Debt, and Higher Future Taxes

As a future taxpayer, this young girl may face "taxation without representation." Explain what this means.

When the government spends more than it collects in tax revenues, it has to borrow the difference. Deficits lead to debt. But what does debt lead to? Some economists argue that it leads to higher taxes in the future. When the government borrows the money to pay for the excess of its spending over tax revenues, it has to borrow that money from people. Those people will have to be repaid one day; the debt has to be paid off. (If you borrowed money from a bank, you would have to repay the money one day, with interest, to pay off your debt.) What happens when the government's debt has to be paid off? Taxes must be used, so taxes have to be higher than they would have been had the debt not been incurred in the first place. Some economists say that as far as future taxpayers are concerned, current budget deficits are a form of "taxation without representation."

Is it ethical for one generation to buy things that another generation ends up partly paying for? Some people say no, but others say it depends on whether what the first generation buys benefits the next generation. For example, suppose the present generation decides to buy an interstate freeway system for $10 billion. The present generation decides to pay $2 billion itself through taxes and to borrow $8 billion. The present generation knows that the future generation will have to pay off the $8 billion (plus interest),

If the budgetary future is one of budget surpluses, what do you think the nature of the political debate will be?

Exhibit 16-9

Federal Budget Projections, 2001–2007

According to the Congressional Budget Office, the federal government will run a surplus in its budget for the near future.

Source: Economic Report of the President, 1999, and the Congressional Budget Office.

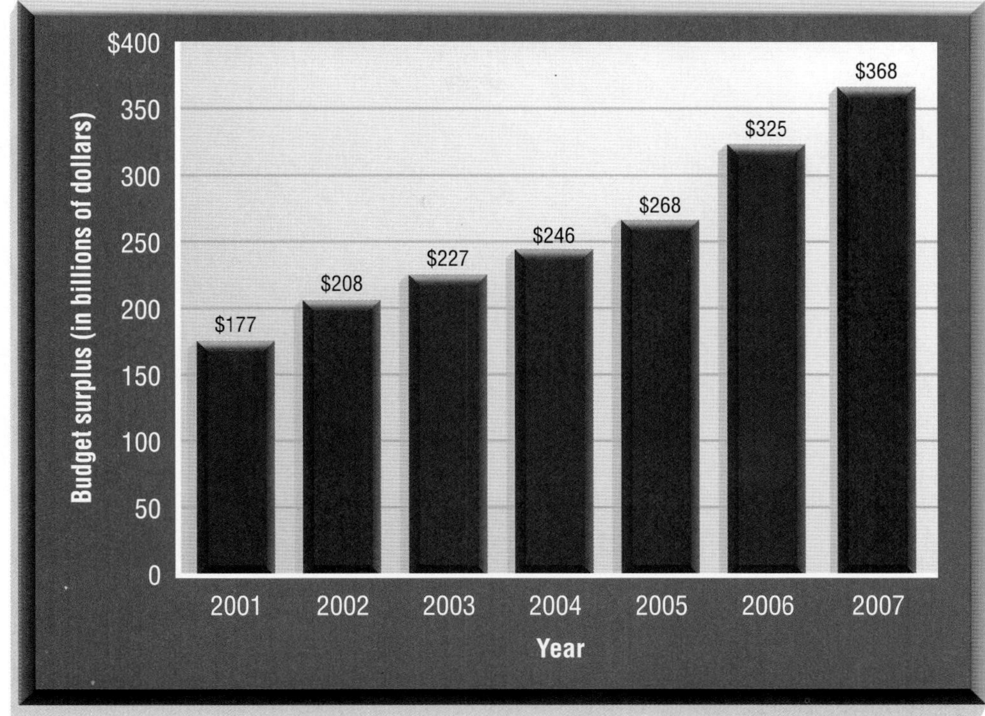

but it reasons that the future generation will use the freeway system, so it should pay for some of it. If the current generation had purchased $10 billion of something from which only it could benefit, the situation would be different.

budget surplus The situation in which federal government expenditures are less than federal government tax revenues.

Balanced Budgets and Surpluses

For the first time in nearly three decades, the federal budget turned from deficit to surplus in 1998. The budget surplus in 1998 was $69 billion.

Will **budget surpluses** be part of the immediate American future? If the economy is healthy and government spending does not increase more rapidly than the GDP increases, there is a good chance that the budgetary future will be one of balanced budgets or surpluses (see Exhibit 16-9).

One of the effects of balanced budgets or surpluses is that interest rates are lower than they would have been under budget deficits. Why are interest rates higher with budget deficits than with balanced budgets or surpluses?

Consider what would happen if the interest rate were 5 percent just before the government runs a $50 billion deficit. The deficit would have to be financed. In other words, the U.S. Treasury would have to borrow the $50 billion, the same way you might borrow funds to buy a car or a house. Because the Treasury would need to borrow the funds to finance the deficit, the overall demand for credit would be greater than it would have been. And if the demand for credit was higher, the price of credit (the interest rate) would be higher, too. In other words, while the interest rate might be 5 percent with a balanced budget or surplus, it would be higher than 5 percent (say, 6 percent) with a budget deficit.

These demonstrators are requesting that the government spend less on the military (national defense) and more on human needs such as housing. How is spending determined?

The Political Aspect of Budget Surpluses

Budget surpluses have political consequences: once a surplus manifests itself, a debate on what should be done with it is sure to follow.

Suppose government spending is $1,500 billion and tax revenues are $1,700 billion, yielding a budget surplus of $200 billion. Some people will say that with the $200 billion in surplus, the federal government can spend more than it is currently spending. In other words, instead of spending only $1,500 billion, the government can increase spending to $1,700 billion. It could spend more on education, modernizing the country's infrastructure, or medical research.

Other people will look at things from a different perspective. Instead of arguing for more spending, they will argue for lower taxes. They might say, "If the government has a surplus of $200 billion, it means that taxes could have been $200 billion lower without cutting any government program even $1. Let's keep spending constant and give back to taxpayers the $200 billion they overpaid in the form of tax cuts."

Still other people will say that we should not spend more, nor should we return the surplus to taxpayers in terms of tax cuts. Instead, we should use any surpluses to retire the national debt. It would be similar to a person who makes a $100 payment on a Visa bill each month deciding to increase the payment to $300 a month so that the debt is eliminated faster.

Section 2 Review

Defining Terms

1. Define
   a. budget deficit
   b. budget surplus

Reviewing Facts and Concepts

2. How are current budget deficits linked to higher taxes in the future?

3. Does expansionary fiscal policy always result in a budget deficit? Explain your answer.

Critical Thinking

4. What do people mean when they say that it is better to balance the economy than to balance the budget?

Applying Economic Concepts

5. Explain how a downturn in the economy can turn a budget surplus into a budget deficit.

Developing Economic

Skills

Thinking Critically in Economics

There is a right and a wrong way to conduct economic analysis. To do it the right way, you must avoid certain fallacies, or errors in thinking. A few common fallacies are examined here.

Confusing Association with Causation

Suppose you are listening to your teacher explain the economic concept of scarcity. You notice that it has started to rain. Three minutes later, your teacher says, "All right, that is enough about scarcity. Let's get out pencil and paper and take a pop quiz."

Two events occurred: (1) it started to rain and (2) your teacher announced a pop quiz. The two events occurred close together in time, so we could say that the two events are associated. But did the first event cause the second event? In other words, is the rain the cause of the quiz? Most likely, the two events are not related by cause and effect. It was just coincidence that they occurred a few minutes apart.

The simple fact that two events are associated in some way does not make one event the cause of the other. In short, association is not causation.

The Fallacy of Composition

John is in the football stadium cheering on his team. Suddenly, John stands up so that he can see better. Does it follow that if everybody stood up, everybody could see better? No. The principle we deduce from this observation is that what is good for the individual is not necessarily good for the group. The *fallacy of composition* is the erroneous view that what is good (or true) for the individual is necessarily good (or true) for the group.

Now suppose Mary moves to the suburbs because she dislikes the crowds in the city. Does it follow that if everyone moved from the city to the suburbs everyone would be better off? If your answer is yes, you have committed the fallacy of composition. If Mary moves to the suburbs because she dislikes crowds, she makes herself better off. But if everyone moved to the suburbs, not everyone would be better off, because the suburbs would become as crowded as the cities were.

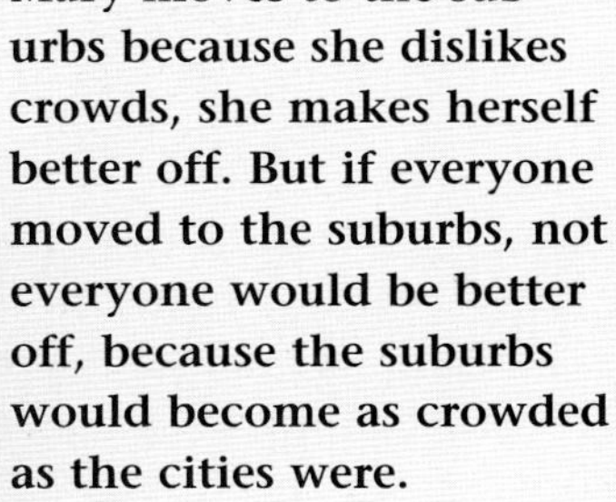

Confusing Fact and Opinion

There is a difference between fact and opinion. A fact is something that is objectively true. It is a fact that you are reading this sentence at this moment. There is no room for doubt. An opinion, in contrast, is not necessarily objectively true. An opinion expresses a subjective, or personal, judgment, preference, or belief. For example, your friend may say that Thomas Jefferson was the most intelligent U.S. president. You may disagree with your friend's statement. The matter can never be proved, because you are both making subjective evaluations.

1. Explain what it means to say that association is not causation.
2. Give an original example that illustrates the fallacy of composition.

CHAPTER 16 Review

Economics Vocabulary

Fill in the following blanks with the appropriate word or phrase.

1. A(n) _____ exists when government spending is greater than tax revenues.
2. A proportional tax is sometimes called a(n) _____ tax.
3. A tax rate that falls as income rises is a(n) _____ tax.
4. The _____ is the idea that each person should pay taxes according to his or her ability to pay.
5. The _____ is the idea that each person should pay taxes according to the benefits that he or she receives from government expenditures.
6. A gas tax is consistent with the _____ principle of taxation.
7. The _____ tax is applied to corporate profits.
8. A(n) _____ exists if federal government spending is greater than federal government tax revenues.
9. A tax rate that rises as income rises is a(n) _____ tax.

Review Questions

1. In what ways can a budget deficit be reduced or eliminated?
2. Explain how a budget deficit can cause a future generation to pay for what a current generation buys.
3. What did Adam Smith mean when he said, "What is prudence in the conduct of every private family, can scarce be folly in that of a great kingdom"?
4. What role does the Congressional Budget Office (CBO) play in the budget process?
5. What is the difference between a calendar year and a fiscal year?
6. In 2000, for what percentage of federal government spending did the combination of national defense, Social Security, and Medicare account?
7. What three federal taxes raise approximately 91 percent of all federal tax revenues?
8. Smith paid $40,000 in federal income taxes, and Abuel paid $20,000. Is the income tax progressive, proportional, or regressive, or is it impossible to tell? Explain your answer.

Calculations

1. According to Exhibit 16-1, on page 419, what percentage of total taxes is the personal income tax projected to account for in 2006?
2. According to Exhibit 16-3, on page 421, what percentage of a year did the representative taxpayer work to pay his or her taxes in 1990?
3. According to Exhibit 16-5, on page 426, how much is government spending expected to grow between 2003 and 2004?

Graphs

1. Look at Exhibit 16-10a below, where you will see bars A, B, and C. Each bar represents a certain type of federal income tax in 2000. Identify the kind of tax that goes with each bar.
2. Look at Exhibit 16-10b. Each bar (A, B, and C) represents a certain federal spending program in 2000. Identify the program that goes with each bar.

Exhibit 16-10

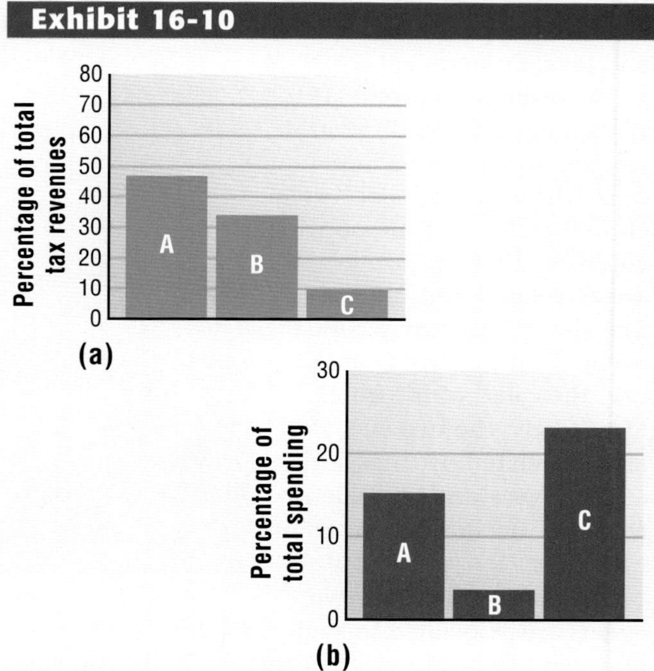

Economics and Thinking Skills

1. **Application.** Suppose a local government were to lower the property tax from 1.25 percent of the assessed value of property to, say, 0.75 percent. How might this affect the price of property? Explain your answer.

2. **Cause and Effect.** Suppose government spending is $1,000 billion. Do you think a balanced budget or a budget surplus is more likely to lead to a rise in government spending? Explain your answer.

Writing Skills

Suppose the federal government is running a budget surplus of $100 billion. Write a one-page paper explaining what you think should be done with the surplus. Give reasons for why you think the surplus should be dealt with the way you suggest.

Economics in the Media

Find an article in the local newspaper that addresses the current state of the federal budget, personal income taxes, sales taxes, or the national debt. Identify the major ideas of the article.

Where's the Economics?

How do the interest payments on the national debt affect your life?

Analyzing Primary Sources

When you discuss government tax and spending decisions, you are usually not far from a discussion of what government should and should not do. What is the proper role of government? What role should government play in our lives? Let's look at what economist Alan Blinder, former member of the Board of Governors of the Federal Reserve System, has to say about the attitudes toward the role of government.

Our market economy can usefully be thought of as a game with winners and losers in varying degrees. But the economic game is no more (and no less) fair than a contest between the New York Giants and your local high-school football team. Some players have advantages. Some of us are born into wealthy families, or with nimble minds that enable us to pursue lucrative and pleasant professions, or with the shrewdness and drive that make for success in business. Some of us are blessed with "good upbringings" that provide high-quality education and instill "the right values," meaning the values that promote success in the economic game. These are the born (or bred) winners. They can be expected to do well in the economic game year after year without help from the government. . . .

Others are born into poverty, or with less intelligence, or into environments where education and economic success are neither prized nor expected. Some remarkable individuals overcome these disadvantages through sheer determination, skill, and guts, but most lack the ability to accomplish that feat. . . . Without help from someone, they [those who lack ability] *will founder and live in penury. . . . What are we to do about this inequality?*

The hard-hearted attitude is that our wonderful market system is so essential, and so fragile, that we must not tamper with it in order to aid the underprivileged, the shortsighted, the indolent, or even the unlucky. Let everyone compete on an equal basis, the argument goes, and let the chips fall where they may. If some of the players are lame or injured, that's a shame. But they must be left to nurse their own wounds, for efforts to assist them would be futile at best and harmful at worst. . . .

The soft-hearted attitude holds that we ought to soften the blows for those who play the economic game and lose, or who cannot play it at all. The objective can be served by making the game less vigorous and risky—which is the rationale for Medicare, Social Security, and unemployment compensation. Or it can be done by making the victors share some of the spoils with the vanquished—via welfare benefits, public housing, Medicaid, and progressive taxation. Liberals generally favor such public generosity. But, of course, society as a whole has no Daddy Warbucks. If benefits are to be provided to the underdogs (or losers), the favorites (or winners) must foot the bill.[2]

1. Do you agree or disagree with Blinder that our market economy can be thought of as a game of winners and losers? Explain your answer.
2. Alexis de Tocqueville, French statesman and author, said that "the major concern of government ought to be to teach the people to gradually do without it." Contrast de Tocqueville's view on the proper role of government with what Blinder has said.

2. *Hard Heads, Soft Hearts* (pp. 22–24), © 1987 by Alan S. Blinder.

UNIT 3

Debate the Issues

Should the Internet Be Governed by the Same Laws as Traditional Businesses?

Caroline Templeton is a junior in high school. She has been saving her money to buy a computer. On Saturday she bought one—online. The total price of the computer, printer, and monitor came to $1,250. Since she bought the computer from an online dealer that does not have a presence in her state, she did not pay the online retailer any sales tax. Do you think that she should have?

Soon after Caroline received her new computer, she went online and began downloading some of her favorite songs. She didn't pay a penny to anyone for any of the songs that she downloaded and now enjoys. Should she have?

People have many different opinions about the ways in which traditional laws and regulations should be applied to the Internet. In Chapter 23, you can read about the Internet's impact on economics and about several controversial issues surrounding use of the Internet. For now, let's listen in as the members of Caroline's family debate two such issues—the Internet and downloadable music.

Mr. Templeton, Caroline's father: In 1997, Congress passed the Internet Tax Freedom Act, which put a moratorium on any Internet taxes. I think it's wrong not to tax Internet transactions, because it ends up hurting the poor guy who is trying to sell computers here in town. If I buy a computer in his store, I pay sales tax. If I buy the same computer online, from a company that's out of state, I don't pay any sales tax.[1] This gives the online computer company a clear advantage over the computer store here in town. That's not fair. We shouldn't give advantages to some companies and hamper others.

Mrs. Templeton, Caroline's mother: It sounds as if you're in favor of taxing sales on the Internet. If that's the case, you and I disagree on this issue. I keep hearing about what the Internet has done for this country. It seems that it has propelled the economy forward. Because of the Internet, there are more jobs, more people working, and generally a stronger economy. Let's not do anything to kill the goose that lays the golden egg. Taxes will hurt the Internet, and if we hurt the Internet, we might end up hurting the economy. Let's leave well enough alone.

Caroline: I agree with Mom. If I had purchased my new computer from our local computer store, I would have had to pay more

1. Online computer companies will often advise customers that they are obligated to pay a sales tax on the computer they buy, but that it is up to them to report the purchase to state authorities and pay the tax. Many people choose not to report the purchase and pay the taxes. When Mr. Templeton, Caroline's father, says that he doesn't pay any sales tax on online computer purchases, he is speaking for what he believes is the usual practice regarding taxes and online purchases.

money because of the sales tax. I don't want to pay more money. With the money I saved on taxes, I can buy something else.

Mr. Templeton: I understand that. But look at it this way. Suppose you owned the computer store down the street. Do you think it is fair that when you sell a computer you have to collect a sales tax from your customer, but when your online competitor sells a computer, it doesn't? It seems to me that either all companies should be required to charge and collect sales taxes, or none of them should. Online retailers and neighborhood retailers should be treated the same.

Wendell, Caroline's brother: I agree with Mom. I don't think we should tax Internet sales. The fact is, I don't want anything to be done to the Internet. I like it just the way it is. I like being able to buy things without paying sales tax. I like being able to go to different sites and read different things. Like Caroline and most of my friends, I like being able to download my favorite songs and play them anytime I want.

Mrs. Templeton: Now that is one thing I don't agree with. I don't think you should be able to download music without paying for it. To me, that's stealing.

Caroline: In a way, I agree with Mom. But since those songs are there to be downloaded, I intend to download them. If I don't, someone else will.

Mr. Templeton: I think that something has to be done about this, or musicians aren't going to write and perform as many songs. The way I look at it, the song is the property of the musician and the company that produces the song. If the musicians and record companies can't prevent people from getting their songs without paying for them, what incentives do they have to keep recording?

Mrs. Templeton: I agree one hundred percent. For example, suppose someone wrote a book. The book sells in the bookstore for $20. Someone buys the book, scans it into his computer, and then puts in on the Internet. Other people simply download the book from the Internet, print it, and read it, or they can simply read it on their computer monitor. People who would have bought the book can now get it for free. The author doesn't earn as much in royalties, and so he decides not to write as many books, if any at all. Then we are denied the benefits of his writing. Unless we can protect people's work, people aren't going to invest the time, energy, and money to create.

Wendell: I see your point, but isn't being able to download music a little like sharing? Suppose I go to the music store and buy a music CD. I come home, play it and then my best friend asks me if he can borrow it. I say yes. Certainly no one would argue that I don't have the right to let a friend borrow my CD.

Mrs. Templeton: There is a difference between sharing your CD with one person and sharing it with millions of people. When you share your CD with one person, you lose the opportunity to play the CD yourself. Only one person at a time can play it. But when you put the songs from the CD on the Internet, that is no longer the case. You can continue to play the CD and, in a way, millions of other people can too.

Wendell: I see your point, but still there is the issue of sharing. Don't I have the right to share what I own with as many people as I want?

Mrs. Templeton: Not when your sharing ends up hurting others.

What Do You Think?

1. If neighborhood retailers are legally required to charge and collect sales taxes, do you believe online retailers should have to do the same? Why or why not?
2. Do you think downloading music that you do not pay for is equivalent to stealing? Why or why not?

UNIT 4

The Global Economy

家鄉雞

美式快餐

Kentucky
Fried Chicken

CHAPTER 17 Economic Development

What This Chapter Is About

When you learn about the different countries of the world, one of the first things you probably notice is that some countries are rich, and others are poor. This chapter, on economic development, explores what causes these differences.

Why This Chapter Is Important

You live in a very rich country. As a resident of the United States, you have one of the highest standards of living in the world. It was not always this way in the United States, and it is not this way in many countries of the world today. A knowledge of economic development will first help you understand why your standard of living is as high as it is. Second, it will help you understand what needs to be done in other countries so that the residents can enjoy a life as rich as yours.

After You Study This Chapter, You Will Be Able To

- explain the difference between economic growth and economic development.
- describe the general economic situation in less-developed countries.
- describe the obstacles to economic development.
- describe the Malthusian view.
- explain some of the ways less-developed countries become developed countries.

You Will Also Learn What Economics Has to Do With

- the one-child policy in China.
- a dictator's lavish palace.
- beans.

Economics Journal

Keep a list of the goods and services you consume during a week. Next to each, identify whether you think that particular good or service is consumed by most people living in a poor country, such as Ghana, Haiti, or India.

SECTION 1 Economic Development

This section considers economic development in terms of the less-developed countries (LDCs). These countries are sometimes called *developing countries, developing economies, underdeveloped countries,* or *third-world countries.* Mainly, we will be concerned with the question, "Why are some nations poor?"

As you read this section, keep these key questions in mind:

- What is a less-developed country?
- What does per-capita GDP have to do with the infant mortality rate?
- How are living conditions related to the GDP?

Key Terms

developed countries (DCs)
less-developed countries (LDCs)
infant mortality rate

Economic Growth versus Economic Development

Chapter 14 discussed economic growth, whereas this chapter discusses economic development. Economic growth and economic development, although similar, are not the same thing. A country can experience economic growth but still not be considered economically developed. For example, consider a country where the per-capita GDP is extremely low, at $400 a year. Most of the roads in the country are dirt roads, there are few hospitals, most people do not have electricity, there is very little indoor plumbing, there are few schools, and so on. It is certainly possible for this country to experience economic growth—say, growth of its per-capita GDP from $400 to $500—but it is doubtful whether a $100 increase in per-capita GDP will change the country fundamentally. Even with growth, the country is still likely to have mostly dirt roads, few hospitals, and little indoor plumbing.

Economic development refers to a rise in the standard of living as measured by some of the things already mentioned: paved roads, electricity, schools, indoor plumbing, and more and higher-quality goods to buy. Certainly economic growth is important to economic development, but economic growth can occur in a country that remains less developed.

Is the country represented in these photos more likely to be experiencing economic growth or economic development? Explain.

developed country (DC) A country with a relatively high per-capita GDP or GNP.

less-developed country (LDC) A country with a relatively low per-capita GDP or GNP.

How Countries Are Classified

The layperson often talks about "rich" countries and "poor" countries. For example, the United States is often said to be a rich country; Ethiopia is said to be a poor country.

Economists talk about rich and poor countries, too, although they do not always use the terms *rich* versus *poor.* More often, they talk about **developed countries (DCs)** or more-developed countries (MDCs) versus **less-developed countries (LDCs).** A developed country is a country that has a relatively high GDP or GNP per capita; a less-developed country is a country with a relatively low GDP or GNP per capita. The United States is a developed country, whereas Haiti and Ethiopia are less-developed countries. Exhibit 17-1 shows the GDP per capita for some of the countries of the world in 1998. In the late-1990s, the ten poorest countries had an average per-capita GDP of $160, while the ten richest countries had an average per-capita GDP of $20,000. As you can see, there is considerable disparity between the poorest of the poor and the richest of the rich.

Economists have established an international poverty line, which is a dollar figure below which people are said to be living in poverty. For most of the 1990s, approximately 1.25 billion people were

ECONOMICS and the INTERNET

The *CIA World Factbook* is a rich source of economic information about most of the countries of the world. Go to its Web site at http://www.odci.gov/cia/publications/factbook/country.html and identify a country that you believe is a less-developed country (in other words, one that has a low per-capita GDP). Then answer these questions about the country.

1. Where is the country located?
2. What is the population?
3. What is the age structure?
4. What is the population growth rate?
5. What is the birthrate?
6. What is the death rate?
7. What is the infant mortality rate?
8. What is the life expectancy for males?
9. What is the life expectancy for females?
10. What is the literacy rate of the total population?
11. What is the growth rate in real GDP?
12. What is the per-capita GDP?
13. What is the inflation rate?
14. What is the unemployment rate?

Exhibit 17-1

Per-Capita GDP, Selected Countries, 1998

Here we show the per-capita GDP in 1998 for selected countries. All amounts are shown in U.S. dollars.

Source: CIA World Factbook, 1999.

This street scene from Ethiopia shows why it is considered to be a less-developed country (LDC).

living in poverty. Sixty-two percent of the people living in sub-Saharan Africa were living in poverty, as were 25 percent of the people in Asia, 35 percent in Latin America, and 28 percent in North America and the Middle East.

Conditions in Many Less-Developed Countries

Differences in per-capita GDP among countries tend to be associated with other differences that reflect the disparity in the standard of living. The **infant mortality rate** (the number of children who die before their first birthday out of every 1,000 live births), for instance, tends to be closely related to a country's per-capita GDP; it is usually higher in less-developed countries than in developed countries. For example, India, a less-developed country, had an infant mortality rate of 71.1 per 1,000 live births in the middle to late 1990s. The infant mortality rate in the United States, by comparison, was 6.7 per 1,000 live births. Of course, only two countries are compared here, but a comparison of many different combinations of developed versus less-developed countries would yield the same results. The infant mortality rate averages 11 (per 1,000 live births) in developed countries and 74 in less-developed countries.

The infant mortality rate is higher in India than in the United States. Why might this be?

infant mortality rate
The number of children who die before their first birthday out of every 1,000 live births.

Also, the calorie intake of the "average" person tends to be lower in less-developed countries than in developed countries. For example, in the mid-1970s, almost 1 billion people in the less-developed countries were living on diets deficient in essential calories. One-third of these billion people were children less than two years old.

Many people around the world, such as this boy in Somalia, go to sleep hungry at night. What events, other than famines, could cause this?

Since the mid-1970s, conditions have improved in some less-developed countries but have become worse in others. For example, in the 1980s and early 1990s, the situation worsened in sub-Saharan Africa, which experienced widespread famine. During this period, more than 60 percent of the population in Asia and Africa barely met basic calorie intake requirements. Millions of people who live in less-developed countries go to sleep hungry each night.

Furthermore, people living in less-developed countries often do not have safe drinking water or adequate medical services. According to the United Nations Development Program, 1.45 billion people living in the less-developed countries do not have access to health care services. In the less-developed countries as a whole, 1.33 billion people do not have access to safe water, 2.25 billion people are without sanitation facilities, and millions of children die each year due to malnourishment and disease.

Our point is simple: a relatively low per-capita GDP or GNP is accompanied by many other things, such as unsafe drinking water, malnourishment, and disease.

W. Arthur Lewis, Economist

W. Arthur Lewis (1915–91) was the co-recipient of the Nobel Prize in Economics in 1979. He won the Nobel Prize for his work in the economics of development. Lewis was born in 1915 in St. Lucia in the West Indies. He entered the London School of Economics at the age of eighteen. At the suggestion of F. A. Hayek, another Nobel Prize-winner in Economics, Lewis started working on the problems of the world economy. In 1963, Lewis was knighted by Queen Elizabeth.

Lewis was best known for his concept of a "dual economy" in less-developed countries. According to Lewis, a poor country's economy consisted of two sectors—a small capitalist sector and a very large traditional sector. For a country to develop, it was necessary to transfer labor from the traditional sector, where labor was not very productive, to the capitalist sector, where it was productive.

Lewis was professor of political economy at Princeton University from 1963 until his death in 1991.

Section 1 Review

Defining Terms

1. Define
   a. less-developed country
   b. developed country
   c. infant mortality rate

Reviewing Facts and Concepts

2. As measured by per-capita GDP, how many times richer are the richest of the rich countries compared with the poorest of the poor countries?
3. Does a less-developed country that experiences economic growth also experience economic development? Explain your answer.

Critical Thinking

4. Do you think you would have a higher standard of living in a country that was experiencing economic growth but was not economically developed, or in a country that was economically developed but not currently experiencing economic growth? Explain your answer.

Applying Economic Concepts

5. So far, this chapter has defined a poor country as a country with a low per-capita GDP. Does it follow that the people in a country with a low per-capita GDP are not as happy as the people in a country with a high per-capita GDP? Explain your answer.

SECTION 2

Obstacles to Economic Development

Why has economic development largely bypassed the people of the less-developed countries? Why are some nations so poor? This section describes five obstacles that some economists believe stifle economic development in less-developed countries.

As you read this section, keep these key questions in mind:

- What are the obstacles to economic development?
- How is the population growth rate calculated?
- What is the dependency ratio?
- What is a criticism of the concept of the vicious circle of poverty?

Rapid Population Growth

It is commonly observed that the **population growth rate** is higher in less-developed countries than in developed countries. The population growth rate in developed countries has been about 0.5 to 1 percent, compared with about 2 to 3 percent for less-developed countries.

The population growth rate is equal to the birthrate minus the death rate.

Population growth rate = Birthrate − Death rate

If in country X the birthrate is 3 percent in a given year and the death rate is 2 percent, the population growth rate is 1 percent. Exhibit 17-2 shows a view of the world according to population.

What has caused the relatively high population growth rate in the less-developed countries? First, the birthrate tends to be higher than in developed nations.

Key Terms

population growth rate
dependency ratio
vicious circle of poverty
status quo

population growth rate The birthrate minus the death rate.

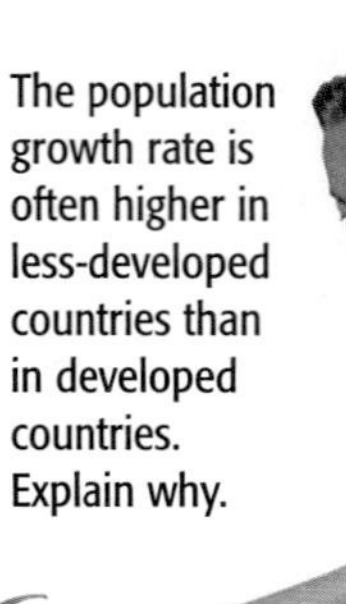

The population growth rate is often higher in less-developed countries than in developed countries. Explain why.

Exhibit 17-2

A View of the World According to Population

This map of the world may be unlike any you have seen before. This type of map is called a cartogram. Countries are drawn according to their populations: a country with a large population, such as India, is drawn larger than a country with a smaller population, such as Russia, although in reality Russia covers a larger landmass than India.

Source: (c) Hammond Incorporated, Maplewood, New Jersey.

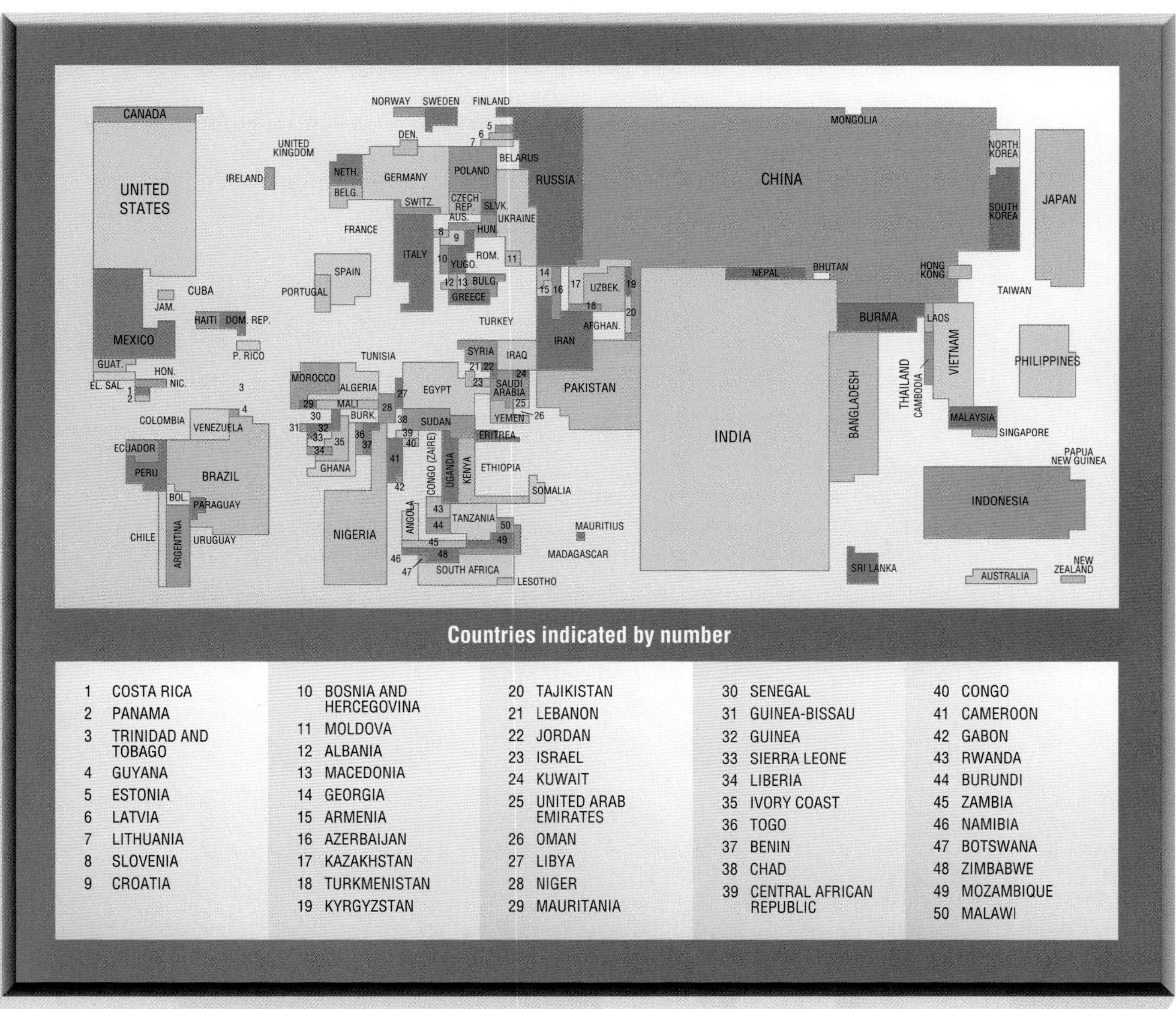

In countries where financial assistance, such as pensions and Social Security does not exist and where the economy revolves around agriculture, children are often seen as essential labor and as security for parents in their old age. In this setting, people tend to have more children.

Second, in the past few decades, the death rate has fallen in the less-developed countries, largely because of medical advances. The combination of higher birthrates and declining death rates explains why the population grows more rapidly in less-developed nations than in developed nations.

dependency ratio
The number of children (under age fifteen) plus the elderly (age sixty-five and over) divided by the total population.

Is a faster population growth rate always an obstacle to economic development? The fact that many of the countries with the fastest-growing populations are relatively poorer on a per-capita basis than those countries with the slowest-growing populations is not proof that rapid population growth *causes* poverty. Many of the developed countries today witnessed faster population growth rates when they were developing than the less-developed countries do today.

Also, when we check population density instead of population growth, we find that a number of countries with high-density populations are much richer than countries with low-density populations. Japan, for example, is more densely populated than India and has a higher per-capita income. The same is true for Taiwan as compared with China.

Nonetheless, some still argue that rapid population growth, though not necessarily a deterrent to economic development, can stifle it because the **dependency ratio** rises. The dependency ratio is the number of children (under fifteen years old) plus the number of elderly (sixty-five years old and over) divided by the total population.

$$\text{Dependency ratio} = \frac{\text{Number of children (under 15)} + \text{Number of elderly (65 and over)}}{\text{Population}}$$

For example, if the number of children and elderly equals 500 and the total population is 1,500, the dependency ratio is 33 percent. The high dependency ratios in less-developed countries such as India, Bangladesh, and Egypt put added burdens on the productive working-age populations.

Low Savings Rate

A farmer with a tractor (which is a capital good) is likely to be more productive than one without a tractor, all other things being equal. Now consider a farmer who cannot afford to buy a tractor. This farmer may decide to borrow the money from a bank. But where does the bank get the

Explain how the savings rate could affect the amount of output produced by the British farmers on the left and the Tibetan farmer on the right.

Beans

This chapter stated that the population growth rate is equal to the birthrate minus the death rate.

Population growth rate = Birthrate − Death rate

In the eighth and ninth centuries, the death rate was high. One reason was that many people had a poor diet and therefore easily became sick. For example, the poor in Europe in the Middle Ages did not eat much meat unless they raised a few chickens. As a result, the population of many European countries was malnourished and sickly. The result was a high death rate.

In the tenth century things began to change as the cultivation of beans, peas, and lentils spread. A dish of lentils or peas

has the protein content of a thick steak. As the cultivation of beans, peas, and lentils spread in the tenth century, the working poor began to eat better, become strong, and therefore live longer and have more years to bear children.

In short, beans, lentils, and peas increased the birthrate, decreased the death rate, and so increased the population growth rate. The fact is that if it had not been for the bean, many of the people living in the United States today would not have been born, because their ancestors would have died from poor nutrition centuries ago.

QUESTION TO ANSWER

1. How might the bean have affected the working poor's productivity?
2. Do you know people who eat foods such as beans and lentils rather than meat? Do their diets seem healthful and nutritious?

SOURCE : Based on Umberto Eco, "How the Bean Saved Civilization," *New York Times Magazine,* 1999, and http://www.nytimes.com/ library/magazine/millennium/m1/eco.html

money to lend? It gets money from the people who have savings accounts at the bank. Savings, then, are important to economic growth and development. If there is a low savings rate, there will not be much money to borrow, and capital goods such as tractors (which increase productivity) will not be produced and purchased.

Some economists argue that the less-developed countries have low savings rates because the people living in them are so poor that they cannot save. In short, they earn only enough income to buy the necessities of life, shelter and food; there is no "extra income" left over to save. This situation is called the **vicious circle of poverty:** less-developed countries are poor because they cannot save and buy capital goods, but they cannot save and buy capital goods because they are poor.

vicious circle of poverty
The idea that countries are poor because they do not save and buy capital goods, but they cannot save and buy capital goods because they are poor.

Other economists argue, though, that being poor is not a barrier to economic development. They say that many nations that are rich today, such as the United States, were poor in the past but still managed to become economically developed.

Cultural Differences

Some less-developed countries may have cultures that retard economic growth and development. For example, some cultures are reluctant to depart from the **status quo** (the existing state of affairs). People may think that things should stay the way they always have been; they view change as dangerous and risky. In such countries, it is not uncommon for people's upward economic and social mobility to depend on who their parents were rather than on who they are or what they do. Furthermore, in some cultures the people are fatalistic by Western standards; that is, they believe that a person's good or bad fortune in life depends more on fate or the spirits than on how hard the person works, how much he or she learns, or how hard he or she strives to succeed.

Peace Corps Volunteer

The motto of the Peace Corps is "The toughest job you'll ever love." The Peace Corps is made up of people who volunteer their time and skills to work in less-developed countries for a period of usually two years. Peace Corps volunteers work in over eighty countries and assist the native population in the areas of education, environment, health, business, and agriculture. The Peace Corps was established March 1, 1961. The toll-free recruitment number is 1-800-424-8580.

QUESTION TO ANSWER Go to the Web site of the Peace Corps (http://www.peacecorps.gov/home.html) and read at least three of the stories written by volunteers. What do you think are the benefits and costs of being a Peace Corps volunteer?

Political Instability and Government Seizure of Private Property

Individuals sometimes do not invest in businesses in the less-developed countries because they are afraid either that the current government leaders will be thrown out of office or that the government will seize their private property. People are not likely to invest their money in places where the risk of losing it is high.

Thomas Malthus believed that many of the people of the world would starve to death because the population would increase at a faster rate than the food supply. Fortunately, he was wrong. Explain.

High Tax Rates

Some economists argue that high tax rates affect economic development. Economist Alvin Rabushka studied the tax structures of fifty-four less-developed countries between 1960 and 1982 and categorized each country as a high-, low-, or medium-tax-rate nation. Rabushka found that Hong Kong, with the lowest tax rates, had the highest growth rate in per-capita income during the period under study. Generally, low-tax countries had an average growth rate in per-capita income of 3.7 percent, and high-tax countries had a per-capita income growth rate of 0.7 percent.

status quo That which exists now; the existing state of affairs.

Thomas Malthus and Economic Development

The economist Thomas Malthus, who lived in England from 1766 to 1834, has been called a prophet of doom. Malthus predicted that the population of the world would increase at a faster rate than the food supply, resulting in mass starvation.

Does China Need More People, Not Fewer?

For many years, China was warned that the greatest problem in its future would be its large population. China, perhaps more than any other country, was headed for a Malthusian nightmare of increasing population and less food per person. This warning appears to have frightened the Chinese Communist leaders. They were determined to raise the living standards of the Chinese people, and they thought they could not do so unless the population growth rate was curbed. After all, they thought, it would be better if ten people could share ten loaves of bread than if 100 people had to share ten loaves of bread.

In an attempt to raise living standards, the Communist leaders passed laws to keep population growth down. One of those laws mandated that couples could have only one child. This one-child policy is beginning to have consequences, not all of which are advantageous to the Chinese people.

If the current population growth rate in China does not change, in 2030 more than one in five Chinese will be sixty years old or older, and the workforce in China will be declining. The consequence will be a financial burden placed upon the working-age population. First, the people who are working will have to pay the bill for health care and pension plans for those not working. Second, a large older population will need to be taken care of by younger people. In China, the family still assumes the major responsibility for caring for the old. Thus, middle-aged women and men will likely soon find themselves having to care for many more old family members than at present, just at the time they will need to be working themselves and saving for their old age.

What can we learn from the one-child policy in China? First, it may have effects that are unintended. The intent of the policy was to raise the standard of living of the Chinese by reducing the population growth rate. The unintended effect is that the composition of the Chinese population is changing toward more elderly people who need to be cared for by the younger population. In other words, one unintended effect of the one-child policy is that it raises the dependency ratio.

Second, it is not clear that the one-child policy was based on solid ground. At its core, it holds that a rising population is contrary to rising living standards, but the history of the world is that a rising population and rising living standards actually go together. Two thousand years ago the population of the world was about 250 million, and today it is over 6 billion. Yet today the standard of living of the "average" person is much higher than it was two thousand years ago. Add to this the following fact: since the 1950s, the world's population has doubled, but food output has tripled.

QUESTION TO ANSWER What do you see as the pros and cons of the government-imposed one-child policy discussed in the feature?

SOURCE: Adapted from "The Ageing of China," *The Economist,* November 21, 1998.

Exhibit 17-3
The Malthusian View in Numbers

Thomas Malthus believed that population increases geometrically, while the food supply increases arithmetically. Accordingly, as time passes, there will be, on average, less food per person. The evidence does not support this Malthusian view, however.

(1) Year	(2) Population (persons)	(3) Food supply (baskets of food)
1	1	1
2	2	2
3	4	3
4	8	4
5	16	5
6	32	6
7	64	7
8	128	8
9	256	9

Specifically, Malthus said that the population increases at a geometric rate. A number that increases at a geometric rate continually multiplies itself by a constant. For example, in the series 1, 2, 4, 8, 16, 32, 64, 128, 256, each number is multiplied by 2, so the series increases at a geometric rate. In contrast, according to Malthus, the food supply increases at an arithmetic rate. When numbers increase by an arithmetic rate, the same number is added at each step—for example, the number *1* in the series 1, 2, 3, 4, 5, 6, 7, 8, 9, 10.

Look at Exhibit 17-3. Column 1 lists the years 1 through 9; column 2, the population in those years; and column 3, the food supply in those years. Notice that the population increases geometrically, and the food supply increases arithmetically. Now notice that in year 4, there are 8 persons and 4 baskets of food, so the average amount of food per person is 0.5 basket. Five years later, in year 9, there are 256 people and 9 baskets of food, so the average amount of food per person has decreased to about 0.035 basket. Malthus warned that if something was not done quickly, the world was headed for dismal times. He proposed that couples put off marriage until later years and have fewer children.

The population in many nations, however, did not increase at the high rate that Malthus predicted, nor did the food supply grow as slowly. For one thing, Malthus did not foresee that major technological changes in agriculture would allow farmers

Some families have chosen to have only one child, something Thomas Malthus did not foresee.

to produce food much more efficiently. Malthus also did not foresee another change. At earlier times in the world's history, most people had just enough to get by—a subsistence living. With a move away from subsistence living in many parts of the world, toward a higher standard of living and increased urbanization, couples naturally chose to have fewer children. (In the poor nations today, however, the birthrate is still relatively high.)

This milking machine is but one of many technological advances that have brought about tremendous gains in agricultural production. What impact has this technology had on Malthus's prediction regarding starvation?

As stated earlier, Malthus predicted that the future would be bleak unless radical changes were made. For this reason, people today who do the same thing are often called Malthusians. What Thomas Malthus did, and what Malthusians do today, is look at what is happening in the present and then assume it will continue into the future. For example, suppose that as the population increases, the demand for oil increases. A Malthusian might argue that if the demand for oil continues to grow, one day there will be no more oil. In fact, however, if the demand for oil continues to grow, the price will rise, people will cut back on their purchases of oil, and entrepreneurs will begin to look for substitutes for oil or additional supplies of oil. The Malthusian view is very static and rigid: what is bad today will be worse tomorrow if something is not done. Some people believe that the evidence does not always support the Malthusian view of things.

Section 2 Review

Defining Terms

1. Define
   - **a.** population growth rate
   - **b.** dependency ratio
   - **c.** vicious circle of poverty
   - **d.** status quo

Reviewing Facts and Concepts

2. Why might people in less-developed countries have more children than people in developed countries?

3. How can a high dependency ratio retard economic development?

Critical Thinking

4. Suppose the average worker in a developed country has to provide for two children and one elderly person, and that the average worker in a less-developed country has to provide for four children and two elderly persons. It has been argued that people in less-developed countries are less productive because they are burdened with a higher dependency ratio. How is a high dependency ratio like a tax?

Applying Economic Concepts

5. Demographers state that the percentage of the U.S. population aged sixty-five and over will grow in the near future. How will this growth affect the dependency ratio? Do you think this growth will have economic consequences for the United States? If so, what are they likely to be?

SECTION 3 How Do Less-Developed Countries Become Developed Countries?

How do poor countries become rich countries? As you read this section, keep these key questions in mind:

- Does foreign aid promote or hinder economic development?
- What factors aid growth and development?

The state of this Haitian village reflects a low per-capita GDP. Explain why foreign aid might not increase the per-capita GDP.

Do Countries That Receive Foreign Aid Grow and Develop?

Some people argue that a less-developed country can grow and develop only if it is assisted through foreign aid. If so, less-developed countries that receive foreign aid should be growing and developing faster than those that do not. This does not appear to be the case, though.

For example, Haiti has received foreign aid from the United States for over fifty years, but in 1965 its per-capita GDP was $360, and in 1994 it was down to $225. Peru has also received foreign aid from the United States for over fifty years, and its per-capita GDP was $1,126 in 1965 and $1,103 in 1994. Somalia, which has received U.S. foreign aid for more than forty-one years, had a per-capita GDP in 1965 of $123 and a per-capita GDP in 1994 of $111.[1] Liberia, Ethiopia, Nicaragua, Madagascar, Togo, Zambia, Chad, and Senegal have all received foreign aid from the United States over a sustained period, and in each country the per-capita GDP was lower in 1994 than it was in 1965.

For the opposite situation, consider both Hong Kong and Singapore. In 1965, Hong Kong had a per-capita GDP of $2,279. A number of international economic agencies then began to withdraw foreign aid from the country. As a result, Hong Kong began to reform its economy by cutting taxes, privatizing banks, cutting regulations, and so on. In 1994, Hong Kong's per-capita GDP had risen to $21,650.

Government actions such as tax cuts and bank privatization allowed Hong Kong to raise its per-capita GDP in spite of also losing foreign aid.

1. These data come from Kim R. Holmes, Bryan T. Johnson, and Melanie Kirkpatrick, eds., *1997 Index of Economic Freedom,* published by the Heritage Foundation and the *Wall Street Journal* (New York: Dow Jones & Company) 1997.

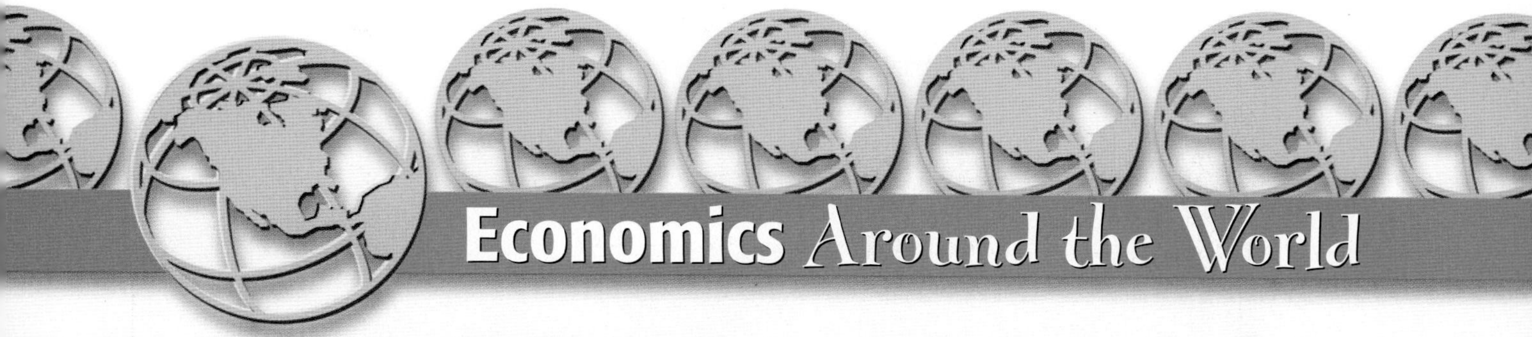

How the United States Can Pay for What It Does Not Want to Pay For

Imagine a less-developed country that is headed by a dictator. The dictator is chauffeured around in big, expensive cars, lives in several palaces; and jets all around the world enjoying himself. Meanwhile, the vast majority of people in his country do not have many of the basic necessities of life, such as food, clothing, or housing.

Suppose the United States wants to provide money for education and housing to help the people of this country. A U.S. representative meets with the dictator and says, "The United States wants to make a contribution to your people. It is willing to pay $100 million to help with education and housing. There is only one stipulation: the money that the United States gives to your country must be used only for education and housing, nothing else. It cannot be used to build roads, airports, or palaces. Do you accept the contribution?"

The dictator immediately says yes, and the U.S. representative starts the process of transferring $100 million from the United States to the country.

Has the United States, by putting stipulations on how the $100 million is to be used, really paid for education and housing and nothing else? Not necessarily. To illustrate, suppose the dictator of the country would like to complete the following list of projects:

1. Build factories for $200 million.
2. Invest $100 million in education and housing.
3. Modernize agriculture for $100 million.
4. Build himself a new and lavish palace for $100 million.

Suppose the dictator currently has only $400 million to spend, which means he will be able to complete only projects 1 through 3. But if the United States contributes $100 million for education and housing (in essence, paying for project 2), it releases $100 million for the dictator to spend as he pleases. He will spend it by completing project 4—that is, by building a new palace for himself.

In the end, then, we have to wonder if the $100 million the United States gave to the country actually went for education and housing, or if it went for a new palace. After all, if the United States had not paid the $100 million for education and housing, the dictator would have spent the $100 million himself for education and housing. Now that he does not have to spend $100 million on education and housing, he has $100 million to spend on a palace.

QUESTION TO ANSWER A father gives his daughter an allowance of $25 a week and tells her that the money can be spent only on books. She abides by his wishes and buys only books with the $25 he gives to her. How is this like the example of the United States and the dictator?

The wheat being loaded onto this ship in Ontario, Canada, could end up almost anywhere in the world. Explain how free trade aids growth and development.

A similar story can be told about Singapore. In 1965, its per-capita GDP was $1,863. Around this time, Singapore was cut off from much of the foreign aid it had previously received. In 1994, its per-capita GDP had risen to $23,360.

Factors That Aid Growth and Development

Economists widely agree on nine factors that aid economic growth and development, which are briefly discussed here.

Free Trade Countries can hinder or promote international trade. For example, they hinder it when they impose tariffs or quotas on imports. They promote it when they eliminate tariffs, quotas, or anything else that prevents the free flow of resources and goods between countries. Free trade promotes the production of goods and services in a country and therefore spurs growth and development in two ways: (1) free trade allows residents of a country to buy inputs from the cheapest supplier, no matter where in the world it is located, and (2) free trade opens up a world market to domestic firms.

Would this money be worth more or less during an inflation?

Low Taxation Generally, a country with relatively low taxes provides a greater incentive to workers to work and more incentive to investors to invest than does a country with relatively high taxes. As discussed earlier in the chapter, economist Alvin Rabushka showed that low-tax countries had an average growth rate in per-capita income that was substantially higher than the average growth rate in per-capita income of high-tax countries.

Stable, Noninflationary Monetary Policy As discussed in Chapter 15, stop-and-go, on-and-off monetary policy can often cause sharp ups and downs in the economy. When monetary policy is on "stop," the economy is likely to slide into a recession. This situation is obviously the opposite of economic growth and development.

What Role Does the Law Play in Economic Development?

It has been said that there are three ways to get something you want. If you want money, for example, first, you can earn it. Second, you can receive it as a gift. Third, you can steal it. Let's ignore receiving what you want as a gift and focus on getting it by earning or stealing it.

Imagine it is a time long ago, when there was no government. There are two farmers, Shouk and Miranda. Both farmers engage in some production and some theft. Suppose Shouk produces 10 bushels of corn each day, and he steals 2 bushels of wheat each day from Miranda. Miranda produces 10 bushels of wheat each day, and she steals 2 bushels of corn each day from Shouk. With both Shouk and Miranda producing and stealing, Shouk ends up with 8 bushels of corn at the end of the day (Miranda stole 2 bushels) and 2 bushels of wheat. Miranda ends up with 8 bushels of wheat (Shouk stole 2 bushels) and 2 bushels of corn.

Suppose government enters the picture and promises to establish and protect private property rights. It states that what Shouk produces is his and that if Miranda steals anything from Shouk, government will come after Miranda and put her in jail. It also states that what Miranda produces is hers and that if Shouk steals anything from Miranda the government will come after him and put him in jail.

By establishing private property rights and promising to protect them, government has raised the cost of stealing to both Shouk and Miranda. It is likely that they will steal less now that the cost of stealing has risen. In fact, they now choose not to steal at all. What can they do with the time that they once spent on stealing? This time can now be used to either consume leisure or produce more goods. Shouk and Miranda each decide to produce more goods. Instead of producing only 10 bushels of corn each day, Shouk produces 12; and instead of producing only 10 bushels of wheat each day, Miranda produces 12.

We can conclude that when there is no government and no way to protect private property, Shouk and Miranda are more likely to devote some of their time and energy to stealing from each other, and thus they have less time to devote to producing goods. But when private property rights are protected, things change. Stealing is not as profitable, and both Shouk and Miranda move away from it, toward more production.

The point is that a government that establishes and protects private property increases the cost of theft (to the thief) and by so doing, gets people to shift from activities of theft toward activities of production. A society that establishes and protects private property ends up producing more goods and services than a society that does not.

Some economists believe that down through history, almost every society that has become economically developed has had a system of laws that protected private property. In other words, the right type of government is a necessary factor in the economic development of a country.

QUESTION TO ANSWER How does law that protects private property rights aid economic growth?

Some countries prevent foreigners from investing in their factories, and businesses. How does this restriction affect growth and development in the country?

Economists often think in terms of *conditions* and *outcomes.* Moreover, the outcomes are often predicated on certain conditions existing. For example, when discussing economic development, economists say that countries will become economically developed if certain conditions exist, such as free trade, property rights, and so on.

Country X is trying to develop economically. It has recently undertaken a number of measures, one of which is to impose wage and price controls. Predict whether country X will develop as quickly with wage and price controls as it would without the controls. Explain your answer.

Consistently high money supply growth rates can be just as bad. When the money economy is expanding rapidly, inflation is likely. In inflationary times, people move resources away from producing goods and services and into hedging (trying to protect themselves) against the ravages of inflation. They often buy gold coins, artwork, and land, which many see as "inflation hedges," instead of building new factories and producing more goods. Only the latter activity, however, promotes economic growth and development.

A stable, noninflationary monetary policy eliminates antigrowth recessions. Such a policy also eliminates the waste of resources that often is part of trying to hedge against inflation.

Absence of Restrictions on Foreign Investment

Some countries prevent foreigners from investing in their countries. For example, country X may pass a law stating that no one from any other country can invest there. Such restrictions on foreign investment often hamper economic growth and development. Allowing foreigners to invest in a country, to start or expand businesses, promotes growth and development.

Absence of Controls on Bank Lending Activity

Banks channel funds from those who save to those who want to invest and produce. In some countries, government tells banks to whom they can and cannot lend. For example, banks may not be able to lend to automobile manufacturers but be permitted to lend to steel manufacturers. Such restrictions may arise because the government in the country is trying to promote a particular industry.

Technology & Innovation

Why Not Use the Technology If It Exists?

This chapter stated that technological advancements promote economic development. Because so much technology exists today, one would think that less-developed countries would simply adopt the technology that exists in developed countries, and then they, too, would be developed countries.

The problem here is that just because technology exists, it does not follow that everyone is going to use it. First, not everyone may know *how* to use it; education may have to come first. Second, even if the knowledge of how to use the technology exists, it may not be used because people are too poor to afford it.

Finally, even if the knowledge of how to use the technology exists and the technology is affordable—in other words, people in less-developed countries could purchase and use it if they wanted—still, people in less-developed countries may not use it. The old ways of doing things may be cheaper. To illustrate, in developed countries, workers use earth-moving equipment to clear the land on which houses are built. In less-developed countries, workers may use axes, shovels, and other hand tools. Why use axes and shovels when earth-moving equipment exists and is affordable? The wages of the people working in the less-developed countries may be so low that it is cheaper to hire a lot of workers than to buy an expensive (yet affordable) piece of equipment.

Consider a personal example. If Hernadez, who is a college student, could have hired someone to type his research papers for 25 cents, he might never have purchased the computer to do it himself, even if he could afford the computer.

QUESTION TO ANSWER Is there some technology that you have chosen not to use even though you can afford to use it? If so, why have you chosen not to use it?

The iron manufacturing plant where these men work in Romania might be able to get a loan when a clothing manufacturer might not. Does this hinder economic growth?

Controls of this type often hinder growth and development. Banks have a monetary incentive to search out those individuals, firms, and industries that can repay any loans received. Often, these individuals, firms, and industries are the ones likely to be the most successful at producing goods and services and at generating employment. Channeling funds to political allies instead of likely successful market participants often stifles growth and development.

Absence of Wage and Price Controls The free market determines equilibrium prices and wages. When government "overrides" the market and imposes controls on prices and wages, production usually suffers. To illustrate, suppose the market wage for workers in a particular industry is $10 an hour, and the market price for the good produced in the industry is $40. At current wages and prices, firms are earning just enough profit to continue in business. Now suppose government says that these firms have to pay a minimum of $12 an hour to their workers and that they cannot charge more than $38 for their goods. It is likely that the firms will go out of business; the goods and services they once produced will no longer exist.

Simple, Easy Business Licensing Procedures Most countries require a person to have a business license before starting a business. In some countries, obtaining a business license is easy, involving the filling out of a few papers and payment of a nominal fee. In other countries it involves visiting government offices, filling out numerous documents, bribing government officials, and so on. The easier and cheaper it is to obtain a business license, the more new businesses will pop up. Historically, new businesses have often promoted economic growth and development.

Protecting Private Property People will not work hard or invest in businesses unless they are reasonably sure that the property they amass from such endeavors is protected from expropriation (seizure by the government). Countries that protect private property often develop faster than those that do not.

Technological Advances Technological advances make it possible to obtain more output from the same amount of resources. For example, compare the amount of work that can be done by a business that uses computers with the amount accomplished by a business that does not. The world has witnessed major technological advances in the past century or so. Consider what your life would have been like if you had lived two hundred years ago, in 1800. Most of the major technological achievements we take for granted today—the car, computer, telephone, electricity, mass production techniques—would not have existed.

Technological advances, such as the computer, have changed the way we do business. Explain.

Section 3 Review

Reviewing Facts and Concepts

1. Identify the nine factors that economists agree aid economic growth and development.
2. Is there any evidence that foreign aid hinders economic development? Explain your answer.
3. What are some of the benefits of free trade to a developing country?

Critical Thinking

4. There are two countries, A and B. In A, the government does not protect private property, taxes are high, and quotas and tariffs are imposed on imported goods. In B, the government does protect private property, taxes are low, and there is free trade. In which country do you expect economic growth and development to be the stronger? Explain your answer.

Applying Economic Concepts

5. Give an example of a technological advancement that has made it possible for you to produce more of something with less effort expended.

Developing Economic

Skills

Thinking In Terms of Functions and Ripple Effects

Economists often think in terms of functions and ripple effects. To illustrate, an economist might say that demand is a function of income, meaning that a change in income can cause a change in the demand for a good. As Sally's income rises, her demand rises for eating out at restaurants.

In this chapter, we have discussed economic growth and development. We said that economic growth and development depended on certain factors, such as free trade, low taxation, and technological advances. Another way of stating this is to say that economic growth and development are a function of free trade, low taxation, technological advances, and so on.

Think about your life. What is getting high grades in school a function of? Some would say getting good grades is a function of how much time you study, how closely you listen in class, and how hard you work. For example, the longer you study, the higher your grades.

Now let's discuss ripple effects. A ripple effect refers to a change in one variable starting a chain reaction, thus causing other changes. Suppose corporate income tax rates are cut by Congress. As a result, businesses find producing and selling goods more profitable. Because of this, they decide to invest more. Because they buy and use more capital goods, the economy begins to grow. Because the economy starts to grow, there are more jobs. Because there are more jobs, Alice, who has been unemployed for six months, finds a job. Because Alice finds a job, she has more income and she buys a computer for her daughter, Maria. Because Maria now has a computer, she ends up surfing the Web more than she would have. In other words, a change in corporate income tax rates has rippled outward far enough to affect what Maria does in her spare time.

Think of a ripple effect in another context. You learned earlier that getting good grades is a function of how much time you study. With this in mind, you decide to study longer. Because you study longer, your grades rise. Because your grades rise, you go to a better college. Because you go to a better college, you get a better job. Because you get a better job, you not only enjoy your work more than you would have, but you also earn more.

Being aware of other ripple effects could save your life. Evan is at a party with his friends. Bob offers him some beer. Evan is not old enough to drink, but his friend keeps hounding him to drink, and against his better judgment, he does. Soon, Evan and Bob are drunk. Will there be any ripple effects of Evan and Bob being drunk? Suppose Bob asks Evan to go for a ride with him. If Evan weren't drunk, he would never get in a car with someone who had been drinking, but his own judgment is impaired. He says okay, let's go. Bob and Evan get into the car. Bob is the driver. Because both young men are drunk, neither of them puts on his seatbelt. Thirty minutes later, Bob drives the car into a tree and they are both hurt.

Neither Bob nor Evan thought things would end up this way. But then perhaps they weren't thinking in terms of ripple effects. The economist reminds us to think in terms of one thing leading to another leading to still another. Often, when you think this way, you can see what the future could hold.

QUESTIONS TO ANSWER

1. What do you think happiness is a function of?
2. Has any change or event in your life had far-reaching ripple effects? If so, what was it? Did you know the initial change or event was going to have such far-reaching effects?

CHAPTER

17 Review

Economics Vocabulary

Fill in the following blanks with the appropriate word or phrase.

1. A _____ is a country with a low per-capita GDP.
2. The existing state of affairs is sometimes called the _____.
3. The _____ ratio is the number of children (under fifteen years old) plus the number of elderly (aged sixty-five and over) divided by the population.
4. The birthrate minus the death rate equals the _____ rate.
5. A _____ is a country with a relatively high per-capita GDP.
6. Countries are poor because they do not save and buy capital goods, but they cannot save and buy capital goods because they are poor. This is descriptive of the _____.

Review Questions

1. What is the difference between economic growth and economic development?
2. What is the international poverty line?
3. What is the vicious circle of poverty?
4. Country X has an infant mortality rate of 45 per 1,000 live births. What does this mean?
5. Explain how a country can experience economic growth and still not be economically developed.
6. Why might couples living in less-developed countries have more children than couples living in developed countries?
7. What are three things with which a low per-capita GDP tends to be associated?
8. What is the population growth rate equal to?
9. How might free trade aid economic development?
10. Describe a culture that would foster economic development. Describe a culture that might hinder economic development.
11. What does it mean if something increases at a geometric rate?
12. According to Thomas Malthus, why was the world headed toward mass starvation?
13. Is a fast-growing population necessarily an obstacle to economic development? Explain your answer.

Calculations

1. If a country's population growth rate is 1 percent and its birthrate is 3 percent, what is its death rate?
2. In year 1 the population is 100, and there are 100 baskets of food. The population doubles each year, and food production increases by 10 baskets each year. What is the amount of food per person in year 10?
3. Country X has a population of 5 million people. In the country, 500,000 persons are under fifteen years of age, and 600,000 persons are sixty-five or over. What is the dependency ratio?

Graphs

1. Using Exhibit 17-1 on page 447, answer the following questions:
   - **a.** Of the countries represented, which has the highest GDP or GNP per capita?
   - **b.** Of the countries represented, which has the lowest GDP or GNP per capita?
   - **c.** What is the average GDP or GNP per capita for the European countries represented (Sweden, Norway, Denmark, Luxembourg, Portugal), *not* including Russia? What is the average if Russia is included?
   - **d.** What is the difference in GDP or GNP per capita between North Korea and South Korea? How might you explain this diffference?
2. Using Exhibit 17-2 on page 451, answer the following questions:.
   - **a.** Which country has a larger population, Canada or Mexico?
   - **b.** In general terms, how would you compare the population of India to all of South America?
   - **c.** Would you say that Russia has about the same population as Japan, twice the population of Japan, or four times the population of Japan?

Economics and Thinking Skills

1. **Application.** Suppose you are paid for certain grades that you earn in school. You receive $50 for an A, $25 for a B, and nothing for any grade lower than a B. Now consider two possible settings. In the first, you have to pay your teacher 10 percent of the grade money you earn: in the second, you have to pay your teacher 40 percent of the grade

money you earn. In short, you can consider what you pay your teacher a tax. In which setting are you more likely to produce more A grades? How is your answer relevant to how quickly or how much a country develops?

2. **Analysis.** This chapter discussed nine factors that contribute to economic development. Suppose country 1 has free trade, and country 2 has a stable, noninflationary monetary policy. Furthermore, suppose country 1 develops at a faster rate than country 2. Does it follow that free trade is a more powerful factor for promoting economic development than a stable, noninflationary monetary policy? Explain your answer.
3. **Cause and Effect.** The problem with the vicious circle of poverty is that it is difficult to establish what is cause and what is effect. Do you agree or disagree? Explain your answer.

Writing Skills

Write a one-page paper describing how you think your life would have been different had you been born and raised in a less-developed country.

Economics in the Media

1. Find an article in the local newspaper that addresses economic development, poor nations, rich nations, Malthusian thought, or foreign aid. Identify the major ideas of the article.
2. Find a story on a television news show that addresses foreign aid, any of the economic problems faced by less-developed countries, or any of the factors that promote economic development. Identify the major ideas of the story.

Where's the Economics?

What does this picture have to do with the vicious circle of poverty?

Analyzing Primary Sources

Thomas Malthus predicted mass starvation unless population growth could be checked. In this regard, he saw as beneficial those acts of nature or of humans that limited the population in some way. Read what he has to say in *An Essay on the Principle of Population:*

It is evident truth that, whatever the increase in the means of subsistence, the increase in population must be limited by it, at least after the food has once been divided into the smallest shares that will support life. All the children born, beyond what would be required to keep up the population at this level, must necessarily perish, unless room be made for them by the deaths of grown persons. . . . To act consistently therefore, we should facilitate, instead of foolishly and vainly endeavoring to impede, the operations of nature in producing mortality; and if we dread the too frequent visitation of the horrid form of famine, we should sedulously encourage the other forms of destruction, which we compel nature to use. Instead of recommending cleanliness to the poor, we should encourage contrary habits. In our towns we should make the streets narrower, crowd more people into the houses, and court the return of the plague. In the country, we should build our villages near stagnant pools, and particularly encourage settlements in all marshy and unwholesome situations. But above all, we should reprobate specific remedies for ravaging diseases; and those benevolent, but much mistaken men, who have thought they were doing a service to mankind by projecting schemes for the total extirpation of particular disorders. If by these and similar means the annual mortality were increased. . . we might probably every one of us marry at the age of puberty, and yet few be absolutely starved.[2]

1. What is Malthus proposing in this passage?
2. What are three of Malthus's proposals?
3. What do you think of Malthus's proposals? Do you agree with them all? Some of them? None of them?

2. Thomas Malthus, *An Essay on the Principle of Population,* 6th ed. (London: 1826), pp. 465–466.

CHAPTER 18

International Trade

What This Chapter Is About

A discussion of international trade, which is this chapter's focus, includes several topics, such as comparative advantage, imports and exports, the benefits of international trade, and exchange rates. The chapter presents the information necessary to answer such questions as, Why do the people in different countries trade with each other? Is it bad economic news if a country buys more from other countries than it sells to other countries? What causes the value of the U.S. dollar to rise and fall on foreign exchange markets?

Why This Chapter Is Important

We live in a global economy. Precision ice hockey equipment is designed in Sweden, financed in Canada, and assembled in Cleveland, Ohio. An advertising campaign is conceived in Great Britain, and footage for it is shot in Canada, dubbed in London, and edited in New York. A sports car is financed in Japan, designed in Italy, and assembled in Indiana, Mexico, and France using advanced electronic components invented in New Jersey and fabricated in Japan. A jet plane is designed in the state of Washington and in Japan and assembled in Seattle, with tail cones from Canada, special tail sections from China and Italy, and engines from England.

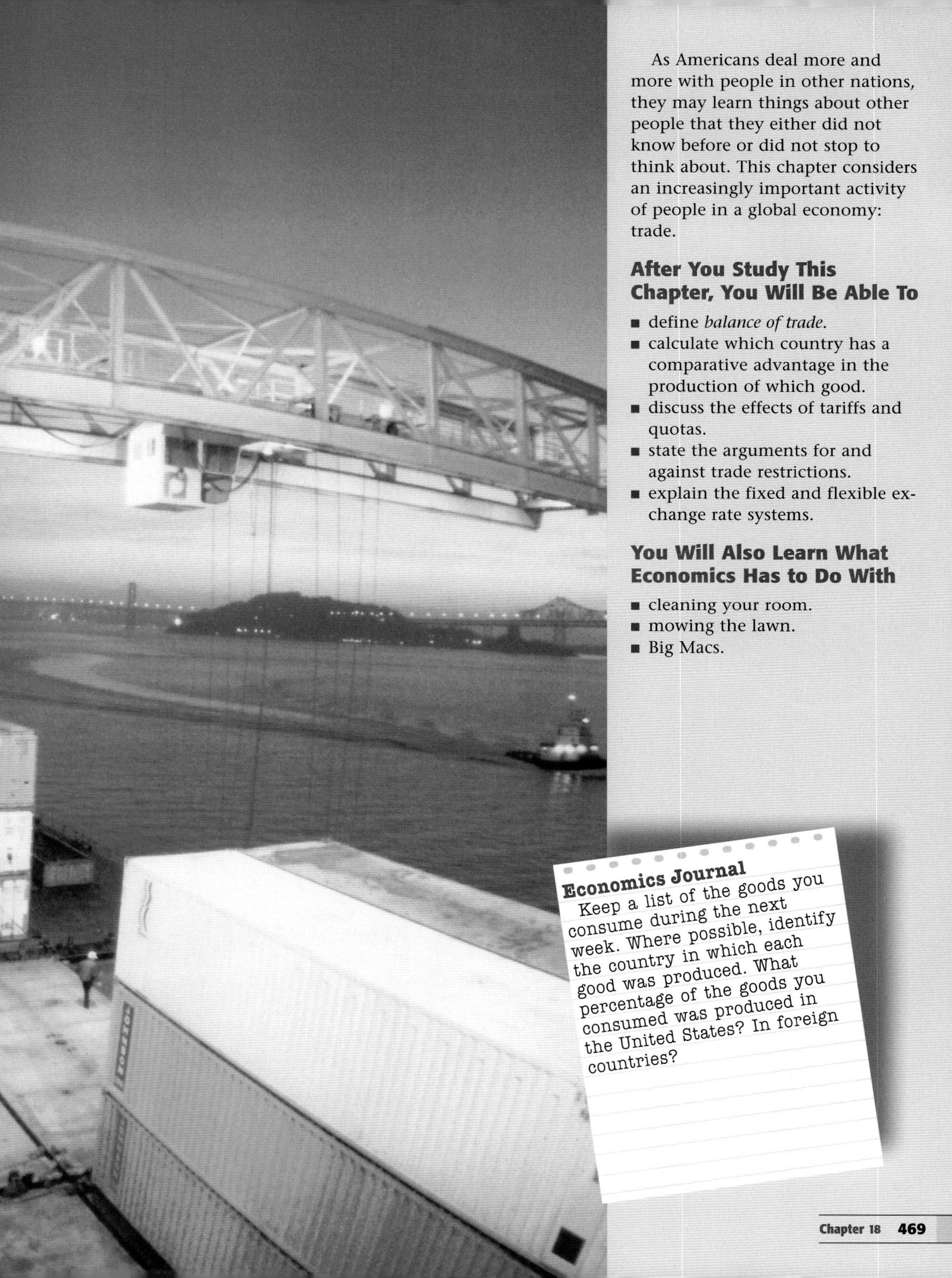

As Americans deal more and more with people in other nations, they may learn things about other people that they either did not know before or did not stop to think about. This chapter considers an increasingly important activity of people in a global economy: trade.

After You Study This Chapter, You Will Be Able To

- define *balance of trade.*
- calculate which country has a comparative advantage in the production of which good.
- discuss the effects of tariffs and quotas.
- state the arguments for and against trade restrictions.
- explain the fixed and flexible exchange rate systems.

You Will Also Learn What Economics Has to Do With

- cleaning your room.
- mowing the lawn.
- Big Macs.

Economics Journal

Keep a list of the goods you consume during the next week. Where possible, identify the country in which each good was produced. What percentage of the goods you consumed was produced in the United States? In foreign countries?

SECTION 1

International Trade

This section discusses some of the facts and figures of international trade, especially as they relate to the United States. It also introduces the important concept of comparative advantage.

As you read this section, keep these key questions in mind:

- What goods are major U.S. exports?
- What goods are major U.S. imports?
- What is comparative advantage?

Why Do People in Different Countries Trade with Each Other?

Key Terms

exports
imports
balance of trade
absolute advantage
specialize
comparative advantage

MINI GLOSSARY

exports Goods produced in the domestic country and sold to residents of a foreign country

We have international trade for the same reason we have trade at any level. Individuals trade to make themselves better off. Frank and Bob, who live in Detroit, trade because both value something the other has more than they value something of their own. For example, perhaps Frank trades $10 for Bob's book. On an international scale, Elaine in the United States trades with Cho in China because Cho has something that Elaine wants and Elaine has something that Cho wants.

Importing bananas is cheaper than growing them in the United States. For what other products is this true?

Obviously, different countries have different terrains, climates, resources, and so on. It follows that some countries will be able to produce some goods that other countries cannot produce or can produce only at extremely high cost. For example, Hong Kong has no oil, and Saudi Arabia has a large supply. Bananas do not grow easily in the United States, but they flourish in Honduras. Americans could grow bananas if they used hothouses, but it is cheaper for them to buy bananas from Honduras than to produce bananas themselves.

Exports and Imports

Exports are goods that are produced in the domestic country and sold to residents of a foreign country. For example, if residents of the United States (the domestic country) produce and sell computers to people in France, Germany, and Mexico, then computers are a U.S. export. In 1999, the value of U.S. exports was $960 billion. This means that U.S. residents produced and sold $960 billion worth of U.S. goods and services to people in other countries. Major U.S. exports include automobiles, computers, aircraft, corn, wheat, soybeans, scientific instruments, coal, machinery, and plastic materials.

This Air India Boeing 747 is just one of many goods manufactured in the United States for sale to other countries.

Exhibit 18-1
Chief Exports of Selected Countries

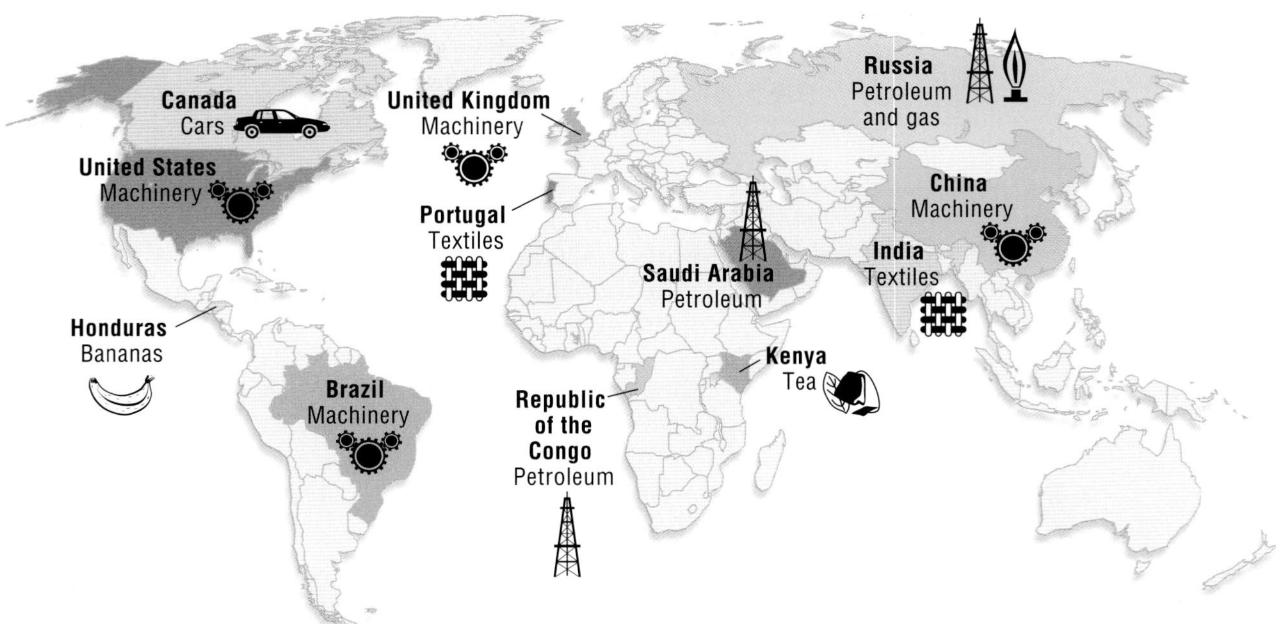

imports
Goods produced in foreign countries and purchased by residents of the domestic country.

Imports are goods produced in foreign countries and purchased by residents of the domestic country. For example, if residents of the United States (the domestic country) buy coffee from Colombia, then coffee is a U.S. import. In 1999, the value of U.S. imports was $1,227 billion. This means that U.S. residents bought $1,227 billion worth of goods and services from people in other countries. Major U.S. imports include petroleum, clothing, iron, steel, office machines, footwear, fish, coffee, and diamonds.

Exhibit 18-2
Exports and Imports of the United States

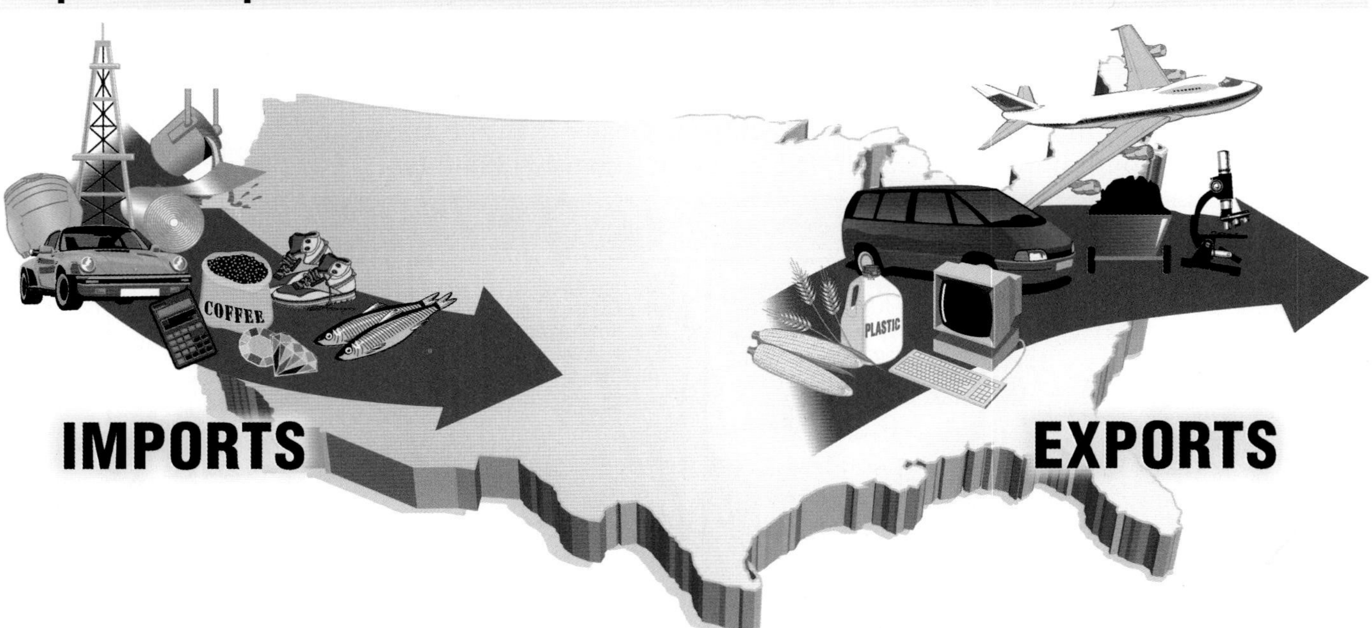

Balance of Trade

A country's **balance of trade** is the difference between the value of its exports and the value of its imports.

balance of trade
The difference between the value of a country's exports and the value of its imports.

absolute advantage
The situation in which a country can produce more of a good than another country can produce with the same quantity of resources.

Balance of trade = Value of exports − Value of imports

Exhibit 18-3
Balance of Trade

For example, if the value of a country's exports is \$300 billion and the value of its imports is \$200 billion, then the country has a positive balance of trade (\$100 billion). If the value of a country's exports is \$100 billion and the value of its imports is \$210 billion, then the country has a negative balance of trade (−\$110 billion).

Absolute and Comparative Advantage

Suppose that using the same quantity of resources as Japan, the United States can produce either of the following two combinations of food and clothing:

- Combination A: 150 units of food and 0 units of clothing.
- Combination B: 100 units of food and 25 units of clothing.

Suppose that Japan, using the same quantity of resources as the United States, can produce either of the two combinations of food and clothing:

- Combination C: 30 units of food and 120 units of clothing.
- Combination D: 0 units of food and 180 units of clothing.

When a country can produce more of a good than another country using the same quantity of resources, it is said to have an **absolute advantage** in the production of that good. In our example, the United States has an absolute advantage in producing food, because the maximum amount of food it can produce (150 units) is greater than the maximum amount of food Japan can produce (30 units). Japan, in contrast, has an absolute advantage in producing clothing, because the maximum amount of clothing it can produce (180 units) is greater than the maximum amount of clothing the United States can produce (25 units).

Reprinted with special permission of King Features Syndicate.

Suppose the United States has a comparative advantage in producing food, and Japan has a comparative advantage in producing clothing. How might these facts affect their production and trade decisions?

specialize
To do only one thing. For example, when a country specializes in the production of a good, it produces only that good.

comparative advantage
The situation in which a country can produce a good at lower opportunity cost than another country.

Suppose that in year 1, Japan and the United States do not trade with each other. Instead, each nation decides to produce some quantity of each good and consume it. The United States produces and consumes combination B (100 units of food and 25 units of clothing), and Japan produces and consumes combination C (30 units of food and 120 units of clothing).

In year 2, things change. Each country decides to **specialize** in the production of one good and then trade some of it for the other good. Which good—clothing or food—should the United States specialize in producing? Which good should Japan specialize in producing?

In general, a country should specialize in the production of the good in which it has a **comparative advantage**—the good it can produce at a *lower opportunity cost.*

Determining Opportunity Cost Recall from Chapter 1 that the opportunity cost of producing a good is what is given up to produce that good. For example, if Julio gives up the opportunity to produce three towels if he produces a blanket, then the opportunity cost of the blanket is three towels.

What is the opportunity cost of producing food for the United States? What is the cost for Japan? We know that the United States can produce either combination A (150 units of food and 0 units of clothing) or combination B (100 units of food and 25 units of clothing). Suppose it is producing combination B. What are the benefits and costs of deciding to produce combination A instead? By producing combination A, the country will make itself better off by 50 additional units of food, but it will have to give up 25 units of clothing to do so. In other words, for every 1 extra unit of food, it will have to give up ½ unit of clothing. In economic terms, for the United States, the opportunity cost of 1 unit of food is ½ unit of clothing.

The process is similar for Japan. We know that Japan can produce either combination C (30 units of food and 120 units of clothing) or combination D (0 units of food and 180 units of clothing). Suppose it is producing combination D. What are the benefits and costs of deciding to produce

Exhibit 18-4
Opportunity Costs

Countries are better off if they specialize in the production of goods for which they have a comparative advantage. Given the opportunity costs shown below, in which good does the United States have a comparative advantage? In which good does Japan have a comparative advantage?

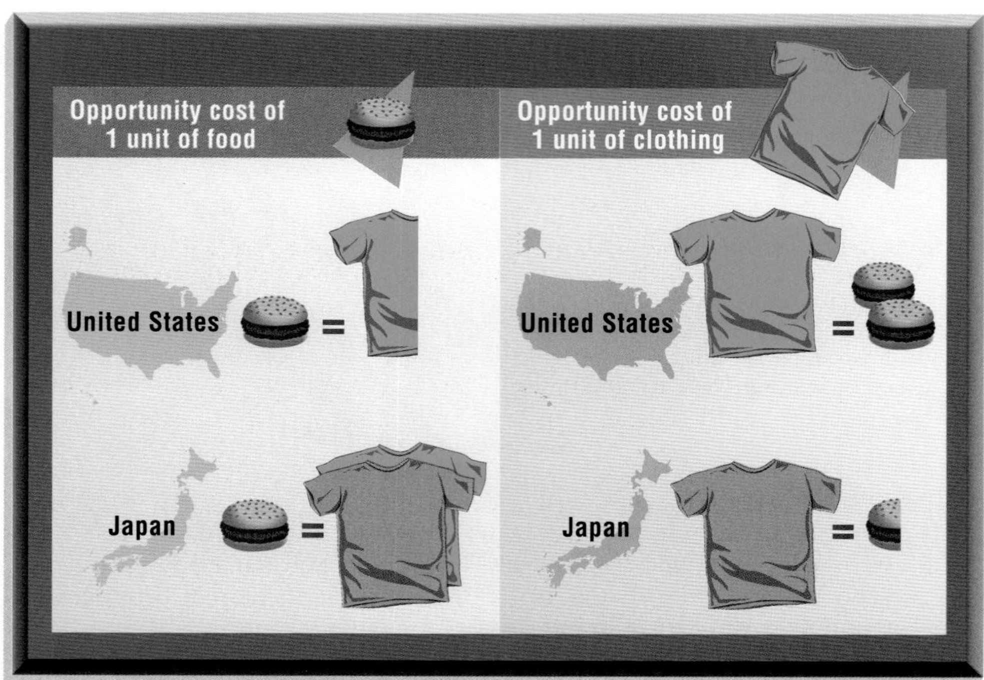

combination C instead? By producing combination C, Japan will make itself better off by 30 additional units of food, but it will have to give up 60 units of clothing to do so. In other words, for every 1 extra unit of food, it will have to give up 2 units of clothing. In economic terms, for Japan, the opportunity cost of 1 unit of food is 2 units of clothing. Thus the opportunity cost of producing 1 unit of food (F) is ½ unit of clothing (C) for the United States and 2 units of clothing for Japan:

Opportunity cost of 1 unit of food

United States: 1F = ½C

Japan: 1F = 2C

We conclude that the United States can produce food more cheaply than Japan. In other words, the United States has a comparative advantage in food production. Food, then, is what the United States should specialize in producing. If we followed this procedure for clothing production, we would find that Japan could produce clothing more cheaply than the United States. The opportunity cost of producing 1 unit of clothing is 2 units of food for the United States and 1/2 unit of food for Japan.

Opportunity cost of 1 unit of clothing

United States: 1C = 2F

Japan: 1C = ½F

Therefore, Japan has a comparative advantage in clothing production. Clothing, then, is what Japan should specialize in producing.

Benefits of Specialization and Trade

Consider two cases, both shown in Exhibit 18-5. In the first case, neither Japan nor the United States specializes in the production of either good (thus, both produce some amount of each good), and the two countries do not trade. In this case, the United States produces combination B (100 units of food and 25 units of clothing), and Japan produces combination C (30 units of food and 120 units of clothing).

No specialization and no trade	
United States:	100F + 25C
Japan:	30F + 120C

Exhibit 18-5

The Benefits of Specialization and Trade

Countries can have more of each good if they specialize in the production of the good for which they have a comparative advantage and then trade some of it for other goods.

No specialization and no trade

A. Without specialization and trade, countries have only what they produce.

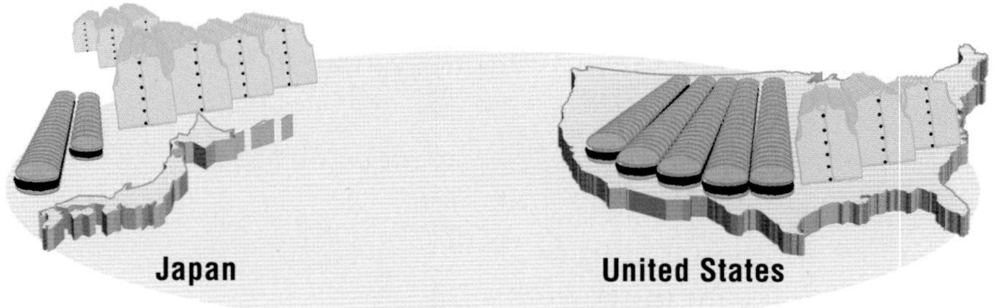

Specialization and trade

B. With specialization, each country can produce more of the good for which it has a comparative advantage.

C. With specialization and trade, each country can have more of *all* goods.

In the second case, each country specializes in the production of the good in which it has a comparative advantage, and then it trades some of that good for the other good. The United States produces combination A (150 units of food and 0 units of clothing), and Japan produces combination D (0 units of food and 180 units of clothing).

The countries decide that the United States will trade 40 units of food to Japan in return for 40 units of clothing.

Countries trade
40F for 40C

After trade, then, the United States ends up with 110 units of food and 40 units of clothing. Japan, in turn, ends up with 40 units of food and 140 units of clothing.

Specialization and trade
United States: 110F + 40C
Japan: 40F + 140C

Carlos and Kim are married. Carlos can wash the dishes in 20 minutes and cut the lawn in 30 minutes. Kim can wash the dishes in 40 minutes and cut the lawn in 40 minutes. If Carlos and Kim decide to specialize in doing certain tasks, who do you predict will cut the lawn? Wash the dishes? Explain your answer.

In which case are Japan and the United States better off? The answer is the second case, where there is specialization and trade. In the first case, the United States ended up with 100 units of food and 25 units of clothing, whereas in the second case, it ended up with 110 units of food and 40 units of clothing. In other words, through specialization and trade, the United States ended up with more of both food and clothing.

Benefits to United States of specialization and trade
10 more units of F
15 more units of C

The same is true for Japan. In the first case, it ended up with 30 units of food and 120 units of clothing, whereas it ended up with 40 units of food and 140 units of clothing in the second case, through specialization and trade.

Benefits to Japan of specialization and trade
10 more units of F
20 more units of C

Thus if countries specialize in the production of the goods in which they have a comparative advantage and then trade some of these goods for other goods, they can make themselves better off.

The International Trade Administration of the U.S. Department of Commerce compiles trade statistics. Go to its Web site at http:// www.ita.doc.gov/ and click on "Trade Statistics," then "U.S. Foreign Trade Highlights," next "U.S. Aggregate Foreign Trade Data," and finally "U.S. International Trade in Goods and Services." What was the U.S. balance of trade for the latest year published?

Cleaning Rooms and Mowing Lawns

Fourteen-year-old Steve and twelve-year-old Danny are brothers. Their father has just told them that each week they must complete two tasks: clean their rooms and mow the lawn. The following table shows how many minutes it takes each brother to do each task:

	Time to clean both rooms	Time to mow lawn
Steve	100 min.	60 min.
Danny	100 min.	300 min.

Steve and Danny wonder how they should go about doing what their father has told them they need to do. They realize they could each do half of each task, or they could simply split the tasks and each do one. Which is the better way to proceed?

Suppose each of the brothers does half of each task. Steve spends 50 minutes on his half of cleaning the rooms, and Danny spends 50 minutes, which is a total of 100 minutes to clean the rooms. Then Steve spends 30 minutes mowing his half of the lawn, and Danny spends 150 minutes mowing, a total of 180 minutes of mowing. To complete both tasks it takes 100 minutes plus 180 minutes, or 280 minutes.

Now suppose that Steve only mows the lawn, and Danny only cleans the rooms. It takes Steve 60 minutes to mow the lawn, and it takes Danny 100 minutes to clean the rooms, which is a total of 160 minutes.

The choice is between 280 minutes or 160 minutes. To save time, the brothers should do what each has a comparative advantage in doing, specialize in one task, and get their duties completed 120 minutes faster. This leaves them much more time to do what they want.

QUESTION TO ANSWER In many families, people have certain things that they do and no one else does. For example, a husband may cook and the wife may wash the dishes; a husband may mow the lawn and the wife may wash the clothes. Do you think the jobs that each family member does are the result of comparative advantage or something else? Explain your answer.

Section 1 Review

Defining Terms

1. Define

a. exports

b. imports

c. balance of trade

d. absolute advantage

e. comparative advantage

f. specialize

Reviewing Facts and Concepts

2. Suppose the United States can produce either 90 apples and 20 oranges or 80 apples and 30 oranges. What is the opportunity cost of producing 1 apple?

3. Suppose Japan can produce either 100 cars and 30 television sets or 80 cars and 60 television sets. What is the opportunity cost of producing 1 television set?

4. What does it mean to say that country A has a comparative advantage in the production of computers?

Critical Thinking

5. Jones is an attorney, and Smith is a gardener. Jones, however, is better at gardening than Smith is at gardening. Essentially, he can do what needs to be done in the garden in thirty minutes, whereas it takes Smith one hour. Does it follow that Jones should do his own gardening instead of hiring Smith to do it? Explain your answer.

Applying Economic Concepts

6. How would you go about computing the opportunity cost (in dollars) of studying for a test?

SECTION 2

Trade Restrictions

The preceding section showed that countries benefit by specializing in the production of goods in which they have a comparative advantage and trading these goods for other goods. In the real world, though, there are numerous trade restrictions. This section discusses why restrictions on trade exist, given that countries gain from free international trade.

As you read this section, keep these key questions in mind:

- What is a tariff?
- What is a quota?
- How do tariffs and quotas affect price?
- What are the arguments for and against trade restrictions?

Trade Restrictions: Tariffs and Quotas

Key Terms

tariff
quota
dumping

Tariffs and quotas are the two major types of trade restrictions. A **tariff** is a tax on imports. For example, currently some Americans buy cars made in Japan, which are considered imports. Let's say each car sells for $22,000. Now suppose the U.S. government places a $1,000 tariff on each car, raising the price of a Japanese car from $22,000 to $23,000. As a result, Americans will buy fewer Japanese cars. (Remember the law of demand: As price rises, quantity demanded falls.)

A **quota** is a legal limit on the amount of a good that may be imported. Suppose Japan is sending 300,000 cars into the United States each year. The U.S. government decides to set a quota, or legal limit, on Japanese cars at 200,000 cars per year. In short, the U.S. government says it is legal for Japan to send 200,000 cars each year to the United States, but not one car more.

How will a tariff on Toyotas affect the price of a Toyota?

The effect of the quota is to raise the price of Japanese cars. With a smaller supply of Japanese cars and with demand for Japanese cars constant, the price of Japanese cars will rise. (Recall that when the supply of a good falls and the demand for the good remains the same, the price of the good rises.) In effect, then, both tariffs and quotas raise the price of the imported good to the U.S. consumer.

MINI GLOSSARY

tariff
A tax on imports.

quota
A legal limit on the amount of a good that may be imported.

The U.S. Government and Producer Interests

If tariffs and quotas result in higher prices for U.S. consumers, why does the government impose them? Government is sometimes more responsive to producer interests than consumer interests. To see why, suppose there are 100 U.S. producers of good X and 20 million U.S. consumers of good X. The producers want to protect themselves from foreign competition, so they lobby for, and receive, tariffs on foreign goods that compete with what they sell. As a result, consumers end up paying higher prices. We'll say that consumers end up paying $40 million more, and producers end up receiving $40 million more, for good X than they would have if the tariffs had not been imposed. If we equally divide the additional $40 million received among the 100 producers, we find that each producer receives $400,000 more as a result of tariffs. If we equally divide the additional $40 million paid among the 20 million consumers, we find that each customer pays $2 more as a result of tariffs. A producer is likely to think, "I should lobby for tariffs, because if I am effective, I will receive $400,000 more." A consumer is likely to think, "Why should I lobby against tariffs? If I am effective, I will save myself only $2. It is not worth my lobbying to save $2." In short, the benefits of tariffs are concentrated on relatively few producers, and the costs of tariffs are spread over relatively many consumers. This situation makes each producer's gain relatively large compared with each consumer's loss. Producers will probably lobby government to obtain the relatively large gains from tariffs, but consumers will not lobby government to avoid paying the small additional amount added by tariffs.

Domestic consumers often lose and domestic producers gain from tariffs. Still, consumers rarely lobby against tariffs as often as producers lobby in favor of them. Do you know why?

Politicians, who generally respond to the most vocal interests, hear from those people who want the tariffs but not from those people who are against them. Politicians may thus mistakenly assume that consumers' silence means that they accept the tariff policy, when in fact they may not. They may simply not find it worthwhile to do anything to fight the policy.

Arguments for Trade Restrictions

Do tariffs and quotas exist only because government is sometimes more responsive to producer interests than consumer interests? Not at all; they exist for other reasons, too, which are discussed here.

What Is It Worth to Save a Job?

Suppose the U.S. government imposes a tariff on imported shoes. As a result, the U.S. (domestic) producers of shoes sell their shoes for higher prices and receive higher incomes. Obviously, the domestic shoe producers are better off with the tariff than without it, as are many of the workers they employ. After all, without the tariffs, foreign shoes might have outcompeted the domestic shoe producers, and some U.S. shoe workers might have lost their jobs. How much should consumers pay to protect U.S. jobs? It is one thing to pay an extra few dollars and quite another to pay many thousands of dollars to save a U.S. worker's job.

In 1977, tariffs and quotas were imposed on foreign footwear, protecting an estimated 21,000 jobs in the domestic footwear industry as a result. The average worker in the industry earned $8,340 (in 1980 dollars). Domestic consumers paid $77,714 for *each* $8,340 domestic footwear job protected.

In 1977, tariffs and quotas were also imposed on imports of carbon steel. An estimated 20,000 domestic jobs in the industry were protected as a result. The average worker in the industry earned $24,329 (again, in 1980 dollars), and in this case domestic consumers paid $85,272 for *each* $24,329 job that was protected.

In 1981, "voluntary" export restraints (which operate like quotas) were placed on Japanese car imports. The U.S. International Trade Commission estimated that 44,000 domestic jobs were protected—at a cost of $193,000 per job.

QUESTION TO ANSWER Should U.S. consumers have to pay higher prices to save U.S. jobs? Why or why not?

The National-Defense Argument It is often argued that certain industries—such as aircraft, petroleum, chemicals, and weapons—are necessary to the national defense and therefore deserve to be protected from foreign competition. For example, suppose the United States has a comparative advantage in the production of wheat, and China has a comparative advantage in the production of weapons. Should the United States specialize in the production of wheat and then trade wheat to China in exchange for weapons? Many Americans would answer no; they maintain it is too dangerous to leave weapons production to another country, whether that country is China, France, or Canada.

If the national defense argument is used, the United States would not buy planes or jets from France. Explain why.

The national-defense argument may have some validity, but even valid arguments may be overused or abused. Industries that are not necessary to the national defense may still argue for trade restrictions placed on imported goods. For example, in the past, the national-defense argument has been used by some firms in the following industries: pens, pottery, peanuts, candles, thumbtacks, tuna fishing, and pencils. It is hard to believe that these goods are necessary to the national defense.

The Infant-Industry Argument Alexander Hamilton, the first U.S. secretary of the Treasury, argued that "infant," or new, industries often need to be protected from older, more established foreign competitors until the new industries are mature enough to compete on an equal basis. Today, some persons voice the same argument. The infant-industry argument is clearly an argument for only temporary protection from foreign producers. Critics charge, however, that once an industry is protected from foreign competition, removing the protection is almost impossible. The once-infant industry will continue to argue that it is not yet old enough to go it alone.

The Antidumping Argument **Dumping** is selling goods in foreign countries at prices below their costs and below the prices charged in the domestic (home) market. For example, if Japan sells a Japanese-made TV set in the United States for a price below the cost to produce the TV set and at a price below what it sells the TV set for in Japan, then Japan is said to be dumping TV sets in the United States. Critics of dumping say that dumpers (in our example, Japan) seek only to get into a market, drive out U.S. competitors, and then raise prices. However, some economists point out that such a strategy is not likely to work. Once the dumpers have driven out their competition and raised prices, their competition is likely to return. The dumpers, in turn, will have obtained only a string of losses (because they have been selling below cost) for their efforts. Second, opponents of the antidumping argument point out that U.S. consumers benefit from dumping by paying lower prices.

dumping
The sale of goods abroad at prices below their costs and below the price charged in domestic (home) markets.

Suppose Japan decides to dump TV sets in the United States. Who gains? Who loses?

The Low-Foreign-Wages Argument Some people argue that U.S. producers can't compete with foreign producers because U.S. producers pay high wages to their workers, and foreign producers pay low wages to their workers. The U.S. producers insist that free trade must be restricted, or they will be ruined.

These Cambodian workers earn much lower wages than workers in similar jobs in the United States. Does it follow that U.S. firms will prefer to hire Cambodian workers instead of U.S. workers? Explain your answer.

What the argument overlooks is the reason U.S. wages are high and foreign wages are low: productivity. High wages and high productivity usually go together, as do low wages and low productivity. Suppose a U.S. worker who receives $20 per hour produces 100 units of good X per hour; the cost per unit is 20 cents. A foreign worker who receives $2 per hour produces 5 units of good X per hour. The cost per unit is 40 cents—twice as high as for the U.S. worker. In short, a country's high-wage disadvantage may be offset by its productivity advantage. (See Exhibit 18-6 for the hourly compensation paid to production workers in different countries.)

Exhibit 18-6

Hourly Compensation for Production Workers, Selected Countries

Hourly compensation includes wages, premiums, bonuses, vacation, holidays and other leave, insurance, and benefit plans. These are 1997 figures. All amounts have been converted to U.S. dollars.
Source: U.S. Bureau of Labor Statistics.

Country	Hourly compensation for production workers (in dollars)
Australia	$16.00
Austria	21.92
Belgium	22.82
Canada	16.55
Denmark	22.02
Finland	21.44
France	17.97
Germany	28.28
Ireland	13.57
Italy	16.74
Japan	19.37
Korea, South	7.22
Mexico	1.75
Netherlands	20.61
New Zealand	11.02
Norway	23.72
Portugal	5.29
Singapore	8.24
Spain	12.16
Sweden	22.24
Switzerland	24.19
Taiwan	5.89
United Kingdom	15.47
United States	18.24

The Tit-for-Tat Argument Some people argue that if a foreign country uses tariffs or quotas against U.S. goods, the United States ought to apply equal tariffs and quotas against that foreign country, in the hope that the foreign country will lower or eliminate its trade restrictions. According to this *tit-for-tat argument,* we should do to them as they do to us.

Critics of this type of policy argue that a tit-for-tat strategy has the potential to escalate into a full-blown trade war. For example, suppose Japan places a tariff on American-made radios. The United States retaliates by placing a tariff on Japanese-made radios. Japan then reacts by placing a tariff on American-made computers, the United States retaliates by placing a tariff on Japanese-made computers, and so on. At some point, it might be difficult to figure out who started what.

International Economic Integration

One of the hallmarks of a global economy is economic integration, the combining of nations to form either a common market or a free-trade area. In a common market, the member nations trade without restrictions, and all share the same trade barriers with the outside world. For example, suppose countries A, B, C, D, E, and F formed a common market. They would eliminate all trade barriers among themselves (free trade would exist), but they would have common trade barriers with all other nations. Thus, any tariffs placed on country Z's goods would apply in all member countries.

These European leaders represent some of the countries that are members of the European Union. How might the EU affect the United States?

A major common market is the European Union (EU), which consists of fifteen countries: Austria, Belgium, Denmark, Finland, France, Germany, Greece, Ireland, Italy, Luxembourg, the Netherlands, Portugal, Spain, Sweden, and the United Kingdom. Members of the EU have eliminated trade barriers among themselves. As discussed in Chapter 10, the euro is a common currency in eleven of the fifteen countries of the EU. On January 1, 1999, these eleven countries irrevocably fixed their national currencies to the euro. Consumers in these eleven countries will begin to use euro notes and coins on July 1, 2002.

In 1992, President Bush, Mexican President Salinas, and Canadian Prime Minister Mulroney signed the North American Free Trade Agreement (NAFTA). NAFTA was signed into law by President Clinton on December 8, 1993, and took effect on January 1, 1994.

Willem (Frederik) Duisenberg, President of the European Central Bank

Just as the United States has a central bank, called the Federal Reserve System, the European Union has a central bank, called the European Central Bank (ECB). The role of the ECB in the world will become extremely important once the euro is circulated in the European Union.

The current president of the ECB is Willem Frederik Duisenberg. He was born on July 9, 1935, in Heerenveen, the Netherlands, and received undergraduate and graduate degrees in economics. Duisenberg has served as a staff member of the International Monetary Fund (IMF), professor of macroeconomics (University of Amsterdam), minister of finance (the Netherlands), and president of the Netherlands Central Bank.

In a free-trade area, in contrast to a common market, trade barriers among the member countries are eliminated, and each country is allowed to set its own trade rules with the rest of the world. Country G might place tariffs on country Z's goods, for instance, but country J might decide not to do so.

A major free-trade area created by the North American Free Trade Agreement (NAFTA) includes Canada, Mexico, and the United States. One of the main arguments against NAFTA was that if it passed, U.S. companies would move their operations to Mexico to benefit from paying lower wages. A counterargument was that although wages were lower in Mexico than in the United States, companies would consider other factors, too, such as the productivity of the workers in the two countries (the amount of output that could be produced in a given amount of time by workers in the two countries).

To illustrate, suppose that in the United States, a worker can produce 30 units of good X an hour, and he or she is paid $10 an hour. In Mexico, a worker can produce 10 units of good X an hour, and he or she is paid $5 an hour. The output per dollar of labor cost (units produced per hour/wage rate) is thus 3 units per $1 in the United States and 2 units per $1 in Mexico. Using these numbers, we conclude that although wages are lower in Mexico than in the United States, it is cheaper to use U.S. workers than Mexican workers to produce good X.

International Organizations

Many economists predict that countries are likely to join in common markets and free-trade areas in the near future. Increasingly, countries of the world are finding that it is in their best interests to lower trade barriers between themselves and their neighbors.

The World Trade Organization (WTO) provides a forum for its member countries (136 countries in mid-2000) to discuss and negotiate trade issues. It also provides a system for adjudicating trade disputes. For example, suppose the United States claimed that the Canadian government was preventing U.S. producers from openly selling their goods in Canada. The WTO would look at the matter, consult trade experts, and then decide the issue. A country that is found engaging in unfair trade can either desist from this practice or face appropriate retaliation from the injured party.

Two other prominent international organizations are the World Bank and the International Monetary Fund (IMF). The World Bank, officially

Joaquin Jacome Diaz, Panama's Minister of Trade, addresses the World Trade Organization. Explain what the WTO does.

known as the International Bank for Reconstruction and Development (IBRD), is the biggest development bank in the world. Its primary function is to lend money to the world's poor and less-developed countries. The money for lending comes from rich member countries, such as the United States, and from selling bonds and lending the money raised through bond sales. The World Bank usually makes loans for economic development projects that are expected to produce a return sufficient to pay back the loan.

The IMF is an international organization that, among other things, provides economic advice and temporary funds to nations with economic difficulties. It has been referred to as a "doctor called in at the last minute." When a country is in economic difficulty, the IMF might submit a list of economic reforms for it to follow, such as cutting excessive government spending to reduce budget deficits or decreasing the growth rate of the money supply. The IMF often lends funds to a country in economic trouble on the condition that its economic advice be followed.

A country's acceptance of IMF reforms is usually a signal to other international organizations, such as the World Bank, that the country is serious about getting its economic house in order. The World Bank may then provide long-term funding.

Section 2 Review

Defining Terms

1. Define
   a. tariff
   b. quota
   c. dumping

Reviewing Facts and Concepts

2. What effect does a tariff have on the price of imported goods?
3. First state, and then criticize, the infant-industry argument for trade restrictions.
4. First state, and then criticize, the tit-for-tat argument for trade restrictions.

Critical Thinking

5. Consider a policy that effectively transfers $100 million from group A to group B. Suppose there are 50 million people in group A. Is the policy more likely to be passed and implemented if the number of people that make up group B is 50 million or 500,000? Explain your answer.

Applying Economic Concepts

6. How might domestic producers of a good abuse the antidumping argument for restricted trade?

SECTION 3

The Exchange Rate

People in different countries have different monies; for example, Americans use dollars, Greeks use drachmas, and Indians use rupees. These differing currencies are related through exchange rates, the topic of this section.

As you read this section, keep these key questions in mind:

- What is an exchange rate?
- What does it mean to say that a currency appreciates in value?
- What does it mean to say that a currency depreciates in value?

An exchange rate is the price of one currency (say dollars) in terms of another currency (say, the Brazilian real).

What Is an Exchange Rate?

Key Terms

exchange rate
flexible exchange rate system
fixed exchange rate system
depreciation
appreciation

The **exchange rate** is the price of one nation's currency in terms of another nation's currency. Suppose you take a trip to Great Britain. To buy goods and services, you will need to have British currency, the basic unit of which is the pound (£). Therefore, you will need to exchange your dollars for pounds.

Suppose you want to exchange $200 for pounds. How many pounds you will get depends on the exchange rate, which may be determined in two ways: by the forces of supply and demand under a **flexible exchange rate system** or by government under a **fixed exchange rate system.** Suppose the exchange rate is currently £1 for $2. For every $2 you have, you will get £1 in exchange, so you will receive £100 in exchange for $200. (Exhibit 18-7 shows the value of the U.S. dollar in terms of eight foreign currencies.)

MINI GLOSSARY

exchange rate The price of one country's currency in terms of another country's currency.

flexible exchange rate system The system whereby currency exchange rates are determined by the forces of supply and demand.

fixed exchange rate system The system whereby currency exchange rates are fixed, or pegged, by countries' governments.

Exhibit 18-7
Exchange Rates

If you travel outside the United States or invest in foreign businesses, you will want to know the exchange rate for your U.S. currency. Below are values for the dollar for selected currencies, as of May 1, 2000. On that day, it took 1.894 German marks to buy one U.S. dollar. The rate is probably different today, as the exchange rates are constantly changing.

Country/region	Currency	Currency units per U.S. dollar
Canada	Dollar	1.463
European Union	Euro	0.9695
France	Franc	6.35
Germany	Mark	1.894
Italy	Lira	1,875.87
Mexico	Peso	9.375
Japan	Yen	105.2
Switzerland	Franc	1.66

Can Big Macs Be Used to Predict Exchange Rates?

Suppose that in New York City a Big Mac costs $3 and in Tokyo it costs ¥400. The exchange rate between the dollar and the yen is $1 = ¥100. Thus, it costs $4 to buy a Big Mac in Tokyo. This means that $1 buys more of a Big Mac in New York City (one-third) than in Tokyo (one-fourth).

In economics, the *purchasing power parity theory* says that a unit of a country's currency (say, $1) will buy the same amount of a good everywhere in the world. In other words, if $1 buys one-third of a Big Mac in the United States, it will buy one-third of a Big Mac in Japan, too.

What would the exchange rate between the dollar and the yen have to be before $1 would buy the same amount of a Big Mac in both the United States and Japan? The exchange rate would have to be $1 = ¥133.33. At this exchange rate, the price of a Big Mac in New York City is $3, and the price of a Big Mac in Tokyo is ¥400, which is the same as $3. The purchasing power parity theory says that this is exactly what will happen. In other words, the exchange rate will adjust so that $1 buys the same amount of a Big Mac everywhere in the world.

The Economist, a well-known economics magazine, publishes what it calls the "Big Mac index" each year. It shows what exchange rates currently are and what a Big Mac costs in different countries, and then it predicts which currencies will appreciate and depreciate based on this information. *The Economist,* using the Big Mac index, does not always predict accurately, but it does do so in many cases. In other words, if you want to predict whether the British pound, Mexican peso, or Japanese yen are going to appreciate or depreciate in the next few months, the Big Mac index may be a useful source of information.

QUESTION TO ANSWER Suppose a Big Mac costs $3 in New York City and 16 francs in Paris. Furthermore, suppose $1 = 4 francs. Based on our discussion, do you expect the franc to appreciate or depreciate? Explain your answer.

Appreciation and Depreciation

Suppose that on Tuesday the exchange rate between pounds and dollars is \$1 for £0.50. By Saturday, the exchange rate has changed to \$1 for £0.45. On Saturday, then, a dollar fetches fewer pounds than it did on Tuesday. When this happens, economists say that the dollar has depreciated relative to the pound. **Depreciation** is a decrease in the value of one currency relative to other currencies. A currency has depreciated if it fetches *less* of another currency.

depreciation
A decrease in the value of one currency relative to other currencies.

appreciation
An increase in the value of one currency relative to other currencies

Appreciation is the opposite—an increase in the value of one currency relative to other currencies. A currency has appreciated if it fetches more of another currency. For example, if the exchange rate goes from \$1 for £0.50 to \$1 for £0.60, the dollar fetches more pounds and therefore has appreciated in value.[1]

These bank employees in Japan keep a close watch on exchange rates. Why would exchange rates be important to a bank?

If the dollar depreciates relative to the British pound, the pound necessarily appreciates relative to the dollar. To illustrate, suppose the dollar-pound exchange rate is \$1 = £0.50 (with \$1, you can get one-half pound [£0.50]). Then £1 can buy \$2. In other words, an exchange rate of \$1 = £0.50 is the same as £1 = \$2.

If:	\$1 = £0.50
Then:	£1 = \$2.00

Now suppose the exchange rate changes from \$1 = £0.50 to \$1 = £0.40. The dollar has depreciated, because \$1 now fetches fewer pounds than it did earlier. As a result of the dollar depreciation, what has happened to the value of the pound? It has appreciated. To see this explicitly, ask yourself what £1 fetches in terms of dollars if the exchange rate is \$1 = £0.40. If \$1 is divided by £0.40, £1 now equals \$2.50. In other words, the pound has appreciated. Again, if the dollar *depreciates* relative to the pound, then it follows that the pound *appreciates* relative to the dollar.

One currency depreciates ➡ Another currency appreciates

Effect of Appreciation and Depreciation on Prices

Suppose you and a friend take a trip to London this summer. In London, you come across a jacket that you want to buy. The price tag reads £50; what is the price in dollars? To find out, you need to know the current exchange rate between the dollar and the pound. Suppose it is \$1 = £0.50; for every dollar you give up, you get £0.50 in return. You divide £50 by £0.50 and learn that you will have to pay \$100 to buy the jacket. In

1. If you have trouble converting from one currency to another, you may want to study the feature "Developing Economics Skills: Converting Currency from One Country's to Another's" on page 491 before you continue to read further.

Does the Value of the Dollar Matter?

The appreciation of the dollar may affect a number of people in the United States, as the following examples illustrate.

The Farmer

Suppose George is a U.S. farmer selling wheat to foreigners. Currently $1 equals 2 German marks, and George's wheat sells for 12 marks in Germany. Thus, he receives $6 for every bushel of wheat he sells in Germany (12 marks/2 marks per dollar = $6). Now the dollar appreciates from 2 to 3 marks. If George's wheat still sells for 12 marks, he will receive only $4 for every bushel. Dollar appreciation lowers George's income.

The Loan Officer

Suppose Micala is a loan officer in a bank. One day, months ago, George went to Micala and asked for a $500,000 loan to modernize his farm. She granted him the loan because his current business looked good. But this was before the dollar appreciated and his income dropped. Now his income has dropped so much that he cannot pay off the loan. Micala's boss, Noriko, comes to Micala and wonders why she gave George the loan in the first place. To Noriko, it looks as if Micala has made one too many bad loans, and she fires her.

The Owner of a Small Shop

Suppose Jerry owns a small shop in a town where many of the inhabitants are employed in the production of goods that are sold in foreign countries. As a result of the dollar appreciation, the firms that employ the inhabitants lose business; they do not need as many workers, so they fire some. These fired workers have less money, so they buy fewer goods in Jerry's shop, thus hurting Jerry's business.

The Shop Owner's Family

Jerry has a family. Because his business is not doing well, he earns less income. His family, in turn, has less money for going to the movies, buying clothes, and perhaps going to college.

QUESTION TO ANSWER The dollar appreciates when you are visiting Mexico City. How will this appreciation affect your trip?

other words, at the current exchange rate, £50 is the same as $100. You decide to buy the jacket.

A week passes, and you and your friend are still in London. Your friend likes your jacket so much that he decides to buy one, too. You and your friend return to the store and find the exact jacket for sale, still for £50. You tell your friend that he will have to pay $100 for the jacket. However, you are wrong, because the dollar-pound exchange rate has changed since last week. Now it is $1 = £0.40. In other words, the dollar has depreciated relative to the pound, because this week each dollar fetches fewer pounds than it did last week.

Currency Trader

National currencies are continuously bought and sold all over the world. A U.S. importer who wants to buy Japanese goods, for example, first buys Japanese yen with U.S. dollars and then uses the Japanese yen to buy the Japanese goods. A large multinational corporation that does business in thirty countries has to buy and sell different national currencies every day.

The person who actually buys and sells currencies for others is called a *currency trader.* Usually, currency traders sit in front of computer screens all day and look at the exchange rates for various currencies. International banks, multinational corporations, and large brokerage houses that deal in different currencies hire currency traders.

Most currency traders have a bachelor's and master's degree in business, finance, or economics, as well as work experience at banks or multinational corporations. The job is often exciting, but it can be quite stressful (for example, buying a currency just before it falls in value).

Some companies advertise on the Internet that anyone with a laptop, a modem, and some money to start with can be a currency trader. These claims are not true. It takes the right kind of education and experience to be a successful currency trader.

If the U.S. dollar appreciates relative to the pound, will a U.S. tourist spend more or fewer U.S. dollars for this coat?

What will the jacket cost in dollars this week? You divide £50 by £0.40 and learn that the jacket will cost \$125. Your friend says that he was willing to buy the jacket for \$100, but that he is not willing to pay \$125 for the jacket. The economic concept illustrated by this example is simply that when one's domestic currency depreciates, it becomes more expensive to buy foreign-produced goods.

Dollar depreciation ➡ Foreign goods become more expensive

The flip side of this concept is that when one's domestic currency appreciates, it becomes cheaper to buy foreign-produced goods. Suppose the dollar-pound exchange rate had changed to \$1 = £0.60. Now a jacket with a price tag of £50 would cost \$83.33.

Dollar appreciation ➡ Foreign goods become cheaper

Section 3 Review

Defining Terms

1. Define
   a. exchange rate
   b. flexible exchange rate system
   c. fixed exchange rate system
   d. depreciation
   e. appreciation

Reviewing Facts and Concepts

2. If the exchange rate is \$1 = ¥129 (yen) and the price of a Japanese good is ¥7,740, what is the equivalent dollar price?
3. If the exchange rate is \$1 = £0.6612 (pounds) and the price of a U.S. good is \$764, what is the equivalent pound price?

Critical Thinking

4. Steve, an American in London, wants to buy a British-made sweater. The current price of the sweater is £40. Would Steve be better off if the exchange rate is \$1 = £0.87 or \$1 = £0.77? Explain your answer.

Applying Economic Concepts

5. Are more Americans likely to travel to Mexico when the peso has appreciated relative to the dollar or when the peso has depreciated relative to the dollar? Explain your answer.

Developing Economic

Skills

Converting Currency from One Country's to Another's

Different nations, of course, have different currencies. In the United States, we have dollars. Mexico has pesos, most countries of the European Union have euros, Japan has yen, and so on. It is important to know how to convert from one currency to another. For example, suppose you are in England and see that a sweater has a price tag of £20. How much does it cost in U.S. dollars? To answer this question, you need to know the exchange rate between dollars and pounds. You can get this information by looking at the business section of many newspapers or calling almost any bank.

Let's say the exchange rate is \$2 for £1. To find out what the English sweater costs in U.S. dollars, simply use this formula:

$$\text{Price of sweater in dollars} = \text{Price of sweater in foreign currency} \times \text{Number of dollars needed to buy 1 unit of foreign currency}$$

Let's find the price in dollars of the sweater costing £20, given an exchange rate of \$2 for £1:

$$\begin{aligned}\text{Price of sweater in dollars} &= £20 \times \$2 \text{ (per £1)}\\ &= \$40\end{aligned}$$

The answer is \$40.

Suppose you knew the price of the sweater in dollars and you wanted to find out its price in some other currency. You could use this formula:

$$\text{Price of sweater in foreign currency} = \text{Price of sweater in dollars} \div \text{Number of dollars needed to buy 1 unit of foreign currency}$$

Let's find the price in pounds of the \$40 sweater, given an exchange rate of \$2 for £1:

$$\begin{aligned}\text{Price of sweater in foreign currency} &= \$40 \div \$2 \text{ (per £1)}\\ &= £20\end{aligned}$$

The answer is £20.

1. The price of an Indian shirt is 4300 rupees and the exchange rate is 1 rupee = \$0.02. What does the Indian shirt cost in dollars?
2. The price of a Swedish lamp is 500 kronor, and the exchange rate is 8 kronor = \$1. What does the lamp cost in dollars?
3. Suppose you are working in Mexico, and you earn 2,000 pesos a week. The exchange rate is 1 peso = \$0.25. What is your weekly pay in dollars?

This South Korean bank employee is exchanging U.S. dollars for Korean won. Do you think you could master the skill of converting currencies? Would you enjoy this type of work?

CHAPTER

18 Review

Economics Vocabulary

Fill in the following blanks with the appropriate word or phrase.

1. A(n) _____ is a tax on imports.
2. A legal limit on the amount of a good that may be imported (into a country) is called a(n) _____.
3. Country A has a(n)_____ in the production of a good if it can produce the good at lower opportunity cost than country B.
4. The _____ is the difference between the value of exports and the value of imports.
5. _____ refers to the sale of goods abroad at prices below their costs and below the price charged in the domestic market.
6. _____ refers to the situation in which a country can produce more of a good than another country can produce with the same quantity of resources.
7. _____ refers to an increase in the value of one currency relative to other currencies.
8. Currency exchange rates are fixed, or pegged, by countries' governments under a(n) _____.
9. If one dollar buys two pesos, then this is the _____ between dollars and pesos.
10. _____ refers to a decrease in the value of one currency relative to other currencies.

Review Questions

1. If exchange rates under a flexible exchange rate system are determined by the forces of supply and demand, will an increase in the demand for pesos cause the peso to appreciate or depreciate? Explain your answer.
2. The United States can produce either combination A (100 units of food and 0 units of clothing) or combination B (80 units of food and 20 units of clothing). Japan can produce combination C (80 units of food and 0 units of clothing) or combination D (75 units of food and 10 units of clothing). Which country has a comparative advantage in the production of food? Which country has a comparative advantage in the production of clothing?
3. State the low-foreign-wages argument for trade restrictions.
4. What does it mean to say that the United States has a comparative advantage in the production of computers?
5. After a tariff is imposed on imported cars, would you expect consumers to buy more or fewer imported cars, all other things remaining the same? Explain your answer.
6. If the pound appreciates relative to the U.S. dollar, the dollar must depreciate relative to the pound. Do you agree or disagree? Explain your answer.
7. What do critics of the low-foreign-wages argument for trade restrictions say?
8. If the value of U.S. exports is $103 billion and the value of U.S. imports is $210 million, what does the balance of trade equal?
9. State the national-defense argument for trade restrictions.

Calculations

1. If the price of a British sweater is £30 and the dollar-pound exchange rate is $1 = £0.66, what does the sweater cost in dollars?
2. If the price of a U.S. car is $20,000 and the dollar-yen exchange rate is $1 = ¥129, what does the car cost in yen?
3. If the United States can produce *either* 20 units of clothing and 40 units of food *or* 60 units of clothing and 0 units of food, what is the opportunity cost of producing 1 unit of food?
4. If Brazil can produce *either* 100 units of clothing and 0 units of food *or* 30 units of clothing and 50 units of food, what is the opportunity cost of producing 1 unit of clothing?

Economics and Thinking Skills

1. **Application.** Suppose the United States buys 1 million cars from Japan each year. If the dollar depreciates relative to the yen, will Americans buy more or fewer than 1 million cars from Japan? Explain your answer.
2. **Analysis.** Suppose that U.S. imports currently equal U.S. exports. Explain how a fall in the value of the dollar vis-à-vis other currencies can affect the current U.S. balance of trade.
3. **Cause and Effect.** Over a six-month period you notice that the dollar appreciates in value vis-à-vis other currencies and that the U.S. balance of trade goes from zero to −$30 billion. You suspect that

there is some relationship between the change in the value of the dollar and the U.S. balance of trade. Did the change in the balance of trade cause the change in the value of the dollar, or did the change in the value of the dollar cause the change in the balance of trade? Explain your answer.

Writing Skills

Consider two U.S. cities, Houston and Los Angeles. Suppose the people in Houston buy more goods from the people in Los Angeles than the people in Los Angeles buy from the people in Houston. Houston has a negative balance of trade with Los Angeles, and Los Angeles has a positive balance of trade with Houston. It is not news when one city has a negative balance of trade with another city in the same country, but it is big news when one country has a negative balance of trade with another country. For example, if the United States has a negative balance of trade with Japan, it is front-page news. Write a one-page paper that answers this question: Why do you think that a city-to-city trade balance is not news but that a country-to-country trade balance is?

Economics in the Media

1. Find an article in the local newspaper that addresses the U.S. balance of trade, exchange rates, or dumping. Identify the major ideas of the article.
2. Find a story on a television news show that addresses the U.S. balance of trade, exchange rates, tariffs, quotas, imports, exports, or dumping. Identify the major ideas of the story.

Where's the Economics?

If the U.S. dollar appreciates, will the next ship carry more or fewer foreign goods? Explain your answer.

Analyzing Primary Sources

The producer interests in a country often lobby government to restrict free trade. They may ask for a tariff or quota to be placed on the imported goods that compete with the goods they produce.

Frederic Bastiat, the nineteenth-century French economist and journalist, wrote an essay on the subject of producer interests and protectionism. The essay is written as a letter from the candle makers of France to the "Honorable Members of the Chamber of Deputies." The following is an excerpt:

Gentlemen:

You are on the right track. You reject abstract theories and have little regard for abundance and low prices. You concern yourselves mainly with the fate of the producer. You wish to free him from foreign competition, that is, to reserve the domestic market *for* domestic industry. . . .

We are suffering from the ruinous competition of a foreign rival who apparently works under conditions so far superior to our own for the production of light that he is flooding the domestic market *with it at an incredibly low price; from the moment he appears, our sales cease, all the consumers turn to him, and a branch of French industry whose ramifications are innumerable is all at once reduced to complete stagnation. This rival, which is none other than the sun, is waging war on us so mercilessly that we suspect he is being stirred up against us by perfidious Albion* [England], *particularly because he has for that haughty island a respect that he does not show for us.*

We ask you to be so good as to pass a law requiring the closing of all windows, dormers, skylights, inside and outside shutters, all openings, holes, chinks, and fissures through which the light of the sun is wont to enter houses, to the detriment of the fair industries with which, we are proud to say, we have endowed the country, a country that cannot, without betraying ingratitude, abandon us today to so unequal a combat.[2]

1. Who or what is the foreign producer that the French candle makers are in competition with?
2. What are the candle makers asking for?

2. Frederic Bastiat, *Economic Sophisms* (Irvington-on-Hudson, N.Y.: Foundation for Economic Education, 1975), pp. 56–57.

CHAPTER 19

Comparative Economic Systems: Past, Present, and Future

What This Chapter Is About

Chapter 2 discussed the free-enterprise economic system, and this text has featured in-depth discussion on the U.S. economy, which is considered a free-enterprise economy. Thus, by now you should have a fairly good understanding of how a free-enterprise economic system works.

Economic systems that are not based on free enterprise can be found around the world. This chapter discusses the major alternative to the free-enterprise system: socialism.

Why This Chapter Is Important

An understanding of this chapter is important to an understanding of the world today. Some formerly socialist countries are currently experimenting with capitalism. The transition away from socialism to capitalism cannot fully be understood without an understanding of each. What is capitalism? What is socialism? What are the major ideas behind each system? This chapter will answer these questions and more, and by so doing will give you a clearer understanding of the world in which you live.

After You Study This Chapter, You Will Be Able To

- discuss the details of both the capitalist vision and the socialist vision.
- outline the major differences between the free-enterprise and socialist economic systems.
- discuss some of the ideas of Adam Smith and Karl Marx.
- give some details of how command-economy socialism worked in the former Soviet Union.
- discuss some of the problems a nation has when it changes from a socialist economic system to a free-enterprise economic system.
- discuss a few of the constraints government can place on an economy.

You Will Also Learn What Economics Has to Do With

- downtown.
- Wal-Mart.
- Mao Zedong.
- a steel furnace in the backyard.
- air-conditioning.

Economics Journal

Aristotle said, "What is common to many is taken least care of, for all men have greater regard for what is their own than for what they possess in common with others." Over the week, identify examples from your daily life in which you find this statement to be true.

SECTION 1

Two Visions Shape Two Economic Systems

Chapter 1 said that a society's economic system is the way society goes about answering the three economic questions: (1) What will be produced? (2) How will the goods be produced? and (3) For whom will the goods be produced? The two major economic systems, free enterprise and socialism, are each based on a certain vision of the way the world works. This section considers these two economic systems and the visions on which they are based.

As you read this section, keep these key questions in mind:

- What is an economic system?
- What are the details of the capitalist vision?
- What are the details of the socialist vision?

Traditional Economic Systems

Key Terms

traditional economy
mixed economy
vision

The hundreds of countries in the world today have differing economic systems. Some have what is called a **traditional economy**—an economic system in which the answers to the three economic questions (What will be produced? How will the goods be produced? For whom will the goods be produced?) are based on customs, traditions, and cultural beliefs.

This page from a thirteenth century illuminated manuscript shows a farmer teaching his son to plow. Explain how this farming method fits with a traditional economy.

MINI GLOSSARY

traditional economy An economic system in which the answers to the three economic questions are based on customs, traditions, and cultural beliefs.

In a traditional economy, customs, skills, and beliefs are passed on from one generation to the next. An example of a traditional economy is the feudal system in Western Europe. Under the feudal system, all land was owned by a king. The king granted land to nobles, who in turn granted small plots of land to peasants to farm. The peasants kept part of what they produced; the remainder went to the nobles and, ultimately, to the king.

Today many traditional economies are found all over the world and are very different from each other, according to their respective customs and traditions. Most people who live in traditional economies live at a subsistence level, working with tools that are relatively primitive compared with those used in countries with modern technology.

One type of traditional economy is the hunting and gathering society. As the name implies, the hunters and gatherers sustain themselves by pursuing game and collecting wild fruits and vegetables. Because they do not cultivate crops, they must travel to find their food supplies, often following the migratory routes of animals. As nomads, hunters and gatherers do not have the same concept of land ownership as people in more settled societies. For example, the Hadza of Tanzania and the Inuit of the North American tundra have no concept of trespassing; all members of these societies are free to collect food wherever they can find it.

Some traditional economies discourage the accumulation of personal wealth by redistributing goods from those who have to those who do not. This redistribution is often accomplished by a tribute paid to a tribal chief, in much the same way that taxes are paid. The chief then gives to those who are in need. In other traditional economies, the redistribution of goods is entirely voluntary, and those who give away their surplus goods attain higher status.

Despite the encroachment of technology, traditional economies in many parts of the world today still resist change and continue to maintain economic relationships going back hundreds of years. The customs and beliefs that sustain these traditional economies continue to be passed from generation to generation. It remains to be seen whether traditional economies can continue to survive into the twenty-first century and, if so, what form they will take.

In the early 1900s, the Inuit hunters used the tools seen here. The Inuit economy was considered a traditional economy.

Free-Enterprise and Socialist Economic Systems

Today there are two dominant economic systems in the world: free enterprise and socialism. The free-enterprise (or capitalist or market) economic system and the socialist economic system are the two major ways of answering the three economic questions today. Some nations' economies fall naturally into one category or the other, but most nations have chosen a mix from both economic systems. Their economies are neither purely free enterprise nor purely socialist; they are called **mixed economies.**

As noted in Chapter 1, it is best to look at the two radically different economic systems—free enterprise and socialism—as occupying opposite ends of an economic spectrum (see Exhibit 1-4 in Chapter 1). The economies of various countries lie along the economic spectrum, some closer to the free-enterprise end and some closer to the socialist end.

MINI GLOSSARY

mixed economy An economy that is neither purely capitalist nor purely socialist; an economy that has some elements of both capitalism and socialism. Most countries in the world have mixed economies.

What economic system is reflected in the billboards on this Shanghai street?

Capitalist and Socialist Visions

The two major and radically different economic systems have arisen because of the existence of two major and radically different visions, or views, of the world. After all, neither free enterprise nor socialism fell from the sky for people to pick up off the ground and put into operation. Both are the products of a certain way of looking at, understanding, and explaining the world. Both are the products of certain visions.

The economist Thomas Sowell defines **vision** as "our sense of how the world works." For example, suppose Michael's vision of the world, as it relates to government, is that our elected officials are endlessly trying to solve society's problems in a way that is good for the general public. Maria's vision may be quite different; she may believe that our elected officials respond to narrowly focused special-interest groups at the expense of the general public. Their different visions of how government works will determine what policies and economic systems Michael and Maria will support. For example, Michael will be much more willing than Maria to argue that government should play a major role in solving society's problems. For this reason, Michael may be much more willing than Maria to support socialism over capitalism.

When a person gives a speech, especially a political speech, he often expresses his vision of how the world works.

For simplicity's sake, we shall call the vision that produces socialism the *socialist vision* and the vision that produces free enterprise, or capitalism, the *capitalist vision*. The purpose of this section is to help you understand each vision and then to understand how these visions could give birth to different economic systems.

vision
A sense of how the world works.

A baker charges a price for six bagels and gives one (bagel) away free. Do socialist and capitalist thinkers look upon *price* differently? Explain.

The Two Visions and the Market

Socialist thinkers and capitalist thinkers—the proponents of the two visions—have different views on a host of topics. This section discusses their views on several market phenomena.

Price When we buy something in a market—whether it is a car, a house, or a loaf of bread—we pay a price. Price is a common market phenomenon. The capitalist thinker sees price as doing a job. Price (1) rations goods and services, (2) conveys information, and (3) serves as an incentive for buyers and sellers to respond to information.

Chapter 1 considered the rationing role of price. Price rations goods and services in that people who are willing and able to pay the price of a good obtain the good. People who are not willing and able to pay the price do not obtain the good. According to capitalist thinkers, because we live in a world of scarcity, we must have some rationing device, whether it is price; first come, first served; brute force; or some other device. There must be some way of determining who gets what part of the available resources, goods, and services, and price serves this purpose.

A socialist thinker views price in a very different light. For example, the rationing function of price is largely invisible to or ignored by the socialist thinker. Whereas the capitalist thinker views price as being determined by the impersonal forces of supply and demand, the socialist thinker views price in a free-enterprise economy as being set by businesses with vast economic power.

Perhaps because of this, the socialist thinker, unlike the capitalist thinker, is ready to "control" price. The socialist is willing to have a law passed stating that "it is unlawful to charge more than a certain price for gasoline or rental homes" or "it is unlawful to pay less than a certain wage to workers." By passing laws that make it unlawful to charge more than a certain price, socialist thinkers seek to reduce some of the economic power that they believe sellers have over consumers. They also try to reduce some of the economic power that they believe the owners of businesses have over workers through the passage of laws that make it illegal to pay workers less than a certain wage.

Competition A capitalist thinker believes that competition is intense under free enterprise and that the competition between producers will force them to offer the highest-quality product to consumers for the lowest price. In contrast, the socialist thinker sees little competition between producers. In the socialist view, the marketplace is controlled by big-business interests dictating to people (through advertising) what they will buy and at what price.

Pepsi and Coke are in competition with each other. Who benefits from this competition? Does anyone lose from this competition?

What Happened to Downtown?

Today, people who want to shop often go to the malls that are located in many U.S. suburbs. Years ago, however, downtown sections of cities did a thriving commercial business. Many of the best clothing, furniture, appliance, and service stores were located downtown.

What happened to downtown? Why is it a mere shadow of what it used to be? One of the reasons relates to Sam Walton, the founder of Wal-Mart. Back in the early 1960s, Sam Walton was the proprietor of a variety store. He was doing well in his business, but not as well as he had hoped. He was feeling some heat from discount merchandisers that were locating near his store and taking a lot of Walton's business away from him with promises of lower prices. Walton decided that the discounters had a good idea. He opened Wal-Mart, a major discount merchandiser, in Rogers, Arkansas, in 1962.

In 1963, Walton decided to expand his business and started opening Wal-Marts in small towns all across the country. So that he could better compete with other stores, he located on the outskirts of town, where the real estate costs were relatively low. By keeping his costs low, he thought, he could better compete with the stores in the downtown area.

Walton's strategy began to work. His big stores, self-service, and low prices were a hit with consumers. Many of them traveled to the outskirts of town to buy from Wal-Mart. In time, the downtown stores began to suffer financially, and many closed.

As would be expected, many of the owners of the downtown stores of yesteryear and even many store owners today dislike Wal-Mart coming to town. They know that Wal-Mart is usually very popular with consumers and that when Wal-Mart comes to town, some businesses go under.

This is the nature of capitalism, though. Capitalism is not a protective system wherein those who are successful and financially well-off will stay that way. With capitalism comes competition, and competition often cuts two ways. It benefits consumers, but it sometimes hurts producers who are not as able or as willing to change in ways that consumers demand.

Some people think capitalism is an economic system that benefits producers at the expense of consumers. However, they need to think again. Capitalism is often a system that benefits consumers at the expense of some producers.

QUESTION TO ANSWER Is there a Wal-Mart in the town in which you live? Do you know what well-established store owners might have said when Wal-Mart first came to town?

How would a capitalist thinker explain the relationship between a factory owner and the products produced in the factory? How would a socialist thinker explain the same relationship?

Private Property The capitalist thinker places high value on private property and agrees with the Greek philosopher Aristotle that "what is common to many is taken least care of, for all men have greater regard for what is their own than for what they possess in common with others." In other words, capitalists believe that if you own something yourself—if, say, your house is your private property—you are more likely to take care of it than if it were owned communally by you and others or owned by the government.

The capitalist thinker also believes that having private property encourages individuals to use their resources in a way that benefits others. For example, suppose Johnson owns a factory that is her private property. If Johnson wants to maximize her income, she will have to use her factory to produce goods that people are willing and able to buy. If she did otherwise and produced something that people were unwilling and unable to buy, she would not benefit the people or earn an income.

The socialist vision of property is very different. The socialist thinker believes that those who own property will end up having more political power than those who do not own it. Furthermore, they will use their greater political power to their advantage and to the disadvantage of others. According to the socialist thinker, it would be better for government to own most of the nonlabor property in the economy (such things as factories, raw materials, and machinery). Government would be more likely than private individuals to make sure this property was used to benefit the many instead of the few.

A person buys an item of clothing for $100. How would a socialist thinker view the purchase? How would a capitalist thinker view the purchase?

Exchange Consider an ordinary, everyday exchange of $100 for some clothes. The capitalist thinker believes that both the buyer and the seller of the clothes benefit from the exchange, or else they would not have entered into it. The socialist thinker often (but not always) believes that one person in an exchange is made better off at the expense of the other person. In our example, perhaps the clothes seller took advantage of the buyer by charging too much money for the clothes.

The Two Visions and Government

Capitalist and socialist thinkers have different visions of government. The socialist thinker believes government decision makers promote what is in the best interest of society as a whole. The capitalist thinker sees this view of how government operates as naive and mistaken. Instead, the capitalist thinks government decision makers respond to well-organized special-interest groups and not to the unorganized members of the general public. For example, government is more likely to respond to the farmers who lobby for higher crop prices than to the consumers who will end up paying higher food prices in the grocery stores. It is more likely to respond to car producers than car consumers.

Do you think government is more responsive to producers or to consumers? Explain your reasoning.

The socialist thinker sees the goal of government decision makers as doing the right thing, whereas the capitalist thinker sees it as getting elected and re-elected to office. According to the socialist thinker, mistakes made by government decision makers occur because the decision makers did not have all the facts. If they are given the facts, they will do the right thing. The capitalist thinker, in contrast, believes that the mistakes of government decision makers are likely politically motivated. When they are given the facts, they may still do what is in the best interest of well-organized special-interest groups at the expense of the general public.

Unintended Consequences and Deliberate Actions: The Two Visions

According to the capitalist thinker, the unintended consequences of individuals' actions sometimes are good. For example, consider the equilibrium price in a market. At the equilibrium price, the quantity of the good that buyers are willing and able to buy equals the quantity of the good that sellers are willing and able to sell. In other words, both buyers and sellers are content at the equilibrium price. Buyers do not want to buy more or less, and sellers do not want to sell more or less.

The important point is that this balance between buyers and sellers came about naturally. There was no blueprint that buyers and sellers followed to get the equilibrium price. No government committee identified the equilibrium price and then directed buyers and sellers to trade at it; the equilibrium price simply emerged as an unintended consequence of buying and selling goods. To a capitalist thinker, things that naturally emerge—such as equilibrium price in a market—are often desirable. It is desirable, for example, that both buyers and sellers be content at equilibrium price.

In contrast to the capitalist, the socialist rarely thinks that unintended consequences of individuals' actions are desirable. The socialist thinker instead focuses on things deliberately created to serve some purpose. For example, the socialist thinker may focus attention on such things as government programs deliberately created and designed to reduce poverty. Here is something tangible, in the socialist's view. A problem (poverty) exists, and a program has been created and designed to deal with it.

F. A. Hayek, Economist

Friedrich August Hayek (1899–1992), a member of the Austrian School of Economics, won the Nobel Prize in economic science in 1974. Although Hayek was mainly an economist, he also made contributions in political theory, philosophy, and psychology.

In the late 1930s and early 1940s Hayek entered the debate about whether socialist planning would work; he believed it would not work, essentially because socialist economic planners would never possess all the relevant information necessary to make good plans. Hayek also argued that although many well-intentioned people advocated socialism, in the end socialism (no matter what its variety) would turn into totalitarianism. Hayek stated, "Economic control is not merely control of a sector of human life which can be separated from the rest; it is the control of the means for all our ends." He outlined his case against socialism in *The Road to Serfdom,* a book that Hayek dedicated to "the socialists of all parties."

How would a government program deliberately created to reduce poverty fit into the socialist vision? the capitalist vision?

Experimenting with Millions of People

One of the things that capitalist thinkers dislike about socialism is that socialism imposes economic plans on millions of people. The problem with an economic plan, according to capitalist thinkers, is that if the plan is no good, many millions of people will be hurt by it.

There is some truth to this view. For example, in the late 1950s the leader of Communist China, Mao Zedong, initiated an economic plan called the Great Leap Forward. The plan sought to revitalize the entire Chinese economy. Almost overnight, the plan changed the lives of 90 percent of the Chinese population, or 700 million people. The model for the economic plan was self-reliant communes, each with its own industrial, agricultural, and service sectors. One major aspect of the plan was that steel production was to be carried out in backyard furnaces.

The Great Leap Forward was a disaster. It did not produce the results Mao had intended, and many millions of people were made worse off. The Great Leap Forward is said to have devastated both the manufacturing and agricultural sectors in China.

In 1959, a few natural disasters, combined with the unnatural disaster of the Great Leap Forward, together caused the starvation of many millions of people. Almost all historians today agree that many millions of people would have lived if it had not been for the disaster of Mao's economic plan imposed on China.

QUESTION TO ANSWER Why might an individual's plan (say, to go to college or start a business) generate consequences different from consequences of an economic plan applied on a massive scale?

Of course, this difference between capitalist and socialist visions has consequences. The capitalist thinker emphasizes that people should not disturb the natural (and often invisible) processes at work in society that bring about desirable outcomes. For example, the capitalist would argue that government should not interfere with the market forces of supply and demand, because to do so would reduce the likelihood that equilibrium price would emerge. The socialist thinker sees this view as fantasy. The socialist sees no good reason for government to avoid involvement in the forces of supply and demand.

The Two Visions: A Summary

The capitalist vision holds that market phenomena—such as prices determined by supply and demand, competition, private property, and exchange—together make up a marvelous system. Within this system, goods are rationed, information is conveyed, high-quality goods are produced at the lowest prices, and people are induced to use their resources in a way that will benefit others and generally raise the standard of living. The socialist vision holds that in the marketplace, some people exploit others—for example, by charging high prices, paying low wages, and manipulating people's preferences through such things as advertising.

The socialist vision holds that government is made up of people who want to, and in most cases will, do the right thing for the general public. The capitalist vision sees government as made up of people who respond more readily to well-organized special-interest groups than to the general public. Socialist thinkers have a higher degree of trust in the intentions and actions of government decision makers than do capitalist thinkers.

Finally, the capitalist vision focuses on the desirable qualities of things that were not deliberately created but that naturally emerged as the unintended consequences of people's actions. The socialist vision focuses on things that were deliberately created to serve a purpose.

THINKING Like an Economist

Many people think that businesses always embrace the capitalist vision, but this belief is not necessarily correct. Businesses often lobby government for legislation that could end up hampering the free-enterprise system. For example, some U.S. business firms lobby government to enact tariffs and quotas on foreign products that compete with the products they produce and sell. As we saw in Chapter 18, U.S. tariffs and quotas end up helping U.S. producers (by reducing the competition they face from foreign producers) and hurting U.S. consumers (because tariffs and quotas end up raising the prices the consumers pay).

Although it is perhaps natural to connect business firms with capitalism and thus the capitalist vision, in reality narrow business interests are not always best served by free enterprise, which emphasizes competition, determination of prices by supply and demand, and free and voluntary exchange (trade). There is sometimes a difference between being pro-business and pro–free enterprise. In fact, the benefits of free enterprise often fall more to consumers than to producers.

Section 1 Review

Defining Terms

1. Define

a. traditional economy

b. mixed economy

c. vision

Reviewing Facts and Concepts

2. What is the difference between the capitalist and socialist visions as they relate to price?

3. What is the difference between the capitalist and socialist visions as they relate to private property?

4. What is the difference between the capitalist and socialist visions as they relate to government?

Critical Thinking

5. Why do you think most economies in the world are mixed economies instead of purely capitalist or purely socialist?

Applying Economic Concepts

6. Choose a current economic issue or policy measure, and then contrast the way a capitalist thinker versus a socialist thinker would discuss it.

SECTION 2

Adam Smith and Karl Marx

As discussed in the previous section, there are two major modern economic systems: capitalism and socialism. Adam Smith, an eighteenth-century economist, is often viewed as the father of capitalism or free enterprise. Nineteenth-century economist Karl Marx is often viewed as the father of socialism. This section discusses the ideas of both Smith and Marx.

As you read this section, keep these key questions in mind:

- What is Adam Smith's position on self-interest?
- According to Adam Smith, what is wealth equal to?
- What is the labor theory of value?
- What are Karl Marx's six stages of economic development?

Adam Smith: Brief Biography

Key Terms

labor theory of value
surplus value

Adam Smith was born in 1723 in Kircaldy, Scotland. His father died before he was born. Smith, a bachelor all his life, lived with his mother until she died in 1784. He died six years later, in 1790.

Smith went to the University of Glasgow (in Scotland) when he was fourteen years old and later attended Balliol College at Oxford University (in England). After Oxford, Smith returned to Scotland and gave public lectures on rhetoric and literature in Edinburgh. He was a professor of logic at the University of Glasgow for nearly twelve years.

Adam Smith is well known for his writing on self-interest, but he also wrote about a moral framework based on reasonable behavior. How would these two concepts work together?

Smith published two major works. The first, published in 1759, was *The Theory of Moral Sentiments*. In this work, Smith discusses the moral forces that restrain selfishness and bind people together in important cooperative endeavors. The second work, published in 1776, was officially titled *An Inquiry into the Nature and Causes of the Wealth of Nations*. More commonly called *The Wealth of Nations,* it is ranked as one of the one hundred most important and influential books in the history of the world.

To fulfill her self-interest, this chef will give us what we want—well-prepared food—to get what she wants—money.

Smith on Self-Interest

Economists today often talk about the four categories of resources: land, labor, capital, and entrepreneurship. Smith would add *self-interest* to this list of resources as a very important component. Self-interest, which for Smith is the desire to better ourselves, is what makes us tick. Smith said that from the minute we enter this world at birth to the day

Cooling Off

Many of the technological marvels that we take for granted today were invented by individuals. What prompted them to do what they did? Were they just smart people who had an idea?

Adam Smith, if he were living today, would not think that intelligence and a good idea were enough to lead individuals to invent things that ended up making other individuals better off. For Smith, there would need to be a big dose of *self-interest* at work, too. In other words, the recipe for a useful invention is one part self-interest, one part intelligence, and one part good idea, mixed together with a lot of hard work.

For example, consider air-conditioning. At one time air-conditioning did not exist, and because it did not, life was not as enjoyable and production was not as high as today. Many of the cities of the hot, dry Southwest (such as Las Vegas, Tucson, and Phoenix) would not be as developed as they are today if air-conditioning had not been invented. (Air-conditioning is sometimes said to have built Las Vegas.)

Moreover, without air-conditioning, the growth of temperature-sensitive industries such as film, tobacco, and textiles would have been difficult, if not impossible. It is unlikely, too, that without air-conditioning the movie industry today would have summer blockbusters. People would not be eager to go by the millions to hot theaters and perspire for two hours to watch a movie.

How did air-conditioning come to be? Was it just someone's good idea? Willis Carrier (of Carrier Engineering Company) is often credited with the development of air-conditioning. In 1922 he patented the "centrifugal chiller," which made it possible to cool off large spaces (such as stores). Carrier was smart and had a few good ideas, but most important, he was motivated by self-interest—the desire to make money. If Carrier and his partners could not have benefited monetarily by their hard work and good ideas—if they could not have benefited from introducing air-conditioning to the world—it is doubtful that they would have risked their time and money to develop the technology that gave birth to air-conditioning.

QUESTION TO ANSWER Do you think William Shakespeare was motivated by self-interest to write plays?

we go to our graves, we have the desire to make ourselves better off. Self-interest thus is a major part of who we are. It is our self-interest, Smith believed, that prompts us to work hard, take risks, and in the end benefit others through our activities.

How can we benefit others through our self-interest? Doesn't a person's self-interest pit the person against the best interests of others? Smith believed that if people wanted to serve their own self-interest, they had to serve others first. In probably the most famous passage of *The Wealth of Nations,* Smith says: "It is not from the benevolence of the butcher, the brewer, or the baker, that we expect our dinner, but from their regard to their own interest. We address ourselves, not to their humanity but to their self-love, and never talk to them of our own necessities but of their advantages." In other words, the butcher, brewer, and baker do not give us our dinner because they love us or because they want to assist us but because they cannot get what they want from us until they first give us what we want. Smith says, "Whoever offers to another a bargain of any kind, proposes to do this. Give me that which I want, and you shall have this which you want."

According to Smith, then, self-interest is not something to look sadly upon or to recoil from in disgust. Much of what we have today that makes our lives better off would not exist if self-interest did not exist.

Wealth: Not Money but Goods

Smith disagreed with the mercantalists, who believed that the more money (gold and silver) a country had, the wealthier it was. Smith believed that the wealth of a nation instead consisted of how many goods and services its people consumed.

A personal example can illustrate Smith's idea. Your wealth consists of those nonmoney and money assets you own that have value. Suppose you own one nonmoney asset, a car, which is worth $20,000, and you have $1,000 in the bank. If we add the monetary value of your car to the money you have in the bank, we would say that your wealth has a money value of $21,000. Stated differently, you could sell your car for $20,000, take the $1,000 out of your bank, and buy $21,000 worth of goods and services. If the average price of a good in society were $1, you could buy 21,000 units of various goods.

What makes a society wealthy—money or goods? Adam Smith's answer: goods.

Now suppose that your personal money supply, along with everyone else's, doubles. Instead of having $1,000 in the bank, you now have $2,000. Are you wealthier? Most of us would answer yes, but it must be remembered that if the money supply doubles in society (remember, you and everyone else has double the money you had the day before), prices are likely to rise. According to the quantity theory of money (discussed in Chapter 13), a doubling of the money supply will lead to a doubling of prices.

What is your new wealth position? You still have a car, worth double ($40,000) what it was worth before, and you have $2,000 in the bank. The money value of your wealth is therefore $42,000, double what your money wealth was before ($21,000). There is one catch, though. Whereas the average price of goods was $1 before, it is now $2. In other words, if you sold your car and got your money out of the bank, you would have $42,000, with which you could buy 21,000 units of various goods— the same number of goods you could buy before the money supply doubled. In other words, you are no better off with double the money supply than you were with half the money supply. More money does not make a society better off; the consumption of more goods and services makes a society better off.

Machines allow more pins to be produced in a day than could be produced by hand. How does this affect the economy?

The Division of Labor

Smith believed that the division of labor was a major factor leading to the wealth of nations. When people specialized in particular tasks, output increased. Consider an example used by Smith, the making of a simple pin. According to Smith, one person, working alone, could make only one pin a day. But ten people, working together and each performing a particular task, could produce about 48,000 pins a day, or 4,800 pins per person.

According to Smith, when we divide up a task and do only one thing, we become proficient at it and do not lose time moving from one task to another. Pin making, for example, involves several different functions. The wire must be drawn out, straightened, cut, ground to a point, and so on. If one person has to do everything, he or she loses time going from one task to another. But several persons who each perform a different function lose very little time going from one task to another. As a result, more can be produced in a given period of time.

Also, said Smith, when we do something over and over, we begin to think of how we can make the task easier. We invent machines to do what

Would more or less of a product be produced if each worker focused on only one task? Explain.

we do—for example, to grind the pin, straighten it, or cut it. Furthermore, we are more likely to develop machinery when we are trying to accomplish one task (say, grind a pin) than to do several tasks (grind a pin, straighten it, cut it, and so on). With the introduction of machinery and tools, the production of output usually rises. For example, we can produce more corn and wheat with tractors; we can produce more houses with drills and electric saws; we can produce more computers with robotic machines.

This Chinese man enjoys an American soft drink. Explain how both this man and the soft drink company benefit.

Voluntary Exchange

Smith believed that both parties to a voluntary exchange must benefit, or they will not enter into the exchange. For Smith, this principle was equally true for two people living in the same country or for two people living in different countries. For example, when a person living in New York City buys something from a person in Los Angeles, both benefit. And when an American buys something from a German, both benefit. Smith was definitely in favor of free international trade; he wanted people in different countries to be able to trade with each other without any government prohibitions (tariffs or quotas).

Self-Interest, Money, the Division of Labor, and Wealth

This chapter discussed the unintended consequences of individuals' actions and the division of labor. According to the capitalist thinker, the unintended consequences of individuals' actions sometimes produce good things.

Adam Smith believed that the division of labor was a major factor leading to the wealth of nations.

According to many economists, the two concepts—the unintended consequences of individuals' actions and the division of labor—together can explain much of the material benefits we enjoy today. As Chapter 10 explained, before there was money, there was only barter. People traded goods and services for other goods and services. In this barter economy trade was difficult and time consuming, because people could never be sure that what they had to trade was acceptable to others. To make trade easier for themselves, individuals started accepting the good that was more widely accepted for purposes of exchange than other goods. In other words, if good A was accepted five out of ten times, and all other goods were accepted only three out of ten times, then there was a natural tendency for more people to accept good A. In time, this good became widely accepted for purposes of exchange and thus became money.

In this story of the emergence of money, no one individual intended for money to exist; each individual only intended that his or her life be made easier. Each person accepted the most widely accepted good to reduce the time and energy it took to make everyday exchanges. In time, this activity generated an outcome no one intended: one good was widely accepted for exchange and became known as money. Money, then, was an unintended consequence of individuals' actions to make trading easier.

With the emergence of money, however, came something else: the division of labor. Once there was money, individuals would specialize in the production of one good, sell it for money, and then use the money to buy whatever they wanted. In a barter economy, where trade is time consuming and difficult, individuals tend to produce many of the goods they wish to consume. But in a money economy, where trade is easy, there is no need to produce some of X, Y, and Z. It is enough to produce only X, sell it for money, and then use the money to buy Y and Z.

With the division of labor, says Adam Smith, comes an increase in the amount of output, which means more wealth. So, the history of the wealth of nations is essentially the history of two economic concepts at play: (1) money emerged as an unintended consequence of individuals' actions, and (2) the existence of money prompted individuals to specialize in the production of one good or service.

QUESTION TO ANSWER What role does self-interest play in the story of money, the division of labor, and wealth?

Competition

Smith thought of competition as a process wherein producers and sellers were in battle with each other for the dollars of the buying public. It is competition, according to Smith, that keeps prices down and quality up. He said that if trade "is divided between two grocers, their competition will tend to make both of them sell cheaper than if it were in the hands of one only; and if it were divided among twenty, their competition would be just so much greater, and the chance of their combining together, in order to raise the price, just so much less."

What Should Government Do?

According to Smith, government has only three duties to perform. Its first duty is to protect society from "the violence and invasion of other societies." In today's language, government has a duty to provide national defense. The second duty is to establish a system of justice—in other words, to establish a court system where disputes between people can be resolved. The third and final duty of government, according to Smith, is to establish certain public works and public institutions (such as roads and bridges).

Smith did not think it proper for government to be involved in the economic affairs of people:

It is the highest impertinence and presumption . . . in kings and ministers, to pretend to watch over the economy of private people, and to restrain their expence. . . . They are themselves always, and without exception, the greatest spendthrifts in the society. Let them look well after their own expence, and they may safely trust private people with theirs. If their own extravagance does not ruin the state, that of their subjects never will.

Karl Marx: Brief Biography

On the opposite end of the economic spectrum from Adam Smith is Karl Marx. Marx was born in 1818 in the German town of Trier, in the Rhineland. Marx studied law, history, and philosophy at the universities of

Adam Smith believed that governments should provide roads and bridges. Do you agree? Explain.

Karl Marx suggested that nations go through six stages of economic development. Name the six stages.

Bonn, Berlin, and Jena but was unable to teach at universities because of his radical views. As a journalist, Marx wrote many articles for the *New York Tribune*. His major work, *Das Kapital,* is one of the most important and influential books in the history of the world. In it he lays out his theory of economics.

Basics of Marx's Thought

Few economists have had as much influence on the world as Karl Marx. Marx, in turn, was influenced by the English economist David Ricardo and the German philosopher Georg Hegel, among others—in particular, by Ricardo's discussion of the labor theory of value.

The **labor theory of value** holds that all value in produced goods is derived from labor. Marx argued that the value of a commodity is determined by the necessary labor time embodied in it. For example, if it takes five hours of labor time to produce good X and ten hours to produce good Y, then Y is twice as valuable as X.

Marx believed that in a capitalist society, the owners of factories and businesses exploited the workers by paying them far less than they were worth. For example, say a worker produced $100 a day worth of value for the factory owner but was only paid $20. Marx used the term **surplus value** to describe the difference between the total value of production and the subsistence wages paid to workers.

Why wouldn't the workers simply refuse to work for less than they were worth? In other words, why wouldn't workers prevent the capitalists from exploiting them? To this question, Marx replied that capitalism creates a large reserve army of the unemployed and that this excess supply of labor keeps wages at the subsistence level. According to Marx, the worker either has to work on the capitalist's terms or not work at all.

Go to the Karl Marx and Fredrick Engels Internet Archive (http://www.marxists.org/archive/marx/index.htm). Once there, click on "Biography" and then "Biographical Overview by F. Engels (1869)." Read the biographical overview of Marx written by Engels.

QUESTIONS TO ANSWER

1. Where was Marx born?
2. When was Marx born?
3. What did Marx do in Paris?
4. What did Marx study in Berlin and Bonn?

Marx on Economic Development

According to Marx, a nation will progress through six stages of economic development, which are discussed here.

labor theory of value
A theory that holds that all value in produced goods is derived from labor.

surplus value
In Marxist terminology, the difference between the total value of production and the subsistence wages paid to workers.

Primitive Communism The first stage of economic development is characterized by common ownership of property; people cooperate to earn a meager living from nature. People generally have to work all day simply to produce the bare necessities for survival. Under these conditions, there is no surplus value and thus no exploitation, because both require workers to produce more than they need to consume for survival.

Slavery At some point, the productive capabilities of people rise to such an extent that they are able to produce more than they need to consume for survival. Now slavery becomes a possibility; some people exploit others and garner the surplus value. When this occurs, class conflict arises.

Feudalism The economic actors in feudalism are lords and serfs, who, in Marx's view, have a relationship that is essentially the same as that between the slave masters and slaves in the preceding stage of economic development. The serfs are permitted to work a few days per week on the land allotted to them, but on other days they are required to till the lord's land.

Capitalism Marx both disliked capitalism and marveled at its ability to greatly increase productivity and output. According to Marx, the means of production become more concentrated under capitalism. For him, the relationship between capitalist and worker is essentially the same as the relationship between slave master and slave or between lord and serf in earlier stages of economic development. The capitalist appears to pay the workers for all the hours they work but in reality pays for only a few hours and appropriates the value produced in the remaining hours to himself or herself. Marx predicted intense class struggles under capitalism between the capitalists and the workers. He believed that capitalists would increasingly exploit workers in the search for higher profits.

In the United States, we don't often see violent struggles between the capitalists and workers. Struggles more often take the form of strikes and boycotts.

Dictatorship of the Workers, or Socialism According to Marx, the intense class struggles under capitalism will eventually result in the state being used as an instrument of oppression by the capitalists against the workers. The workers will rise in revolt, overthrow the capitalist state, and establish in its place the dictatorship of the workers, in which capital and land are owned by the worker government. Exploitation of the workers will then cease.

Pure Communism The dictatorship of the workers will eventually "wither away," and only pure communism will remain. In this, the highest, stage of economic development, individuals will produce according to their abilities and receive according to their

Reprinted with special permission of King Features Syndicate.

needs. In pure communism, selfishness and greed are largely a thing of the past, and there is no need for a formal government apparatus.

Critics of Marx

Is labor the sole source of value, as Marx believed, or are there other parts to the equation?

The following are some of the criticisms that have been raised against Marx's ideas.

1. *The labor theory of value is faulty.* Most modern economists agree that labor is not the sole source of value. They argue that land, capital, and entrepreneurship are independent factors of production and, like labor, are capable of creating value. Marxists sometimes reply that capital is created by labor, thus making it *indirect* labor. The critics agree that capital is in part past labor (and note that labor is paid its contribution to the production of capital), but they point out that capital is capable of creating value beyond the value of the labor employed to produce it.
2. *There is no large reserve army of the unemployed.* Marx maintained that capitalism produced a large reserve army of the unemployed that capitalists could use to hold wages down to a subsistence level. Massive unemployment has indeed occurred under capitalism, but this has been the exception rather than the rule.
3. *Most workers earn an above-subsistence wage.* Critics argue that the competition for workers among business firms puts upward pressure on wages and causes firms to improve working conditions, shorten working hours, provide fringe benefits, and so forth.
4. *Marxist revolutions have not appeared in the places Marx expected.* Marx expected worker revolutions to appear in advanced capitalist nations where capitalism had had the longest time to intensify. According to Marx, countries such as Great Britain and the United States were far more likely to experience revolutions than were countries such as Russia and China.

Section 2 Review

Defining Terms

1. Define
   - **a.** labor theory of value
   - **b.** surplus value

Reviewing Facts and Concepts

2. According to Adam Smith, how does our self-interest work to the advantage of others?
3. According to Adam Smith, if a country has more money, does it necessarily have more wealth, too? Explain your answer.
4. Karl Marx believed in a labor theory of value. Explain.

Applying Economic Concepts

5. Do you believe that Adam Smith and Karl Marx would view self-interest in the same way? Explain your answer.

SECTION 3

Socialism in the Former Soviet Union

Many countries experimented with socialism during the twentieth century. A list of these nations includes the former Soviet Union, China, Poland, Sweden, the former Yugoslavia, and Cuba. This section discusses one twentieth-century variety of socialism: the command-economy socialism that was practiced in the former Soviet Union.

As you read this section, keep these key questions in mind:

- What is central economic planning, and what is the case against it?
- How were prices set in the former Soviet Union?

Vladimir Ilich Lenin headed the socialist regime in the Soviet Union for many years.

Command-Economy Socialism

Key Terms

command-economy socialism
Gosplan

What today makes up much of the Commonwealth of Independent States used to be the Union of Soviet Socialist Republics (USSR), commonly called the Soviet Union. Between approximately 1917 and 1991, the Soviet economy was described as **command-economy socialism.** This version of socialism is as extreme as can be found: government is involved in almost every aspect of the economy. Government owns all the nonlabor resources (such as land and capital), it decides what will be produced and in what quantities, it sets prices and wages, and much more.

Under command-economy socialism, the government virtually controls the economy. Who controls the economy in a democracy?

Gosplan In the former Soviet Union, under command-economy socialism, **Gosplan** was the central planning agency. It had the responsibility of drafting the economic plan for the Soviet economy with input from high government officials in the Politburo (parliament).

Gosplan constructed two types of plans: five-year (long-range) plans and one-year (short-range) plans. The five-year plans allocated the nation's resources. They determined how much would go into producing investment goods (such as factories and machinery), how much would go into pro-

MINI GLOSSARY

command-economy socialism An economic system characterized by government ownership of the nonlabor factors of production, government allocation of resources, and centralized decision making. Most economic activities take place in the public sector, and government plays a very large role in the economy.

Gosplan Under Soviet command-economy socialism, the planning agency that had the responsibility of drafting the economic plan for the country.

ducing military goods (such as bombers and tanks), and how much would go into producing consumer goods (such as television sets and washing machines). The one-year plans were much more detailed than the five-year plans. They outlined what each of the more than 200,000 Soviet enterprises under Gosplan's supervision was to produce, the amounts of labor and raw materials each would be allocated, the amount and type of machinery that would be installed, and so on.

To get a sense of how this process worked, let's translate it to the U.S. scene. If there were a U.S. Gosplan, it would probably be located in Washington, D.C. It would issue orders to Pepsico, Dell Computers, Ford Motor Company, and other companies stating what each was to produce. For example, it might direct Ford Motor Company to produce 300,000 cars. Then it would direct the companies supplying Ford to send so much steel, so much plastic, and so many tires to the company. It would also tell Ford whether it could expect to have its factories updated, what type of new capital goods would be arriving, and other crucial information.

Critics of command-economy socialism point out that a central planning committee cannot anticipate the needs and wants of consumers months in advance.

The Case against Central Economic Planning Central economic planning—planning done by the government—is commonplace in a nation that practices command-economy socialism. The critics of central economic planning say that the economic planners cannot take into account as much relevant information as a market does. Therefore, economic plans cannot coordinate economic activity or satisfy consumer demand as well as market forces.

Consider an economic planning board composed of thirty or forty persons who must decide how many houses, apartment buildings, buses, cars, and pizza restaurants should be built within the next year. Where would the planners start? Would they know about people's changing demands for houses, apartment buildings, and the rest? The critics of central economic planning argue that they would not. At best, the planners would be making a guess about what goods and services consumers would demand and how much they would buy at different prices. If they guessed wrong, resources would be wasted, and demands would go unfulfilled.

Private individuals, guided by rising and falling prices and by the desire to earn profits, are better at satisfying consumer demand.

Economic planners risk little themselves when they draw up economic plans for others to follow (after all, they do not put their own money on the line). Therefore, they are not as likely to avoid costly economic mistakes as are the risk-taking entrepreneurs in a free market.

Question: *Everybody makes plans. Individuals make plans for their lives. A business may draw up a plan for the next five years. If individuals and firms plan, why not let government plan for the economy?*

Answer: *The critics of central planning argue that there are two major distinctions to be made between a plan that an individual or business firm makes and an economic plan for all of society. First, if an individual or a firm makes a plan that fails, only the individual or the firm suffers. For the most part, the rest of society is unaffected. If a central economic plan fails, however, one mistake can have major consequences for many people.*

Second, if one person makes a personal plan, others can still make and follow their own plans. In contrast, an economic plan that encompasses all of society might prohibit people from following their own plans.

Setting Prices As discussed earlier, a planning agency determines the total quantity of goods produced in a command economy—that is, how many radios, television sets, cars, refrigerators, toasters, and so forth will be produced. In other words, it controls the supply side of the market. There is also a demand side to every market, and supply and demand determine price.

Under command-economy socialism in the former Soviet Union, economic planners not only determined the supply of a particular good but also set its price. For example, they might decide to sell 11 million toasters for a price of 25 rubles each. Unless 25 rubles happened to be the equilibrium price, though, either a surplus or a shortage of toasters would result.

Say that economic planners have set the price of toasters at 25 rubles (see Exhibit 19-1), an example of a *price ceiling.* A price ceiling is a government-

Exhibit 19-1
Prices in a Command-Economy Socialist Nation

You can see in this example that the planners set the price for toasters too low. A government-mandated maximum price, above which legal trades cannot be made, is referred to as a price ceiling. One consequence of a price ceiling is a shortage. Toasters will be rationed by some combination of price and waiting in line.

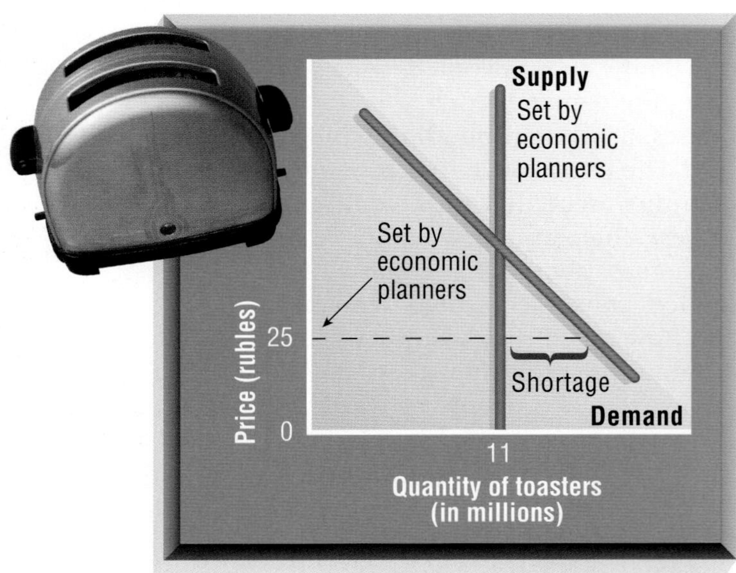

mandated maximum price above which legal trades cannot be made. In the example, it would be illegal to buy or sell toasters at a price higher than 25 rubles (the price ceiling). As the exhibit illustrates, the price ceiling of 25 rubles does not equate supply with demand, and there are consequences: a shortage of toasters. At this point in a free-enterprise economic system, the price of toasters would be bid up to the equilibrium price, where the quantity demanded of toasters would equal the quantity supplied. But in the former Soviet Union under command-economy socialism, it was illegal to bid up the ruble price of a good. Instead, toasters were rationed by some combination of ruble price and waiting in line. (That is, the rationing device was first come, first served.)

Western travelers to the former Soviet Union observed long lines of people in front of some stores—the result of shortages. They also observed no people at all in front of other stores. What accounted for this difference? Just as some prices were set below the equilibrium price, producing shortages and long lines of people, some prices were set above the equilibrium price, producing surpluses and relatively empty stores. As long as price is centrally imposed, shortages or surpluses are likely. It would be most unusual if the planners could correctly guess equilibrium prices.

Here we see long lines of people waiting to buy consumer items in the former Soviet Union. What caused long lines like these?

Section 3 Review

Defining Terms

1. Define

a. command-economy socialism

b. Gosplan

Reviewing Facts and Concepts

2. State the case against central planning.

3. How were prices determined in the former Soviet Union under command-economy socialism?

Critical Thinking

4. Some people believe that long lines of people waiting to buy bread, milk, and meat is indicative of buying behavior in a poor country. They argue that there can never be long lines of people waiting to buy goods in a rich country. Do you agree or disagree? Explain your answer.

SECTION 4

Moving from Socialism to Free Enterprise

In the early 1990s, many formerly socialist nations began trying to throw off their socialist economic ways and move toward a free-enterprise economic system. This movement was most notable in the nations of Eastern Europe and Russia. This section discusses some of the problems encountered in moving from socialism to free enterprise.

As you read this section, keep these key questions in mind:

- In the move from socialism to free enterprise, what is likely to happen at first to prices and jobs?
- What is infrastructure?

The move from socialism to free enterprise often comes with a difficult transition period in prices.

The Rise in Prices

Key Terms

infrastructure
rule of law

Remember that prices are set by government officials in a nation that practices command-economy socialism. When a nation moves away from command-economy socialism to free enterprise, prices are no longer set by government. Instead, buyers and sellers together—through demand and supply—determine prices. If many prices were previously set at levels below the equilibrium price, prices can clearly be expected to rise as the economy moves from socialism to free enterprise.

This rise in prices is exactly what happened in Russia, Poland, the former Yugoslavia, Czechoslovakia, Hungary, and other countries in the early 1990s as they moved from socialism toward free enterprise. Unfortunately, it takes time for the benefits of free enterprise to be seen, and meanwhile the peoples of these formerly socialist nations were experiencing pain caused by the economic mistakes of the past. Government officials had controlled prices—stated differently, they had prevented supply and demand from working—for too long. The higher prices caused a good deal of discontent in these nations, because people expected free enterprise to make their lives easier, not harder.

In a free enterprise economy, this Polish woman is able to have her own produce stand and sell her goods at market-determined prices.

The Elimination of Certain Firms and Jobs

A change in economic systems is often accompanied by a reallocation of workers from some businesses to others.

In a free-enterprise economic system, consumers have a large say in which firms survive and which firms fail. For example, firm A produces goods that consumers are willing and able to buy, and firm B produces goods that consumers do not want to buy. In a free-enterprise economic system, firm A will survive, and firm B will go out of business.

Under command-economy socialism, however, a firm will go out of business only if the government economic planners say that it will go out of business. Consumers have little power in this regard. As we might expect, then, there will be a number of firms that consumers care little about and buy little from. In the transition from socialism to free enterprise, these firms will go out of business, and the workers will lose their jobs.

In time, the resources used by these firms will be bought by surviving firms, and the workers who lost their jobs will end up finding new jobs. In the meantime, however, output production will probably go down, and the unemployment rate will rise. Here, then, are two additional reasons for people to get upset about the transition from socialism to a market economy.

Private Property

In a free-enterprise economic system, business firms compete with each other. For example, General Motors, Ford, and Chrysler, along with other car companies, compete with each other for consumers' car dollars. Competition is a necessary part of free enterprise.

To have competition, however, there must be private property. If individuals are not allowed to own businesses, land, capital, and so on, they cannot compete with each other. Clearly, a nation that wants to move away from socialism, where the government owns the nonlabor resources, to free enterprise must make it possible for people to have private property. Thus, a socialist nation that wants to move toward free enterprise must have a way of turning government property into private property.

Under free enterprise, this car company in Poland will have to compete with other car companies. Who must own the companies for competition to work?

When the former Soviet Union operated under command-economy socialism, the government owned the stores, factories, apartment buildings, and more. Once the government chose to move toward free enterprise, it had to decide how to turn government property into private property. It mainly did this by selling government properties and by issuing shares of stock in various businesses to former managers and employees.

MINI GLOSSARY

infrastructure The basic structures and facilities on which the continuance and growth of a community depend. Interstate highways, bridges, and communication networks are some of the things that make up a country's infrastructure.

Infrastructure

Infrastructure refers to the basic structures and facilities on which the continuance and growth of a community depend. Interstate highways, bridges, and communication networks are some of the things that make up a nation's infrastructure.

As countries change their economic systems, their infrastructure needs (roads, telephones, etc.) change, too.

Many of the nations attempting to move from socialism to free enterprise lack infrastructure, which makes the move difficult. For example, the former Soviet Union had a low-quality telephone system compared with that in the United States. In the former Soviet Union, where the managers of firms were simply given orders as to what to produce, where to ship it, and so on, telephones were not as important as in a free-enterprise system. In a market economy, materials have to be bought and sold daily, and the owners and managers of firms need to find out who has the materials and what their prices are. Currently, many Eastern European nations and the independent countries of the Commonwealth of Independent States lack the infrastructure necessary for full-blown free enterprise.

Attitudes

If you were raised in the United States, with its free-enterprise economic system, you have probably developed certain attitudes. For example, you probably believe that it is worthwhile for people to start their own businesses, work hard, and save to get ahead. People who have lived their lives in a free-enterprise economic system more readily accept the ideas that you have to take some risk to succeed, that you have to produce goods that people want to buy, and that government is not there to take care of you.

People who have lived much of their lives under socialism, however, have different attitudes. For example, they are not accustomed to taking business risks, because government has not let them start their own businesses. They are not used to the idea of having to produce goods that people want to buy; many of them have been simply producing whatever goods the government told them to produce. They also feel that government should take care of them. In short, people who have lived under free enterprise have attitudes that are different from the attitudes of people who have lived under socialism.

For free enterprise to get started, a certain attitude must exist. Some people have to be willing to take business risks and accept that they may lose their jobs if they do not produce what consumers want to buy. The people of the formerly socialist nations are sometimes reported to lack ini-

An economic system often influences people's work ethic, initiative, and degree of risk-taking. Might these Russians exhibit different work behavior living under free enterprise than command-economy socialism? Explain.

tiative, to not want to take risks, and to be used to having government take care of them. This attitude has grown up over years of living under socialism, and it will not change overnight.

Rule of Law

Free enterprise cannot survive without the **rule of law.** The term *rule of law* takes into account many important things, including the protection of private property and a fair and impartial judiciary that enforces fair and reasonable contracts. Most important, the rule of law holds that no one is above the laws of the country. Rich and poor, strong and weak, privileged and unprivileged are all treated alike before the law. The alternative to the rule of law is rule by men.

A country can allow prices to be set by the forces of supply and demand. It can let entrepreneurs easily and freely start new businesses without being burdened by excessive government taxation or regulation, and it can promote consumer sovereignty. However, a country is unlikely to flourish as a free-enterprise economy unless it abides by the rule of law.

rule of law
A governing by law or laws (instead of by men and women).

Since the late 1980s and early 1990s, there has been a global movement toward free enterprise and away from socialism. Countries such as Russia and China, as well as many of the countries of Eastern Europe, have moved toward free enterprise. Do you think this move toward free enterprise will continue in the near future? Why or why not?

Section 4 Review

Defining Terms

1. Define
   a. infrastructure
   b. rule of law

Reviewing Facts and Concepts

2. When a country moves from command-economy socialism to free enterprise, why will some people lose their jobs in the transition?

Critical Thinking

3. Explain the link between private property and competition between sellers.

Applying Economic Concepts

4. In country A, supply and demand determine prices, but there is no rule of law. Is it likely that free enterprise will flourish in the country? Explain your answer.

SECTION 5

Government and the Economy

Some governments place greater constraints on economic activity than others. One way to discuss different economies of the world is according to how severely government constrains economic activity. Economies with only mild governmental constraints on economic activity are usually thought of as free-enterprise economies, whereas economies with severe governmental constraints on economic activity are usually considered to be socialist economies. This section discusses the degree of constraint that various governments impose on their economies.

Fidel Castro visits a factory near Havana, Cuba. Who do you think makes decisions about what and how many goods this factory will produce?

As you read this section, keep these key questions in mind:

- What are the ways in which government can constrain or hamper economic activity?
- What are some of the economic policies in Argentina, Canada, Cuba, Germany and many other countries?

Governmental Economic Constraints

Government can constrain economic activity in many different ways, a few of which are discussed here.

- *International trade.* Government can limit the free flow of goods and services between countries by imposing high tariffs and quotas.
- *Taxation.* Government limits entrepreneurship and dampens incentives to work and assume risk if it imposes a high tax rate on the average taxpayer.
- *Government ownership of business.* Government ownership of many businesses or entire industries is generally considered a constraint on the ability of private individuals to own and operate businesses.
- *Banking.* Government ownership of banks, government control over the allocation of credit, and restrictions on the ability of foreign banks to open branches are considered constraints on economic activity. Such constraints inhibit people from making the kinds of economic decisions that promote economic freedom and economic efficiency.
- *Government expropriation of property.* Individuals lose a large degree of economic freedom and are severely constrained in their economic activities when government willfully and without just cause expropriates (seizes) their property.
- *Business licensing.* Government can constrain individuals from starting new businesses by making it difficult to obtain a business license.

- *Wage and price controls.* When government imposes controls on wages and prices, it prevents individuals from making trades at mutually agreed-upon prices determined by the forces of supply and demand.

Economies of Selected Countries

This section looks at the economic environment in a few selected countries in terms of some of the governmental constraints described in the previous section (taxation, government ownerships, banking, business licensing, and wage and price controls).[1]

Argentina Argentina has low to moderate tariffs. The top income tax rate is 35 percent, and the rate for the average taxpayer is 6 percent (a relatively low tax rate). Argentina has been privatizing many industries (selling public properties to the private sector) in recent years, including even some nuclear power plants. In short, government ownership of business is minimal. Most banks in Argentina are now in private hands. Also, in recent years most barriers to foreign banking have been reduced. Opening a business in Argentina is relatively easy. No major goods or services are subject to price controls. Most wages are market determined; however, the government sets wages for public-sector employees, and there is a legislatively mandated minimum wage.

Canada Canada has very low tariffs. Its top income tax rate is 51.645 percent; the average taxpayer pays a tax rate of 17 percent. Since 1984, Canada has

College or University Professor

College and university professors teach students and conduct research in their fields. They also meet with colleagues to keep up with developments in their fields and consult with business, government, nonprofit, and community organizations.

College and university faculty are organized into departments or divisions based on their fields of study. For example, an economics professor is likely to be in the Economics Department in the College of Arts and Sciences or in the College of Business. College faculty members usually have flexible schedules. They usually teach and meet with students two or three days a week and conduct research and have committee meetings on the other days.

Teachers in a four-year college or university are usually required to have a Ph.D. A master's degree, and sometimes a Ph.D., is required to teach at a two-year college.

1. Most of the information in this section comes from Bryan Johnson, Kim Holmes, and Melanie Kirkpatrick, *1999 and 2000 Index of Economic Freedom,* published jointly by the *Wall Street Journal* (New York) and The Heritage Foundation (Washington, D.C., 1999 and 2000).

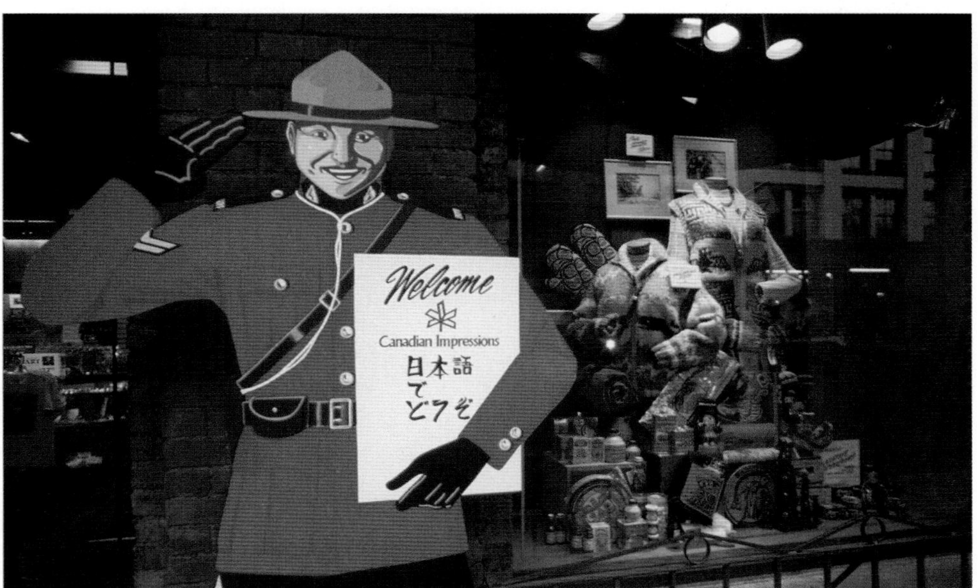

In Canada it is relatively easy to establish a new business. Do you think it should be easy to establish new businesses? Explain.

This steel mill worker in Beijing, China, likely works for a government-owned company. Explain.

undertaken substantial privatization of business and industry. Canada's banking system prohibits foreign-owned bank branches. It is relatively easy to establish a business in Canada. Most prices and wages are determined by the market. There are some exceptions, though—for example, on certain agricultural goods and on services in the health care industry.

People's Republic of China China has relatively high tariffs, with an average tariff rate of 20.9 percent. China's top marginal income tax rate (the tax rate on the additional dollar earned) is 45 percent, and the average taxpayer pays a rate of 15 percent. The government plays a big part in business and industry in China. State-owned enterprises produce about 34 percent of all industrial output. This percentage rises to 75 percent if joint government enterprises are counted. The government controls the financial sector principally through its ownership of four major commercial banks. It is moderately difficult to start a business in China. In 1993, government imposed price controls on foodstuffs and utilities, but it later removed the controls on foodstuffs.

Cuba In Cuba, the government inspects and then approves or disapproves of all imports. It is reported that in many cases customs officials confiscate imports for their personal use. Many businesses in Cuba complain that they cannot import the goods and services they need to produce their products. The top marginal income tax rate in Cuba is 50 percent, although some argue that since the government owns the fruits of everyone's labor, the effective tax rate is 100 percent. The government owns and runs most of the economy. For example, if a foreign company in Cuba hires Cubans to work for it, it must pay the wages of the Cubans to the government in hard currency (such as U.S. dollars). The Cuban government then pays the Cuban workers in pesos at a fraction of the wages it received from the foreign companies. Banks are owned and operated by the government. It is difficult to start a business in Cuba. The government sets almost all prices and wages.

Germany Germany has low tariffs on imports. Income tax rates are high, with the top marginal tax rate at 53 percent and the average taxpayer paying 35 percent in income taxes. Government does not own or operate many

The Volkswagon Beetle is just one example of the quality of manufacturing for which Germany is known.

businesses. Many of the banks in Germany are publicly owned. Establishing a business is relatively easy. With the exception of some agricultural goods and some rents, prices are market determined.

Hong Kong Hong Kong has almost no tariffs on imports. Income tax rates are low, topping off at 17 percent. The average taxpayer pays an income tax rate of 2 percent. Government does not own many businesses. Banks in Hong Kong are independent of the government. It is easy to start a business in Hong Kong. Most prices and wages are market determined, but there are price controls on rent, public transport, and electricity.

Japan Tariffs are low in Japan, but some significant nontariff barriers to importing goods into the country exist. In recent years, Japan has tried to dismantle many of these nontariff barriers. Japan's top marginal income tax rate is 37 percent, and average taxpayers pay an income tax rate of 20 percent. Government does not own many businesses. Banks are in private hands, but the government regulates them heavily. It is fairly easy to start a business in Japan. With only few exceptions, there are no price and wage controls.

Mexico Mexico has low tariffs on imports. The top marginal income tax rate is 35 percent, with an average income tax rate of 17 percent. In recent years, Mexico has privatized many formerly government-owned businesses. Most banks are privately owned; however, in recent years the government has bailed out some banks, giving it a major voice in those banks. It is difficult to start a new business in Mexico. Price controls have become less prominent in recent years, but a significant amount still exists.

North Korea The North Korean government inspects all imports into the country and bans imports from many countries. North Korea is a communist state, and the government owns all property. Government confiscates all output, making the effective tax rate 100 percent. The

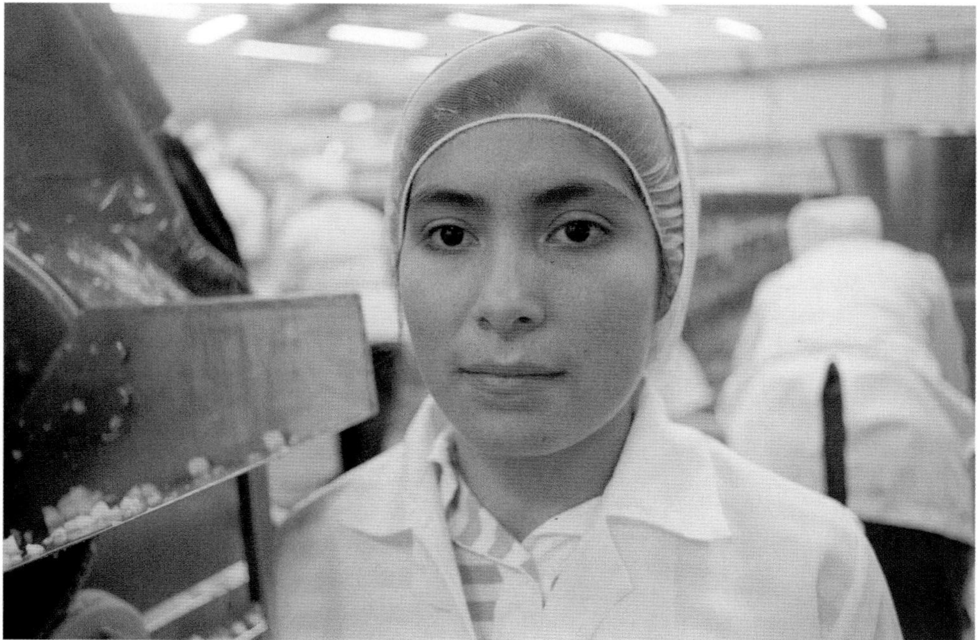

Mexico initiated a series of economic reforms in the late 1980s and 1990s. Mexico exports more goods to the United States than to any other country in the world.

government owns all businesses, and state-owned businesses account for nearly all the gross domestic product. The government also controls all banks. It is difficult to start a business in North Korea. The government sets most wages and prices.

Russia Russia has relatively high tariffs on imports, ranging from 5 percent to 30 percent; the average tariff is 13.4 percent. The top marginal income tax rate is 35 percent, with an average of 12 percent. Even though Russia has made a move toward free enterprise in recent years, state-controlled enterprises still account for a significant part of industrial output. Many of Russia's banks have been privatized in recent years. It is moderately difficult to start a new business in Russia. Most wages and prices are market determined; about 5 percent of all prices are set by the government.

United States Tariffs on imports are low. The top marginal income tax rate is 39.6 percent; the average taxpayer faces a 28 percent marginal tax rate. Government owns very few businesses. Banks are in private hands, and the federal, state, and local governments only minimally regulate them. It is relatively easy to start a new U.S. business. There are price controls on a few agricultural products, as well as a minimum wage. Mostly, though, wages and prices are determined by the market.

This business woman in the United States can count on little, if any, interference from the government in her company.

Section 5 Review

Reviewing Facts and Concepts

1. How can government constrain international trade?
2. How might individual economic freedom be limited by government expropriation of private property?
3. How do wage and price controls limit individual freedom?
4. In which country do you think government constrains economic activity to a greater degree, Cuba or Argentina? Explain your answer.

Critical Thinking

5. Why do you think some governments constrain economic activity more than governments in other countries?
6. Do you think that over the next 25 years, government constraints on economic activity (around the world) will lessen or become greater? Explain your answer.

Applying Economic Concepts

7. What do you think Russia should do differently in the economic arena? For example, do you think it should lower its tariffs, increase or decrease taxes, etc. Give reasons why you believe Russia would be better off if it followed your suggestions.
8. What do you think the United States should do differently in the economic arena? Give reasons why you believe the United States would be better off if it followed your suggestions.

Developing Economic Skills

Comparing International Statistics

When we compare the data of one country with the data of another country, we can get an idea about where the two countries stand in relationship to each other. In other words, we can put things in *relative terms.* A simple example can illustrate this point. In 2000, the GDP of the United States was over $9 trillion. Although $9 trillion sounds like a lot of production, is it? We do not know for sure unless we compare the figure with the production of other countries. Maybe all countries produce $9 trillion worth of goods and services, or even more. Once we learn the GDP figures for other countries, however, we realize that the GDP for the United States is very large; in fact, the U.S. has the largest GDP of any country in the world. The point is that this knowledge came by making a *comparison.* Through comparisons we learn things that we cannot learn in any other way.

Now suppose someone tells you that the inflation rate in the United States in a particular year was 5.0 percent. Was this a high or low inflation rate? If most other countries in the world had an inflation rate of, say, 1 percent, a comparison would lead you to surmise that an inflation rate of 5.0 percent was high. However, if most countries in the world had an inflation rate much higher than 5.0 percent, you would conclude that the 5.0 percent inflation rate was low.

An even better way to look at things is to compute the average inflation rate and compare it with the U.S. inflation rate. For example, suppose there are three countries, X, Y, and Z. The inflation rate is 3 percent in X, 25 percent in Y, and 50 percent in Z. Does X have a relatively low inflation rate? The average inflation rate is 3 percent + 25 percent + 50 percent divided by 3, or 26 percent. In comparison, the inflation rate of X is only 3 percent, so X has a relatively low inflation rate.

In looking at international statistics, we also need to consider whether countries being compared are alike. For example, even if the dollar amounts of a particular economic variable are the same in two countries, it does not necessarily mean that the two countries are alike. Suppose two countries had nearly the same GDP in a year. Would this mean that the two countries were alike in terms of the composition of the goods and services they produced? Not at all. One country could be producing houses, cars, bookshelves, and desks, whereas the other country might be producing oranges, apples, carpets, and computers. Thus, it is important to use numbers accurately and to read in them only what they tell us and no more.

In terms of the GDP example, we know that two countries that have the same GDP have identical total market value for the goods and services they produced in a year. We cannot compare such things as the quality of the goods the two countries produced or the types of goods they produced. Making the mistake of thinking that two countries with an identical GDP are alike in other respects is similar to assuming that if two people are both 5 feet 7 inches tall, their weights are also identical. This is not necessarily the case, of course.

1. Country X has a GDP of $3,000 billion. Given no other information, would you know if country X's GDP was relatively large or small? Explain your answer.
2. In 1996, the United States spent 12.8 cents of every dollar on health care. How would you go about determining whether this was a relatively large percentage of each dollar spent?

CHAPTER

19 Review

Economics Vocabulary

Fill in the following blanks with the appropriate word or phrase.

1. A(n) _____ is an economy based on customs and beliefs that have been handed down from one generation to the next.
2. The economist Thomas Sowell defines a(n) _____ as a sense of how the world works.
3. A(n) _____ is an economy that has a mixture of capitalist and socialist elements.
4. According to the _____, all value in produced goods is derived from direct and indirect (embodied) labor.
5. In Marxist terminology, the difference between the total value of production and the subsistence wages paid to workers is called _____.
6. The _____ refers to governing by law or laws, where no person is above the law.
7. Under Soviet command-economy socialism, the planning agency that had the responsibility of drafting the economic plan of the country was _____.
8. _____ is an economic system characterized by government ownership of the nonlabor factors of production, government allocation of resources, and centralized decision making. Most economic activities take place in the public sector, and government plays a very large role in the economy.
9. Interstate highways, bridges, and communication networks are part of a country's _____.

Review Questions

1. What is Adam Smith's position on voluntary exchange?
2. Explain the case against central economic planning.
3. Identify the six stages of economic development according to Karl Marx.
4. Give an example to illustrate the division of labor.
5. According to Adam Smith, what are the three duties of government?
6. What does the capitalist thinker say about prices, competition, private property, and exchange?
7. What was Karl Marx's position on capitalism?
8. What does the socialist thinker say about prices, competition, private property, and exchange?
9. Why would we expect to see numerous shortages and surpluses in an economy that is centrally planned and sets prices by government edict?
10. Give the highest income tax rate in each of the following countries:
    a. Argentina
    b. Hong Kong
    c. United States
11. Explain the difference between the capitalist vision and the socialist vision as they relate to government and unintended consequences.
12. A capitalist thinker would be much less likely to support controls on prices than would a socialist thinker. Why?
13. Is equilibrium price in a free market an unintended consequence? Explain your answer.
14. The capitalist thinker believes that private property encourages individuals to use their resources in a way that benefits others. Construct an example to explain what this means.
15. According to Adam Smith, what constitutes the wealth of a nation?
16. In the former Soviet Union, what task or tasks did Gosplan perform?
17. What do the critics of the labor theory of value say?
18. Why would we expect to see an initial sharp rise in prices in economies moving from socialism to free enterprise?

Calculations

1. Give a numerical example that illustrates how you can be no better off with double the money.
2. Give a numerical example that illustrates that output can increase through the division of labor.

Graphs

1. Exhibit 19-2 shows the consequences of economic planning in a command-economy. Identify each of the following points:

   a. point A

   b. point B

   c. point C

Exhibit 19-2

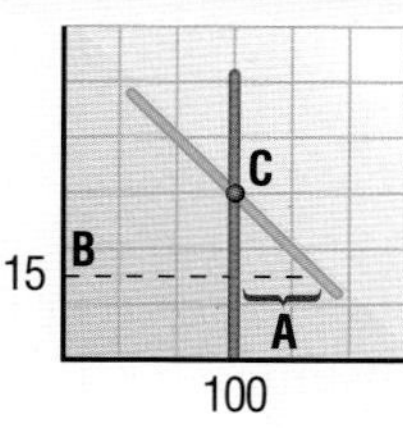

Economics and Thinking Skills

1. **Application.** Aristotle said, "What is common to many is taken least care of, for all men have greater regard for what is their own than for what they possess in common with others." Give an example that illustrates the essence of what Aristotle is saying.
2. **Analysis.** Clark buys a computer from Wilson for $1,200. Adam Smith would say that both Clark and Wilson are made better off by the trade of money for a computer, but how do we know this is true?
3. **Cause and Effect.** According to Karl Marx, what is the cause of socialism?

Writing Skills

Research one of the following topics: (1) the life of Adam Smith, (2) the life of Karl Marx, (3) the economic situation in Russia today, (4) capitalism, or (5) socialism. Next, write a two-page paper discussing some of the most interesting points of your topic.

Economics in the Media

1. Find a newspaper article that addresses the current economic condition of one of the countries discussed in Section 5 of the chapter. Identify the major ideas of the article.
2. Find a story on a television news show that addresses capitalism, socialism, private property rights, competition, the division of labor, or central economic planning. Identify the major ideas of the story.

Where's the Economics?

What does this picture have to do with price?

Analyzing Primary Sources

The chapter's discussion of Karl Marx introduced the concept of *surplus value,* a focus of much of Marx's writing. Here is an excerpt from his work *Das Kapital:*

The directing motive, the end and aim of capitalist production, is to extract the greatest possible amount of surplus-value, and consequently to exploit labour-power to the greatest possible extent. As the number of co-operating labourers increases, so too does their resistance to the domination of capital, and with it, the necessity for capital to overcome this resistance by counter-pressure. The control exercised by the capitalist is not only a special function, due to the nature of the social labour-process, and peculiar to that process, but it is, at the same time, a function of the exploitation of a social labour-process, and is consequently rooted in the unavoidable antagonism between the exploiter and the living and labouring raw material he exploits.[2]

1. What is the aim of capitalist production?
2. What happens as the number of laborers increases?

2. Karl Marx, *Capital,* vol. 1, New York: International Publishers, 1975, p. 331.

UNIT 4

Debate the Issues

Is Free Trade the Best Policy for the United States?

Oklahoma can't impose a tariff or quota on goods produced in Wisconsin, but the United States can and does impose tariffs and quotas on goods produced in other countries. For example, the United States currently imposes tariffs on garments, textiles, sugar, and many other goods produced in other countries. In other words, free trade exists among the states of the United States, but not among countries of the world. Do you think there should be free trade among countries, as there is among states? The issue has both opponents and proponents.

One day in November, two high school debate teams met and debated the issue of free trade. The question before each team was, Is free trade the best policy for the United States? Here is what four of the debaters, two from each team, had to say.

Alycyn Waldrop, Addison High School Debate Team: When I go to the store to buy something new, whether it be a pair of running shoes or a portable telephone, I want to buy the best product for the lowest price. That's my objective, plain and simple. I have a better chance of meeting that objective living in a world of free trade than living in a world where countries impose tariffs and quotas on each other's goods. Free trade maximizes competition, which is what guarantees me the highest quality goods at the lowest possible price.

Suppose there are forty running shoe companies in the world, ten in the United States and thirty in other countries. Am I, as a consumer, better off if all forty companies sell their shoes in the United States, or if only the ten U.S. companies sell their shoes in the United States? The answer is obvious. I am better off when forty companies, domestic and foreign alike, compete for my business, than when only ten domestic companies compete for it. Free trade is the policy that maximizes choice for the consumer. It guarantees high quality goods at reasonable prices.

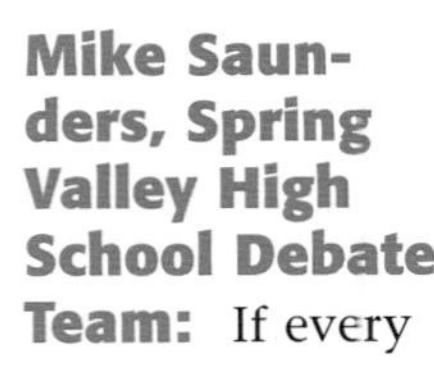

Mike Saunders, Spring Valley High School Debate Team: If every country in the world practiced free trade, then perhaps free trade would be the best policy for the United States. But that's not the world we live in, and we shouldn't pretend that it is. When other countries impose tariffs and quotas on our goods, that hurts our industries and our workers, and we should retaliate in kind.

Suppose the German government places a tariff on American cars imported into Germany. As a result, the price of American cars rises in Germany and Germans buy more German cars and fewer American cars. Since U.S. car companies sell fewer cars, they will have to lay off some of their workers. The people who are laid off are Americans, not Germans.

In other words, some Americans will lose their jobs because the German government decided to impose tariffs on American cars. Is this fair? Should the U.S. government practice free trade when another country doesn't? Should our government sit back and do nothing as the German government puts Americans out of work? I don't think so. A policy of "give and take" would be more acceptable. If Germany practices free trade with us, then we should practice free trade with Germany. But if Germany doesn't practice free trade with us, then we shouldn't practice free trade with them.

Sylvia Minors, Addison High School Debate Team: I disagree. I think that practicing free trade is a little like practicing honesty—you should do it even if others don't. If ten people tell lies, it doesn't follow that the best thing you can do is tell a lie, too. If most countries impose tariffs and quotas, it doesn't follow that the United States should do likewise. The United States should practice free trade even if every other country in the world does not. That's because the United States prospers through free trade, even when other countries do not practice it.

Suppose there are five countries in the world. Four of the countries impose tariffs and quotas; one country, the United States, does not. Certainly foreign tariffs and quotas hurt U.S. producers and workers, but the U.S. government can't make things better for our producers and workers by making our consumers worse off. And that is exactly what the U.S. government would be doing if it retaliated by imposing tariffs and quotas on foreign goods. Then, not only would U.S. producers and workers be hurt by foreign tariffs and quotas, but U.S. consumers would also be hurt by U.S. tariffs and quotas on foreign goods. If the choice is between hurting producers and workers or hurting producers, workers, and consumers, it is better to hurt as few people as possible.

Here's what it comes down to: The best policy is for every country in the world to practice free trade. The second best policy is for the United States to practice free trade, even if no other country in the world practices it. The worst policy is for the United States to impose tariffs and quotas on foreign goods simply because other countries impose tariffs and quotas on our goods.

Madison Golecke, Spring Valley High School Debate Team: United States policy shouldn't protect the interests only of consumers; it should protect the interests of consumers, producers, and workers. When other countries impose tariffs and quotas on U.S.-produced goods, those countries hurt our producers and our workers. These countries should bear the economic consequences. There must be a price for such actions, or these countries will continue to make themselves better off at the expense of American producers and workers. The higher the price of imposing tariffs and quotas on U.S.-produced goods, the less likely foreign countries will do so.

The way to ensure free trade is for the United States to give other countries a taste of their own medicine. If they practice free trade with us, then we should practice free trade with them. If they impose tariffs and quotas on our goods, we should do the same to their goods.

What Do You Think?

1. Should the United States practice free trade even if other countries do not?
2. Is the world moving toward or away from greater free trade?

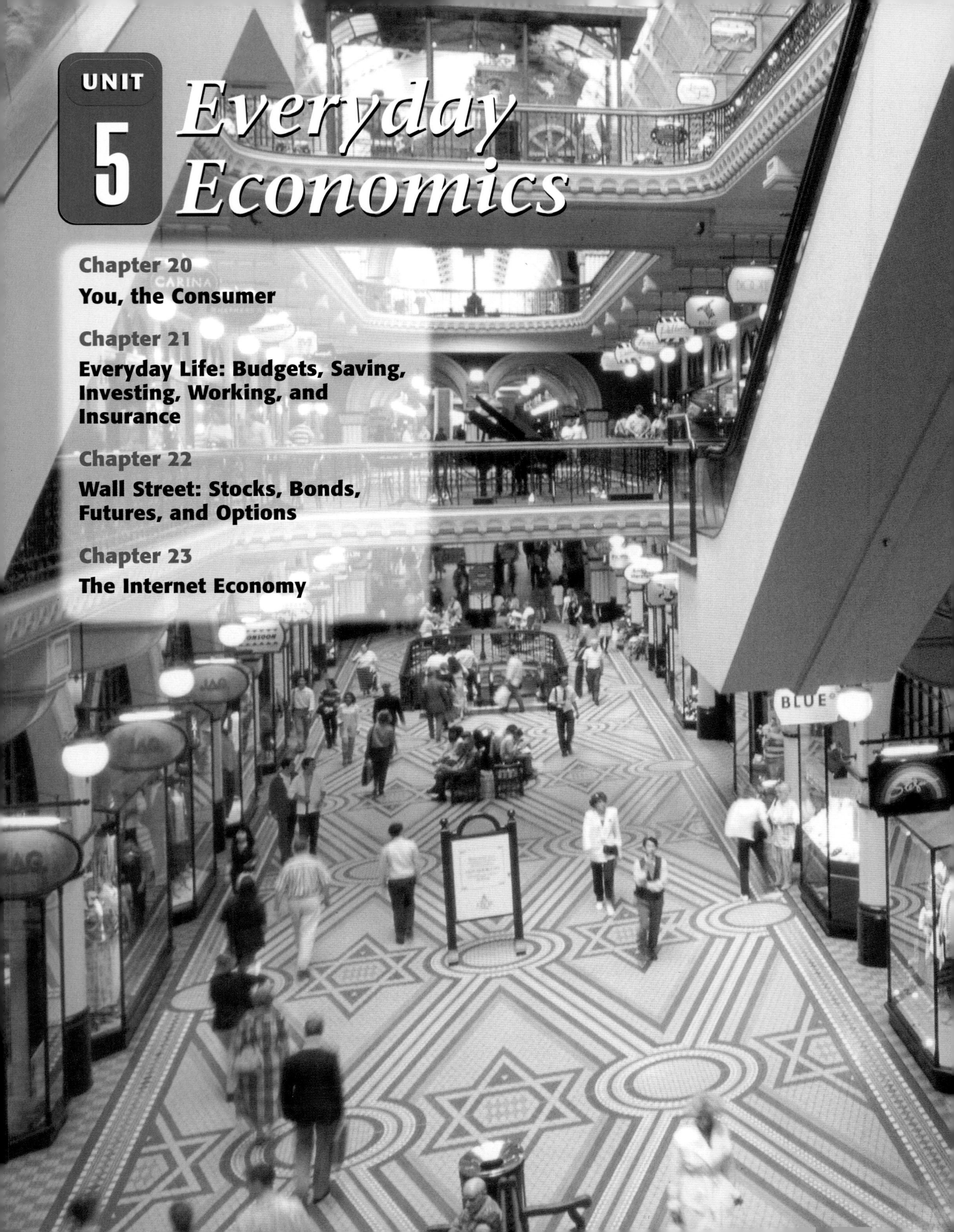

UNIT 5 Everyday Economics

Chapter 20
You, the Consumer

Chapter 21
Everyday Life: Budgets, Saving, Investing, Working, and Insurance

Chapter 22
Wall Street: Stocks, Bonds, Futures, and Options

Chapter 23
The Internet Economy

Ginger
BOUTIQUE

CHAPTER

20 You, the Consumer

What This Chapter Is About

As a consumer, you will buy many products in your life. Some of those products, such as clothes and food, will be relatively inexpensive. Others, such as a car, a house, and an education, will be relatively expensive. This chapter discusses your everyday purchases, along with some of the major purchases you will make only a few times in your life.

Why This Chapter Is Important

We think we know a lot about things that we do each day. For example, we buy goods and services almost every day, and almost all of us feel we know how to buy things. But it is often important to put our daily activities under a microscope to see and understand what we are really doing. Maybe we have been doing some things incorrectly, and we can do them better. Or perhaps we thought we were doing some things that we were not really doing. This chapter will put our buying behavior—ourselves as consumers—under the microscope. We will probably not only be startled by what we see but also will learn from it.

After You Study This Chapter, You Will Be Able To:

- discuss some of the trade-offs involved in buying clothes.
- compute the unit price for food.
- discuss the signs of telemarketing fraud.
- explain the details of renting an apartment and buying a house.
- describe in detail how to buy a car.
- outline the rights and responsibilities of a consumer.
- discuss federal government programs that might help you pay for a college education.

You Will Also Learn What Economics Has to Do With

- telephone swindlers.
- George Mason and Rosa Parks.
- Beanie Babies and tulips.

Economics Journal

Write out a list of the goods or services that you have purchased in the last month. Next to each item, identify whether you are currently pleased or disappointed that you purchased it. If you are disappointed, try to identify the reason you are disappointed.

SECTION 1 Buying Clothes

This section discusses some of the things you should keep in mind when you buy clothes. As you read this section, keep these key questions in mind:

- What are some of the trade-offs involved in buying clothes?
- Can a person shop too long for clothes?

MINI GLOSSARY

trade-off: A balancing of factors that are not all available at the same time. The nature of a trade-off is that one must give up one thing that is desirable to get something else that is desirable.

Be Aware of Trade-Offs

Key Term

trade-off

When you buy clothes, it is important to be aware of dollar price and durability. *Durability* refers to how long the clothing item will remain in good condition. Sometimes the more durable an item is, the higher its price. Suppose you want to buy a shirt. You see two shirts that appeal to you. One is priced at $30 and the other at $40. If you buy the $30 shirt, you may not get the durability you could get with the $40 shirt. For example, the $40 shirt may be made of a stronger, more durable cloth than the $30 shirt and thus last longer.

A person buying clothes should think about more than simply price. Durability is important, as are other qualities. In short, there are **trade-offs** to be considered.

You probably would not expect $50 shoes to be as durable as $75 shoes. Is there a trade-off here?

You might not be able to get the service you want at a price you are willing to pay. Which would be more important to you, service or price?

Different Places to Shop

Today, we can buy clothes in a variety of places that differ in terms of selection, price, quality, and service. For example, consider both the upscale department store and the manufacturer's outlet. In the upscale department store, you will likely find high-quality clothing items at relatively high prices with good to excellent service. At the manufacturer's outlet you will find many items of the same quality at lower prices with little service. You have to be aware of the price you pay for the service and decide whether the service is worth this price.

Cartoon by Randy Glasbergen, © 2000

"They've made online shopping so much like the real thing, after visiting 20 stores I'm exhausted and my feet hurt!"

Suppose the same shirt can be purchased in an upscale department store and a manufacturer's outlet. At the department store it is priced at $40, and at the outlet, at $32. You need to decide whether buying the shirt in the upscale department store with the good service (and fashionable displays, a generally nice atmosphere, and close proximity to other stores and places to eat) is worth $8 to you. Maybe it is worth it; you must decide once you know how much you pay for the extras.

Can a Person Shop Too Long?

An economist would never advise you to shop for clothes for as long as it takes to find exactly what you want at the lowest possible price. Some comparison shopping is good, but too much can be costly for you in terms of what else you could be doing.

To illustrate, suppose it is Monday afternoon, and you want to do two things before Tuesday morning: buy a pair of shoes and study for your English test. You shop for the shoes first, going from store to store to find the "perfect" shoes. It is getting late, but you have not yet found the perfect shoes. You continue to search. Finally, hours later, you find the perfect shoes, purchase them, and rush home to study. However, you do not end up studying as long as you needed to, so you get a lower grade than you would have if you had studied longer. Was getting the lower grade worth getting the perfect shoes? Or would an average pair of shoes and a higher grade have been better?

Would you shop as long as necessary to find the "perfect" item? Why or why not?

Section 1 Review

Defining Terms

1. Define
   a. trade-off

Applying Economic Concepts

2. "It is always better to buy a cheaper shirt than a more expensive one." Do you agree or disagree? Explain your answer.
3. The same shirt can be purchased for $40 in an upscale store and for $25 at a manufacturer's outlet. Is it necessarily better to buy the shirt at the manufacturer's outlet?
4. "You should always shop until you find exactly what you are looking for at the lowest possible price." Do you agree or disagree? Explain your answer.

SECTION 2 Food

Food buying involves many decisions and strategies. This section discusses a few of them. As you read this section, keep these key questions in mind:

- From what types of stores do people buy food?
- What is impulse buying, and how can people guard against it?
- How is unit price computed?
- What is the difference between national brands, private brands, and generic brands?

Key Terms

impulse buying
unit price
national brand
private brand
generic brand

Where to Shop

People buy food from three principal types of stores: supermarkets, discount warehouse food stores, and convenience stores.

Is there a trade-off between buying food at a supermarket and at a discount warehouse food store?

Supermarket The supermarket is where most people buy their food. Supermarkets often run "specials" on certain products. There may be a special on a particular soft drink this week and a special on tomatoes next week. Supermarkets in an area often differ in the prices they charge for specific items. A loaf of brand X bread may be $1.25 at one supermarket and $1.55 at the supermarket down the road. Therefore, it is a good idea to make a list of the food items you buy on a regular weekly basis and check the prices at different supermarkets to find out which gives you the lowest weekly total for the same quality of service and convenience.

Discount Warehouse Food Store Discount warehouse food stores do not usually carry as large a variety of foods as supermarkets, but they do sell most items for less. Also, they tend to sell things in large quantities. For example, whereas you can buy a 1-pound jar of mayonnaise at a supermarket, you can buy a 5-pound jar of mayonnaise at a discount warehouse food store at a lower price per pound. Of course, the

impulse buying
Buying goods that one did not intend to buy. The impulse to buy something strikes quickly, and the consumer reacts by buying it.

unit price
The total price of an item divided by its weight.

5-pound jar may not be your best buy if you normally use only a small amount of mayonnaise. It might become spoiled or rancid and thus be a waste of money.

Convenience Store Convenience stores, such as 7-Eleven and Quik-Stop, are prominent in the U.S. landscape. Most are open twenty-four hours a day. They charge more than supermarkets, and they do not carry as large a selection. But for some people, what they lack in selection and price, they make up for in convenience. Do you need to pick up a few food items in a hurry? The nearest convenience store could be your best bet.

Make a Prediction

Chapter 1 discussed the economic concept of *opportunity cost.* Would a person be more likely to buy a quart of milk and a loaf of bread from a convenience store instead of a regular supermarket when the opportunity cost of time is relatively high or relatively low? Explain your answer.

What to Consider While Shopping

You should think about a number of things while you are shopping at the supermarket. These considerations are explored next.

Pitfalls of Shopping without a List and When Hungry You are walking down a supermarket aisle when you notice a brand of cookies that was recently advertised on television. You think, "They look good," and toss them into your basket. Going food shopping without a written list of things to buy often leads to this sort of **impulse buying** (buying what you did not plan to buy). Writing out a list takes time and thought, but it can cut down on impulse buying and thus help you get some control over your food budget. A list can also help if you are trying to cut down on buying junk food, which you are more likely to buy when you do not make and follow a list.

Making a shopping list can help cut down on the amount of junk food you buy.

It is also a good idea to do your food shopping on a full stomach. If you are hungry, many foods will look good to you, and you may end up buying more than you should.

Unit Price Your supermarket offers two sizes of the same laundry detergent, one small (40 ounces) and the other large (120 ounces). The small one is priced at \$1.97, and the large one at \$5.45. To compute the **unit price**—the price per ounce, in this case—you need to divide the price of each item by its weight.

$$\text{Unit price} = \frac{\text{Price}}{\text{Weight}}$$

In this case, the small size costs 4.9 cents per ounce, while the large size costs 4.5 cents per ounce. Many supermarkets list the unit price, along with the total price for a product. If your supermarket does not, you may want to carry a calculator to compute unit prices.

Exhibit 20-1
Calculating Unit Price

To make the best buying decisions, you often need to determine unit prices for two or more packages of the same type of good. You can do this easily by dividing the price by the unit of measurement.

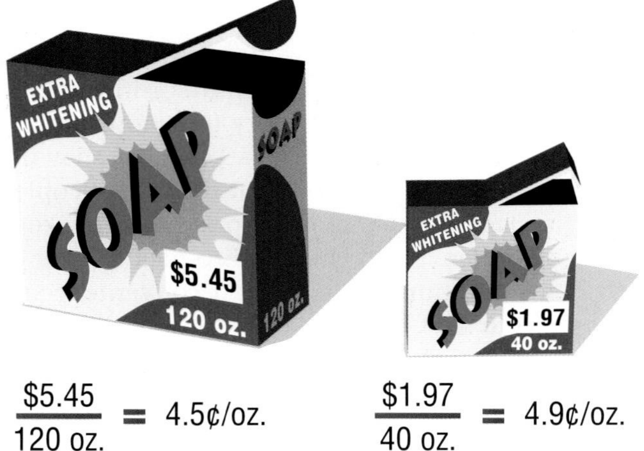

$\frac{\$5.45}{120 \text{ oz.}} = 4.5¢/\text{oz.}$ $\frac{\$1.97}{40 \text{ oz.}} = 4.9¢/\text{oz.}$

Coupons Food coupons often appear in newspapers, magazines, and shopping circulars. Using them can lower your grocery bill. Keep in mind, though, that a time cost is involved in clipping the coupons out of the newspaper and gathering them before your shopping trip. You have to decide whether having a lower grocery bill is worth spending this time.

National Brands, Private Brands, and Generic Brands Products in food stores may carry national brand names, private brand names, or generic brand names. A **national brand** is a brand name owned by the maker of a product. Many national brands are known across the country, such as Kellogg's and Coca-Cola. A **private brand** is a brand name often produced for a specific supermarket chain and includes the name of that

national brand A brand name that is owned by the maker of a product. Many national brands are known across the country, such as Kellogg's and Coca-Cola.

private brand A brand name owned by a seller rather than by the maker of the product. For example, products are often produced for a specific supermarket chain and carry the name of that chain on the label.

generic brand A brand name that does not use the name of any company; it uses only the product name.

Coupon shopping can save money but cost additional time. What would be more important to you, saving money or saving time?

chain. A **generic brand** is simply a brand name that identifies the product (for example, "Corn Flakes"). National brands are more expensive than private brands, and private brands are more expensive than generic brands.

Should you try a private-brand product or a generic-brand product? Many people think these brands are worth a try. National-brand products have instant name recognition, usually because they have been widely advertised on television. Often, however, they are no better in quality and taste than the private-brand or generic-brand products.

A Quick Review of Food Selections before the Checkout Line It is a good idea to quickly look over the food selections in your cart before you enter the checkout line. Nutritionists say that to maintain a good diet we should regularly eat lots of grains, fruits, and vegetables. If you find that most of the items in your grocery cart are snacks, you may decide that for your health you should exchange potato chips for fresh fruit or ice cream for yogurt.

Name brands cost more than private brands and generic brands, but do they taste better?

Section 2 Review

Defining Terms

1. Define
   a. impulse buying
   b. unit price
   c. national brand
   d. private brand
   e. generic brand

Applying Economic Concepts

2. You are deciding whether to buy food from a discount warehouse food store or a supermarket. What is the trade-off in terms of price and variety?
3. How can you cut down on impulse buying?
4. The large size of brand X detergent is priced at $6.25 and contains 150 ounces. The small size is priced at $1.50 and contains 30 ounces. What is the unit price for each size?
5. "Coupons may lower the dollar price of food but increase the time cost of shopping for food." Do you agree or disagree? Explain your answer.

SECTION 3

Telemarketing

Each day in the United States, thousands of telephone calls are made in attempts to sell something. Direct sales of products by telephone is called **telemarketing.** Some of the offers are legitimate, whereas others are not. It is important to be able to separate the two.

As you read this section, keep these key questions in mind:

- What are the signs of telemarketing fraud?
- What are the signs that a telemarketing salesperson is trying to swindle you?

Identifying Telemarketing Fraud

Key Term

telemarketing

When dealing with telemarketers, companies that sell products or services over the telephone, you should be alert to identify telemarketing fraud. You can spot phone swindlers in the following ways:

MINI GLOSSARY

telemarketing
Direct sales of products by telephone.

1. *Telephone swindlers are likely to know more about you than you know about them.* Where did the phone caller get your name and telephone number? If the telephone book was the source, the caller may not know much about you. But if your name and number came from a company that sells mailing lists, the caller may know such personal information as your age, income, and occupation. Telephone callers may tailor their comments to what they know about you in an attempt to hold your interest and perhaps gain your trust.
2. *Telephone swindlers will say anything to get a sale.* They are always ready with an answer. Don't assume that every telephone salesperson is as honest as you are. Telephone swindlers are often coached to misrepresent the truth in order to make a sale. Furthermore, they are often coached to sound believable.
3. *Telephone swindlers often sound as if they work for legitimate businesses.* Good telephone swindlers do not sound like telephone swindlers. In a polished presentation they tell you about their company, how many employees work for the company, and so on. In fact, they may tell you so many details about the company that you are convinced that they could not be making it up. However,

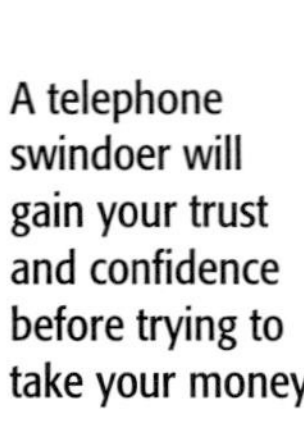

A telephone swindoer will gain your trust and confidence before trying to take your money.

The U.S. Postal Service has a Web site at which it discusses telemarketing fraud. (http://www.usps.gov/websites/depart/inspect/fonetact.htm). According to the U.S. Postal Service, if you think you have been taken advantage of by a telemarketer, what should you do?

they could indeed be lying; they may have told the same lies a hundred times before they called you. If they sound believable, it may be because they have had a lot of practice.

4. *Telephone swindlers often advertise in reputable magazines.* You may read an advertisement for a product in a magazine. You return the attached postcard to request "additional information." Days later, you receive a telephone call. Do not assume that because you requested the information, the person calling is representing a legitimate business. Many telephone swindlers will imitate the marketing practices of legitimate businesses by advertising in reputable publications.
5. *Victims of telephone fraud rarely get their money back.* You may realize that you have been swindled and try to get your money back, but usually your efforts will be of little use. Even if regulatory bodies and law enforcement agencies get involved, you are not likely to get your money back, because the telephone swindlers will have probably spent the money already.

Telephone Tactics of Swindlers

Not every person involved in telemarketing sales is a crook. However, the following are some telltale signs of a telemarketing swindler:

1. *High-pressure sales tactics.* The call may begin politely enough, but if the caller senses that you are not eager to buy, he or she may try to pressure you into buying. Legitimate salespersons, on the other hand, respect your right to be uninterested in what they have to sell.

You have the right to say, "No, thank you," to a telemarketer and then to hang up.

Financial Scams

One week, Alice Lakeland received a letter from Jay Quentin, a financial adviser who owned his own company. The letter said that Quentin had an excellent record of predicting whether the price of gold would go up or down. In the letter to Lakeland, he predicted that by week's end, the price of gold would have risen. The end of the week came, and sure enough the price of gold had risen.

For each of the next five weeks, Lakeland received a letter from Quentin in which he correctly predicted the change in the price of gold.

In the seventh week Lakeland received another letter from Quentin, but this time there was no prediction. He wrote that he had proved he could correctly predict the direction of the price of gold and that for $500, he would send her his financial newsletter each week for the next thirty months. The newsletter would make weekly predictions about the direction for the price of gold. He told Lakeland that she would soon become rich by buying gold before its price rose and then selling it before its price fell. Buy low, sell high—that is the way to make tremendous profits, he said.

Lakeland sent Quentin a check for $500. She wondered how she could lose. After all, the man was always right. She would simply read the newsletter, and if it said the price of gold was going to rise, she would buy gold. Then, after the price had risen, she would sell the gold and take her profits. It would be easy, wouldn't it?

Not exactly. Quentin was running a scam (a fraudulent scheme). In the first week, he sent out letters to 5,000 people. In 2,500 of the 5,000 letters, he predicted that the price of gold would rise; and in the remaining 2,500 letters, he predicted that the price of gold would fall. At the end of the first week, when Quentin learned that the price of gold had risen, he took the names of the 2,500 people he had told that the price would rise and sent them another letter. To all 2,500 people, he pointed out that his first prediction had been correct. To 1,250 of them, he again predicted that the price of gold would rise. To the remaining 1,250, he predicted that the price would fall. The price of gold had risen by week's end.

Quentin repeated the procedure for four more weeks. Lakeland happened to be one of the people who received a correct "prediction" from Quentin for six consecutive weeks. The only problem, of course, was that Quentin was not really predicting.

Consumer beware: What looks like a special ability to predict the future may be something quite different. Looks can be deceiving.

Furthermore, consumers may actually want to believe things that seem too good to be true. In our story, Lakeland might have wanted to believe that Quentin had some special talent or gift for predicting the direction of the price of gold. If he did, perhaps she could become rich—and she might have wanted that very badly. Con artists know that a person's wish to become rich, beautiful, or smart often works to a swindler's advantage. It is when you want something badly that you are most vulnerable to the words and actions of others.

QUESTION TO ANSWER An astrologer writes, "In March, someone you know will bring you happiness." How is this like or unlike the scam that Jay Quentin was running?

Telemarketers often call at inconvienient times or when you are distracted.

2. *Insistence on an immediate decision.* Sometimes telemarketers will say "there are only a few left" in order to get you to make a fast decision. Be wary of this tactic. Telephone swindlers do not want you to have time to think through what they have told you or to check with others.
3. *An offer that sounds too good to be true.* If the offer of a telemarketer sounds too good to be true, you have to wonder why someone has to call you on the telephone to offer it. Be careful, though. Many telephone swindlers are getting more sophisticated. Instead of making their offers sound "too good to be true," they are making the offers sound more realistic.
4. *Unwillingness to provide written information or references (such as the names of satisfied customers in your area) for you to contact.* Telephone swindlers usually have a list of reasons why they cannot provide you with written information or references. They may say, "The written material hasn't been published yet," or "Giving out the names of satisfied customers is unethical."
5. *A request for your credit card number.* Telephone swindlers will often ask for your credit card number for identification or verification purposes. Be wary of giving out your credit card number over the telephone, especially if you do not know the company. If you do give out the number, you can have the charge removed from your credit card bill if you do not receive the goods or services or if your order was obtained through misrepresentation or fraud. You must notify the credit card company in writing, at its billing inquiries/disputes address, within sixty days after the charge first appears on your bill.

Section 3 Review

Defining Terms

1. Define
   a. telemarketing

Applying Economic Concepts

2. What are two tip-offs that a telemarketing caller may be trying to swindle you?
3. How should you go about having a credit card charge that was made through misrepresentation or fraud removed from your credit card bill?
4. If a telemarketer's offer sounds too good to be true, what should you think?

SECTION 4

Housing

This section discusses the types of housing and what is involved in renting or buying an apartment or house. As you read this section, keep these key questions in mind:

- What is a security deposit?
- How can you find out the crime rate in the area in which you are planning to live?
- What kinds of things are involved in buying and financing a house?
- Taking out a loan to buy a house often involves paying points. What are points?
- What is the difference between a fixed-rate loan and an adjustable-rate loan?

There are different types of housing: apartments, manufactured homes, condominiums and single-family homes.

Types of Housing

Key Terms

security deposit
lease
subleasing
down payment
mortgage note
point

Different types of housing are available, including apartments, manufactured homes (mobile homes), condominiums, and single-family homes.

Apartments An apartment is a room or suite of rooms in which to live. A number of apartments together make up an apartment building or apartment house. Most people who live in apartments rent them on a six-month or one-year basis, although it is sometimes possible to rent from month to month. A person who rents an apartment is usually required to pay the rent for the first and last months up front and to put down a **security deposit** before actually taking up residence in the apartment.

Manufactured Homes A manufactured home, or mobile home, is a movable dwelling with no permanent foundation; it is connected to utility lines and set more or less permanently at one location. Today it is more accurate to call these dwellings *manufactured homes,* because most of them are never moved. Manufactured homes are built in a factory in sections, towed to the homesite, and then assembled.

Condominiums A condominium is a single unit in a multiunit building or complex. Condominiums may be built either upon each other (going up) or side by side (going to the left and right). Condominiums built side by side often have front yards and backyards. A condominium owner holds full title to the unit and also owns a proportionate share in common areas, such as recreational facilities and grounds.

security deposit An amount of money a renter pays a landlord before moving into an apartment (or other rental property). The money is to be returned when the renter moves out, but the landlord may keep a part or all of it to make repairs or compensate for rent not paid.

Single-Family Homes A single-family home is a dwelling that is separate from dwellings around it and is located on a lot that surrounds the dwelling on all sides.

Renting an Apartment

Many young adults rent apartments. Here are some things to consider if you are thinking of renting an apartment in the near future.

Would living near school or work be important to you? Why?

Location Most people consider it important to rent an apartment near their workplaces or schools. A convenient location cuts down on transportation costs.

Neighbors As a renter of an apartment, you will likely have a common wall with neighbors on both sides. If you live in a multistory apartment complex, your ceiling may be someone else's floor, and your floor may be someone else's ceiling. In many cases, you will hear the noises made by your close neighbors; for example, someone in the apartment above you may play his CD player loudly when you are trying to sleep.

For this reason, it is important to know something about the people who will be your close neighbors before you move into an apartment. Simply asking the apartment manager to tell you about your neighbors may yield information. If quiet is particularly important to you, you should tell the apartment manager, who then may be more likely to rent you an apartment among some of the quieter tenants.

Making sure in advance that safety features such as smoke detectors and fire escapes are in proper working condition could save your life.

Safety Features Before you rent an apartment, make sure the apartment complex has fire escapes, smoke detectors, and safe stairs. Also important are such safety features as good lighting outside, good locks on the doors and windows, and no large shrubbery near windows where people can hide.

Crime in the Area You may want to know the amount and nature of crime in the area where an apartment is located. The local police department will usually provide this information.

As the crime rate in an area rises, do you think the rent for an apartment is likely to rise or fall? Explain your answer.

Common Areas Most apartment complexes have common areas—areas that are shared by the tenants, such as a common television area, recreational facilities, or meeting rooms. Check the condition of common areas. You may not want to live in an apartment complex that does not keep these areas in good repair.

lease
A contract that conveys property (such as an apartment) for a specific time period for a fee.

sublease
To rent out an apartment when one is a renter rather than the owner.

Lease A **lease** is a contract that specifies the terms under which property is rented. The lease sets the rent for a period of time. The apartment owner or manager will ask you to sign a lease. Read it carefully—every word. Leases often contain formal language that you might find difficult to understand if you have not read many leases before. If you do not understand the terms of the lease, ask the apartment owner or manager to carefully explain them to you. If you do not believe that the apartment manager will correctly explain the lease, seek out a friend, relative, or attorney.

All leases should indicate the following:

1. The amount of monthly rent and the date it is due.
2. The amount of the late fee (penalty) for turning in your rent after it is due.
3. The amount of the security deposit and the conditions under which it will be returned.
4. Who pays for utilities (electricity and water), repairs, insurance, and so on.
5. Conditions under which a tenant may be evicted, or legally forced to leave. (For example, tenants may be evicted for making too much noise or for **subleasing** the apartment—that is, renting the apartment to someone else.)
6. Conditions under which the lease can be renewed. (For example, will it be renewed at the same rent, or will the rate be renegotiated?)

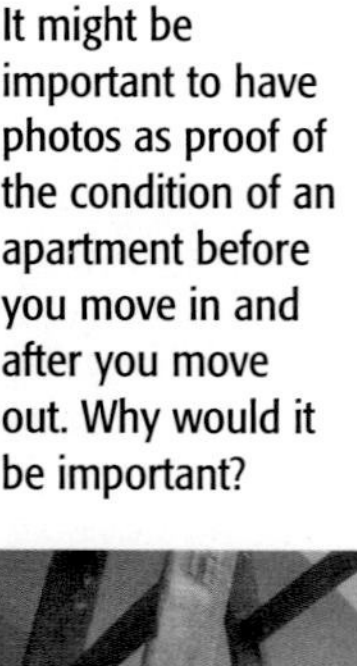

A lease should spell out who is responsible to pay for utilities and repairs to the apartment.

It might be important to have photos as proof of the condition of an apartment before you move in and after you move out. Why would it be important?

Condition of the Apartment Before you accept an apartment and begin paying rent, carefully inspect the premises with the owner or manager. If things need to be fixed (such as a shower rod or stove), urge the owner or manager to fix them promptly, and ask the manager to state in the lease that the repair will be made by a specified date. It is also a good idea to take a few pictures of the inside of the apartment before you move in (as well as after you move out). Get the pictures developed by a company that prints the date on photos. The photos can be important if, after you move out, you and the apartment owner or manager disagree on the state of the apartment when you moved in or out. Without photos, you may find that you get back less of your security deposit than you think you should.

Buying a Single-Family Home

Buying a single-family home will probably be the largest single purchase you ever make. Here are some things to do and know.

Spending the time and money necessary to have a house inspected before buying can prevent problems in the future.

Real Estate Broker Most home buyers seek out a real estate broker to help them locate a suitable house. If you are looking for a house, the broker will ask you the type of house you want to buy (number of bedrooms, size of lot, and so on), your price range, and other information. The broker will then take you around to look at the houses for sale that may suit you. As the buyer of a house, you do not pay the real estate broker a fee; the fee is paid by the seller of the house. The broker's fee amounts to 3 to 6 percent of the price of the home. For example, if you buy a house for $110,000 and the broker's fee is 6 percent, the broker receives $6,600 ($\$110{,}000 \times 0.06 = \$6{,}600$).

House Inspection If you are like most people, when you enter a house you may notice the size of the rooms, the color of the carpets, and the number of windows. The house may have a particularly attractive staircase that you marvel about or large windows that allow in plenty of sunlight. Outside, you may notice how big the backyard is and what the neighborhood is like. But you may not have the expertise to determine such things as whether the house has termites or is solidly built.

Many house buyers like to hire a house inspector to check the house they are thinking about buying. Suppose you do this and learn that the house you want to buy has a plumbing problem. You then may offer to buy the house only on the condition that the seller correct this problem. Your real estate broker will inform the seller of this condition.

Real Estate Agent

A real estate agent or real estate broker matches home buyers with sellers, assists in finding mortgage lenders, and handles the paperwork necessary. Most real estate agents and brokers sell residential property (houses). A few, usually in large firms or small specialized firms, sell commercial, industrial, agricultural, or other types of properties.

An agent works with prospective home buyers to locate properties that fit the needs of the customers at prices they can afford. When someone wants to sell a house, the agent figures out the market price of the house (market conditions change), advertises it, and finds potential buyers.

In every state, real estate agents must be licensed, must be high school graduates, be at least eighteen years old, and pass a written examination on real estate transactions and laws. Most states require between sixty and ninety hours of classroom instruction as well. To prepare for a career as a real estate agent today, it is a good idea to obtain a college degree in business administration and take courses in real estate, business law, finance, economics, statistics, computer science, and English.

QUESTION TO ANSWER Some say that a real estate agent or broker is simply a "middleman" who brings buyers and sellers together and doesn't really produce anything. They claim that agents or brokers do not provide a valuable service. Do you agree or disagree? Explain your answer.

The Down Payment The **down payment** is the amount of money a person pays at the time of purchase toward the price of a house. The difference between the down payment and the purchase price is the amount the person needs to borrow to purchase the house. For example, suppose the price of a house is $110,000, and the down payment is $20,000. The loan amount is then $90,000. In return for the loan, the borrower signs a **mortgage note,** a written agreement to repay the loan. Each month the borrower makes a mortgage payment to the lender.

Writing a check for the down payment on a house can be both exciting and frightening. Explain.

Costs to Consider When Buying a House The down payment is not the only cost of buying a house. Some of the additional costs are as follows:

1. *Closing costs.* Closing costs are costs incurred in transferring property (the house and lot) from one person to another. They include such things as a fee for a title search (to make sure the property really belongs to the person who is selling it), a fee for house inspection, and a loan application fee. A major component of the closing costs are points (see below).
2. *Points.* When a person takes out a loan to buy a house, the lender usually charges **points.** For example, a loan for $90,000 may come with 2 points. Each point amounts to 1 percent of the loan, so 2 points on a $90,000 loan equal $1,800. The borrower pays this amount to the lender. Lenders charge points when they believe the interest rate they are charging for the loan may turn out to be too low to allow them to make a profit. It is typical for lenders to charge between 1 and 4 points.
3. *Real estate (or property) taxes.* Homeowners have to pay real estate (or property) taxes each year on their homes. Much of the tax money goes to finance public education. Different localities set different real estate tax rates. For example, a locality may charge 1 percent of the market price of the house: if the market price is $200,000, the real estate taxes are $2,000 each year.
4. *Homeowner's insurance.* A person who owns a home will want to insure it against theft and fire. Depending on where the home is located, the homeowner may also purchase insurance against hurricanes, tornadoes, or earthquakes.

In some parts of the United States, it is necessary to have insurance against hurricanes, tornadoes, and earthquakes. Do you live in one of these areas?

MINI GLOSSARY

down payment Cash paid at the time of a purchase, with the rest of the purchase price to be paid later.

mortgage note A written agreement by which a buyer of property agrees to repay a loan taken out to purchase the property. If the loan is not repaid, the lender can take the property.

point One percentage point of a loan amount. Points are paid by the borrower to the lender.

5. *Mortgage insurance.* A lender often requires a borrower to buy mortgage insurance, especially if the down payment is less than 20 percent of the purchase price of the home. Mortgage insurance insures the lender against a loss if the borrower does not pay back the loan.
6. *Mortgage life insurance.* Some home buyers purchase mortgage life insurance so that if they die, their mortgage loans will be paid off. For example, suppose a husband and wife borrow $90,000 to buy a house. The wife is working, and the husband is attending school. Each month, the wife meets the monthly mortgage payment out of her salary. The couple decides to buy mortgage life insurance so that if the wife dies, the insurance company will pay the full amount of the loan.
7. *Utilities.* A homeowner must pay for electricity, water, garbage pickup, heat, and air-conditioning.
8. *Miscellaneous costs.* Most first-time home buyers do not have everything they will need to make the house livable. For example, they may need to buy furniture, curtains, and a refrigerator.

Utility costs, such as trash pickup, are in addition to the cost of the home.

Taking Out a Loan

Interest Rates A lender that lends money to a borrower charges an interest rate. For example, suppose Jim takes out a simple loan for one year. The loan amount is $1,000, and the interest rate charged for the loan is 10 percent. Jim's interest payment is $100. The interest payment is computed by multiplying the amount Jim borrows times the interest rate: Obviously, the higher the interest rate, the higher the interest payments.

$$\text{Interest payment} = \text{Amount borrowed} \times \text{Interest rate}$$

Thus, people who are borrowing money to buy houses are interested not only in the price of the houses but also in the interest rates. Often, when interest rates are dropping, home sales pick up; and when interest rates are rising, home sales slow down or drop. When interest rates are dropping, people realize that they will have to pay less to borrow the money to buy a house, so they are more likely to want to buy a house. But when interest rates are rising, people realize that they will have to pay more to borrow the money and they are less likely to want to purchase a house.

In addition to the interest rate, home buyers must consider two other things. First, how long do they have to pay off the loan? Second, will the interest rate change during this time? We consider these issues next.

Time Period Lenders usually allow borrowers fifteen or thirty years to pay off their mortgage loans. Most borrowers choose thirty years.

Interest Rate Change Mortgage loans may be fixed-rate loans or adjustable-rate loans. On a fixed-rate loan, the interest rate stays the same

Most borrowers choose to pay off a house loan over thirty years. Why wouldn't they choose to pay it off in fifteen years?

over the entire period of the loan. For example, you might hear of a "9 percent, fixed-rate, thirty-year loan." The interest rate on the loan is fixed at 9 percent for all thirty years. On an adjustable-rate loan, the interest may change, but it can go up only to some ceiling level. For example, a person may have an adjustable-rate loan starting at an interest rate of "6 percent, with a ceiling cap of 12 percent, for thirty years." Here, the borrower begins paying off the loan at an interest rate of 6 percent. The interest rate may rise as high as 12 percent, but no higher, during the thirty-year period. (Adjustments in the interest rate may be made after a period of months or years, depending on the specification of the lender and the acceptance of the borrower.)

Lenders who offer adjustable-rate loans cannot simply choose any interest rate they wish. Rates are ultimately governed by a particular economic index. For example, a lender may tie the interest rate to the interest rate the federal government pays people who buy U.S. Treasury bonds. If the interest rate on U.S. Treasury bonds rises, so does the interest rate on the loan.

Is it better to get a loan with a fixed interest rate or an adjustable interest rate? The answer depends on the individual obtaining the loan. A fixed rate offers more certainty, because the person knows exactly what the interest payments will be for the duration of the loan. An adjustable-rate loan, however, usually comes with a lower initial interest rate. For example, suppose you want to borrow $90,000 for thirty years. The lender may offer you (1) a fixed-rate loan at 9 percent or (2) an adjustable-rate loan starting at 5 percent with a cap of 12 percent. You may find it worthwhile to choose the adjustable-rate loan if you cannot currently afford the payments at a 9 percent interest rate. Understand, though, that your adjustable rate may rise from 5 percent and make it difficult for you to make your payments.

Economics and the Internet

Numerous calculators are available online. For example, if you want to calculate your mortgage payments for a house loan, go to Bloomberg.com (http://www.bloomberg.com/welcome.html). Once there, click on "mortgage calculator." Suppose you borrow $150,000 at an interest rate of 7.00 percent. What is your monthly mortgage payment?

Section 4 Review

Defining Terms

1. Define
   a. security deposit
   b. lease
   c. down payment
   d. mortgage note
   e. points
   f. sublease

Applying Economic Concepts

2. Name five safety features you should check before renting an apartment.
3. How would you determine the crime rate in the area in which you plan to rent an apartment?
4. The broker's fee is between ___ and ___ percent of the sales price of a home.
5. Carmen takes out a simple loan for one year. The loan amount is $5,000, and the interest rate is 5 percent. How much is her interest payment?
6. What is the difference between a fixed-rate loan and an adjustable-rate loan?

SECTION 5

Buying a Car

There are 571 cars per every 1,000 persons in the United States—1 car for every 1.75 persons. This section discusses the details involved in buying a car.

As you read this section, keep these key questions in mind:

- What is lowballing? Highballing?
- Where can you find out the value of a used car?
- What is the difference between a warranty and a service contract?
- Where can a person buy a car other than from a car dealership?

What to Consider When Buying a Car

Key Term

warranty

Before you buy a car, you should carefully think about and research many things, as described here.

Think about the Type of Car You Want before You Go Shopping It is a good idea to think about the type of car you want before you set out to shop for one. Otherwise, a salesperson may sell you a car that does not really meet your needs—perhaps one that costs too much, is not fuel efficient, or does not have the safety features you want. If you like to window-shop for cars before you start talking to a salesperson, then tell the salesperson that you are only looking so you can walk around the lot viewing cars at your leisure. Study the April issue of *Consumer Reports*, a consumer publication that tests and rates products, before setting out to shop for a car. It is full of information about new cars that relates to safety, maintenance, fuel economy, and so on. Some people take their April *Consumer Reports* with them to car dealerships so the car salespersons will know that they have done their homework and are serious about getting a good car at a reasonable price.

Doing some homework, such as checking *Consumer Reports*, before buying a car can help make the experience more satisfying.

Investigate the Competition Suppose you have decided that you want to buy a Ford. If there are two Ford dealerships in your town, you may want to visit both of them instead of only one. Two dealerships then may compete for your business, perhaps by offering you a better price or more features on the car.

Watch Out for Certain Sales Tactics Some car salespersons practice what is known as *lowballing* by quoting an unusually low price to get you interested. Later, when you sit down to do business, they say they made a "mistake" and forgot to include some costs, or their managers won't let them sell the car for that price, or something of the sort. Lowballing is most often used by salespersons who think you are only shopping around right now and are also going to look around at other car dealerships. They want you to remember their "low price" as you shop around, and they hope that the price they quoted will bring you back, as it often does.

Also watch out for *highballing*. Here, salespersons promise you an unusually high price for a trade-in (the used car you give in partial payment for the car you are buying). Later, they say that the car has been checked out and is not really worth as much as they thought.

Check to see that the car you want to purchase has all of the safety features you need for the type of driving you do.

Salespersons often try to find out what a person does for a living. For example, a salesperson who learns that a customer is a physician may be less likely to bargain on price on the assumption that physicians are wealthy. If you are a teenager looking for a car, the salesperson might ask you what your parents do for a living.

Salespersons may also try to find out where you live. If you live nearby, they may be less likely to offer you a lower price than if you live farther away. The farther away you live, the less likely it is that you will return after shopping around.

Finally, if you are a teenager seeking to buy a car, watch out for intimidating sales tactics. Salespersons may think they can take advantage of you because they are older and because this is the first time you have bought a car. Remember, though, that you are the customer, and you are in charge. The salesperson wants your business. Do not act intimidated (even if you

Car salesmen sell cars everyday, but most shoppers buy new cars only once every few years. Who do you think would be the most skillful in negotiating a deal?

feel that way), and do not be afraid to walk out of the car dealership at any time. There are other places you can buy a car.

Your Attitude Matters When you are talking to a salesperson about a car, your attitude matters. If you act thrilled at seeing exactly the car you have always wanted, the salesperson is not very likely to lower the price. If you act as if you could take the car or leave it, you are in a better position. Thus, do not give the impression that there is only one car in the world for you. Let the salesperson know that you are shopping around, and maybe that you are not quite sure you are going to buy a car right now. You want your attitude to say to the salesperson, "If you want my business, you're going to have to give me a fair deal."

Determine the Wholesale Price (Dealer Cost) of the Car You Want to Buy Some newsstands carry publications that list the wholesale price, or dealer cost, of most makes of cars. This information is also available on the Internet. Find out what the wholesale price is for the car you want to buy. If you cannot find the information, you can make a reasonable guess by discounting the sticker price of the car by 10 to 15 percent. Knowing the wholesale price of a car lets you know how much negotiating room you and the dealer have.

Know the Worth of a Trade-In You may have an old car that you want to trade in when you buy your new car. To find out its value, look in the *Kelley Blue Book Market Report.* Car dealerships have this information, but they will not give it to you. Banks, credit unions, and libraries usually carry the *Blue Book* and will let you see it. You can also find it on the Internet. Remember that it is advisable to make the best deal you can on a new car before discussing the possibility of making a trade-in.

Drive the Car Make sure you drive the car you are thinking about buying. Test-drive it without using the radio or air conditioner, which can

You can find out what the dealer pays for a car and what your trade in is worth on the Internet.

sometimes mask car sounds of which you need to be aware. Salespersons often accompany you on a test-drive and talk to you while you're driving. If you want to drive in silence so you can hear the car, tell them so.

warranty
A guarantee or assurance given by a seller stating that a product is in good working order and that the seller will provide certain types of service for a period of time.

The Warranty New cars, as well as some used cars, come with warranties. A **warranty** is a guarantee or an assurance given by a seller stating that a product is in good working order. It may also state that the seller will provide certain types of service for a period of time. For example, a car seller may provide a warranty specifying that if anything goes wrong with the engine in the next five years, the seller will fix it free of charge.

Read the warranty carefully. Know what it covers and what it doesn't cover. If you have questions about specifics, be sure to ask.

It is important to know what the warranty says, so make sure to ask about it and to read it carefully. If you have any problems in getting the car seller to live by the words of the warranty, you may have to call the manufacturer's representative in your area. The telephone number should be in your car manual. If you are still unsatisfied, call company headquarters, and talk with someone in customer service.

Service Contracts Service contracts, which you may buy with a new car, provide for the repair of certain parts or problems. Service contracts are usually offered by car manufacturers or car dealerships. Remember, you already have a warranty with a new car, so you need to find out what the service contract provides that the warranty does not. Keep the following questions in mind when considering whether to buy a service contract:

1. What is the difference between the coverage under the warranty and the coverage under the service contract?
2. What repairs are covered?
3. Who pays for the labor? The parts?
4. Who performs the repairs?
5. How long does the service contract last?
6. What is the policy on cancellation and refund?

Your car dealership's service department might not give you the best deal on repairs. It might pay to check around.

Financing a Car If you decide to borrow money to finance a new-car purchase, be sure to compare the interest rate the car dealership offers you with the rates offered by banks, credit unions, and savings and loan institutions. Interest rates on car loans vary, so shop around for the best rate. Keep in mind that car dealerships sometimes offer very low interest rates on specific cars or models but may not be willing to negotiate on the price of these cars. Also, to qualify for the low interest rate, you may be required to make a large down payment. You may find that it is less expensive to pay the higher financing charges on a car that is lower in price or to purchase a car that requires a smaller down payment.

Technology & Innovation

Making Things Just For You

Once you know exactly what you want, you'll be able to get it that way. Computers will enable goods that today are mass produced to be both mass produced and custom-made for particular consumers.

—Bill Gates, cofounder of Microsoft Corporation

Henry Ford is often credited for introducing mass production to the United States. At his car assembly plant in Highland Park, Michigan, Model T cars rolled off the assembly line at a rate of one every twenty-four seconds. There was only one problem: every Model T was the same as every other Model T; they were all black. In fact, Henry Ford once said, "The consumer can have any color [Model T] he wants so long as it's black."

That world exists no more. Today's products come in a multitude of different designs and colors. For example, today the Ford Motor Company offers six models of its Explorer, each with choices of power train, exterior, interior, audio, wheels, tires, and other options. There are 2.5 million different combinations for the Explorer alone.

While the important thing in Henry Ford's time was mass production (producing a large quantity of a given good), today the important thing seems to be mass customization, or producing a large quantity of a good that has been individualized to meet a particular person's preferences. You can get an online newspaper easily customized for you, for example. If you are interested only in sports, health, and current events, you can have a newspaper produced for you that deals only with these topics. Alternatively, a newspaper that covers only sports, business, education, and lifestyle can be easily created thanks to the powerful search engine technology that now exists.

Consider the entertainment field. Online CD companies allow you to choose sound bites from over ten thousand titles and then choose a dozen or so "cuts" for a CD to be shipped to you.

Recent advances in biotechnology (most important, the cracking of the DNA code) allows physicians to individualize drugs and treatments for their patients. No doubt this will be even more common in the future. Once computers were mass produced, but today companies allow you to customize your computer with the hard drive capacity, processor speed, and size of monitor screen that you want.

Customization is prevalent today because technology has made it cheaper than in the past. For example, because search engine software can customize a newspaper for much less than a penny, there are many customized newspapers. Furthermore, computer-guided machinery today allows production to change from one style to another with only a change in a few lines of computer code. For example, at Motorola's pager factory in Florida, the specifications for different pagers can be translated into bar code instructions so the factory can turn out 29 million different pagers on the same production line without the expense of retooling.

Is customization the wave of the future? It certainly looks like recent advances have made it so.

QUESTION TO ANSWER What goods or services have you bought that were customized for you?

Buying a new car can be intimidating unless you have done your homework.

Leasing a Car Leasing a car has become popular in recent years. Whether it is better to buy or to lease depends on your preferences and circumstances. Some people do not have the purchase price of the car and therefore decide to lease it instead. Some people like to lease cars because they like to drive new cars every three years (most leases are three years long), and they do not want the inconvenience of selling one car and buying another every three years. Instead, they want to drive a new car for three years and then turn it in for another new car.

When deciding whether to lease or buy a car, you should first decide how long you plan to keep the car. If you plan to keep it more than three or four years, it is generally less expensive to buy the car.

The best course of action is to ask your car dealer how much it will cost to lease the car and how much it will cost to buy it. Once you have the real figures for both a lease and a purchase in front of you, you can make an informed decision.

Car-Buying Services and Automobile Brokers You are not limited to buying a car from a car dealership. You can go to a car-buying service or an automobile broker. For a fee, you can buy a new car from a car-buying service or an automobile broker at factory cost and save perhaps hundreds of dollars.[1] You may have to wait a month or two for your new car, but the wait may be worth the dollar savings. To find out about car-buying services and automobile brokers, consult the Yellow Pages of the telephone book or a credit union. In addition, the American Automobile Association (AAA), an automobile club, can help you contact a car-buying service or an automobile broker.

Buying a Used Car

A new car loses about 25 percent of its value the first year. Therefore, used cars are much less expensive than new cars. Buying a used car always involves some risk, however. The buyer usually does not know why the original owner sold or traded in the car. Was it because the owner wanted to buy a new car or because the car was always in the shop? You need to be especially careful if you are planning to buy a used car. Here are some things to keep in mind:

1. It is typical for an automobile broker to charge (as a fee) a percentage of the sales price or a flat fee, whichever is higher. For example, an automobile broker might charge 2.5 percent of the sales price of the car or a flat fee of $250, whichever is higher.

Beware when buying a used car. Sellers won't always tell you if a car has been in an accident.

1. Do not buy a used car that is no longer in production. It will be hard to get parts for the car.
2. Do not buy a used car without taking it for a test-drive.
3. Watch out for used cars that are loaded with options, such as power windows, power seats, and so on. Such things need replacing as a car gets older.
4. Find out if the used car you want to buy has been recalled. A manufacturer will recall a car model if it finds out something is wrong with it. The owners of the cars are notified of the recall and asked to bring their cars in to be fixed (at no charge). Almost half the owners do not respond to a recall, however, so a used car you want to buy might have been recalled but never fixed. To learn about recalls and other safety information, call the Department of Transportation Auto Safety Hotline at 1-800-424-9393.
5. Have an auto mechanic inspect a used car you are thinking about buying. This inspection is particularly important, because a $50 inspection fee may save you hundreds of dollars and endless problems later on. In addition, it may put your mind at ease.
6. Look for the Buyer's Guide sticker on the window of the used car. The sticker, which is required by the Federal Trade Commission, gives you important information on the car, such as whether it comes with a warranty and what major problems may occur in any used car.
7. Be alert to those things on the car that you can check. For example, are the tires slick, with very little tread? Are there oil spots under the car?

Section 5 Review

Defining Terms

1. Define
   a. warranty

Applying Economic Concepts

2. Why might a car salesperson try to find out what a potential buyer does for a living?
3. Explain how your attitude can help or hinder you in getting a good price when shopping for a car.
4. How can you find out the value of a car you want to trade in?
5. How can you find out whether a used car you are thinking about buying has been recalled by the manufacturer?

SECTION 6

The Rights and Responsibilities of Consumers

As a consumer, you have some rights and responsibilities. The information on these rights and duties described in this section will be particularly important to you, because you will make thousands of consumer purchases in your lifetime.

As you read this section, keep these key questions in mind:

- What are the rights of a consumer?
- What are the responsibilities of a consumer?

Consumer Rights

In general, a consumer has four rights: the right to be informed, the right to be safe, the right to choose, and the right to be heard.

The Right to Be Informed You have the right to the information you need to make a good consumer decision. For example, suppose you walk into a grocery store and pick up a box of cookies. You turn to the back of the box and read the ingredients, but the label is inaccurate. The cookies contain more of one ingredient than is listed, and one ingredient in the product is not listed at all. Your right to have the information you need to make a good consumer decision has been violated. Or suppose you are shopping for a car, and the salesperson tells you that the car you are looking at has six cylinders, when it actually has only four cylinders. You have been misled by the car salesperson and given inaccurate information. Again, your right to accurate information has been violated.

As a consumer, you have the right to accurate information on food labels. What problems could arsie from inaccurate labels?

These consumers, both the baby and the mother, have the right to a safe baby backpack.

The Right to Be Safe Consumers have the right to a safe product—one that will not harm their health or lives. For example, a consumer has the right to a safe car (for example, one without defective brakes), a safe home (one that is not built on a toxic waste dump), and safe toys (ones that will not harm children).

The Right to Choose A consumer has the right to choose among a variety of products offered at competitive prices. Choice is not usually present if competition is prohibited, so firms cannot legally band together to prevent consumers from paying a lower price for a good. For example, suppose U.S. car manufacturers got together and decided not to compete on price. Instead, they would sell cars for a certain agreed-on price. If that happened, the consumer's right to choose would have been violated. Or suppose grocery stores got together and tried to prevent any new grocery stores from entering the market. This act would violate the

Boycotts: From George Mason to Rosa Parks

Throughout history, consumers have showed their dissatisfaction with either the producers of goods and services or the goods or services themselves by boycotting. When consumers boycott a good or service, they choose not to buy it. Often the boycott serves to call attention to an important issue that deals with human rights.

For example, George Mason (1725–1792) was a Virginia planter and political leader. He helped George Washington prepare the Fairfax Resolves of July 1774, which were written in response to the way England was treating the American colonists at the time. The Fairfax Resolves called for an economic boycott of all English goods—in other words, for all colonists to stop buying English goods. This action, it was thought, would not only communicate the colonists' dissatisfaction with English treatment but also impose a trading cost on the English that would ultimately lead to their changing their behavior in a desirable way.

A more recent important boycott was the Montgomery, Alabama, bus boycott of 1955 and 1956. In 1955, Montgomery had a law that required African American citizens to ride in the back of the city's buses. On December 1, 1955, Rosa Parks, a forty-two-year old African American seamstress, boarded a bus and sat in the first row of seats in the black section of the bus. When some white men got on the bus, the bus driver told Rosa Parks to move to the back of the bus. She refused, the bus driver called the police, and she was arrested.

At the time, the leaders in Montgomery's African American community saw the incident as an opportunity to stage a protest against the city's segregation laws. On December 3 and 4, Martin Luther King, Jr., and other leaders in the African American community met and decided to stage a boycott against the bus system in Montgomery. They requested that all African Americans stop riding the buses. The boycott, which began on December 5, 1955, and lasted about a year, was a success. About 90 percent of the African Americans who usually rode the buses participated, and the boycott brought much attention to the plight of African Americans in the United States. In November 1956, the U.S. Supreme Court declared that segregation on public buses was unconstitutional, and the boycott ended.

QUESTION TO ANSWER There is a problem with some boycotts that was not a problem with the Montgomery bus boycott. The problem is that when a large number of people are asked to boycott a good or service, each individual can think this way: "I agree with the boycott in principle, but as long as most people boycott the good or service, I don't have to. I am only one of hundreds or thousands. The success of the boycott does not depend on my boycotting the good or service. Therefore, I don't think I will go along with the boycott." Of course, if many people act this way, the boycott will not be successful. Why do you think this problem did not apply to the Montgomery bus boycott?

Ralph Nader, Consumer Advocate

Ralph Nader is perhaps the best-known U.S. consumer advocate today. Although not everyone agrees with his ideas or tactics, Nader has made a lifetime career of pushing and prodding companies to make better and safer products.

Nader was born in 1934 to Lebanese immigrants. During his youth he was very interested in politics and public issues and even read back issues of the *Congressional Record.* In 1951 he went to Princeton University. While walking across campus, Nader came across some dead birds on the ground. Believing that they had died as a result of campus gardeners' spraying the trees with DDT, he tried to get Princeton to ban the use of the insecticide on campus. After graduating in 1955, he went on to Harvard Law School, which he described as "a high-priced tool factory, only instead of tools and dies, they were producing hired advocates for corporate law firms and corporations."

Nader gained public recognition when he wrote that the sporty Corvair, a popular General Motors car, was unsafe and pushed for congressional action to legislate car safety. In the years since then, Nader has taken on numerous other consumer causes.

QUESTION TO ANSWER Are there any consumer advocates on the local news shows in your town or city? What types of issues do they discuss?

consumer's right to choose and thus would be illegal. Finally, suppose a store chose to sell products only to men and not to women. This policy would violate female consumers' right to choose and would be illegal.

The Right to Be Heard Consumers with complaints have the right to be heard. They can address complaints to various government and private agencies that deal with consumer affairs, or they can go to small-claims court.

Consumers who make purchases by telephone or online have the same rights and responsibilities as those who shop in stores.

Consumer Responsibilities

Just as consumers have rights, they have responsibilities. We consider them next.

The Responsibility to Get Information Yourself

If you are going to buy a car, a pair of shoes, or anything else, you have to ask questions to get the information you need. You cannot simply wait for the seller to tell you everything there is to know about the subject. For example, if you are concerned about a car's safety, you need to ask the salesperson about the safety features of the car, or find out about its safety features from consumer organizations and publications. If you are at a restaurant and need to know how much salt is in the food you are eating, you need to ask. As a consumer, you also have the responsibility to pursue something until you get a satisfactory answer. For example, if a waiter at the restaurant tells you that he does not know the salt content of the food, ask that he check with the cook.

Also, when you are planning to make a purchase, especially a large one, it is your responsibility to call the Better Business Bureau and ask whether it has received any complaints about the seller from whom you are planning to buy. For example, you may be thinking about getting the trees in your yard trimmed by Frank's Tree Service. It is a good idea to call the Better Business Bureau and ask whether Frank's Tree Service is a reputable company and whether any consumers have complained about it.

The Better Business Bureau can help you find out whether a seller, such as this jeweler, has received any complaints.

Guidelines for a Wise Consumer

Nanette, age sixteen, attends high school in Columbus, Ohio. Recently, she has noticed that she has been buying a lot of the goods she sees advertised on television. Consequently, she has been spending more of her part-time earnings and saving less. She admits she has become a compulsive buyer, a person who feels driven to buy things. She wants to change, but how can she go about it?

Becoming a wise consumer requires us to think before we buy; it requires us to follow some basic rules. As buyers, keep the following rules and thoughts in mind:

1. *Think of the opportunity cost of what you plan to buy.* Suppose your friend has recently purchased a new style of coat. You think the coat looks good on him, and you want to buy one for yourself. Before you do, however, ask yourself, What can't I buy or do if I spend the money to buy the coat? In other words, you need to determine the opportunity cost of buying the coat—what you will give up, or forfeit, if you buy it. In the end, you have to ask yourself if the coat is worth what you would give up to buy it.
2. *Ask yourself if there are substitutes for what you plan to buy.* Ramona's friend Sujinta has recently purchased a computer. Ramona is seriously thinking about buying the same kind of computer, but she has not yet saved enough money to do so. Before Ramona buys the same kind of computer, she should consider whether there are substitutes. What about a different brand name? Considering the substitutes opens the door to a wider range of choice, and price, quality, and other things then can be more fully considered.
3. *Keep your long-term goals in mind.* Brian, age sixteen, has a long-term goal of buying a car. He currently attends high school in Arlington, Virginia, and works part-time stocking shelves at a building supplies store after school and on the weekends.

   During the course of a week, Brian sees many things that he would like to buy—new clothes, new CDs, and so on. If he buys these things, however, it will become harder for him to accomplish his long-term goal of buying a car. Brian needs to make a choice: buy more of what he wants now and decrease the probability of buying a car, or buy less of what he wants now and increase the probability of buying a car.

   Should long-term goals always take precedence over short-term goals? There is no absolute answer. It's not that long-term goals should always take precedence over short-term goals or vice versa. It's simply that our short-term goals sometimes conflict with our long-term goals, and we should be aware of this fact.

QUESTION TO ANSWER Think of a time when you purchased something priced at more than $15 and failed to consider one or more of the consumer guidelines. Would you still have made the purchase had you considered the guidelines? Explain why or why not.

Beanie Babies and Tulips

What causes you to buy something? You often buy something because you want to consume it. For example, you might buy a pen because you want to write with it, a CD because you want to listen to it, or a car because you want to drive it.

People buy things not only to consume them but sometimes with the expectation of selling them at a later date. For example, a person might buy a painting today for $10,000 in the hopes of selling it next year for $15,000; or someone might buy 100 shares of stock at a per-share price of $120 in the hopes of selling the stock next year for a per-share price of $180.

In the spring and summmer of 1998 many people in the United States were buying Beanie Babies, not so much to keep them for themselves but in the expectation that someone in a week or a month would pay them more for the Beanie Babies than they paid for them. The prices of many Beanie Babies rose into the hundreds and thousands of dollars. A year later, many of those Beanie Babies were selling for one-tenth of what they sold for the year before.

Something similar happened in the 1600s in Holland. The tulip, which was originally a wildflower named by the Turks, came to Holland by way of Carolus Clusius, the director of the Royal Medicinal Garden in Vienna. Clusius fled to Holland for religious sanctuary, taking many tulip bulbs with him from Vienna to Holland.

Historians do not know the reason why, but tulips became a craze in Holland. No doubt, tulips are beautiful to look at, and they were new to the country, but people began buying them like nothing else mattered. Tulip bulbs were bought for the tulips they would produce, their rarity, their status, and because the people who bought them thought they could sell them later for a much higher price. It was the Beanie Babies phenomenon, only slightly less than four hundred years earlier.

The tulip craze became so frenzied that some people sold their businesses and family jewels just to buy a few tulip bulbs. Prices rose so high that some people earned $44,000 a month just by buying and selling tulips. (Think of what $44,000 a month could buy in the 1600s.)

As with all buying crazes, the day came when things began to fall apart. In 1637, a group of tulip bulb merchants could not sell their bulbs for more than they had paid for them. Word spread rapidly, the tulip bulb market crashed, and prices quickly fell by large percentages. Thousands of Dutch businesspeople were ruined in only weeks or months.

QUESTION TO ANSWER In the late 1990s, some people thought that buying certain Internet stocks had become as foolish as buying tulip bulbs in Holland in the 1600s or buying Beanie Babies in the United States in 1998. Do you think some stocks are subject to the type of buying described in the feature? Explain why or why not.

The Responsibility to Learn How to Assemble or Use the Products You Buy Some consumer goods come with instructions. In particular, most items that can be used incorrectly come with instructions telling you what to watch out for, how to use the product safely, and so on. Read the instructions carefully, and learn how to assemble or use the product. For example, let's say you buy a microwave oven for your kitchen. You do not read the instructions that came with the oven, so you do not learn what can be cooked safely in the oven. One day, you put a metal pan in the oven and start a fire. If you had read the instructions, you would not have made this mistake.

The Responsibility to Make Fair Complaints and to Be Honest Consumers feel they have a right to expect honesty from sellers. In turn, sellers feel they have a right to expect honesty from consumers. For example, suppose you purchase a CD player from a store but drop it on the way into your house. Because you dropped it, it does not play as well as it would have. You could, of course, go back to the store and tell the seller that the CD player you bought does not work properly—without mentioning the fact that you dropped it—but that would be dishonest. You have a responsibility, when making consumer complaints, to provide the seller, or any government agency or court that gets involved, with the whole truth as you know it. This consumer responsibility should not be taken lightly.

The Responsibility to Act Courteously A consumer has the responsibility to be courteous. You have probably seen people in restaurants who treat servers rudely, order them about, and complain when their every request is not instantly fulfilled. Remember that a seller is simply there to sell you a product, not to be put down, to be argued with unnecessarily, or to do your full bidding.

What is the buyer's responsibility when making a complaint? What is the seller's responsibility when a complaint has been made?

The Responsibility to Seek Action through Government Organizations That Deal with Consumer Complaints If you have a complaint that you cannot settle with the seller, you have a responsibility to report this fact to the appropriate government agency. Do not hesitate to report a seller to a government agency if you feel that you have been wronged. Remember, as a consumer, you have the right to voice your complaints, and you also have a responsibility to exercise it.

Section 6 Review

Applying Economic Concepts

1. "Choice is not usually present where competition is prohibited." Explain.
2. List the responsibilities of a consumer.
3. Which of the consumer responsibilities do you think is the most important? Why?

SECTION 7

Paying for a College Education

If you plan to attend college but do not have the resources to pay for it, you may want to apply for financial aid. Federal grants, student loans, and college work-study programs are described in this section.

As you read this section, keep these key questions in mind:

- What is the difference between a grant, a loan, and a work-study arrangement?
- How can a person obtain information on financial aid for college?
- In terms of federal financial aid, what is the significance of a college's default rate?

Grants, Loans, and Work-Study Programs

Key Term

default rate

The U.S. Department of Education offers the following major student financial aid programs: (1) Pell Grants; (2) Federal Supplemental Educational Opportunity Grants (FSEOG); (3) Federal Work- Study (FWS), (4) Federal Perkins Loans, formerly called National Direct Student Loans (NDSL); (5) Stafford Loans, formerly called Guaranteed Student Loans (GSL); and (6) PLUS Loans (Parent Loans for Undergraduate Students).

These six programs fall into three categories: grants, loans, and work-study programs. A grant is financial aid that you do not have to pay back. For example, if you receive a Pell Grant for $2,400 to attend college for a year, you do not have to pay back any of the money. A loan is borrowed money that you must pay back with interest. A work-study program gives you the chance to work and earn money to help you pay for your college education.

There are many ways to finance a college education. Be sure to check out all of the possibilities.

Exhibit 20-2
Types of Financial Aid Programs

Type of program	Example
Grants	• Pell Grant • Supplemental Education Opportunity Grants (SEOG)
Loans	• Perkins Loan • Stafford Loan • Plus Loans
Work-study programs	• College Work-Study (CWS)

If you need more information on the different kinds of grants, loans, and work-study programs than is given in this section, you can go to the U.S. Department of Education site on the World Wide Web (http://www.ed.gov/finaid.html). Once there, click on "Student Financial Assistance."

Pell Grants A Pell Grant is an award to help first-time undergraduates pay for their education after high school. A first-time undergraduate is a person who has not earned a bachelor's or first professional degree. (Professional degrees include degrees in such fields as pharmacy and dentistry.) To obtain a Pell Grant, a person must show financial need and must be attending school at least half-time, which for most colleges means being registered for at least six semester hours. Applications for Pell Grants can be obtained from financial aid offices of colleges and universities and sometimes from high school guidance counselors' offices.

The amount of a Pell Grant award depends on the degree of financial need and the cost of the school. In the late 1990s, the maximum Pell Grant was about $3,000 per year.

Which type of financial aid would best fit your circumstances: a grant, a loan, or a work-study program?

Federal Supplemental Educational Opportunity Grants (FSEOG) A Federal Supplemental Educational Opportunity Grant (FSEOG) is an award to help first-time undergraduates with exceptional financial need, as determined by the school. Like a Pell Grant, an FSEOG does not have to be paid back. The monetary amount of FSEOGs ranges between $100 and $4,000 a year.

Unfortunately, colleges and universities are not crime free. If you are thinking of attending a certain college or university in the future, you may be interested in the crimes that have been committed at that institution in the past. One place to obtain this information is CampusSafety.Org, whose URL is http://campussafety.org/ STATS/. Once there, click on "Campus Crime Stats, F.B.I. Uniform Crime Reporting." Next, click on the crime report of the most recent year. You will find the crime statistics for various colleges and universities in the fifty states. How many robberies were there at the college you may be thinking of attending?

Federal Work-Study (FWS) The Federal Work-Study (FWS) program provides jobs for first-time undergraduates; it lets students earn money to help pay for their education. The student's job may be on or off campus, and the student receives at least the federal minimum wage. A student's work schedule and number of hours worked are determined by the school, not the student.

Federal Perkins Loans Federal Perkins Loans are low-interest loans for first-time undergraduates with exceptional financial need, as determined by the school. The student can borrow up to $4,000 per year for each year of undergraduate study. The student must repay this loan but may be allowed up to ten years to do so.

Stafford Loans Stafford Loans are low-interest loans to students attending school at least half-time. These loans must be repaid.

PLUS Loans PLUS Loans (Parent Loans for Undergraduate Students) are for parents who want to borrow to help pay for their children's education. These loans must be repaid.

Getting Needed Information

The federal government has a toll-free number to call with questions about financial aid: 1-800-4-FED-AID. Hearing-impaired individuals can call 1-800-730-8913. It is a good idea to call this number and inquire about the **default rate** of the college you are thinking about attending (the percentage of loans that are not repaid), because there may be restrictions on borrowing money to attend a college with a default rate of 30 percent or more. Other places to obtain information on financial aid are the financial aid office of the college you want to attend, the guidance counselor's office at your high school, and the Internet.

default rate
The percentage of loans that are not repaid.

Section 7 Review

Defining Terms

1. Define *default rate.*

Applying Economic Concepts

2. What are the major student financial aid programs offered by the U.S. Department of Education?
3. What is the difference between a student grant and a student loan?
4. What are PLUS Loans?

Developing Economic

Skills

Figuring Your Monthly Car Payments

Suppose you buy a car for $12,000. You make a down payment of $3,000 and take out a $9,000 loan at an annual interest rate of 9 percent for

three years. What are your monthly payments? It is easy to find out with the help of Exhibit 20-3.

The table in Exhibit 20-3 shows (1) the dollar amount a person pays each month for a $1,000 loan (2) at different interest rates (3) over different time periods from three to five years. The example involved a $9,000 loan at an annual interest rate of 9 percent for three years. The dollar amount in the 9 percent row and the three-year column is $31.80. Therefore, under these conditions, for every $1,000 borrowed, $31.80 a month must be paid back. The loan in the example is for $9,000, so we must multiply $31.80 by 9 to find the monthly payment. The total is $286.20 per month.

Here's the procedure in step-by-step form:

Step 1. Write down the loan amount.
Step 2. Write down the annual interest rate for the loan.
Step 3. Write down the length of the loan, in years.
Step 4. Consult Exhibit 20-3 to find the monthly payment for every $1,000 borrowed. Write down this amount.
Step 5. Divide the loan amount (from step 1) by 1,000. Write down this number.
Step 6. Multiply the dollar amount in step 4 by the number in step 5 to obtain the monthly payment.

Exhibit 20-3

Calculating Monthly Payments on a $1,000 Loan

Annual interest rate (%)	Length of the loan		
	3 years	4 years	5 years
5%	$29.98	$23.03	$18.88
6	30.43	23.49	19.34
7	30.88	23.95	19.81
8	31.34	24.42	20.28
9	31.80	24.89	20.76
10	32.27	25.37	21.25
11	32.74	25.85	21.75
12	33.22	26.34	22.25
13	33.70	26.83	22.76
14	34.18	27.33	23.27
15	34.67	27.84	23.79

For example, suppose you want to borrow $10,500 at an annual interest rate of 10 percent for five years. Here's how you would figure out your monthly payments:

Step 1. The loan amount is $10,500.
Step 2. The annual interest rate is 10 percent.
Step 3. The loan is for five years.
Step 4. Exhibit 20-3 says that the dollar amount that corresponds to 10 percent for five years is $21.25.
Step 5. The loan amount in step 1 ($10,500) divided by 1,000 is 10.5.
Step 6. The dollar amount in step 4 ($21.25) multiplied by the number in step 5 (10.5) is $223.13, which is the monthly payment.

1. Victor borrows $11,000 at an annual interest rate of 8 percent for five years. What are his monthly payments?
2. Keesha borrows $8,000 at an annual interest rate of 9 percent for four years. What are her monthly payments?
3. Marcos borrows $10,000 at an annual interest rate of 7 percent for three years. What are his monthly payments?

CHAPTER 20

Review

Economics Vocabulary

Fill in the following blanks with the appropriate word or phrase.

1. Buying goods that you bought on the spur of the moment, and which you really did not intend to buy, is called ____.
2. The total price of an item divided by its weight gives us the item's ____.
3. Kellogg's is a(n) ____, not a generic brand.
4. A(n) ____ is a contract that conveys property for a specific item period for a fee.
5. Cash paid at the time of a purchase, with the rest of the purchase price to be paid later, is called a(n) ____.
6. ____ refers to direct sales of products by telephone.
7. Products produced for a specific supermarket chain and which carry the name of that chain on the label are referred to as ____ products.
8. An amount of money a renter pays a landlord before moving into the apartment (or rental property) is called a(n) ____.
9. The nature of a(n) ____ is that one must give up one thing that is desirable to get something else that is desirable.
10. One percentage of a loan amount is called a(n) ____.
11. The percentage of loans that are not repaid is referred to as the ____.
12. A written agreement by which a buyer of property agrees to repay a loan taken out to purchase the property is called a(n) ____.
13. A guarantee or assurance given by a seller stating that a product is in good working order is called a(n) ____.

Review Questions

1. Give an example of a national brand, a private brand, and a generic brand.
2. What is the cost of shopping? (Keep in mind that the cost of shopping is not the cost of a particular item you may purchase while shopping.)
3. What is the purpose of a security deposit?
4. How can you guard against impulse buying when shopping for groceries?
5. Give an example of a consumer trade-off.
6. Identify three signs that a telemarketer may be trying to swindle you.
7. What are the differences between a discount warehouse food store and a supermarket?
8. You are thinking about renting an apartment in a certain area of town. How can you find out how safe the area is?
9. What are points? Who pays points?
10. Why wouldn't an economist advise consumers to shop until they found the perfect item at the best price?
11. Why would a car salesperson want to lowball?
12. What is the difference between a grant and a student loan? Between a work-study arrangement and a student loan?
13. What makes it possible for convenience stores to charge higher prices than supermarkets for the same items?
14. "Coupons lower the dollar price of buying groceries but increase the time cost." What does this statement mean?

Calculations

1. Calculate the unit price for each of the following items.
   - **a.** Total price = \$3.33; size = 11 ounces.
   - **b.** Total price = \$5.22; size = 1 pound 3 ounces.
   - **c.** Total price = \$2.29; size = 1 pound 1 ounce.
2. Calculate the monthly payment for each of the following car loans.
   - **a.** Loan amount = \$13,200; annual interest rate = 7 percent; length of loan = 4 years.
   - **b.** Loan amount = \$9,900; annual interest rate = 6 percent; length of loan = 3 years.
   - **c.** Loan amount = \$8,000; annual interest rate = 9 percent; length of loan = 5 years.
3. Compute the amount paid in points on each of the following loans.
   - **a.** Points = 2; loan amount = \$90,000.
   - **b.** Points = 1.75; loan amount = \$144,000.
   - **c.** Points = 0.5; loan amount = \$249,000.
4. Compute the real estate broker's commission for each of the following sales.
   - **a.** Commission fee = 4 percent; sales price = \$169,000.
   - **b.** Commission fee = 6 percent; sales price = \$321,000.

c. Commission fee = 6 percent; sales price = $248,500.

Graphs

Using the table of information on a $1,000 loan in Exhibit 20-3 on page 571, graph the monthly payments for five separate annual interest rates over three, four, and five years. See the graph below as an example.

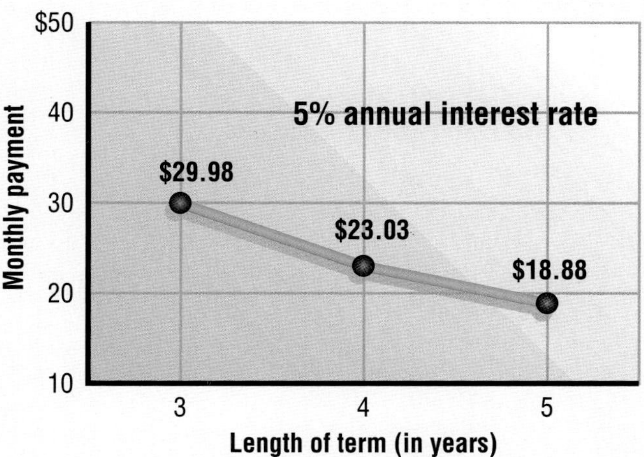

Economics and Thinking Skills

1. **Application.** What are some of the trade-offs encountered when buying a car?
2. **Analysis.** Why would a new-car salesperson ask the following questions?
   a. What are you driving now?
   b. Where do you attend high school?
   c. Do you have a part-time job?
   d. Is there a work telephone number where we could reach one of your parents?
3. **Cause and Effect.** A telemarketer calls George on the phone and offers to sell him a good product at an excellent price. It sounds good to George; George buys the product without seeing it. When he receives the product in the mail, he believes the telemarketer tricked him into buying something that was not worth one-fourth what he paid for it. Whose fault is it that George was tricked—the telemarketer's, George's, or both? Explain your answer.

Writing Skills

1. Write out a conversation between you and a telemarketer who is trying to swindle you. What does the telemarketer say? What do you say to protect yourself?
2. Write a one-page paper outlining what you see as the costs and benefits of attending college.

Economics in the Media

Find an article in the newspaper that deals with one of the following: telemarketing, college loans, car loans, buying a house, renting an apartment, or the rights of consumers. Describe the contents of the article.

Where's the Economics?

In what way do coupons make buying goods cheaper? More expensive?

CHAPTER 21

Everyday Life: Budgets, Saving, Investing, Working, and Insurance

What This Chapter Is About

The economic concepts, theories, and policies discussed in much of this book are all very important and make up the bulk of any substantive economics course. But economics is more than concepts, theories, and policies. It deals with some of our most fundamental everyday concerns, such as budgeting, saving, getting a job, and buying insurance. This chapter discusses many of the economic issues that affect us all in our everyday lives.

Why This Chapter Is Important

Life is easier if you know how to do certain things. For example, if you did not know how to do such things as write out a budget, save, invest, write a job résumé, or buy insurance, life could be difficult indeed. This chapter discusses some of the things you need to know in order to make your current and future personal economic life more comfortable and rewarding.

After You Study This Chapter, You Will Be Able To

- write out a budget.
- explain the benefits of saving.
- discuss what the Federal Deposit Insurance Corporation does.
- determine the capital ratio of a bank.
- discuss the important factors that relate to personal investing.
- discuss the ins and outs of joining the workforce.
- prepare a job résumé.
- discuss in detail the different types of insurance, such as health, life, and automobile.

You Will Also Learn What Economics Has to Do With

- education and income.
- bank runs.
- helping others through saving.

Economics Journal

Keep a list of the things that you buy in a week. At the end of the week, identify each item as something you needed or something you simply wanted. Finally, make a reasonable estimate of how much money you saved during the week. Ask yourself if you would have been better off at the end of the week had you spent less and saved more.

SECTION 1

Budgeting

Most people do not take the time to draw up a budget. Perhaps they think budgeting is burdensome and complex. In fact, it is neither. Writing out and following a budget can be of immense value to you.

As you read this section, keep these key questions in mind:

- What is a budget?
- How do you make a budget?
- When you save, what do you "buy"?

What Is a Budget?

Key Term

budget

A **budget** is an organized plan for spending and saving money. Years ago, many people used a budget that worked this way: On payday, they would cash their checks. Then they would take the cash and divide it up among different labeled envelopes. On one envelope might be written "House Payments"; on another, "Food"; and on another, "Eating Out at Restaurants." In this way people controlled their expenditures. After all, once the proper amount of money had been put into the envelope marked "House Payments," it was difficult to use it to go to the movies or buy clothes.

budget An organized plan for spending and saving money.

You might think you don't earn enough income to need a budget. You would probably be surprised, however, to learn how much farther your money goes when you budget.

The Steps in Making a Budget

Let's consider a five-step process for making a budget.

Step 1. Determine Your Income and Expenditures Over the Past Year You need to figure out dollar amounts for both your income and your expenditures over a year. To find your annual income, you may want to check your pay stubs. Suppose Marion, seventeen years old, has been working part-time at a department store for the past year. She checks her pay stubs and learns that she earned $2,125 last year.

To figure out your expenditures, you need to keep a list of what you spend for a month or two. An easy way to

Keeping the receipts for what you buy can help you make a budget.

keep track of your spending is simply to ask for receipts for everything you buy and keep them in one place. Another way is to record your expenditures in a journal each night. You might want to break your expenditures down into four or five categories, such as (1) school; (2) clothes; (3) entertainment, including movies, CD purchases, eating out, and so on; (4) transportation; and (5) miscellaneous. Each day, register the dollar amount you spent in each category. After you have done this for a month or two, compute the dollar amounts you spent.

Next, you need to decide whether your expenses for the month or two you have recorded are typical. For example, suppose Marion spent $20 in school costs and $30 for clothes in the month of November. She has to ask herself if $20 is a typical monthly cost for school and if $30 is a typical monthly cost for clothes. If these costs are not typical, she must adjust accordingly. For example, if Marion believes she usually spends less than $20 each month on school-related items and more each month for clothing, she needs to adjust the figures for this fact. Let's say she thinks that $10 is closer to her typical monthly school costs and that $33 is closer to her typical monthly cost for clothes.

Once you have found your typical monthly cost in each category, multiply by 12 to find your yearly cost in each category. For example, Marion's typical monthly cost for clothes is $33. If she multiplies $33 by 12, she finds that her cost for clothes for a year is $396. Marion does this for each spending category and then sums the figures to get her estimated dollar expenditures for the year (see Exhibit 21-1 below).

Computing your income and estimated expenditures on an annual basis gives you an idea of (1) how much money is coming in and (2) how much money is going out. In addition, it tells you how you spend the money. For example, Marion can see from Exhibit 21-1 that she spent $396 for clothing.

Step 2. Determine How Much You Are Saving It is important to know whether you are saving or not and, if you are, how much you are saving. How much you are saving relates to your future goals. For example, Marion earned $2,125 from her part-time job last year and spent approximately $1,650 (see Exhibit 21-1). The difference between earnings and spending was $475, which she saved.

Exhibit 21-1

Marion's Income and Estimated Expenditures for the Year

Income for the year	Estimated expenditures for the year						
$2,125	a. School costs	=	$10 per month	×	9 months	=	$90
	b. Clothing costs	=	$33 per month	×	12 months	=	$396
	c. Entertainment costs	=	$25 per month	×	12 months	=	$300
	d. Transportation costs	=	$60 per month	×	12 months	=	$720
	e. Miscellaneous costs	=	$12 per month	×	12 months	=	$144
					Total estimated expenditures	**=**	**$1,650**

How much Marion needs to save all depends on her future plans. For example, if she intends to go to college or take a vacation, she may need to save more than $475 a year, or $39.58 a month.

List your income, expenditures, and savings for the past year. Do you need to make any adjustments to be able to meet your goals?

Step 3. View Your Income, Expenditures, and Savings, and Decide If You Want to Make Any Adjustments Keep in mind that your savings relate to your future goals. At this point, you have condensed your "money life" into three dollar amounts: income, expenditures, and savings. As mentioned, Marion's three dollar amounts are $2,125 for income, $1,650 for expenditures, and $475 for savings.

Once you see things on paper, it is easier to figure out if you want to make changes or continue the same way. For example, Marion may decide to increase her savings and decrease her expenditures because she plans to go to college. To do so, she will need more money.

Step 4. Change the Way You View Saving Think of saving as a regular "expenditure" item; think of what you "buy" with it. Many people simply save what is left over at the end of the month if they have not spent their entire paycheck. This attitude relegates saving to a less important position than purchasing goods and services. ("If I have any money left over after I've purchased everything I need, I'll save it.") Some economists think that many Americans need to change the way they view saving. Instead of seeing it as something "left over"—as something less important than buying—they need to see it as the equal of buying.

In fact, when we save, we do buy something—both in the present and in the future. What we buy in the present is security. When Antonio saves 10

When we save, we often have enough money to take care of certain unforeseen events–such as a needed car repair or an emergency trip across the country.

percent of his paycheck each month, he "buys" the comfortable feeling of knowing that if an emergency arises tomorrow, he can meet it. If his car breaks down and he needs to get it repaired, or if he needs to take an emergency trip across the country, he can do it. He sleeps easier each night knowing that he will be better equipped to handle any surprises that arise.

Furthermore, when Sally saves 8 percent of her paycheck each month, she is "buying" the ability to purchase something in the future that she would not have been able to buy if she had not saved. Saving today makes it easier for her to buy certain things tomorrow. Saving is really consumption postponed:

Saving = Consumption postponed

You would do well to develop the habit of saving early in life and to view it as equal in importance to buying. Think of savings as an expenditure item, much as you would think about school costs or transportation costs. What do you buy each month? Let it be food, clothing, books, entertainment—and savings.

Step 5. Write Out a Monthly Budget Exhibit 21-2 below shows the main elements of a monthly budget. Column 1, which lists expenditure categories, can contain as many or as few categories as you want. Often, a person's stage of life determines the number of categories in this column. For example, a high school student may have fewer expenditure items than a woman in her thirties who is employed. The woman may have such expenditures as health insurance and mortgage insurance that the high school student does not have. Notice that "Savings" is listed in this column; it is an expenditure item.

Exhibit 21-2
The Main Elements of a Monthly Budget

This budget shows (1) a student's expenditure categories (school, clothing, for example); (2) how much has been budgeted in each category; (3) how much has actually been spent in each category; and (4) the difference between the budgeted amount and the actual amount spent.

(1) Expenditure	(2) Budgeted	(3) Actual	(4) Difference
School	$10	$15	+$5
Clothing	$33	$37	+$4
Entertainment	$25	$30	+$5
Transportation	$60	$62	+$2
Savings	$37	$20	–$17
Miscellaneous	$12	$13	+$1
Total	**$177**	**$177**	**$0**

Does Your Saving Help Others As Well As You?

Most of us probably do not think much about the social aspects of saving money or about how our saving affects the economy. We simply think about how it affects us. For example, Robert may simply think that saving $100 each month will make it possible for him to make a down payment on a car in eighteen months.

Saving does affect us as savers, but it also affects the economy. To illustrate, take two people, Tammy and Catalina. Catalina works as a physician. Each month she saves approximately $1,000, and she now has $54,000 in a savings account. Until recently, Tammy was working as a cook in a restaurant, but she has now decided to open a restaurant of her own. The problem is that building and running a restaurant take money, and Tammy does not have all the money that is needed. She needs a loan.

One day, she goes to a bank to ask for a loan to start her new restaurant. The loan officer asks her how much money she needs, how she plans to spend it, where she wants to locate the restaurant, how many customers she thinks she will have each day, and other questions related to the business. After gathering Tammy's answers and doing some further checking, the loan officer grants Tammy a loan. Where does the loan officer get the money to lend to Tammy? He gets it from the savings of people who have savings accounts at the bank—from people like Catalina. In other words, the bank has channeled some of Catalina's saved funds to Tammy in the form of a loan, so that she can start a new business.

As Catalina is driving to work one day, she is stopped at a light at the corner of the street where Tammy's new restaurant is being built. Catalina observes the construction for a few seconds and thinks to herself that there are a lot of new businesses starting up in town. Then the light turns green, and she proceeds on her way. She does not think about what we, as students of economics, know: that her own savings have much to do with these new businesses. The dollars she saves end up as credit for people like Tammy who want to start new businesses.

QUESTION TO ANSWER Some people have suggested that banks do not serve any social purpose. Do you agree or disagree? Explain your answer.

Column 2 lists the dollar amounts the person plans to spend in each expenditure category—the budgeted amounts. Column 3 lists the actual dollar amounts the person ended up spending in each category. Column 4 records the difference between the budgeted and actual expenditures. To get this difference, subtract the dollar amount in column 2 from the dollar amount in column 3. A plus sign before the dollar amount means the person spent more in this category than planned. A minus sign means he or she spent less.

A quick look back at Exhibit 21-2 on page 579 shows that the person spent more than planned in five categories (school, clothing, entertainment, transportation, and miscellaneous). Less money than the budgeted amount was spent in one category (savings).

What a Budget Can and Cannot Do

What you do with the information in a budget is up to you. No one can force you to spend less on, say, clothing and entertainment and more on savings if you do not want to. Writing out a budget is not a cure-all for money problems; it is simply an organized way of looking at your expenditures and goals and at what you are doing about them. Your budget records your efforts, successes, and failures, much as a thermometer records your body temperature.

If you write out a budget and do not follow it successfully at first—if you do not save as much as you wanted to, perhaps—do not despair. Few people immediately succeed at following a budget. Like practicing good study habits, following a budget takes willpower. Only you can decide whether your goals are important enough for you to exercise the willpower necessary to achieve them. All an economist can do is point out the opportunity costs and the trade-offs involved. For example, what is the cost to Marion if she buys too many clothes now and does not save enough for her college career tomorrow? What is the cost to Antonio of buying an expensive television now and not being able to afford the car repair tomorrow?

These questions must be raised and answered by the individual making the budget. As a student of economics, however, you may have a better understanding than others that current actions mean trade-offs have been made and opportunity costs incurred.

Section 1 Review

Defining Terms

1. Define *budget*

Applying Economic Concepts

2. Explain how you can determine what your income and expenditures were over the past year.

3. What might a person "buy" when he or she saves?

4. "Writing out a budget does not guarantee that you will be successful at solving your money problems." Do you agree or disagree? Explain your answer.

SECTION 2

Savings and Banks

For many people, saving means opening up a savings account at a bank. There is more to it, though, as this section shows.

As you read this section, keep these key questions in mind:

- How can I start the habit of saving?
- What is the Federal Deposit Insurance Corporation?
- What makes a bank safe or unsafe?

Key Terms

asset
liability
net worth (equity, capital)
capital ratio
insolvent

How to Get in the Habit of Saving

It is difficult for many people to get in the habit of saving, because it is just too easy to spend money. Advertisements for things to buy are everywhere: television, billboards, magazines, the Internet, newspapers, and so on. Hundreds of people tell you where you can spend your money. ("Buy it from us. We're at the corner of Park and Main!") Although few people argue the benefits of saving some money, it is no wonder that spending comes so much easier than saving.

One way to get in the habit of saving is simply to pretend that you earn less than you do. Consider a married couple with children. Both the husband and wife work, and their combined income is approximately $50,000 a year. These people could simply pretend that their combined income was $45,000 and save the remaining $5,000. That is, instead of consuming like a family earning $50,000 a year, they could consume like a family earning $45,000 a year.

It is not likely that this trick will be so convincing that you will not remember your actual income, of course, but that does not matter. The point

Most people find it much easier to spend money than save it. How about you?

Exhibit 21-3
Buying and Saving

There are many opportunities to buy things, but it is important to get into the habit of saving.

is to get in the habit of thinking and acting as if you earned less income than you actually did to make saving easier in the beginning. Once the saving habit is established, you may have no further need for the trick.

Banks sometimes make "bad" loans and end up going out of business. What protection do depositors have in the event of a bank failure?

Bank Failure and the FDIC Many people place their savings in a bank. Sometimes banks fail. To understand what it means for a bank to fail, we need to look at the banking business more closely. A bank makes most of its income from loans. For example, suppose a person puts $40,000 into a savings account in a bank, and the bank turns around and lends the $40,000 to someone. The borrower has to pay interest for the $40,000 loan, and the interest payments constitute income for the bank.

Now suppose a bank makes many loans that borrowers cannot repay. Say the person who borrowed the $40,000 needed the money to start a small business. The business ended up doing poorly, and the owner can pay neither the interest on the loan nor the loan amount itself.

As far as the bank is concerned, the $40,000 it lent to this person was a "bad" loan (a loan that was not repaid). If the bank has many other bad loans, it may not be able to survive. After all, banks are successful only when they get back the loan money plus interest. If they are consistently unable to do so, they fail and go out of business.

Bank Runs and Failures during the Great Depression

A bank fails when its assets are less than its liabilities. A bank run, or a run on a bank, occurs when the bank's depositors think their bank either has failed or is going to fail and they will not be able to get their money back. Thus, they "run" to the bank, hoping to get their money before it is too late. Today there are almost no bank runs, largely because of the Federal Deposit Insurance Corporation (FDIC) that stands behind deposits up to $100,000.

Of course, the FDIC only came into existence with the Banking Act of 1933. Before 1933, deposits were not insured. During the 1920s and 1930s there were not only numerous bank failures but also many bank runs, which fostered even more bank failures.

How can a bank run foster a bank failure? Suppose bank A is financially sound. Somehow, though, a rumor spreads that bank A is in financial trouble and that it will not be able to pay all its depositors should they all ask for their money. Without deposit insurance, this rumor could cause a run on the bank. So many depositors could ask for their money that the bank could run out of money and fail.

In the worst years of the Great Depression, 1930 through 1933, there were over two thousand bank failures a year. At the end of 1933 fewer than 15,000 banks remained out of the 30,000 that had existed in 1920.

It is widely accepted among economists that the Federal Reserve could have prevented many of the bank failures had it acted properly as "lender of last resort." The Fed could have lent the banks enough funds to pay off all their deposits. As fewer banks failed, fewer people would panic about an impending bank failure, and most would leave their money in the banks.

Historians and economists have wondered why the Fed did not act this way and thus prevent many bank runs and failures. Three reasons are often given.

First, some say that the Fed was still a young institution (it became operational in 1914) and that it still did not know how important it was to prevent massive bank failures.

Second, some say that at the time, certain members of the Board of Governors of the Federal Reserve System thought that the banks that failed deserved to fail. They believed that if the bank managers had not made wise lending decisions, they deserved to fail.

Third, some people suggest that the Fed policy of standing back and letting banks fail was a conscious decision. Many of the first banks to fail in the 1930s were small banks in the Midwest and South. The large city banks felt that these banks were in competition with them and that they would be better off if they did not exist. It is thought that these big-city bankers might have been able to influence certain Fed officials to sit back and watch the competition die off.

QUESTION TO ANSWER Deposit insurance, on the one hand, prevents bank runs and therefore can avert bank failures. On the other hand, when depositors have deposit insurance, they may not monitor their bank as closely to see that it is making wise lending decisions. Do you see this as a problem with deposit insurance? Why or why not?

asset
In reference to a bank, a thing that the bank owns that has value.

liability
In reference to a bank, its debts.

If you were the original depositor of the $40,000, what will happen to your money? What are you going to do? Your money is insured through the Federal Deposit Insurance Corporation (FDIC), which was set up by Congress in 1933 to insure bank deposits. You will get your money back, but not necessarily as soon as you would like. Having to wait may or may not be a problem for depositors, depending on when and why they need their money.

Keeping Your Savings Safe Here are some things to keep your savings safe in a bank.

Never place over $100,000 in an account at any one bank. The government insures accounts only up to $100,000. Of course, you're probably thinking that placing more than $100,000 in an account is not a problem you are likely to have. It is true that having such a large amount of savings is rare, but it does happen, even to middle-income earners. For example, a family may sell its home and place the proceeds in a bank for a month or more.

When a person does have more than $100,000 to put into a savings account, the money should be split up between two or more banks. If the person opens up an account at two different branches of the same bank, the savings are still insured for only $100,000. For example, suppose a person places $70,000 in an account at one branch of bank A and $50,000 in an account at another branch of bank A. He or she may think that both accounts are insured by the FDIC, because neither account contains over $100,000. In the eyes of the FDIC, however, this person has deposited $120,000 in bank A, so $20,000 is not insured at all. It is better for this person to open up accounts at different banks.

Accounts over $100,000 should be split between two or more banks. Explain why.

Check the capital ratio of the bank. The **assets** of a bank are those things the bank owns that have value. The **liabilities** of a bank are its debts. Subtracting the liabilities from the assets yields the **net worth** of the bank (also called **equity** or **capital**). The net worth is the value of the bank to its owners. For example,

Donna Tanoue, Chair of the Federal Deposit Insurance Corporation (FDIC)

As chair of the Federal Deposit Insurance Corporation (FDIC), Donna Tanoue oversees the agency that provides $100,000 in insurance for accounts at banks. Under Tanoue's leadership, the FDIC took aggressive steps to insure its readiness for the Y2K (year 2000) computer date change. Tanoue has also focused attention on emerging risks in the banking industry. Before she became FDIC chair, she was a partner in the Hawaii law firm of Goodsill Anderson Quinn & Stifel, specializing in banking, real estate finance, and governmental affairs.

Tanoue was commissioner of financial institutions for the state of Hawaii from 1983 to 1987 and special deputy attorney general to the Department of Commerce and Consumer Affairs for Hawaii from 1981 to 1983. She received a bachelor's degree from the University of Hawaii in 1977 and a law degree from Georgetown University in 1981.

The Federal Deposit Insurance Corporation (FDIC) insures many deposits. Go to its Web site (http://www.fdic.gov/index.html). Once at the site, click on "Are My Deposits Insured?" Then click on "Your Insured Deposit" and "General Questions 1–9." Read the information presented, and answer the following questions.

QUESTIONS TO ANSWER

1. Are mutual funds insured by the FDIC?
2. Are Treasury securities insured by the FDIC?
3. Do you have to be a U.S. citizen to be FDIC insured?

suppose bank C's assets total $130 million, and its liabilities total $120 million. The $10 million difference is the equity of the bank—the value of the bank to its owners.

The equity of a bank divided by the assets of the bank is the **capital ratio.** For example, for bank C—which has equity of $10 million and assets of $130 million—the capital ratio is 7.7 percent. The average capital ratio for all banks is roughly 6.5 percent. It is generally thought that a bank must have a capital ratio of at least 5 percent to be considered healthy. To be considered a strong bank, a bank should have a capital ratio between 6 and 7.5 percent. An exceptionally strong bank has a capital ratio higher than 7.5 percent. A bank with a ratio below 5 percent is considered weak, and a bank with a ratio below 3 percent is very weak. In addition, if you subtract liabilities from assets and get a negative number, the bank has no equity and is therefore **insolvent.**

It is relatively easy to find out a bank's assets and equity if shares of the bank's stock are traded on the stock exchange. A stockbroker, for example, would have this information. Once you know the bank's assets and equity, you can simply do the division yourself to calculate the capital ratio.

MINI GLOSSARY

net worth (equity, capital) The difference between assets and liabilities.

capital ratio Equity divided by assets.

insolvent Having more liabilities than assets

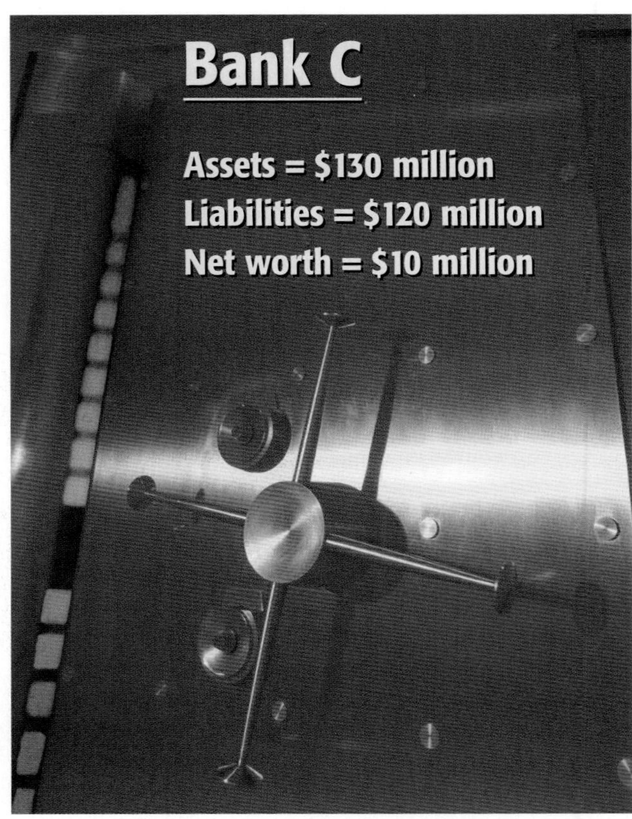

Section 2 Review

Defining Terms

1. Define
   a. asset
   b. liability
   c. net worth (equity, capital)
   d. capital ratio
   e. insolvent

Applying Economic Concepts

2. What does it mean to say that a bank has made a "bad" loan?
3. Jones has $40,523 in an account with branch 1 of bank A and $64,213 in an account with branch 2 of bank A. How much of her money is not insured?
4. Calculate the net worth in each of the following cases.
   a. Assets = $1.2 million; liabilities = $800,000.
   b. Assets = $44 million; liabilities = $39 million.
   c. Assets = $10.45 million; liabilities = $8.45 million.
5. You are searching for an exceptionally strong bank in which to place your money. For what capital ratio will you look?
6. What does it mean to say that a bank is insolvent?

SECTION 3

Investing

As noted in an earlier chapter, the words *invest* and *investment* mean something different to economists than to many others. An economist who talks about investing is talking about what a business firm does when it buys new machinery for its factories or increases the size of its present factory. She might say, "Business firms in the United States have invested heavily in the last year. They have built new factories and purchased new machinery in record amounts." The noneconomist who talks about investing usually means buying stocks and bonds, real estate, and so on. For example, a person might say, "My investments in real estate and the stock market are really paying off." This section uses the words *invest* and *investment* the way the noneconomist uses them.

As you read this section, keep these key questions in mind:

- What are some of the incorrect things people say and believe about buying stocks?
- What is a mutual fund?

Key Term

mutual fund

Buying Stocks: Fact versus Fiction

Buying stocks in the stock market has an exciting appeal for many people. Many view buying stocks as far more exciting than buying bonds or putting money in a passbook savings account, for example. Remember, however, that excitement and profit sometimes go together, but sometimes they do not.

The New York Stock Exchange, in existence for over 200 years, is a trading center for thousands of companies with a total market value of over $12 trillion.

Perhaps because the stock market does hold a fascination for so many people, a number of things are said about it that are not true. Here are some of those statements:

1. *"The stock has gone down so much already that it can't possibly go down any more."* People often make this statement about the stocks of well-known and respectable companies, but the price of the stocks of such companies can indeed continue to go down. In a period of one year, the stock price of Polaroid went from $143 to $14. No doubt, when the stock's price was $100, $50, $25, some people were saying, "The stock has gone down so much already that it can't possibly go down any more." They were wrong.
2. *"The stock has gone up so far that it can't possibly go higher."* This assumption is, of course, the opposite of the previous assumption. The prices of plenty of stocks continue to go

higher even as people are saying that they cannot. McDonald's, Stop & Shop, Subaru, Philip Morris, Dell, Yahoo, and Amazon.com are examples.

If stock prices go down, should an investor sell immediately? Explain.

3. *"It's only a dollar a share. How can I lose?"* Look at the stock listings in a newspaper, and you will find different prices for different stocks. Some prices are relatively low. It may be natural to think that you cannot lose your money if you pay only $1 per share of stock. However, even a stock that sells for $1 a share can go down in price.
4. *"The stock has gone down in price, but eventually it will come back up."* Investors are inclined to think that if a stock goes down in price, it will eventually move back up. This belief is not always true, however. The stock of some companies has gone down in price and never come back up. In fact, the companies went out of business.
5. *"I can't sell now; the price has gone down."* Suppose a person buys a stock at $20 a share, and the stock's price falls to $10 a share. The person says, "I can't sell the stock now, because I'd take a loss. I have to wait until the price goes back up to at least $20 a share." This person obviously thinks that a stock will eventually rebound to whatever price he paid for it. Unfortunately, this belief may not hold up to reality. There is nothing to prevent a stock's price from continuing to fall.
6. *"I've had this stock for a very long time and nothing has happened. Nothing will ever happen. I'm selling it."* The stock of a number of companies has hardly moved in price for five to ten years and then has moved sharply upward. A few examples include Merck, GAF Corporation, and Lukens. The fact that a stock is quiet today does not mean it will be quiet tomorrow.

THINKING Like an Economist

The economist believes that what people do in the present can influence their future, but that what they do in the present can never change their past. For this reason, the economist would not say, "I can't sell my stock now, because the price has gone down." This present action (choosing not to sell the stock) cannot change the past (the fall in the stock's price). The stockholder may take a bigger loss by waiting than by selling the stock now. Again, you can affect the future through your present actions, but you cannot change the past. Thinking otherwise will only lead you to make mistakes that you could have avoided.

Mutual Funds

Many people today invest their money in **mutual funds,** financial organizations that pool people's money and invest it in various ways. Suppose you invested in a stock mutual fund. You would buy shares in this fund, and the fund manager would invest your money, along with the money of other people, in various stocks. She might invest the money in twenty to thirty stocks. Alternatively, you could put your money in a bond mutual fund, which invests in different bonds, such as corporate and government bonds. Finally, you could put the money in a money market fund, which invests in short-term government or U.S. Treasury securities. Putting your money in a money market fund that invests in short-term U.S. Treasury securities is an extremely safe investment; there is little doubt that the U.S. government is going to pay what it owes on those securities.

mutual fund
A financial organization that pools people's money and invests it.

Research Past Performance and Fees Mutual fund companies regularly advertise in business publications, and many business publications report

Mutual fund managers invest people's money in various stocks.

on how well certain mutual fund companies are doing. It is important to order and read the prospectus of any fund company in which you are interested. In the prospectus, the company outlines its investment philosophy and its results over the past five to ten years. Be sure to check whether the same management team that produced the described results is managing the fund today. A mutual fund company may have invested well a few years ago, but if a different management team is making investments for the company today, past results may not be meaningful.

It is also important to check the fees of the mutual fund company. Usually, the fee is a small percentage of the total amount of funds you invest. Fees can change periodically, so keep in touch with your mutual fund company.

Look for Prompt, Courteous Service Suppose Maya turns over $10,000 to the XYZ Mutual Fund Company in Boston. She has her money in three funds: $5,000 in a stock fund, $3,000 in a bond fund, and $2,000 in a money market fund. One of the options XYZ Mutual Fund Company offers is the ability to switch money from one fund to another. Suppose Maya thinks that over the next two months the value of most stocks is going to fall and the value of most bonds is going to rise. She may want to switch $4,000 from the stock fund to the bond fund. When she calls the mutual fund company to issue this order, the person she talks to on the telephone should offer prompt, courteous service. If the person does not do so, Maya might want to consider putting her money elsewhere. An investor needs to be able to switch money between funds easily when economic conditions change. Anything that gets in the way, such as discourteous or uncooperative employees, should be a signal that the mutual fund company is not all the investor might want it to be.

Section 3 Review

Defining Terms

1. Define *mutual fund.*

Applying Economic Concepts

2. Wu owns 100 shares of stock, which he purchased for $32 a share. Currently, the stock is selling for $23 a share. Wu says that he cannot sell the stock now, because he would take too big a loss. Is he exhibiting sensible behavior? Explain your answer.
3. What type of information will you find in a mutual fund company's prospectus?
4. What is the difference between the way an economist and a noneconomist use the word *investment?*
5. Suppose the stock market has gone down by 20 percent in a few weeks. Someone says, "The stock market can't possibly fall any more." Do you agree or disagree? Explain your answer.

SECTION 4

Joining the Workforce

This section discusses some important topics that relate to the work world. As you will probably be involved in this world for a large portion of your life, this section should be of interest and assistance.

As you read this section, keep these key questions in mind:

- Do an individual's chances of becoming unemployed decline as he or she acquires more education?
- What is the relationship between education and income?
- What are the things to keep in mind when filling out a job application, writing a résumé, and being interviewed for a job?

Education, Income, and Unemployment

Key Term

résumé

Can a good education help keep you out of the unemployment line? Explain.

As you probably already know, education and income are related. A recent edition of the *Economic Report of the President* says, "Educational attainment is one of the primary characteristics that distinguishes high-income from low-income workers." In other words, high-income workers generally have more education than low-income workers. (See Exhibit 21-4 on page 591.) Specifically, high school dropouts earn less than high school graduates, high school graduates earn less than college graduates, and so on. For example, in the late 1990s, the average annual income of a person (eighteen years old or more) without a high school diploma was $15,011. For a person with only a high school diploma, it was $22,154. For a person with some college but no degree, the average annual income was $23,937. For a person with a college degree it was $38,112, and with a master's degree, $50,162. Finally, the average annual income for a person with a Ph.D. was $72,464.

Not only is it likely that income will rise with further education, but also the chances of becoming unemployed are reduced. For example, in the late 1990s, the unemployment rate for high school dropouts was 13.5 percent; for persons with a high school diploma, 7.7 percent; for persons with one to three years of college, 5.9 percent; and for persons with four years of college or more, 2.9 percent. In summary, if you want to increase your chances of earning a high income and of not being unemployed, one of the surest ways is to get an education.

Exhibit 21-4

Income Relative to Educational Level

Here we see the average annual income at different educational levels in the late 1990s. Numbers on the vertical axis are in thousands of dollars.

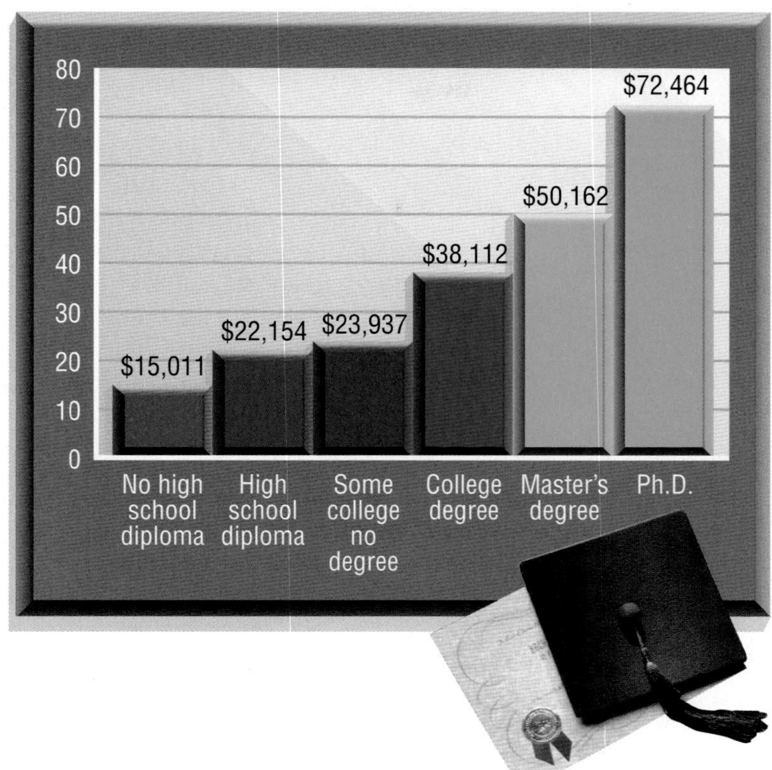

Sabrina went to college for two years; she did not receive a degree. Goro went to college and received both a bachelor's and a master's degree. Predict whose income will be higher over a lifetime. Explain your answer.

Matching Your Abilities, Educational Interests, and Job

Ideally, we all would like to work at a job that is interesting, that we are able to do, and that pays relatively well. For example, let's say Brenda has a natural ability in mathematics, and she works hard in school to learn as much about the subject as possible. She goes on to get a college degree in mathematics and ends up working for a company that pays her extremely well. For Brenda, everything has come together. She is doing something that she likes, that she is good at, and that earns her a very good income.

If you look forward to your biology class, you might want to pursue science as a profession.

It may not work this way for everyone. Jorge, for example, may be a natural when it comes to music and may go on to study music at college. But when he graduates, he may learn that as a musician he cannot earn the income that he would like to earn. This fact does not mean that Jorge should not have been a music major in college. His love of, and ability in, music may give him so much pleasure that he is willing to earn less as a musician than he would as, say, an accountant or a chemist. After all, there are other things in life than earning more income.

Protecting your future requires you to be aware of many things. When it comes to getting a job, you must consider what you are good at doing, what you are interested in, and what pays an income with which you can be comfortable. For example, you do not protect your future when you focus only on what you are interested in and ignore what you are good at doing. You may end up not being able to do what you are interested in. For example, not everyone who is interested in being a professional ballet dancer can become one.

What are some of the things you should consider if you're planning a career as an artist?

The Job and Earnings Outlook

How do you know if what you are interested in will be in demand and pay well when it is time for you to go job hunting? You may be thinking of becoming an accountant, actor, teacher, or advertising executive, but you may be unsure whether there will be a job for you when the time comes, or how much that job will pay.

In a quickly changing economy, such as the U.S. economy, it is impossible to know exactly what skills and talents will be in demand in future years or what they will be worth. However, the U.S. Department of Labor attempts to predict the job and earnings outlook for the future. Two sources of career guidance are the *Occupational Outlook Handbook* (which is found in nine out of ten high schools) and *Occupational Projections and Training Data.*[1] The *Handbook* contains detailed information on the outlook for hundreds of occupations, as well as information about the nature of the work, qualifications, average earnings, and so on. *Occupational Projections and Training Data,* a statistical supplement to the *Handbook,* contains current and projected employment estimates for about five hundred occupations.

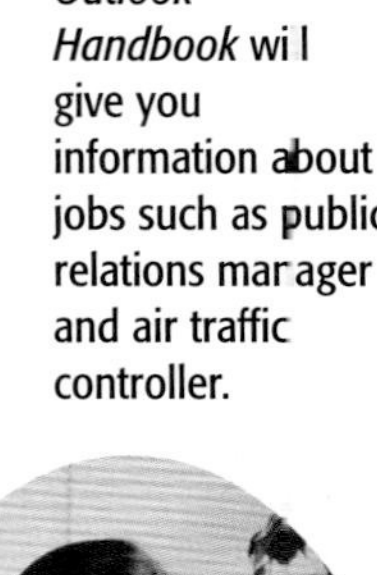

The *Occupational Outlook Handbook* will give you information about jobs such as public relations manager and air traffic controller.

Additional information can be obtained from state job service centers, which can be found in the telephone book in the state government section. These centers provide information on local job markets, which is important because the outlook for any occupation may vary considerably from place to place. For example, sections of the country where population growth is slow have less need for elementary school teachers than do regions experiencing growth.

1. These publications are available from the Bureau of Labor Statistics Publication Sales Center, P.O. Box 2145, Chicago, IL 60690, and the Superintendent of Documents, U.S. Government Printing Office, Washington, D.C. 20402.

Application Forms, Résumés, and Interviews

When you apply for a job, you will have to fill out an application form, submit a résumé, or both. You will also be interviewed.

The Application Form The following are some things to consider when filling out an application form:

1. *Before you start to fill out the application form, photocopy it.* Most people make mistakes when filling out application forms. When they erase the errors, scratch through them with pen, or type over them, the finished application comes out looking ragged and dirty. A neat, clean application is what you want. Therefore, fill out the photocopy of the application first, check it for mistakes, rewrite it where necessary, and then use it as a guide to fill out the actual application form that you will submit to the employer.
2. *Be neat and type the form, if possible.* Suppose an employer reviews two application forms. One is neatly typed, and the other is filled in with pencil or pen, has a few scribbles and dark eraser marks, and generally looks shabby. The often-subtle message that an employer receives from a messy application form is that the applicant is untidy, impatient, and unlikely to take the time to do a job correctly.
3. *Be prepared to fill in an application form when you visit the employer's premises.* Suppose you visit a local company to ask if it is hiring. The personnel manager says yes and hands you an application form to fill out immediately. You need to be prepared with some information about yourself. For example, you may need (1) the names, addresses, and telephone numbers of former employers; (2) your Social Security number; and (3) previous home addresses. Keep this information with you when you visit prospective employers.
4. *Do not leave anything blank.* If something does not apply to you, simply write "n/a," which stands for "not applicable." If you leave some lines of an application form blank, the person reading the form will not know if you missed something.
5. *If there is a place on the application form to write down comments, do so.* Many application forms end with a space for you to make some

It's almost impossible to remember all of the information you need to fill out an application form. Be sure to write down the information and take it with you.

FBI Agent

The Federal Bureau of Investigation (FBI) enforces more than 260 federal statutes and conducts investigations for national security issues. The FBI investigates organized crime, white-collar crime, financial crime, bribery, fraud against the government, bank robbery, terrorism, and extortion, among other things. FBI employees include special agents, scientists and lab technicians, forensic specialists, accountants, lawyers, language specialists, and engineers.

To qualify to become an FBI agent, you need a degree from a four-year college (and an advanced degree if you plan to work in forensics or behavior profiling). You must be a citizen between the ages of twenty-three and thirty-six and be able to relocate.

When applying for a job with the FBI, you complete an application, take a number of tests (physical, background, credit, and so on), and go through numerous interviews. If you are accepted, you will go to the FBI academy for four months of training.

QUESTION TO ANSWER What do you see as the benefits and costs of becoming an FBI special agent?

Some information you'll need to fill in an application

- ✓ Names, addresses, and telephone numbers of former employers
- ✓ Your Social Security number
- ✓ Previous home address

HELP WANTED

comments if you choose. For example, a form might read: "In the space below, please provide any information about yourself that you feel is relevant to your doing this job."

Do not view this part of the application as a stumbling block to filling in the form in under five minutes. Instead, take your time; look at the comment section as an opportunity to separate yourself from the many others who may be applying for the same job. Tell your potential employer why you think you are right for the job.

résumé
A statement of a job applicant's previous employment, education, and other relevant information.

The Résumé A **résumé** is a document you create that contains the following information : (1) your name, address, and telephone number; (2) the job you are seeking or your career goal; (3) your education; (4) your work experience; (5) honors you have received; and (6) any other information relevant to your ability to do the job you are seeking. A résumé should be well organized, easy to read, and no longer than two pages. Exhibit 21-5 on page 595 shows a standard way to organize a résumé. The two major parts identify the person's education and work experience in a matter-of-fact way.

Some persons use a different format for their résumés. For example, instead of simply listing their former workplaces and stating what jobs they held, they discuss the talents they exhibited and the skills they acquired working at previous jobs. Exhibit 21-6 shows a résumé of this kind.

The Interview The job interview is your best opportunity to present yourself in a favorable light to an employer. Keep in mind that you represent a risk to the employer, who does not know what type of employee you will be. Will you be consistently late to work, or on time? Will you be a good worker or not? Will you get along with others?

To be equipped for an interview, keep these things in mind:

1. *Learn about the employer before the interview.* Suppose you have an interview with the AAA Company on Monday. Before the interview, you should learn something about that company, such as what it produces, how long it has been in business, and how many employees it has. The information need not be detailed, but you do not want to walk into an interview knowing nothing about the company for which you hope to work. After all, you want to be able to give a knowledgeable answer if an interviewer asks, "Do you know what it is we do here at our company?"

   You can usually obtain general information on a company at the local library or from persons who work for the company. You can also call the company before the interview and ask a few questions.

A trip to the library to research potential employers can give you the edge you need in a competitive job market.

Exhibit 21-5
Résumé A

This résumé emphasizes education and work experience. See Exhibit 21-6 for a résumé with a different emphasis.

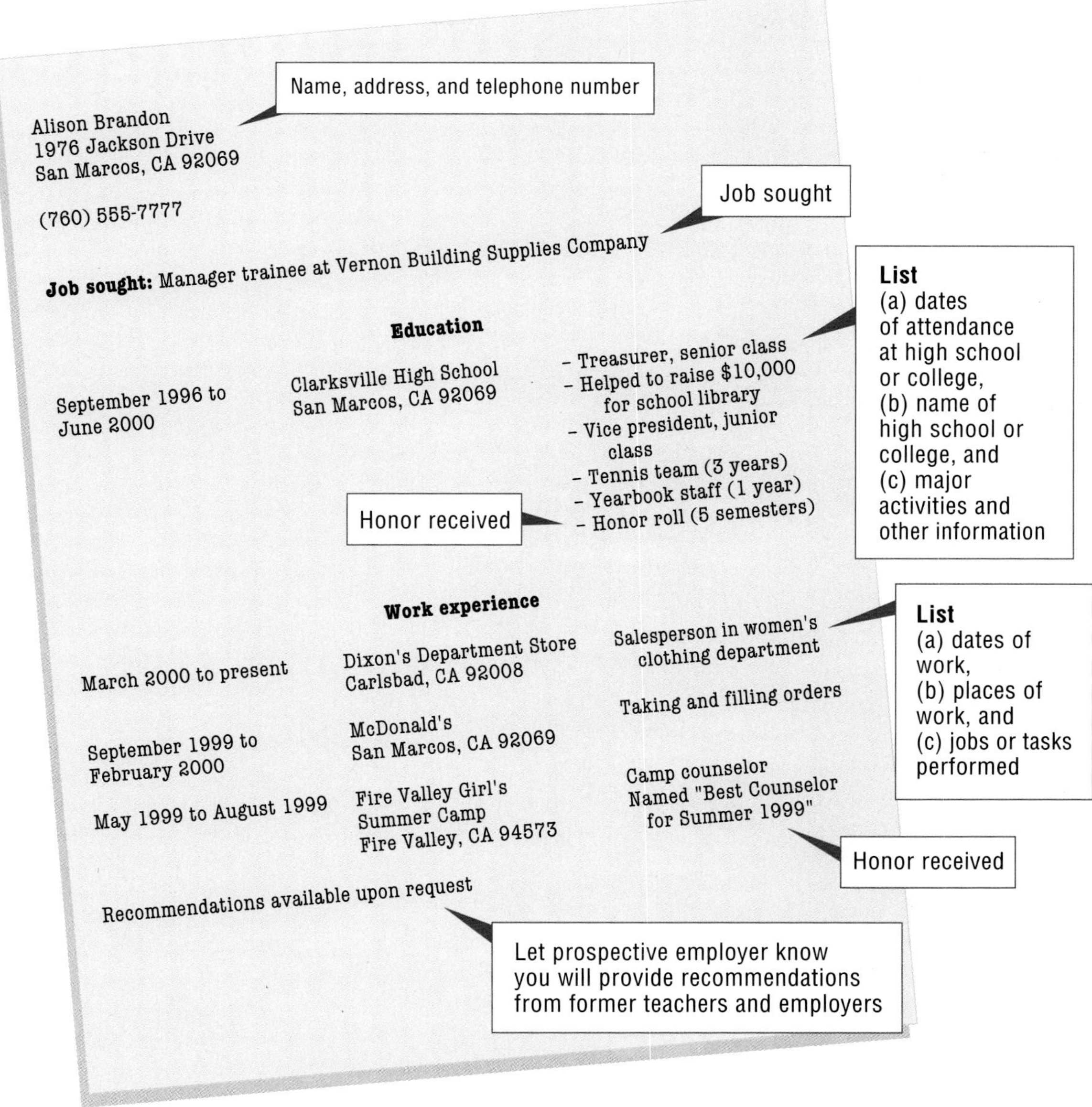
Alison Brandon
1976 Jackson Drive
San Marcos, CA 92069

(760) 555-7777

Job sought: Manager trainee at Vernon Building Supplies Company

Education

September 1996 to June 2000	Clarksville High School San Marcos, CA 92069	- Treasurer, senior class - Helped to raise $10,000 for school library - Vice president, junior class - Tennis team (3 years) - Yearbook staff (1 year) - Honor roll (5 semesters)

Work experience

March 2000 to present	Dixon's Department Store Carlsbad, CA 92008	Salesperson in women's clothing department
September 1999 to February 2000	McDonald's San Marcos, CA 92069	Taking and filling orders
May 1999 to August 1999	Fire Valley Girl's Summer Camp Fire Valley, CA 94573	Camp counselor Named "Best Counselor for Summer 1999"

Recommendations available upon request

2. *Rehearse the interview.* One of the best ways to prepare for an interview is to rehearse it with a friend or two. Let your friend be the interviewer and you be the interviewee. Before you start the rehearsal, write down a list of questions the real interviewer is likely to ask you. Here is a possible list:
   - Why did you apply for this job?
   - What do you know about this job or company?
   - Why should I hire you?
   - What are your strengths and weaknesses?
   - What would you like to tell me about yourself?
   - What accomplishment has given you the greatest satisfaction?
   - What courses did you like best in school?
   - What courses did you like least in school?

Exhibit 21-6
Résumé B

This résumé emphasizes talents and skills. Contrast it with the résumé in Exhibit 21-5.

Alison Brandon
1976 Jackson Drive
San Marcos, CA 92069

(760) 555-7777

Job sought: Manager trainee at Vernon Building Supplies Company

Skills, education, and experience

Working with people: Both in high school and in my jobs, I have worked well with people. As treasurer of the senior class, and as vice president of the junior class, I worked on school projects that required me to argue my positions convincingly, listen to the arguments advanced by others, and find suitable compromise positions. I realize that I cannot always get my way, but I continue to state what I believe, accept that people may disagree with me, and move on to see if we can work together.

In my work experience I have enjoyed dealing with the public. I have learned to be patient, listen attentively, and recognize that if people get "hot under the collar," I should try to work things out in a cordial way.

Effective communication: In high school, I played a leadership role in my junior and senior classes. I learned that a part of good leadership is being able to communicate your views and opinions to others in a cordial way. I have developed this skill, which I believe will help me throughout my life.

Hard work and attention to detail: In my school courses, activities, and jobs, I have learned the need to work hard and attentively. I have learned that it is better to do something right the first time than have to re-do it.

Chronology

September 1996 to June 2000	Attended Clarksville High School in San Marcos, California. I was treasurer of the senior class and vice president of the junior class, played on the tennis team for 3 years, worked as a member of the yearbook staff for 1 year, helped to raise $10,000 for the school library, and was on the honor roll for 5 semesters.
March 2000 to present	I worked as a salesperson in the women's clothing department at Dixon's Department Store in Carlsbad, California.
September 1999 to February 2000	I worked taking and filling orders at McDonald's in San Marcos, California.
May 1999 to August 1999	I was camp counselor at Fire Valley Girl's Summer Camp in Fire Valley, California. I was voted "Best Counselor for Summer 1999."

Recommendations available upon request

- Why did you leave your last job?
- What do you hope to be doing in three to five years?
- What are your hobbies?
- What would you change about yourself?
- How do your education and work experience relate to this job?
- What salary do you expect?

3. *Arrive for the interview on time.* Arriving early or late makes a bad impression. When you arrive early, you may interrupt the person who expected you later. When you arrive late, you signal that you are not dependable.
4. *Do not brag, but do not ignore your strong points.* Sometime during the interview, tell the interviewer why you think you would be a good person to hire. The interviewer may give you this chance by simply asking, "Why do you think you are right for this job?" If not, then you should work this information into the conversation somehow. You might say, "I believe you are looking for a person who is hardworking, conscientious, and works well with people. I am all of these things. Let me give you a few examples. . . ." Then you could describe how, in past jobs or at school, you have shown these characteristics.

   You have to be careful, however. It is one thing to state the truth and tell someone that you are a good person for the job; it is another thing to brag. No one wants to hire a bragger, but almost everyone wants to hire people who are confident about themselves and know how to tell others of their strengths in a positive, polite manner.

Showing poise and confidence are essential during an interview.

5. *Ask questions when you have a chance.* At the end of the interview, the interviewer will often ask if you have any questions. Here are some suggestions:
   - What would a day on this job be like?
   - To whom would I report?
   - Would I supervise anyone?
   - Why did the last person leave this job?
   - What is that person doing now?
   - What is the greatest challenge of this job?
   - Is this company growing?
6. *Listen carefully.* Many people get nervous in interviews. They wonder if they look right, if they are smiling enough, if they should not have said what they just said, or if the interviewer likes them. Feeling nervous is natural, but try your best to put such concerns aside and listen to what the interviewer is saying and asking. If you do not listen carefully—and if you do not respond directly and specifically—the interviewer may get the feeling that your mind is somewhere else and that perhaps you really do not want the job.
7. *Write a thank-you letter.* Soon after the interview, send a letter to the interviewer expressing your appreciation for the interview. If you need to follow up on something you said during the interview, do it in this letter.

Section 4 Review

Defining Terms

1. Define *résumé.*

Applying Economic Concepts

2. Name two government publications that attempt to predict the job and earnings outlook for the future.

3. Why shouldn't you leave anything blank on a job application?

4. List five questions you may be asked in an interview.

5. Why is it important to arrive on time to a job interview?

SECTION 5

Health Insurance

Some people buy insurance and then, when they don't use it, say that they spent their money for nothing. The fact is, everyone buys insurance and hopes not to use it. No one buys car insurance hoping to have an accident; no one buys fire insurance hoping that his or her house will catch on fire; and no one buys health insurance hoping to get sick and go to the hospital. The best we can hope for is not to have to use the insurance we buy. But we do buy it because it usually gives us peace of mind. We buy it because we are not sure what the future holds. In this section we discuss one type of insurance—health insurance.

As you read this section, keep these key questions in mind.

- What is covered by basic health insurance? By major medical insurance?
- What is a health maintenance organization (HMO)?

Basic Health Insurance

Basic health insurance is composed of three different types of insurance: hospital-expense insurance, surgical-expense insurance, and physician-expense insurance.

Hospital-Expense Insurance Daily hospital room and board and routine nursing care are covered by hospital-expense insurance. It also provides for laboratory tests, X-ray examinations, the use of an operating room, drugs and medication, anesthesia, and so on. The insurance policy usually limits the number of hospital days covered and the daily costs. For example, a policy may state that a person's hospital stay is covered for up to 180 days at a rate of up to $250 a day.

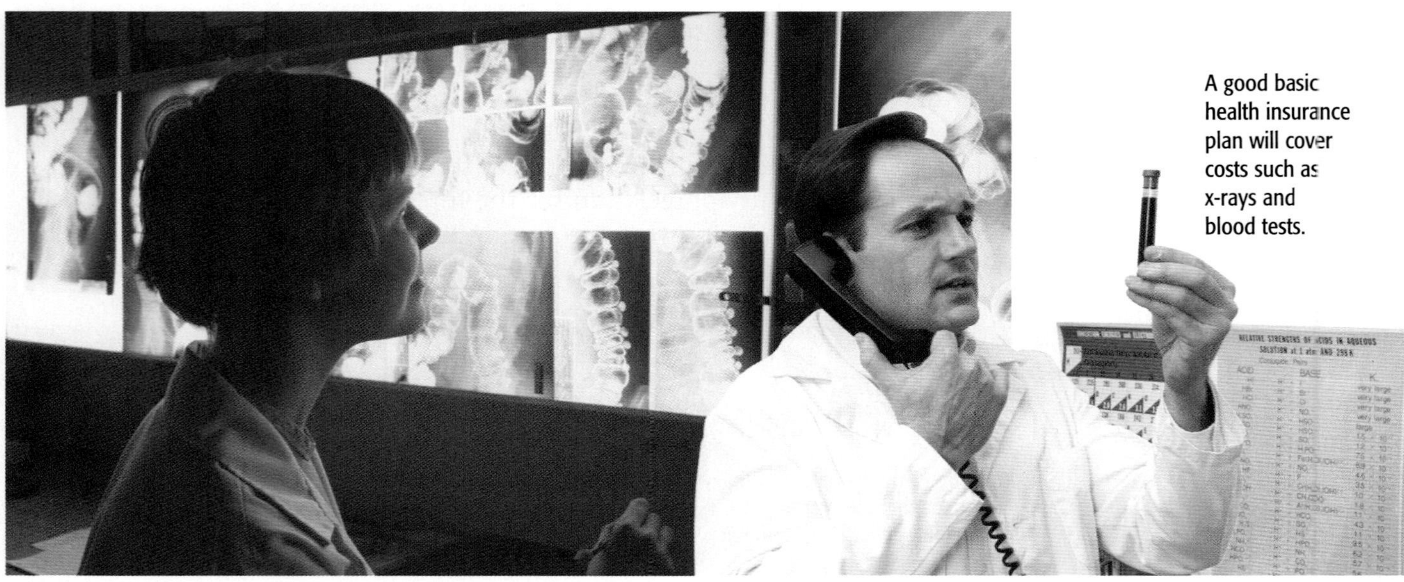

A good basic health insurance plan will cover costs such as x-rays and blood tests.

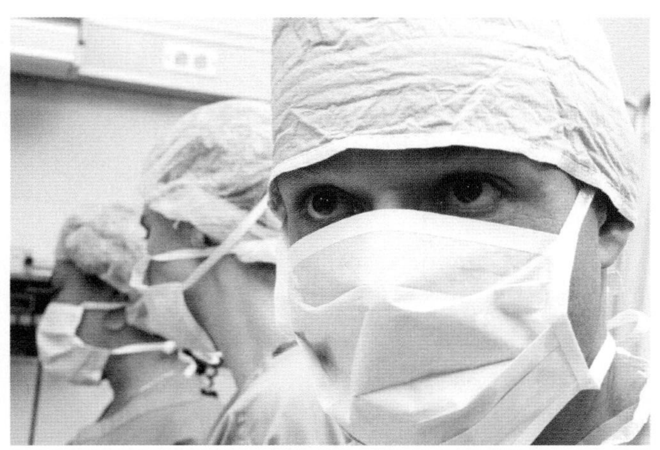

Without insurance coverage, most people would have difficulty paying the high costs associated with a major surgery.

Surgical-Expense Insurance The fees of the surgeon are covered by surgical-expense insurance. There is a limit to what is covered and how much is paid out. For example, cosmetic surgery (say, a face-lift) is not covered, and usually there is a set fee for specific procedures (say, $600 for gallstone removal).

Physician-Expense Insurance Doctors' fees for nonsurgical care in the hospital, the home, or the office are covered by physician-expense insurance.

Major Medical Insurance

Major medical insurance is designed to pick up where basic health insurance leaves off. It covers large, catastrophic, and unpredictable medical expenses. Major medical insurance usually comes with a deductible and a co-payment. The deductible is the amount of a bill that you must pay before you are eligible for benefits. For example, suppose there is a $200 deductible on your policy. If you go into the hospital and the bill comes to $12,000, you have to pay the first $200. You may also have to pay a percentage of the remainder as your co-payment. For example, if you have an 80/20 co-payment plan, the insurance company pays 80 percent of everything after you have met the deductible, and you pay 20 percent. Finally, some major medical insurance policies place limits on what will be paid per illness (say, $300,000 for cancer) or over the lifetime of the insured person (say, $1 million over the person's lifetime). A person who has both basic health insurance and major medical insurance is said to have comprehensive health insurance.

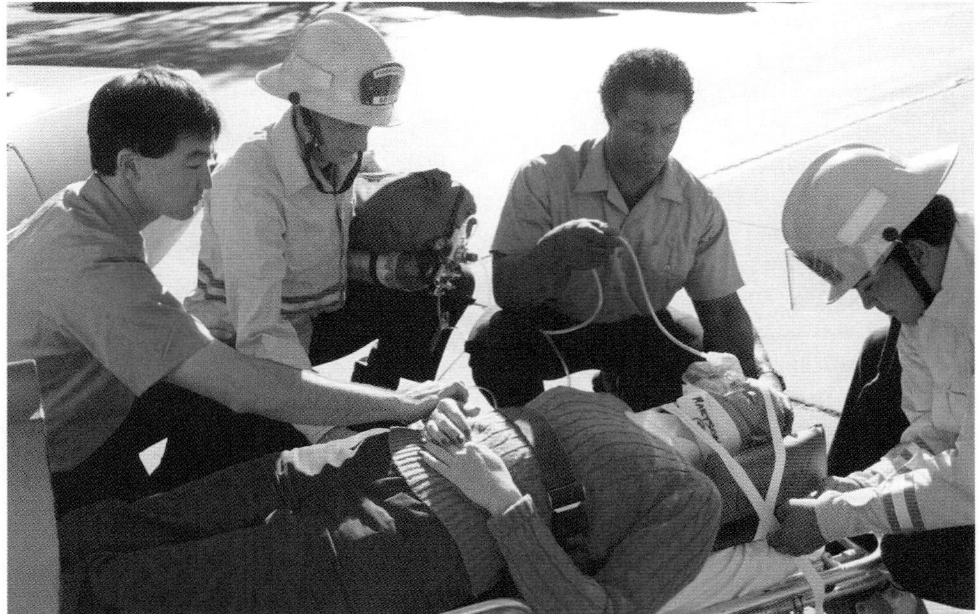

Major medical coverage, which covers emergencies such as you see here, is a type of insurance we pay for but hope we never use.

Health Maintenance Organizations

A health maintenance organization (HMO) offers its members comprehensive medical care for a monthly or yearly fee. First, members pay a monthly or yearly fee no matter how much medical attention they receive. When they go to a doctor or hospital, there are no deductibles, copayments, or insurance forms to fill out.

Second, members usually receive medical attention from a selected group of doctors and hospitals. In other words, if you are a member of an HMO, you must choose your doctor and hospital from the ones offered by the HMO. You cannot be treated by just any doctor or at just any hospital if you want your HMO to pay for the services you receive. In contrast, when you buy regular health care insurance, you can go to any doctor you wish.

The growth in HMOs has been explosive. In 1971 there were 41 HMOs in the United States. In the late 1990s there were about 550. This growth has been caused by the lower costs of HMOs, which have been estimated to be 10 to 40 percent lower than the costs of regular health care plans. Of course, we need to remember that there are always trade-offs. Lower health care costs may come with less flexibility in choosing a doctor and possibly longer waits to see the doctor. Still, many millions of people are deciding the trade-off is worthwhile.

What should you look for in an HMO? First, be sure the HMO has a variety of doctors and specialists. Second, make sure the HMO-affiliated hospital or hospitals has up-to-date facilities and technology. Third, find out how long it takes, on average, to see a doctor for a nonemergency. In some HMOs you may wait six weeks to two months and get to see a doctor right away in others.

It is important to many people that they have the freedom to choose their doctors. However, members of a HMO do not always have that freedom.

Section 5 Review

Applying Economic Concepts

1. What does basic health insurance cover?
2. What does major medical insurance cover?
3. "When you join an HMO, you can choose any doctor you want." State whether this statement is true or false, and explain your answer.

SECTION 6

Life Insurance

You have probably seen advertisements for life insurance on television and in newspapers and magazines. This section discusses life insurance.

As you read this section, keep these key questions in mind:

- What is the difference between term life insurance and whole life insurance?
- What is universal life insurance?
- What is variable life insurance?

Young, healthy people often question the value of life insurance. As they mature, get married, and begin families, their attitudes about insurance usually change.

Two Major Types of Life Insurance

Key Term

beneficiary

Life insurance guarantees payment if a person dies or reaches a certain age (depending on the type of life insurance policy the person has). There are two major types of life insurance: term and whole life.

Term Life Insurance With term life insurance, you pay premiums to the insurance company, and in turn the **beneficiaries** you name are paid a certain sum of money if you die during a specific period. When the specific period ends, your coverage ends. For example, you may buy a five-year term policy for $250,000 worth of coverage for an annual premium of $430. If you die within the five-year period and your premiums are paid up, your beneficiaries will receive $250,000.

The price of term life insurance varies according to how much coverage you want and your age and health. For example, the premiums are higher for a thirty-year-old than for a twenty-five-year-old. Your premiums are raised if you renew your policy; for example, your premiums would be higher when you renewed your policy at age thirty than when you took out the policy at age twenty-five.

Typically, a young married couple with a new house and children would purchase term life insurance, because the husband and wife would want to protect themselves against each other's death. If one died, the insurance payment would help the other with house payments, everyday expenses, college costs for the children in future years, and so on. They might simply want term life insurance for ten to fifteen years while the children are growing up.

Purchasing life insurance that provides for their children gives parents a feeling of security.

MINI GLOSSARY

beneficiary
A person named to receive benefits from an insurance policy.

Whole Life Insurance As the name implies, whole life insurance covers a person for his or her whole life, until death. The premiums under whole life insurance stay the same as long as the policy is in effect. (Recall that with term life insurance, the monthly or yearly premiums rise as one gets older.)

One important feature of whole life insurance is its cash value, the amount of money policyholders would receive if they decided to redeem, or cash in, their policy. Some people see the cash value that is accumulated in a whole life policy as a form of savings to be drawn on (borrowed) in later years. When policyholders make a withdrawal from the cash value in their insurance account, however, they give up insurance protection. A withdrawal, either partial or total, ends the whole life policy. Alternatively, policyholders can take out a loan against the cash value of their policies. For example, suppose you have a cash value of $10,000 and you want to borrow $5,000. The insurance company will give you this loan at an interest rate that is usually low.

Many people view their whole life policies as investments that will help to finance their retirement years.

Whole life insurance is often costly. For example, a thirty-five-year-old nonsmoking man might pay $2,000 annually for a $200,000 whole life policy, whereas he would pay about $300 annually (until renewal) for a $200,000 term policy. Of course, the term policy premium (payment) would increase with each renewal period, whereas the whole life premium would stay the same. Only after many years would the term premium be greater than the whole life premium.

Other Types of Life Insurance

Two other types of life insurance are universal life and variable life.

Universal Life Insurance Universal life insurance is similar to whole life insurance in that it allows you to build up a cash value for the policy and allows you to borrow against the cash value or completely withdraw it. It is different, though, in that you may withdraw part of the cash value without ending your insurance protection. However, if you do withdraw part of the cash value, your death benefit is reduced.

Variable Life Insurance Variable life insurance is similar to universal life insurance, with one exception. With universal life insurance, the money in your cash value account is invested by the insurance company. Under a variable life insurance policy, you decide how your money is invested. You may choose to invest in stocks, bonds, money market funds, or a combination.

Section 6 Review

Defining Terms

1. Define *beneficiary.*

Applying Economic Concepts

2. What is the cash value of a whole life insurance policy?
3. What is a major difference between whole life insurance and universal life insurance?
4. What is a major difference between universal life insurance and variable life insurance?

SECTION 7 Homeowner's and Renter's Insurance

Homes and the personal possessions in them represent major investments. Protecting those investments is the purpose of homeowner's and renter's insurance, the topic of this section.

As you read this section, keep these key questions in mind:

- What should every homeowner's insurance policy cover?
- In buying homeowner's insurance, why is it a mistake to insure only up to the value of the mortgage?
- How does inflation affect the replacement cost of a house?
- What are the benefits and costs of renter's insurance?

Considerations in Buying Homeowner's Insurance

There are many things to consider when you purchase homeowner's insurance. Here are a few:

1. *Make certain your homeowner's insurance policy covers (a) damage to the house, (b) personal property, (c) personal liability, and (d) loss of use.* Homeowners rarely think of all the things that need to be covered by insurance. What they do think of is coverage for any damage done to the house itself—for example, damage caused by a fire or by a car crashing into the house. But other things need to be considered, too. For example, if you are shopping for homeowner's insurance, make sure personal property (such things as clothes, jewelry, and computers) is covered. Also, if someone falls down your porch stairs, his or her medical expenses should be covered by what is referred to as *personal liability insurance.* Finally, make sure that if your house is damaged and you have to live elsewhere while the damage is being repaired, your homeowner's insurance will pay you for the "loss of use" of your house.

Few people could afford to replace a beautiful home such as this if it were to be severely damaged or destroyed. This is why people buy homeowner's insurance.

You increase your chances of being reimbursed for valuable personal belongings if you have sales receipts and photos.

2. *Keep sales slips, and photograph your personal belongings.* Suppose you come home one night to find that your home has been burglarized and a number of things are missing. You report the missing items to your insurance agent, who asks for evidence that you actually owned those items. The best way to show proof of ownership is to show the agent either a sales slip for the item or an actual photograph of the item in your home.
3. *Don't make the mistake of insuring only up to the value of your mortgage.* Suppose your house cost you $150,000. You made a $50,000 down payment and took out a mortgage loan of $100,000. Do not make the mistake of simply insuring your house for the mortgage amount ($100,000). You need to insure the house for its replacement cost—that is, the amount of money that you would need to replace the house if it were destroyed.
4. *Consider inflation when you estimate the replacement cost of your house.* Suppose that in 1997 you insured your house for its replacement cost. You found out that if your house were completely destroyed, it would cost you $135,000 to rebuild it, so you insured your house for $135,000. It is now 2001. Between 1997 and 2001, building supplies and labor have become more expensive because of inflation. Can you still replace your home for $135,000 if it is destroyed? Because of inflation, the answer is probably no. The best thing to do, then, is to increase your insurance coverage to adjust for the inflation that has made rebuilding your home more costly.
5. *Be aware that most insurance companies will reduce your insurance premiums if you install certain safeguards in your home.* Most insurance companies will reduce your insurance premiums if you install a smoke detector, dead bolts on the doors, a security system, and so on. Make sure you tell your insurance agent about what you have done to reduce the chance of crime or fire in your home.

THE BORN LOSER ® by Art and Chip Sansom

THE BORN LOSER reprinted by permission of Newspaper Enterprise Association, Inc.

To make sure you have the protection you need, check out the financial stability of the insurance company before you buy a policy. Also be sure to read the policy carefully to determine what is and is not covered.

6. *Inform yourself of what your policy does not cover.* You may assume that your policy covers flood damage done to your house. However, if you live in an area prone to floods, it may not. When it comes to homeowner's insurance, *do not assume anything.* Ask questions. You may need to buy some supplemental insurance to protect yourself against floods and other natural disasters.
7. *Be aware that the higher the deductible, the less expensive the policy.* The deductible is the amount of money you must pay for losses before the insurance company begins to pay. The more you are willing to pay before the insurance company has to pay (that is, the higher your deductible), the lower your premiums will be. If your insurance agent tells you that your premium will be $500 a year with a deductible of $200, ask what the premium would be if the deductible were $500 or $1,000. You may or may not prefer to pay a higher deductible and lower premiums, but you should be aware of this trade-off.
8. *Consider the financial stability of the insurance company.* In recent years, some insurance companies have had financial problems, so make sure your insurance company is financially stable. The Consumers Union, which publishes *Consumer Reports,* advises that you buy insurance only from firms that have an A+ or A rating from *Best's Insurance Reports,* a publication of the Best Company, an independent rating organization. Check with a library for the publication, or ask your insurance agent for written documentation of the insurance company's rating.

Renter's Insurance

If you rent an apartment, the landlord probably has insurance on the apartment building itself. But the landlord's insurance will probably not cover you if, say, you are robbed or if a friend comes over to your apartment and slips and hurts herself on the stairs going from the first floor of your apartment to the second floor. Renters often mistakenly think that because they pay monthly rent, they do not have to worry about such things as insurance against loss of personal possessions or personal liability. However, renters need insurance, too. Renter's insurance is widely available and usually modest in cost. If you rent an apartment, you should strongly consider having it.

Section 7 Review

Applying Economic Concepts

1. Against what does personal liability insurance (as a part of homeowner's insurance) protect you?
2. Why is it important to photograph the personal belongings in your house?
3. What does inflation do to the replacement cost of a house?
4. What happens to your insurance premiums as the deductible rises? As it falls?

SECTION 8

Automobile Insurance

This section discusses automobile insurance. As you will learn, automobile insurance protects more than just the money invested in the automobile.

As you read this section, keep these key questions in mind:

- What does bodily injury liability insurance pay for?
- What does property damage liability insurance pay for?
- What is the purpose of buying uninsured motorist protection insurance?
- What is no-fault insurance?
- What should you do if you have an automobile accident?

The Automobile Insurance Policy

An automobile insurance policy is a package of several types of coverage, each with its own premium. The sum of these premiums is what you pay for the policy. This section examines a few of the most important types of coverage.

In many states the law requires drivers to have liability coverage.

Bodily Injury Liability Insurance Bodily injury liability insurance pays for losses due to death or injury in a car accident that is the insured driver's fault. It covers people both inside and outside the car. Injured persons can make a claim against this coverage to pay for medical bills, lost wages, and damages due to pain and suffering.

Many bodily injury liability policies are referred to as *split-limit policies.* These policies contain provisions that set (1) the maximum dollar amount paid per injured person and (2) the maximum dollar amount paid per accident. A typical split-limit policy might read "25/50," which means that the policy pays a maximum of $25,000 per injured person and not more than $50,000 per accident. For example, if one person was injured in an accident and had damages of $30,000, the policy would pay $25,000 to this person. Most experts recommend carrying bodily injury liability insurance of 100/300—a maximum of $100,000 per person and $300,000 per accident.

Property Damage Liability Insurance Property damage liability insurance covers damage done to another person's car, buildings, fences, and so on. Experts recommend coverage of between $25,000 and $50,000. Keep in mind that sometimes only a small increase in your premium can dramatically increase the coverage.

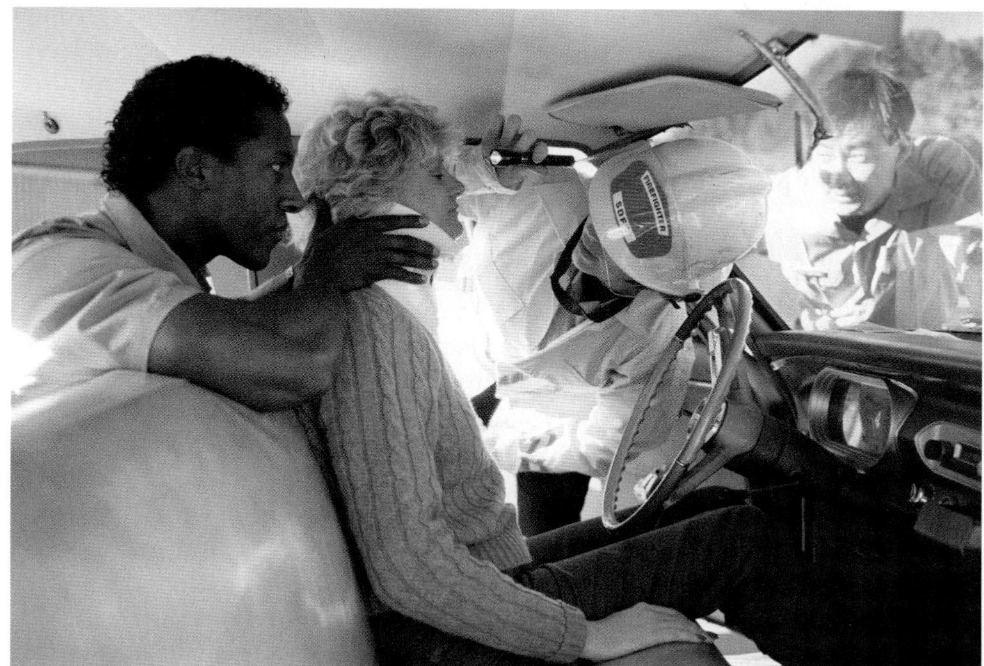

If your health insurance policy provides medical and hospital coverage, you may not need to purchase this coverage as part of your automobile insurance.

Medical Payments Insurance Medical payments insurance pays for medical expenses resulting from a car accident, no matter who is at fault. Some people do not purchase medical payments insurance because their health insurance pays for injuries sustained in an accident. However, health insurance does not usually pay funeral benefits, whereas medical payments insurance usually does.

Uninsured Motorist Protection Insurance Some people drive their cars without having any automobile insurance. If one of them hits you with his or her car and you or your car suffers damages, you may not be able to collect any money from the person. To guard against this possibility, you may choose to purchase uninsured motorist coverage. This insurance would cover you if you were in an accident with an uninsured motorist or harmed by a hit-and-run driver.

Collision Insurance Collision insurance pays for the damage to your car if it is in an accident, no matter who is responsible for the accident. Your coverage is limited by the amount of the deductible, which usually ranges from $100 to $250. As always, the higher the deductible, the lower the premiums.

Comprehensive Insurance Comprehensive insurance is the companion of collision insurance. While collision insurance covers damage to your car if it is in an accident, comprehensive insurance covers just about everything else that can happen to a car. For example, it covers the damage if the car is stolen, is vandalized, or catches fire. As with collision insurance, the coverage is limited by the deductible.

No-Fault Insurance

No-fault insurance, which began to be adopted in some states in the early 1970s, was designed to eliminate the need to sue the other driver to gain compensation for injuries suffered in a car accident. Instead, a

If she lives in a no-fault state, this woman's auto insurance will pay for the costs of any injuries resulting from an accident, whether she was at fault or not.

person's own insurance company pays him or her for injuries suffered, no matter who is at fault. Usually, no-fault insurance covers you and the passengers in your car, as well as pedestrians hit by your car.

Determination of Automobile Insurance Premiums

People pay different premiums for their automobile insurance. The following are some of the factors that determine how much you will pay.

Your Age In most but not all states, a person's age affects his or her automobile insurance premium. Statistics show that drivers under the age of twenty-five have a higher accident rate than drivers between the ages of twenty-five and thirty-five. For this reason, their premiums are higher.

Where You Live If you live in a densely populated area where vandalism and car theft are common, you will pay a higher premium than if you live in a sparsely populated area where these things are relatively uncommon.

You will pay significantly less in insurance premiums if you drive defensively and within the speed limit.

Your Driving Record If you have a history of car accidents and speeding tickets, your premium is likely to be higher than if you do not have such a history.

The Car You Drive If you drive a new, expensive car that is difficult and costly to repair, you will pay a higher premium than if you drive an older car that is easy and inexpensive to repair.

How Much You Drive If you drive only a few miles a week, you are likely to pay a lower premium than a person who drives many miles a week.

Whether or Not You Have Had a Driver Education Course Many insurance companies will give you a discount on your

Installing antitheft devices can lower your insurance premiums.

premium if you have taken a driver education course. The discount is usually 5 to 10 percent.

Whether or Not You Have Air Bags in Your Car Some insurance companies will give you a discount on the medical insurance part of your automobile insurance coverage if you have air bags in your car.

Whether or Not You Have Antitheft Devices in Your Car Many insurance companies will discount the comprehensive part of your automobile insurance coverage if you have installed antitheft devices in your car.

What to Do in an Automobile Accident

The steps to take if you have a car accident are listed here:

1. *Check to see if anyone is injured. Next, call the police.* When you call the police, state where the accident occurred (the nearest cross streets). If someone has been injured, ask that an ambulance or rescue squad be sent immediately.
2. *Do not move injured persons.* If you move injured persons, you could harm them. Cover an injured person with a blanket or coat if one is handy.
3. *When police officers arrive, cooperate fully.* Be sure to answer police officers' questions honestly, but state only what you know to be the facts. It is natural to be shaken up after an accident, and some people in this condition quickly conclude that they must have been at fault. Remember to stay calm and state only the facts rather than guesses, assumptions, or beliefs.
4. *Ask a police officer where you can obtain a copy of the police report.* You may need a copy of the police report for insurance purposes or for a court case. Ask a police officer on the scene where you should go to obtain the report.
5. *Make sure you obtain the following information: the names and addresses of all drivers and passengers in the accident; the license plate numbers, makes, and models of the cars involved; other drivers' license identification numbers; insurance identification numbers; the names, addresses, and telephone numbers of any witnesses to the accident; and the names of the police officers at the scene.* This information may come in handy later, and your insurance agent may ask for it. Get into the habit of carrying a pencil or pen and paper in the glove compartment of your car so that you are always ready to write down the information you may need.
6. *If you have a camera in the car, take pictures of the accident scene.* Photograph the damage done to the cars; skid marks, if there are any; and

If you are involved in an automobile accident, call the police and cooperate fully in their investigation. At the first opportunity you should also call your insurance agent.

so on. If you do not have a camera, make a rough sketch of the accident. You may need it later to refresh your memory.

7. *If you run into an unattended car, leave your name and telephone number on the car's windshield so that the owner can get in touch with you.* This response is simply the right thing to do.
8. *Get in touch with your insurance company as soon as possible.* Make sure you tell your insurance agent exactly what happened, and let the agent advise you as to what to do next. The insurance company will probably want to have an insurance adjuster inspect your car before you get it repaired. It is a good idea to keep the name and telephone number of your insurance agent in the glove compartment of your car. That way, if you are out of town and have an accident, you can easily and quickly get in touch.
9. *Keep a record of your expenses.* Make sure to keep a record of all the expenses you incur as a result of an accident. This list might include lost wages, the cost of a rental car, and so on.
10. *Keep copies of all your paperwork.* There is a good chance that you will have to refer to certain papers later.

These are general guidelines. It is important to know the laws of your own state in dealing with motor vehicle accidents.

Section 8 Review

Applying Economic Concepts

1. What does a split-limit policy that reads "100/300" mean?
2. How much property damage liability coverage do experts recommend that people have?
3. When it comes to medical expenses incurred in an automobile accident, what is the difference between bodily injury liability insurance and medical payments insurance?
4. Which of the following is covered by collision insurance? Comprehensive insurance? Property damage liability insurance?
   a. Your car is vandalized.
   b. The driver of a Honda Accord runs into and damages your Ford Escort.
   c. Your car is stolen.
   d. You accidentally drive your car off the road and into a wall, causing damage.

Developing Economic **Skills**

Building Your Decision-Making Skills

As a consumer, citizen, and voter, you will make many economic decisions every day. One of the best ways to improve your decision-making skills is by learning and using a decision-making model.

The steps in the decision-making model are listed and described below using the hypothetical example of choosing a major for college.

Step 1. Define Your Need or Want

The first step in the decision-making process is to define the need or want that requires a decision. When working through this step, it is important to be as specific as possible. Say you define your need or want as follows: I want to choose a major that I will enjoy and that will help me to fulfill my long-range goal of a happy, productive career.

Step 2. Analyze Your Resources

Your resources will vary according to the decision you have to make. In this case, your resources might include your parents and guidance counselors. For example, many guidance counselors can provide you with an interest inventory that can help you to determine your main areas of interest. You might also want to talk with college representatives or any friends or family members who are attending college.

Step 3. Identify Your Choices

The very fact that a decision needs to be made implies that choices exist. Suppose that you determine that you are most interested in art, art history, and history.

Step 4. Compare the Choices

At this point, you need to determine which choice is the best by using your available resources to gather information. Let's say that your guidance counselor tells you that you should look at the career opportunities that each major allows. Then you should try to imagine the outcome of each choice.

Step 5. Choose the Best Alternative

After you have compared your choices, it is time to choose the best one. This can be difficult if no one alternative stands out as the best. Suppose, for example, that all three majors have basically the same appeal. You finally choose art history because it seems to combine your three interests and because it might lead to a career as a museum curator, which sounds exciting and rewarding.

Step 6. Make a Plan to Get Started

You must make a plan of action. Your plan of action might include obtaining college catalogs, completing applications, and writing letters to art history departments for information about curricula.

Step 7. Evaluate Your Decision

Just because you have made a decision does not mean that you cannot change your mind. Look at the results of your decision. If the outcome is not what you had hoped it would be, perhaps it is time to start over with step 1.

Notice that the decision-making model contains words like *choices, wants,* and *resources.* As you have learned, scarcity exists and, as a result, choices have to be made. Decision making is part of economics, and using the decision-making model is a good example of thinking like an economist.

Identify the seven steps in the decision-making model.

CHAPTER 21

Review

Economics Vocabulary

Fill in the following blanks with the appropriate word or phrase.

1. A(n) ____ is an organized plan for spending and saving money.
2. If a bank has no equity, it is ____.
3. Equity divided by assets equals ____.
4. A(n) ____ is a statement of a job applicant's previous employment, education, and so on.
5. John received the benefits from his wife's insurance policy. John is a(n) ____.
6. Something that a bank owns that has value is called a(n) ____.
7. The difference between assets and liabilities is referred to as ____.
8. A(n) ____ is a financial organization that pools and invests people's money.

Review Questions

1. Why is it important not to leave anything blank when filling out a job application?
2. "It is possible to 'buy' something in both the present and the future when we save." Explain this statement.
3. What is no-fault insurance?
4. What is a mutual fund?
5. What three things do you learn from computing your income and estimated expenditures on an annual basis?
6. Explain what a health maintenance organization is and how it works.
7. You are in a car accident. You are not hurt, but the other person is. What should you do?
8. What capital ratio indicates that a bank is weak? Exceptionally strong?
9. What factors determine how much a person will pay for automobile insurance?
10. What does savings buy?
11. Schweitzer buys 100 shares of stock X for $10 a share. The next week the share price drops to $5. Schweitzer says, "I can't sell the stock now; I'd lose too much money." What is wrong with her statement?
12. What is the difference between term life insurance and whole life insurance? Between whole life insurance and universal life insurance?

Calculations

1. You make a down payment of $30,000 on a house that costs $135,000. Your mortgage is the difference between the purchase price and your down payment, or $105,000. If the house is destroyed in a fire, you will need $105,000 to pay off your mortgage loan, so you decide to insure your house for $105,000. What is wrong with this amount?
2. Calculate the capital ratio in the following cases.
   a. Assets = $50 million; liabilities = $47 million.
   b. Assets = $43 million; liabilities = $38 million.
   c. Assets = $32 million; liabilities = $29 million.
3. Calculate net worth in the following cases.
   a. Assets = $49.68 million; liabilities = $37.65 million.
   b. Assets = $21.54 million; liabilities = $19.54 million.
   c. Assets = $10.69 million; liabilities = $11.34 million.

Graphs

Obviously the value of a quality education cannot be shown strictly in monetary amounts. When considering the total value of an individual's education, one must take into account the value of the knowledge that is gained, the experiences that are shared, the influence and power that can be attached by furthering your education, the prestige, and so on. We can, however, determine the average salary of a person with a certain level of education. Refer back to Exhibit 21-4 on page 591 to answer the following questions.

1. What is the difference between the average salary of a person without a high school diploma and the average salary of a person with a high school diploma?
2. Is there a significant difference between the average salary of a person with a high school diploma and a person with some college but no degree?
3. Which increase in education brings the greatest increase in average annual income?

Economics and Thinking Skills

1. **Application.** Gonzalez is a twenty-five-year-old woman who works for a large media company. She earns a good income and spends almost everything she earns. How would you go about convincing her that it is important to save?
2. **Analysis.** What is the capital ratio of a bank? Why is it important to check out the capital ratio of a bank?
3. **Cause and Effect.** The *Economic Report of the President* states, "Educational attainment is one of the primary characteristics that distinguishes high-income from low-income workers." Which is cause, and which is effect? Does more education lead to more income, or does more income lead to more education?

Writing Skills

1. Write a one-page paper in which you describe the job you would like to have when you are thirty years old. Next, explain what you need to do to get the job.
2. Use you imagination to create the résumé that you would submit to the employer when applying for the ideal job that you described in number one above. Create the fictitious work experiences and educational background that would make you the "dream" candidate for the job.

Economics in the Media

Find an article in the newspaper or a story on television news that mentions one of the following: an insolvent bank, savings, capital ratio, equity, a mutual fund, a job interview, an HMO, term life insurance, or whole life insurance. Outline the context of the article or story.

Where's the Economics?

These students are attending college. What does this picture have to do with income and future consumption?

CHAPTER

22

Wall Street: Stocks, Bonds, Futures, and Options

What This Chapter Is About

Wall Street is the southern section of the borough of Manhattan in New York City. A narrow street extending only seven blocks from Broadway to the East River, it is the location of some of the chief financial institutions in the United States. It was named for a wall built by Dutch settlers in 1653 to repel an expected English invasion. Wall Street is the home of the New York Stock Exchange, the American Stock Exchange, investment banks, government bond dealers, trust companies, the Federal Reserve Bank of New York, commodity exchanges, and much more.

Why This Chapter Is Important

Many people will come to this chapter and think, "Great, if I just read this chapter carefully and understand everything, I will be able to invest my money in the stock and bond markets and get rich!" Unfortunately, it does not work that way. You can read and understand every word of this chapter and still lose a bundle in the stock and bond markets.

What, then, is the point of this chapter? If it won't make you rich, why should you read it? Even though this chapter will not make you rich, it can keep you from losing more money than you might lose without it. After having read this chapter, you will be more knowledgeable about stocks and bonds, much less likely to make rash movements in your investments, and much less likely to be taken advantage of by a get-rich-quick con artist.

After You Study This Chapter, You Will Be Able To

- identify the major stock exchanges.
- discuss the Dow Jones Industrial Average.
- explain what influences the Dow Jones Industrial Average.
- describe how the stock market works.
- know the difference between buying a stock and "buying the stock market."
- read the stock market page of the newspaper.
- explain the components of a bond.
- discuss the different types of bonds.
- read the bond market page of the newspaper.
- know what futures and options are.
- explain the difference between a call option and a put option.

You Will Also Learn What Economics Has to Do With

- dart-throwing monkeys.
- the Dow.
- "Spyders."
- junk bonds.
- Winston Churchill.

Economics Journal

Read at least two articles in the newspaper each day that involve either the stock market, the bond market, or both. Keep a list of the articles. Beside the title of each article, write a paragraph that explains what the article was about.

SECTION 1 Stocks

This section discusses stocks—how to buy them, how to sell them, what it means when the stock market goes up, what it means when the stock market goes down, and much more.

As you read this section, keep these key questions in mind:

- What are stocks?
- Where are stocks bought and sold?
- What is the Dow Jones Industrial Average?
- What does it mean to "buy the market"?

Key Terms

stock
Dow Jones Industrial Average (DJIA)
initial public offering (IPO)
investment bank
dividend

What Are Stocks?

If someone says that she owns 100 shares of a particular stock, what does that mean? If Bicek owns 100 shares of Yahoo stock, it means he is a part owner in Yahoo, Inc., a global Internet media company that offers a network of World Wide Web programming. A **stock** is a claim on the assets of a corporation that gives the purchaser a share in the corporation.

What does it mean to own stock in a company?

Bicek is not an owner in the sense that he can walk into Yahoo headquarters in Santa Clara, California, and start issuing orders. He cannot hire or fire anyone, and he cannot decide what the company will or will not do over the next few months or years. Still, he is an owner, and as an owner he can, if he wants, sell his ownership rights in Yahoo. All he has to do is find a buyer for his 100 shares of stock. Most likely, he could do so in a matter of minutes, if not seconds.

stock
A claim on the assets of a corporation that gives the purchaser a share in the corporation.

Where Is Stock Bought and Sold?

Most stocks in the United States are bought on the New York Stock Exchange, the American Stock Exchange, or on an electronic stock market.

New York Stock Exchange The New York Stock Exchange (NYSE) is the largest marketplace for the sale and purchase of stocks in the world. The NYSE evolved from a meeting of twenty-four men under a buttonwood tree in 1792 on what is now Wall Street in New York City. It was earlier called the New York Stock and Exchange Board and in 1863 was renamed the New York Stock Exchange.

To buy and sell stock on the NYSE, you must be a member of the exchange. Membership has been limited to 1,366 since 1953. To become a

At the New York Stock Exchange and the American Stock Exchange, the trading takes place on the floor of the exchange.

member, you must purchase a seat on the exchange from an existing member. The price of a seat fluctuates according to supply and demand conditions. For example, the more profitable the stock-brokerage business, the greater the demand for a seat on the exchange and the higher the price of a seat. In the late 1990s, a seat sold within the range of $1.2 million to a high of $2 million.

A person or firm with a seat on the exchange can sell and buy stock for its own account or for others. If you own, say, 100 shares of stock and want to sell it but do not have a seat on the exchange, you might contact a stockbrokerage firm that does have a seat on the exchange. A broker would sell your stock on your behalf.

American Stock Exchange The American Stock Exchange (AMEX) was originally known as "the Curb" because its transactions took place outdoors during its early days of existence. The AMEX is thought to have started around 1840. By 1908 it was officially known as the New York Curb Agency. In 1953 its name was changed to the American Stock Exchange. The exchange moved indoors in 1921 to its present location in New York City, on Wall Street. In its early history, it was known as a marketplace for stocks not considered reputable enough to be listed on the NYSE. Today, this is not the case.

What is the difference between the NASDAQ Stock Market and the New York Stock Exchange?

NASDAQ Stock Market Both the New York Stock Exchange and the American Stock Exchange are considered floor-based exchanges, because the buying and selling of stocks on these exchanges take place in a particular location (on the floor of the exchange on Wall Street). The NASDAQ is different. (NASDAQ is pronounced "Nas-dak" and stands for National Association of Securities Dealers Automated Quotations.) Trading on the NASDAQ does not take place in one location. The NASDAQ, established in 1971, is an electronic stock market with trades executed through a sophisticated computer and telecommunications network. The NASDAQ stock market trades more stock shares per day than any other stock market in the United States.

MINI GLOSSARY

Dow Jones Industrial Average (DJIA) The most popular, most widely cited indicator of day-to-day stock market activity. The DJIA is a weighted average of the thirty most widely traded stocks on the New York Stock Exchange.

Dow Jones Industrial Average (DJIA or the Dow)

You may have heard news commentators say, "The market is down today. The Dow Jones Industrial Average fell 102 points on heavy trading." The **Dow Jones Industrial Average (DJIA** or the "Dow") first appeared

Charles Dow, Cofounder of Dow Jones & Company, Inc., and Creator of the Dow Jones Industrial Average

Charles Henry Dow was born on November 6, 1851, in Sterling, Connecticut. He began his journalism career at age twenty-one as a reporter with the *Springfield* (Mass.) *Daily Republican* and soon became an assistant editor. In 1875 he left Springfield to join the *Providence* (R.I.) *Morning Star and Evening Press.* There he met Edward Jones, and in 1882 they formed Dow Jones & Company. The first office of Dow Jones & Company was 15 Wall Street, adjacent to the New York Stock Exchange.

Today Dow Jones & Company owns two premier business publications, the *Wall Street Journal* and *Barron's* (a magazine). The first edition of the *Wall Street Journal* appeared on July 8, 1889, with Dow as editor. Dow also came up with the idea for the Dow Jones Industrial Average, which debuted on May 26, 1896. He died in his Brooklyn, New York, home on December 4, 1902.

It has just been announced that personal income in the United States is higher than expected. Do you predict that this announcement will have any effect on the Dow? Explain your answer.

on the scene over a hundred years ago, on May 26, 1896. It was devised by Charles Henry Dow, who took eleven stocks, summed their prices on a particular day, and then divided by 11. This average price was the DJIA. (Some of the companies included American Cotton Oil, Chicago Gas, National Lead, and U.S. Rubber.)

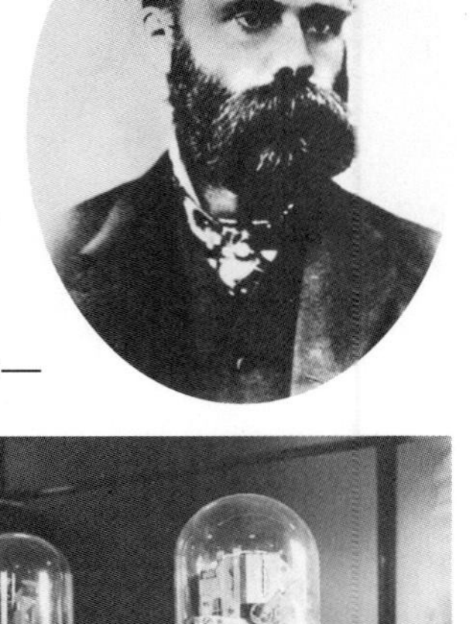

When Dow first computed the DJIA, the stock market was not highly regarded in the United States. Prudent investors bought bonds—not stocks, which were thought to be the area in which speculators and conniving Wall Street operators plied their trade. Wall Streeters were seen as managing stock prices to make themselves better off at the expense of others.

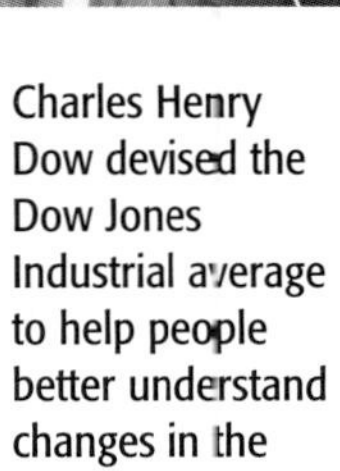

Charles Henry Dow devised the Dow Jones Industrial average to help people better understand changes in the stock market.

Dow devised the DJIA to convey some information about what was happening in the stock market, which at the time was the object of gossip and rumor. Before the DJIA existed, people had a hard time figuring out whether the stock market, on average, was rising or falling. They knew only that a particular stock went up a quarter of a point, another stock fell half a point, and so on. Dow decided to find the average price of a certain number of stocks (eleven) that he thought would largely mirror what was happening in the stock market as a whole. With this number, people could then have some sense of what the stock market was doing on any given day.

Today, the DJIA consists of thirty stocks (see Exhibit 22-1).[1] The average is no longer computed by simply summing the prices of stocks and dividing by thirty. A special divisor is used to avoid certain distortions that arise from events such as companies splitting their stock shares. The thirty stocks that make up the Dow are widely held by individuals and institutional investors. These thirty stocks represent about one-fifth of the $8 trillion market value of all U.S. stocks and about one-quarter of the value of stocks listed on the New York Stock Exchange.

Exhibit 22-2 tracks the course of the DJIA over most of the 1990s. As you can see, there were sharp increases during this time. Exhibit 22-3 on page 620 shows the best years for the Dow in terms of annual increases, and Exhibit 22-4 shows the Dow's worst years.

In addition to the DJIA, other prominent stock indexes are cited in the United States. Two of the most widely cited indexes are the NASDAQ Composite and the Standard & Poor's (S&P) 500.

1. Today, the thirty stocks that make up the Dow Jones Industrial Average are chosen by the editors of the *Wall Street Journal.*

Exhibit 22-1
The Thirty Stocks of the Dow Jones Industrial Average

Alcoa	Intel Corp.
American Express Co.	International Business Machines Corp.
AT&T Corp.	International Paper Co.
Boeing Co.	J. P. Morgan & Company
Caterpillar Inc.	Johnson & Johnson
Citigroup, Inc.	McDonald's Corp.
Coca-Cola Co.	Merck & Co. Inc.
DuPont Co.	Microsoft Corp.
Eastman Kodak Co.	Minnesota Mining & Manufacturing Co.
Exxon Mobil Corp.	Philip Morris Companies Inc.
General Electric Co.	Proctor & Gamble Co.
General Motors Corp.	SBC Communications Inc.
Hewlett-Packard Co.	United Technologies Corp.
Home Depot, Inc.	Wal-Mart Stores Inc.
Honeywell International Inc.	Walt Disney Co.

Different economic consulting firms have attempted to find out what influences the Dow. What causes it to go up, and what causes it to go down?

According to many economists, the Dow is closely connected to changes in such things as consumer credit, the previous close of the Dow, exports and imports, personal income, and the money supply. For example, increases in consumer credit (greater availability of loans) are expected to push up the Dow, the thought being that when consumer credit

Exhibit 22-2
The Course of the Dow over Most of the 1990s

As is evident, the Dow had sharp increases during this period.

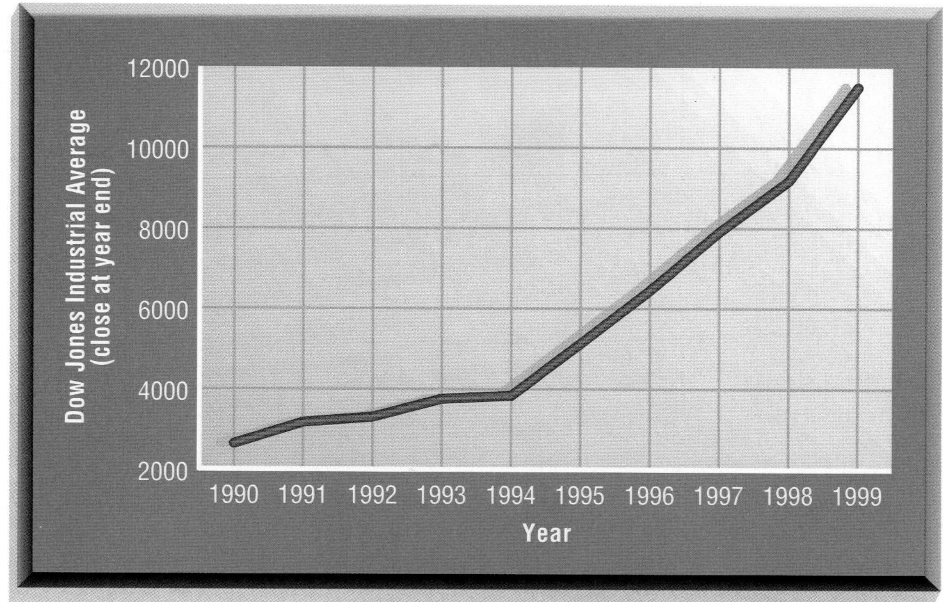

Exhibit 22-3

The Dow's Best Years

The exhibit shows the ten years in which the DJIA increased the most.

Rank	Year	Close	% change
1	1915	99.15	81.66
2	1933	99.90	66.69
3	1928	300.00	48.22
4	1908	86.15	46.64
5	1954	404.39	43.96
6	1904	69.61	41.74
7	1935	144.13	38.53
8	1975	852.41	38.32
9	1905	96.20	38.20
10	1958	583.65	33.96

Exhibit 22-4

The Dow's Worst Years

The exhibt shows the ten years in which the DJIA decreased the most.

Rank	Year	Close	% change
1	1931	77.90	–52.67
2	1907	58.75	–37.73
3	1930	164.58	–33.77
4	1920	71.95	–32.90
5	1937	120.85	–32.82
6	1914	54.58	–30.72
7	1974	616.24	–27.57
8	1903	49.11	–23.61
9	1932	59.93	–23.07
10	1917	74.38	–21.71

rises, people will buy more goods and services, which benefits the companies that sell goods and services. When consumer credit falls, the reverse happens. Oddly enough, neither the savings rate in the economy (whether people are saving or not) nor the state of the government budget (surplus or deficit) seems to have much influence on the Dow.

Stock Indexes around the World

Just as the Dow is closely watched in the United States, so are stock indexes in other countries of the world watched closely. For example, the Hang Seng is watched in Hong Kong, the Nikkei 225 in Japan, and the Shanghai Composite in China. Exhibit 22-5 shows some of the major stock indexes in selected countries.

ECONOMICS and the INTERNET

Plenty of news about stocks, bonds, futures, and options can be found online. A good site to find much information is Bloomberg.com at http://www.bloomberg.com/welcome.html. Once there, answer the following questions:

1. What was the Dow at the time you checked?
2. What was the Standard & Poor's 500 at the time you checked?
3. Click on "News," and read three of the many financial news items. For each news item, write a paragraph explaining it.

This man is checking the closing stock index in Hong Kong. Was it a good day for this stock index?

How the Stock Market Works

Suppose a company wants to raise money so that it can invest in a new product or a new manufacturing technique. In short, the company needs money, and it can get it in one of three ways. First, the company can go to a bank and borrow the money. Second, it can borrow the money by issuing a bond (a promise to repay the borrowed money with interest). Third, it can sell or issue stock in the company (in other words, sell part of the company). Stocks are also called *equity,* because the buyer of the stock has part ownership of the company.

When a company is initially formed, the owners set up a certain amount of stock, which is worth very little. The owners of the company try to find people (usually friends and associates) who would be willing to buy the stock (in hopes that one day it will be worth something). It is nearly impossible in these early days of the company for anyone who owns stock to sell it. For example, if Mendez owned 100 shares of some new company that almost no one had heard of, hardly anyone would be willing to pay any money to buy the stock.

As the company grows and needs more money, it may decide to offer its stock on the open market—in other words, to anyone who wants to buy it. By this time, the company may be known well enough that there will be people who are willing to buy its stock. The company's first offering of stock to the public is called an **initial public offering (IPO),** a simple process. Usually an **investment bank** is the intermediary between the company and the public and sells the stock for the company for an initial price (say, $10 a share). IPOs are announced in the *Wall Street Journal.*

Once there is an IPO for a stock, the stock is usually traded on an exchange or in an electronic stock market like NASDAQ. Sometimes a stock that initially sold for $10 will rise in price, and sometimes it will fall like a rock. It all depends on what people in the stock market think the company that initially issued the stock will do in the future. If they think the company is destined for big earnings, the stock will likely rise in price. If they think the company is destined for losses or only marginal earnings, the stock will probably fall in price.

In October 1999, Martha Stewart and Bill Johnson (president of the New York Stock Exchange) celebrated the initial public offering of stock in her company, Martha Stewart Living Omnimedia, Inc.

MINI GLOSSARY

initial public offering (IPO) A company's first offering of stock to the public.

investment bank A firm that acts as an intermediary between a company that issues a stock and the public that wishes to buy the stock.

Exhibit 22-5
Major Stock Indexes in Selected Countries

Country	Index	Symbol
Brazil	Bovespa Index	BVSP
Canada	TSE 300 Composite	TSE
Mexico	IPC	MXX
Venezuela	IBC	IBC
Australia	All Ordinaries	AORD
Hong Kong	Hang Seng	HSI
Japan	Nikkei 225	N225
Taiwan	Taiwan Weighted	TWII
Finland	Helsinki General	HEX
France	CAC 40	FCHI
Russia	Moscow Times	MTMS
Germany	Deutscher Aktienindex	DAX

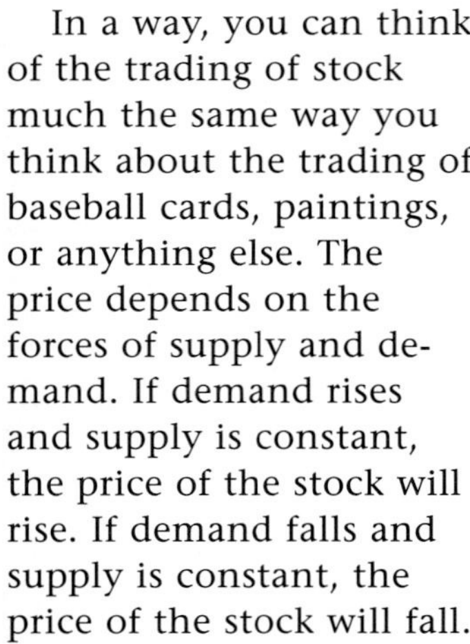

In a way, you can think of the trading of stock much the same way you think about the trading of baseball cards, paintings, or anything else. The price depends on the forces of supply and demand. If demand rises and supply is constant, the price of the stock will rise. If demand falls and supply is constant, the price of the stock will fall.

Sometimes people buy certain stocks because they hear that other people are buying the stock and because they think that the stock is "hot." In other words, the stock is very popular, and everyone wants it. In the 1990s, some of the Internet stocks fit this description. Stocks such as Yahoo!, Amazon.com, and eBay were bought because people thought the Internet was the wave of the future and that almost anything connected with the Internet was destined for great profit.

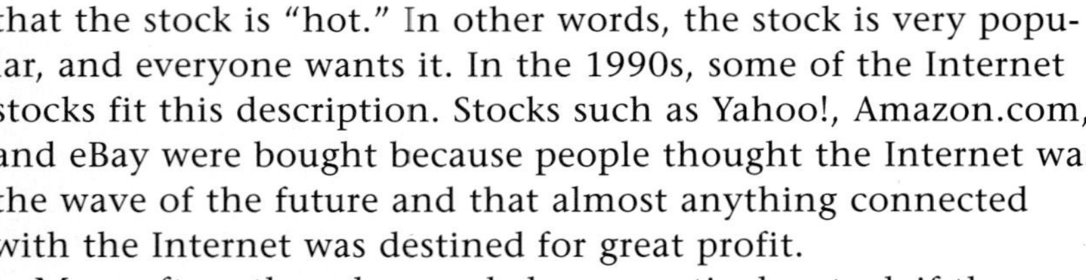

More often, though, people buy a particular stock if they think the earnings of the company that initially issued it are likely to rise. Remember that a share of stock represents ownership in a company. The more profitable that company is expected to be, the more likely people are going to want to own that company, and therefore the greater the demand for its stock.

MINI GLOSSARY

dividend
A share of the profits of a corporation distributed to stockholders

Yahoo chief Jerry Yang (top photo, right) and *Time* magazine's Person of the Year, Jeff Bezos of Amazon.com, benefited from the popularity of Internet stocks in the late 1990s.

Why Do People Buy and Sell Stock?

Many millions of people all over the world buy stock every day. They do it either to get the dividends that many companies pay on outstanding stock or for the expected gain in the stock's price. To illustrate the concept of dividends, suppose company X has issued 1 million shares of stock, which are owned by different people. Each year the company tabulates its profit and loss, and any profits are divided up among the owners of the company as **dividends.** If this year's dividend is $1 for each share of stock a person owns and Kallas owns 50,000 shares of stock, she will receive a dividend check for $50,000.

The other reason to buy stock is for the expected gain in its price. Gerald buys 100 shares of Microsoft stock today because he thinks that one year from now he will be able to sell the stock for $50 more a share than he purchased it. In other words, he hopes to earn $5,000 on his stock purchase.

People also sell stock for many reasons. Smith might sell his 100 shares of IBM because he currently needs the money to help his son pay for college or to help put together a down payment for a house. Alternatively, someone might sell stock because she thinks the stock is likely to go down in price soon. In other words, she feels it is better to sell at $25 a share today than to sell one week from now at $18 a share.

Is a Dart-Throwing Monkey As Good As a Wall Street Analyst at Picking Stocks?

Compare two methods of selecting stock. In the first, a monkey throws darts at the stock market page of the newspaper, and we put $1,000 in each stock "hit." In the second, we put $1,000 in each stock chosen by a Wall Street analyst. Which method of picking stocks will earn us a higher return? The inclination is to say that the Wall Street analyst will earn us a higher return than the monkey. After all, she has a degree in business or economics and reads the financial pages every day. All the monkey does is eat bananas and hang around. Who couldn't beat a monkey at picking stocks?

Often, however, the Wall Street analysts do not beat the monkey. Of course, monkeys do not really throw darts at the stock market page, but people do. And often the Wall Street analyst does no better, and sometimes worse, than the person who simply throws darts. To explain why, consider two stocks, IBM stock and Ford Motor stock. Suppose that on a given day each stock sells for $100 a share. One day individuals learn that IBM has made a major breakthrough in computer technology and that it is headed for good times. On the same day, individuals learn that Ford has to recall one of its cars. In other words, the news about IBM is good, and the news about Ford is bad. This difference in news will change the prices of IBM and Ford Motor stock. We would expect the price of IBM stock to be bid up and the price of Ford Motor stock to fall. At the end of the day, IBM will be selling for more than $100 a share, and Ford Motor will be selling for less than $100 a share.

After the price of each stock has changed, which is the better stock to buy? Actually, one stock is as good as the other. If the price of the two stocks were the same, certainly the IBM stock would be better to buy, but the price of the stocks is not the same. Ford Motor stock is a cheaper stock. Given the future earnings, likely dividends, and future corporate earnings, Ford Motor stock at a price of less than $100 a share is probably as good as IBM stock at a price of more than $100 a share. As long as stock prices adjust quickly to good and bad news—and they do—it is not likely that IBM stock will be any better a buy than Ford Motor stock. If one stock is better than another, its price will rise so that it is no longer better. If one stock is worse than another, its price will fall so that it is no longer worse.

This example helps explain why Wall Street analysts are often no better than, and sometimes are worse than, monkeys when picking stocks. If all stocks are alike once prices have adjusted, then certainly a monkey can pick stocks as well as a Wall Street analyst.

QUESTION TO ANSWER In 1999, Barbra Streisand, the singer and actor, decided to play the stock market. She picked the stocks she thought would rise in value, invested some money in the stocks, and did very well. At the time Streisand was making stock picks, the stock market was rising substantially. Do you believe Streisand had an instinct for picking stocks, or do you think it is hard not to look good in the stock market when the market is rising?

In April 2000, people watch as Nasdaq stocks drop sharply. Why might they be concerned?

How to Buy and Sell Stock

Buying and selling stock is relatively easy. You can buy or sell stock through a full-service stockbrokerage firm, a discount broker, or an online broker. With all varieties of brokers, you usually open an account by depositing a certain dollar amount into it, most commonly between $1,000 and $2,500. Once you have opened an account, you can begin to trade (buy and sell stock).

You may call a full-service broker on the telephone and ask him or her to recommend some good stock. The broker, usually called an *account representative,* might say that you should buy X, Y, or Z stock, because the research department in the brokerage firm has looked closely at these stocks and believes they are headed for good times based on such factors as the current economic situation in the country, the level of exports, and the new technology that is coming to market.

A stockbrokerage firm carefully researches stocks and their histories before recommending them to customers. Why would a stock's history be important?

If you do not require help with buying stocks, you can go to either a discount broker or an online broker. You can telephone a discount broker the same way you called up a full-service broker and tell the broker that you want to buy or sell so many shares of a given stock. The broker will simply execute the trade for you; he or she is not there to offer any advice.

The same process can be undertaken online. You go to your broker's Web site, log in, enter your username and password, and then submit an order to buy, say, 100 shares of stock X. Your online broker will register your buy request and then note when it has been executed. Your account, easily visible online, will show how much cash you have in it, how many shares of a particular stock you hold, and so on.

Online trading has caused many people to become their own stockbrokers.

The Stock Market: Good Long-Term Investment

If you have some money to invest and will not need the money for a long time, a good place to put it is in the stock market. To see why, consider the average annual return on different investments. Exhibit 22-6 shows that between 1926 and 1997, the average annual return on U.S. Treasury bills was 3.8 percent, 5.3 percent on intermediate-term government bonds, and 5.7 percent on long-term government bonds. In contrast, it would have been 11.0 percent if you had purchased the five hundred stocks that make up the Standard & Poor's 500. In short, the stock market would have given you a substantially higher average annual return than the bond market.

To put things differently, if you had invested $1 in the stocks that make up the Standard & Poor's 500 in 1926, your $1 investment would be worth $1,828 in

If you want to determine how a stock is doing, go to Yahoo! at http://www.yahoo.com and click on "Stock Quotes." Then put in the symbol of the stock you want to check. If you do not know the symbol, you can look it up at this page. For example, the symbol for Microsoft stock is *MSFT;* see what it is selling for today.

Exhibit 22-6

Average annual return, 1926–1997

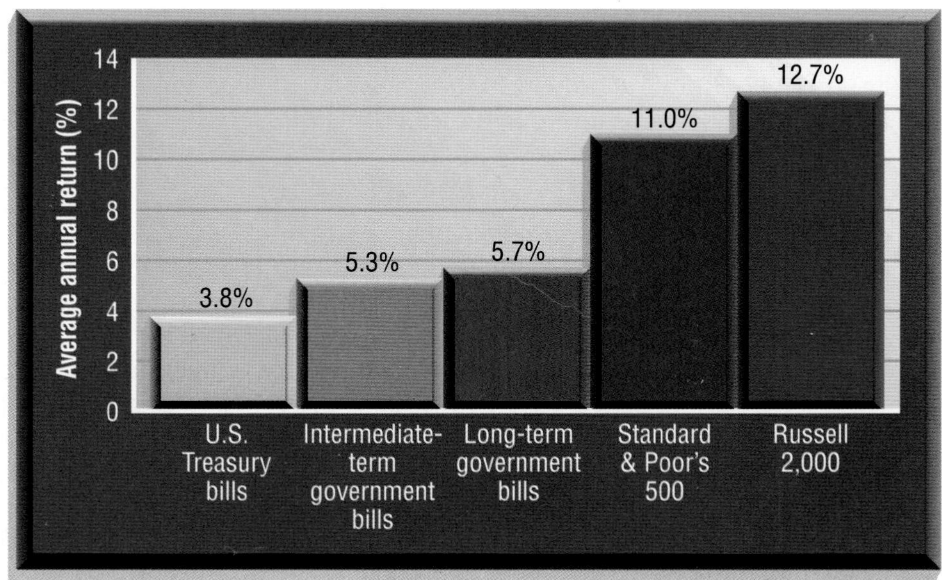

Reprinted by permission of Copley News Service © 2000 The Birmingham News. All rights reserved.

1997. But $1 invested in long-term government bonds would have been worth $55.38. There is a big difference between $1,828 and $55.38.

Remember, the stock market is a good place to invest if you do not need the money for a long time. There is no guarantee that if you put, say, $1,000 in the stock market this year that you will get a positive return in a year. Your stock might be worth half that in a year, or even less. The stock market goes up, and it goes down. For example, look back at Exhibit 22-4 on page 620. If you had purchased the thirty stocks that made up the Dow in 1974, you would have lost over 27 percent of your money. Of course, a look at Exhibit 22-3 shows that if you had purchased the thirty stocks that made up the Dow one year later, in 1975, you would have gained a whopping 38.32 percent return.

Thus, the stock market goes up and down on a short-term basis, but it usually goes up on a long-term basis. If you look back at Exhibit 22-2 on page 619, you will note that the Dow was under 3,000 in 1990 and over 11,000 in 1999. From 1990 to 1999, however, there were some daily, weekly, and monthly ups and downs along the way.

Buying Stocks or Buying the Market

You can use various methods to decide which stocks to purchase. The first way is simply to buy shares of a stock that you think is going to rise in price. You might buy 50 shares of Microsoft, 100 shares of General Electric, and 500 shares of Amazon.com.

Another way is to invest in a stock mutual fund, a collection of stocks managed by a fund manager who works for a mutual fund company. For example, Pearson may operate mutual fund Z at mutual fund company Z. If you put $10,000 in mutual fund Z, you are in effect buying the stocks in that fund. Let's say the fund consists of stocks A, B, C, W, and X at the current time. The fund manager, on any given day, may buy more of A and sell some of B, or sell all of C and add stock D to the fund portfolio.

The reputation and success of a mutual fund company depends on how well their mutual fund managers choose stocks.

It is up to the fund manager to do what he or she thinks will maximize the overall returns from the fund. As a buyer of the fund, you put your money in the fund manager's hands to do what he or she thinks will be best. Mutual fund companies often advertise the records of their fund managers. They might say, "Our fund managers have the best record on Wall Street. Invest with us, and get the highest returns you can." You may be prompted to put your money in the hands of the "experts" because you feel they know better than you what stocks to buy and sell and when to do each.

You could use another strategy, though, and buy the stocks that make up a stock index. As already discussed, the DJIA is a stock index that gives information on the performance of the thirty stocks of which it is made up. Another index, the Standard & Poor's 500 index, is a broad index of stock market activity made up of five hundred of the largest U.S. companies, representing about 75 percent of U.S. stock market values. Another broad-based stock index is the Wilshire 5000, which consists of the stocks of about 7,600 firms.

A particularly easy way to buy a stock index fund is to buy what are called "Spyders." The term *Spyders* comes from *Standard & Poor's Depository Receipts,* or *SPDRs,* which are securities representing ownership in the

In May 1996, the Dow Jones Industrial Average celebrated its 100th anniversary.

SPDR Trust. The SPDR Trust buys the stocks that make up the S&P 500 index. Spyders are traded on the American Stock Exchange under the symbol *SPY.* They cost one-tenth the S&P index. For example, if the S&P index is 1,000, a Spyder will sell for $100. When this text was being written, Spyders were selling for about $146 a share.

When you buy Spyders, you are buying the stock of five hundred companies—so many companies that you are said to be "buying the market." Is it better to simply buy the market or to buy a mutual fund that is managed by a high-paid fund manager? In recent years, numerous articles in business and financial publications have stated that it is better to buy the market than to buy a mutual fund managed by a fund manager. For example, one article states: "Since 1993, index funds that mirror the Standard & Poor's 500 have posted higher returns than 80 percent of all actively managed mutual funds."[2] An article in the *Wall Street Journal* stated, "Active fund managers are struggling to beat the indexes. As of Friday, just 26 percent of actively managed U.S. stock mutual funds were beating the S&P 500 so far this year [1998]."[3]

The lesson seems to be that it is harder to do better in the stock market than simply buying the market. Simply buying the S&P 500, for example, is likely to earn you a higher return than buying the best financial advice that money can buy.

How to Read the Stock Market Page

Suppose you have purchased some stock, and now you want to find out how it is doing. Is it rising or falling in price? Is it paying a dividend? How many shares were traded today? You can find the answers to these questions and more in the newspaper. Turn to the stock market page to see something similar to Exhibit 22-7. We discuss each item in each column here.

52-Week Hi The highest price of the stock during the past year or past fifty-two weeks appears in the "52-Week Hi" column. For the stock in the exhibit, the number "101 1/16" translates into $101.06. In other words, the highest share price paid for this stock during the past year was $101.06.

52-Week Lo The "52-Week Lo" column gives the lowest price of the stock during the past fifty-two weeks: "74 11/16," which translates into $74.68. In other words, the lowest share price paid for this stock during the past year was $74.68.

Stock In the "Stock" column is *DowChem,* an abbreviation of the name of the company whose stock we are looking at. *DowChem* stands for *Dow Chemical.*

Symbol In the "Symbol" column you see *DOW,* which is the stock or ticker symbol for Dow Chemical.

Div *Div* stands for *dividend.* The number 3.48 in this column means that the last annual dividend per share of stock was $3.48. For example, a

2. Laura Casteneda, "Hassle-Free Way to Make Money: Investors Flocking to Index Funds, but There Can Be Pitfalls," *San Francisco Chronicle,* February 17, 1997, p. B1.

3. Greg Ip, "Why Index Funds Aren't As Mighty As Some May Think," *Wall Street Journal,* March 11, 1998, p. C1.

Exhibit 22-7
Reading the Stock Market Page of a Newspaper

Using an excerpt from the stock market page of a newspaper, the text explains what each number in each column means. Many, but not all, newspapers will present the information as we have presented it here. Some newspapers will convert fractions into decimals.

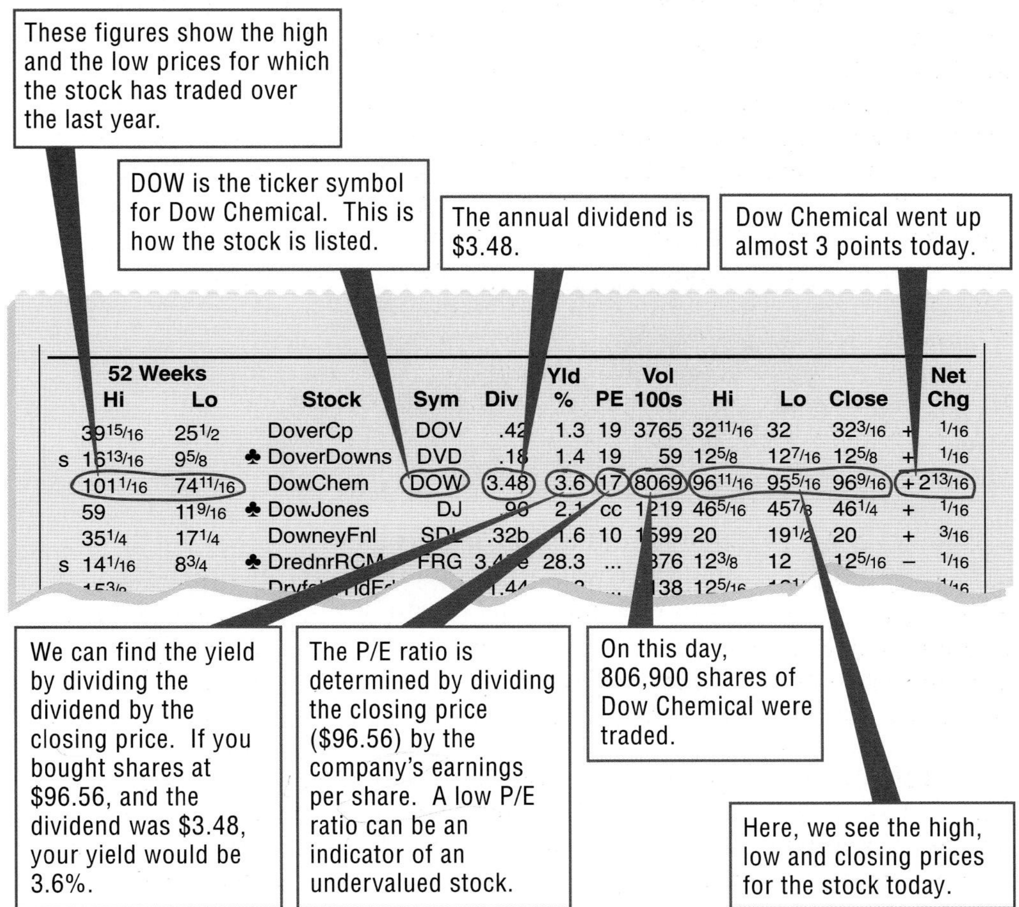

	52 Weeks Hi	Lo	Stock	Sym	Div	Yld %	PE	Vol 100s	Hi	Lo	Close	Net Chg
	39 15/16	25 1/2	DoverCp	DOV	.42	1.3	19	3765	32 11/16	32	32 3/16	+ 1/16
s	16 13/16	9 5/8	♣ DoverDowns	DVD	.18	1.4	19	59	12 5/8	12 7/16	12 5/8	+ 1/16
	101 1/16	74 11/16	DowChem	DOW	3.48	3.6	17	8069	96 11/16	95 5/16	96 9/16	+2 13/16
	59	11 9/16	♣ DowJones	DJ	.96	2.1	cc	1219	46 5/16	45 7/8	46 1/4	+ 1/16
	35 1/4	17 1/4	DowneyFnl	SDL	.32b	1.6	10	1599	20	19 1/2	20	+ 3/16
s	14 1/16	8 3/4	♣ DrednrRCM	FRG	3.4[illegible]e	28.3	...	376	12 3/8	12	12 5/16	− 1/16
	[illegible]		[illegible]		1.44	[illegible]	...	138	12 5/16	[illegible]		[illegible]

person who owned 5,000 shares of Dow Chemical stock would have received $3.48 per share, or $17,400 in dividends.

Yld % *Yld* means the yield of a stock, or the dividend divided by the closing price, which is a percentage.

$$\text{Yield} = \frac{\text{Dividend per share}}{\text{Closing price per share}}$$

The closing price of the stock (shown in one of the later columns) is 96 9/16, or $96.56. If we divide the dividend ($3.48) by the closing price ($96.56), we get a yield of 3.6 percent. The higher the yield the better, all other things being the same. For example, a stock that yields 5 percent is better than a stock that yields 3 percent, if all other things between the two stocks are the same.

The Great Crash

On Thursday, October 24, 1929, the *New York Times* ran a headline that read, "Prices of Stocks Crash in Heavy Liquidation." Elsewhere in the *Times* a headline read, "Many Accounts Wiped Out." These headlines referred to the stock market crash (sometimes simply called the Great Crash) that began on that October day in 1929 and continued on October 28 and 29.

In some historical accounts and in the minds of many members of the public, the stock market crash in 1929 was what caused the Great Depression that followed. However, this is not true, and it points out the *post hoc ergo propter hoc* logical fallacy. *Post hoc ergo propter hoc* is Latin for "After this, therefore as a result of this." Stated differently, it means "That which comes before another must be its cause." For example, if X comes before Y, then X is the cause of Y. This statement is not true.

Think of very simple examples. The teacher gives you a test before it rains, but the teacher's giving you a test does not cause the rain. Similarly, just because the stock market crash came before the many years of the Great Depression does not necessarily mean that the stock market crash caused the Great Depression. In fact, most economists believe that both the stock market crash and the Great Depression (with such things as rising unemployment and falling incomes) were effects of the same causes. In other words, the same factors caused both the stock market crash and the Great Depression.

Be that as it may, the stock market crash did change the psychological mind-set of the people living in the late 1920s. Gone were the good times of the Roaring Twenties; a dark economic cloud seemed to have descended. It is interesting how many people failed to see the dark economic cloud on the horizon. Irving Fisher, perhaps the best-known American economist of the day, said just a week before the crash, "Stock prices have reached what looks like a permanently high plateau. I expect to see the stock market a good deal higher than it is today within a few months." Fisher ended up losing a fortune in the stock market crash.

Other people who did not see the Crash coming were Myron Forbes, who was president of Pierce Arrow Motor Company, and E.H.H. Simmons, president of the New York Stock Exchange. There was also Winston Churchill, who until earlier that year had served as chancellor of the exchequer, a very important financial position, in Great Britain for five years.[a] Just a few weeks before the Crash, he had written his wife from America telling her how well they were doing in the stock market. On October 24, 1929, when word got out that the stock market was crashing, thousands of people gathered on Wall Street to witness events. One of those people was Winston Churchill, who watched from the visitors' gallery of the New York Stock Exchange as his fortune disappeared on the trading floor below.

QUESTION TO ANSWER Predicting stock market movements is often very difficult. Why do you think it is so difficult?

a. Churchill became prime minister of Great Britain in 1940.

PE *PE* stands for *P-E ratio* or *price-earnings ratio.* The number here, 17, is obtained by taking the latest closing price per share and dividing it by the latest available net earnings per share. In other words,

$$PE = \frac{\text{Closing price per share}}{\text{Net earnings per share}}$$

A stock with a PE ratio of 17 means that the stock is selling for a share price that is 17 times its earnings per share.

Suppose that most stocks have a PE ratio of 20. In other words, most stocks sell for a share price that is 20 times their earnings per share. In comparison, stock X has a PE ratio of 50. What would make stock X have a PE ratio so much higher than most stocks? Obviously, the people buying stock X expect that its future earnings will somehow warrant the higher prices they are paying for the stock today. In other words, a high PE ratio usually indicates that people believe there will be higher-than-average growth in earnings. Whether or not they are right remains to be seen.

Vol 100s The "Vol 100s" column shows volume in the hundreds. The number is 8069, which translates into 806,900. In other words, 806,900 shares of this stock were traded (bought and sold) on this particular day.

Hi The "Hi" column shows the highest price the stock traded for on this particular day. The number is $96\frac{11}{16}$, which translates into approximately $96.69.

Lo The lowest price the stock traded for on this particular day is found in the "Lo" column. Here $95\frac{5}{16}$ translates into approximately $95.31.

Close The number in the "Close" column is $96\frac{9}{16}$, which translates into $96.56. This figure is the share price of the stock when trading stopped this particular day.

Net Chg *Net Chg* stands for *net change.* The number here, $+2\frac{13}{16}$, translates into $2.81. The price of the stock on this particular day closed $2.81 *higher* than it did the day before.

Section 1 Review

Defining Terms

1. Define
   a. stock
   b. Dow Jones Industrial Average
   c. investment bank
   d. dividend
   e. initial public offering (IPO)

Reviewing Facts and Concepts

2. What was the price range for a seat on the New York Stock Exchange in the late 1990s?
3. What is the difference between a floor-based stock market and an electronic stock market?
4. What information did Charles Dow convey with the Dow Jones Industrial Average?

Critical Thinking

5. Suppose that there are 500 stocks and that the share price of each stock rises on Monday. Does it follow that everyone in the stock market believes that stocks are headed even higher, because no one would buy a stock if he or she thought share prices were headed lower?

Applying Economic Concepts

6. Which of the following two stocks has a bigger gap between its closing price and net earnings per share: stock A with a PE ratio of 17 or stock B with a PE ratio of 45?

SECTION 2

Bonds

What are bonds? What types of bonds exist? How do you buy and sell bonds? This section explores these and other questions.

As you read this section, keep these key questions in mind:

- What are bonds?
- How are bonds rated?
- What is the relationship between interest rates and the price of bonds?
- What are the various types of bonds?

Key Terms

bond
face value (par value)
junk bond

What Is a Bond?

Suppose a company in St. Louis wants to build a new factory. It gets the money to build the factory in three principal ways. First, it can go to a bank and take out a loan. Second, it can issue some stock in the company—in other words, sell ownership rights in the company. Third, it can issue bonds. A **bond** is simply an IOU, or a promise to pay. Typically, bonds are issued by companies, governments, or government agencies to borrow money. Thus, the issuer of a bond is a borrower, and the person who buys a bond is a lender.

The Chicago Mercantile Exchange trades in domestic and foreign bonds.

The Components of a Bond

There are three major components of a bond: face (par) value, maturity date, and coupon rate.

Face Value The **face value,** or **par value,** is the dollar amount specified on the "face" (front) of the bond; it is the amount the issuer of the bond promises to pay the buyer of the bond on the maturity date. For example, suppose Lewis buys a bond from company Z, and its face value is $10,000. It follows that company Z promises to pay Lewis $10,000 at some point in the future.

Maturity Date The maturity date is the day when the issuer of the bond must pay the buyer of the bond the face value of the bond. For example, Kieso buys a bond with a face value of $10,000 that matures on December 31, 2005. On December 31, 2005, he will receive $10,000 from the issuer of the bond.

Coupon Rate The coupon rate of a bond is the percentage of the face value that the bondholder receives each year until the bond matures. For example, suppose Wright buys a bond with a face value of $10,000 that matures in five years, and has a coupon rate of 10 percent. He will receive a coupon payment of $1,000 each year for five years. It follows, then, that

MINI GLOSSARY

bond
An IOU, a promise to pay.

face value (par value)
The dollar amount specified on the "face" (front) of the bond; it is the amount the issuer of the bond promises to pay the buyer of the bond on the maturity date.

junk bond
A bond with a high default risk.

the coupon rate is equal to the annual coupon payment divided by the face value of the bond.

$$\text{Coupon rate} = \frac{\text{Annual coupon payment}}{\text{Face value of the bond}}$$

Bond Ratings

Bonds are rated or evaluated. The more likely the bond issuer will pay the face value of the bond at maturity and will meet all scheduled coupon payments, the higher the bond's rating. The two best-known ratings are Standard & Poor's and Moody's. If a bond gets a rating of AAA from Standard & Poor's or a rating of Aaa from Moody's, it has received the highest rating possible. You can be sure that it is one of the most secure bonds you can buy; there is little doubt that the bond issuer will pay the face value of the bond at maturity and meet all scheduled coupon payments.

Bonds with a rating of BB, Ba, or below are considered **junk bonds,** which are bonds with a high default risk. In other words, they may not be paid off. Exhibit 22-8 discusses the ratings of the two major rating services, Standard & Poor's and Moody's.

Exhibit 22-8
Bond Ratings

The two major bond-rating services, Standard & Poor's and Moody's, give these ratings to bonds.

Standard & Poor's rating	Moody's rating	What the rating signifies
AAA	Aaa	Best-quality bond. Issuer's ability to pay interest and face value (at time of maturity) is extremely strong.
AA	Aa	High-quality bond. Issuer's ability to pay is very strong. Bonds with this rating or higher are considered high-grade bonds.
A	A	Upper-medium-quality bond. Issuer has strong ability to pay, but bond is somewhat more susceptible to economic changes than bonds with a higher rating.
BBB	Baa	Medium-quality bond. Issuer has satisfactory ability to pay, but negative economic conditions can diminish ability to pay. Some economists say that these bonds are too risky for individuals to invest in.
BB	Ba	Speculative bonds. May not be repaid. Anything with the rating of BB/Ba or lower is considered a junk bond.
B	B	Low-grade bond. May not be repaid.
CCC	Caa	Poor-quality bond. May not be repaid.
CC	Ca	Highly speculative bond. May not be repaid or may be in default.
C	C	Lowest-grade bond. May not be repaid or may be in default.
D	D	Entity that issued the bond is in default. It owes money to bondholders.

Bond Prices

A person can buy a bond for a price equal to, less than, or greater than the face value, depending on market conditions. The greater the demand for the bond relative to the supply, the higher the price.

Suppose a bond has a face value of $1,000 and a coupon rate of 5 percent. Alexander buys this bond for $950. He knows that the coupon payment on this bond will be 5 percent of $1,000 each year, or $50. The yield on the bond is the coupon payment divided by the bond's price:

$$\text{Yield} = \frac{\text{Annual coupon payment}}{\text{Price paid for the bond}}$$

In this example, the yield is $50/$950, or 5.26 percent. From the perspective of the bond buyer, the higher the yield, the better.

Now suppose that Alexander had paid $1,100 for the bond instead of $950. In this case, the yield would have been $50/$1,100, or 4.54 percent. In other words, as the price paid for the bond rose, the yield declined.

When are the coupon rate and the yield the same? Obviously, they are the same when the price paid for the bond equals the face value. For example, consider a bond with a face value of $1,000 and a coupon rate of 5 percent. If the bond is purchased for $1,000, then the yield ($50/$1,000), which is the 5 percent, is equal to the coupon rate.

Trading activity at the Chicago Mercantile Exchange.

Interest Rates and Bond Prices

It is year 1, and a company wants to borrow funds by issuing bonds. Before it issues its bonds, the company checks interest rates in the market and finds that people who simply put their money in a savings account earn an interest rate of 5 percent. The company knows that the coupon rate for its bonds will have to be 5 percent, or no one will buy them. It sets the coupon rate at 5 percent on its $10,000 bond that matures in five years. Vera buys the bond for face value, or $10,000. Her coupon rate and yield are the same at 5 percent.

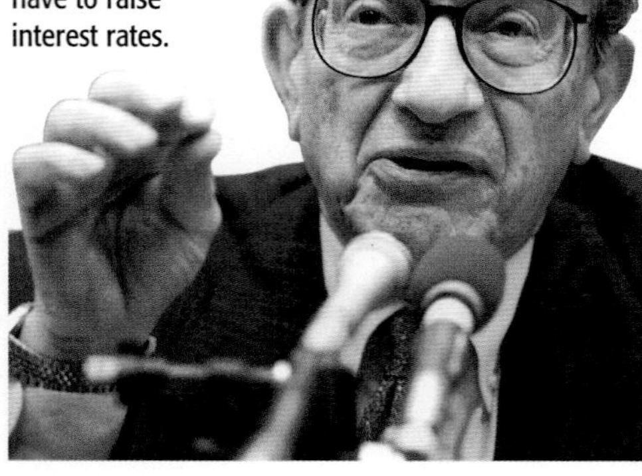

In February 2000, Alan Greenspan, Chairman of the Board of Governors of the Federal Reserve System, told the House Banking Committee that the Fed may have to raise interest rates.

Now it is year 2, and the same company wants to borrow more money. This time, when it checks interest rates in the market, it learns that people who put their money in a savings account can earn an interest rate of 7 percent. To get people to buy its bonds, the company now sets its coupon rate on its new bonds, with a face value of $10,000 and a maturity rate of five years, at 7 percent.

Consider what such a rise in interest rates in the market will do to the price of old bonds (year 1 bonds). If Vera wants to sell her bond before it matures (perhaps she needs the money for an emergency), no one is going to pay her what she paid for it, $10,000, because they can buy bonds with the same face value ($10,000) that pay a higher coupon rate (7 percent instead of 5 percent). The only way Vera can possibly sell her year 1 bond is to lower its price.

What, then, is the relationship between market interest rates and the price of old or existing bonds? As interest rates rise, the price of old or existing bonds falls. In other words, interest rates and the price of old or existing bonds move in the opposite directions.

Bonds: Timing Is Everything

To become rich, buy low and sell high. With this rule in mind, consider the buying and selling of bonds. Suppose it is January, and you expect interest rates in February to be higher than they are today. Should you buy or sell bonds? If you expect interest rates to rise, then you must expect the price of existing bonds to fall. In other words, you believe the price of bonds will be lower in February than in January. (Remember, interest rates and the price of existing bonds are inversely related.)

To be successful in buying and selling bonds, you must buy low and sell high. How does the interest rate affect the sale of bonds?

If your objective is to earn profit and you expect the price of a good to be lower next month than this month, you will sell the good if you have it—before it goes down in price. Then, once it has gone down in price, you will buy it back.

The same strategy works for bonds. If you own bonds in January, sell them, before they fall in price. You can always buy them back at the lower price if you want. The rule is that if you expect interest rates to rise, sell bonds now (before the price of the bonds falls).

Now suppose it is March, and you expect interest rates in April to be lower than they are today. Should you buy or sell bonds? If you expect interest rates to fall, then it follows that you expect the price of existing bonds to rise (the price of bonds to be higher in April than in March). Now is the time to buy bonds. Buy when they are relatively low in price, and then wait for the rise in price to sell. If you expect interest rates to fall, buy bonds now (before the price of the bonds rises).

All economists know that investors should sell bonds if they expect interest rates to rise and should buy bonds if they expect interest rates to fall. Why, then, aren't all economists rich? Is their advice on bonds incorrect?

Expect interest rates to rise ➡ Sell bonds
Expect interest rates to fall ➡ Buy bonds

Financial Journalist

Financial journalists work at newspapers, magazines, television networks, cable television stations, and many other places. Most have attended college and majored in journalism, with perhaps a second major or a minor in business or economics.

Networking is an important part of getting a job in the field, so many financial journalists first serve as interns at places such as newspapers or television networks while in college. They also work on college newspapers to gain experience and publish work that can be submitted when interviewing for their first postcollege jobs. Employers interviewing financial journalists look for an ability to write well, a knowledge of economics and business, initiative, good ideas, and the ability to be part of a team.

The advice is not incorrect; it is just difficult to accurately predict interest rates over a long period of time. An interest rate is a price—specifically, the price of credit—and as such it is determined by the forces of supply and demand. The demand for and supply of credit determine the interest rate. To predict interest rates accurately, then, one would have to predict changes in all those factors that affect the demand for and supply of credit. That is a difficult, if not impossible, task to complete accurately on a consistent basis.

Types of Bonds

As stated earlier, bonds are typically issued by companies, governments, and government agencies. This section briefly describes some of the many types of bonds that these entities issue.

Corporate Bonds A corporate bond is a bond issued by a private corporation, typically with a $10,000 face value. Corporate bonds may sell for a price above or below face value, depending on current supply and demand conditions for the bond. The interest that corporate bonds pay is fully taxable.

Municipal Bonds Municipal bonds are issued by state and local governments. A state may issue a bond to help pay for a new highway; a local government may issue a bond to finance a civic auditorium or a water park. Many people purchase municipal bonds because the interest paid on them is not subject to federal taxes.

Municipal bonds are often used to build community buildings. Why are municipal bonds popular with bond buyers?

A group of congresswomen discuss government spending programs that will require the government to borrow funds.

Treasury Bills, Notes, and Bonds When the federal government wants to borrow funds, it can issue Treasury bills (T-bills), Treasury notes, or Treasury bonds. Although called by different names, all are bonds; the only difference is the time to maturity. Treasury bills mature in 13, 26, or 52 weeks. Treasury notes mature in 2 to 10 years, and Treasury bonds mature in more than 10 to 30 years. Treasury bills, notes, and bonds are considered very safe investments, because it is not likely that the federal government will be unable to meet its bond obligations. After all, it has the power of taxation to pay off bondholders.

Inflation-Indexed Treasury Bonds In 1997, the federal government began to issue inflation-indexed bonds. The first indexed bonds issued matured in ten years and were available with a face value as small as $1,000. An inflation-indexed Treasury bond guarantees the purchaser a certain real rate of return, but a nonindexed Treasury bond does not. For example, suppose you purchase an inflation-indexed, ten-year, $1,000 bond that pays a 4 percent coupon rate. If there is no inflation, the annual interest payment will be $40. But if the inflation rate is, say, 3 percent, the government will "mark up" the value of the bond by 3 percent—from $1,000 to $1,030—and pay 4 percent on this higher dollar amount. Thus, instead of paying $40 each year, it pays $41.20. By increasing the monetary value of the security by the rate of inflation, the government guarantees the bondholder a real return of 4 percent.

How to Read the Bond Market Page

The bond market page of the newspaper looks similar to Exhibit 22-9. The following discussion explains how to read the corporate bond market page.

Exhibit 22-9
Reading the Bond Market Page of a Newspaper

The bond under consideration is a corporate bond. The text explains what each number in each column means. Many, but not all, newspapers will present the information as we have presented it here. Some newspapers will convert fractions into decimals.

Bonds	Cur Yld	Vol	Close	Net Chg
OffDep zr08	...	28	83	– 7/8
OreStl 11s03	10.4	79	106	– 5/8
Oryx 7½14	cv	56	98½	– 1/8
PacBell 6¼05	6.2	136	101½	– 3/4
PacBell 7½33	7.3	137	103	– 1⅛
PacBell 6⅝34	6.8	110	98⅛	– 1⅜
[illegible]	[illegible]	[illegible]	87	½

Bonds The "Bonds" column lists the name of the company that issued the bonds or its abbreviation. The company here is Pacific Bell. Next to the name you see "6¼05," which means the bond has a coupon rate of 6¼ percent and matures in 2005. Most corporate bonds have a face value of $1,000.

Cur Yld *Cur Yld* stands for *current yield.* Here the current yield is listed as 6.2, which means that if the bond is purchased today at the closing price, it will provide a yield (effective interest rate) of 6.2 percent. Keep in mind that the coupon rate and the yield are not necessarily the same. The coupon rate equals the annual coupon payment divided by the face value of the bond, while the yield equals the annual coupon payment divided by the price paid for the bond.

Vol The "Vol" column shows volume. The number here is 136, so the dollar volume for the day was $136,000.

Close The "Close" column lists the closing price for the company's bonds on this day, or 101½. Bond prices are quoted in points and fractions; each point is $10. Thus, 101½ is $1,015 (101½ = $101.50 × 10 = $1,015).

Net Chg *Net Chg* stands for *net change.* The number here is –¾, which means the price of the bond on this day was $7.50 lower than on the previous trading day.

The newspaper listing for Treasury bonds does not look the same as the listing for corporate bonds. Exhibit 22-10 shows information that relates to Treasury notes and bonds, as explained in the text that follows.

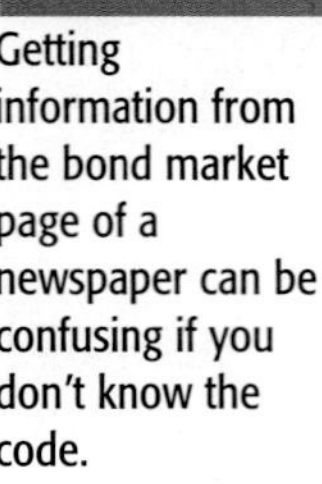

Getting information from the bond market page of a newspaper can be confusing if you don't know the code.

Rate The "Rate" column gives the coupon rate of the bond. In other words, the bond in Exhibit 22-10 pays 9⅜ percent of the face value of the bond in annual interest payments.

Maturity Mo/Yr The "Maturity Mo/Yr" column tells when the bond matures. This Treasury bond matures in February 2006.

Exhibit 22-10

Treasury Notes and Bonds

In this excerpt from the bond market page of the newspaper, the bond under consideration is a U.S. Treasury bond. The text explains what each number in each column means.

Rate	Maturity Mo/Yr	Bid	Asked	Chg	Ask Yld
9 3/8	Feb 06	122:17	122:23	-26	5.42
6 7/8	May 06n	108:08	108:18	-23	5.42
7	Jul 06n	109:08	109:12	-23	5.44
6 1/2	Oct 06n	106:13	106:15	-23	5.45
3 3/8	Jan 07I	96:03	96:13	-13	3.91
7 5/8	Feb 02-07	105:29	105:31	-12	5.42
[illegible]	[illegible] 07[illegible]	107[illegible]	[illegible]07:21	[illegible]	5.45

Bid The "Bid" column shows how much the buyer offered to pay for the bond—in other words, the price you will receive if you sell the bond. The number here is 122:17. The number after the colon stands for 32nds of $10. So, if the buyer has offered to pay 122:17 for the bond, how much is this in dollars and cents? We break the problem down into two parts. First, look at the number in front of the colon in the price—122. Since bond prices are quoted in points, and each point is $10, we multiply 122 times $10 to get $1,220. Second, we look at the number after the colon—17. This represents 17/32nds of $10, which amounts to $5.31. When we add $5.31 to $1,220 we get $1,225.31. This is the bid price of the bond. In other words, 122:17 translates into $1,225.31.

Asked The "Asked" number is how much the seller asked for in order to sell the bond—in other words, the price you will pay if you buy the bond. In the exhibit, this is 122:23, which is $1,227.19.

Chg *Chg* is the change in the price of the bond from the previous trading day, in 32nds. It follows, then, that –26 means that the price of the bond fell by 26/32nds of $10, or approximately $8.12, from the previous day.

Ask Yld *Ask Yld* stands for *ask yield,* or yield to maturity. This yield is based on the ask price. It means that a person who buys the bond today (at the ask price) and holds it to maturity will reap a return of 5.42 percent.

Section 2 Review

Defining Terms

1. Define
   a. bond
   b. face value (par value)
   c. junk bond

Reviewing Facts and Concepts

2. a. Is an issuer of a bond a lender or a borrower? b. Is a buyer of a bond a lender or a borrower?
3. If the face value of a bond is $10,000 and the annual coupon payment is $600, then what is the coupon rate?
4. If the annual coupon payment is $500 and the price paid for the bond is $9,544, then what is the yield?

Critical Thinking

5. "If you can predict interest rates, then you can earn a fortune buying and selling bonds." Do you agree or disagree? Explain your answer.

Applying Economic Concepts

6. What is the difference between the coupon rate and the current yield of a bond?

SECTION 3

Futures and Options

This section discusses futures and options. As you read this section, keep these key questions in mind:

- What is a futures contract?
- What is a currency futures contract?
- What is an option?
- What is a call option?
- What is a put option?

Futures

Key Terms

futures contract
option

Myers is a miller. He buys wheat from a wheat farmer, turns the wheat into flour, and then sells the flour to a baker. Obviously, he wants to earn a profit for what he does. How much, if any, profit he earns depends on the price at which he can buy the wheat and the price at which he can sell the flour.

Now suppose Myers enters into a contract with a baker. Myers promises to deliver to the baker 1,000 pounds of flour in six months. At the current wheat price, $3 a bushel, Myers knows he can earn a profit on his deal with the baker. However, he does not need the wheat now; he needs it in about six months. What will the price of wheat be then? If it is $2 a bushel, Myers will earn more profit on the deal with the baker. But if it is $4 a bushel, he will lose money. Myers's problem is that he does not know what a bushel of wheat will sell for in six months.

A miller can buy a futures contract from a speculator who hopes to earn profit on the sale. Explain how the speculator would earn profit.

Myers is a miller, not a speculator in the price of wheat. He decides to buy a futures contract in wheat. A **futures contract** is an agreement in which someone agrees to buy or sell a particular good (in this case, wheat) on a specified future date at an agreed-upon price. For example, Myers might buy a specific number of bushels of wheat now, for a price of $3 a bushel, to be delivered to him in six months.

Who would sell Myers the futures contract? The seller would be someone who does not mind assuming the risk of a change in wheat prices. Smith, the speculator, may look at things this way: "The price of wheat today is $3 a bushel. I think the price of wheat in six months will be close to $2 a bushel. Why not promise the miller that I will deliver a certain amount of wheat to him in six months if, in return, he pays me $3 a bushel today? Then, in six months, I will buy the wheat for $2 a bushel, earning myself $1 profit per bushel."

Myers, the miller, and Smith, the speculator, enter into a futures contract. Myers buys so many bushels of wheat for delivery in six months; Smith sells so many bushels of wheat for delivery in six months.

MINI GLOSSARY

futures contract An agreement to buy or sell a specific amount of something (a commodity, currency, or financial instrument) at a particular price on a stipulated future date.

option A contract that gives the owner the right, but not the obligation, to buy or sell shares of a stock at a specified price on or before a specified date.

What does each person get out of the deal? Myers gets peace of mind. He knows that he will be able to buy the wheat at a price that will let him earn a profit on his deal with the baker. Smith takes a chance that she is willing to take for the prospect of earning a profit.

Currency Futures

A futures contract can be written for wheat, as we have seen, or for a currency, a stock index, or even bonds. A currency futures contract works as follows.

Suppose Tyrone owns a Toyota dealership in Tulsa, Oklahoma. It is currently May, and Tyrone is thinking about a shipment of Toyotas he plans to buy in August. He knows he must buy the Toyotas from Japan with yen, which have a current dollar price of $0.012. Tyrone wonders what the price of yen will be in August, when he plans to make his purchase. Suppose the dollar price of yen rises to $0.018 in August; instead of paying $30,000 for a Toyota priced at 2.5 million yen, Tyrone would then have to pay $45,000.[4]

Tyrone can purchase a futures contract today for the needed quantity of yen in August from someone who thinks the dollar price of yen will go down between now and August. For example, Julie may reason, "I think the dollar price of yen will go down between now and August. Therefore, I will enter into a contract with Tyrone stating that I will give him 2.5 million yen in August for $30,000, the exchange rate specified in the contract being 1 yen = $0.012. If I am right and the actual exchange rate in August is 1 yen = $0.011, then I can purchase the 2.5 million yen for $27,500 and fulfill my contract with Tyrone by turning the yen over to him for $30,000. I will earn $2,500 profit."

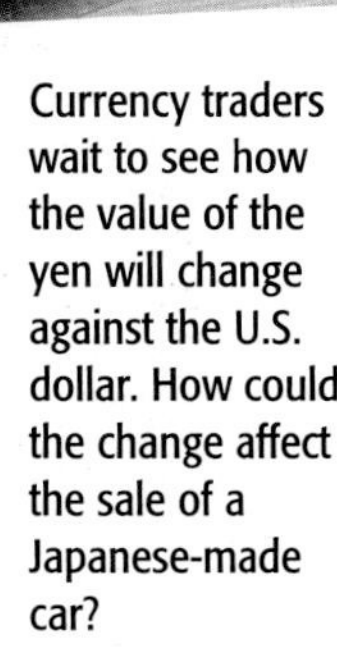

Currency traders wait to see how the value of the yen will change against the U.S. dollar. How could the change affect the sale of a Japanese-made car?

Options

An **option** is a contract that gives the owner the right, but not the obligation, to buy or sell shares of a stock at a specified price on or before a specified date. There are two types of options—call options and put options.

Call Option Call options give the owner the right to buy shares of a stock at a specified price within the time limits of the contract. The specified price at which the buyer can buy shares of a stock is called the *strike price*. For example, suppose Brown buys a call option for $20. The call option specifies that he can buy 100 shares of IBM stock at a strike price of $150 within the next month. If the price of IBM stock falls below $150, Brown does not exercise his call option; he simply tears it up and buys at the lower price. But if the price rises above $150, he exercises his call option. He buys the stock at $150 a share and then turns around and sells it for the higher market price.

4. If a yen equals $0.012, then a Toyota with a price of 2.5 million yen costs $30,000 ($0.012 × 2.5 million = $30,000). If a yen equals $0.018, then a Toyota with a price of 2.5 million yen costs $45,000 ($0.018 × 2.5 million = $45,000).

If Brown buys a call option, there has to be someone who sells it to him. A call option would be sold by a person who thought the option would not be exercised by the buyer. For example, if Nieves believed that the price of IBM was going to fall below $150, he would gladly sell a call option to Brown for $20, thinking that the option would never be exercised and he would make $20.

When would a buyer exercise a call option? a put option?

Put Options Put options give the owner the right, but not the obligation, to sell shares of a stock at a strike price during some period of time. For example, suppose Martin buys a put option to sell 100 shares of IBM stock at $130 during the next month. If the share price rises above $130, Martin will not exercise her put option. Instead, she will tear it up and sell the stock for more than $130. In contrast, if the price drops below $130, she will exercise her option to sell the stock for $130 a share. People who think the price of the stock is going to decline buy put options.

Who sells put options? Obviously, it is the people who think the price of the stock is going to rise. They would want to sell a put option for, say, $20, if they believed that the price of the stock was going to rise and the buyer of the put option was not going to exercise the option.

How You Can Use Options

Suppose you think a particular stock is going to rise in price during the next few months. Currently, the stock sells for $250 a share. You do not have enough money to buy many shares of stock, but you would like to benefit an expected rise in the price of the stock. To do so, you can buy a call option, which will sell for a fraction of the cost of the stock. In this case, you might buy a call option that gives you the right to buy 100 shares of the stock at $250 anytime during the next three months.

If you do not have the money to buy the stock at $250 a share now, however, why would anyone think you will have the money to buy the stock at $250 in a few months? The answer is that you do not have to buy the stock. If you are right that the price of the stock will rise, then the call option you are holding becomes worth more to people. You will be able to sell it and benefit from the uptick (increase) in the price of the stock.

Alternatively, if you expect the price of a stock to fall, you can buy a put option. In other words, you can buy the right to sell the stock for $250 anytime during the next three months. If the price does fall, your option becomes more valuable. People who have the stock and want to sell it for a price higher than it currently fetches will be willing to buy your put option for some price higher than you paid.

Section 3 Review

Defining Terms

1. Define

- **a.** futures contract
- **b.** option

Reviewing Facts and Concepts

2. Why might a person buy a futures contract?

3. Why might a person buy a call option?

Critical Thinking

4. "The currency speculator who sells futures contracts assumes the risk that someone else does not want to assume." Do you agree or disagree? Explain your answer.

Applying Economic Concepts

5. If you thought the share price of a stock was going to fall, would you buy a call option or a put option?

Developing Economic

Skills

Foresight versus Hindsight

Many different investment avenues are available. A person can invest in stocks, bonds, gold, silver, real estate, and so on. At the close of the twentieth century, the editors of the financial magazine, the *Economist,* identified the highest returning investment for each year, beginning in 1900 and ending in 1999. For example, in 1974, the highest returning investment was gold, in 1902 it was U.S. Treasury bills, in 1900 it was the U.S. stock market, and in 1979 it was silver.

Now the editors of the *Economist* asked how much income a person would have earned at the end of 1999, if she had invested $1 in the highest returning investment in 1900, and then taken the returns from that investment and invested it in the highest-returning investment in 1901, and so on for each year through the century. In other words, they were asking what amount of income a person would have earned, starting with $1 in 1900, if she had perfect investment foresight. After taxes and dealer costs, she would have earned $1.3 quadrillion—or 15,000 times more money than Bill Gates has. In other words, with perfect foresight a person can be rich beyond his or her imagination.

After the editors of the *Economist* had identified the dollar worth of foresight ($1.3 quadrillion), they went back and asked how much income the typical investor would have earned over the century. The typical investor does not have perfect foresight, of course. According to the editors of the *Economist,* the typical investor is a person who follows fashion. He buys silver because silver is a popular investment; he buys high tech stocks because high tech stocks are all the rage. The typical investor buys what people currently are talking about. The problem is that by the time people start talking about an investment, it has usually already reaped the highest percentage of the gains it will reap. Remember, people start talking about an investment because it has outperformed other investments, but a great past performance does not indicate a great future performance. To put this in context, while the person with perfect foresight would have invested in the Polish stock market in 1993, when no one was talking about it, and reaped a 754 percent gain, the typical investor would have invested in it one year later, in 1994, when everyone was talking about it. The problem is that the Polish stock market fell by 55 percent in 1994.

So, what would a person, starting with $1 in 1900, have earned by 1999, if he had missed the highest-earning investment of each year by one year? In other words, given that gold was the highest-earning investment in 1974, he had invested in gold in 1975, and so on? After taxes and dealing costs, it is $290.

We conclude that with perfect foresight $1 in 1900 turns into $1.3 quadrillion, but getting in on the highest-earning investment one year later earns only $290.

What are the economic lessons to be learned? First, the best investments are often the ones that you don't hear about until it is too late. Second, ignoring the first lesson, and thinking that a popular investment is a good investment, is often the way to low returns.

1. If gold is a good investment in year 1, it follows that it will be a good investment in year 2, too. Do you agree or disagree? Explain your answer.
2. You read the following ad in the newspaper: "Gold has gone up by 50 percent in the last six months. Isn't it time your money earned high returns? Isn't it time you bought gold?" What does the advertiser want you to believe?

CHAPTER

22 Review

Economics Vocabulary

Fill in the following blanks with the appropriate word or phrase.

1. The most widely cited indicator of day-to-day stock market activity is the ____.
2. A(n) ____ is a firm that acts as an intermediary between a company that issues a stock and the public that wishes to buy the stock.
3. A bond with a high default risk is a(n) ____.
4. A(n) ____ is an IOU, or promise to pay.
5. A company's first offering of stock to the public is a(n) ____.
6. ____ is a claim on the assets of a corporation.
7. The dollar amount specified on a bond is called the ____ of the bond.
8. An agreement to buy or sell a specific amount of something at a particular price on a stipulated future date is a(n) ____.
9. A(n) ____ is a contract that gives the owner the right, but not the obligation, to buy or sell shares of a stock at a specified price on or before a specified date.

Review Questions

1. "The stock market may not be the best place to put your money in the short run, but it is a pretty good place to put your money in the long run." What does this statement mean?
2. What does it mean if the Dow Jones Industrial Average rises by 100 points in a day?
3. What are the two reasons to buy stock?
4. What is a call option?
5. What is the origin of the New York Stock Exchange (NYSE)?
6. What is the yield of a bond?
7. List and define the three major components of a bond.
8. What is a Treasury bill?
9. What are junk bonds?
10. What does it mean when we say the PE ratio of a stock is 33?
11. Who usually issues bonds?
12. Would you buy or sell bonds if you expected the interest rate to rise? Explain your answer.
13. What does a bond's rating depend upon?
14. What is the ask yield of a bond?
15. What is a futures contract?
16. What does it mean if you invest in a mutual fund? In a stock index fund?
17. What services to investors are provided by a full-service stockbroker? By a discount broker?
18. What is a speculator? Give an example.

Calculations

1. The face value of a bond is $10,000, and the annual coupon payment is $850. What is the coupon rate?
2. The closing price of a stock is 90$\frac{9}{16}$, and the dividend is 3.50. What is the yield of the stock?
3. You buy a $10,000 inflation-indexed Treasury bond that pays a 5 percent coupon rate. If the inflation rate is 2 percent, what is the coupon payment?
4. You own 1,250 shares of stock X. You read in the newspaper that the dividend for the stock is "3.88." What do you earn in dividends?
5. A person buys a bond that matures in ten years and pays a coupon rate of 10 percent. The face value of the bond is $10,000. How much money will the bondholder receive in the tenth year?
6. The closing price of a stock is 66$\frac{3}{16}$, and the net earnings per share is $2.50. What is the stock's PE ratio?

Economics and Thinking Skills

1. **Application.** Chapter 11 discussed how the Fed changes the money supply. Suppose the Fed increases the money supply. How do you think this increase will affect the stock market?
2. **Analysis.** If bonds and stocks are substitutes, then what should we see as bonds offer higher returns?
3. **Cause and Effect.** If there is no cause-effect relationship between the state of the federal budget (deficit, balance, or surplus) and the Dow, what should we see in the real world?
4. **Analysis.** Why might a corporation decide to issue bonds to build a new factory instead of issuing stock or borrowing money?

Writing Skills

1. Write a one-page paper discussing the factors that you think influence the stock market. Explain how the factors that you identify will

cause people to want to buy more stocks or sell more stocks.

2. Imagine you are a business reporter for your local newspaper. Write a short article outlining the basic steps for selecting and purchasing stock.
3. Investigate projects funded by municipal bonds that were issued by your local government. Write a brief report about one of them. Include a discussion of the purpose of the bond, its face value, maturity date, and coupon rate. Find the bond rating on the Internet or in the newspaper.

Economics in the Media

1. Look in the newspaper to find the Dow Jones Industrial Average (DJIA) for the most recent date.
2. In the newspaper, find the current stock price for five of the thirty companies that make up the DJIA. Next, use the Internet to research one of the five companies. What kind of business is it? What is its history? Print out its latest quarterly report.
3. Find an article in the newspaper or a story on television news that mentions one of the following: stock market, bond market, put option, call option, DJIA, S&P 500, or NASDAQ. Discuss the contents of the article or story.
4. Log on to the Standard & Poor's Web site to find the current S&P 500 list. What kinds of companies are listed?
5. Find the history and track record of Moody's using their Web site. What other information is available on this Web site?

Where's the Economics?

This is the floor of the New York Stock Exchange. If good (but unexpected) economic news is reported, what is likely to happen to the buying activity here?

CHAPTER 23

The Internet Economy

What This Chapter Is About

As long as there have been people, there has been trade. Think back to the days when money did not exist. In the days of barter, there was trade. People traded goods and services for other goods and services. An apple for an orange or a loaf of bread for some meat.

Money emerged out of a barter economy and the world would never be the same. As we learned in an earlier chapter, the introduction of money changed our economy in fundamental ways. No longer did people have to spend so much time making everyday exchanges. The transaction costs of making exchanges fell dramatically and so people had more time to consume leisure and to produce.

Today, we not only live in a money economy, we also live in a new Internet economy. Has the introduction of the Internet changed the world in much the same way that the introduction of money changed the world? Some economists think that it has. We will discuss the many facets of the Internet economy, and the effects of the Internet economy, in this chapter.

Why This Chapter Is Important

In Chapter 6 we introduced the topic of business firms with these words: "To understand the life you are living, it is important to understand the institutions that play a big role in society. One of those institutions is business."

With only a slight modification, the same sentiment holds for what we will discuss in this chapter. To understand the life you are living, it is important to understand the Internet.

After You Study This Chapter, You Will Be Able To

- define *Internet.*
- list several key steps in the growth of the Internet.
- describe how the Internet has revolutionized the global economy.
- define *E-commerce.*
- explain the nature of *exchange.*
- identify ways in which the Internet has facilitated exchange.
- discuss both sides of key issues related to the development of the Internet.

You Will Also Learn What Economics Has to Do With

- Pez dispensers.
- science fiction.
- counterfeiting.
- Internet addiction.
- the Love Bug.

Economics Journal

For the next week or more, make a list of the tasks you complete or activities you enjoy online. For example, you may go online to buy a book, chat with a friend, or search for some information to help you write your history paper. Next to each activity or task, identify what you would have done to complete the task or activity had you not been able to go online. Would you have bought the book from a brick-and-mortar bookstore? Would you have called a friend on the telephone?

SECTION 1

The Internet and Its Impact

The Internet has given birth to an economic revolution, creating a new and exciting global economy. Just ten years ago, the expression *dot.com* was unknown, and only a very few people had heard of—let alone visited—cyberspace. The Internet was primarily a tool for a small group of scientists and researchers. Few at that time could have predicted what was about to happen. What did happen transformed our economy forever.

As you read this section, keep these key questions in mind:

- What is the Internet?
- What were some key developments in the growth of the Internet?
- How has the Internet changed the way businesses sell their products?
- What are some advantages of buying over the Internet?

What Is the Internet?

Key Terms

Internet
World Wide Web
Web site
cyberspace
E-commerce

Long ago, the invention of the steam engine unleashed great economic changes. These changes revolutionized the way products were made and sold. At the same time, they revolutionized economic theory. We refer to these changes today as the *Industrial Revolution.*

In the same way, the Internet has created a totally new way of doing business. This modern economic revolution has been called by many different names, such as the *New Economy* or the *Internet Economy.* More generally, the great changes created by the widespread use of computers, including the Internet, are often referred to as the *Digital Revolution.* You may have heard it said that we live in the *Information Age.* This is yet another term related to broad changes in our society involving computers and other ways of exchanging information.

These people graduated from Carnegie Mellon University with Master of Science degrees in Electronic Commerce.

Internet is a term familiar to almost everyone today, but what exactly does it refer to? The **Internet** is an international "network of networks" that links computers and computer systems of many types for the purpose of communicating data. Through the Internet, computer users can:

MINI GLOSSARY

Internet
A system of linked computer networks that facilitates data communication in a way that expands the reach of each participating system.

World Wide Web
Global system of interlinked Web sites or locations.

Web site
A home or location on the World Wide Web. A Web site is made up of a page or pages that may contain text, graphics, video and audio sources.

cyberspace The digital world constructed by computer networks.

- send and receive electronic mail, or *E-mail.*
- use their computers to access different computers at distant locations.
- transfer computer files to other Internet users.
- participate in discussion groups, or *chat groups.*
- access the **World Wide Web**—the global system of interlinked **Web sites** or locations, we most often think of when we think of the Internet.

The term *Internet* did not appear until the early 1980s, but the Internet had its start much earlier.

Growth of the Internet

What we know today as the Internet began as a small government program in the 1960s. The Cold War was a major national concern, and the government needed a way to link large computers involved in national defense projects. The job of creating the link went to the Advanced Research Projects Agency (ARPA), a part of the U.S. Department of Defense. In 1969, ARPA launched a network linking research computers at four universities. The new network was called *ARPAnet.*

The Cold War with the former Soviet Union prompted the development of what we now know as the Internet, a network that links computers all over the world.

ARPAnet quickly began to expand to include other networks. For some time, however, using it remained the privilege of scientists and researchers working on government projects. This situation began to change in the mid-1970s. In 1974, the first commercial version of ARPAnet, called *Telenet,* made its appearance. But further changes would have to take place before using the Internet would become practical for most people.

One important change involved the computer itself. In the earliest days of ARPAnet, computers were very large—and very expensive. Computers were found at research sites, such as universities, and in large businesses, not in people's homes. The first personal computers appeared in the late 1970s. Apple Computer, formed in 1976, introduced the popular Apple II in 1977. IBM, already a giant company, marketed its first PC in 1981. During the following years, personal computers became more affordable and powerful. At the same time, software was developed to give them new capabilities and make them easier to use.

The Man Who Brought Us Into Cyberspace

"Cyberpunk" is a genre of science fiction that examines the futuristic impact of new, far-out technologies. One of the first and most influential authors in this genre was William Gibson. In fact, Gibson was the one who coined the term **cyberspace**, today's popular term for the digital world of computer networks, in particular the Internet. The word first appeared in his 1984 novel *Neuromancer.* In this book, Gibson's characters explored uses of advanced technologies that, at the time, were completely unknown. His "cyborg" characters were part human and part machine—completely virtual. It was this virtual community that he called "cyberspace." Gibson's imaginative narrative described uses of technology that at the time were unthinkable. Widely read, and now considered a cult classic, *Neuromancer* stimulated many to explore the possibilities of actually realizing the world Gibson had described. Today, *cyberspace* is not considered a futuristic term. Rather, it is something in which almost all of us have traveled at one time or another. Some of us spend a lot of time there. Have you met any "cyborgs" recently? Are you sure?

In spite of the increasing numbers of computers in businesses and households, Internet use grew slowly in the 1980s. That would change in the 1990s, when several important developments took place. One was the birth of the *World Wide Web.* The Web introduced a way for computers to display files that contained links to other files in other locations. The files could also include pictures or sounds. Soon after, *Web browsers* began to appear. Web browsers were a new kind of *user interface*—that is, a new way for users to interact with their computers. Rather than typing commands on their keyboards, they could "point and click" to get where they wanted to go. It became possible to travel among Web sites by simply clicking on links—easy even for beginners. Mosaic, developed in 1993 at the University of Illinois, was a groundbreaking Web browser that included the ability to display pictures. Mosaic formed the basis for Netscape Navigator, the first commercial Web browser. Shortly after Navigator appeared on the market, Microsoft introduced its browser, Internet Explorer.

Web sites such as MyFamily.com allow Internet users to access information in seconds that might have taken months to find without the Internet.

The Internet exlosion was now underway. In 1994, there were about 3 million Internet users. In 2000, there were over 120 million. As the Internet's growth rate skyrocketed, many individuals and organizations began to think about its commercial possibilities.

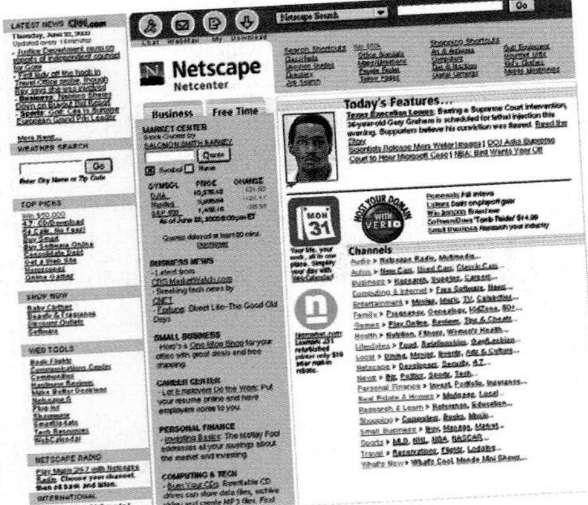

Netscape was the first commercial browser for the World Wide Web. What does a browser do?

Economic Growth and Internet Companies

The Internet of the 1990s soon emerged as a source of revenue. Netscape, the company that introduced the first Web browser, was formed in 1994. In its first year, its earnings exceeded $75 million. The company "went public" by selling stock for the first time in 1995. Buyers paid far more for Netscape shares than stock market experts had expected. Its founders became multimillionaires overnight.

The Internet offered other possibilities as well. The emerging service providers, portals, and search engines offer just a few examples. America Online (1989), which originated as a private computer network, like CompuServe and Prodigy, became the leading Internet *service provider.* Charging a monthly fee for access to the Internet, similar to the way phone companies charge for phone service, AOL generated billions of dollars in revenue. Another new company achieving tremendous success was Yahoo (1994), one of the first successful *portals.* Serving as a gateway to the Internet, portals such as Yahoo offered users collections of links to popular Web sites, giving them a convenient jumping-off place for exploring the Internet. Alta Vista (1995) was one of the first *search engines,* software programs that allow a user to look for a Web site on a particular topic.

Sites such as AOL and Yahoo soon became popular destinations for Internet users. As a result, they began to attract large amounts of advertising revenue. Companies raced to become leading portals and search engines. Newcomers emerged with names such as Excite and WebCrawler. Like Netscape, many of these companies went public with great success.

By the late 1990s, then, Internet-related companies had come into the economic mainstream. Venture capitalists, who provide funds for companies starting up or expanding, eagerly sought out the next Netscape or Yahoo. Internet-related stocks in general were extremely popular among stock traders. Partly because of this new area of investment, the stock market reached increasingly greater heights over the decade of the 1990s.

The Internet and E-Commerce

Entrepreneurs have made money on the Internet by selling online advertising and by taking their companies public. But more importantly, the Internet has become the delivery system for a new economy, one in which we can buy goods and services in the privacy of our homes. **E-commerce** is the term used to describe this use of the Internet for direct buying and selling, both business to consumer and business to business. Today, because of E-commerce, starting a new business no longer requires a traditional store. (In fact, "brick-and-mortar" became a popular term for distinguishing traditional businesses from the new online, E-commerce businesses.) A bookseller anywhere in the world with a World Wide Web site and a warehouse, for example, can compete with the largest bookstores in your community.

The Amazon.com distribution warehouse in Seattle is a busy place. How has E-commerce changed the way people shop?

E-commerce Business conducted online. Electronic commerce.

Exhibit 23-1
Popular Web Sites

Web Site	Unique visitors per month
1. yahoo.com	3,339,800
2. aol.com	2,933,300
3. msn.com	2,807,900
4. geocities.com	2,138,900
5. netscape.com	1,980,900
6. go.com	1,849,600
7. microsoft.com	1,803,100
8. lycos.com	1,485,700
9. excite.com	1,414,900
10. hotmail.com	1,386,800
11. passport.com	1,367,700
12. angelfire.com	1,215,600
13. amazon.com	1,161,800
14. tripod.com	1,126,100
15. altavista.com	918,500

E-commerce offers many advantages to consumers. We can find what we want quickly and easily, at any hour of the night or day. Long drives to the mall are replaced by online shopping. Using a simple search, we can locate the CD we've been looking for without scrambling through bins in store after store. We can shop in Paris or London, price Italian art, and even purchase collectibles in Japan, all from our Internet-connected computer. Exhibit 23-1 lists some of the most popular Web sites.

Another advantage of E-commerce relates to price. If we find one seller's price too high, we can quickly and easily shop for better prices elsewhere. Furthermore, prices tend to be lower on the Internet. We will see why this is so in Section 2, where we examine in more detail the exchanges between buyers and sellers on the Internet.

Just how much business is actually done on the Internet? Like the growth of the Internet itself, the growth of E-commerce was at first somewhat cautious. Its potential, however, has become clear. In 1999, one-third of all those connected to the Internet in the United States made an online purchase—twice as many as in the preceding year. Plane tickets and car rentals accounted for $7 billion of those sales. Books, music, and entertainment accounted for almost $4 billion. Durable goods, such as computers, accounted for $100 billion. Exhibit 23-2 on page 654 lists some of the most successful E-commerce businesses.

In South Korea, major companies such as Samsung have online shopping malls. How might online catalogs change the way a company sells products?

Is Internet Addiction a Big Joke?

Anyone who has used the Internet knows how easy it is to lose track of time. Surfing the Web is effortless, absorbing, and consuming. The Internet has so much to offer—help with homework, interesting Web pages, chat rooms, and interactive gaming areas. You can E-mail your friends or develop online relationships with people you have never met. Many parents see this as a better activity than passively watching TV.

Now it seems that surfing the Web may also be addictive. Internet Addiction Disorder (IAD), according to psychologist Dr. Ivan Goldberg, has many clear symptoms. He should know; he coined the name of this new disorder. These symptoms include psychomotor agitation, anxiety, obsessive thinking about the Internet, fantasies, dreams about the Internet, and involuntary typing movements. His diagnostic work has received much attention. Psychologists all over the world have read his online newsletters and have prescribed his suggested treatment for IAD. His research is quoted in many Internet books and manuals.

There is one problem, however, with Dr. Goldberg's work. He has admitted that the whole thing was a joke. He first wrote about IAD as a parody. He did not think that any serious doctor would believe that IAD truly existed and was amazed that so many responded to the mailing list he established.

The lesson here is more serious than one might at first realize. The ability to pass bogus information across the Internet may not always be funny, and it is not always harmless. It may be dangerous if the information is taken seriously, and it is becoming far too common these days. That truly is an addiction to worry about.

Furthermore, Internet addiction may not be such a joke after all. An increasing number of psychologists have expressed concern about the long-term effects of overusing the Internet. Many believe that it results in social isolation. This isolation, in turn, may have a harmful effect on our culture. Addiction to the Internet, according to these experts, is a true medical problem. Dr. Kimberly Young has founded the Center for On-Line Addiction. Dr. Maressa Orzack runs a computer addiction center at McLean Hospital.

What are the true symptoms? Although there are horror stories of children and adults spending as much as 80 hours a week online, most would agree that less than 1 percent of Internet users could be classified as addicted. There is a definite difference between enjoying the Internet and being addicted to it. Signs of addiction might include continuing to use the Internet despite suffering personal loss from such use or feeling an obsessive need to check your E-mail many times throughout the day.

While some believe that Internet addiction is a growing problem, Dr. Sherry Turkle, a sociology professor at M.I.T. and a clinical psychologist, disagrees. She argues that "the Internet offers experiences in which people discover things about themselves, good and bad, usually complicated and hard to sort out. People grow and learn and discover new potential. People also discover preoccupations and fantasies that they may have never dealt with before and which may be very troubling. . . . I think that many of our anxieties about the Internet are a displacement of other anxieties about the power of technology in our lives."

QUESTION TO ANSWER Do you think Internet addiction can occur? What are the signs? What are the solutions?

Exhibit 23-2
Market Value of Selected E-companies

E-company	2000 market value (millions of dollars)
1. Amazon.com	$17,428
2. eBay	15,666
3. Priceline.com	7,080
4. E*Trade	4,485
5. eToys Inc.	761
6. Open Market, Inc.	377
7. ShopNow.com	292
8. Barnesandnoble.com	261
9. Egghead.com	159
10. Beyond.com	78

This exciting new marketplace is attracting many businesses, as well as consumers. In 2000, four hundred thousand companies were conducting business on the Internet, and the number grows daily. It appears that E-commerce is poised for tremendous global growth. The resulting changes are likely to affect all parts of the business community. No industry will remain untouched. Bill Gates, cofounder of Microsoft, states in his book *The Road Ahead:* "We are watching something historic happen, and it will affect the world seismatically, rocking us in the same way that the discovery of the scientific method, the invention of printing, and the arrival of the Industrial Age did."

Other observers, though, have suggested that "some important things haven't changed." In their book *Clicks and Mortar,* David S. Pottruck and Terry Pearce argue that the success of E-commerce will depend on its willingness to follow the successful formulas of the past. "In a world where companies are rushing to add an 'e' to everything they do—e-commerce, e-tailing—the real key to success still lies off-line." Success, they say, lies in looking beyond quick fixes and short-term profit.

Section 1 Review

Defining Terms

1. Define

a. cyberspace

b. E-commerce

c. Internet

d Web site

e. World Wide Web

Reviewing Facts and Concepts

2. Describe the development of the Internet.

3. Name several developments that have been essential to the growth of E-commerce.

4. What are some advantages of E-commerce for consumers?

Critical Thinking

5. How does E-commerce differ from the traditional economy? How is it similar to the traditional economy?

Applying Economic Concepts

6. Using the economic principles that you have learned in this text, predict the way in which "brick-and-mortar" businesses will be affected by the Internet in the next twenty years. Will they disappear? Will they change? Explain your answer.

SECTION 2 The Internet and Exchange

For the student writing a report on the Roman Empire, the Internet is an encyclopedia. For the person who wants to talk about music, politics, or food, it is a chat room. For the person who wants to listen to music, it is a radio. For an economist, the Internet is, as you learned in Section 1, a tool that is increasingly being used to create new markets and to facilitate exchange. It is the Internet as the facilitator of exchange and the creator of new markets that we discuss in this section.

As you read this section, keep these key questions in mind:

- What is the nature of exchange?
- How does money facilitate exchange?
- How does the Internet facilitate exchange?
- Does the Internet create new markets?

Key Term

reverse auction

The Nature of Exchange

In Chapter 2, we said that "individuals make themselves better off by entering into exchanges—by trading what they value less for what they value more." To illustrate, John has $10, and Steve has a book. John values the book more than his $10; Steve values the $10 more than the book. John trades his $10 for Steve's book. Through exchange, each person gives up what he values less for what he values more. Each person is made better off through exchange.

If you doubt that exchange makes you better off, think of what your life would be like if you lived in a world where no one traded. In this world, the only goods you have are the goods you produce for yourself. If you produce only apples and oranges, then apples and oranges are all that you have. Would you be better off living in this world, or would you prefer living in a world where you could trade your apples and oranges for other goods? The answer is obvious. All of us are made better off through exchange.

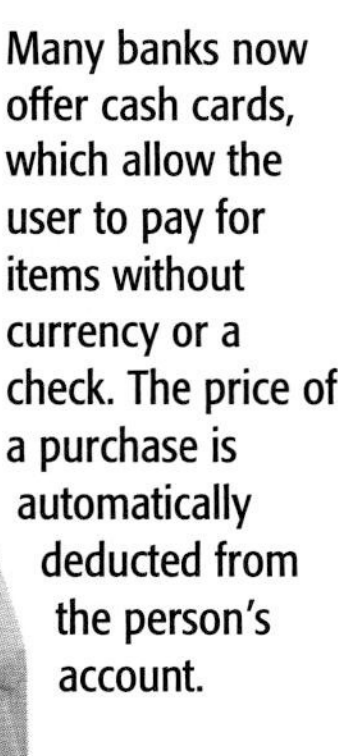

Many banks now offer cash cards, which allow the user to pay for items without currency or a check. The price of a purchase is automatically deducted from the person's account.

Money and Exchange

In Chapter 10, we discussed the emergence of money from a barter economy. As you may recall, in a barter economy, making exchanges was often difficult and time-consuming because not everyone had a *double coincidence of wants* with everyone else. You have a double coincidence of wants with Smith if Smith has what you want and you have what Smith wants. In a barter

How does exchange make people better off?

(moneyless) economy, you may have apples and want oranges, but the person who has oranges may not want your apples. There will be no trade. Obviously, then, before an exchange can be made, two people *must* have a double coincidence of wants.

In a money economy, the probability of having a double coincidence of wants with others increases dramatically. Therefore, exchange becomes more likely. The person who wouldn't trade oranges for apples in a barter economy will gladly trade oranges for money in a money economy.

Let's summarize. First, through exchange we make ourselves better off—we trade what we value less for what we value more. Second, the use of money makes exchange more likely. Conclusion: The use of money, in that it makes exchanges more likely, makes us better off.

The Internet and Exchange

The Internet is a little like money—it makes exchanges more likely. Because it does, it makes us better off.

Think of things this way. Say that in a barter economy there were 100 exchanges each day. When money emerged on the scene, the number of exchanges increased to 200 exchanges each day. Now, with the Internet, the number of exchanges rises to 250 exchanges each day. Stated differently, in the Internet economy, more people are making themselves better off each day through exchange than they did in the money economy. Our economic history is one of evolving toward increasingly more exchanges.

But just how does the Internet promote exchange? How does it make exchange more likely? What exchanges are taking place today with the Internet that did not take place before the Internet existed? We begin to answer these questions next.

The Internet, Transaction Costs, and Exchange

Sometimes exchanges are not made because the transaction costs of making them are too high. In Chapter 10, we defined *transaction costs* as the costs you have to incur before you can actually make an exchange or trade. For example, think of the transaction costs you incur when you buy a CD from a store. You have to drive to the store to buy the CD, which means you have to spend some gas money and incur a time cost of driving. You have to search for the CD once you get to the store. You have to wait as the store clerk rings up the sale. You have to drive home, which means you have to spend additional gas money and incur an additional

eBay: So You Want to Buy a Bulldozer?

In 1995, a software developer named Pierre Omidyar had a problem. His fiancée was having difficulty finding a particular Pez dispenser. She was not interested in the candy inside. Her hobby involved collecting these quirky candy holders. Yet due to time and location, she had reached a dead end. How could she network to find others who shared in her hobby? Omidyar imagined that the Internet might be able to help. He wanted to develop an online, one-stop, buy-and-sell flea market. First, he developed a software package designed to make the marketplace more efficient. His idea was quite simple. His program would allow people to list items for sale and would allow others to bid on and buy the items. The result was an online auction site called eBay. Today, eBay is the global leader in this sort of online trading.

In pure business terms, eBay is an amazing story. After only four years, eBay was averaging over $8 million a day in gross merchandise. This translated to over 1.5 million interested visitors every single day. For the first quarter of 2000, eBay reported net revenues of over $85 million.

According to recent company figures, more than 60 million auctions have been completed since eBay first opened its doors in 1995. Pez dispensers can still be found at eBay, but so can expensive art and valuable antiques. Anyone with any hobby is welcome to use eBay's market to sell his or her wares. One of the company's favorite sales involved a $7 purchase of knickknacks found underneath an old sofa. Another favorite is the sale of a used bulldozer for $23,000.

This e-commerce business has clearly found its niche. Many other companies are racing to compete in the auction market, including Amazon.com and Yahoo.

According to Kevin Pursglove, senior director of communications for eBay, the key to eBay's success is not in its software or even in its convenience. eBay could not have succeeded without "creating trust and confidence among users." This comfort level is critical, he says. If E-commerce is going to thrive, the industry must rely on "some old principles that carry over from the traditional world." The old principle most talked about at eBay these days is customer service.

QUESTIONS TO ANSWER

1. What is unqiue about Pierre Omidyar? What personal qualities have contributed to his creation of such a successful new Internet company?
2. Have you traded at eBay or similar sites? If so, describe your experiences. Have you found this new type of exchange rewarding?

SOURCE: Adapted from Matthew Beale, "E-Commerce Success Story: eBay," *E-Commerce Times,* May 12, 2000.

time cost of driving—you may even have to spend time in a traffic jam. Might these transaction costs be high enough to prevent some exchanges from being made?

With this in mind, consider Mario, who wants to buy a CD. The highest price that he is willing to pay for the CD is $16. Suppose the price of the CD is $14. One would think that since Mario is willing to pay more ($16) than the price of the CD ($14), he will definitely buy the CD. But not so fast! We haven't yet taken into account the transaction costs connected with the purchase.

Suppose Mario says that the transaction costs for him of driving to the store, searching for the CD, and so on, amount to $5. This means that Mario would have to spend a total of $19 to buy the CD—$14 for the CD itself and $5 in transaction costs. This is $3 more than the highest price he is willing to pay for the CD. In other words, the transaction costs are high enough to prevent an exchange from happening.

Would lower transaction costs entice you to shop online? If not, what might entice you to shop online?

If someone or something could lower the transaction costs of purchasing the CD, Mario may buy the CD. Enter the Internet. Today, Mario can go online and buy the CD. By purchasing the CD online, Mario eliminates many of the transaction costs he would have to incur if he purchased the CD from a (brick-and-mortar) store. He doesn't have to incur the time cost driving to the store, the cost of gas, and so on. Essentially, the only transaction cost he incurs online is mailing cost. Suppose the online store charges $14 for the CD and the mailing cost is $1.50. Will Mario buy the CD? He certainly will.

Let's recap. The transaction costs of buying the CD from a store were $5 at a local store versus $1.50 online. In other words, the Internet was able to lower Mario's transaction costs by $3.50. In that the Internet lowers or eliminates transaction costs (for buying CDs, books, flowers, watches, and so on), it makes exchanges more likely. In short, sometimes the only thing that stands between a buyer and a seller transacting business are high transaction costs. By lowering transaction costs, the Internet makes it more likely that buyers and sellers will get together, making each other better off in the process.

The Internet, Reverse Auctions, and Exchange

Suppose the price of an airline ticket from Los Angeles to New York is $600 (round trip). At this price, Jones decides not to buy the ticket because it is not worth it to him. The highest dollar amount Jones is willing and able to pay for the ticket is $500.

It is easy to conclude that there will be no exchange. After all, if the price the seller is asking ($600) is more than the buyer is willing and able to pay ($500), how can there be an exchange? What we don't know, though, is whether or not the $600 price is negotiable. When an airline company posts a ticket price of $600, does this mean that it *will not* sell the ticket for less, or does it mean that it *may* sell the ticket for less?

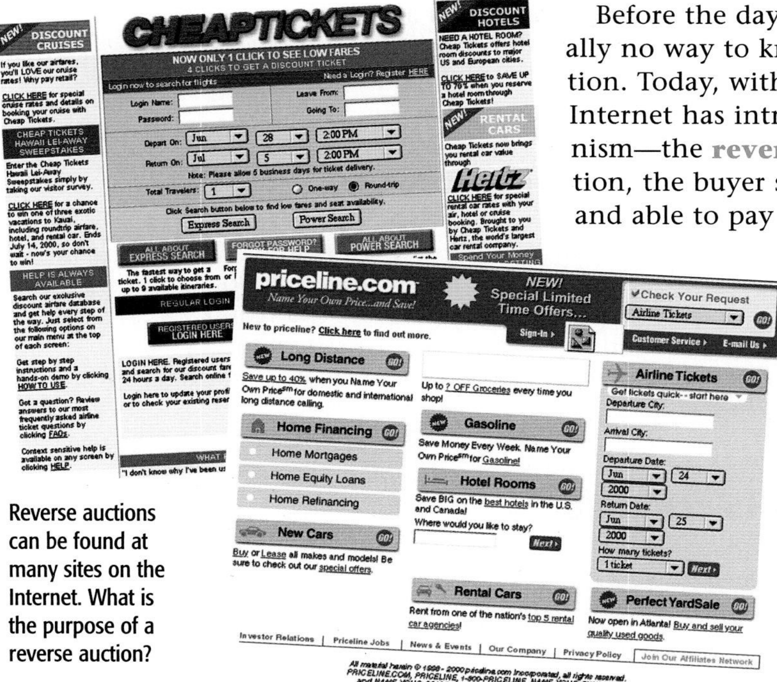

Reverse auctions can be found at many sites on the Internet. What is the purpose of a reverse auction?

Before the days of the Internet, there was really no way to know the answer to this question. Today, with the Internet, there is. The Internet has introduced a new pricing mechanism—the **reverse auction.** In a reverse auction, the buyer states the price he is willing and able to pay for a good or service. Then, it is up to the seller to either take it or leave it.

The Internet has made the reverse auction commonplace. Today, if you want to buy an airline ticket, you can do so at a reverse auction. You can go to one of many reverse auction sites—for example, Priceline.com. There, you can identify what you want to buy and the price you are willing to pay. You might say you are willing to pay $500 for an airline ticket, $18,000 for a particular car, or $80 a night for a hotel room in Washington, D.C.

Are there more exchanges being made today with online reverse auctions than were made in the days before online reverse auctions? The answer is yes. Thousands of people say they would not have purchased the airline ticket, the car, or the hotel room if they could not have purchased it at "their" price.

We are left with only one nagging question: Why didn't reverse auctions (for airline tickets, cars, and so on) exist before the Internet? It is because there was really no cheap way for a broker to collect bids from people from all over the world and then communicate them to sellers all over the world. With the Internet, there is. In short, the Internet made it inexpensive to collect and submit bids, and so the online reverse auction (for buying many goods) was born.

reverse auction
An auction in which the buyer states the price he or she is willing to pay for a good or service, and the seller decides whether or not to sell at those terms.

The Internet, New Markets, and Exchange

Stella has an old tea set that she would like to sell. Beverly has a 100-year-old desk to sell. Mark has an antique telephone. Ask yourself where a person goes to sell old tea sets, desks, and telephones. Today the answer is "to the Internet." Before the existence of the Internet, answering this question was difficult. To a large degree, the Internet has created markets for goods where none existed before.

Markets cannot exist without information. A seller has an old tea set but doesn't know if a buyer is willing to buy it. The seller lacks information. One way to obtain that information is to take a megaphone and shout into it, "Anyone want to buy an old tea set?" No matter how loudly you shout, not many people will hear. The Internet, however, is a giant megaphone. You can just "whisper" words on the Internet, and people in Brazil, Japan, Russia, and New Zealand can hear them. Through the Internet, sellers who couldn't previously find buyers can now find them. Once they do, exchanges are made.

Take a look at any of the online auction sites. How many of the items on that site would have been sold if there were no Internet? Would Jerry's old guitar find a buyer without the Internet? Would Maria's gold necklace find a buyer without the Internet? If the answer is no, then we must conclude that the Internet, once again, is making exchange much more likely.

This young woman in Tehran, Iran, might be willing and able to buy an antique tea set from a woman in Iowa. It is possible for her to do so using the Internet.

The Internet, Costs, and Exchange

The greater the number of exchanges, the greater the equilibrium quantity of a good. For example, there are more exchanges if the equilibrium quantity of television sets is 100,000 than if it is 20,000.

One of the things that will increase the equilibrium quantity of a good is an increase in the supply of the good. For example, if the supply of houses rises and the demand for houses is constant, the equilibrium price of houses will fall, and the equilibrium quantity of houses will rise. This is simple supply and demand analysis.

A decrease in resource prices will increase the supply of a good. To illustrate, suppose wood is needed to produce desks. A decrease in the price of wood will lead to an increase in the supply of desks. An increase in the supply of desks will lead to lower desk prices and more desks bought and sold—more exchange.

Is there a link between the Internet and lower costs? If there is, then there is also a link between the Internet, increased supply, lower prices, and more exchanges.

One of the ways the Internet reduces costs is by enabling firms to find the cheapest supplier of the resources they need to produce their goods. This business-to-business (B2B) marketplace is a big part of the Internet. Hundreds of thousands of resource suppliers have sites on the Internet. Now a firm can simply key in what it is looking for—pulp, paper, chemicals, wire, cable—and in seconds have the names of firms all over the world that are willing and able to sell it what it needs. Such intense competition has led to lower resource prices, which translate into lower costs for the firm. From there, it is but one step to greater supply, lower product prices, and more exchanges.

How might the Internet change the way this logging company finds buyers for its logs?

The Internet, the Cost of Entering a Market, and Exchange

This online publishing company doesn't have nearly as many startup and overhead costs as a brick-and-mortar publishing house.

The Internet can lower a firm's cost of entering a market. As a consequence, it increases the supply of a good, lowers price, and brings about more exchange. To illustrate, consider the costs of entering the book market if you have to buy land and build a store. The cost of buying the land, building the store, stocking the store with books, and hiring employees can be many millions of dollars. Enter the Internet. Instead of buying a piece of land and putting up a bricks-and-mortar store, you can enter the book market through cyberspace. Instead of a store on a parcel of land, you have a Web site. Instead of bookshelves with books on them, you have a list of books that appear on a computer screen. In short, the cost of entering the book market is cheaper now that the Internet exists than it would be if it did not exist.

Would you prefer to shop for books in an online store or in a "real," brick-and-mortar store?

How does this help the average book buyer? As the costs of entering the book market decline, more sellers will enter the book market. There will be a greater supply of books available for sale, book prices will decline, and more books will be bought and sold—hence, more exchanges.

Section 2 Review

Define Terms

1. Define reverse auction.

Reviewing Facts and Concepts

2. Give an example of how the Internet lowers transaction costs.
3. Before the Internet, a person could have called up an airline company and said, "I am willing to pay only $200 for a ticket to New York. Are you willing to sell the ticket to me at this price?" However, not many people did this. Today, hundreds of thousands of people make such offers online. Why are so many people willing to do today online what they weren't willing to do years ago over the telephone?
4. Can the Internet affect the supply of a good? Explain your answer.

Critical Thinking

5. If Suzanne can produce more with the same amount of resources, or if she can produce the same amount with fewer resources, economists say her productivity has increased. For example, suppose Suzanne can produce 100 units of good X this week with the same resources and in the same time it took her to produce 90 units of good X last week. Suzanne's productivity has increased. Can you think of examples of how the Internet can raise productivity?

SECTION 3

Conflicting Views: Challenges to the New Internet Economy

Few would deny that the new Internet economy has permanently changed the way business is conducted around the world. The Internet is not, however, without controversy. In this section, we discuss a few of the major conflicts and issues regarding the Internet and its uses. As you read this section, evaluate for yourself the arguments on both sides, and determine where you stand on each issue. Keep these key questions in mind:

- Who controls the Internet?
- What is the digital divide?
- Should the Internet be taxed?
- Why is the issue of protecting intellectual property a problem for the Internet?

Key Terms

digital divide
hacker
computer virus
intellectual property

Who Controls the Internet?

Some economists and political scientists argue that the Internet represents the purest form of democracy we have yet experienced in America. It is made up of thousands of independent sites. No single institution manages or monitors its content. Any and all viewpoints are welcome. Anyone can create a Web site and put anything he or she wants on that site. Furthermore, a sense of anonymity has made the posting of information and the participation in various chat rooms seem easy and safe. As a result, images and opinions of all kinds are placed on the Internet. This complete lack of restriction and regulation has prompted calls to impose controls.

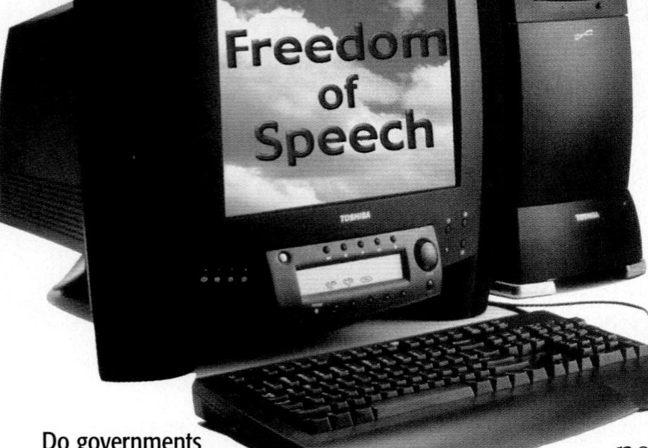

Do governments have the right to control the Internet? Should anyone have the power to control the Internet? Explain your answer.

As more and more people are connected to the Internet, concerns grow about the effect of its content on children. In 1996, the United States Congress agreed that it was time to establish standards for the Internet. In an effort to "protect the children," Congress overwhelmingly passed the Communications Decency Act. This law made it a crime to send "indecent" material over the Internet. But when President Bill Clinton signed the bill into law, there was an immediate outcry. The Center for Democracy and Technology organized a 48-hour Internet blackout. Over those two days, thousands of World Wide Web pages went black in protest in order to show the far-reaching impact of the new law. It was an amazing show of Internet solidarity.

To block enforcement of the new law, the American Civil Liberties Union (ACLU) filed a lawsuit against the Department of Justice and Attorney General Reno. At issue was whether the First Amendment's guarantee of free speech applied to the Internet community. Despite America's commitment to the right of free speech, the courts have often argued that this right has limits. A "clear and present danger" standard has been applied to public speech. This standard holds that speech that endangers others is not protected by the First Amendment. Would the courts hold the Internet to this standard?

Who has the responsibility to keep this child "safe" while using the Internet?

On June 26, 1997, the United States Supreme Court handed down its unanimous decision in the case of *Reno v. ACLU*. The Court declared that the Communications Decency Act violated the guarantee of freedom of speech and ruled that the law was unconstitutional. The Court argued that the Internet was not yet an "invasive" medium, like TV and radio. Furthermore, it asserted that this law threatened "to torch a large segment of the Internet community." Rachel Chong, at that time a commissioner in the Federal Communications Commission (FCC), commented:

> The Internet has been the tremendous success that it's been because the government has kept its mitts off it. I'm in the camp that government should not regulate unless it has to. For example, the Communications Decency Act was not the right way to regulate the Internet. The better way to control the Internet is with software controls, and, frankly, parental responsibility has got to be the key.

The fight over the regulation of the Internet did not end with the Supreme Court decision in 1997. Many individuals, media outlets, interest groups, and government officials have continued to pursue efforts to curb unlimited transmission of material across the Internet. Recent Congresses have tried to re-address the issue with the Children's Online Protection Act (COPA) and the Juvenile Justice Reform Act. Both would require schools and libraries that receive federal funding to filter minors' access to the Internet. Disputes over these acts are still pending in the courts. The courts will be busy sorting out these legal questions: Who should control the Internet? Does it need control? How does, or should, the First Amendment, with its guarantee of free speech, affect Internet content and use?

The Haves and Have Nots—The Digital Divide

The Internet has become an important part of the economy and of life, but not everyone has access to the Internet. According to a Department of Commerce report, "Falling Through the Net," whites and Asian Americans have Internet access in larger proportions than African Americans, Hispanics, and Native Americans. Individuals in higher-income households are more likely to be connected than those in lower-income households. Highly educated individuals are more likely to have Internet access than poorly educated individuals. People who reside in suburban areas are more likely to have Internet access than people who reside in central cities or in rural areas. These inequities have been labeled the **digital divide**.

digital divide
The economic gap between those who have access to computers and the Internet, and those who do not.

The digital divide has prompted many across the political and social spectrum to ask a basic question, "If the Internet is creating a new society of haves and have nots, what should be done? Predictably, as computer

Internet-connection costs come down, the gap between information haves and have nots becomes smaller. Another positive factor is the presence of the Internet in schools, libraries, and community centers, where people can access this technology free of charge. The private sector has also tried to help bridge the gap. At a recent press conference, Ameritech Corporation pledged $350,000 to build new Internet community centers in five urban areas. The 3Com Corporation has donated $1 million in hardware and support to 10 different cities. Individuals like Microsoft cofounder Bill Gates have offered scholarships and large gifts to underprivileged persons and communities. But are these efforts too little and too late?

This native American girl is able to access the Internet on a computer at the school she attends.

The situation in many other nations is worse than that in the United States. There are few, if any, Internet connections in Iraq, in North Korea, or in the nations of Africa. In many countries, Internet access is a privilege for a very limited few. For most, the expense associated with the Internet is too great. Furthermore, in many countries, government censors put the Internet out of reach. In Laos, for instance, the government considers the Internet a corrupting influence and keeps connections scarce.

The Internet Society, a nonprofit international group that coordinates Internet-related projects around the world, has the motto "Internet is for everyone." But is the Internet for everyone? Should it be? Is the digital divide a political issue, a social issue, a racial issue, or just an economic issue? Who should be involved in addressing the digital divide? These are important questions that need to be answered in into the Internet economy.

This after-school computer training program gives many students an Internet opportunity they don't have at home.

Technological Gridlock

One of the most immediate problems for the Internet is technological gridlock. In 1995, only 16 million computers had access to the World Wide Web. Today, over 250 million computers around the globe have the potential to log in to the information superhighway. Can the Internet and its infrastructure withstand this traffic? When people cannot get online to conduct business or buy goods, and businesses cannot contact each other because of gridlock, time and money are lost.

Technology is always changing to improve the accessibility and speed of the Internet.

Gridlock is an increasing problem, particularly for E-commerce. America Online in its early days discovered that its public relations were adversely affected each time one of its members was unable to make an online connection. Other online businesses have learned from those early lessons. Roadblocks on the information superhighway cause grief and frustration. Perhaps the most important cost is lost profits. Computer engineers are, and will continue to be, in great demand to overcome these network roadblocks.

Taxing the Internet

What might happen to local businesses if more people shop online to avoid paying sales taxes?

If you buy a computer from the computer store down the street, you are likely to pay a state or local sales tax. If you go online and buy a computer from a company that doesn't have a physical presence in your state, you may not pay a sales tax. The owner of the computer store down the street thinks this is unfair. She wonders how she can effectively compete against a company that does not have to charge sales tax to its customers.

Should the Internet be taxed like every other business? The owner of the computer store down the street says yes, but there are plenty of people who say no. The opponents of a tax on Internet trade argue that the Internet is in its infancy, that it is the growth engine for the U.S. economy, and that it should not be restrained by taxes.

Currently, a government-imposed *moratorium,* or waiting period, prohibits state and local taxes targeting the Internet. Congress recently showed an interest in extending the moratorium for five more years. It would appear, then, that the Internet is safe from taxation for the time being. National and state politicians worry, however, about the equity of such a moratorium, especially because related telecommunication industries would like to share in these tax-free benefits. Others argue that if certain sectors of the economy are exempt from paying taxes, those taxes will have to be paid by someone else. State governors see the moratorium as an infringement on their powers to raise revenue. Some estimate that the moratorium reduces state and local revenue potential by $30 billion annually. As E-commerce profits soar in the future, the debate over taxing the Internet will surely grow even more intense.

What do you think? Should E-commerce be given a tax advantage? Would taxation at this point kill the industry in its infancy, as some believe? If states or the U.S. Congress were to tax the Internet, could it be done fairly? How would such taxes be administered and collected?

Cybercrime, Cybercriminals, and Cyberterrorism

Among the greatest concerns facing the new Internet economy are the potential pitfalls associated with *cybercrime,* or computer crime, and *cyberterrorism,* which involves invasions of computer systems with such weapons as computer viruses. A recent *New York Times* editorial put it this way: "Cyberspace is a chaotic Wild West frontier full of highway bandits." Recently a spokesperson from America Online warned, "the online world is not immune to people with less than good intentions any more than the offline world is." How bad is the situation? Is the Internet a dangerous place? Or is it, as Bill Gates has tried to assure us, "a reasonably reliable communications channel for millions of people"?

A cybercriminal could break into this designer's computer and steal her design. How can cybercrime be combatted?

Certainly, crime is no stranger to the online world. Probably the predominant crime is *fraud*—intentionally misleading people to get their money. In total, consumers lost over $4 billion to Internet fraud in 2000. People are becoming more willing to report problems, and Internet fraud complaints have risen dramatically. Nevertheless, the Federal Trade Commission (FTC) has estimated that losses could actually be much higher than reported—perhaps as high as $40 billion per year.

Internet fraud may involve purchases of goods or investments. For example, in 2000, consumers lost an average $600 per transaction purchasing computer equipment and software from nonexistent companies. The consumers placed their orders online, but the merchandise never arrived. The Web sites where they placed the orders had disappeared before the companies and the purchases could be tracked.

Online auction sales account for more than 90 percent of reported cases of Internet fraud. And Internet investment fraud costs consumers millions of dollars each year. What can we do about such problems? The FTC has issued regulations to help consumers, and consumer groups offer education programs and advice. Clearly, it is up to us to be cautious and well-informed when we shop online.

Cybercriminals often steal credit card numbers for their own use. How can you protect your credit card number?

Linked to the issue of fraud is the problem of ensuring the security of credit card numbers provided by consumers when they make purchases on the Internet. Cybercriminals have stolen credit card numbers and used them to make their own purchases, creating an economic nightmare for credit card companies and for consumers. It is estimated that there are over 30,000 credit card numbers "floating" around the Internet, numbers that were stolen either when commercial sites were "hacked" into or when their security systems failed. Although companies are working with Internet security firms and software manufacturers to help protect consumers, the problem has yet to be resolved.

Security is indeed one of the most serious problems for the Internet. The FBI estimates that U.S. businesses lose hundreds of millions of dollars every year to **hackers**. Hackers have become more than an annoyance. They pose a serious threat to E-commerce. Although 90 percent of hackers are reportedly amateurs, the threat they pose has become increasingly sophisticated.

Originally, a hacker was a person who possessed unique computer skills. Today, however, hacker generally refers to a person who breaks into another person's computer, violating that person's private space online. Once hackers enter secure networks, they can change or delete files, steal or change information, and remove the evidence of those activities. Many hackers, however, merely enjoy the challenge of breaking into secure systems.

A hacker who breaks into a network and prevents it from functioning correctly is called a *cracker.* Crackers tend to be more sinister in their goals. They may seek to compromise secure files and steal protected credit card numbers. These activities cost E-commerce millions each year.

Worms are self-duplicating programs that hackers use to snowball through multiple systems automatically. The most talked-about worms come in the form of **computer viruses**, programs created to disrupt computer systems. The results of a computer virus vary from simple attention-getting notes to system crashes. Worse yet, some viruses erase data files and destroy saved information. Virtually all of us who conduct activities online have been confronted by the legitimate threat of cyberterrorism in the form of computer viruses.

hacker
A person who, using highly sophisticated programming techniques, breaks into secured computer systems.

computer virus
A program created to disrupt computer systems.

The Not So Endearing Love Bug

Time magazine described it this way: "It came. It flattered. It wreaked havoc on the Internet" (May 15, 2000). At issue is the now infamous virus known as the "Love Bug." This seemingly harmless E-mail attachment was disguised with a simple "I love you" title. When it was opened, an Internet worm was unleashed—a worm that caused an estimated $10 billion in worldwide damage. The virus spread throughout Asia, Europe, and the Americas with lightning speed. No continent was untouched. Unfortunately, much of the damage occurred before those most vulnerable could be warned.

It did not take long to find the perpetrator of the Love Bug virus. Contained within every virus is a blueprint that provides unique clues about its author. These clues pointed to a student attending a computer college in the Philippines. To some, this made the Love Bug even more frightening. It meant that someone living in a distant country could reach us very quickly, with devastating results.

Beyond the immediate damages is the question "What will prevent these deadly viruses from striking again, and again, and again?" The Internet was brought to its knees by a young, seemingly innocent hacker. Could the next devastating worm be sent by a third-grader living down the street? Many computer analysts think so. Government officials think that stricter laws will best address the problem. "Not so," says computer security guru Jeff Carpenter. Without improvements within computers themselves, Carpenter warns, "we will see this again."

If the Internet economy someday will connect us all, we'd better learn how to defend against these random acts of cyberterrorism. If not, our love of the Internet will come crashing down.

QUESTION TO ANSWER Do you think it is possible for unchecked viruses to bring about the demise of the Internet? Why or why not?

Companies such as Clear Commerce Solutions provide retailers with software to help protect them against credit card fraud.

Businesses have already spent billions of dollars researching and developing ways to prevent the type of terror caused by hackers and viruses. This financial commitment to a secure Internet is bound to grow. Many antivirus programs are now available in the marketplace, and many new jobs have been created in this emerging field. Although antivirus programs can be successful in the short run, these security devices generally challenge the more talented hackers to work even harder to break the new codes.

Big business is not alone in the need to worry about hackers and viruses. Anyone who uses a computer network needs to be aware of the potential danger. In 1996, in response to heightened awareness of the potential for cyberterrorism, President Clinton created the Commission of Critical Infrastructure Protection. The CIA, the FBI, and the Secret Service have all created their own groups to monitor and police computer hackers, crackers, and viruses. In May 2000, the Economic Group of Eight (G-8) held a special three-day conference on Internet crime. Recognizing that cybercrime is a serious threat to global commerce, G-8 is calling for the business world to work with government agencies to help police the Internet. Numerous high-profile hackers have been caught and prosecuted in criminal court. In many cases, however, prosecution is difficult because of the global nature of the crime.

Passwords, firewalls, and encryption systems have all been used to protect our computer systems. Each has its own strengths and weaknesses. Passwords can be easily uncovered. *Firewalls,* barriers that inhibit network communication and often slow down transactions, are not fail-safe. *Encryption* involves scrambling information before it is sent across the Internet. At first, encryption was effective in protecting businesses and consumers. Now, however, cybercriminals have found encryption programs useful in covering up their own activities. This kind of developing technology gives law enforcement even more problems and challenges. Lawmakers in the United States have made it a crime to export encryption programs, but these laws apply only within the United States. Ironically, rather than protecting us from criminal hacking, encryption programs have aided the criminal.

Currently, there are no foolproof protections against cyberterrorism. French Prime Minister Lionel Jospin has called "for mobilization and collective responses on a global scale." For now, however, our greatest protection may be to constantly be aware of and monitor these threats. We need to be vigilant in our pursuit of a secure Internet. Perhaps we need to treat hackers the same as we would those who break into our homes. Whatever the case, cyberterrorists will continue to challenge the growth of the new Internet economy. What do you think we should do about them?

"High-Tech" Counterfeiting

Until recently, counterfeiting was an expensive, highly technical, time-consuming process. Advanced reprographic technology has, however, made counterfeiting easier and cheaper. Although new technology has increased the amount of counterfeiting, counterfeit U.S. paper currency is still a tiny percentage of total U.S. currency. In 2000, counterfeit currency composed only three one-hundredths of one percent of the total.

Is there reason for alarm when such a small percentage of our total currency is counterfeit? The answer is yes. In recent years, much of the counterfeit U.S. paper currency has been found overseas.

When people begin to suspect that money is being counterfeited, they do not accept it, and this lowers the usefulness of money. For government authorities to ignore counterfeiting is to invite a decline in the acceptability of one's money—something no one wants.

In its attempt to combat counterfeiting in the digital age, the U.S. Treasury has printed and circulated newly designed $100, $50, $20, $10, and $5 notes. The exhibit below describes the security features of the newly redesigned paper currency.

QUESTION TO ANSWER Someone hands you a redesigned $10 note. What would you look at to determine whether it is a real or a counterfeit note?

New $10 note

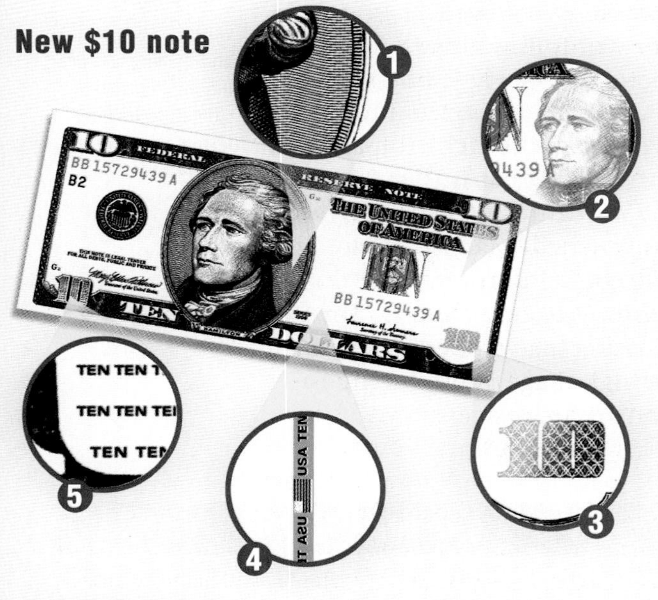

Old $10 note

1. **Fine-line printing.** A fine-line pattern is printed behind the portrait of Hamilton on the front of the note and behind the building on the back of the note. The fine lines are clean and parallel to each other. When copied, they usually become splotchy or create new patterns.

2. **Watermark.** If you hold a redesigned $10 note up to the light, you will see a watermark of Hamilton's image on the front right of the note. Watermarks are difficult to reproduce.

3. **Color-shifting ink.** Take a look at the numeral in the lower right corner on the front of the $10 note. It looks green when viewed straight on, but black when viewed at an angle.

4. **Security thread.** There is a security thread to the right of Hamilton's portrait. In the thread, the words "USA TEN" and a flag are repeatedly printed. Using an ultraviolet light, the security thread glows orange.

5. **Micro-printing.** Micro-printed words are difficult to replicate. The micro-printed word "TEN" is continually repeated in the numeral in the left corner on the front of the note. Above Hamilton's name, "THE UNITED STATES OF AMERICA" is continually repeated.

Yours, Mine, and Ours: Protecting Intellectual Property on the Internet

Another Internet debate involves **intellectual property**—a person's or company's ideas or inventions that have special ownership protection. Creations such as books, songs, and even computer programs are considered intellectual property and are protected by copyright law. They are owned by their creators or publishers, and others do not have the right to use them without permission. The Internet, however, makes copyright law very easy to break.

The FBI has established several computer crime units throughout the country. These cybercops track cybercriminals across the Internet.

At the center of the debate about intellectual property are entertainers, authors, and film producers who find their work being passed over the Internet without their permission—and more specifically, without payment by customers. Sites such as MP3.com allow users to share and download music, which is often pirated. Many believe that traditional copyright laws will have to be changed to protect artists, musicians, and actors from such practices. Others argue that the entertainment industry should change the way it does business. Some musical artists have already accommodated. Artists like Prince have chosen to bypass traditional stores and sell their music directly online. Many believe that soon the whole music industry will follow this trend. Perhaps the way intellectual property is bought and sold will need to be changed. When you buy a book or CD, don't you have the right to pass that book or CD on to a friend? What if that friend is on the Internet? The new Internet economy will leave no industry untouched. Many traditional practices may need to be reinterpreted for this new economy. According to one expert, "For the moment, at least, intellectual property's troubled encounter with the digital age is producing many more questions than answers."

Many believe that sites such as MP3.com are costing musicians money. How would you feel if you wrote a popular song and someone else gave it away for free?

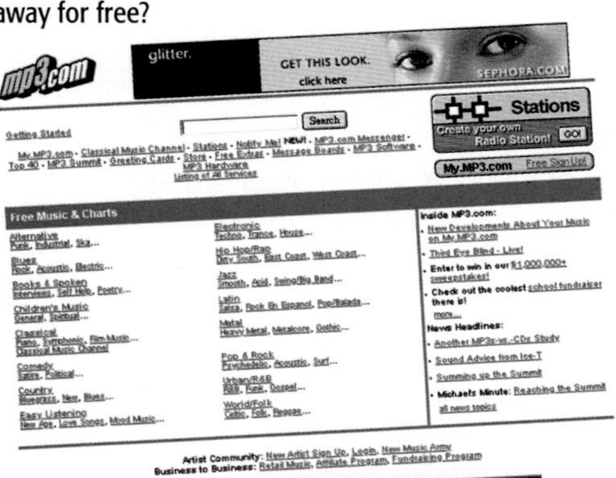

intellectual property Intangible materials that are legally recognized as owned by an individual or a company. Software, databases, and mailing lists are among items considered to be intellectual property.

Section 3 Review

Defining Terms

1. Define
   a. digital divide
   b. hacker
   c. computer virus
   d. intellectual property

Reviewing Facts and Concepts

2. How has the government involved itself in controlling the Internet?
3. Who has been left behind in the new Internet economy? Explain.
4. Are Internet transactions taxed?
5. Who are hackers, and what are viruses?
6. List five security features of the newly designed U.S. paper currency.

Critical Thinking

7. For each of the following topics discussed in this section, develop your own policy. How would you address each issue so as to assist in the expansion of the new Internet economy?
   a. controlling the Internet
   b. haves and have nots
   c. taxing the Internet
   d. keeping the Internet secure
   e. safeguarding intellectual property
   f. Internet addiction

Developing Economic

Skills

Understanding Contracts

Whether you buy a good or service by traditional means or over the Internet, you are protected by a contract. Contracts do provide legal recourse against Internet fraud.

A contract is a legal agreement involving an exchange of promises between two people or groups of people. Each party to the contract promises either to perform or to refrain from performing certain actions. Throughout your life, you will form contracts. If you shop on line and buy a car, a CD, or even an airline ticket, a contract is involved.

Contracts may be written or verbal, although a written contract is easier to enforce. In some cases, such as the purchase of goods worth $500 or more, unwritten contracts are normally not enforceable.

A contract contains several parts. First, the party writing the contract makes an offer, usually involving the exchange of goods or services. For example, a health club offers an individual the use of its facilities. The second part of the contract is the recipient's acceptance of the offer. Most contracts are enforceable only if each party receives something of value, which is called consideration. For example, the health club in the contract receives an initiation fee and monthly fees. The customer in turn gets use of the club's facilities. The offer, the acceptance, and the consideration must all be included in the deal. If one or more of these parts is left out, the contract is not legally binding.

Each party must understand and accept the terms of the contract. After the terms of the contract have been fulfilled, the contract is completed. The contract must be agreed to, without force or bribery, by persons of legal age and sound mind. If all of these conditions are not met, the contract can be canceled.

A breached, or broken, contract is one that has been violated, or one in which one or both parties did not fulfill the terms of the contract. Legal action to enforce a breached contract may be taken by either party. The dispute may be settled out of court, or the injured party can sue for damages.

Always remember that you need to fully understand all parts of any contract that you are asked to sign. Especially when you shop online, it is critical to read and agree to all the parts of the contract before you buy.

QUESTIONS TO ANSWER

1. Go online to a car rental or airline site and read the contracts that appear for buyers. Are the contracts clear and easy to understand? How does the consumer indicate approval?
2. Write down a summary of the three main parts in the contract.

CHAPTER

23 Review

Economics Vocabulary

1. The _____ economy has changed the world of commerce as much as the change from a barter to a money economy changed the world many years ago.
2. Business conducted online or purchases made online are considered part of _____.
3. The _____ refers to an international network of computers that are linked for the purpose of communicating data.
4. The digital world that has been constructed though linked computer networks is known as _____.
5. The _____ is the global system of interlinked, individual Web sites or locations.
6. Software programs that allow a user to look for a Web site that contains material on a particular topic are called _____ engines.
7. A(n) _____ may contain multiple pages, including the home page for an individual or a particular business.
8. The Internet has introduced a new pricing mechanism, a(n) _____ in which the buyer states the price he is willing to pay for a service and the seller then decides whether to sell that service for the stated price.
9. With the Internet, _____ costs for businesses are lower than in the traditional economy.
10. Some believe that the Internet is creating a society of "haves" and "have nots", or a _____.
11. _____ are those individuals who are able to break into another person's computer system.
12. A computer _____ can cause data files to be erased and valuable information stored in a computer to be destroyed.
13. A significant problem yet to be solved is theft of a company's ideas, songs, and books, that is, their _____, stored on the Internet.

Review Questions

1. List five common uses of the Internet.
2. Explain how the Internet began.
3. Describe the importance of Apple Computer and IBM in the development of the computer industry.
4. Why were Web browsers developed, and which were the first Web browsers?
5. Explain why companies such as Yahoo and America OnLine became so successful so quickly.
6. Explain why E-commerce offers advantages to both consumers and to those businesses that decide to conduct their business online.
7. How do economists view the Internet? Is the view of an economist different from that of a consumer? Of a business?
8. Explain how the Internet reduces transaction costs for businesses.
9. Explain how a reverse auction works and why so many people now participate in reverse auction.
10. What is the impact of the Internet on economic productivity?
11. Describe the legislative act and the background incidents that led to the Supreme Court case of *Reno v. ACLU*. What was the Supreme Court ruling in this case? What was the reasoning of the Court in this case?
12. Why is it important that schools, libraries, and community centers provide free access to the Internet to their communities?
13. Describe some of the arguments against taxing purchases made via the Internet. What are some of the principal arguments that support taxing purchases made over the Internet?
14. What is the predominant crime on the Internet today, and how does it occur?
15. Why has intellectual property become a problematic area for the Internet?

Calculations

1. In 1994 there were about 3 million Internet users. In 2000, there were approximately 120 million. If the growth rate is steady, approximately how many Internet users will there by in 2010?
2. If a sports team of 35 members buys its shoes from the local sporting goods stores, the cost will be \$56.50 plus 7.5% sales tax. The team can buy the same shoes online for \$52.75. How much money will the team save if the members buy their shoes online? How much in sales tax will the team save if it purchases the shoes online?

Economics and Thinking Skills

1. **Application.** Radio and television are regulated by the Federal Communications Commission, but the Internet is not. Rachel Chong, who has served as a commissioner with the Federal Communications Commission, has argued that the Internet is a completely different medium, that regulation would stifle its success, and that it should not be regulated by the government. She has commented that the way to control the Internet is through software controls and parental control. What kinds of controls could be successfully implemented to protect children from financial scams, fraud, and viewing inappropriate material? Is parental control the best solution? Why or why not?
2. **Analysis.** Shopping online is often more effective in terms of both time and money. What are the drawbacks or disadvantages to shopping online for both businesses and the consumer? If more people shop online than at their local stores, what will be the impact on the local economies? Explain your answers with logic and reasoning.
3. **Cause and Effect.** The growth of E-commerce has been staggering. In the year 2000, approximately 120 million people in the United States had access to the Internet, 400,000 companies conducted their business online, and online sales totaled over $100 billion. These are amazing figures for a technology that was unknown just two decades ago. What might account for the phenomenal growth in this particular area of the economy?

Writing Skills

Research one of the following topics using either traditional print sources or the Internet: (1) ARPAnet, (2) Apple Computers, (3) Microsoft, (4) Web browsers, (5) a new dot.com company. Prepare a two-page paper or a PowerPoint presentation discussing what you have learned and the impact of your subject on the Internet Economy.

Economics in the Media

1. Find an online or newspaper article that discusses recent hacking or cracking attempts. Identify what sites were hacked, if the hackers were identified, and what, if any punishment, was given to them.
2. Find a story on a television news show that discusses *dot.com* companies and their impact on the economy or the stock market. Summarize the story and explain the viewpoint of the commentator.

Where's the Economics?

How many different aspects of E-commerce can you identify in the photo below?

UNIT 5

Debate the Issues

Advertising: Is it Helpful or Harmful?

How are you affected by the hundreds of advertisements you encounter each day on television and radio, in magazines and newspapers, and on signs and billboards? Does advertising inform you of the availability of goods, or does it trick you into buying what you might not want to buy? Are advertisers informers or tricksters? Let's listen to a consumer advocate argue the case with an advertising executive.

Carlin Jenkins, consumer advocate: It seems to me that advertising can be used for good or bad. An advertisement that truthfully informs you about a product is a good advertisement. An advertisement that tries to trick you into buying something you may not want is a bad advertisement. I'm thinking about the ad that has a beautiful person in an exotic setting sipping a cola, or a famous athlete biting into a hamburger, or a famous actor driving a car. Are we selling colas, hamburgers, and cars here or are we selling an image? The ad lulls some people into thinking they can live the life of gorgeous, rich, and famous people if they buy the good being advertised. This is deceptive advertising that plays on people's emotions and tricks them into doing things they may not want to do. Government needs to make sure that advertisers use their skills to inform people, not to trick them.

Martin Smith, advertising executive: You give advertisers too much credit. Advertising is not as powerful as you seem to believe. Advertising cannot sell people a good they don't want to buy. A few years ago the Coca-Cola Company heavily advertised New Coke and it didn't sell. Many years before that, the Ford Motor Company advertised the Edsel, and it didn't sell. Every day products are advertised that flop. The truth is, advertising simply informs people of what is available in the marketplace. It says, "Here is our product, you might not have known it was here. We think it is a good product. Why not give it a chance?" That's all that advertising really does.

Carl Jenkins: You have to be kidding. How many commercials on prime time television do you see that simply say, "Here is our product, we hope you use it." I don't see those commercials. I see commercials with beautiful people, music, special effects, and more. Companies spend millions if not billions of dollars each year on their advertising. If the purpose of advertising were simply to provide us with information, companies wouldn't need to spend so much money. They could just take out a 15-second commercial, show their product, put the price below it on the screen, and call it a day.

Martin Smith: Companies spend millions of advertising dollars because before you can inform people, you must get their attention. Your 15-second commercial wouldn't get anyone's attention. You have to have the music, the special effects, and the celebrities to get people's attention. But once you have their attention, all you are really doing is informing them about a product. Sure, you may inform them in the best possible way you can, but what's wrong with that?

Carl Jenkins: What's wrong with it is that people end up buying things they don't really want to buy. When advertisers imply that if you buy their products you will be one of the beautiful people, or you will be happy, or you will be smart, they are essentially telling a lie. It is wrong to use lies to entice people to buy things.

Martin Smith: Well, who should decide if it is a lie or not? You? I hope not. Suppose a company advertises its jeans by having some movie stars wear them. Sandra buys the jeans because of the feeling she gets from the ad. She wears the jeans and every time she does, she feels special. Perhaps she would not have felt special without the ad. Is there anything wrong with that? I don't think so. What's so wrong with feeling special?

Carl Jenkins: I am not against feeling special. I am against lies. If you have to lie to make someone feel special, it's wrong. Let me give you an example. At one time in this country, the tobacco companies could advertise cigarettes using images that directly appealed to young kids. Basically they told the kids that it was cool to smoke. Some kids started smoking because they believed the ads and thought they were being cool. I'm sure many of them felt pretty cool when they were puffing away on their cigarettes. But you know what happened to those kids? When they grew up, some of them died of lung cancer.

Martin Smith: You shouldn't generalize from cigarettes to everything else. I agree that cigarettes are harmful to one's health and that cigarettes should not be advertised in a way that appeals to kids. But there is a big difference between advertising cigarettes and advertising a vacation, restaurant, soft drink, car, pair of jeans, jewelry, and so many other things. The rule should be that we cannot advertise (in an appealing way) those goods that have been proved unhealthful. But beyond that, we should let advertisers do what they want.

Carl Jenkins: I don't agree. I think certain things should be off limits. Anything that smacks of advertisers trying to trick people into buying something should be off limits.

Martin Smith: What you are asking for is the end of free speech. Are you going to have government officials decide what is and what is not acceptable speech when it comes to advertising?

Carl Jenkins: Better to have government officials decide this than to let advertising executives fool us into buying things we don't need or want. Better to let government officials decide these things than to let the tobacco companies advertise their cigarettes in ways that end up causing thousands of deaths.

Martin Smith: I guess we just don't see things the same way.

Carl Jenkins: You're right about that.

What Do You Think?

1. Do you think most advertising informs people or tricks them? Explain your answer.
2. Do you think advertisers should be able to advertise products any way they deem desirable? Why or why not?
3. Are there different types of advertising? Do you think some types of advertising inform more than they manipulate? Do some types manipulate more than they inform? Explain your answers.
4. Do you think you were ever "tricked" into buying something you didn't want to buy because of an advertisement? Explain your answer.

Resource Center

On the following pages you will find historical data for selected economic and economic-related topics, such as GDP, money supply, business revenue, personal income, and population. The data included in the Resource Center will be interesting and helpful throughout your economics course. For updated information, visit the learningeconomics Web site.

The following exhibits are included in this Resource Center:

Exhibit R1 Map of United States

Exhibit R2 United States GDP, 1990-1999

Year	GDP (billions of current dollars)
1990	$5,803.2
1991	5,986.2
1992	6,318.9
1993	6,642.3
1994	7,054.3
1995	7,400.5
1996	7,813.2
1997	8,300.8
1998	8,759.9
1999	9,256.1

SOURCE: Bureau of Economic Analysis

Exhibit R3 United States Real GDP, 1990-2000

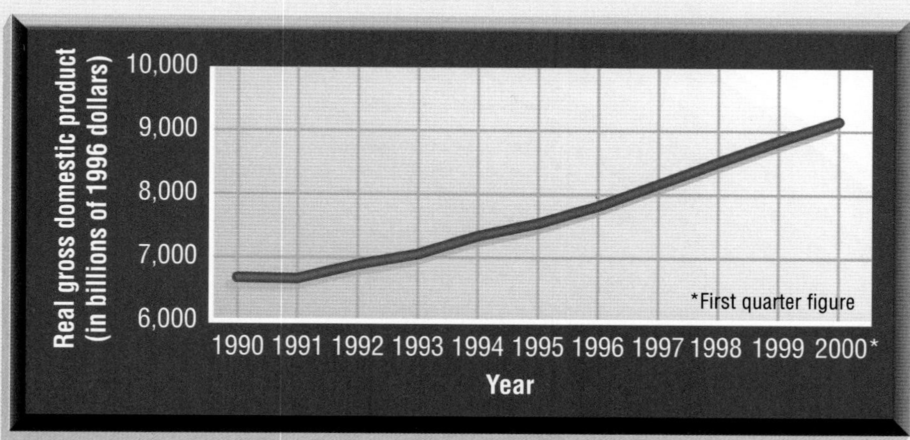

SOURCE: Economic Report of the President

Go to . . . learningeconomics.com *for updated information*

Exhibit R4 United States per-capita Real GDP, 1990-2000

Year	Real GDP (per capita)
1990	$26,794
1991	26,451
1992	27,024
1993	27,368
1994	28,190
1995	28,684
1996	29,463
1997	30,496
1998	31,507
1999	32,432
2000	33,332*

*First quarter figure

SOURCE: Economic Report of the President

Exhibit R5 U.S. Population and Personal per-capita Income, Selected Years

Year	U.S. population	Per-capita personal income
1950	151,871,000	$ 1,509
1960	179,972,000	2,276
1970	203,798,722	4,077
1980	227,224,719	10,062
1990	249,438,712	19,156
2000	276,000,000	29,458*

*First quarter figure

SOURCE: Bureau of Economic Analysis

Exhibit R6 Money Supply, 1985-2000

SOURCE: Federal Reserve

Exhibit R7 Percentage Change in Prices for Various Expenditure Items, 1990-1999

Percentage change in prices 1990–1999

80
70
60
50
40
30
20
10
0

27.5%
24.6%
5.8%
27.5%
19.8%
53.9%
62.5%
4.4%

All items
Food & beverage
Apparel
Housing
Transportation
Medical
Other goods & services
Energy

SOURCE: Economic Report of the President

Exhibit R8 State of Federal Budget, 1990-2001

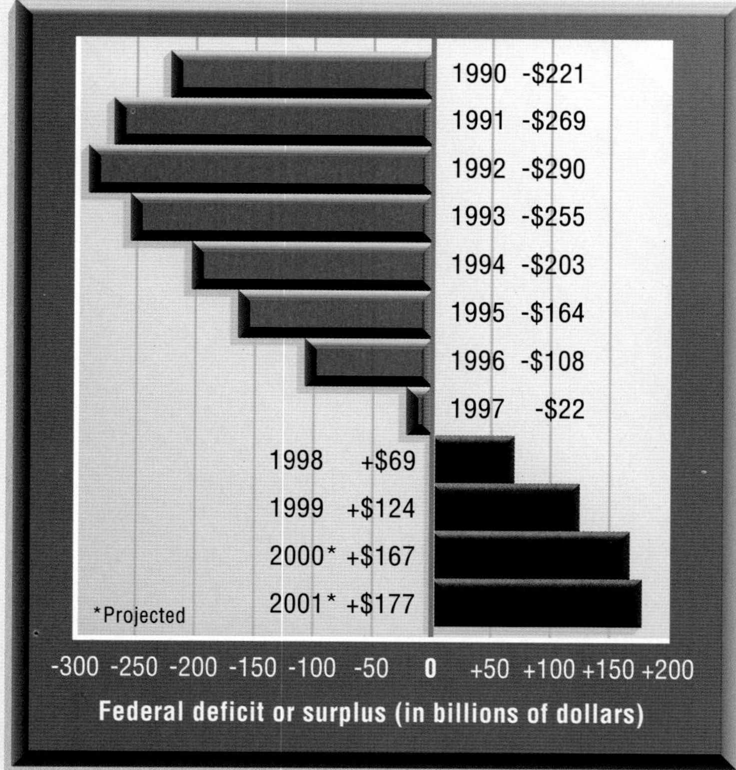

SOURCE: Economic Report of the President

Exhibit R9 Gross Federal Debt, 1990-2001

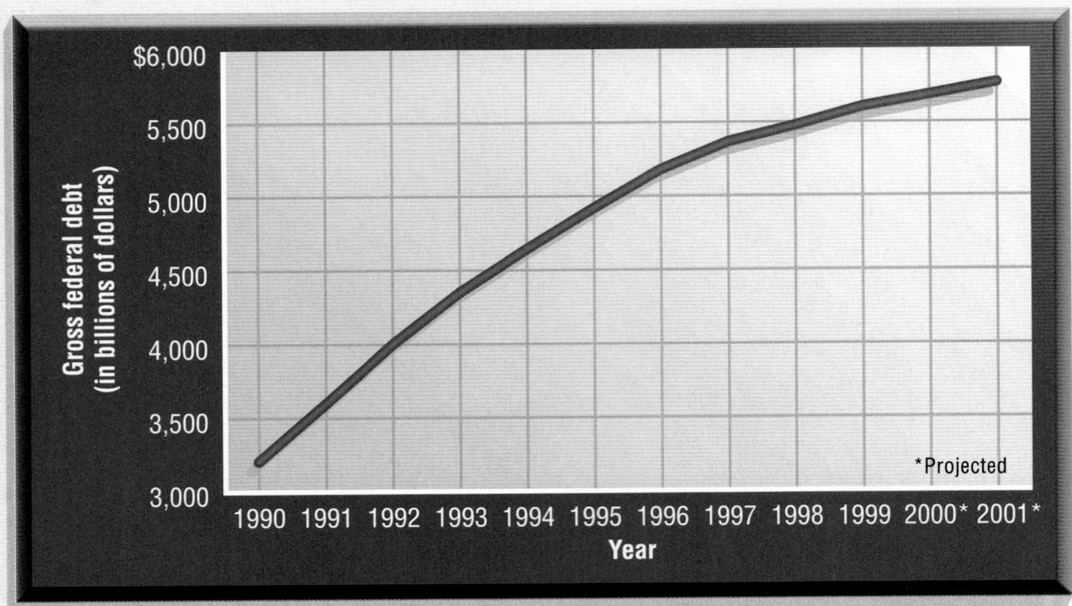

SOURCE: Economic Report of the President

Exhibit R10 Consumer Price Index, 1970-2000

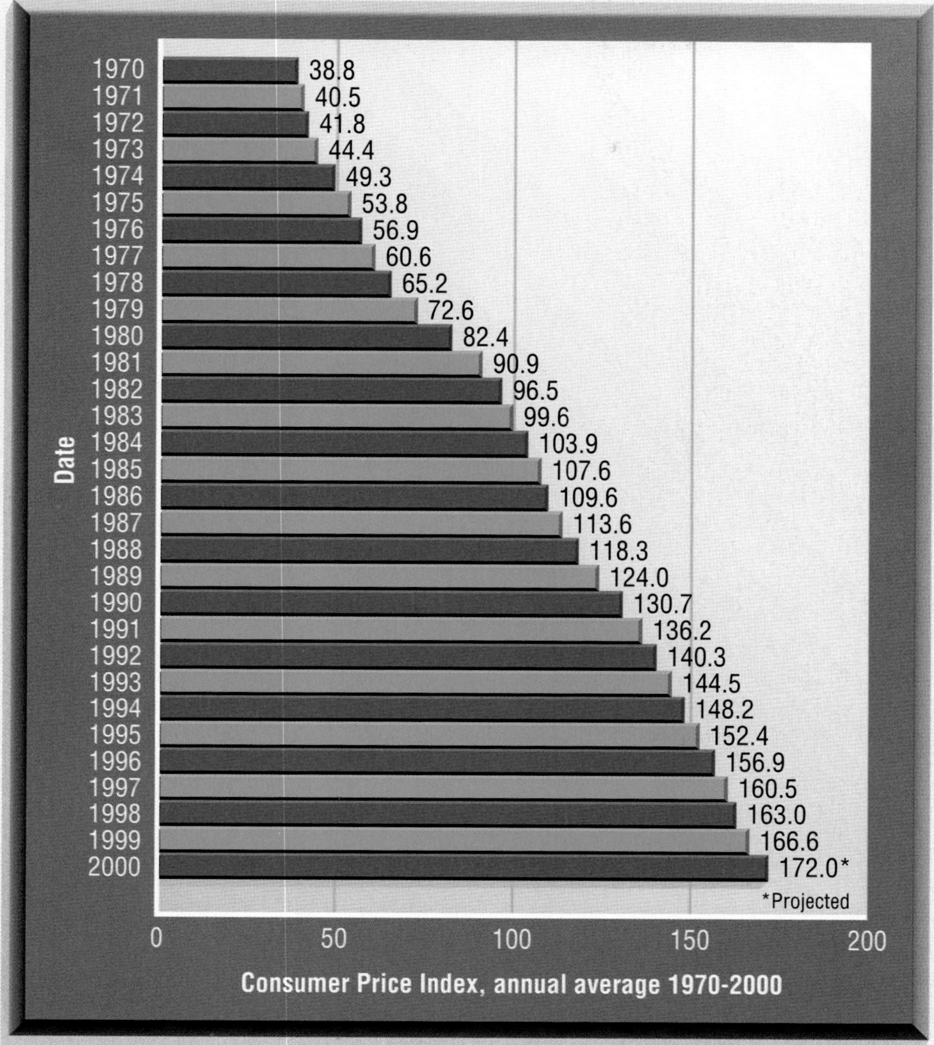

SOURCE: Bureau of Economic Analysis

Exhibit R11 Composition of Federal Receipts, Selected Years

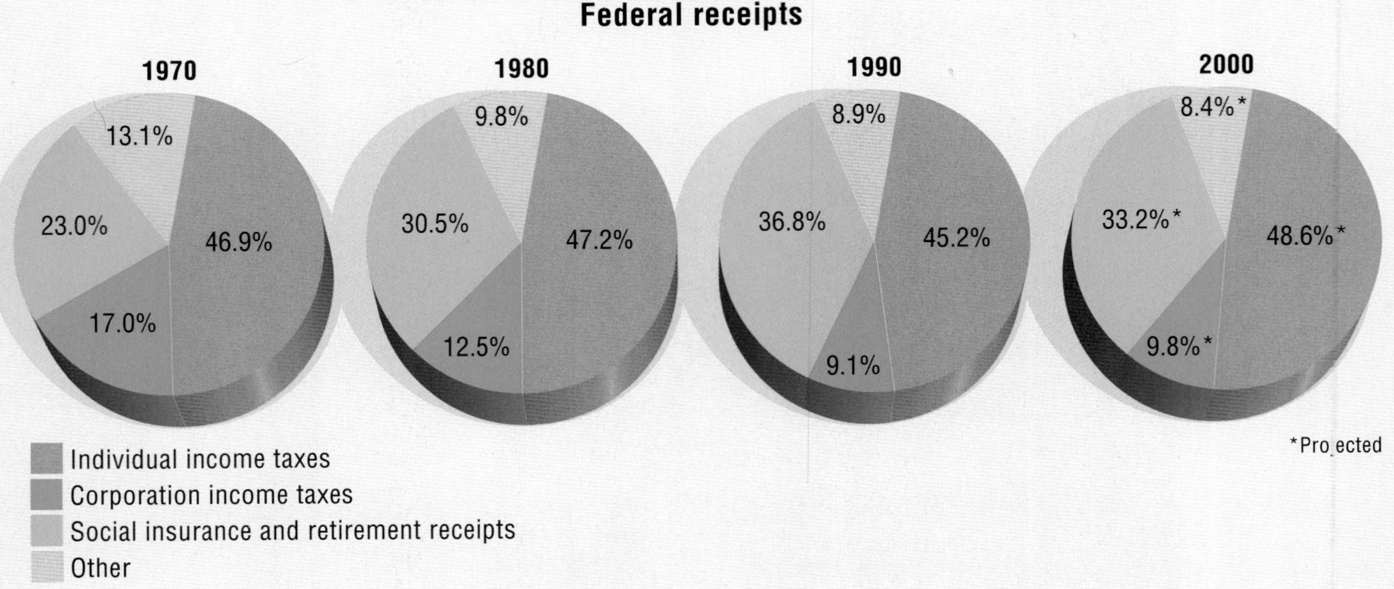

SOURCE: Economic Report of the President

Exhibit R12 Value of Exports and Imports, 1990-1999

Year	Exports	Imports
1990	389.3	498.3
1991	416.9	491.0
1992	440.4	536.5
1993	456.8	589.4
1994	502.4	686.6
1995	575.8	749.6
1996	612.1	803.3
1997	679.7	876.4
1998	670.2	914.2
1999	789.0	969.0

SOURCE: Economic Report of the President

Exhibit R13 State Population, Gross State Product, and Real Gross State Product

State	Population (thousands)	Gross State Product (GSP) (millions of dollars)	Real GSP (millions of 1992 dollars)
Alabama	4,320	$ 103,109	$ 92,845
Alaska	609	24,494	21,848
Arizona	4,552	121,239	110,466
Arkansas	2,525	58,479	53,209
California	32,218	1,033,016	927,521
Colorado	3,891	126,084	112,733
Connecticut	3,269	134,565	118,537
Delaware	735	31,585	27,407
Florida	14,683	380,607	338,059
Georgia	7,486	229,473	206,139
Hawaii	1,189	38,024	33,736
Idaho	1,211	29,149	27,287
Illinois	12,012	393,532	358,136
Indiana	5,872	161,701	148,020
Iowa	2,854	80,479	74,304
Kansas	2,616	71,737	64,589
Kentucky	3,908	100,076	92,617
Louisiana	4,351	124,350	109,840
Maine	1,245	30,156	26,754
Maryland	5,093	153,797	135,048
Massachusetts	6,115	221,009	197,798
Michigan	9,785	272,607	246,368
Minnesota	4,688	149,394	133,810
Mississippi	2,732	58,314	52,873
Misssouri	5,407	152,100	136,732
Montana	879	$ 19,160	$ 17,244
Nebraska	1,656	48,812	44,228
Nevada	1,676	57,407	50,237
New Hampshire	1,173	38,106	35,188
New Jersey	8,054	294,055	260,940
New Mexico	1,723	45,242	43,519
New York	18,143	651,652	579,680
North Carolina	7,429	218,888	202,108
North Dakota	641	15,786	14,355
Ohio	11,212	320,506	291,380
Oklahoma	3,314	76,642	69,232
Oregon	3,243	98,367	90,225
Pennsylvania	12,016	339,940	305,266
Rhode Island	987	27,806	24,695
South Carolina	3,790	93,259	85,171
South Dakota	731	20,186	17,915
Tennessee	5,378	146,999	132,646
Texas	19,355	601,643	543,987
Utah	2,065	55,417	49,562
Vermont	589	15,214	13,934
Virginia	6,733	211,331	189,703
Washington	5,604	172,253	152,288
West Virginia	1,816	38,228	35,269
Wisconsin	5,200	147,325	134,600
Wyoming	480	17,561	16,480

SOURCE: Economic Report of the President

Exhibit R14 State per-capita Income, per-capita Disposable Personal Income, and Median Income

State	Per capita income	Per capita disposable personal income	Median income
Alabama	$21,260	$18,728	$32,436
Alaska	26,990	23,733	48,742
Arizona	22,839	19,880	33,250
Arkansas	20,342	17,972	26,569
California	26,779	22,859	40,312
Colorado	28,070	24,088	43,906
Connecticut	35,636	29,312	44,670
Delaware	27,605	23,285	43,703
Florida	25,645	22,386	32,961
Georgia	24,594	21,204	37,234
Hawaii	26,299	23,064	41,572
Idaho	21,013	18,385	33,924
Illinois	28,468	24,385	41,926
Indiana	23,909	20,568	39,495
Iowa	23,882	20,859	34,309
Kansas	24,406	21,118	37,039
Kentucky	21,286	18,472	33,973
Louisiana	21,254	18,768	33,778
Maine	22,394	19,542	33,282
Maryland	29,112	24,409	47,412
Massachusetts	31,592	26,378	42,678
Michigan	25,780	22,086	39,345
Minnesota	27,536	23,306	43,227
Mississippi	18,873	16,914	28,943
Misssouri	24,368	21,200	37,122
Montana	$20,130	$17,728	$29,667
Nebraska	24,769	21,649	35,232
Nevada	28,216	24,564	39,459
New Hampshire	27,746	24,175	41,637
New Jersey	32,582	27,656	48,769
New Mexico	20,288	17,910	30,555
New York	30,538	25,637	36,356
North Carolina	24,210	20,934	36,398
North Dakota	20,876	18,572	32,154
Ohio	24,998	21,467	36,697
Oklahoma	21,080	18,454	31,839
Oregon	24,987	21,282	37,827
Pennsylvania	26,211	22,625	38,101
Rhode Island	26,855	23,378	35,339
South Carolina	21,416	18,737	34,796
South Dakota	22,410	20,173	30,157
Tennessee	23,445	20,875	31,113
Texas	23,998	21,172	35,621
Utah	21,192	18,305	44,299
Vermont	23,382	20,333	39,372
Virginia	26,810	23,059	43,354
Washington	27,018	23,598	47,421
West Virginia	19,406	17,187	26,704
Wisconsin	24,941	21,258	41,327
Wyoming	23,601	20,375	35,250

SOURCE: Bureau of Economic Analysis

Exhibit R15 The Top 10 Corporations (in terms of revenues)

1997			2000		
Rank	Company	Revenues (dollars)	Rank	Company	Revenues (dollars)
1	General Motors	$178,174,000,000	1	General Motors	$189,058,000,000
2	Ford Motor	153,627,000,000	2	Wal-Mart Stores	166,809,000,000
3	Exxon	122,379,000,000	3	Exxon Mobil	163,881,000,000
4	Wal-Mart Stores	99,299,000,000	4	Ford Motor	162,558,000,000
5	General Electric	90,840,000,000	5	General Electric	111,630,000,000
6	IBM	78,508,000,000	6	IBM	87,548,000,000
7	Chrysler	61,147,000,000	7	Citigroup	82,005,000,000
8	Mobil	59,978,000,000	8	AT&T	62,391,000,000
9	Philip Morris	56,114,000,000	9	Philip Morris	61,751,000,000
10	AT&T	53,261,000,000	10	Boeing	57,993,000,000

SOURCE: Fortune Magazine

Exhibit R16 Domestic Corporate Profits, by Industry, 1990-1998

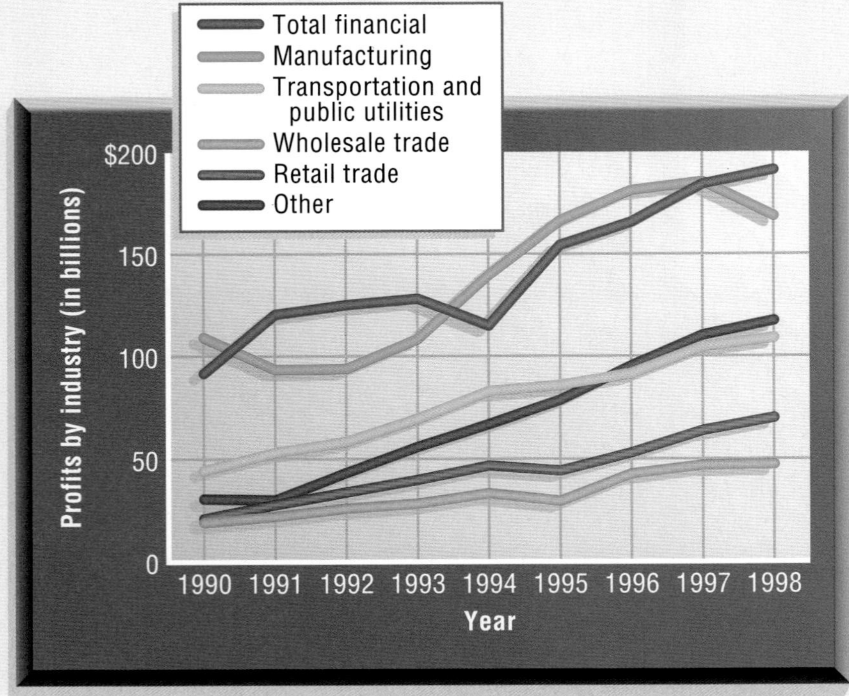

SOURCE: Economic Report of the President

Exhibit R17 Various Interest Rates, 1970-1999

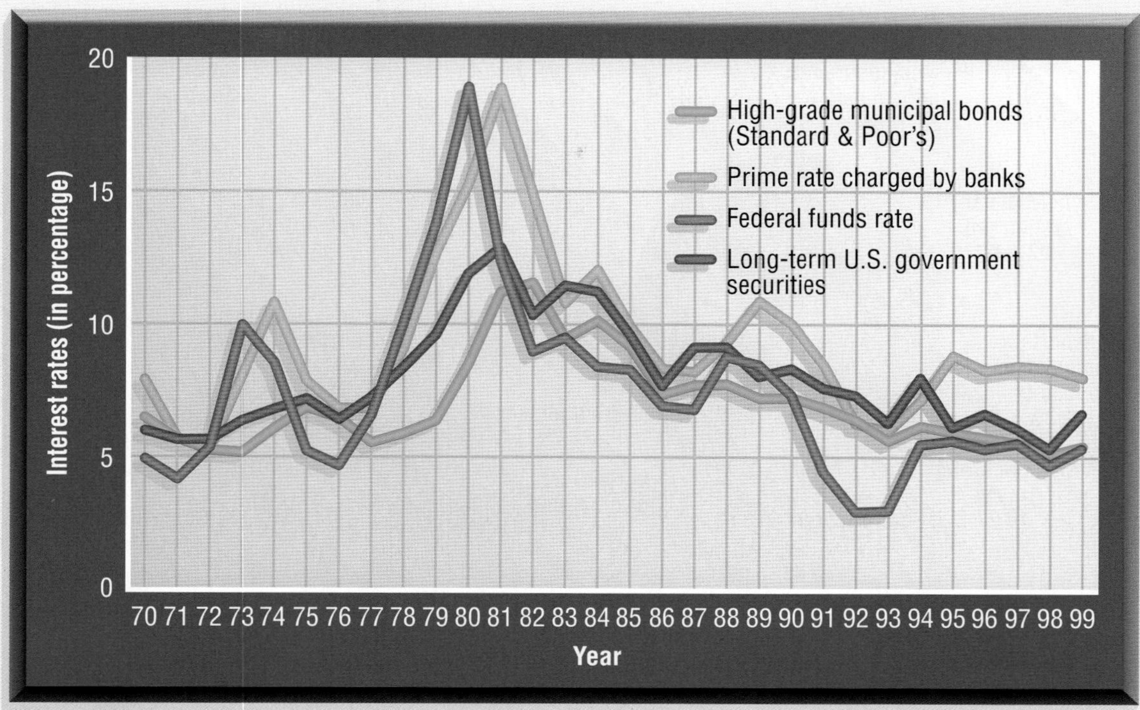

SOURCE: Economic Report of the President

Exhibit R18 Percentage of Total Employment in Various Industries, 1998 and (Projected) 2008

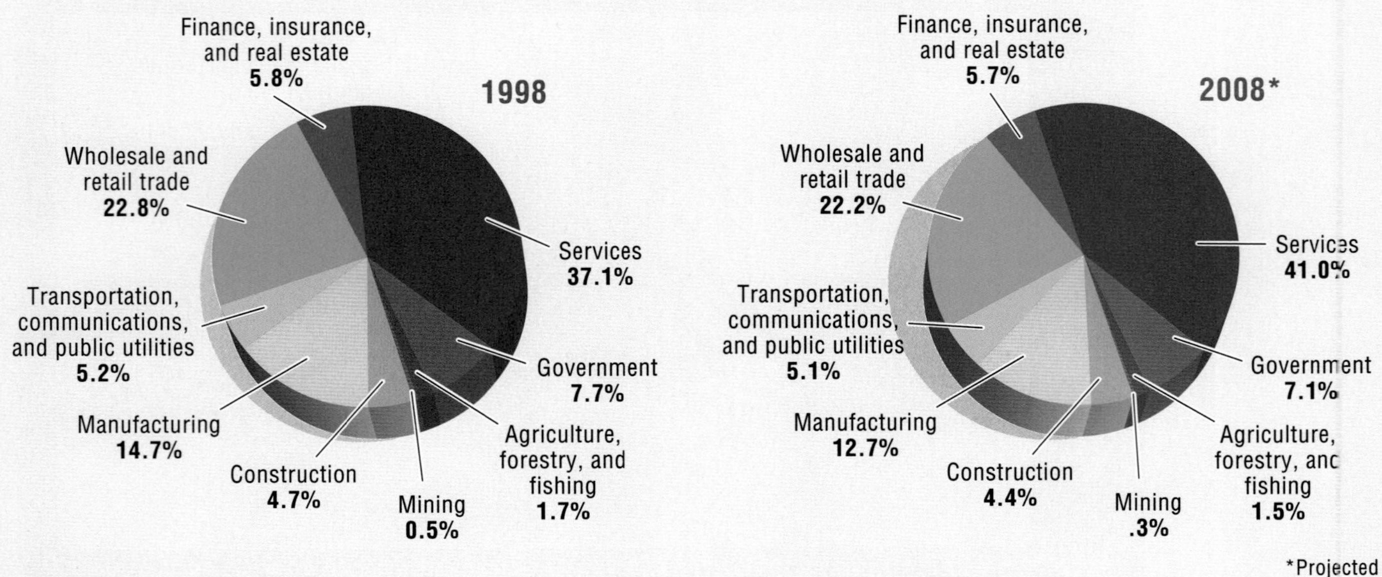

SOURCE: Bureau of Labor Statistics

Exhibit R19 Poverty Status, 1998

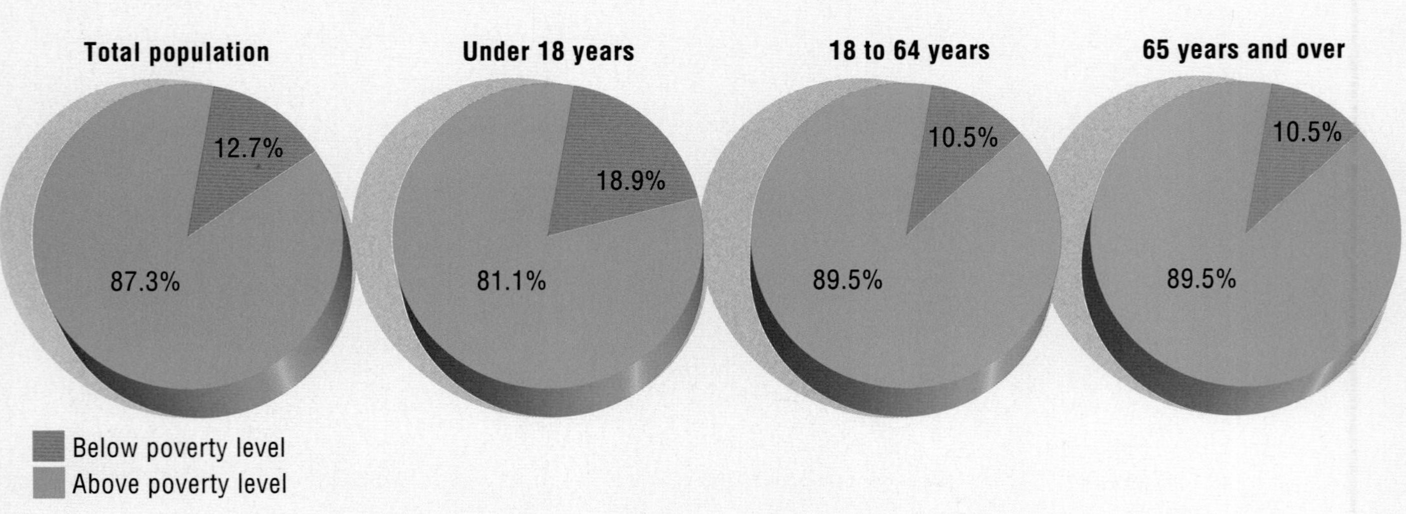

SOURCE: U. S. Census Bureau

Exhibit R20 Personal Income, Disposable Personal Income, and Consumption Expenditures

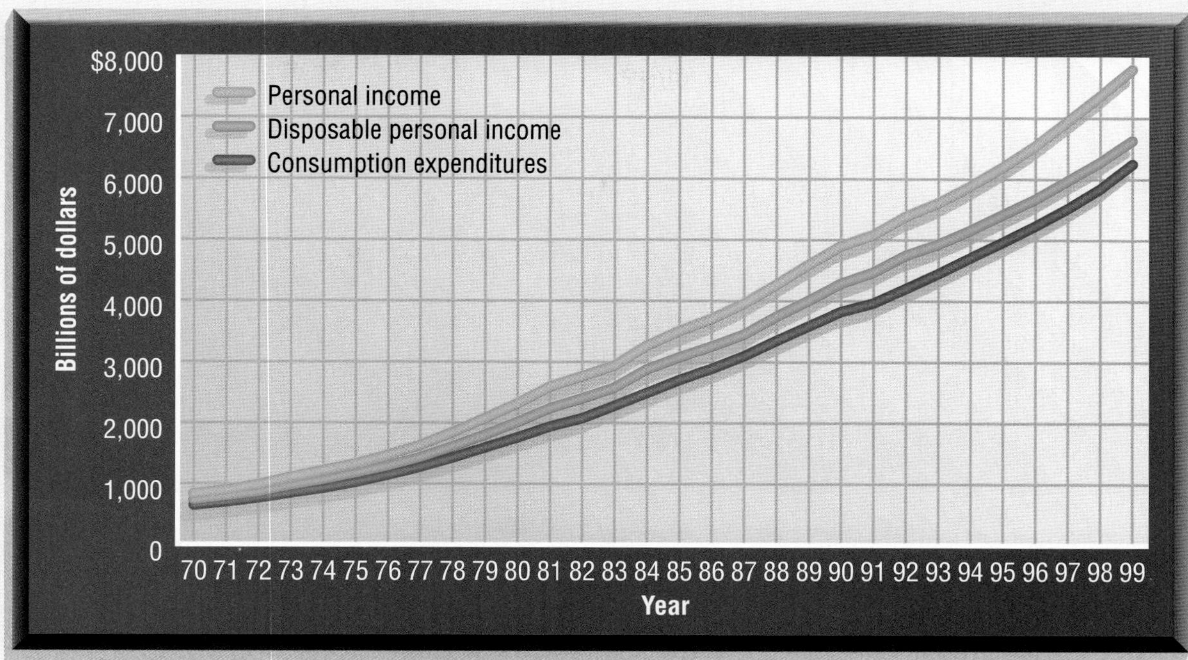

SOURCE: Economic Report of the President

Exhibit R21 Personal Savings as a Percentage of Disposable Personal Income, 1970-2000

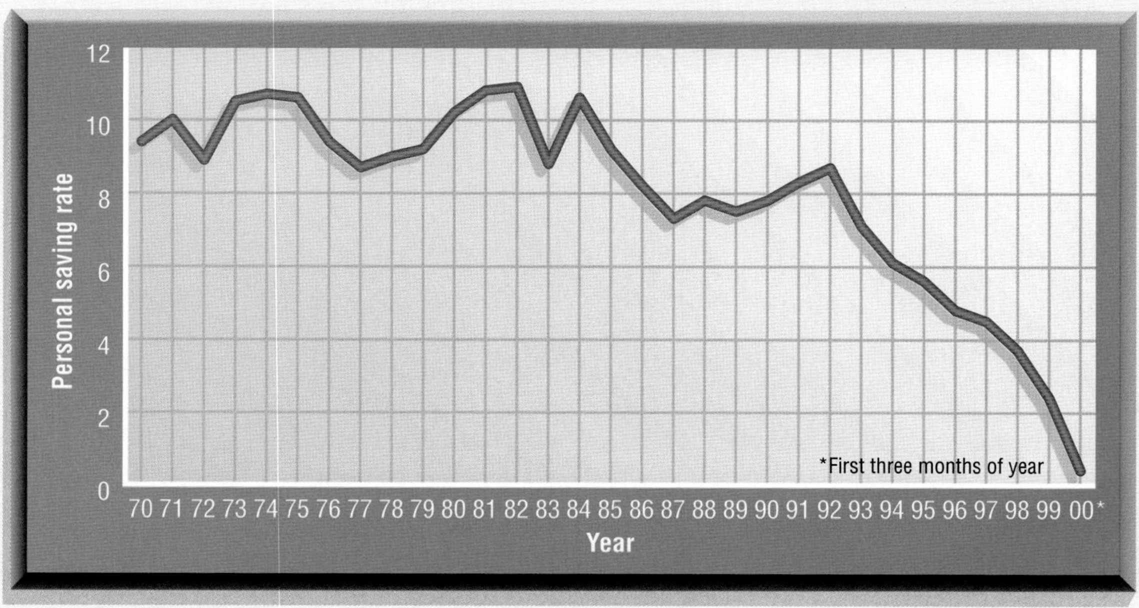

SOURCE: Bureau of Economic Analysis

Exhibit R22 Mean Income by Race

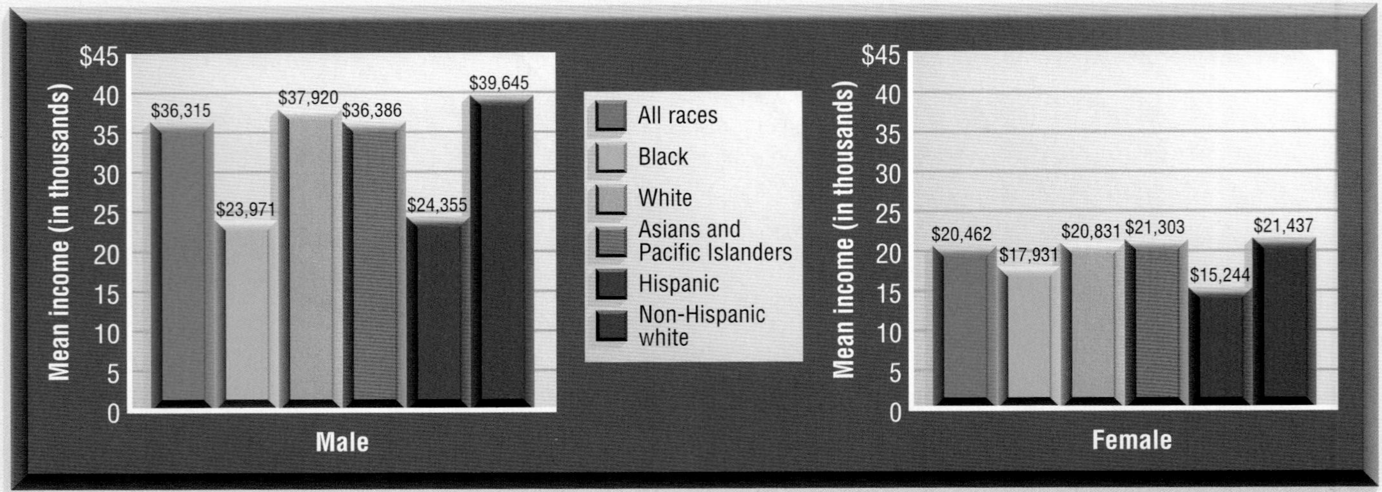

SOURCE: U.S. Census Bureau

Exhibit R23 Average Weekly Earnings, 1990-2000

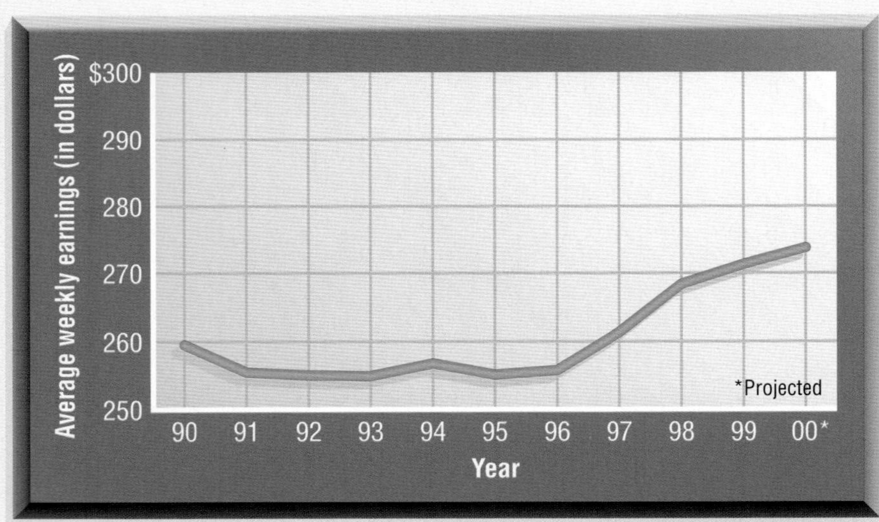

SOURCE: Bureau of Labor Statistics

Exhibit R24 Average Weekly Work Hours, 1990-2000

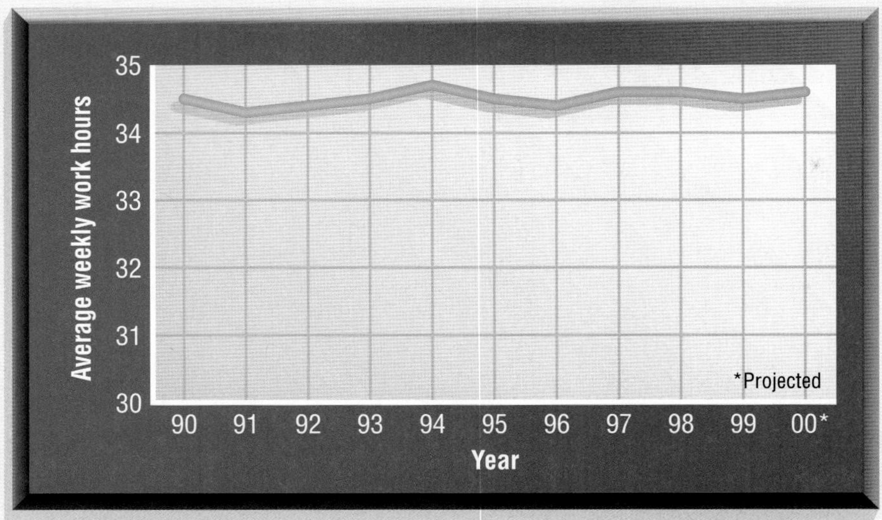

SOURCE: Bureau of Labor Statistics

Exhibit R25 Median Earnings by Educational Level and by Gender, 1998

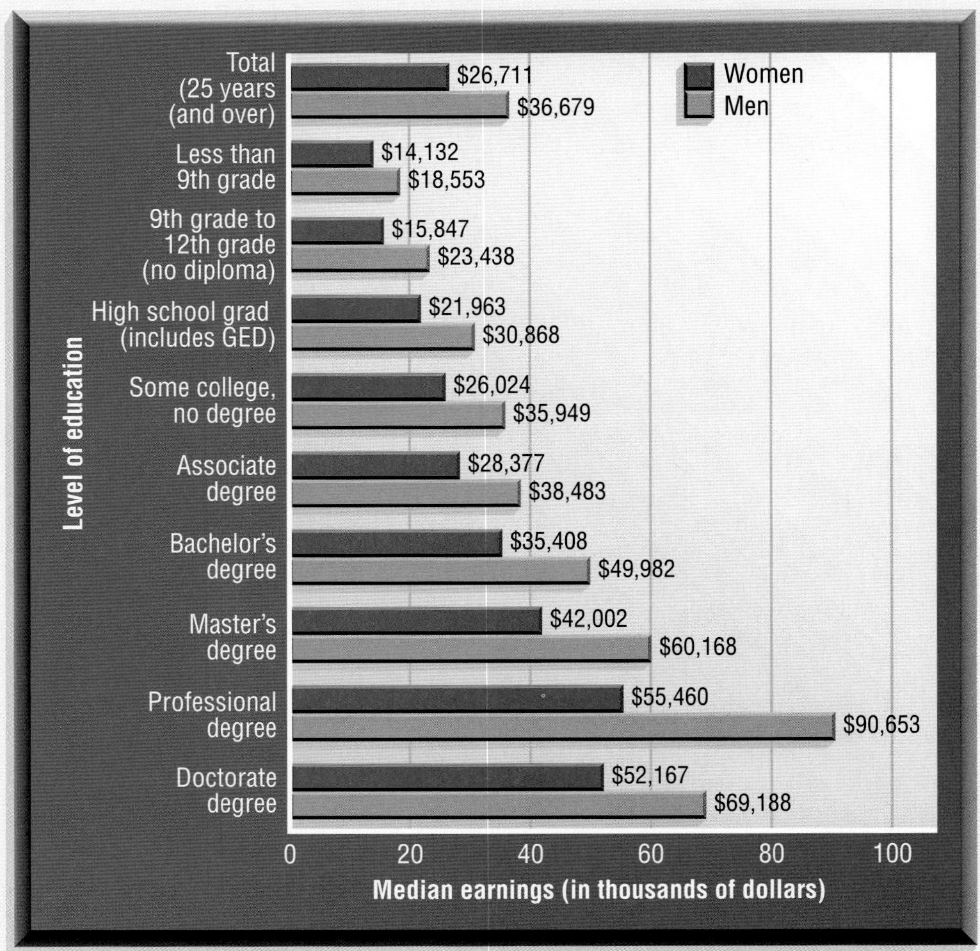

SOURCE: U.S. Census Bureau

Exhibit R26 Median Earnings in Selected Occupations and by Gender, 1998

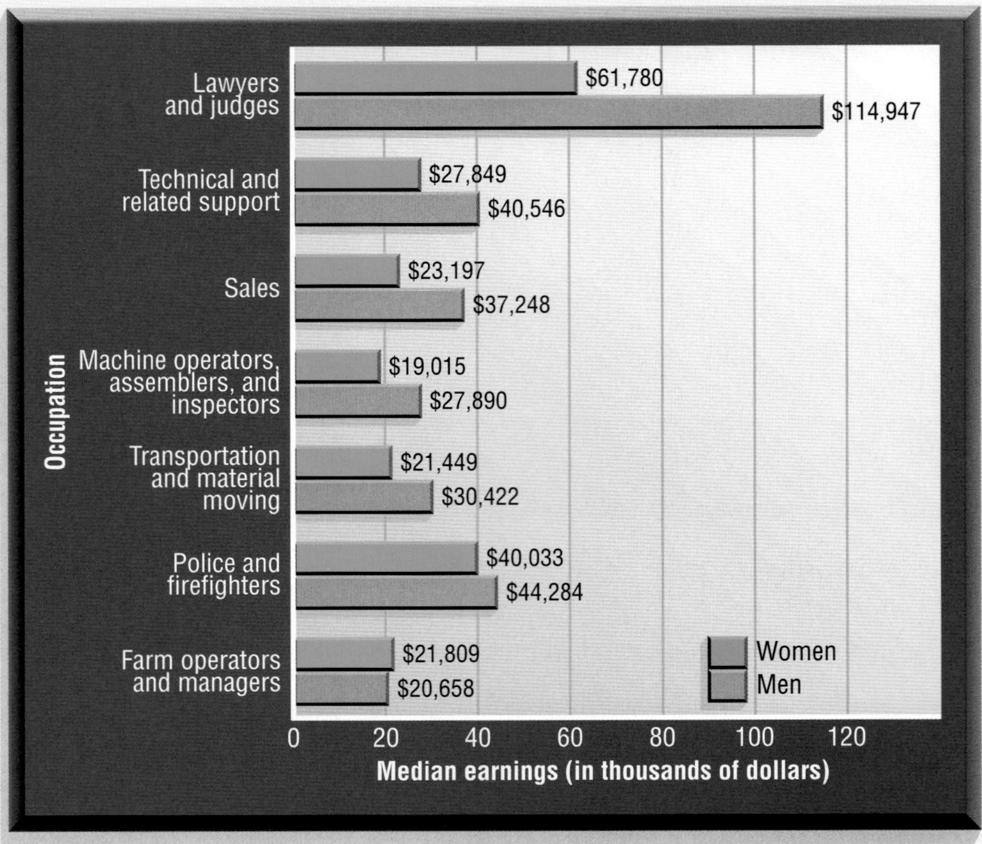

SOURCE: U.S. Census Bureau

Exhibit R27 United States Unemployment Rate, 1990-2000

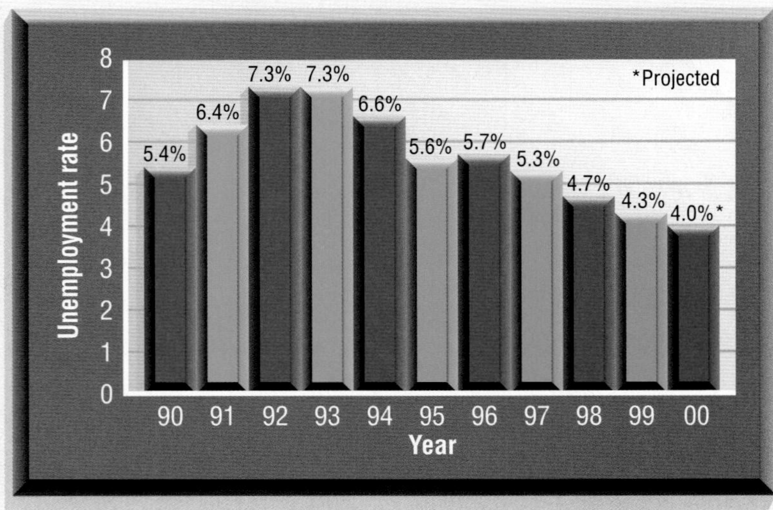

SOURCE: Bureau of Economic Analysis

Exhibit R28 Percentage Change in Industry Employment, 1996-2001

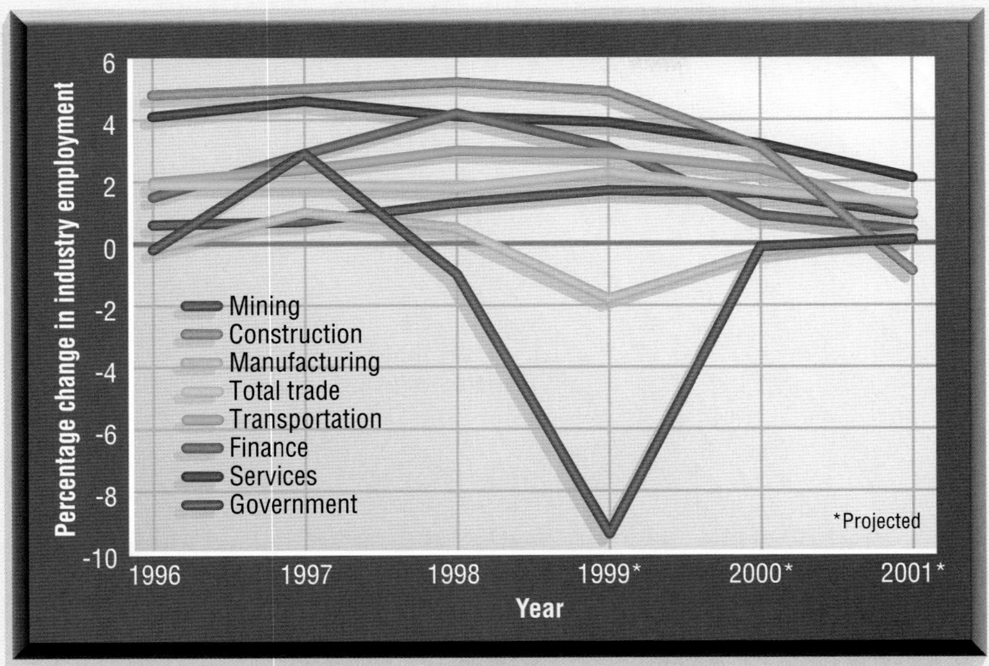

SOURCE: The Dismal Scientist

Exhibit R29 Hourly Earnings in Various Industries, 1996-2001

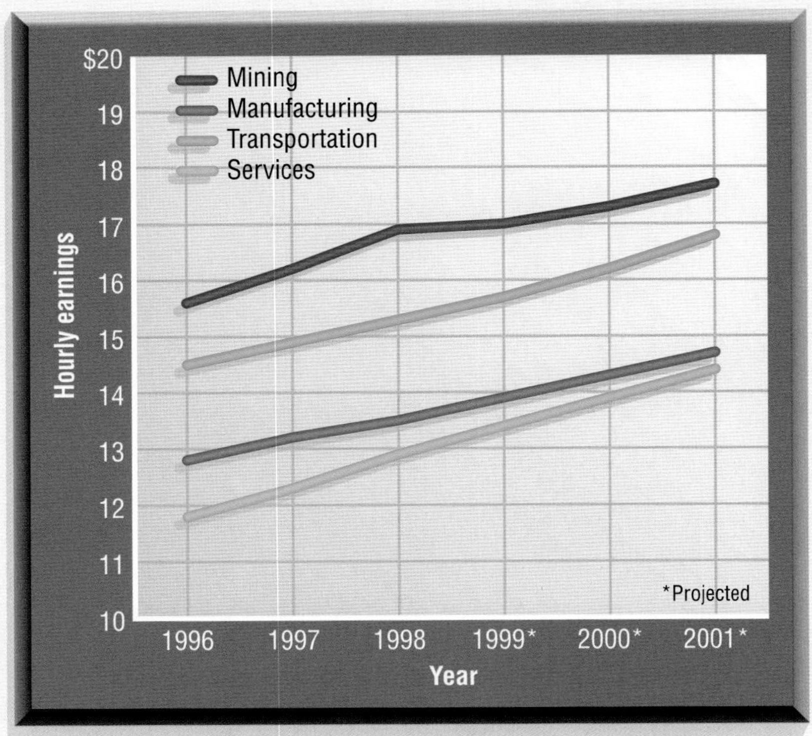

SOURCE: The Dismal Scientist

Go to . . . learningeconomics.com for updated information

Exhibit R30 World Map

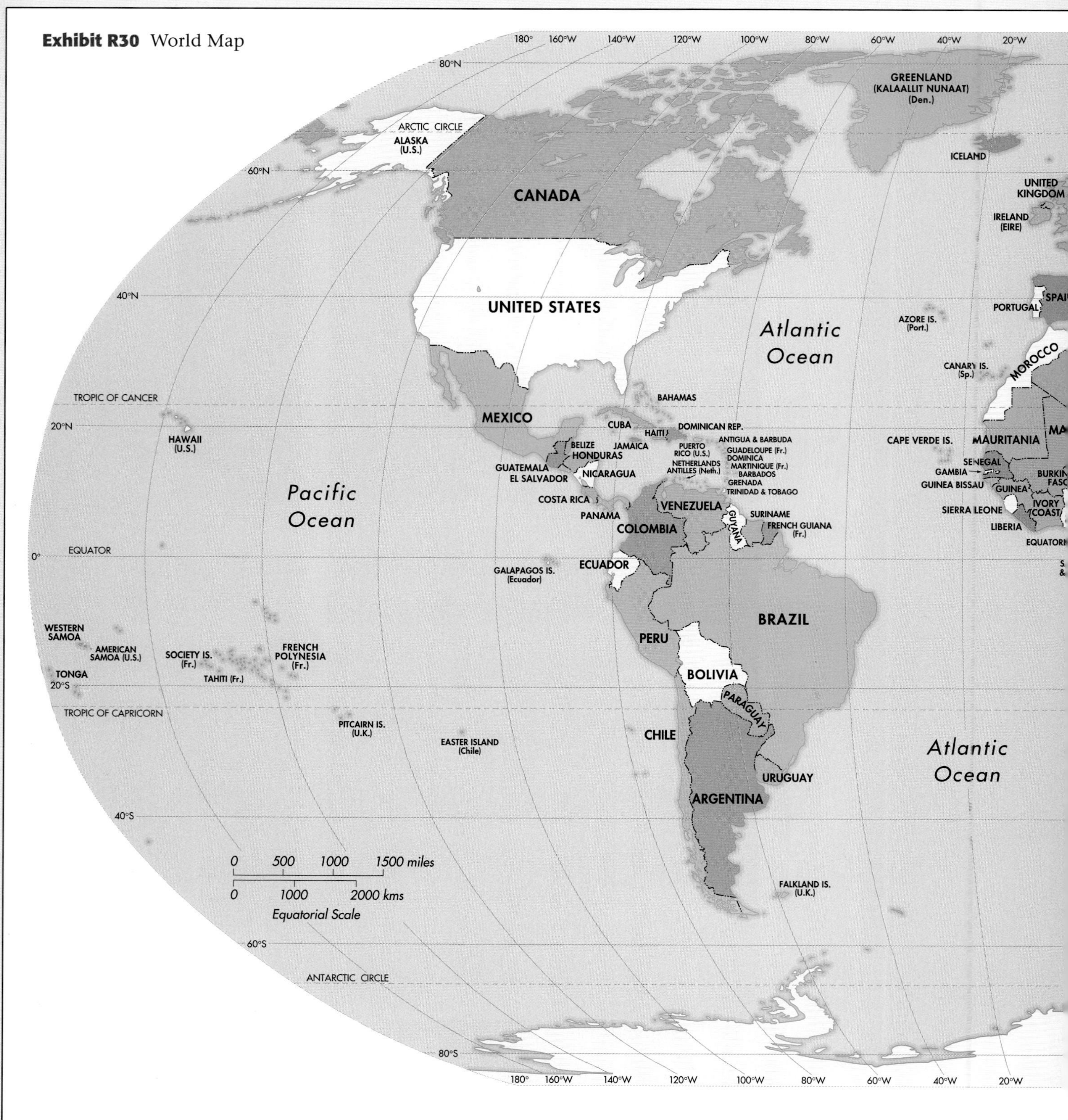

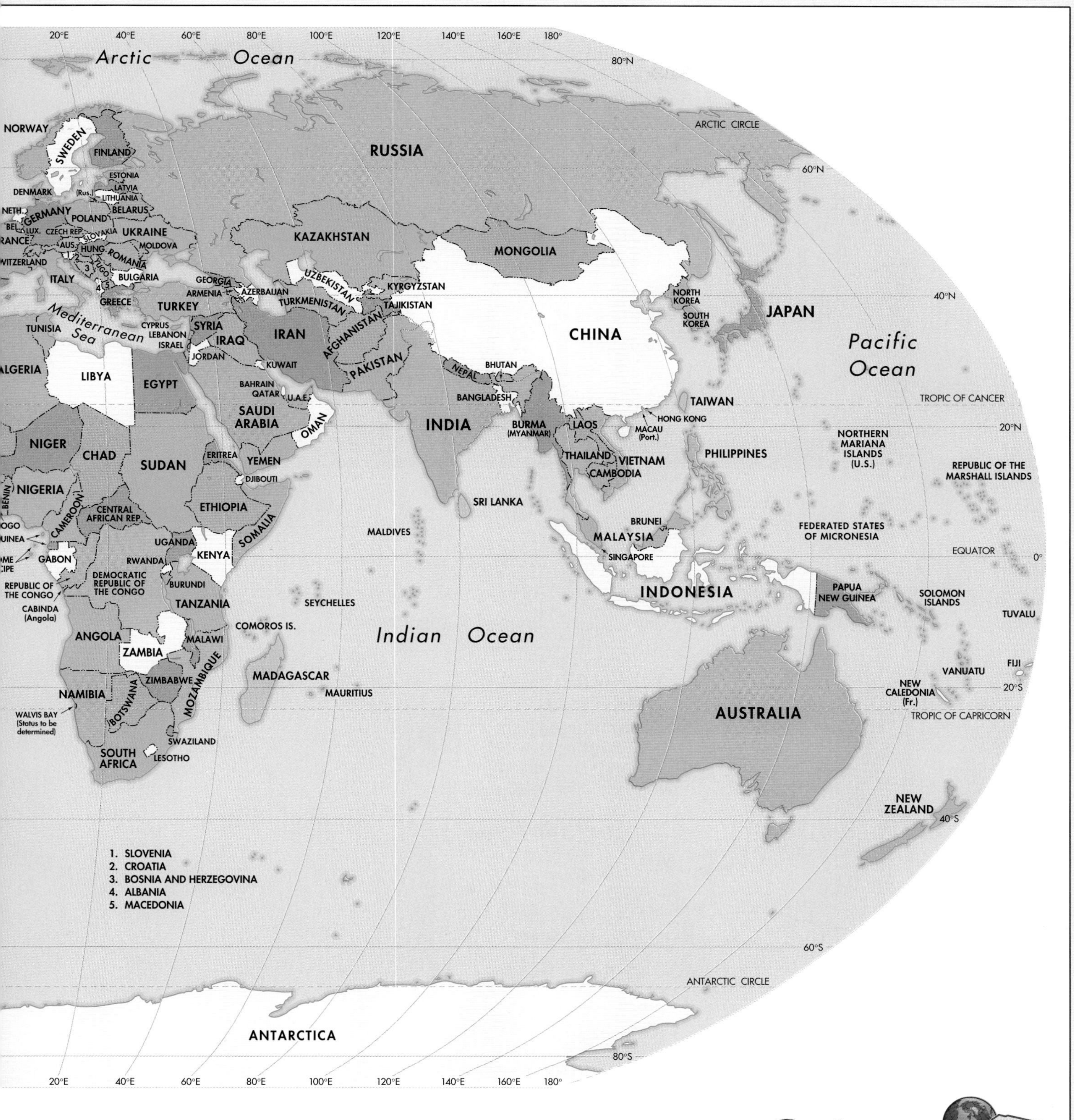

Go to . . .
learningeconomics.com
for updated information

Exhibit R31 Top 25 Countries by Population

Rank	Country	Population	Rank	Country	Population
1	China	1,250,463,856	14	Vietnam	77,600,713
2	India	997,892,285	15	Egypt	67,178,624
3	United States	273,131,194	16	Iran	65,045,410
4	Indonesia	221,110,775	17	Turkey	64,819,580
5	Brazil	171,155,221	18	Ethiopia	62,361,042
6	Russia	146,515,771	19	Thailand	60,652,737
7	Pakistan	138,496,052	20	United Kingdom	59,357,096
8	Bangladesh	127,146,060	21	France	59,100,912
9	Japan	126,314,453	22	Italy	57,577,963
10	Nigeria	120,051,679	23	Congo (Kinshasa)	50,428,273
11	Mexico	98,806,793	24	Ukraine	49,565,699
12	Germany	82,561,399	25	South Korea	47,026,322
13	Philippines	79,483,021			

SOURCE: U.S. Census Bureau

Exhibit R32 Unemployment Rate, Selected Countries, 1995-1998

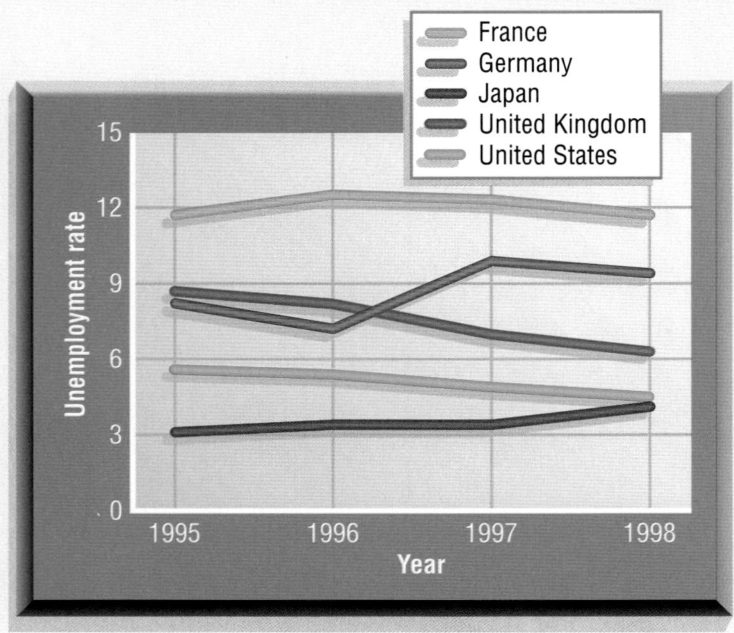

SOURCE: U.S. Census Bureau

Exhibit R33 Percentage Change in Prices, Selected Countries, 1994-1998

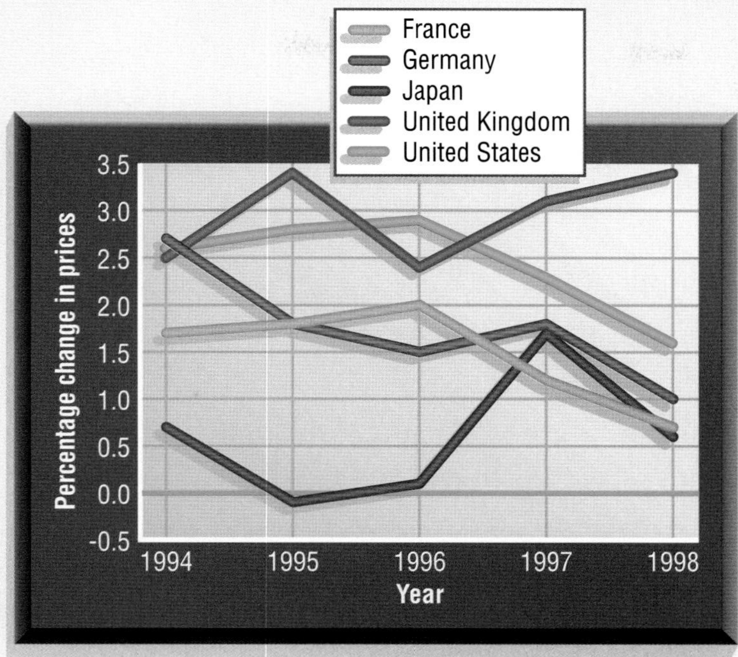

SOURCE: U.S. Census Bureau

Glossary

A

absolute advantage The situation in which a country can produce more of a good than another country can produce with the same quantity of resources.

absolute real economic growth An increase in real GDP from one period to the next.

advancement in technology The ability to produce more output with a fixed amount of resources.

after-tax income The part of income that's left over after taxes are paid.

aggregate demand curve A curve that shows the quantity of goods and services that buyers are willing and able to buy at different price levels.

aggregate supply curve A curve that shows the quantity of goods and services that producers are willing and able to supply at different price levels.

antitrust law Legislation passed for the stated purpose of controlling monopoly power and preserving and promoting competition.

appreciation An increase in the value of one currency relative to other currencies.

asset In reference to a bank, a thing that the bank owns that has value. Anything of value to which a firm has legal claim.

average cost Total cost divided by quantity. For example, if the total cost is $100 and the quantity is 10, then the average total cost is $10. Average total cost is often called *per-unit cost.*

average total cost (or per-unit cost) *See **average cost.***

B

balance of trade The difference between the value of a country's exports and the value of its imports.

barrier to entry Anything that prohibits a firm from entering a market.

barter economy An economy in which trades are made in goods and services instead of in money.

base year In general, a benchmark year—a year chosen as a point of reference for comparison. When real GDP is computed, the outputs of different years are priced at base-year levels.

beneficiary A person named to receive benefits from an insurance policy.

board of directors An important decision-making body in a corporation. It decides corporate policies and goals, among other things.

Board of Governors of the Federal Reserve System The governing body of the Federal Reserve System.

bond A statement of debt issued by a corporation; the corporation promises to pay a certain sum of money at maturity and also to pay periodic fixed sums until that date. An IOU, a promise to pay.

budget An organized plan for spending and saving money.

budget deficit The situation in which federal government expenditures are greater than federal government tax revenues.

budget surplus The situation in which federal government expenditures are less than federal government tax revenues.

business cycle Recurrent swings (up and down) in real GDP.

business firm An organization that uses resources to produce goods and services, which are sold to consumers, other firms, or the government.

bylaws Internal rules of a corporation.

C

capital Produced goods that can be used as resources for further production. Such things as factories, machines, and farm tractors are capital.

capital ratio Equity divided by assets.

cartel agreement An agreement that specifies that the firms that entered into the agreement will act in a coordinated way to reduce the competition among them.

circular flow of economic activity The economic relationships that exist between different economic groups in an economy.

closed shop An organization that hires only union members.

command-economy socialism An economic system characterized by government ownership of the nonlabor factors of production, government allocation of resources, and centralized decision making. Most economic activities take place in the public sector, and government plays a very large role in the economy.

comparative advantage The situation in which a country can produce a good at lower opportunity cost than another country.

complement A good that is consumed jointly with another good. With complements, the price of one and the demand for the other move in opposite directions.

computer virus A program created to disrupt computer systems.

consumer price index (CPI) The most widely cited price index.

consumption Expenditures made by the household sector.

contract An agreement between two or more people to do something.

contractionary fiscal policy A decrease in government spending or an increase in taxes.

contractionary monetary policy A decrease in the money supply.

cooperative A business that provides services to its members and is not run for profit. Usually, a cooperative is formed when a group of persons (the members) want to pool their resources to gain some benefit that they, as individuals, could not otherwise obtain.

corporate income tax A tax paid on a corporation's profits.

corporation A legal entity that can conduct business in its own name in the same way that an individual does. Ownership of the corporation resides with the stockholders.

coupon rate A percentage of the face value of a bond that is paid out regularly (usually quarterly or annually) to the holder of the bond.

crowding in The situation in which decreases in government spending lead to increases in private spending.

crowding out The situation in which increases in government spending lead to reductions in private spending.

currency Coins issued by the U.S. Treasury and paper money (called Federal Reserve notes) issued by the Federal Reserve System.

cyberspace The digital world constructed by computer networks.

cyclical unemployment The difference between actual or official unemployment and natural unemployment.

D

debit card A card that can be used to withdraw funds at automated teller machines and to pay for purchases by electronically transferring funds from one account to another (where the seller has the appropriate equipment). Debit cards look like credit cards.

default rate The percentage of loans that are not repaid.

deflation A decrease in the price level, or average level of prices.

demand The willingness and ability of buyers to purchase a good or service.

demand curve The graphical representation of the law of demand.

demand deposit A deposit that can be withdrawn in currency or transferred by a check to a third party on the initiative of the owner.

demand schedule The numerical representation of the law of demand.

demand-side inflation An increase in the price level that originates on the demand side of the economy.

dependency ratio The number of children (under age fifteen) plus the elderly (age sixty-five and over) divided by the total population.

depreciation A decrease in the value of one currency relative to other currencies.

derived demand A demand that is the result of some other demand.

developed country (DC) A country with a relatively high per-capita GDP or GNP.

digital divide The economic gap between those who have access to computers and the Internet, and those who do not.

direct relationship A relationship between two factors in which the factors move in the same direction; for example, as one factor rises, the other rises, too.

discount rate The interest rate the Fed charges a bank for a loan.

dividend A share of the profits of a corporation distributed to stockholders.

double coincidence of wants The situation in which each of two parties to an exchange has what the other wants. In a barter economy, it is a requirement that must be met before a trade can be made.

double-counting Counting a good more than once in computing GDP.

Dow Jones Industrial Average (DJIA) The most popular, most widely cited indicator of day-to-day stock market activity. The DJIA is a weighted average of the thirty most widely traded stocks on the New York Stock Exchange.

down payment Cash paid at the time of a purchase, with the rest of the purchase price to be paid later.

dumping The sale of goods abroad at prices below their costs and below the price charged in domestic (home) markets.

E

E-commerce Business conducted online. Electronic commerce.

economic plan A government program specifying economic activities, such as what goods are to be produced and what prices will be charged.

economic system The way in which a society decides what goods to produce, how to produce them, and for whom goods will be produced.

economics The science that studies the choices of people trying to satisfy their wants in a world of scarcity.

elastic demand The type of demand that exists when the percentage change in quantity demanded is greater than the percentage change in price.

elastic supply The kind of supply that exists when the percentage change in quantity supplied is greater than the percentage change in price.

elasticity of demand The relationship between the percentage change in quantity demanded and the percentage change in price.

elasticity of supply The relationship between the percentage change in quantity supplied and the percentage change in price.

employment rate The percentage of the noninstitutional adult civilian population that is employed. Employment rate = employed persons ÷ noninstitutional adult civilian population.

entrepreneur A person who has a special talent for searching out and taking advantage of new business opportunities, as well as for developing new products and new ways of doing things.

entrepreneurship The special talent that some people have for searching out and taking advantage of new business opportunities and for developing new products and new ways of doing things.

equilibrium The condition of being at rest or balanced. Equilibrium in a market exists when the quantity of a good that buyers are willing and able to buy is equal to the quantity of the good that sellers are willing and able to produce and offer for sale (that is, quantity demanded equals quantity supplied). Graphically, equilibrium in a market is shown as the intersection point of the supply and demand curves.

equilibrium price The price at which a good is bought and sold in a market that is in equilibrium.

equilibrium quantity The quantity of a good that is bought and sold in a market that is in equilibrium.

ethics The principles of conduct, such as right and wrong, morality and immorality, good and bad.

excess reserves Any reserves held beyond the required amount; the difference between total reserves and required reserves.

exchange rate The price of one country's currency in terms of another country's currency.

excludable public good A public good that individuals can be excluded (physically prohibited) from consuming.

expansionary fiscal policy An increase in government spending or a reduction in taxes.

expansionary monetary policy An increase in the money supply.

export spending The amount spent by the residents of other countries for goods produced in the United States.

exports Goods produced in the domestic country and sold to residents of a foreign country.

externality A side effect of an action that affects the well-being of third parties.

F

face value The stated denomination on paper money or coins. For example, the face value of a nickel is 5 cents, and the words *five cents* actually appear on a nickel.

face value (par value) The dollar amount specified on the "face" (front) of the bond; it is the amount the issuer of the bond promises to pay the buyer of the bond on the maturity date.

federal funds rate The interest rate one bank charges another bank for a loan.

Federal Open Market Committee (FOMC) The 12-member policy-making group within the Fed. This committee has the authority to conduct open market operations.

Federal Reserve note Paper money issued by the Federal Reserve System.

Federal Reserve System (The Fed) The central bank of the United States.

fiscal policy Changes government makes in spending or taxation to achieve particular economic goals.

fixed cost A cost, or expense, that is the same no matter how many units of a good are produced.

fixed exchange rate system The system whereby currency exchange rates are fixed, or pegged, by countries' governments.

flexible exchange rate system The system whereby currency exchange rates are determined by the forces of supply and demand.

fractional reserve banking A banking arrangement in which banks hold only a fraction of their deposits and lend out the remainder.

franchise A contract by which a firm (usually a corporation) lets a person or group use its name and sell its goods in exchange for certain payments being made and certain requirements being met.

franchisee The person or group that buys a franchise.

franchiser The entity that offers a franchise.

free enterprise An economic system in which individuals (not government) own most, if not all, the resources and control their use. Government plays a very small role in the economy.

free rider A person who receives the benefits of a good without paying for it.

frictional unemployment The condition of workers who have lost their jobs because of changing market (demand) conditions and who have transferable skills.

full employment The situation that exists when the official unemployment rate equals the natural unemployment rate.

futures contract An agreement to buy or sell a specific amount of something (a commodity, currency, or financial instrument) at a particular price on a stipulated future date.

G

general partner A partner who is responsible for the management of the firm and who has unlimited liability.

generic brand A brand name that does not use the name of any company; it uses only the product name.

global economy An economy in which economic actions taken anywhere in the world may affect an individual's standard of living.

good A tangible item that gives a person utility or satisfaction. Sometimes a good is referred to as a *product.*

Gosplan Under Soviet command-economy socialism, the planning agency that had the responsibility of drafting the economic plan for the country.

government purchases Expenditures made by the government sector. Government purchases do not include government transfer payments.

Gresham's law An economic law stating that bad money drives good money out of circulation. (Bad money has the same face value as good money, but a lower precious metal content.)

gross domestic product (GDP) The total market value of all final goods and services produced annually in an economy.

H

hacker A person who, using highly sophisticated programming techniques, breaks into secured computer systems.

hedge To try to avoid or lessen a loss by taking some counterbalancing action.

household An economic unit of one person or more that sells resources and buys goods and services.

I

import spending The amount spent by Americans for foreign-produced goods.

imports Goods produced in foreign countries and purchased by residents of the domestic country.

impulse buying Buying goods that one did not intend to buy. The impulse to buy something strikes quickly, and the consumer reacts by buying it.

incentive Something that encourages or motivates a person toward an action.

income distribution The way all the income earned in a country is divided among different groups of income earners.

inelastic demand The type of demand that exists when the percentage change in quantity demanded is less than the percentage change in price.

inelastic supply The kind of supply that exists when the percentage change in quantity supplied is less than the percentage change in price.

infant mortality rate The number of children who die before their first birthday out of every 1,000 live births.

inferior good A good the demand for which falls as income rises and rises as income falls.

inflation An increase in the price level, or average level of prices.

infrastructure The basic structures and facilities on which the continuance and growth of a community depend. Interstate highways, bridges, and communication networks are some of the things that make up a country's infrastructure.

initial public offering (IPO) A company's first offering of stock to the public.

insolvent Having more liabilities than assets.

intangible Not able to be felt by touch. For example, an economics lecture is intangible.

intellectual property Intangible materials that are legally recognized as owned by an individual or a company. Software, databases, and mailing lists are among items considered to be intellectual property.

interest The payment to the resource capital.

Internet A system of linked computer networks that facilitates data communication in a way that expands the reach of each participating system.

inventory The stock of goods that a business or store has on hand.

inverse relationship A relationship whereby two variables move in opposite directions. When one variable rises, the other falls.

investment Expenditures made by the business sector.

investment bank A firm that acts as an intermediary between a company that issues a stock and the public that wishes to buy the stock.

J

junk bond A bond with a high default risk.

L

labor The physical and mental talents that people contribute to the production of goods and services.

labor theory of value A theory that holds that all value in produced goods is derived from labor.

labor union An organization that seeks to increase the wages and improve the working conditions of its members.

Laffer curve The curve, named after economist Arthur Laffer, that shows the relationship between tax rates and tax revenues. According to the Laffer curve, as tax rates rise from zero, tax revenues rise, reach a maximum at some point, and then fall with further increases in tax rates.

land All the natural resources found in nature. An acre of land, mineral deposits, and water in a stream are all considered land.

law of demand A law stating that as the price of a good increases, the quantity demanded of the good decreases, and that as the price of a good decreases, the quantity demanded of the good increases.

law of diminishing marginal returns A law that states that if additional units of a resource (such as labor) are added to another resource (such as capital) that is fixed in supply, eventually the additional output produced (as a result of hiring an additional worker) will decrease.

law of diminishing marginal utility A law stating that as a person consumes additional units of a good, eventually the utility gained from each additional unit of the good decreases.

law of supply A law stating that as the price of a good increases, the quantity supplied of the good increases, and as the price of a good decreases, the quantity supplied of the good decreases.

lease A contract that conveys property (such as an apartment) for a specific time period for a fee.

less-developed country (LDC) A country with a relatively low per-capita GDP or GNP.

liability In reference to a bank, its debts.

limited liability A condition in which an owner of a business firm can lose only the amount he or she has invested (in the firm). Stockholders of a corporation have limited liability.

limited partner A partner who cannot participate in the management of the firm and who has limited liability.

loss The amount of money by which total cost exceeds total revenue.

M

macroeconomics The branch of economics that deals with human behavior and choices as they relate to the entire economy.

marginal cost The additional cost of producing an additional unit of a good; the change in total cost that results from producing an additional unit of output.

marginal revenue The additional revenue from selling an additional unit of a good; the change in total revenue that results from selling an additional unit of output.

market Any place where people come together to buy and sell goods or services.

market structure The setting in which a seller finds itself. Market structures are defined by their characteristics, such as the number of sellers in the market, the product that sellers produce and sell, and how easy or difficult it is for new firms to enter the market.

medium of exchange Anything that is generally acceptable in exchange for goods and services.

merger A joining of two companies that occurs when one company buys more than half the stock in the other company. As a result, the companies come to act as one.

microeconomics The branch of economics that deals with human behavior and choices as they relate to relatively small units—an individual, a business firm, or a single market.

minimum wage law A federal law that specifies the lowest hourly wage rate that can be paid to workers.

mixed economy An economy that is neither purely capitalist nor purely socialist; an economy that has some elements of both capitalism and socialism. Most countries in the world have mixed economies.

monetary policy The deliberate control of the money supply by the Fed.

money A good that is widely accepted for purposes of exchange and in the repayment of debt.

money supply The total supply of money in circulation, composed of currency, checking accounts, and traveler's checks.

monitor The person in a business who coordinates team production and reduces shirking.

monopolistic competition A market structure in which (1) there are many buyers and many sellers, (2) sellers produce and sell slightly differentiated products, and (3) there is easy entry into and easy exit from the market.

monopoly A market structure in which (1) there is a single seller, (2) the seller sells a product for which there are no close substitutes, and (3) there are extremely high barriers to entry.

mortgage note A written agreement by which a buyer of property agrees to repay a loan taken out to purchase the property. If the loan is not repaid, the lender can take the property.

mutual fund A financial organization that pools people's money and invests it.

N

national brand A brand name that is owned by the maker of a product. Many national brands are known across the country, such as Kellogg's and Coca-Cola.

national debt The sum total of what the federal government owes its creditors.

natural monopoly A firm with such a low average total cost (per-unit cost) that only it can survive in the market.

natural unemployment Unemployment that is caused by frictional and structural factors in the economy.

near-money Assets, such as nonchecking savings accounts, that can be easily and quickly turned into money.

negative externality An adverse side effect of an action that is felt by others.

net worth (equity, capital) The difference between assets and liabilities.

neutral good A good the demand for which remains unchanged as income rises or falls.

nonexcludable public good A public good that individuals cannot be excluded (physically prohibited) from consuming.

normal good A good the demand for which rises as income rises and falls as income falls.

O

oligopoly A market structure in which (1) there are few sellers, (2) sellers produce and sell either identical or slightly differentiated products, and (3) there are significant barriers to entry.

open market operations Buying and selling of government securities by the Fed.

opportunity cost The most highly valued opportunity or alternative forfeited when a choice is made.

option A contract that gives the owner the right, but not the obligation, to buy or sell shares of a stock at a specified price on or before a specified date.

P

par value *See* ***face value (par value)***

partnership A business that is owned by two or more co-owners called partners, who share any profits the business earns and are legally responsible for any debts incurred by the firm.

per-capita real economic growth An increase from one period to the next in per-capita real GDP, which is real GDP divided by population.

per-unit cost The average total cost of a good. For example, if $400,000 is spent to produce 100 cars, the average, or per-unit, cost is $4,000.

perfect competition A market structure in which (1) there are many buyers and many sellers, (2) all firms sell identical goods, (3) buyers and sellers have all relevant information about buying and selling activities, and (4) there is easy entry into the market and easy exit out of the market.

personal income tax A tax paid on a person's income.

point One percentage point of a loan amount. Points are paid by the borrower to the lender.

population growth rate The birthrate minus the death rate.

positive externality A beneficial side effect of an action that is felt by others.

price discrimination What occurs when a seller charges different buyers different prices for the same product when the price differences are not related to cost differences.

price index A measure of the price level, or the average level of prices.

price searcher A seller that can sell some of its output at various prices.

price taker A seller that can sell all its output at the equilibrium price but can sell none of its output at any other price.

private brand A brand name owned by a seller rather than by the maker of the product. For example, products are often produced for a specific supermarket chain and carry the name of that chain on the label.

private good A good of which one person's consumption takes away from another person's consumption. A car is a private good.

private property Any good that is owned by an individual or a business.

production possibilities frontier (PPF) All possible combinations of two goods that an economy can produce in a certain period of time, under the conditions of a given state of technology, no unemployed resources, and efficient production.

profit The amount of money left over after all the costs of production have been paid. Also, the payment to the resource entrepreneurship. Profit exists whenever total revenue is greater than total cost.

progressive income tax An income tax whose rate increases as income level rises. Progressive income tax structures are usually capped at some rate.

proportional income tax An income tax that everyone pays at the same rate, whatever the income level.

public franchise A right granted to a firm by government that permits the firm to provide a particular good or service and excludes all others from doing so.

public good A good of which one person's consumption does not take away from another person's consumption. National defense is a public good.

public property Any good that is owned by the government.

public utility commission A government group that regulates public utility companies (such as electric, water, and gas companies).

Q

quantity demanded The number of units of a good purchased at a specific price.

quantity supplied The number of units of a good produced and offered for sale at a specific price.

quota A legal limit on the number of units of a foreign-produced good (import) that can enter a country.

R

rationing device A means for deciding who gets what portion of the available resources and goods.

real GDP Gross domestic product (GDP) that has been adjusted for price changes; GDP measured in base-year, or constant, prices.

recession A slowdown in the economy marked by real GDP falling for two consecutive quarters.

regressive income tax An income tax whose rate decreases as income level rises.

rent The payment to the resource land.

required reserves The minimum amount of reserves a bank must hold against its deposits as mandated by the Fed.

reserve account A bank's checking account with its Federal Reserve district bank.

reserve requirement A regulation which requires a bank to keep a certain percentage of each dollar deposited in the bank in its reserve account with the Fed or in its vault (as vault cash).

residual claimant A person who shares in the profits of a business firm.

resource Anything that is used to produce goods or services. For example, a person's labor may be used to produce computers, TV sets, and much more, and therefore a person's labor is a resource. There are four categories of resources: land, labor, capital, and entrepreneurship.

résumé A statement of a job applicant's previous employment, education, and so on.

reverse auction An auction in which the buyer states the price he or she is willing to pay for a good or service, and the seller decides whether or not to sell at those terms.

right-to-work law A state law that prohibits the practice of requiring employees to join a union in order to work.

rule of law A governing by law or laws (instead of by men and women).

S

savings account An interest-earning account.

scarcity The condition in which our wants are greater than the resources available to satisfy those wants.

security deposit An amount of money a renter pays a landlord before moving into an apartment (or other rental property). The money is to be returned when the renter moves out, but the landlord may keep a part or all of it to make repairs or compensate for rent not paid.

service An intangible item that gives a person utility or satisfaction.

shirking The behavior of a worker who is putting forth less than the agreed-to effort.

shortage The condition in which the quantity demanded of a good is greater than the quantity supplied. Shortages occur only at prices below equilibrium price.

simple quantity theory of money A theory that predicts that changes in the price level will be strictly proportional to changes in the money supply.

socialism An economic system in which government controls and may own many of the resources. Government plays a major role in the economy.

sole proprietorship A business that is owned by one individual, who makes all business decisions, receives all the profits or incurs all the losses of the firm, and is legally responsible for the debts of the firm.

specialize To do only one thing. For example, when a country specializes in the production of a good, it produces only that good.

stagflation The occurrence of inflation and high unemployment at the same time.

status quo That which exists now; the existing state of affairs.

stock A claim on the assets of a corporation that gives the purchaser a share of the ownership of the corporation.

stockholder A person who owns shares of stock in a corporation. The stockholders of a corporation are the owners of the corporation.

stop-and-go, on-and-off monetary policy An erratic monetary policy. The money supply is increased, then decreased, then increased, and so on. It is similar to driving a car by putting the accelerator to the floor, then slamming on the brakes, then putting the accelerator to the floor, then slamming on the brakes again, and so on.

store of value Something with the ability to hold value over time.

strike A work stoppage called by members of a union to place pressure on an employer.

structural unemployment The condition of workers who have lost their jobs because of changing market (demand) conditions and whose skills do not match the requirements of available jobs.

sublease To rent out an apartment when one is a renter rather than the owner.

subsidy A financial payment made by government for certain actions.

substitute A similar good. With substitutes, the price of one and the demand for the other move in the same direction.

supply The willingness and ability of sellers to produce and offer to sell a good or service.

supply curve A graph that shows the amount of a good sellers are willing and able to sell at various prices. Only the upward-sloping supply curve is a graphic representation of the law of supply.

supply schedule A numerical chart that illustrates the law of supply.

supply-side inflation An increase in the price level that originates on the supply side of the economy.

surplus The condition in which the quantity supplied of a good is greater than the quantity demanded. Surpluses occur only at prices above equilibrium price.

surplus value In Marxist terminology, the difference between the total value of production and the subsistence wages paid to workers.

T

Taft-Hartley Act An act, passed in 1947 by the U.S. Congress, which made the closed shop illegal and gave states the right to pass right-to-work laws. These right-to-work laws prohibit employers from establishing union membership as a condition of employment.

tangible Able to be felt by touch. For example, a book is tangible: you can touch and feel it.

tariff A tax on imports.

technology The body of skills and knowledge concerning the use of resources in production.

telemarketing Direct sales of products by telephone.

theory An explanation of how something works, designed to answer a question for which there is no obvious answer.

total cost The average cost (or expense) of a good times the number of units of the good sold. Total cost = average cost × number of units sold. Also, the sum of the fixed costs plus variable costs.

total reserves The sum of a bank's deposits in its reserve account at the Fed and its vault cash.

total revenue The price of a good times the number of units of the good sold. Total revenue = price × number of units sold.

trade-off A situation in which more of one thing necessarily means less of something else. The nature of a trade-off is that one must give up one thing that is desirable to get something else that is desirable.

traditional economy An economic system in which the answers to the three economic questions are based on customs, traditions, and cultural beliefs.

transaction costs The costs associated with the time and effort needed to search out, negotiate, and consummate an exchange.

trust A combination of firms that come together to act as a monopolist.

U

unemployment rate The percentage of the civilian labor force that is unemployed. Unemployment rate = unemployed persons ÷ civilian labor force.

union shop An organization that requires employees to join the union within a certain period after being hired.

unit of account A common measurement in which values are expressed.

unit price The total price of an item divided by its weight.

unit-elastic demand The type of demand that exists when the percentage change in quantity demanded is the same as the percentage change in price.

unit-elastic supply The kind of supply that exists when the percentage change in quantity supplied is the same as the percentage change in price.

unlimited liability The legal responsibility of a sole proprietor of a business or of partners in a business to pay any money owed by the business. The proprietor's or partners' personal assets may be used to pay these debts.

V

variable cost A cost, or expense, that changes with the number of units of a good produced.

velocity The average number of times a dollar is spent to buy final goods and services in a year.

vicious circle of poverty The idea that countries are poor because they do not save and buy capital goods, but they cannot save and buy capital goods because they are poor.

vision A sense of how the world works.

W

wage rate The price of labor.

wages The payment to the resource labor.

want A thing that we desire to have.

warranty A guarantee or assurance given by a seller stating that a product is in good working order and that the seller will provide certain types of service for a period of time.

Web site A home or location on the World Wide Web. A Web site is made up of a page or pages that may contain text, graphics, video and audio sources.

World Wide Web Global system of interlinked Web sites or locations.

Glosario

A

absolute advantage – ventaja absoluta Situación en la cual un país puede producir mayor cantidad de un bien que el que puede producir otro país con la misma cantidad de recursos.

absolute real economic growth – crecimiento económico real absoluto Un incremento en el Producto Doméstico Bruto de un periodo al siguiente.

advancement in technology – adelanto tecnológico Habilidad de incrementar la producción con una cantidad fija de recursos.

after-tax income – ingresos después de impuestos La porción del ingreso que queda luego de pagar los impuestos.

aggregate demand curve – curva de demanda agregada Curva que muestra la cantidad de bienes y servicios que los compradores desean y pueden comprar en los diferentes niveles de precios.

aggregate supply curve – curva de oferta agregada Curva que muestra la cantidad de bienes y servicios que los productores desean y pueden suministrar en los diferentes niveles de precios.

antitrust law – ley antimonopolio Legislación aprobada con el expreso propósito de controlar el poder monopólico y preservar y estimular la competencia.

appreciation – valoración Aumento en el valor de una moneda con relación a otras.

asset – activo En lenguaje bancario, cosa que posee un banco y que tiene valor. Cualquier cosa de valor que la empresa puede reclamar legalmente.

average cost – costo promedio El costo total dividido por la cantidad. Por ejemplo, si el costo total es \$100 y la cantidad es \$10, el costo promedio total es \$10. A menudo se llama al costo promedio total costo por unidad.

average total cost – promedio de costo total (o costo por unidad) *Ver costo promedio.*

B

balance of trade – balanza comercial La diferencia entre el valor de las exportaciones de un país y el valor de sus importaciones.

barrier to entry – barrera al ingreso Cualquier cosa que impide a una empresa ingresar al mercado.

barter economy – economía de trueque Economía en la cual el comercio se efectúa intercambiando bienes y servicios en lugar de dinero.

base year – año base En general, un año de referencia - un año elegido como punto de referencia para comparación. Cuando se calcula el Producto Doméstico Bruto, el total de los diferentes años se valora con relación a los niveles del año base.

beneficiary – beneficiario Persona nominada para recibir los beneficios de una póliza de seguros.

board of directors – junta de directores Un organismo importante de toma de decisiones en una empresa. Decide, entre otras cosas, las políticas y las metas de la empresa.

Board of Governors of the Federal Reserve System – Junta de Gobernadores del Sistema de Reservas Federales La entidad que gobierna el Sistema de Reservas Federales.

bond – bono Un estado de cuenta emitido por una corporación; la corporación se compromete a pagar cierta suma de dinero al vencimiento y tambien a pagar sumas periodicamente hasta dicha fecha. Pagaré de débito. Promesa de pago.

budget – presupuesto Un plan organizado para gastar y ahorrar dinero.

budget deficit – déficit presupuestario Situación en la cual los desembolsos del gobierno federal son mayores que sus entradas por concepto tributario.

budget surplus – superávit presupuestario Situación en la cual los desembolsos del gobierno federal son menores que sus entradas por concepto tributario.

business cycle – ciclo comercial Oscilaciones recurrentes (alzas y bajas) en el Producto Doméstico Bruto real.

business firm – firma comercial Organización que usa recursos para producir bienes y servicios, los que son vendidos a los consumidores, a otras firmas o al gobierno.

bylaws – Estatutos normas internas de una empresa.

C

capital – capital Bienes producidos que pueden utilizarse como recursos para una mayor producción. Cosas tales como las fábricas, la maquinaria y los tractores agrícolas son capital

capital ratio – proporción de capital El capital social dividido por los activos.

cartel agreement – convenio monopólico Un convenio que especifica que las firmas que suscribieron el convenio van a actuar en forma coordinada para reducir la competencia entre ellas.

circular flow of economic activity – flujo circular de la actividad económica La relación económica que existe entre los diferentes grupos económicos de una economía.

closed shop – empresa cerrada Organización que sólo contrata a miembros de un sindicato.

command-economy socialism – socialismo que gobierna a la economía Sistema económico caracterizado por la propiedad gubernamental de los factores no laborales de la producción, de la asignación de recursos, y con una toma de decisiones centralizada. La mayor parte de la actividad económica se lleva a cabo en el sector público, y el gobierno desempeña un papel muy importante en la economía.

comparative advantage – ventaja comparativa Situación en la cual un país puede producir un bien a un costo de oportunidad menor que otro país.

complement – complementario Un bien que se consume juntamente con otro. En el caso de los bienes complementarios, el precio de uno y la demanda por el otro se mueven en direcciones opuestas.

computer virus – virus computacional Un programa creado para interrumpir sistemas computacionales.

consumer price index (CPI) – índice de precios al consumidor El índice de precios más ampliamente citado.

consumption – consumo Gastos efectuados por el sector doméstico.

contract – contrato Convenio entre dos o más personas para hacer algo.

contractionary fiscal policy – política fiscal contractiva Disminución en los gastos gubernamentales o aumento de impuestos.

contractionary monetary policy – política monetaria contractiva Disminución de la cantidad de dinero circulante.

cooperative – cooperativa Una empresa sin fines de lucro que proporciona servicios a sus miembros. Generalmente, una cooperativa se forma cuando un grupo de personas (los miembros) desean unir sus recursos para algún tipo de beneficio que de otro modo no podrían obtener como personas particulares.

corporate income tax – impuesto a la renta corporativa Impuestos pagados sobre las ganancias de una sociedad anónima.

corporation – sociedad anónima Entidad legal que puede llevar a cabo negocios a su nombre y de la misma manera en que lo hace un individuo. La propiedad de una sociedad anónima reside en los accionistas.

coupon rate – interés nominal de un bono El porcentaje del valor nominal de un bono que se paga en forma regular al tenedor (generalmente en forma trimestral o anual).

crowding in – presión hacia dentro Situación en la cual la disminución de los gastos gubernamentales lleva a aumentos en los gastos privados.

crowding out – presión hacia fuera La situación en la cual el aumento de los gastos gubernamentales lleva a una reducción de los gastos privados.

currency – dinero circulante Monedas emitidas por el Tesoro de los Estados Unidos y papel moneda (llamado pagarés de la Reserva Federal) emitidas por el Sistema de Reserva Federal.

cyberspace – ciberespacio El mundo digital creado por las redes computacionales.

cyclical unemployment – desempleo cíclico La diferencia entre el desempleo real u oficial y el desempleo natural.

D

debit card – tarjeta de débito Tarjeta que se puede utilizar para retirar fondos en máquinas de cajeros automáticos y cancelar compras mediante la transferencia de fondos de una cuenta bancaria a otra (cuando el vendedor cuenta con el equipo apropiado). Las tarjetas de débito se parecen a las tarjetas de crédito.

default rate – tasa de incumplimiento El porcentaje de préstamos que no son pagados.

deflation – deflación Disminución del nivel de precios o del nivel promedio de precios.

demand – demanda El deseo y capacidad de los compradores para adquirir un bien o un servicio.

demand curve – curva de la demanda Representación gráfica de la ley de demanda.

demand deposit – depósito de retiro instantáneo Un depósito que puede ser retirado en efectivo o transferido por cheque a un tercero por iniciativa de su dueño.

demand schedule – programa de demanda La representación numérica de la ley de demanda.

demand-side inflation – inflación por demanda Aumento del nivel de precios que se origina en el sector de demanda de la economía.

dependency ratio – porcentaje de dependientes El número de niños (menores de 15 años) más las personas de edad (de sesenta y cinco años) o más dividido por la población total.

depreciation – depreciación La disminución del valor de una moneda en relación con las otras.

derived demand – demanda derivada Demanda que es el resultado de otra demanda.

developed country – país desarrollado País con un Producto Nacional Bruto o Producto Doméstico Bruto per cápita relativamente alto.

digital divide – brecha digital El vacío o laguna que existe entre aquellos que tienen acceso a las computadoras y al Internet y aquellos que no lo tienen.

direct relationship – relación directa Relación entre dos factores en la cual ambos factores se mueven en la misma dirección; por ejemplo, cuando un factor sube, el otro también sube.

discount rate – tasa de descuento La tasa de interés que el banco federal cobra a un banco por un préstamo.

dividend – dividendo Porcentaje de las ganancias de una sociedad anónima que se distribuye entre los accionistas.

double coincidence of wants – doble coincidencia de necesidades La situación en que cada una de las partes de un intercambio tiene lo que el otro desea. En una sociedad de trueque, es un requisito que se debe cumplir antes de poder efectuar un negocio.

double counting – doble verificación El contar mucho más de una vez al calcular el Producto Doméstico Bruto.

double counting – doble verificación El contar un producto más de una vez al calcular el Producto Doméstico Bruto.

Dow Jones Industrial Average (DJIA) – Promedio Industrial Dow Jones El indicador más popular y más ampliamente citado de la actividad bursátil diaria. El DJIA es un promedio estadístico de las treinta acciones de mayor transacción en la Bolsa de Comercio de Nueva York.

down payment – pago inicial, pie Dinero cancelado en el momento de la compra, el resto del precio de compra será pagado posteriormente.

dumping – devaloración La venta de productos en el exterior bajo su costo y bajo el precio que se cobra en los mercados domésticos (nacionales).

E

E-commerce – Comercio electrónico Comercio que se realiza en línea.

economic plan – plan económico Plan gubernamental que especifica las actividades económicas, como ser cuales bienes producir y a que precio se van a vender.

economic system – sistema económico La forma en que una sociedad decide cuales bienes producir, como producirlos y para quien se producirán los bienes.

economics – economía Ciencia que estudia las opciones de las personas que tratan de satisfacer sus necesidades en un mundo de escasez.

elastic demand – demanda elástica El tipo de demanda que existe cuando el cambio de porcentaje en la cantidad demandada es mayor al cambio de porcentaje en el precio.

elastic supply – oferta elástica El tipo de oferta que existe cuando el cambio de porcentaje en la cantidad ofertada es mayor al cambio de porcentaje en el precio.

elasticity of demand – elasticidad de demanda La relación entre cambio de porcentaje en la cantidad demandada y el cambio de porcentaje en el precio.

elasticity of supply – elasticidad de oferta La relación entre cambio de porcentaje en la cantidad suministrada y el cambio de porcentaje en el precio.

employment rate – tasa de empleo El porcentaje de población civil adulta no institucional que tiene un empleo. La tasa de empleo es el resultado del personal empleado dividido por la población civil adulta no institucional.

entrepreneur – empresario Persona que posee un talento especial para buscar y sacar ventaja de nuevas oportunidades de negocios, así como de desarrollar nuevos productos y nuevas formas de hacer las cosas.

entrepreneurship – espíritu empresarial Talento especial que poseen algunas personas para buscar y sacar ventaja de nuevas oportunidades de negocios, así como de desarrollar nuevos productos y nuevas formas de hacer las cosas.

equilibrium – equilibrio La condición de estar en reposo o equilibrado. El equilibrio existe en un mercado cuando la cantidad de un bien que los compradores desean y pueden adquirir es igual a la cantidad que los vendedores desean y pueden producir y ofrecer a la venta (esto es, la cantidad de demanda es igual a la cantidad de oferta). Gráficamente, el equilibrio de un mercado se muestra como el punto de intersección de las curvas de oferta y demanda.

equilibrium price – precio de equilibrio Precio de compra y de venta de un bien en un mercado en equilibrio.

equilibrium quantity – cantidad de equilibrio La cantidad de un bien que se compra y vende en un mercado en equilibrio.

ethics – ética Principios de conducta, tales como corrección e incorrección, moralidad e inmoralidad, bien y mal.

excess reserves – exceso de reservas Cualquier reserva que se mantiene por sobre la cantidad requerida; la diferencia entre las reservas totales y las reservas requeridas.

exchange rate – tasa de cambio El precio de la moneda de un país con relación a la moneda de otro país.

excludable public good – bien público excluible Un bien público de cuyo consumo se puede excluir (prohibir físicamente) a los individuos.

expansionary fiscal policy – política fiscal expansionista Aumento de los gastos fiscales o reducción de impuestos.

expansionary monetary policy – política monetaria expansionista Aumento en el suministro de dinero circulante.

export spending – gastos de exportación La cantidad gastada por los residentes de otros países en bienes producidos en los Estados Unidos.

exports – exportaciones Bienes producidos en el país y vendidos a residentes de otro país.

externality – externalidad Efecto lateral de una acción que afecta el bienestar de terceros.

F

face value – valor nominal La denominación indicada en el papel moneda o las monedas. Por ejemplo, el valor nominal de una moneda de cinco centavos es cinco centavos, y las palabras cinco centavos aparecen efectivamente en la moneda.

face value (par value) – valor nominal (valor a la par) La cantidad de dólares especificados en la "cara" (parte delantera) de un bono; es la cantidad que el emisor del bono promete pagar al comprador del mismo en la fecha de vencimiento.

federal funds rate – tasa de fondos federales La tasa de interés que un banco cobra a otro banco por un préstamo.

Federal Open Market Committee (FOMC) – Comité Federal de Mercado Abierto Grupo de doce miembros que establece las políticas dentro de la entidad federal. Este comité tiene autoridad para conducir las operaciones de mercado abierto.

Federal Reserve note – pagaré de la Reserva Federal Papel moneda emitido por el Sistema de Reserva Federal.

Federal Reserve System – Sistema de Reserva Federal El Banco Central de los Estados Unidos de América.

fiscal policy – política fiscal Cambios llevados a cabo por un gobierno o tributación para lograr metas económicas específicas.

fixed cost – costo fijo Un costo o gasto que se mantiene sin importar cuántas unidades se produzcan.

fixed exchange rate system – sistema de tasa fija de cambio El sistema mediante el cual las tasas de cambio monetario se mantienen rígidas o "fijadas" por los gobiernos de los países.

flexible exchange rate system – sistema de tasa flexible de cambio El sistema mediante el cual las tasas de cambio monetario se determinan por las fuerzas de la oferta y demanda.

fractional reserve banking – reserva bancaria fraccionada Medidas bancarias mediante las cuales los bancos conservan sólo una fracción de sus depósitos y prestan el saldo.

franchise – concesión Un contrato mediante el cual una empresa (generalmente una sociedad anónima) otorga a una persona o a un grupo el derecho de utilizar su nombre y de vender sus productos a cambio de que se realicen ciertos pagos y que se cumplan ciertos requisitos.

franchisee – concesionario La persona o grupo que adquiere una concesión.

franchiser – franquiciador La entidad que otorga una concesión.

free enterprise – libre empresa Sistema económico en el cual los individuos (no el gobierno) poseen la mayor parte, sino la totalidad, de los recursos y controlan su uso. El gobierno desempeña un papel muy pequeño en la economía.

free rider – a la cochiguagua, a la berlina Persona que recibe los beneficios de un bien sin pagar por él.

frictional unemployment – desempleo friccional Condición de los trabajadores que han perdido su empleo a causa de cambios en las condiciones del mercado (demanda) y que poseen habilidades transferibles.

full employment – empleo pleno La situación que existe cuando la tasa oficial de desempleo es igual a la tasa natural de desempleo.

futures contract – contrato a futuro Convenio de comprar o vender una cantidad específica de algo (mercancía, moneda o instrumento financiero) a un precio determinado o a una fecha futura determinada.

G

general partner – socio general Socio responsable de la administración de la firma y que tiene responsabilidad ilimitada

generic brand – marca genérica Nombre de marca que no usa el nombre de ninguna compañía, y sólo utiliza el nombre del producto.

global economy – economía global Economía en la cual las acciones económicas que se tomen en cualquier punto del mundo pueden afectar el estándar de vida de un individuo.

good – bien Item tangible que presta servicio o satisfacción a un individuo. Algunas veces el bien es llamado producto.

Gosplan – Gosplan Durante el socialismo Soviético de gobierno de la economía, la agencia de planificación que tenía la responsabilidad de delinear el plan económico de la nación,

government purchases – compras fiscales Gastos efectuados por el sector gubernamental. Las compras fiscales no incluyen los pagos gubernamentales de transferencias.

Gresham's law – ley de Gresham Ley económica que sostiene que el dinero malo saca al dinero bueno de circulación. (Dinero malo es aquél que tiene el mismo valor nominal que el dinero bueno pero con un contenido de metal precioso más bajo.)

gross domestic product (GDP) – Producto Doméstico Bruto El valor total de mercado de todos los bienes elaborados y servicios producidos anualmente en una economía.

H

hacker – pirata informático Una persona que interrumpe sistemas computacionales mediante el uso de técnicas de programación altamente complejas.

hedge – eludir Tratar de impedir o disminuir una pérdida llevando a cabo una acción compensatoria.

household – familia Unidad económica compuesta de una o más personas que vende recursos y compra bienes y servicios.

I

import spending – gastos de importación La cantidad gastada por los Americanos en bienes producidos en el exterior.

imports – importaciones Bienes producidos en países extranjeros y comprados por los residentes de un determinado país.

impulse buying – compra compulsiva La compra de productos que no se tenía la intención de comprar. El impulso de comprar sobreviene en forma rápida y el consumidor reacciona comprando el producto.

incentive – incentivo Algo que alienta o motiva a una persona hacia cierta acción.

income distribution – distribución del ingreso La forma en que el ingreso ganado en un país se divide entre los diferentes grupos que perciben ingresos.

inelastic demand – demanda inelástica El tipo de demanda que existe cuando el cambio de porcentaje en la cantidad demandada es menor al cambio de porcentaje en el precio.

inelastic supply – oferta inelástica El tipo de oferta que existe cuando el cambio de porcentaje en la cantidad ofrecida es menor al cambio de porcentaje en el precio.

infant mortality rate – tasa de mortalidad infantil el número anual de muertes de niños que fallecen antes de su primer cumpleaños por cada mil nacimientos vivos.

inferior good – producto inferior Un producto cuya demanda decae en la medida en que sube el ingreso y aumenta en la medida que cae el ingreso.

infrastructure – infraestructura Las estructuras básicas y servicios públicos de cuya continuidad y crecimiento depende una comunidad. Las carreteras interestatales, los puentes y las redes de comunicación son algunos de los ítems que forman la infraestructura de un país.

initial public offering (IPO) – oferta inicial pública La primera oferta pública de acciones de una compañía.

insolvent – insolvente Cuando la suma de pasivos es más alta que la de activos.

intangible – intangible Incapaz de ser percibido al tacto. Por ejemplo, una conferencia de economía es intangible.

intellectual property – propiedad intelectual Material intangible que está legalmente reconocido como propiedad de un individuo o empresa. Los programas de software, las bases de datos y las listas de correspondencia están entre los ítems que se consideran propiedad intelectual.

interest – interés El pago por el recurso capital.

Internet – Internet Un sistema de redes computacionales enlazadas que facilita la comunicación de datos de modo que cada sistema participante puede ampliar su alcance.

inventory – inventario Las existencias de bienes que un negocio o tienda tiene a mano.

inverse relationship – relación inversa Una relación mediante la cual dos variables se mueven en sentido contrario. Cuando sube una variable la otra baja.

investment – inversión Gastos efectuados por el sector empresarial.

investment bank – banco de inversiones Firma que actúa de intermediario entre una compañía que emite acciones y el público que desea adquirir dichos valores.

J

junk bond – bono chatarra Un bono con un alto riesgo de incumplimiento.

L

labor – trabajo Los talentos físicos e intelectuales de personas que contribuyen a la producción de bienes y servicios.

labor theory of value – teoría del valor laboral Teoría que sostiene que todo el valor de los bienes producidos se deriva del trabajo.

labor union – sindicato laboral Organización que busca incrementar los salarios y mejorar las condiciones laborales de sus miembros.

Laffer curve – curva de Laffer Esta curva, que lleva el nombre del economista Arthur Laffer, muestra la relación entre las tasas de impuestos y los ingresos tributarios. De acuerdo con la curva de Laffer, cuando las tasas de impuestos suben de cero, los ingresos tributarios crecen, llegan a un máximo en un punto determinado, y luego caen si se siguen elevando los impuestos.

land – tierra Todos los recursos naturales encontrados en la naturaleza. Se considera tierra a un terreno de un acre, a un depósito de minerales, o al agua de un arroyo.

law of demand – ley de demanda Ley que enuncia que a medida que aumenta el precio de un bien, disminuye su demanda y que a medida que disminuye su precio, aumenta la demanda por ese bien.

law of diminishing marginal returns – ley de rendimientos desscrecientes Una ley que estipula que si se agregan unidades adicionales de un recurso (tal como los trabajadores) a otro recurso fijo (tal como el capital), a la larga el rendimiento disminuirá (debido a la contratación de un trabajador adicional).

law of diminishing marginal utility – ley de disminución de utilidad marginal Ley que enuncia que a medida que una persona consume unidades adicionales de un bien, las utilidades ganadas por cada unidad adicional del bien, eventualmente disminuirán.

law of supply – ley de oferta Ley que enuncia que a medida que aumenta el precio de un producto, la cantidad ofertada aumenta, y a medida que disminuye el precio de un bien la cantidad ofertada disminuye.

lease – contrato de arriendo Contrato que cede una propiedad (por ejemplo, un departamento) por un período específico de tiempo a cambio de una suma de dinero.

less-developed country (LDC) – país menos desarrollado País con un Producto Doméstico Bruto o Producto Nacional Bruto per cápita relativamente bajo.

liability – pasivo Con respecto a un banco, sus deudas.

limited liability - responsabilidad limitada Una condición por medio de la cual el propietario de una empresa sólo puede perder el monto de dinero que él o ella ha invertido (en la empresa). Los accionistas de una sociedad anónima tienen responsabilidad limitada.

limited partner – socio comanditario Socio que no puede participar en la administración de la firma y que tiene responsabilidad limitada.

loss – pérdida La cantidad de dinero en que los costos totales exceden a los ingresos totales.

M

macroeconomics – macroeconomía La rama de la economía que se ocupa del comportamiento y opciones humanas en cuanto se relacionan a la economía global.

marginal cost – costo límite o marginal El gasto adicional que significa producir una unidad adicional de un artículo; la variación del costo total como resultado de la producción de una unidad adicional de un producto.

marginal revenue – ingresos marginales Los ingresos adicionales que se obtienen de la venta de una unidad adicional de un artículo; la variación de los ingresos totales como resultado de la venta de una unidad adicional de un producto.

market – mercado Cualquier lugar en que la gente se reúne para comprar o vender bienes o servicios.

market structure – estructura de mercado El medio en que se encuentra un vendedor. Las estructuras de mercado están definidas por sus características, tales como el número de vendedores en el mercado, el producto que los vendedores producen y venden, y cuan fácil o difícil es para las nuevas firmas ingresar al mercado.

medium of exchange – medio de intercambio Cualquier cosa que sea generalmente aceptable como intercambio por bienes y servicios.

merger – fusión La unión de dos compañías que ocurre cuando una de las compañías adquiere más de la mitad de las acciones de la otra compañía. Tiene como resultado el que ambas compañías actúen como si fueran una.

microeconomics – microeconomía El ramo de la economía que se ocupa del comportamiento y opciones humanas en lo que se refiere a unidades pequeñas - un individuo, una firma comercial o un solo mercado.

minimum wage law – ley de salario mínimo Ley federal que especifica el salario mínimo por hora que puede ser pagado a un trabajador.

mixed economy – economía mixta Economía que no es puramente capitalista ni puramente socialista, una economía que tiene elementos tanto de capitalismo como de socialismo. La mayoría de los países del mundo tienen economías mixtas.

monetary policy – política monetaria El control deliberado de la cantidad de dinero circulante por parte de la entidad federal.

money – dinero Bien ampliamente aceptado para propósitos de intercambio y pago de deudas.

money supply – suministro de dinero La cantidad total de dinero en circulación, compuesto de efectivo, cuentas bancarias, y cheques viajeros.

monitor – monitor La persona en una empresa que coordina la producción de equipos y reduce las evasiones al trabajo.

monopolistic competition – competencia monopólica Estructura de mercado en la cual (1) existen muchos compradores y muchos vendedores, (2) los vendedores producen y venden productos con pequeñas diferencias, y (3) existe fácil ingreso y fácil salida del mercado.

monopoly – monopolio Estructura de mercado en la que (1) existe un solo vendedor, (2) el vendedor vende un producto para el que no existen sustitutos similares, y (3) existen barreras sumamente altas para ingresar.

mortgage note – pagaré hipotecario Convenio escrito por medio del cual el comprador de una propiedad accede a pagar una deuda contraída para comprar la propiedad. Si no se cancela la deuda, el prestamista puede tomar la propiedad.

mutual fund – fondo mutuo Organización financiera que junta el dinero de sus clientes y lo invierte.

N

national brand – marca nacional Un nombre de marca de propiedad del fabricante de un producto. Muchas marcas nacionales son conocidas por todo el país, como son Kellogg's y Coca-Cola.

national debt – deuda nacional La suma total de lo que el gobierno federal debe a sus acreedores.

natural monopoly – monopolio natural Una firma cuyo promedio de costo total es tan bajo (costo por unidad) que sólo ella puede subsistir en el mercado.

natural unemployment – desempleo natural Desempleo causado por factores friccionales y estructurales de la economía.

near-money – cuasi dinero Activos, como ser cuentas de ahorro sin cheques que pueden ser fácil y rápidamente convertidos en dinero.

negative externality – externalidad negativa Efecto lateral adverso de una acción que es sentido por terceros.

net worth (equity, capital) – valor neto (capital social, capital) La diferencia entre activos y pasivos.

neutral good – producto neutro Producto cuya demanda permanece estable, aunque suba o baje el ingreso.

nonexcludable public good – bien público no excluible Un bien público de cuyo consumo no se puede excluir (prohibir físicamente) a los individuos.

normal good – producto normal Un producto cuya demanda sube cuando aumenta el ingreso y baja si el ingreso baja.

O

oligopoly – oligopolio Estructura de mercado en la cual (1) hay pocos vendedores, (2) los vendedores producen y venden productos idénticos o con muy ligeras diferencias, y (3) existen barreras significativas para ingresar.

open market operations – operaciones de libre mercado La compra y venta de valores gubernamentales por parte de la entidad federal.

opportunity cost – costo de oportunidad La pérdida de la oportunidad o alternativa más altamente valuada cuando se hace una elección.

option – opción Contrato que da el derecho al propietario, pero no la obligación, de comprar o vender acciones de un capital comercial a un precio específico en o antes de una fecha determinada.

P

par value *Miré* ***face value (par value)***

partnership – sociedad Empresa de propiedad de dos o más co-dueños, llamados socios, que comparten las ganancias que obtiene la empresa y que son legalmente responsables de cualquier deuda en que incurra la empresa.

per-capita real economic growth – crecimiento económico real per cápita Aumento de un período a otro en el Producto Doméstico Bruto real per cápita, que lo constituye el Producto Doméstico Bruto real dividido por la población.

per unit cost – costo por unidad El costo promedio total de un producto. Por ejemplo, si se gastan $400.000 para producir 100 automóviles, el costo promedio o por unidad es de $4.000.

perfect competition – competencia perfecta Estructura de mercado en la cual (1) existen muchos compradores y vendedores, (2) todas las firmas venden productos idénticos, (3) los compradores y vendedores poseen toda la información relevante acerca de las actividades de compra y venta, y (4) existe facilidad de ingreso al mercado y facilidad de retiro del mismo.

personal income tax – impuesto personal a la renta Impuesto pagado sobre los ingresos de una persona.

point – punto Punto porcentual de la cifra de un préstamo. Los puntos son pagados por el prestatario al prestamista.

population growth rate – tasa de crecimiento de la población La tasa de nacimiento menos la tasa de mortalidad.

positive externality – externalidad positiva Efecto lateral benéfico de una acción que es sentido por terceros.

price discrimination – discriminación de precios Lo que ocurre cuando un vendedor cobra precios diferentes a diferentes compradores del mismo producto y estas diferencias de precios no están relacionadas a diferencias en los costos.

price index – índice de precios Medida del nivel de precios, o el nivel promedio de los precios.

price searcher – vendedor con libertad de fijar precios Vendedor que puede vender parte de su producción a precios diferentes.

price taker – vendedor sin libertad de fijar precios Vendedor que puede vender toda su producción al precio de equilibrio pero que no puede vender ninguna parte de su producción a cualquier otro precio.

private brand – marca privada Marca de propiedad del vendedor en vez del productor del bien. Por ejemplo, a veces se producen algunos productos para una cadena determinada de supermercados y llevan el nombre de esa cadena en la etiqueta.

private good – bien privado Un producto que al ser consumido por una persona, excluye de su consumo a terceros. Un automóvil es un bien privado.

private property – propiedad privada Cualquier bien que es poseído por un individuo o una empresa.

production possibilities frontier (PPF) – frontera de posibilidades de producción Todas las combinaciones posibles de dos productos que puede producir una economía en un determinado período de tiempo, bajo condiciones de un estado tecnológico dado, sin desempleo de recursos y producción eficiente.

profit – ganancia La suma de dinero que queda tan pronto como todos los costos de producción han sido pagados. También el pago al recurso empresarial. La ganancia existe toda vez que el ingreso total es mayor que el costo total.

progressive income tax – impuesto a la renta progresivo Impuesto a la renta cuya tasa sube cuando sube el nivel de ingreso. Las estructuras de impuesto a la renta progresivo están generalmente limitadas en cierta tasa.

proportional income tax – impuesto a la renta proporcional Impuesto a la renta en que todos pagan la misma tasa, sin importar el nivel.

public franchise – franquicia pública Derecho otorgado a una firma por el gobierno que permite a dicha firma suministrar un determinado producto o servicio y excluye a todos los demás de hacer lo mismo.

public good – bien público Un bien cuyo consumo no excluye a los demás de su consumo. La defensa nacional es un bien público.

public property – propiedad pública Cualquier bien de propiedad del gobierno.

public utility commission – comisión de servicios públicos Grupo gubernamental que regula a las compañías de servicios públicos (como ser las compañías de electricidad, de agua y de gas).

Q

quantity demanded – cantidad demandada Número de unidades de un bien comprado a un precio específico.

quantity supplied – cantidad ofertada El número de unidades de un bien producido y ofrecido a la venta a un precio específico.

quota – cuota Límite legal al número de unidades de un bien producido en el extranjero (importado) que puede ingresar al país.

R

rationing device – dispositivo de racionamiento Un medio para decidir quien obtiene cual porción de los recursos y bienes disponibles.

real GDP – Producto Doméstico Bruto real Producto Doméstico Bruto que ha sido ajustado según la variación de precios; el Producto Doméstico Bruto se mide en precios constantes o de año base.

recession – recesión Una desaceleración de la economía marcada por la caída del Producto Doméstico Bruto durante dos trimestres consecutivos.

regressive income tax – impuesto a la renta regresivo Impuesto a la renta cuya tasa disminuye a medida que sube el ingreso.

rent – alquiler El pago al recurso tierra.

required reserves – reservas exigidas Cantidad mínima de reservas que un banco debe mantener como respaldo de sus depósitos en conformidad con lo estipulado por la entidad federal.

reserve account – cuenta de reservas Cuenta corriente de un banco con el banco de la Reserva Federal de su distrito.

reserve requirement – exigencia de reservas Reglamento que exige que un banco mantenga un cierto porcentaje de cada dólar depositado en el banco en su cuenta de reservas con la entidad federal o en su bóveda (como efectivo de bóveda).

residual claimant – derecho residual Persona que tiene participación en las ganancias de una firma comercial.

resource – recurso Cualquier cosa que se utiliza para producir bienes o servicios. Por ejemplo, el trabajo de una persona puede ser utilizado para producir computadoras, receptores de televisión, y mucho más, y por lo tanto, el trabajo de una persona es un recurso. Existen cuatro categorías de recursos: tierra, trabajo, capital y espíritu empresarial.

résumé – curriculum vitae Informe sobre los empleos anteriores, la educación, y otros datos de un candidato a un puesto de trabajo.

reverse auction - subasta invertida Una subasta en donde el comprador declara el precio que está dispuesto a pagar a cambio de un artículo o de un servicio y en donde el vendedor decide si desea realizar la venta de acuerdo a esos términos.

right-to-work law - ley de derecho al trabajo Ley estatal que prohibe la práctica de exigir a los empleados ingresar a un sindicato para poder obtener un trabajo.

rule of law - gobierno de la ley El hecho de gobernar mediante la ley o leyes (en lugar de mediante hombres y mujeres).

S

savings account - cuenta de ahorro Cuenta que gana intereses.

scarcity - escasez La condición en la cual nuestras necesidades son mayores que los recursos disponibles para satisfacer esas necesidades.

security deposit - depósito de garantía Suma de dinero que un arrendatario paga al dueño de una propiedad al mudarse a un departamento (o a otra propiedad de renta). El dinero debe ser devuelto cuando el arrendatario deje la propiedad, pero el dueño puede quedarse con parte o la totalidad del depósito para efectuar reparaciones o como compensación por renta no pagada.

service - servicio Item intangible que presta utilidad o satisfacción a una persona.

shirking - evasión Comportamiento de un trabajador que hace un esfuerzo de trabajo menor al acordado.

shortage - escasez Condición en la cual la cantidad demandada de un producto es mayor que la cantidad ofertada. La escasez ocurre solamente cuando los precios están por debajo del precio de equilibrio.

simple quantity theory of money - teoría monetaria de cantidad simple Teoría que predice que los cambios en el nivel de precios serán estrictamente proporcionales a los cambios en el suministro de dinero.

socialism - socialismo Sistema económico en el cual el gobierno posee y controla gran parte de los recursos. El gobierno representa un papel muy importante en la economía.

sole propietorship - único dueño Empresa perteneciente a un solo individuo, quien efectúa todos los negocios y decisiones y recibe todas las ganancias o sufre todas las pérdidas de la firma, y es legalmente responsable de todas las deudas de la firma.

specialize - especialización Hacer sólo una cosa. Por ejemplo, cuando un país se especializa en la producción de un producto, produce solamente ese producto.

stagflation - estagflación La ocurrencia de inflación y de un alto nivel de desempleo al mismo tiempo.

status quo - status quo Lo que existe en este momento; el estado actual de las cosas.

stock - acciones Derecho sobre los activos de una sociedad anónima que otorga el comprador una participación en la propiedad de la sociedad.

stockholder - accionista Persona que posee acciones de una sociedad anónima. Los accionistas de una sociedad anónima son los dueños de la sociedad.

stop-and-go, on-and-off monetary policy - política monetaria de pare-siga, conecte-desconecte Política económica errática. Se aumenta el suministro de dinero, luego se disminuye, se vuelve a incrementar y así sucesivamente. Es similar a manejar un auto apretando el acelerador hasta el piso, luego apretar el freno, luego volver a acelerar a fondo para volver a pegar una frenada, y así sucesivamente.

store of value - conservar su valor Algo que conserva su valor a través del tiempo.

strike - huelga Paro laboral convocado por un sindicato para presionar a un empleador.

structural unemployment - desempleo estructural Condición de los trabajadores que han perdido sus trabajos a causa de las condiciones cambiantes del mercado (demanda) y cuyas habilidades no coinciden con los requerimientos de los trabajos disponibles.

sublease - subarrendar Arrendar un departamento a un arrendatario en lugar de al dueño.

subsidy - subsidio Pago financiero efectuado por el gobierno para determinadas acciones.

substitute - substituto Producto similar. En el caso de los sustitutos, el precio de uno y la demanda por el otro se mueven en la misma dirección.

supply - oferta El deseo y capacidad de los vendedores de producir y ofrecer a la venta un producto o servicio.

supply curve - curva de oferta Gráfico que muestra la cantidad de un producto que los vendedores desean y son capaces de vender a diferentes precios. Sólo una curva de oferta inclinada hacia arriba, constituye una representación gráfica de la ley de oferta.

supply schedule - plan de oferta Cuadro numérico que ilustra la ley de oferta.

supply-side inflation – inflación por oferta Aumento del nivel de precios que se origina en el sector de oferta de la economía.

surplus – excedente Condición en la cual la cantidad ofertada de un producto es mayor que la cantidad demandada. Los excedentes ocurren solamente con precios sobre el precio de equilibrio.

surplus value – valor de excedente En terminología Marxista, la diferencia entre el valor total de la producción y los salarios de subsistencia pagados a los trabajadores.

T

Taft-Hartley Act – Ley Taft-Hartley Ley aprobada en 1947 por el Congreso de los Estados Unidos, que convirtió a la empresa cerrada en ilegal, y dio el derecho a los Estados a aprobar leyes de derecho al trabajo. Estas leyes de derecho al trabajo prohiben a los empleadores el convertir la asociación a un sindicato en condición de empleo.

tangible – tangible Capaz de ser sentido por el tacto. Por ejemplo, un libro es tangible: se puede tocar y sentir.

tariff – tarifa, derecho Impuesto sobre las importaciones.

technology – tecnología El conjunto de habilidades y conocimientos relativos al uso de recursos en la producción.

telemarketing – mercado telefónico Ventas directas de productos por vía telefónica.

theory – teoría Explicación sobre el funcionamiento de una cosa. Diseñada para responder a una pregunta sobre la cual no existe una respuesta obvia.

total cost – costo total El costo (o gasto) promedio de un producto multiplicado por el número de unidades vendidas de ese producto. El costo total es el resultado del costo promedio multiplicado por el número de unidades vendidas. La suma de los costos fijos y los costos variables.

total reserves – total de reservas La suma de los depósitos bancarios en la cuenta de reservas de la entidad federal y del efectivo de bóveda.

total revenue – total de ingreso El precio de un producto multiplicado por el número de unidades vendidas. El total de ingresos es el resultado del precio multiplicado por el número de unidades vendidas.

trade-off – negociación Equilibrio de factores que no están todos disponibles al mismo tiempo. La naturaleza de la negociación es que uno debe renunciar a algo deseable para obtener otra cosa que es deseable. Una situación en la cual más de una cosa necesariamente significa menos de otra cosa.

traditional economy – economía tradicional Sistema económico en el cual las respuestas a las tres preguntas económicas están basadas en las costumbres, las tradiciones y las creencias culturales.

transaction costs – costos de transacción Los costos asociados con el tiempo y esfuerzo necesarios para buscar, negociar y consumar un intercambio.

trust – consorcio Combinación de firmas que se unen para actuar como monopolistas.

U

unemployment rate – tasa de desempleo Porcentaje de la fuerza laboral civil que está desempleada. La tasa de desempleo es el resultado de las personas desempleadas dividido por la fuerza laboral civil.

union shop – negocio sindicado Organización que exige a los empleados ingresar al sindicato dentro de un período de tiempo posterior a su contratación.

unit of account – unidad de cuenta Medida común en la cual se expresan los valores.

unit price – precio por unidad El precio total de un producto dividido por su peso.

unit-elastic demand – demanda elástica de unidad El tipo de demanda que existe cuando el porcentaje de cambio en la cantidad pedida es igual al porcentaje de cambio en el precio.

unit-elastic supply – oferta elástica de unidad El tipo de oferta que existe cuando el porcentaje del cambio en la cantidad ofertada es igual al porcentaje del cambio en el precio.

unlimited liability – responsabilidad ilimitada La responsabilidad legal de un único dueño de un negocio o de los socios de un negocio de pagar cualquier dinero adeudado por la firma. Los bienes personales del dueño o de los socios se pueden utilizar para pagar estas deudas.

V

variable cost – costo o gasto variable Un costo o gasto que cambia de acuerdo al número de unidades de un artículo que se produzca.

velocity – rotación de circulante El número promedio de veces en que se utiliza un dólar para comprar productos elaborados y servicios durante un año.

vicious circle of poverty – círculo vicioso de la pobreza La idea de que los países son pobres porque no ahorran para adquirir bienes de capital, pero ellos no pueden ahorrar y comprar bienes de capital porque son pobres.

vision – visión Un sentido acerca de cómo funciona el mundo.

W

wage rate – tasa de salario El precio del trabajo.

wages – salarios El pago al recurso trabajo.

want – necesidad Algo que deseamos tener.

warranty – garantía Garantía o seguridad que da el vendedor aseverando que un producto está en buenas condiciones de funcionamiento y que el vendedor va a proporcionar cierto tipo de servicios por un período de tiempo.

Web site - sitio Web Un sitio o ubicación en la Red Mundial. Un sitio Web está compuesto de una página o páginas que pueden contener texto, gráficos, videos y fuentes de audio.

World Wide Web - Red Mundial Sistema global de sitios Web o ubicaciones.

Index

C

D

E

F

G

H

I

J

K

L

M

N

O

P

T

U

V

W

Y

Z

Photo Credits

Unit Openers **2** Richard Cummins/ CORBIS; **136** © Roman Eschel/CORBIS; **262** © Michael S. Yamashita/CORBIS; **442** © The Purcell Team/CORBIS; **534** © Paul A. Souders/CORBIS.

Chapter 1 **4** © Davy Crockett/CORBIS; **6** © Chris Briscoe/Index Stock; **7 (bottom)** © Paul Barton/The Stock Market; **9** © The Purcell Team/CORBIS; **10** © PhotoDisc; **11** © SW Production/Index Stock; **12** © Michael Keller/Index Stock; **14 (top)** © Bob Rowan/CORBIS; **14 (bottom)** © Stock Index; **15** © Chris Sorenson/The Stock Market; **16** © PhotoDisc; **17 (top)** © PhotoDisc; **17 (bottom)** © AFP/ CORBIS; **19** © Elizabeth Hathon/The Stock Market; **21** Reuters Newmedia Inc./CORBIS; **22 (top)** © David Young–Wolff/PhotoEdit; **22 (bottom left)** © CORBIS; **22 (bottom right)** © CORBIS; **23** © Steve Chenn/ CORBIS; **24 (top)** © Digital Stock; **24 (Inset)** © Anthony Bannister; Gallo Images/CORBIS; **24 (bottom)** © Index Stock; **25 (top)** © Digital Stock; **25 (bottom)** © Associated Press AP; **26** © Bettmann/CORBIS; **27 (top)** © Tom Nebbia/CORBIS; **27 (bottom)** © Richard Hamilton Smith/CORBIS; **29** © Vince Streano/CORBIS.

Chapter 2 **36** © Michael S. Yamashita/ CORBIS; **35** © PhotoDisc; **38 (top)** © PhotoDisc; **38 (bottom)** © Kevork Djansezian Associated Press; **39** © Index Stock; **40** © Bettmann/CORBIS; **41** © PhotoDisc; **42** © PhotoDisc; **44** © David Tumley/CORBIS; **47 (top)** © RNT Productions/CORBIS; **47 (bottom)** © Catherine Kamow/CORBIS; **48** © Joseph Sohm; ChromoSohm Inc./CORBIS; **48 (inset)** © Scott T. Smith/CORBIS; **49** © SW Production/Index Stock; **50** © PhotoDisc and © Image Club Graphics; **51** © Index Stock; **52** © PhotoDisc; **54** © PhotoDisc; **55 (top)** © Digital Stock; **55 (bottom)** © PhotoDisc; **56 (top)** © Jim Sugar Photography/CORBIS; **56 (bottom)** © Jim Winkley; Ecoscene/CORBIS; **57** © PhotoDisc; **58** © PhotoDisc and © Digital Stock; **60** © PhotoDisc; **61** © PhotoDisc; **63** © PhotoDisc.

Chapter 3 **64** © Owen Franken/CORBIS; **66** © PhotoDisc; **67** Digital Stock; **68** © Ted Streshinsky/CORBIS; **69** © AFP/CORBIS; **72** © Nik Wheeler/CORBIS; **74** © PhotoDisc; **78** © Digital Stock; **79 (top)** © Digital Stock; **79 (bottom)** © PhotoDisc; **80** © Duomo/CORBIS; **82** © Benjamin Randel/ The Stock Market; **82 (inset)** © FPG International; **83** © PhotoDisc; **85** © Owen Franken/CORBIS; **87** © Digital Stock.

Chapter 4 **88** © Jim Sugar Photography/ CORBIS; **90** © Dan Lamont/CORBIS; **91** © Dan Lamont/CORBIS; **91 (inset)** © Digital Stock; **92** © PhotoDisc; **97** © Steve Strickland/CORBIS; **98** © PhotoDisc; **99** © Philip Richardson; Gallo Images/CORBIS; **100** © Bettmann/CORBIS; **101** © Minnesota Historical Society/ CORBIS; **107** © PhotoDisc.

Chapter 5 **108** © Michael S. Yamashita/ CORBIS; **110** © PhotoDisc; **112** © R. W. Jones/CORBIS; **114 (top)** © Bettmann/ CORBIS; **114 (middle)** © Bettmann/ CORBIS; **114 (bottom)** © AFP/CORBIS; **116** © Paul A. Souders/CORBIS; **117** © PhotoDisc; **120** AFP/CORBIS; **121** © AFP/CORBIS; **122** © Shelley Gazin/ CORBIS; **122 (inset)** © Digital Stock; **123** © Dave G. Houser/CORBIS; **123 (inset)** © Robert Holmes/CORBIS; **124 (top)** © Robert Holmes/CORBIS; **124 (bottom)** © AFP/ CORBIS; **125** © Owen Franken/ CORBIS; **127** © Robert Holmes/CORBIS; **128** © Digital Stock; **129** © Laura Dwight/CORBIS; **131 (top)** © PhotoDisc; **131 (bottom)** © Walley McNamee/ CORBIS; **133** © Digital Stock; **134** © PhotoDisc; **135** © PhotoDisc.

Chapter 6 **138** © Reuters Newmedia Inc./ CORBIS; **140** © CORBIS; **141** © Dean Conger/CORBIS; **142 (top)** © Jonathan Blair/CORBIS; **142 (bottom)** © James P. Blair/CORBIS; **143** © Richard Hamilton Smith/CORBIS; **144 (top)** © Bill Varie/ CORBIS; **144 (bottom)** © Ariel Skelley/The Stock Market; **145 (top)** © Reuters Newmedia Inc./CORBIS; **145 (bottom)** © Lee Snider/CORBIS; **146** © Stewart Cohen/ Index Stock; **147 (left)** © AP Photo/Stevan Morgian; **147 (right)** © Bettmann/ CORBIS; **149 (top)** © Adamsmith Productions/CORBIS; **149 (bottom)** © The Stock Market; **151** © Index Stock; **152** © Bettmann/CORBIS; **153** © Philip Gould/ CORBIS; **154** © Gary Conner/Index Stock; **155** © Lynn Edoice/Index Stock; **156** © MacDuff Everton/CORBIS; **158** © Associated Press/AP; **160** © Jonathan Blair/ CORBIS; **160 (inset)** © PhotoDisc; **161** © George Lepp/CORBIS; **163** © Digital Stock; **164** © PhotoDisc; **166** © AP/Wide World Photos; **167** © PhotoDisc; **169** © Index Stock.

Chapter 7 **170** © Kevin Fleming/CORBIS; **172 (top)** © Ted Streshinsky/CORBIS; **172 (bottom)** © Peter Tumley/CORBIS; **173** © Michael Lewis/CORBIS; **174 (top)** © James P. Blair/CORBIS; **174 (middle)** © Reuter Newmedia Inc./CORBIS; **174 (bottom)** © PhotoDisc; **175 (top)** © Digital Stock; **175 (inset)** © Digital Stock; **175 (bottom)** © Photo Disc; **176** © Photo Disc; **177** © Digital Stock; **177 (inset)** © PhotoDisc; **178** © Robert Maass/CORBIS; **178 (inset)** John-Marshall Mantel/ CORBIS; **179** © Bettmann/CORBIS; **181** © R. W. Jones/ CORBIS; **182** © Robert Trubia/CORBIS; **183** © Roger Wood/CORBIS; **184** © Digital Stock; **185** © Reuters Newmedia Inc./ CORBIS; **185 (inset)** © Alisca Crandall/ CORBIS; **186** © Wolfgang Kaehler/ CORBIS; **186 (inset)** © Digital Stock; **186 (bottom)** © Michael S. Yamashita/CORBIS; **187** © PhotoDisc; **188 (top)** © Steve Raymer/CORBIS; **187** © PhotoDisc; **188 (top)** © Steve Raymer/CORBIS; **188 (bottom)** © Digital Stock; **190** © Kevin Fleming/CORBIS; **191** © Digital Stock; **191 (inset)** © Reuters Newmedia Inc./ CORBIS; **192 (top)** © Joseph Sohm; ChromoSohm Inc./CORBIS; **192 (bottom)** © John-marshall Mantel/CORBIS;**193 (top)** © PhotoDisc; **193 (bottom)** © Digital Stock; **194** © Digital Stock; **195** © Bob Kast/ CORBIS; **196** © PhotoDisc; **197** © Index Stock; **199** © Reuters Newmedia Inc./ CORBIS.

Chapter 8 **200** © Bill Varie/CORBIS; **202** © Reuters Newmedia Inc./CORBIS; **204 (top)** © Digital Stock; **204 (bottom)** © PhotoDisc; **205** © Reuters Newmedia Inc./ CORBIS; **206** © PhotoDisc; **208** © AFP/ CORBIS; **209** © Kevin Morris/CORBIS; **210 (top)** © Michael Pole/CORBIS; **210 (middle)** © PhotoDisc; **210 (bottom)** © PhotoDisc; **211** © Reuters Newmedia Inc./CORBIS; **212** © PhotoDisc; **213 (left)** © PhotoDisc; **213 (right)** © PhotoDisc; **214** © Digital Stock; **216 (left)** © David H. Wells/CORBIS; **217 (right)** © Cathy Crawford/CORBIS; **218 (left)** © Roger Ressmeyer/CORBIS; **218 (right)** © PhotoDisc; **220 (top)** © AFP/CORBIS; **220 (bottom)** © Galen Rowell/CORBIS; **221** © AFP/CORBIS; **222 (top)** © Bettmann/ CORBIS; **222 (bottom)** © Bettmann/ CORBIS; **223 (top)** © Museum of Flight/ CORBIS; **223 (inset)** © Bettmann/ CORBIS; **223 (bottom)** © Bettmann/ CORBIS; **224** © PhotoDisc; **226 (top)** © PhotoDisc; **226 (bottom)** © PhotoDisc; **227** © Philip Gould/CORBIS; **228 (left)** © PhotoDisc; **228 (right)** © PhotoDisc; **229** © PhotoDisc; **231** © Paul A Souders/ CORBIS.

Chapter 9 **232** © CORBIS; **234** © Bettmann/CORBIS; **234 (inset)** © Bettmann/CORBIS; **235** © Steve Chenn/ CORBIS; **236 (top)** © PhotoDisc; **236 (bottom)** © Bob Rowan; Progressive Image/CORBIS; **237 (top)** © Bettmann/ CORBIS; **237 (bottom)** © Horace Bristol/CORBIS; **238** © AFP/CORBIS; **239** © CORBIS; **240** © Kevin Fleming/CORBIS; **241** © AFP/CORBIS; **245 (top)** © Layne Kennedy/CORBIS; **245 (bottom)** © Tim Wright/CORBIS; **245 (inset)** © Patrick Ward/CORBIS; **246 (top)** © PhotoDisc; **246 (bottom)** © PhotoDisc; **247 (top)** © PhotoDisc; **247 (bottom)** © Danny Lehman/CORBIS; **248** © Joseph Sohm; ChromoSohm Inc./CORBIS; **250 (top)** © Kevin P. Morris/CORBIS; **250 (inset)** © PhotoDisc; **250 (bottom)** © Roger Chester; Eye Ubiquitious/CORBIS; **251** © Digital Stock; **252** © PhotoDisc; **254 (top)** © Philip Gould/CORBIS; **254 (bottom)** ©

Paul Souders/CORBIS; **255 (inset)** © PhotoDisc; **255** © PhotoDisc; **256** © Richard Hamilton Smith/CORBIS; **257** © PhotoDisc; **259** © PhotoDisc; **260** © PhotoDisc; **261** © PhotoDisc.

Chapter 10 **264** © Reuters Newmedia Inc./ CORBIS; **266** © Bettmann/CORBIS; **267 (left)** © Mimmo Jodice/CORBIS; **267 (middle)** © Wolfgang Kaehler/CORBIS; **267 (right)** © Charles & Josette Lenars/ CORBIS; **269 (top)** © Hulton-Deutsch Collection/CORBIS; **269 (bottom)** © Bettmann/CORBIS; **270** © PhotoDisc; **271** © Ted Spiegel/CORBIS; **271 (inset)** © Bettmann/CORBIS; **272** © Neal Preston/ CORBIS; **274 (left)** © Nathan Benn/ CORBIS; **274 (right)** © Adam Woolhill/ CORBIS; **275** © D. Boone/CORBIS; **276** © D. Boone/CORBIS; **277** © PhotoEdit; **279** © PhotoEdit; **280** © Digital Art/CORBIS; **285** © PhotoDisc.

Chapter 11 **286** © Sandy Felsenthal/ CORBIS; **288** © Reuters Newmedia Inc./ CORBIS; **289** © Reuters Newmedia Inc./ CORBIS; **290** © PhotoDisc; **291 (left)** © Henry Diltz/CORBIS; **291 (right)** Bettmann/ CORBIS; **293** © Michael S. Yamashita/ CORBIS; **295 (top)** © Bettmann/CORBIS; **295 (bottom)** © CORBIS; **296** © Reuters Newmedia Inc./ CORBIS; **298 (left)** © B. Franklin/CORBIS; **298 (right)** © Bob Rowan; Progressive Image/CORBIS; **299** © Steve Chenn/ CORBIS; **300** © PhotoDisc; **302** © Joseph Sohm/ ChromoSohm Inc./ CORBIS; **302** © Roger Ressmeyer/CORBIS; **302 (inset)** © Bettmann/CORBIS; **307** © Richard Hamilton Smith/CORBIS; **309** © William Taufic/The Stock Market.

Chapter 12 **310** © Reuters Newmedia Inc./ CORBIS; **312** © PhotoDisc; **313** © RNT Productions/CORBIS; **314** © Digital Stock; **315** © PhotoDisc; **316 (top)** © Tim Wright/CORBIS; **316 (bottom)** © PhotoDisc; **317 (left)** © Owen Franken/CORBIS; **317 (right)** © Paul A. Souders/CORBIS; **319** © Stephanie Maze/CORBIS; **320** © Owen Franken/CORBIS; **321** © Owen Franken/CORBIS; **322 (left)** © Amanda Gazidis/CORBIS; **322 (right)** © Karen Huntt Mason/CORBIS; **323** © Richard T. Nowitz/CORBIS; **324** © Hulton-Deutsch Collection/CORBIS; **327** © AFP/CORBIS; **330** © Digital Stock; **332 (left)** © George Kleiman/CORBIS/ **332 (right)** © AFP/ CORBIS; **333** © Kevin Fleming/CORBIS; **333 (inset)** © Reuters Newmedia Inc./ CORBIS; **335** © Richard Hamilton Smith/ CORBIS; **337** © PhotoDisc.

Chapter 13 **338** © Lee White/CORBIS; **340** © W. Wayne Lockwood, M.D./ CORBIS; **342 (top)** © Christine Osborne/CORBIS; **342 (bottom)** © PhotoDisc; **343** © PhotoDisc; **347** © Hulton/ Deutsch Collection/ CORBIS; **347 (inset)** © Archive Iconografico, S.A./CORBIS; **348** © Bob Rowan; Progressive Image/CORBIS; **349** © Richard Bickel/CORBIS; **350** © AFP/CORBIS; **350 (inset)** © World Films Enterprise/CORBIS; **351** © Kevin P. Morris/CORBIS; **353** © Kevin P. Morris/ CORBIS; **353 (left inset)** © Charles O'Rear/CORBIS; **353 (bottom inset)** © PhotoDisc; **354** © Philip Gould/ CORBIS; **355 (top)** © Richard Hamilton Smith/CORBIS; **355 (bottom)** © Reuters Newmedia Inc./CORBIS; **355 (bottom inset)** © Richard Hamilton Smith/ CORBIS; **356** © PhotoDisc; **356 (inset)** © Digital Stock; **358** © Tony Arruza/CORBIS; **359** © PhotoDisc; **363** © Todd Gipstein/ CORBIS.

Chapter 14 **364** © Patrick Bennett/ CORBIS; **366** © Richard Cummins/ CORBIS; **367 (top)** © Bettmann/CORBIS; **367 (bottom)** © Underwood & Underwood/CORBIS; **368 (top)** © PhotoDisc; **368 (bottom)** © PhotoDisc; **369 (top)** © USA Today; **369 (bottom)** © Reuters Newmedia Inc./CORBIS; **371 (top)** © Digital Stock; **371 (bottom)** © PhotoDisc; **372** © Bettmann/CORBIS; **373** © Peter Turnley/CORBIS; **374** © AFP/ CORBIS; **375 (left)** © Paul Almasy/ CORBIS; **375 (right)** © Ali Meyer/ CORBIS; **378** © Steve Chenn/CORBIS; **379** © Reuters Newmedia, Inc./CORBIS; **380 (top left)** © Jack Fields/CORBIS; **380 (top right)** © Dean Conger/CORBIS; **380 (bottom)** © Janet Wishnelsky/CORBIS; **382** © Roger Ressmeyer/CORBIS; **383** © Steve Raymer/CORBIS; **384** © AFP/ CORBIS; **387** © Charles O'Rear/CORBIS.

Chapter 15 **388** © Reuters Newmedia Inc./ CORBIS; **390 (left)** © CORBIS; **390 (right)** © Wally McNamee/CORBIS; **391** © James P. Blair/CORBIS; **392 (top)** © PhotoDisc; **392 (bottom)** © PhotoDisc; **393** © AFP/ CORBIS; **394** © Hulton-Deutsch Collection/ CORBIS; **395 (top left)** © Paul A. Souders/CORBIS; **395 (top right)** © AFP/ CORBIS; **395 (bottom)** © Bob Krist/ CORBIS; **396** © Philip Gould/CORBIS; **398** © Roger Ressmeyer/CORBIS; **399** © R. W. Jones/ CORBIS; **400** © Davy Crockett/ CORBIS; **401** © PhotoDisc; **402** © Bettmann/ CORBIS; **404** © Robert Maass/ CORBIS; **405** © Nick Gunderson/CORBIS; **407** © CORBIS; **408** © H. David Seawell/ CORBIS; **409** © Reuters Newmedia Inc./ CORBIS; **410 (top)** © PhotoDisc; **410 (bottom)** © Tim Sugar Photography/ CORBIS; **411 (top)** © Pablo Corral V/CORBIS; **411 (bottom)** © Nik Wheeler/CORBIS; **412** © Lowell Georgia/CORBIS; **413** © Joseph Sohm/ChromoSohm Inc./CORBIS; **415** © Wally McNamee/CORBIS.

Chapter 16 **416** © Adam Woolfitt/ CORBIS; **418 (bottom)** © AFP/CORBIS; **420 (top)** © Danny Lehman/CORBIS; **420 (bottom)** © Kevin P. Morris/CORBIS; **422** © Paul A. Souders/CORBIS; **423 (top)** © Peter Turnley/CORBIS; **423 (bottom)** © PhotoDisc; **424** © AFP/CORBIS; **426 (top)** © Wally McNamee/CORBIS; **426 (bottom)** © Reuters Newmedia Inc./CORBIS; **427 (top)** © AFP/CORBIS; **427** (bottom) © Richard T. Nowitz/CORBIS; **428** © George Hall/CORBIS; **429 (left)** © Yogi, Inc./ CORBIS; **429 (right)** © PhotoDisc; **431** © Bettmann/CORBIS; **432** © CORBIS; **432 (inset)** © Bettmann/CORBIS; **433** © PhotoDisc; **434** © Jim Zukerman/CORBIS; **436** © David H. Wells/CORBIS; **437** © PhotoDisc; **439** © AP/Wide World Photos; **440** © AP/ Wide World Photos; **441** © Lee White/ CORBIS.

Chapter 17 **444** © Peter Turnley/CORBIS; **446 (left)** © Pablo Corral/CORBIS; **446 (right)** © Jonathan Blair/CORBIS; **448 (top)** © Francoise de Mulder/CORBIS; **448 (bottom)** © Richard Powers/CORBIS; **449** © Peter Turnley/CORBIS; **450 (left)** © Jeremy Horner/CORBIS; **450 (right)** © Howard Davies/CORBIS; **452 (left)** © James L. Amos/CORBIS; **452 (right)** © Brian Vikander/CORBIS; **453** © Neil Beer/ CORBIS; **454** © Bettmann/CORBIS; **455** © Vittonano Rastelli/CORBIS; **456** © Walter Hodges/CORBIS; **457** © Peter Turnley/ CORBIS; **458 (left)** © Bill Gentile/ CORBIS; **458 (right)** © Vince Streano/ CORBIS; **459** © Francoise de Mulder/ CORBIS; **460 (top)** © Paul A. Souders/ CORBIS; **460 (bottom)** © Brian Leng/CORBIS; **461** © Owen Franken/ CORBIS; **462** © Bojan Brecel/ CORBIS; **463 (top)** © Jonathan Blair/ CORBIS; **463 (bottom)** © Peter Turnley/ CORBIS; **464** © R. W. Jones/CORBIS; **465** © Gerrit Grevel/CORBIS; **467** © Peter Turnley/ CORBIS.

Chapter 18 **468** © Robert Holmes/ CORBIS; **470 (top left)** © Martin Rogers/ CORBIS; **470 (bottom right)** © George Hall/CORBIS; **470 (cutout)** © PhotoDisc; **473 (left)** © Catherine Karnow/CORBIS; **473 (right)** © The Purcell Team/CORBIS; **477** © Philip Gould/CORBIS; **478** © Wolfgang Kaehler/CORBIS; **479 (top)** © PhotoDisc; **479 (bottom)** © Catherine Karnow/ CORBIS; **480 (top)** © Kevin Fleming/ CORBIS; **480 (bottom)** © AFP/CORBIS; **481** © Catherine Karnow/CORBIS; **482** © Reuters Newmedia Inc./CORBIS; **483 (top)** © Reuters Newmedia Inc./CORBIS; **483 (bottom)** © Bettmann/CORBIS; **485** © AFP/CORBIS; **486** © Reuters Newmedia Inc./CORBIS; **487 (top)** © Ric Ergenbright/ CORBIS; **487 (bottom)** © Reuters Newmedia Inc./CORBIS; **488** © AFP/CORBIS; **489** © Digital Art/CORBIS; **490** © Michael S. Yamashita/CORBIS; **491** © Reuters Newmedia Inc./CORBIS; **493** © Judy Griesedieck/CORBIS.

Chapter 19 **494** © Farrell Grehan/ CORBIS; **496** © Gianni Dagli Orti/CORBIS; **497 (top)** © Wolfgang Kaehler/CORBIS; **497 (top inset)** © Peter Harholdt/ CORBIS; **497 (bottom)** © Owen Franken/ CORBIS; **498 (top)** © AFP/CORBIS; **498 (bottom)** © PhotoDisc; **499** © Neil Rabinowitz/ CORBIS; **499 (inset)** © Kevin Fleming/ CORBIS; **500** © AFP/CORBIS; **501 (top)** © PhotoDisc; **501 (middle)** © PhotoDisc; **501 (bottom)** © PhotoDisc; **502 (top)** © Wally McNamee/CORBIS; **502 (bottom)** © PhotoDisc; **503** © Stephanie Maze/ CORBIS; **504** © Hulton-Deutsch Collection/ CORBIS; **506 (left)** © Bettmann/CORBIS; **506 (right)** © PhotoDisc; **507** © Bettmann/CORBIS; **508 (left)** © PhotoDisc; **508 (right)** © PhotoDisc; **509** © Hulton-Deutsch Collection/ CORBIS; **509 (inset)** © Cydney Conger/CORBIS; **510 (top)** © PhotoDisc; **510 (bottom)** © Owen Franken/CORBIS; **511** © PhotoDisc; **511 (inset)** © Phil Schermeister/CORBIS; **512** © Jonathan Blair/ CORBIS; **513** © Archive IconograFico, S. A./CORBIS; **514** © AFP/ CORBIS; **515** © Craig Aurness/CORBIS; **516 (top)** © Novosti/CORBIS; **516 (bottom left)** ©

Galen Rowell/CORBIS; **516 (bottom right)** © Peter Turnley/CORBIS; **517 (top)** © Peter Turnley/CORBIS; **517 (bottom)** © Peter Turnley/CORBIS; **519** © Peter Turnley/CORBIS; **520 (top)** © Peter Turnley/CORBIS; **520 (bottom)** © Steve Raymer/CORBIS; **521 (top)** © David Turnley/CORBIS; **523** © Peter Turnley/CORBIS; **524 (bottom)** © Wolfgang Kaehler/ CORBIS; **522** © Francoise de Mulder/ CORBIS; **525** © Buddy Mays/ CORBIS; **526 (top)** © Wally McNamee/ CORBIS; **526 (bottom)** © AFP/CORBIS; **527** © David Turnley/ CORBIS; **528** © R. W. Jones/CORBIS; **529** © W. Cody/ CORBIS; **531** © David H. Wells/CORBIS; **532** © Philip Gould/ CORBIS; **533 (top)** © Reuters Newmedia Inc./CORBIS; **533 (bottom)** © Reuters Newmedia Inc./ CORBIS.

Chapter 20 **536** © Nik Wheeler/CORBIS; **538 (top)** © PhotoDisc; **538 (bottom left)** © Judy Griesedieck/CORBIS; **538 (bottom right)** © PhotoDisc; **539** © Digital Stock; **540** © PhotoDisc; **541** © David Young-Wolff/PhotoEdit; **542** © PhotoDisc; **543** © Felicia Martinez/PhotoEdit; **544** © Wally McNamee/CORBIS; **545** © PhotoDisc; **546** © PhotoDisc; **547** © PhotoDisc; **548** © Dennis Degnan/CORBIS; **549 (top)** Digital Stock; **549 (bottom)** © George Hall/ CORBIS; **549 (inset)** © PhotoDisc; **550 (bottom left)** Digital Stock; **550 (right)** © Lee White/CORBIS; **550 (cutouts)** © Image Club Graphics; **551** © PhotoDisc; **552 (top)** © PhotoDisc; **552 (bottom)** © Jim Sugar Photography/ CORBIS; **553** © Catherine Karnow/ CORBIS; **554** © Digital Stock; **555** © Mary Kate Denny/PhotoEdit; **556 (top)** © Tim Wright/CORBIS; **556 (top inset)** © Alex Fevzer/CORBIS; **556 (bottom)** © PhotoDisc; **557** © Digital Stock; **558 (top)** © PhotoDisc; **558 (bottom)** © Jim Sugar Photography/CORBIS; **559** © Bettmann/ CORBIS; **560** © Charles O'Rear/ CORBIS; **561** © Raymond Gehman/ CORBIS; **561 (inset)** © PhotoDisc; **562 (top)** © PhotoDisc; **562 (bottom)** © PhotoDisc; **563** © Bettmann/CORBIS; **564 (top)** © PhotoDisc; **564 (bottom)** © PhotoDisc; **565** © Richard Hutchings, InfoEdit; **566** © AFP/CORBIS; **567** © Michael Newman/ PhotoEdit; **568** © PhotoDisc; **569** © PhotoDisc; **571** © The Purcell Team/ CORBIS; **573** © Michelle Bridwell/PhotoEdit.

Chapter 21 **574** © Fotografia, Inc./ CORBIS; **576 (top)** © Dana White Productions; **576 (bottom)** © Bob Krist/CORBIS; **578 (top right)** © PhotoDisc; **578 (top inset)** © CORBIS; **578 (bottom)** © PhotoDisc; **578 (bottom inset)** © Bob Rowan/ Progressive Image/CORBIS; **580** © PhotoDisc; **582** © PhotoDisc; **583** © AP/Wide World Photos; **584** © CORBIS; **585** © AP/ Wide World Photos; **586** © Bill Varie/ CORBIS; **587** © José F. Poblete/CORBIS; **588** © James Marshall/CORBIS; **589** © AP/Wide World Photos; **590** © PhotoDisc; **591** © PhotoDisc; **592 (top left)** © PhotoDisc; **592 (top right)** © PhotoDisc; **593 (bottom)** © PhotoDisc; **593 (inset)** © PhotoDisc; **593** © PhotoDisc; **594** © Jeff Greenberg/Index Stock; **597** © George White, Jr./CORBIS; **598 (left)** © PhotoDisc; **598 (right)** © PhotoDisc; **599 (top)** © PhotoDisc; **599 (bottom)** © PhotoDisc; **599 (bottom inset)** © PhotoDisc; **600** © PhotoDisc; **601 (top)** © Digital Stock; **601 (bottom)** © Warren Morgan/CORBIS; **602** © PhotoDisc; **603** © Morton Beebe, S.F./ CORBIS; **604** © Vince Streano/CORBIS; **604 (inset)** © Steve Chenn/CORBIS; **605 (top)** © AFP/CORBIS; **605 (bottom)** © Roger Ressmeyer/CORBIS; **606** © Mark Stephenson/CORBIS; **607** © PhotoDisc; **608 (top)** © PhotoDisc; **608 (bottom)** © PhotoDisc; **608 (bottom inset)** © PhotoDisc; **609** © Philip Gould/CORBIS; **610** © PhotoDisc; **611** © PhotoDisc; **613** © Digital Stock.

Chapter 22 **614** © James Marshall/ CORBIS; **616** © D. Boone/CORBIS; **617 (top)** © Reuters Newmedia Inc./CORBIS; **617 (bottom)** © AFP/CORBIS; **618 (top)** © Bettmann/CORBIS; **618 (bottom)** © Bettmann/CORBIS; **620** © Reuters Newmedia Inc./CORBIS; **621** © Reuters Newmedia Inc./CORBIS; **622 (top)** © Reuters Newmedia Inc./CORBIS; **622 (bottom)** © Associated Press/TIME MAGAZINE; **623** ©Randy Faris/CORBIS; **624 (top)** © AFP/ CORBIS; **624 (bottom)** © PhotoDisc; **625** Digital Stock; **627 (top)** Digital Stock; **627 (bottom)** © Richard Drew/Associated Press AP; **630 (left)** © Bettmann/CORBIS; **630 (right)** © CORBIS; **632** © AP Photo/David Barnes; **634 (top)** © Reuters Newmedia Inc./CORBIS; **634 (bottom)** © AFP/ CORBIS; **635** © R. W. Jones/CORBIS; **636** © Charles O'Rear/CORBIS; **637** © AP Photo/Wilfredo Lee; **638** © Jim Cornfield/CORBIS; **640 (top)** © Vince Streano/CORBIS; **640 (bottom)** © Richard Hamilton Smith/CORBIS; **641 (top)** © AFP/CORBIS; **641 (bottom)** © Naokazu Oinuma/Associated Press AP; **642** © Reuters Newmedia Inc./CORBIS; **643** © CORBIS; **645** © Reuters Newmedia Inc./ CORBIS.

Chapter 23 **646** © AFP/CORBIS; **648** © Keith Srakocie/AP Wide World Photos; **649 (top)** © Dean Conger/CORBIS; **649 (bottom)** © Wally McNamee/CORBIS; **650** © Douglas C. Pizac/AP Wide World Photos; **651** © Barry Sweet/AP Wide World Photos; **652** © Ahn Young-Joon/AP Wide World Photos; **653** © Pat Sullivan/AP Wide World Photos; **655** © Michael Schmelling/AP Wide World Photos; **656** © PhotoDisc; **658** © Digital Stock; **660 (top)** © Kamran Jebreili/AP Wide World Photos; **660 (bottom)** © Robert F. Bukaty/AP Wide World Photos; **661 (top)** © Cris Yarborough/AP Wide World Photos; **661 (bottom)** © Ricardo Figueroa/AP Wide World Photos; **662** © AP Wide World Photos; **663** © Morry Gash/AP Wide World Photos; **664 (top)** © Marc F. Henning/AP Wide World Photos; **664 (middle)** © Linda Radin/AP Wide World Photos; **664 (bottom)** © Nancy Palmieri/AP Wide World Photos; **665 (top)** © Vin Catania/AP Wide World Photos; **665 (bottom)** © Jeff T. Green/AP Wide World Photos; **666** © Todd Gipstein/CORBIS; **667** © Ed Wray/AP Wide World Photos; **668** © Bill Janscha/ AP Wide World Photos; **670** © Todd Sumlin/AP Wide World Photos; **671** © AP Wide World Photos; **673** © AP Wide World Photos; **675** © PhotoDisc; **676 (top)** © PhotoDisc; **676 (bottom)** © Nathan Benn/ CORBIS; **677 (top)** © Sandy Felsenthal/ CORBIS; **677 (bottom)** © Reuters Newmedia Inc./CORBIS.